Featured Applications in This Book

Cross-Chapter Analyses

Microeconomics

FIFTH EDITION

The Addison-Wesley Series in Economics

Abel/Bernanke/Croushore
*Macroeconomics**

Bade/Parkin
*Foundations of Economics**

Bierman/Fernandez
Game Theory with Economic Applications

Binger/Hoffman
Microeconomics with Calculus

Boyer
Principles of Transportation Economics

Branson
Macroeconomic Theory and Policy

Bruce
Public Finance and the American Economy

Byrns/Stone
Economics

Carlton/Perloff
Modern Industrial Organization

Caves/Frankel/Jones
World Trade and Payments: An Introduction

Chapman
Environmental Economics: Theory, Application, and Policy

Cooter/Ulen
Law & Economics

Downs
An Economic Theory of Democracy

Ehrenberg/Smith
Modern Labor Economics

Ekelund/Ressler/Tollison
*Economics**

Fusfeld
The Age of the Economist

Gerber
International Economics

Ghiara
Learning Economics

Gordon
Macroeconomics

Gregory
Essentials of Economics

Gregory/Stuart
Russian and Soviet Economic Performance and Structure

Hartwick/Olewiler
The Economics of Natural Resource Use

Hoffman/Averett
Women and the Economy: Family, Work, and Pay

Holt
Markets, Games, and Strategic Behavior

Hubbard
Money, the Financial System, and the Economy

Hughes/Cain
American Economic History

Husted/Melvin
International Economics

Jehle/Reny
Advanced Microeconomic Theory

Johnson-Lans
A Health Economics Primer

Klein
Mathematical Methods for Economics

Krugman/Obstfeld
*International Economics**

Laidler
The Demand for Money

Leeds/von Allmen
The Economics of Sports

Leeds/von Allmen/Schiming
*Economics**

Lipsey/Ragan/Storer
*Economics**

Melvin
International Money and Finance

Miller
*Economics Today**

Miller
Understanding Modern Economics

Miller/Benjamin
The Economics of Macro Issues

Miller/Benjamin/North
The Economics of Public Issues

Mills/Hamilton
Urban Economics

Mishkin
*The Economics of Money, Banking, and Financial Markets**

Mishkin
*The Economics of Money, Banking, and Financial Markets, Alternate Edition**

Murray
Econometrics: A Modern Introduction

Parkin
*Economics**

Perloff
*Microeconomics**

Perloff
Microeconomics: Theory and Applications with Calculus

Perman/Common/McGilvray/Ma
Natural Resources and Environmental Economics

Phelps
Health Economics

Riddell/Shackelford/Stamos/Schneider
Economics: A Tool for Critically Understanding Society

Ritter/Silber/Udell
Principles of Money, Banking, and Financial Markets

Rohlf
Introduction to Economic Reasoning

Ruffin/Gregory
Principles of Economics

Sargent
Rational Expectations and Inflation

Scherer
Industry Structure, Strategy, and Public Policy

Sherman
Market Regulation

Stock/Watson
Introduction to Econometrics

Stock/Watson
Introduction to Econometrics, Brief Edition

Studenmund
Using Econometrics

Tietenberg/Lewis
Environmental and Natural Resource Economics

Tietenberg
Environmental Economics and Policy

Todaro/Smith
Economic Development

Waldman
Microeconomics

Waldman/Jensen
Industrial Organization: Theory and Practice

Weil
Economic Growth

Williamson
Macroeconomics

**denotes myeconlab titles*

Go to www.myeconlab.com to learn more.

Microeconomics

FIFTH EDITION

JEFFREY M. PERLOFF

University of California, Berkeley

Boston San Francisco New York
London Toronto Sydney Tokyo Singapore Madrid
Mexico City Munich Paris Cape Town Hong Kong Montreal

To my mother, Mimi Perloff

Editor in Chief:	*Donna Battista*
Senior Acquisitions Editor:	*Adrienne D'Ambrosio*
Development Editor:	*Deepa Chungi*
Assistant Editor:	*Margaret Beste*
Managing Editor:	*Nancy Fenton*
Senior Production Supervisor:	*Meredith Gertz*
Cover Designer:	*Gillian Hall, The Aardvark Group*
Senior Designer:	*Barbara Atkinson*
Supplements Editor:	*Heather McNally*
Senior Marketing Manager:	*Roxanne McCarley*
Marketing Assistant:	*Ashlee Clevenger*
Senior Media Producer:	*Melissa Honig*
Content Lead, MyEconLab:	*Douglas Ruby*
Senior Author Support/Technology Specialist:	*Joe Vetere*
Photo Researcher:	*Beth Anderson*
Senior Prepress Supervisor:	*Caroline Fell*
Senior Manufacturing Buyer:	*Carol Melville*
Production Coordination, Composition, Illustrations, and Text Design:	*Gillian Hall, The Aardvark Group*
Copyeditor:	*Rebecca Greenberg*
Proofreader:	*Holly McLean-Aldis*
Indexer:	*Jack Lewis*
Cover images:	*©Andrew Swaine Photography (foreground image)/Big Stock Photo (background image)*

Photo credits appear on page A-78, which constitutes a continuation of this copyright page.

Library of Congress Cataloging-in-Publication Data

Perloff, Jeffrey M.
Microeconomics / Jeffrey Perloff. -- 5th ed.
p. cm.
Includes index.
ISBN 978-0-321-55849-7
1. Microeconomics. I. Title.

HB172.P39 2009
338.5--dc22 2008016612

ISBN-13: 978-0-321-55849-7
ISBN-10: 0-321-55849-9

1 2 3 4 5 6 7 8 9 10—CRK—12 11 10 09 08

Brief Contents

Contents

PART SEVEN
Uncertainty, Missing Markets, and Limited Information

Preface

When I was a student, I fell in love with microeconomics because it cleared up many mysteries about the world and provided the means to answer new questions. I wrote this book to show students that economic theory has practical, problem-solving uses and is not an empty academic exercise.

This book shows how individuals, policy makers, and firms can use microeconomic tools to analyze and resolve problems. For example, students learn that

- individuals can draw on microeconomic theories when deciding about issues such as whether to invest and whether to sign a contract that pegs prices to the government's measure of inflation;
- policy makers (and voters) can employ microeconomics to predict the impact of taxes, regulations, and other measures before they are enacted;
- lawyers and judges use microeconomics in antitrust, discrimination, and contract cases;
- firms apply microeconomic principles to produce at minimum cost and maximize profit, select strategies, decide whether to buy from a market or to produce internally, and write contracts to provide optimal incentives for employees.

My experience in teaching microeconomics for the departments of economics at MIT, the University of Pennsylvania, and the University of California, Berkeley; the Department of Agricultural and Resource Economics at Berkeley; and the Wharton Business School has convinced me that students prefer this emphasis on real-world issues.

Features

This book differs from other microeconomics texts in three main ways. First, it integrates real-world "widget-free" examples throughout the exposition, in addition to offering extended applications. Second, it places greater emphasis than other texts on modern theories—such as industrial organization theories, game theory, transaction cost theory, information theory, and contract theory—that are useful in analyzing actual markets. Third, it employs a step-by-step approach to demonstrate how to use microeconomic theory to solve problems and analyze policy issues.

Widget-Free Economics

To convince students that economics is practical and useful, not just a textbook exercise, this text presents theories using real-world examples rather than made-up analyses of widgets, those nonexistent products beloved by earlier generations of textbook writers. These real economic "stories" are integrated into the formal presentation of many economic theories, discussed in featured Applications, and analyzed in what-if policy discussions.

Integrated Real-World Examples. The book uses real-world examples throughout the narrative to illustrate many basic theories of microeconomics. Students learn the basic model of supply and demand using estimated supply and demand curves for Canadian processed pork and U.S. sweetheart roses. They analyze consumer choice employing typical consumers' estimated indifference curves between beer and wine or CDs and DVDs and mill workers' indifference curves between income and leisure. They learn about production and cost functions using evidence from a U.S. furniture manufacturer and Intel's learning by doing in chip manufacturing. Students see monopoly theory applied to a patented pharmaceutical, Botox. They use oligopoly theories to analyze the rivalry between United Airlines and American Airlines on the Chicago–Los Angeles route and between Coke and Pepsi in the cola industry.

Applications. The text also includes many featured Applications to illustrate the versatility of microeconomic theory. One such Application derives an isoquant for semiconductors using actual data. Other Applications look at measures of the pleasure consumers get from television and the amount by which recipients value Christmas presents relative to the cost to gift givers. Applications analyze how auction houses that provide more information achieve higher prices than sellers on eBay, the debate on drilling in the Arctic National Wildlife Refuge, and how Disneyland price discriminates. One Application investigates whether buying flight insurance makes sense.

What-If Policy Analysis. In addition, the book uses economic models to probe the likely outcomes of changes in public policies. Students learn how to conduct what-if analyses of policies such as taxes, subsidies, barriers to entry, price floors and ceilings, quotas and tariffs, zoning, pollution controls, and licensing laws. The text analyzes the effects of taxes on virtually every type of market.

The book also reveals the limits of economic theory for policy analysis. For example, to illustrate why attention to actual institutions is important, the text uses three different models to show how the effects of minimum wages vary across types of markets and institutions. Similarly, the text illustrates that a minimum wage law that is harmful in a competitive market may be desirable in certain noncompetitive markets.

Modern Theories

The first half of the book (Chapters 1–10) examines competitive markets and shows that competition has very desirable properties. The second half (Chapters 11–20) concentrates on imperfectly competitive markets, where firms have market power, firms and consumers are uncertain about the future and have limited information, and there are externalities and public goods.

The book goes beyond basic microeconomic theory to look at theories and applications from many important contemporary fields of economics. Extensive coverage of problems from behavioral economics, resource economics, labor economics, international trade, public finance, and industrial organization is featured throughout.

This book differs from other microeconomics texts by using game theory in several chapters in the second half. Game theory and decision trees are used to study oligopoly quantity and price setting, strategic trade policy, strategic behavior in multiperiod games (such as collusion and preventing entry), strategic advertising, investing when there's uncertainty about the future, and pollution (the Coase Theorem). Unlike most texts, this book covers pure and mixed strategies and analyzes both normal-form and extensive-form games.

The last two chapters draw from modern contract theory to analyze adverse selection and moral hazard extensively, instead of (as other texts do) mentioning these topics only in passing, if at all. The text covers lemons markets, signaling, preventing shirking, and the revelation of information (including through contract choice).

Step-by-Step Problem Solving

Many professors report that their biggest challenge in teaching microeconomics is helping students learn to solve new problems. This book is based on the belief that the best way to teach this important skill is to demonstrate problem solving repeatedly and then to give students exercises to do on their own. Each chapter after Chapter 1 provides several Solved Problems showing students how to answer qualitative and quantitative problems using a step-by-step approach. Rather than empty arithmetic exercises demanding no more of students than to employ algebra or a memorized mathematical formula, the Solved Problems focus on important economic issues such as analyzing government policies and determining firms' optimal strategies.

One Solved Problem examines how bad incentives lead to bad decisions by mortgage lenders (and an associated Application discusses the subprime mortgage crisis). Another shows how a monopolistically competitive airline equilibrium would change if fixed costs (such as fees for landing slots) rise. Others examine why firms charge different prices at factory stores than elsewhere, and when markets for lemons exist, among many other topics.

The Solved Problems illustrate how to approach the two sets of formal end-of-chapter problems. The first set of questions can be solved using graphs or verbal arguments; the second set of problems requires the use of math. The answers to selected end-of-chapter problems appear at the end of the book, and the solutions to the remaining problems may be found in the Instructor's Manual.

Changes in the Fifth Edition

The Fifth Edition is substantially updated and modified based on the extremely helpful suggestions of faculty and students who used the first four editions. I have rewritten two chapters, added sections to others, updated material throughout the text, increased the references to exercises within the text, and added more real-world questions and problems at the end of chapters.

New Chapters and Material

The most significant changes to the book are the two new chapters on oligopoly and on game theory and the new material on behavioral economics. Chapters 13 and 14 have been substantially changed at the request of a number of faculty members. Chapter 13 now presents the traditional models of oligopoly and monopolistic competition without using game theory. Chapter 14 is entirely new. It introduces game theory formally and applies game theory to many strategic problems, including a reexamination of the traditional oligopoly models.

The material of behavioral economics has been substantially expanded. Indeed, there is the equivalent of a chapter on this topic spread across four chapters. Section 4.5 in Chapter 4 examines how consumers' behavior deviates from the traditional models. Section 11.8 in Chapter 11—Network Externalities, Behavioral Economics, and Monopoly Decisions over Time—discusses how a consumer is influenced by the purchasing behavior of others. The material in Section 16.2 of Chapter 16 on why many people lack self-control has been revised. Chapter 17, has a new section, 17.5, on how psychology affects decision making under uncertainty.

In addition, several sections have been revised, including Sections 4.2 on utility, Section 5.3 on the effect of price changes, Section 6.6 on technical change, and the material in Section 7.4 on learning by doing. Two of these changes involve new, estimated models. Section 5.3 uses a new estimate of consumers' choices between CDs and DVDs. The section on learning by doing incorporates a new analysis based on an estimate of Intel's learning by doing in producing its central processing units.

I have also updated statistics and discussions throughout the text. For example, Chapter 2 has new discussions on nicotine and cigarette demand and the history of U.S. price controls. Similarly, Chapter 5 has new statistics on taxes, alcohol use, and inflation. New statistics or other material were also added to Chapters 6, 8, 9, 10, 11, 12, 16, 18, and 19.

Applications

Two-thirds of the Applications are new, updated, or revised. The Applications stress current issues: 62% cover events in 2007 or 2008 and 80% concern events in the twenty-first century (a couple deal with historical events and most of the rest examine timeless material).

To make room for the new applications, some older Applications from the Fourth Edition were moved to MyEconLab, at **www.myeconlab.com/perloff.** In addition, two new Applications have been added to MyEconLab. With these additions, MyEconLab has nearly 200 applications.

There are five Cross-Chapter Analyses, which combine the features of an Application and a Solved Problem. All the Cross-Chapter Analyses were updated to include 2007 or 2008 information.

Solved Problems and Exercises

This edition continues to use the well-received Solved Problems, which show the student how to address economic questions using a step-by-step approach. Nearly half of these Solved Problems are tied to real-world events. Many of these are associated with an adjacent Application. Examples of a paired Application and Solved Problem include Apple's iPod pricing and "smuggling" Canadian pharmaceuticals into the United States.

Starting with Chapter 2, at the end of each chapter and Cross-Chapter Analysis there are a large number of additional exercises, divided into verbal or graphical Questions and mathematical Problems. This edition has nearly 700 exercises—an average of 36 per chapter—of which 40% are based on recent real-life issues drawn from newspapers and other sources. This edition adds 58 new exercises—an average of 3 per chapter—of which nearly half are based on recent real-world events.

In this edition, virtually every exercise is referenced within the chapters. These references in the margins indicate to the student which material is particularly relevant to solving the exercise.

Alternative Organizations

Because instructors differ as to the order in which they cover material, this text has been designed for maximum flexibility. The most common approach to teaching microeconomics is to follow the sequence of the chapters in the first half of this book: supply and demand (Chapters 2 and 3), consumer theory (Chapters 4 and 5), the theory of the firm (Chapters 6 and 7), and the competitive model (Chapters 8 and 9). Many instructors then cover monopoly (Chapter 11), price discrimination

(Chapter 12), oligopoly (Chapter 13), input markets (Chapter 15), uncertainty (Chapter 17), and externalities (Chapter 18).

A common variant is to present uncertainty (Sections 17.1 through 17.3) immediately after consumer theory. Many instructors like to take up welfare issues between discussions of the competitive model and noncompetitive models, as Chapter 10, on general equilibrium and economic welfare, does. Alternatively, that chapter may be covered at the end of the course. Faculty can assign material on factor markets earlier (Section 15.1 could follow the chapters on competition, and the remaining sections could follow Chapter 11). The material in Chapters 14–20 can be presented in a variety of orders, though Chapter 20 should follow Chapter 19 if both are covered, and Section 17.4 should follow Chapter 16.

Many business school courses skip consumer theory (and possibly some aspects of supply and demand, such as Chapter 3) to allow more time for consideration of the topics covered in the second half of this book. Business school faculty may want to place particular emphasis on game and theory strategies (Chapter 14), vertical integration (Section 15.4), capital markets (Chapter 16), and modern contract theory (Chapters 19 and 20).

Technically demanding sections are marked with a green star (★). Subsequent sections and chapters can be understood even if these sections are skipped.

MyEconLab

MyEconLab—is the premier online assessment and tutorial system, pairing rich online content with innovative learning tools. The **MyEconLab** course for the Fifth Edition of *Microeconomics* includes select end-of-chapter questions and problems from the text, which can be easily assigned and automatically graded.

Students and MyEconLab

This online homework and tutorial system puts students in control of their own learning through a suite of study and practice tools correlated with the online, interactive version of the textbook and other media tools. Within **MyEconLab**'s structured environment, students practice what they learn, test their understanding, and pursue a study plan that **MyEconLab** generates for them based on their performance on practice tests.

Instructors and MyEconLab

MyEconLab provides flexible tools that allow instructors to easily and effectively customize online course materials to suit their needs. Instructors can create and assign tests, quizzes, or graded homework assignments. **MyEconLab** saves time by automatically grading all questions and tracking results in an online gradebook. **MyEconLab** can even grade assignments that require students to draw a graph.

After registering for **MyEconLab**, instructors have access to downloadable supplements such as an Instructor's Manual, microeconomics experiments, PowerPoint lecture notes, and a Test Bank. The Test Bank can also be used within **MyEconLab**, giving instructors ample material from which they can create assignments.

Additional **MyEconLab** resources:

- **Animated Figures.** Key figures from the textbook are presented in step-by-step animations with audio explanations of the action.
- **Audio Answers Using Slides.** James Dearden of Lehigh University wrote over 60 of these exercises. Starting with Chapter 2, each chapter has at least two of

Professor Dearden's exercises, and some chapters have as many as ten. The majority of exercises are based on real-world events, many taken from newspapers, and most are multipart exercises. Professor Dearden walks you through the answer for each exercise using slides at **www.myeconlab.com/perloff.**

- **eThemes of the Times.** Archived articles from *The New York Times*, correlated to each chapter of the textbook and paired with critical thinking questions.
- **Research Navigator (CourseCompass version only).** Extensive help on the research process and four exclusive databases of accredited and reliable source material including *The New York Times*, *The Financial Times*, and peer-reviewed journals.

The enhanced **MyEconLab** problems for Microeconomics were created by Bert G. Wheeler at Cedarville University and Charles L. Baum II at Middle Tennesee State University. For more information about **MyEconLab**, or to request an Instructor Access Code, visit **http://www.myeconlab.com.**

Supplements to Accompany *Microeconomics*

A full range of additional supplementary materials to support teaching and learning accompanies this book.

- The *Study Guide*, by Charles F. Mason of the University of Wyoming and Léonie Stone of the State University of New York at Geneseo, provides students with a quick guide to Key Concepts and Formulas, as well as additional Applications, and it walks them through the solution of many problems. Students can then work through a large number of Practice Problems on their own and check their answers against those in the Guide. At the end of each Study Guide chapter is a set of Exercises suitable for homework assignments.
- The *Online Instructor's Manual*, revised by Ali Toossi-Ardakani of the University of Illinois, Urbana-Champaign, has many useful and creative teaching ideas. It also offers additional Applications, as well as extra problems and answers, and it provides solutions for all the end-of-chapter text problems.
- The *Online Test Bank*, revised by Craig Depken of the University of North Carolina, Charlotte, features problems of varying levels of complexity, suitable for homework assignments and exams. Many of these multiple choice questions draw on current events.
- The *Computerized Test Bank* reproduces the Test Bank material in the TestGen software that is available for Windows and Macintosh. With TestGen, instructors can easily edit existing questions, add questions, generate tests, and print the tests in a variety of formats.
- The *Online PowerPoint Presentation with Art, Figures, and Lecture Notes* was written by José Vasquez of the University of Illinois, Urbana-Champaign. This resource contains text figures and tables, as well as lecture notes and click-animated graphs. These layered slides allow instructors to walk through examples from the text during in-class presentations.

The Instructor's Resource CD-ROM contains electronic files of all Instructor's Resources, including the Instructor's Manual, Test Bank, Computerized Test Bank, and PowerPoint slides. A PowerPoint viewer is provided for those who do not have the full software program. The CD-ROM also contains TestGen-EQ and QuizMaster-EQ software programs. These programs can be used to easily create multiple-choice tests.

Instructors can download supplements from a secure, instructor-only source via the Addison-Wesley Web page (**www.pearsonhighered.com/irc**).

Acknowledgments

My greatest debt is to my students and to the two best development editors in the business, Jane Tufts and Sylvia Mallory. My students at MIT, the University of Pennsylvania, and the University of California, Berkeley, patiently dealt with my various approaches to teaching them microeconomics and made useful (and generally polite) suggestions. I received constructive student and faculty comments on early versions of this book when it was used by faculty members at Berkeley and by Jerome Culp at the Duke University Law School.

Jane Tufts reviewed drafts of the first edition of this book for content and presentation. By showing me how to present the material as clearly, orderly, and thoroughly as possible, she greatly strengthened this text. Sylvia Mallory worked valiantly to improve my writing style and helped to shape and improve every aspect of the book's contents and appearance in each of the first four editions.

I am very grateful to Adrienne D'Ambrosio, Senior Acquisitions Editor, and Deepa Chungi, Development Editor, at Addison-Wesley, who helped me plan this revision and made very valuable suggestions at each stage of the process. In addition, Deepa worked hard on making sure that the new material in this edition is clear.

My excellent research assistants—Hayley Chouinard, R. Scott Hacker, Nancy McCarthy, Enrico Moretti, Lisa Perloff, Asa Sajise, Hugo Salgado, Gautam Sethi, Edward Shen, Klaas van 't Veld, and Ximing Wu—worked hard to collect facts, develop examples, and check material. I am particularly grateful to Hugo, Klaas, Scott, and Edward for helping to produce many of the best examples in the book and on the Web site. Nancy, Enrico, Hayley, Ximing, and Asa showed flair in collecting facts. Hayley and Gautam carefully checked the book and made very helpful suggestions.

Many people were very generous in providing me with data, models, and examples, including the following: Peter Berck, University of California, Berkeley: exhaustible resources and investments; James Brander, University of British Columbia: American Airlines and United Airlines; Richard Garbaccio, Brandeis University: China; Farid Gasmi, Université des Sciences Sociales, Toulouse: Coke and Pepsi; Claudia Goldin, Harvard University: income distribution; Rachel Goodhue, University of California, Davis: incentives; William Greene, New York University: power plants; Nile Hatch, University of Illinois: semiconductors and learning by doing; Charles Hyde, University of Melbourne: demand estimates; Fahad Khalil, University of Washington: contract theory; Jean-Jacques Laffont, Université des Sciences Sociales, Toulouse: Coke and Pepsi; Karl D. Meilke, University of Guelph: pork; Giancarlo Moschini, Iowa State University: pork; Michael Roberts, U.S. Department of Agriculture: exhaustible resources; Peter von Allmen, Moravian College: various applications; Quang Vuong, Université des Sciences Sociales, Toulouse, and University of Southern California: Coke and Pepsi.

Writing a textbook is hard work for everyone involved. I am grateful to the many teachers of microeconomics who spent untold hours reading and commenting on proposals and chapters. Many of the best ideas in this book are due to them. I particularly thank W. Bruce Allen of the Wharton School of Business, who read every single word in the First Edition at least twice (and commented productively on nearly each one) and James Brander, University of British Columbia, who made insightful comments on the first two editions and Chapter 14 in this edition. Peter Berck made major contributions to Chapter 16. Charles F. Mason made particularly helpful comments on chapters, and he authored one and coauthored another of the major supplements to this textbook. Larry Karp helped me to develop two of the sections and carefully reviewed the content of several others. One of my two major debts is to Robert Whaples, Wake Forest University, who has read many chapters, offered particularly useful comments, and coauthored two of the major supplements to this textbook; he also wrote the first draft of one of my favorite Applications. My other biggest debt is to James Dearden, Lehigh University, who has made insightful comments on all editions. Even more important, he developed and brilliantly executed the idea of writing topical questions with audio-slide show answers—a very valuable feature.

I also thank the following reviewers, who provided valuable comments at various stages:

M. Shahid Alam, Northeastern University
Anne Alexander, University of Wyoming
Richard K. Anderson, Texas A & M University
Niels Anthonisen, University of Western Ontario
Wilma Anton, University of Central Florida
Emrah Arbak, State University of New York at Albany
Scott E. Atkinson, University of Georgia
Raymond G. Batina, Washington State University
Anthony Becker, St. Olaf College
Gary Biglaiser, University of North Carolina, Chapel Hill
S. Brock Blomberg, Wellesley College
Vic Brajer, California State University, Fullerton
Bruce Brown, Cal Polytech Pomona and UCLA
Cory S. Capps, University of Illinois, Urbana-Champaign
John Cawley, Cornell University
Indranil Chakraborty, University of Oklahoma
Leo Chan, University of Kansas
Joni S. Charles, Southwest Texas State University
Kwang Soo Cheong, University of Hawaii at Manoa
Joy L. Clark, Auburn University, Montgomery
Dean Croushore, Federal Reserve Bank of Philadelphia
Douglas Dalenberg, University of Montana
Andrew Daughety, Vanderbilt University
Carl Davidson, Michigan State University
Ronald Deiter, Iowa State University
Manfred Dix, Tulane University
John Edgren, Eastern Michigan University
Patrick Emerson, University of Colorado, Denver
Bernard Fortin, Université Laval
Tom Friedland, Rutgers University
Roy Gardner, Indiana University
Rod Garratt, University of California, Santa Barbara
Wei Ge, Bucknell University
J. Fred Giertz, University of Illinois, Urbana-Champaign
Haynes Goddard, University of Cincinnati
Steven Goldman, University of California, Berkeley
Julie Gonzalez, University of California, Santa Cruz
Rachel Goodhue, University of California, Davis
Srihari Govindan, University of Western Ontario
Gareth Green, Seattle University
Thomas A. Gresik, Pennsylvania State University
Jonathan Gruber, MIT
Steffan Habermalz, University of Nebraska, Kearney
Claire Hammond, Wake Forest University
John A. Hansen, State University of New York, Fredonia
Philip S. Heap, James Madison University
L. Dean Hiebert, Illinois State University
Kathryn Ierulli, University of Illinois, Chicago
Mike Ingham, University of Salford, U.K.
Samila Islam, Boise State University
D. Gale Johnson, University of Chicago
Charles Kahn, University of Illinois, Urbana-Champaign
Alan Kessler, Providence College
Kate Krause, University of New Mexico
Robert Lemke, Lake Forest College
Jing Li, University of Pennsylvania
Fred Luk, University of California, Los Angeles
Robert Main, Butler University
David Malueg, Tulane University
Steve Margolis, North Carolina State University
Kate Matraves, Michigan State University
James Meehan, Colby College
Claudio Mezzetti, University of North Carolina, Chapel Hill
Janet Mitchell, Cornell University
Babu Nahata, University of Louisville
Kathryn Nantz, Fairfield University
Jawwad Noor, Boston University
Yuka Ohno, Rice University
Patrick B. O'Neil, University of North Dakota
John Palmer, University of Western Ontario
Christos Papahristodoulou, Uppsala University
Silve Parviainen, University of Illinois, Urbana-Champaign

Sharon Pearson, University of Alberta
Ingrid Peters-Fransen, Wilfrid Laurier University
Jaishankar Raman, Valparaiso University
Sunder Ramaswamy, Middlebury College
Lee Redding, University of Michigan, Dearborn
David Reitman, Department of Justice
Luca Rigotti, Tillburg University
S. Abu Turab Rizvi, University of Vermont
Bee Yan Aw Roberts, Pennsylvania State University
Richard Rogers, Ashland University
Nancy Rose, Sloan School of Business, MIT
Joshua Rosenbloom, University of Kansas
Roy Ruffin, University of Houston
George Santopietro, Radford College
David Sappington, University of Florida
Richard Sexton, University of California, Davis
Jacques Siegers, Utrecht University, The Netherlands
William Doyle Smith, University of Texas at El Paso
Philip Sorenson, Florida State University
Peter Soule, Park College
Robert Stearns, University of Maryland
Shankar Subramanian, Cornell University
Beck A. Taylor, Baylor University
Wade Thomas, State University of New York, Oneonta
Judith Thornton, University of Washington
Vitor Trindade, Syracuse University
Nora Underwood, University of California, Davis
Burcin Unel, University of Florida
Kay Unger, University of Montana
Bas van der Klaauw, Free University Amsterdam and Tinbergen Institute
Jacob L. Vigdor, Duke University
Alan van der Hilst, University of Washington
Peter von Allmen, Moravian College
Eleanor T. von Ende, Texas Tech University
Curt Wells, Lund University
Lawrence J. White, New York University
John Whitehead, East Carolina University
Colin Wright, Claremont McKenna College
Bruce Wydick, University of San Francisco
Peter Zaleski, Villanova University
Artie Zillante, Florida State University
Mark Zupan, University of Arizona

In addition, I thank Bob Solow, the world's finest economics teacher, who showed me how to simplify models without losing their essence. I've also learned a great deal over the years about economics and writing from my coauthors on other projects, especially Dennis Carlton (my coauthor on *Modern Industrial Organization*), Jackie Persons, Steve Salop, Michael Wachter, Larry Karp, Peter Berck, Amos Golan, and Dan Rubinfeld (whom I thank for still talking to me despite my decision to write this book).

It was a pleasure to work with the good people at Addison-Wesley, who were incredibly helpful in producing this book. Marjorie Williams and Barbara Rifkin signed me to write it. Denise Clinton, Publisher for Economics, was instrumental in making the entire process work. Meredith Gertz supervised the production process, assembled the extended publishing team and managed the design of the handsome interior and cover. Gillian Hall and the rest of the team at The Aardvark Group Publishing Services have my sincere thanks for designing the book and keeping the project on track and on schedule. I also want to acknowledge, with gratitude, the efforts of Melissa Honig, Douglas Ruby, and Noel Lotz in developing **MyEconLab**, the online assessment and tutorial system for the book. Additional thanks go to to Roxanne McCarley, for her work in marketing the entire program and to Mathew Dorsey for his efforts in marketing **MyEconLab**.

Finally, I thank my family, Mimi Perloff, Jackie Persons, and Lisa Perloff for their great patience and support during the nearly endless writing process. And I apologize for misusing their names—and those of my other relatives and friends—in the book!

J. M. P.

1

Introduction

I've often wondered what goes into a hot dog. Now I know and I wish I didn't.
—William Zinsser

If each of us could get all the food, clothing, and toys we want without working, no one would study economics. Unfortunately, most of the good things in life are scarce—we can't all have as much as we want. Thus scarcity is the mother of economics.

microeconomics
the study of how individuals and firms make themselves as well off as possible in a world of scarcity and the consequences of those individual decisions for markets and the entire economy

Microeconomics is the study of how individuals and firms make themselves as well off as possible in a world of scarcity and the consequences of those individual decisions for markets and the entire economy. In studying microeconomics, we examine how individual consumers and firms make decisions and how the interaction of many individual decisions affects markets.

Microeconomics is often called *price theory* to emphasize the important role that prices play. Microeconomics explains how the actions of all buyers and sellers determine prices and how prices influence the decisions and actions of individual buyers and sellers.

In this chapter, we examine three main topics

1. **Microeconomics: Allocation of Scarce Resources.** Microeconomics is the study of the allocation of scarce resources.
2. **Models.** Economists use models to make testable predictions.
3. **Uses of Microeconomic Models.** Individuals, governments, and firms use microeconomic models and predictions in decision making.

1.1 Microeconomics: Allocation of Scarce Resources

Individuals and firms allocate their limited resources to make themselves as well off as possible. Consumers pick the mix of goods and services that makes them as happy as possible given their limited wealth. Firms decide which goods to produce, where to produce them, how much to produce to maximize their profits, and how to produce those levels of output at the lowest cost by using more or less of various inputs such as labor, capital, materials, and energy. The owners of a depletable natural resource such as oil decide when to use it. Government decision makers—to benefit consumers, firms, or government bureaucrats—decide which goods and services the government produces and whether to subsidize, tax, or regulate industries and consumers.

Trade-Offs

People make trade-offs because they can't have everything. A society faces three key trade-offs:

- **Which goods and services to produce.** If a society produces more cars, it must produce fewer of other goods and services, because there are only so many *resources*—workers, raw materials, capital, and energy—available to produce goods.
- **How to produce.** To produce a given level of output, a firm must use more of one input if it uses less of another input. Cracker and cookie manufacturers switch between palm oil and coconut oil, depending on which is less expensive.
- **Who gets the goods and services.** The more of society's goods and services you get, the less someone else gets.

Who Makes the Decisions

These three allocation decisions may be made explicitly by the government or may reflect the interaction of independent decisions by many individual consumers and firms. In the former Soviet Union, the government told manufacturers how many cars of each type to make and which inputs to use to make them. The government also decided which consumers would get a car.

In most other countries, how many cars of each type are produced and who gets them are determined by how much it costs to make cars of a particular quality in the least expensive way and how much consumers are willing to pay for them. More consumers would own a handmade Rolls-Royce and fewer would buy a mass-produced Ford Taurus if a Rolls were not 21 times more expensive than a Taurus.

APPLICATION

Flu Vaccine Shortage

In 2004, the U.S. government expected a record 100 million flu vaccine doses to be available, but one vaccine maker, Chiron, could not ship 46 million doses because of contamination.[1] As a consequence, the government expected a shortage at the traditional price.

In response, government and public health officials urged young, healthy people to forgo getting shots until the sick, the elderly, and other high-risk populations, such as health care providers and pregnant women, were inoculated. Public spirit failed to dissuade enough healthy people. Perversely, de Janvry et al. (2007) found that the high-priority adult population was the group most likely to show self-control and not ask for a shot. Consequently, federal, state, and local governments restricted access to the shots to high-risk populations.

In most non-health-related goods markets, prices adjust to prevent shortages. In contrast, during the flu shot shortage, governments didn't increase the price to reduce demand, but relied on exhortation and formal allocation schemes.

[1] Sources for applications appear at the end of the book.

Prices Determine Allocations

An Economist's Theory of Reincarnation: If you're good, you come back on a higher level. Cats come back as dogs, dogs come back as horses, and people—if they've been real good like George Washington—come back as money.

Prices link the decisions about *which goods and services to produce*, *how to produce them*, and *who gets them*. Prices influence the decisions of individual consumers and firms, and the interactions of these decisions by consumers, firms, and the government determine price.

market
an exchange mechanism that allows buyers to trade with sellers

Interactions between consumers and firms take place in a **market**, which is an exchange mechanism that allows buyers to trade with sellers. A market may be a town square where people go to trade food and clothing, or it may be an international telecommunications network over which people buy and sell financial securities. Typically, when we talk about a single market, we refer to trade in a single good or group of goods that are closely related, such as soft drinks, movies, novels, or automobiles.

Most of this book concerns how prices are determined within a market. We show that the *number of buyers and sellers* in a market and the amount of *information* they have help determine whether the price equals the cost of production. We also show that if there is no market—and hence no market price—serious problems, such as high levels of pollution, result.

APPLICATION

Twinkie Tax

Many U.S., Canadian, New Zealand, U.K., and Australian jurisdictions are proposing a "Twinkie tax" on unhealthful fatty and sweet foods to reduce obesity and cholesterol problems, particularly among children. One survey found that 45% of adults would support a 1¢ tax per pound of soft drinks, chips, and butter, with the revenues used to fund health education programs.

Many proponents and opponents of these proposed laws seem unaware that at least 25 states and 3 cities differentially tax soft drinks, candy, chewing gum, or snack foods such as potato chips (Chouinard et al., 2007). By 2007, many school districts throughout the United States banned soft drink vending machines. This ban discourages consumption, as would an extremely high tax.

New taxes will affect *which foods are produced*, as firms offer new low-fat and low-sugar programs, and *how fast-foods are produced*, as manufacturers reformulate their products to lower their tax burden. These taxes will also influence *who gets these goods* as consumers, especially children, substitute to less expensive, untaxed products.

1.2 Models

Everything should be made as simple as possible, but not simpler.
—Albert Einstein

model
a description of the relationship between two or more economic variables

To *explain* how individuals and firms allocate resources and how market prices are determined, economists use a **model**: a description of the relationship between two or more economic variables. Economists also use models to *predict* how a change in one variable will affect another.

APPLICATION

Income Threshold Model and China

According to an *income threshold model*, no one who has an income level below a threshold buys a particular consumer durable, which is a good that can be used for long periods of time such as a refrigerator or car. The theory also holds that almost everyone whose income is above the threshold does buy the durable.

If this theory is correct, we predict that, as most people's incomes rise above that threshold in less-developed countries, consumer durable purchases will go from near zero to large numbers virtually overnight. This prediction is consistent with evidence from Malaysia, where the income threshold for buying a car is about $4,000.

Given such evidence from other countries, many firms believed that this model's predictions will apply to China. Incomes are rising rapidly in China and are exceeding the threshold levels for many types of durable goods. As a result, these companies predicted that the greatest consumer durable goods sales boom in history would take place there over the next decade. Anticipating this boom, these companies greatly increased their investments in durable goods manufacturing plants in China. Annual foreign direct investments went from $916 million a year in 1983 to $82.7 billion in 2007. In expectation of this growth potential, even traditional political opponents of the People's Republic—Taiwan, South Korea, and Russia—invested in China.

Simplifications by Assumption

We stated the income threshold model in words, but we could have presented it using graphs or mathematics. Regardless of how the model is described, an economic model is a simplification of reality that contains only its most important features. Without simplifications, it is difficult to make predictions because the real world is too complex to analyze fully.

By analogy, if the manual accompanying your new DVD recorder has a diagram showing the relationships between all the parts in the DVD, the diagram will be overwhelming and useless. In contrast, if it shows a photo of the buttons on the front of the machine with labels describing the purpose of each button, the manual is useful and informative.

Economists make many *assumptions* to simplify their models.[2] When using the income threshold model to explain car purchasing behavior in Malaysia, we *assume* that factors other than income, such as the color of cars, are irrelevant to the decision to buy cars. Therefore, we ignore the color of cars that are sold in Malaysia in describing the relationship between average income and the number of cars consumers want. If this assumption is correct, by ignoring color, we make our analysis of the auto market simpler without losing important details. If we're wrong and these ignored issues are important, our predictions may be inaccurate.

Throughout this book, we start with strong assumptions to simplify our models. Later, we add complexities. For example, in most of the book, we assume that consumers know the price each firm charges. In many markets, such as the New York Stock Exchange, this assumption is realistic. It is not realistic in other markets, such as the market for used automobiles, in which consumers do not know the prices

[2]An economist, an engineer, and a physicist are stranded on a desert island with a can of beans but no can opener. How should they open the can? The engineer proposes hitting the can with a rock. The physicist suggests building a fire under it to build up pressure and burst the can open. The economist thinks for a while and then says, "*Assume* that we have a can opener. . . ."

each firm charges. To devise an accurate model for markets in which consumers have limited information, we add consumer uncertainty about price into the model in Chapter 19.

Testing Theories

> *Blore's Razor: When given a choice between two theories, take the one that is funnier.*

Economic *theory* is the development and use of a model to test *hypotheses*, which are predictions about cause and effect. We are interested in models that make clear, testable predictions, such as "If the price rises, the quantity demanded falls." A theory that said "People's behavior depends on their tastes, and their tastes change randomly at random intervals" is not very useful because it does not lead to testable predictions.

Economists test theories by checking whether predictions are correct. If a prediction does not come true, they may reject the theory.[3] Economists use a model until it is refuted by evidence or until a better model is developed.

A good model makes sharp, clear predictions that are consistent with reality. Some very simple models make sharp predictions that are incorrect, and other more complex models make ambiguous predictions—any outcome is possible—which are untestable. The skill in model building is to chart a middle ground.

The purpose of this book is to teach you how to think like an economist in the sense that you can build testable theories using economic models or apply existing models to new situations. Although economists think alike in that they develop and use testable models, they often disagree. One may present a logically consistent argument that prices will go up next quarter. Another, using a different but equally logical theory, may contend that prices will fall. If the economists are reasonable, they agree that pure logic alone cannot resolve their dispute. Indeed, they agree that they'll have to use empirical evidence—facts about the real world—to find out which prediction is correct.

Although one economist's model may differ from another's, a key assumption in most microeconomic models is that individuals allocate their scarce resources so as to make themselves as well off as possible. Of all affordable combinations of goods, consumers pick the bundle of goods that gives them the most possible enjoyment. Firms try to maximize their profits given limited resources and existing technology. That resources are limited plays a crucial role in these models. Were it not for scarcity, people could consume unlimited amounts of goods and services, and sellers could become rich beyond limit.

As we show throughout this book, the maximizing behavior of individuals and firms determines society's three main allocation decisions: which goods are produced, how they are produced, and who gets them. For example, diamond-studded pocket combs will be sold only if firms find it profitable to sell them. The firms will make and sell these combs only if consumers value the combs at least as much as it costs the firm to produce them. Consumers will buy the combs only if they get more

[3]We can use evidence on whether a theory's predictions are correct to *refute* the theory but not to *prove* it. If a model's prediction is inconsistent with what actually happened, the model must be wrong, so we reject it. Even if the model's prediction is consistent with reality, however, the model's prediction may be correct for the wrong reason. Hence we cannot prove that the model is correct—we can only fail to reject it.

pleasure from the combs than they would from the other goods they could buy with the same resources.

Positive Versus Normative

The use of models of maximizing behavior sometimes leads to predictions that seem harsh or heartless. For instance, a World Bank economist predicted that if an African government used price controls to keep the price of food low during a drought, food shortages would occur and people would starve. The predicted outcome is awful, but the economist was not heartless. The economist was only making a scientific prediction about the relationship between cause and effect: Price controls (cause) lead to food shortages and starvation (effect).

positive statement
a testable hypothesis about cause and effect

Such a scientific prediction is known as a **positive statement**: a testable hypothesis about cause and effect. "Positive" does not mean that we are certain about the truth of our statement—it only indicates that we can test the truth of the statement.

If the World Bank economist is correct, should the government control prices? If the government believes the economist's predictions, it knows that the low prices help those consumers who are lucky enough to be able to buy as much food as they want while hurting both the firms that sell food and the people who are unable to buy as much food as they want, some of whom may die. As a result, the government's decision whether to use price controls turns on whether the government cares more about the winners or the losers. In other words, to decide on its policy, the government makes a value judgment.

Instead of first making a prediction and testing it and then making a value judgment to decide whether to use price controls, the government could make a value judgment directly. The value judgment could be based on the belief that "because people *should* have prepared for the drought, the government *should* not try to help them by keeping food prices low." Alternatively, the judgment could be based on the view that "people *should* be protected against price gouging during a drought, so the government *should* use price controls."

normative statement
a conclusion as to whether something is good or bad

These two statements are *not* scientific predictions. Each is a value judgment or **normative statement**: a conclusion as to whether something is good or bad. A normative statement cannot be tested because a value judgment cannot be refuted by evidence. It is a prescription rather than a prediction. A normative statement concerns what somebody believes *should* happen; a positive statement concerns what *will* happen.

Although a normative conclusion can be drawn without first conducting a positive analysis, a policy debate will be more informed if positive analyses are conducted first.[4] Suppose your normative belief is that the government should help the poor. Should you vote for a candidate who advocates a higher minimum wage (a law that requires that firms pay wages at or above a specified level), a European-style welfare system (guaranteeing health care, housing, and other basic goods and services), an end to our current welfare system, a negative income tax (in which the less income a person has, the more the government gives that person), or job training programs? Positive economic analysis can be used to predict whether these programs will benefit poor people but not whether they are good or bad. Using these predictions and your value judgment, you can decide for whom to vote.

[4]Some economists draw the normative conclusion that, as social scientists, we economists *should* restrict ourselves to positive analyses. Others argue that we shouldn't give up our right to make value judgments just like the next person (who happens to be biased, prejudiced, and pigheaded, unlike us).

Economists' emphasis on positive analysis has implications for what we study and even our use of language. For example, many economists stress that they study people's *wants* rather than their *needs*. Although people need certain minimum levels of food, shelter, and clothing to survive, most people in developed economies have enough money to buy goods well in excess of the minimum levels necessary to maintain life. Consequently, in wealthy countries, calling something a "need" is often a value judgment. You almost certainly have been told by some elder that "you *need* a college education." That person was probably making a value judgment—"you *should* go to college"—rather than a scientific prediction that you will suffer terrible economic deprivation if you do not go to college. We can't test such value judgments, but we can test a hypothesis such as "One-third of the college-age population *wants* to go to college at current prices."

1.3 Uses of Microeconomic Models

Have you ever imagined a world without hypothetical situations?
—Steven Wright

Because microeconomic models *explain* why economic decisions are made and allow us to make *predictions*, they can be very useful for individuals, governments, and firms in making decisions. Throughout this book, we consider examples of how microeconomics aids in actual decision making. Here we briefly look at some uses by individuals and governments and then examine a series of recent decisions by General Motors.

Individuals use microeconomics to make purchasing and other decisions. In Chapter 5, we examine how inflation and adjustments for inflation affect individuals. In Chapter 16, we show how to determine whether it pays financially to go to college. Another use of microeconomics is helping you decide for whom to vote based on candidates' views on economic issues.

Your government's elected and appointed officials use (or could use) economic models in many ways. Recent administrations have placed increased emphasis on economic analysis. Today, economic and environmental impact studies are required before many projects can commence. The President's Council of Economic Advisers and other federal economists analyze and advise national government agencies on the likely economic effects of all major policies.

Indeed, probably the major use of microeconomic models by governments is to predict the probable impact of a policy before it is adopted. In Chapter 3, we show how to predict the likely impact of a tax on the prices consumers pay and on the tax revenues raised.

APPLICATION

Putting Saturn in Orbit

Many firms have staffs of economists to make predictions and evaluate policies. Microeconomic analysis was particularly important to GM when it started selling its line of Saturn cars in 1991. The company broke a lot of its old rules. It built Saturns differently from the way it built its other cars and changed its relationship with its dealers so that they would sell and service the cars in a new way. Did GM's gamble work?

Manufacturing Costs. Starting up the Saturn line was a major risk; GM spent an estimated $5 billion to get Saturn going. (We examine investment policies in Chapter 16.) To keep manufacturing costs down, GM built a new plant that uses modern technology and a team approach and other Japanese-style management methods to assemble cars. One of these, just-in-time inventories (Chapter 6), allows GM to keep its inventory costs down by having suppliers ready to deliver parts almost immediately when needed. The Saturn plant produces relatively few models, and its sharing of engines and other major parts reduces production costs. (We analyze how firms minimize costs in Chapter 7.)

In building its new plant and designing its new car, GM had to take into account the federal government's emissions standards and other pollution regulations. (In Chapter 18, we analyze how firms react to such regulations and the effects of the regulations.)

Some industry experts believe that GM lost $500 million a year in the first few years because it couldn't make enough cars to cover its investment. Does it make sense to run a plant at a loss for a while? (We first examine shut-down decisions in Chapter 8.) In keeping the plant operating, GM was counting on Saturn managers and workers gaining experience in producing cars, which would lower the costs of production in the future (Chapter 7).

GM's Saturn division struck a new, separate deal with its union, the United Auto Workers. (In Chapter 15, we discuss relations between an input supplier, the union, and a manufacturer.)

Pricing. GM does not sell Saturns the way it sells its other cars. Knowing consumers' tastes with respect to the cars' features, service, and purchasing negotiations was an essential part of GM's new strategy. (Consumer decision making is analyzed in Chapters 4 and 5.)

Saturn's most striking marketing innovation was the "no-dicker sticker." Saturn dealers charge a fixed price for a car—they don't negotiate with customers as do most dealers. Why? One reason is that, according to a J. D. Power survey, 78% of American car buyers dislike negotiating for a new car. At the very least, this negotiation process is time consuming.

Why do traditional firms want to bargain with customers? It allows them to charge customers different prices. Such price discrimination can raise a firm's profits. (We address price discrimination in Chapter 12.)

In the past, some consumers who did not bargain well or had little information about costs and prices paid substantially more than the dealer's cost for a car. One dealer claims that car dealers often marked up their price over cost by 24% in the 1960s compared to under 7% today. Now, information about dealers' costs is available on the Internet, allowing some consumers to strike better deals than they could previously. (In Chapter 19, we examine the roles of unequal information on the prices consumers pay.)

Dealers. GM wanted its Saturn dealers not only to charge a fixed price, but also to provide superior service. With superior service, they could compete more effectively with dealers of high-quality imported cars and attract repeat customers. (Chapter 20 discusses how one firm gives another incentives to ensure the desired behavior.) Because of its pricing method and its emphasis on service, by the end of the millennium, Saturn was one of consumers' top-rated brands for service, along with Cadillac, Jaguar, Volvo, Land Rover, Mercedes-Benz, and Lexus.

GM ensured that its dealers would earn unusually high profits by limiting the number of Saturn dealers. Initially, GM had only 230 Saturn dealers nationally, compared with 5,000 Chevy dealers. As a result, a Saturn dealer's markup of its price above its costs is greater than it would be if the dealer had to compete with many other local Saturn dealers (see Chapter 13). According to one expert, the typical Saturn price markup is 13% over dealer costs, whereas traditional dealer markups average about half that.

Are higher dealer prices and profits good for GM? On the one hand, the higher retail price cuts current sales of Saturns, which hurts GM. On the other hand, the resulting high profits give dealers an incentive to provide superior service. As one dealer said, "If there were more Saturn dealers, with more competition among ourselves, we couldn't afford to give extra service. The trouble with non-Saturn GM dealers is that they cut their own throats by charging too little and taking most profit out of deals." Extra service should increase the demand for Saturns, which helps GM.

Because its sales staff does not have to spend time negotiating with each customer, Saturn dealers need fewer salespeople. Some dealers calculate that traditional dealers need 30% to 40% more sales staff. Thus the ratio of labor to capital in traditional dealers is different from that in fixed-price dealers. (Chapters 6 and 7 analyze substitution between inputs.)

At traditional dealerships, a salesperson gets a commission of about a quarter of the markup on a final sale. Because they make money from each extra sale, these salespeople use cold calls (phone calls to strangers) and personal contacts to attract customers. In contrast, Saturn sales staff are paid a salary. As a result, Saturn salespeople have less incentive to pursue customers aggressively than salespeople who earn a commission (see Chapter 20). To offset this effect, some Saturn dealers boost advertising to generate showroom traffic (see Chapter 14).

Strategy. Why did GM change the way it did business? The reason was that its old approach was not working: GM was losing business and profits to other auto manufacturers.

By the very way it designed the Saturn, GM went after a particular type of customer. Only relatively short customers can fit comfortably in a Saturn. Customers who want sporty or other special features were not going to buy a Saturn. Saturn was apparently designed for customers who want to minimize the hassles in their life. A Saturn customer does not have to negotiate over price and is assured a well-built, well-serviced car—with a loaner available if repairs take a long time. (Chapter 13 discusses how firms aim at specific market niches.)

Other dealers and auto manufacturers did not stand still. In picking its strategies, a firm forms beliefs about how its rival will react to its actions. When GM drops its wholesale price, Ford and Honda respond to prevent the loss of sales and profits. When GM started selling Saturns and some of its other cars at fixed prices, Ford began using fixed prices on two of its vehicles. The 2007 Saturn Aura sedan used a new gear box that GM jointly developed with Ford. In 2008, GM struck a deal with the company that makes the Segway two-wheeled personal transporters so that the Saturn Flextreme electric concept car will integrate an onboard storage and charging system for two Segways. (Chapter 13 examines how large firms compete with each other in setting their prices or quantities. Chapter 14 looks at more complex investment strategies that firms use to gain at the expense of their competitors.)

Thus GM made many production, marketing, and strategy decisions based on microeconomic models and predictions. The test that GM uses to determine whether its models and predictions are correct is whether Saturn makes a profit.

SUMMARY

1. **Microeconomics: Allocation of Scarce Resources.** Microeconomics is the study of the allocation of scarce resources. Consumers, firms, and the government must make allocation decisions. The three key trade-offs a society faces are which goods and services to produce, how to produce them, and who gets them. These decisions are interrelated and depend on the prices that consumers and firms face and on government actions. Market prices affect the decisions of individual consumers and firms, and the interaction of the decisions of individual consumers and firms determines market prices. The organization of the market, especially the number of firms in the market and the information consumers and firms have, plays an important role in determining whether the market price is equal to or higher than marginal cost.
2. **Models.** Models based on economic theories are used to predict the future or to answer questions about how some change, such as a tax increase, affects various sectors of the economy. A good theory is simple to use and makes clear, testable predictions that are not refuted by evidence. Most microeconomic models are based on maximizing behavior. Economists use models to construct *positive* hypotheses concerning how a cause leads to an effect. These positive questions can be tested. In contrast, *normative* statements, which are value judgments, cannot be tested.
3. **Uses of Microeconomic Models.** Individuals, governments, and firms use microeconomic models and predictions to make decisions. For example, to maximize its profits, a firm needs to know consumers' decision-making criteria, the trade-offs between various ways of producing and marketing its product, government regulations, and other factors. For large companies, beliefs about how a firm's rivals will react to its actions play a critical role in how it forms its business strategies.

2 Supply and Demand

Talk is cheap because supply exceeds demand.

When asked, "What is the most important thing you know about economics?" many people reply, "Supply equals demand." This statement is a shorthand description of one of the simplest yet most powerful models of economics. The supply-and-demand model describes how consumers and suppliers interact to determine the *quantity* of a good or service sold in a market and the *price* at which it is sold. To use the model, you need to determine three things: buyers' behavior, sellers' behavior, and how they interact. After reading this chapter, you should be adept enough at using the supply-and-demand model to analyze some of the most important policy questions facing your country today, such as those concerning international trade, minimum wages, and price controls on health care.

After reading that grandiose claim, you may ask, "Is that all there is to economics? Can I become an expert economist that fast?" The answer to both these questions is no (of course). In addition, you need to learn the limits of this model and what other models to use when this one does not apply. (You must also learn the economists' secret handshake.)

Even with its limitations, the supply-and-demand model is the most widely used economic model. It provides a good description of how many markets function and works particularly well in markets in which there are many buyers and many sellers, such as in most agriculture and labor markets. Like all good theories, the supply-and-demand model can be tested—and possibly shown to be false. But in markets where it is applicable, it allows us to make accurate predictions easily.

In this chapter, we examine six main topics

1. **Demand.** The quantity of a good or service that consumers demand depends on price and other factors such as consumers' incomes and the price of related goods.
2. **Supply.** The quantity of a good or service that firms supply depends on price and other factors such as the cost of inputs firms use to produce the good or service.
3. **Market Equilibrium.** The interaction between consumers' demand and firms' supply determines the market price and quantity of a good or service that is bought and sold.
4. **Shocking the Equilibrium.** Changes in a factor that affect demand (such as consumers' incomes), supply (such as a rise in the price of inputs), or a new government policy (such as a new tax) alter the market price and quantity of a good.
5. **Effects of Government Interventions.** Government policies may alter the equilibrium and cause the quantity supplied to differ from the quantity demanded.
6. **When to Use the Supply-and-Demand Model.** The supply-and-demand model applies only to competitive markets.

2.1 Demand

Potential consumers decide how much of a good or service to buy on the basis of its price and many other factors, including their own tastes, information, prices of other goods, income, and government actions. Before concentrating on the role of price in determining demand, let's look briefly at some of the other factors.

Consumers' *tastes* determine what they buy. Consumers do not purchase foods they dislike, artwork they hate, or clothes they view as unfashionable or uncomfortable. Advertising may influence people's tastes.

Similarly, *information* (or misinformation) about the uses of a good affects consumers' decisions. A few years ago when many consumers were convinced that oatmeal could lower their cholesterol level, they rushed to grocery stores and bought large quantities of oatmeal. (They even ate some of it until they remembered that they couldn't stand how it tastes.)

The *prices of other goods* also affect consumers' purchase decisions. Before deciding to buy Levi's jeans, you might check the prices of other brands. If the price of a close *substitute*—a product that you view as similar or identical to the one you are considering purchasing—is much lower than the price of Levi's jeans, you may buy that brand instead. Similarly, the price of a *complement*—a good that you like to consume at the same time as the product you are considering buying—may affect your decision. If you eat pie only with ice cream, the higher the price of ice cream, the less likely you are to buy pie.

Income plays a major role in determining what and how much to purchase. People who suddenly inherit great wealth may purchase a Rolls-Royce or other luxury items and would probably no longer buy do-it-yourself repair kits.

Government rules and regulations affect purchase decisions. Sales taxes increase the price that a consumer must spend for a good, and government-imposed limits on the use of a good may affect demand. If a city's government bans the use of skateboards on its streets, skateboard sales fall.

Other factors may also affect the demand for specific goods. Consumers are more likely to have telephones if most of their friends have telephones. The demand for small, dead evergreen trees is substantially higher in December than in other months.

Although many factors influence demand, economists usually concentrate on how price affects the quantity demanded. The relationship between price and quantity demanded plays a critical role in determining the market price and quantity in a supply-and-demand analysis. To determine how a change in price affects the quantity demanded, economists must hold constant other factors such as income and tastes that affect demand.

The Demand Curve

quantity demanded
the amount of a good that consumers are willing to buy at a given price, holding constant the other factors that influence purchases

demand curve
the *quantity demanded* at each possible price, holding constant the other factors that influence purchases

The amount of a good that consumers are *willing* to buy at a given price, holding constant the other factors that influence purchases, is the **quantity demanded**. The quantity demanded of a good or service can exceed the quantity *actually* sold. For example, as a promotion, a local store might sell music CDs for $1 each today only. At that low price, you might want to buy 25 CDs, but because the store ran out of stock, you can buy only 10 CDs. The quantity you demand is 25—it's the amount you *want*, even though the amount you *actually buy* is only 10.

We can show the relationship between price and the quantity demanded graphically. A **demand curve** shows the quantity demanded at each possible price, holding constant the other factors that influence purchases. Figure 2.1 shows the estimated

Figure 2.1 A Demand Curve.

The estimated demand curve, D^1, for processed pork in Canada (Moschini and Meilke, 1992) shows the relationship between the quantity demanded per year and the price per kg. The downward slope of the demand curve shows that, holding other factors that influence demand constant, consumers demand less of a good when its price is high and more when the price is low. A change in price causes a *movement along the demand curve.*

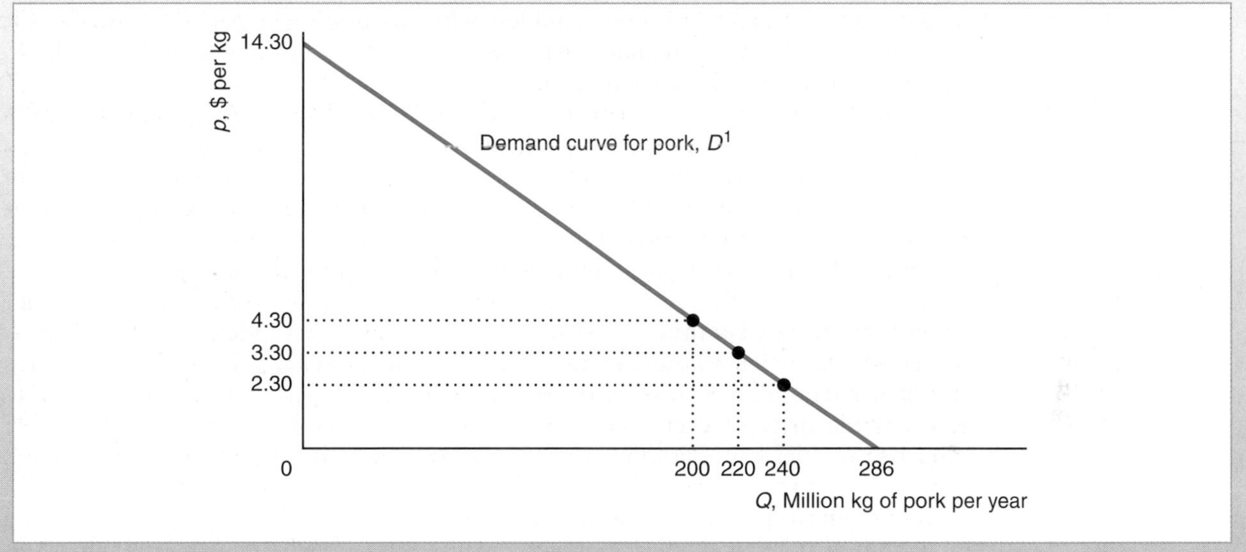

demand curve, D^1, for processed pork in Canada (Moschini and Meilke, 1992). (Although this demand curve is a straight line, demand curves may also be smooth curves or wavy lines.) By convention, the vertical axis of the graph measures the price, p, per unit of the good—here dollars per kilogram (kg). The horizontal axis measures the quantity, Q, of the good, which is usually expressed in some *physical measure* (million kg of dressed cold pork carcass weight) *per time period* (per year).

The demand curve hits the vertical axis at $14.30, indicating that no quantity is demanded when the price is $14.30 (or higher). The demand curve hits the horizontal quantity axis at 286 million kg—the amount of pork that consumers want if the price is zero. To find out what quantity is demanded at a price between these extremes, pick that price on the vertical axis—say, $3.30 per kg—draw a horizontal line across until you hit the demand curve, and then draw a line straight down to the horizontal quantity axis: 220 million kg of pork per year is demanded at that price.

One of the most important things to know about a graph of a demand curve is what is *not* shown. All relevant economic variables that are not explicitly shown on the demand curve graph—tastes, information, prices of other goods (such as beef and chicken), income of consumers, and so on—are held constant. Thus the demand curve shows how quantity varies with price but not how quantity varies with tastes, information, the price of substitute goods, or other variables.[1]

[1]Because prices, quantities, and other factors change simultaneously over time, economists use statistical techniques to hold the effects of factors other than the price of the good constant so that they can determine how price affects the quantity demanded (see Appendix 2A). Moschini and Meilke (1992) used such techniques to estimate the pork demand curve. As with any estimate, their estimates are probably more accurate in the observed range of prices ($1 to $6 per kg) than at very high or very low prices.

Law of Demand
consumers demand more of a good the lower its price, holding constant tastes, the prices of other goods, and other factors that influence consumption

Effect of Prices on the Quantity Demanded. Many economists claim that the most important *empirical* finding in economics is the **Law of Demand**: Consumers demand more of a good the lower its price, holding constant tastes, the prices of other goods, and other factors that influence the amount they consume. According to the Law of Demand, *demand curves slope downward*, as in Figure 2.1.[2]

A downward-sloping demand curve illustrates that consumers demand more of this good when its price is lower and less when its price is higher. What happens to the quantity of pork demanded if the price of pork drops and all other variables remain constant? If the price of pork falls by \$1 from \$3.30 to \$2.30 in Figure 2.1, the quantity consumers want to buy increases from 220 to 240.[3] Similarly, if the price increases from \$3.30 to \$4.30, the quantity consumers demand decreases from 220 to 200. These changes in the quantity demanded in response to changes in price are *movements along the demand curve*. Thus the demand curve is a concise summary of the answers to the question "What happens to the quantity demanded as the price changes, when all other factors are held constant?"

Effects of Other Factors on Demand. If a demand curve measures the effects of price changes when all other factors that affect demand are held constant, how can we use demand curves to show the effects of a change in one of these other factors, such as the price of beef? One solution is to draw the demand curve in a three-dimensional diagram with the price of pork on one axis, the price of beef on a second axis, and the quantity of pork on the third axis. But just thinking about drawing such a diagram probably makes your head hurt.

Economists use a simpler approach to show the effect on demand of a change in a factor that affects demand other than the price of the good. A change in any factor other than price of the good itself causes a *shift of the demand curve* rather than a *movement along the demand curve*.

Many people view beef as a close substitute for pork. Thus at a given price of pork, if the price of beef rises, some people will switch from beef to pork. Figure 2.2 shows how the demand curve for pork shifts to the right from the original demand curve D^1 to a new demand curve D^2 as the price of beef rises from \$4.00 to \$4.60 per kg. (The quantity axis starts at 176 instead of 0 in the figure to emphasize the relevant portion of the demand curve.) On the new demand curve, D^2, more pork is demanded at any given price than on D^1. At a price of pork of \$3.30, the quantity of pork demanded goes from 220 on D^1, before the change in the price of beef, to 232 on D^2, after the price change.

Similarly, a change in information can shift the demand curve. Reinstein and Snyder (2005) find that movie reviews affect the demand for some types of movies. Holding price constant, they determined that if Siskel and Ebert gave a movie a two-thumbs-up review, the opening weekend demand curve shifted to the right by 25% for a drama, but the demand curve did not significantly shift for an action film or a comedy.

---

[2]Theoretically, a demand curve could slope upward (Chapter 5); however, available empirical evidence strongly supports the Law of Demand.

[3]Economists typically do not state the relevant physical and time period measures unless they are particularly useful. They refer to *quantity* rather than something useful such as "metric tons per year" and *price* rather than "cents per pound." I'll generally follow this convention, usually referring to the price as \$3.30 (with the "per kg" understood) and the quantity as 220 (with the "million kg per year" understood).

Figure 2.2 A Shift of the Demand Curve.

The demand curve for processed pork shifts to the right from D^1 to D^2 as the price of beef rises from \$4 to \$4.60. As a result of the increase in beef prices, more pork is demanded at any given price.

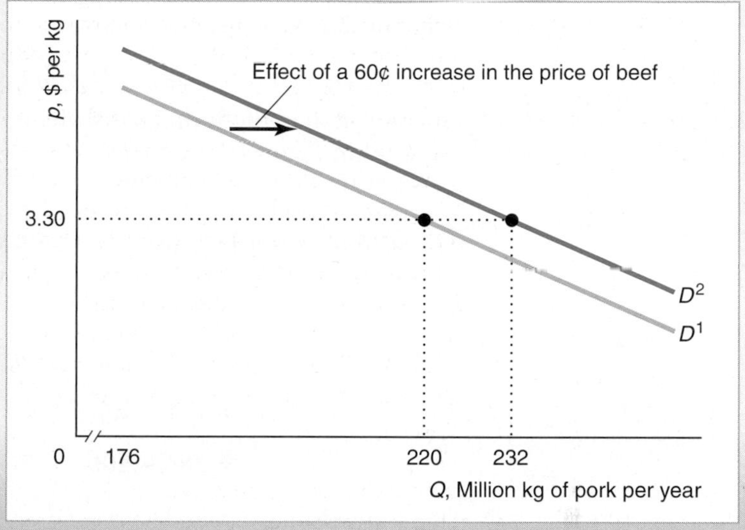

Increased nicotine levels in cigarettes may cause the demand curve for cigarettes of existing smokers to shift to the right. A 2007 Harvard School of Public Health study concluded that cigarette manufacturers raised nicotine levels in cigarettes by 11% over the last decade to make them more addictive. Although some cigarette makers denied such actions, the Massachusetts Department of Public Health issued a study citing the industry's own reports that the amount of nicotine that could be inhaled from cigarettes had risen by an average of 10% from 1998 through 2004. Presumably, if cigarettes have become more addictive, the demand curve of existing smokers would shift to the right.[4]

To properly analyze the effects of a change in some variable on the quantity demanded, we must distinguish between a *movement along a demand curve* and a *shift of a demand curve.* A change in the *price of a good* causes a *movement along a demand curve.* A change in *any other factor besides the price of the good* causes a *shift of the demand curve.*

The Demand Function

In addition to drawing the demand curve, you can write it as a mathematical relationship called the *demand function.* The processed pork demand function is

$$Q = D(p, p_b, p_c, Y), \tag{2.1}$$

where Q is the quantity of pork demanded, p is the price of pork, p_b is the price of beef, p_c is the price of chicken, and Y is the income of consumers. This expression says that the amount of pork demanded varies with the price of pork, the price of substitutes (beef and chicken), and the income of consumers. Any other factors that are not explicitly listed in the demand function are assumed to be irrelevant (the price of llamas in Peru) or held constant (the price of fish).

[4]Gardiner Harris, "Study Showing Boosted Nicotine Levels Spurs Calls for Controls," *San Francisco Chronicle*, January 19, 2007, A-4.

By writing the demand function in this general way, we are not explaining exactly how the quantity demanded varies as p, p_b, p_c, or Y changes. Instead, we can rewrite Equation 2.1 as a specific function:

$$Q = 171 - 20p + 20p_b + 3p_c + 2Y. \quad (2.2)$$

See Problems 22 and 23.

Equation 2.2 is the estimated demand function that corresponds to the demand curve D^1 in Figures 2.1 and 2.2.[5]

When we drew the demand curve D^1 in Figures 2.1 and 2.2, we held p_b, p_c, and Y at their typical values during the period studied: $p_b = 4$ (dollars per kg), $p_c = 3\frac{1}{3}$ (dollars per kg), and $Y = 12.5$ (thousand dollars). If we substitute these values for p_b, p_c, and Y in Equation 2.2, we can rewrite the quantity demanded as a function of only the price of pork:

$$\begin{aligned} Q &= 171 - 20p + 20p_b + 3p_c + 2Y \\ &= 171 - 20p + (20 \times 4) + \left(3 \times 3\tfrac{1}{3}\right) + (2 \times 12.5) \\ &= 286 - 20p \end{aligned} \quad (2.3)$$

The straight-line demand curve D^1 in Figures 2.1 and 2.2—where we hold the price of beef, the price of chicken, and disposable income constant at these typical values—is described by the *linear* demand function in Equation 2.3.

The constant term, 286, in Equation 2.3 is the quantity demanded if the price is zero. Setting the price equal to zero in Equation 2.3, we find that the quantity demanded is $Q = 286 - (20 \times 0) = 286$. Figure 2.1 shows that $Q = 286$ where D^1 hits the quantity axis at a price of zero.

This equation also shows us how quantity demanded changes with a change in price: a movement *along* the demand curve. If the price increases from p_1 to p_2, the change in price, Δp, equals $p_2 - p_1$. (The Δ symbol, the Greek letter delta, means "change in" the following variable, so Δp means "change in price.") As Figure 2.1 illustrates, if the price of pork increases by \$1 from $p_1 = \$3.30$ to $p_2 = \$4.30$, $\Delta p = \$1$ and $\Delta Q = Q_2 - Q_1 = 200 - 220 = -20$ million kg per year.

More generally, the quantity demanded at p_1 is $Q_1 = D(p_1)$, and the quantity demanded at p_2 is $Q_2 = D(p_2)$. The change in the quantity demanded, $\Delta Q = Q_2 - Q_1$, in response to the price change (using Equation 2.3) is

$$\begin{aligned} \Delta Q &= Q_2 - Q_1 \\ &= D(p_2) - D(p_1) \\ &= (286 - 20p_2) - (286 - 20p_1) \\ &= -20(p_2 - p_1) \\ &= -20\Delta p. \end{aligned}$$

Thus the change in the quantity demanded, ΔQ, is -20 times the change in the price, Δp. If $\Delta p = \$1$, $\Delta Q = -20\Delta p = -20$.

The slope of a demand curve is $\Delta p/\Delta Q$, the "rise" (Δp, the change along the vertical axis) divided by the "run" (ΔQ, the change along the horizontal axis). The slope of demand curve D^1 in Figures 2.1 and 2.2 is

$$\text{Slope} = \frac{\text{rise}}{\text{run}} = \frac{\Delta p}{\Delta Q} = \frac{\$1 \text{ per kg}}{-20 \text{ million kg per year}} = -\$0.05 \text{ per million kg per year.}$$

[5]The numbers are rounded slightly from the estimates to simplify the calculation. For example, the estimate of the coefficient on the price of beef is 19.5, not 20, as the equation shows.

The negative sign of this slope is consistent with the Law of Demand. The slope says that the price rises by \$1 per kg as the quantity demanded falls by 20 million kg per year. Turning that statement around: The quantity demanded falls by 20 million kg per year as the price rises by \$1 per kg.

Thus we can use the demand curve to answer questions about how a change in price affects the quantity demanded and how a change in the quantity demanded affects price. We can also answer these questions using demand functions.

Solved Problem 2.1

How much would the price have to fall for consumers to be willing to buy 1 million more kg of pork per year?

Answer

1. *Express the price that consumers are willing to pay as a function of quantity.* We use algebra to rewrite the demand function as an *inverse demand function,* where price depends on the quantity demanded. Subtracting Q from both sides of Equation 2.3 and adding $20p$ to both sides, we find that $20p = 286 - Q$. Dividing both sides of the equation by 20, we obtain the inverse demand function:

$$p = 14.30 - 0.05Q \qquad (2.4)$$

2. *Use the inverse demand curve to determine how much the price must change for consumers to buy 1 million more kg of pork per year.* We take the difference between the inverse demand function, Equation 2.4, at the new quantity, $Q_2 + 1$, and at the original quantity, Q_1, to determine how the price must change:

$$\begin{aligned}\Delta p &= p_2 - p_1 \\ &= (14.30 - 0.05Q_2) - (14.30 - 0.05Q_1) \\ &= -0.05(Q_2 - Q_1) \\ &= -0.05\Delta Q.\end{aligned}$$

The change in quantity is $\Delta Q = Q_2 - Q_1 = (Q_1 + 1) - Q_1 = 1$, so the change in price is $\Delta p = -0.05$. That is, for consumers to demand 1 million more kg of pork per year, the price must fall by 5¢ a kg, which is a *movement along the demand curve.*

Summing Demand Curves

If we know the demand curve for each of two consumers, how do we determine the total demand for the two consumers combined? The total quantity demanded *at a given price* is the sum of the quantity each consumer demands at that price.

We can use the demand functions to determine the total demand of several consumers. Suppose that the demand function for Consumer 1 is

$$Q_1 = D^1(p)$$

and the demand function for Consumer 2 is

$$Q_2 = D^2(p).$$

At price p, Consumer 1 demands Q_1 units, Consumer 2 demands Q_2 units, and the total demand of both consumers is the sum of the quantities each demands separately:

See Problems 24 and 25.

$$Q = Q_1 + Q_2 = D^1(p) + D^2(p).$$

We can generalize this approach to look at the total demand for three or more consumers.

It makes sense to add the quantities demanded only when all consumers face the same price. Adding the quantity Consumer 1 demands at one price to the quantity Consumer 2 demands at another price would be like adding apples and oranges.

APPLICATION

Aggregating the Demand for Broadband Service

We illustrate how to combine individual demand curves to get a total demand curve graphically using estimated demand curves of broadband (high-speed) Internet service (Duffy-Deno, 2003). The figure shows the demand curve for small firms (1–19 employees), the demand curve for larger firms, and the total demand curve for all firms, which is the horizontal sum of the other two demand curves.

At the current average rate of 40¢ per kilobyte per second (Kbps), the quantity demanded by small firms is $Q_s = 10$ (in millions of Kbps) and the quantity demanded by larger firms is $Q_l = 11.5$. Thus, the total quantity demanded at that price is $Q = Q_s + Q_l = 10 + 11.5 = 21.5$.

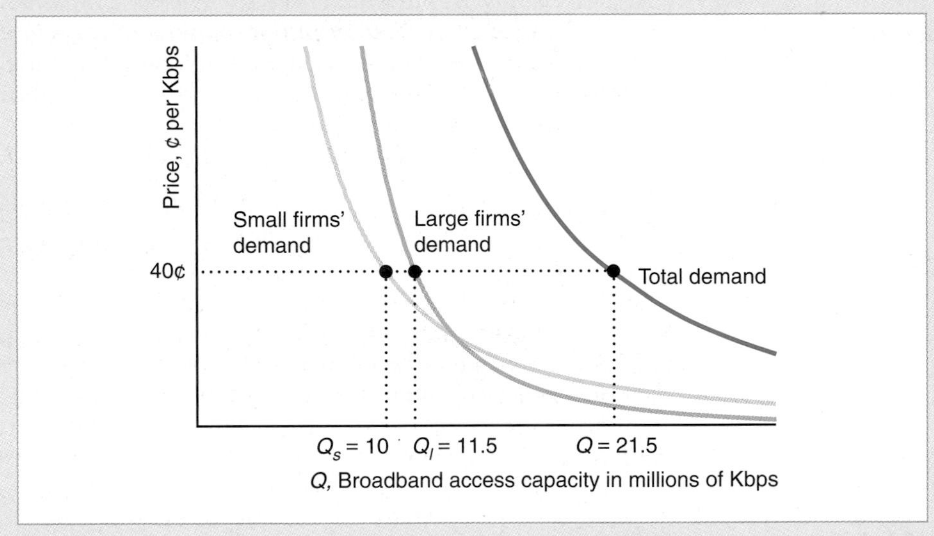

See Problem 26.

2.2 Supply

Knowing how much consumers want is not enough, by itself, to tell us what price and quantity are observed in a market. To determine the market price and quantity, we also need to know how much firms want to supply at any given price.

Firms determine how much of a good to supply on the basis of the price of that good and other factors, including the costs of production and government rules and regulations. Usually, we expect firms to supply more at a higher price. Before concentrating on the role of price in determining supply, we'll briefly describe the role of some of the other factors.

Costs of production affect how much firms want to sell of a good. As a firm's cost falls, it is willing to supply more, all else the same. If the firm's cost exceeds what it can earn from selling the good, the firm sells nothing. Thus, factors that affect costs, also affect supply. A technological advance that allows a firm to produce a good at lower cost leads the firm to supply more of that good, all else the same.

Government rules and regulations affect how much firms want to sell or are allowed to sell. Taxes and many government regulations—such as those covering pollution, sanitation, and health insurance—alter the costs of production. Other regulations affect when and how the product can be sold. In Germany, retailers may not sell most goods and services on Sundays or during evening hours. In the United States, the sale of cigarettes and liquor to children is prohibited. New York, San Francisco, and many other cities restrict the number of taxicabs.

The Supply Curve

quantity supplied
the amount of a good that firms *want* to sell at a given price, holding constant other factors that influence firms' supply decisions, such as costs and government actions

supply curve
the *quantity supplied* at each possible price, holding constant the other factors that influence firms' supply decisions

The **quantity supplied** is the amount of a good that firms *want* to sell at a given price, holding constant other factors that influence firms' supply decisions, such as costs and government actions. We can show the relationship between price and the quantity supplied graphically. A **supply curve** shows the quantity supplied at each possible price, holding constant the other factors that influence firms' supply decisions. Figure 2.3 shows the estimated supply curve, S^1, for processed pork (Moschini and Meilke, 1992). As with the demand curve, the price on the vertical axis is measured in dollars per physical unit (dollars per kg), and the quantity on the horizontal axis is measured in physical units per time period (millions of kg per year). Because we hold fixed other variables that may affect the supply, such as costs and government rules, the supply curve concisely answers the question "What happens to the quantity supplied as the price changes, holding all other factors constant?"

Effect of Price on Supply. We illustrate how price affects the quantity supplied using the supply curve for processed pork in Figure 2.3. The supply curve for pork is upward sloping. As the price of pork increases, firms supply more. If the price is \$3.30, the market supplies a quantity of 220 (million kg per year). If the price rises to \$5.30, the quantity supplied rises to 300. An increase in the price of pork causes a *movement along the supply curve*, resulting in more pork being supplied.

Although the Law of Demand requires that the demand curve slope downward, there is *no* "Law of Supply" that requires the market supply curve to have a particular slope. The market supply curve can be upward sloping, vertical, horizontal, or downward sloping. Many supply curves slope upward, such as the one for pork. Along such supply curves, the higher the price, the more firms are willing to sell, holding costs and government regulations fixed.

Effects of Other Variables on Supply. A change in a variable other than the price of pork causes the entire *supply curve to shift*. Suppose the price, p_h, of hogs—the main factor used to produce processed pork—increases from \$1.50 per kg to \$1.75 per kg. Because it is now more expensive to produce pork, the supply curve shifts to the left, from S^1 to S^2 in Figure 2.4.[6] Firms want to supply less pork at any given price than before the price of hogs rose. At a price of processed pork of \$3.30, the

[6]Alternatively, we may say that the supply curve shifts up because firms' costs of production have increased, so they will supply a given quantity only at a higher price.

Figure 2.3 A Supply Curve.

The estimated supply curve, S^1, for processed pork in Canada (Moschini and Meilke, 1992) shows the relationship between the quantity supplied per year and the price per kg, holding cost and other factors that influence supply constant. The upward slope of this supply curve indicates that firms supply more of this good when its price is high and less when the price is low. An increase in the price of pork causes a movement *along the supply curve*, resulting in a larger quantity of pork supplied.

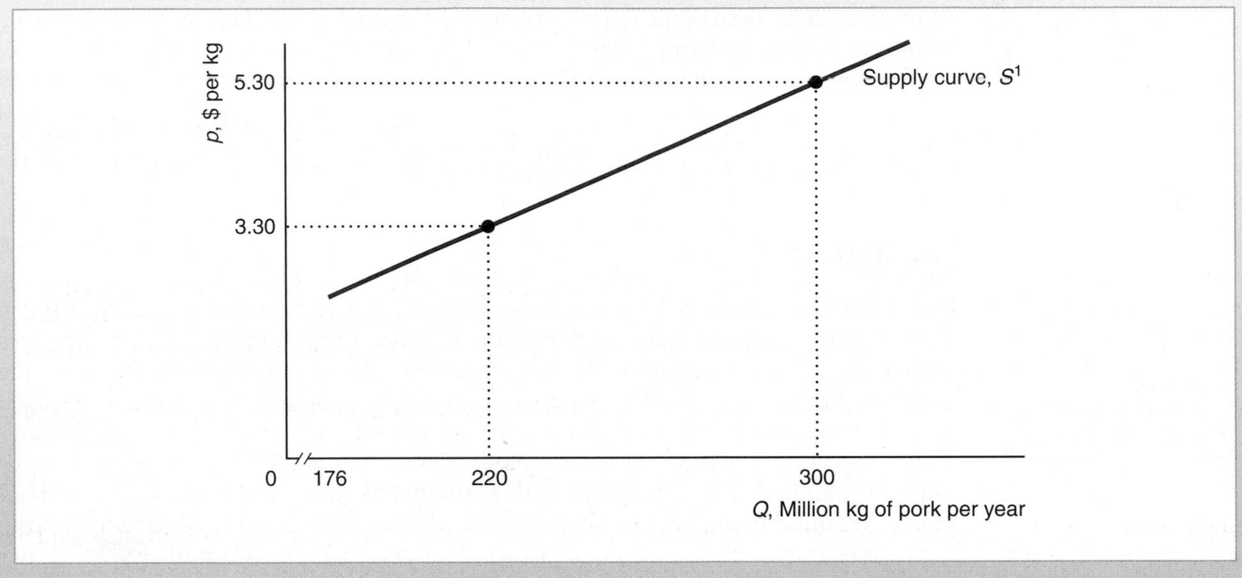

Figure 2.4 A Shift of a Supply Curve.

An increase in the price of hogs from \$1.50 to \$1.75 per kg causes the supply curve for processed pork to shift from S^1 to S^2. At the price of processed pork of \$3.30, the quantity supplied falls from 220 on S^1 to 205 on S^2.

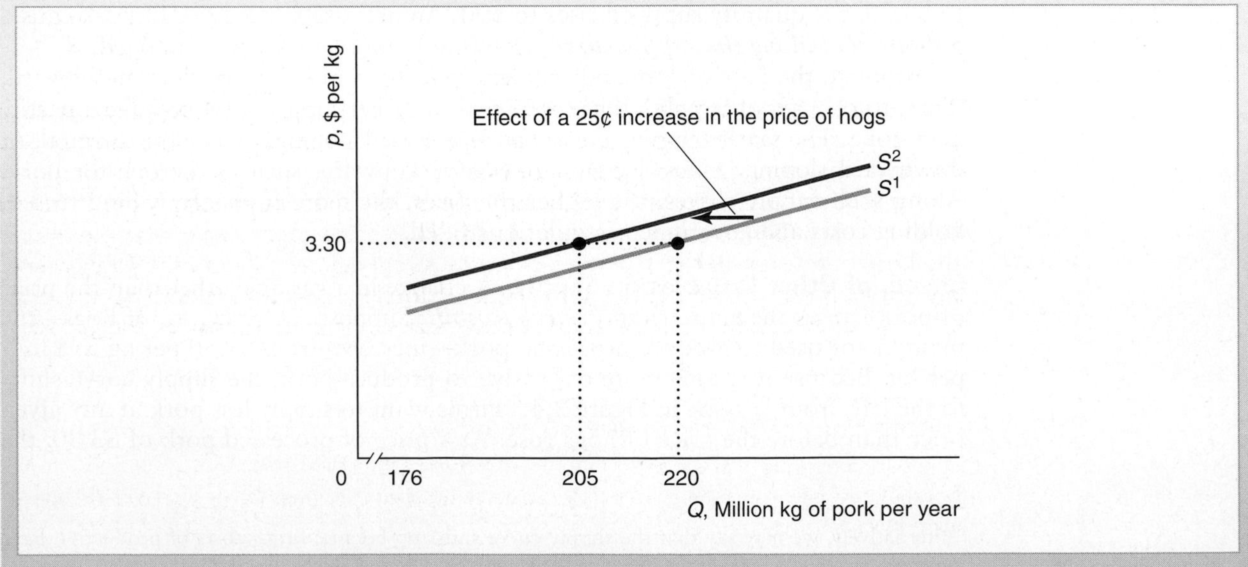

quantity supplied falls from 220 on S^1, before the increase in the hog price, to 205 on S^2, after the increase in the hog price.

Again, it is important to distinguish between a *movement along a supply curve* and a *shift of the supply curve*. When the price of pork changes, the change in the quantity supplied reflects a *movement along the supply curve*. When costs, government rules, or other variables that affect supply change, the entire *supply curve shifts*.

The Supply Function

We can write the relationship between the quantity supplied and price and other factors as a mathematical relationship called the *supply function*. Written generally, the processed pork supply function is

$$Q = S(p, p_h), \tag{2.5}$$

where Q is the quantity of processed pork supplied, p is the price of processed pork, and p_h is the price of a hog. The supply function, Equation 2.5, may also be a function of other factors such as wages, but by leaving them out, we are implicitly holding them constant.

Based on Moschini and Meilke (1992), the linear pork supply function in Canada is

$$Q = 178 + 40p - 60p_h, \tag{2.6}$$

where quantity is in millions of kg per year and the prices are in Canadian dollars per kg. If we hold the price of hogs fixed at its typical value of \$1.50 per kg, we can rewrite the supply function in Equation 2.6 as[7]

$$Q = 88 + 40p. \tag{2.7}$$

What happens to the quantity supplied if the price of processed pork increases by $\Delta p = p_2 - p_1$? Using the same approach as before, we learn from Equation 2.7 that $\Delta Q = 40\Delta p$.[8] A \$1 increase in price ($\Delta p = 1$) causes the quantity supplied to increase by $\Delta Q = 40$ million kg per year. This change in the quantity of pork supplied as p increases is a *movement along the supply curve*.

Summing Supply Curves

The total supply curve shows the total quantity produced by all suppliers at each possible price. For example, the total supply of rice in Japan is the sum of the domestic and foreign supply curves of rice.

Suppose that the domestic supply curve (panel a) and foreign supply curve (panel b) of rice in Japan are as Figure 2.5 shows. The total supply curve, S in panel c, is the horizontal sum of the Japanese *domestic* supply curve, S^d, and the *foreign* supply curve, S^f. In the figure, the Japanese and foreign supplies are zero at any price equal to or less than $\underline{p}$, so the total supply is zero. At prices above $\underline{p}$, the Japanese

---

[7]Substituting $p_h = \$1.50$ into Equation 2.6, we find that

$$Q = 178 + 40p - 60p_h = 178 + 40p - (60 \times 1.50) = 88 + 40p.$$

[8]As the price increases from p_1 to p_2, the quantity supplied goes from Q_1 to Q_2, so the change in quantity supplied is

$$\Delta Q = Q_2 - Q_1 = (88 + 40p_2) - (88 + 40p_1) = 40(p_2 - p_1) = 40\Delta p.$$

Figure 2.5 Total Supply: The Sum of Domestic and Foreign Supply.

If foreigners may sell their rice in Japan, the total Japanese supply of rice, S, is the horizontal sum of the domestic Japanese supply, S^d, and the imported foreign supply, S^f. With a ban on foreign imports, the foreign supply curve, $\bar{S}^f$ is zero at every price, so the total supply curve, $\bar{S}$ is the same as the domestic supply curve, S^d.

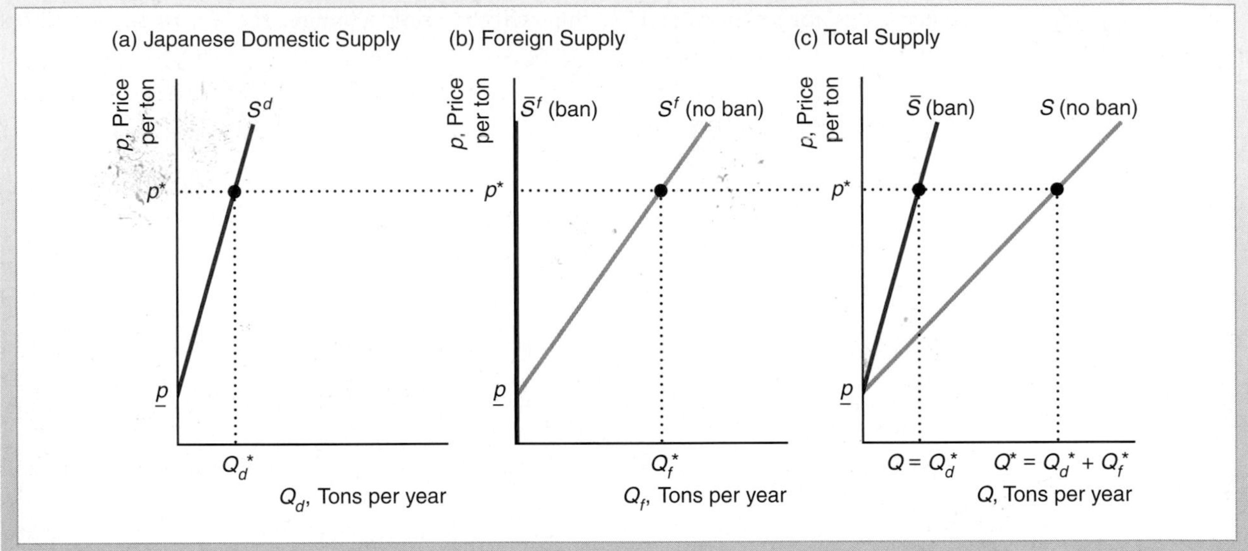

and foreign supplies are positive, so the total supply is positive. For example, when price is p^*, the quantity supplied by Japanese firms is Q_d^* (panel a), the quantity supplied by foreign firms is Q_f^* (panel b), and the total quantity supplied is $Q^* = Q_d^* + Q_f^*$ (panel c). Because the total supply curve is the horizontal sum of the domestic and foreign supply curves, the total supply curve is flatter than either of the other two supply curves.

Effects of Government Import Policies on Supply Curves

We can use this approach for deriving the total supply curve to analyze the effect of government policies on the total supply curve. Traditionally, the Japanese government banned the importation of foreign rice. We want to determine how much less is supplied at any given price to the Japanese market because of this ban.

Without a ban, the foreign supply curve is S^f in panel b of Figure 2.5. A ban on imports eliminates the foreign supply, so the foreign supply curve after the ban is imposed, $\bar{S}^f$, is a vertical line at $Q_f = 0$. The import ban has no effect on the domestic supply curve, S^d, so the supply curve is the same as in panel a.

Because the foreign supply with a ban, $\bar{S}^f$, is zero at every price, the total supply with a ban, $\bar{S}$, in panel c is the same as the Japanese domestic supply, S^d, at any given price. The total supply curve under the ban lies to the left of the total supply curve without a ban, S. Thus the effect of the import ban is to rotate the total supply curve toward the vertical axis.

quota
the limit that a government sets on the quantity of a foreign-produced good that may be imported

The limit that a government sets on the quantity of a foreign-produced good that may be imported is called a **quota**. By absolutely banning the importation of rice, the Japanese government sets a quota of zero on rice imports. Sometimes governments set positive quotas, $\bar{Q} > 0$. The foreign firms may supply as much as they want, Q_f, as long as they supply no more than the quota: $Q_f \le \bar{Q}$.

We investigate the effect of such a quota in Solved Problem 2.2. In most of the solved problems in this book, you are asked to determine how a *change* in a variable or policy *affects* one or more variables. In this problem, the policy *changes* from no quota to a quota, which *affects* the total supply curve.

Solved Problem 2.2

How does a quota set by the United States on foreign steel imports of $\bar{Q}$ affect the total American supply curve for steel given the domestic supply, S^d in panel a of the graph, and foreign supply, S^f in panel b?

Answer

1. *Determine the American supply curve without the quota.* The *no-quota* total supply curve, S in panel c, is the horizontal sum of the U.S. domestic supply curve, S^d, and the no-quota foreign supply curve, S^f.

2. *Show the effect of the quota on foreign supply.* At prices less than $\bar{p}$ foreign suppliers want to supply quantities less than the quota, $\bar{Q}$. As a result, the foreign supply curve under the quota, $\bar{S}^f$, is the same as the no-quota foreign supply curve, S^f, for prices less than $\bar{p}$. At prices above $\bar{p}$, foreign suppliers want to supply more but are limited to $\bar{Q}$. Thus the foreign supply curve with a quota, $\bar{S}^f$, is vertical at $\bar{Q}$ for prices above $\bar{p}$.

3. *Determine the American total supply curve with the quota.* The total supply curve with the quota, $\bar{S}$ is the horizontal sum of S^d and $\bar{S}^f$. At any price above $\bar{p}$, the total supply equals the quota plus the domestic supply. For example at p^*, the domestic supply is Q_d^* and the foreign supply is $\bar{Q}_f$ so the total supply is $Q_d^* + \bar{Q}_f$. Above $\bar{p}$, $\bar{S}$, is the domestic supply curve shifted $\bar{Q}$ units to the right. As a result, the portion of $\bar{S}$ above $\bar{p}$ has the same slope as S^d.

4. *Compare the American total supply curves with and without the quota.* At prices less than or equal to $\bar{p}$, the same quantity is supplied with and without the quota, so $\bar{S}$ is the same as S. At prices above $\bar{p}$, less is supplied with the quota than without one, so $\bar{S}$ is steeper than S, indicating that a given increase in price raises the quantity supplied by less with a quota than without one.

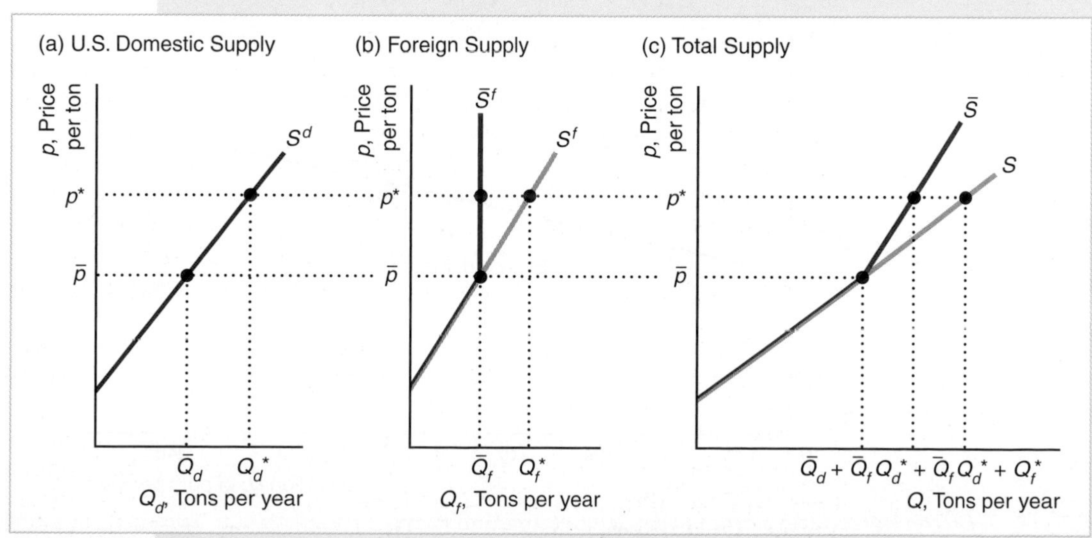

2.3 Market Equilibrium

The supply and demand curves determine the price and quantity at which goods and services are bought and sold. The demand curve shows the quantities consumers want to buy at various prices, and the supply curve shows the quantities firms want to sell at various prices. Unless the price is set so that consumers want to buy exactly the same amount that suppliers want to sell, either some buyers cannot buy as much as they want or some sellers cannot sell as much as they want.

equilibrium
a situation in which no one wants to change his or her behavior

When all traders are able to buy or sell as much as they want, we say that the market is in **equilibrium**: a situation in which no participant wants to change its behavior. A price at which consumers can buy as much as they want and sellers can sell as much as they want is called an *equilibrium price*. The quantity that is bought and sold at the equilibrium price is called the *equilibrium quantity*.

Using a Graph to Determine the Equilibrium

This little piggy went to market. . .

To illustrate how supply and demand curves determine the equilibrium price and quantity, we use our old friend, the processed pork example. Figure 2.6 shows the supply, *S*, and demand, *D*, curves for pork. The supply and demand curves intersect at point *e*, the market equilibrium, where the equilibrium price is \$3.30 and the equilibrium quantity is 220 million kg per year, which is the quantity firms want to sell *and* the quantity consumers want to buy.

Figure 2.6 Market Equilibrium.

The intersection of the supply curve, *S*, and the demand curve, *D*, for processed pork determines the market equilibrium point, *e*, where p = \$3.30 per kg and Q = 220 million kg per year. At the lower price of p = \$2.65, the quantity supplied is only 194, whereas the quantity demanded is 233, so there is excess demand of 39. At p = \$3.95, a price higher than the equilibrium price, there is excess supply of 39 because the quantity demanded, 207, is less than the quantity supplied, 246. When there is excess demand or supply, market forces drive the price back to the equilibrium price of \$3.30.

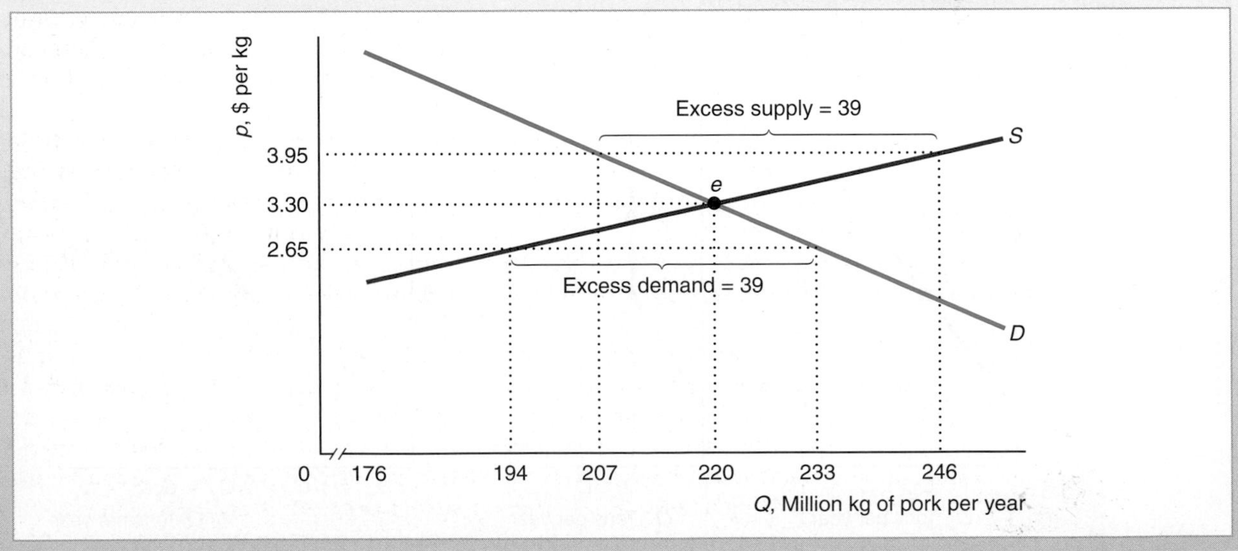

Using Math to Determine the Equilibrium

We can determine the processed pork market equilibrium mathematically, using the supply and demand functions. We use these two functions to solve for the equilibrium price at which the quantity demanded equals the quantity supplied (the equilibrium quantity).

The demand function, Equation 2.3, shows the relationship between the quantity demanded, Q_d, and the price:

$$Q_d = 286 - 20p.$$

The supply function, Equation 2.7, tells us the relationship between the quantity supplied, Q_s, and the price:

$$Q_s = 88 + 40p.$$

We want to find the p at which $Q_d = Q_s = Q$, the equilibrium quantity. Because the left sides of the two equations are equal in equilibrium, $Q_s = Q_d$, the right sides of the two equations must be equal:

$$286 - 20p = 88 + 40p.$$

Adding $20p$ to both sides of this expression and subtracting 88 from both sides, we find that $198 = 60p$. Dividing both sides of this last expression by 60, we learn that the equilibrium price is $p = \$3.30$. We can determine the equilibrium quantity by substituting this p into either the supply or the demand equation:

$$\begin{aligned} Q_d &= Q_s \\ 286 - (20 \times 3.30) &= 88 + (40 \times 3.30) \\ 220 &= 220. \end{aligned}$$

See Problems 27–33.

Thus the equilibrium quantity is 220.

Forces That Drive the Market to Equilibrium

A market equilibrium is not just an abstract concept or a theoretical possibility. We can observe markets in equilibrium. Indirect evidence that a market is in equilibrium is that you can buy as much as you want of the good at the market price. You can almost always buy as much as you want of such common goods as milk and ballpoint pens.

Amazingly, a market equilibrium occurs without any explicit coordination between consumers and firms. In a competitive market such as that for agricultural goods, millions of consumers and thousands of firms make their buying and selling decisions independently. Yet each firm can sell as much as it wants; each consumer can buy as much as he or she wants. It is as though an unseen market force, like an *invisible hand*, directs people to coordinate their activities to achieve a market equilibrium.

What really causes the market to move to an equilibrium? If the price is not at the equilibrium level, consumers or firms have an incentive to change their behavior in a way that will drive the price to the equilibrium level, as we now illustrate.

If the price were initially lower than the equilibrium price, consumers would want to buy more than suppliers want to sell. If the price of pork is \$2.65 in Figure 2.6, firms are willing to supply 194 million kg per year but consumers demand 233 million kg. At this price, the market is in *disequilibrium*, meaning that the quantity

excess demand
the amount by which the *quantity demanded* exceeds the *quantity supplied* at a specified price

demanded is not equal to the quantity supplied. There is **excess demand**—the amount by which the quantity demanded exceeds the quantity supplied at a specified price—of 39 (= 233 – 194) million kg per year at a price of $2.65.

Some consumers are lucky enough to buy the pork at $2.65. Other consumers cannot find anyone who is willing to sell them pork at that price. What can they do? Some frustrated consumers may offer to pay suppliers more than $2.65. Alternatively, suppliers, noticing these disappointed consumers, may raise their prices. Such actions by consumers and producers cause the market price to rise. As the price rises, the quantity that firms want to supply increases and the quantity that consumers want to buy decreases. This upward pressure on price continues until it reaches the equilibrium price, $3.30, where there is no excess demand.

excess supply
the amount by which the *quantity supplied* is greater than the *quantity demanded* at a specified price

If, instead, the price is initially above the equilibrium level, suppliers want to sell more than consumers want to buy. For example, at a price of pork of $3.95, suppliers want to sell 246 million kg per year but consumers want to buy only 207 million, as the figure shows. At $3.95, the market is in disequilibrium. There is an **excess supply**—the amount by which the quantity supplied is greater than the quantity demanded at a specified price—of 39 (= 246 – 207) at a price of $3.95. Not all firms can sell as much as they want. Rather than incur storage costs (and possibly have their unsold pork spoil), firms lower the price to attract additional customers. As long as the price remains above the equilibrium price, some firms have unsold pork and want to lower the price further. The price falls until it reaches the equilibrium level, $3.30, where there is no excess supply and hence no more pressure to lower the price further.

See Question 1.

In summary, at any price other than the equilibrium price, either consumers or suppliers are unable to trade as much as they want. These disappointed people act to change the price, driving the price to the equilibrium level. The equilibrium price is called the *market clearing price* because it removes from the market all frustrated buyers and sellers: There is no excess demand or excess supply at the equilibrium price.

2.4 Shocking the Equilibrium

Once an equilibrium is achieved, it can persist indefinitely because no one applies pressure to change the price. *The equilibrium changes only if a shock occurs that shifts the demand curve or the supply curve. These curves shift if one of the variables we were holding constant changes.* If tastes, income, government policies, or costs of production change, the demand curve or the supply curve or both shift, and the equilibrium changes.

Effects of a Shift in the Demand Curve

Suppose that the price of beef increases by 60¢, and so consumers substitute pork for beef. As a result, the demand curve for pork shifts outward from D^1 to D^2 in panel a of Figure 2.7. At any given price, consumers want more pork than they did before the price of beef rose. In particular, at the original equilibrium price of pork, $3.30, consumers now want to buy 232 million kg of pork per year. At that price, however, suppliers still want to sell only 220. As a result, there is excess demand of 12. Market pressures drive the price up until it reaches a new equilibrium at $3.50. At that price, firms want to sell 228 and consumers want to buy 228, the new equilibrium quantity. Thus the pork equilibrium goes from e_1 to e_2 as a result of the

Figure 2.7 Equilibrium Effects of a Shift of a Demand or Supply Curve.

(a) An increase in the price of beef by 60¢ causes the demand curve for processed pork to shift outward from D^1 to D^2. At the original equilibrium, e_1, price, \$3.30, there is excess demand of 12. Market pressures drive the price up until it reaches \$3.50 at the new equilibrium, e_2. (b) An increase in the price of hogs by 25¢ causes the supply curve for processed pork to shift to the left from S^1 to S^2, driving the market equilibrium from e_1 to e_2.

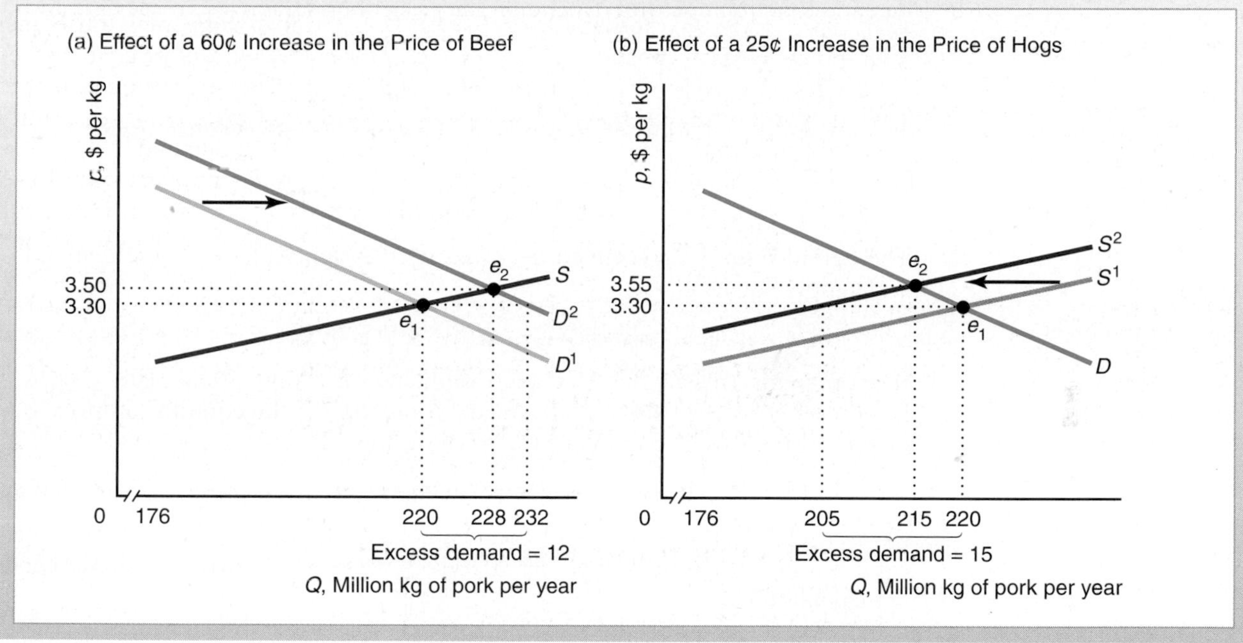

increase in the price of beef. Both the equilibrium price and the equilibrium quantity of pork rise as a result of the outward shift of the pork demand curve. Here the increase in the price of beef causes a *shift of the demand curve*, causing a *movement along the supply curve*.

See Question 2.

Effects of a Shift in the Supply Curve

Now suppose that the price of beef stays constant at its original level but the price of hogs increases by 25¢. It is now more expensive to produce pork because the price of a major input, hogs, has increased. As a result, the supply curve for pork shifts to the left from S^1 to S^2 in panel b of Figure 2.7. At any given price, firms want to supply less pork than they did before the price of hogs increased. At the original equilibrium price of pork of \$3.30, consumers still want 220, but suppliers are now willing to supply only 205, so there is excess demand of 15. Market pressure forces the price of pork up until it reaches a new equilibrium at e_2, where the equilibrium price is \$3.55 and the equilibrium quantity is 215. The increase in the price of hogs causes the equilibrium price to rise but the equilibrium quantity to fall. Here a *shift of the supply curve* results in a *movement along the demand curve*.

In summary, a change in an underlying factor, such as the price of a substitute or the price of an input, shifts the demand or supply curve. As a result of this shift in the demand or supply curve, the equilibrium changes. To describe the effect of this change in the underlying factor on the market, we compare the original equilibrium price and quantity to the new equilibrium values.

See Questions 3–5 and Problem 34.

Solved Problem 2.3

Mathematically, how does the equilibrium price of pork vary as the price of hogs changes if the variables that affect demand are held constant at their typical values?

Answer

1. *Solve for the equilibrium price of pork in terms of the price of hogs.* The demand function does not depend on the price of hogs, so we can use Equation 2.3 from before,

$$Q_d = 286 - 20p.$$

To see how the equilibrium depends on the price of hogs, we use supply function Equation 2.6:

$$Q_s = 178 + 40p - 60p_h.$$

The equilibrium is determined by equating the right sides of these demand-and-supply equations:

$$286 - 20p = 178 + 40p - 60p_h.$$

Rearranging terms in this last expression, we find that $60p = 108 + 60p_h$. Dividing both sides by 60, we have an expression for the equilibrium price of processed pork as a function of the price of hogs:

$$p = 1.8 + p_h. \tag{2.8}$$

(As a check, when p_h equals its typical value, \$1.50, Equation 2.8 says that the equilibrium price of pork is p = \$3.30, which we know is correct from our earlier calculations.)

We find the equilibrium quantity as a function of the price of hogs by substituting this expression for the equilibrium price, Equation 2.8, into the demand equation (though we could use the supply function instead):

$$Q = 286 - 20p = 286 - 20(1.8 + p_h) = 250 - 20p_h.$$

(Again, as a check, if p_h equals its typical value of \$1.50, $Q = 220$, which we know is the original equilibrium quantity.)

2. *Show how the equilibrium price of pork varies with the price of hogs.* We know from Equation 2.8 that $\Delta p = \Delta p_h$. Any increase in the price of hogs causes an equal increase in the price of processed pork. As panel b of Figure 2.7 illustrates, if the price of hogs increases by Δp_h = \$0.25 (from \$1.50 to \$1.75), the price of pork, p, increases by $\Delta p = \Delta p_h$ = \$0.25 (from \$3.30 to \$3.55).

Effects of a Shift in the Supply and Demand Curves

Some events cause both the supply curve and the demand curve to shift. If both shift, then the qualitative effect on the equilibrium price and quantity may be difficult to predict, even if we know the direction in which each curve shifts. Changes in the equilibrium price and quantity depend on exactly how the curves shift—see the following application and solved problem and the related questions at the end of the chapter.

See Questions 6–8.

APPLICATION

Mad Cow: Shifting Supply and Demand Curves

Government announcements that the fatal disease known as mad cow (bovine spongiform encephalopathy, or BSE) has been found in a country's cattle affect both supply and demand curves. Humans who consume beef products made from diseased animal parts can develop the new variant Creutzfeldt-Jakob disease, a deadly affliction that slowly eats holes in sufferers' brains. Mad cow disease can take years to develop in cattle, and symptoms in its human version may not appear for decades. Consequently, identifying the presence of the disease has been difficult.

In 1986, the British government disclosed a case of mad cow disease, but initially asserted that humans were not at risk from eating infected beef. Since then, 180,000 cases of mad cow have been reported in the United Kingdom. Not until 1996 did the British government announce that people were falling victim to a degenerative new brain disease linked to BSE. Following this announcement and similar reports in France, Italy, and Germany, many British and other European consumers stopped buying beef, causing the beef demand curves in European countries to shift to the left. Over time, many cattle were removed from the food chain as European beef producers reduced their herds, so that the supply curves also shifted to the left. Consequently, beef consumption plummeted in Europe in the 1990s.

Japan announced that it had found its first case of mad cow in 2001. Two-thirds of beef sold in Japan in 2001 was imported: 49% of it from Australia and 46% from the United States. Immediately following the domestic mad cow discovery, beef consumption in Japan fell by 60% (including a 30% drop in imports, which were not implicated). To protect and reassure consumers, Japan began conducting BSE tests on all 1.2 million domestic cattle that are slaughtered. By mid-2002, Japan's beef consumption recovered to within 10% to 15% of its pre-announcement levels.

Canada announced its first indigenous case in May 2003 (Canada reported a case in 1993 for a cow imported from Europe). The first U.S. case, in a cow imported from Canada, was reported in December 2003 (and the second in 2005). These announcements affected supply curves and demand curves throughout the world. As soon as the United States revealed the discovery of the single mad cow, more than 40 countries slapped an embargo on U.S. beef, causing beef supply curves to shift to the left in those importing countries. The loss of U.S. producers' largest export market, Japan, cost beef suppliers $1 billion worth of sales; Canadian exporters lost about $55 million worth of sales to Japan. U.S. exports fell from 1,143 thousand metric tons in 2003 to 209 thousand metric tons in 2004. At least initially, a few people in the United States and Canada stopped consuming beef, causing demand curves in these countries to move slightly to the left. Strangely, the National Cattlemen's Beef Association reported that 89% of U.S. consumers expressed confidence in the safety of U.S. beef after the mad cow announcement, compared to 88% in September 2003. Schlenker and Villas-Boas (2007) found that U.S. consumers regained confidence and resumed their earlier levels of beef buying within three months.

The immediate supply effects in the United States and Canada were larger than the long-run effects. The United States was exporting about 10% of its total production (about $3.8 billion in sales), while the Canadians were exporting 40% of their domestic production. When they were unable to ship the beef abroad, U.S. and Canadian producers had to sell their beef only in their domestic markets, causing domestic supply curves to shift to the right. Thereafter, U.S. and Canadian producers reduced their herds, so that the supply curves shifted to the left in the longer run. Japan allowed U.S. beef to be imported again starting in 2006; however, it suspended imports from at least one U.S. slaughterhouse in 2007 for failing to maintain safety standards.[9]

Solved Problem 2.4

In the first few weeks after the U.S. ban, the quantity of beef sold in Japan fell substantially, and the price rose. In contrast, three weeks after the first discovery, the U.S. price in January 2004 fell by about 15% and the quantity sold increased by 43% over the last week in October 2003. Use supply-and-demand diagrams to explain why these events occurred.

Answer

1. *Show how a shift of the Japanese supply curve affects the Japanese equilibrium.* When Japan banned U.S. imports, the supply curve of beef in Japan shifted to the left from S^1 to S^2 in panel a of the figure. (The figure shows a parallel shift, for the sake of simplicity.) Presumably, the Japanese demand curve, D, was unaffected as Japanese consumers had no increased risk of consuming tainted meat. Thus the shift of the supply curve caused the equilibrium to move along the demand curve from e_1 to e_2. The equilibrium price rose from p_1 to p_2 and the equilibrium quantity fell from Q_1 to Q_2.
2. *Show how shifts of both the U.S. supply and U.S. demand curves affect the U.S. equilibrium.* U.S. beef consumers' fear of mad cow disease caused their demand curve in panel b of the figure to shift slightly to the left from D^1 to D^2. In the short run, total U.S. production was essentially unchanged. Because of the ban on exports, beef that would have been sold in Japan and elsewhere was sold in the United States, causing the U.S. supply curve to shift to the right

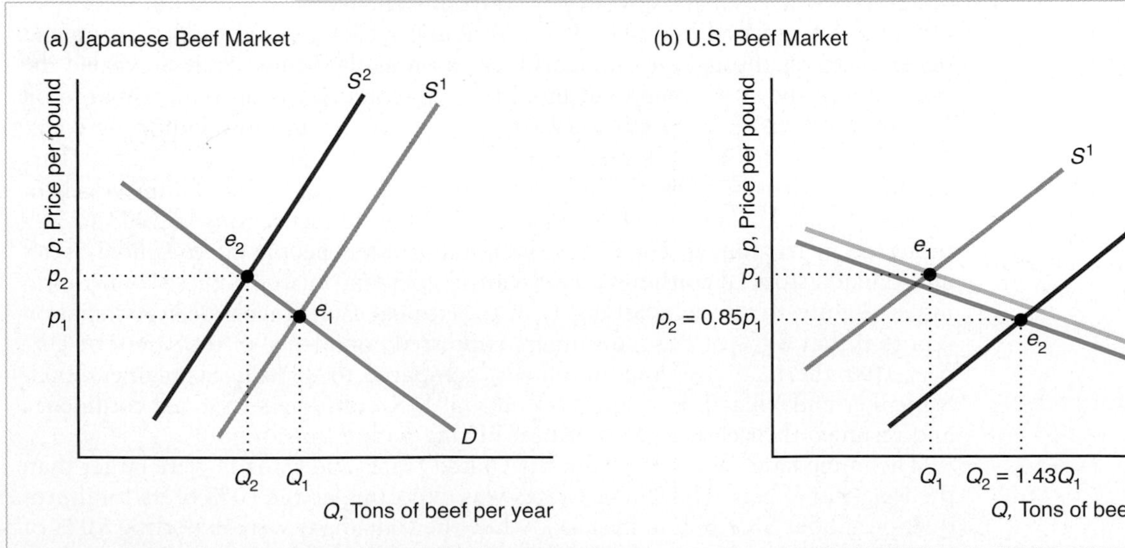

[9]Sources for applications appear at the back of the book.

from S^1 to S^2. As a result, the U.S. equilibrium changed from e_1 (where S^1 intersects D^1) to e_2 (where S^2 intersects D^2). The U.S. price fell 15% from p_1 to $p_2 = 0.85p_1$, while the quantity rose 43% from Q_1 to $Q_2 = 1.43Q_1$.

See Questions 9–12.

Comment: Depending on exactly how the U.S. supply and demand curves had shifted, it would have been possible for the U.S. price and quantity to have both fallen. For example, if D^2 had shifted far enough left, it could have intersected S^2 to the left of Q_1, so that the equilibrium quantity would have fallen.

2.5 Effects of Government Interventions

A government can affect a market equilibrium in many ways. Sometimes government actions cause a shift in the supply curve, the demand curve, or both curves, which causes the equilibrium to change. Some government interventions, however, cause the quantity demanded to differ from the quantity supplied.

Policies That Shift Supply Curves

As we saw earlier, quotas on imports affect the supply curve. We illustrate the effect of quotas on market equilibrium.

The Japanese government's ban on rice imports raised the price of rice in Japan substantially. Figure 2.8 shows the Japanese demand curve for rice, D, and the total supply curve without a ban, S. The intersection of S and D determines the equilibrium, e_1, if rice imports are allowed.

What is the effect of a ban on foreign rice on Japanese supply and demand? The ban has no effect on demand if Japanese consumers do not care whether they eat

Figure 2.8 A Ban on Rice Imports Raises the Price in Japan.

A ban on rice imports shifts the total supply of rice in Japan without a ban, S, to $\bar{S}$ which equals the domestic supply alone. As a result, the equilibrium changes from e_1 to e_2. The ban causes the price to rise from p_1 to p_2 and the equilibrium quantity to fall to Q_1 from Q_2.

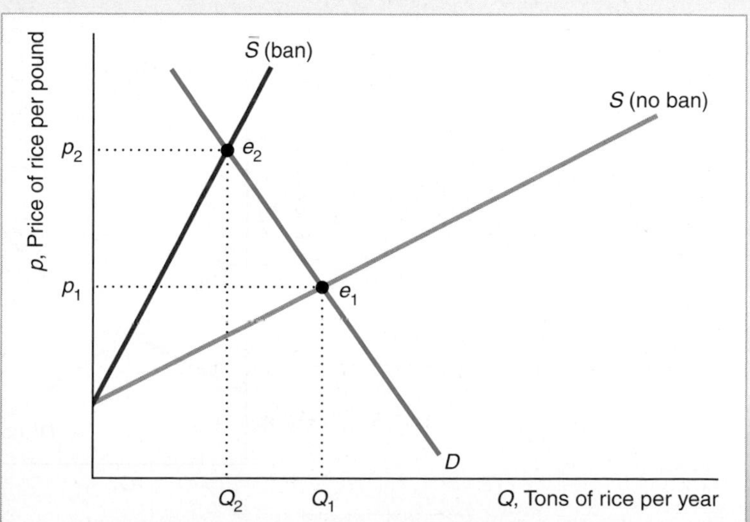

domestic or foreign rice. The ban causes the total supply curve to rotate toward the origin from S (total supply is the horizontal sum of domestic and foreign supply) to $\bar{S}$ (total supply equals the domestic supply).

The intersection of $\bar{S}$ and D determines the new equilibrium, e_2, which lies above and to the left of e_1. The ban causes a shift of the supply curve and a movement along the demand curve. It leads to a fall in the equilibrium quantity from Q_1 to Q_2 and a rise in the equilibrium price from p_1 to p_2. Because of the Japanese ban on imported rice, the price of rice in Japan was 10.5 times higher than the price in the rest of the world in 2001.

A quota of $\bar{Q}$ may have a similar effect to an outright ban; however, a quota may have no effect on the equilibrium if the quota is set so high that it does not limit imports. We investigate this possibility in Solved Problem 2.5 and the application that follows it.

Solved Problem 2.5

What is the effect of a United States quota on steel of $\bar{Q}$ on the equilibrium in the U.S. steel market? *Hint:* The answer depends on whether the quota binds (is low enough to affect the equilibrium).

Answer

1. *Show how a quota, $\bar{Q}$, affects the total supply of steel in the United States.* The graph reproduces the no-quota total American supply curve of steel, S, and the total supply curve under the quota, $\bar{S}$ (which we derived in Solved Problem 2.2). At a price below $\bar{p}$ the two supply curves are identical because the quota is not binding: It is greater than the quantity foreign firms want to supply. Above $\bar{p}$, $\bar{S}$ lies to the left of S.

See Questions 13–16.

2. *Show the effect of the quota if the original equilibrium quantity is less than the quota so that the quota does not bind.* Suppose that the American demand is relatively *low* at any given price so that the demand curve, D^l, intersects both the supply curves at a price below $\bar{p}$. The equilibria both before and after the quota is imposed are at e_1, where the equilibrium price, p_1, is less than $\bar{p}$. Thus if the demand curve lies near enough to the origin that the quota is not binding, the quota has no effect on the equilibrium.

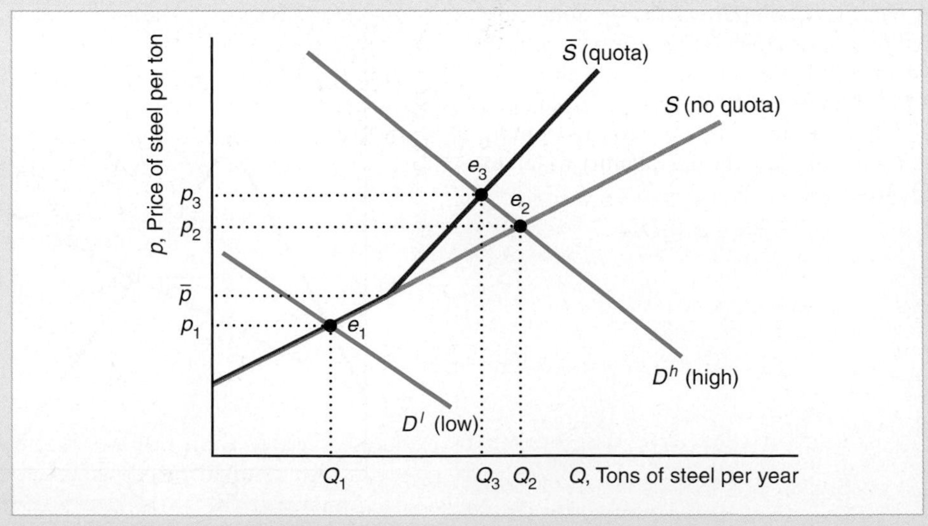

3. *Show the effect of the quota if the quota binds.* With a relatively *high* demand curve, D^h, the quota affects the equilibrium. The no-quota equilibrium is e_2, where D^h intersects the no-quota total supply curve, S. After the quota is imposed, the equilibrium is e_3, where D^h intersects the total supply curve with the quota, $\bar{S}$. The quota raises the price of steel in the United States from p_2 to p_3 and reduces the quantity from Q_2 to Q_3.

APPLICATION

American Steel Quotas

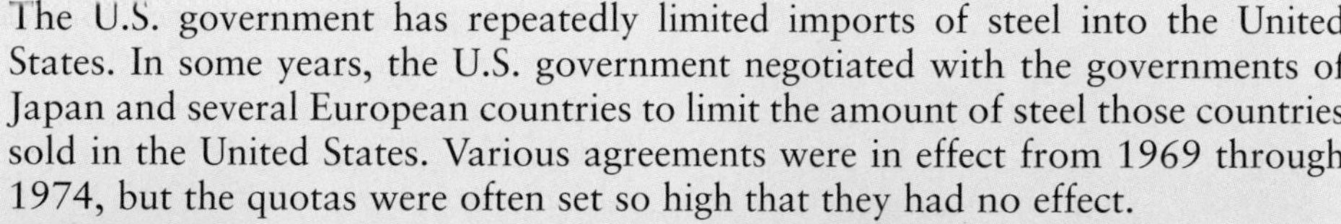

The U.S. government has repeatedly limited imports of steel into the United States. In some years, the U.S. government negotiated with the governments of Japan and several European countries to limit the amount of steel those countries sold in the United States. Various agreements were in effect from 1969 through 1974, but the quotas were often set so high that they had no effect.

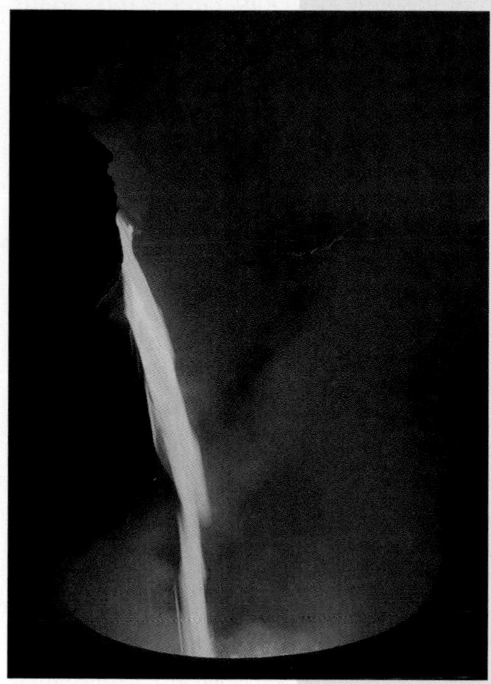

However, in 1971 and 1972, the quotas were binding for most steel products. These quotas raised average U.S. steel prices between 1.2% and 3.5%.

In 1984, President Ronald Reagan negotiated *voluntary* quotas, which covered most steel-exporting countries and limited finished steel imports into the United States to 18.5% of the total U.S. sales for 1985–1989. These limits on imports drove up prices. In 1979–1980, in the absence of quotas, the average U.S. price of steel was approximately the same as the market price in Antwerp, Belgium. In 1984 and 1985, under the Reagan quotas, the average U.S. price was about 25% higher than the corresponding price in Antwerp.

In 1980, pig iron and semifinished steel imports accounted for only 3.5% of domestic steel use, a share that remained virtually unchanged through 1992. Thereafter, in the absence of quotas, imports rose substantially, and the share of imports reached 26.4% by 1998.

Tariffs, taxes on imported goods, also restrict imports. The U.S. government has imposed tariffs on steel goods from certain countries since 1933. In 2006, the U.S. government ended tariffs on carbon steel plate for 16 countries, but kept them for Germany and Korea. In 2007, the U.S. government extended the tariffs on hot-rolled steel from Indonesia, Taiwan, Thailand, Ukraine, China, and India but eliminated them for Argentina, Kazakhstan, Romania, and South Africa. Thus, U.S. restrictions on steel products continue to evolve over time.

Policies That Cause Demand to Differ from Supply

Some government policies do more than merely shift the supply or demand curve. For example, governments may control prices directly, a policy that leads to either excess supply or excess demand if the price the government sets differs from the equilibrium price. We illustrate this result with two types of price control programs.

When the government sets a *price ceiling* at $\bar{p}$ the price at which goods are sold may be no higher than $\bar{p}$. When the government sets a *price floor* at $\underline{p}$, the price at which goods are sold may not fall below $\underline{p}$.

Price Ceilings. Price ceilings have no effect if they are set above the equilibrium price that would be observed in the absence of the price controls. If the government says that firms may charge no more than $\bar{p} = \$5$ per gallon of gas and firms are actually charging $p = \$1$, the government's price control policy is irrelevant. However, if the equilibrium price, p, would be above the price ceiling $\bar{p}$ the price that is actually observed in the market is the price ceiling.

The United States used price controls during both world wars, the Korean War, and in 1971–1973 during the Nixon administration, among other times. Gasoline price controls were imposed in 1973 and 1979. Hawaii limited the price of wholesale gasoline from 2005–2006. In the aftermath of Hurricane Katrina and the run up in gasoline prices in 2006–2007, many legislators called for price controls on gasoline, but no bills have been passed so far.

The U.S. experience with gasoline illustrates the effects of price controls. In the 1970s, the Organization of Petroleum Exporting Countries (OPEC) reduced supplies of oil (which is converted into gasoline) to Western countries. As a result, the total supply curve for gasoline in the United States—the horizontal sum of domestic and OPEC supply curves—shifted to the left from S^1 to S^2 in Figure 2.9. Because of this shift, the equilibrium price of gasoline would have risen substantially, from p_1 to p_2. In an attempt to protect consumers by keeping gasoline prices from rising, the U.S. government set price ceilings on gasoline in 1973 and 1979.

Figure 2.9 Price Ceiling on Gasoline.

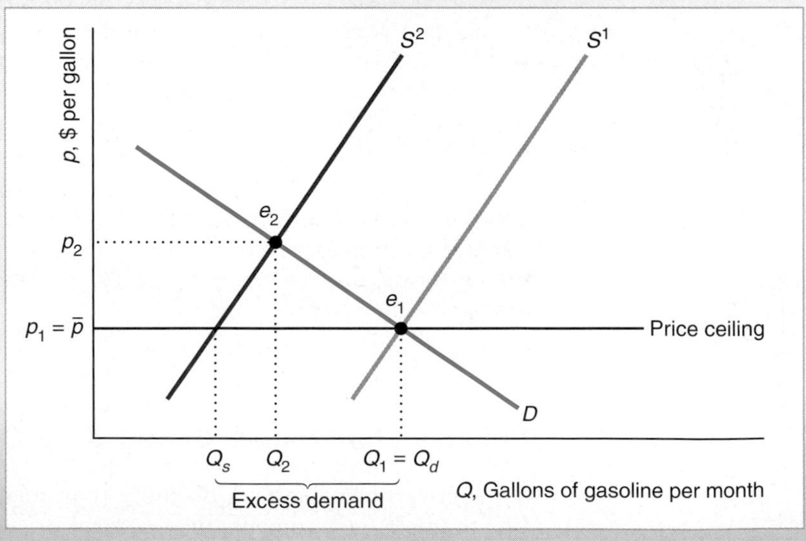

Supply shifts from S^1 to S^2. Under the government's price control program, gasoline stations may not charge a price above the price ceiling $\bar{p} = p_1$. At that price, producers are willing to supply only Q_s, which is less than the amount $Q_1 = Q_d$ that consumers want to buy. The result is excessive demand, or a shortage of $Q_d - Q_s$.

The government told gas stations that they could charge no more than $p = p_1$. Figure 2.9 shows the price ceiling as a solid horizontal line extending from the price axis at $\bar{p}$. The price control is binding because $p_2 > \bar{p}$. The observed price is the price ceiling. At $\bar{p}$ consumers want to buy $Q_d = Q_1$ gallons of gasoline, which is the equilibrium quantity they bought before OPEC acted. However, firms supply only Q_s gallons, which is determined by the intersection of the price control line with S^2. As a result of the binding price control, there is excess demand of $Q_d - Q_s$.

Were it not for the price controls, market forces would drive up the market price to p_2, where the excess demand would be eliminated. The government price ceiling prevents this adjustment from occurring. As a result, an enforced price ceiling causes a **shortage**: a persistent excess demand.

shortage
a persistent excess demand

At the time of the controls, some government officials argued that the shortages were caused by OPEC's cutting off its supply of oil to the United States, but that's not true. Without the price controls, the new equilibrium would be e_2. In this equilibrium, the price, p_2, is much higher than before, p_1; however, there is no shortage. Moreover, without controls, the quantity sold, Q_2, is greater than the quantity sold under the control program, Q_s.

With a binding price ceiling, the supply-and-demand model predicts an *equilibrium with a shortage*. In this equilibrium, the quantity demanded does not equal the quantity supplied. The reason that we call this situation an equilibrium, even though a shortage exists, is that no consumers or firms want to act differently, given the law. Without the price controls, consumers facing a shortage would try to get more output by offering to pay more, or firms would raise prices. With effective government price controls, they know that they can't drive up the price, so they live with the shortage.

What happens? Some lucky consumers get to buy Q_s units at the low price of $\bar{p}$ Other potential customers are disappointed: They would like to buy at that price, but they cannot find anyone willing to sell gas to them.

What determines which consumers are lucky enough to find goods to buy at the low price when there are price controls? With enforced price controls, sellers use criteria other than price to allocate the scarce commodity. Firms may supply their friends, long-term customers, or people of a certain race, gender, age, or religion. They may sell their goods on a first-come, first-served basis. Or they may limit everyone to only a few gallons.

Another possibility is for firms and customers to evade the price controls. A consumer could go to a gas station owner and say, "Let's not tell anyone, but I'll pay you twice the price the government sets if you'll sell me as much gas as I want." If enough customers and gas station owners behaved that way, no shortage would occur. A study of 92 major U.S. cities during the 1973 gasoline price controls found no gasoline lines in 52 of them. However, in cities such as Chicago, Hartford, New York, Portland, and Tucson, potential customers waited in line at the pump for an hour or more.[10] Deacon and Sonstelie (1989) calculated that for every dollar consumers saved during the 1980 gasoline price controls, they lost \$1.16 in waiting time and other factors.

See Questions 17-20 and Problem 35.

[10]See **www.myeconlab.com/perloff**, Chapter 2, "Gas Lines," for a discussion of the effects of the 1973 and 1979 gasoline price controls.

APPLICATION

Price Controls Kill

Robert G. Mugabe, who has ruled Zimbabwe with an iron fist for more than 27 years, is using price controls to try to stay in power by currying favor among the poor. Price controls imposed during the 2001 election year caused severe problems, but more draconian measures in 2007 have brought the economy to a dead stop and emptied grocery shelves.[11] Zimbabweans are dying from starvation and lack of medical care.

Zimbabwe's 2001 price controls on many basic commodities, including foods (about a third of citizens' daily consumption), soap, and cement led to shortages of these goods at retail outlets. A thriving *black* or *parallel market*, where controls were ignored, developed. Prices on the black market were two or three times higher than the controlled prices.

With the much more extreme controls in 2007, many people's hope for survival vanished. A government edict cut prices of 26 essential items by up to 70%, and a subsequent edict imposed price controls on a much wider range of goods. Gangs of price inspectors patrol shops and factories, imposing arbitrary price reductions. State-run newspapers exhort citizens to turn in store owners whose prices exceed the limits. Shop owners who refuse to comply are to be jailed, and stores that close or refuse to restock goods are to be taken over by the government.

The Zimbabwean police report that they arrested at least 4,000 businesspeople for not complying with the price controls. The government took over the nation's slaughterhouses after meat disappeared, but in a typical week, butchers killed and dressed only 32 cows for the entire city. Farmers are unwilling to sell their cows at a loss, so meat is virtually nonexistent, even for members of the middle class who have money to buy it on the black market.

Ordinary citizens initially greeted the price cuts with euphoria, as they had been unable to buy even basic necessities—such as bread, sugar, and cornmeal—because of hyperinflation and past price controls. Yet most ordinary citizens were unable to obtain much food, as most of the cut-rate merchandise was grabbed by the police, soldiers, and members of Mr. Mugabe's governing party, who were tipped off to the price inspectors' rounds. Store shelves are empty.

Manufacturing has slowed to a crawl as firms cannot buy raw materials and the prices firms receive are less than their costs of production. Businesses are laying off workers or reducing their hours, bringing new poverty to the 15% or 20% of adult Zimbabweans who still have jobs.

Many people, including the former middle class, live on nothing but *sadza* (a cornmeal porridge) and are suffering from diseases of poverty, such as tubercu-

[11] Mr. Mugabe justifies price controls as a means to deal with profiteering businesses that he says are part of a Western conspiracy to reimpose colonial rule. Actually, they are a vain attempt to slow the 10,000% per year hyperinflation that has resulted from his printing Zimbabwean money rapidly.

losis and malnutrition. Hospitals lack drugs and other critical supplies. At one urban public hospital, an accident victim recently underwent successful surgery but died due to dehydration because there was not enough saline solution. Most of Zimbabwe's medical practitioners have long fled the country.

Wealthier people used to drive across the border to Zambia, South Africa, and Botswana for supplies, but now gasoline is nearly impossible to find. For years, Zimbabwe's poorest citizens, the majority of its 10 or 11 million people, have been unable to afford most foods. The rural poor survive on whatever they can grow. Outside aid from the two million Zimbabweans who have fled abroad and international relief agencies have helped keep some alive.

In 2007, the World Food Program made an urgent appeal for $118 million in donations to feed Zimbabweans, stating that drought and political upheaval would soon exhaust the organization's stockpiles. The program provided emergency food aid to one-third of the nation's 12 million people in January, 2008.

Price Floors. Governments also commonly use price floors. One of the most important examples of a price floor is the minimum wage in labor markets.

The minimum wage law forbids employers from paying less than the minimum wage, $\underline{w}$. Minimum wage laws date from 1894 in New Zealand, 1909 in the United Kingdom, and 1912 in Massachusetts. The Fair Labor Standards Act of 1938 set a federal U.S. minimum wage of 25¢. The U.S. federal minimum wage is currently $5.85 an hour and will rise to $6.55 July 24, 2008 and to $7.25 on July 24, 2009. The statutory monthly minimum wage ranges from the equivalent of 19€ in the Russian Federation to 375€ in Portugal, 1,154€ in France, and 1,466€ in Luxembourg. If the minimum wage binds—exceeds the equilibrium wage, w^*—the minimum wage creates *unemployment*, which is a persistent excess supply of labor.[12]

For simplicity, suppose that there is a single labor market in which everyone is paid the same wage. Figure 2.10 shows the supply and demand curves for labor services (hours worked). Firms buy hours of labor service—they hire workers. The quantity measure on the horizontal axis is hours worked per year, and the price measure on the vertical axis is the wage per hour.

With no government intervention, the market equilibrium is e, where the wage is w^* and the number of hours worked is L^*. The minimum wage creates a price floor, a horizontal line, at $\underline{w}$. At that wage, the quantity demanded falls to L_d and the quantity supplied rises to L_s. As a result, there is an excess supply or unemployment of $L_s - L_d$. The minimum wage prevents market forces from eliminating this excess supply, so it leads to an equilibrium with unemployment. The original 1938 U.S. minimum wage law caused massive unemployment in Puerto Rico (see **www.myeconlab.com/perloff**, Chapter 2, "Minimum Wage Law in Puerto Rico").

---

[12]Where the minimum wage applies to only a few labor markets (Chapter 10) or where only a single firm hires all the workers in a market (Chapter 15), a minimum wage may not cause unemployment (see Card and Krueger, 1995, for empirical evidence). The U.S. Department of Labor maintains at its Web site (**www.dol.gov**) an extensive history of the minimum wage law, labor markets, state minimum wage laws, and other information. For European countries, see **www.fedee.com/minwage.html**.

Figure 2.10 Minimum Wage.

In the absence of a minimum wage, the equilibrium wage is w^* and the equilibrium number of hours worked is L^*. A minimum wage, $\underline{w}$, set above w^*, leads to unemployment—persistent excess supply—because the quantity demanded, L_d, is less than the quantity supplied, L_s.

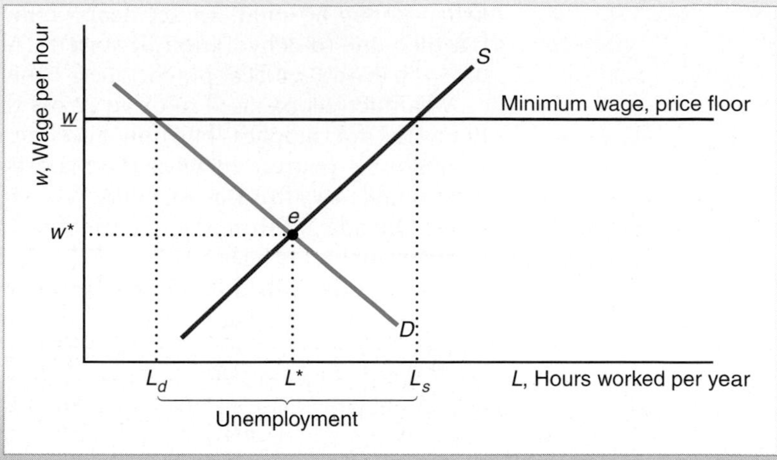

It is ironic that a law designed to help workers by raising their wages may harm some of them by causing them to become unemployed. A minimum wage law benefits only those who remain employed.[13]

Why Supply Need Not Equal Demand

The price ceiling and price floor examples show that the quantity supplied does not necessarily equal the quantity demanded in a supply-and-demand model. The quantity supplied need not equal the quantity demanded because of the way we defined these two concepts. We defined the quantity supplied as the amount firms *want to sell* at a given price, holding other factors that affect supply, such as the price of inputs, constant. The quantity demanded is the quantity that consumers *want to buy* at a given price, if other factors that affect demand are held constant. The quantity that firms want to sell and the quantity that consumers want to buy at a given price need not equal the *actual* quantity that is bought and sold.

When the government imposes a binding price ceiling of $\bar{p}$ on gasoline, the quantity demanded is greater than the quantity supplied. Despite the lack of equality between the quantity supplied and the quantity demanded, the supply-and-demand model is useful in analyzing this market because it predicts the excess demand that is actually observed.

We could have defined the quantity supplied and the quantity demanded so that they must be equal. If we were to define the quantity supplied as the amount firms *actually* sell at a given price and the quantity demanded as the amount consumers *actually* buy, supply must equal demand in all markets because the quantity demanded and the quantity supplied are *defined* to be the same quantity.

It is worth pointing out this distinction because many people, including politicians and newspaper reporters, are confused on this point. Someone insisting that "demand *must* equal supply" must be defining supply and demand as the *actual* quantities sold.

[13]The minimum wage could raise the wage enough that total wage payments, wL, rise despite the fall in demand for labor services. If the workers could share the unemployment—everybody works fewer hours than he or she wants—all workers could benefit from the minimum wage.

Because we define the quantities supplied and demanded in terms of people's *wants* and not *actual* quantities bought and sold, the statement that "supply equals demand" is a theory, not merely a definition. This theory says that the equilibrium price and quantity in a market are determined by the intersection of the supply curve and the demand curve if the government does not intervene. Further, we use the model to predict excess demand or excess supply when a government does control price. The observed gasoline shortages during the period when the U.S. government controlled gasoline prices are consistent with this prediction.

2.6 When to Use the Supply-and-Demand Model

As we've seen, supply-and-demand theory can help us to understand and predict real-world events in many markets. Through Chapter 10, we discuss competitive markets in which the supply-and-demand model is a powerful tool for predicting what will happen to market equilibrium if underlying conditions—tastes, incomes, and prices of inputs—change. The types of markets for which the supply-and-demand model is useful are described at length in these chapters, particularly in Chapter 8. Briefly, this model is applicable in markets in which:

- **Everyone is a price taker.** Because no consumer or firm is a very large part of the market, no one can affect the market price. Easy entry of firms into the market, which leads to a large number of firms, is usually necessary to ensure that firms are price takers.
- **Firms sell identical products.** Consumers do not prefer one firm's good to another.
- **Everyone has full information about the price and quality of goods.** Consumers know if a firm is charging a price higher than the price others set, and they know if a firm tries to sell them inferior-quality goods.
- **Costs of trading are low.** It is not time consuming, difficult, or expensive for a buyer to find and trade with a seller or for a seller to find and trade with a buyer.

Markets with these properties are called *perfectly competitive markets*.

Where there are many firms and consumers, no single firm or consumer is a large enough part of the market to affect the price. If you stop buying bread or if one of the many thousands of wheat farmers stops selling the wheat used to make the bread, the price of bread will not change. Consumers and firms are *price takers*: They cannot affect the market price.

In contrast, if there is only one seller of a good or service—a *monopoly* (see Chapter 11)—that seller is a *price setter* and can affect the market price. Because demand curves slope downward, a monopoly can increase the price it receives by reducing the amount of a good it supplies. Firms are also price setters in an *oligopoly*—a market with only a small number of firms—or in markets where they sell differentiated products so that a consumer prefers one product to another (see Chapter 13). In markets with price setters, the market price is usually higher than that predicted by the supply-and-demand model. That doesn't make the model generally wrong. It means only that the supply-and-demand model does not apply to markets with a small number of sellers or buyers. In such markets, we use other models.

If consumers have less information than a firm, the firm can take advantage of consumers by selling them inferior-quality goods or by charging a much higher price than that charged by other firms. In such a market, the observed price is usually higher than that predicted by the supply-and-demand model, the market may not exist at all (consumers and firms cannot reach agreements), or different firms may charge different prices for the same good (see Chapter 19).

transaction costs
the expenses of finding a trading partner and making a trade for a good or service beyond the price paid for that good or service

The supply-and-demand model is also not entirely appropriate in markets in which it is costly to trade with others because the cost of a buyer finding a seller or of a seller finding a buyer are high. **Transaction costs** are the expenses of finding a trading partner and making a trade for a good or service other than the price paid for that good or service. These costs include the time and money spent to find someone with whom to trade. For example, you may have to pay to place a newspaper advertisement to sell your gray 1999 Honda with 137,000 miles on it. Or you may have to go to many stores to find one that sells a shirt in exactly the color you want, so your transaction costs includes transportation costs and your time. The cost of a long-distance call to place an order is a transaction cost. Other transaction costs include the costs of writing and enforcing a contract, such as the cost of a lawyer's time. Where transaction costs are high, no trades may occur, or if they do occur, individual trades may occur at a variety of prices (see Chapters 12 and 19).

Thus the supply-and-demand model is not appropriate in markets in which there are only one or a few sellers (such as electricity), firms produce differentiated products (music CDs), consumers know less than sellers about quality or price (used cars), or there are high transaction costs (nuclear turbine engines). Markets in which the supply-and-demand model has proved useful include agriculture, finance, labor, construction, services, wholesale, and retail.

SUMMARY

1. **Demand.** The quantity of a good or service demanded by consumers depends on their tastes, the price of a good, the price of goods that are substitutes and complements, their income, information, government regulations, and other factors. The *Law of Demand*—which is based on observation—says that *demand curves slope downward.* The higher the price, the less of the good is demanded, holding constant other factors that affect demand. A change in price causes a *movement along the demand curve.* A change in income, tastes, or another factor that affects demand other than price causes a *shift of the demand curve.* To get a total demand curve, we horizontally sum the demand curves of individuals or types of consumers or countries. That is, we add the quantities demanded by each individual at a given price to get the total demanded.

2. **Supply.** The quantity of a good or service supplied by firms depends on the price, costs, government regulations, and other factors. The market supply curve need not slope upward but usually does. A change in price causes a *movement along the supply curve.* A change in the price of an input or government regulation causes a *shift of the supply curve.* The total supply curve is the horizontal sum of the supply curves for individual firms.

3. **Market Equilibrium.** The intersection of the demand curve and the supply curve determines the equilibrium price and quantity in a market. Market forces—actions of consumers and firms—drive the price and quantity to the equilibrium levels if they are initially too low or too high.

4. **Shocking the Equilibrium.** A change in an underlying factor other than price causes a shift of the supply curve or the demand curve, which alters the equilibrium. For example, if the price of beef rises, the demand curve for pork shifts outward, causing a movement along the supply curve and leading to a new equilibrium at a higher price and quantity. If changes in these underlying factors follow one after the other, a market that adjusts slowly may stay out of equilibrium for an extended period.

5. **Effects of Government Interventions.** Some government policies—such as a ban on imports—cause a shift in the supply or demand curves, thereby altering the equilibrium. Other government policies—such as price controls or a minimum wage—cause the quantity supplied to be greater or less than the quantity demanded, leading to persistent excesses or shortages.

6. **When to Use the Supply-and-Demand Model.** The supply-and-demand model is a powerful tool to explain what happens in a market or to make predictions about what will happen if an underlying factor in a market changes. This model, however, is applicable only in markets with many buyers and sellers; identical goods; certainty and full information about price, quantity, quality, incomes, costs, and other market characteristics; and low transaction costs.

QUESTIONS

If you ask me anything I don't know, I'm not going to answer. —Yogi Berra

■ = *exercise is available on MyEconLab;* * = *answer appears at the back of this book;* C = *use of calculus may be necessary;* W = *audio-slideshow answer by James Dearden is available in Textbook Resources on MyEconLab.*

*1. Use a supply-and-demand diagram to explain the statement "Talk is cheap because supply exceeds demand." At what price is this comparison being made?

2. Increased outsourcing to India by firms in the United States and other developed countries has driven up the wage of some Indian skilled workers by 10% to 15% (Adam Geller, "Offshore Savings Can Be Iffy," *San Francisco Chronicle,* June 21, 2005: D1, D4). Use a supply-and-demand diagram to explain why, and discuss the effect on the number of people employed.

3. The U.S. supply of frozen orange juice comes from Florida and Brazil. What is the effect of a freeze that damages oranges in Florida on the price of frozen orange juice in the United States and on the quantities of orange juice sold by Floridian and Brazilian firms?

4. The Federation of Vegetable Farmers Association of Malaysia reported that a lack of workers caused a 25% drop in production that drove up vegetable prices by 50% to 100% in 2005 ("Vegetable Price Control Sought," **thestar.com.my**, June 6, 2005). Consumers called for price controls on vegetables. Show why the price increased, and predict the effects of a binding price control. W

5. Increasingly, instead of advertising in newspapers, individuals and firms use Web sites that offer free or inexpensive classified ads, such as Classifiedads.com, Craigslist.org, Realtor.com, Jobs.com, Monster.com, and portals like Google and Yahoo. Using a supply-and-demand model, explain what will happen to the equilibrium levels of newspaper advertising as the use of the Internet grows. Will the growth of the Internet affect the supply curve, the demand curve, or both? Why?

6. When he was the top American administrator in Iraq, L. Paul Bremer III set a rule that upheld Iraqi law: anyone 25 years and older with a "good reputation and character" could own one firearm, including an AK-47 assault rifle. Iraqi citizens quickly began arming themselves. Akram Abdulzahra has a revolver handy at his job in an Internet cafe. Haidar Hussein, a Baghdad bookseller, has a new fully automatic assault rifle. After the bombing of a sacred Shiite shrine in Samarra at the end of February 2006 and the subsequent rise in sectarian violence, the demand for guns increased, resulting in higher prices. The average price of a legal, Russian-made Kalashnikov AK-47 assault rifle jumped from $112 to $290 from February to March 2006. The price of bullets shot up from 24¢ to 33¢ each. (Jeffrey Gettleman, "Sectarian Suspicion in Baghdad Fuels a Seller's Market for Guns," *New York Times*, April 3, 2006.) This increase occurred despite the hundreds of thousands of firearms and millions of rounds of ammunition that American troops had been providing to Iraqi security forces, some of which eventually ended up in the hands of private citizens. Use a graph to illustrate why prices rose.

7. The prices received by soybean farmers in Brazil, the world's second-largest soybean producer and exporter, tumbled 30%, in part because of China's decision to cut back on imports and in part because of a bumper soybean crop in the United States, the world's leading exporter (Todd Benson, "A Harvest at Peril," *New York Times,* January 6, 2005, C6). In addition, Asian soy rust, a deadly crop fungus, is destroying large quantities of the Brazilian crops.
   a. Use a supply-and-demand diagram to illustrate why Brazilian farmers are receiving lower prices.
   b. If you knew only the *direction* of the shifts in both the supply and the demand curves, could you predict that prices would fall? Why or why not? W

8. Due to a slight recession that lowered incomes, the 2002 market prices for last-minute rentals of U.S. beachfront properties were lower than usual (June Fletcher, "Last-Minute Beach Rentals Offer Summer's Best Deals," *Wall Street Journal,* June 21, 2002, D1).
   a. How does a recession affect the demand curve and the supply curve for rental properties? In answering the supply curve question, consider the two options of owners of beach homes: staying in the homes or renting them to others.
   b. Use a supply-and-demand analysis to show the effect of decreased income on the price of rental homes. W

9. In Solved Problem 2.4, we illustrated why the mad cow announcement initially caused the U.S. equilibrium price of beef to fall and the quantity to rise. Show that if the supply and demand curves had

shifted in the same directions as in the Solved Problem but to greater or lesser degrees, the equilibrium quantity might have fallen. Could the equilibrium price have risen?

10. Japan stopped importing animal feed from Britain in 1996, beef imports and processed beef products from 18 countries including EU members starting in 2001, and similar imports from Canada and the United States in 2003. After U.S. beef imports were banned, McDonald's Japan and other Japanese importers replaced much of the banned U.S. beef with Australian beef, causing an export boom for Australia ("China Bans U.S. Beef," **cnn.com**, December 24, 2003; "Beef Producers Are on the Lookout for Extra Demand," **abc.net.au**, June 13, 2005). Use supply and demand curves to show the impact of these events on the domestic Australian beef market.

11. In December 2000, Japan reported that test shipments of U.S. corn had detected StarLink, a genetically modified corn that is not approved for human consumption in the United States. As a result, Japan and some other nations banned U.S. imports. Use a graph to illustrate why this ban, which caused U.S. corn exports to fall 4%, resulted in the price of corn falling 11.1% in the United States in 2001–2002.

12. In 2002, the U.S. Fish and Wildlife Service proposed banning imports of beluga caviar to protect the beluga sturgeon in the Caspian and Black seas, whose sturgeon population had fallen 90% in the last two decades. The United States imports 60% of the world's beluga caviar. On the world's legal wholesale market, a kilogram of caviar costs an average of $500, and about $100 million worth is sold per year. What effect would the U.S. ban have on world prices and quantities? Would such a ban help protect the beluga sturgeon? (In 2005, the service decided not to ban imports.)

13. On January 1, 2005, a three-decades-old system of global quotas that had limited how much China and other countries could ship to the United States and other wealthy nations ended. Over the next four months, U.S. imports of Chinese-made cotton trousers rose by more than 1,505% and their price fell 21% in the first quarter of the year (Tracie Rozhon, "A Tangle in Textiles," *New York Times*, April 21, 2005, C1). The U.S. textile industry demanded quick action, saying that 18 plants had already been forced to close that year and 16,600 textile and apparel jobs had been lost. The Bush administration reacted to the industry pressure. The United States (and Europe, which faced similar large increases in imports) pressed China to cut back its textile exports, threatening to restore quotas on Chinese exports or to take other actions. Illustrate what happened, and show how the U.S. quota reimposed in May 2005 affected the equilibrium price and quantity in the United States.

14. What is the effect of a quota $\bar{Q} > 0$ on equilibrium price and quantity? (*Hint*: Carefully show how the total supply curve changes.)

*15. Is it possible that an outright ban on foreign imports will have no effect on the equilibrium price? (*Hint*: Suppose that imports occur only at relatively high prices.)

16. In 1996, a group of American doctors called for a limit on the number of foreign-trained physicians permitted to practice in the United States. What effect would such a limit have on the equilibrium quantity and price of doctors' services in the United States? How are American-trained doctors and consumers affected?

17. Usury laws place a ceiling on interest rates that lenders such as banks can charge borrowers. Low-income households in states with usury laws have significantly lower levels of consumer credit (loans) than comparable households in states without usury laws (Villegas, 1989). Why? (*Hint*: The interest rate is the price of a loan, and the amount of the loan is the quantity measure.)

18. Argentines love a sizzling steak, consuming twice as much per capita as U.S. citizens. Thus, when the price of beef started to shoot up, Argentina's President Néstor Kirchner took dramatic action to force down beef prices. (Larry Rohter, "For Argentina's Sizzling Economy, a Cap on Steak Prices," *New York Times*, April 3, 2006.) He ordered government ministries to cease their purchases, prohibited the export of most cuts of beef, and urged consumers to boycott beef. But beef-loving Argentines, benefiting from higher wages due to a growing economy, largely ignored his call. When these actions failed to lower prices substantially, he turned to "voluntary" price controls ("encouraging" grocery chains and others not to raise prices for extended periods of time). Use graphs to illustrate this sequence of events.

19. In 1999, after nearly 20 years of rent control in Berkeley, California, the elimination of the law led to an estimated rise in rents of nearly 40%. Using supply-and-demand models, illustrate how the law and then its elimination affected the rental housing market. Discuss the effects on the equilibrium rental price and the quantity of housing rented.

*20. After a major earthquake struck Los Angeles in January 1994, several stores raised the price of milk to over $6 a gallon. The local authorities announced that they would investigate and that they would enforce a law prohibiting price increases of more than 10% during an emergency period. What is the likely effect of such a law?

21. Suppose that cotton is produced only in the United States and China. The U.S. government says that if an American farmer sells a bale of cotton at the world price, p, the government will give the farmer $(p^* - p)$ per bale, where $p^* > p$. What happens to the quantities sold by American and Chinese growers and the world price of cotton?

PROBLEMS

*22. Using the estimated demand function for processed pork in Canada (Equation 2.2), show how the quantity demanded at a given price changes as per capita income, Y, increases by $100 a year.

23. In Equation 2.2, suppose that the price of beef, p_b, in Canada increased by 30%, from $4 to $5.20. How does the demand curve for processed pork shift?

*24. Suppose that the inverse demand function for movies is $p = 120 - Q_1$ for college students and $p = 120 - 2Q_2$ for other town residents. What is the town's total demand function ($Q = Q_1 + Q_2$ as a function of p)? Use a diagram to illustrate your answer.

25. The demand function for movies is $Q_1 = 120 - p$ for college students and $Q_2 = 120 - 2p$ for other town residents. What is the total demand function? Use a diagram to illustrate your answer. (*Hint*: By looking at your diagram, you'll see that some care must be used in writing the demand function.)

26. In the application "Aggregating the Demand for Broadband Service" (based on Duffy-Deno, 2003), the demand function is $Q_s = 15.6p^{-0.563}$ for small firms and $Q_l = 16.0p^{-0.296}$ for larger ones, where price is in cents per kilobyte per second and quantity is in millions of kilobytes per second (Kbps). What is the total demand function for all firms?

*27. The demand function for a good is $Q = a - bp$, and the supply function is $Q = c + ep$, where a, b, c, and e are positive constants. Solve for the equilibrium price and quantity in terms of these four constants.

28. If the supply of corn by the United States is $Q_a = a + bp$, and the supply by the rest of the world is $Q_r = c + ep$, what is the world supply?

29. Using the equations for processed pork demand (Equation 2.2) and supply (Equation 2.6), solve for the equilibrium price and quantity in terms of the price of hogs, p_h; the price of beef, p_b; the price of chicken, p_c; and income, Y. If $p_h = 1.5$ (dollars per kg), $p_b = 4$ (dollars per kg), $3\frac{1}{3}$ (dollars per kg), and $Y = 12.5$ (thousands dollars), what are the equilibrium price and quantity?

30. The demand function for roses is $Q = a-bp$, and the supply function is $Q = c + ep + ft$, where a, b, c, e, and f are positive constants and t is the average temperature in a month. Show how the equilibrium quantity and price vary with temperature.

31. Use Equations 2.2 and 2.7 and other information in the chapter to show how the equilibrium quantity of pork varies with income.

32. Suppose that the supply curve for broadband service is horizontal at 40¢ Kbps (firms will supply as much service as desired at that price). Using the information in Problem 31, what is the quantity demanded by small firms, large firms, and all firms?

*33. Green et al. (2005) estimate the supply and demand curves for California processed tomatoes. The supply function is $\ln(Q) = 0.2 + 0.55 \ln(p)$, where Q is the quantity of processing tomatoes in millions of tons per year and p is the price in dollars per ton. The demand function is $\ln(Q) = 2.6 - 0.2 \ln(p) + 0.15 \ln(p_t)$, where p_t is the price of tomato paste (which is what processing tomatoes are used to produce) in dollars per ton. In 2002, $p_t = 110$. What is the demand function for processing tomatoes, where the quantity is solely a function of the price of processing tomatoes? Solve for the equilibrium price and quantity of processing tomatoes (explain your calculations, and round to two digits after the decimal point). Draw the supply and demand curves (note that they are not straight lines), and label the equilibrium and axes appropriately.

34. Using the information in Problem 33, determine how the equilibrium price and quantity of processing tomatoes change if the price of tomato paste falls by 10%.

35. Suppose that the government imposes a price support (price floor) on processing tomatoes at $65 per ton. The government will buy as much as farmers want to sell at that price. Thus processing firms pay $65. Use the information in Problem 33 to determine how many tons firms buy and how many tons the government buys. Illustrate your answer in a supply-and-demand diagram.

36. Use the information in Problem 33 to show how the quantity of processing tomatoes supplied varies with the price (dQ/dp). (*Hint*: It might be easier for you to exponentiate both sides of the equation first.) C

3 Applying the Supply-and-Demand Model

Few of us ever test our powers of deduction, except when filling out an income tax form. —Laurence J. Peter

How large a tax would be necessary to reduce the number of teenagers who smoke by half? If the government were to intercept half the cocaine smuggled into New York City, how much would the price of cocaine rise in the short run and in the long run? We can use supply-and-demand analysis to answer such questions.

When an underlying factor that affects the demand or supply curve changes, the equilibrium price and quantity also change. Chapter 2 showed that you can predict the direction of the change—the *qualitative* change—in equilibrium price and quantity even without knowing the exact shape of the supply and demand curves. In most of the examples in Chapter 2, all you needed to know to give a qualitative answer was the direction in which the supply curve or demand curve shifted when an underlying factor changed.

To determine the exact amount the equilibrium quantity and price change—the *quantitative* change—you can use estimated equations for the supply and demand functions, as we demonstrated using the pork example in Chapter 2. This chapter shows how to use a single number to describe how sensitive the quantity demanded or supplied is to a change in price and how to use these summary numbers to obtain quantitative answers to what-if questions.

In this chapter, we examine five main topics

1. **How Shapes of Supply and Demand Curves Matter.** The effect of a shock (such as a new tax or an increase in the price of an input) on market equilibrium depends on the shape of supply and demand curves.
2. **Sensitivity of Quantity Demanded to Price.** The sensitivity of the quantity demanded to price is summarized by a single measure called the *price elasticity of demand.*
3. **Sensitivity of Quantity Supplied to Price.** The sensitivity of the quantity supplied to price is summarized by a single measure called the *price elasticity of supply.*
4. **Long Run Versus Short Run.** The sensitivity of the quantity demanded or supplied to price varies with time.
5. **Effects of a Sales Tax.** How a sales tax increase affects the equilibrium price and quantity of a good and whether the tax falls more heavily on consumers or suppliers depend on the shape of the supply and demand curves.

3.1 How Shapes of Supply and Demand Curves Matter

The shapes of the supply and demand curves determine by how much a shock affects the equilibrium price and quantity. We illustrate the importance of the shape of the demand curve using the processed pork example (Moschini and Meilke, 1992) from Chapter 2. The supply of pork depends on the price of pork and the price of hogs, the major input in producing processed pork. A 25¢ increase in the price of hogs causes the supply curve of pork to shift to the left from S^1 to S^2 in panel a of Figure 3.1. The *shift of the supply curve* causes a *movement along the demand curve*, D^1, which is downward sloping. The equilibrium quantity falls from 220 to 215 million kg per year, and the equilibrium price rises from \$3.30 to \$3.55 per kg. Thus this supply shock—an increase in the price of hogs—hurts consumers by raising the equilibrium price 25¢ per kg. Customers buy less (215 instead of 220).

A supply shock would have different effects if the demand curve had a different shape. Suppose that the quantity demanded were not sensitive to a change in the price, so the same amount is demanded no matter what the price is, as in vertical demand curve D^2 in panel b. A 25¢ increase in the price of hogs again shifts the supply curve from S^1 to S^2. Equilibrium quantity does not change, but the price consumers pay rises by 37.5¢ to \$3.675. Thus the amount consumers spend rises by more when the demand curve is vertical instead of downward sloping.

Now suppose that consumers are very sensitive to price, as in the horizontal demand curve, D^3, in panel c. Consumers will buy virtually unlimited quantities of pork at \$3.30 per kg (or less), but, if the price rises even slightly, they stop buying pork. Here an increase in the price of hogs has *no* effect on the price consumers pay;

Figure 3.1 How the Effect of a Supply Shock Depends on the Shape of the Demand Curve.

An increase in the price of hogs shifts the supply of processed pork upward. (a) Given the actual downward-sloping linear demand curve, the equilibrium price rises from \$3.30 to \$3.55 and the equilibrium quantity falls from 220 to 215. (b) If the demand curve were vertical, the supply shock would cause price to rise to \$3.675 while quantity would remain unchanged. (c) If the demand curve were horizontal, the supply shock would not affect price but would cause quantity to fall to 205.

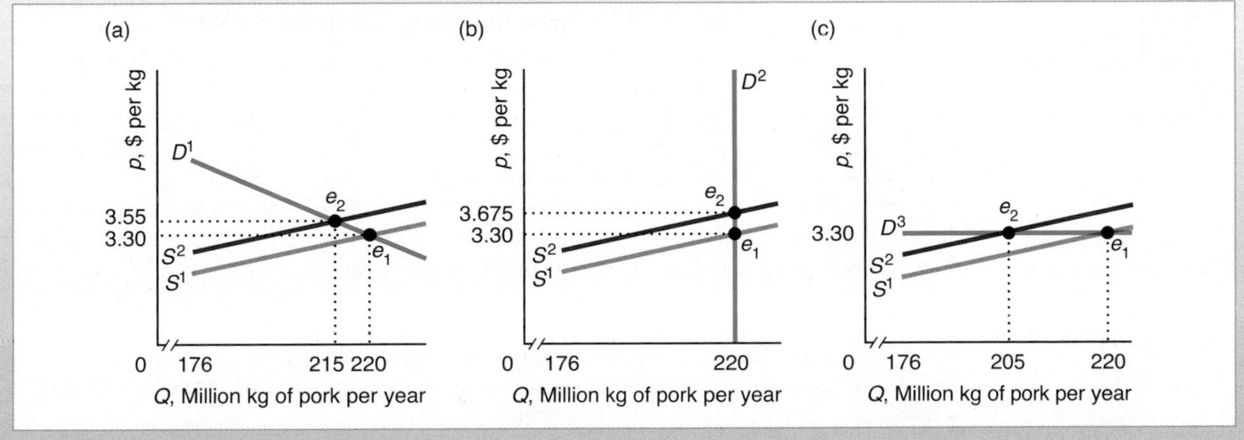

however, the equilibrium quantity drops substantially to 205 million kg per year. Thus how much the equilibrium quantity falls and how much the equilibrium price of processed pork rises when the price of hogs increases depend on the shape of the demand curve.

See Questions 1–4.

3.2 Sensitivity of Quantity Demanded to Price

Knowing how much quantity demanded falls as the price increases, holding all else constant, is therefore important in predicting the effect of a shock in a supply-and-demand model. We can determine how much quantity demanded falls as the price rises using an accurate drawing of the demand curve or the demand function (the equation that describes the demand curve). It is convenient, however, to be able to summarize the relevant information to answer what-if questions without having to write out an equation or draw a graph. Armed with such a summary statistic, the pork firms can predict the effect on the price of pork and their revenues from a shift in the market supply curve.

In this section, we discuss a summary statistic that describes how much the quantity demanded changes in response to an increase in price at a given point. In the next section, we discuss a similar statistic for the supply curve. At the end of the chapter, we show how the government can use these summary measures for supply and demand to predict the effect of a new sales tax on the equilibrium price, firms' revenues, and tax receipts.

Price Elasticity of Demand

elasticity
the percentage change in a variable in response to a given percentage change in another variable

price elasticity of demand (or *elasticity of demand*, ε)
the percentage change in the *quantity demanded* in response to a given percentage change in the price

The most commonly used measure of the sensitivity of one variable, such as the quantity demanded, to another variable, such as price, is an **elasticity**, which is the percentage change in one variable in response to a given percentage change in another variable. The **price elasticity of demand** (or simply *elasticity of demand*) is the percentage change in the quantity demanded, Q, in response to a given percentage change in the price, p, at a particular point on the demand curve. The price elasticity of demand (represented by ε, the Greek letter epsilon) is

$$\varepsilon = \frac{\text{percentage change in quantity demanded}}{\text{percentage change in price}} = \frac{\Delta Q/Q}{\Delta p/p}, \tag{3.1}$$

where the symbol Δ (the Greek letter delta) indicates a change, so ΔQ is the change in the quantity demanded; $\Delta Q/Q$ is the percentage change in the quantity demanded; Δp is the change in price; and $\Delta p/p$ is the percentage change in price.[1] For example, if a 1% increase in the price results in a 3% decrease in the quantity demanded, the elasticity of demand is $\varepsilon = -3\%/1\% = -3$.[2] Thus the elasticity of demand is a pure number (it has no units of measure).

See Questions 5 and 6.

[1]When we use calculus, we use infinitesimally small changes in price (Δp approaches zero), so we write the elasticity as $(dQ/dp)(p/Q)$. When discussing elasticities, we assume that the change in price is small.

[2]Because demand curves slope downward according to the Law of Demand, the elasticity of demand is a negative number. Realizing that, some economists ignore the negative sign when reporting a demand elasticity. In the example, instead of saying the elasticity is –3, they would say that the elasticity is 3 (with the negative sign understood).

It is often more convenient to calculate the elasticity of demand using an equivalent expression,

$$\varepsilon = \frac{\Delta Q/Q}{\Delta p/p} = \frac{\Delta Q}{\Delta p}\frac{p}{Q}, \tag{3.2}$$

where $\Delta Q/\Delta p$ is the ratio of the change in quantity to the change in price (the inverse of the slope of the demand curve).

We can use Equation 3.2 to calculate the elasticity of demand for a linear demand curve, which has a demand function (holding fixed other variables that affect demand) of

$$Q = a - bp,$$

where a is the quantity demanded when price is zero, $Q = a - (b \times 0) = a$, and $-b$ is the ratio of the fall in quantity to the rise in price, $\Delta Q/\Delta p$.[3] Thus for a linear demand curve, the elasticity of demand is

$$\varepsilon = \frac{\Delta Q}{\Delta p}\frac{p}{Q} = -b\frac{p}{Q}. \tag{3.3}$$

As an example, we calculate the elasticity of demand for the linear pork demand curve D in panel a of Figure 3.1. The estimated linear demand function for pork, which holds constant other factors that influence demand besides price (Equation 2.3, based on Moschini and Meilke, 1992), is

$$Q = 286 - 20p,$$

where Q is the quantity of pork demanded in million kg per year and p is the price of pork in dollars per kg. For this demand equation, $a = 286$ and $b = 20$. Using Equation 3.3, we find that the elasticity of demand at the equilibrium e_1 in panel a, where $p = \$3.30$ and $Q = 220$, is

See Problem 27.

$$\varepsilon = b\frac{p}{Q} = -20 \times \frac{3.30}{220} = -0.3.$$

The negative sign on the elasticity of demand of pork illustrates the Law of Demand: Less quantity is demanded as the price rises. The elasticity of demand concisely answers the question, "How much does quantity demanded fall in response to a 1% increase in price?" A 1% increase in price leads to an ε% change in the quantity demanded. At the equilibrium, a 1% increase in the price of pork leads to a −0.3% fall in the quantity of pork demanded: A price increase causes a less than proportionate fall in the quantity of pork demanded.

APPLICATION

Turning Off the Faucet

Many cities, states, and countries are having trouble providing households with adequate supplies of clean water. Typically, governments supply water at prices below its cost of providing the last unit of water. During droughts, governments often ration water rather than raise the price.

Is it feasible to cut the demand for water substantially by raising prices, or will households pay "virtually anything" for water? Many political leaders think that

[3]As the price increases from p_1 to p_2, the quantity demanded goes from Q_1 to Q_2, so the change in quantity demanded is $\Delta Q = Q_2 - Q_1 = (a - bp_2) - (a - bp_1) = -b(p_2 - p_1) = -b\Delta p$. Thus $\Delta Q/\Delta p = -b$. (The slope of the demand curve is $\Delta p/\Delta Q = -1/b$.)

water usage is not sensitive to price. Thus they keep the price low to help the poor (and others), figuring that it doesn't greatly affect usage.

Shanthi Nataraj (2007), a student at the University of California, Berkeley, used a natural experiment to determine the sensitivity of water demand to price. Like many cities, Santa Cruz, California, sells water using increasing block pricing (see Chapter 12 for more details on block pricing). Initially, the city charged 65¢ per unit for the first 8 units of water (a unit = 100 cubic feet), and $1.55 per unit for extra units. However, after a drought, it raised its rates and added a third block, so that it charged 69¢ per unit for the first 8 units, $1.64 per unit for units 9–39, and $3.14 per unit for 40 or more units.

Nataraj used statistics to control for other effects occurring at the same time and concluded that this nearly 100% increase in price for 40 and more units led to a 15% to 25% decrease in consumption among heavy users. Thus the demand for water is inelastic, but not literally zero. Consequently, by substantially raising prices, a government can cut water demand by heavy users significantly.

Elasticity Along the Demand Curve

The elasticity of demand varies along most demand curves. The elasticity of demand is different at every point along a downward-sloping linear demand curve; however, the elasticities are constant along horizontal and vertical linear demand curves.

Downward-Sloping Linear Demand Curve. On strictly downward-sloping linear demand curves—those that are neither vertical nor horizontal—the elasticity of demand is a more negative number the higher the price is. Consequently, even though the slope of the linear demand curve is constant, the elasticity varies along the curve. A 1% increase in price causes a larger percentage fall in quantity near the top (left) of the demand curve than near the bottom (right).

The linear pork demand curve in Figure 3.2 illustrates this pattern. Where this demand curve hits the quantity axis ($p = 0$ and $Q = a = 286$ million kg per year), the elasticity of demand is $\varepsilon = -b(0/a) = 0$, according to Equation 3.3. Where the price is zero, a 1% increase in price does not raise the price, so quantity does not change. At a point where the elasticity of demand is zero, the demand curve is said to be *perfectly inelastic*. As a physical analogy, if you try to stretch an inelastic steel rod, the length does not change. The change in the price is the force pulling at demand; if the quantity demanded does not change in response to this pulling, it is perfectly inelastic.

For quantities between the midpoint of the linear demand curve and the lower end where $Q = a$, the demand elasticity lies between 0 and −1: $0 > \varepsilon > -1$. A point along the demand curve where the elasticity is between 0 and −1 is *inelastic* (but not perfectly inelastic). Where the demand curve is inelastic, a 1% increase in price leads to a fall in quantity of less than 1%. For example, at the competitive pork equilibrium, $\varepsilon = -0.3$, so a 1% increase in price causes quantity to fall by −0.3%. A physical analogy is a piece of rope that does not stretch much—is inelastic—when you pull on it: Changing price has relatively little effect on quantity.

See Question 7.

At the midpoint of the linear demand curve,

$$p = a/(2b) \text{ and } Q = a/2, \text{ so } \varepsilon = -bp/Q = -b(a/[2b])/(a/2) = -1.$$

Such an elasticity of demand is called a *unitary elasticity*: A 1% increase in price causes a 1% fall in quantity.

Figure 3.2 Elasticity Along the Pork Demand Curve.

With a linear demand curve, such as the pork demand curve, the higher the price, the more elastic the demand curve (ε is larger in absolute value—a larger negative number). The demand curve is perfectly inelastic (ε = 0) where the demand curve hits the horizontal axis, is perfectly elastic where the demand curve hits the vertical axis, and has unitary elasticity (ε = –1) at the midpoint of the demand curve.

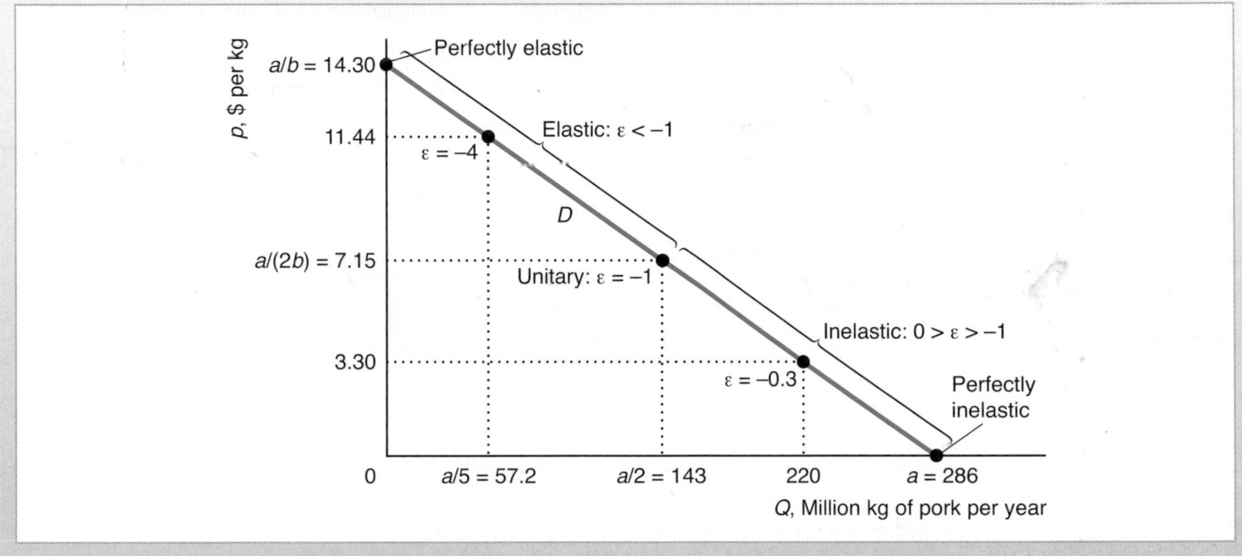

At prices higher than at the midpoint of the demand curve, the elasticity of demand is less than negative one, $\varepsilon < -1$. In this range, the demand curve is called *elastic*. A physical analogy is a rubber band that stretches substantially when you pull on it. A 1% increase in price causes a more than 1% fall in quantity. The figure shows that the elasticity is –4 where $Q = a/5$: A 1% increase in price causes a 4% drop in quantity.

As the price rises, the elasticity gets more and more negative, approaching negative infinity. Where the demand curve hits the price axis, it is *perfectly elastic*.[4] At the price a/b where $Q = 0$, a 1% decrease in p causes the quantity demanded to become positive, which is an infinite increase in quantity.

See Question 8.

The elasticity of demand varies along most demand curves, not just downward-sloping linear ones. Along a special type of demand curve, called a *constant-elasticity demand curve*, however, the elasticity is the same at every point along the curve.[5] Two extreme cases of these constant-elasticity demand curves are the strictly vertical and the strictly horizontal linear demand curves.

See Problems 28 and 29.

Horizontal Demand Curve. The demand curve that is horizontal at p^* in panel a of Figure 3.3 shows that people are willing to buy as much as firms sell at any price less than or equal to p^*. If the price increases even slightly above p^*, however,

[4]The demand curve hits the price axis at $p = a/b$ and $Q = 0$, so the elasticity is $-bp/0$. As the price approaches a/b, the elasticity approaches negative infinity. An intuition for this convention is provided by looking at a sequence, where –1 divided by 1/10 is –10, –1 divided by 1/100 is –100, and so on. The smaller the number we divide by, the more negative is the result, which goes to $-\infty$ (negative infinity) in the limit.

[5]Constant-elasticity demand curves all have the form $Q = Ap^{\varepsilon}$, where A is a positive constant and ε, a negative constant, is the demand elasticity at every point along these demand curves.

Figure 3.3 Vertical and Horizontal Demand Curves.

(a) A horizontal demand curve is perfectly elastic at p^*. (b) A vertical demand curve is perfectly inelastic at every price. (c) The demand curve of an individual who is diabetic is perfectly inelastic below p^* and perfectly elastic at p^*, which is the maximum price the individual can afford to pay.

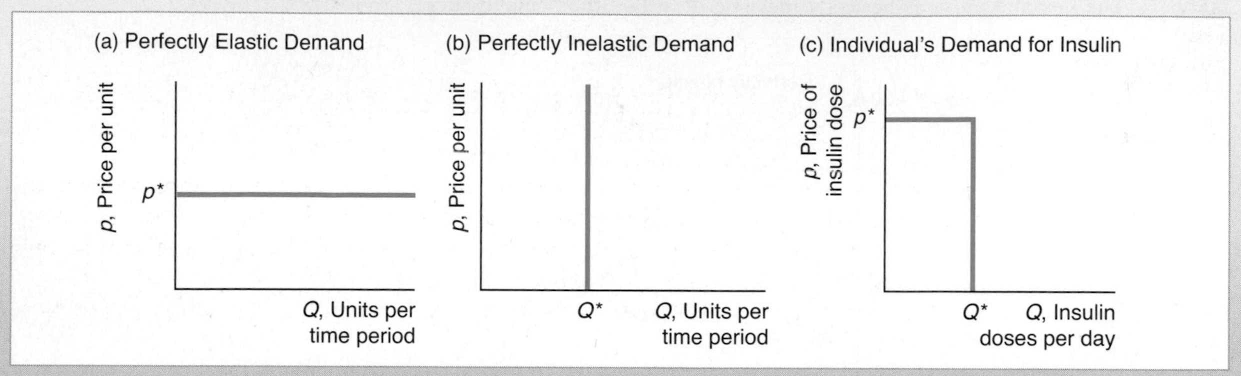

demand falls to zero. Thus a small increase in price causes an infinite drop in quantity, so the demand curve is perfectly elastic.

Why would a demand curve be horizontal? One reason is that consumers view this good as identical to another good and do not care which one they buy. Suppose that consumers view Washington apples and Oregon apples as identical. They won't buy Washington apples if these sell for more than apples from Oregon. Similarly, they won't buy Oregon apples if their price is higher than that of Washington apples. If the two prices are equal, consumers do not care which type of apple they buy. Thus the demand curve for Oregon apples is horizontal at the price of Washington apples.

Vertical Demand Curve. A vertical demand curve, panel b in Figure 3.3, is perfectly inelastic everywhere. Such a demand curve is an extreme case of the linear demand curve with an infinite (vertical) slope. If the price goes up, the quantity demanded is unchanged ($\Delta Q/\Delta p = 0$), so the elasticity of demand must be zero: $(\Delta Q/\Delta p)(p/Q) = 0(p/Q) = 0$.

A demand curve is vertical for *essential goods*—goods that people feel they must have and will pay anything to get. Because Jerry is a diabetic, his demand curve for insulin could be vertical at a day's dose, Q^*. More realistically, he may have a demand curve (panel c of Figure 3.3) that is perfectly inelastic only at prices below p^*, the maximum price he can afford to pay. Because he cannot afford to pay more than p^*, he buys nothing at higher prices. As a result, his demand curve is perfectly elastic up to Q^* units at a price of p^*.

Other Demand Elasticities

We refer to the price elasticity of demand as *the* elasticity of demand. However, there are other demand elasticities that show how the quantity demanded changes in response to changes in variables other than price that affect the quantity demanded. Two such demand elasticities are the income elasticity of demand and the cross-price elasticity of demand.

Income Elasticity. As income increases, the demand curve shifts. If the demand curve shifts to the right, a larger quantity is demanded at any given price. If instead the demand curve shifts to the left, a smaller quantity is demanded at any given price.

income elasticity of demand (or *income elasticity*)
the percentage change in the *quantity demanded* in response to a given percentage change in income

We can measure how sensitive the quantity demanded at a given price is to income by using an elasticity. The **income elasticity of demand** (or *income elasticity*) is the percentage change in the quantity demanded in response to a given percentage change in income, Y. The income elasticity of demand may be calculated as

$$\xi = \frac{\text{percentage change in quantity demanded}}{\text{percentage change in income}} = \frac{\Delta Q/Q}{\Delta Y/Y} = \frac{\Delta Q}{\Delta Y}\frac{Y}{Q},$$

where ξ is the Greek letter xi. If quantity demanded increases as income rises, the income elasticity of demand is positive. If the quantity does not change as income rises, the income elasticity is zero. Finally, if the quantity demanded falls as income rises, the income elasticity is negative.

We can calculate the income elasticity for pork using the demand function, Equation 2.2:

$$Q = 171 - 20p + 20p_b + 3p_c + 2Y, \tag{3.4}$$

where p is the price of pork, p_b is the price of beef, p_c is the price of chicken, and Y is the income (in thousands of dollars). Because the change in quantity as income changes is $\Delta Q/\Delta Y = 2$,[6] we can write the income elasticity as

$$\xi = \frac{\Delta Q}{\Delta Y}\frac{Y}{Q} = 2\frac{Y}{Q}.$$

At the equilibrium, quantity $Q = 220$ and income is $Y = 12.5$, so the income elasticity is $2 \times (12.5/220) \approx 0.114$. The positive income elasticity shows that an increase in income causes the pork demand curve to shift to the right. Holding the price of pork constant at \$3.30 per kg, a 1% increase in income causes the demand curve for pork to shift to the right by 0.25 ($= \xi \times 220 \times .01$) million kg, which is about one-ninth of 1% of the equilibrium quantity.

See Question 12 and Problem 32.

Income elasticities play an important role in our analysis of consumer behavior in Chapter 5. Typically, goods that society views as necessities, such as food, have income elasticities near zero. Goods that society considers to be luxuries generally have income elasticities greater than one.

cross-price elasticity of demand
the percentage change in the *quantity demanded* in response to a given percentage change in the price of another good

Cross-Price Elasticity. The **cross-price elasticity of demand** is the percentage change in the quantity demanded in response to a given percentage change in the price of another good, p_o. The cross-price elasticity may be calculated as

$$\frac{\text{percentage change in quantity demanded}}{\text{percentage change in price of another good}} = \frac{\Delta Q/Q}{\Delta p_o/p_o} = \frac{\Delta Q}{\Delta p_o}\frac{p_o}{Q}.$$

When the cross-price elasticity is negative, the goods are *complements* (Chapter 2). If the cross-price elasticity is negative, people buy less of the good when the price of the other good increases: The demand curve for this good shifts to the left. For example, if people like cream in their coffee, as the price of cream rises, they consume less coffee, so the cross-price elasticity of the quantity of coffee with respect to the price of cream is negative.

---

[6]At income Y_1, the quantity demanded is $Q_1 = 171 - 20p + 20p_b + 3p_c + 2Y_1$. At income Y_2, $Q_2 = 171 - 20p + 20p_b + 3p_c + 2Y_2$. Thus $\Delta Q = Q_2 - Q_1 = 2(Y_2 - Y_1) = 2(\Delta Y)$, so $\Delta Q/\Delta Y = 2$.

If the cross-price elasticity is positive, the goods are *substitutes* (Chapter 2). As the price of the other good increases, people buy more of this good. For example, the quantity demanded of pork increases when the price of beef, p_b, rises. From Equation 3.4, we know that $\Delta Q/\Delta p_b = 20$. As a result, the cross-price elasticity between the price of beef and the quantity of pork is

$$\frac{\Delta Q}{\Delta p_b}\frac{p_b}{Q} = 20\frac{p_b}{Q}.$$

See Questions 14 and 15 and Problem 31.

At the equilibrium where $p = \$3.30$ per kg, $Q = 220$ million kg per year, and $p_b = \$4$ per kg, the cross-price elasticity is $20 \times (4/220) \approx 0.364$. As the price of beef rises by 1%, the quantity of pork demanded rises by a little more than one-third of 1%.

Taking account of cross-price elasticities is important in making business and policy decisions. For example, General Motors wants to know how much a change in the price of a Toyota affects the demand for its Chevy.

APPLICATION

Substitution May Save Endangered Species

One reason that many species—including tigers, rhinoceroses, pinnipeds, green turtles, geckos, sea horses, pipefish, and sea cucumbers—are endangered, threatened, or vulnerable to extinction is that certain of their body parts are used as aphrodisiacs in traditional Chinese medicine. Is it possible that consumers will switch from such potions to Viagra, a less expensive and almost certainly more effective alternative treatment, and thereby help save these endangered species?

We cannot directly calculate the substitution elasticity between Viagra and these endangered species because their trade is illicit and not reported. However, harp seal and hooded seal genitalia are also used as aphrodisiacs in Asia, and they may be legally traded. Before 1998, Viagra was unavailable (effectively, it had an infinite price). When it became available at about \$15 to \$20 Canadian per pill, the demand curve for seal sex organs shifted substantially to the left. According to von Hippel and von Hippel (2002, 2004), 30,000 to 50,000 seal organs were sold at between \$70 and \$100 Canadian in the years just before 1998. In 1998, the price per unit fell to \$15 to \$20, and only 20,000 organs were sold. By 1999–2000 (and thereafter), virtually none were sold. A survey of older Chinese males confirms that, after the introduction of Viagra, they were much more likely to use a Western medicine than traditional Chinese medicines for erectile dysfunction. However, they were not more likely to use Western medicines for other problems (von Hippel et al., 2005).

This evidence suggests a strong willingness to substitute at current prices: a positive cross-price elasticity between seal organs and the price of Viagra. Thus Viagra can perhaps save more than marriages.

See Question 13.

3.3 Sensitivity of Quantity Supplied to Price

To answer many what-if questions, we need information about the sensitivity of the quantity supplied to changes in price. For example, to determine how a sales tax will affect market price, a government needs to know the sensitivity to price of both the quantity supplied and the quantity demanded.

Elasticity of Supply

price elasticity of supply (or *elasticity of supply*, η) the percentage change in the *quantity supplied* in response to a given percentage change in the price

Just as we can use the elasticity of demand to summarize information about the shape of a demand curve, we can use the elasticity of supply to summarize information about the supply curve. The **price elasticity of supply** (or *elasticity of supply*) is the percentage change in the quantity supplied in response to a given percentage change in the price. The price elasticity of supply (η, the Greek letter eta) is

$$\eta = \frac{\text{percentage change in quantity supplied}}{\text{percentage change in price}} = \frac{\Delta Q/Q}{\Delta p/p} = \frac{\Delta Q}{\Delta p}\frac{p}{Q}, \quad (3.5)$$

where Q is the *quantity supplied*. If $\eta = 2$, a 1% increase in price leads to a 2% increase in the quantity supplied.

The definition of the elasticity of supply, Equation 3.5, is very similar to the definition of the elasticity of demand, Equation 3.1. The key distinction is that the elasticity of supply describes the movement along the *supply* curve as price changes, whereas the elasticity of demand describes the movement along the *demand* curve as price changes. That is, in the numerator, supply elasticity depends on the percentage change in the *quantity supplied*, whereas demand elasticity depends on the percentage change in the *quantity demanded.*

If the supply curve is upward sloping, $\Delta p/\Delta Q > 0$, the supply elasticity is positive: $\eta > 0$. If the supply curve slopes downward, the supply elasticity is negative: $\eta < 0$.

To show how to calculate the elasticity of supply, we use the supply function for pork (based on Moschini and Meilke, 1992), Equation 2.7,

$$Q = 88 + 40p,$$

where Q is the quantity of pork supplied in million kg per year and p is the price of pork in dollars per kg. This supply function is a straight line in Figure 3.4. (The horizontal axis starts at 176 rather than at the origin.) The number multiplied by p in the supply function, 40, shows how much the quantity supplied rises as the price

Figure 3.4 Elasticity Along the Pork Supply Curve.

The elasticity of supply, η, varies along the pork supply curve. The higher the price, the larger is the supply elasticity.

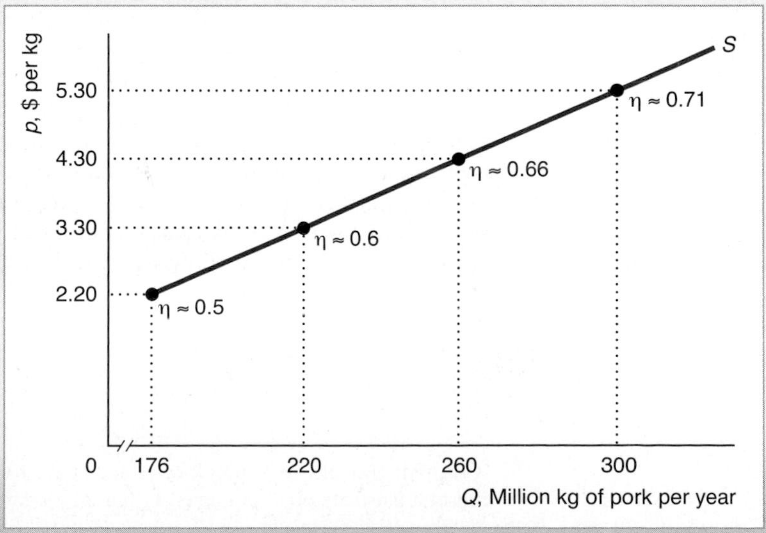

increases: $\Delta Q/\Delta p = 40$. At the equilibrium where $p = \$3.30$ and $Q = 220$, the elasticity of supply of pork is

$$\eta = \frac{\Delta Q}{\Delta p}\frac{p}{Q} = 40 \times \frac{3.30}{220} = 0.6.$$

As the price of pork increases by 1%, the quantity supplied rises by slightly less than two-thirds of a percent.

We use the terms *inelastic* and *elastic* to describe *upward-sloping* supply curves, just as we did for demand curves. If $\eta = 0$, we say that the supply curve is *perfectly inelastic*: The supply does not change as price rises. If $0 < \eta < 1$, the supply curve is *inelastic* (but not perfectly inelastic): A 1% increase in price causes a less than 1% rise in the quantity supplied. If $\eta = 1$, the supply curve has a *unitary elasticity*: A 1% increase in price causes a 1% increase in quantity. If $\eta > 1$, the supply curve is *elastic*. If η is infinite, the supply curve is *perfectly elastic*.

Elasticity Along the Supply Curve

The elasticity of supply may vary along the supply curve. The elasticity of supply varies along most linear supply curves.

The supply function of a linear supply curve is

$$Q = g + hp,$$

where g and h are constants. By the same reasoning as before, $\Delta Q = h\Delta p$, so $h = \Delta Q/\Delta p$ shows the change in the quantity supplied as price changes.

The supply curve for pork is $Q = 88 + 40p$, so $g = 88$ and $h = 40$. Because $h = 40$ is positive, the quantity of pork supplied increases as the price of pork rises.

The elasticity of supply for a linear supply function is $\eta = h(p/Q)$. The elasticity of supply for the pork is $\eta = 40p/Q$. As the ratio p/Q rises, the supply elasticity rises. Along most linear supply curves, the ratio p/Q changes as p rises.

See Problem 30.

The pork supply curve, Figure 3.4, is inelastic at each point shown. The elasticity of supply varies along the pork supply curve: It is 0.5 when $p = \$2.20$, 0.6 when $p = \$3.30$, and about 0.71 when $p = \$5.30$.

Only *constant elasticity of supply curves* have the same elasticity at every point along the curve.[7] Two extreme examples of both constant elasticity of supply curves and linear supply curves are the vertical and the horizontal supply curves.

The supply curve that is vertical at a quantity, Q^*, is perfectly inelastic. No matter what the price is, firms supply Q^*. An example of inelastic supply is a perishable item such as fresh fruit. If the perishable good is not sold, it quickly becomes worthless. Thus the seller accepts any market price for the good.

A supply curve that is horizontal at a price, p^*, is perfectly elastic. Firms supply as much as the market wants—a potentially unlimited amount—if the price is p^* or above. Firms supply nothing at a price below p^*, which does not cover their cost of production.

[7]Constant elasticity of supply curves are of the form $Q = Bp^{\eta}$, where B is a constant and η is the constant elasticity of supply at every point along the curve.

APPLICATION

The Big Freeze

From January 11 through January 17, 2007, a major freeze hit the fruit and vegetable fields of California, which supply most of the nation's grocery stores. Early reports said that half of many crops were destroyed. A spokesperson for the Western Growers Association, which represents 3,000 growers and shippers in California and Arizona, said that the damage could affect some tree crops and prices into 2008. Other crops, like celery and lettuce, have a new harvest every week, so the effect was short term.

Newspapers, quoting alleged industry experts, confidently made three predictions about the next several months. First, there would be shortages. Second, prices would zoom up and remain high. Third, industry revenue (price times quantity) would plummet.

This example shows why economists take newspaper stories and claims of "industry experts" with a grain of salt (Carmen and Sexton, 2007). The first two predictions are inconsistent: If prices can adjust freely, no shortages will occur.

The prediction of large price increases was true for some crops—only those that are grown primarily in California. Compared to the previous year, the January price for celery increased 352% and that of broccoli, 215%. These large increases occurred because the California supply curves are relatively vertical or inelastic, and the freeze shifted these vertical supply curves substantially to the left, causing a movement along the steeply downward-sloping demand curve, which is inelastic at the equilibria.

However, price increases were more moderate for those crops that can be imported from elsewhere. The total supply curve for such commodities is relatively flat—relatively elastic—where it intersects the demand curve. Before the freeze, experts expected that 58% of avocados would be imported from Mexico and Chile, whereas two-thirds of the avocados were imported. January imports from Chile alone were almost 5 times greater than 2006 imports, even though the freeze didn't occur in mid-month. Thus almost instantly, nearly half the forecast loss of California avocados was offset by increased imports. As a result, avocado price increases were small during January and February when Chilean imports were available. The price increased by about a third from mid-February to mid-March.

The prediction of massive industry losses due to the freeze was completely false for crops that experienced large price increases. Early reports based on a survey of citrus growers said that they expected to lose $800 million of a crop that was valued at $1.3 billion. However, these calculations were based on the prices from just before the freeze and neglected the increase in prices due to smaller crops.

For example, the freeze caused the steep supply curve for iceberg lettuce to shift to the left, causing a movement along the demand curve, which is relatively inelastic at the equilibrium price. Given the estimated elasticity of demand of –0.43, as price increases 10%, quantity falls 4.3%. We can use this estimated elasticity to calculate how much the equilibrium price would rise as the freeze causes a movement along the demand curve. To calculate this price change, we use the inverse of the elasticity, called the *price flexibility*, which is the percentage change in price divided by the percentage change in quantity. The price flexibility for lettuce is –2.3 ($\approx$ 1/–0.43). That is, a 10% decrease in the quantity of lettuce results in a 23% increase in price.

Because the price rises by more than the quantity falls, the remaining crop will bring in *more* revenue than would the original, larger lettuce crop. Suppose that 100 units of lettuce were originally produced and would have sold at $10, so that the revenue would have been $1,000. The freeze destroys 10% of the crop so that only 90 units are sold. Based on the price flexibility estimate, the equilibrium price rises to $12.30 so that the revenue is $1,107, which is nearly 11% more than would have been received without the freeze.

See Question 16 and Problem 34.

Similarly, the forecasts of dramatic drops in revenue for citrus and many other crops that experienced large price effects turned out to be false. Only crops whose prices remain relatively unchanged experienced large drops in industry revenue due to the freeze.

3.4 Long Run Versus Short Run

The shapes of supply and demand curves depend on the relevant time period. Short-run elasticities may differ substantially from long-run elasticities. The duration of the *short run* depends on how long it takes consumers or firms to adjust for a particular good.

Demand Elasticities over Time

Two factors that determine whether short-run demand elasticities are larger or smaller than long-run elasticities are ease of substitution and storage opportunities. Often one can substitute between products in the long run but not in the short run.

When oil prices rose rapidly in the 1970s and 1980s because of actions by OPEC, most Western consumers did not greatly alter the amount of oil they demanded. Someone who drove 27 miles to and from work every day in a 1969 Chevy could not easily reduce the amount of gasoline purchased. In the long run, however, this person could buy a smaller car, get a job closer to home, join a car pool, or in other ways reduce the amount of gasoline purchased.

Gallini (1983) estimated long-run demand elasticities that are more elastic than the short-run elasticity for gasoline in Canada. She found that the short-run elasticity is –0.35; the 5-year intermediate-run elasticity is nearly twice as elastic, –0.7; and the 10-year, long-run elasticity is approximately –0.8, which is slightly more elastic. Thus a 1% increase in price lowers the quantity demanded by only about a 0.35% in the short run but by more than twice as much, 0.8%, in the long run. Similarly, Grossman and Chaloupka (1998) estimate that a rise in the street price of cocaine has a larger long-run than short-run effect on cocaine consumption by young adults (aged 17–29). The long-run demand elasticity is –1.35, whereas the short-run elasticity is –0.96.

For goods that can be stored easily, short-run demand curves may be more elastic than long-run curves. If frozen orange juice goes on sale this week at your local supermarket, you may buy large quantities and store the extra in your freezer. As a result, you may be more sensitive to price changes for frozen orange juice in the short run than in the long run.

Supply Elasticities over Time

Supply curves too may have different elasticities in the short run than in the long run. If a manufacturing firm wants to increase production in the short run, it can do so by hiring workers to use its machines around the clock, but how much it can expand its output is limited by the fixed size of its manufacturing plant and the number of machines it has. In the long run, however, the firm can build another plant and buy or build more equipment. Thus we would expect this firm's long-run supply elasticity to be greater than its short-run elasticity.

See Question 17.

Similarly, Adelaja (1991) found that the short-run elasticity of supply of milk is 0.36, whereas the long-run supply elasticity is 0.51. Thus, the long-run quantity response to a 1% increase in price is about 42% (= [0.51 – 0.36]/0.36) more than in the short run.

APPLICATION

Oil Drilling in the Arctic National Wildlife Refuge

We can use information about supply and demand elasticities to answer an important public policy question: Would selling oil from the Arctic National Wildlife Refuge (ANWR) substantially affect the price of oil? ANWR, established in 1980, covers 20 million acres, is the largest of Alaska's 16 national wildlife refuges, and is believed to contain large deposits of petroleum (about the amount consumed in the United States in 2005). For decades, a debate has raged over whether the owners of ANWR—the citizens of the United States—should keep it undeveloped or permit oil drilling.[8]

In the simplest form of this complex debate, environmentalists stress that drilling would harm the wildlife refuge and pollute the environment, while President George W. Bush and other drilling proponents argue that extracting this oil would substantially reduce the price of petroleum (as well as decrease U.S. dependence on foreign oil and bring in large royalties). Recent large increases in the price of gasoline and the war in Iraq have heightened this intense debate.

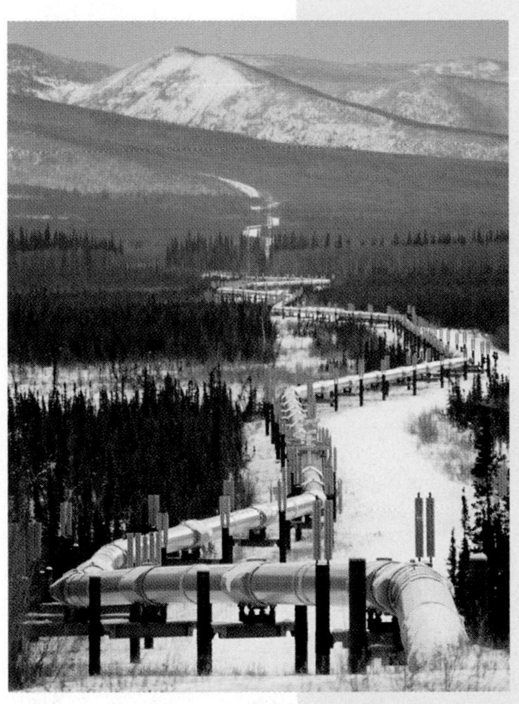

The effect of selling ANWR on the world price of oil is a key element of this debate. We can combine oil production information with supply and demand elasticities to make a "back of the envelope" estimate of the price effects.

A number of studies estimate that the long-run elasticity of demand, ε, for oil is about –0.4 and the long-run supply elasticity, η, is about 0.3. Analysts agree less about how much ANWR oil will be produced. The Department of Energy's Energy Information Service predicts that production from ANWR would average about 800,000 barrels per day. That production would be about 1% of the worldwide oil production, which averaged about 82 million barrels per day in 2004 and 84 million barrels per day in 2007.

A report of the U.S. Department of Energy predicted that ANWR drilling could lower the price of oil by about 1%, which was 50¢ a barrel given that the price of a barrel of oil was about $50 at the beginning of 2007, or $1 given the price of a barrel of $100 at the beginning of 2008. Severin Borenstein, an economist who is the director of the U.C. Energy Institute, concluded that ANWR might reduce oil prices by up to a few percentage points, so that "drilling in ANWR will never noticeably affect gasoline prices." In Solved Problem 3.1, we can make our own calculations of the price effect of drilling in ANWR.

[8] I am grateful to Robert Whaples, who wrote an earlier version of this analysis. In the following discussion, we assume for simplicity that the oil market is competitive, and use current values of price and quantities even though drilling in ANWR could not take place for at least a decade.

Solved Problem 3.1

What would be the effect of ANWR production on the world price of oil given that $\varepsilon = -0.4$, $\eta = 0.3$, the pre-ANWR daily world production of oil is $Q_1 = 82$ million barrels per day, the pre-ANWR world price is $p_1 = \$100$ per barrel, and daily ANWR production would be 0.8 million barrels per day? For simplicity, assume that the supply and demand curves are linear and that the introduction of ANWR oil would cause a parallel shift in the world supply curve to the right by 0.8 million barrels per day.

Answer

1. *Determine the long-run linear demand function that is consistent with pre-ANWR world output and price.* At the original equilibrium, e_1, in the figure, $p_1 = \$100$ and $Q_1 = 82$. There the elasticity of demand is $\varepsilon = (\Delta Q/\Delta p)(p_1/Q_1) = (\Delta Q/\Delta p)(50/100) = -0.4$. Using algebra, we find that $\Delta Q/\Delta p$ equals $-0.4(82/100) = -0.328$, which is the inverse of the slope of the demand curve, D, in the figure. Knowing this slope and that demand equals 82 at \$100 per barrel, we can solve for the intercept, because the quantity demanded rises by 0.328 for each dollar by which the price falls. The quantity demanded when price is zero is $82 + (0.328 \times 100) = 114.8$. Thus the equation for the demand curve is $Q = 114.8 - 0.328p$.

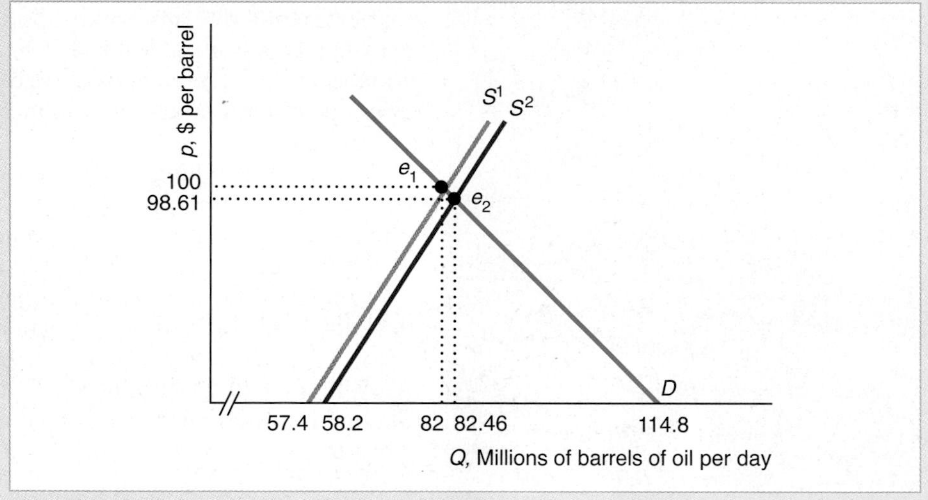

2. *Determine the long-run linear supply function that is consistent with pre-ANWR world output and price.* Where S^1 intercepts D at the original equilibrium, e_1, the elasticity of supply is

$$\eta = (\Delta Q/\Delta p)(p_1/Q_1) = (\Delta Q/\Delta p)(100/82) = 0.3.$$

Solving this, we find that $\Delta Q/\Delta p = 0.3(82/100) = 0.246$. Because the quantity supplied falls by 0.246 for each dollar by which the price drops, the quantity supplied when price is zero is $82 - (0.246 \times 100) = 57.4$. Thus the equation for the pre-ANWR supply curve, S^1 in the figure, is $Q = 57.4 + 0.246p$.

3. *Determine the post-ANWR long-run linear supply function.* The oil pumped from ANWR would cause a parallel shift in the supply curve, moving S^1 to the right by 0.8 to S^2. That is, the slope remains the same, but the intercept on the quantity axis increases by 0.8. Thus the supply function for S^2 is $Q = 58.2 + 0.246p$.

4. *Use the demand curve and the post-ANWR supply function to calculate the new equilibrium price and quantity:* The new equilibrium, e_2, occurs where S^2 intersects D. Setting the right sides of the demand function and the post-ANWR supply function equal, we obtain an expression in the new price, p_2:

$$58.2 + 0.246p_2 = 114.8 - 0.328p_2.$$

We can solve this expression for the new equilibrium price: $p_2 \approx \$98.61$. That is, the price drops about \$1.39, about 1.4%. If we substitute this new price into either the demand curve or the post-ANWR supply curve, we find that the new equilibrium quantity is 82.46 million barrels per day. That is, equilibrium output rises by 0.46 million barrels per day (0.56%), which is only a little more than half of the predicted daily ANWR supply, because other suppliers will decrease their output slightly in response to the lower price.

Comment: Our estimate of a small drop in the world oil price if ANWR oil is sold would not change substantially if our estimates of the elasticities of supply and demand were moderately larger or smaller. The main reason for this result is that the ANWR output would be a very small portion of worldwide supply—the new supply curve is only slightly to the right of the initial supply curve. Thus drilling in ANWR cannot insulate the American market from international events that roil the oil market. A new war in the Persian Gulf could shift the worldwide supply curve to the left by 3 million barrels a day or more (nearly four times the ANWR production). Such a shock would cause the price of oil to soar whether or not we drill in ANWR.

See Question 10 and Problem 35.

3.5 Effects of a Sales Tax

Before voting for a new sales tax, legislators want to predict the effect of the tax on prices, quantities, and tax revenues. If the new tax will produce a large increase in the price, legislators who vote for the tax may lose their jobs in the next election. Voters' ire is likely to be even greater if the tax does not raise significant tax revenues.

In this section, we examine three questions about the effects of a sales tax:

1. What effect does a sales tax have on equilibrium prices and quantity?
2. Is it true, as many people claim, that taxes assessed on producers are *passed along* to consumers? That is, do consumers pay for the entire tax?
3. Do the equilibrium price and quantity depend on whether the tax is assessed on consumers or on producers?

How much a tax affects the equilibrium price and quantity and how much of the tax falls on consumers depend on the shape of the supply and demand curves, which is summarized by the elasticities. Knowing only the elasticities of supply and demand, we can make accurate predictions about the effects of a new tax and determine how much of the tax falls on consumers.

Two Types of Sales Taxes

Governments use two types of sales taxes. The most common sales tax is called an *ad valorem* tax by economists and *the* sales tax by real people. For every dollar the consumer spends, the government keeps a fraction, α, which is the *ad valorem* tax rate. Since 1997, Japan's national sales tax has been $\alpha = 5\%$. If a Japanese consumer buys a CD player for \$100, the government collects $\alpha \times \$100 = 5\% \times \$100 = \$5$ in taxes, and the seller receives $(1 - \alpha) \times \$100 = \$95$.[9]

The other type of sales tax is a *specific* or *unit* tax, where a specified dollar amount, τ, is collected per unit of output. The federal government collects $\tau = 18.4$¢ on each gallon of gas sold in the United States. Many communities charge a fixed filing fee or tax on every house sold.

Equilibrium Effects of a Specific Tax

To answer our three questions, we must extend the standard supply-and-demand analysis to take taxes into account. Let's start by assuming that the specific tax is assessed on firms at the time of sale. If the consumer pays p for a good, the government takes τ and the seller receives $p - \tau$.

Specific Tax Effects in the Pork Market. Suppose that the government collects a specific tax of $\tau = \$1.05$ per kg of processed pork from pork producers. Because of the tax, suppliers keep only $p - \tau$ of price p that consumers pay. Thus at every possible price paid by consumers, firms are willing to supply less than when they received the full amount consumers paid. Before the tax, firms were willing to supply 206 million kg per year at a price of \$2.95 as the pretax supply curve S^1 in Figure 3.5 shows. After the tax, firms receive only \$1.90 if consumers pay \$2.95, so they are not willing to supply 206. For firms to be willing to supply 206, they must receive \$2.95 after the tax, so consumers must pay \$4. As a result, the after-tax supply curve, S^2, is $\tau = \$1.05$ above the original supply curve S^1 at every quantity, as the figure shows.

We can use this figure to illustrate the answer to our first question concerning the effects of the tax on the equilibrium. *The specific tax causes the equilibrium price consumers pay to rise, the equilibrium quantity to fall, and tax revenue to rise.*

The intersection of the pretax pork supply curve S^1 and the pork demand curve D in Figure 3.5 determines the pretax equilibrium, e_1. The equilibrium price is $p_1 = \$3.30$, and the equilibrium quantity is $Q_1 = 220$. The tax shifts the supply curve to S^2, so the after-tax equilibrium is e_2, where consumers pay $p_2 = \$4$, firms receive $p_2 - \$1.05 = \$2.95$, and $Q_2 = 206$. Thus the tax causes the price that consumers pay to increase ($\Delta p = p_2 - p_1 = \$4 - \$3.30 = 70$¢) and the quantity to fall ($\Delta Q = Q_2 - Q_1 = 206 - 220 = -14$).

See Problem 36.

Although the consumers and producers are worse off because of the tax, the government acquires new tax revenue of $T = \tau Q = \$1.05$ per kg $\times$ 206 million kg per year = \$216.3 million per year. The length of the shaded rectangle in Figure 3.5 is $Q_2 = 206$ million kg per year, and its height is $\tau = \$1.05$ per kg, so the area of the rectangle equals the tax revenue. (The figure shows only part of the length of the rectangle because the horizontal axis starts at 176.)

How Specific Tax Effects Depend on Elasticities. The effects of the tax on the equilibrium prices and quantity depend on the elasticities of supply and demand.

[9]For specificity, we assume that the price firms receive is $p = (1 - \alpha)p^*$, where p^* is the price consumers pay and α is the *ad valorem* tax rate on the price consumers pay. Many governments, however, set the *ad valorem* sales tax, β, as an amount added to the price sellers charge, so consumers pay $p^* = (1 + \beta)p$. By setting α and β appropriately, the taxes are equivalent. Here $p = p^*/(1 + \beta)$, so $(1 - \alpha) = 1/(1 + \beta)$. For example, if $\beta = \frac{1}{3}$, then $\alpha = \frac{1}{4}$.

Figure 3.5 Effect of a $1.05 Specific Tax on the Pork Market Collected from Producers.

The specific tax of τ = $1.05 per kg collected from producers shifts the pretax pork supply curve from S^1 to the posttax supply curve, S^2. The tax causes the equilibrium to shift from e_1 (determined by the intersection of S^1 and D) to e_2 (intersection of S^2 with D). The equilibrium price increases from $3.30 to $4.00. Two-thirds of the incidence of the tax falls on consumers, who spend 70¢ more per unit. Producers receive 35¢ less per unit after the tax. The government collects tax revenues of $T = \tau Q_2$ = $216.3 million per year.

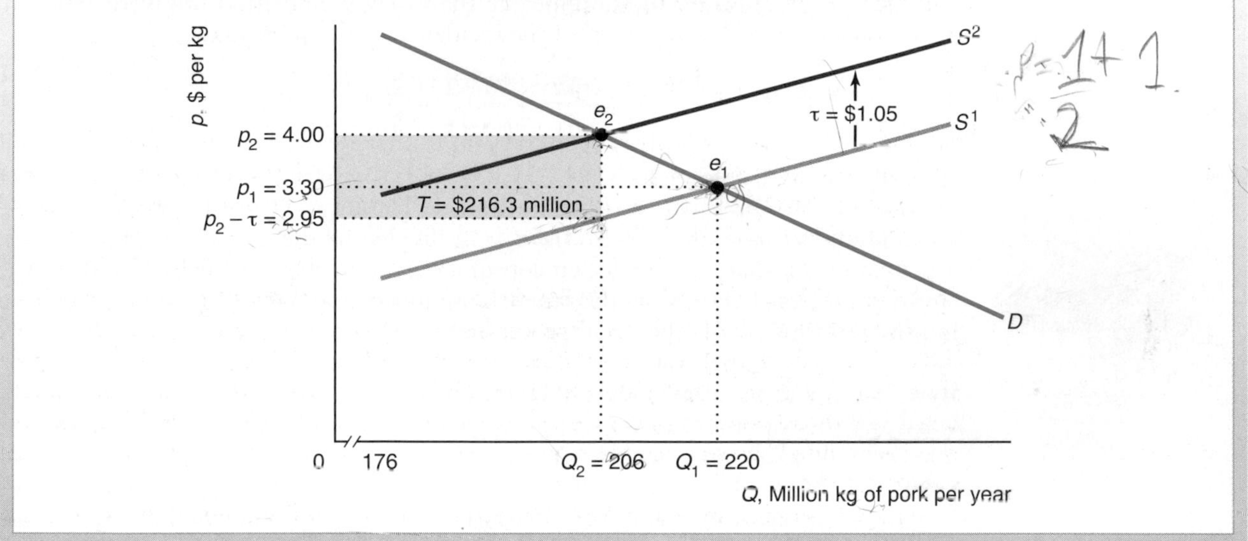

The government raises the tax from zero to τ, so the change in the tax is $\Delta\tau = \tau - 0 = \tau$. In response to this change in the tax, the price consumers pay increases by

$$\Delta p = \left(\frac{\eta}{\eta - \varepsilon}\right)\Delta\tau, \tag{3.6}$$

where ε is the demand elasticity and η is the supply elasticity at the equilibrium (this equation is derived in Appendix 3A). The demand elasticity for pork is $\varepsilon = -0.3$, and the supply elasticity is $\eta = 0.6$, so a change in the tax of $\Delta\tau$ = $1.05 causes the price consumers pay to rise by

$$\Delta p = \left(\frac{\eta}{\eta - \varepsilon}\right)\Delta\tau = \frac{0.6}{0.6 - [-0.3]} \times \$1.05 = 70¢,$$

as Figure 3.5 shows.

For a given supply elasticity, the more elastic demand is, the less the equilibrium price rises when a tax is imposed. In the pork equilibrium in which the supply elasticity is $\eta = 0.6$, if the demand elasticity were $\varepsilon = -2.4$ instead of -0.3 (that is, the linear demand curve had a less steep slope through the original equilibrium point), the consumer price would rise only $0.6/(0.6 - [-2.4]) \times \$1.05 = 21¢$ instead of 70¢.

Similarly, for a given demand elasticity, the greater the supply elasticity, the larger the increase in the equilibrium price consumers pay when a tax is imposed. In the pork example, in which the demand elasticity is $\varepsilon = -0.3$, if the supply elasticity were $\eta = 1.2$ instead of 0.6, the consumer price would rise $1.2/(1.2 - [-0.3]) \times \$1.05 = 84¢$ instead of 70¢.

Tax Incidence of a Specific Tax

incidence of a tax on consumers
the share of the tax that falls on consumers

We can now answer our second question: Who is hurt by the tax? The **incidence of a tax on consumers** is the share of the tax that falls on consumers. The incidence of the tax that falls on consumers is $\Delta p/\Delta\tau$, the amount by which the price to consumers rises as a fraction of the amount the tax increases.

In our pork example in Figure 3.5, a $\Delta\tau = \$1.05$ increase in the specific tax causes consumers to pay Δp = 70¢ more per kg than they would if no tax were assessed. Thus consumers bear two-thirds of the incidence of the pork tax:

$$\frac{\Delta p}{\Delta\tau} = \frac{\$0.70}{\$1.05} = \frac{2}{3}.$$

Firms receive $(p_2 - \tau) - p_1 = (\$4 - \$1.05) - \$3.30 = \$2.95 - \$3.30 = -35¢$ less per kg than they would in the absence of the tax. The incidence of the tax on firms—the amount by which the price to them falls, divided by the tax—is $\$0.35/\$1.05 = \frac{1}{3}$. The sum of the share of the tax on consumers, $\frac{2}{3}$, and that on firms, $\frac{1}{3}$, adds to the entire tax effect, 1. Equivalently, the increase in price to consumers minus the drop in price to firms equals the tax: 70¢ − (−35¢) = \$1.05 = τ.

How Tax Incidence Depends on Elasticities. If the demand curve slopes downward and the supply curve slopes upward, as in Figure 3.5, the incidence of the tax *does not* fall solely on consumers. Firms do not pass along the entire tax in higher prices.

Firms can pass along the full cost of the tax only when the demand or supply elasticities take on certain extreme values. To determine the conditions under which firms can pass along the full tax, we need to know how the incidence of the tax depends on the elasticities of supply and demand at the pretax equilibrium. By dividing both sides of Equation 3.6 by $\Delta\tau$, we can write the incidence of the tax that falls on consumers as

$$\frac{\Delta p}{\Delta\tau} = \frac{\eta}{\eta - \varepsilon}. \tag{3.7}$$

Because the demand elasticity for pork is $\varepsilon = -0.3$ and the supply elasticity is $\eta = 0.6$, the incidence of the pork tax that falls on consumers is

$$\frac{0.6}{0.6 - (-0.3)} = \frac{2}{3}.$$

See Question 25 and Problems 39, 40, and 43.

The more elastic the demand at the equilibrium, holding the supply elasticity constant, the lower the burden of the tax on consumers. Similarly, the greater the supply elasticity, holding the demand elasticity constant, the greater the burden on consumers. Thus as the demand curve becomes relatively inelastic (ε approaches zero) or the supply curve becomes relatively elastic (η becomes very large), the incidence of the tax falls mainly on consumers.

Solved Problem 3.2

If the supply curve is perfectly elastic and demand is linear and downward sloping, what is the effect of a \$1 specific tax collected from producers on equilibrium price and quantity, and what is the incidence on consumers? Why?

Even at current tax rates, cigarette tax revenue is substantial. The U.S. government collected cigarette tax revenues of $7.7 billion (2005 fiscal year), and state governments raised $13 billion (2005 calendar year). Tobacco tax revenues as a share of total government revenues range from 9.1% in China, 7.7% in Greece, 5.4% in Nepal, 4.9% in Brazil, 4.0% in Argentina, 3.4% in Australia, 3.2% in the United Kingdom, and 1.6% in Sweden, to only 0.44% in the United States. In short, given the inelastic demand for cigarettes at current prices, the U.S. government could raise substantially more tax revenue by increasing the tax rate on cigarettes.

See Problem 42.

The Same Equilibrium No Matter Who Is Taxed

Our third question is, "Does the equilibrium or the incidence of the tax depend on whether the tax is collected from suppliers or demanders?" Surprisingly, in the supply-and-demand model, the equilibrium and incidence of the tax are the same regardless of whether the government collects the tax from consumers or producers.

See Question 34.

We've already seen that firms are able to pass on some or all of the tax collected from them to consumers. We now show that, if the tax is collected from consumers, they can pass the producer's share back to the firms.

Suppose the specific tax $\tau = \$1.05$ on pork is collected from consumers rather than from sellers. Because the government takes τ from each p consumers spend, sellers receive only $p - \tau$. Thus the demand curve as seen by firms shifts downward by $1.05 from D^1 to D^2 in Figure 3.6.

See Problem 37.

Figure 3.6 Effect of a $1.05 Specific Tax on Pork Collected from Consumers.

The tax shifts the demand curve down by $\tau = \$1.05$ from D^1 to D^2. The new equilibrium is the same as when the tax is applied to suppliers in Figure 3.5. We can also determine the after-tax equilibrium by sticking a wedge with length $\tau = \$1.05$ between S and D^1.

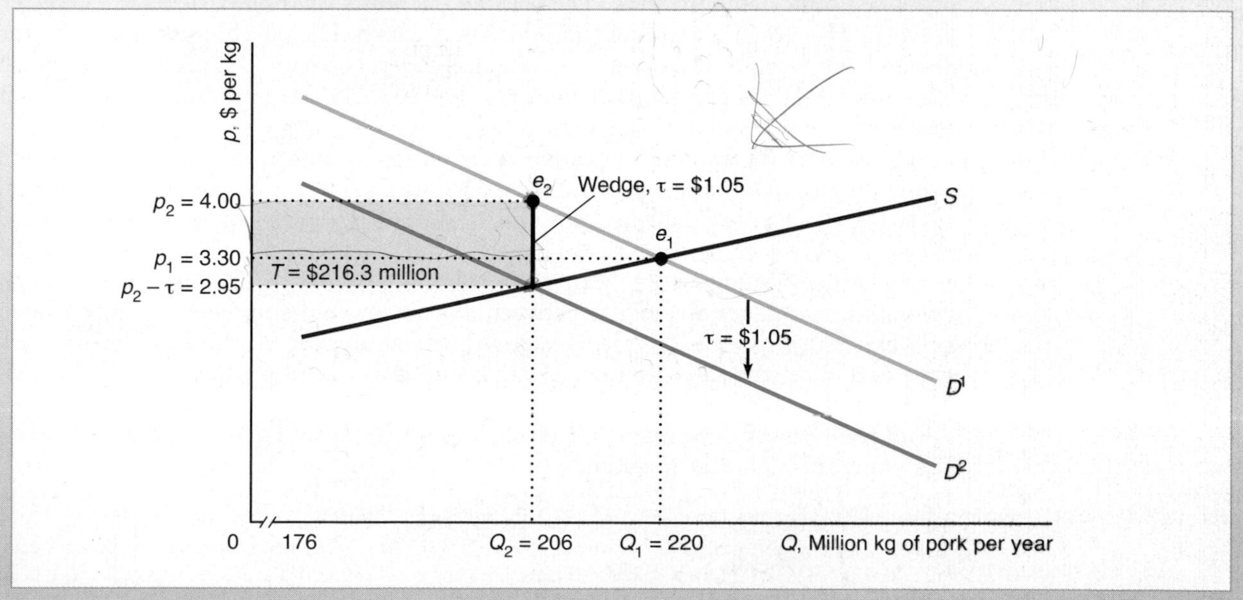

The intersection of D^2 and the supply curve S determines the after-tax equilibrium, e_2, where the equilibrium quantity is Q_2 and the price received by producers is $p_2 - \tau$. The price paid by consumers, p_2 (on the original demand curve D^1 at Q_2), is τ above the price received by producers.

Comparing Figure 3.6 to Figure 3.5, we see that the after-tax equilibrium is the same regardless of whether the tax is imposed on the consumers or the sellers. The price to consumers rises by the same amount, Δp, so the incidence of the tax, $\Delta p/\Delta\tau$, is also the same.

A specific tax, regardless of whether the tax is collected from consumers or producers, creates a *wedge* equal to the per-unit tax of τ between the price consumers pay, p, and the price suppliers receive, $p - \tau$. Indeed, we can insert a wedge—the vertical line labeled $\tau = \$1.05$ in the figure—between the original supply and demand curves to determine the after-tax equilibrium.

In short, regardless of whether firms or consumers pay the tax to the government, you can solve tax problems by shifting the supply curve, shifting the demand curve, or using a wedge. All three approaches give the same answer.

The Similar Effects of *Ad Valorem* and Specific Taxes

In contrast to specific sales taxes, governments levy *ad valorem* taxes on a wide variety of goods. Most states apply an *ad valorem* sales tax to most goods and services, exempting only a few staples such as food and medicine. There are 6,400 different *ad valorem* sales tax rates across the United States, which can go as high as 8.5% (Besley and Rosen, 1999).

Suppose that the government imposes an *ad valorem* tax of α, instead of a specific tax, on the price that consumers pay for processed pork. We already know that the equilibrium price is \$4 with a specific tax of \$1.05 per kg. At that price, an *ad valorem* tax of $\alpha = \$1.05/\$4 = 26.25\%$ raises the same amount of tax per unit as a \$1.05 specific tax.

It is usually easiest to analyze the effects of an *ad valorem* tax by shifting the demand curve. Figure 3.7 shows how a specific tax and an *ad valorem* tax shift the processed pork demand curve. The specific tax shifts the pretax demand curve, D, down to D^s, which is parallel to the original curve. The *ad valorem* tax shifts the demand curve to D^a. At any given price p, the gap between D and D^a is αp, which is greater at high prices than at low prices. The gap is \$1.05 ($= 0.2625 \times \$4$) per unit when the price is \$4, and \$2.10 when the price is \$8.

Imposing an *ad valorem* tax causes the after-tax equilibrium quantity, Q_2, to fall below the original quantity, Q_1, and the after-tax price, p_2, to rise above the original price, p_1. The tax collected per unit of output is $\tau = \alpha p_2$. The incidence of the tax that falls on consumers is the change in price, $\Delta p = (p_2 - p_1)$, divided by the change in the per unit tax, $\Delta\tau = \alpha p_2 - 0$, collected, $\Delta p/(\alpha p_2)$. The incidence of an *ad valorem* tax is generally shared between consumers and suppliers. Because the *ad valorem* tax of $\alpha = 26.25\%$ has exactly the same impact on the equilibrium pork price and raises the same amount of tax per unit as the \$1.05 specific tax, the incidence is the same for both types of taxes. (As with specific taxes, the incidence of the *ad valorem* tax depends on the elasticities of supply and demand, but we'll spare you going through that in detail.)

See Questions 22 and 23.

Figure 3.7 Comparison of an *Ad Valorem* and a Specific Tax on Pork.

Without a tax, the demand curve is D and the supply curve is S. The *ad valorem* tax of $\alpha = 26.25\%$ shifts the demand curve facing firms to D^a. The gap between D and D^a, the per-unit tax, is larger at higher prices. In contrast, the demand curve facing firms given a specific tax of \$1.05 per kg, D^s, is parallel to D. The after-tax equilibrium is the same with both of these taxes.

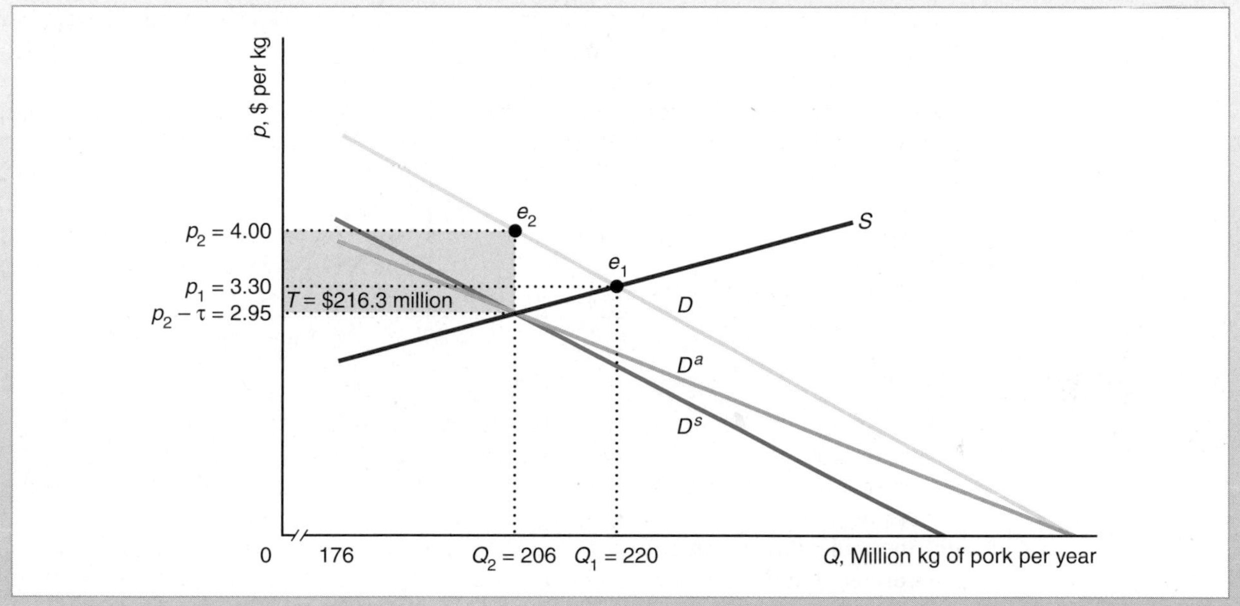

Solved Problem 3.3

If the short-run supply curve for fresh fruit is perfectly inelastic and the demand curve is a downward-sloping straight line, what is the effect of an *ad valorem* tax on equilibrium price and quantity, and what is the incidence on consumers? Why?

Answer

1. *Determine the before-tax equilibrium.* The perfectly inelastic supply curve, S, is vertical at Q^* in the graph. The pretax demand curve, D^1, intersects S at e_1, where the equilibrium price to both consumers and producers is p^* and the equilibrium quantity is Q^*.

2. *Show how the tax shifts the demand curve, and determine the after-tax equilibrium.* When the government imposes an *ad valorem* tax with a rate of α, the demand curve as seen by the firms rotates down to D^2, where the gap between the two demand curves is αp. The intersection of S and D^2 determines the after-tax equilibrium, e_2. The equilibrium quantity remains unchanged at Q^*. Consumers continue to pay p^*. The government collects αp^* per unit, so firms receive less, $(1 - \alpha)p^*$, than the p^* they received before the tax.

3. *Determine the incidence of the tax on consumers.* The consumers continue to pay the same price, so $\Delta p = 0$ when the tax increases by αp^* (from 0), and the incidence of the tax that falls on consumers is $\$0/(\alpha p^*) = 0\%$.

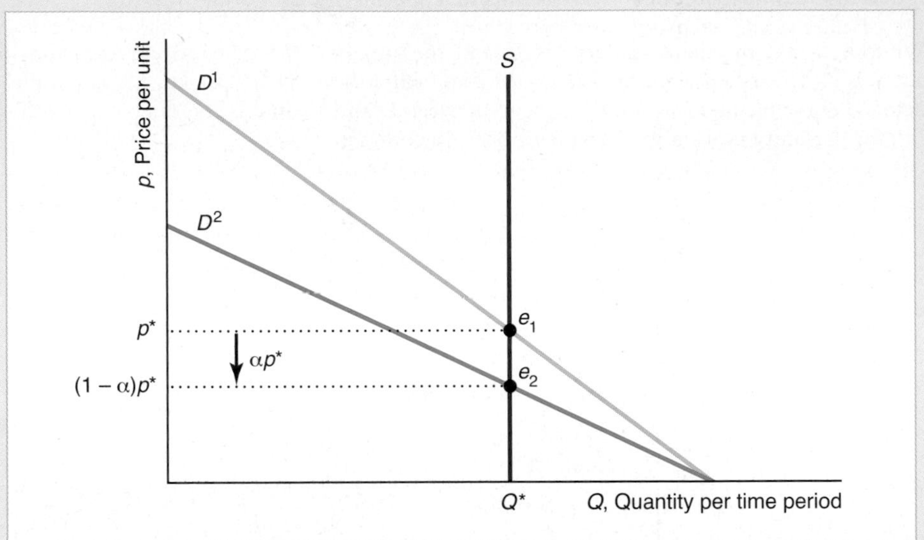

4. *Explain why the incidence of the tax falls entirely on firms.* The reason why firms absorb the entire tax is that firms supply the same amount of fruit, Q^*, no matter what tax the government sets. If firms were to raise the price, consumers would buy less fruit and suppliers would be stuck with the essentially worthless excess quantity, which would spoil quickly. Thus because suppliers prefer to sell their produce at a positive price rather than a zero price, they absorb any tax-induced drop in price.

SUMMARY

1. **How Shapes of Supply and Demand Curves Matter.** The degree to which a shock (such as an increase in the price of a factor) shifts the supply curve and affects the equilibrium price and quantity depends on the shape of the demand curve. Similarly, the degree to which a shock (such as an increase in the price of a substitute) shifts the demand curve and affects the equilibrium depends on the shape of the supply curve.

2. **Sensitivity of Quantity Demanded to Price.** The price elasticity of demand (or elasticity of demand), ε, summarizes the shape of a demand curve at a particular point. The elasticity of demand is the percentage change in the quantity demanded in response to a given percentage change in price. For example, a 1% increase in price causes the quantity demanded to fall by ε%. Because demand curves slope downward according to the Law of Demand, the elasticity of demand is always negative.

   The demand curve is perfectly inelastic if $\varepsilon = 0$, inelastic if $0 > \varepsilon > -1$, unitary elastic if $\varepsilon = -1$, elastic if $\varepsilon < -1$, and perfectly elastic when ε approaches negative infinity. A vertical demand curve is perfectly inelastic at every price. A horizontal demand curve is perfectly elastic.

   The income elasticity of demand is the percentage change in the quantity demanded in response to a given percentage change in income. The cross-price elasticity of demand is the percentage change in the quantity demanded of one good when the price of a related good increases by a given percentage.

3. **Sensitivity of Quantity Supplied to Price.** The price elasticity of supply (or elasticity of supply), η, is the percentage change in the quantity supplied in response to a given percentage change in price. The elasticity of supply is positive if the supply curve has an upward slope. A vertical supply curve is perfectly inelastic. A horizontal supply curve is perfectly elastic.

4. **Long Run Versus Short Run.** Long-run elasticities of supply and demand may differ from the corresponding short-run elasticities. Where consumers can substitute between goods more readily in the long run, long-run demand curves are more elastic than short-run demand curves. However, if goods can be stored easily, short-run demand curves are more elastic than long-run curves. If producers can increase output at lower extra cost in the long run than in the short run, the long-run elasticity of supply is greater than the short-run elasticity.

5. **Effects of a Sales Tax.** The two common types of sales taxes are *ad valorem* taxes, by which the government collects a fixed percent of the price paid per unit, and specific taxes, by which the government collects a fixed amount of money per unit sold. Both types of sales taxes typically raise the equilibrium price and lower the equilibrium quantity. Both usually raise the price consumers pay and lower the price suppliers receive, so consumers do not bear the full burden or incidence of the tax. The effects on quantity, price, and the incidence of the tax that falls on consumers depend on the supply and demand elasticities. In competitive markets, for which supply-and-demand analysis is appropriate, the effect of a tax on equilibrium quantities, prices, and the incidence of the tax is unaffected by whether the tax is collected from consumers or producers.

QUESTIONS

■ = *exercise is available on MyEconLab;* * = *answer appears at the back of this book;* C = *use of calculus may be necessary;* W = *audio-slideshow answer by James Dearden is available in Textbook Resources on MyEconLab.*

1. Using graphs similar to those in Figure 3.1, illustrate how the effect of a demand shock depends on the shape of the supply curve. Consider supply curves that are horizontal, linear upward sloping, linear downward sloping, and vertical.

2. For years, Anthony Gallis, his wife, and their four children traveled from Dallas, Pennsylvania to South Bend, Indiana where they rented a house for $1,200 a weekend so that they could see Notre Dame football games. On the weekend of the 2006 home opener against Penn State, someone else arranged to rent his house months earlier, and another house recommended to him at $3,000 was also taken. A parking pass sold for $500, and a pair of tickets with face prices of $59 went for $3,200 for the Penn State game on eBay. Hotel prices and the cost of restaurant meals are also much higher on football weekends than during the other 341 days of the year—particularly in years when Notre Dame is expected to have a winning season. (Ilan Brat, "Why Fans Pay Through the Nose to See Notre Dame," *Wall Street Journal*, September 7, 2006.) Use a supply-and-demand diagram to illustrate why, when the demand curve shifts to the right, the prices of hotel rooms and rental apartments shoot up. (*Hint*: Carefully explain the shape of the supply curve, taking into account what happens when capacity is reached, such as occurs when all hotel rooms are filled.)

3. Six out of ten teens no longer use watches to tell time—they've turned to cell phones and iPods. Sales of inexpensive watches dropped 12% from 2004 to 2005, and sales of teen favorite, Fossil, Inc, fell 19%. (Leslie Earnest, "Wristwatches Get the Back of the Hand," *Los Angeles Times*, April 16, 2006.) On the other hand, the price of inexpensive watches has not changed substantially. What can you conclude about the shape of the supply curve? Illustrate these events using a graph.

4. The 9/11 terrorist attacks caused the U.S. airline travel demand curve to shift left by an estimated 30% (Ito and Lee, 2005). Use a supply-and-demand diagram to show the likely effect on price and quantity (assuming that the market is competitive). Indicate the magnitude of the likely equilibrium price and quantity effects—for example, would you expect that equilibrium quantity changes by about 30%? Show how the answer depends on the shape and location of the supply and demand curves.

■ *5. According to Duffy-Deno (2003), when the price of broadband access capacity (the amount of information one can send over an Internet connection) increases 10%, commercial customers buy about 3.8% less capacity. What is the elasticity of demand for broadband access capacity for firms? Is demand at the current price inelastic?

■ 6. The United States Tobacco Settlement between the major tobacco companies and 46 states caused the price of cigarettes to jump 45¢ (21%) in November 1998. Levy and Meara (2005) find only a 2.65% drop in prenatal smoking 15 months later. What is the elasticity of demand for this group? Is demand for this group more or less elastic than that of other groups discussed in the application "Taxing to Stop Smoking and Raise Revenue?"

7. According to Agcaoli-Sombilla (1991), the elasticity of demand for rice is –0.47 in Austria; –0.8 in Bangladesh, China, India, Indonesia, and Thailand; –0.25 in Japan; –0.55 in the European Union and the United States; and –0.15 in Vietnam. In which countries is the demand for rice inelastic? In which country is it the least elastic?

8. What section of a straight-line demand curve is elastic?

9. Suppose that the demand curve for wheat in each country is inelastic up to some "choke" price p^*—a price so high that nothing is bought—so that the demand curve is vertical at Q^* at prices below p^* and horizontal at p^*. If p^* and Q^* vary across countries, what does the world's demand curve look like? Discuss how the elasticity of demand varies with price along the world's demand curve.

10. According to Borjas (2003), immigration into the United States increased the labor supply of working men by 11.0% from 1980 to 2000 and reduced the wage of the average native worker by 3.2%. From these results, can we make any inferences about the elasticity of supply or demand? Which curve (or curves) changed, and why? Draw a supply-and-demand diagram and label the axes to illustrate what happened.

11. The U.S. Bureau of Labor Statistics reports that the average salary for postsecondary economics teachers in the Raleigh-Durham-Chapel Hill metropolitan area, which has many top universities, rose to $105,200 (based on a 52-week work year) in 2003. According to the *Wall Street Journal* (Timothy Aeppel, "Economists Gain Star Power," February 22, 2005, A2), the salary increase resulted from an outward shift in the demand curve for academic economists due to the increased popularity of the economics major, while the supply curve of Ph.D. economists did not shift.
    a. If this explanation is correct, what is the short-run price elasticity of supply of academic economists?
    b. If these salaries are expected to remain high, will more people enter doctoral programs in economics? How would such entry affect the long-run price elasticity of supply? W

12. In 1997, the shares of consumers who had cable television service were 59% for people with incomes of $25,000 or less; 66%, $25,000–$34,999; 67%, $35,000–$49,999; 71%, $50,000–$74,999; and 78%, $75,000 or more. What can you say about the income elasticity for cable television?

13. The application "Substitution May Save Endangered Species" describes how the equilibrium changed in the market for seal genitalia (used as an aphrodisiac in Asia) when Viagra was introduced. Use a supply-and-demand diagram to illustrate what happened. Show whether the following is possible: A positive quantity is demanded at various prices, yet nothing is sold in the market.

14. According to industry experts, low-priced conventional TVs are generic commodities, and the market is not affected by any single manufacturer (Saul Hansell and Eric A. Taub, "No End in Sight to Supply of Cheap TVs," *New York Times*, January 4, 2005, C1, C4). Typically, 20″ sets sell for from $89 to $100. The low end of the television market was shaken as the U.S. government phased in a requirement by 2007 that all new sets over 13″ have a tuner that can receive digital broadcasts. Some predicted that this digital tuner, mainly meant for high-definition televisions, would add several hundred dollars in cost, at least at first, to sets so small that they could not display high-definition signals effectively.
    a. Why? (*Hint*: Answer in terms of cross-elasticities of demand with higher-quality sets.)
    b. Use supply and demand curves to show the likely effect of this new requirement on small televisions. Explain how your prediction depends on the shapes of the supply and demand curves. Speculate about those shapes.

15. Traditionally, the perfectly round, white saltwater pearls from oysters have been prized above small, irregularly shaped, and strangely colored freshwater pearls from mussels. By 2002, scientists in China (where 99% of freshwater pearls originate) had perfected a means of creating bigger, rounder, and whiter freshwater pearls. These superior mussel pearls now sell well at Tiffany's and other prestigious jewelry stores (though at slightly lower prices than saltwater pearls). What is the likely effect of this innovation on the cross-elasticity of demand for saltwater pearls given a change in the price of freshwater pearls?

16. Using the information in the application "The Big Freeze" about lettuce industry revenue, create a graph to illustrate why industry revenue may rise after a freeze destroyed some of the crop. Draw a flatter demand curve to show that a freeze could cause revenue to fall. (*Hint*: Because revenue = price × quantity, you can show the revenue as a rectangle on the supply-and-demand diagram, where the height is the equilibrium price and the length is the equilibrium quantity.)

17. Will Mexico stop producing tequila? Because of record-low industry prices for the agave azul plant, from which tequila is distilled, farmers in Jalisco and other Mexican states are switching to more lucrative plants like corn, which is used for the now-trendy ethanol fuel alternative. (Kyle Arnold, "No Mas Tequila," *The Monitor*, September 17, 2007.) Planting of agave rose substantially from 2000 through 2004, and then started to plummet as the price of inexpensive tequila fell. The number of agave planted went from 60 million in 2000, to 93 million in 2002, to 12.8 million in 2006, and the downward trend continued in 2007. It takes seven years for an agave plant to be ready for harvesting. The price of inexpensive tequila has dropped 35% to 40% in recent years, but the price of high-end tequilas, which has been growing in popularity, has remained stable. Discuss the relative sizes of the short-run and long-run supply elasticities of tequila. What do you think the supply elasticity of high-quality tequila is? Why? If the demand curve for inexpensive tequila has remained relatively unchanged, is the demand curve relatively elastic or inelastic at the equilibrium? Why?

18. What is the effect of a $1 specific tax on equilibrium price and quantity if demand is perfectly inelastic? What is the incidence on consumers? Explain.

19. What is the effect of a $1 specific tax on equilibrium price and quantity if demand is perfectly elastic? What is the incidence on consumers? Explain.

20. What is the effect of a $1 specific tax on equilibrium price and quantity if supply is perfectly inelastic? What is the incidence on consumers? Explain.

21. What is the effect of a $1 specific tax on equilibrium price and quantity if demand is perfectly elastic and supply is perfectly inelastic? What is the incidence on consumers? Explain.

22. On July 1, 1965, the federal *ad valorem* taxes on many goods and services were eliminated. Comparing prices before and after this change, we can determine how much the price fell in response to the tax's elimination. When the tax was in place, the tax per unit on a good that sold for p was αp. If the price fell by αp when the tax was eliminated, consumers must have been bearing the full incidence of the tax. Consequently, consumers got the full benefit of removing the tax from those goods. The entire amount of the tax cut was passed on to consumers for all commodities and services Brownlee and Perry (1967) studied for which the taxes were collected at the retail level (except motion picture admissions and club dues) and most commodities for which excise taxes were imposed at the manufacturer level, including face powder, sterling silverware, wristwatches, and handbags. List the conditions (in terms of the elasticities or shapes of supply or demand curves) that are consistent with 100% pass-through of the taxes. Use graphs to illustrate your answer.

*23. Essentially none of the savings from removing the federal *ad valorem* tax were passed on to consumers for motion picture admissions and club dues (Brownlee and Perry, 1967; see Question 22). List the conditions (in terms of the elasticities or shapes of supply or demand curves) that are consistent with 0% pass-through of the taxes. Use graphs to illustrate your answer.

*24. Do you care whether a 15¢ tax per gallon of milk is collected from milk producers or from consumers at the store? Why?

25. California supplies the United States with 80% of its eating oranges. In late 1998, four days of freezing temperatures in the state's Central Valley substantially damaged the orange crop. In early 1999, Food Lion, with 1,208 grocery stores mostly in the Southeast, said its prices for fresh oranges would rise by 20% to 30%, which was less than the 100% increase it had to pay for the oranges. Explain why the price to consumers did not rise by the full amount of Food Lion's price increase. What can you conclude about the elasticities of supply and demand for oranges? (*Hint*: Use the relationship between elasticities and the incidence of a tax, Equation 3.7.)

26. Consider the market for labor services. The state collects a tax of α percent (where $0 < \alpha < 100$) of every dollar a worker earns. If the state raises its minimum wage, what happens to the amount of tax revenues it collects? Must tax revenue necessarily rise or fall?

PROBLEMS

27. In a commentary piece on the rising cost of health insurance ("Healthy, Wealthy, and Wise," *Wall Street Journal*, May 4, 2004, A20), economists John Cogan, Glenn Hubbard, and Daniel Kessler state, "Each percentage-point rise in health-insurance costs increases the number of uninsured by 300,000 people." Assuming that their claim is correct, demonstrate that the price elasticity of demand for health

insurance depends on the number of people who are insured. What is the price elasticity if 200 million people are insured? What is the price elasticity if 220 million people are insured? W

*28. Use calculus to prove that the elasticity of demand is ε everywhere along the demand curve whose demand function is $Q = Ap^{\varepsilon}$. C

29. In the application "Aggregating the Demand for Broadband Service" in Chapter 2 (based on Duffy-Deno, 2003), the demand function for broadband service is $Q_s = 15.6p^{-0.563}$ for small firms and $Q_l = 16.0p^{-0.296}$ for larger ones. As the graph in the application shows, the two demand functions cross. What can you say about the elasticities of demand on the two demand curves at the point where they cross? What can you say about the elasticities of demand more generally (at other prices)? (*Hint*: The question about the crossing point may be a red herring. Explain why.)

*30. The supply curve is $Q = g + hp$. Derive a formula for the elasticity of supply in terms of p (and not Q). Now give one entirely in terms of Q.

*31. Calculate the price and cross-price elasticities of demand for coconut oil. The coconut oil demand function (Buschena and Perloff, 1991) is

$$Q = 1{,}200 - 9.5p + 16.2p_p + 0.2Y,$$

where Q is the quantity of coconut oil demanded in thousands of metric tons per year, p is the price of coconut oil in cents per pound, p_p is the price of palm oil in cents per pound, and Y is the income of consumers. Assume that p is initially 45¢ per pound, p_p is 31¢ per pound, and Q is 1,275 thousand metric tons per year.

32. Using the coconut oil demand function from Problem 31, calculate the income elasticity of demand for coconut oil. (If you do not have all the numbers necessary to calculate numerical answers, write your answers in terms of variables.)

*33. When the U.S. government announced that a domestic mad cow was found in December 2003, analysts estimated that domestic supplies would increase in the short run by 10.4% as many other countries barred U.S. beef. An estimate of the price elasticity of beef demand is –1.6 (Henderson, 2003). Assuming that only the domestic supply curve shifted, how much would you expect the price to change? Compare your analysis and result with those in Solved Problem 2.4.

*34. The application "The Big Freeze" argued that a freeze that causes the supply curve to shift to the left may cause the market price to rise if the demand curve is inelastic at the equilibrium price. Use calculus to demonstrate this result by showing how the elasticity of revenue with respect to quantity depends on the elasticity of demand. C

35. Solved Problem 3.1 claims that a new war in the Persian Gulf could shift the world supply curve to the left by 3 million barrels a day or more, causing the world price of oil to soar regardless of whether we drill in ANWR. How accurate is that claim? Use the same type of analysis as in the solved problem to calculate how much such a shock would cause the price to rise with and without the ANWR production.

36. In Figure 3.5, applying a \$1.05 specific tax causes the equilibrium price to rise by 70¢ and the equilibrium quantity to fall by 14 million kg of pork per year. Using the estimated pork demand function and the original and after-tax supply functions, derive these results using algebra.

37. In Figure 3.6, applying a \$1.05 specific tax causes the equilibrium price to rise by 70¢ and the equilibrium quantity to fall by 14 million kg of pork per year. Using the pork supply function and the original and after-tax demand functions, derive these results using algebra.

38. Besley and Rosen (1998) find that a 10¢ increase in the federal tax on a pack of cigarettes leads to an average 2.8¢ increase in state cigarette taxes. What implications does their result have for calculating the effects of an increase in the federal cigarette tax on the quantity demanded? Given the current federal tax (see the application "Taxing to Stop Smoking and Raise Revenue") and an elasticity of demand for the U.S. population of –0.3, what is the effect of a 10¢ increase in the federal tax? How would your answer change if the state tax does not change?

39. Green et al. (2005) estimate that the demand elasticity is –0.47 and the long-run supply elasticity is 12.0 for almonds. The corresponding elasticities are –0.68 and 0.73 for cotton and –0.26 and 0.64 for processing tomatoes. If the government were to apply a specific tax to each of these commodities, what incidence would fall on consumers?

40. A constant elasticity supply curve, $Q = Bp^{\eta}$, intersects a constant elasticity demand curve, $Q = Ap^{\varepsilon}$, where A, B, η, and ε are constants. What is the incidence of a \$1 specific tax? Does your answer depend on where

the supply curve intersects the demand curve? Interpret your result.

***41.** Use math to show that, as the supply curve at the equilibrium becomes nearly perfectly elastic, the entire incidence of the tax falls on consumers.

***42.** Use calculus to show that an increase in a specific sales tax τ reduces quantity by less and raises tax revenue more, the less elastic the demand curve. (*Hint*: The quantity demanded depends on its price, which in turn depends on the specific tax, $Q(p(\tau))$, and tax revenue is $R = pQ(p(\tau))$.) C

43. If the inverse demand function is $p = a - bQ$ and the inverse supply function is $p = c + dQ$, show that the incidence of a specific tax of τ per unit falling on consumers is $b/(b + d) = \eta/(\eta - \varepsilon)$. C

4 Consumer Choice

If this is coffee, please bring me some tea; but if this is tea, please bring me some coffee. —Abraham Lincoln

Alexx's employer wants to transfer him to the firm's Paris office. Although Alexx likes the idea of living in Paris, he's concerned about the high cost of living there. The firm offers to pay him enough in euros that he can buy the same combination of goods in Paris that he is buying currently in the United States. In terms of what he can consume, will this higher income undercompensate, fully compensate, or overcompensate Alexx for the higher prices in Paris?

The U.S. government gives poor people food stamps, which they may use in retail stores only to buy food. Would the benefit to recipients be greater if they were given cash instead of food stamps? Would they buy less food?

As we saw in Chapters 2 and 3, the supply-and-demand model is useful for analyzing economic questions concerning markets. We could use the supply-and-demand model to examine the market price of croissants in Paris and New York or the effect of food stamps on the market price of donuts. However, the supply-and-demand model cannot be used to answer questions concerning individuals, such as Alexx's problem about whether to move to Paris or whether cash or food stamps would be better for a given individual.

To answer questions about individual decision making, we need a model of individual behavior. Our model of consumer behavior is based on the following premises:

- Individual *tastes* or *preferences* determine the amount of pleasure people derive from the goods and services they consume.
- Consumers face *constraints* or limits on their choices.
- Consumers *maximize* their well-being or pleasure from consumption, subject to the constraints they face.

Consumers spend their money on the bundle of products that give them the most pleasure. If you like music and don't have much of a sweet tooth, you spend a lot of your money on concerts and CDs and relatively little on candy. By contrast, your chocoholic friend with the tin ear may spend a great deal on Hershey's Kisses and very little on music.

All consumers must choose which goods to buy because limits on wealth prevent them from buying everything that catches their fancy. In addition, government rules restrict what they may buy: Young consumers can't buy alcohol or cigarettes legally, and people of all ages are prohibited from buying crack and other "recreational" drugs. Therefore, consumers buy the goods that give them the most pleasure, subject to the constraints that they cannot spend more money than they have and that they cannot spend it in ways that the government prevents.

In economic analyses designed to explain behavior (positive analysis—see Chapter 1) rather than judge it (normative statements), economists assume that *the consumer is the boss*. If your brother gets pleasure from smoking, economists don't argue with him that it is bad for him any more than they'd tell your sister, who likes reading Stephen King, that she should read Adam Smith's *The Wealth of Nations* instead. Accepting each consumer's tastes is not the same as condoning the resulting behaviors. Economists want to predict behavior. They want to know, for example, whether your brother will smoke more next year if the price of cigarettes decreases 10%. The prediction is unlikely to be correct if economists say, "He shouldn't smoke; therefore, we predict he'll stop smoking next year." A prediction based on your brother's actual tastes is more likely to be correct: "Given that he likes cigarettes, he is likely to smoke more of them next year if the price falls."

In this chapter, we examine five main topics

1. **Preferences.** We use three properties of preferences to predict which combinations, or bundle, of goods an individual prefers to other combinations.
2. **Utility.** Economists summarize a consumer's preferences using a *utility* function, which assigns a numerical value to each possible bundle of goods, reflecting the consumer's relative ranking of these bundles.
3. **Budget Constraint.** Prices, income, and government restrictions limit a consumer's ability to make purchases by determining the rate at which a consumer can trade one good for another.
4. **Constrained Consumer Choice.** Consumers maximize their pleasure from consuming various possible bundles of goods given their income, which limits the amount of goods they can purchase.
5. **Behavioral Economics.** Experiments indicate that people sometimes deviate from rational, maximizing behavior.

4.1 Preferences

Do not unto others as you would that they would do unto you. Their tastes may not be the same. —George Bernard Shaw

We start our analysis of consumer behavior by examining consumer preferences. Using three basic assumptions, we can make many predictions about preferences. Once we know about consumers' preferences, we can add information about the constraints consumers face so that we can answer many questions, such as the ones posed at the beginning of this chapter, or derive demand curves, as is done in the next chapter.

As a consumer, you choose among many goods. Should you have ice cream or cake for dessert? Should you spend most of your money on a large apartment or rent a single room and use the savings to pay for trips and concerts? In short, you must allocate your money to buy a *bundle* (*market basket* or combination) of goods.

How do consumers choose the bundle of goods they buy? One possibility is that consumers behave randomly and blindly choose one good or another without any thought. However, consumers appear to make systematic choices. For example, you probably buy more or less the same specific items each time you go to the grocery store.

To explain consumer behavior, economists *assume* that consumers have a set of tastes or preferences that they use to guide them in choosing between goods. These tastes differ substantially among individuals. Three out of four European men prefer colored underwear, while three out of four American men prefer white underwear.[1] Let's start by specifying the underlying assumptions in the economist's model of consumer behavior.

Properties of Consumer Preferences

> *I have forced myself to contradict myself in order to avoid conforming to my own taste.* —Marcel Duchamp, Dada artist

Economists make three critical assumptions about the properties of consumers' preferences. For brevity, these properties are referred to as *completeness*, *transitivity*, and *more is better*.

Completeness. The completeness property holds that, when facing a choice between any two bundles of goods, a consumer can rank them so that one and only one of the following relationships is true: The consumer prefers the first bundle to the second, prefers the second to the first, or is indifferent between them. This property rules out the possibility that the consumer cannot decide which bundle is preferable.

It would be very difficult to predict behavior if consumers' rankings of bundles were not logically consistent. The next property eliminates the possibility of certain types of illogical behavior.

Transitivity. The transitivity (or what some people refer to as *rationality*) property is that a consumer's preferences over bundles is consistent in the sense that, if the consumer *weakly prefers* Bundle z to Bundle y (likes z at least as much as y) and weakly prefers Bundle y to Bundle x, the consumer also weakly prefers Bundle z to Bundle x.[2]

If your sister told you she preferred a scoop of ice cream to a piece of cake, a piece of cake to a bar of candy, and a bar of candy to a scoop of ice cream, you'd probably think she'd lost her mind. At the very least, you wouldn't know which of these desserts to serve her.

More Is Better. The more-is-better property holds that, all else being the same, more of a commodity is better than less of it (always wanting more is known as *nonsatiation*). Indeed, economists define a **good** as a commodity for which more is preferred to less, at least at some levels of consumption. In contrast, a **bad** is something for which less is preferred to more, such as pollution. We now concentrate on goods.

good
a commodity for which more is preferred to less, at least at some levels of consumption

bad
something for which less is preferred to more, such as pollution

Although the completeness and transitivity properties are crucial to the analysis that follows, the more-is-better property is included to simplify the analysis—our most important results would follow even without this property.

---

[1] L. M. Boyd, "The Grab Bag," *San Francisco Examiner*, September 11, 1994, p. 5.

[2] The assumption of transitivity of weak preferences is sufficient for the following analysis. However, it is easier (and plausible) to assume that other preference relations—strict preference and indifference between bundles—are also transitive.

So why do economists assume that the more-is-better property holds? The most compelling reason is that it appears to be true for most people.[3] A second reason is that if consumers can freely dispose of excess goods, a consumer can be no worse off with extra goods. (We examine a third reason later in the chapter: Consumers buy goods only when this condition is met.)

Preference Maps

Surprisingly enough, with just these three properties, we can tell a lot about a consumer's preferences. One of the simplest ways to summarize information about a consumer's preferences is to create a graphical interpretation—a map—of them. For graphical simplicity, we concentrate throughout this chapter on choices between only two goods, but the model can be generalized to handle any number of goods.

Each semester, Lisa, who lives for fast food, decides how many pizzas and burritos to eat. The various bundles of pizzas and burritos she might consume are shown in panel a of Figure 4.1, with (individual-size) pizzas per semester on the horizontal axis and burritos per semester on the vertical axis.

At Bundle *e*, for example, Lisa consumes 25 pizzas and 15 burritos per semester. By the more-is-better property, all the bundles that lie above and to the right (area *A*) are preferred to Bundle *e* because they contain at least as much of both pizzas and burritos as Bundle *e*. Thus, Bundle *f* (30 pizzas and 20 burritos) in that region is preferred to *e*. By the same reasoning, Lisa prefers *e* to all the bundles that lie in area *B*, below and to the left of *e*, such as Bundle *d* (15 pizzas and 10 burritos).

Bundles such as *b* (30 pizzas and 10 burritos), in the region below and to the right of *e*, or *c* (15 pizzas and 25 burritos), in the region above and to the left, may or may not be preferred to *e*. We can't use the more-is-better property to determine which bundle is preferred because these bundles each contain more of one good and less of the other than *e* does.

Indifference Curves. Suppose we asked Lisa to identify all the bundles that gave her the same amount of pleasure as consuming Bundle *e*. Using her answers, we draw curve *I* in panel b of Figure 4.1 through all bundles she likes as much as *e*. Curve *I* is an **indifference curve**: the set of all bundles of goods that a consumer views as being equally desirable.

indifference curve
the set of all bundles of goods that a consumer views as being equally desirable

Indifference curve *I* includes Bundles *c*, *e*, and *a*, so Lisa is indifferent about consuming Bundles *c*, *e*, and *a*. From this indifference curve, we also know that Lisa prefers *e* (25 pizzas and 15 burritos) to *b* (30 pizzas and 10 burritos). How do we know that? Bundle *b* lies below and to the left of Bundle *a*, so Bundle *a* is preferred to Bundle *b* by the more-is-better property. Both Bundle *a* and Bundle *e* are on indifference curve *I*, so Lisa likes Bundle *e* as much as Bundle *a*. Because Lisa is indifferent between *e* and *a* and she prefers *a* to *b*, she must prefer *e* to *b* by transitivity.

---

[3]When teaching microeconomics to Wharton MBAs, I told them about a cousin of mine who had just joined a commune in Oregon. His worldly possessions consisted of a tent, a Franklin stove, enough food to live on, and a few clothes. He said that he didn't need any other goods—that he was *satiated*. A few years later, one of these students bumped into me on the street and said, "Professor, I don't remember your name or much of anything you taught me in your course, but I can't stop thinking about your cousin. Is it really true that he doesn't want *anything* else? His very existence is a repudiation of my whole way of life." Actually, my cousin had given up his ascetic life and was engaged in telemarketing, but I, for noble pedagogical reasons, responded, "Of course he still lives that way—you can't expect everyone to have the tastes of an MBA."

Figure 4.1 Bundles of Pizzas and Burritos Lisa Might Consume.

Pizzas per semester are on the horizontal axis, and burritos per semester are on the vertical axis. (a) Lisa prefers more to less, so she prefers Bundle *e* to any bundle in area *B*, including *d*. Similarly, she prefers any bundle in area *A*, including *f*, to *e*. (b) The indifference curve, I^1, shows a set of bundles (including *c*, *e*, and *a*) among which she is indifferent. (c) The three indifference curves, I^0, I^1, and I^2, are part of Lisa's preference map, which summarizes her preferences.

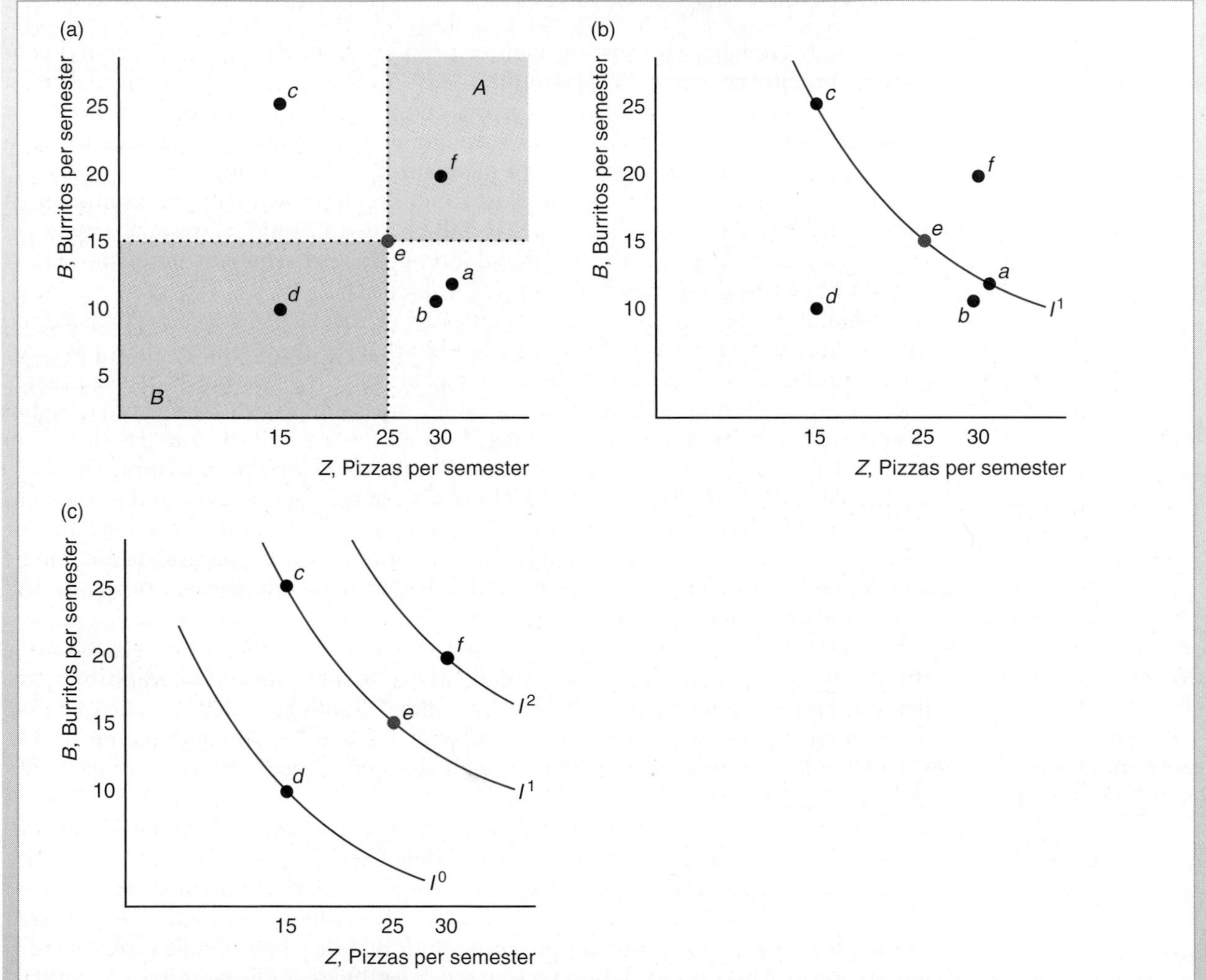

indifference map (or *preference map*)
a complete set of indifference curves that summarize a consumer's tastes or preferences

If we asked Lisa many, many questions, in principle, we could draw an entire set of indifference curves through every possible bundle of burritos and pizzas. Lisa's preferences are summarized in an **indifference map** or *preference map*, which is a complete set of indifference curves that summarize a consumer's tastes. Panel c of Figure 4.1 shows three of Lisa's indifference curves: I^0, I^1, and I^2.

We assume that indifference curves are continuous—have no gaps—as the figure shows. The indifference curves are parallel in the figure, but they need not be. All indifference curve maps must have four important properties:

1. Bundles on indifference curves farther from the origin are preferred to those on indifference curves closer to the origin.

2. There is an indifference curve through every possible bundle.
3. Indifference curves cannot cross.
4. Indifference curves slope downward.

First, we show that bundles on indifference curves farther from the origin (zero units of both goods) are preferred to those on indifference curves closer to the origin. By the more-is-better property, Lisa prefers Bundle *f* to Bundle *e* in panel c of Figure 4.1. She is indifferent among all the bundles on indifference curve I^2 and Bundle *f*, just as she is indifferent among all the bundles, such as Bundle *c*, on indifference curve I^1, and Bundle *e*. By the transitivity property, she prefers Bundle *f* to Bundle *e*, which she likes as much as Bundle *c*, so she prefers Bundle *f* to Bundle *c*. By this type of reasoning, she prefers all bundles on I^2 to all bundles on I^1.

Second, we show that there is an indifference curve through every possible bundle as a consequence of the completeness property: The consumer can compare any bundle to another. Compared to a given bundle, some bundles are preferred, some are enjoyed equally, and some are inferior. Connecting the bundles that give the same pleasure produces an indifference curve that includes the given bundle.

Third, we show that indifference curves cannot cross: A given bundle cannot be on two indifference curves. Suppose that two indifference curves crossed at Bundle *e* as in panel a of Figure 4.2. Because Bundles *e* and *a* lie on the same indifference curve I^0, Lisa is indifferent between *e* and *a*. Similarly, she is indifferent between *e* and *b* because both are on I^1. By transitivity, if Lisa is indifferent between *e* and *a*

Figure 4.2 Impossible Indifference Curves.

(a) Suppose that the indifference curves cross at Bundle *e*. Lisa is indifferent between *e* and *a* on indifference curve I^0 and between *e* and *b* on I^1. If Lisa is indifferent between *e* and *a* and she is indifferent between *e* and *b*, she must be indifferent between *a* and *b* by transitivity. But *b* has more of both pizzas and burritos than *a*, so she *must* prefer *a* to *b*. Because of this contradiction, indifference curves cannot cross. (b) Suppose that indifference curve *I* slopes upward. The consumer is indifferent between *b* and *a* because they lie on *I* but prefers *b* to *a* by the more-is-better assumption. Because of this contradiction, indifference curves cannot be upward sloping. (c) Suppose that indifference curve *I* is thick enough to contain both *a* and *b*. The consumer is indifferent between *a* and *b* because both are on *I* but prefers *b* to *a* by the more-is-better assumption because *b* lies above and to the right of *a*. Because of this contradiction, indifference curves cannot be thick.

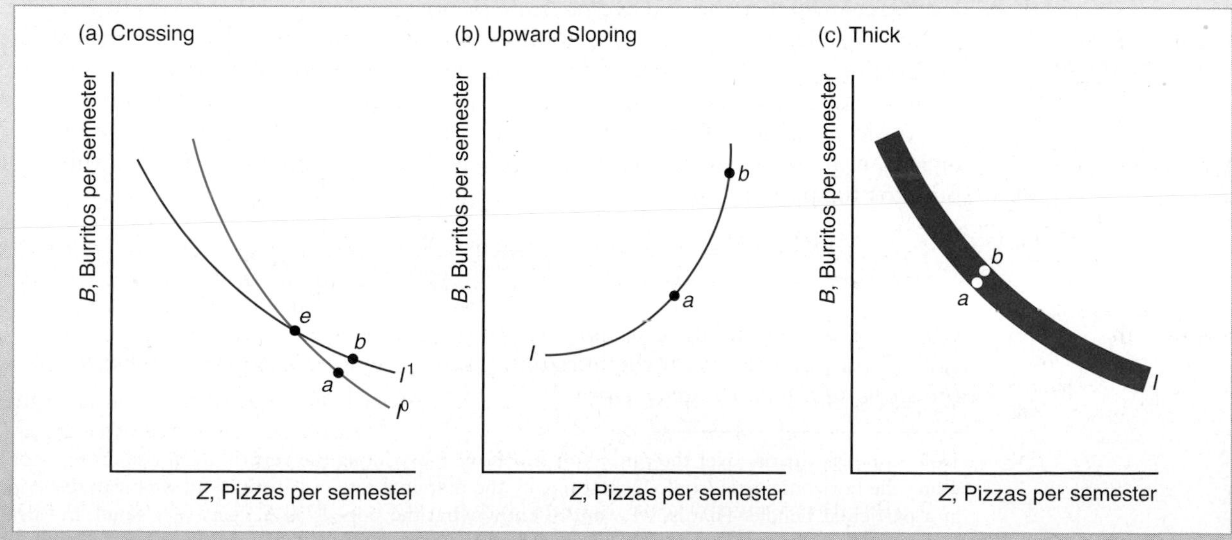

and she is indifferent between e and b, she must be indifferent between a and b. But that's impossible! Bundle b is above and to the right of bundle a, so Lisa *must* prefer b to a by the more-is-better property. Thus, because preferences are transitive and more is better than less, indifference curves cannot cross.

Fourth, we show that indifference curves must be downward sloping. Suppose to the contrary that an indifference curve sloped upward, as in panel b of Figure 4.2. The consumer is indifferent between Bundles a and b because both lie on the same indifference curve, I. But the consumer prefers b to a by the more-is-better property: Bundle a lies strictly below and to the left of Bundle b. Because of this contradiction—the consumer cannot both be indifferent between a and b and strictly prefer b to a—indifference curves cannot be upward sloping. For example, if Lisa views pizza and burritos as goods, she can't be indifferent between a bundle of one pizza and one burrito and another bundle with six of each.

Solved Problem 4.1

Can indifference curves be thick?

Answer

Draw an indifference curve that is at least two bundles thick, and show that a preference property is violated. Panel c of Figure 4.2 shows a thick indifference curve, I, with two bundles, a and b, identified. Bundle b lies above and to the right of a: Bundle b has more of both burritos and pizza. Thus, by the more-is-better property, Bundle b must be strictly preferred to Bundle a. But the consumer must be indifferent between a and b because both bundles are on the same indifference curve. Because both relationships between a and b cannot be true, there is a contradiction. Consequently, indifference curves cannot be thick. (We illustrate this point by drawing indifference curves with very thin lines in our figures.)

Willingness to Substitute Between Goods. Lisa is willing to make some trades between goods. The downward slope of her indifference curves shows that Lisa is willing to give up some burritos for more pizza or vice versa. She is indifferent between Bundles a and b on her indifference curve I in panel a of Figure 4.3. If she initially has Bundle a (eight burritos and three pizzas), she could get to Bundle b (five burritos and four pizzas) by trading three burritos for one more pizza. She is indifferent whether she makes this trade or not.

marginal rate of substitution (*MRS*) the maximum amount of one good a consumer will sacrifice to obtain one more unit of another good

Lisa's willingness to trade one good for another is measured by her **marginal rate of substitution** (*MRS*): the maximum amount of one good a consumer will sacrifice to obtain one more unit of another good. The marginal rate of substitution refers to the trade-off (rate of substitution) of burritos for a marginal (small additional or incremental) change in the number of pizzas. Lisa's marginal rate of substitution of burritos for pizza is

$$MRS = \frac{\Delta B}{\Delta Z},$$

where ΔZ is the number of pizzas Lisa will give up to get ΔB, more burritos, or vice versa, and pizza (Z) is on the horizontal axis. *The marginal rate of substitution is the slope of the indifference curve.*[4]

[4]The *slope* is "the rise over the run": how much we move along the vertical axis (rise) as we move along the horizontal axis (run). Technically, by the marginal rate of substitution, we mean the slope at a particular bundle. That is, we want to know what the slope is as ΔZ gets very small. In calculus terms, the relevant slope is a derivative. See Appendix 4A.

Figure 4.3 Marginal Rate of Substitution.

(a) At Bundle *a*, Lisa is willing to give up three burritos for one more pizza; at *b*, she is willing to give up only two burritos to obtain another pizza. That is, the relatively more burritos she has, the more she is willing to trade for another pizza. (b) An indifference curve of this shape is unlikely to be observed. Lisa would be willing to give up more burritos to get one more pizza, the fewer the burritos she has. Moving from Bundle *c* to *b*, she will trade one pizza for three burritos, whereas moving from *b* to *a*, she will trade one pizza for two burritos, even though she now has relatively more burritos to pizzas.

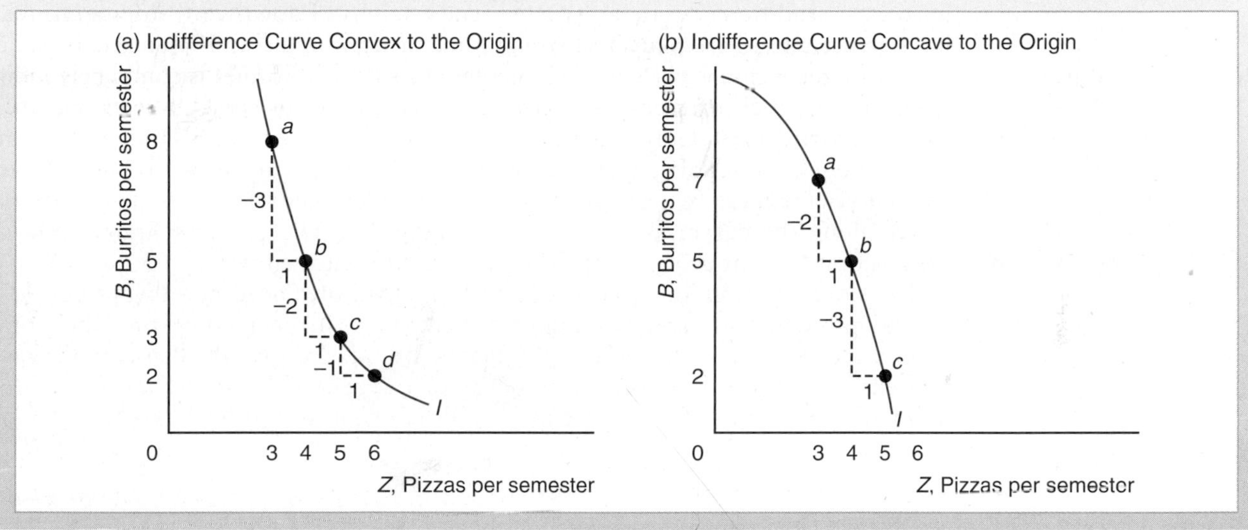

Moving from Bundle *a* to Bundle *b* in panel a of Figure 4.3, Lisa will give up three burritos, $\Delta B = -3$, to obtain one more pizza, $\Delta Z = 1$, so her marginal rate of substitution is $-3/1 = -3$. That is, the slope of the indifference curve is -3. The negative sign shows that Lisa is willing to give up some of one good to get more of the other: Her indifference curve slopes downward.

Curvature of Indifference Curves. Must an indifference curve, such as *I* in panel a of Figure 4.3, be *convex* to the origin (that is, must the middle of the curve be closer to the origin than if the indifference curve were a straight line)? An indifference curve doesn't have to be convex, but casual observation suggests that most people's indifference curves are convex. When people have a lot of one good, they are willing to give up a relatively large amount of it to get a good of which they have relatively little. However, after that first trade, they are willing to give up less of the first good to get the same amount more of the second good.

Lisa is willing to give up three burritos to obtain one more pizza when she is at *a* in panel a of Figure 4.3. At *b*, she is willing to trade only two burritos for a pizza. At *c*, she is even less willing to trade; she will give up only one burrito for another pizza. This willingness to trade fewer burritos for one more pizza as we move down and to the right along the indifference curve reflects a *diminishing marginal rate of substitution*: The marginal rate of substitution approaches zero as we move down and to the right along an indifference curve. That is, the indifference curve becomes flatter (less sloped) as we move down and to the right.

It is hard to imagine that Lisa's indifference curves are *concave*, as in panel b of Figure 4.3, rather than *convex*, as in panel a. If her indifference curve is concave, Lisa would be willing to give up more burritos to get one more pizza, the fewer the burritos she has. In panel b, she trades one pizza for three burritos moving from Bundle *c* to *b*, and she trades one pizza for only two burritos moving from *b* to *a*, even though her ratio of burritos to pizza is greater. Though it is difficult to imagine concave indifference curves, two extreme versions of downward-sloping, convex indifference curves are plausible: straight-line or right-angle indifference curves.

See *Question 1*.

perfect substitutes
goods that a consumer is completely indifferent as to which to consume

One extreme case is **perfect substitutes**: goods that a consumer is completely indifferent as to which to consume. Because Bill cannot taste any difference between Coca-Cola and Pepsi-Cola, he views them as perfect substitutes: He is indifferent between one additional can of Coke and one additional can of Pepsi. His indifference curves for these two goods are straight, parallel lines with a slope of –1 everywhere along the curve, as in panel a of Figure 4.4. Thus, Bill's marginal rate of substitution is –1 at every point along these indifference curves.

The slope of indifference curves of perfect substitutes need not always be –1; it can be any constant rate. For example, Ben knows from reading the labels that Clorox bleach is twice as strong as a generic brand. As a result, Ben is indifferent between one cup of Clorox and two cups of the generic bleach. The slope of his indifference curve is –2 where the generic bleach is on the vertical axis.[5]

Figure 4.4 Perfect Substitutes, Perfect Complements, Imperfect Substitutes.

(a) Bill views Coke and Pepsi as perfect substitutes. His indifference curves are straight, parallel lines with a marginal rate of substitution (slope) of –1. Bill is willing to exchange one can of Coke for one can of Pepsi. (b) Maureen likes pie à la mode but does not like pie or ice cream by itself: She views ice cream and pie as perfect complements. She will not substitute between the two; she consumes them only in equal quantities. (c) Lisa views burritos and pizza as imperfect substitutes. Her indifference curve lies between the extreme cases of perfect substitutes and perfect complements.

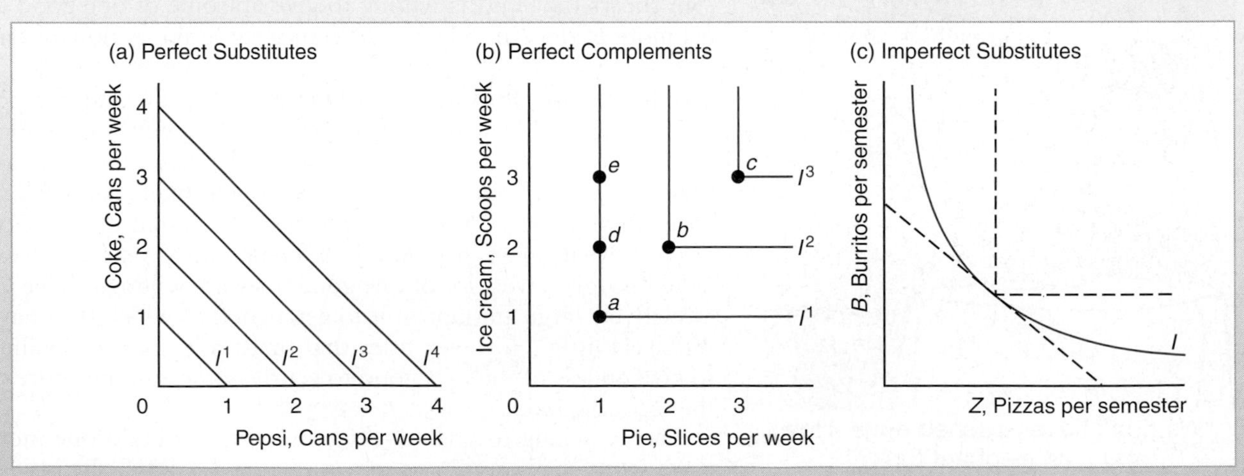

[5]Sometimes it is difficult to guess which goods are close substitutes. According to Harper's Index 1994, flowers, perfume, and fire extinguishers rank 1, 2, and 3 among Mother's Day gifts that Americans consider "very appropriate."

perfect complements goods that a consumer is interested in consuming only in fixed proportions

The other extreme case is **perfect complements**: goods that a consumer is interested in consuming only in fixed proportions. Maureen doesn't like pie by itself or ice cream by itself but loves pie à la mode: a slice of pie with a scoop of vanilla ice cream on top. Her indifference curves have right angles in panel b of Figure 4.4. If she has only one piece of pie, she gets as much pleasure from it and one scoop of ice cream, Bundle *a*, as from it and two scoops, Bundle *d*, or as from it and three scoops, Bundle *e*. That is, she won't eat the extra scoops because she does not have pieces of pie to go with the ice cream. Therefore, she consumes only bundles like *a*, *b*, and *c* in which pie and ice cream are in equal proportions.

With a bundle like *a*, *b*, or *c*, she will not substitute a piece of pie for an extra scoop of ice cream. For example, if she were at *b*, she would be unwilling to give up an extra slice of pie to get, say, two extra scoops of ice cream, as at point *e*. Indeed, she wouldn't give up the slice of pie for a virtually unlimited amount of extra ice cream because the extra ice cream is worthless to her.

See Questions 2–7.

The standard-shaped, convex indifference curve in panel c of Figure 4.4 lies between these two extreme examples. Convex indifference curves show that a consumer views two goods as imperfect substitutes.

APPLICATION

Indifference Curves Between Food and Clothing

Using the estimates of Eastwood and Craven (1981), the figure shows the indifference curves of the average U.S. consumer between food consumed at home and clothing. The food and clothing measures are weighted averages of various goods. At relatively low quantities of food and clothing, the indifference curves, such as I^1, are nearly right angles: perfect complements. As we move away from the origin, the indifference curves become flatter: closer to perfect substitutes.

One interpretation of these indifference curves is that there are minimum levels of food and clothing necessary to support life. The consumer cannot trade one good for the other if it means having less than these critical levels. As the consumer obtains more of both goods, however, the consumer is increasingly willing to trade between the two goods. According to these estimates, food and clothing are perfect complements when the consumer has little of either good and perfect substitutes when the consumer has large quantities of both goods.

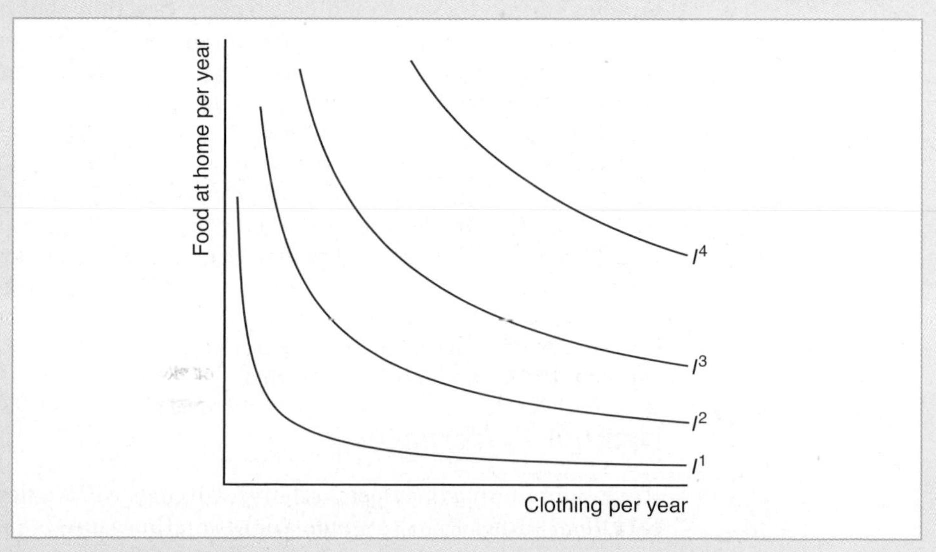

4.2 Utility

Underlying our model of consumer behavior is the belief that consumers can compare various bundles of goods and decide which gives them the greatest pleasure. We can summarize a consumer's preferences by assigning a numerical value to each possible bundle to reflect the consumer's relative ranking of these bundles.

utility
a set of numerical values that reflect the relative rankings of various bundles of goods

Following Jeremy Bentham, John Stuart Mill, and other nineteenth-century British economist-philosophers, economists apply the term **utility** to this set of numerical values that reflect the relative rankings of various bundles of goods. The statement that "Bonnie prefers Bundle x to Bundle y" is equivalent to the statement that "consuming Bundle x gives Bonnie more utility than consuming Bundle y." Bonnie prefers x to y if Bundle x gives Bonnie 10 *utils* (the name given to a unit of utility) and Bundle y gives her 8 utils.

Utility Function

utility function
the relationship between *utility* values and every possible bundle of goods

If we knew the **utility function**—the relationship between utility measures and every possible bundle of goods—we could summarize the information in indifference maps succinctly. Lisa's utility function, $U(B, Z)$, tells us how many utils she gets from B burritos and Z pizzas. Given that her utility function reflects her preferences, if Lisa prefers Bundle 1, (B_1, Z_1), to Bundle 2, (B_2, Z_2), then the utils she gets from the first bundle exceeds that from the second bundle: $U(B_1, Z_1) > U(B_2, Z_2)$.

For example, suppose that the utility, U, that Lisa gets from burritos and pizzas is

$$U = \sqrt{BZ}.$$

From this function, we know that the more she consumes of either good, the greater the utility that Lisa receives. Using this function, we can determine whether she would be happier if she had Bundle x with 9 burritos and 16 pizzas or Bundle y with 13 of each. The utility she gets from x is $12(=\sqrt{9 \times 16})$ utils. The utility she gets from y is $13(=\sqrt{13 \times 13})$ utils. Therefore, she prefers y to x.

The utility function is a concept that economists use to help them think about consumer behavior; utility functions do not exist in any fundamental sense. If you asked your mother what her utility function is, she would be puzzled—unless, of course, she is an economist. But if you asked her enough questions about choices of bundles of goods, you could construct a function that accurately summarizes her preferences. For example, by questioning people, Rousseas and Hart (1951) constructed indifference curves between eggs and bacon, and MacCrimmon and Toda (1969) constructed indifference curves between French pastries and money (which can be used to buy all other goods).

Typically, consumers can easily answer questions about whether they prefer one bundle to another, such as "Do you prefer a bundle with one scoop of ice cream and two pieces of cake to another bundle with two scoops of ice cream and one piece of cake?" But they have difficulty answering questions about how much more they prefer one bundle to another because they don't have a measure to describe how their pleasure from two goods or bundles differs. Therefore, we may know a consumer's rank-ordering of bundles, but we are unlikely to know by how much more that consumer prefers one bundle to another.

Ordinal Preferences

If we know only consumers' relative rankings of bundles, our measure of pleasure is *ordinal* rather than *cardinal*. An ordinal measure is one that tells us the relative ranking of two things but not how much more one rank is than another.

If a professor assigns only letter grades to an exam, we know that a student who receives a grade of A did better than a student who received a B, but we can't say how much better from that ordinal scale. Nor can we tell whether the difference in performance between an A student and a B student is greater or less than the difference between a B student and a C student.

A cardinal measure is one by which absolute comparisons between ranks may be made. Money is a cardinal measure. If you have \$100 and your brother has \$50, we know not only that you have more money than your brother but also that you have exactly twice as much money as he does.

See Problem 33.

Because utility is an ordinal measure, we should not put any weight on the absolute differences between the utility associated with one bundle and another.[6] We care only about the relative utility or ranking of the two bundles.

Utility and Indifference Curves

We can use Lisa's utility function to construct a three-dimensional diagram that shows how utility varies with changes in the consumption of B and Z. Imagine that you are standing with your back against a corner of a room. Walking away from the corner along the wall to your left, you are tracing out the B axis: The farther you get from the corner, the more burritos Lisa has. Similarly, starting back at the corner and walking along the wall to your right, you are moving along the Z axis. When you stand in the corner, you are leaning against the utility axis, where the two walls meet. The higher the point along your back, the greater Lisa's utility. Because her utility is increasing (more is preferred to less) in both B and Z, her utility rises as you walk away from the corner (origin) along either wall or into the room, where Lisa has more B or Z or both. Lisa's utility or *hill of happiness* rises as you move away from the corner.

What is the relationship between Lisa's utility and one of her indifference curves, those combinations of B and Z that give Lisa a particular level of utility? Imagine that the hill of happiness is made of clay. If you were to cut the hill parallel to the floor at a particular height on the wall—a given level of utility—you'd get a smaller hill above the cut. Now suppose that you place that smaller hill directly on the floor and trace the outside edge of the hill. Looking down at the floor, the traced outer edge of the hill represents an indifference curve on the two-dimensional floor. By making other parallel cuts in the hill of happiness, placing the smaller hills on the floor, and then tracing their outside edges you could obtain a map of indifference curves on which each indifference curve reflects a different level of utility.

Utility and Marginal Utility

Using Lisa's utility function over burritos and pizza, we can show how her utility changes if she gets to consume more of one of the goods. We now suppose that Lisa has the utility function in Figure 4.5. The curve in panel a shows how Lisa's utility

[6]Let $U(Z, B)$ be the original utility function and $V(Z, B)$ be the new utility function after we have applied a *positive monotonic transformation*: a change that increases the value of the function at every point. These two utility functions give the same ordinal ranking to any bundle of goods. (Economists often express this idea by saying that a *utility function is unique only up to a positive monotonic transformation*.) Suppose that $V(Z, B) = \alpha + \beta U(Z, B)$, where $\beta > 0$. The rank ordering is the same for these utility functions because $V(Z, B) = \alpha + \beta U(Z, B) > V(Z^*, B^*) = \alpha + \beta U(Z^*, B^*)$ if and only if $U(Z, B) > U(Z^*, B^*)$.

Figure 4.5 Utility and Marginal Utility.

As Lisa consumes more pizza, holding her consumption of burritos constant at 10, her total utility, U, increases and her marginal utility of pizza, MU_Z, decreases (though it remains positive).

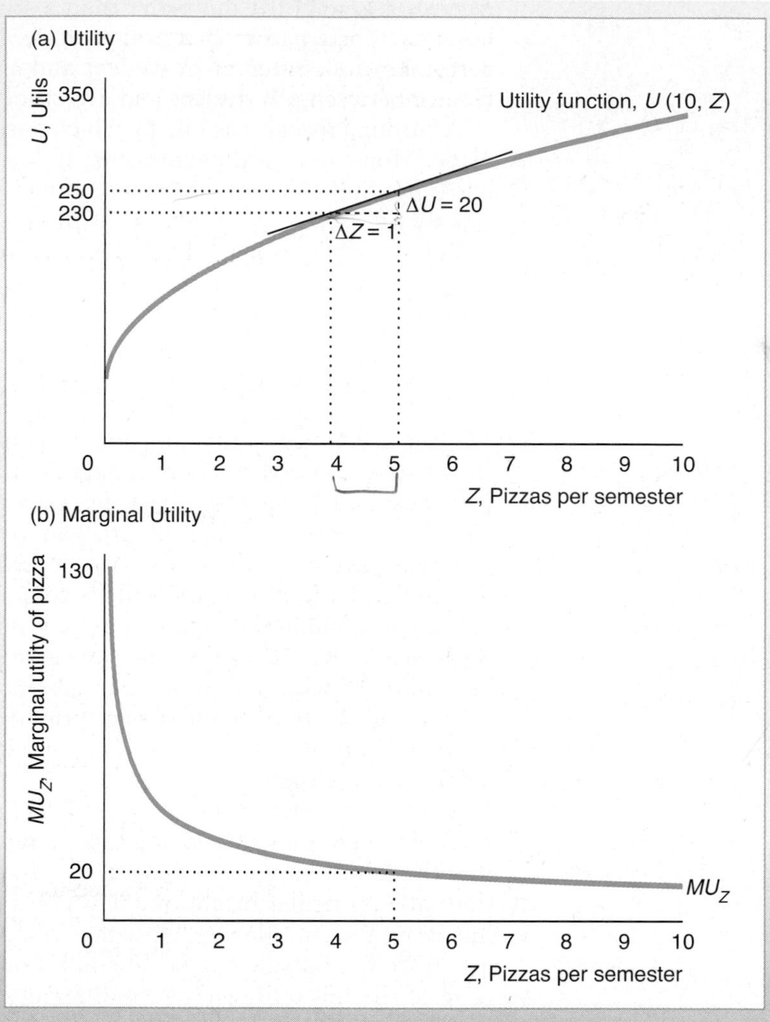

rises as she consumes more pizzas while we hold her consumption of burritos fixed at 10. Because pizza is a *good*, Lisa's utility rises as she consumes more pizza.

marginal utility
the extra utility that a consumer gets from consuming the last unit of a good

If her consumption of pizzas increases from $Z = 4$ to 5, $\Delta Z = 5 - 4 = 1$, her utility increases from $U = 230$ to 250, $\Delta U = 250 - 230 = 20$. The extra utility ($\Delta U$) that she gets from consuming the last unit of a good ($\Delta Z = 1$) is the **marginal utility** from that good. Thus, marginal utility is the slope of the utility function as we hold the quantity of the other good constant. (Appendix 4A):

$$MU_Z = \frac{\Delta U}{\Delta Z}.$$

Lisa's marginal utility from increasing her consumption of pizza from 4 to 5 is

$$MU_Z = \frac{\Delta U}{\Delta Z} = \frac{20}{1} = 20.$$

Panel b in Figure 4.5 shows that Lisa's marginal utility from consuming one more pizza varies with the number of pizzas she consumes, holding her consumption of burritos constant. Her marginal utility of pizza curve falls as her consumption of pizza increases, but the marginal utility remains positive: Each extra pizza gives Lisa pleasure, but it gives her less pleasure than the previous pizza relative to other goods.

Utility and Marginal Rates of Substitution

Earlier we learned that the marginal rate of substitution (MRS) is the slope of the indifference curve. The marginal rate of substitution can also be expressed in terms of marginal utilities. If Lisa has 10 burritos and 4 pizzas in a semester and gets one more pizza, her utility rises. That extra utility is the marginal utility from the last pizza, MU_Z. Similarly, if she received one extra burrito instead, her marginal utility from the last burrito is MU_B.

Suppose that Lisa trades from one bundle on an indifference curve to another by giving up some burritos to gain more pizza. She gains marginal utility from the extra pizza but loses marginal utility from fewer burritos. As Appendix 4A shows, the marginal rate of substitution can be written as

$$MRS = \frac{\Delta B}{\Delta Z} = -\frac{MU_Z}{MU_B}. \tag{4.1}$$

See Problems 35 and 41.

The MRS is the negative of the ratio of the marginal utility of another pizza to the marginal utility of another burrito.

4.3 Budget Constraint

You can't have everything.... Where would you put it? —Steven Wright

Knowing an individual's preferences is only the first step in analyzing that person's consumption behavior. Consumers maximize their well-being subject to constraints. The most important constraint most of us face in deciding what to consume is our personal budget constraint.

If we cannot save and borrow, our budget is the income we receive in a given period. If we can save and borrow, we can save money early in life to consume later, such as when we retire; or we can borrow money when we are young and repay those sums later in life. Savings is, in effect, a good that consumers can buy. For simplicity, we assume that each consumer has a fixed amount of money to spend now, so we can use the terms *budget* and *income* interchangeably.

For graphical simplicity, we assume that consumers spend their money on only two goods. If Lisa spends all her budget, Y, on pizza and burritos, then

$$p_B B + p_Z Z = Y, \tag{4.2}$$

where $p_B B$ is the amount she spends on burritos and $p_Z Z$ is the amount she spends on pizzas. Equation 4.2 is her budget constraint. It shows that her expenditures on burritos and pizza use up her entire budget.

How many burritos can Lisa buy? Subtracting $p_Z Z$ from both sides of Equation 4.2 and dividing both sides by p_B, we determine the number of burritos she can purchase to be

$$B = \frac{Y - p_Z Z}{p_B}. \tag{4.3}$$

According to Equation 4.3, she can buy more burritos with a higher income, a lower price of burritos or pizza, or the purchase of fewer pizzas.[7] For example, if she has one more dollar of income (Y), she can buy $1/p_B$ more burritos.

If $p_Z = \$1$, $p_B = \$2$, and $Y = \$50$, Equation 4.2 is

$$B = \frac{\$50 - (\$1 \times Z)}{\$2} = 25 - \tfrac{1}{2}Z. \tag{4.4}$$

As Equation 4.4 shows, every two pizzas cost Lisa one burrito. How many burritos can she buy if she spends all her money on burritos? By setting $Z = 0$ in Equation 4.3, we find that $B = Y/p_B = \$50/\$2 = 25$. Similarly, if she spends all her money on pizza, $B = 0$ and $Z = Y/p_Z = \$50/\$1 = 50$.

Instead of spending all her money on pizza or all on burritos, she can buy some of each. Table 4.1 shows four possible bundles she could buy. For example, she can buy 20 burritos and 10 pizzas with \$50.

See *Question 9.*

budget line (or *budget constraint*)
the bundles of goods that can be bought if the entire budget is spent on those goods at given prices

opportunity set
all the bundles a consumer can buy, including all the bundles inside the budget constraint and on the budget constraint

Equation 4.4 is plotted in Figure 4.6. This line is called a **budget line** or *budget constraint*: the bundles of goods that can be bought if the entire budget is spent on those goods at given prices. This budget line shows the combinations of burritos and pizzas that Lisa can buy if she spends all of her \$50 on these two goods. The four bundles in Table 4.1 are labeled on this line.

Lisa could, of course, buy any bundle that cost less than \$50. The **opportunity set** is all the bundles a consumer can buy, including all the bundles inside the budget constraint and on the budget constraint (all those bundles of positive Z and B such that $p_B B + p_Z Z \le Y$). Lisa's opportunity set is the shaded area in Figure 4.6. She could buy 10 burritos and 15 pieces of pizza for \$35, which falls inside the constraint. Unless she wants to spend the other \$15 on some other good, though, she might as well spend all of it on the food she loves and pick a bundle on the budget constraint rather than inside it.

Slope of the Budget Constraint

marginal rate of transformation (*MRT*)
the trade-off the market imposes on the consumer in terms of the amount of one good the consumer must give up to obtain more of the other good

Every extra unit of Z that Lisa purchases reduces B by $-p_Z/p_B$, according to Equation 4.3, so the slope of the budget line is $\Delta B/\Delta Z = -p_Z/p_B$. The slope of the budget line is called the **marginal rate of transformation** (MRT): the trade-off the market imposes on the consumer in terms of the amount of one good the consumer must give up to obtain more of the other good. The marginal rate of transformation is the rate at which Lisa can trade burritos for pizza in the marketplace:

$$MRT = \frac{\Delta B}{\Delta Z} = -\frac{p_Z}{p_B}. \tag{4.5}$$

Table 4.1 Allocations of a \$50 Budget Between Burritos and Pizza.

Bundle	Burritos	Pizza
a	25	0
b	20	10
c	10	30
d	0	50

[7]Using calculus, we find that $dB/dY = 1/p_B > 0$, $dB/dZ = -p_Z/p_B < 0$, $dB/dp_Z = -Z/p_B < 0$, and $dB/dp_B = -(Y - p_Z Z)/(p_B)^2 = -B/p_B < 0$.

Figure 4.6 Budget Constraint.

If $Y = \$50$, $p_Z = \$1$, and $p_B = \$2$, Lisa can buy any bundle in the opportunity set, the shaded area, including points on the *budget line*, L^1, which has a slope of $-\frac{1}{2}$.

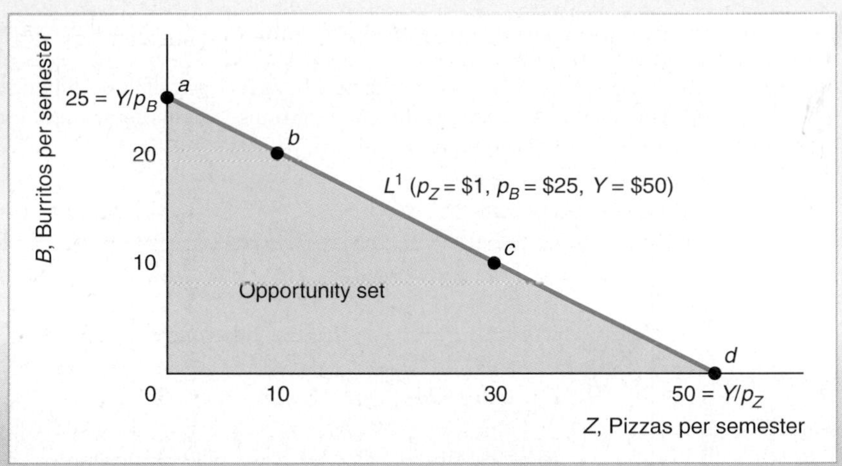

Because the price of pizza is half that of a burrito ($p_Z = \$1$ and $p_B = \$2$), the marginal rate of transformation Lisa faces is

$$MRT = -\frac{p_Z}{p_B} = -\frac{\$1}{\$2} = -\frac{1}{2}.$$

An extra pizza costs her half an extra burrito—or, equivalently, an extra burrito costs her two pizzas.

Purchasing Fractional Quantities

The budget constraint in Figure 4.6 is a smooth, continuous line, and the opportunity set includes all the points inside that constraint. Implicitly, this drawing implies that Lisa can buy fractional numbers of burritos and pizzas. Is that true? Do you know of a restaurant that will sell you a quarter of a burrito? Probably not.

Why then don't we draw the opportunity set and the budget constraint as points (bundles) of whole numbers of burritos and pizzas? The reason is that Lisa can buy a burrito at a *rate* of one-half per time period. If Lisa buys one burrito every other week, she buys an average of one-half burrito every week. Thus, it is plausible that she could purchase fractional amounts over time, and this diagram concerns her behavior over a semester.

Effect of a Change in Price on Consumption

If the price of pizza doubles but the price of burritos is unchanged, the budget constraint swings in toward the origin in panel a of Figure 4.7. If Lisa spends all her money on burritos, she can buy as many burritos as before, so the budget line still hits the burrito axis at 25. If she spends all her money on pizza, however, she can now buy only half as many pizzas as before, so the budget line intercepts the pizza axis at 25 instead of at 50.

Figure 4.7 Changes in the Budget Constraint.

(a) If the price of pizza increases from \$1 to \$2 a slice, Lisa's budget constraint rotates from L^1 to L^2 around the intercept on the burrito axis. The slope of the new budget line, L^2, is –1. The shaded area shows the combinations of pizza and burritos that she can no longer afford. (b) At the original prices, her new budget constraint moves from L^1 to L^3 if Lisa's income increases by \$50. This shift is parallel: Both budget lines have the same slope of $-\frac{1}{2}$. The new opportunity set is larger by the shaded area.

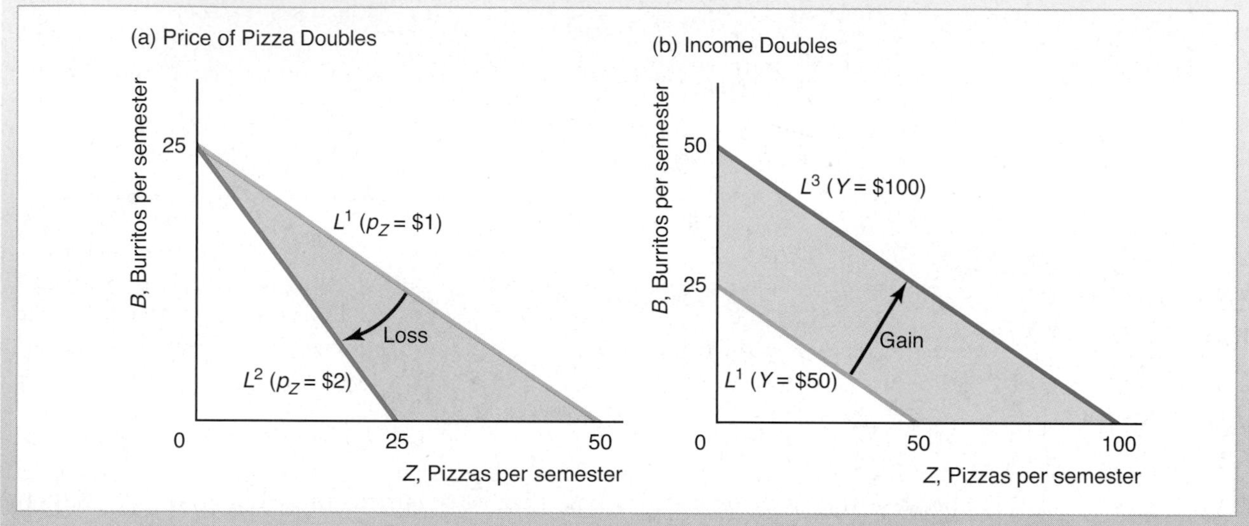

The new budget constraint is steeper and lies inside the original one. As the price of pizza increases, the slope of the budget line, *MRT*, changes. On the original line, L^1, $MRT = -\frac{1}{2}$. On the new line, L^2, $MRT = p_Z/p_B = -\$2/\$2 = -1$. Lisa is unambiguously worse off (unless she wants to eat burritos only), because she can no longer afford the combinations of pizza and burritos in the shaded area.

See Question 8.

A decrease in the price of pizza would have the opposite effect: The budget line would rotate outward around the intercept of the line and the burrito axis. As a result, the opportunity set would increase.

Effect of a Change in Income on Consumption

If the consumer's income increases, the consumer can buy more of all goods. Suppose that Lisa's income increases by \$50 per semester to $Y = \$100$. Her budget constraint shifts outward—away from the origin—and is parallel to the original constraint in panel b of Figure 4.7. Why is the new constraint parallel to the original one? The intercept of the budget line on the burrito axis is Y/p_B, and the intercept on the pizza axis is Y/p_Z. Thus, holding prices constant, the intercepts shift outward in proportion to the change in income. Originally, if she spent all her money on pizza, Lisa could buy $50 = \$50/\$1$ pizzas; now she can buy $100 = \$100/\$1$. Similarly, the burrito axis intercept goes from $25 = \$50/\$2$ to $50 = \$100/\$2$.

See Question 10.

A change in income affects only the position and not the slope of the budget line. The slope is determined solely by the relative prices of pizza and burritos. If the prices of both pizza and burritos fall by half, Lisa can buy twice as much as previously with the same budget. The budget line shifts outward parallel by the same amount as if her income doubles. Thus, her opportunity set is identical if both prices drop by half *or* her budget doubles.

APPLICATION
Rationing

During emergencies, governments frequently ration food, gas, and other staples rather than let their prices rise, as the United States and the United Kingdom did during World War II. Cuban citizens receive a ration book that limits their purchases of staples such as rice, legumes, potatoes, bread, eggs, and meat. China also rations food. The United States and many other countries limit fishing, and there's an international agreement that restricts whaling. In 2007, Canadians were debating setting quotas on electricity.

Water rationing is common during droughts. In 2007, water quotas were imposed in areas of the United Kingdom, North Carolina, Massachusetts, Georgia, most major Australian cities, and many Californian cities. Rationing affects consumers' opportunity sets because they cannot necessarily buy as much as they want at market prices.

Solved Problem 4.2

A government rations water, setting a quota on how much a consumer can purchase. If a consumer can afford to buy 12 thousand gallons a month but the government restricts purchases to no more than 10 thousand gallons a month, how does the consumer's opportunity set change?

Answer

1. *Draw the original opportunity set using a budget line between water and all other goods.* In the graph, the consumer can afford to buy up to 12 thousand gallons of water a week if not constrained. The opportunity set, areas *A* and *B*, is bounded by the axes and the budget line.

2. *Add a line to the figure showing the quota, and determine the new opportunity set.* A vertical line at 10 thousand on the water axis indicates the quota. The new opportunity set, area *A*, is bounded by the axes, the budget line, and the quota line.

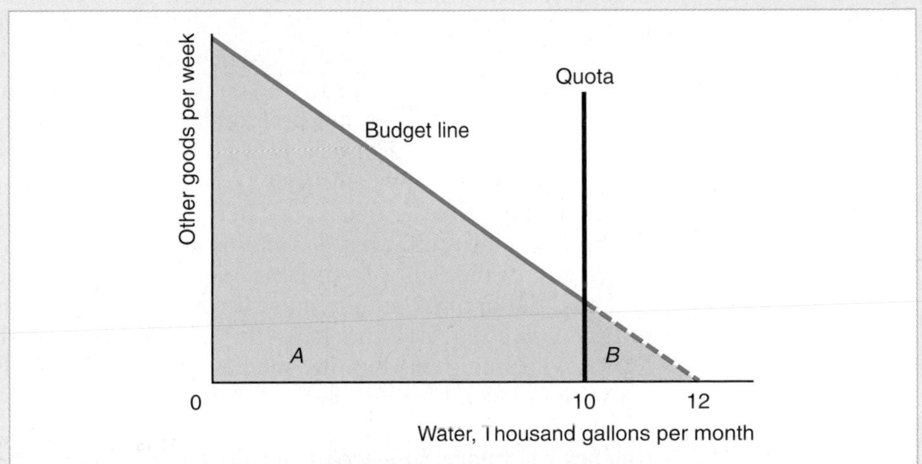

3. *Compare the two opportunity sets.* Because of the rationing, the consumer loses part of the original opportunity set: the triangle *B* to the right of the 10 thousand gallons line. The consumer has fewer opportunities because of rationing.

4.4 Constrained Consumer Choice

My problem lies in reconciling my gross habits with my net income.
—Errol Flynn

Were it not for the budget constraint, consumers who prefer more to less would consume unlimited amounts of all goods. Well, they can't have it all! Instead, consumers maximize their well-being subject to their budget constraints. Now, we have to determine the bundle of goods that maximizes well-being subject to the budget constraint.

The Consumer's Optimal Bundle

Veni, vidi, Visa. (We came, we saw, we went shopping.) —Jan Barrett

To determine which of the points on the budget constraint gives Lisa the highest level of pleasure, we use her indifference curves in panel a of Figure 4.8.[8] We will show that her optimal bundle lies on an indifference curve that touches the budget constraint at only one point (e on I^2)—hence the indifference curve does not cross the constraint. We show this result by rejecting the possibility that the optimal bundle could be located off the budget constraint or that it lies on an indifference curve that intersects the budget constraint.

The optimal bundle must be on the budget constraint. Bundles that lie on indifference curves above the constraint, such as those on I^3, are not in the opportunity set. So even though Lisa prefers f on indifference curve I^3 to e on I^2, f is too expensive and she can't purchase it. Although Lisa could buy a bundle inside the budget constraint, she does not want to do so, because more is better than less: For any bundle inside the constraint (such as d on I^1), there is another bundle on the constraint with more of at least one of the two goods, and hence she prefers that bundle. Therefore, the optimal bundle must lie on the budget constraint.

Bundles that lie on indifference curves that cross the budget constraint (such as I^1, which crosses the constraint at a and c) are less desirable than certain other bundles on the constraint. Only some of the bundles on indifference curve I^1 lie within the opportunity set: Bundles a and c and all the points on I^1 between them, such as d, can be purchased. Because I^1 crosses the budget constraint, the bundles between a and c on I^1 lie strictly inside the constraint, so there are bundles in the opportunity set (area $A + B$) that are preferable to these bundles on I^1 and are affordable. By the more-is-better property, Lisa prefers e to d because e has more of both pizza and burritos than d. By transitivity, e is preferred to a, c, and all the other points on I^1—even those, like g, that Lisa can't afford. Because indifference curve I^1 crosses the budget constraint, area B contains at least one bundle that is preferred to—lies above and to the right of—at least one bundle on the indifference curve.

Thus, the optimal bundle must lie on the budget constraint and be on an indifference curve that does not cross it. Such a bundle is the *consumer's optimum*. If Lisa is consuming this bundle, she has no incentive to change her behavior by substituting one good for another.

So far we've shown that the optimal bundle must lie on an indifference curve that touches the budget constraint but does not cross it. There are two ways that outcome can be reached. The first is an *interior solution*, in which the optimal bundle

[8]Appendix 4B uses calculus to determine the bundle that maximizes utility subject to the budget constraint.

Figure 4.8 Consumer Maximization.

(a) *Interior solution:* Lisa's optimal bundle is *e* (10 burritos and 30 pizzas) on indifference curve I^2. Any bundle that is preferred to *e* (such as points on indifference curve I^3) lies outside of the opportunity set—it can't be purchased. Bundles inside the opportunity set, such as *d*, are less desirable than *e*. (b) *Corner solution:* Spenser's indifference curves are relatively flat (he'll give up many pizzas for one more burrito), so his optimal bundle occurs at a corner of the opportunity set at Bundle *e*: 25 burritos and 0 pizzas.

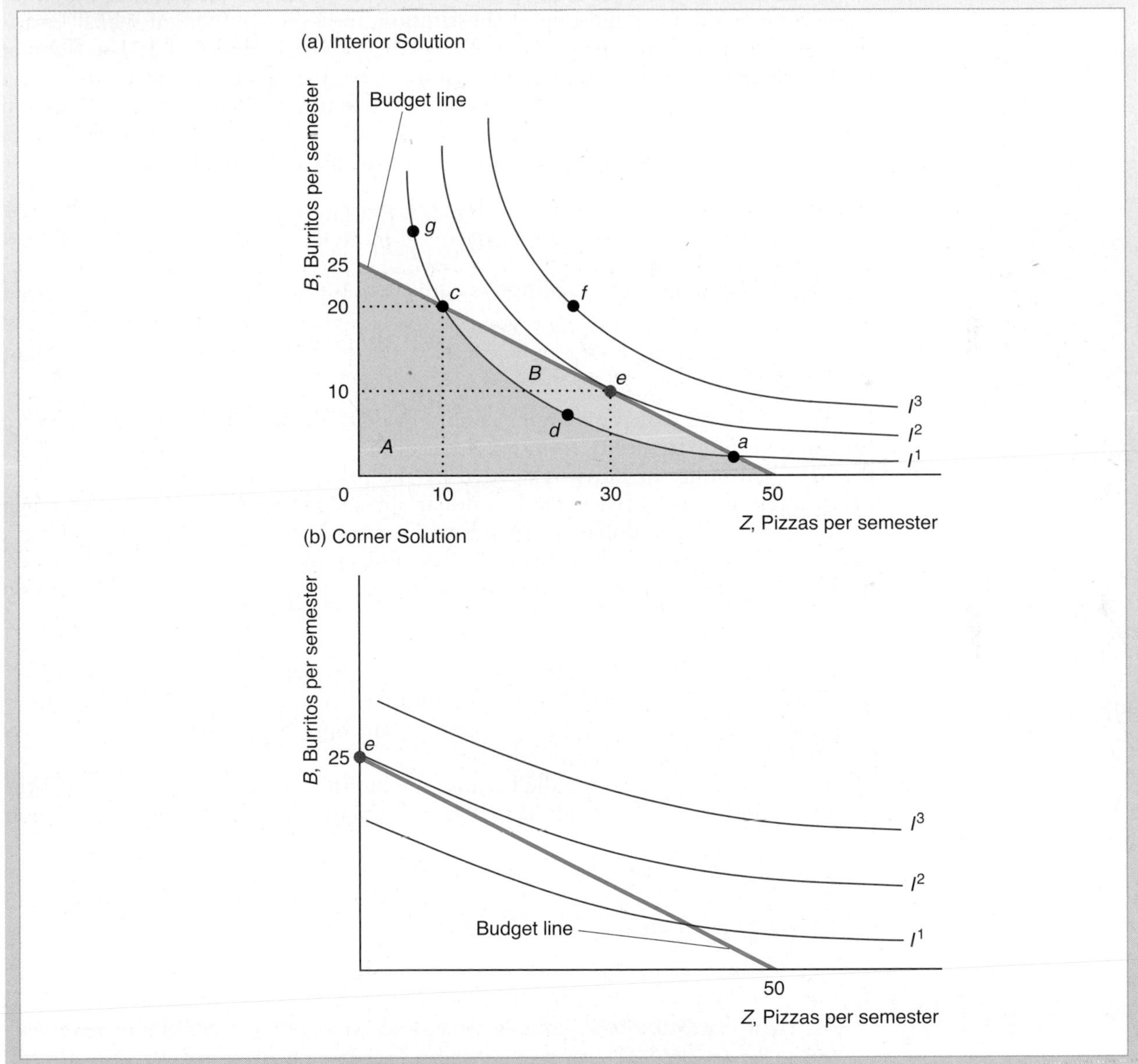

has positive quantities of both goods: The optimal bundle is on the budget line other than at one end or the other. The other possibility is called a *corner solution*, where the optimal bundle is at one end or the other of the budget line: It is at a corner with one of the axes.

Interior Solution. In panel a of Figure 4.8, Bundle *e* on indifference curve I^2 is the optimum bundle. It lies in the interior of the budget line away from the corners. Lisa prefers consuming a balanced diet, *e*, of 10 burritos and 30 pizzas, to eating only one type of food or the other.

For the indifference curve I^2 to touch the budget constraint but not cross it, it must be *tangent* to the budget constraint: The budget constraint and the indifference curve have the same slope at the point *e* where they touch. The slope of the indifference curve, the marginal rate of substitution, measures the rate at which Lisa is *willing* to trade burritos for pizza: $MRS = -MU_Z/MU_B$, Equation 4.1. The slope of the budget line, the marginal rate of transformation, measures the rate at which Lisa *can* trade her money for burritos or pizza in the market: $MRT = -p_Z/p_B$, Equation 4.5. Thus, Lisa's utility is maximized at the bundle where the rate at which she is willing to trade burritos for pizza equals the rate at which she can trade:

$$MRS = -\frac{MU_Z}{MU_B} = -\frac{p_Z}{p_B} = MRT.$$

Rearranging terms, this condition is equivalent to

$$\frac{MU_Z}{p_Z} = \frac{MU_B}{p_B}. \tag{4.6}$$

Equation 4.6 says that the marginal utility of pizza divided by the price of a pizza (the amount of extra utility from pizza per dollar spent on pizza), MU_Z/p_Z, equals the marginal utility of burritos divided by the price of a burrito, MU_B/p_B. Thus, Lisa's utility is maximized if the last dollar she spends on pizza gets her as much extra utility as the last dollar she spends on burritos. If the last dollar spent on pizza gave Lisa more extra utility than the last dollar spent on burritos, Lisa could increase her happiness by spending more on pizza and less on burritos. Her cousin Spenser is a different story.

See Questions 11, 15–17, and Problems 36–40.

Corner Solution. Spenser's indifference curves in panel b of Figure 4.8 are flatter than Lisa's. His optimal bundle lies on an indifference curve that touches the opportunity set only once, at the upper-left corner of the opportunity set, *e*, where he buys only burritos (25 burritos and 0 pizzas).

Bundle *e* is the optimal bundle because the indifference curve does not cross the constraint into the opportunity set. If it did, another bundle would give Spenser more pleasure.

See Questions 14 and 18.

Spenser's indifference curve is not tangent to his budget line. It would cross the budget line if both the indifference curve and the budget line were continued into the "negative pizza" region of the diagram, on the other side of the burrito axis.

Solved Problem 4.3

Nigel, a Brit, and Bob, a Yank, have the same tastes, and both are indifferent between a sports utility vehicle (SUV) and a luxury sedan. Each has a budget that will allow him to buy and operate one vehicle for a decade. For Nigel, the price of owning and operating an SUV is greater than that for the car. For Bob, an SUV is a relative bargain because he benefits from lower gas prices and can qualify for an SUV tax break. Use an indifference curve–budget line analysis to explain why Nigel buys and operates a car while Bob chooses an SUV.

Answer

1. *Describe their indifference curves.* Because Nigel and Bob view the SUV and the car as perfect substitutes, each has an indifference curve for buying one vehicle that is a straight line with a slope of –1 and that hits each axis at 1 in the figure.

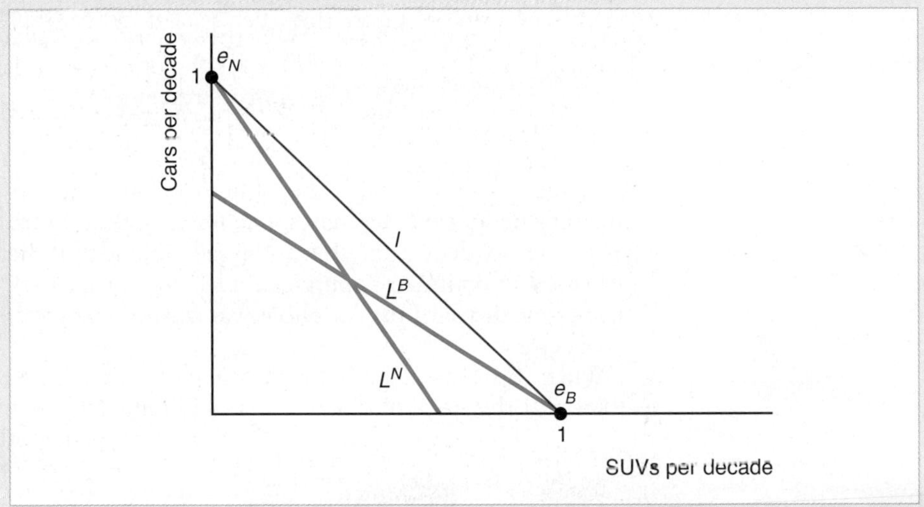

2. *Describe the slopes of their budget line.* Nigel faces a budget line, L^N, that is flatter than the indifference curve, and Bob faces one, L^B, that is steeper.
3. *Use an indifference curve and a budget line to show why Nigel and Bob make different choices.* As the figure shows, L^N hits the indifference curve, I, at 1 on the car axis, e_N, and L^B hits I at 1 on the SUV axis, e_N. Thus, Nigel buys the relatively inexpensive car and Bob scoops up a relatively cheap SUV.

See Questions 12 and 13.

Comment: If Nigel and Bob were buying a bundle of cars and SUVs for their large families or firms, the analysis would be similar—Bob would buy relatively more SUVs than would Nigel.

APPLICATION

U.S. Versus EU SUVs

If you believe what newspapers report, Americans have a love affair with SUVs and Europeans see no reason to drive a vehicle nearly the size of Luxembourg. SUVs are derided as "Chelsea tractors" in England and "Montessori wagons" in Sweden. News stories point to this difference in tastes to explain why SUVs account for less than a twentieth of total car sales in Western Europe but a quarter in the United States. Maybe the narrower European streets or Europeans' greater concern for the environment is the explanation. The analysis in Solved Problem 4.3 provides an alternative explanation: The price of owning and operating an SUV is much less in the United States than in Europe, so people with identical tastes are more likely to buy an SUV in the United States than in Europe.

Higher European gasoline taxes make gas-guzzling SUVs more expensive to operate in Europe than in the United States. In 2007, gas taxes as a percentage of the final gas price were 12% in the United States and 29% in Canada, compared to 60% in the Netherlands, 61% in Sweden, 62% in France and Germany, and 63% in the United Kingdom.

Europeans are calling for taxes against SUVs. The French government is considering raising taxes by up to $3,900 on heavy vehicles while giving discounts on smaller, lighter cars. The United Kingdom added an extra tax on SUVs of £45 ($90) per year and is proposing additional, substantial taxes for polluting vehicles. London's mayor slammed SUV drivers as "complete idiots" and, in 2008, increased the daily congestion fee for the privilege of driving around the city center to £25-per-day while efficient cars travel free.

In contrast, the U.S. government subsidizes SUV purchases. Under the 2003 Tax Act, people who use a vehicle that weighs more than 6,000 pounds—such as the biggest, baddest SUVs and Hummers—in their business at least 50% of the time may deduct the purchase price up to $100,000 from their taxes. They might get a state tax deduction, too. Originally intended to help self-employed ranchers, farmers, and contractors purchase a heavy pickup truck or van necessary for their businesses, the SUV tax loophole was quickly exploited by accountants, lawyers, and doctors.

When this bizarre boondoggle was reduced from $100K to $25K in October 2004 and the price of gas rose, sales plummeted for many brands of SUVs and behemoths such as Hummers. Sales of SUVs fell significantly in 2005 and 2006 (but picked up slightly in 2007). The *Boston Globe* concluded that this drop in relative SUV sales proved that U.S. consumers' "tastes are changing again." A more plausible, alternative explanation to differences in tastes for the difference in SUVs' share of sales in Europe and the United States (or over time in the United States) is variations in the relative costs of owning and operating SUVs.

★ Optimal Bundles on Convex Sections of Indifference Curves[9]

Earlier we argued, on the basis of introspection, that most indifference curves are convex to the origin. Now that we know how to determine a consumer's optimal bundle, we can give a more compelling explanation about why we assume that indifference curves are convex. We can show that, if indifference curves are smooth, optimal bundles lie either on convex sections of indifference curves or at the point where the budget constraint hits an axis.

Suppose that indifference curves were strictly concave to the origin as in panel a of Figure 4.9. Indifference curve I^1 is tangent to the budget line at d, but that bundle is not optimal. Bundle e on the corner between the budget constraint and the

[9]Starred sections are optional.

Figure 4.9 Optimal Bundles on Convex Sections of Indifference Curves.

(a) Indifference curve I^1 is tangent to the budget line at Bundle d, but Bundle e is superior because it lies on a higher indifference curve, I^2. If indifference curves are strictly concave to the origin, the optimal bundle, e, is at a corner. (b) If indifference curves have both concave and convex sections, a bundle such as d, which is tangent to the budget line in the concave portion of indifference curve I^1, cannot be an optimal bundle because there must be a preferable bundle in the convex portion of a higher indifference curve, e on I^2 (or at a corner).

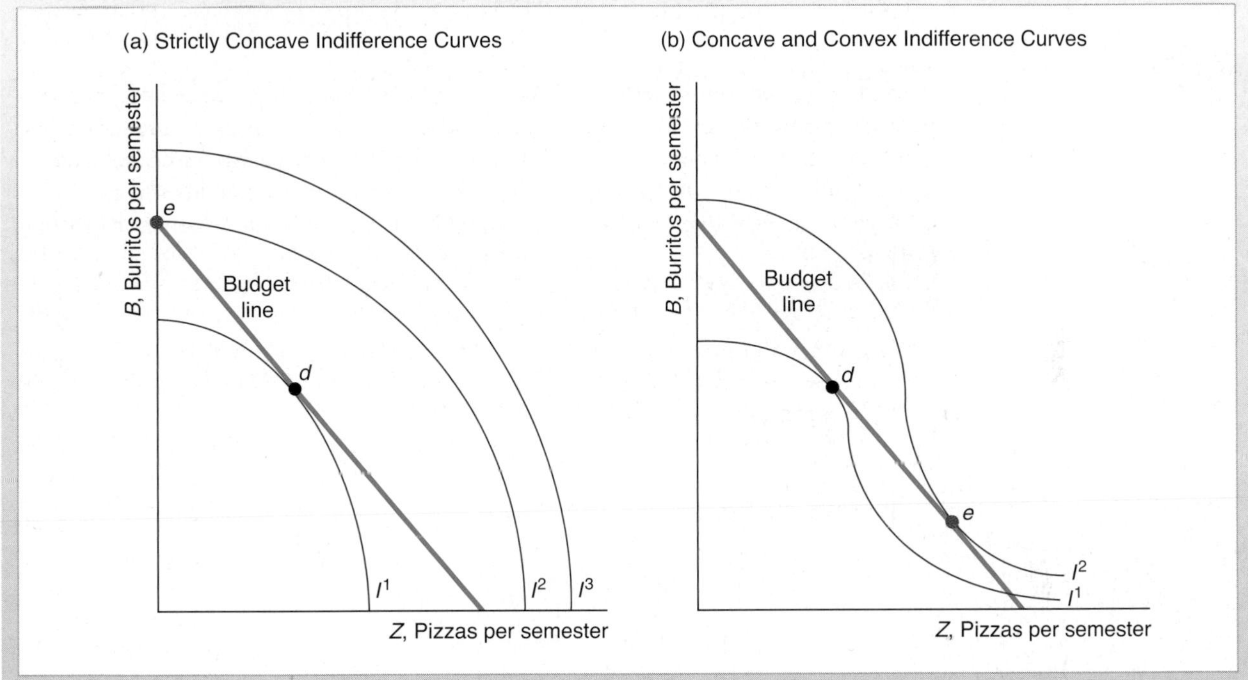

burrito axis is on a higher indifference curve, I^2, than d is. Thus, if a consumer had strictly concave indifference curves, the consumer would buy only one good—here, burritos. Similarly, as we saw in Solved Problem 4.3, consumers with straight-line indifference curves buy only the cheapest good. Because we do not see consumers buying only one good, indifference curves must have convex sections.

If indifference curves have both concave and convex sections as in panel b of Figure 4.9, the optimal bundle lies in a convex section or at a corner. Bundle d, where a concave section of indifference curve I^1 is tangent to the budget line, cannot be an optimal bundle. Here, e is the optimal bundle and is tangent to the budget constraint in the convex portion of the higher indifference curve I^2. *If a consumer buys positive quantities of two goods, the indifference curve is convex and tangent to the budget line at that optimal bundle.*

Buying Where More Is Better

Whoever said money can't buy happiness didn't know where to shop.

A key assumption in our analysis of consumer behavior is that more is preferred to less: Consumers are not satiated. We now show that, if both goods are consumed in positive quantities and their prices are positive, more of either good must be preferred to less. Suppose that the opposite were true and that Lisa prefers fewer burritos to more. Because burritos cost her money, she could increase her well-being by reducing the amount of burritos she consumes until she consumes no burritos—a scenario that violates our assumption that she consumes positive quantities of both goods.[10] Though it is possible that consumers prefer less to more at some large quantities, we do not observe consumers making purchases where that occurs.

See Question 7.

In summary, we do not observe consumer optima at bundles where indifference curves are concave or consumers are satiated. Thus, we can safely assume that indifference curves are convex and that consumers prefer more to less in the ranges of goods that we actually observe.

Solved Problem 4.4

Alexx doesn't care about where he lives, but he does care about what he eats. Alexx spends all his money on restaurant meals at either American or French restaurants. His firm offers to transfer him from its Miami office to its Paris office, where he will face different prices. The firm will pay him a salary in euros such that he can buy the same bundle of goods in Paris that he is currently buying in Miami.[11] Will Alexx benefit by moving to Paris?

Answer

1. *Show Alexx's optimum in the United States:* Alexx's optimal bundle, a, in the United States is determined by the tangency of his indifference curve I^1 and his American budget constraint L^A in the graph.

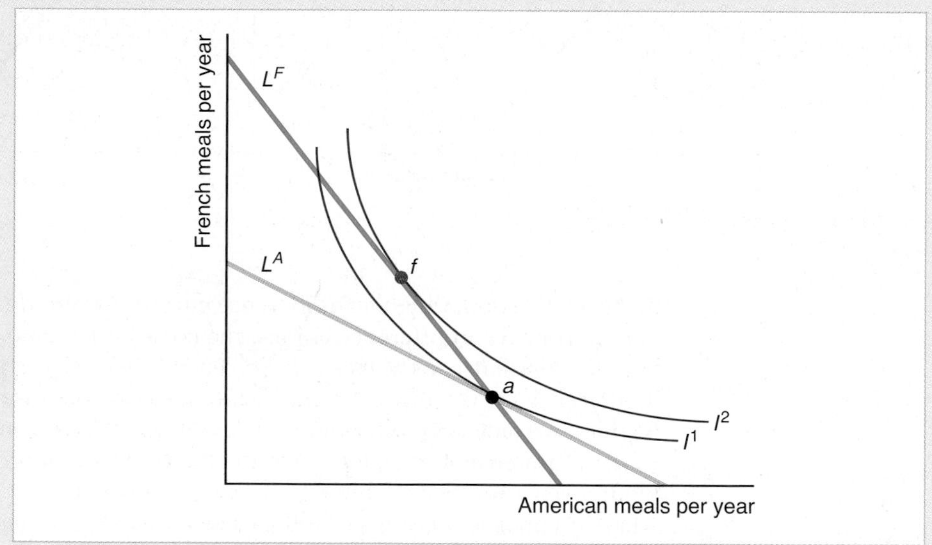

2. *Discuss what happens if prices are higher in France but the relative prices between American and French meals are the same:* If the prices of both French and American meals are x times higher in France than in the United States, the

[10]Similarly, at her optimal bundle, Lisa cannot be *satiated*—indifferent between consuming more or fewer burritos. Suppose that her budget is obtained by working and that Lisa does not like working at the margin. Were it not for the goods she can buy with what she earns, she would not work as many hours as she does. Thus, if she were satiated and did not care if she consumed fewer burritos, she would reduce the number of hours she worked, thereby lowering her income, until her optimal bundle occurred at a point where more was preferred to less or she consumed none.

[11]According to Organization Resource Counselors, Inc., 79% of international firms surveyed report that they provide their workers with enough income abroad to maintain their home lifestyle.

relative costs of French and American meals are the same. If the firm raises Alexx's income x times, his budget line does not change. Thus, if relative prices are the same in Miami and Paris, his budget line and optimal bundle are unchanged, so his level of utility is unchanged.

3. *Show the new optimum if relative prices in France differ from those in the United States:* Alexx's firm adjusts his income so that Alexx can buy the same bundle, a, as in the United States, so his new budget line in France, L^F, must go through a. Suppose that French meals are relatively less expensive than American meals in Paris. If Alexx spends all his money on French meals, he can buy more in Paris than in the United States, and if he spends all his money on American meals, he can buy fewer in Paris than in the United States. As a result, L^F hits the vertical axis at a higher point than the L^A line and cuts the L^A line at Bundle a. Alexx's new optimal bundle, f, is determined by the tangency of I^2 and L^F. Thus, if relative prices are different in Paris and Miami, Alexx is better off with the transfer. He was on I^1 and is now on I^2. Alexx could buy his original bundle, a, but chooses to substitute toward French meals, which are relatively inexpensive in France, thereby raising his utility.

See Question 27.

Food Stamps

I've known what it is to be hungry, but I always went right to a restaurant.
—Ring Lardner

We can use the theory of consumer choice to analyze whether poor people are better off receiving food stamps or a comparable amount of cash. Currently, federal, state, and local governments work together to provide a food subsidy for poor Americans. Nearly 11% of U.S. households worry about having enough money to buy food and 3.3% report that they suffer from inadequate food (Sullivan and Choi, 2002). Households that meet income, asset, and employment eligibility requirements receive coupons that can be used to purchase food from retail stores. The Food Stamps Program is one of the nation's largest social welfare programs with expenditures of \$33.1 billion for nearly 29.1 million people in 2006.

Since the food stamp programs started in the early 1960s, economists, nutritionists, and policymakers have debated "cashing out" food stamps by providing checks or cash instead of coupons that can be spent only on food. Legally, food stamps may not be sold, though a black market for them exists. Because of technological advances in electronic fund transfers, switching from food stamps to a cash program would lower administrative costs and reduce losses due to fraud and theft.

Would a switch to a comparable cash subsidy increase the well-being of food stamp recipients? Would the recipients spend less on food and more on other goods?

Why Cash Is Preferred to Food Stamps. Poor people who receive cash have more choices than those who receive a comparable amount of food stamps. With food stamps, only extra food can be obtained. With cash, either food or other goods can be purchased. As a result, a cash grant raises a recipient's opportunity set by more than food stamps of the same value do, as we now show.

In Figure 4.10, the price of a unit of food and the price of all other goods are both \$1, with an appropriate choice of units. A person with a monthly income of Y has a budget line that hits both axes at Y: The person can buy Y units of food per month, Y units of all other goods, or any linear combination. The opportunity set is area A.

Figure 4.10 Food Stamps Versus Cash.

The lighter line shows the original budget line of an individual with Y income per month. The heavier line shows the budget constraint with \$100 worth of food stamps. The budget constraint with a grant of \$100 in cash is a line between $Y + 100$ on both axes. The opportunity set increases by area B with food stamps but by $B + C$ with cash. An individual with these indifference curves consumes Bundle d (with less than 100 units of food) with no subsidy, e (Y units of all other goods and 100 units of food) with food stamps, and f (more than Y units of all other goods and less than 100 units of food) with a cash subsidy. This individual's utility is greater with a cash subsidy than with food stamps.

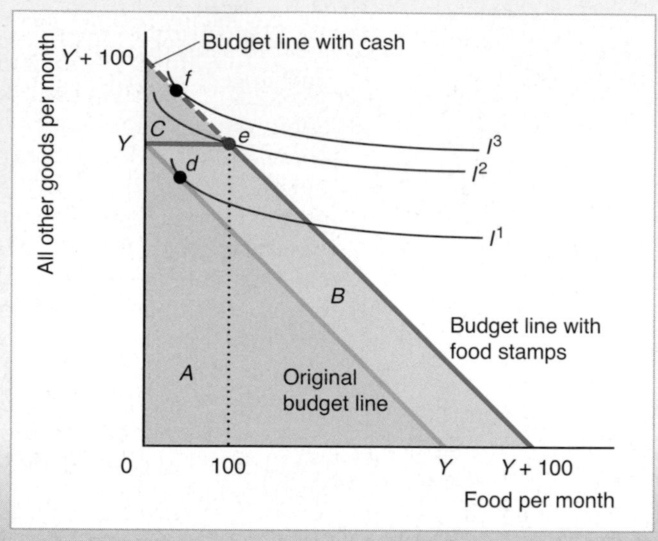

If that person receives a subsidy of \$100 in cash per month, the person's new monthly income is $Y + \$100$. The budget constraint with cash hits both axes at $Y + 100$ and is parallel to the original budget constraint. The opportunity set increases by $B + C$ to $A + B + C$.

If the person receives \$100 worth of food stamps, the food stamp budget constraint has a kink. Because the food stamps can be spent only on food, the budget constraint shifts 100 units to the right for any quantity of other goods up to Y units. For example, if the recipient buys only food, now $Y + 100$ units of food can be purchased. If the recipient buys only other goods with the original Y income, that person can get Y units of other goods plus 100 units of food. However, the food stamps cannot be turned into other goods, so the recipient can't buy $Y + 100$ units of other goods, as can be done under the cash transfer program. The food stamps opportunity set is areas $A + B$, which is larger than the presubsidy opportunity set by B. The opportunity set with food stamps is smaller than that with the cash transfer program by C.

See Questions 19–21.

A recipient benefits as much from cash or an equivalent amount of food stamps if the recipient would have spent at least \$100 on food if given cash. In other words, the individual is indifferent between cash and food stamps if that person's indifference curve is tangent to the downward-sloping section of the food stamp budget constraint.

Conversely, if the recipient would not spend at least \$100 on food if given cash, the recipient prefers receiving cash to food stamps. Figure 4.10 shows the indifference curves of an individual who prefers cash to food stamps. This person chooses Bundle e (Y units of all other goods and 100 units of food) if given food stamps but Bundle f (more than Y units of all other goods and less than 100 units of food) if given cash. This individual is on a higher indifference curve, I^2 rather than I^1, if given cash rather than food stamps.

See Questions 22–26, 28, and 30.

One other advantage of cash over food stamps is that it avoids the stigma of presenting food stamps at a grocery store, which discourages some poor people from using the program. To make participating easier and to reduce the stigma, the federal government required that by 2005, all states replace paper food stamps with ATM-like cards such as shown in the photo.[12] However, this change may not have completely eliminated the stigma problem: Only about two-thirds of individuals—25 million out of the 38 million—who were eligible for food stamp benefits in an average month of 2005 participated.

APPLICATION

Effects of Food Stamps

Your food stamps will be stopped effective March 1992 because we received notice that you passed away. May God bless you. You may reapply if there is a change in your circumstances.

—Department of Social Services, Greeneville, South Carolina

According to consumer theory, if recipients of food stamps received cash instead of the stamps, their utility would remain the same or rise, some recipients would consume less food and more of other goods, potential recipients would be more likely to participate, and the administrative costs of these welfare programs would fall.

Consistent with these predictions, Hoynes and Schanzenbach (2007) reports that the introduction of food stamps leads to a decrease in out-of-pocket food spending and an increase in overall food expenditures. However, Kaushale (2007) concludes that food stamps do not lead to obesity.

Whitmore (2002) found that a sizeable minority of food stamp recipients would be better off if they were given cash instead of an equivalent value in food stamps. She estimated that between 20% to 30% of food stamp recipients would spend less on food than their food stamp benefit amount if they received cash instead of stamps, and therefore would be better off with cash. Of those who would trade their food stamps for cash, the average food stamp recipient values it at 80% of its face value (the average price on the underground market is only 65%, however). Thus, she concluded that across all such recipients, $500 million is wasted by using food stamps rather than cash.

Why We Give Food Stamps. Two groups in particular object to giving cash instead of food stamps: some policymakers, because they fear that cash might be spent on booze or drugs, and some nutritionists, who worry that poor people will spend the money on housing or other goods and get too little nutrition.

In response, many economists argue that poor people are the best judges of how to spend their scarce resources. The question of whether it is desirable to let poor people choose what to consume is normative (a question of values), and economic theory cannot answer it. How poor people will change their behavior, however, is a positive (scientific) question, which we can analyze. Experiments to date find that cash recipients consume slightly lower levels of food but receive at least adequate levels of nutrients and that they prefer receiving cash.

Given that recipients are as well off or better off receiving cash than food stamps, why do we have food stamp programs instead of providing cash? The introduction to a report by the U.S. Department of Agriculture's Food and Nutrition Service,

[12]Using cards instead of stamps also cut administrative costs in half in some states.

which administers the food stamp program (Fasciano, Hall, and Beebout, 1993, p. 6), offers this explanation:

> *From the perspective of recipient households, cash is more efficient than coupons in that it permits each household to allocate its resources as it sees fit.... But in a more general sense, recipients' welfare clearly depends on public support for the program. And what evidence we have suggests that taxpayers are more comfortable providing in-kind, rather than cash, benefits and may consequently be more generous in their support of a coupon-based program. The question of which benefit form best promotes the welfare of financially needy households is therefore more complex than it might appear.*

4.5 Behavioral Economics

behavioral economics by adding insights from psychology and empirical research on human cognition and emotional biases to the rational economic model, economists try to better predict economic decision making

So far, we have assumed that consumers are rational, maximizing individuals. A new field of study, **behavioral economics**, adds insights from psychology and empirical research on human cognition and emotional biases to the rational economic model to better predict economic decision making.[13] We discuss three applications of behavioral economics in this section: tests of transitivity, the endowment effect, and salience. Later in the book, we examine whether a consumer is influenced by the purchasing behavior of others (Chapter 11), why many people lack self-control (Chapter 16), and the psychology of decision making under uncertainty (Chapter 17).

Tests of Transitivity

In our presentation of the basic consumer choice model at the beginning of this chapter, we assumed that consumers make transitive choices. But do consumers actually make transitive choices?

A number of studies of both humans and animals show that preferences usually are transitive. Weinstein (1968) used an experiment to determine how frequently people give intransitive responses. None of the subjects knew the purpose of the experiment. They were given choices between ten goods, offered in pairs, in every possible combination. To ensure that monetary value would not affect their calculations, they were told that all of the goods had a value of \$3. Weinstein found that 93.5% of the responses of adults—people over 18 years old—were transitive. However, only 79.2% of children aged 9–12 gave transitive responses.

Psychologists have also tested for transitivity using preferences for colors, photos of faces, and so forth. Bradbury and Ross (1990) found that, given a choice of three colors, nearly half of 4–5 year olds are intransitive, compared to 15% for 11–13 year olds, and 5% for adults. Bradbury and Ross showed that novelty (a preference for a new color) is responsible for most intransitive responses, and that this effect is especially strong in children.

Based on these results, one might conclude that it is appropriate to assume that adults exhibit transitivity for most economic decisions. On the other hand, one might modify the theory when applying it to children or when novel goods are introduced.

Economists normally argue that rational people should be allowed to make their own consumption choices so as to maximize their well-being. However, some might conclude that children's lack of transitivity or rationality provides a justification for political and economic restrictions and protections placed on young people.

[13]The introductory chapter of Camerer et al. (2004) and DellaVigna (2007) are excellent surveys of the major papers in this field and heavily influenced the following discussion.

APPLICATION

Should Youths Be Allowed to Drink?

Should young adults be allowed to decide whether or not to drink, or do they lack judgment and need to have their decisions restricted by older adults? Carpenter and Dobkin (2007) find that when youths start drinking alcohol legally at age 21, there is a 21% increase in the number of days on which they drink, which results in a 9% increase in their mortality rate.[14] This substantial jump in deaths at 21 is due to a 30% increase in alcohol overdoses and alcohol-related deaths, a 14% increase in deaths due to motor vehicle accidents, and a 15% increase in suicides.

Other research shows that when the minimum legal drinking age is raised to 21, younger people drink less overall, and people continue to drink less through their early twenties. Moreover, mortality due to external causes peaks at about 21.

Thus, to save young lives, many Congressional leaders felt justified in passing the Minimum National Drinking Age Act of 1984, which raised the national minimum age to 21 from 18, 19, or 20 years of age formerly used in 29 states. However, not all countries' leaders agree: Most other countries set the minimum drinking age between 16 and 18. It is 16 in Belgium, Denmark, and France; 18 in Australia, Sweden, and the United Kingdom; 18 or 19 in Canada; and 20 in Japan. Even in the United States, alcohol consumption by youths under 21 is not specifically illegal in 19 states.

Endowment Effect

endowment effect people place a higher value on a good if they own it than they do if they are considering buying it

Experiments show that people have a tendency to stick with the bundle of goods that they currently possess. One important reason for this tendency is called the **endowment effect**, which occurs when people place a higher value on a good if they own it than they do if they are considering buying it.

We normally assume that an individual can buy or sell goods at the market price. Rather than rely on income to buy some mix of two goods, an individual who was *endowed* with several units of one good could sell some and use that money to buy units of another good.

We assume that a consumer's endowment does not affect the indifference curve map. In a classic buying and selling experiment, Kahneman et al. (1990) challenged this assumption. In an undergraduate law and economics class at Cornell University, 44 students were divided randomly into two groups. Members of one group were given a coffee mug, which were available at the student store for $6. Those students *endowed* with a mug were told that they could sell it and were asked the minimum price that they would accept for the mug. The subjects in the other group, who did not receive a mug, were asked how much they would pay to buy the mug. Given the standard assumptions of our model and that the subjects were chosen randomly, we would expect no difference between the selling and buying prices. However, the median selling price was $5.75 and the median buying price was $2.25, so sellers wanted more than twice what buyers would pay. This type of experiment has been repeated with many variations and typically an endowment effect is found.

However, some economists believe that this result has to do with the experimental design. Plott and Zeiler (2005) argued that if you take adequate care to train the subjects in the procedures and make sure they understand them, we no longer find this result. List (2003) examined the actual behavior of sports memorabilia collectors and found that amateurs who do not trade frequently exhibited an endowment

[14]A word to the wise: Carpenter and Dobkin's (2007) statistical study indicates that a 10% increase in the number of days that a young adult drinks per year raises the probability of dying by 4%.

effect, unlike professionals and amateurs who traded a lot. Thus, experience may minimize or eliminate the endowment effect, and people who buy goods for resale may be less likely to become attached to these goods.

Others accept the results and have considered how to modify the standard model to reflect the endowment effect (Knetsch, 1992). One implication of these experimental results is that people will only trade away from their endowments if prices change substantially. This resistance to trade could be captured by having a kink in the indifference curve at the endowment bundle. (We showed indifference curves with a kink at a 90° angle in panel b of Figure 4.4.) These indifference curves could have an angle greater than 90°, and the indifference curve could be curved at points other than at the kink. If the indifference curve has a kink, the consumer does not shift to a new bundle in response to a small price change, but may shift if the price change is large.

See Question 31.

APPLICATION

How You Ask the Question Matters

One practical implication of the endowment effect is that consumers' behavior may differ depending on how a choice is posed. Many workers are offered the choice of enrolling in their firm's voluntary tax-deferred retirement plan, called a 401(k) plan. The firm can pose the choice in two ways: It can automatically sign employees up for the program and let them opt out, or it can tell them that they must sign up (opt in) to participate. These two approaches may seem identical, but they are not.

Madrian and Shea (2001, 2002) find that many more workers participate with the automatic enrollment than when they have to opt in: 86% versus 37%. In short, inertia matters. As a consequence of this type of evidence, federal law was changed in 2006 and 2007 to make it easier for employers to automatically enroll their employees in their 401(k) plans. Labor Department officials estimate that retirement savings in 401(k) plans could increase by as much as $134 billion by 2034 as a consequence of these changes.

Salience

Except in the last three chapters of this book, we examine economic theories that are based on the assumption that decision makers are aware of all the relevant information. In this chapter, we assume that consumers know their own income or endowment, the relevant prices, and their own tastes, and hence they make informed decisions.

Behavioral economists and psychologists have demonstrated that people are more likely to consider information if it is presented in a way that grabs their attention or if it takes relatively little thought or calculation to understand. Economists use the term *salience*, in the sense of *striking* or *obvious*, to describe this idea. For example, *tax salience* is awareness of a tax.

If a store's posted price includes the sales tax, consumers observe a change in the price as the tax rises. On the other hand, if a store posts the pretax price and collects the tax at the cash register, consumers are less likely to note that the posttax price has increased when the tax rate increases. Chetty et al. (2007) compare consumers' response to a rise in an *ad valorem* sales tax on beer (called an *excise tax*) that is included in the posted price to an increase in a general *ad valorem* sales tax, which is collected at the cash register but not reflected in the posted price. An increase in either tax has the same effect on the final price, so an increase in either tax should have the same effect on purchases if consumers pay attention to both taxes.[15] However, a 10% increase in the posted price, which includes the excise tax, reduces beer consumption by 9%, whereas a 10% increase in the price due to a rise in the sales tax that is not posted reduces consumption by only 2%. Chetty et al. also conducted an experiment where they posted tax-inclusive prices for 750 products in a grocery store and found that demand for these products fell by about 8% relative to control products in that store and comparable products at nearby stores.

One explanation for the lack of an effect of a tax on consumer behavior is consumer ignorance. For example, Furnham (2005) found that even by the age of 14 or 15 children do not fully understand the nature and purpose of taxes. Similarly, unless the tax-inclusive price is posted, many consumers ignore or forget about taxes.

bounded rationality
people have a limited capacity to anticipate, solve complex problems, or enumerate all options

An alternative explanation for ignoring taxes is **bounded rationality**: people have a limited capacity to anticipate, solve complex problems, or enumerate all options. To avoid having to perform hundreds of calculations when making purchasing decisions at a grocery store, many people chose not to calculate the tax-inclusive price. However, when that posttax price information is easily available to them, consumers make use of it. One way to modify the standard model is to assume that people incur a cost to making calculations—such as the time taken or the mental strain—and that deciding whether to incur this cost is part of their rational decision-making process.

People incur this calculation cost only if they think the gain from a better choice of goods exceeds the cost. More people pay attention to a tax when the tax rate is high or when their demand for the good is elastic (they are sensitive to price). Similarly, some people are more likely to pay attention to taxes when making large, one-time purchases—such as for a computer or car—rather than small, repeated purchases—such as for a bar of soap.

Tax salience has important implications for tax policy. In Chapter 3, where we assumed that consumers pay attention to prices and taxes, we showed that the tax incidence on consumers is the same regardless of whether the tax is collected from consumers or sellers. However, if consumers are inattentive to taxes, they're more likely to bear the tax burden if they're taxed. If a tax on consumers rises and consumers don't notice, their demand for the good becomes relatively inelastic, causing consumers to bear more of the tax incidence (see Equation 3.7). In contrast, if the tax is placed on sellers and the sellers want to pass at least some of the tax on to consumers, they raise their price, which consumers observe.

---

[15]The final price consumers pay is $p^* = p(1 + \beta)(1 + \alpha)$, where p is the pretax price, α is the general sales tax, and β is the excise tax on beer.

SUMMARY

Consumers maximize their utility (well-being) subject to constraints based on their income and the prices of goods.

1. **Preferences.** To predict consumers' responses to changes in these constraints, economists use a theory about individuals' preferences. One way of summarizing consumers' preferences is with a family of indifference curves. An indifference curve consists of all bundles of goods that give the consumer a particular level of utility. On the basis of observations of consumers' behavior, economists assume that consumers' preferences have three properties: completeness, transitivity, and more is better. Given these three assumptions, indifference curves have the following properties:
   - Consumers get more pleasure from bundles on indifference curves the farther from the origin the curves are.
   - Indifference curves cannot cross.
   - There is an indifference curve through any given bundle.
   - Indifference curves have no thickness.
   - Indifference curves slope downward.
   - Consumers are observed purchasing positive quantities of all relevant goods only where their indifference curves are convex to the origin.

2. **Utility.** Economists call the set of numerical values that reflect the relative rankings of bundles of goods *utility*. Utility is an ordinal measure: By comparing the utility a consumer gets from each of two bundles, we know that the consumer prefers the bundle with the higher utility, but we can't tell by how much the consumer prefers that bundle. The marginal utility from a good is the extra utility a person gets from consuming one more unit of that good, holding the consumption of all other goods constant. The rate at which a consumer is willing to substitute Good 1 for Good 2, the marginal rate of substitution, *MRS*, depends on the relative amounts of marginal utility the consumer gets from each of the two goods.

3. **Budget Constraint.** The amount of goods consumers can buy at given prices is limited by their income. As a result, the greater their income and the lower the prices of goods, the better off they are. The rate at which they can exchange Good 1 for Good 2 in the market, the marginal rate of transformation, *MRT*, depends on the relative prices of the two goods.

4. **Constrained Consumer Choice.** Each person picks an affordable bundle of goods to consume so as to maximize his or her pleasure. If an individual consumes both Good 1 and Good 2 (an interior solution), the individual's utility is maximized when the following four equivalent conditions hold:
   - The indifference curve between the two goods is tangent to the budget constraint.
   - The consumer buys the bundle of goods that is on the highest obtainable indifference curve.
   - The consumer's marginal rate of substitution (the slope of the indifference curve) equals the marginal rate of transformation (the slope of the budget line).
   - The last dollar spent on Good 1 gives the consumer as much extra utility as the last dollar spent on Good 2.

   However, consumers do not buy some of all possible goods (corner solutions). The last dollar spent on a good that is actually purchased gives more extra utility than would a dollar's worth of a good the consumer chose not to buy.

5. **Behavioral Economics.** Using insights from psychology and empirical research on human cognition and emotional biases, economists are starting to modify the rational economic model to better predict economic decision making. While adults tend to make transitive choices, children are less likely to do so, especially when novelty is involved. Consequently, some would argue that children's ability to make economic choices should be limited. If consumers have an endowment effect, such that they place a higher value on a good if they own it than they do if they are considering buying it, they are less sensitive to price changes and hence less likely to trade than would be predicted by the standard economic model. Many consumers ignore sales taxes and do not take them into account when making decisions.

QUESTIONS

■ = *exercise is available on MyEconLab;* * = *answer appears at the back of this book;* C = *use of calculus may be necessary;* W = *audio-slideshow answer by James Dearden is available in Textbook Resources on MyEconLab.*

1. Give as many reasons as you can why we believe that indifference curves are convex.

2. Don is altruistic. Show the possible shape of his indifference curves between charity and all other goods.

■ *3. Arthur spends his income on bread and chocolate. He views chocolate as a good but is neutral about bread, in that he doesn't care if he consumes it or not. Draw his indifference curve map.

4. Miguel considers tickets to the Houston Grand Opera and to Houston Astros baseball games to be perfect substitutes. Show his preference map. What is his utility function?

*5. Sofia will consume hot dogs only with whipped cream. Show her preference map. What is her utility function?

6. If Joe views two candy bars and one piece of cake as perfect substitutes, what is his marginal rate of substitution between candy bars and cake?

■ 7. Which of the following pairs of goods are complements and which are substitutes? Are the goods that are substitutes likely to be perfect substitutes for some or all consumers?
   a. A popular novel and a gossip magazine
   b. A camera and film
   c. A gun and a stick of butter
   d. A Panasonic DVD player and a JVC DVD player

■ 8. What happens to the budget line if the government applies a specific tax of $1 per gallon on gasoline but does not tax other goods? What happens to the budget line if the tax applies only to purchases of gasoline in excess of 10 gallons per week?

9. Suppose Gregg consumes chocolate candy bars and oranges. He is given four candy bars and three oranges. He can buy or sell a candy bar for $2 each. Similarly, he can buy or sell an orange for $1. If he has no other source of income, draw his budget constraint and write the equation. What is the most he can spend, Y, on these goods?

*10. What is the effect of a 50% income tax on Dale's budget line and opportunity set?

11. What happens to a consumer's optimum if all prices and income double? (*Hint*: What happens to the intercepts of the budget line?)

*12. Gasoline was once less expensive in the United States than in Canada, but now gasoline costs less in Canada than in the United States due to a change in taxes. How will the gasoline-purchasing behavior of a Canadian who lives equally close to gas stations in both countries change? Answer using an indifference curve and budget line diagram.

13. Suppose that Solved Problem 4.3 were changed so that Nigel and Bob are buying a bundle of several cars and SUVs for their large families or business and have identical tastes, with the usual-shaped indifference curves. Use a figure to discuss how the different slopes of their budget lines affect the bundles of SUVs and cars that each chooses. Can you make any unambiguous statements about how much each can buy? Can you make an unambiguous statement if you know that Bob's budget line goes through Nigel's optimal bundle?

■ 14. Max chooses between water and all other goods. If he spends all his money on water, he can buy 12 thousand gallons per week. At current prices, his optimal bundle is e_1. Show e_1 in a diagram. During a drought, the government limits the number of gallons per week that he may purchase to 10 thousand. Using diagrams, discuss under which conditions his new optimal bundle, e_2, will be the same as e_1. If the two bundles differ, can you state where e_2 must be located?

15. Some of the largest import tariffs, the tax on imported goods, are on shoes. Strangely, the higher the tariff, the cheaper the shoes. The highest U.S. tariff, 67%, is on a pair of $3 canvas sneakers, while the tariff on $12 sneakers is 37%, and that on $300 Italian leather imports is 0%. (Adam Davidson, "U.S. Tariffs on Shoes Favor Well-Heeled Buyers," National Public Radio, June 12, 2007, **www.npr.org/templates/story/story.php?storyId=10991519**.) Laura buys either inexpensive, canvas sneakers ($3 before the tariff) or more expensive gym shoes ($12 before the tariff) for her many children. Use an indifference

curve-budget line analysis to show how imposing these unequal tariffs affects the bundle of shoes that she buys compared to what she would have bought in the absence of tariffs. Can you confidently predict whether she'll buy relatively more expensive gym shoes after the tariff? Why or why not?

16. Suppose that Boston consumers pay twice as much for avocados as for tangerines, whereas San Diego consumers pay half as much for avocados as for tangerines. Assuming that consumers maximize their utility, which city's consumers have a higher marginal rate of substitution of avocados for tangerines? Explain your answer.

17. Minnesota customers of Earthlink, Inc., a high-speed Internet service provider, who obtained broadband access from a cable modem paid no tax, but Earthlink customers who use telephone digital subscribers lines paid $3.10 a month in state and local taxes and other surcharges (Matt Richtel, "Cable or Phone? Difference Can Be Taxing," *New York Times*, April 5, 2004, C1, C6). Suppose that were it not for the tax, Earthlink would set its prices for the two services so that Sven would be indifferent between using cable or phone service. Describe his indifference curves. Given the tax, Earthlink raised its price for the phone service but not its cable service. Use a figure to show how Sven chooses between the two services.

18. Ralph usually buys one pizza and two colas from the local pizzeria. The pizzeria announces a special: All pizzas after the first one are half-price. Show the original and new budget constraint. What can you say about the bundle Ralph will choose when faced with the new constraint?

19. A poor person who has an income of $1,000 receives $100 worth of food stamps. Draw the budget constraint if the food stamp recipient can sell these coupons on the black market for less than their face value.

20. Show how much an individual's opportunity set increases if the government gives food stamps rather than sells them at subsidized rates.

21. Since 1979, recipients have been given food stamps. Before 1979, however, people bought food stamps at a subsidized rate. For example, to get $1 worth of food stamps, a household paid about 15¢ (the exact amount varied by household characteristics and other factors). What is the budget constraint facing an individual if that individual may buy up to $100 per month in food stamps at 15¢ per each $1 coupon?

22. Is a poor person more likely to benefit from $100 a month worth of food stamps (that can be used only to buy food) or $100 a month worth of clothing stamps (that can be used only to buy clothing)? Why?

*23. Is a wealthy person more likely than a poor person to prefer to receive a government payment of $100 in cash to $100 worth of food stamps? Why or why not?

24. Federal housing assistance programs provide allowances that can only be spent on housing. Several empirical studies find that recipients increase their nonhousing expenditures by 10% to 20% (cited in Harkness and Newman, 2003). Show that recipients might (but do not necessarily) increase their spending on nonhousing, depending on their tastes.

25. Federal housing and food stamp subsidy programs are two of the largest in-kind transfer programs for the poor. President George W. Bush's 2006 budget allocated the Food Stamp Program (FSP) approximately $33.1 billion in benefits and the housing program another $38.4 billion. Many poor people are eligible for both programs: 30% of housing assistance recipients also used food stamps, and 38% of FSP participants also received housing assistance (Harkness and Newman, 2003). Suppose Jill's income is $500 a month, which she spends on food and housing. The price of food and of housing is each $1 per unit. Draw her budget line. If she receives $100 in food stamps and $200 in a housing subsidy (which she can spend only on housing), how do her budget line and opportunity set change?

26. The local swimming pool charges nonmembers $10 per visit. If you join the pool, you can swim for $5 per visit but you have to pay an annual fee of F. Use an indifference curve diagram to find the value of F such that you are indifferent between joining and not joining. Suppose that the pool charged you exactly that F. Would you go to the pool more or fewer times than if you did not join? For simplicity, assume that the price of all other goods is $1.

27. In Solved Problem 4.4, suppose that French meals are relatively more expensive than American meals in Paris, so that the L^F budget line cuts the L^A budget line from below rather than from above as in the solved problem's figure. Show that the conclusion that Alexx is better off after his move still holds. Explain the logic behind the following statement: "The analysis holds as long as the relative prices differ in the two cities. Whether both prices, one price, or neither price in Paris is higher than in Miami is irrelevant to the analysis."

28. Jim spends most of his time in Jazzman's, a coffee shop in south Bethlehem, Pennsylvania. Jim has $12 a week to spend on coffee and muffins. Jazzman's sells muffins for $2 each and coffee for $1.20 per cup. He consumes q_c cups of coffee per week and q_m muffins per week.
    a. Draw Jim's budget line.
    b. Now Jazzman's introduces a frequent-buyer card: For every five cups of coffee purchased at the regular price of $1.20 per cup, Jim receives a free sixth cup. Draw Jim's new budget line.
    c. Does the introduction of the frequent-buyer card necessarily encourage Jim to consume more coffee? Show how your answer depends on Jim's preference map.
    d. Use a budget line–indifference curve map analysis to explain which pricing scheme Jim prefers. W

29. Jackie likes playing sports—all types—and also likes to earn A's in school. Jackie figures that by participating in sports, she learns about competition, hard work, and time management, skills that lead to better grades. Jackie also knows that if she spends more time participating in sports, she has less time to study. If Jackie participates in no sports, her grade point average is 3.5. Considering only the psychological and sociological benefits of sports, Jackie's grade point average improves by 0.5 points for the first sport and by 0.02 for each additional sport. Jackie has six hours each day to participate in sports and to study. Each sport in which Jackie participates takes $1\frac{1}{2}$ hours per day. Jackie figures that for each additional hour that she studies, her grade point average improves by 0.1 points.
    a. What is the maximum grade point average that Jackie can earn? To earn that GPA, in how many sports does Jackie participate?
    b. Draw Jackie's budget line where the axes are GPA and number of sports.
    c. Based on the budget line, can you conclude that Jackie will participate in at least one sport? W

30. In 2002, the Supreme Court ruled that school-voucher programs do not violate the Establishment Clause of the First Amendment, provided that parents, not the state, direct where the money goes. Educational vouchers are increasingly used in various parts of the United States. Suppose that the government offers poor people a $5,000 education voucher, which can be used only to pay for education. Doreen would be better off with $5,000 in cash than with the educational voucher. In a graph, determine the cash value, *V*, Doreen places on the education voucher (that is, the amount of cash that would leave her as well off as with the educational voucher). Show how much education and "all other goods" she would consume with the educational voucher or with a cash payment of *V*. (*Hint*: If you can't solve this problem, look at the Cross-Chapter Analysis, "Child-Care Subsidies," following Chapter 5.)

31. Illustrate the logic of the endowment effect using a kinked indifference curve. Let the angle be greater than 90°. Suppose that the prices change, so the slope of the budget line through the endowment changes. Use the diagram to explain why an individual will only trade from the endowment point if the price change is substantial.

32. Goolsbee (2000) found that people who live in high sales tax areas are much more likely than other consumers to purchase over the Internet, where they are generally exempt from the sales tax if the firm is located in another state. The National Governors Association (NGA) proposed a uniform tax of 5% on all Internet sales. Goolsbee estimates that the NGA's flat 5% tax would lower the number of online customers by 18% and total sales by 23%. Alternatively, if each state could impose its own taxes (which average 6.33%), the number of buyers would fall by 24% and spending by 30%. Use an indifference curve-budget line diagram to illustrate the reason for his results. (*Hint*: Review Solved Problem 4.3.)

PROBLEMS

33. Does the utility function $V(Z, B) = \alpha + [U(Z, B)]^2$ give the same ordering over bundles as does $U(Z, B)$?

34. Fiona requires a minimum level of consumption, a *threshold*, to derive additional utility: $U(X, Z)$ is 0 if $X + Z \leq 5$ and is $X + Z$ otherwise. Draw Fiona's indifference curves. Which of our usual assumptions are violated by this example?

35. Julia consumes cans of anchovies, *A*, and boxes of biscuits, *B*. Each of her indifference curves reflects strictly diminishing marginal rates of substitution. Where $A = 2$ and $B = 2$, her marginal rate of substitution between cans of anchovies and boxes of biscuits equals -1 ($= MU_A/MU_B$). Will she prefer a bundle with three cans of anchovies and a box of biscuits to a bundle with two of each? Why?

*36. Andy purchases only two goods, apples (a) and kumquats (k). He has an income of \$40 and can buy apples at \$2 per pound and kumquats at \$4 per pound. His utility function is $U(a, k) = 3a + 5k$. That is, his (constant) marginal utility for apples is 3 and his marginal utility for kumquats is 5. What bundle of apples and kumquats should he purchase to maximize his utility? Why?

*37. David's utility function is $U = B + 2Z$. Describe the location of his optimal bundle (if possible) in terms of the relative prices of B and Z. C

38. Linda loves buying shoes and going out to dance. Her utility function for pairs of shoes, S, and the number of times she goes dancing per month, T, is $U(S, T) = 2ST$, so $MU_S = 2T$ and $MU_T = 2S$. It costs Linda \$50 to buy a new pair of shoes or to spend an evening out dancing. Assume that she has \$500 to spend on clothing and dancing.

   a. What is the equation for her budget line? Draw it (with T on the vertical axis), and label the slope and intercepts.

   b. What is Linda's marginal rate of substitution? Explain.

   c. Solve mathematically for her optimal bundle. Show how to determine this bundle in a diagram using indifference curves and a budget line.

39. Vasco's utility function is $U = 10X^2Z$. The price of X is $p_X = \$10$, the price of Z is $p_z = \$5$, and his income is $Y = \$150$. What is his optimal consumption bundle? (*Hint*: See Appendix 4B.) Show this bundle in a graph. C

*40. Diogo has a utility function $U(B, Z) = AB^{\alpha}Z^{\beta}$, where A, α, and β are constants, B is burritos, and Z is pizzas. If the price of burritos, p_B, is \$2 and the price of pizzas, p_Z, is \$1, and Y is \$100, what is Diogo's optimal bundle? C

41. If José Maria's utility function is $U(B, Z) = B + AB^{\alpha}Z^{\beta} + Z$, what is his marginal utility of Z? What is his marginal rate of substitution between these two goods? C

Applying Consumer Theory

5

I have enough money to last me the rest of my life, unless I buy something.
—Jackie Mason

We used consumer theory in Chapter 4 to show how a consumer chooses a bundle of goods, subject to a budget constraint, so as to maximize happiness. Here we apply consumer theory to derive demand curves and examine their properties.

We start by using consumer theory to show how to determine the shape of a demand curve for a good by varying the price of a good, holding other prices and income constant. Firms use information about the shape of demand curves when setting prices. Governments apply this information in predicting the impact of policies such as taxes and price controls.

We then use consumer theory to show how an increase in income causes the demand curve to shift. Firms use information about the relationship between income and demand to predict which less-developed countries will substantially increase their demand for the firms' products.

Next, we show that an increase in the price of a good has two effects on demand. First, consumers would buy less of the now relatively more expensive good even if they were compensated with cash for the price increase. Second, consumers' incomes can't buy as much as before because of the higher price, so consumers buy less of at least some goods.

We use this analysis of these two demand effects of a price increase to show why the government's measure of inflation, the Consumer Price Index (CPI), overestimates the amount of inflation. Because of this bias in the CPI, some people gain and some lose from contracts that adjust payment on the basis of the government's inflation index. If you signed a long-term lease for an apartment in which your rent payments increase over time in proportion to the change in the CPI, you lose and your landlord gains from this bias.

Finally, we show how we can use the consumer theory of demand to determine an individual's labor *supply* curve. Knowing the shape of workers' labor supply curves is important in analyzing the effect of income tax rates on work and on tax collections. Many politicians, including Presidents John F. Kennedy, Ronald Reagan, and George W. Bush, have argued that if the income tax rates were cut, workers would work so many more hours that tax revenues would increase. If so, everyone could be made better off by a tax cut. If not, the deficit could grow to record levels. Economists use empirical studies based on consumer theory to predict the effect of the tax rate cut on tax collections, as we discuss at the end of this chapter.

In this chapter, we examine five main topics

1. **Deriving Demand Curves.** We use consumer theory to derive demand curves, showing how a change in price causes a shift along a demand curve.
2. **How Changes in Income Shift Demand Curves.** We use consumer theory to determine how a demand curve shifts because of a change in income.
3. **Effects of a Price Change.** A change in price has two effects on demand, one having to do with a change in relative prices and the other concerning a change in the consumer's opportunities.
4. **Cost-of-Living Adjustments.** Using this analysis of the two effects of price changes, we show that the CPI overestimates the rate of inflation.
5. **Deriving Labor Supply Curves.** Using consumer theory to derive the demand curve for leisure, we can derive workers' labor supply curves and use them to determine how a reduction in the income tax rate affects labor supply and tax revenues.

5.1 Deriving Demand Curves

We use consumer theory to show by how much the quantity demanded of a good falls as its price rises. An individual chooses an optimal bundle of goods by picking the point on the highest indifference curve that touches the budget line (Chapter 4). When a price changes, the budget constraint the consumer faces shifts, so the consumer chooses a new optimal bundle. By varying one price and holding other prices and income constant, we determine how the quantity demanded changes as the price changes, which is the information we need to draw the demand curve. After deriving an individual's demand curve, we show the relationship between consumer tastes and the shape of the demand curve, which is summarized by the elasticity of demand (Chapter 3).

We derive a demand curve using the information about tastes from indifference curves (see Appendix 4B for a mathematical approach). To illustrate how to construct a demand curve, we estimated a set of indifference curves between wine and beer, using data for American consumers. Panel a of Figure 5.1 shows three of the estimated indifference curves for a typical U.S. consumer, whom we call Mimi.[1] These indifference curves are convex to the origin: Mimi views beer and wine as imperfect substitutes (Chapter 4). We can construct Mimi's demand curve for beer by holding her budget, her tastes, and the price of wine constant at their initial levels and varying the price of beer.

The vertical axis in panel a measures the number of gallons of wine Mimi consumes each year, and the horizontal axis measures the number of gallons of beer she drinks per year. Mimi spends $Y = \$419$ per year on beer and wine. The price of beer, p_b, is \$12 per unit, and the price of wine, p_w, is \$35 per unit.[2] The slope of her bud-

[1]My 93-year-old mother, Mimi, wanted the most degenerate character in the book named after her. She and I hope that you do not consume as much beer or wine as the typical American in this example.

[2]To ensure that the prices are whole numbers, we state the prices with respect to an unusual unit of measure (not gallons).

Figure 5.1 Deriving an Individual's Demand Curve.

If the price of beer falls, holding the price of wine, the budget, and tastes constant, the typical American consumer buys more beer, according to our estimates. (a) At the actual budget line, L^1, where the price of beer is \$12 per unit and the price of wine is \$35 per unit, the average consumer's indifference curve I^1 is tangent at Bundle e_1, 26.7 gallons of beer per year and 2.8 gallons of wine per year. If the price of beer falls to \$6 per unit, the new budget constraint is L^2, and the average consumer buys 44.5 gallons of beer per year and 4.3 gallons of wine per year. (b) By varying the price of beer, we trace out the individual's demand curve, D_1. The beer price-quantity combinations E_1, E_2, and E_3 on the demand curve for beer in panel b correspond to optimal Bundles e_1, e_2, and e_3 in panel a.

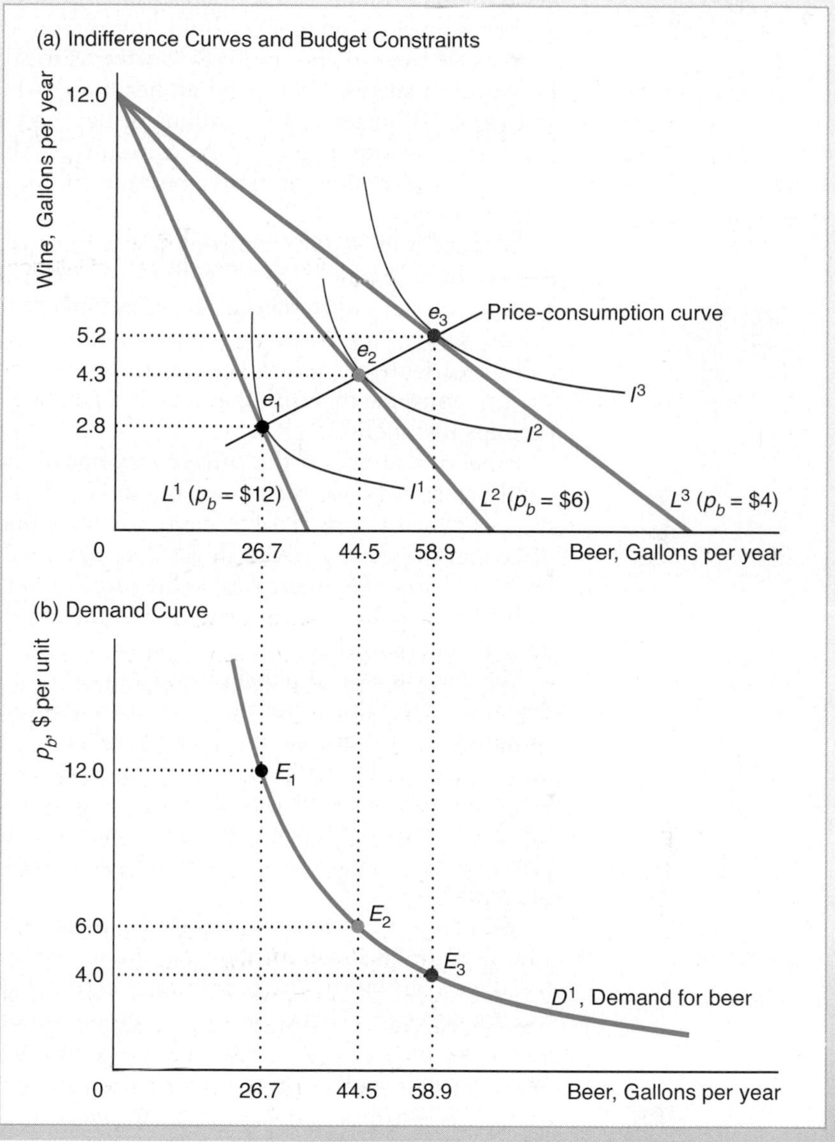

get line, L^1, is $-p_b/p_w = -12/35 \approx -\frac{1}{3}$. At those prices, Mimi consumes bundle e_1, 26.7 gallons of beer per year and 2.8 gallons of wine per year, a combination that is determined by the tangency of indifference curve I^1 and budget line L^1.[3]

[3]These figures are the U.S. average annual per capita consumption of wine and beer. These numbers are startlingly high given that they reflect an average that includes teetotalers and (apparently heavy) drinkers. According to the World Health Organization in 2007, consumption of liters of pure alcohol per capita for people 15 years and older is 4.6 in Mexico, 5.5 in Norway, 7.0 in Iceland, 7.8 in Canada, 8.0 in Italy, 8.6 in the United States, 9.0 in Australia, 9.7 in New Zealand, 11.8 in the United Kingdom, 12.0 in Germany, 12.9 in France, 13.0 in Portugal and the Czech Republic, 13.7 in Ireland, and 15.6 in Luxembourg. The average U.S. adult drinks the equivalent of 228 beers, a dozen bottles of wine, and 2 quarts of distilled spirits (such as vodka or single malt Scotch).

If the price of beer falls in half to \$6 per unit while the price of wine and her budget remain constant, Mimi's budget line rotates outward to L^2. If she were to spend all her money on wine, she could buy the same 12 ($\approx$ 419/35) gallons of wine per year as before, so the intercept on the vertical axis of L^2 is the same as for L^1. However, if she were to spend all her money on beer, she could buy twice as much as before (70 instead of 35 gallons of beer), so L^2 hits the horizontal axis twice as far from the origin as L^1. As a result, L^2 has a flatter slope than L^1, about $-\frac{1}{6}(\approx -6/35)$. The slope is flatter because the price of beer has fallen relative to the price of wine.

Because beer is now relatively less expensive, Mimi drinks relatively more beer. She chooses Bundle e_2, 44.5 gallons of beer per year and 4.3 gallons of wine per year, where her indifference curve I^2 is tangent to L^2. If the price of beer falls again, say, to \$4 per unit, Mimi consumes Bundle e_3, 58.9 gallons of beer per year and 5.2 gallons of wine per year.[4] The lower the price of beer, the happier Mimi is because she can consume more on the same budget: She is on a higher indifference curve (or perhaps just higher).

Panel a also shows the *price-consumption curve*, which is the line through the equilibrium bundles, such as e_1, e_2, and e_3, that Mimi would consume at each price of beer, when the price of wine and Mimi's budget are held constant. Because the price-consumption curve is upward sloping, we know that Mimi's consumption of both beer and wine increases as the price of beer falls.

We can use the same information in the price-consumption curve to draw Mimi's demand curve for beer, D^1, in panel b. Corresponding to each possible price of beer on the vertical axis of panel b, we record on the horizontal axis the quantity of beer demanded by Mimi from the price-consumption curve.

Points E_1, E_2, and E_3 on the demand curve in panel b correspond to Bundles e_1, e_2, and e_3 on the price-consumption curve in panel a. Both e_1 and E_1 show that when the price of beer is \$12, Mimi demands 26.7 gallons of beer per year. When the price falls to \$6 per unit, Mimi increases her consumption to 44.5 gallons of beer, point E_2. The demand curve, D^1, is downward sloping as predicted by the Law of Demand.

See Question 1 and Problems 29–32.

We can use the relationship between the points in panels a and b to show that Mimi's utility is lower at point E_1 on D^1 than at point E_2. Point E_1 corresponds to Bundle e_1 on indifference curve I^1, whereas E_2 corresponds to Bundle e_2 on indifference curve I^2, which is farther from the origin than I^1, so Mimi's utility is higher at E_2 than at E_1. Mimi is better off at E_2 than at E_1 because the price of beer is lower at E_2, so she can buy more goods with the same budget.

5.2 How Changes in Income Shift Demand Curves

To trace out the demand curve, we looked at how an increase in the good's price—holding income, tastes, and other prices constant—causes a downward *movement along the demand curve*. Now we examine how an increase in income, when all prices are held constant, causes a *shift of the demand curve*.

[4]These quantity numbers are probably higher than they would be in reality because we are assuming that Mimi continues to spend the same total amount of money on beer and wine as the price of beer drops.

Businesses routinely use information on the relationship between income and the quantity demanded. For example, in deciding where to market its products, Whirlpool wants to know which countries are likely to spend a relatively large percentage of any extra income on refrigerators and washing machines.

Effects of a Rise in Income

We illustrate the relationship between the quantity demanded and income by examining how Mimi's behavior changes when her income rises while the prices of beer and wine remain constant.[5] Figure 5.2 shows three ways of looking at the relationship between income and the quantity demanded. All three diagrams have the same horizontal axis: the quantity of beer consumed per year. In the consumer theory diagram, panel a, the vertical axis is the quantity of wine consumed per year. In the demand curve diagram, panel b, the vertical axis is the price of beer per unit. Finally, in panel c, which shows the relationship between income and quantity directly, the vertical axis is Mimi's budget, Y.

A rise in Mimi's income causes the budget constraint to shift outward in panel a, which increases Mimi's opportunities. Her budget constraint L^1 at her original income, $Y = \$419$, is tangent to her indifference curve I^1 at e_1.

As before, Mimi's demand curve for beer is D^1 in panel b. Point E_1 on D^1, which corresponds to point e_1 in panel a, shows how much beer, 26.7 gallons per year, Mimi consumes when the price of beer is \$12 per unit (and the price of wine is \$35 per unit).

Now suppose that Mimi's beer and wine budget, Y, increases by roughly 50% to \$628 per year. Her new budget line, L^2 in panel a, is farther from the origin but parallel to her original budget constraint, L^1, because the prices of beer and wine are unchanged. Given this larger budget, Mimi chooses Bundle e_2. The increase in her income causes her demand curve to shift to D^2 in panel b. Holding Y at \$628, we can derive D^2 by varying the price of beer, in the same way as we derived D^1 in Figure 5.1. When the price of beer is \$12 per unit, she buys 38.2 gallons of beer per year, E_2 on D^2. Similarly, if Mimi's income increases to \$837 per year, her demand curve shifts to D^3.

The *income-consumption curve* through Bundles e_1, e_2, and e_3 in panel a shows how Mimi's consumption of beer and wine increases as her income rises. As Mimi's income goes up, her consumption of both wine and beer increases.

Engel curve
the relationship between the quantity demanded of a single good and income, holding prices constant

We can show the relationship between the quantity demanded and income directly rather than by shifting demand curves to illustrate the effect. In panel c, we plot an **Engel curve**, which shows the relationship between the quantity demanded of a single good and income, holding prices constant. Income is on the vertical axis, and the quantity of beer demanded is on the horizontal axis. On Mimi's Engel curve for beer, points E_1^*, E_2^*, and E_3^* correspond to points E_1, E_2, and E_3 in panel b and to e_1, e_2, and e_3 in panel a.

[5]How much wealth do you need to live comfortably? In a survey of wealthy people (*Business Week*, February 28, 2005, 13), those with a net worth of over \$1 million said that they needed \$2.4 million to live comfortably, those with at least \$5 million in net worth said that they need \$10.4 million, and those with at least \$10 million wanted \$18.1 million. Apparently, people never have enough.

Figure 5.2 Effect of a Budget Increase on an Individual's Demand Curve.

As the annual budget for wine and beer, Y, increases from \$419 to \$628 and then to \$837, holding prices constant, the typical consumer buys more of both products, as shown by the upward slope of the income-consumption curve (a). That the typical consumer buys more beer as income increases is shown by the outward shift of the demand curve for beer (b) and the upward slope of the Engel curve for beer (c).

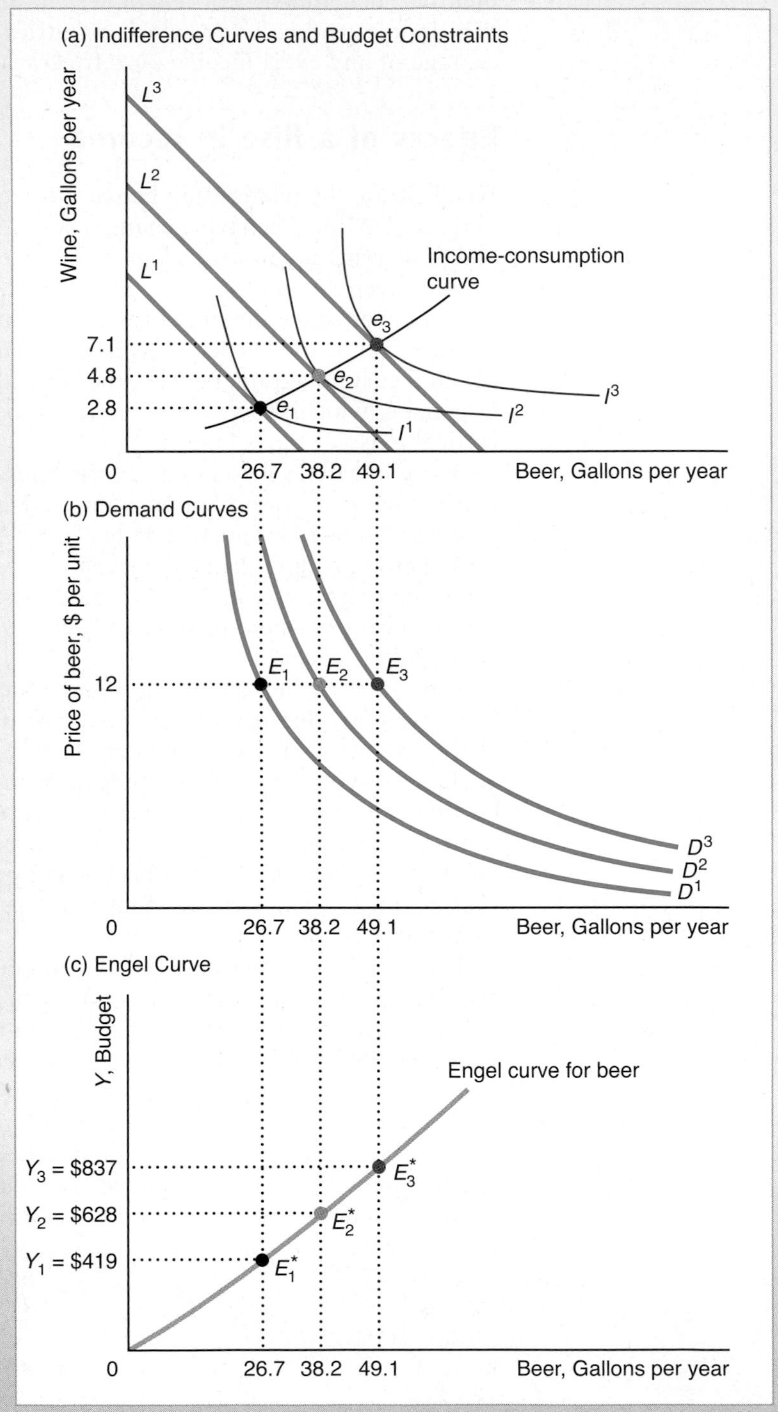

Solved Problem 5.1

Mahdu views Cragmont and Canada Dry ginger ales as perfect substitutes: He is indifferent as to which one he drinks. The price of a 12-ounce can of Cragmont, p, is less than the price of a 12-ounce can of Canada Dry, p^*. What does Mahdu's Engel curve for Cragmont ginger ale look like? How much does his weekly ginger ale budget have to rise for Mahdu to buy one more can of Cragmont ginger ale per week?

Answer

1. *Use indifference curves to derive Mahdu's equilibrium choice.* Because Mahdu views the two brands as perfect substitutes, his indifference curves, such as I^1 and I^2 in panel a of the graphs, are straight lines with a slope of −1 (see Chapter 4). When his income is Y_1, his budget line hits the Canada Dry axis at Y_1/p^* and his Cragmont axis at Y_1/p. Mahdu maximizes his utility by consuming Y_1/p cans of the less expensive Cragmont ginger ale and no Canada Dry (corner solution). As his income rises, say, to Y_2, his budget line shifts outward and is parallel to the original one, with the same slope of $-p/p^*$. Thus, at each income level, his budget lines are flatter than his indifference curves, so his equilibria lie along the Cragmont axis.

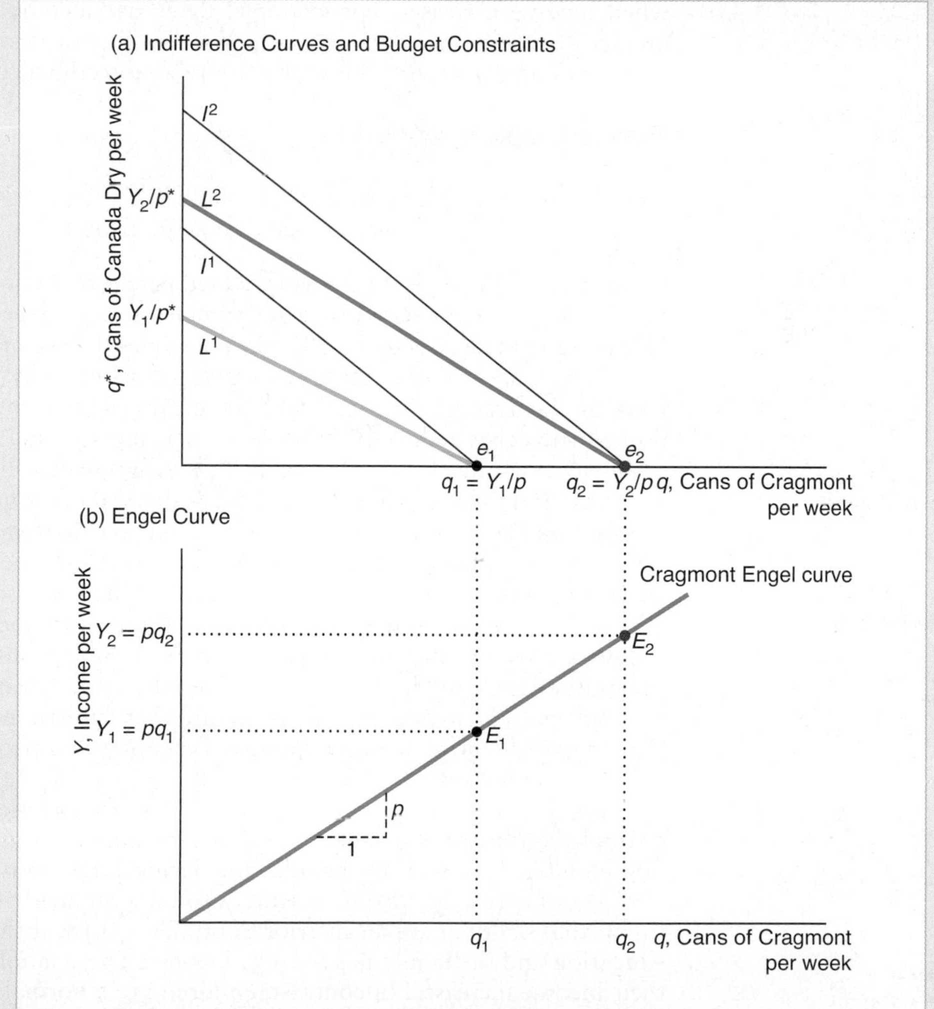

2. *Use the first figure to derive his Engel curve.* Because his entire budget, Y, goes to buying Cragmont, Mahdu buys $q = Y/p$ cans of Cragmont ginger ale. This expression, which shows the relationship between his income and the quantity of Cragmont ginger ale he buys, is Mahdu's Engel curve for Cragmont. The points E_1 and E_2 on the Engel curve in panel b correspond to e_1 and e_2 in panel a. We can rewrite this expression for his Engel curve as $Y = pq$. This relationship is drawn in panel b as a straight line with a slope of p. As q increases by one can ("run"), Y increases by p ("rise"). Because all his ginger ale budget goes to buying Cragmont, his income needs to rise by only p for him to buy one more can of Cragmont per week.

See Questions 2 and 3 and Problems 33–35.

Consumer Theory and Income Elasticities

Income elasticities tell us how much the quantity demanded changes as income increases. We can use income elasticities to summarize the shape of the Engel curve, the shape of the income-consumption curve, or the movement of the demand curves when income increases. For example, firms use income elasticities to predict the impact of income taxes on consumption. We first discuss the definition of income elasticities and then show how they are related to the income-consumption curve.

Income Elasticities. We defined the income elasticity of demand in Chapter 3 as

$$\xi = \frac{\text{percentage change in quantity demanded}}{\text{percentage change in income}} = \frac{\Delta Q \,/\, Q}{\Delta Y \,/\, Y}$$

where ξ is the Greek letter xi. Mimi's income elasticity of beer, ξ_b, is 0.88, and that of wine, ξ_w, is 1.38 (based on our estimates for the average American consumer). When her income goes up by 1%, she consumes 0.88% more beer and 1.38% more wine. Thus, according to these estimates, as income falls, consumption of beer and wine by the average American falls—contrary to frequent (unsubstantiated) claims in the media that people drink more as their incomes fall during recessions.

normal good
a commodity of which as much or more is demanded as income rises

inferior good
a commodity of which less is demanded as income rises

Most goods, like beer and wine, have positive income elasticities. A good is called a **normal good** if as much or more of it is demanded as income rises. Thus, a good is a normal good if its income elasticity is greater than or equal to zero: $\xi \geq 0$.

Some goods, however, have negative income elasticities: $\xi < 0$. A good is called an **inferior good** if less of it is demanded as income rises. No value judgment is intended by the use of the term *inferior*. An inferior good need not be defective or of low quality. Some of the better-known examples of inferior goods are foods such as potatoes and cassava that very poor people typically eat in large quantities. Some economists—apparently seriously—claim that human meat is an inferior good: Only when the price of other foods is very high and people are starving will they turn to cannibalism.

A good that is inferior for some people may be superior for others. One strange example concerns treating children as a consumption good. Even though they can't buy children in a market, people can decide how many children to have. Willis (1973) estimated the income elasticity for the number of children in a family. He found that children are an inferior good, $\xi = -0.18$, if the wife has relatively little education and the family has average income: These families have fewer children as their income increases. In contrast, children are a normal good, $\xi = 0.044$, in families in which the wife is relatively well educated. For both types of families, the income elasticities are close to zero, so the number of children is not very sensitive to income.

Income-Consumption Curves and Income Elasticities. The shape of the income-consumption curve for two goods tells us the sign of the income elasticities: whether the income elasticities for those goods are positive or negative. We know that Mimi's income elasticities of beer and wine are positive because the income-consumption curve in panel a of Figure 5.2 is upward sloping. As income rises, the budget line shifts outward and hits the upward-sloping income-consumption line at higher levels of both goods. Thus, as her income rises, Mimi demands more beer and wine, so her income elasticities for beer and wine are positive. Because the income elasticity for beer is positive, the demand curve for beer shifts to the right in panel b of Figure 5.2 as income increases.

To illustrate the relationship between the slope of the income-consumption curve and the sign of income elasticities, we examine Peter's choices of food and housing. Peter purchases Bundle *e* in Figure 5.3 when his budget constraint is L^1. When his income increases, so that his budget constraint is L^2, he selects a bundle on L^2. Which bundle he buys depends on his tastes—his indifference curves.

Figure 5.3 Income-Consumption Curves and Income Elasticities.

At the initial income, the budget constraint is L^1 and the optimal bundle is *e*. After income rises, the new constraint is L^2. With an upward sloping income-consumption curve such as ICC^2, both goods are normal. With an income-consumption curve such as ICC^1 that goes through the upper-left section of L^2 (to the left of the vertical dotted line through *e*), housing is normal and food is inferior. With an income-consumption curve such as ICC^3 that cuts L^2 in the lower-right section (below the horizontal dotted line through *e*), food is normal and housing is inferior.

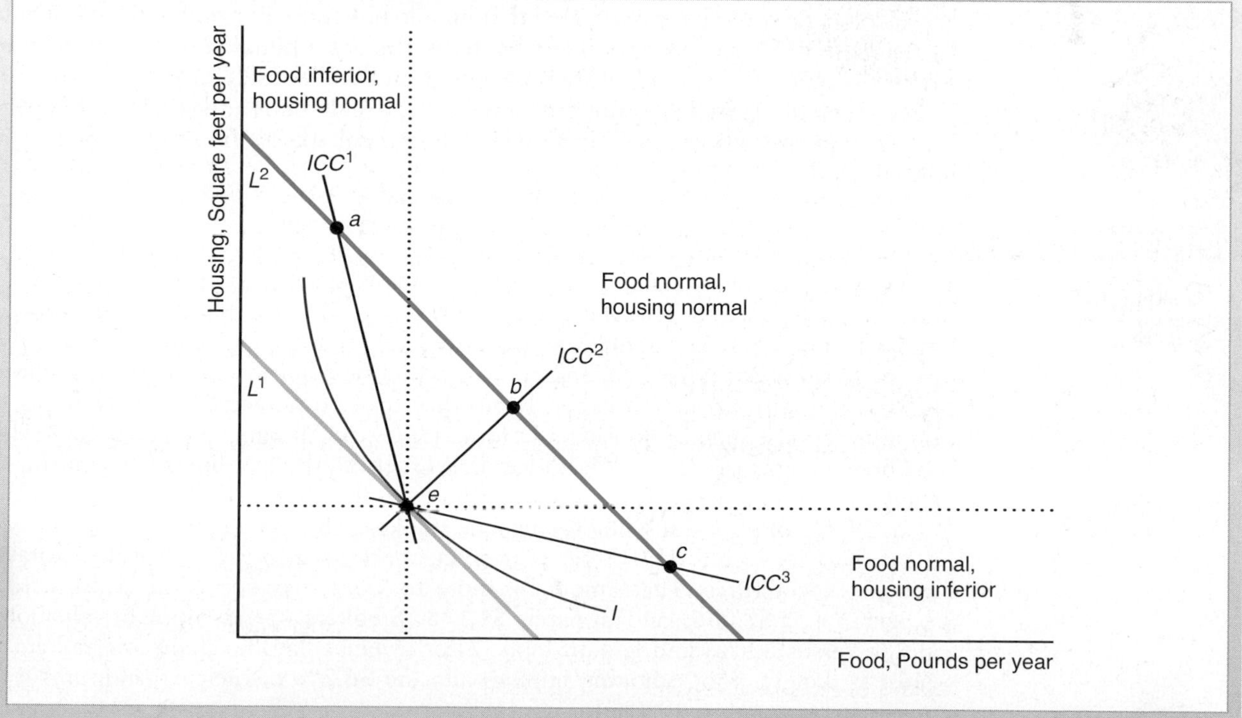

The horizontal and vertical dotted lines through e divide the new budget line, L^2, into three sections. In which of these three sections the new optimal bundle is located determines Peter's income elasticities of food and clothing.

Suppose that Peter's indifference curve is tangent to L^2 at a point in the upper-left section of L^2 (to the left of the vertical dotted line that goes through e) such as a. If Peter's income-consumption curve is ICC^1, which goes from e through a, he buys more housing and less food as his income rises. (We draw the possible ICC curves as straight lines for simplicity. In general, they may curve.) Housing is a normal good, and food is an inferior good.

If instead the new optimal bundle is located in the middle section of L^2 (above the horizontal dotted line and to the right of the vertical dotted line), such as at b, his income-consumption curve ICC^2 through e and b is upward sloping. He buys more of both goods as his income rises, so both food and housing are normal goods.

Third, suppose that his new optimal bundle is in the bottom-right segment of L^2 (below the horizontal dotted line). If his new optimal bundle is c, his income-consumption curve ICC^3 slopes downward from e through c. As his income rises, Peter consumes more food and less housing, so food is a normal good and housing is an inferior good.

See Problem 37.

Some Goods Must Be Normal. It is impossible for all goods to be inferior. We illustrate this point using Figure 5.3. At his original income, Peter faced budget constraint L^1 and bought the combination of food and housing e. When his income goes up, his budget constraint shifts outward to L^2. Depending on his tastes (the shape of his indifference curves), he may buy more housing and less food, such as Bundle a; more of both, such as b; or more food and less housing, such as c. Therefore, either both goods are normal or one good is normal and the other is inferior.

If both goods were inferior, Peter would buy less of both goods as his income rises—which makes no sense. Were he to buy less of both, he would be buying a bundle that lies inside his original budget constraint L^1. Even at his original, relatively low income, he could have purchased that bundle but chose not to, buying e instead. By the more-is-better assumption of Chapter 4, there is a bundle on the budget constraint that gives Peter more utility than any given bundle inside the constraint.

Even if an individual does not buy more of the usual goods and services, that person may put the extra money into savings. Empirical studies find that savings is a normal good.

APPLICATION

Going Up in Smoke

A tax on cigarettes discourages some people from smoking (see the application "Taxing to Stop Smoking and Raise Revenue" in Chapter 3). U.S. per capita consumption of cigarettes fell from 2,445 in1996 to 1,592 in 2006. Lower-income, minority, and younger populations are more likely than others to quit smoking if the price rises. But what happens to those who don't quit or cut back on smoking substantially? To pay for their habit, they have to reduce their expenditures on other goods, such as housing and food. (Similarly, in panel a of Figure 5.1, if the price of beer rises from \$4, budget line L^3, to \$6, budget line L^2, Mimi substantially reduces her consumption of wine as well as beer.)

In 29.1% of poor households, someone smokes. The average low-income family of smokers spends \$1,018 per year on cigarettes, which is 5.1% of their total annual expenditures. That amount is close to what they spend on health care expenditures, \$1,056, and apparel, \$1,138. Smokers spend more on alcohol (1.2% versus 0.5%) and less on food (21.5% versus 22.3%) than nonsmokers. Most strikingly, poor, smoking families allocate 36.2% of their expenditures to housing compared to 40.4% for nonsmokers.

Busch et al. (2004) estimated the elasticities of demand for cigarettes and the cross-elasticities of other goods when the price of cigarettes rises. They concluded that a 10% increase in the price of cigarettes causes poor, smoking families to cut back on cigarettes by 9% (a higher estimate than other studies), alcohol and transportation by 11%, food by 17%, and health care by 12%. Thus, to continue to smoke, these people cut back on many basic goods.

Income Elasticities May Vary with Income. A good may be normal at some income levels and inferior at others. When Gail was poor and her income increased slightly, she ate meat more frequently, and her meat of choice was hamburger. Thus, when her income was low, hamburger was a normal good. As her income increased further, however, she switched from hamburgers to steak. Thus, at higher incomes, hamburger is an inferior good.

We show Gail's choice between hamburger (horizontal axis) and all other goods (vertical axis) in panel a of Figure 5.4. As Gail's income increases, her budget line

Figure 5.4 A Good That Is Both Inferior and Normal.

When she was poor and her income increased, Gail bought more hamburger; however, when she became wealthier and her income rose, she bought less hamburger and more steak. (a) The forward slope of the income-consumption curve from e_1 to e_2 and the backward bend from e_2 to e_3 show this pattern. (b) The forward slope of the Engel curve at low incomes, E_1 to E_2, and the backward bend at higher incomes, E_2 to E_3, also show this pattern.

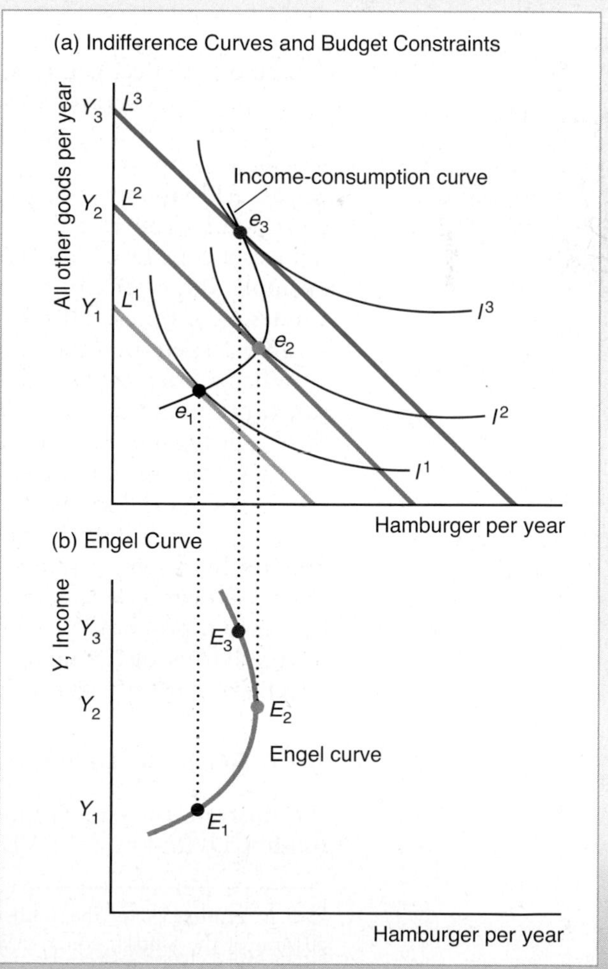

shifts outward, from L^1 to L^2, and she buys more hamburger: Bundle e_2 lies to the right of e_1. As her income increases further, shifting her budget line outward to L^3, Gail reduces her consumption of hamburger: Bundle e_3 lies to the left of e_2.

Gail's Engel curve in panel b captures the same relationship. At low incomes, her Engel curve is upward sloping, indicating that she buys more hamburger as her income rises. At higher incomes, her Engel curve is backward bending.

As their incomes rise, many consumers switch between lower-quality (hamburger) and higher-quality (steak) versions of the same good. This switching behavior explains the pattern of income elasticities across different-quality cars. For example, the income elasticity of demand for a Jetta is 2.1, an Accord is 2.2, a BMW 700 Series is 4.4, and a Jaguar X-Type is 4.5 (see **www.myeconlab.com/perloff**, Chapter 5, "Income Elasticities of Demand for Cars").

5.3 Effects of a Price Change

substitution effect
the change in the quantity of a good that a consumer demands when the good's price changes, holding other prices and the consumer's utility constant

income effect
the change in the quantity of a good a consumer demands because of a change in income, holding prices constant

Holding tastes, other prices, and income constant, an increase in a price of a good has two effects on an individual's demand. One is the **substitution effect**: the change in the quantity of a good that a consumer demands when the good's price rises, holding other prices and the consumer's utility constant. If utility is held constant, as the price of the good increases, consumers *substitute* other, now relatively cheaper goods, for that one.

The other effect is the **income effect**: the change in the quantity of a good a consumer demands because of a change in income, holding prices constant. An increase in price reduces a consumer's buying power, effectively reducing the consumer's *income* or opportunity set and causing the consumer to buy less of at least some goods. A doubling of the price of all the goods the consumer buys is equivalent to a drop in income to half its original level. Even a rise in the price of only one good reduces a consumer's ability to buy the same amount of all goods as previously. For example, if the price of food increases in China, the effective purchasing power of a Chinese consumer falls substantially because one-third of Chinese consumers' income is spent on food (*Statistical Yearbook of China*, 2006).

When a price goes up, the total change in the quantity purchased is the sum of the substitution and income effects.[6] When estimating the effects of a price change on the quantity an individual demands, economists decompose this combined effect into the two separate components. By doing so, they gain extra information that they can use to answer questions about whether inflation measures are accurate, whether an increase in tax rates will raise tax revenue, and what the effects are of government policies that compensate some consumers. For example, President Jimmy Carter, when advocating a tax on gasoline, and President Bill Clinton, when calling for an energy tax, proposed providing an income compensation for poor consumers to offset the harms of the taxes. We can use knowledge of the substitution and income effects from a price change of energy to evaluate the effect of these policies.

Income and Substitution Effects with a Normal Good

To illustrate the substitution and income effects, we examine the choice between music CDs and movie DVDs. In 2005, a typical owner of a home theater (a televi-

[6]See Appendix 5A for the mathematical relationship, called the *Slutsky equation*. See also the discussion of the Slutsky equation at **www.myeconlab.com/Perloff**, "Measuring the Substitution and Income Effects."

sion and a DVD player), whom we call Laura, bought 12 music CDs, C, and 6 movie DVDs, D, per year.[7] We estimated Laura's utility function and used it to draw Laura's indifference curves in Figure 5.5.[8]

Because Laura's entertainment budget for the year is $Y = \$300$, the price of a DVD is $p_D = \$20$, and the price of a CD is $p_C = \$15$, her original budget constraint is L^1 in Figure 5.5. She can afford to buy 15 DVDs and no CDs, 20 CDs and no DVDs, or any combination between these extremes.

Figure 5.5 Substitution and Income Effects with Normal Goods.

An increase in the price of music CDs from \$15 to \$30 causes Laura's budget line to rotate from L^1 to L^2. The imaginary budget line L^* has the same slope as L^2 and is tangent to indifference curve I^1. The shift of the optimal bundle from e_1 to e_2 is the *total effect* of the price change. The total effect can be decomposed into the *substitution effect*—movement from e_1 to e^*—and the *income effect*—movement from e^* to e_2.

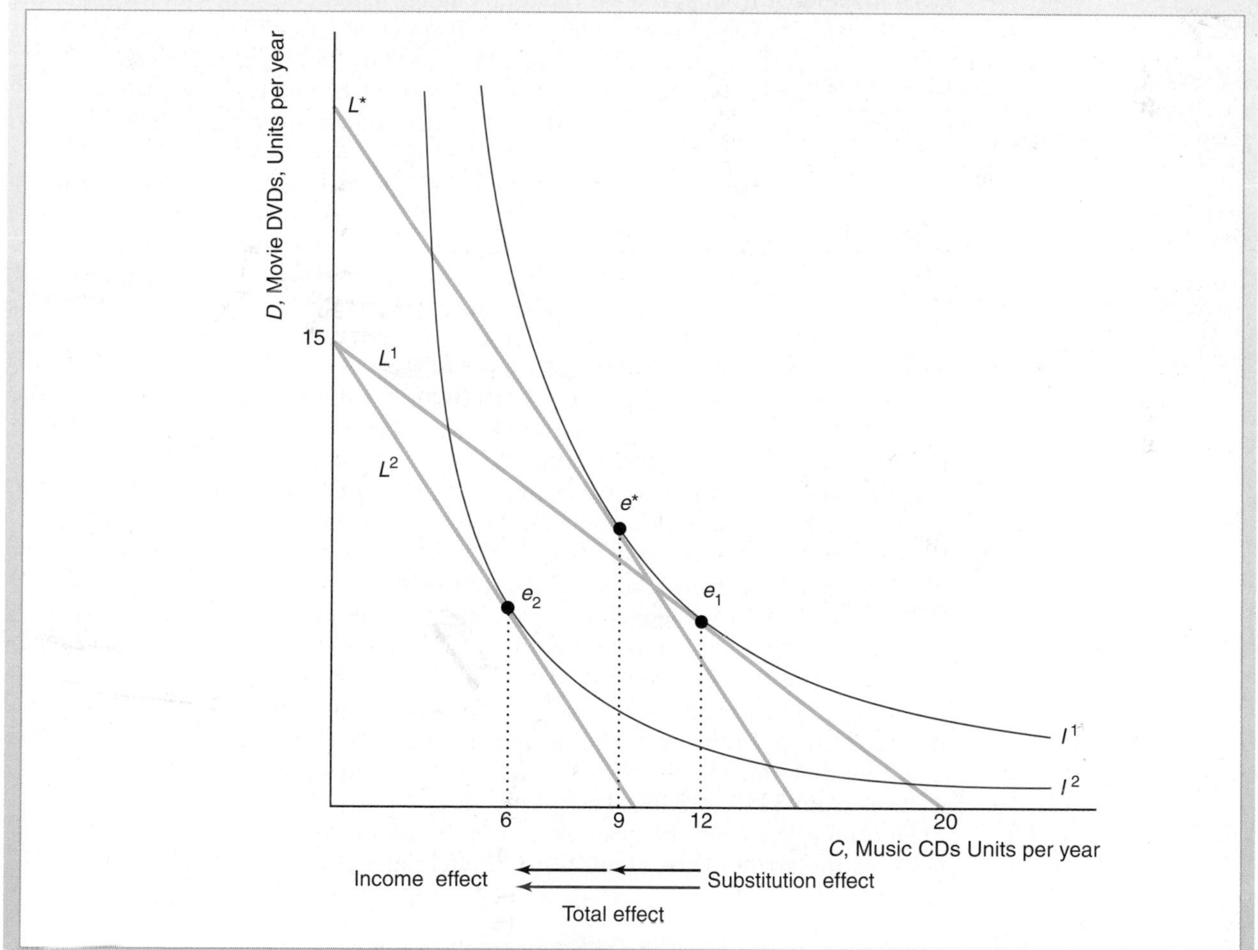

[7]Using budget information from **www.ce.org/Press/CEA_Pubs/834.asp** and prices, we calculated the average number of units purchased.

[8]Laura's estimated utility function is $U = C^{0.6}D^{0.4}$, which is a type of Cobb-Douglas utility function (Appendix 4A).

Now suppose that the price of CDs doubles to \$30, causing Laura's budget constraint to rotate inward from L^1 to L^2 in Figure 5.5. The new budget constraint, L^2, is twice as steep, $-p_C/p_D = -30/20 = -1.5$, as is L^1, $-p_C/p_D = -15/20 = -0.75$, because CDs are now twice as expensive.

Laura's opportunity set is smaller, so she can choose between fewer CD-DVD bundles than she could at the lower CD price. The area between the two budget constraints reflects the decrease in her opportunity set owing to the increase in the price of CDs.

Given her estimated utility function, Laura's demand functions for CDs, C, and DVDs, D, are $C = 0.6Y/p_C$ and $D = 0.4Y/p_D$ (see Appendix 4B). At the original price of CDs and with an entertainment budget of Y = \$300 per year, Laura chooses Bundle e_1, $C = 0.6 \times 300/15 = 12$ CDs and $D = 0.4 \times 300/20 = 6$ DVDs per year, where her indifference curve I^1 is tangent to her budget constraint L^1. When the price of CDs rises, Laura's new equilibrium bundle is e_2 (where she buys $C = 0.6 \times 300/30 = 6$ CDs), which occurs where her indifference curve I^2 is tangent to L^2.

The movement from e_1 to e_2 is the total change in her consumption owing to the rise in the price of CDs. In particular, the *total effect* on Laura's consumption of CDs from the rise in the price of CDs is that she now buys 6 (= 12 – 6) fewer CDs per year. In the figure, the red arrow pointing to the left and labeled "Total effect" shows this decrease. We can break the total effect into a substitution effect and an income effect.

The *substitution effect* is the change in the quantity demanded from a *compensated change in the price* of CDs, which occurs when we increase Laura's income by enough to offset the rise in the price of CDs so that her utility stays constant. To determine the substitution effect, we draw an imaginary budget constraint, L^*, that is parallel to L^2 and tangent to Laura's original indifference curve, I^1. This imaginary budget constraint, L^*, has the same slope, –1.5, as L^2 because both curves are based on the original, lower price of CDs. For L^* to be tangent to I^1, we need to increase Laura's budget from \$300 to \$450 to offset the harm of the higher price of CDs. If Laura's budget constraint were L^*, she would choose Bundle e^*, where she buys $C = 0.6 \times 450/30 = 9$ CDs.

Thus, if the price of CDs rises relative to that of DVDs and we hold Laura's utility constant by raising her income, Laura's optimal bundle shifts from e_1 to e^*, which is the substitution effect. She buys 3 (= 12 – 9) fewer CDs per year, as the arrow pointing to the left labeled "Substitution effect" shows.

The *income effect* is the change in the quantity of a good a consumer demands because of a change in income, holding prices constant. The change in income is due to the change in the price of CDs, which allows Laura to buy fewer units with her same budget. The parallel shift of the budget constraint from L^* to L^2 captures this effective decrease in income. The movement from e^* to e_2 is the income effect, as the arrow pointing to the left labeled "Income effect" shows. As her budget decreases from \$450 to \$300, Laura consumes 3 (= 9 – 6) fewer CDs per year.

The *total effect* from the price change is the *sum of the substitution and income effects*, as the arrows show. Laura's total effect in CDs per year from a rise in the price of CDs is

$$\begin{array}{ccccc} \text{Total effect} & = & \text{substitution effect} & + & \text{income effect} \\ -6 & = & -3 & + & (-3). \end{array}$$

Because indifference curves are convex to the origin, *the substitution effect is unambiguous:* Less of a good is consumed when its price rises. A consumer always substitutes a less expensive good for a more expensive one, holding utility constant. The substitution effect causes a *movement along an indifference curve.*

The income effect causes a shift to another indifference curve due to a change in the consumer's opportunity set. The direction of the income effect depends on the income elasticity. Because a CD is a normal good for Laura, her income effect is negative. Thus, both Laura's substitution effect and her income effect go in the same direction, so the total effect of the price rise must be negative.

See Questions 4 and 5.

Income and Substitution Effects with an Inferior Good

If a good is inferior, the income effect goes in the opposite direction from the substitution effect. For most inferior goods, the income effect is smaller than the substitution effect. As a result, the total effect moves in the same direction as the substitution effect, but the total effect is smaller. However, the income effect can more than offset the substitution effect in extreme cases. We now examine such a case.

Dennis chooses between spending his money on Chicago Bulls basketball games and on movies, as Figure 5.6 shows. When the price of movies falls, Dennis' budget line shifts from L^1 to L^2. The total effect of the price fall is the movement from e_1 to e_2. We can break this total movement into an income effect and a substitution effect.

Dennis' income effect, the movement to the left from Bundle e^* to Bundle e_2, is negative, as the arrow pointing left labeled "Income effect" shows. The income effect is negative because Dennis regards movies as an inferior good.

Figure 5.6 Giffen Good.

Because a movie ticket is an inferior good for Dennis, the income effect, the movement from e^* to e_2, resulting from a drop in the price of movies is negative. This negative income effect more than offsets the positive substitution effect, the movement from e_1 to e^*, so the total effect, the movement from e_1 to e_2, is negative. Thus, a movie ticket is a Giffen good because as its price drops, Dennis consumes less of it.

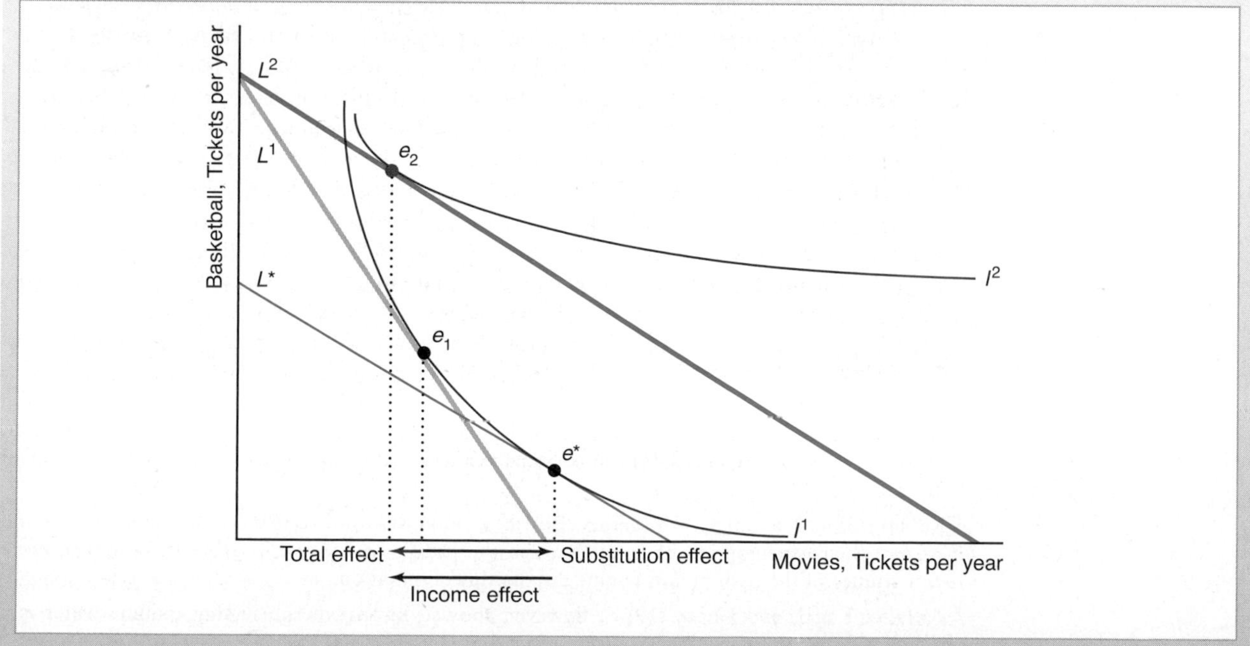

Dennis' substitution effect for movies is positive because movies are now less expensive than they were before the price change. The substitution effect is the movement to the right from e_1 to e^*.

The total effect of a price change, then, depends on which effect is larger. Because Dennis' negative income effect for movies more than offsets his positive substitution effect, the total effect of a drop in the price of movies is negative.[9]

Giffen good
a commodity for which a decrease in its price causes the quantity demanded to fall

A good is called a **Giffen good** if a decrease in its price causes the quantity demanded to fall.[10] Thus, going to the movies is a Giffen good for Dennis. The price decrease has an effect that is similar to an income increase: His opportunity set increases as the price of movies drops. Dennis spends the money he saves on movies to buy more basketball tickets. Indeed, he decides to increase his purchase of basketball tickets even further by reducing his purchase of movie tickets.

The demand curve for a Giffen good has an upward slope! Dennis' demand curve for movies is upward sloping because he goes to more movies at the high price, e_1, than at the low price, e_2.

The Law of Demand (Chapter 2), however, says that demand curves slope downward. You're no doubt wondering how I'm going to worm my way out this apparent contradiction. The answer is that I claimed that the Law of Demand was an empirical regularity, not a theoretical necessity. Although it's theoretically possible for a demand curve to slope upward, economists have found few, if any, real-world examples of Giffen goods.[11]

Solved Problem 5.2

Next to its plant, a manufacturer of dinner plates has an outlet store that sells plates of both first quality (perfect plates) and second quality (plates with slight blemishes). The outlet store sells a relatively large share of seconds. At its regular stores elsewhere, the firm sells many more first-quality plates than second-quality plates. Why? (Assume that consumers' tastes with respect to plates are the same everywhere and that there is a cost, s, of shipping each plate from the factory to the firm's other stores.)

Answer

1. *Determine how the relative prices of plates differ between the two types of stores.* The slope of the budget line consumers face at the factory outlet store is $-p_1/p_2$, where p_1 is the price of first-quality plates and p_2 is the price of the seconds. It costs the same, s, to ship a first-quality plate as a second because they weigh the same and have to be handled in the same way. At all other stores, the firm adds the cost of shipping to the price it charges at its factory outlet store, so the price of a first-quality plate is $p_1 + s$ and the price of a second is $p_2 + s$. As a result, the slope of the budget line consumers face at the other retail stores is $-(p_1 + s)/(p_2 + s)$. The seconds are relatively less expensive at the factory outlet than at other stores. For example, if $p_1 = \$2$, $p_2 = \$1$, and

[9]Economists mathematically decompose the total effect of a price change into substitution and income effects to answer various business and policy questions: see **www.myeconlab.com/perloff**, Chapter 5, "Measuring the Substitution and Income Effects" and "International Comparison of Substitution and Income Effects."

[10]Robert Giffen, a nineteenth-century British economist, argued that poor people in Ireland increased their consumption of potatoes when the price rose because of a blight. However, more recent studies of the Irish potato famine dispute this observation.

[11]Battalio, Kagel, and Kogut (1991), however, showed in an experiment that quinine water is a Giffen good for lab rats!

s = \$1 per plate, the slope of the budget line is –2 at the outlet store and –3/2 elsewhere. Thus, the first-quality plate costs twice as much as a second at the outlet store but only 1.5 times as much elsewhere.

2. *Use the relative price difference to explain why relatively more seconds are bought at the factory outlet.* Holding a consumer's income and tastes fixed, if the price of seconds rises relative to that of firsts (as we go from the factory outlet to other retail shops), most consumers will buy relatively more firsts. The substitution effect is unambiguous: Were they compensated so that their utilities were held constant, consumers would unambiguously substitute firsts for seconds. It is possible that the income effect could go in the other direction; however, as most consumers spend relatively little of their total budget on plates, the income effect is presumably small relative to the substitution effect. Thus, we expect relatively fewer seconds to be bought at the retail stores than at the factory outlet.

See Questions 7 and 8.

APPLICATION

Shipping the Good Stuff Away

According to the economic theory discussed in Solved Problem 5.2, we expect that the relatively larger share of higher-quality goods will be shipped, the greater the per-unit shipping fee. Is this theory true, and is the effect large? To answer these questions, Hummels and Skiba (2004) examined shipments between 6,000 country pairs for more than 5,000 goods. They found that doubling per-unit shipping costs results in a 70% to 143% increase in the average price (excluding the cost of shipping) as a larger share of top-quality products are shipped.

The greater the distance between the trading countries, the higher the cost of shipping. Hummels and Skiba speculate that the relatively high quality of Japanese goods is due to that country's relatively great distance to major importers.

5.4 Cost-of-Living Adjustments

In spite of the cost of living, it's still popular. —Kathleen Norris

By knowing both the substitution and income effects, we can answer questions that we could not if we knew only the total effect. For example, if firms have an estimate of the income effect, they can predict the impact of a negative income tax (a gift of money from the government) on the consumption of their products. Similarly, if we know the size of both effects, we can determine how accurately the government measures inflation.

Many long-term contracts and government programs include *cost-of-living adjustments (COLAs)*, which raise prices or incomes in proportion to an index of inflation. Not only business contracts but also rental contracts, alimony payments, salaries, pensions, and Social Security payments are frequently adjusted in this manner over time. We will use consumer theory to show that a cost-of-living measure that governments commonly use overestimates how the true cost of living changes over time. Because of this overestimate, you overpay your landlord if the rent on your apartment rises with this measure. (See the Cross-Chapter Analysis "Child-Care Subsidies," which follows this chapter, for an analogous problem.)

Inflation Indexes

The prices of most goods rise over time. We call the increase in the overall price level *inflation*.

Real Versus Nominal Prices. The actual price of a good is called the *nominal price*. The price adjusted for inflation is the *real price*.

Because the overall level of prices rises over time, nominal prices usually increase more rapidly than real prices. For example, the nominal price of a McDonald's hamburger rose from 15¢ in 1955 to 89¢ in 2008, nearly a six-fold increase. However, the real price of a burger fell because the prices of other goods rose more rapidly than that of a burger.

How do we adjust for inflation to calculate the real price? Governments measure the cost of a standard bundle of goods for use in comparing prices over time. This measure, as mentioned earlier in this chapter, is called the Consumer Price Index (CPI). Each month, the government reports how much it costs to buy the bundle of goods that an average consumer purchased in a *base* year (with the base year changing every few years).

By comparing the cost of buying this bundle over time, we can determine how much the overall price level has increased. In the United States, the CPI was 26.8 in 1955 and 211.1 in January 2008.[12] The cost of buying the bundle of goods increased 788% ($\approx$ 211.1/26.8) from 1955 to 2008.

We can use the CPI to calculate the real price of a hamburger over time. In terms of 2008 dollars, the real price of a hamburger in 1955 was

$$\frac{\text{CPI for 2008}}{\text{CPI for 1955}} \times \text{price of a burger} = \frac{211.1}{26.8} \times 15¢ \approx 1.18.$$

If you could have purchased the hamburger in 1955 with 2008 dollars—which are worth less than 1955 dollars—the hamburger would have cost \$1.18. The real price in 2008 dollars (and the nominal price) of a hamburger in 2008 was only 89¢. Thus, the real price of a hamburger fell by about a quarter. If we compared the real prices in both years using 1955 dollars, we would reach the same conclusion that the real price of hamburgers fell by about a fifth.

Calculating Inflation Indexes. The government collects data on the quantities and prices of 364 individual goods and services, such as housing, dental services, watch and jewelry repairs, college tuition fees, taxi fares, women's hairpieces and wigs, hearing aids, slipcovers and decorative pillows, bananas, pork sausage, and funeral expenses. These prices rise at different rates. If the government merely reported all these price increases separately, most of us would find this information overwhelming. It is much more convenient to use a single summary statistic, the CPI, which tells us how prices rose *on average*.

---

[12]The number 211.1 is not an actual dollar amount. Rather, it is the actual dollar cost of buying the bundle divided by a constant. That constant was chosen so that the average expenditure in the period 1982–1984 was 100.

We can use an example with only two goods, clothing and food, to show how the CPI is calculated. In the first year, consumers buy C_1 units of clothing and F_1 units of food at prices p_C^1 and p_F^1. We use this bundle of goods, C_1 and F_1, as our base bundle for comparison. In the second year, consumers buy C_2 and F_2 units at prices p_C^2 and p_F^2.

The government knows from its survey of prices each year that the price of clothing in the second year is p_C^2 / p_C^1 times as large as the price the previous year and the price of food is p_F^2 / p_F^1 times as large. If the price of clothing was \$1 in the first year and \$2 in the second year, the price of clothing in the second year is $\frac{2}{1} = 2$ times, or 100%, larger than in the first year.

One way we can average the price increases of each good is to weight them equally. But do we really want to do that? Do we want to give as much weight to the price increase for skateboards as to the price increase for automobiles? An alternative approach is to give a larger weight to the price change of a good as we spend more of our income on that good, its budget share. The CPI takes this approach to weighting, using budget shares.[13]

The CPI for the first year is the amount of income it takes to buy the market basket actually purchased that year:

$$Y_1 = p_C^1 C_1 + p_F^1 F_1. \tag{5.1}$$

The cost of buying the first year's bundle in the second year is

$$Y_2 = p_C^2 C_1 + p_F^2 F_1. \tag{5.2}$$

To calculate the rate of inflation, we determine how much more income it would take to buy the first year's bundle in the second year, which is the ratio of Equation 5.1 to Equation 5.2:

$$\frac{Y_2}{Y_1} = \frac{p_C^2 C_1 + p_F^2 F_1}{p_C^1 C_1 + p_F^1 F_1}.$$

For example, from 1996 to 1997, the U.S. CPI rose by $1.023 \approx Y_2/Y_1$ from $Y_1 = 156.9$ to $Y_2 = 160.5$. Thus, it cost 2.3% more in 1997 than in 1996 to buy the same bundle of goods.

The ratio Y_2/Y_1 reflects how much prices rise on average. By multiplying and dividing the first term in the numerator by p_C^1 and multiplying and dividing the second term by p_F^1 we find that this index is equivalent to

$$\frac{Y_2}{Y_1} = \frac{\left(\frac{p_C^2}{p_C^1}\right) p_C^1 C_1 + \left(\frac{p_F^2}{p_F^1}\right) p_F^1 F_1}{Y_1} = \left(\frac{p_C^2}{p_C^1}\right)\theta_C + \left(\frac{p_F^2}{p_F^1}\right)\theta_F,$$

where $\theta_C = p_C^1 C_1/Y_1$ and $\theta_F = p_F^1 F_1/Y_1$ are the budget shares of clothing and food in the first or base year. The CPI is a *weighted average* of the price increase for each good, p_C^2 / p_C^1 and p_F^2 / p_F^1 where the weights are each good's budget share in the base year, θ_C and θ_F.

See Question 12.

[13]This discussion of the CPI is simplified in a number of ways. Sophisticated adjustments are made to the CPI that are ignored here, including repeated updating of the base year (chaining). See Pollak (1989) and Diewert and Nakamura (1993).

Effects of Inflation Adjustments

A CPI adjustment of prices in a long-term contract overcompensates for inflation. We use an example involving an employment contract to illustrate the difference between using the CPI to adjust a long-term contract and using a true cost-of-living adjustment, which holds utility constant.

CPI Adjustment. Klaas signed a long-term contract when he was hired. According to the COLA clause in his contract, his employer increases his salary each year by the same percentage as that by which the CPI increases. If the CPI this year is 5% higher than the CPI last year, Klaas' salary rises automatically by 5% over last year's.

Klaas spends all his money on clothing and food. His budget constraint in the first year is $Y_1 = p_C^1 C + p_F^1 F$, which we rewrite as

$$C = \frac{Y_1}{p_C^1} - \frac{p_F^1}{p_C^1} F.$$

The intercept of the budget constraint, L^1, on the vertical (clothing) axis in Figure 5.7 is Y_1 / p_C^1 and the slope of the constraint is $-p_F^1 / p_C^1$. The tangency of his indifference curve I^1 and the budget constraint L^1 determine his equilibrium consumption bundle in the first year, e_1, where he purchases C_1 and F_1.

In the second year, his salary rises with the CPI to Y_2, so his budget constraint, L^2, in that year is

$$C = \frac{Y_2}{p_C^2} - \frac{p_F^2}{p_C^2} F.$$

The new constraint, L^2, has a flatter slope, $-p_F^2 / p_C^2$, than L^1 because the price of clothing rose more than the price of food. The new constraint goes through the original equilibrium bundle, e_1, because, by increasing his salary using the CPI, the firm ensures that Klaas can buy the same bundle of goods in the second year that he chose in the first year.

He *can* buy the same bundle, but *does* he? The answer is no. His optimal bundle in the second year is e_2, where indifference curve I^2 is tangent to his new budget constraint L^2. The movement from e_1 to e_2 is the *total effect* from the changes in the real prices of clothing and food. *This adjustment to his income does not keep him on his original indifference curve,* I^1.

Indeed, Klaas is better off in the second year than in the first. The CPI adjustment *overcompensates* for the change in inflation in the sense that his utility increases.

Klaas is better off because the prices of clothing and food did not increase by the same amount. Suppose that the price of clothing and food had both increased by *exactly* the same amount. After a CPI adjustment, Klaas' budget constraint in the second year, L^2, would be exactly the same as in the first year, L^1, so he would choose exactly the same bundle, e_1, in the second year as in the first year.

Because the price of food rose by less than the price of clothing, L^2 is not the same as L^1. Food became cheaper relative to clothing, so by consuming more food and less clothing Klaas has higher utility in the second year.

Had clothing become relatively less expensive, Klaas would have raised his utility in the second year by consuming relatively more clothing. Thus, it doesn't matter which good becomes relatively less expensive over time—it's only necessary for one of them to become a relative bargain for Klaas to benefit from the CPI compensation.

See Questions 9–11.

Figure 5.7 The Consumer Price Index.

In the first year, when Klaas has an income of Y_1, his optimal bundle is e_1, where indifference curve I^1 is tangent to his budget constraint, L^1. In the second year, the price of clothing rises more than the price of food. Because his salary increases in proportion to the CPI, his second-year budget constraint, L^2, goes through e_1, so he can buy the same bundle as in the first year. His new optimal bundle, however, is e_2, where I^2 is tangent to L^2. The CPI adjustment overcompensates him for the increase in prices: Klaas is better off in the second year because his utility is greater on I^2 than on I^1. With a smaller true cost-of-living adjustment, Klaas' budget constraint, L^*, is tangent to I^1 at e^*.

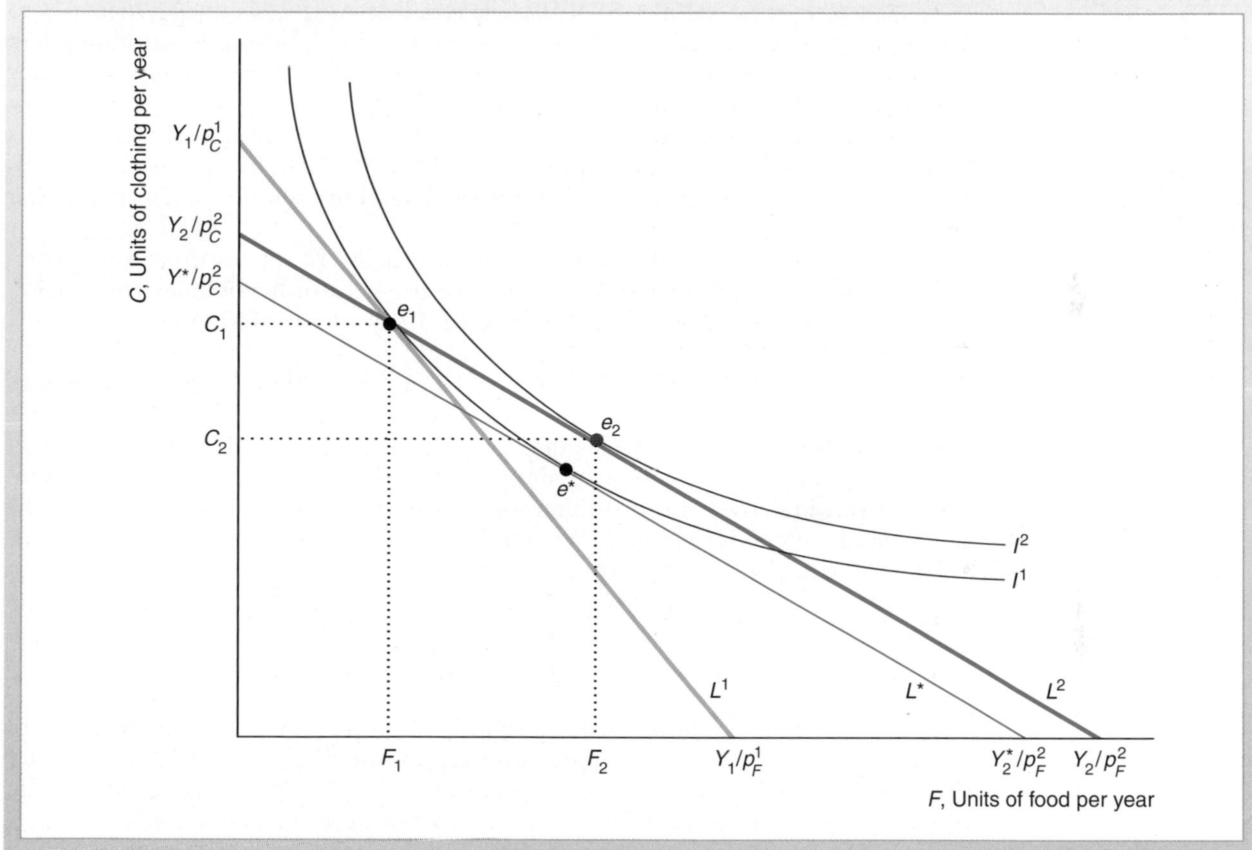

True Cost-of-Living Adjustment. We now know that a CPI adjustment overcompensates for inflation. What we want is a *true cost-of-living index*: an inflation index that holds utility constant over time.

How big an increase in Klaas' salary would leave him exactly as well off in the second year as in the first? We can answer this question by applying the same technique we use to identify the substitution and income effects. We draw an imaginary budget line, L^* in Figure 5.7, that is tangent to I^1, so that Klaas' utility remains constant but has the same slope as L^2. The income, Y^*, corresponding to that imaginary budget constraint, is the amount that leaves Klaas' utility constant. Had Klaas received Y^* in the second year instead of Y_2, he would have chosen Bundle e^* instead of e_2. Because e^* is on the same indifference curve, I^1, as e_1, Klaas' utility would be the same in both years.

The numerical example in Table 5.1 illustrates how the CPI overcompensates Klaas.[14] Suppose that p_C^1 is \$1, p_C^2 is \$2, p_F^1 is \$4, and p_F^2 is \$5. In the first year, Klaas spends his income, Y_1, of \$400 on $C_1 = 200$ units of clothing and $F_1 = 50$ units of food and has a utility of 2,000, which is the level of utility on I^1. If his income did not increase in the second year, he would substitute toward the relatively inexpensive food, cutting his consumption of clothing in half but reducing his consumption of food by only a fifth. His utility would fall to 1,265.

If his second-year income increases in proportion to the CPI, he can buy the same bundle, e_1, in the second year as in the first. His second-year income is $Y_2 = \$650$ $(= p_C^2 C_1 + p_F^2 F_1 = \$2 \times 200 + \$5 \times 50)$. Klaas is better off if his budget increases to Y_2. He substitutes toward the relatively inexpensive food, buying less clothing than in the first year but more food, e_2. His utility rises from 2,000 to approximately 2,055 (the level of utility on I^2).

How much would his income have to rise to leave him only as well off as he was in the first year? If his second-year income is $Y^* \approx \$632.50$, by appropriate substitution toward food, e^*, he can achieve the same level of utility, 2,000, as in the first year.

We can use the income that just compensates Klaas, Y^*, to construct a true cost-of-living index. In our numerical example, the true cost-of-living index rose 58.1% $(\approx [632.50 - 400]/400)$, while the CPI rose 62.5% $(= [650 - 400]/400)$.

See Question 6.

Size of the CPI Substitution Bias. We have just demonstrated that the CPI has an *upward bias* in the sense that an individual's utility rises if we increase that person's income by the same percentage as that by which the CPI rises. If we make the CPI adjustment, we are implicitly assuming—incorrectly—that consumers do not substitute toward relatively inexpensive goods when prices change but keep buying the same bundle of goods over time. We call this overcompensation a *substitution bias*.

The CPI calculates the increase in prices as Y_2/Y_1. We can rewrite this expression as

$$\frac{Y_2}{Y_1} = \frac{Y^*}{Y_1}\frac{Y_2}{Y^*}.$$

The first term to the right of the equal sign, Y^*/Y_1, is the increase in the true cost of living. The second term, Y_2/Y^*, reflects the substitution bias in the CPI. It is greater than one because $Y_2 > Y^*$. In the example in Table 5.1, $Y_2/Y^* = 650/632.50 \approx 1.028$, so the CPI overestimates the increase in the cost of living by about 2.8%.

There is no substitution bias if all prices increase at the same rate so that relative prices remain constant. The faster some prices rise relative to others, the more pronounced is the upward bias caused by substitution to now less expensive goods.

Table 5.1 Cost-of-Living Adjustments.

	p_C	p_F	Income, Y	Clothing	Food	Utility, U
First year	\$1	\$4	$Y_1 = \$400$	200	50	2,000
Second year	\$2	\$5				
No adjustment			$Y_1 = \$400$	100	40	≈1,265
CPI adjustment			$Y_2 = \$650$	162.5	65	≈2,055
True COLA			$Y^* \approx \$632.50$	≈158.1	≈63.2	2,000

[14]We assume that Klaas has a utility function $U = 20\sqrt{CF}$, which we used to draw Figure 5.7.

APPLICATION

Fixing the CPI Substitution Bias

Several studies estimate that, due to the substitution bias, the CPI inflation rate is about half a percentage point too high per year. What can be done to correct this bias? One approach is to estimate utility functions for individuals and to use that data to calculate a true cost-of-living index. However, given the wide variety of tastes across individuals, as well as various technical estimation problems, this approach is not practical.

A second method is to use a *Paasche* index, which weights prices using the current quantities of goods purchased. In contrast, the CPI (which is also called a *Laspeyres* index) uses quantities from the earlier, base period. A Paasche index is likely to overstate the degree of substitution and thus to understate the change in the cost-of-living index. Hence, replacing the traditional Laspeyres index with the Paasche would merely replace an overestimate with an underestimate of the rate of inflation.

See Question 13.

A third compromise approach is to take an average of the Laspeyres and Paasche indexes, because the true cost-of-living index lies between the two indexes. The most widely touted average is the *Fisher* index, which is the geometric mean of the Laspeyres and Paasche indexes (the square root of their product). If we use the Fisher index, we are implicitly assuming that there is a unitary elasticity of substitution among goods, so that the share of consumer expenditures on each item remains constant as relative prices change (in contrast to the Laspeyres approach, where we assume that the quantities remain fixed).

Not everyone agrees that averaging the Laspeyres and Paasche indexes would be an improvement. For example, if people do not substitute, the CPI (Laspeyres) index is correct and the Fisher index, based on the geometric average, would underestimate the rate of inflation.

Nonetheless, in recent years, the Bureau of Labor Statistics (BLS), which calculates the CPI, has made several adjustments to its CPI methodology, including using this averaging approach. Starting in 1999, the BLS replaced the Laspeyres index with a Fisher approach to calculate almost all of its 200 basic indexes (such as "ice cream and related products") within the CPI. It still uses the Laspeyres approach for a few of the categories where it does not expect much substitution, such as utilities (electricity, gas, cable television, and telephones), medical care, and housing, and it uses the Laspeyres method to combine the basic indexes to obtain the final CPI.

Now the BLS updates the CPI weights (the market basket shares of consumption) every two years instead of only every decade or so as the bureau had done before 2002. More frequent updating reduces the substitution bias in a Laspeyres index because market basket shares are frozen for a shorter period of time. According to the BLS, had it used updated weights between 1989 and 1997, the CPI would have increased by only 31.9% rather than the reported 33.9%. Thus, the BLS predicts that this change will reduce the rate of increase in the CPI by approximately 0.2 percentage points per year.

Overestimating the rate of inflation has important implications for U.S. society because Social Security, various retirement plans, welfare, and many other programs include CPI-based cost-of-living adjustments. According to one estimate, the bias in the CPI alone makes it the fourth-largest "federal program" after Social Security, health care, and defense. For example, the U.S. Postal Service (USPS) has a CPI-based COLA in its union contracts. In 2005, a typical employee earned $48,000 a year, including benefits. A substitution bias of half a percent a year costs the USPS nearly $240 per employee. Because the USPS has about 764,000 employees in 2008, the bias costs the USPS over $182 million per year—and benefits its employees by the same amount.

5.5 Deriving Labor Supply Curves

The human race is faced with a cruel choice: work or daytime television.

Throughout this chapter, we've used consumer theory to examine consumers' *demand* behavior. Perhaps surprisingly, we can use the consumer theory model to derive the *supply curve* of labor. We are going to do that by deriving a demand curve for time spent *not* working and then using that demand curve to determine the supply curve of hours spent working.

Labor-Leisure Choice

People choose between working to earn money to buy goods and services and consuming *leisure*: all time spent not working. In addition to sleeping, eating, and playing, leisure includes time spent cooking meals and fixing things around the house. The number of hours worked per day, H, equals 24 minus the hours of leisure or nonwork, N, in a day:

$$H = 24 - N.$$

Using consumer theory, we can determine the demand curve for leisure once we know the price of leisure. What does it cost you to watch TV or go to school or do anything for an hour other than work? It costs you the wage, w, you could have earned from an hour's work: The price of leisure is forgone earnings. The higher your wage, the more an hour of leisure costs you. For this reason, taking an afternoon off costs a lawyer who earns \$250 an hour much more than it costs someone who earns the minimum wage.

We use an example to show how the number of hours of leisure and work depends on the wage, unearned income (such as inheritances and gifts from parents), and tastes. Jackie spends her total income, Y, on various goods. For simplicity, we assume that the price of these goods is \$1 per unit, so she buys Y goods. Her utility, U, depends on how many goods and how much leisure she consumes:

$$U = U(Y, N).$$

Initially, we assume that Jackie can choose to work as many or as few hours as she wants for an hourly wage of w. Jackie's earned income equals her wage times the number of hours she works, wH. Her total income, Y, is her earned income plus her unearned income, Y^*:

$$Y = wH + Y^*.$$

Panel a of Figure 5.8 shows Jackie's choice between leisure and goods. The vertical axis shows how many goods, Y, Jackie buys. The horizontal axis shows both hours of leisure, N, which are measured from left to right, and hours of work, H, which are measured from right to left. Jackie maximizes her utility given the *two* constraints she faces. First, she faces a time constraint, which is a vertical line at 24 hours of leisure. There are only 24 hours in a day; all the money in the world won't buy her more hours in a day. Second, Jackie faces a budget constraint. Because Jackie has no unearned income, her initial budget constraint, L^1, is $Y = w_1H = w_1(24 - N)$. The slope of her budget constraint is $-w_1$, because each extra hour of leisure she consumes costs her w_1 goods.

Jackie picks her optimal hours of leisure, $N_1 = 16$, so that she is on the highest indifference curve, I^1, that touches her budget constraint. She works $H_1 = 24 - N_1 = 8$ hours per day and earns an income of $Y_1 = w_1H_1 = 8w_1$.

Figure 5.8 Demand for Leisure.

(a) Jackie chooses between leisure, N, and other goods, Y, subject to a time constraint (vertical line at 24 hours) and a budget constraint, L^1, which is $Y = w_1H = w_1(24 - N)$, with a slope of $-w_1$. The tangency of her indifference curve, I^1, with her budget constraint, L^1, determines her optimal bundle, e_1, where she has $N_1 = 16$ hours of leisure and works $H_1 = 24 - N_1 = 8$ hours. If her wage rises from w_1 to w_2, Jackie shifts from optimal bundle e_1 to e_2. (b) Bundles e_1 and e_2 correspond to E_1 and E_2 on her leisure demand curve.

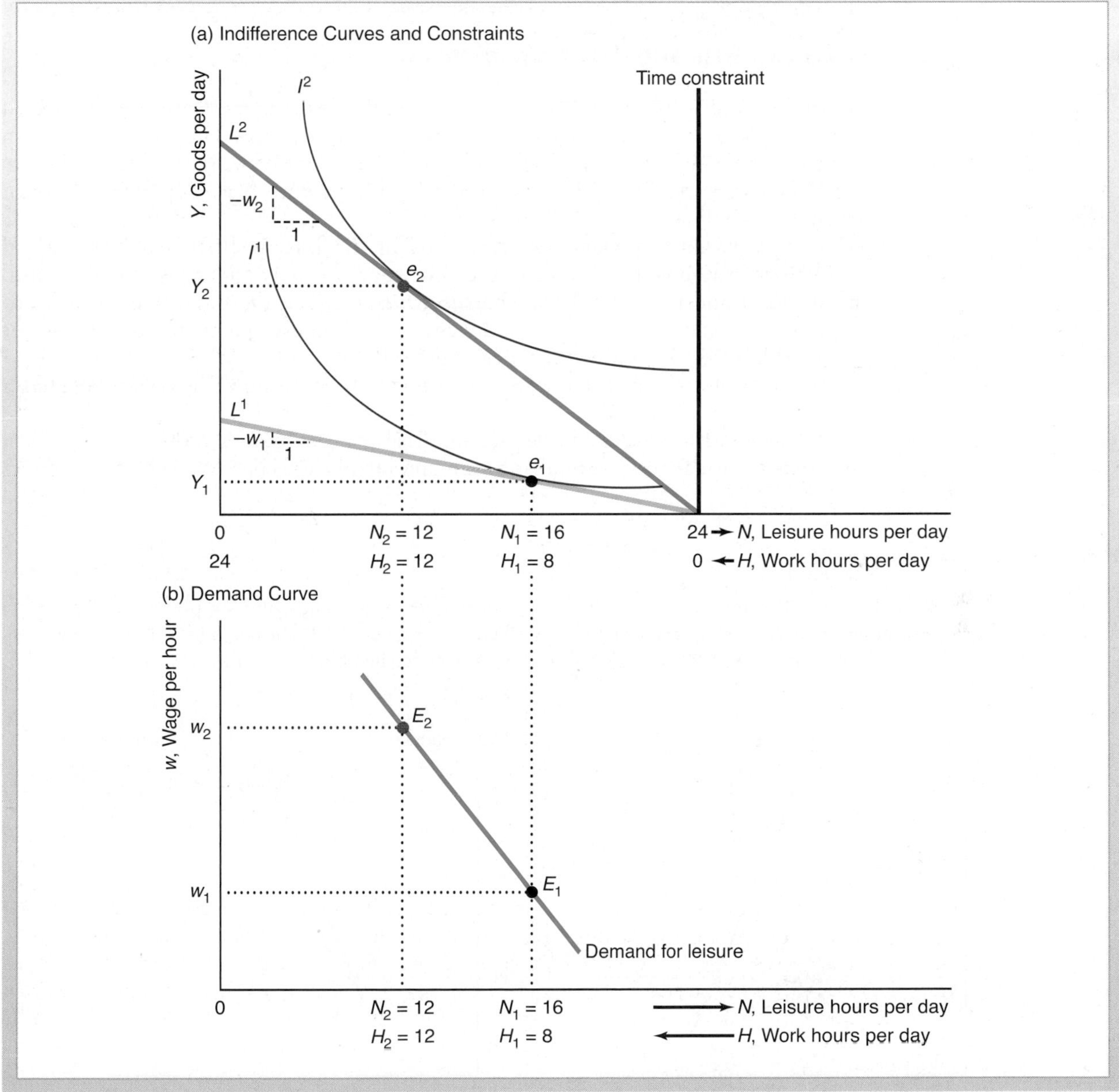

We derive Jackie's demand curve for leisure using the same method that we used to derive Mimi's demand curve for beer. We raise the price of leisure—the wage—in panel a of Figure 5.8 to trace out Jackie's demand curve for leisure in panel b. As the wage increases from w_1 to w_2, leisure becomes more expensive, and Jackie demands less of it.

By subtracting her demand for leisure at each wage—her demand curve for leisure in panel a of Figure 5.9—from the 24, we construct her labor supply curve—the hours she is willing to work as a function of the wage—in panel b.[15] Her supply curve for hours worked is the mirror image of the demand curve for leisure: For every extra hour of leisure that Jackie consumes, she works one hour less.

Income and Substitution Effects

An increase in the wage causes both income and substitution effects, which alter an individual's demand for leisure and supply of hours worked. The *total effect* of an increase in Jackie's wage from w_1 to w_2 is the movement from e_1 to e_2 in Figure 5.10. Jackie works $H_2 - H_1$ fewer hours and consumes $N_2 - N_1$ more hours of leisure.

By drawing an imaginary budget constraint, L^*, that is tangent to her original indifference curve with the slope of the new wage, we can divide the total effect into substitution and income effects. The *substitution effect*, the movement from e_1 to e^*, must be negative: A compensated wage increase causes Jackie to consume fewer hours of leisure, N^*, and work more hours, H^*.

As the wage rises, if Jackie works the same number of hours as before, she has a higher income. The *income effect* is the movement from e^* to e_2. Because leisure is a normal good for Jackie, as her income rises, she consumes more leisure. When leisure is a normal good, the substitution and income effects work in opposite direc-

Figure 5.9 Supply Curve of Labor.

(a) Jackie's demand for leisure is downward sloping. (b) At any given wage, the number of hours that Jackie works, H, and the number of hours of leisure, N, that she consumes add to 24. Thus, her supply curve for hours worked, which equals 24 hours minus the number of hours of leisure she demands, is upward sloping.

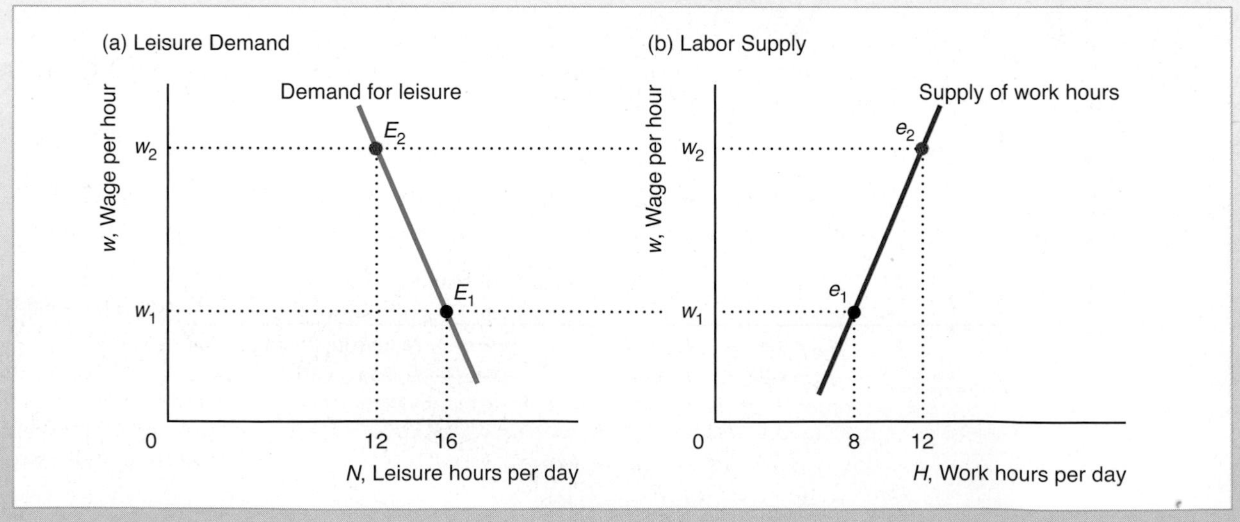

[15]Appendix 5B shows how to derive the labor supply curve using calculus.

Figure 5.10 Income and Substitution Effects of a Wage Change.

A wage change causes both a substitution and an income effect. The movement from e_1 to e^* is the substitution effect, the movement from e^* to e_2 is the income effect, and the movement from e_1 to e_2 is the total effect.

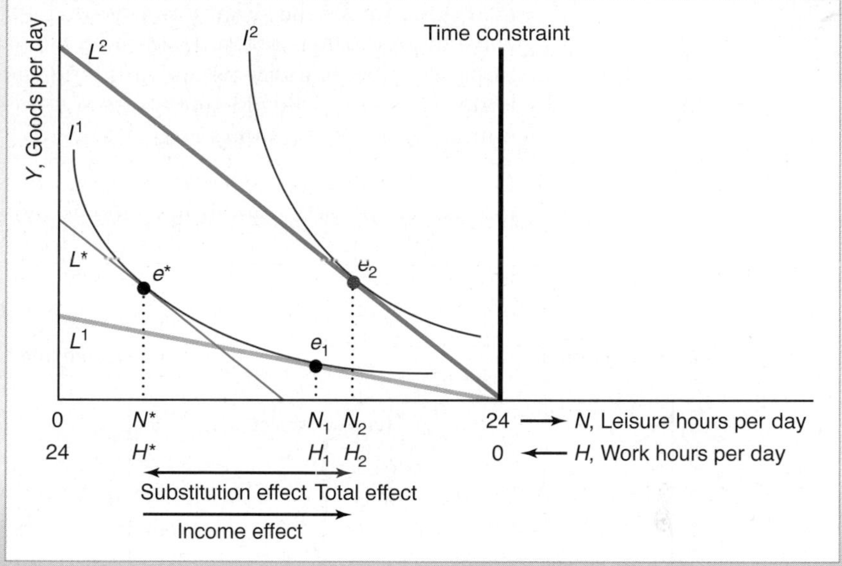

tions, so whether leisure demand increases or not depends on which effect is larger. Jackie's income effect dominates the substitution effect, so the total effect for leisure is positive: $N_2 > N_1$. Jackie works fewer hours as the wage rises, so her labor supply curve is backward bending.

See Problem 38.

If leisure is an inferior good, both the substitution effect and the income effect work in the same direction, and hours of leisure definitely fall. As a result, if leisure is an inferior good, a wage increase unambiguously causes the hours worked to rise.

Solved Problem 5.3

Enrico receives a no-strings-attached scholarship that pays him an extra Y^* per day. How does this scholarship affect the number of hours he wants to work? Does his utility increase?

Answer

1. *Show his consumer equilibrium without unearned income.* When Enrico had no unearned income, his budget constraint, L^1 in the graphs, hit the hours-leisure axis at 0 hours and had a slope of $-w$.

2. *Show how the unearned income affects his budget constraint.* The extra income causes a parallel upward shift of Y^*. His new budget constraint, L^2, has the same slope as before because his wage does not change. The extra income cannot buy Enrico more time, of course, so L^2 cannot extend to the right of the time constraint. As a result, L^2 is vertical at 0 hours up to Y^*: His income is Y^* if he works no hours. Above Y^*, L^2 slants toward the goods axis with a slope of $-w$.

3. *Show that the relative position of the new to the original equilibrium depends on his tastes.* The change in the number of hours he works depends on Enrico's tastes. Panels a and b show two possible sets of indifference curves.

In both diagrams, when facing budget constraint L^1, Enrico chooses to work H_1 hours. In panel a, leisure is a normal good, so as his income rises, Enrico consumes more leisure than originally: He moves from Bundle e_1 to Bundle e_2. In panel b, he views leisure as an inferior good and consumes fewer hours of leisure than originally: He moves from e_1 to e_3. (Another possibility is that the number of hours he works is unaffected by the extra unearned income.)

See Questions 17–28.

4. *Discuss how his utility changes.* Regardless of his tastes, Enrico has more income in the new equilibrium and is on a higher indifference curve after receiving the scholarship. In short, he believes that more money is better than less.

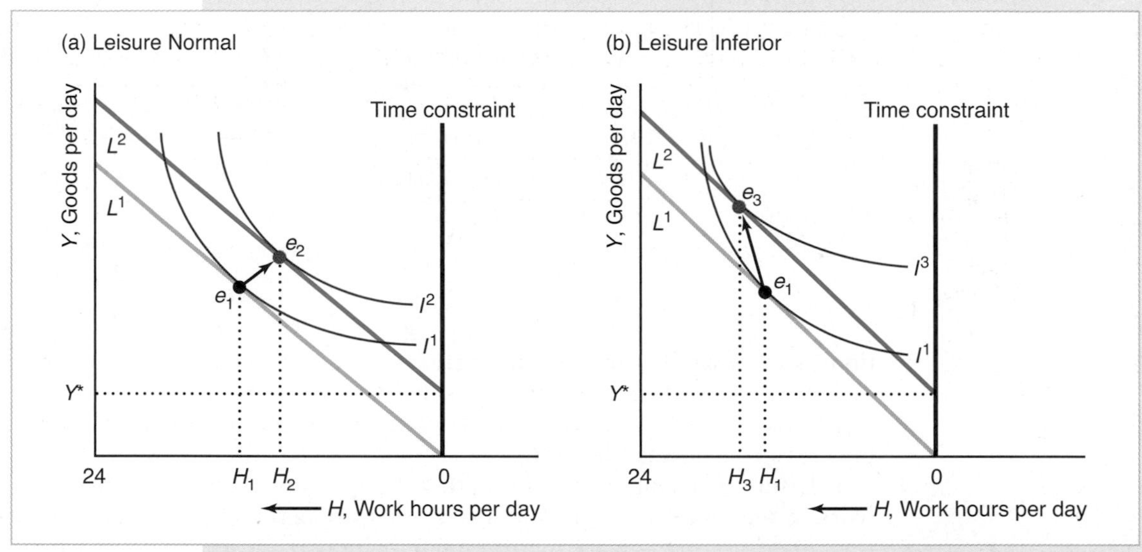

APPLICATION

Leisure-Income Choices of Textile Workers

Dunn (1977, 1978, 1979), using data obtained by questioning Southern cotton mill workers and examining their behavior, determined their indifference curves, which we can use to examine income and substitution effects. A typical worker's indifference curves are close to right angles (see the graph), indicating that leisure and all other goods are nearly perfect complements: The worker is relatively unwilling to substitute goods for leisure.

At the original wage, \$2.09 per hour, the budget constraint is L^1 and a typical worker chooses to work 42.4 hours per week (assuming that there are 100 total hours to be allocated between work and

leisure), Bundle e_1. An increase in the wage of \$1 per hour causes the budget constraint to rotate outward to L^2. An uncompensated increase in the wage increases the demand for leisure and reduces the hours worked to 29.5 per week, Bundle e_2. Thus, workers' labor supply curves are backward bending: Workers decrease their hours as their wage rises. An increase in the wage from \$2.09 to \$3.09 leads to weekly earnings rising only from \$88.69 to \$91.18 because of the offsetting reduction in the hours worked.

What would happen if, when the wage increased, workers' incomes were reduced so that they remained on the original indifference curve, I^1? That is, what is the substitution effect for this \$1 wage increase? The imaginary budget constraint L^* is parallel to L^2 but tangent to indifference curve I^1 at e^*. Therefore, the substitution effect—the movement from e_1 to e^*—due to a compensated wage increase is an increase in weekly hours by half an hour a week to 42.9 hours. The income effect (the movement from e^* to e_2) is to work 13.4 (= 29.5 – 42.9) fewer hours a week.

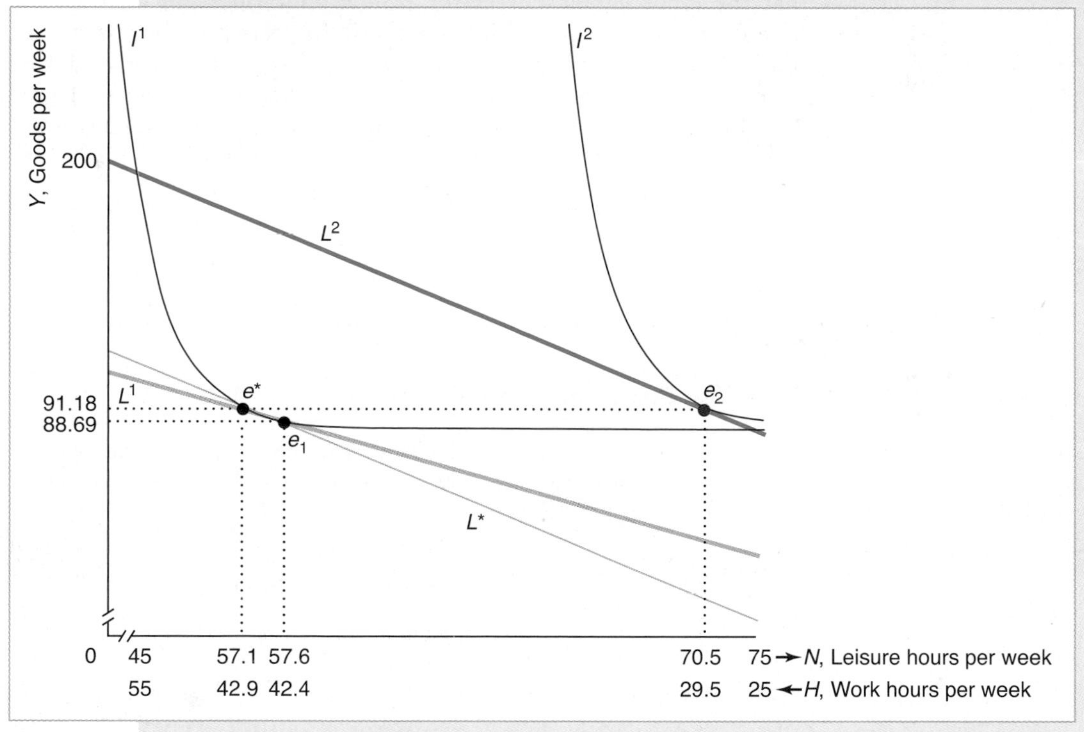

Shape of the Labor Supply Curve

Whether the labor supply curve slopes upward, bends backward, or has sections with both properties depends on the income elasticity of leisure. Suppose that a worker views leisure as an inferior good at low wages and a normal good at high wages. As the wage increases, the demand for leisure first falls and then rises, and the hours supplied to the market first rise and then fall. (Alternatively, the labor supply curve may slope upward and then backward even if leisure is normal at all wages: At low wages, the substitution effect—work more hours—dominates the income effect—work fewer hours—while the opposite occurs at higher wages.)

The budget line rotates upward from L^1 to L^2 as the wage rises in panel a of Figure 5.11. Because leisure is an inferior good at low incomes, in the new optimal bundle, e_2, this worker consumes less leisure and more goods than at the original bundle, e_1.

At higher incomes, however, leisure is a normal good. At an even higher wage, the new equilibrium is e_3, on budget line L^3, where the quantity of leisure demanded is higher and the number of hours worked is lower. Thus, the corresponding supply curve for labor slopes upward at low wages and bends backward at higher wages in panel b.

Do labor supply curves slope upward or backward? Economic theory alone cannot answer this question: Both forward-sloping and backward-bending supply curves are *theoretically* possible. Empirical research is necessary to resolve this question.

Most studies (Killingsworth, 1983; MaCurdy, Green, and Paarsch, 1990) find that the labor supply curves for British and American men are virtually vertical because both the income and substitution effects are about zero. Studies find that wives' labor supply curves are also virtually vertical: slightly backward bending in Canada and the United States and slightly forward sloping in the United Kingdom and Germany. In contrast, studies of the labor supply of single women find relatively large positive supply elasticities of 4.0 and even higher. Thus, only single women tend to work substantially more hours when their wages rise.

Figure 5.11 Labor Supply Curve That Slopes Upward and Then Bends Backward.

At low incomes, an increase in the wage causes the worker to work more: the movement from e_1 to e_2 in panel a or from E_1 to E_2 in panel b. At higher incomes, an increase in the wage causes the worker to work fewer hours: the movement from e_2 to e_3 or from E_2 to E_3.

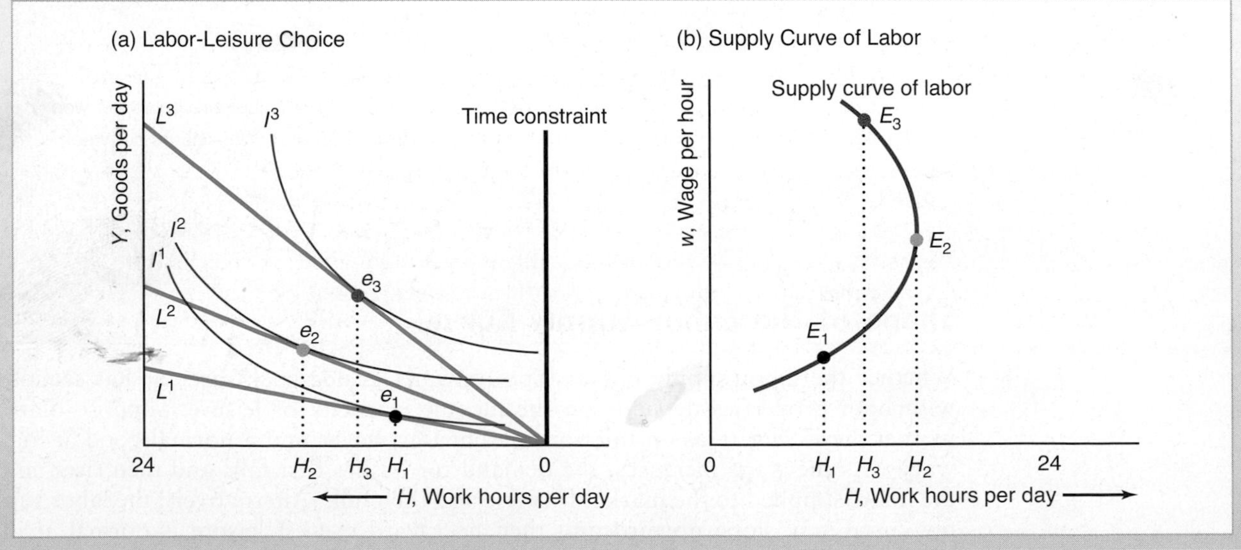

APPLICATION

Winning the Good Life

See Question 16.

Would you stop working if you won a lottery jackpot or inherited a large sum? Economists want to know how unearned income affects labor supply because this question plays a crucial role in many government debates on taxes and welfare. For example, some legislators oppose negative income tax and welfare programs because they claim that giving money to poor people will stop them from working. Is that assertion true?

We could clearly answer this question if we could observe the behavior of a large group of people of whom only some were randomly selected to receive varying large payments of unearned income each year for decades. Luckily for us, governments conduct such experiments by running lotteries.

Imbens, Rubin, and Sacerdote (2001) compared the winners of major prizes and others who played the Massachusetts Megabucks lottery. Major prizes ranged from $22,000 to $9.7 million, with an average of $1.1 million, and were paid in yearly installments over two decades.

A typical player in this lottery earned $16,100. The average winner received $55,200 in prize money per year and chose to work slightly fewer hours so that his or her labor earnings fell by $1,877 per year. That is, winners increased their consumption and savings but did not substantially decrease how much they worked.

For every dollar of unearned income, winners reduced their work effort and hence their labor earnings by 11¢ on average. Men and women, big and very big prize winners, and people of all education levels behaved the same. However, there were differences by age of the winner and by income groups. People 55 to 65 reduced their effort by about a third more than younger people, presumably because they decided to retire early. Most important, people with no earnings in the year before winning the lottery tended to increase their labor earnings after winning.

Income Tax Rates and Labor Supply

The wages of sin are death, but by the time taxes are taken out, it's just sort of a tired feeling. —Paula Poundstone

Why do we care about the shape of labor supply curves? One reason is that we can tell from the shape of the labor supply curve whether an increase in the income tax rate—a percent of earnings—will cause a substantial reduction in the hours of work.[16] Taxes on earnings are an unattractive way of collecting money for the government if supply curves are upward sloping because the taxes cause people to work fewer hours, reducing the amount of goods society produces and raising less tax revenue than if the supply curve were vertical or backward bending. On the other hand, if supply curves are backward bending, a small increase in the tax rate increases tax revenue *and* boosts total production (but reduces leisure).

Although unwilling to emulate Lady Godiva's tax-fighting technique—allegedly, her husband, Leofric, the Earl of Mercia, agreed to eliminate taxes if she rode naked through the Coventry marketplace—various U.S. presidents have advocated tax

[16]Although taxes are ancient, the income tax is a relatively recent invention. William Pitt the Younger introduced the British income tax (10% on annual incomes above £60) in 1798 to finance the war with Napoleon. The U.S. Congress followed suit in 1861, using the income taxes (3% on annual incomes over $800) to pay for the Civil War.

cuts. Presidents John Kennedy, Ronald Reagan, and George W. Bush argued that cutting the marginal tax rate (the percentage of the last dollar earned that the government takes in taxes) would stimulate people to work longer and produce more, both desirable effects. President Reagan claimed that tax receipts would increase due to the additional work.

Because tax rates have changed substantially over time, we have a natural experiment to test this hypothesis. The Kennedy tax cuts lowered the top personal marginal tax rate from 91% to 70%. Due to the Reagan tax cuts, the maximum rate fell to 50% from 1982 to 1986, 38.5% in 1987, and 28% in 1988–1990. The rate rose to 31% in 1991–1992 and 39.6% from 1993 to 2000. The Bush administration's Tax Relief Act of 2001 tax cut reduced this rate to 38.6% for 2001–2003, 37.6% for 2004–2005, and 35% for 2006 and thereafter.

Many other countries' central governments also lowered their top marginal tax rates in recent years. For example, Japan's rate fell from 88% in 1986 to 65% in 1994 and to 50% in 1999.

In 2006, according to the Organization for Economic Co-operation and Development (OECD), the highest marginal tax rate (including central government, local government, and Social Security taxes) in the United States was 43% (though there's substantial variation across states). In other relatively developed OECD countries, this rate ranges from 24% in Mexico to 61% in Belgium (which was 71% in 1988). This rate is 37% in Iceland, 39% in New Zealand, 40% in the United Kingdom, 46% in Canada, 48% in Japan, 49% in Australia, 52% in the Netherlands (72% in 1988), and 57% in Sweden (87% in 1979).

The effect of a tax rate of $\tau = 0.28$ is to reduce the effective wage from w to $(1 - \tau)w = 0.72w$.[17] The tax reduces the after-tax wage by 28%, so a worker's budget constraint rotates downward, similar to rotating the budget constraint downward from L^2 to L^1, in Figure 5.11.

As we discussed, if the budget constraint rotates downward, the hours of work may increase or decrease, depending on whether leisure is a normal or an inferior good. The worker in panel b has a labor supply curve that at first slopes upward and then bends backward, as in panel b. If the worker's wage is very high, the worker is in the backward-bending section of the labor supply curve.

If so, the relationship between the marginal tax rate, τ, and tax revenue, τwH, is bell-shaped, as in Figure 5.12. At a zero tax rate, a small increase in the tax rate *must* increase the tax revenue, because no revenue was collected when the tax rate was zero. However, if the tax rate rises a little more, tax revenue must rise even higher, for two reasons. First, the government collects a larger percentage of every dollar earned because the tax rate is higher. Second, employees work more hours as the tax rate rises because workers are in the backward-bending section of their labor supply curves.

As the tax rate rises far enough, however, the workers are in the upward-sloping section of their labor supply curves. In this section, an increase in the tax rate reduces the number of hours worked. When the tax rate rises high enough, the

[17]Under a progressive income tax system, the marginal tax rate increases with income. The average tax rate differs from the marginal tax rate. People in the top 1% of income have a marginal rate of 35% but an average rate of 26%. Suppose that the marginal tax rate is 20% on the first \$10,000 earned and 30% on the second \$10,000. Someone who earned \$20,000 would pay \$2,000 (= 0.2 × \$10,000) on the first \$10,000 of earnings and \$3,000 on the next \$10,000. That taxpayer's average tax rate is 25% (= [\$2,000 + \$3,000]/\$20,000). For simplicity in the following analysis, we assume that the marginal tax rate is a constant, τ, so that the average tax rate is also τ. To see your marginal and average tax rates, use the calculator at **www.smartmoney.com/tax/filing/index.cfm?story=taxbracket.**

Figure 5.12 Relationship of Tax Revenue to Tax Rates.

At marginal tax rates below τ^*, an increase in the rate leads to larger tax collections. At rates above τ^*, however, an increase in the marginal rate decreases tax revenue. These calculations (Fullerton, 1982, Table 1, p. 15) are based on the assumption that the labor supply elasticity with respect to the after-tax wage is 0.15 and that the labor demand curve is horizontal.

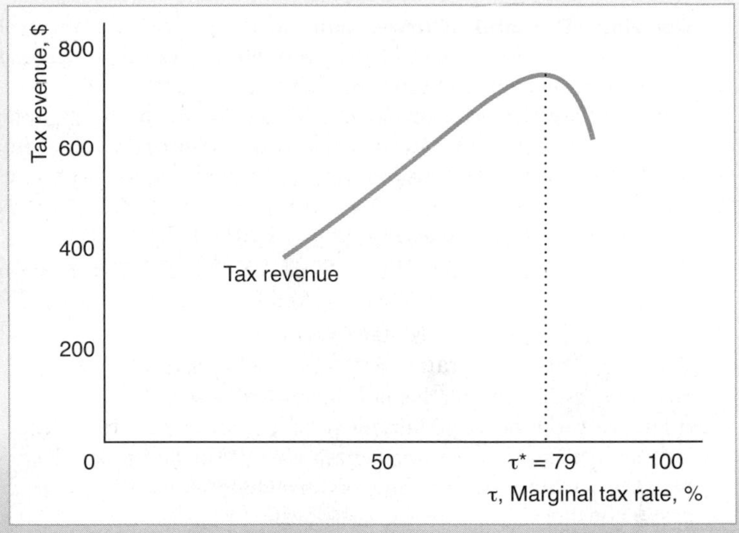

reduction in hours worked more than offsets the gain from the higher rate, so tax revenue falls.

It makes little sense for a government to operate at very high marginal tax rates in the downward-sloping portion of this bell-shaped curve. The government could get more output *and* more tax revenue by cutting the marginal tax rate.

APPLICATION

Effect of a Tax Cut on Tax Revenue

The marginal tax rate τ^*, that maximizes tax revenue is estimated to be very high for the United States: Estimates range from 79% (Fullerton, 1982) to 85% (Stuart, 1984). Thus, the Kennedy era tax cuts from 91% to 70% raised tax revenue and increased the work effort of top-income-bracket workers, but the Reagan tax cut (in which the actual rate was only about half that of τ^*) and the Bush tax cut had the opposite effect. Goolsbee (2000) examined the effect of higher taxes on corporate executives and found that even this extremely high-income group has little long-run response to tax changes. Fullerton and Gan (2004) estimated that the 2001 Bush tax cut caused almost no change in expected working hours of married women between the ages of 25 and 55 and lowered their tax revenue by an average of $843 per person.

Heijman and van Ophem (2005) reported the following typical marginal tax rate (including all taxes, not just income taxes) and their simulations of τ^* for various countries:

	Sweden	France	Ireland	Spain	Switzerland	U.K.	Japan
Marginal tax rate, τ	65	47	41	37	35	26	24
Optimal tax rate, τ^*	58	59	57	59	58	54	54

According to their calculations, τ^* is well above the actual marginal tax rate, τ, in all countries except Sweden. Thus, in these countries, tax rate increases would raise total tax revenue.

SUMMARY

1. **Deriving Demand Curves.** Individual demand curves can be derived by using the information about tastes contained in a consumer's indifference curve map. Varying the price of one good, holding other prices and income constant, we find how the quantity demanded varies with that price, which is the information we need to draw the demand curve. Consumers' tastes, which are captured by the indifference curves, determine the shape of the demand curve.
2. **How Changes in Income Shift Demand Curves.** The entire demand curve shifts as a consumer's income rises. By varying income, holding prices constant, we show how quantity demanded shifts with income. An Engel curve summarizes the relationship between income and quantity demanded, holding prices constant.
3. **Effects of a Price Change.** An increase in the price of a good causes both a substitution effect and an income effect. The *substitution effect* is the amount by which a consumer's demand for the good changes as a result of a price increase when we compensate the consumer for the price increase by raising the individual's income by enough that his or her utility does not change. The substitution effect is unambiguous: A compensated rise in a good's price *always* causes consumers to buy less of that good. The *income effect* shows how a consumer's demand for a good changes as the consumer's income falls. The price rise lowers the consumer's opportunities, because the consumer can now buy less than before with the same income. The income effect can be positive or negative. If a good is normal (income elasticity is positive), the income effect is negative.
4. **Cost-of-Living Adjustments.** The government's major index of inflation, the Consumer Price Index, overestimates inflation by ignoring the substitution effect. Though on average small, the substitution bias may be substantial for particular individuals or firms.
5. **Deriving Labor Supply Curves.** Using consumer theory, we can derive the daily demand curve for leisure, which is time spent on activities other than work. By subtracting the demand curve for leisure from 24 hours, we obtain the labor supply curve, which shows how the number of hours worked varies with the wage. Depending on whether leisure is an inferior good or a normal good, the supply curve of labor may be upward sloping or backward bending. The shape of the supply curve for labor determines the effect of a tax cut. Empirical evidence based on this theory shows why tax cuts in the 1980s did not increase the tax revenue of individuals as predicted by the Reagan administration.

QUESTIONS

■ = *exercise is available on MyEconLab;* * = *answer appears at the back of this book;* C = *use of calculus may be necessary;* W = *audio-slideshow answer by James Dearden is available in Textbook Resources on MyEconLab.*

1. Draw diagrams similar to Figure 5.1 showing that the price-consumption curve can be horizontal or downward sloping.
2. ■ *2. Don spends his money on food and on operas. Food is an inferior good for Don. Does he view an opera performance as an inferior or a normal good? Why? In a diagram, show a possible income-consumption curve for Don.
3. Have your folks given you cash or promised to leave you money after they're gone? If so, your parents may think of such gifts as a good. They must decide whether to spend their money on fun, food, drink, cars, or on transfers to you. Hmmm. Altonji and Villanueva (2007) estimate that, for every extra dollar of expected lifetime resources, parents give their adult offspring between 2¢ and 3¢ in bequests and about 3¢ in transfers. Those gifts are about one-fifth of what they give their children under 18 and spend on college. Illustrate how an increase in your parents' income affects their allocations between bequests to you and all other goods ("fun") in two related graphs, where you show an income-consumption curve in one and an Engel curve for bequests in the other.
4. ■ Under what conditions does the income effect reinforce the substitution effect? Under what conditions does it have an offsetting effect? If the income effect more than offsets the substitution effect for a good, what do we call that good?
5. ■ Michelle spends all her money on food and clothing. When the price of clothing decreases, she buys more clothing.

a. Does the substitution effect cause her to buy more or less clothing? Explain. (If the direction of the effect is ambiguous, say so.)

b. Does the income effect cause her to buy more or less clothing? Explain. (If the direction of the effect is ambiguous, say so.)

*6. Alix consumes only coffee and coffee cake and consumes them only together (they are complements). By how much will a CPI over these two goods differ from the true cost-of-living index?

7. Relatively more high-quality navel oranges are sold in California than in New York. Why?

*8. Draw a figure to illustrate the verbal answer given in Solved Problem 5.2. Use math and a figure to show how adding an *ad valorem* tax changes the analysis. (See the application "Shipping the Good Stuff Away.")

9. During his first year at school, Ximing buys eight new college textbooks at a cost of $50 each. Used books cost $30 each. When the bookstore announces a 20% price increase in new texts and a 10% increase in used texts for the next year, Ximing's father offers him $80 extra. Is Ximing better off, the same, or worse off after the price change? Why?

10. Jean views coffee and cream as perfect complements. In the first period, Jean picks an optimal bundle of coffee and cream, e_1. In the second period, inflation occurs, the prices of coffee and cream change by different amounts, and Jean receives a cost-of-living adjustment (COLA) based on the Consumer Price Index (CPI) for these two goods. After the price changes and she receives the COLA, her new optimal bundle is e_2. Show the two equilibria in a figure. Is she better off, worse off, or equally well off at e_2 compared to e_1? Explain why.

11. Ann's only income is her annual college scholarship, which she spends exclusively on gallons of ice cream and books. Last year when ice cream cost $10 and used books cost $20, Ann spent her $250 scholarship on five gallons of ice cream and ten books. This year, the price of ice cream rose to $15 and the price of books increased to $25. So that Ann can afford the same bundle of ice cream and books that she bought last year, her college raised her scholarship to $325. Ann has the usual-shaped indifference curves. Will Ann change the amount of ice cream and books that she buys this year? If so, explain how and why. Will Ann be better off, as well off, or worse off this year than last year? Why?

12. The *Economist* magazine publishes the Big Mac Index for various countries, based on the price of a Big Mac hamburger at McDonald's over time. Under what circumstances would people find this index to be as useful as or more useful than the Consumer Price Index in measuring how their true cost of living changes over time?

13. Illustrate that the Paasche cost-of-living index (see the application "Fixing the CPI Substitution Bias") underestimates the rate of inflation when compared to the true cost-of-living index.

14. Because people dislike commuting to work, homes closer to employment centers tend to be more expensive. The price of a home in a given employment center is $60 per day. The housing price drops by $2.50 per mile for each mile farther from the employment center. The price of gasoline per mile of the commute is p_g (which is less than $2.50). Thus, the net cost of traveling an extra mile to work is $p_g - 2.5$. Lan chooses the distance she lives from the job center, D (where D is at most 50 miles), and all other goods, A. The price of A is $1 per unit. Lan's utility function is $U = D^{-0.5}A^{0.5}$, and her income is Y, which for technical reasons is between $60 and $110.

a. Is D an economic bad (the opposite of a good)?

b. Draw Lan's budget constraint.

c. Derive Lan's demand functions for A and D.

d. Show that as the price of gasoline increases, Lan chooses to live closer to the employment center.

e. Show that as Lan's income increases, she chooses to live closer to the employment center. Reportedly, increases in gasoline prices hit the poor especially hard because they live farther from their jobs, consume more gasoline in commuting, and spend a greater fraction of their income on gasoline ("For Many Low-Income Workers, High Gasoline Prices Take a Toll," *Wall Street Journal*, July 12, 2004, A1). Demonstrate that as Lan's income decreases, she spends more per day on gasoline. W

15. Recent research by economists David Cutler, Edward Glaeser, and Jesse Shapiro on Americans' increasing obesity points to improved technology in the preparation of tasty and more caloric foods as a possible explanation of weight gain. Before World War II, people rarely prepared French fries at home because of the significant amount of peeling, cutting, and cooking required. Today, French fries are prepared in factories using low-cost labor, shipped frozen, and then simply reheated in homes. Paul consumes two goods: potatoes and leisure, N. The number of potatoes Paul consumes does not vary, but their tastiness, T, does. For each extra unit of tastiness, he must spend p_t hours in the kitchen. Thus, Paul's time constraint is $N + p_t T = 24$. Paul's utility function is $U = TN^{1/2}$.

a. What is Paul's marginal rate of substitution, MU_T/MU_N?

b. What is the marginal rate of transformation, p_T/p_N?

c. What is Paul's optimal choice, (T^*, N^*)?

d. With a decrease in the price of taste (the ability to produce a given level of tastiness faster), does Paul consume more taste (and hence gain weight) or spend more of his time in leisure? Does a decrease in the price of taste contribute to weight gain? W

16. Joe won \$365,000 a year for life in the state lottery. Use a labor-leisure choice analysis to answer the following questions:

a. Show how Joe's lottery winnings affect the position of his budget line.

b. After winning the lottery, Joe continues to work the same number of hours each day. What is the income effect of Joe's lottery gains?

c. Suppose Joe's employer the same week increases Joe's hourly wage rate. Use the income effect you derived in part b as well as the substitution effect to analyze whether Joe chooses to work more hours per week. W

17. Under a welfare plan, poor people are given a lump-sum payment of \$$L$. If they accept this welfare payment, they must pay a high tax, $\tau = \frac{1}{2}$, on anything they earn. If they do not accept the welfare payment, they do not have to pay a tax on their earnings. Show that whether an individual accepts welfare depends on the individual's tastes.

18. If an individual's labor supply curve slopes forward at low wages and bends backward at high wages, is leisure a Giffen good? If so, at high or low wage rates?

19. Bessie, who can currently work as many hours as she wants at a wage of w, chooses to work ten hours a day. Her boss decides to limit the number of hours that she can work to eight hours per day. Show how her budget constraint and choice of hours change. Is she unambiguously worse off as a result of this change? Why?

20. Suppose that Roy could choose how many hours to work at a wage of w and chose to work seven hours a day. The employer now offers him time-and-a-half wages ($1.5w$) for every hour he works beyond a minimum of eight hours per day. Show how his budget constraint changes. Will he choose to work more than seven hours a day?

21. Jerome moonlights: He holds down two jobs. The higher-paying job pays w, but he can work at most eight hours. The other job pays w^*, but he can work as many hours as he wants. Show how Jerome determines how many hours to work.

22. Suppose that the job in Question 21 that had no restriction on hours was the higher-paying job. How do Jerome's budget constraint and behavior change?

23. Suppose that Joe's wage varies with the hours he works: $w(H) = \alpha H$, $\alpha > 0$. Show how the number of hours he chooses to work depends on his tastes.

24. Taxes during the fourteenth century were very progressive. The 1377 poll tax on the Duke of Lancaster was 520 times the tax on a peasant. A poll tax is a lump-sum (fixed amount) tax per person, which does not vary with the number of hours a person works or how much that person earns. Use a graph to show the effect of a poll tax on the labor-leisure decision. Does knowing that the tax was progressive tell us whether a nobleman or a peasant—assuming they have identical tastes—worked more hours?

25. Today most developed countries have progressive income taxes. Under such a taxation program, is the marginal tax higher than, equal to, or lower than the average tax?

26. Several political leaders, including some recent candidates for the U.S. presidency, have proposed a flat income tax, where the marginal tax rate is constant.

a. Show that if each person is allowed a "personal deduction" where the first \$10,000 is untaxed, the flat tax can be a progressive tax.

b. Proponents of the flat tax claim that it will stimulate production (relative to the current progressive income tax where marginal rates increase with income). Discuss the merits of their claim.

27. Inheritance taxes are older than income taxes. Caesar Augustus instituted a 5% tax on all inheritances (except gifts to children and spouses) to provide retirement funds for the military. During the Bush administration, congressional Republicans and Democrats have vociferously debated the wisdom of cutting income taxes and inheritance taxes (which the Republicans call the death tax) to stimulate the economy by inducing people to work harder. Presumably the government cares about a tax's effect on work effort and tax revenues.

a. Suppose George views leisure as a normal good. He works at a job that pays w an hour. Use a labor-leisure analysis to compare the effects on the hours he works from a marginal tax rate on his wage, τ, or a lump-sum tax (a tax collected regardless of the number of hours he works), T. If the per-hour tax is used, he works 10 hours and earns $10w(1 - \tau)$. The government sets $T = 10w\tau$, so that it earns the same from either tax.

b. Now suppose that the government wants to raise a given amount of revenue through taxation with either an inheritance tax or an income (wage) tax. Which is likely to reduce George's hours of work more, and why?

*28. Prescott (2004) argues that U.S. employees 50% more than do German, French, and Itali employees because they face lower marginal tax rates. Assuming that workers in all four countries have the same tastes toward leisure and goods, must it necessarily be true that U.S. employees will work longer hours? Use graphs to illustrate your answer, and explain why. Does Prescott's evidence indicate anything about the relative sizes of the substitution and income effects? Why or why not?

PROBLEMS

*29. Derive Madeline's demand curve for Coke if she views Coke and Pepsi as perfect substitutes. (*Hint:* The quantity of Coke consumed where the budget line hits the Coke axis is Y/p_c, where p_c = the price of Coke.)

30. Derive and plot Olivia's demand curve for pie if she eats pie only à la mode and does not eat either pie or ice cream alone (pie and ice cream are complements).

*31. Nadia likes spare ribs, R, and fried chicken, C. Her utility function is

$$U = 10R^2C.$$

Her marginal utilities are $MU_R = 20RC$ and $MU_C = 10R^2$. Her weekly income is \$90, which she spends on only ribs and chicken.

a. If she pays \$10 for a slab of ribs and \$5 for a chicken, what is her optimal consumption bundle? Show her budget line, indifference curve, and optimal bundle, e_1, in a diagram.

b. Suppose the price of chicken doubles to \$10. How does her optimal consumption of chicken and ribs change? Show her new budget line and optimal bundle, e_2, in your diagram.

32. Roger's utility function is Cobb-Douglas,

$$U = B^{0.25}Z^{0.75},$$

his income is Y, the price of B is p_B, and the price of Z is p_Z. Derive his demand curves. (*Hint:* See Appendixes 4A and 4B.)

33. Derive Roger's Engel curve for B for the utility given in Problem 32. C

34. Steve's utility function is $U = BC$, where B = veggie burgers per week and C = packs of cigarettes per week. Here, $MU_B = C$ and $MU_C = B$. What is his marginal rate of substitution if veggie burgers are on the vertical axis and cigarettes are on the horizontal axis? Steve's income is \$120, the price of a veggie burger is \$2, and that of a pack of cigarettes is \$1. How many burgers and how many packs of cigarettes does Steve consume to maximize his utility? When a new tax raises the price of a burger to \$3, what is his new optimal bundle? Illustrate your answers in a graph. In a related graph, show his demand curve for burgers with after-tax price on the vertical axis and show the points on the demand curve corresponding to the before- and after-tax equilibria.

35. Hugo views donuts and coffee as perfect complements: He always eats one donut with a cup of coffee and will not eat a donut without coffee or drink coffee without a donut. Derive and plot Hugo's Engel curve for donuts. How much does his weekly budget have to rise for Hugo to buy one more donut per week?

36. Cori eats eggs and toast for breakfast and insists on having three pieces of toast for every two eggs she eats. Derive her utility function. If the price of eggs increases but we compensate Cori to make her just as "happy" as she was before the price change, what happens to her consumption of eggs? Draw a graph and explain your diagram. Does the change in her consumption reflect a substitution or an income effect?

*37. Using calculus, show that not all goods can be inferior. (*Hint:* Start with the identity that $y = p_1q_1 + p_2q_2 + \ldots + p_nq_n$.) C

38. Using calculus, show the effect of a change in the wage on the amount of leisure an individual wants to consume. (*Hint:* See Appendix 5A.) C

CROSS-CHAPTER ANALYSIS

Child-Care Subsidies

Laws passed during the Clinton administration aimed to double the number of children from poor families receiving federal child care between 1997 and 2003. Under the Bush administration, Congress reauthorized these programs twice. Congress has to decide whether to extend the program again. Suppose that your employer, a member of Congress, asks you to appraise the effect of the program on how much recipients benefit, the cost to taxpayers, and how other consumers of day-care services are affected.

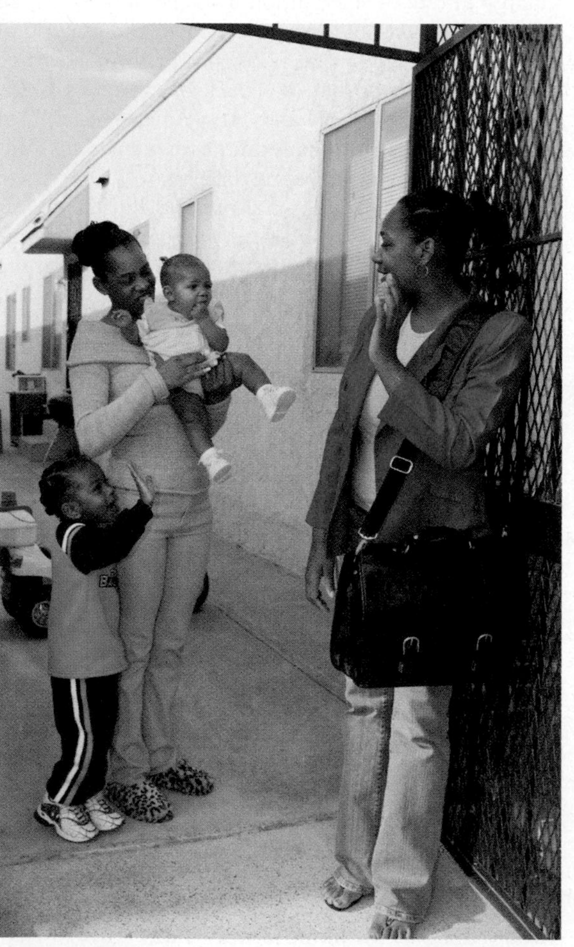

Background

The increased employment of mothers outside the home has led to a steep rise in the use of child care over the past several decades. In the United States, nearly seven out of ten mothers work today—more than twice the rate in 1970. Six out of ten children under the age of six are in child care, as are 45% of children under age one. Eight of ten employed mothers with children under age six are likely to have some form of nonparental child-care arrangement.

Child care is a major burden for the poor and may prevent poor mothers from working. Child-care expenses for children under the age of five absorbed 25% of the earnings for families with annual incomes under $14,400 but only 6% for families with incomes of $54,000 or more.

A 1996 U.S. welfare law, the Personal Responsibility and Work Opportunity Reconciliation Act (PRWORA), sought to facilitate the transition from welfare to work and to help keep low-income parents employed. Up to 30% of the funding came from the major welfare program, Temporary Assistance for Needy Families (TANF), which provided relatively unrestricted lump-sum funds to poor families. Passed during the Clinton administration, PRWORA was intended to double the number of children from poor families receiving federal child care between 1997 and 2003.

The amount spent on child care rose from $10.4 billion in 2001 to $12.3 billion in 2003, but fell to $11.9 billion in 2004 and to $11.7 billion in 2005, while the average number of children served has remained essentially constant over this period. Child-care programs vary substantially across states in their generosity and in the form of the subsidy. A family's maximum child-care fee is currently 85% of the cost of care in Nevada and 70% in Louisiana; \$72.50 per week in Alabama; 10% of gross income in Maine; and \$153 per month plus \$5 per month for each extra child in Mississippi. The reimbursement rate for infants and toddlers is \$2.51 per hour in Kansas, \$16 per day in Kentucky, and \$125 per week in Minnesota. Some states provide an *ad valorem* subsidy, while others use a specific subsidy (see Chapter 3) to lower the hourly rate that a poor family pays for day care.

Rather than subsidizing the price of child care, the government, under the major welfare program, can provide an unrestricted lump-sum payment that could be spent on day care or on all other goods, such as food and housing. Since 2006, Canada has provided such lump-sum payments. The government mails a monthly cash payment of \$100 (Canadian) to parents for every child younger than six years old, whether or not the parents pay for child-care services.

Child care subsidies increase the probability that a single mother will work at a standard job by 7% (Tekin, 2007). As one would expect, the subsidies have larger impacts on welfare recipients than on wealthier mothers.

Task

Congress must decide how to aid poor families. The child-care program could provide an *ad valorem* or a specific subsidy (see Chapter 3), as many states currently do, to lower the hourly rate that a poor family pays for day care. Alternatively, the government could provide an unrestricted lump-sum payment under the major welfare program that could be spent on day care or on all other goods, such as food and housing, as Canada does.

For a given government expenditure, consider the price subsidy and the lump-sum subsidy. Which provides greater benefit to recipients? Which increases the demand for day-care services by more? Which inflicts less cost on other consumers of day care?

Analysis

To determine which program benefits recipients more, we employ a model of consumer choice (Chapters 4 and 5). We use an approach similar to the one with which we analyzed food stamps (in Figure 4.10). As the day-care figure here shows, a poor family chooses between *hours of day care per day* (Q) and *all other goods per day.*

Given that its initial budget constraint is L^o, a poor family chooses Bundle e_1 on indifference curve I^1. The family consumes Q_1 hours of day-care services.

If the government gives a day-care price subsidy, the new budget line L^{PS} rotates out along the day-care axis. Now the family consumes Bundle e_2 on (higher) indifference curve I^2. The family consumes more hours of day care, Q_2, because day care is now less expensive and it is a normal good (Chapter 5).

One way to measure the value of the subsidy the family receives is to calculate how many *other goods* the family could buy before and after the subsidy. (Given that the price of other goods is \$1 per unit, these other goods are essentially income, Y.) If the family consumes Q_2 hours of day care, the family could have consumed Y_o other goods with the original budget constraint and Y_2 with the price-subsidy budget constraint. Given that Y_2 is the family's income after paying for child care, the family buys Y_2 units of all other goods. Thus, the value to the family of the day-care price subsidy is $Y_2 - Y_o$.

If, instead of receiving a day-care price subsidy, the family were to receive a lump-sum payment of $Y_2 - Y_o$, taxpayers' costs for the two programs would be the same.

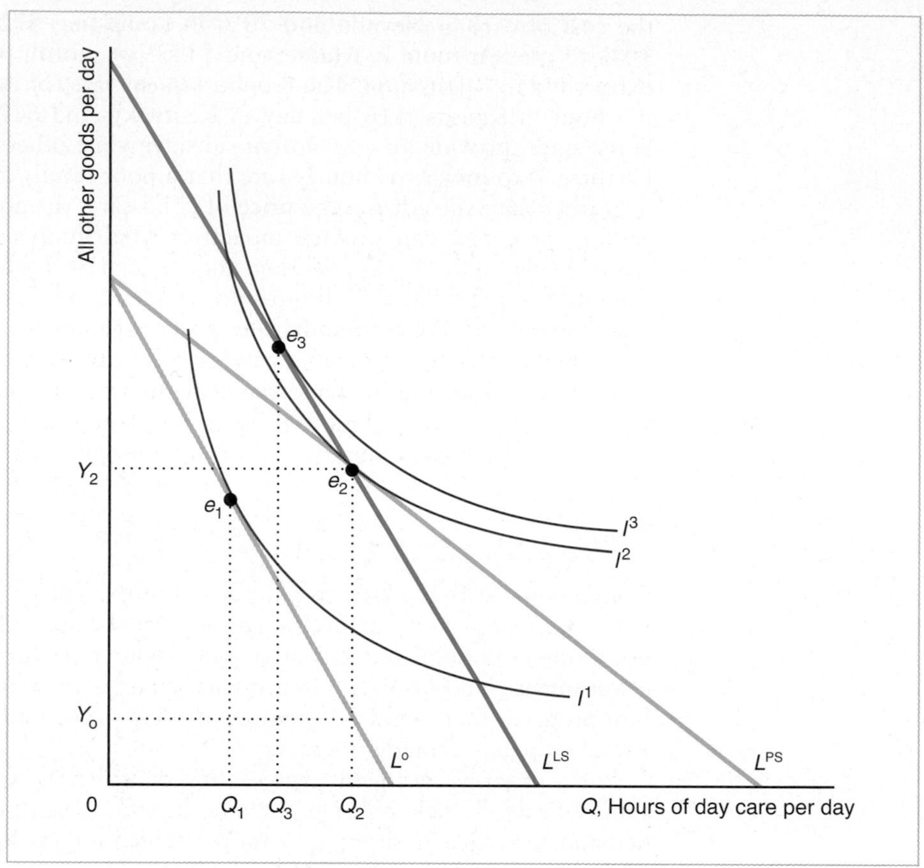

The family's budget constraint after receiving a lump-sum payment, L^{LS}, has the same slope as the original one, L^o, because the relative prices of day care and all other goods are the same as originally (see Section 4.3). This budget constraint must go through e_2 because the family has just enough money to buy that bundle. However, the family will be better off if it buys Bundle e_3 on indifference curve I^3 (the reasoning is the same as that in Solved Problem 4.4 and the Consumer Price Index analysis in Figure 5.7). The family consumes less day care with the lump-sum subsidy: Q_3 rather than Q_2.

Poor families prefer the lump-sum payment to the price subsidy because indifference curve I^3 is above I^2. Taxpayers are indifferent between the two programs because they both cost the same. The day-care industry prefers the price subsidy because the demand curve for its service is farther to the right: At any given price, more is demanded by poor families who receive a price subsidy rather than a lump-sum subsidy. (In the following questions, you are asked to show that parents who do not receive subsidies may prefer the lump-sum approach.)

Given that most of the directly affected groups should prefer lump-sum payments to price subsidies, why are price subsidies so heavily used? One possible explanation is that the day-care industry has very effectively lobbied for price supports, but there is little evidence that occurred. Second, politicians might believe that poor families will not make intelligent choices about day care, and so they might see price subsidies as a way of getting such families to consume relatively more (or better-quality) day care than they would otherwise choose. Third, politicians may prefer that poor people consume more day care so that they can work more hours, thereby increasing society's wealth. Fourth, politicians may not understand this analysis.

Questions

Answers appear at the back of the book.

1. How do parents who do not receive subsidies feel about the two programs? (*Hint*: Use a demand-and-supply analysis from Chapters 2 and 3.)
2. How could the government set a smaller lump-sum subsidy that would make poor parents as well off as the hourly subsidy yet cost less? Given the tastes shown in the figure, what would be the effect on the number of hours of child-care service that these parents buy? (*Hint*: Use a consumer theory analysis from Chapters 4 and 5.)

6 Firms and Production

Hard work never killed anybody, but why take a chance?
—Charlie McCarthy

The Ghirardelli Chocolate Company converts chocolate and other inputs into an output of 144,000 wrapped chocolate bars and 340,000 wrapped chocolate squares a day. The *material inputs* include chocolate, other food products, and various paper goods for wrapping and boxing the candy. The *labor inputs* include chefs, assembly-line workers, and various mechanics and other technicians. The *capital inputs* are the manufacturing plant, the land on which the plant is located, conveyor belts, molds, wrapping machines, and various other types of equipment.

Over time, Ghirardelli has changed how it produces its finished product, increasing the ratio of machines to workers. Several years ago, to minimize employees' risk of repetitive motion injuries, the company spent $300,000 on robots, which pack the wrapped chocolate and put it on pallets. The use of robotic arms resulted in greatly reduced downtime, increased production, and improved working conditions.

This chapter looks at the types of decisions that the owners of firms have to make. First, a decision must be made as to how a firm is owned and managed. Ghirardelli, for example, is a corporation—it is not owned by an individual or partners—and is run by professional managers. Second, the firm must decide how to produce. Ghirardelli now uses relatively more machines and robots and fewer workers than in the past. Third, if a firm wants to expand output, it must decide how to do that in both the short run and the long run. In the short run, Ghirardelli can expand output by extending the workweek to six or seven days and using extra materials. To expand output more, Ghirardelli would have to install more equipment (such as extra robotic arms), hire more workers, and eventually build a new plant, all of which take time. Fourth, given its ability to change its output level, a firm must determine how large to grow. Ghirardelli determines its current investments on the basis of its beliefs about demand and costs in the future.

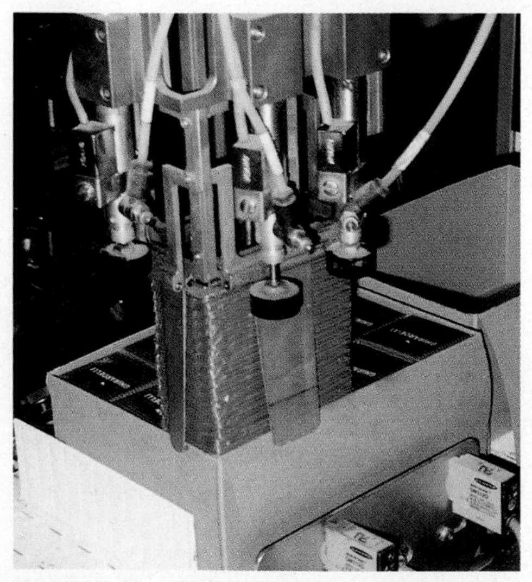

By using robotic equipment to pack finished, wrapped chocolate, the Ghirardelli Chocolate Company benefits from reduced downtime and increased production.

In this chapter, we examine the nature of a firm and how a firm chooses its inputs so as to produce efficiently. In Chapter 7, we examine how the firm chooses the least costly among all possible efficient production processes. In Chapter 8, we combine this information about costs with information about revenues to determine how a firm picks the output level that maximizes profit.

The main lesson of this chapter and the next is that firms are not black boxes that mysteriously transform inputs (such as labor, capital, and material) into outputs. Economic theory explains how firms make decisions about production processes, types of inputs to use, and the volume of output to produce.

In this chapter, we examine six main topics

1. **The Ownership and Management of Firms.** Decisions must be made as to how a firm is owned and run.
2. **Production.** A firm converts inputs into outputs using one of possibly many available technologies.
3. **Short-Run Production: One Variable and One Fixed Input.** In the short run, only some inputs can be varied, so the firm changes its output by adjusting its variable inputs.
4. **Long-Run Production: Two Variable Inputs.** The firm has more flexibility in how it produces and how it changes its output level in the long run when all factors can be varied.
5. **Returns to Scale.** How the ratio of output to input varies with the size of the firm is an important factor in determining the size of a firm.
6. **Productivity and Technical Change.** The amount of output that can be produced with a given amount of inputs varies across firms and over time.

6.1 The Ownership and Management of Firms

firm
an organization that converts inputs such as labor, materials, energy, and capital into outputs, the goods and services that it sells

A **firm** is an organization that converts *inputs* such as labor, materials, and capital into *outputs*, the goods and services that it sells. U.S. Steel combines iron ore, machinery, and labor to create steel. A local restaurant buys raw food, cooks it, and serves it. A landscape designer hires gardeners and machines, buys trees and shrubs, transports them to a customer's home, and supervises the work.

Most goods and services produced in Western countries are produced by firms. In the United States, firms produce 77% of national production (U.S. gross domestic product); the government, 11%; nonprofit institutions (such as some universities and hospitals), 5%; and households, 6% (*Survey of Current Business*, 2007). In developing countries, the government's share of total national production can be much higher, reaching 37% in Ghana, 38% in Zambia, 40% in Sudan, and 90% in Algeria, though it is as low as 3% in Bangladesh, Paraguay, and Nepal (United Nations, *Industry and Development: Global Report 1992/93*). In this book, we focus on production by for-profit firms rather than by nonprofit organizations and governments.

The Ownership of Firms

In most countries, for-profit firms have one of three legal forms: sole proprietorships, partnerships, and corporations.

Sole proprietorships are firms owned and run by a single individual.

Partnerships are businesses jointly owned and controlled by two or more people. The owners operate under a partnership agreement. If any partner leaves, the partnership agreement ends. For the firm to continue to operate, a new partnership agreement must be written.

Corporations are owned by *shareholders* in proportion to the numbers of shares of stock they hold. The shareholders elect a board of directors who run the firm. In turn, the board of directors usually hires managers who make short-term decisions and long-term plans.

Corporations differ from the other two forms of ownership in terms of personal liability for the debts of the firm. Sole proprietors and partners are personally responsible for the debts of their firms. All of an owner's personal wealth—not just that invested in the firm—is at risk if the business becomes bankrupt and is unable to pay its bills. Even the assets of partners who are not responsible for the failure can be taken to cover the firm's debts.

limited liability
condition whereby the personal assets of the owners of the corporation cannot be taken to pay a corporation's debts if it goes into bankruptcy

Corporations have **limited liability**: The personal assets of the corporate owners cannot be taken to pay a corporation's debts if it goes into bankruptcy. Because of the limited liability of corporations, the most that shareholders can lose if the firm goes bankrupt is the amount they paid for their stock, which becomes worthless if the corporation fails. Sole proprietors have unlimited liability—that is, even their personal assets can be taken to pay the firm's debts. Partners share liability: Even the assets of partners who are not responsible for the failure can be taken to cover the firm's debts. General partners can manage the firm but have unlimited liability. Limited partners are prohibited from managing but are liable only to the extent of their investment in the business.[1]

In the United States, 84% of business sales are made by corporations, even though only 20% of all firms are corporations. Nearly 72% of all firms are sole proprietorships. Sole proprietorships tend to be small, however, so they are responsible for only 4% of all sales. Partnerships account for 8% of all firms and make 11% of sales (*Statistical Abstract of the United States*, 2007).

The Management of Firms

In a small firm, the owner usually manages the firm's operations. In larger firms, typically corporations and larger partnerships, a manager or team of managers usually runs the company. In such firms, owners, managers, and lower-level supervisors are all decision makers.

As recent revelations about Enron and WorldCom illustrate, the various decision makers may have conflicting objectives. What is in the best interest of the owners may not be the same as what is in the best interest of managers or other employees. For example, a manager may want a fancy office, a company car, a company jet, and other perks, but the owner would likely oppose these drains on profit.

The owner replaces the manager if the manager pursues personal objectives rather than the firm's objectives. In a corporation, the board of directors is supposed to ensure that managers do not stray. If the manager and the board of directors run the firm badly, the shareholders can fire both or directly change some policies through votes at the corporation's annual meeting for shareholders. Until Chapter 20, we'll ignore the potential conflict between managers and owners and assume that the owner *is* the manager of the firm and makes all the decisions.

What Owners Want

> *Organized crime in America takes in over $40 billion a year and spends very little on office supplies.* —Woody Allen

Economists usually assume that a firm's owners try to maximize profit. Presumably, most people invest in a firm to make money—lots of money, they hope. They want

[1]Due to changes in corporate and tax laws over the last decade, *limited liability companies* (LLCs) have become common in the United States. Owners are liable only to the extent of their investment (as in a corporation) and can play an active role in management (as in a partnership or sole proprietorship). When an owner leaves, the LLC does not have to dissolve as with a partnership.

profit (π)
the difference between revenues, R, and costs, C: $\pi = R - C$

the firm to earn a positive profit rather than make a loss (a negative profit). A firm's **profit**, π, is the difference between its revenue, R, which is what it earns from selling the good, and its cost, C, which is what it pays for labor, materials, and other inputs:

$$\pi = R - C.$$

Typically, revenue is p, the price, times q, the firm's quantity: $R = pq$.

In reality, some owners have other objectives, such as having as big a firm as possible or a fancy office or keeping risks low. In Chapter 8, however, we show that a competitive firm is likely to be driven out of business if it doesn't maximize profits.

efficient production or technological efficiency
situation in which the current level of output cannot be produced with fewer inputs, given existing knowledge about technology and the organization of production

To maximize profits, a firm must produce as efficiently as possible as we will consider in this chapter. A firm engages in **efficient production** (achieves **technological efficiency**) if it cannot produce its current level of output with fewer inputs, given existing knowledge about technology and the organization of production. Equivalently, the firm produces efficiently if, given the quantity of inputs used, no more output could be produced using existing knowledge.

If the firm does not produce efficiently, it cannot be profit maximizing—so efficient production is a *necessary condition* for profit maximization. Even if a firm produces a given level of output efficiently, it is not maximizing profit if that output level is too high or too low or if it is using excessively expensive inputs. Thus, efficient production alone is not a *sufficient condition* to ensure that a firm's profit is maximized.

A firm may use engineers and other experts to determine the most efficient ways to produce with a known method or technology. However, this knowledge does not indicate which of the many technologies, each of which uses different combinations of inputs, allows for production at the lowest cost or with the highest possible profit. How to produce at the lowest cost is an economic decision, typically made by the firm's manager (Chapter 7).

6.2 Production

A firm uses a *technology* or *production process* to transform *inputs* or *factors of production* into *outputs*. Firms use many types of inputs. Most of these inputs can be grouped into three broad categories:

- **Capital (K).** Long-lived inputs such as land, buildings (factories, stores), and equipment (machines, trucks)
- **Labor (L).** Human services such as those provided by managers, skilled workers (architects, economists, engineers, plumbers), and less-skilled workers (custodians, construction laborers, assembly-line workers)
- **Materials (M).** Raw goods (oil, water, wheat) and processed products (aluminum, plastic, paper, steel)

The output can be a *service*, such as an automobile tune-up by a mechanic, or a *physical product*, such as a computer chip or a potato chip.

Production Functions

Firms can transform inputs into outputs in many different ways. Candy-manufacturing companies differ in the skills of their workforce and the amount of equipment they use. While all employ a chef, a manager, and relatively unskilled workers, some candy firms also use skilled technicians and modern equipment. In small candy companies, the relatively unskilled workers shape the candy, decorate it, package it, and box it by hand. In slightly larger firms, the relatively unskilled workers use conveyor belts and other equipment that was invented decades ago. In modern, large-scale plants, the relatively unskilled laborers work with robots and other state-of-the-art machines, which are maintained by skilled technicians. Before deciding which production process to use, a firm needs to consider its various options.

production function
the relationship between the quantities of inputs used and the maximum quantity of output that can be produced, given current knowledge about technology and organization

The various ways inputs can be transformed into output are summarized in the **production function**: the relationship between the quantities of inputs used and the *maximum* quantity of output that can be produced, given current knowledge about technology and organization. The production function for a firm that uses only labor and capital is

$$q = f(L, K), \tag{6.1}$$

where q units of output (wrapped candy bars) are produced using L units of labor services (days of work by relatively unskilled assembly-line workers) and K units of capital (the number of conveyor belts).

The production function shows only the *maximum* amount of output that can be produced from given levels of labor and capital, because the production function includes only efficient production processes. A profit-maximizing firm is not interested in production processes that are inefficient and waste inputs: Firms do not want to use two workers to do a job that can be done as efficiently by one worker.

Time and the Variability of Inputs

A firm can more easily adjust its inputs in the long run than in the short run. Typically, a firm can vary the amount of materials and of relatively unskilled labor it uses comparatively quickly. However, it needs more time to find and hire skilled workers, order new equipment, or build a new manufacturing plant.

short run
a period of time so brief that at least one factor of production cannot be varied practically

fixed input
a factor of production that cannot be varied practically in the short run

variable input
a factor of production whose quantity can be changed readily by the firm during the relevant time period

long run
a lengthy enough period of time that all inputs can be varied

The more time a firm has to adjust its inputs, the more factors of production it can alter. The **short run** is a period of time so brief that at least one factor of production cannot be varied practically. A factor that cannot be varied practically in the short run is called a **fixed input**. In contrast, a **variable input** is a factor of production whose quantity can be changed readily by the firm during the relevant time period. The **long run** is a lengthy enough period of time that all inputs can be varied. There are no fixed inputs in the long run—all factors of production are variable inputs.

Suppose that a painting company gets more work than usual one day. Even if it wanted to do so, the firm does not have time to buy or rent an extra truck and buy another compressor to run a power sprayer; these inputs are fixed in the short run. To get the work done that afternoon, the firm uses the company's one truck to drop off a temporary worker, equipped with only a brush and a can of paint, at the last job. In the long run, however, the firm can adjust all its inputs. If the firm wants to paint more houses every day, it hires more full-time workers, gets a second truck, purchases more compressors to run the power sprayers, and buys a computer to keep track of all its projects.

How long it takes for all inputs to be variable depends on the factors a firm uses. For a janitorial service whose only major input is workers, the long run is a very brief period of time. In contrast, an automobile manufacturer may need many years to build a new manufacturing plant or to design and construct a new type of machine. A pistachio farmer needs the better part of a decade before newly planted trees yield a substantial crop of nuts.

For many firms, materials and often labor are variable inputs over a month. However, labor is not always a variable input. Finding additional highly skilled workers may take substantial time. Similarly, capital may be a variable or fixed input. A firm can rent small capital assets (trucks and personal computers) quickly, but it may take the firm years to obtain larger capital assets (buildings and large, specialized pieces of equipment).

To illustrate the greater flexibility that a firm has in the long run than in the short run, we examine the production function in Equation 6.1, in which output is a function of only labor and capital. We look at first the short-run and then the long-run production process.

6.3 Short-Run Production: One Variable and One Fixed Input

In the short run, we assume that capital is a fixed input and labor is a variable input, so the firm can increase output only by increasing the amount of labor it uses. In the short run, the firm's production function is

$$q = f(L, \bar{K}), \tag{6.2}$$

where q is output, L is workers, and $\bar{K}$ is the fixed number of units of capital.

To illustrate the short-run production process, we consider a firm that assembles computers for a manufacturing firm that supplies it with the necessary parts, such as computer chips and disk drives. The assembly firm cannot increase its capital—eight workbenches fully equipped with tools, electronic probes, and other equipment for testing computers—in the short run, but it can hire extra workers or pay current workers extra to work overtime so as to increase production.

Total Product

The exact relationship between *output* or *total product* and *labor* can be illustrated by using a particular function, Equation 6.2, a table, or a figure. Table 6.1 shows the relationship between output and labor when capital is fixed for a firm. The first column lists the fixed amount of capital: eight fully equipped workbenches. As the number of workers, the amount of labor (second column), increases, total output, the number of computers assembled in a day (third column), first increases and then decreases.

With zero workers, no computers are assembled. One worker with access to the firm's equipment assembles five computers in a day. As the number of workers increases, so does output: 1 worker assembles 5 computers in a day, 2 workers assemble 18, 3 workers assemble 36, and so forth. The maximum number of computers that can be assembled with the capital on hand, however, is limited to 110 per day. That maximum can be produced with 10 or 11 workers. Adding extra workers beyond 11 lowers production as workers get in each other's way. The dashed line in the table indicates that a firm would not use more than 11 workers, as to do so would be inefficient. We can show how extra workers affect the total product by using two additional concepts: the marginal product of labor and the average product of labor.

Table 6.1 Total Product, Marginal Product, and Average Product of Labor with Fixed Capital.

Capital, $\bar{K}$	Labor, L	Output, Total Product of Labor, Q	Marginal Product of Labor, $MP_L = \Delta Q/\Delta L$	Average Product of Labor, $AP_L = Q/L$
8	0	0		
8	1	5	5	5
8	2	18	13	9
8	3	36	18	12
8	4	56	20	14
8	5	75	19	15
8	6	90	15	15
8	7	98	8	14
8	8	104	6	13
8	9	108	4	12
8	10	110	2	11
8	11	110	0	10
8	12	108	–2	9
8	13	104	–4	8

Marginal Product of Labor

marginal product of labor (MP_L)
the change in total output, Δq, resulting from using an extra unit of labor, ΔL, holding other factors constant: $MP_L = \Delta q/\Delta L$

Before deciding whether to hire one more worker, a manager wants to determine how much this extra worker, $\Delta L = 1$, will increase output, Δq. That is, the manager wants to know the **marginal product of labor** (MP_L): the change in total output resulting from using an extra unit of labor, holding other factors (capital) constant. If output changes by Δq when the number of workers increases by ΔL, the change in output per worker is[2]

$$MP_L = \frac{\Delta q}{\Delta L}.$$

As Table 6.1 shows, if the number of workers increases from 1 to 2, $\Delta L = 1$, output rises by $\Delta q = 13 = 18 - 5$, so the marginal product of labor is 13.

Average Product of Labor

average product of labor (AP_L)
the ratio of output, q, to the number of workers, L, used to produce that output: $AP_L = q/L$

Before hiring extra workers, a manager may also want to know whether output will rise in proportion to this extra labor. To answer this question, the firm determines how extra workers affect the **average product of labor** (AP_L): the ratio of output to the number of workers used to produce that output,

$$AP_L = \frac{q}{L}.$$

See Question 1.

Table 6.1 shows that 10 workers can assemble 110 computers in a day, so the average product of labor for 10 workers is 11 computers. The average product of labor for 9 workers is 12 computers per day; thus increasing from 9 to 10 workers lowers the average product per worker.

[2]The calculus definition of the marginal product of labor is $MP_L = \partial q/\partial L = \partial f(L, \bar{K})/\partial L$, where capital is fixed at $\bar{K}$.

Graphing the Product Curves

Figure 6.1 and Table 6.1 show how output, the average product of labor, and the marginal product of labor vary with the number of workers. (The figures are smooth curves because the firm can hire a "fraction of a worker" by employing a

Figure 6.1 Production Relationships with Variable Labor.

(a) The total product of labor curve shows how many computers, q, can be assembled with eight fully equipped workbenches and a varying number of workers, L, who work an eight-hour day (see columns 2 and 3 in Table 6.1). Where extra workers reduce the number of computers assembled, the total product curve is a dashed line, which indicates that such production is inefficient production and not part of the production function. The slope of the line from the origin to point B is the average product of labor for six workers. (b) The marginal product of labor ($MP_L = \Delta q/\Delta L$, column 4 of Table 6.1) equals the average product of labor ($AP_L = q/L$, column 5 of Table 6.1) at the peak of the average product curve.

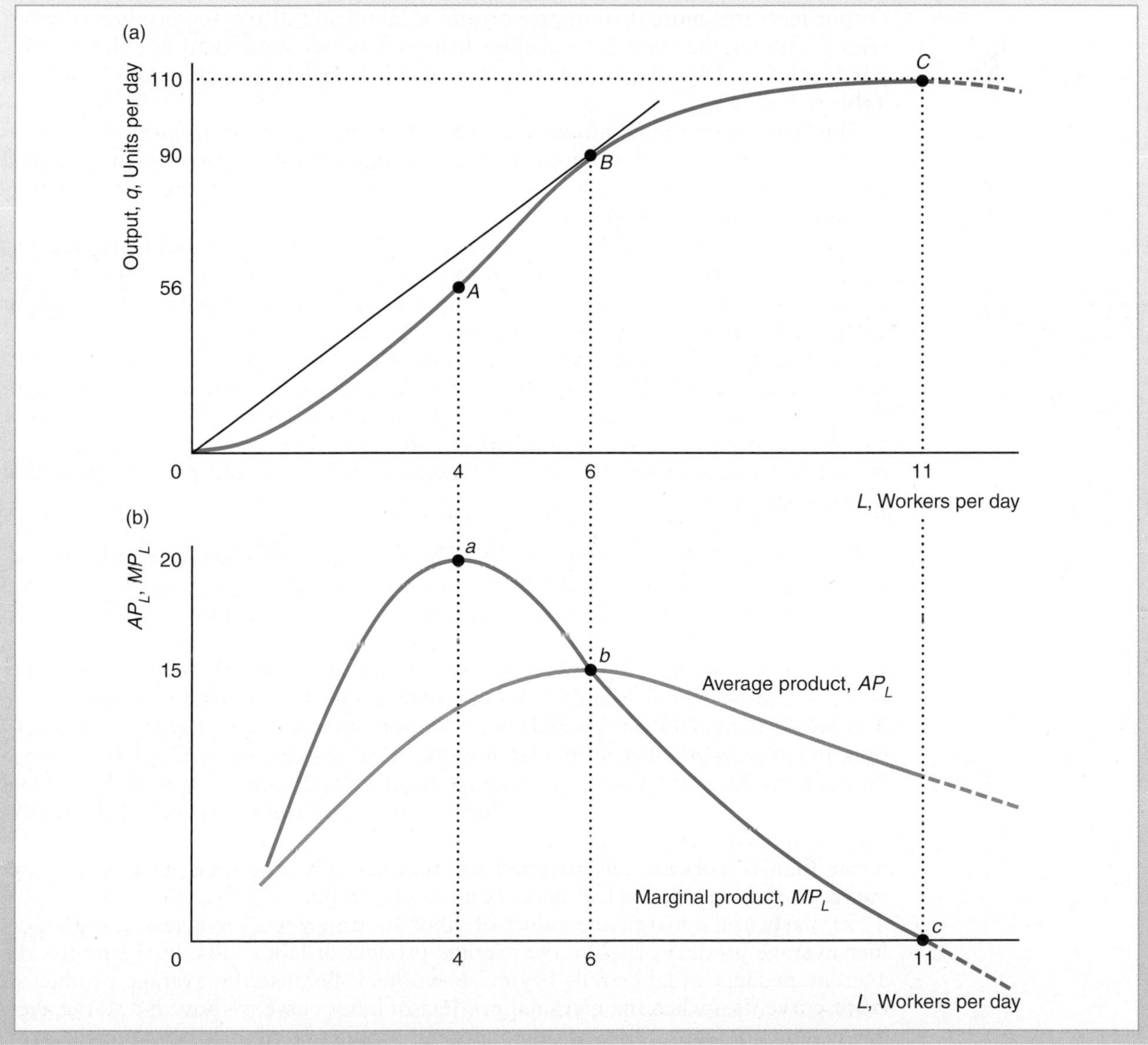

worker for a fraction of a day.) The curve in panel a of Figure 6.1 shows how a change in labor affects the **total product of labor**—the amount of output (or *total product*) that can be produced by a given amount of labor. Output rises with labor until it reaches its maximum of 110 computers at 11 workers, point C; with extra workers, the number of computers assembled falls.

total product of labor the amount of output (or total product) that can be produced by a given amount of labor

Panel b of the figure shows how the average product of labor and marginal product of labor vary with the number of workers. We can line up the figures in panels a and b vertically because the units along the horizontal axes of both figures, the number of workers per day, are the same. The vertical axes differ, however. The vertical axis is total product in panel a and the average or marginal product of labor—a measure of output per unit of labor—in panel b.

Effect of Extra Labor. In most production processes, the average product of labor first rises and then falls as labor increases. One reason the AP_L curve initially rises in Figure 6.1 is that it helps to have more than two hands when assembling a computer. One worker holds a part in place while another one bolts it down. As a result, output increases more than in proportion to labor, so the average product of labor rises. Doubling the number of workers from one to two more than doubles the output from 5 to 18 and causes the average product of labor to rise from 5 to 9, as Table 6.1 shows.

Similarly, output may initially rise more than in proportion to labor because of greater specialization of activities. With greater specialization, workers are assigned to tasks at which they are particularly adept, and time is saved by not having workers move from task to task.

As the number of workers rises further, however, output may not increase by as much per worker as they have to wait to use a particular piece of equipment or get in each other's way. In Figure 6.1, as the number of workers exceeds 6, total output increases less than in proportion to labor, so the average product falls.

If more than 11 workers are used, the total product curve falls with each extra worker as the crowding of workers gets worse. Because that much labor is not efficient, that section of the curve is drawn with a dashed line to indicate that it is not part of the production function. Similarly, the dashed portions of the average and marginal product curves are irrelevant because no firm would produce with that many workers.

See Question 2.

Relationship of the Product Curves. The three curves are geometrically related. First we use panel b to illustrate the relationship between the average and marginal product of labor curves. Then we use panels a and b to show the relationship between the total product of labor curve and the other two curves.

The average product of labor curve slopes upward where the marginal product of labor curve is above it and slopes downward where the marginal product curve is below it. If an extra worker adds more output—that worker's marginal product—than the average product of the initial workers, the extra worker raises the average product. As Table 6.1 shows, the average product of 2 workers is 9. The marginal product for a third worker is 18—which is above the average product for 2 workers—so the average product rises from 9 to 12. As panel b shows, when there are fewer than 6 workers, the marginal product curve is above the average product curve, so the average product curve is upward sloping.

Similarly, if the marginal product of labor for a new worker is less than the former average product of labor, the average product of labor falls. In the figure, the average product of labor falls beyond 6 workers. Because the average product of labor curve rises when the marginal product of labor curve is above it and the average product of labor falls when the marginal product of labor is below it, the average product of labor curve reaches a peak, point *b* in panel b, where the marginal product of labor curve crosses it. (See Appendix 6A for a mathematical proof.)

The geometric relationship between the total product curve and the average and marginal product curves is illustrated in panels a and b of Figure 6.1. We can determine the average product of labor using the total product of labor curve. The average product of labor for L workers equals the slope of a straight line from the origin to a point on the total product of labor curve for L workers in panel a. The slope of this line equals output divided by the number of workers, which is the definition of the average product of labor. For example, the slope of the straight line drawn from the origin to point B ($L = 6$, $q = 90$) is 15, which equals the "rise" of $q = 90$ divided by the "run" of $L = 6$. As panel b shows, the average product of labor for 6 workers at point *b* is 15.

The marginal product of labor also has a geometric interpretation in terms of the total product curve. The slope of the total product curve at a given point, $\Delta q/\Delta L$, equals the marginal product of labor. That is, the marginal product of labor equals the slope of a straight line that is tangent to the total output curve at a given point. For example, at point C in panel a where there are 11 workers, the line tangent to the total product curve is flat, so the marginal product of labor is zero: A little extra labor has no effect on output. The total product curve is upward sloping when there are fewer than 11 workers, so the marginal product of labor is positive. If the firm is foolish enough to hire more than 11 workers, the total product curve slopes downward (dashed line), so the MP_L is negative: Extra workers lower output. Again, this portion of the MP_L curve is not part of the production function.

When there are 6 workers, the average product of labor equals the marginal product of labor. The reason is that the line from the origin to point B in panel a is tangent to the total product curve, so the slope of that line, 15, is the marginal product of labor and the average product of labor at point *b* in panel b.

Law of Diminishing Marginal Returns

Next to "supply equals demand," probably the most commonly used phrase of economic jargon is the "law of diminishing marginal returns." This law determines the shapes of the total product and marginal product of labor curves as the firm uses more and more labor.

The *law of diminishing marginal returns* (or *diminishing marginal product*) holds that *if a firm keeps increasing an input, holding all other inputs and technology constant, the corresponding increases in output will become smaller eventually.* That is, if only one input is increased, *the marginal product of that input will diminish eventually.*

In Table 6.1, if the firm goes from 1 to 2 workers, the marginal product of labor is 13. If 1 or 2 more workers are used, the marginal product rises: The marginal product for 3 workers is 18, and the marginal product for 4 workers is 20. However, if the firm increases the number of workers beyond 4, the marginal product falls: The marginal product of 5 workers is 19, and that for 6 workers is 15. Beyond 4 workers, each extra worker adds less and less extra output, so the total product of labor curve rises by smaller increments. At 11 workers, the marginal product is zero. In short, the law of diminishing marginal returns says that if a firm keeps adding one more unit of an input, the extra output it gets grows smaller and smaller. This diminishing return to extra labor may be due to too many workers sharing too few machines or to crowding, as workers get in each other's way. Thus, as the amount of labor used grows large enough, the marginal product curve approaches zero and the corresponding total product of labor curve becomes nearly flat.

Unfortunately, many people, when attempting to cite this empirical regularity, overstate it. Instead of talking about "diminishing *marginal* returns," they talk about "diminishing returns." The two phrases have different meanings. Where there are "diminishing marginal returns," the MP_L curve is falling—beyond 4 workers in panel b of Figure 6.1—but it may be positive, as the solid MP_L curve between 4 and 11 workers shows. With "diminishing returns," extra labor causes *output* to fall. There are diminishing (total) returns for more than 11 workers—a dashed MP_L line in panel b.

Thus, saying that there are diminishing returns is much stronger than saying that there are diminishing marginal returns. We often observe firms producing where there are diminishing marginal returns to labor, but we rarely see firms operating where there are diminishing total returns. Only a firm that is willing to lose money would operate so inefficiently that it has diminishing returns. Such a firm could produce more output by using fewer inputs.

A second common misinterpretation of this law is to claim that marginal products must fall as we increase an input without requiring that technology and other inputs stay constant. If we increase labor while simultaneously increasing other factors or adopting superior technologies, the marginal product of labor may rise indefinitely. Thomas Malthus provided the most famous example of this fallacy.

See Questions 11, 12, 14, and 17–19 and Problem 23.

APPLICATION

Malthus and the Green Revolution

In 1798, Thomas Malthus—a clergyman and professor of modern history and political economy—predicted that (unchecked) population would grow more rapidly than food production because the quantity of land was fixed. The problem, he believed, was that the fixed amount of land would lead to diminishing marginal product of labor, so output would rise less than in proportion to the increase in farmworkers. Malthus grimly concluded that mass starvation would result. Brander and Taylor (1998) argue that such a disaster may have occurred on Easter Island around 500 years ago.

Since Malthus' day, world population has increased nearly 800%. Why haven't we starved to death? The simple explanation is that fewer workers using less land can produce much more food today than was possible when Malthus was alive. Two hundred years ago, most of the population had to work in agriculture to prevent starvation. Today, less than 2% of the U.S. population works in agriculture, and the share of land devoted to farming is constantly falling. Yet U.S. food production continues to grow faster than the U.S. population. Since World War II, world population doubled but food production tripled.

The average farm worker produced 100 units of output in 1948, but 215 units by 2004. From 1948 to 2004, the amount of labor used on farms fell 76%, an index of all inputs used fell by 4%, yet total output was 2.66 times larger, so we are producing much more output from many fewer inputs (U.S. Department of Agriculture, 2007).

Two key factors (in addition to birth control) are responsible for the rapid increase in food production per capita in most countries. First, agricultural technology—such as disease-resistant seeds and better land management practices—has improved substantially, so more output can be produced with the same inputs. Second, although the amounts of land and labor used have remained constant or fallen in most other countries in recent years, the use of other inputs such as fertilizer and tractors has increased significantly, so output per acre of land has risen.[3]

[3]See **www.myeconlab.com/perloff**, Chapter 6, "Does That Compute Down on the Farm?" on the technical progress of farms due to their increased use of computers.

In 1850, it took more than 80 hours of labor to produce 100 bushels of corn. Introducing mechanical power cut the labor required in half. Labor needs were again cut in half by the introduction of hybrid seed and chemical fertilizers, and then by the advent of herbicides and pesticides. Biotechnology, with the recent introduction of herbicide-tolerant and insect-resistant crops in 1996, has reduced the labor requirement today to about two hours of labor.

Of course, the risk of starvation is more severe in developing countries. Luckily, one man decided to defeat the threat of Malthusian disaster personally. Do you know anyone who saved a life? A hundred lives? *Do you know the name of the man who probably saved the most lives in history?* According to some estimates, Norman Borlaug and his fellow scientists prevented a *billion deaths* with their green revolution that resulted in a spectacular increase in wheat, rice, and maize production in the developing world.

Starting in Mexico, they developed new seeds and new approaches involving fertilizer, tractors, irrigation, soil treatments, and anything else that would increase production. Anything. (Hear Dr. Borlaug's story in his own words: **webcast.berkeley.edu/event_details.php?webcastid=9955**)

In the late 1960s, Dr. Borlaug and his colleagues brought the techniques he developed in Mexico to India and Pakistan because of the risk of mass starvation there. The results were stunning. Pakistan's wheat crop in 1968 soared to 146% of the 1965 pre-green revolution crop. By 1970, it was 183% of the 1965 crop. The comparable outputs for India were 134% and 163%.

Dr. Borlaug explained why Malthus was wrong:

Biotechnology helps farmers produce higher yields on less land. This is a very environmentally favorable benefit. For example, the world's grain output in 1950 was 692 million tons. Forty years or so later, the world's farmers used about the same amount of acreage but they harvested 1.9 billion tons—a 170% increase! We would have needed an additional 1.8 billion hectares of land, instead of the 600 million used, had the global cereal harvest of 1950 prevailed in 1999 using the same conventional farming methods.

However, as Dr. Borlaug noted in his 1970 Nobel Prize speech, superior science is not the complete answer to preventing starvation. A sound economic system is needed too. It is the lack of a sound economic system that has doomed many Africans. Per capita food production has fallen in parts of Africa over the past two decades. Worse, in several recent years, mass starvation has plagued some African countries. Although droughts have contributed, these tragedies appear to be primarily due to political problems such as wars and a breakdown of economic production and distribution systems. If these economic and political problems cannot be solved, Malthus may prove to be right for the wrong reason.

6.4 Long-Run Production: Two Variable Inputs

Eternity is a terrible thought. I mean, where's it going to end?
—Tom Stoppard

We started our analysis of production functions by looking at a short-run production function in which one input, capital, was fixed, and the other, labor, was variable. In the long run, however, both of these inputs are variable. With both factors variable, a firm can usually produce a given level of output by using a great deal of labor and very little capital, a great deal of capital and very little labor, or moderate amounts of both. That is, the firm can substitute one input for another while continuing to produce the same level of output, in much the same way that a consumer can maintain a given level of utility by substituting one good for another.

Typically, a firm can produce in a number of different ways, some of which require more labor than others. For example, a lumberyard can produce 200 planks an hour with 10 workers using hand saws, with 4 workers using handheld power saws, or with 2 workers using bench power saws.

We illustrate a firm's ability to substitute between inputs in Table 6.2, which shows the amount of output per day the firm produces with various combinations of labor per day and capital per day. The labor inputs are along the top of the table, and the capital inputs are in the first column. The table shows four combinations of labor and capital that the firm can use to produce 24 units of output: The firm may employ (a) 1 worker and 6 units of capital, (b) 2 workers and 3 units of capital, (c) 3 workers and 2 units of capital, or (d) 6 workers and 1 unit of capital.

Isoquants

isoquant
a curve that shows the efficient combinations of labor and capital that can produce a single (*iso*) level of output (*quantity*)

These four combinations of labor and capital are labeled *a*, *b*, *c*, and *d* on the "q = 24" curve in Figure 6.2. We call such a curve an **isoquant**, which is a curve that shows the efficient combinations of labor and capital that can produce a single (*iso*) level of output (*quantity*). If the production function is $q = f(L, K)$, then the equation for an isoquant where output is held constant at $\bar{q}$ is

$$\bar{q} = f(L, K).$$

See Question 7.

An isoquant shows the flexibility that a firm has in producing a given level of output. Figure 6.2 shows three isoquants corresponding to three levels of output. These isoquants are smooth curves because the firm can use fractional units of each input.

We can use these isoquants to illustrate what happens in the short run when capital is fixed and only labor varies. As Table 6.2 shows, if capital is constant at 2 units, 1 worker produces 14 units of output (point *e* in Figure 6.2), 3 workers produce 24 units (point *c*), and 6 workers produce 35 units (point *f*). Thus, if the firm holds one factor constant and varies another factor, it moves from one isoquant to another. In contrast, if the firm increases one input while lowering the other appropriately, the firm stays on a single isoquant.

Table 6.2 Output Produced with Two Variable Inputs.

	Labor, L					
Capital, K	1	2	3	4	5	6
1	10	14	17	20	22	**24**
2	14	20	**24**	28	32	35
3	17	**24**	30	35	39	42
4	20	28	35	40	45	49
5	22	32	39	45	50	55
6	**24**	35	42	49	55	60

Figure 6.2 Family of Isoquants.

These isoquants show the combinations of labor and capital that produce various levels of output. Isoquants farther from the origin correspond to higher levels of output. Points a, b, c, and d are various combinations of labor and capital the firm can use to produce $q = 24$ units of output. If the firm holds capital constant at 2 and increases labor from 1 (point e) to 3 (c) to 6 (f), it shifts from the $q = 14$ isoquant to the $q = 24$ isoquant and then to the $q = 35$ isoquant.

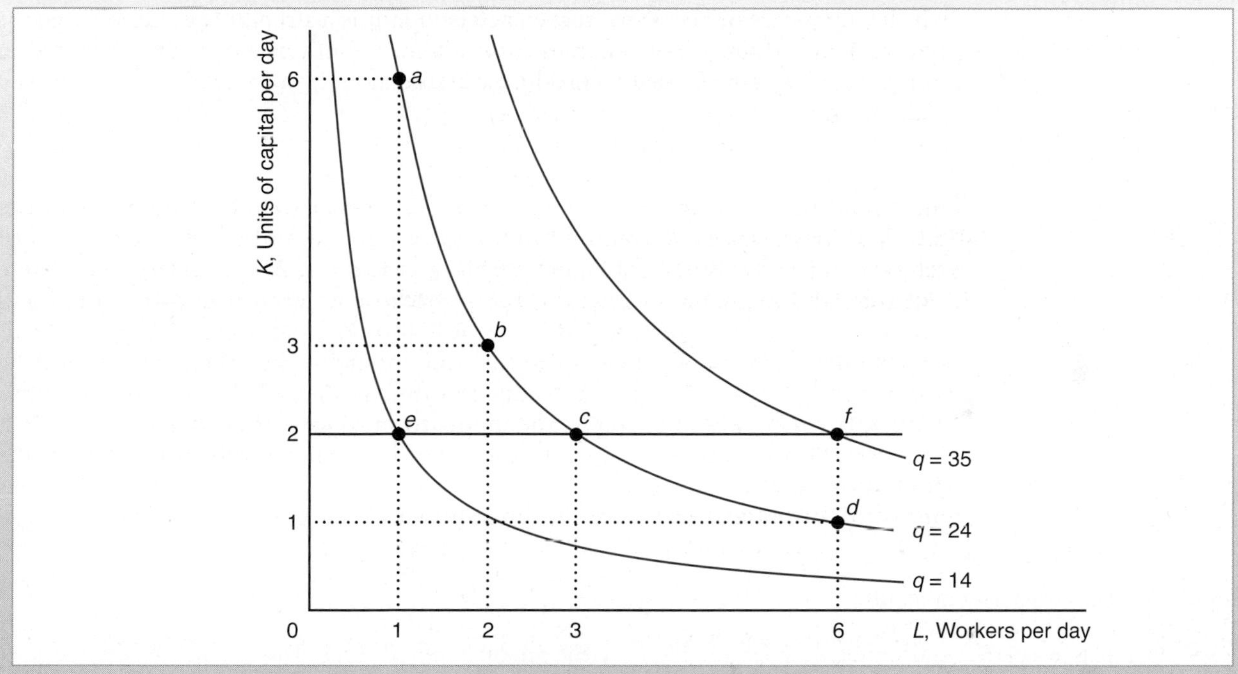

Properties of Isoquants. Isoquants have most of the same properties as indifference curves. The biggest difference between indifference curves and isoquants is that an isoquant holds quantity constant, whereas an indifference curve holds utility constant. We now discuss three major properties of isoquants. Most of these properties result from firms' producing efficiently.

See Question 3.

First, *the farther an isoquant is from the origin, the greater the level of output.* That is, the more inputs a firm uses, the more output it gets if it produces efficiently. At point e in Figure 6.2, the firm is producing 14 units of output with 1 worker and 2 units of capital. If the firm holds capital constant and adds 2 more workers, it produces at point c. Point c must be on an isoquant with a higher level of output—here, 24 units—if the firm is producing efficiently and not wasting the extra labor.

Second, *isoquants do not cross.* Such intersections are inconsistent with the requirement that the firm always produces efficiently. For example, if the $q = 15$ and $q = 20$ isoquants crossed, the firm could produce at either output level with the same combination of labor and capital. The firm must be producing inefficiently if it produces $q = 15$ when it could produce $q = 20$. So that labor-capital combination should not lie on the $q = 15$ isoquant, which should include only efficient combinations of inputs. Thus, efficiency requires that isoquants do not cross.

Third, *isoquants slope downward.* If an isoquant sloped upward, the firm could produce the same level of output with relatively few inputs or relatively many inputs. Producing with relatively many inputs would be inefficient. Consequently, because isoquants show only efficient production, an upward-sloping isoquant is

See Question 4.

impossible. Virtually the same argument can be used to show that isoquants must be thin.

Shape of Isoquants. The curvature of an isoquant shows how readily a firm can substitute one input for another. The two extreme cases are production processes in which inputs are perfect substitutes or in which they cannot be substituted for each other.

If the inputs are perfect substitutes, each isoquant is a straight line. Suppose either potatoes from Maine, x, or potatoes from Idaho, y, both of which are measured in pounds per day, can be used to produce potato salad, q, measured in pounds. The production function is

$$q = x + y.$$

See Questions 5, 6, and 8–10.

One pound of potato salad can be produced by using 1 pound of Idaho potatoes and no Maine potatoes, 1 pound of Maine potatoes and no Idahoes, or $\frac{1}{2}$ pound of each type of potato. Panel a of Figure 6.3 shows the $q = 1$, 2, and 3 isoquants. These isoquants are straight lines with a slope of -1 because we need to use an extra pound of Maine potatoes for every pound fewer of Idaho potatoes used.[4]

Sometimes it is impossible to substitute one input for the other: Inputs must be used in fixed proportions. Such a production function is called a *fixed-proportions production function*. For example, the inputs to produce a 12-ounce box of cereal, q, are cereal (in 12-ounce units per day) and cardboard boxes (boxes per day). If the firm has one unit of cereal and one box, it can produce one box of cereal. If it has one unit of cereal and two boxes, it can still make only one box of cereal. Thus, in

Figure 6.3 Substitutability of Inputs.

(a) If the inputs are perfect substitutes, each isoquant is a straight line. (b) If the inputs cannot be substituted at all, the isoquants are right angles (the dashed lines show that the isoquants would be right angles if we included inefficient production). (c) Typical isoquants lie between the extreme cases of straight lines and right angles. Along a curved isoquant, the ability to substitute one input for another varies.

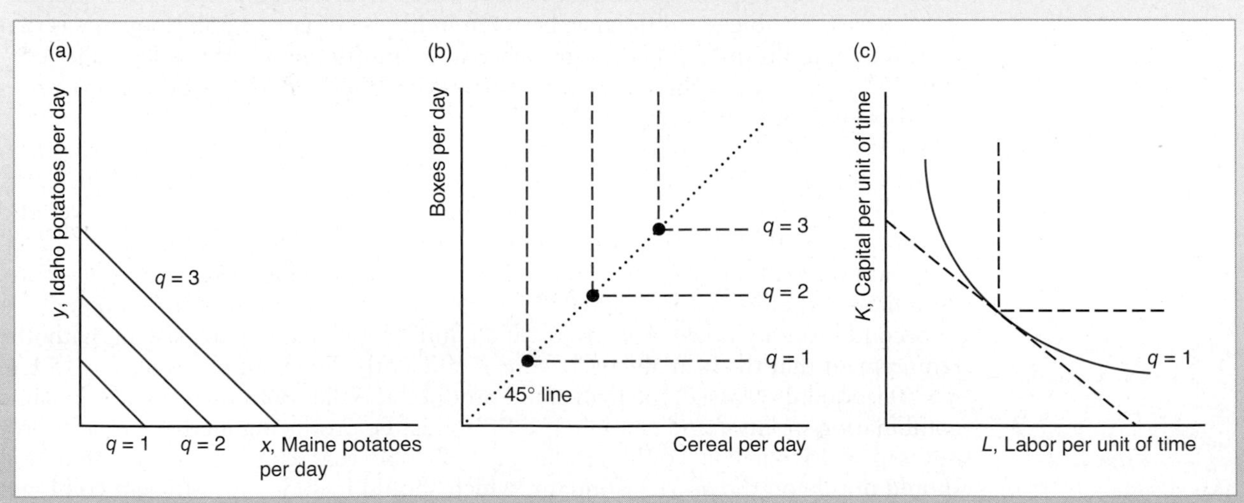

[4]The isoquant for $\bar{q} = 1$ pound of potato salad is $1 = x + y$, or $y = 1 - x$. This equation shows that the isoquant is a straight line with a slope of -1.

panel b, the only efficient points of production are the large dots along the 45° line.[5] Dashed lines show that the isoquants would be right angles if isoquants could include inefficient production processes.

Other production processes allow imperfect substitution between inputs. The isoquants are convex (so the middle of the isoquant is closer to the origin than it would be if the isoquant were a straight line). They do not have the same slope at every point, unlike the straight-line isoquants. Most isoquants are smooth, slope downward, curve away from the origin, and lie between the extreme cases of straight lines (perfect substitutes) and right angles (nonsubstitutes), as panel c illustrates.

APPLICATION

A Semiconductor Integrated Circuit Isoquant

We can show why isoquants curve away from the origin by deriving an isoquant for semiconductor integrated circuits (ICs, or "chips"). ICs—the "brains" of computers and other electronic devices—are made by building up layers of conductive and insulating materials on silicon wafers. Each wafer contains many ICs, which are subsequently cut into individual chips, called *dice*.

Semiconductor manufacturers ("fabs") buy the silicon wafers and then use labor and capital to produce the chips. A semiconductor IC's several layers of conductive and insulating materials are arranged in patterns that define the function of the chip.

During the manufacture of ICs, a track moves a wafer into a machine where it is spun, and a light-sensitive liquid called *photoresist* is applied to its whole surface. The photoresist is then hardened. The wafer advances along the track to a point where photolithography is used to define patterns in the photoresist. In photolithography, light transfers a pattern from a template, called a *photomask*, to the photoresist, which is then "developed" like film, creating a pattern by removing the resist from certain areas. A subsequent process then can either add to or etch away those areas not protected by the resist.

In a repetition of this entire procedure, additional layers are created on the wafer. Because the conducting and insulating patterns in each layer interact with those in the previous layers, the patterns must line up correctly.

To align layers properly, firms use combinations of labor and equipment. In the least capital-intensive technology, employees use machines called *aligners*. Operators look through microscopes and line up the layers by hand and then expose the entire surface. An operator running an aligner can produce 250 layers a day, or 25 ten-layer chips.

A second, more capital-intensive technology uses machines called *steppers*. The stepper picks a spot on the wafer, automatically aligns the layers, and then exposes that area to light. Then the machine moves—*steps* to other sections—lining up and exposing each area in turn until the entire surface has been aligned and exposed. This technology requires less labor: A single worker can run two steppers and produce 500 layers, or 50 ten-layer chips, per day.

A third, even more capital-intensive technology uses a stepper with wafer-handling equipment, which reduces the amount of labor even more. By linking the tracks directly to a stepper and automating the chip transfer process, human handling can be greatly reduced. A single worker can run four steppers with wafer-handling equipment and produce 1,000 layers, or 100 ten-layer chips, per day.

---

[5]This fixed-proportions production function is $q = \min(g, b)$, where g is the number of 12-ounce measures of cereal, b is the number of boxes used in a day, and the min function means "the minimum number of g or b." For example, if g is 4 and b is 3, q is 3.

Only steppers can be used if the chip requires line widths of 1 micrometer or less. We show an isoquant for producing 200 ten-layer chips that have lines more than 1 micrometer wide, for which any of the three technologies can be used.

All three technologies use labor and capital in fixed proportions. To produce 200 chips takes 8 workers and 8 aligners, 3 workers and 6 steppers, or 1 worker and 4 steppers with wafer-handling capabilities. The accompanying graph shows the three right-angle isoquants corresponding to each of these three technologies.

Some fabs, however, employ a combination of these technologies; some workers use one type of machine while others use different types. By doing so, the fabs can produce using intermediate combinations of labor and capital, as the solid-line, kinked isoquant illustrates. The firm does *not* use a combination of the aligner and the wafer-handling stepper technologies because those combinations are less efficient than using the plain stepper (the line connecting the aligner and wafer-handling stepper technologies is farther from the origin than the lines between those technologies and the plain stepper technology).

New processes are constantly being invented. As they are introduced, the isoquant will have more and more kinks (one for each new process) and will begin to resemble the smooth, usual-shaped isoquants we've been drawing.

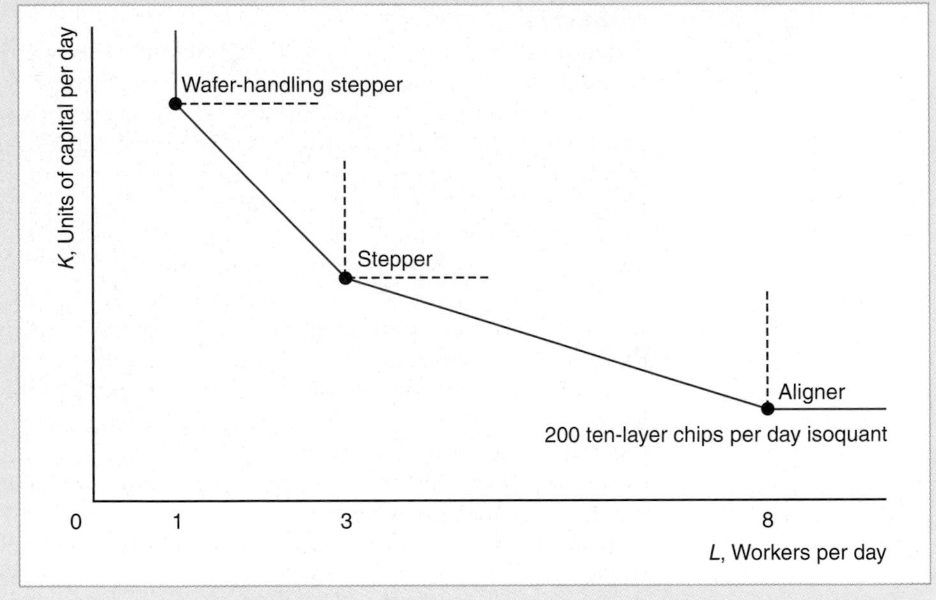

Substituting Inputs

The slope of an isoquant shows the ability of a firm to replace one input with another while holding output constant. Figure 6.4 illustrates this substitution using an estimated isoquant for a U.S. printing firm, which uses labor, L, and capital, K, to print its output, q.[6] The isoquant shows various combinations of L and K that the firm can use to produce 10 units of output.

[6]This isoquant for $\bar{q} = 10$ is based on the estimated production function $q = 2.35L^{0.5}K^{0.4}$ (Hsieh, 1995), where different units of measure are used. A unit of labor, L, is a worker-day. Because capital, K, includes various types of machines, and output, q, reflects different types of printed matter, their units cannot be described by any common terms. This production function is an example of a Cobb-Douglas (Appendix 4A) production function, whose properties are examined in Appendix 6B.

Figure 6.4 How the Marginal Rate of Technical Substitution Varies Along an Isoquant.

Moving from point a to b, a U.S. printing firm (Hsieh, 1995) can produce the same amount of output, $q = 10$, using six fewer units of capital, $\Delta K = -6$, if it uses one more worker, $\Delta L = 1$. Thus, its $MRTS = \Delta K/\Delta L = -6$. Moving from point b to c, its $MRTS$ is -3. If it adds yet another worker, moving from c to d, its $MRTS$ is -2. Finally, if it moves from d to e, its $MRTS$ is -1. Thus, because it curves away from the origin, this isoquant exhibits a diminishing marginal rate of technical substitution. That is, each extra worker allows the firm to reduce capital by a smaller amount as the ratio of capital to labor falls.

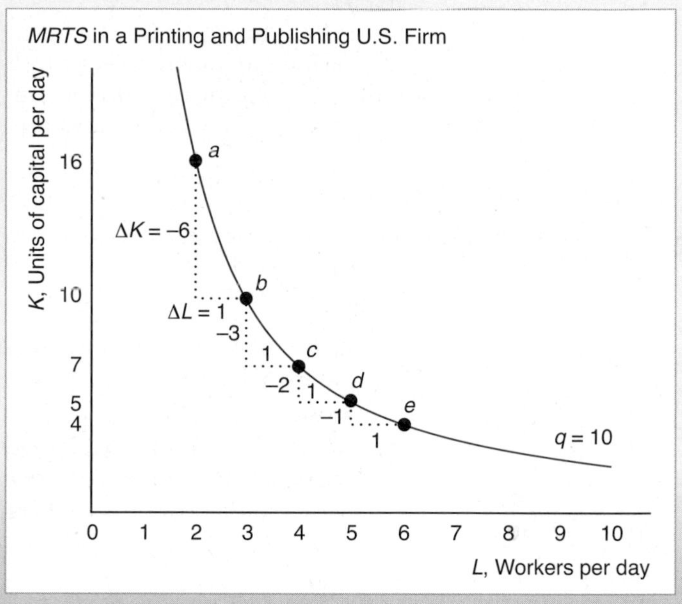

The firm can produce 10 units of output using the combination of inputs at a or b. At point a, the firm uses 2 workers and 16 units of capital. The firm could produce the same amount of output using $\Delta K = -6$ fewer units of capital if it used one more worker, $\Delta L = 1$, point b. If we drew a straight line from a to b, its slope would be $\Delta K/\Delta L = -6$. Thus, this slope tells us how many fewer units of capital (6) the firm can use if it hires one more worker.[7]

The slope of an isoquant is called the *marginal rate of technical substitution* (*MRTS*):

$$MRTS = \frac{\text{change in capital}}{\text{change in labor}} = \frac{\Delta K}{\Delta L}.$$

marginal rate of technical substitution
the number of extra units of one input needed to replace one unit of another input that enables a firm to keep the amount of output it produces constant

The **marginal rate of technical substitution** tells us how many units of capital the firm can replace with an extra unit of labor while holding output constant. Because isoquants slope downward, the *MRTS* is negative.

Substitutability of Inputs Varies Along an Isoquant. The marginal rate of technical substitution varies along a curved isoquant, as in Figure 6.4 for the printing firm. If the firm is initially at point a and it hires one more worker, the firm gives up 6 units of capital and yet remains on the same isoquant at point b, so the $MRTS$ is -6. If the firm hires another worker, the firm can reduce its capital by 3 units and yet stay on the same isoquant, moving from point b to c, so the $MRTS$ is -3. If the firm moves from point c to d, the $MRTS$ is -2; and if it moves from point d to e, the $MRTS$ is -1. This decline in the $MRTS$ (in absolute value) along an isoquant as the firm increases labor illustrates *diminishing marginal rates of technical substitution.*

The curvature of the isoquant away from the origin reflects diminishing marginal rates of technical substitution. The more labor the firm has, the harder it is to

[7] The slope of the isoquant at a point equals the slope of a straight line that is tangent to the isoquant at that point. Thus, the straight line between two nearby points on an isoquant has nearly the same slope as that of the isoquant.

replace the remaining capital with labor, so the *MRTS* falls as the isoquant becomes flatter.

In the special case in which isoquants are straight lines, isoquants do not exhibit diminishing marginal rates of technical substitution because neither input becomes more valuable in the production process: The inputs remain perfect substitutes. Solved Problem 6.1 illustrates this result.

Solved Problem 6.1

Does the marginal rate of technical substitution vary along the isoquant for the firm that produced potato salad using Idaho and Maine potatoes? What is the *MRTS* at each point along the isoquant?

Answer

1. *Determine the shape of the isoquant.* As panel a of Figure 6.3 illustrates, the potato salad isoquants are straight lines because the two types of potatoes are perfect substitutes.
2. *On the basis of the shape, conclude whether the MRTS is constant along the isoquant.* Because the isoquant is a straight line, the slope is the same at every point, so the *MRTS* is constant.
3. *Determine the MRTS at each point.* Earlier, we showed that the slope of this isoquant was –1, so the *MRTS* is –1 at each point along the isoquant. That is, because the two inputs are perfect substitutes, 1 pound of Idaho potatoes can be replaced by 1 pound of Maine potatoes.

Substitutability of Inputs and Marginal Products. The marginal rate of technical substitution—the degree to which inputs can be substituted for each other—equals the ratio of the marginal products of labor to the marginal product of capital, as we now show. The marginal rate of technical substitution tells us how much a firm can increase one input and lower the other while still staying on the same isoquant. Knowing the marginal products of labor and capital, we can determine how much one input must increase to offset a reduction in the other.

Because the marginal product of labor, $MP_L = \Delta q/\Delta L$, is the increase in output per extra unit of labor, if the firm hires ΔL more workers, its output increases by $MP_L \times \Delta L$. For example, if the MP_L is 2 and the firm hires one extra worker, its output rises by 2 units.

A decrease in capital alone causes output to fall by $MP_K \times \Delta K$, where $MP_K = \Delta q/\Delta K$ is the marginal product of capital—the output the firm loses from decreasing capital by one unit, holding all other factors fixed. To keep output constant, $\Delta q = 0$, this fall in output from reducing capital must exactly equal the increase in output from increasing labor:

$$(MP_L \times \Delta L) + (MP_K \times \Delta K) = 0.$$

Rearranging these terms, we find that[8]

$$-\frac{MP_L}{MP_K} = \frac{\Delta K}{\Delta L} = MRTS. \tag{6.3}$$

[8]We can derive this result directly by totally differentiating an isoquant, $\bar{q} = f(L, K)$. As we change labor and capital, the output doesn't change, so

$$d\bar{q} = 0 = \frac{\partial f}{\partial L} dL + \frac{\partial f}{\partial K} dK \equiv MP_L\, dL + MP_K\, dK.$$

Rearranging this expression, we find that $-MP_L/MP_K = dK/dL = MRTS$.

That is, the marginal rate of technical substitution, which is the change in capital relative to the change in labor, equals the ratio of the marginal products.

We can use Equation 6.3 to explain why marginal rates of technical substitution diminish as we move to the right along the isoquant in Figure 6.4. As we replace capital with labor (shift downward and to the right along the isoquant), the marginal product of capital increases—when there are few pieces of equipment per worker, each remaining piece is more useful—and the marginal product of labor falls, so the $MRTS = -MP_L/MP_K$ falls in absolute value.[9]

See Problem 24.

6.5 Returns to Scale

So far, we have examined the effects of increasing one input while holding the other input constant (the shift from one isoquant to another) or decreasing the other input by an offsetting amount (the movement along an isoquant). We now turn to the question of *how much output changes if a firm increases all its inputs proportionately.* The answer helps a firm determine its *scale* or size in the long run.

In the long run, a firm can increase its output by building a second plant and staffing it with the same number of workers as in the first one. Whether the firm chooses to do so depends in part on whether its output increases less than in proportion, in proportion, or more than in proportion to its inputs.

Constant, Increasing, and Decreasing Returns to Scale

constant returns to scale (*CRS*)
property of a production function whereby when all inputs are increased by a certain percentage, output increases by that same percentage

If, when all inputs are increased by a certain percentage, output increases by that same percentage, the production function is said to exhibit **constant returns to scale** (*CRS*). A firm's production process has constant returns to scale if, when the firm doubles its inputs—builds an identical second plant and uses the same amount of labor and equipment as in the first plant—it doubles its output:

$$f(2L, 2K) = 2f(L, K).$$

We can check whether the potato salad production function has constant returns to scale. If a firm uses x_1 pounds of Idaho potatoes and y_1 pounds of Maine potatoes, it produces $q_1 = x_1 + y_1$ pounds of potato salad. If it doubles both inputs, using $x_2 = 2x_1$ Idaho and $y_2 = 2y_1$ Maine potatoes, it doubles its output:

$$q_2 = x_2 + y_2 = 2x_1 + 2y_1 = 2q_1.$$

Thus, the potato salad production function exhibits constant returns to scale.

increasing returns to scale (*IRS*)
property of a production function whereby output rises more than in proportion to an equal increase in all inputs

If output rises more than in proportion to an equal percentage increase in all inputs, the production function is said to exhibit **increasing returns to scale** (*IRS*). A technology exhibits increasing returns to scale if doubling inputs more than doubles the output:

$$f(2L, 2K) > 2f(L, K).$$

Why might a production function have increasing returns to scale? One reason is that, although it could duplicate a small factory and double its output, the firm

[9]Figure 6.4 shows the effects of fairly large changes in labor and capital along a printing firm's isoquant. Calculated exactly for small changes (see Appendix 6B), the printing firm's $MRTS = -1.25K/L$. As we move to the right along this isoquant, the amount of capital decreases and the amount of labor increases, so the capital-labor ratio falls, causing the $MRTS$ to fall in absolute value.

might be able to more than double its output by building a single large plant, thereby allowing for greater specialization of labor or capital. In the two smaller plants, workers have to perform many unrelated tasks such as operating, maintaining, and fixing the machines they use. In the large plant, some workers may specialize in maintaining and fixing machines, thereby increasing efficiency. Similarly, a firm may use specialized equipment in a large plant but not in a small one.

If output rises less than in proportion to an equal percentage increase in all inputs, the production function exhibits **decreasing returns to scale** (*DRS*). A technology exhibits decreasing returns to scale if doubling inputs causes output to rise less than in proportion:

decreasing returns to scale (*DRS*) property of a production function whereby output increases less than in proportion to an equal percentage increase in all inputs

$$f(2L, 2K) < 2f(L, K).$$

One reason for decreasing returns to scale is that the difficulty of organizing, coordinating, and integrating activities increases with firm size. An owner may be able to manage one plant well but may have trouble running two plants. In some sense, the owner's difficulties in running a larger firm may reflect our failure to take into account some factor such as management in our production function. When the firm increases the various inputs, it does not increase the management input in proportion. If so, the "decreasing returns to scale" is really due to a fixed input. Another reason is that large teams of workers may not function as well as small teams, in which each individual takes greater personal responsibility.

See Questions 13, 15, and 17 and Problems 27 and 28.

One of the most widely estimated production functions is the Cobb-Douglas (Appendix 6B):

$$q = AL^{\alpha}K^{\beta}, \tag{6.4}$$

where A, α, and β are all positive constants. Solved Problem 6.2 shows that $\gamma = \alpha + \beta$ determines the returns to scale in a Cobb-Douglas production function.

Solved Problem 6.2

Under what conditions does a Cobb-Douglas production function, Equation 6.4, exhibit decreasing, constant, or increasing returns to scale?

See Problems 22 and 26.

Answer

1. *Show how output changes if both inputs are doubled:* If the firm initially uses L and K amounts of inputs, it produces

$$q_1 = AL^{\alpha}K^{\beta}.$$

When the firm doubles the amount of both labor and capital it uses, it produces

$$q_2 = A(2L)^{\alpha}(2K)^{\beta} = 2^{\alpha+\beta}AL^{\alpha}K^{\beta}.$$

Thus, its output increases by

$$\frac{q_2}{q_1} = \frac{2^{\alpha+\beta}AL^{\alpha}K^{\beta}}{AL^{\alpha}K^{\beta}} = 2^{\alpha+\beta} \equiv 2^{\gamma}, \tag{6.5}$$

where $\gamma \equiv \alpha + \beta$.

2. *Give a rule for determining the returns to scale:* The Cobb-Douglas production function has decreasing, constant, or increasing returns to scale as γ is less than, equal to, or greater than 1. For example, if $\gamma = 1$, doubling inputs doubles output, $q_2/q_1 = 2^{\gamma} = 2^1 = 2$, so the production function exhibits constant returns to scale.

APPLICATION

Returns to Scale in U.S. Manufacturing

Increasing, constant, and decreasing returns to scale are commonly observed. The table shows estimates of Cobb-Douglas production functions and rates of returns in various U.S. manufacturing industries (based on Hsieh, 1995). The returns to scale measure in the table, γ, is an elasticity. It represents the percentage change in output for a 1% increase in all the inputs. Because the estimated returns to scale measure for an electronics firm is virtually 1, a 1% increase in the inputs causes a 1% increase in output. Thus, an electronics firm's production function exhibits constant returns to scale.

	Labor, α	Capital, β	Scale, $\gamma = \alpha + \beta$
Decreasing Returns to Scale			
Tobacco products	0.18	0.33	0.51
Food and kindred products	0.43	0.48	0.91
Transportation equipment	0.44	0.48	0.92
Constant Returns to Scale			
Apparel and other textile products	0.70	0.31	1.01
Furniture and fixtures	0.62	0.40	1.02
Electronic and other electric equipment	0.49	0.53	1.02
Increasing Returns to Scale			
Paper and allied products	0.44	0.65	1.09
Petroleum and coal products	0.30	0.88	1.18
Primary metal	0.51	0.73	1.24

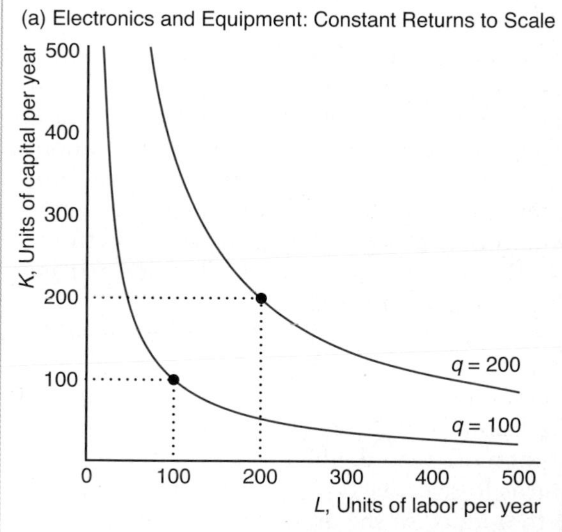

The estimated returns to scale measure for a tobacco firm is 0.51: A 1% increase in the inputs causes output to rise by 0.51%. Because output rises less than in proportion to the inputs, the tobacco production function exhibits decreasing returns to scale. In contrast, firms that manufacture primary metals have increasing returns to scale production functions, in which a 1% increase in all inputs causes output to rise by 1.24%.

The accompanying graphs use isoquants to illustrate the returns to scale for the electronics, tobacco, and primary metal firms. We measure the units of labor, capital, and output so that, for all three firms, 100 units of labor and 100 units of capital produce 100 units of output on the $q = 100$ isoquant in the three panels. For the constant returns to scale electronics firm, panel a, if both labor and capital are doubled from 100 to 200 units, output doubles to 200 ($= 100 \times 2^1$, multiplying the original output by the rate of increase using Equation 6.5). That same doubling of inputs causes output to rise to only 142 ($\approx 100 \times 2^{0.51}$) for the tobacco firm, panel b. Because output rises less than in proportion to inputs, the production function has decreasing returns to scale. If the primary metal firm doubles its inputs, panel c, its output more than doubles, to 236 ($\approx 100 \times 2^{1.24}$), so the production function has increasing returns to scale.

These graphs illustrate that the spacing of the isoquant determines the returns to scale. The closer together the $q = 100$ and $q = 200$ isoquants, the greater the returns to scale.

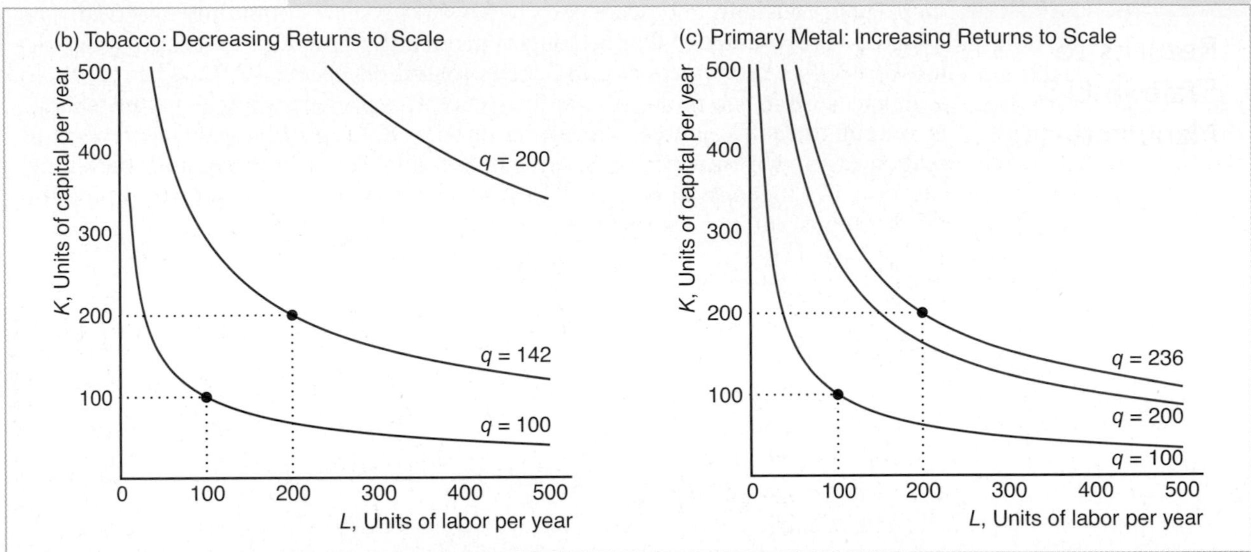

The returns to scale in these industries are estimated to be the same at all levels of output. A production function's returns to scale may vary, however, as the scale of the firm changes.

See Problem 28.

Varying Returns to Scale

Many production functions have increasing returns to scale for small amounts of output, constant returns for moderate amounts of output, and decreasing returns for large amounts of output. When a firm is small, increasing labor and capital allows for gains from cooperation between workers and greater specialization of workers and equipment—*returns to specialization*—so there are increasing returns to scale. As the firm grows, returns to scale are eventually exhausted. There are no more returns to specialization, so the production process has constant returns to scale. If the firm continues to grow, the owner starts having difficulty managing everyone, so the firm suffers from decreasing returns to scale.

We show such a pattern in Figure 6.5. Again, the spacing of the isoquants reflects the returns to scale. Initially, the firm has one worker and one piece of equipment, point a, and produces 1 unit of output on the $q = 1$ isoquant. If the firm doubles its inputs, it produces at b, where $L = 2$ and $K = 2$, which lies on the dashed line through the origin and point a. Output more than doubles to $q = 3$, so the production function exhibits increasing returns to scale in this range. Another doubling of inputs to c causes output to double to 6 units, so the production function has constant returns to scale in this range. Another doubling of inputs to d causes output to increase by only a third, to $q = 8$, so the production function has decreasing returns to scale in this range.

6.6 Productivity and Technical Change

Because firms may use different technologies and different methods of organizing production, the amount of output that one firm produces from a given amount of inputs may differ from that produced by another firm. Moreover, after a technical

Figure 6.5 Varying Scale Economies.

This production function exhibits varying returns to scale. Initially, the firm uses one worker and one unit of capital, point a. It repeatedly doubles these inputs to points b, c, and d, which lie along the dashed line. The first time the inputs are doubled, a to b, output more than doubles from $q = 1$ to $q = 3$, so the production function has increasing returns to scale. The next doubling, b to c, causes a proportionate increase in output, constant returns to scale. At the last doubling, from c to d, the production function exhibits decreasing returns to scale.

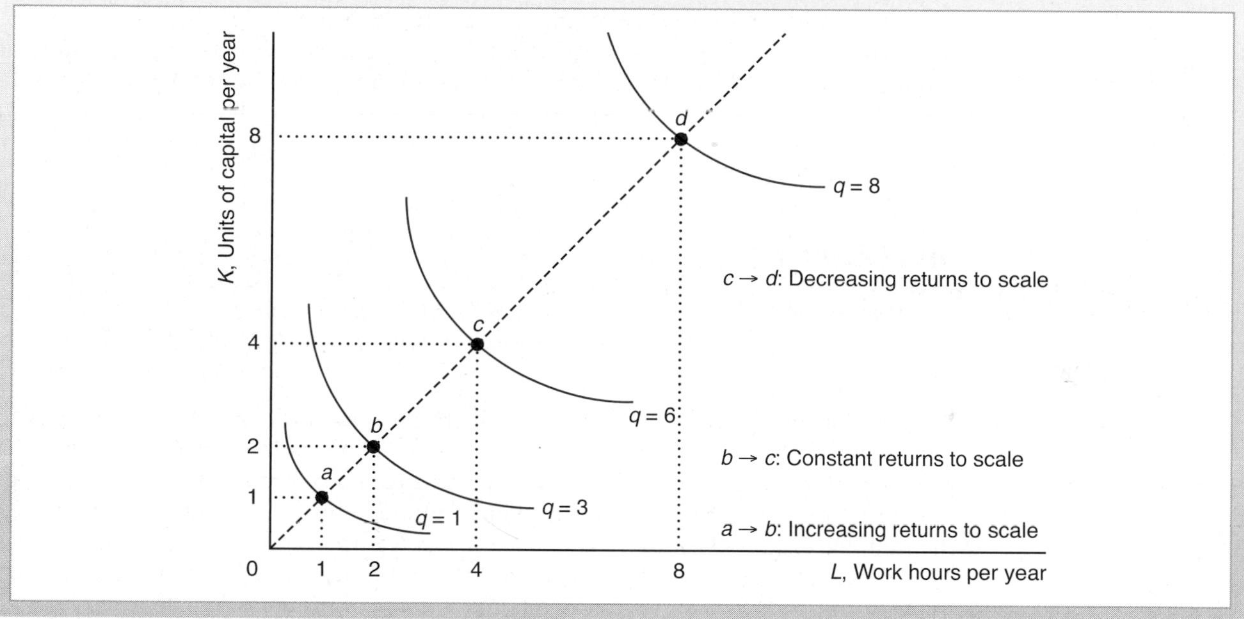

or managerial innovation, a firm can produce more today from a given amount of inputs than it could in the past.

Relative Productivity

Throughout this chapter, we've assumed that firms produce efficiently. A firm must produce efficiently if it is to maximize its profit. Even if each firm in a market produces as efficiently as possible, however, firms may not be equally *productive*, in the sense that one firm can produce more than another from a given amount of inputs.

A firm may be more productive than others if its manager knows a better way to organize production or if it is the only firm with access to a new invention. Union-mandated work rules, government regulations, other institutional restrictions, or racial or gender discrimination that affect only some firms may lower the relative productivity of those firms.

We can measure the *relative productivity* of a firm by expressing the firm's actual output, q, as a percentage of the output that the most productive firm in the industry could have produced, q^*, from the same amount of inputs: $100q/q^*$. The most productive firm in an industry has a relative productivity measure of 100% (= $100q^*/q^*$ percent).

Caves and Barton (1990) report that the average productivity of firms across U.S. manufacturing industries ranges from 63% to 99%. That is, in the manufacturing industry with the most diverse firms, the average firm produces slightly less than two-thirds as much as the most productive firm, whereas in the manufacturing industry with the most homogeneous firms, all firms are nearly equally productive.

Differences in productivity across markets may be due to differences in the degree of competition. In competitive markets, in which many firms can enter and exit the market easily, less productive firms lose money and are driven out of business, so the firms that are actually producing are equally productive (as Chapter 8 shows). In a less competitive oligopoly market, with few firms and no possibility of entry by new firms, a less productive firm may be able to survive, so firms with varying levels of productivity are observed.

See Question 20 and Problem 30.

In communist and other government-managed economies, in which firms are not required to maximize profits, inefficient firms may survive. For example, a study of productivity in 48 medium-size, machine-building state enterprises in China (Kalirajan and Obwona, 1994) found that the productivity measure ranges from 21% to 100%, with an average of 55%. See **www.myeconlab.com/perloff**, Chapter 6, "German Versus British Productivity."

Innovations

Maximum number of miles that Ford's most fuel-efficient 2003 car could drive on a gallon of gas: 36. Maximum number its 1912 Model T could: 35.
—Harper's Index 2003

technical progress
an advance in knowledge that allows more output to be produced with the same level of inputs

In its production process, a firm tries to use the best available technological and managerial knowledge. An advance in knowledge that allows more output to be produced with the same level of inputs is called **technical progress**. The invention of new products is a form of technical innovation. The use of robotic arms increases the number of automobiles produced with a given amount of labor and raw materials. Better *management or organization of the production process* similarly allows the firm to produce more output from given levels of inputs.

Technical Progress. A technological innovation changes the production process. Last year a firm produced

$$q_1 = f(L, K)$$

units of output using L units of labor services and K units of capital service. Due to a new invention that the firm uses, this year's production function differs from last year's, so the firm produces 10% more output with the same inputs:

$$q_2 = 1.1f(L, K).$$

This firm has experienced *neutral technical change*, in which it can produce more output using the same ratio of inputs. For example, a technical innovation in the form of a new printing press may allow more output to be produced using the same ratio of inputs as before: one worker to one printing press.

In our neutral technical change example, the firm's rate of growth of output was $10\% = \Delta q/q_1 = [1.1f(L, K) - f(L, K)]/f(L, K)$ in one year due to the technical change. Table 6.3 shows estimates for several countries of the annual rate at which computer and related goods output grew, holding the levels of inputs constant.

Neutral technical progress leaves the shapes of the isoquants unchanged. However, each isoquant is now associated with more output. For example, if there was neutral technical progress in Figure 6.5 that doubled output for any combination of inputs, then we would relabel the isoquants from lowest to highest as $q = 2$, $q = 6$, $q = 12$, and $q = 16$.

Nonneutral technical changes are innovations that alter the proportion in which inputs are used. If a printing press that required two people to operate is replaced by one that can be run by a single worker, the technical change is *laborsaving*. The

Table 6.3 Annual Percentage Rates of Neutral Productivity Growth for Computer and Related Capital Goods.

	1990–1995	1995–2002
Australia	1.4	1.5
Canada	0.4	1.0
France	0.8	1.4
Japan	0.8	0.6
United Kingdom	1.2	0.9*
United States	0.8	1.3

*United Kingdom rate is for 1995–2001.
Source: OECD Productivity Database, December 17, 2004.

ratio of labor to other inputs used to produce a given level of output falls after the innovation. Similarly, the ratio of output to labor, the average product of labor, rises. Here, technical progress changes the shapes of isoquants.

See Question 21.

Organizational Change. Organizational changes may also alter the production function and increase the amount of output produced by a given amount of inputs. Organizational innovations have been very important in automobile manufacturing.

In the early 1900s, Henry Ford revolutionized mass production through two organizational innovations. First, he introduced interchangeable parts, which cut the time required to install parts because workers no longer had to file or machine individually made parts to get them to fit.

Second, Ford introduced a conveyor belt and an assembly line to his production process. Before Ford, workers walked around the car, and each worker performed many assembly activities. In Ford's plant, each worker specialized in a single activity such as attaching the right rear fender to the chassis. A conveyor belt moved the car at a constant speed from worker to worker along the assembly line. Because his workers gained proficiency from specializing in only a few activities and because the conveyor belts reduced the number of movements workers had to make, Ford could produce more automobiles with the same number of workers. By the early 1920s, Ford had cut the cost of a car by more than two-thirds and had increased production from fewer than a thousand cars per year to two million per year.

APPLICATION

Dell Computer's Organizational Innovations

Michael Dell, the president of Dell Computer, has become rich by innovating in organizational practices rather than by producing the most technologically advanced computers. Dell Computer is probably the world's most efficient personal computer manufacturer due in large part to two organizational innovations: building to order and just-in-time delivery. Dell made its name by selling directly to customers and allowing them to specify the features they wanted on their personal computer. It has adopted and extended the use of just-in-time inventories, a practice developed by Toyota and other Japanese auto manufacturers. Upon getting an order, Dell uses the Internet to tell its suppliers which parts it needs, and receives delivery within an hour and a half. As Michael Dell writes, "Keep your friends close, and your suppliers closer." Its just-in-time strategy virtually eliminates the need for Dell to maintain any inventory of parts and finished products.

Twelve years ago, Dell had 30 days of parts in inventory, and its main competitors still maintain 12–16 weeks of inventory. In 2005, Dell had just two hours' worth of inventories at its Limerick plant. Consequently, Dell has eliminated warehouses in its factories, cutting the number of buildings it needs in each factory from two to one.

To further facilitate its manufacturing process, the company uses special hydraulic tools, conveyor belts, and tracks, cutting human intervention in half. Workers snap computer components into place, rarely having to use screwdrivers. Every screw and every sticker they remove by design from a machine saves four seconds of assembly time. To build a PC took 2 workers 14 minutes in 1999 but only a single worker roughly 5 minutes in 2004.

Dell started selling computers in retail stores in 2007 and acts to keep inventories low there as well. Dell uses automatic replenishing: If a Staples store sells three Dell notebooks, Dell automatically sends three replacements. In contrast, many of its rivals build a large number of machines at once and ship them by boat to a distribution center, which then redirects a large number of them to a store.

SUMMARY

1. **The Ownership and Management of Firms.** Firms are either sole proprietorships, partnerships, or corporations. In smaller firms (particularly sole proprietorships and partnerships), the owners usually run the company. In large firms (such as most corporations), the owners hire managers to run the firms. Owners want to maximize profits. If managers have different objectives than owners, owners must keep a close watch over managers to ensure that profits are maximized.

2. **Production.** Inputs, or factors of production—labor, capital, and materials—are combined to produce output using the current state of knowledge about technology and management. To maximize profits, a firm must produce as efficiently as possible: It must get the maximum amount of output from the inputs it uses, given existing knowledge. A firm may have access to many efficient production processes that use different combinations of inputs to produce a given level of output. New technologies or new forms of organization can increase the amount of output that can be produced from a given combination of inputs. A production function shows how much output can be produced efficiently from various levels of inputs. A firm can vary all its inputs in the long run but only some of them in the short run.

3. **Short-Run Production: One Variable and One Fixed Input.** In the short run, a firm cannot adjust the quantity of some inputs, such as capital. The firm varies its output by adjusting its variable inputs, such as labor. If all factors are fixed except labor, and a firm that was using very little labor increases its use of labor, its output may rise more than in proportion to the increase in labor because of greater specialization of workers. Eventually, however, as more workers are hired, the workers get in each other's way or wait to share equipment, so output increases by smaller and smaller amounts. This latter phenomenon is described by the law of diminishing marginal returns: The marginal product of an input—the extra output from the last unit of input—eventually decreases as more of that input is used, holding other inputs fixed.

4. **Long-Run Production: Two Variable Inputs.** In the long run, when all inputs are variable, firms can substitute between inputs. An isoquant shows the combinations of inputs that can produce a given level of output. The marginal rate of technical substitution is the absolute value of the slope of the isoquant. Usually, the more of one input the firm uses, the more difficult it is to substitute that input for another input. That is, there are diminishing marginal rates of

technical substitution as the firm uses more of one input.

5. **Returns to Scale.** If, when a firm increases all inputs in proportion, its output increases by the same proportion, the production process is said to exhibit constant returns to scale. If output increases less than in proportion to inputs, the production process has decreasing returns to scale; if it increases more than in proportion, it has increasing returns to scale. All three types of returns to scale are commonly seen in actual industries. Many production processes exhibit first increasing, then constant, and finally decreasing returns to scale as the size of the firm increases.

6. **Productivity and Technical Change.** Although all firms in an industry produce efficiently, given what they know and the institutional and other constraints they face, some firms may be more productive than others: They can produce more output from a given bundle of inputs. Due to innovations such as technical progress or new means of organizing production, a firm can produce more today than it could in the past from the same bundle of inputs. Such innovations change the production function.

QUESTIONS

■ = *exercise is available on MyEconLab;* * = *answer appears at the back of this book;* C = *use of calculus may be necessary;* W = *audio-slideshow answer by James Dearden is available in Textbook Resources on MyEconLab.*

*1. If each extra worker produces an extra unit of output, how do the total product of labor, average product of labor, and marginal product of labor vary with labor?

2. Each extra worker produces an extra unit of output up to six workers. After six, no additional output is produced. Draw the total product of labor, average product of labor, and marginal product of labor curves.

3. What is the difference between an isoquant and an indifference curve?

4. Why must isoquants be thin? (*Hint*: See the explanation of why indifference curves must be thin in Chapter 4.)

5. Suppose that a firm has a fixed-proportions production function, in which one unit of output is produced using one worker and two units of capital. If the firm has an extra worker and no more capital, it still can produce only one unit of output. Similarly, one more unit of capital does the firm no good.
   a. Draw the isoquants for this production function.
   b. Draw the total product, average product, and marginal product of labor curves (you will probably want to use two diagrams) for this production function.

■*6. To produce a recorded CD, $q = 1$, a firm uses one blank disk, $D = 1$, and the services of a recording machine, $M = 1$, for one hour. Draw an isoquant for this production process. Explain the reason for its shape.

7. Draw a diagram with labor services on one axis and capital services on the other. Draw a circle in the middle of this figure. This circle represents all the combinations of labor and capital that produce 100 units of output. Now draw the isoquant for 100 units of output. (*Hint*: Remember that the isoquant includes only the efficient combinations of labor and capital.)

8. The production function at Ginko's Copy Shop is $q = 1{,}000 \times \min(L, 3K)$, where q is the number of copies per hour, L is the number of workers, and K is the number of copy machines. As an example, if $L = 2$ and $K = 1$, then $\min(L, 3K) = 3$, and $q = 3{,}000$.
   a. Draw the isoquants for this production function.
   b. Draw the total product, average product, and marginal product of labor curves for this production function for some fixed level of capital.

■9. What is the production function if L and K are perfect substitutes and each unit of q requires 1 unit of L or 1 unit of K (or a combination of these inputs that adds up to 1)?

■*10. Mark launders his white clothes using the production function $q = B + 2G$, where B is the number of cups of Clorox bleach and G is the number of cups of a generic bleach that is half as potent. Draw an isoquant. What is the marginal product of B? What is the marginal rate of technical substitution at each point on an isoquant?

11. Why might we expect the law of diminishing marginal product to hold?

■12. Ben swims 50,000 yards per week in his practices. Given this amount of training, he will swim the 100-yard butterfly in 52.6 seconds and place tenth in a big upcoming meet. Ben's coach calculates that if Ben increases his practice to 60,000 yards per week, his time will decrease to 50.7 seconds and he will place eighth in the meet. If Ben practices 70,000 yards per week, his time will be 49.9 and he will win the meet.

a. In terms of Ben's *time* in the big meet, what is his marginal productivity of the number of yards he practices? Is there diminishing marginal productivity of practice yards?

b. In terms of Ben's *place* in the big meet, what is his marginal productivity of the number of yards he practices? Is there diminishing marginal productivity of practice yards?

c. Does Ben's marginal productivity of the number of yards he practices depend on how he measures his productivity, either place or time, in the big meet? W

13. To speed relief to isolated South Asian communities that were devastated by the December 2004 tsunami, the U.S. government doubled the number of helicopters from 45 to 90 in early 2005. Navy admiral Thomas Fargo, head of the U.S. Pacific Command, was asked if doubling the number of helicopters would "produce twice as much [relief]." He predicted, "Maybe pretty close to twice as much." (Vicky O'Hara, *All Things Considered,* National Public Radio, January 4, 2005, **www.npr.org/dmg/dmg.php?prgCode=ATC&showDate=04-Jan-2005&segNum=10&NPRMediaPref=WM&getAd=1**)
Identify the outputs and inputs and describe the production process. Is the admiral discussing a production process with nearly constant returns to scale, or is he referring to another property of the production process?

14. Michelle's business produces ceramic cups using labor, clay, and a kiln. She can manufacture 25 cups a day with one worker and 35 with two workers. Does her production process illustrate *diminishing returns to scale* or *diminishing marginal returns to scale*? What is the likely explanation for why output doesn't increase proportionately with the number of workers?

15. From the ninth century B.C. until the proliferation of gunpowder in the fifteenth century A.D., the ultimate weapon of mass destruction was the catapult (John N. Wilford, "How Catapults Married Science, Politics and War," *New York Times,* February 24, 2004, D3). As early as the fourth century B.C., rulers set up research and development laboratories to support military technology. Research on improving the catapult was by trial and error until about 200 B.C., when the engineer Philo of Byzantium reports that by using mathematics, it was determined that each part of the catapult was proportional to the size of the object it was designed to propel. For example, the weight and length of the projectile was proportional to the size of the torsion springs (bundles of sinews or ropes that were tightly twisted to store enormous power). Mathematicians devised precise tables of specifications for reference by builders and by soldiers on the firing line. The Romans had catapults capable of delivering 60-pound boulders at least 500 feet. (Legend has it that Archimedes' catapults used stones that were three times heavier.) If the output of the production process is measured as the weight of a projectile delivered, how does the amount of capital needed vary with output? If the amount of labor to operate the catapult did not vary substantially with the projectile's size, what can you say about the marginal productivity of capital and scale economies?

16. In a manufacturing plant, workers use a specialized machine to produce belts. A new machine is invented that is laborsaving. With the new machine, the firm can use fewer workers and still produce the same number of belts as it did using the old machine. In the long run, both labor and capital (the machine) are variable. From what you know, what is the effect of this invention on the AP_L, MP_L, and returns to scale? If you require more information to answer this question, specify what you need to know.

17. Show in a diagram that a production function can have diminishing marginal returns to a factor and constant returns to scale.

18. If a firm lays off workers during a recession, how will the firm's marginal product of labor change?

*19. During recessions, American firms lay off a larger proportion of their workers than Japanese firms do. (It has been claimed that Japanese firms continue to produce at high levels and store the output or sell it at relatively low prices during the recession.) Assuming that the production function remains unchanged over a period that is long enough to include many recessions and expansions, would you expect the average product of labor to be higher in Japan or the United States? Why?

20. Does it follow that because we observe that the average product of labor is higher for Firm 1 than for Firm 2, Firm 1 is more productive in the sense that it can produce more output from a given amount of inputs? Why?

21. Until the mid-eighteenth century when spinning became mechanized, cotton was an expensive and relatively unimportant textile (Virginia Postrel, "What Separates Rich Nations from Poor Nations?" *New York Times,* January 1, 2004). Where it used to take an Indian hand-spinner 50,000 hours to hand-spin 100 pounds of cotton, an operator of a 1760s-

era hand-operated cotton mule-spinning machine could produce 100 pounds of stronger thread in 300 hours. When the self-acting mule spinner automated the process after 1825, the time dropped to 135 hours, and cotton became an inexpensive, common cloth. Was this technological progress neutral? In a figure, show how these technological changes affected isoquants.

PROBLEMS

*22. Suppose that the production function is $q = L^{0.75}K^{0.25}$.

a. What is the average product of labor, holding capital fixed at $\bar{K}$?

b. What is the marginal product of labor? (*Hint*: Calculate how much q changes as L increases by 1 unit, use calculus, or see Appendix 6B.)

c. Does this production function have increasing, constant, or decreasing returns to scale?

23. In the short run, a firm cannot vary its capital, $K = 2$, but can vary its labor, L. It produces output q. Explain why the firm will or will not experience diminishing marginal returns to labor in the short run if its production function is

a. $q = 10L + K$

b. $q = L^{0.5}K^{0.5}$

24. By studying, Will can produce a higher grade, G_W, on an upcoming economics exam. His production function depends on the number of hours he studies marginal analysis problems, A, and the number of hours he studies supply-and-demand problems, R. Specifically, $G_W = 2.5A^{0.36}R^{0.64}$. His roommate David's grade-production function is

$$G_D = 2.5A^{0.25}R^{0.75}.$$

a. What is Will's marginal productivity of studying supply-and-demand problems? What is David's? (*Hint*: See Appendix 6B.)

b. What is Will's marginal rate of technical substitution between studying the two types of problems? What is David's?

c. Is it possible that Will and David have different marginal productivity functions but the same marginal rate of technical substitution functions? Explain. W, C

*25. At $L = 4$, $K = 4$, the marginal product of labor is 2 and the marginal product of capital is 3. What is the marginal rate of technical substitution?

*26. The production function for the automotive and parts industry is $q = L^{0.27}K^{0.16}M^{0.61}$, where M is energy and materials (based loosely on Klein, 2003). What kind of returns to scale does this production function exhibit? What is the marginal product of materials?

27. Under what conditions do the following production functions exhibit decreasing, constant, or increasing returns to scale?

a. $q = L + K$

b. $q = L^{\alpha}K^{\beta}$

c. $q = L + L^{\alpha}K^{\beta} + K$

28. Is it possible that a firm's production function exhibits increasing returns to scale while exhibiting diminishing marginal productivity of each of its inputs? To answer this question, calculate the marginal productivities of capital and labor for the production of electronics and equipment, tobacco, and primary metal using the information listed in the "Returns to Scale in U.S. Manufacturing" application. (*Hint*: See Appendix 6B.) W, C

29. A production function is said to be homogeneous of degree γ if $f(xL, xK) = x^{\gamma}f(L, K)$, where x is a positive constant. That is, the production function has the same returns to scale for every combination of inputs. For such a production function, show that the marginal product of labor and marginal product of capital functions are homogeneous of degree $\gamma - 1$. C

*30. Firm 1 and Firm 2 use the same type of production function, but Firm 1 is only 90% as productive as Firm 2. That is, the production function of Firm 2 is $q_2 = f(L, K)$, and the production function of Firm 1 is $q_1 = 0.9f(L, K)$. At a particular level of inputs, how does the marginal product of labor differ between the firms? C

7 Costs

An economist is a person who, when invited to give a talk at a banquet, tells the audience there's no such thing as a free lunch.

A semiconductor manufacturer can produce a chip using many pieces of equipment and relatively few workers' labor or many workers and relatively few machines. How does the firm make its choice?

The firm uses a two-step procedure in determining how to produce a certain amount of output efficiently. It first determines which production processes are *technologically efficient* so that it can produce the desired level of output with the least amount of inputs. As we saw in Chapter 6, the firm uses engineering and other information to determine its production function, which summarizes the many technologically efficient production processes available.

economically efficient minimizing the cost of producing a specified amount of output

The firm's second step is to pick from these technologically efficient production processes the one that is also **economically efficient**, minimizing the cost of producing a specified amount of output. To determine which process minimizes its cost of production, the firm uses information about the production function and the cost of inputs.

By reducing its cost of producing a given level of output, a firm can increase its profit. Any profit-maximizing competitive, monopolistic, or oligopolistic firm minimizes its cost of production.

In this chapter, we examine five main topics

1. **Measuring Costs.** Economists count both explicit costs and implicit (opportunity) costs.
2. **Short-Run Costs.** To minimize its costs in the short run, a firm adjusts its variable factors (such as labor), but it cannot adjust its fixed factors (such as capital).
3. **Long-Run Costs.** In the long run, a firm adjusts all its inputs because usually all inputs are variable.
4. **Lower Costs in the Long Run.** Long-run cost is as low as or lower than short-run cost because the firm has more flexibility in the long run, technological progress occurs, and workers and managers learn from experience.
5. **Cost of Producing Multiple Goods.** If the firm produces several goods simultaneously, the cost of each may depend on the quantity of all the goods produced.

Businesspeople and economists need to understand the relationship between costs of inputs and production to determine the least costly way to produce. Economists have an additional reason for wanting to know about costs. As we'll see in later chapters, the relationship between output and costs plays an important role in determining the nature of a market—how many firms are in the market and how high price is relative to cost.

7.1 Measuring Costs

How much would it cost you to stand at the wrong end of a shooting gallery?
—S. J. Perelman

To show how a firm's cost varies with its output, we first have to measure costs. Businesspeople and economists often measure costs differently.

Economic Cost

Economists include all relevant costs. To run a firm profitably, a manager acts like an economist and considers all relevant costs. However, this same manager may direct the firm's accountant or bookkeeper to measure cost in ways that are consistent with tax laws and other laws to make the firm's financial statement look good to stockholders or to minimize the firm's taxes this year.

Economists consider both explicit costs and implicit costs. *Explicit costs* are a firm's direct, out-of-pocket payments for inputs to its production process during a given time period, such as a year. These costs include production workers' wages, managers' salaries, and payments for materials. However, firms use inputs that may not have an explicit price. These *implicit costs* include the value of the working time of the firm's owner and the value of other resources used but not purchased in a given period.

economic cost or opportunity cost the value of the best alternative use of a resource

The **economic cost** or **opportunity cost** is the value of the best alternative use of a resource. The economic or opportunity cost includes both explicit and implicit costs. If a firm purchases and uses an input immediately, that input's opportunity cost is the amount the firm pays for it. If the firm uses an input from its inventory, its opportunity cost is not necessarily the price it paid for the input years ago. Rather, the opportunity cost is what it could buy or sell that input for today.

The classic example of an implicit opportunity cost is captured in the phrase "There's no such thing as a free lunch." Suppose that your parents offer to take you to lunch tomorrow. You know that they'll pay for the meal, but you also know that this lunch is not free for you. Your opportunity cost for the lunch is the best alternative use of your time. Presumably, the best alternative use of your time is studying this textbook, but other possible alternatives include what you could earn at a job or the value you place on watching TV. Often such opportunity costs are a substantial portion of total costs. (See **www.myeconlab.com/perloff**, Chapter 7, "Waiting for the Doctor.")

If you start your own firm, you should be very concerned about opportunity costs. Suppose that your explicit cost is $40,000, including the rent for your work space, the cost of materials, and the wage payments to your employees. Because you do not pay yourself a salary—instead, you keep any profit at the end of the year—the explicit cost does not include the value of your time. According to an economist, your firm's full economic cost is the sum of the explicit cost plus the opportunity value of your time. If the highest wage you could have earned working for some other firm is $25,000, your full economic cost is $65,000.

In deciding whether to continue running your firm or to work for someone else, you must consider both explicit and opportunity costs. If your annual revenue is $60,000, after you pay your explicit cost of $40,000, you keep $20,000 at the end of the year. The opportunity cost of your time, $25,000, exceeds $20,000, so you can earn more working for someone else. (What are you giving up to study opportunity costs?)

See Question 1.

APPLICATION

Opportunity Cost of Going to Church

One-fifth of the U.S. population goes to religious services in a typical week, and half attend at least once a month. Presumably people engage in an activity if they view the benefits as outweighing the costs. What are the costs of going to church? The largest one is the opportunity cost of time—the value that one places on engaging in the best alternative activity.

Gruber and Hungerman (2006) developed a clever method to estimate the effects on church attendance from an increase in their opportunity cost of time. In the middle of the twentieth century, most areas of the United States except the west had "blue laws" that forbade shopping (particularly for alcohol or a hair cut) on Sunday, when most churches hold services. These laws were eliminated in most states between the mid-1960s and mid-1980s. The repeal of these laws increased the opportunities of many to work, shop, and engage in additional leisure activities, such as watching a movie at the mall.

Controlling for secular trends and for differences across demographic groups, Gruber and Hungerman found that eliminating a blue law reduced church attendance by Christians by about 5%. It caused a 15% drop in attendance by those who had previously attended services weekly, but had little effect on people who attended more or less frequently. Thus, an increase in opportunity cost has significant effects on church attendance by some but not all people.

Capital Costs

durable good
a product that is usable for years

Determining the opportunity cost of capital, such as land or equipment, requires special considerations. Capital is a **durable good**: a product that is usable for years. Two problems may arise in measuring the cost of capital. The first is how to allocate the initial purchase cost over time. The second is what to do if the value of the capital changes over time.

Allocating Capital Costs over Time. Capital may be rented or purchased. For example, a firm may rent a truck for $200 a month or buy it outright for $18,000.

If the firm rents the truck, the rental payment is the relevant opportunity cost. By using the rental rate, we avoid the two measurement problems. The truck is rented period by period, so the firm does not have to worry about how to allocate the purchase cost of a truck over time. Moreover, the rental rate adjusts if the cost of a new truck changes over time.

Suppose, however, that the firm buys the truck. The firm's bookkeeper may *expense* the cost by recording the full $18,000 when it's made or may *amortize* the cost by spreading the $18,000 over the life of the truck according to an arbitrary rule set by the relevant government authority, such as the Internal Revenue Service (IRS). If the IRS approves of several approaches to amortizing expenses, a bookkeeper or an accountant may use whichever arbitrary rule minimizes the firm's taxes.

See Questions 2 and 3.

An economist amortizes the cost of the truck on the basis of its opportunity cost at each moment of time, which is the amount that the firm could charge others to rent the truck. That is, regardless of whether the firm buys or rents the truck, an economist views the opportunity cost of this capital good as a rent per time period: the amount the firm will receive if it rents its truck to others at the going rental rate.[1]

[1]If trucks cannot be rented, an economist calculates an implicit rental rate for trucks taking account of both explicit and opportunity costs. If the firm could sell the truck for $5,000, the opportunity cost of keeping it is the interest that could be earned on $5,000 (Chapter 16). In addition, the firm incurs direct maintenance costs and the opportunity cost due to *depreciation*: the drop in value from wear and tear.

If the value of an older truck is less than that of a newer one, the rental rate for the truck falls over time.

Actual and Historical Costs. Not only may the rental rate for a piece of capital fall over time as the capital ages, but it may also change because of shifts in supply and demand in the market for capital goods or for other reasons. A piece of capital may be worth much more or much less today than it was when it was purchased.

To maximize its profit, a firm must properly measure the cost of a piece of capital—its current opportunity cost of the capital good—and not what the firm paid for it—its historical cost. Suppose that a firm paid $30,000 for a piece of land that it can resell for only $20,000. Also suppose that it uses the land itself and the current value of the land to the firm is only $19,000. Should the firm use the land or sell it? As any child can tell the firm, there's no point in crying over spilt milk. The firm should ignore how much it paid for the land in making its decision. As the value of the land to the firm, $19,000, is less than the opportunity cost of the land, $20,000, the firm can make more by selling the land.

The firm's current opportunity cost of capital may be less than what it paid if the firm cannot resell the capital. A firm that bought a specialized piece of equipment with no alternative use cannot resell the equipment. Because the equipment has no alternative use, the historical cost of buying that capital is a **sunk cost**: an expenditure that cannot be recovered. Because this equipment has no alternative use, the current or opportunity cost of the capital is zero. In short, when determining the rental value of capital, economists use the opportunity value and ignore the historical price.

sunk cost
an expenditure that cannot be recovered

APPLICATION

Swarthmore College's Cost of Capital

Many nonprofit institutions such as universities and governmental agencies are notorious for ignoring the implicit cost of their capital. When setting tuition and making other plans, Swarthmore College in Pennsylvania estimates its annual cost at $90,000 per student, based on the cost of salaries, academic and general institutional support, food, maintenance and additions to the physical plant, and other annual expenses such as student aid. This cost calculation is a gross underestimate, however, because it ignores the opportunity cost of the campus—the amount the college could earn by renting out its land and buildings. Including that opportunity cost of its land and buildings raises its true economic cost to about $115,000 annually per student.

7.2 Short-Run Costs

To make profit-maximizing decisions, a firm needs to know how its cost varies with output. A firm's cost rises as it increases its output. A firm cannot vary some of its inputs, such as capital, in the short run (Chapter 6). As a result, it is usually more costly for a firm to increase output in the short run than in the long run, when all inputs can be varied. In this section, we look at the cost of increasing output in the short run.

Short-Run Cost Measures

We start by using a numerical example to illustrate the basic cost concepts. We then examine the graphic relationship between these concepts.

fixed cost (F)
a production expense that does not vary with output

variable cost (VC)
a production expense that changes with the quantity of output produced

cost (total cost, C)
the sum of a firm's variable cost and fixed cost: $C = VC + F$

Cost Levels. To produce a given level of output in the short run, a firm incurs costs for both its fixed and variable inputs. A firm's **fixed cost** (F) is its production expense that does not vary with output. The fixed cost includes the cost of inputs that the firm cannot practically adjust in the short run, such as land, a plant, large machines, and other capital goods. The fixed cost for a capital good a firm owns and uses is the opportunity cost of not renting it to someone else. The fixed cost is $48 per day for the firm in Table 7.1.

A firm's **variable cost** (VC) is the production expense that changes with the quantity of output produced. The variable cost is the cost of the variable inputs—the inputs the firm can adjust to alter its output level, such as labor and materials. Table 7.1 shows that the firm's variable cost changes with output. Variable cost goes from $25 a day when 1 unit is produced to $46 a day when 2 units are produced.

A firm's **cost** (or **total cost**, C) is the sum of a firm's variable cost and fixed cost:

$$C = VC + F.$$

The firm's total cost of producing 2 units of output per day is $94 per day, which is the sum of the fixed cost, $48, and the variable cost, $46. Because variable cost changes with the level of output, total cost also varies with the level of output, as the table illustrates.

To decide how much to produce, a firm uses several measures of how its cost varies with the level of output. Table 7.1 shows four such measures that we derive using the fixed cost, the variable cost, and the total cost.

Table 7.1 Variation of Short-Run Cost with Output.

Output, q	Fixed Cost, F	Variable Cost, VC	Total Cost, C	Marginal Cost, MC	Average Fixed Cost, $AFC = F/q$	Average Variable Cost, $AVC = VC/q$	Average Cost, $AC = C/q$
0	48	0	48				
1	48	25	73	25	48	25	73
2	48	46	94	21	24	23	47
3	48	66	114	20	16	22	38
4	48	82	130	16	12	20.5	32.5
5	48	100	148	18	9.6	20	29.6
6	48	120	168	**20**	8	**20**	28
7	48	141	189	21	6.9	20.1	27
8	48	168	216	**27**	6	21	**27**
9	48	198	246	30	5.3	22	27.3
10	48	230	278	32	4.8	23	27.8
11	48	272	320	42	4.4	24.7	29.1
12	48	321	369	49	4.0	26.8	30.8

marginal cost (*MC*) the amount by which a firm's cost changes if the firm produces one more unit of output

Marginal Cost. A firm's **marginal cost** (*MC*) is the amount by which a firm's cost changes if the firm produces one more unit of output. The marginal cost is[2]

$$MC = \frac{\Delta C}{\Delta q},$$

where ΔC is the change in cost when output changes by Δq. Table 7.1 shows that, if the firm increases its output from 2 to 3 units, $\Delta q = 1$, its total cost rises from \$94 to \$114, $\Delta C = \$20$, so its marginal cost is $\$20 = \Delta C/\Delta q$.

Because only variable cost changes with output, we can also define marginal cost as the change in variable cost from a one-unit increase in output:

$$MC = \frac{\Delta VC}{\Delta q}.$$

As the firm increases output from 2 to 3 units, its variable cost increases by $\Delta VC = \$20 = \$66 - \$46$, so its marginal cost is $MC = \Delta VC/\Delta q = \$20$. A firm uses marginal cost in deciding whether it pays to change its output level.

average fixed cost (*AFC*) the fixed cost divided by the units of output produced: $AFC = F/q$

average variable cost (*AVC*) the variable cost divided by the units of output produced: $AVC = VC/q$

average cost (*AC*) the total cost divided by the units of output produced: $AC = C/q$

Average Costs. Firms use three average cost measures. The **average fixed cost** (*AFC*) is the fixed cost divided by the units of output produced: $AFC = F/q$. The average fixed cost falls as output rises because the fixed cost is spread over more units. The average fixed cost falls from \$48 for 1 unit of output to \$4 for 12 units of output in Table 7.1.

The **average variable cost** (*AVC*) is the variable cost divided by the units of output produced: $AVC = VC/q$. Because the variable cost increases with output, the average variable cost may either increase or decrease as output rises. The average variable cost is \$25 at 1 unit, falls until it reaches a minimum of \$20 at 6 units, and then rises. As we show in Chapter 8, a firm uses the average variable cost to determine whether to shut down operations when demand is low.

The **average cost** (*AC*)—or *average total cost*—is the total cost divided by the units of output produced: $AC = C/q$. The average cost is the sum of the average fixed cost and the average variable cost:[3]

$$AC = AFC + AVC.$$

In Table 7.1, as output increases, average cost falls until output is 8 units and then rises. The firm makes a profit if its average cost is below its price, which is the firm's average revenue. See **www.myeconlab.com/perloff**, Chapter 7, "Lowering Transaction Costs for Used Goods at eBay and Abebooks," for a discussion of transaction, fixed, and variable shopping costs for consumers.

See Questions 4–6 and Problems 23 and 24.

Short-Run Cost Curves

We illustrate the relationship between output and the various cost measures using curves in Figure 7.1. Panel a shows the variable cost, fixed cost, and total cost curves that correspond to Table 7.1. The fixed cost, which does not vary with output, is a horizontal line at \$48. The variable cost curve is zero at zero units of output and

[2]If we use calculus, the marginal cost is $MC = dC(q)/dq$, where $C(q)$ is the cost function that shows how cost varies with output. The calculus definition says how cost changes for an infinitesimal change in output. To illustrate the idea, however, we use larger changes in the table.

[3]Because $C = VC + F$, if we divide both sides of the equation by q, we obtain

$$AC = C/q = F/q + VC/q = AFC + AVC.$$

Figure 7.1 Short-Run Cost Curves.

(a) Because the total cost differs from the variable cost by the fixed cost, *F*, of $48, the total cost curve, *C*, is parallel to the variable cost curve, *VC*. (b) The marginal cost curve, *MC*, cuts the average variable cost, *AVC*, and average cost, *AC*, curves at their minimums. The height of the *AC* curve at point *a* equals the slope of the line from the origin to the cost curve at *A*. The height of the *AVC* at *b* equals the slope of the line from the origin to the variable cost curve at *B*. The height of the marginal cost is the slope of either the *C* or *VC* curve at that quantity.

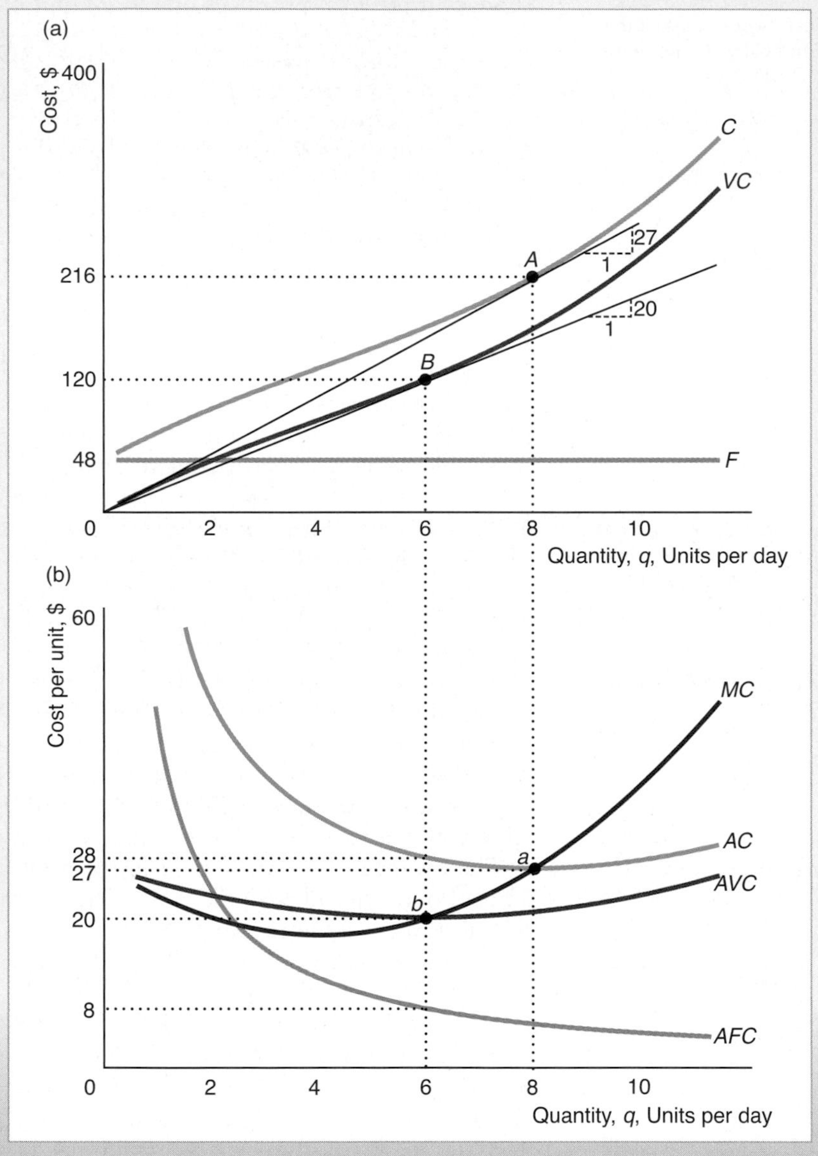

rises with output. The total cost curve, which is the vertical sum of the variable cost curve and the fixed cost line, is $48 higher than the variable cost curve at every output level, so the variable cost and total cost curves are parallel.

Panel b shows the average fixed cost, average variable cost, average cost, and marginal cost curves. The average fixed cost curve falls as output increases. It approaches zero as output gets large because the fixed cost is spread over many units of output. The average cost curve is the vertical sum of the average fixed cost and average variable cost curves. For example, at 6 units of output, the average variable cost is 20 and the average fixed cost is 8, so the average cost is 28.

The relationships between the average and marginal curves to the total curves are similar to those between the total product, marginal product, and average product curves, which we discussed in Chapter 6. The average cost at a particular output level is the slope of a line from the origin to the corresponding point on the cost curve. The slope of that line is the rise—the cost at that output level—divided by the run—the output level—which is the definition of the average cost. In panel a, the slope of the line from the origin to point A is the average cost for 8 units of output. The height of the cost curve at A is 216, so the slope is $216/8 = 27$, which is the height of the average cost curve at the corresponding point a in panel b.

Similarly, the average variable cost is the slope of a line from the origin to a point on the variable cost curve. The slope of the dashed line from the origin to B in panel a is 20—the height of the variable cost curve, 120, divided by the number of units of output, 6—which is the height of the average variable cost at 6 units of output, point b in panel b.

The marginal cost is the slope of either the cost curve or the variable cost curve at a given output level. As the cost and variable cost curves are parallel, they have the same slope at any given output. The difference between cost and variable cost is fixed cost, which does not affect marginal cost.

The dashed line from the origin is tangent to the cost curve at A in panel a. Thus, the slope of the dashed line equals both the average cost and the marginal cost at 8 units of output. This equality occurs at the corresponding point a in panel b, where the marginal cost curve intersects the average cost. (See Appendix 7A for a mathematical proof.)

Where the marginal cost curve is below the average cost, the average cost curve declines with output. Because the average cost of 47 for 2 units is greater than the marginal cost of the third unit, 20, the average cost for 3 units falls to 38. Where the marginal cost is above the average cost, the average cost curve rises with output. At 8 units, the marginal cost equals the average cost, so the average is unchanging, which is the minimum point, a, of the average cost curve.

We can show the same results using the graph. Because the dashed line from the origin is tangent to the variable cost curve at B in panel a, the marginal cost equals the average variable cost at the corresponding point b in panel b. Again, where marginal cost is above average variable cost, the average variable cost curve rises with output; where marginal cost is below average variable cost, the average variable cost curve falls with output. Because the average cost curve is above the average variable cost curve everywhere and the marginal cost curve is rising where it crosses both average curves, the minimum of the average variable cost curve, b, is at a lower output level than the minimum of the average cost curve, a.

See Question 7 and Problems 25 and 26.

Production Functions and the Shape of Cost Curves

The production function determines the shape of a firm's cost curves. The production function shows the amount of inputs needed to produce a given level of output. The firm calculates its cost by multiplying the quantity of each input by its price and summing the costs of the inputs.

If a firm produces output using capital and labor, and its capital is fixed in the short run, the firm's variable cost is its cost of labor. Its labor cost is the wage per hour, w, times the number of hours of labor, L, employed by the firm: $VC = wL$.

In the short run, when the firm's capital is fixed, the only way the firm can increase its output is to use more labor. If the firm increases its labor enough, it reaches the point of *diminishing marginal return to labor*, at which each extra worker increases output by a smaller amount. We can use this information about the relationship between labor and output—the production function—to determine the shape of the variable cost curve and its related curves.

Shape of the Variable Cost Curve. If input prices are constant, the production function determines the shape of the variable cost curve. We illustrate this relationship for the firm in Figure 7.2. The firm faces a constant input price for labor, the wage, of $5 per hour.

The total product of labor curve in Figure 7.2 shows the firm's short-run production function relationship between output and labor when capital is held fixed. For example, it takes 24 hours of labor to produce 6 units of output. Nearly doubling labor to 46 hours causes output to increase by only two-thirds to 10 units of output. As labor increases, the total product of labor curve increases less than in proportion. This flattening of the total product of labor curve at higher levels of labor reflects the diminishing marginal return to labor.

This curve shows both the production relation of output to labor and the variable cost relation of output to cost. Because each hour of work costs the firm $5, we can relabel the horizontal axis in Figure 7.2 to show the firm's variable cost, which is its cost of labor. To produce 6 units of output takes 24 hours of labor, so the firm's variable cost is $120. By using the variable cost labels on the horizontal axis, the total product of labor curve becomes the variable cost curve, where each worker costs the firm $120 per day in wages. The variable cost curve in Figure 7.2 is the same as the one in panel a of Figure 7.1, in which the output and cost axes are reversed. For example, the variable cost of producing 6 units is $120 in both figures.

Diminishing marginal returns in the production function cause the variable cost to rise more than in proportion as output increases. Because the production function determines the shape of the variable cost curve, it also determines the shape of the marginal, average variable, and average cost curves. We now examine the shape

Figure 7.2 Variable Cost and Total Product of Labor.

The firm's short-run variable cost curve and its total product of labor curve have the same shape. The total product of labor curve uses the horizontal axis measuring hours of work. The variable cost curve uses the horizontal axis measuring labor cost, which is the only variable cost.

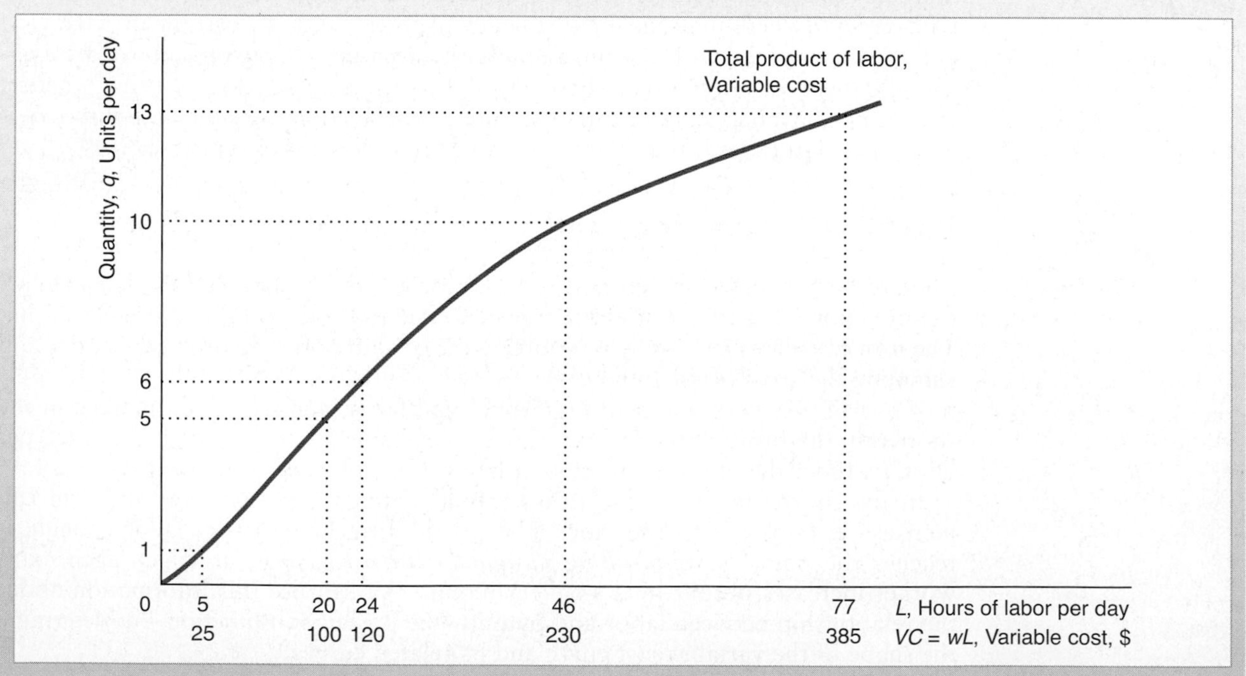

See Question 8 and Problem 27.

of each of these cost curves in detail because in making decisions, firms rely more on these per-unit cost measures than on total variable cost.

Shape of the Marginal Cost Curve. The marginal cost is the change in variable cost as output increases by one unit: $MC = \Delta VC/\Delta q$. In the short run, capital is fixed, so the only way the firm can produce more output is to use extra labor. The extra labor required to produce one more unit of output is $\Delta L/\Delta q$. The extra labor costs the firm w per unit, so the firm's cost rises by $w(\Delta L/\Delta q)$. As a result, the firm's marginal cost is

$$MC = \frac{\Delta VC}{\Delta q} = w\frac{\Delta L}{\Delta q}.$$

The marginal cost equals the wage times the extra labor necessary to produce one more unit of output. To increase output by one unit from 5 to 6 units takes 4 extra workers in Figure 7.2. If the wage is $5 per hour, the marginal cost is $20.

How do we know how much extra labor we need to produce one more unit of output? That information comes from the production function. The marginal product of labor—the amount of extra output produced by another unit of labor, holding other inputs fixed—is $MP_L = \Delta q/\Delta L$. Thus, the extra labor we need to produce one more unit of output, $\Delta L/\Delta q$, is $1/MP_L$, so the firm's marginal cost is

$$MC = \frac{w}{MP_L}. \tag{7.1}$$

Equation 7.1 says that the marginal cost equals the wage divided by the marginal product of labor. If the firm is producing 5 units of output, it takes 4 extra hours of labor to produce 1 more unit of output in Figure 7.2, so the marginal product of an hour of labor is $\frac{1}{4}$. Given a wage of $5 an hour, the marginal cost of the sixth unit is $5 divided by $\frac{1}{4}$ or $20, as panel b of Figure 7.1 shows.

Equation 7.1 shows that the marginal cost moves in the direction opposite that of the marginal product of labor. At low levels of labor, the marginal product of labor commonly rises with additional labor because extra workers help the original workers and they can collectively make better use of the firm's equipment (Chapter 6). As the marginal product of labor rises, the marginal cost falls.

Eventually, however, as the number of workers increases, workers must share the fixed amount of equipment and may get in each other's way, so the marginal cost curve slopes upward because of diminishing marginal returns to labor. Thus, the marginal cost first falls and then rises, as panel b of Figure 7.1 illustrates.

Shape of the Average Cost Curves. Diminishing marginal returns to labor, by determining the shape of the variable cost curve, also determine the shape of the average variable cost curve. The average variable cost is the variable cost divided by output: $AVC = VC/q$. For the firm we've been examining, whose only variable input is labor, variable cost is wL, so average variable cost is

$$AVC = \frac{VC}{q} = \frac{wL}{q}.$$

Because the average product of labor is q/L, average variable cost is the wage divided by the average product of labor:

$$AVC = \frac{w}{AP_L}. \tag{7.2}$$

In Figure 7.2, at 6 units of output, the average product of labor is $\frac{1}{4}$ (= q/L = 6/24), so the average variable cost is \$20, which is the wage, \$5, divided by the average product of labor, $\frac{1}{4}$.

With a constant wage, the average variable cost moves in the opposite direction of the average product of labor in Equation 7.2. As we discussed in Chapter 6, the average product of labor tends to rise and then fall, so the average cost tends to fall and then rise, as in panel b of Figure 7.1.

The average cost curve is the vertical sum of the average variable cost curve and the average fixed cost curve, as in panel b. If the average variable cost curve is U-shaped, adding the strictly falling average fixed cost makes the average cost fall more steeply than the average variable cost curve at low output levels. At high output levels, the average cost and average variable cost curves differ by ever smaller amounts, as the average fixed cost, F/q, approaches zero. Thus, the average cost curve is also U-shaped.

See Problems 28 and 30.

APPLICATION

Short-Run Cost Curves for a Furniture Manufacturer

The short-run average cost curve for a U.S. furniture manufacturer is U-shaped, even though its average variable cost is strictly upward sloping. The graph (based on the estimates of Hsieh, 1995) shows the firm's various short-run cost curves, where the firm's capital is fixed at $\bar{K} = 100$. Appendix 7B derives the firm's short-run cost curves mathematically.

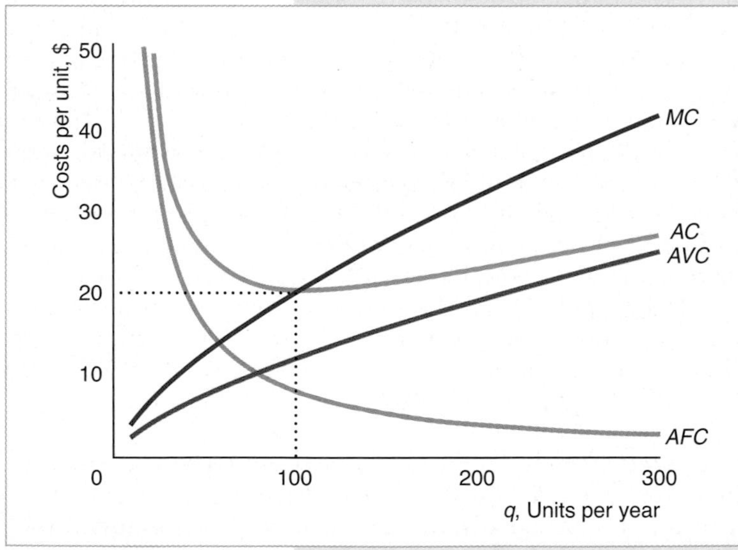

The firm's average fixed cost (AFC) falls as output increases. The firm's average variable cost curve is strictly increasing. The average cost (AC) curve is the vertical sum of the average variable cost (AVC) and average fixed cost curves. Because the average fixed cost curve falls with output and the average variable cost curve rises with output, the average cost curve is U-shaped. The firm's marginal cost (MC) lies above the rising average variable cost curve for all positive quantities of output and cuts the average cost curve at its minimum.

Effects of Taxes on Costs

Taxes applied to a firm shift some or all of the marginal and average cost curves. For example, suppose that the government collects a specific tax of \$10 per unit of output from the firm. This tax, which varies with output, affects the firm's variable cost but not its fixed cost. As a result, it affects the firm's average cost, average variable cost, and marginal cost curves but not its average fixed cost curve.

At every quantity, the average variable cost and the average cost rise by the full amount of the tax. The second column of Table 7.2 (based on Table 7.1) shows the firm's average variable cost before the tax, AVC^b. For example, if it sells 6 units of output, its average variable cost is \$20. After the tax, the firm must pay the government \$10 per unit, so the firm's after-tax average variable cost rises to \$30. More generally, the firm's after-tax average variable cost, AVC^a, is its average variable cost of production—the before-tax average variable cost—plus the tax per unit, \$10: $AVC^a = AVC^b + \$10$.

The average cost equals the average variable cost plus the average fixed cost. Because the tax increases average variable cost by \$10 and does not affect the average fixed cost, the tax increases average cost by \$10.

The tax also increases the firm's marginal cost. Suppose that the firm wants to increase output from 7 to 8 units. The firm's actual cost of producing the third unit—its before-tax marginal cost, MC^b—is \$27. To produce an extra unit of output, the cost to the firm is the marginal cost of producing the extra unit plus \$10, so its after-tax marginal cost is $MC^a = MC^b + \$10$. In particular, its after-tax marginal cost of producing the eighth unit is \$37.

A specific tax shifts the marginal cost and the average cost curves upward in Figure 7.3 by the amount of the tax, \$10 per unit. The after-tax marginal cost intersects the after-tax average cost at its minimum. Because both the marginal and average cost curves shift upward by exactly the same amount, the after-tax average cost curve reaches its minimum at the same level of output, 8 units, as the before-tax average cost, as both panel a and Table 7.2 show. At 8 units, the minimum of the before-tax average cost curve is \$27 and that of the after-tax average cost curve is \$37. So even though a specific tax increases a firm's average cost, it does not affect the output at which average cost is minimized.

Similarly, we can analyze the effect of a franchise tax on costs. A *franchise tax*—also called a *business license fee*—is a lump sum that a firm pays for the right to operate a business. An \$800-per-year tax is levied "for the privilege of doing business in California." A three-year license to sell hot dogs in front of New York City's Metropolitan Museum of Art costs \$978,000. These taxes do not vary with output, so they affect firms' fixed costs only—not their variable costs.

Table 7.2 Effect of a Specific Tax of \$10 per Unit on Short-Run Costs.

Q	AVC^b	$AVC^a = AVC^b + \$10$	$AC^b = C/q$	$AC^a = C/q + \$10$	MC^b	$MC^a = MC^b + \$10$
1	25	35	73	83	25	35
2	23	33	47	57	21	31
3	22	32	38	48	20	30
4	20.5	30.5	32.5	42.5	16	26
5	20	30	29.6	39.6	18	28
6	20	30	28	38	20	30
7	20.1	30.1	27	37	21	31
8	21	31	27	37	27	37
9	22	32	27.3	37.3	30	40
10	23	33	27.8	37.8	32	42
11	24.7	34.7	29.1	39.1	42	52
12	26.8	36.8	30.8	40.8	49	59

Figure 7.3 Effect of a Specific Tax on Cost Curves.

A specific tax of \$10 per unit shifts both the marginal cost and average cost curves upward by \$10. Because of the parallel upward shift of the average cost curve, the minimum of both the before-tax average cost curve, AC^b, and the after-tax average cost curve, AC^a, occurs at the same output, 8 units.

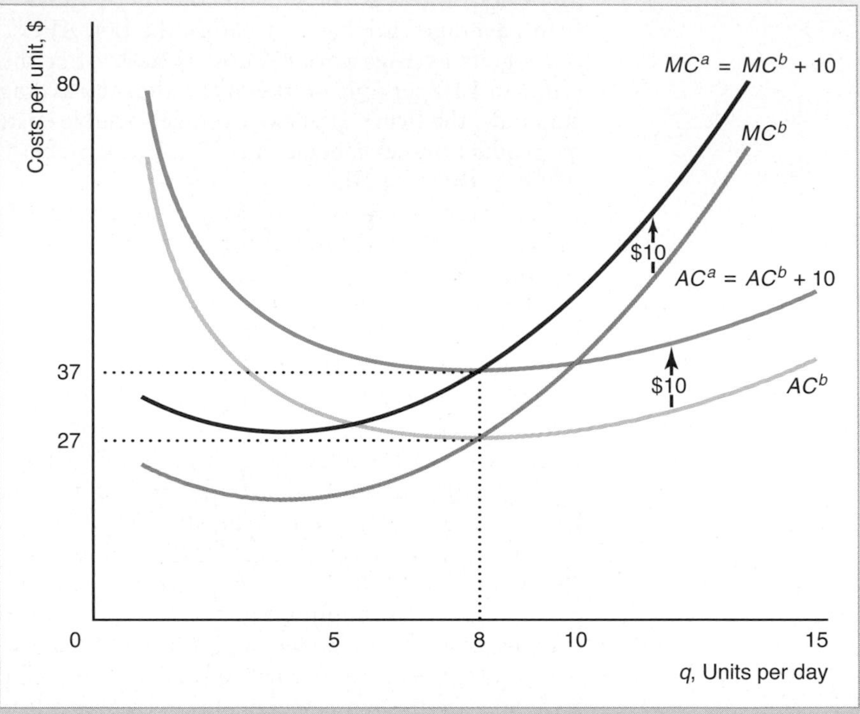

Solved Problem 7.1

What is the effect of a lump-sum franchise tax $\mathcal{L}$ on the quantity at which a firm's after-tax average cost curve reaches its minimum? (Assume that the firm's before-tax average cost curve is U-shaped.)

Answer

1. *Determine the average tax per unit of output.* Because the franchise tax is a lump-sum payment that does not vary with output, the more the firm produces, the less tax it pays per unit. The tax per unit is $\mathcal{L}/q$. If the firm sells only 1 unit, its cost is $\mathcal{L}$; however, if it sells 100 units, its tax payment per unit is only $\mathcal{L}/100$.
2. *Show how the tax per unit affects the average cost.* The firm's after-tax average cost, AC^a, is the sum of its before-tax average cost, AC^b, and its average tax payment per unit, $\mathcal{L}/q$. Because the average tax payment per unit falls with output, the gap between the after-tax average cost curve and the before-tax average cost curve also falls with output on the graph.
3. *Determine the effect of the tax on the marginal cost curve.* Because the franchise tax does not vary with output, it does not affect the marginal cost curve.
4. *Compare the minimum points of the two average cost curves.* The marginal cost curve crosses from below both average cost curves at their minimum points. Because the after-tax average cost lies above the before-tax average cost curve, the quantity at which the after-tax average cost curve reaches its minimum, q_a, is larger than the quantity, q_b, at which the before-tax average cost curve achieves a minimum.

See Question 9.

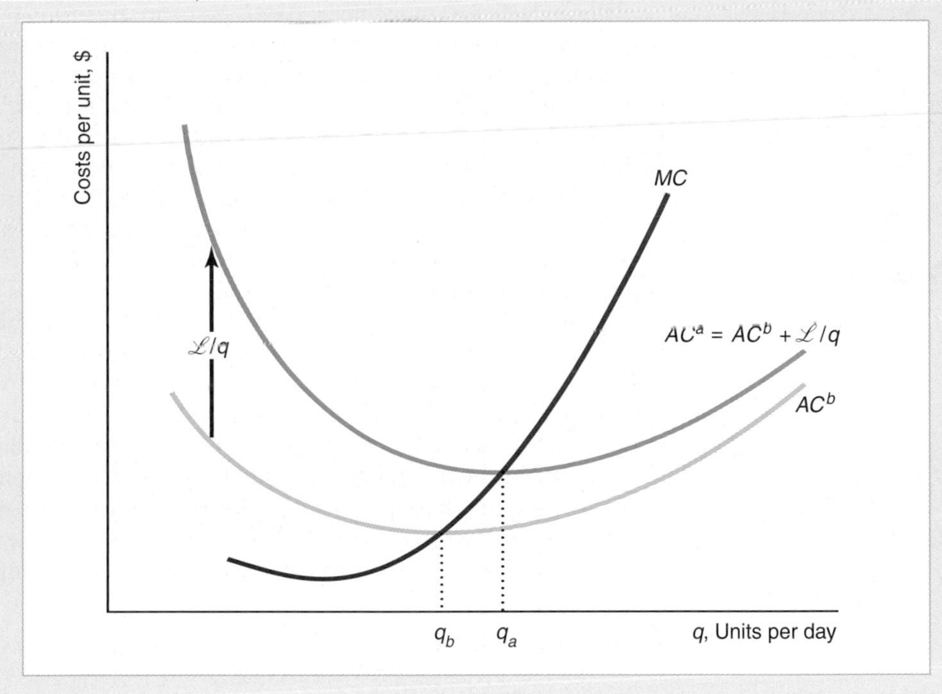

Short-Run Cost Summary

We discussed three cost-level curves—total cost, fixed cost, and variable cost—and four cost-per-unit curves—average cost, average fixed cost, average variable cost, and marginal cost. Understanding the shapes of these curves and the relationships between them is crucial to understanding the analysis of firm behavior in the rest of this book. Fortunately, we can derive most of what we need to know about the shapes and the relationships between the curves using four basic concepts:

- In the short run, the cost associated with inputs that cannot be adjusted is fixed, while the cost from inputs that can be adjusted is variable.
- Given that input prices are constant, the shapes of the variable cost and cost curves are determined by the production function.
- Where there are diminishing marginal returns to a variable input, the variable cost and cost curves become relatively steep as output increases, so the average cost, average variable cost, and marginal cost curves rise with output.
- Because of the relationship between marginals and averages, both the average cost and average variable cost curves fall when marginal cost is below them and rise when marginal cost is above them, so the marginal cost cuts both these average cost curves at their minimum points.

7.3 Long-Run Costs

In the long run, the firm adjusts all its inputs so that its cost of production is as low as possible. The firm can change its plant size, design and build new machines, and otherwise adjust inputs that were fixed in the short run.

Although firms may incur fixed costs in the long run, these fixed costs are *avoidable* (rather than *sunk*, as in the short run). The rent of F per month that a restaurant pays is a fixed cost because it does not vary with the number of meals (output) served. In the short run, this fixed cost is sunk: The firm must pay F even if the restaurant does not operate. In the long run, this fixed cost is avoidable: The firm does not have to pay this rent if it shuts down. The long run is determined by the length of the rental contract during which time the firm is obligated to pay rent.

In our examples throughout this chapter, we assume that all inputs can be varied in the long run so that there are no long-run fixed costs ($F = 0$). As a result, the long-run total cost equals the long-run variable cost: $C = VC$. Thus, our firm is concerned about only three cost concepts in the long run—total cost, average cost, and marginal cost—instead of the seven cost concepts that it considers in the short run.

To produce a given quantity of output at minimum cost, our firm uses information about the production function and the price of labor and capital. The firm chooses how much labor and capital to use in the long run, whereas the firm chooses only how much labor to use in the short run when capital is fixed. As a consequence, the firm's long-run cost is lower than its short-run cost of production if it has to use the "wrong" level of capital in the short run. In this section, we show how a firm picks the cost-minimizing combinations of inputs in the long run.

Input Choice

A firm can produce a given level of output using many different *technologically efficient* combinations of inputs, as summarized by an isoquant (Chapter 6). From among the technologically efficient combinations of inputs, a firm wants to choose the particular bundle with the lowest cost of production, which is the *economically efficient* combination of inputs. To do so, the firm combines information about technology from the isoquant with information about the cost of labor and capital.

We now show how information about cost can be summarized in an *isocost line*. Then we show how a firm can combine the information in an isoquant and isocost lines to pick the economically efficient combination of inputs.

Isocost Line. The cost of producing a given level of output depends on the price of labor and capital. The firm hires L hours of labor services at a wage of w per hour, so its labor cost is wL. The firm rents K hours of machine services at a rental rate of r per hour, so its capital cost is rK. (If the firm owns the capital, r is the implicit rental rate.) The firm's total cost is the sum of its labor and capital costs:

$$C = wL + rK. \qquad (7.3)$$

The firm can hire as much labor and capital as it wants at these constant input prices.

The firm can use many combinations of labor and capital that cost the same amount. Suppose that the wage rate, w, is \$5 an hour and the rental rate of capital, r, is \$10. Five of the many combinations of labor and capital that the firm can use that cost \$100 are listed in Table 7.3. These combinations of labor and capital are plotted on an **isocost line**, which is all the combinations of inputs that require the same (*iso*-) total expenditure (*cost*). Figure 7.4 shows three isocost lines. The \$100 isocost line represents all the combinations of labor and capital that the firm can buy for \$100, including the combinations *a* through *e* in Table 7.3.

isocost line
all the combinations of inputs that require the same (*iso*-) total expenditure (*cost*)

Along an isocost line, cost is fixed at a particular level, $\bar{C}$, so by setting cost at $\bar{C}$ in Equation 7.3, we can write the equation for the $\bar{C}$ isocost line as

$$\bar{C} = wL + rK.$$

Table 7.3 Bundles of Labor and Capital That Cost the Firm $100.

Bundle	Labor, L	Capital, K	Labor Cost, $wL = \$5L$	Capital Cost, $rK = \$10K$	Total Cost, $wL + rK$
a	20	0	$100	$0	$100
b	14	3	$70	$30	$100
c	10	5	$50	$50	$100
d	6	7	$30	$70	$100
e	0	10	$0	$100	$100

Using algebra, we can rewrite this equation to show how much capital the firm can buy if it spends a total of $\bar{C}$ and purchases L units of labor:

$$K = \frac{\bar{C}}{r} - \frac{w}{r}L. \tag{7.4}$$

By substituting $\bar{C} = \$100$, $w = \$5$, and $r = \$10$ in Equation 7.4, we find that the $100 isocost line is $K = 10 - \frac{1}{2}L$. We can use Equation 7.4 to derive three properties of isocost lines.

First, where the isocost lines hit the capital and labor axes depends on the firm's cost, $\bar{C}$, and on the input prices. The $\bar{C}$ isocost line intersects the capital axis where

Figure 7.4 A Family of Isocost Lines.

An isocost line shows all the combinations of labor and capital that cost the firm the same amount. The greater the total cost, the farther from the origin the isocost lies. All the isocosts have the same slope, $-w/r = -\frac{1}{2}$. The slope shows the rate at which the firm can substitute capital for labor holding total cost constant: For each extra unit of capital it uses, the firm must use two fewer units of labor to hold its cost constant.

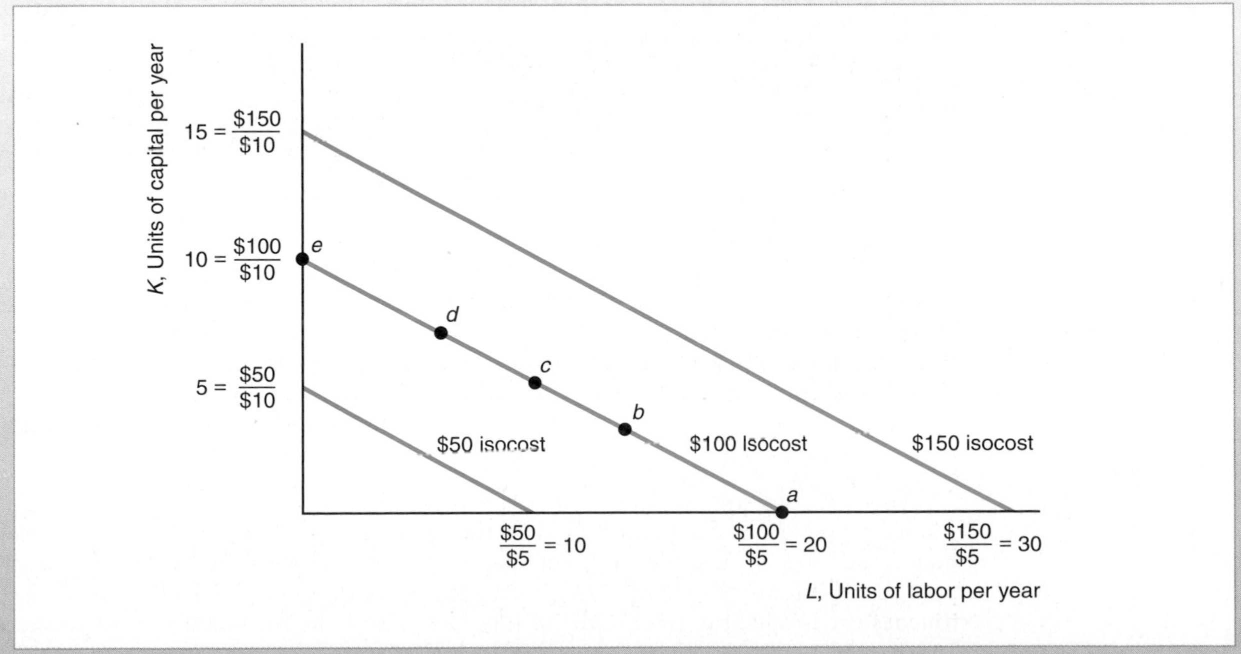

the firm is using only capital. Setting $L = 0$ in Equation 7.4, we find that the firm buys $K = \bar{C}/r$ units of capital. In the figure, the \$100 isocost line intersects the capital axis at \$100/\$10 = 10 units of capital. Similarly, the intersection of the isocost line with the labor axis is at $\bar{C}/w$, which is the amount of labor the firm hires if it uses only labor. In the figure, the intersection of the \$100 isocost line with the labor axis occurs at $L = 20$, where $K = 10 - \frac{1}{2} \times 20 = 0$.

Second, isocosts that are farther from the origin have higher costs than those that are closer to the origin. Because the isocost lines intersect the capital axis at $\bar{C}/r$ and the labor axis at $\bar{C}/w$, an increase in the cost shifts these intersections with the axes proportionately outward. The \$50 isocost line hits the capital axis at 5 and the labor axis at 10, whereas the \$100 isocost line intersects at 10 and 20.

Third, the slope of each isocost line is the same. From Equation 7.4, if the firm increases labor by ΔL, it must decrease capital by

$$\Delta K = -\frac{w}{r}\Delta L.$$

Dividing both sides of this expression by ΔL, we find that the slope of an isocost line, $\Delta K/\Delta L$, is $-w/r$. Thus, the slope of the isocost line depends on the relative prices of the inputs. The slope of the isocost lines in the figure is $-w/r = -\$5/\$10 = -\frac{1}{2}$. If the firm uses two more units of labor, $\Delta L = 2$, it must reduce capital by one unit, $\Delta K = -\frac{1}{2}\Delta L = -1$, to keep its total cost constant. Because all isocost lines are based on the same relative prices, they all have the same slope, so they are parallel.

The isocost line plays a similar role in the firm's decision making as the budget line does in consumer decision making. Both an isocost line and a budget line are straight lines whose slopes depend on relative prices. There is an important difference between them, however. The consumer has a single budget line determined by the consumer's income. The firm faces many isocost lines, each of which corresponds to a different level of expenditures the firm might make. A firm may incur a relatively low cost by producing relatively little output with few inputs, or it may incur a relatively high cost by producing a relatively large quantity.

Combining Cost and Production Information. By combining the information about costs contained in the isocost lines with information about efficient production summarized by an isoquant, a firm chooses the lowest-cost way to produce a given level of output. We examine how our furniture manufacturer picks the combination of labor and capital that minimizes its cost of producing 100 units of output. Figure 7.5 shows the isoquant for 100 units of output (based on Hsieh, 1995) and the isocost lines where the rental rate of a unit of capital is \$8 per hour and the wage rate is \$24 per hour.

The firm can choose any of three equivalent approaches to minimize its cost:

- **Lowest-isocost rule.** Pick the bundle of inputs where the lowest isocost line touches the isoquant.
- **Tangency rule.** Pick the bundle of inputs where the isoquant is tangent to the isocost line.
- **Last-dollar rule.** Pick the bundle of inputs where the last dollar spent on one input gives as much extra output as the last dollar spent on any other input.

Using the *lowest-isocost rule*, the firm minimizes its cost by using the combination of inputs on the isoquant that is on the lowest isocost line that touches the isoquant. The lowest possible isoquant that will allow the furniture manufacturer to produce 100 units of output is tangent to the \$2,000 isocost line. This isocost line touches the isoquant at the bundle of inputs x, where the firm uses $L = 50$ workers and $K = 100$ units of capital.

Figure 7.5 Cost Minimization.

The furniture manufacturer minimizes its cost of producing 100 units of output by producing at x ($L = 50$ and $K = 100$). This cost-minimizing combination of inputs is determined by the tangency between the $q = 100$ isoquant and the lowest isocost line, $2,000, that touches that isoquant. At x, the isocost is tangent to the isoquant, so the slope of the isocost, $-w/r = -3$, equals the slope of the isoquant, which is the negative of the marginal rate of technical substitution. That is, the rate at which the firm can trade capital for labor in the input markets equals the rate at which it can substitute capital for labor in the production process.

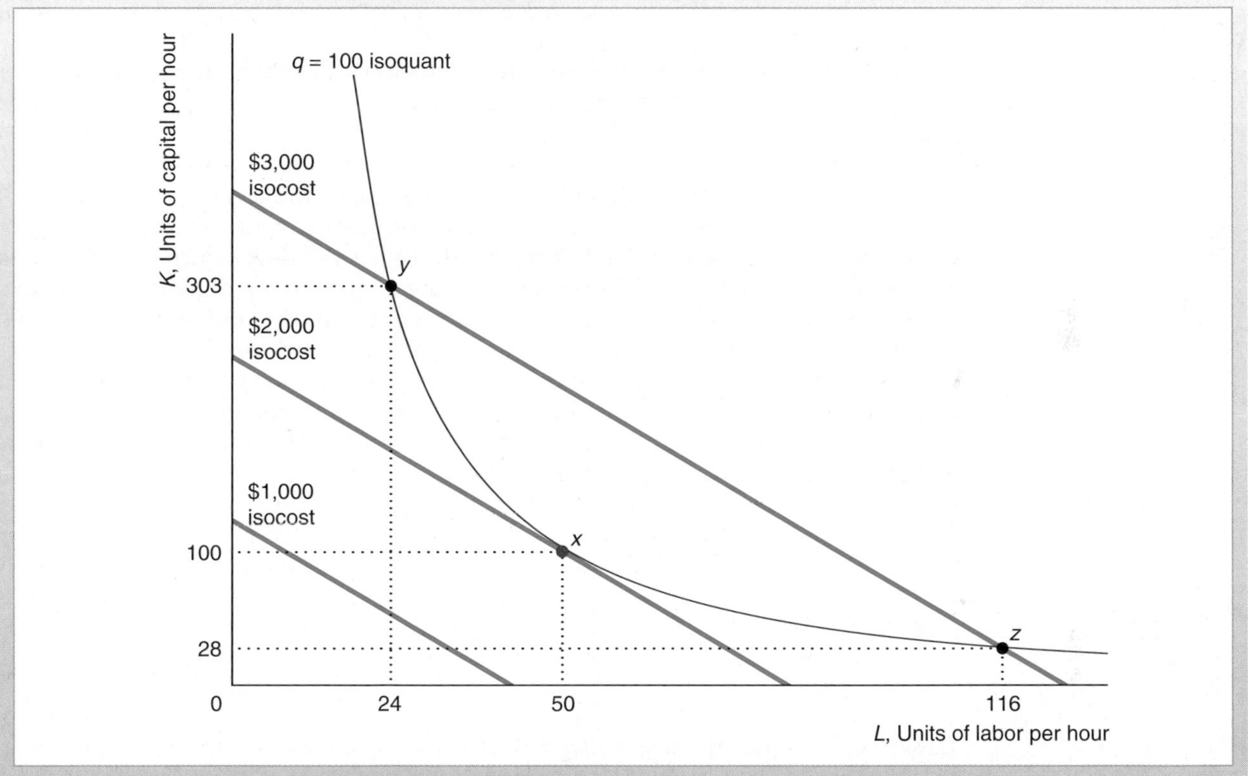

How do we know that x is the least costly way to produce 100 units of output? We need to demonstrate that other practical combinations of input produce less than 100 units or produce 100 units at greater cost.

If the firm spent less than $2,000, it could not produce 100 units of output. Each combination of inputs on the $1,000 isocost line lies below the isoquant, so the firm cannot produce 100 units of output for $1,000.

The firm can produce 100 units of output using other combinations of inputs beside x; however, using these other bundles of inputs is more expensive. For example, the firm can produce 100 units of output using the combinations y ($L = 24$, $K = 303$) or z ($L = 116$, $K = 28$). Both these combinations, however, cost the firm $3,000.

If an isocost line crosses the isoquant twice, as the $3,000 isocost line does, there must be another lower isocost line that also touches the isoquant. The lowest possible isocost line that touches the isoquant, the $2,000 isocost line, is tangent to the isoquant at a single bundle, x. Thus, the firm may use the *tangency rule*: The firm chooses the input bundle where the relevant isoquant is tangent to an isocost line to produce a given level of output at the lowest cost.

We can interpret this tangency or cost minimization condition in two ways. At the point of tangency, the slope of the isoquant equals the slope of the isocost. As we showed in Chapter 6, the slope of the isoquant is the marginal rate of technical substitution (*MRTS*). The slope of the isocost is the negative of the ratio of the wage to the cost of capital, $-w/r$. Thus, to minimize its cost of producing a given level of output, a firm chooses its inputs so that the marginal rate of technical substitution equals the negative of the relative input prices:

$$MRTS = -\frac{w}{r}. \tag{7.5}$$

The firm picks inputs so that the rate at which it can substitute capital for labor in the production process, the *MRTS*, exactly equals the rate at which it can trade capital for labor in input markets, $-w/r$.

The furniture manufacturer's marginal rate of technical substitution is $-1.5K/L$. At $K = 100$ and $L = 50$, its *MRTS* is -3, which equals the negative of the ratio of the input prices it faces, $-w/r = -24/8 = -3$. In contrast, at y, the isocost cuts the isoquant so the slopes are not equal. At y, the *MRTS* is -18.9375, which is greater than the ratio of the input price, 3. Because the slopes are not equal at y, the firm can produce the same output at lower cost. As the figure shows, the cost of producing at y is \$3,000, whereas the cost of producing at x is only \$2,000.

We can interpret the condition in Equation 7.5 in another way. We showed in Chapter 6 that the marginal rate of technical substitution equals the negative of the ratio of the marginal product of labor to that of capital: $MRTS = -MP_L/MP_K$. Thus, the cost-minimizing condition in Equation 7.5 (taking the absolute value of both sides) is

$$\frac{MP_L}{MP_K} = \frac{w}{r}. \tag{7.6}$$

This expression may be rewritten as

$$\frac{MP_L}{w} = \frac{MP_K}{r}. \tag{7.7}$$

Equation 7.7 states the *last-dollar rule*: Cost is minimized if inputs are chosen so that the last dollar spent on labor adds as much extra output as the last dollar spent on capital.

The furniture firm's marginal product of labor is $MP_L = 0.6q/L$, and its marginal product of capital is $MP_K = 0.4q/K$.[4] At Bundle x, the furniture firm's marginal product of labor is 1.2 ($= 0.6 \times 100/50$) and its marginal product of capital is 0.4. The last dollar spent on labor gets the firm

$$\frac{MP_L}{w} = \frac{1.2}{24} = 0.05$$

more output. The last dollar spent on capital also gets the firm

$$\frac{MP_K}{r} = \frac{0.4}{8} = 0.05$$

extra output. Thus, spending one more dollar on labor at x gets the firm as much extra output as spending the same amount on capital. Equation 7.6 holds, so the firm is minimizing its cost of producing 100 units of output.

---

[4]The furniture manufacturer's production function, $q = 1.52L^{0.6}K^{0.4}$, is a Cobb-Douglas production function. The marginal product formula for Cobb-Douglas production functions is derived in Appendix 6B.

If instead the firm produced at y, where it is using more capital and less labor, its MP_L is 2.5 (= $0.6 \times 100/24$) and the MP_K is approximately 0.13 ($\approx 0.4 \times 100/303$). As a result, the last dollar spent on labor gets $MP_L/w \approx 0.1$ more unit of output, whereas the last dollar spent on capital gets only a fourth as much extra output, $MP_K/r \approx 0.017$. At y, if the firm shifts one dollar from capital to labor, output falls by 0.017 because there is less capital but also increases by 0.1 because there is more labor for a net gain of 0.083 more output at the same cost. The firm should shift even more resources from capital to labor—which increases the marginal product of capital and decreases the marginal product of labor—until Equation 7.6 holds with equality at x.

To summarize, we demonstrated that there are three equivalent rules that the firm can use to pick the lowest-cost combination of inputs to produce a given level of output when isoquants are smooth: the lowest-isocost rule, the tangency rule (Equations 7.5 and 7.6), and the last-dollar rule (Equation 7.7). If the isoquant is not smooth, the lowest-cost method of production cannot be determined by using the tangency rule or the last-dollar rule. The lowest-isocost rule always works—even when isoquants are not smooth—as **www.myeconlab.com/perloff**, Chapter 7, "Rice Milling on Java," illustrates.

Factor Price Changes. Once the furniture manufacturer determines the lowest-cost combination of inputs to produce a given level of output, it uses that method as long as the input prices remain constant. How should the firm change its behavior if the cost of one of the factors changes? Suppose that the wage falls from \$24 to \$8 but the rental rate of capital stays constant at \$8.

The firm minimizes its new cost by substituting away from the now relatively more expensive input, capital, toward the now relatively less expensive input, labor. The change in the wage does not affect technological efficiency, so it does not affect the isoquant in Figure 7.6. Because of the wage decrease, the new isocost lines have a flatter slope, $-w/r = -8/8 = -1$, than the original isocost lines, $-w/r = -24/8 = -3$.

Figure 7.6 Change in Factor Price.

Originally, the wage was \$24 and the rental rate of capital was \$8, so the lowest isocost line (\$2,000) was tangent to the $q = 100$ isoquant at $x(L = 50, K = 100)$. When the wage fell to \$8, the isocost lines became flatter: Labor became relatively less expensive than capital. The slope of the isocost lines falls from $-w/r = -24/8 = -3$ to $-8/8 = -1$. The new lowest isocost line (\$1,032) is tangent at v ($L = 77$, $K = 52$). Thus, when the wage falls, the firm uses more labor and less capital to produce a given level of output, and the cost of production falls from \$2,000 to \$1,032.

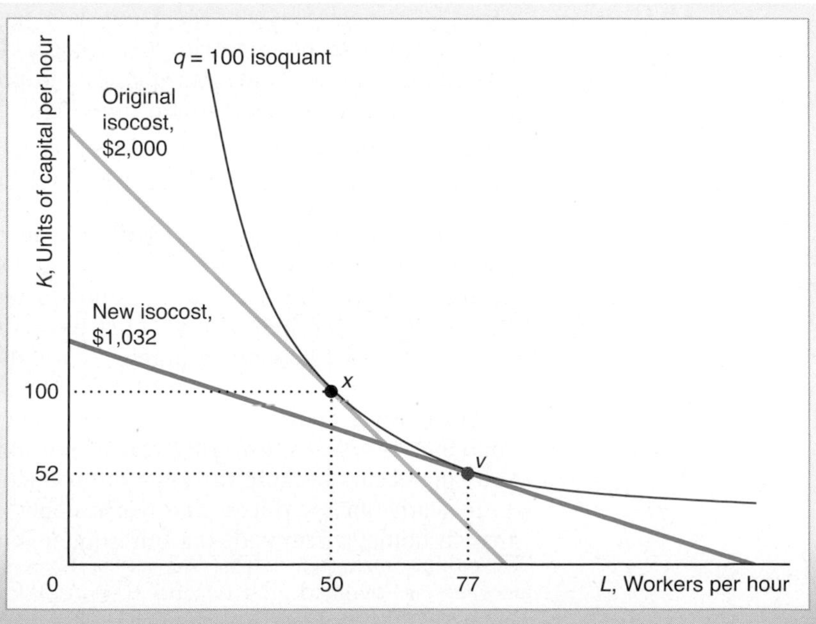

The relatively steep original isocost line is tangent to the 100-unit isoquant at Bundle x ($L = 50$, $K = 100$). The new, flatter isocost line is tangent to the isoquant at Bundle v ($L = 77$, $K = 52$). Thus, the firm uses more labor and less capital as labor becomes relatively less expensive. Moreover, the firm's cost of producing 100 units falls from \$2,000 to \$1,032 because of the fall in the wage. This example illustrates that a change in the relative prices of inputs affects the mix of inputs that a firm uses.

See Questions 10–15 and Problems 31–33.

APPLICATION

The Internet and Outsourcing

To start a children's pajama business, Philip Chigos and Mary Domenico are designing, choosing fabrics, and searching for low-cost workers in China or Mexico from an office in the basement below their San Francisco apartment. Increasingly, such mom-and-pop operations are sending their clothing, jewelry, and programming work to Sri Lanka, China, India, Mexico, and Eastern Europe.

A firm *outsources* if it retains others to provide services that the firm had previously performed itself. Firms have always used outsourcing. For example, a restaurant buys goods such as butter and flour or finished products such as bread and pies from other firms or contracts with another firm to provide cleaning services. A firm outsources if others can produce a good or service for less than the firm's own cost. Though all domestic firms face the same factor prices, some firms can produce at lower cost than others because they specialize in a good or service.

Newspapers and politicians have been wringing their hands about outsourcing to other countries. The different factor prices that foreign firms face may allow them to produce at lower cost.

In the past, outsourcing to other countries was not practical because of the high transaction costs of finding partners abroad and communicating with them, and the high transportation costs of quickly sending goods vast distances. The Internet and other communication technologies have made outsourcing abroad much easier. Without the Internet and modern telecommunications, small U.S. firms would not be able to find foreign suppliers in countries they will never visit. Using e-mail, fax, and phone, they can inexpensively communicate with foreign factories, transmit images and design specifications, and track inventory.

Mr. Chigos used the Internet to find potential Chinese and Mexican manufacturers for the pajamas that Ms. Domenico designed. Hiring foreign workers is crucial to their nascent enterprise. Mr. Chigos claims, "We'd love it to say 'Made in the U.S.A.' and use American textiles and production." However, if they did so, their cost would rise four to ten times, and "We didn't want to sell our pajamas for \$120." One result of easy access to cheap manufacturing, he said, is that more American entrepreneurs may be able to turn an idea into a product.

The would-be pajama tycoons plan to outsource to U.S. firms as well. They will use a Richmond, California, freight management company to receive the shipments, check the merchandise's quality, and ship it to customers. They will market their clothes on the Internet and through boutique retailers. Indeed, their business will be entirely virtual: They have no manufacturing plant, storefront, or warehouse. As Mr. Chigos notes, "With the technology available today, we'll never touch the product."

Thus, lower communication and transportation costs have made foreign outsourcing feasible by lowering transaction costs. Ultimately, however, such outsourcing occurs because the costs of production are lower abroad.

If relative factor prices (and hence slopes of isocost lines) are different abroad than at home, a firm with smooth isoquants uses a different factor mix when producing abroad, as Figure 7.6 illustrates. However, the firm does not necessarily use a different factor mix. Solved Problem 7.2 shows that if all foreign factor prices are proportionally lower than domestic prices, the firm will use the same technology as at home. Solved Problem 7.3 shows that small differences in factor prices may not induce the firm to change technologies or factor mixes if isoquants have kinks. Three problems at the end of the chapter ask you to show what happens in the typical case with smooth isoquants.

Solved Problem 7.2

If it manufactures at home, a firm faces input prices for labor and capital of $\hat{w}$ and $\hat{r}$ and produces $\hat{q}$ units of output using $\hat{L}$ units of labor and $\hat{K}$ units of capital. Abroad, the wage and cost of capital are half as much as at home. If the firm manufactures abroad, will it change the amount of labor and capital it uses to produce $\hat{q}$? What happens to its cost of producing $\hat{q}$?

Answer

1. *Determine whether the change in factor prices affects the slopes of the isoquant or the isocost lines.* The change in input prices does not affect the isoquant, which depends only on technology (the production function). Moreover, cutting the input prices in half does not affect the slope of the isocost lines. The original slope was $-\hat{w}/\hat{r}$, and the new slope is $-(\hat{w}/2)/(\hat{r}/2) = -\hat{w}/\hat{r}$.
2. *Using a rule for cost minimization, determine whether the firm changes its input mix.* A firm minimizes its cost by producing where its isoquant is tangent to the lowest possible isocost line. That is, the firm produces where the slope of its isoquant, *MRTS*, equals the slope of its isocost line, $-w/r$. Because the slopes of the isoquant and the isocost lines are unchanged after input prices are cut in half, the firm continues to produce $\hat{q}$ using the same amount of labor, $\hat{L}$, and capital, $\hat{K}$, as originally.
3. *Calculate the original cost and the new cost and compare them.* The firm's original cost of producing $\hat{q}$ units of output was $\hat{w}\hat{L} + \hat{r}\hat{K} = \hat{C}$. Its new cost of producing the same amount of output is $(\hat{w}/2)\hat{L} + (\hat{r}/2)\hat{K} = \hat{C}/2$. Thus, its cost of producing $\hat{q}$ falls by half when the input prices are halved. The isocost lines have the same slope as before, but the cost associated with each isocost line is halved.

Solved Problem 7.3

A U.S. semiconductor manufacturing company plans to move its production abroad (according to the Semiconductor Industry Association, worldwide semiconductor billings from the Americas dropped to 17% in 2007 from 33% in 1998). Its technologies are described in the application "A Semiconductor Integrated Circuit Isoquant" (Chapter 6). The firm currently produces using a wafer-handling stepper. The cost of equipment is the same everywhere; however, the wage is lower abroad. Will the firm necessarily use a different technology when it produces abroad? Why might it use a different technology?

Answer

1. *Show the isoquant and the relevant domestic isoquant.* The figure shows the same isoquant as in Chapter 6. We are told that the firm produces at home

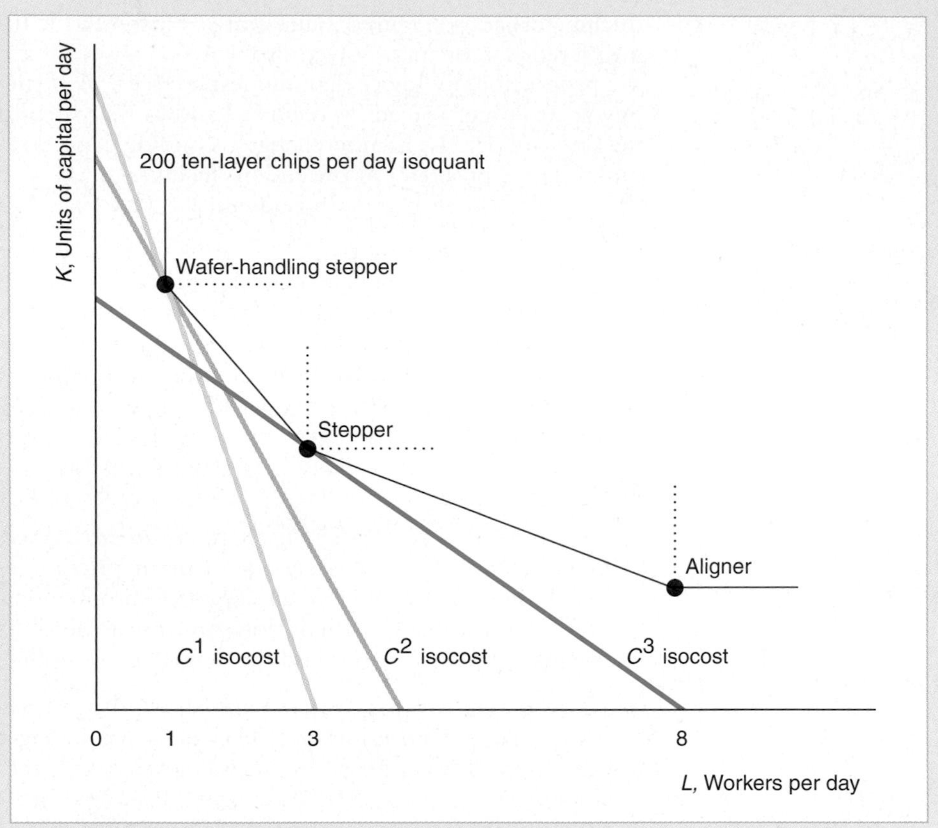

using the wafer-handling stepper technology, so its C^1 isocost must hit the isoquant at that technology. Because the isoquant is not smooth, the C^1 isoquant could have any of several different slopes.

2. *State what happens to the slope of the isocost line if the firm produces abroad.* The firm's new isocost line will be flatter than the C^1 isocost. The slope of the isocost is $-w/r$, where w is the wage and r is the rental cost of the machine. Thus, the smaller w is, the less steeply sloped is the isocost curve.

3. *Show that a flatter isocost might but does not necessarily hit the isoquant at a different technology.* Because the isoquant has kinks, a small change in the relative input prices does not necessarily lead to a change in technique. The C^2 and C^3 isocost curves are both flatter than the C^1 isocost. If the wage drops only slightly, so that the C^2 isocost is only slightly flatter, the firm still uses the capital-intensive wafer-handling stepper technology. However, with a larger drop in the wage, the much flatter C^3 isocost curve hits the isoquant at the stepper technology (if it were even flatter, it could hit at the aligner technology).

See Question 16.

Comment: The firm's cost will drop due to the lower wage even if it uses the same technology: $C^2 < C^1$. However, if the wage is low enough that it can shift to a more labor-intensive technology, its costs will be even lower: $C^3 < C^2$. If the isoquant were smooth (without kinks), any change in relative factor costs would induce the firm to change the technology (labor–capital ratio) that it uses.

How Long-Run Cost Varies with Output

We now know how a firm determines the cost-minimizing output for any given level of output. By repeating this analysis for different output levels, the firm determines how its cost varies with output.

expansion path
the cost-minimizing combination of labor and capital for each output level

Panel a of Figure 7.7 shows the relationship between the lowest-cost factor combinations and various levels of output for the furniture manufacturer when input prices are held constant at $w = \$24$ and $r = \$8$. The curve through the tangency points is the long-run **expansion path**: the cost-minimizing combination of labor and capital for each output level. The lowest-cost way to produce 100 units of output is to use the labor and capital combination $x(L = 50$ and $K = 100)$, which lies on the \$2,000 isocost line. Similarly, the lowest-cost way to produce 200 units is to use z, which is on the \$4,000 isocost line. The expansion path goes through x and z.

The expansion path of the furniture manufacturer in the figure is a straight line through the origin with a slope of 2: At any given output level, the firm uses twice as much capital as labor.[5] To double its output from 100 to 200 units, the firm doubles the amount of labor from 50 to 100 workers and doubles the amount of capital from 100 to 200 units. Because both inputs double when output doubles from 100 to 200, cost also doubles.

The furniture manufacturer's expansion path contains the same information as its long-run cost function, $C(q)$, which shows the relationship between the cost of production and output. From inspection of the expansion path, to produce q units of output takes $K = q$ units of capital and $L = q/2$ units of labor. Thus, the long-run cost of producing q units of output is

$$C(q) = wL + rK = wq/2 + rq = (w/2 + r)q = (24/2 + 8)q = 20q.$$

That is, the long-run cost function corresponding to this expansion path is $C(q) = 20q$. This cost function is consistent with the expansion path in panel a: $C(100) = \$2,000$ at x on the expansion path, $C(150) = \$3,000$ at y, and $C(200) = \$4,000$ at z.

Panel b plots this long-run cost curve. Points X, Y, and Z on the cost curve correspond to points x, y, and z on the expansion path. For example, the \$2,000 isocost line goes through x, which is the lowest-cost combination of labor and capital that can produce 100 units of output. Similarly, X on the long-run cost curve is at \$2,000 and 100 units of output. Consistent with the expansion path, the cost curve shows that as output doubles, cost doubles.

Solved Problem 7.4

What is the long-run cost function for a fixed-proportions production function (Chapter 6) when it takes one unit of labor and one unit of capital to produce one unit of output? Describe the long-run cost curve.

Answer

See Questions 17–20 and Problems 29 and 34.

Multiply the inputs by their prices, and sum to determine total cost. The long-run cost of producing q units of output is $C(q) = wL + rK = wq + rq = (w + r)q$. Cost rises in proportion to output. The long-run cost curve is a straight line with a slope of $w + r$.

[5]In Appendix 7C, we show that the expansion path for a Cobb-Douglas production function is $K = [\beta w/(\alpha r)]L$. The expansion path for the furniture manufacturer is

$$K = [(0.4 \times 24)/(0.6 \times 8)]L = 2L.$$

Figure 7.7 Expansion Path and Long-Run Cost Curve.

(a) The curve through the tangency points between isocost lines and isoquants, such as x, y, and z, is called the expansion path. The points on the expansion path are the cost-minimizing combinations of labor and capital for each output level. (b) The furniture manufacturer's expansion path shows the same relationship between long-run cost and output as the long-run cost curve.

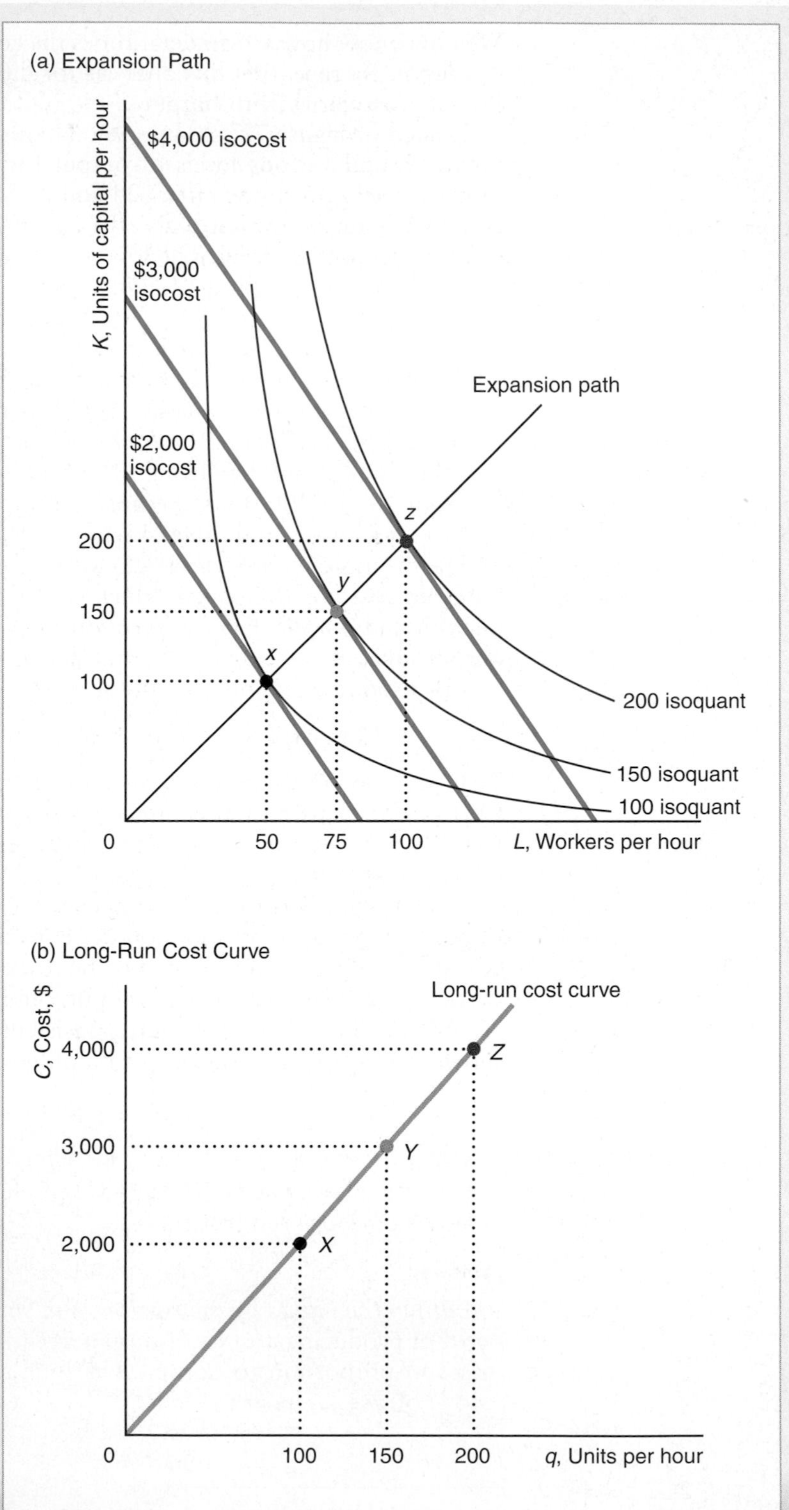

The Shape of Long-Run Cost Curves

The shapes of the average cost and marginal cost curves depend on the shape of the long-run cost curve. To illustrate these relationships, we examine the long-run cost curves of a typical firm that has a U-shaped long-run average cost curve.

The long-run cost curve in panel a of Figure 7.8 corresponds to the long-run average and marginal cost curves in panel b. Unlike the straight-line long-run cost curves of the printing firm and the firm with fixed-proportions production, the long-run cost curve of this firm rises less than in proportion to output at outputs below q^* and then rises more rapidly.

Figure 7.8 Long-Run Cost Curves.

(a) The long-run cost curve rises less rapidly than output at output levels below q^* and more rapidly at higher output levels. (b) As a consequence, the marginal cost and average cost curves are U-shaped. The marginal cost crosses the average cost at its minimum at q^*.

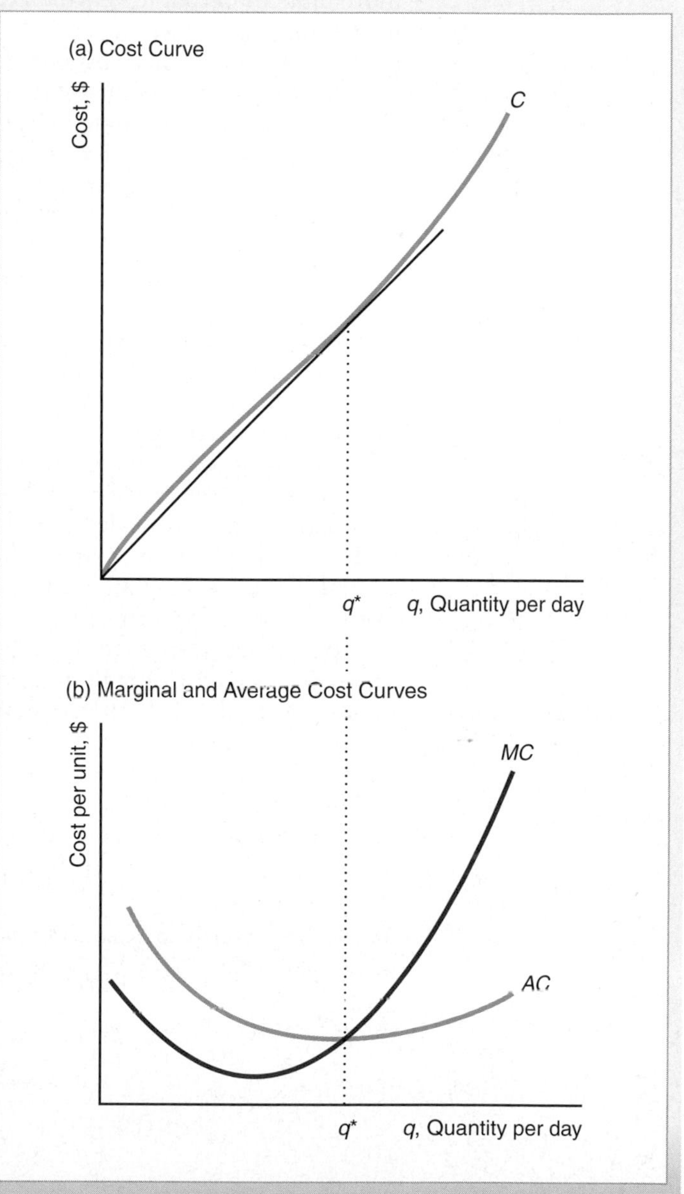

We can apply the same type of analysis that we used to study short-run curves to look at the geometric relationship between long-run total, average, and marginal curves. A line from the origin is tangent to the long-run cost curve at q^*, where the marginal cost curve crosses the average cost curve, because the slope of that line equals the marginal and average costs at that output. The long-run average cost curve falls when the long-run marginal cost curve is below it and rises when the long-run marginal cost curve is above it. Thus, the marginal cost crosses the average cost curve at the lowest point on the average cost curve.

Why does the average cost curve first fall and then rise, as in panel b? The explanation differs from those given for why short-run average cost curves are U-shaped.

A key reason why the short-run average cost is initially downward sloping is that the average fixed cost curve is downward sloping: Spreading the fixed cost over more units of output lowers the average fixed cost per unit. There are no fixed costs in the long run, however, so fixed costs cannot explain the initial downward slope of the long-run average cost curve.

A major reason why the short-run average cost curve slopes upward at higher levels of output is diminishing marginal returns. In the long run, however, all factors can be varied, so diminishing marginal returns do not explain the upward slope of a long-run average cost curve.

Ultimately, as with the short-run curves, the shape of the long-run curves is determined by the production function relationship between output and inputs. In the long run, returns to scale play a major role in determining the shape of the average cost curve and other cost curves. As we discussed in Chapter 6, increasing all inputs in proportion may cause output to increase more than in proportion (increasing returns to scale) at low levels of output, in proportion (constant returns to scale) at intermediate levels of output, and less than in proportion (decreasing returns to scale) at high levels of output. If a production function has this returns-to-scale pattern and the prices of inputs are constant, long-run average cost must be U-shaped.

To illustrate the relationship between returns to scale and long-run average cost, we use the returns-to-scale example of Figure 6.5, the data for which are reproduced in Table 7.4. The firm produces one unit of output using a unit each of labor and capital. Given a wage and rental cost of capital of \$6 per unit, the total cost and average cost of producing this unit are both \$12. Doubling both inputs causes output to increase more than in proportion to 3 units, reflecting increasing returns to scale. Because cost only doubles and output triples, the average cost falls. A cost function is said to exhibit **economies of scale** if the average cost of production falls as output expands.

economies of scale
property of a cost function whereby the average cost of production falls as output expands

Doubling the inputs again causes output to double as well—constant returns to scale—so the average cost remains constant. If an increase in output has no effect on average cost—the average cost curve is flat—there are *no economies of scale*.

Table 7.4 Returns to Scale and Long-Run Costs.

Output, Q	Labor, L	Capital, K	Cost, $C = wL + rK$	Average Cost, $AC = C/q$	Returns to Scale
1	1	1	12	12	
3	2	2	24	8	Increasing
6	4	4	48	8	Constant
8	8	8	96	12	Decreasing

$w = r = \$6$ per unit.

diseconomies of scale
property of a cost function whereby the average cost of production rises when output increases

Doubling the inputs once more causes only a small increase in output—decreasing returns to scale—so average cost increases. A firm suffers from **diseconomies of scale** if average cost rises when output increases.

Returns to scale in the production function are a sufficient but not necessary condition for economies of scale in the average cost curve. In the long run, a firm may change the ratio of capital to labor that it uses as it expands output. As a result, the firm could have economies of scale in costs without increasing returns to scale in production or could have diseconomies of scale in costs without decreasing returns to scale in production.

Consider a firm that has constant returns to scale in production at every output level. At small levels of output, the firm uses lots of labor and commonly available tools. At large levels of output, the firm designs and builds its own specialized equipment and uses relatively few workers, thereby lowering its average cost. Such a firm has economies of scale in cost despite having constant returns to scale in production.

Average cost curves can have many different shapes. Competitive firms typically have U-shaped average cost curves. Average cost curves in noncompetitive markets may be U-shaped, L-shaped (average cost at first falls rapidly and then levels off as output increases), everywhere downward sloping, or everywhere upward sloping or have other shapes. The shapes of the average cost curves indicate whether the production process has economies or diseconomies of scale.

Table 7.5 summarizes the shapes of average cost curves of firms in various Canadian manufacturing industries (as estimated by Robidoux and Lester, 1992). The table shows that U-shaped average cost curves are the exception rather than the rule in Canadian manufacturing and that nearly one-third of these average cost curves are L-shaped. Some of these apparently L-shaped average cost curves may be part of a U-shaped curve with long, flat bottoms, where we don't observe any firm producing enough to exhibit diseconomies of scale.

Table 7.5 Shape of Average Cost Curves in Canadian Manufacturing.

Scale Economies	Share of Manufacturing Industries, %	
Economies of scale: initially downward-sloping *AC*	57	
Everywhere downward-sloping *AC*		18
L-shaped *AC* (downward-sloping, then flat)		31
U-shaped *AC*		8
No economies of scale: flat *AC*	23	
Diseconomies of scale: upward-sloping *AC*	14	

Source: Robidoux and Lester (1992).

APPLICATION

Innovations and Economies of Scale

Before the introduction of robotic assembly lines in the tire industry, firms had to produce large runs of identical products to take advantage of economies of scale and thereby keep their per-unit costs low. A traditional plant might be half a mile in length and be designed to produce popular models in batches of a thousand or more. To change to a different model, workers in traditional plants labored for eight hours or more to switch molds and set up the machinery.

In contrast, in its modern plant in Rome, Georgia, Pirelli Tire uses its modular integrated robotized system (MIRS) to produce small batches of a large number of products without driving up the cost per tire. A MIRS production unit has a dozen robots feeding a group of rubber-extruding and ply-laying machines. MIRS fabricates tires around metal drums that the robotic arms powerfully grip. The robots hand the tire-in-progress to extruding machinery at various angles, where strips of rubber and reinforcing materials are built up to form the tire's structure. One MIRS system can simultaneously build 12 different tire models. At the end of the process, robots load the unfinished tires into molds that emboss the tread pattern and sidewall lettering. By being able to produce as needed, Pirelli avoids the inventory cost of storing large quantities of expensive raw materials and finished tires.

Because Pirelli can practically produce as few as four tires at a time, it can build some wild variations. "We make tires for ultra-big bling-bling wheels in small numbers, but they are quite profitable," brags Gaetano Mannino, the president of Pirelli Tire North America.

Estimating Cost Curves Versus Introspection

Economists use statistical methods to estimate a cost function. Sometimes, however, we can infer the shape by casual observation and deductive reasoning.

For example, in the good old days, the Good Humor company sent out fleets of ice-cream trucks to purvey its products. It seems likely that the company's production process had fixed proportions and constant returns to scale: If it wanted to sell more, Good Humor dispatched one more truck and one more driver. Drivers and trucks are almost certainly nonsubstitutable inputs (the isoquants are right angles). If the cost of a driver is w per day, the rental cost is r per day, and q quantity of ice cream is sold in a day, then the cost function is $C = (w + r)q$.

Such deductive reasoning can lead one astray, as I once discovered. A water heater manufacturing firm provided me with many years of data on the inputs it used and the amount of output it produced. I also talked to the company's engineers about the production process and toured the plant (which resembled a scene from Dante's *Inferno*, with staggering noise levels and flames everywhere).

A water heater consists of an outside cylinder of metal, a liner, an electronic control unit, hundreds of tiny parts (screws, washers, etc.), and a couple of rods that slow corrosion. Workers cut out the metal for the cylinder, weld it together, and add the other parts. "Okay," I said to myself, "this production process must be one of fixed proportions because the firm needs one of everything to produce a water heater. How could you substitute a cylinder for an electronic control unit? Or how can you substitute labor for metal?"

I then used statistical techniques to estimate the production and cost functions. Following the usual procedure, however, I did not assume that I knew the exact form of the functions. Rather, I allowed the data to "tell" me the type of production and cost functions. To my surprise, the estimates indicated that the production process was not one of fixed proportions. Rather, the firm could readily substitute between labor and capital.

"Surely I've made a mistake," I said to the plant manager after describing these results. "No," he said, "that's correct. There's a great deal of substitutability between labor and metal."

"How can they be substitutes?"

"Easy," he said. "We can use a lot of labor and waste very little metal by cutting out exactly what we want and being very careful. Or we can use relatively little labor, cut quickly, and waste more metal. When the cost of labor is relatively high, we waste more metal. When the cost of metal is relatively high, we cut more carefully." This practice minimizes the firm's cost.

7.4 Lower Costs in the Long Run

In its long-run planning, a firm chooses a plant size and makes other investments so as to minimize its long-run cost on the basis of how many units it produces. Once it chooses its plant size and equipment, these inputs are fixed in the short run. Thus, the firm's long-run decision determines its short-run cost. Because the firm cannot vary its capital in the short run but can vary it in the long run, short-run cost is at least as high as long-run cost and is higher if the "wrong" level of capital is used in the short run.

Long-Run Average Cost as the Envelope of Short-Run Average Cost Curves

As a result, the long-run average cost is always equal to or below the short-run average cost. Suppose, initially, that the firm in Figure 7.9 has only three possible plant sizes. The firm's short-run average cost curve is $SRAC^1$ for the smallest possible plant. The average cost of producing q_1 units of output using this plant, point *a* on $SRAC^1$, is \$10. If instead the plant used the next larger plant size, its cost of producing q_1 units of output, point *b* on $SRAC^2$, would be \$12. Thus, if the firm knows that it will produce only q_1 units of output, it minimizes its average cost by using the smaller plant size. If it expects to be producing q_2, its average cost is lower on the $SRAC^2$ curve, point *e*, than on the $SRAC^1$ curve, point *d*.

In the long run, the firm chooses the plant size that minimizes its cost of production, so it picks the plant size that has the lowest average cost for each possible out-

Figure 7.9 Long-Run Average Cost as the Envelope of Short-Run Average Cost Curves.

If there are only three possible plant sizes, with short-run average costs $SRAC^1$, $SRAC^2$, and $SRAC^3$, the long-run average cost curve is the solid, scalloped portion of the three short-run curves. *LRAC* is the smooth and U-shaped long-run average cost curve if there are many possible short-run average cost curves.

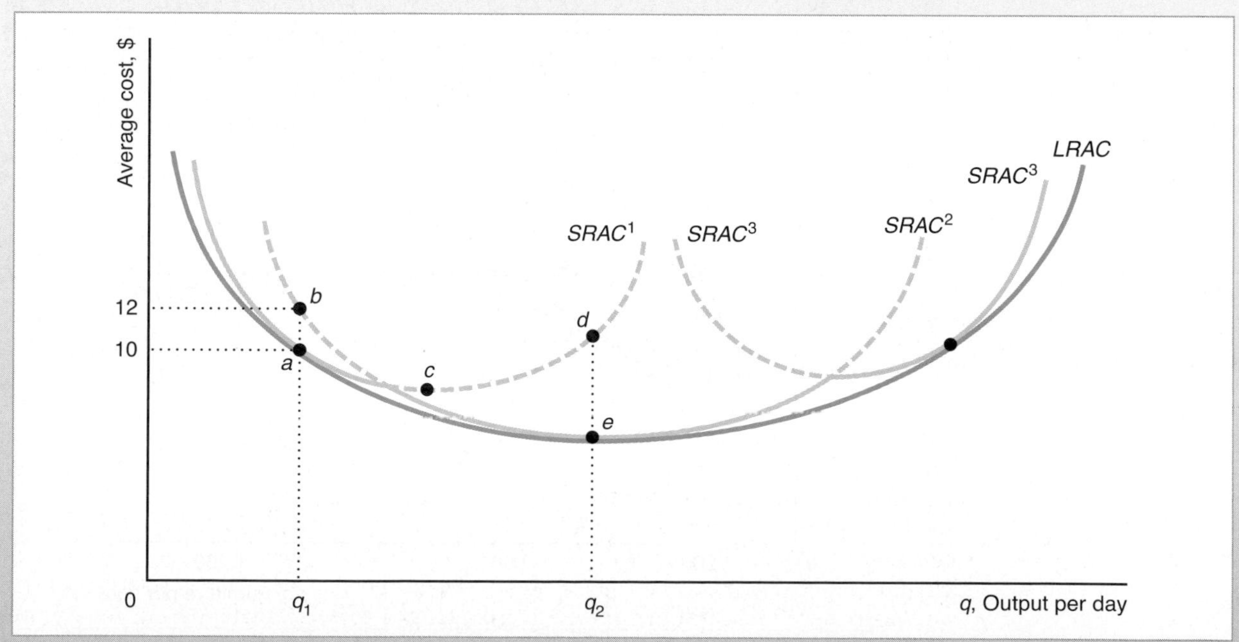

put level. At q_1, it opts for the small plant size, whereas at q_2, it uses the medium plant size. Thus, the long-run average cost curve is the solid, scalloped section of the three short-run cost curves.

See Question 21.

If there are many possible plant sizes, the long-run average curve, *LRAC*, is smooth and U-shaped. The *LRAC* includes one point from each possible short-run average cost curve. This point, however, is not necessarily the minimum point from a short-run curve. For example, the *LRAC* includes *a* on $SRAC^1$ and not its minimum point, *c*. A small plant operating at minimum average cost cannot produce at as low an average cost as a slightly larger plant that is taking advantage of economies of scale.

APPLICATION

Long-Run Cost Curves in Furniture Manufacturing and Oil Pipelines

Here we illustrate the relationship between long-run and short-run cost curves for our furniture manufacturing firm and for oil pipelines. In the next application, we show the long-run cost when you choose between a laser printer and an ink-jet printer.

Furniture Manufacturer. The first graph shows the relationship between short-run and long-run average cost curves for the furniture manufacturer. Because this production function has constant returns to scale, doubling both inputs doubles output, so the long-run average cost, *LRAC*, is constant at $20, as we saw earlier. If capital is fixed at 200 units, the firm's short-run average cost curve is $SRAC^1$. If the firm produces 200 units of output, its short-run and long-run average costs are equal. At any other output, its short-run cost is higher than its long-run cost.

The short-run marginal cost curves, $SRMC^1$ and $SRMC^2$, are upward sloping and equal the corresponding U-shaped short-run average cost curves, $SRAC^1$ and $SRAC^2$, only at their minimum points, $20. In contrast, because the long-run average cost is horizontal at $20, the long-run marginal cost curve, *LRMC*, is hori-

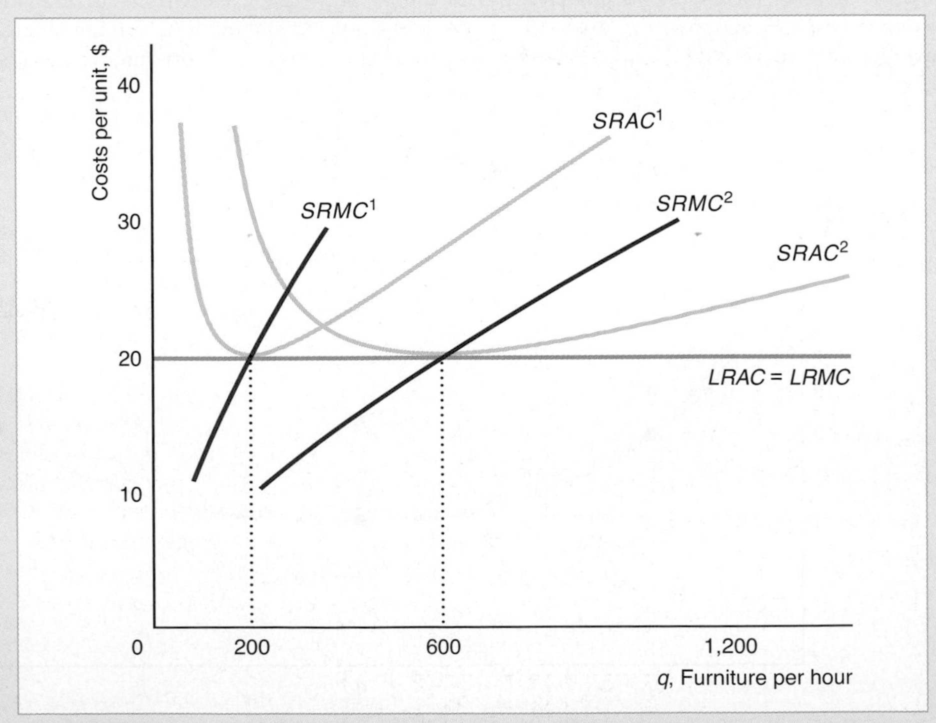

zontal at $20. Thus, the long-run marginal cost curve is *not* the envelope of the short-run marginal cost curves.

Oil Pipelines. Oil companies use the information in the second graph[6] to choose what size pipe to use to deliver oil. In the figure, the 8″ *SRAC* is the short-run average cost curve of a pipe with an 8-inch diameter. The long-run average cost curve, *LRAC*, is the envelope of all possible short-run average cost curves. It is more expensive to lay larger pipes than smaller ones, so a firm does not want to install unnecessarily large pipes. The average cost of sending a substantial quantity through a single large pipe is lower than that of sending it through two smaller pipes. For example, the average cost per barrel of sending 200,000 barrels per day through two 16-inch pipes is 1.67 (= $50/$30) greater than through a single 26-inch pipe.

Because the company incurs large fixed costs in laying miles and miles of pipelines and because pipes last for years, it does not vary the size of pipes in the short run. In the long run, the oil company installs the ideal pipe size to handle its "throughput" of oil. As Exxon notes, several oil companies share interstate pipelines because of the large economies of scale.

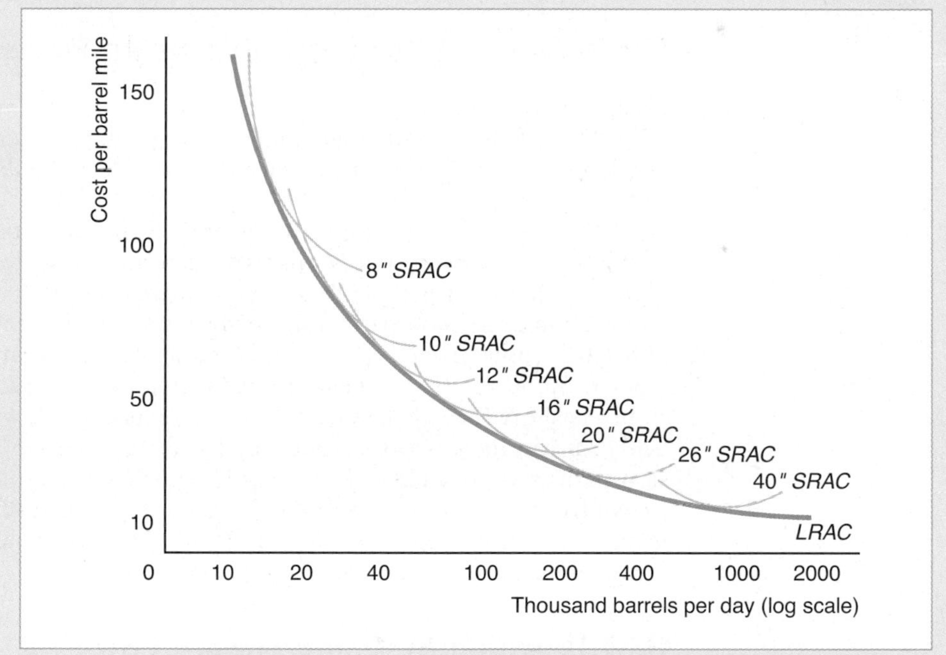

APPLICATION

Choosing an Ink-Jet or a Laser Printer

You decide to buy a printer for your college assignments. You need to print in black and white. In 2008, you can buy a personal laser printer for $150 or an ink-jet printer for $75 that prints 20 pages a minute.

If you buy the ink jet, you save $75 right off the bat. The laser costs less per page to operate, however. The cost of ink and paper is about 4¢ per page for a

[6]Exxon Company, U.S.A., *Competition in the Petroleum Industry*, 1975, p. 30. Reprinted with permission.

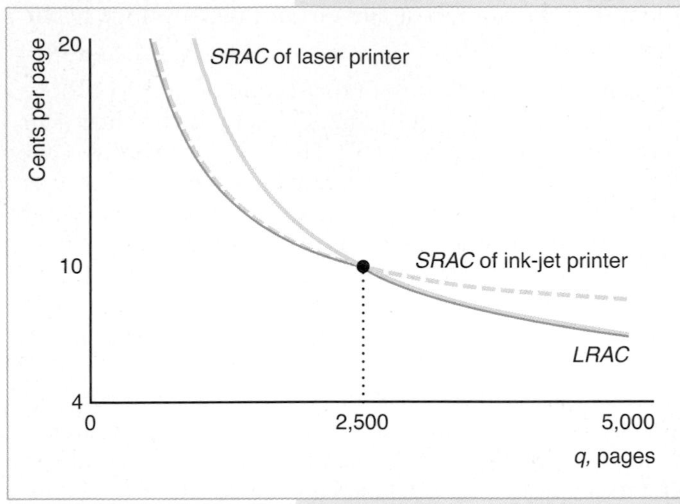

laser compared to about 7¢ per page for an ink jet. That means that the average cost per page of operating a laser ($\$150/q + 0.04$, where q is the number of pages) is less than that of an ink jet ($\$75/q + 0.07$) after q reaches about 2,500 pages.

The graph shows the short-run average cost curves for the laser printer and the ink-jet printer. The lower-cost choice is the ink jet if you're printing fewer than 2,500 pages and the laser if you're printing more.

So should you buy the laser printer? If you print more than 2,500 pages over its lifetime, the laser is less expensive to own and operate than the ink jet. If the printers last two years and you print 25 or more pages per week, then the laser printer is cost effective.

Short-Run and Long-Run Expansion Paths

Long-run cost is lower than short-run cost because the firm has more flexibility in the long run. To show the advantage of flexibility, we can compare the short-run and long-run expansion paths, which correspond to the short-run and long-run cost curves.

The furniture manufacturer has greater flexibility in the long run. The tangency of the firm's isoquants and isocost lines determines the long-run expansion path in Figure 7.10. The firm expands output by increasing both its labor and its capital, so its long-run expansion path is upward sloping. To increase its output from 100 to 200 units (move from x to z), it doubles its capital from 100 to 200 units and its labor from 50 to 100 workers. Its cost increases from \$2,000 to \$4,000.

In the short run, the firm cannot increase its capital, which is fixed at 100 units. The firm can increase its output only by using more labor, so its short-run expansion path is horizontal at $K = 100$. To expand its output from 100 to 200 units (move from x to y), the firm must increase its labor from 50 to 159 workers, and its cost rises from \$2,000 to \$4,616. Doubling output increases long-run cost by a factor of 2 and short-run cost by approximately 2.3.

How Learning by Doing Lowers Costs

learning by doing the productive skills and knowledge that workers and managers gain from experience

Two reasons why long-run cost is lower than short-run cost are that firms have more flexibility in the long run and that technical progress (Chapter 6) may lower cost over time. A third reason is **learning by doing**: the productive skills and knowledge of better ways to produce that workers and managers gain from experience.

In some firms, learning by doing is a function of the time since the product was introduced. In others, learning by doing is a function of *cumulative output*: the total number of units of output produced since the product was introduced. Learning is connected to cumulative output if workers become increasingly adept the more times they perform a task. As a consequence, workers become more productive if they make many units over a short period than if they produce a few units over a longer period. For example, the average labor cost of producing an Intel central pro-

Figure 7.10 Long-Run and Short-Run Expansion Paths.

In the long run, the furniture manufacturer increases its output by using more of both inputs, so its long-run expansion path is upward sloping. In the short run, the firm cannot vary its capital, so its short-run expansion path is horizontal at the fixed level of output. That is, it increases its output by increasing the amount of labor it uses. Expanding output from 100 to 200 raises the furniture firm's long-run cost from $2,000 to $4,000 but raises its short-run cost from $2,000 to $4,616.

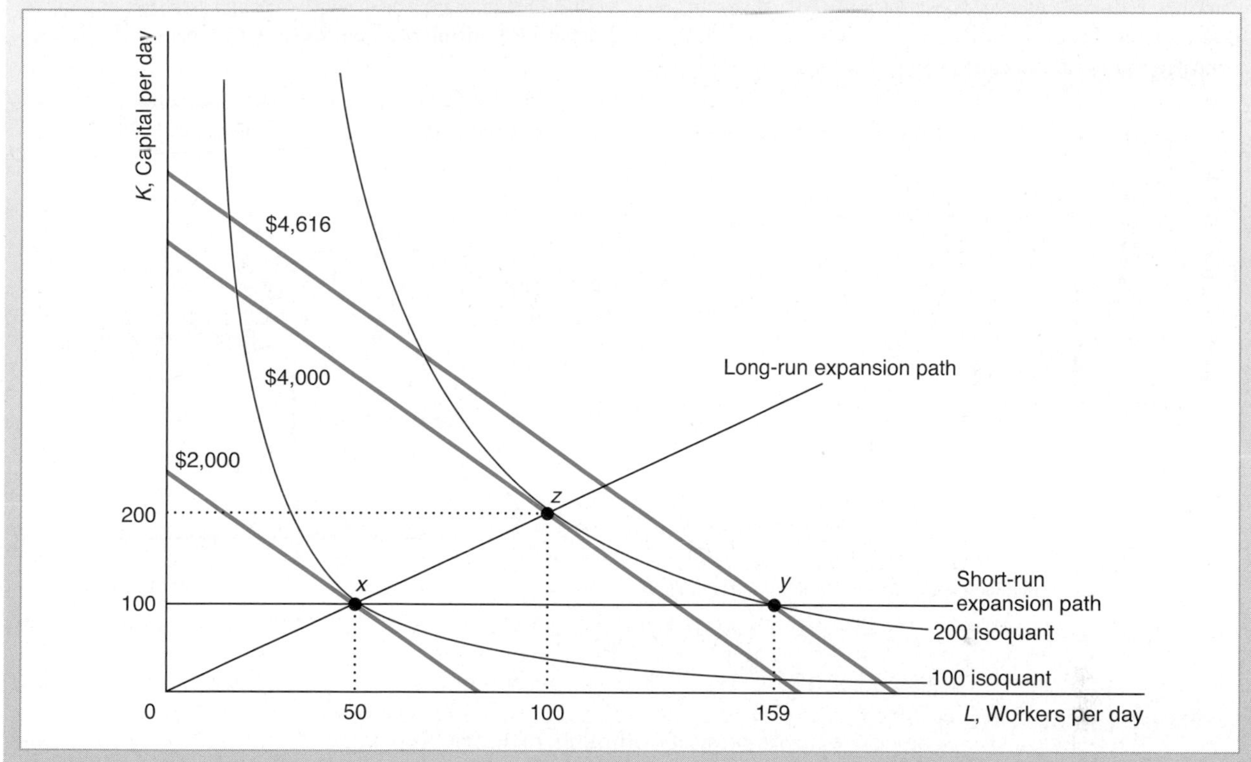

cessing unit or CPU (panel a of Figure 7.11) fell with cumulative output (based on Salgado, 2007).

If a firm is operating in the economies of scale section of its average cost curve, expanding output lowers its cost for two reasons. Its average cost falls today because of economies of scale, and for any given level of output, its average cost is lower in the next period due to learning by doing.

In panel b of Figure 7.11, the firm is currently producing q_1 units of output at point *A* on average cost curve AC^1. If it expands its output to q_2, its average cost falls in this period to *B* because of economies of scale. The learning by doing in this period results in a lower average cost, AC^2, in the next period. If the firm continues to produce q_2 units of output in the next period, its average cost falls to *b* on AC^2.

If instead of expanding output to q_2 in this period, the firm expands to q_3, its average cost is even lower in this period (*C* on AC^1) due to even more economies of scale. Moreover, its average cost in the next period is even lower, AC^3, due to the extra experience in this period. If the firm continues to produce q_3 in the next period, its average cost is *c* on AC^3. Thus, all else being the same, if learning by doing depends on cumulative output, firms have an incentive to produce more in the short run than they otherwise would to lower their costs in the future.

Figure 7.11 Learning by Doing.

(a) As Intel produced more cumulative CPUs, the average cost of production fell (Salgado, 2007). (b) In the short run, extra production reduces a firm's average cost owing to economies of scale: because $q_1 < q_2 < q_3$, A is higher than B, which is higher than C. In the long run, extra production reduces average cost because of learning by doing. To produce q_2 this period costs B on AC^1, but to produce that same output in the next period would cost only b on AC^2. If the firm produces q_3 instead of q_2 in this period, its average cost in the next period is AC^3 instead of AC^2 because of additional learning by doing. Thus, extra output in this period lowers the firm's cost in two ways: It lowers average cost in this period due to economies of scale and lowers average cost for any given output level in the next period due to learning by doing.

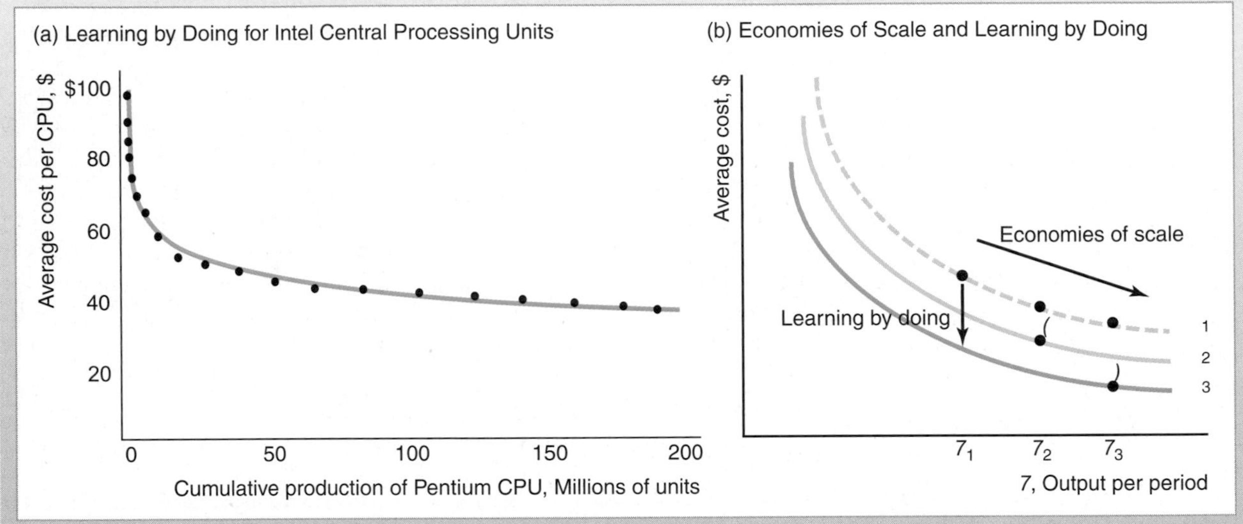

APPLICATION

Learning by Doing in Computer Chips

The cost of producing a computer memory chip falls substantially due to learning by doing. There are several different types of MOS (metal oxide on silicon) memory chips: EPROM (erasable programmable read-only memory), DRAM (dynamic random-access memory), and fast SRAM (static random-access memory). From one generation to another, EPROM's storage capacity doubles, whereas the storage capacity of DRAM and SRAM increases by a factor of 4. Like clockwork, a new EPROM generation appears every 18 months; a new DRAM, every 3 years.

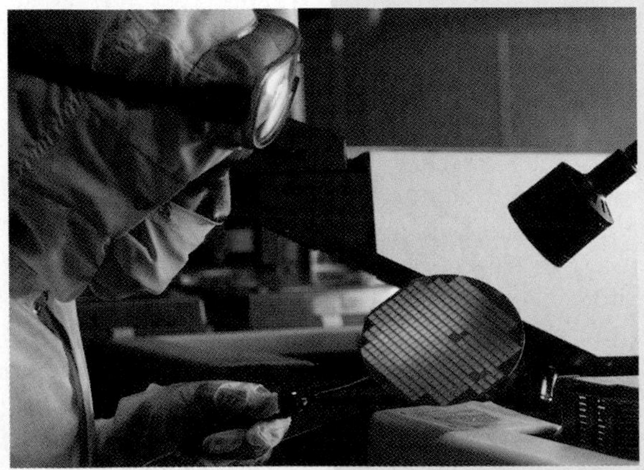

Gruber (1992) finds that the average cost of EPROM chips falls with cumulative output but does not decrease over time or with the scale of production. With each doubling in the cumulative output of an EPROM chip, its average cost falls by 22%. This effect may encourage firms to produce more EPROM chips in the first few months after a new generation is introduced than they would without learning. By doing so, the firm gains experience more rapidly, which causes its average cost to fall more rapidly.

Irwin and Klenow (1994) find an average of 20% learning curve effect on cumulative output for DRAMs. Chung (2001) reports 17% learning for 64K DRAM and 9% for 256K DRAM in Korea.

Although the type and speed of learning by doing vary across chips, they are the same across generations of the same chip. Thus, firms know that they can count on their costs falling and build these predictable cost reductions into their planning over time.

7.5 Cost of Producing Multiple Goods

Few firms produce only a single good, but we discuss single-output firms for simplicity. If a firm produces two or more goods, the cost of one good may depend on the output level of the other.

Outputs are linked if a single input is used to produce both of them. For example, mutton and wool both come from sheep, cattle provide beef and hides, and oil supplies both heating fuel and gasoline. It is less expensive to produce beef and hides together than separately. If the goods are produced together, a single steer yields one unit of beef and one hide. If beef and hides are produced separately (throwing away the unused good), the same amount of output requires two steers and more labor.

economies of scope situation in which it is less expensive to produce goods jointly than separately

We say that there are **economies of scope** if it is less expensive to produce goods jointly than separately (Panzar and Willig, 1977, 1981). A measure of the degree to which there are economies of *scope* (*SC*) is

$$SC = \frac{C(q_1, 0) + C(0, q_2) - C(q_1, q_2)}{C(q_1, q_2)},$$

where $C(q_1, 0)$ is the cost of producing q_1 units of the first good by itself, $C(0, q_2)$ is the cost of producing q_2 units of the second good, and $C(q_1, q_2)$ is the cost of producing both goods together. If the cost of producing the two goods separately, $C(q_1,0) + C(0,q_2)$, is the same as producing them together, $C(q_1, q_2)$, then *SC* is zero. If it is cheaper to produce the goods jointly, *SC* is positive. If *SC* is negative, there are diseconomies of scope, and the two goods should be produced separately.

production possibility frontier the maximum amount of outputs that can be produced from a fixed amount of input

To illustrate this idea, suppose that Laura spends one day collecting mushrooms and wild strawberries in the woods. Her **production possibility frontier**—the maximum amounts of outputs (mushrooms and strawberries) that can be produced from a fixed amount of input (Laura's effort during one day)—is PPF^1 in Figure 7.12. The production possibility frontier summarizes the trade-off Laura faces: She picks fewer mushrooms if she collects more strawberries in a day.

If Laura spends all day collecting only mushrooms, she picks 8 pints; if she spends all day picking strawberries, she collects 6 pints. If she picks some of each, however, she can harvest more total pints: 6 pints of mushrooms and 4 pints of strawberries. The product possibility frontier is concave (the middle of the curve is farther from the origin than it would be if it were a straight line) because of the diminishing marginal returns to collecting only one of the two goods. If she collects only mushrooms, she must walk past wild strawberries without picking them. As a result, she has to walk farther if she collects only mushrooms than if she picks both. Thus, there are economies of scope in jointly collecting mushrooms and strawberries.

If instead the production possibility frontier were a straight line, the cost of producing the two goods jointly would not be lower. Suppose, for example, that mushrooms grow in one section of the woods and strawberries in another section. In that case, Laura can collect only mushrooms without passing any strawberries. That production possibility frontier is a straight line, PPF^2 in Figure 7.12. By allocating her time between the two sections of the woods, Laura can collect any combination of

Figure 7.12 Joint Production.

If there are economies of scope, the production possibility frontier is bowed away from the origin, PPF^1. If instead the production possibility frontier is a straight line, PPF^2, the cost of producing both goods does not fall if they are produced together.

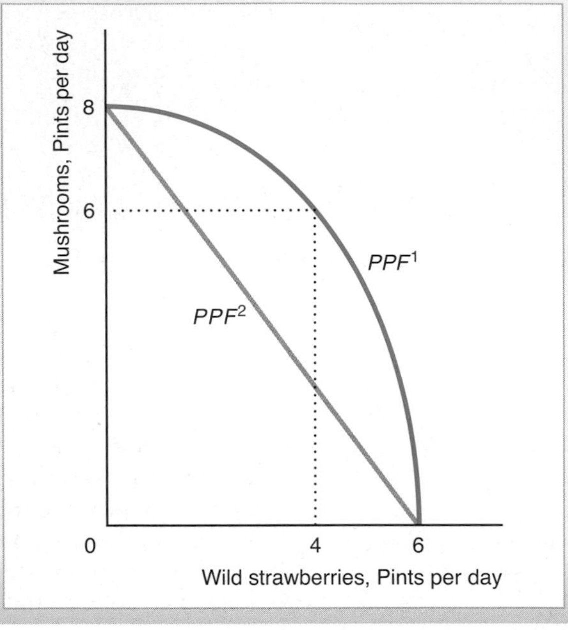

mushrooms and strawberries by spending part of her day in one section of the woods and part in the other.

See Question 22.

APPLICATION
Scope

Empirical studies show that some processes have economies of scope, others have none, and some have diseconomies of scope. In Japan, there are substantial economies of scope in producing and transmitting electricity, $SC = 0.2$ (Ida and Kuwahara, 2004), and broadcasting television and radio, $SC = 0.12$ (Asai 2006).

Friedlaender, Winston, and Wang (1983) found that for American automobile manufacturers, it is 25% less expensive ($SC = 0.25$) to produce large cars together with small cars and trucks than to produce large cars separately and small cars and trucks together. However, there are no economies of scope from producing trucks together with small and large cars. Producing trucks separately from cars is efficient.

Kim (1987) found substantial diseconomies of scope in using railroads to transport freight and passengers together. It is 41% less expensive ($SC = -0.41$) to transport passengers and freight separately than together. In the early 1970s, passenger service in the United States was transferred from the private railroad companies to Amtrak, and the services are now separate. Kim's estimates suggest that this separation is cost effective.

SUMMARY

From all technologically efficient production processes, a firm chooses the one that is economically efficient. The economically efficient production process is the technologically efficient process for which the cost of producing a given quantity of output is lowest, or the one that produces the most output for a given cost.

1. **Measuring Costs.** The economic or opportunity cost of a good is the value of its next best alternative use. Economic cost includes both explicit and implicit costs.
2. **Short-Run Costs.** In the short run, the firm can vary the costs of the factors that it can adjust, but the costs of other factors are fixed. The firm's average fixed cost falls as its output rises. If a firm has a short-run average cost curve that is U-shaped, its marginal cost curve is below the average cost curve when average cost is falling and above the average cost when it is rising, so the marginal cost curve cuts the average cost curve at its minimum.
3. **Long-Run Costs.** In the long run, all factors can be varied, so all costs are variable. As a result, average cost and average variable cost are identical. The firm chooses the combination of inputs it uses to minimize its cost. To produce a given output level, it chooses the lowest isocost line that touches the relevant isoquant, which is tangent to the isoquant. Equivalently, to minimize cost, the firm adjusts inputs until the last dollar spent on any input increases output by as much as the last dollar spent on any other input. If the firm calculates the cost of producing every possible output level given current input prices, it knows its cost function: Cost is a function of the input prices and the output level. If the firm's average cost falls as output expands, it has economies of scale. If its average cost rises as output expands, there are diseconomies of scale.
4. **Lower Costs in the Long Run.** The firm can always do in the long run what it does in the short run, so its long-run cost can never be greater than its short-run cost. Because some factors are fixed in the short run, to expand output, the firm must greatly increase its use of other factors, which is relatively costly. In the long run, the firm can adjust all factors, a process that keeps its cost down. Long-run cost may also be lower than short-run cost if there is technological progress or learning by doing.
5. **Cost of Producing Multiple Goods.** If it is less expensive for a firm to produce two goods jointly rather than separately, there are economies of scope. If there are diseconomies of scope, it is less expensive to produce the goods separately.

QUESTIONS

■ = *exercise is available on MyEconLab;* * = *answer appears at the back of this book;* C = *use of calculus may be necessary;* W = *audio-slideshow answer by James Dearden is available in Textbook Resources on MyEconLab.*

1. Executives at Leonesse Cellars, a premium winery in Southern California, were surprised to learn that shipping wine by sea to some cities in Asia was less expensive than sending it to the East Coast of the United States, so they started shipping to Asia (David Armstrong, "Discount Cargo Rates Ripe for the Taking," *San Francisco Chronicle*, August 28, 2005). Because of the large U.S. trade imbalance with major Asian nations, cargo ships arrive at West Coast seaports fully loaded but return to Asia half to completely empty. Use the concept of opportunity cost to help explain the differential shipping rates.

*2. "There are certain fixed costs when you own a plane," [Andre] Agassi explained during a break in the action at the Volvo/San Francisco tennis tournament, "so the more you fly it, the more economic sense it makes.... The first flight after I bought it, I took some friends to Palm Springs for lunch." (Scott Ostler, "Andre Even Flies like a Champ," *San Francisco Chronicle*, February 8, 1993, C1.) Discuss whether Agassi's statement is reasonable.

3. Many corporations allow CEOs to use the firm's corporate jet for personal travel. The Internal Revenue Service (IRS) requires that the firm report personal use of its corporate jet as taxable executive income, and the Securities and Exchange Commission (SEC) requires that publicly traded corporations report the value of this benefit to shareholders. An important issue is the determination of the value of this benefit. The *Wall Street Journal* (Mark Maremont, "Amid Crackdown, the Jet Perk Suddenly Looks a Lot Pricier," May 25, 2005, A1) reports three valuation techniques. The IRS values a CEO's personal flight at or below the price of a first-class ticket. The SEC values the flight at the "incremental" cost of the flight: the additional costs to the corporation of the flight.

The third alternative is the market value of chartering an aircraft. Of the three methods, the first-class ticket is least expensive and the chartered flight is most expensive.

a. What factors (such as fuel) determine the marginal explicit cost to a corporation of an executive's personal flight? Does any one of the three valuation methods correctly determine the marginal explicit cost?

b. What is the marginal opportunity cost to the corporation of an executive's personal flight? W

4. In the twentieth century, department stores and supermarkets largely replaced smaller specialty stores, as consumers found it more efficient to go to one store rather than many stores. Consumers incur a transaction or search cost to shop, primarily the opportunity cost of their time. This transaction cost consists of a fixed cost of traveling to and from the store and a variable cost that rises with the number of different types of items the consumer tries to find on the shelves. By going to a supermarket that carries meat, fruits and vegetables, and other items, consumers can avoid some of the fixed transaction costs of traveling to a separate butcher shop, produce mart, and so forth. Use math or figures to explain why a shopper's average costs are lower when buying at a single supermarket than from many stores. (*Hint*: Define the goods as the items purchased and brought home.)

5. Using the information in Table 7.1, construct another table showing how a lump-sum franchise tax of $30 affects the various average cost curves of the firm.

*6. A firm builds shipping crates out of wood. How does the cost of producing a 1-cubic-foot crate (each side is 1-foot square) compare to the cost of building an 8-cubic-foot crate if wood costs $1 a square foot and the firm has no labor or other costs? More generally, how does cost vary with volume?

7. In 1796, Gottfried Christoph Härtel, a German music publisher, calculated the cost of printing music using an engraved plate technology and used these estimated cost functions to make production decisions. Härtel figured that the fixed cost of printing a musical page—the cost of engraving the plates—was 900 pfennings. The marginal cost of each additional copy of the page is 5 pfennings (Scherer, 2001).

a. Graph the total cost, average total cost, average variable cost, and marginal cost functions.

b. Is there a cost advantage to having only one music publisher print a given composition? Why?

c. Härtel used his data to do the following type of analysis. Suppose he expects to sell exactly 300 copies of a composition at 15 pfennings per page of the composition. What is the greatest amount the publisher is willing to pay the composer per page of the composition? W

8. The only variable input a janitorial service firm uses to clean offices is workers who are paid a wage, w, of $8 an hour. Each worker can clean four offices in an hour. Use math to determine the variable cost, the average variable cost, and the marginal cost of cleaning one more office. Draw a diagram like Figure 7.1 to show the variable cost, average variable cost, and marginal cost curves.

9. Suppose in Solved Problem 7.1 that the government charges the firm a franchise tax each year (instead of only once). Describe the effect of this tax on the marginal cost, average variable cost, short-run average cost, and long-run average cost curves.

10. Suppose that the government subsidizes the cost of workers by paying for 25% of the wage (the rate offered by the U.S. government in the late 1970s under the New Jobs Tax Credit program). What effect will this subsidy have on the firm's choice of labor and capital to produce a given level of output?

*11. You have 60 minutes to take an exam with 2 questions. You want to maximize your score. Toward the end of the exam, the more time you spend on either question, the fewer extra points per minute you get for that question. How should you allocate your time between the two questions? (*Hint*: Think about producing an output of a score on the exam using inputs of time spent on each of the problems. Then use Equation 7.6.)

*12. The all-American baseball is made using cork from Portugal, rubber from Malaysia, yarn from Australia, and leather from France, and it is stitched (108 stitches exactly) by workers in Costa Rica. To assemble a baseball takes one unit each of these inputs. Ultimately, the finished product must be shipped to its final destination—say, Cooperstown, New York. The materials used cost the same anywhere. Labor costs are lower in Costa Rica than in a possible alternative manufacturing site in Georgia, but shipping costs from Costa Rica are higher. What production function is used? What is the cost function? What can you conclude about shipping costs if it is less expensive to produce baseballs in Costa Rica than in Georgia?

*13. A bottling company uses two inputs to produce bottles of the soft drink Sludge: bottling machines (K) and workers (L). The isoquants have the usual smooth shape. The machine costs \$1,000 per day to run: the workers earn \$200 per day. At the current level of production, the marginal product of the machine is an additional 200 bottles per day, and the marginal product of labor is 50 more bottles per day. Is this firm producing at minimum cost? If it is minimizing cost, explain why. If it is not minimizing cost, explain how the firm should change the ratio of inputs it uses to lower its cost. (*Hint*: Examine the conditions for minimizing cost: Equations 7.5, 7.6, or 7.7.)

14. Rosenberg (2004) reports the invention of a new machine that serves as a mobile station for receiving and accumulating packed flats of strawberries close to where they are picked, reducing workers' time and burden of carrying full flats of strawberries. A machine-assisted crew of 15 pickers produces as much output, q^*, as that of an unaided crew of 25 workers. In a 6-day, 50-hour workweek, the machine replaces 500 worker-hours. At an hourly wage cost of \$10, a machine saves \$5,000 per week in labor costs, or \$130,000 over a 26-week harvesting season. The cost of machine operation and maintenance expressed as a daily rental is \$200, or \$1,200 for a six-day week. Thus, the net savings equal \$3,800 per week, or \$98,800 for 26 weeks.
   a. Draw the q^* isoquant assuming that only two technologies are available (pure labor and labor-machine). Label the isoquant and axes as thoroughly as possible.
   b. Add an isocost line to show which technology the firm chooses (be sure to measure wage and rental costs on a comparable time basis).
   c. Draw the corresponding cost curves (with and without the machine), assuming constant returns to scale, and label the curves and the axes as thoroughly as possible.

15. In February 2003, Circuit City Stores, Inc. replaced skilled sales representatives who earn up to \$54,000 per year with relatively unskilled workers who earn \$14 to \$18 per hour (Carlos Tejada and Gary McWilliams, "New Recipe for Cost Savings: Replace Highly Paid Workers," *Wall Street Journal*, June 11, 2003). Suppose that sales representatives sell one particular Sony high-definition TV model. Let q represent the number of TVs sold per hour, s the number of skilled sales reps per hour, and u the number of unskilled reps per hour. Working eight hours per day, each skilled worker sells six TVs per day, and each unskilled worker sells four. The wage rate of the skilled workers is w_s = \$26 per hour, and the wage rate of the unskilled workers is w_u = \$16 per hour.
   a. Using a graph similar to Figure 6.3, show the isoquant for $q = 4$ with both skilled and unskilled sales representatives. Are they substitutes?
   b. Draw a representative isocost for c = \$104 per hour.
   c. Using an isocost-isoquant diagram, identify the cost-minimizing number of skilled and unskilled reps to sell $q = 4$ TVs per hour. W

*16. In Solved Problem 7.3, show that there are a wage and cost of capital services such that the firm is indifferent between using the wafer-handling stepper technology and the stepper technology. How does this wage/cost of capital ratio compare to those in the C^2 and C^3 isocosts?

17. Boxes of cereal are produced by using a fixed-proportion production function: One box and one unit (eight ounces) of cereal produce one box of cereal. What is the expansion path?

18. Suppose that your firm's production function has constant returns to scale. What is the long-run expansion path?

19. The Bouncing Ball Ping Pong Co. sells table tennis sets that consist of two paddles and one net. What is the firm's long-run expansion path if it incurs no costs other than what it pays for paddles and nets, which it buys at market prices? How does its expansion path depend on the relative prices of paddles and nets?

20. The production process of the firm you manage uses labor and capital services. How does the long-run expansion path change when the wage increases while the rental rate of capital stays constant?

21. A U-shaped long-run average cost curve is the envelope of U-shaped short-run average cost curves. On what part of the curve (downward sloping, flat, or upward sloping) does a short-run curve touch the long-run curve? (*Hint*: Your answer should depend on where on the long-run curve the two curves touch.)

22. What can you say about Laura's economies of scope if her time is valued at \$5 an hour and her production possibility frontier is PPF^1 in Figure 7.12?

PROBLEMS

23. Give the formulas for and plot *AFC*, *MC*, *AVC*, and *AC* if the cost function is

a. $C = 10 + 10q$

b. $C = 10 + q^2$

c. $C = 10 + 10q - 4q^2 + q^3$

24. Gail works in a flower shop, where she produces ten floral arrangements per hour. She is paid $10 an hour for the first eight hours she works and $15 an hour for each additional hour she works. What is the firm's cost function? What are its *AC*, *AVC*, and *MC* functions? Draw the *AC*, *AVC*, and *MC* curves.

25. A firm's cost curve is $C = F + 10q - bq^2 + q^3$, where $b > 0$.

a. For what values of b are cost, average cost, and average variable cost positive? (From now on, assume that all these measures of cost are positive at every output level.)

b. What is the shape of the *AC* curve? At what output level is the *AC* minimized?

c. At what output levels does the *MC* curve cross the *AC* and the *AVC* curves?

d. Use calculus to show that the *MC* curve must cross the *AVC* at its minimum point. C

26. A firm has two plants that produce identical output. The cost functions are $C_1 = 10q - 4q^2 + q^3$ and $C_2 = 10q - 2q^2 + q^3$.

a. At what output levels does the average cost curve of each plant reach its minimum?

b. If the firm wants to produce four units of output, how much should it produce in each plant?

***27.** What is the long-run cost function if the production function is $q = L + K$?

28. A firm has a Cobb-Douglas production function, $Q = AL^{\alpha}K^{\beta}$, where $\alpha + \beta < 1$. On the basis of this information, what properties does its cost function have?

29. For a Cobb-Douglas production function, how does the expansion path change if the wage increases while the rental rate of capital stays the same? (*Hint*: See Appendix 7C.)

30. A U.S. chemical firm has a production function of $q = 10L^{0.32}K^{0.56}$ (based on Hsieh, 1995). It faces factor prices of $w = 10$ and $r = 20$. What are its short-run marginal and average variable cost curves? (*Hint*: See Appendix 7B.)

31. A U.S. electronics firm is considering moving its production abroad. Its production function is $q = L^{0.5}K^{0.5}$ (based on Hsieh, 1995), so its $MP_L = \frac{1}{2}K^{0.5}/L^{0.5}$ and its $MP_K = \frac{1}{2}L^{0.5}/K^{0.5}$. The U.S. factor prices are $w = r = 10$. In Mexico, the wage is half that in the United States but the firm faces the same cost of capital: $w^* = 5$ and $r^* = r = 10$. What are L and K, and what is the cost of producing $q = 100$ units in both countries?

32. A U.S. electronics firm is considering moving its production abroad. Its production function is $q = L^{0.5}K^{0.5}$ (based on Hsieh, 1995), so its $MP_L = \frac{1}{2}q/L$ and its $MP_K = \frac{1}{2}q/K$. In the United States, $w = 10 = r$. At its Asian plant, the firm will pay a 10% lower wage and a 10% higher cost of capital: $w^* = 10/1.1$ and $r^* = 1.1 \times 10 = 11$. What are L and K, and what is the cost of producing $q = 100$ units in both countries? What would the cost of production be in Asia if the firm had to use the same factor quantities as in the United States?

***33.** A U.S. apparel manufacturer is considering moving its production abroad. Its production function is $q = L^{0.7}K^{0.3}$ (based on Hsieh, 1995), so its $MP_L = 0.7q/L$ and its $MP_K = 0.3q/K$. In the United States, $w = 7$ and $r = 3$. At its Asian plant, the firm will pay a 50% lower wage and a 50% higher cost of capital: $w = 10/1.1$ and $r = 1.1 \times 10 = 11$. What are L and K, and what is the cost of producing $q = 100$ units in both countries? What would the cost of production be in Asia if the firm had to use the same factor quantities as in the United States?

34. A glass manufacturer's production function is $q = 10L^{0.5}K^{0.5}$ (based on Hsieh, 1995). Its marginal product functions are $MP_L = 5K^{0.5}/L^{0.5} = \frac{1}{2}q/L$ and $MP_K = 5L^{0.5}/K^{0.5} = \frac{1}{2}q/K$ (as Appendix 6B shows). Suppose that its wage, w, is $1 per hour and the rental cost of capital, r, is $4.

a. Draw an accurate figure showing how the glass firm minimizes its cost of production.

b. What is the equation of the (long-run) expansion path for a glass firm? Illustrate this path in a graph.

c. Derive the long-run total cost curve equation as a function of q.

***35.** A firm's average cost is $AC = \alpha q^{\beta}$, where $\alpha > 0$. How can you interpret α? (*Hint*: Suppose that $q = 1$.) What sign must β have if there is learning by doing? What happens to average cost as q gets large? Draw the average cost curve as a function of output for a particular set of α and β.

Competitive Firms and Markets

8

The love of money is the root of all virtue. —George Bernard Shaw

One of the major questions firms face is "How much should we produce?" To pick a level of output that maximizes its profit, a firm must consider its cost function and how much it can sell at a given price. The amount the firm thinks it can sell depends in turn on the market demand of consumers and its beliefs about how other firms in the market will behave. The behavior of firms depends on the **market structure**: the number of firms in the market, the ease with which firms can enter and leave the market, and the ability of firms to differentiate their products from those of their rivals.

market structure
the number of firms in the market, the ease with which firms can enter and leave the market, and the ability of firms to differentiate their products from those of their rivals

In this chapter, we look at a competitive market structure, one in which many firms produce identical products and firms can easily enter and exit the market. Because each firm produces a small share of the total market output and its output is identical to that of other firms, each firm is a *price taker* that cannot raise its price above the market price. If it were to try to do so, this firm would be unable to sell any of its output because consumers would buy the good at a lower price from the other firms in the market. The market price summarizes all a firm needs to know about the demand of consumers *and* the behavior of its rivals. Thus a competitive firm can ignore the specific behavior of individual rivals in deciding how much to produce.[1]

In this chapter, we examine five main topics

1. **Competition.** A competitive firm is a price taker, and as such it faces a horizontal demand curve.
2. **Profit Maximization.** To maximize profit, any firm must make two decisions: how much to produce and whether to produce at all.
3. **Competition in the Short Run.** Variable costs determine a profit-maximizing, competitive firm's supply curve, the market supply curve, and with the market demand curve, the competitive equilibrium in the short run.
4. **Competition in the Long Run.** Firm supply, market supply, and competitive equilibrium are different in the long run than in the short run because firms can vary inputs that were fixed in the short run.
5. **Zero Profit for Competitive Firms in the Long Run.** In the long-run competitive market equilibrium, profit-maximizing firms break even, so firms that do not try to maximize profits lose money and leave the market.

[1]In contrast, each oligopolistic firm must consider the behavior of each of its small number of rivals, as we discuss in Chapter 13.

8.1 Competition

Competition is a common market structure that has very desirable properties, so it is useful to compare other market structures to competition. In this section, we describe the properties of competitive firms and markets. Next, we examine how competitive firms maximize profit to derive the short-run and long-run supply curves of competitive firms and competitive markets. Then we reexamine the competitive equilibrium.

Price Taking

When most people talk about "competitive firms," they mean firms that are rivals for the same customers. By this interpretation, any market that has more than one firm is competitive. However, to an economist, only some of these multifirm markets are competitive.

Economists say that a market is *competitive* if each firm in the market is a *price taker*: a firm that cannot significantly affect the market price for its output or the prices at which it buys its inputs. If any one of the more than 107,000 soybean farms in the United States were to stop producing soybeans or to double its production, the market price of soybeans would not change appreciably. Similarly, by stopping production or doubling its production, a soybean farm would have little or no effect on the price for soybean seeds, fertilizer, and other inputs.

Why would a competitive firm be a price taker? It has no choice. The firm *has* to be a price taker if it faces a demand curve that is horizontal at the market price. If the demand curve is horizontal at the market price, the firm can sell as much as it wants at the market price, so it has no incentive to lower its price. Similarly, the firm cannot increase the price at which it sells by restricting its output because it faces an infinitely elastic demand (see Chapter 3): A small increase in price results in its demand falling to zero.

Why the Firm's Demand Curve Is Horizontal

Firms are likely to be price takers in markets that have some or all of four properties:

- Consumers believe that all firms in the market sell *identical products*.
- Firms *freely enter and exit* the market.
- *Buyers and sellers know the prices* charged by firms.
- *Transaction costs*—the expenses of finding a trading partner and making a trade for a good or service other than the price paid for that good or service—*are low*.

When the products of all firms are seen as perfect substitutes, no firm can sell its product if it charges more than others because no consumer is willing to pay a premium for that product. Consumers don't ask which farm grew a Granny Smith apple because they view apples as *homogeneous* or *undifferentiated* products. In contrast, consumers who know that the characteristics of a Jaguar and a Civic differ substantially view automobiles as *heterogeneous* or *differentiated* products. If some customers prefer one firm's product to those of other firms, the firm's demand curve has a downward slope. One firm can charge more than other firms without losing all its customers.

No firm can raise its price above the market price if other firms are able and eager to undercut another firm's high price to attract more customers. Even in markets with only a few firms, if other firms can quickly and easily enter, a firm cannot raise its price without other firms entering the market and undercutting its price. Moreover, ease of entry may cause the number of firms in a market to be large. The more firms there are in a market, the less the effect of a change in one firm's output on total market output and hence on the market price. If one of the 107,000 soybean growers drops out of the market, market supply falls by only 0.00093% (assuming that the firms are of equal size), so the market price is unaffected.

If buyers know the prices other firms charge—the market price—a firm cannot raise its price without losing its customers. In contrast, if consumers do not know the prices other firms charge, a firm can charge more than other firms without losing all its customers, so its demand curve is downward sloping.

If transaction costs are low, it is easy for a customer to buy from a rival firm if the customer's usual supplier raises its price. Transaction costs are low if buyers and sellers do not have to spend time and money finding each other or hiring lawyers to write contracts in order to make a trade. The higher the transaction costs, the more likely that a firm's demand curve is downward sloping. Because finding a new, competent auto mechanic is very time consuming or involves traveling a great distance, some consumers continue to use their current auto repair shop even if it charges more than other firms. In some markets, buyers and sellers are brought together in a single room, so transaction costs are virtually zero. For example, transaction costs are very low at the auction in Amsterdam that the Bloemenveiling Aalsmeer cooperative holds daily for 10,000 sellers who ship 16,000 types of flowers and plants from Zimbabwe, Colombia, Israel, Thailand, and Europe to 5,000 buyers around the world with over 100,000 transactions per day—60% of world trade.

We call a market in which all these conditions hold a *perfectly competitive market*. In such a market, if a firm raised its price above the market price, the firm would be unable to make any sales. Its former customers would know that other firms sell an identical product at a lower price. These customers can easily find those other firms and buy from them without incurring extra transaction costs. If firms that are currently in the market cannot meet the demand of this firm's former customers, new firms can quickly and easily enter the market. Thus, firms in such a market must be price takers.

The market for wheat is an example of an almost perfectly competitive market. Many farmers produce identical products, and transaction costs are negligible. Wheat is sold in a formal exchange or market such as the Chicago Commodity Exchange. Using a formal exchange, buyers and sellers can easily place buy or sell orders in person, over the telephone, or electronically, so transaction costs are negligible. No time is wasted in finding someone who wants to trade, and the transactions are made virtually instantaneously without much paperwork. Moreover, every buyer and seller in the market knows the market prices, quantities, and qualities of wheat available at any moment.

Even if some of these conditions are violated, firms and consumers may still be price takers. For example, even if entry of new firms is limited but the market has a very large number of firms and each can produce much more than its current output at about the same cost, firms are price takers. If one of these firms tries to raise its price, it will be unable to sell to consumers because other firms will expand their output if necessary to meet demand. A firm's demand curve is essentially horizontal as long as there are many firms in the market. (See **www.myeconlab.com/perloff**, Chapter 8, "Competitive Firm's Demand Curve.")

Derivation of a Competitive Firm's Demand Curve

Are the demand curves faced by individual competitive firms actually flat? To answer this question, we use a modified supply-and-demand diagram to derive the demand curve an individual firm faces.

residual demand curve the market demand that is not met by other sellers at any given price.

The demand curve that an individual firm faces is called the **residual demand curve**: the market demand that is not met by other sellers at any given price. The firm's residual demand function, $D^r(p)$, shows the quantity demanded from the firm at price p. A firm sells only to people who have not already purchased the good from another seller. We can determine how much demand is left for a particular firm at each possible price using the market demand curve and the supply curve for all *other* firms in the market. The quantity the market demands is a function of the price: $Q = D(p)$. The supply curve of the other firms is $S^o(p)$. The residual demand function equals the market demand function, $D(p)$, minus the supply function of all other firms:

$$D^r(p) = D(p) - S^o(p). \tag{8.1}$$

At prices so high that the amount supplied by other firms, $S^o(p)$, is greater than the quantity demanded by the market, $D(p)$, the residual quantity demanded, $D^r(p)$, is zero.

In Figure 8.1 we derive the residual demand for a Canadian manufacturing firm that produces metal chairs. Panel b shows the market demand curve, D, and the

Figure 8.1 Residual Demand Curve.

The residual demand curve, $D^r(p)$, that a single office furniture manufacturing firm faces is the market demand, $D(p)$, minus the supply of the other firms in the market, $S^o(p)$. The residual demand curve is much flatter than the market demand curve.

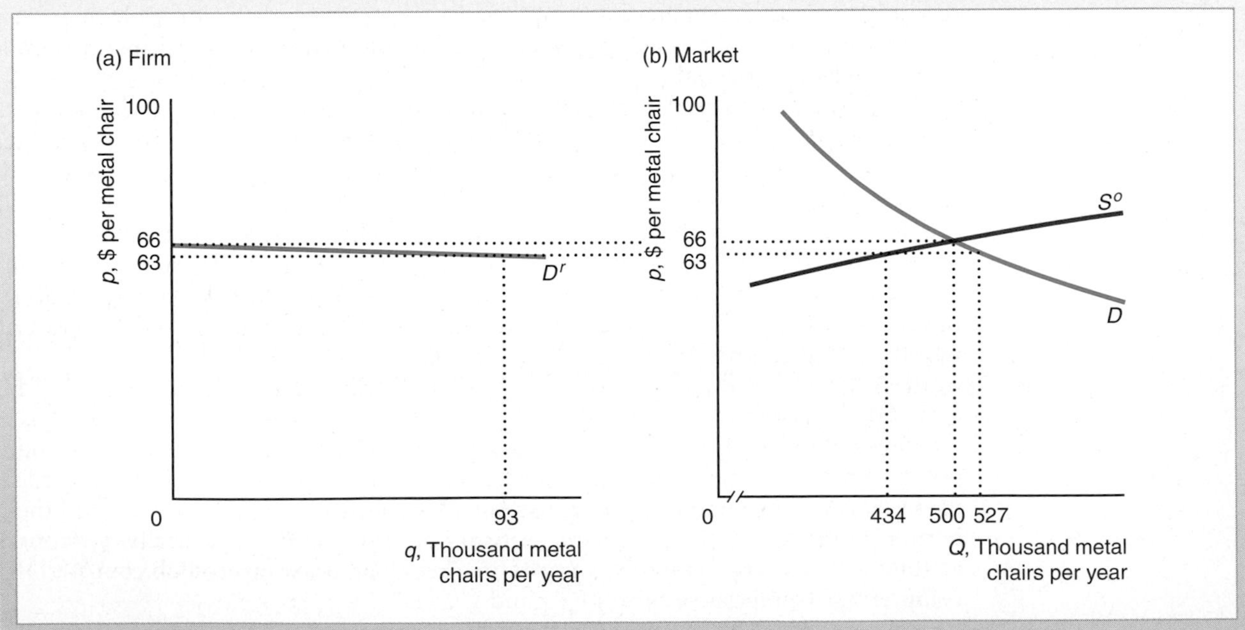

supply of all but one manufacturing firm, S^o.[2] At p = \$66 per chair, the supply of other firms, 500 units (one unit being 1,000 metal chairs) per year, exactly equals the market demand (panel b), so the residual quantity demanded of the remaining firm (panel a) is zero.

At prices below \$66, the other chair firms are not willing to supply as much as the market demands. At p = \$63, for example, the market demand is 527 units, but other firms want to supply only 434 units. As a result, the residual quantity demanded from the individual firm at p = \$63 is 93 (= 527 – 434) units. Thus, the residual demand curve at any given price is the horizontal difference between the market demand curve and the supply curve of the other firms.

The residual demand curve the firm faces, panel a, is much flatter than the market demand curve, panel b. As a result, the elasticity of the residual demand curve is much higher than the market elasticity.

If there are n identical firms in the market, the elasticity of demand, ε_i, facing Firm i is

$$\varepsilon_i = n\varepsilon - (n-1)\eta_o, \tag{8.2}$$

where ε is the market elasticity of demand (a negative number), η_o is the elasticity of supply of each of the other firms (typically a positive number), and $n - 1$ is the number of other firms (see Appendix 8A for the derivation).

There are n = 78 firms manufacturing metal chairs in Canada. If they are identical, the elasticity of demand facing a single firm is

$$\varepsilon_i = n\varepsilon - (n-1)\eta_o = [78 \times (-1.1)] - [77 \times 3.1] = -85.8 - 238.7 = -324.5.$$

That is, a typical firm faces a residual demand elasticity, –324.5, that's nearly 300 times the market elasticity, –1.1. If a firm raises its price by one-tenth of a percent, the quantity it could sell would fall by nearly one-third. Therefore, the competitive model assumption that this firm faces a horizontal demand curve with an infinite price elasticity is not much of an exaggeration.

As Equation (8.2) shows, a firm's residual demand curve is more elastic the more firms, n, in the market, the more elastic the market demand, ε, and the larger the elasticity of supply of the other firms, η_o. If the supply curve slopes upward, the residual demand elasticity, ε_i, must be at least as elastic as $n\varepsilon$ (because the second term only makes the estimate more elastic), so using $n\varepsilon$ as an approximation is conservative. For example, even though the market elasticity of demand for soybeans is very inelastic, about –0.2, because there are roughly 107,000 soybean farms, the residual demand facing a single firm must be at least $n\varepsilon$ = 107,000 × (–0.2) = –21,400, which is extremely elastic.

See Question 1.

Why We Study Perfect Competition

Economists spend a great deal of time discussing perfect competition, which takes place in markets in which firms are price takers because products are homogeneous, firms enter and exit the market freely, buyers and sellers know the prices charged by firms, and transaction costs are low.[3]

---

[2]The figure uses constant elasticity demand and supply curves. The elasticity of supply, 3.1, is based on the estimated cost function from Robidoux and Lester (1988) for Canadian office furniture manufacturers. I estimate that the elasticity of demand is –1.1 using data from Statistics Canada, *Office Furniture Manufacturers.*

[3]In addition, a perfectly competitive market has no externalities such as pollution (see Chapter 18).

Perfectly competitive markets are important for two reasons. First, many markets can be reasonably described as competitive. Many agricultural and other commodity markets, stock exchanges, retail and wholesale markets, building construction markets, and others have many or all of the properties of a perfectly competitive market. The competitive supply-and-demand model works well enough in these markets that it accurately predicts the effects of changes in taxes, costs, incomes, and other factors on market equilibrium.

Second, a perfectly competitive market has many desirable properties. Economists use this model as the ideal against which real-world markets are compared. Throughout the rest of this book, we show that society as a whole is worse off if the properties of the perfectly competitive market fail to hold. From this point on, for brevity, we use the phrase *competitive market* to mean a *perfectly competitive market* unless we explicitly note an imperfection.

8.2 Profit Maximization

"Too caustic?" To hell with the cost. If it's a good picture, we'll make it.
—Samuel Goldwyn

Economists usually assume that *all* firms—not just competitive firms—want to maximize their profits. One reason is that many businesspeople say that their objective is to maximize profits. A second reason is that firms—especially competitive firms—that do not maximize profit are likely to lose money and be driven out of business.

In this section, we discuss how any type of firm—not just a competitive firm—maximizes its profit. We then examine how a competitive firm in particular maximizes profit.

Profit

A firm's *profit*, π, is the difference between a firm's revenues, R, and its cost, C:

$$\pi = R - C.$$

If profit is negative, $\pi < 0$, the firm makes a *loss*.

Economists and businesspeople often measure profit differently. Because both economists and businesspeople measure revenue the same way—revenue is price times quantity—the difference in their profit measures is due to the way they measure costs (see Chapter 7). Some businesses use only explicit costs: a firm's out-of-pocket expenditures on inputs such as workers' wage payments, payments for materials, and payments for energy. *Economic cost* includes both explicit and implicit costs. Economic cost is the *opportunity cost*: the value of the best alternative use of any asset the firm employs.

economic profit
revenue minus *economic* cost

Economic profit is revenue minus economic cost. Because explicit cost is less than economic cost, *business profit*—based on only explicit cost—is often larger than economic profit. The reason that this distinction is important is that a firm may make a costly mistake if it mismeasures profit by ignoring relevant opportunity costs.

A couple of examples illustrate the difference in the two profit measures and the importance of this distinction. First, let's return to the scenario in Chapter 7 in which you start your own firm.[4] You have to pay explicit costs such as workers' wages and the price of materials. Like many owners, you do not pay yourself a salary. Instead, you take home a business profit of $20,000 per year.

[4]Michael Dell started a mail-order computer company while he was in college. Today, it is the world's largest personal computer company. By 2007, his wealth reached $15.8 billion.

Economists (well-known spoilsports) argue that your profit is less than $20,000. Economic profit is business profit minus any additional opportunity cost. Suppose that you could have earned $25,000 a year working for someone else instead of running your business. The opportunity cost of your time working in your business is $25,000—your forgone salary. So even though your firm made a business profit of $20,000, you had an economic loss (negative economic profit) of $5,000. Put another way, the price of being your own boss is $5,000.

By looking at only the business profit and ignoring opportunity cost, you conclude that running your business is profitable. However, if you consider economic profit, you realize that working for others maximizes your income.

Similarly, when a firm decides whether to invest in a new venture, it must consider its next best alternative use of its funds. A firm that is considering setting up a new branch in Tucson must consider all the alternatives—placing the branch in Santa Fe, putting the money that the branch would cost in the bank and earning interest, and so on. If the best alternative use of the money is to put it in the bank and earn $10,000 per year in interest, the firm should build the new branch in Tucson only if it expects to make $10,000 or more per year in business profits. That is, the firm should create a Tucson branch only if its economic profit from the new branch is zero or positive. If its economic profit is zero, then it is earning the same return on its investment as it would from putting the money in its next best alternative, the bank. From this point on, when we use the term *profit*, we mean *economic profit* unless we specifically refer to business profit.

APPLICATION

Breaking Even on Christmas Trees

On the day after Thanksgiving each year, Tom Ruffino begins selling Christmas trees in Lake Grove, New York. The table summarizes his seasonal explicit costs.

Mr. Ruffino sells trees for 29 days at the market price of $25 each. To break even, he has to sell an average of 45 trees per day, so his average cost is $25. If he can sell 1,500 trees (an average of nearly 52 trees per day), he makes an accounting profit of $5,090 for the season.

To calculate his economic profit, he has to subtract his forgone earnings at another job and the interest he would have earned on the money he paid at the beginning of the month (on his fixed costs and the price of the trees, $27,110) if he had invested that money elsewhere, such as in a bank, for a month. Although the forgone interest is small, his alternative earnings could be a large proportion of his business profit.

Fixed Costs	
Permit	$ 300
Security (guard patrol when the lot is closed to prevent theft)	360
Insurance	700
Electricity	1,000
Lot rental (undeveloped land across from a major shopping mall)	2,500
Miscellaneous (fences, lot cleanup, snow removal)	2,000
Total fixed costs:	$6,860
Variable Costs	
Labor (two full-time employees at $12 an hour for 50 hours a week, plus some part-time workers)	$ 5,500
Trees (1,500 trees bought from a Canadian tree farm at $11.50 each)	17,250
Shipping (1,500 trees at $2 each)	3,000
Total variable costs:	$25,750
Total accounting costs:	$32,610

Two Steps to Maximizing Profit

A firm's profit varies with its output level. The firm's profit function is

$$\pi(q) = R(q) - C(q).$$

A firm decides how much output to sell to maximize its profit. To maximize its profit, any firm (not just competitive, price-taking firms) must answer two questions:

- **Output decision.** If the firm produces, what output level, q^*, maximizes its profit or minimizes its loss?
- **Shutdown decision.** Is it more profitable to produce q^* or to shut down and produce no output?

The profit curve in Figure 8.2 illustrates these two basic decisions. This firm makes losses at very low and very high output levels and positive profits at moderate output levels. The profit curve first rises and then falls, reaching a maximum profit of π^* when its output is q^*. Because the firm makes a positive profit at that output, it chooses to produce q^* units of output.

Output Rules. A firm can use one of three equivalent rules to choose how much output to produce. All types of firms maximize profit using the same rules.

The most straightforward rule is

Output Rule 1: The firm sets its output where its profit is maximized.

The profit curve in Figure 8.2 is maximized at π^* when output is q^*. If the firm knows its entire profit curve, it can immediately set its output to maximize its profit.

Even if the firm does not know the exact shape of its profit curve, it may be able to find the maximum by experimenting. The firm slightly increases its output. If profit increases, the firm increases the output more. The firm keeps increasing output until profit does not change. At that output, the firm is at the peak of the profit curve. If profit falls when the firm first increases its output, the firm tries decreasing its output. It keeps decreasing its output until it reaches the peak of the profit curve.

marginal profit
the change in profit a firm gets from selling one more unit of output

What the firm is doing is experimentally determining the slope of the profit curve. The slope of the profit curve is the firm's **marginal profit**: the change in the profit

Figure 8.2 Maximizing Profit.

By setting its output at q^*, the firm maximizes its profit at π^*.

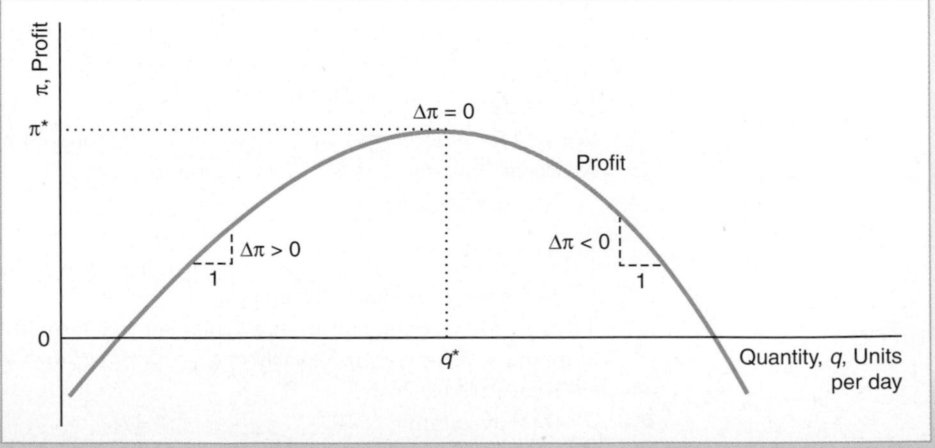

the firm gets from selling one more unit of output, $\Delta\pi/\Delta q$.[5] In the figure, the marginal profit or slope is positive when output is less than q^*, zero when output is q^*, and negative when output is greater than q^*. Thus,

Output Rule 2: A firm sets its output where its marginal profit is zero.

marginal revenue (*MR*) the change in revenue a firm gets from selling one more unit of output

A third way to express this profit-maximizing output rule is in terms of cost and revenue. The marginal profit depends on a firm's *marginal cost* and *marginal revenue*. A firm's *marginal cost* (MC) is the amount by which a firm's cost changes if it produces one more unit of output (Chapter 7): $MC = \Delta C/\Delta q$, where ΔC is the change in cost when output changes by Δq. Similarly, a firm's **marginal revenue**, MR, is the change in revenue it gets from selling one more unit of output: $\Delta R/\Delta q$, where ΔR is the change in revenue.[6] If a firm that was selling q units of output sells one more unit of output, the extra revenue, $MR(q)$, raises its profit, but the extra cost, $MC(q)$, lowers its profit. The change in the firm's profit is[7]

$$\text{Marginal profit}(q) = MR(q) - MC(q).$$

Does it pay for a firm to produce one more unit of output? If the marginal revenue from this last unit of output exceeds its marginal cost, $MR(q) > MC(q)$, the firm's marginal profit is positive, $MR(q) - MC(q) > 0$, so it pays to increase output. The firm keeps increasing its output until its marginal profit $= MR(q) - MC(q) = 0$. There, its marginal revenue equals its marginal cost: $MR(q) = MC(q)$. If the firm produces more output where its marginal cost exceeds its marginal revenue, $MR(q) < MC(q)$, the extra output reduces the firm's profit. Thus, a third, equivalent rule is (Appendix 8B):

Output Rule 3: A firm sets its output where its marginal revenue equals its marginal cost:

$$MR(q) = MC(q).$$

Shutdown Rule. The firm chooses to produce if it can make a profit. If the firm is making a loss, however, does it shut down? The answer, surprisingly, is "It depends." The general rule, which holds for all types of firms in both the short run and in the long run, is

Shutdown Rule 1: The firm shuts down only if it can reduce its loss by doing so.

In the short run, the firm has variable and sunk fixed costs (Chapter 7). By shutting down, it can eliminate the variable cost, such as labor and materials, but usually not the fixed cost, the amount it paid for its factory and equipment. By shutting down, the firm stops receiving revenue and stops paying the avoidable costs, but it is still stuck with its fixed cost. Thus, it pays for the firm to shut down only if its revenue is less than its avoidable cost.

---

[5]The marginal profit is the derivative of the profit function, $\pi(q)$, with respect to quantity, $d\pi(q)/dq$.

[6]The marginal revenue is the derivative of the revenue function with respect to quantity:

$$MR(q) = dR(q)/dq.$$

[7]Because profit is $\pi(q) = R(q) - C(q)$, marginal profit is the difference between marginal revenue and marginal cost:

$$\frac{d\pi(q)}{dq} = \frac{dR(q)}{dq} - \frac{dC(q)}{dq} = MR - MC.$$

Suppose that the weekly firm's revenue is R = \$2,000, its variable cost is VC = \$1,000, and its fixed cost is F = \$3,000, which is the price it paid for a machine that it cannot resell or use for any other purpose. This firm is making a short-run loss:

$$\pi = R - VC - F = \$2{,}000 - \$1{,}000 - \$3{,}000 = -\$2{,}000.$$

See Questions 2 and 3.

If the firm shuts down, it loses its fixed cost, \$3,000, so it is better off operating. Its revenue more than covers its avoidable, variable cost and offsets some of the fixed cost.

However, if its revenue is only \$500, its loss is \$3,500, which is greater than the loss from the fixed cost alone of \$3,000. Because its revenue is less than its avoidable, variable cost, the firm reduces its loss by shutting down.

In conclusion, the firm compares its revenue to its variable cost only when deciding whether to stop operating. Because the fixed cost is *sunk*—the expense cannot be avoided by stopping operations (Chapter 7)—the firm pays this cost whether it shuts down or not. Thus, the sunk fixed cost is irrelevant to the shutdown decision.[8]

In the long run, all costs are avoidable because the firm can eliminate them all by shutting down. Thus, in the long run, where the firm can avoid all losses by not operating, it pays to shut down if the firm faces any loss at all. As a result, we can restate the shut-down rule as:

See Question 4.

Shutdown Rule 2: The firm shuts down only if its revenue is less than its avoidable cost.

This rule holds for all types of firms in both the short run and the long run.

8.3 Competition in the Short Run

Having considered how firms maximize profit in general, we now examine the profit-maximizing behavior of competitive firms, first in the short run and then in the long run. In doing so, we pay careful attention to the firm's shutdown decision.

Short-Run Competitive Profit Maximization

A competitive firm, like other firms, first determines the output at which it maximizes its profit (or minimizes its loss). Second, it decides whether to produce or to shut down.

Short-Run Output Decision. We've already seen that *any* firm maximizes its profit at the output where its marginal profit is zero or, equivalently, where its marginal cost equals its marginal revenue. Because it faces a horizontal demand curve, a competitive firm can sell as many units of output as it wants at the market price, p. Thus, a competitive firm's revenue, $R = pq$, increases by p if it sells one more unit of output, so its marginal revenue is p.[9] For example, if the firm faces a market price

---

[8]We usually assume that fixed cost is sunk. However, if a firm can sell its capital for as much as it paid, its fixed cost is avoidable and should be taken into account when the firm is considering whether to shut down. A firm with a fully avoidable fixed cost always shuts down if it makes a short-run loss. If a firm buys a specialized piece of machinery for \$1,000 that can be used only in its business but can be sold for scrap metal for \$100, then \$100 of the fixed cost is avoidable and \$900 is sunk. Only the avoidable portion of fixed cost is relevant for the shutdown decision.

[9]Because $R(q) = pq$, $MR = dR(q)/dq = d(pq)/dq = p$.

of \$2 per unit, its revenue is \$10 if it sells 5 units and \$12 if it sells 6 units, so its marginal revenue for the sixth unit is \$2 = \$12 − \$10 (the market price). Because a competitive firm's marginal revenue equals the market price, *a profit-maximizing competitive firm produces the amount of output at which its marginal cost equals the market price:*

$$MC(q) = p. \tag{8.3}$$

To illustrate how a competitive firm maximizes its profit, we examine a typical Canadian lime manufacturing firm. Lime is a nonmetallic mineral used in mortars, plasters, cements, bleaching powders, steel, paper, glass, and other products. The lime plant's estimated cost curve, C, in panel a of Figure 8.3 rises less rapidly with output at low quantities than at higher quantities.[10] If the market price of lime is p = \$8, the competitive firm faces a horizontal demand curve at \$8 (panel b), so the revenue curve, $R = pq$ = \$8q, in panel a is an upward-sloping straight line with a slope of 8.

By producing 284 units (one unit being 1,000 metric tons), the firm maximizes its profit at π^* = \$426,000, which is the height of the profit curve and the difference between the revenue and cost curves at that quantity in panel a. At the competitive firm's profit-maximizing output, its marginal cost equals the market price of \$8 (Equation 8.3) at point e in panel b.

Point e is the competitive firm's equilibrium. Were the firm to produce less than the equilibrium quantity, 284 units, the market price would be above its marginal cost. As a result, the firm could increase its profit by expanding output because the firm earns more on the next ton, p = \$8, than it costs to produce it, MC < \$8. If the firm were to produce more than 284 units, so market price was below its marginal cost, MC > \$8, the firm could increase its profit by reducing its output. Thus, the firm does not want to change its quantity only at output when its marginal cost equals the market price.

The firm's maximum profit, π^* = \$426,000, is the shaded rectangle in panel b. The length of the rectangle is the number of units sold, $q = 284$ units. The height of the rectangle is the firm's average profit, which is the difference between the market price, or average revenue, and its average cost:

$$\frac{\pi}{q} = \frac{R - C}{q} = \frac{pq}{q} - \frac{C}{q} = p - AC. \tag{8.4}$$

Here the average profit per unit is \$1.50 = $p - AC(284)$ = \$8 − \$6.50.

As panel b illustrates, the firm chooses its output level to maximize its total profit rather than its profit per ton. By producing 140 units, where its average cost is minimized at \$6, the firm could maximize its average profit at \$2. Although the firm gives up 50¢ in profit per ton when it produces 284 units instead of 140 units, it more than makes up for that by selling an extra 144 units. The firm's profit is \$146,000 higher at 284 units than at 140 units.

See Questions 5 and 6 and Problems 36 and 37.

Using the $MC = p$ rule, a firm can decide how much to alter its output in response to a change in its cost due to a new tax. For example, one of the many lime plants in Canada is in the province of Manitoba. If that province taxes that lime firm, the Manitoba firm is the only one in the lime market affected by the tax, so the tax will not affect market price. Solved Problem 8.1 shows how a profit-maximizing competitive firm would react to a tax that affected only it.

[10]Robidoux and Lester (1988) estimate the variable cost function. In the figure, we assume that the minimum of the average variable cost curve is \$5 at 50,000 metric tons of output. Based on information from Statistics Canada, we set the fixed cost so that the average cost is \$6 at 140,000 tons.

Figure 8.3 How a Competitive Firm Maximizes Profit.

(a) A competitive lime manufacturing firm produces 284 units of lime so as to maximize its profit at $\pi^* = \$426,000$ (Robidoux and Lester, 1988). (b) The firm's profit is maximized where its marginal revenue, *MR*, which is the market price, $p = \$8$, equals its marginal cost, *MC*.

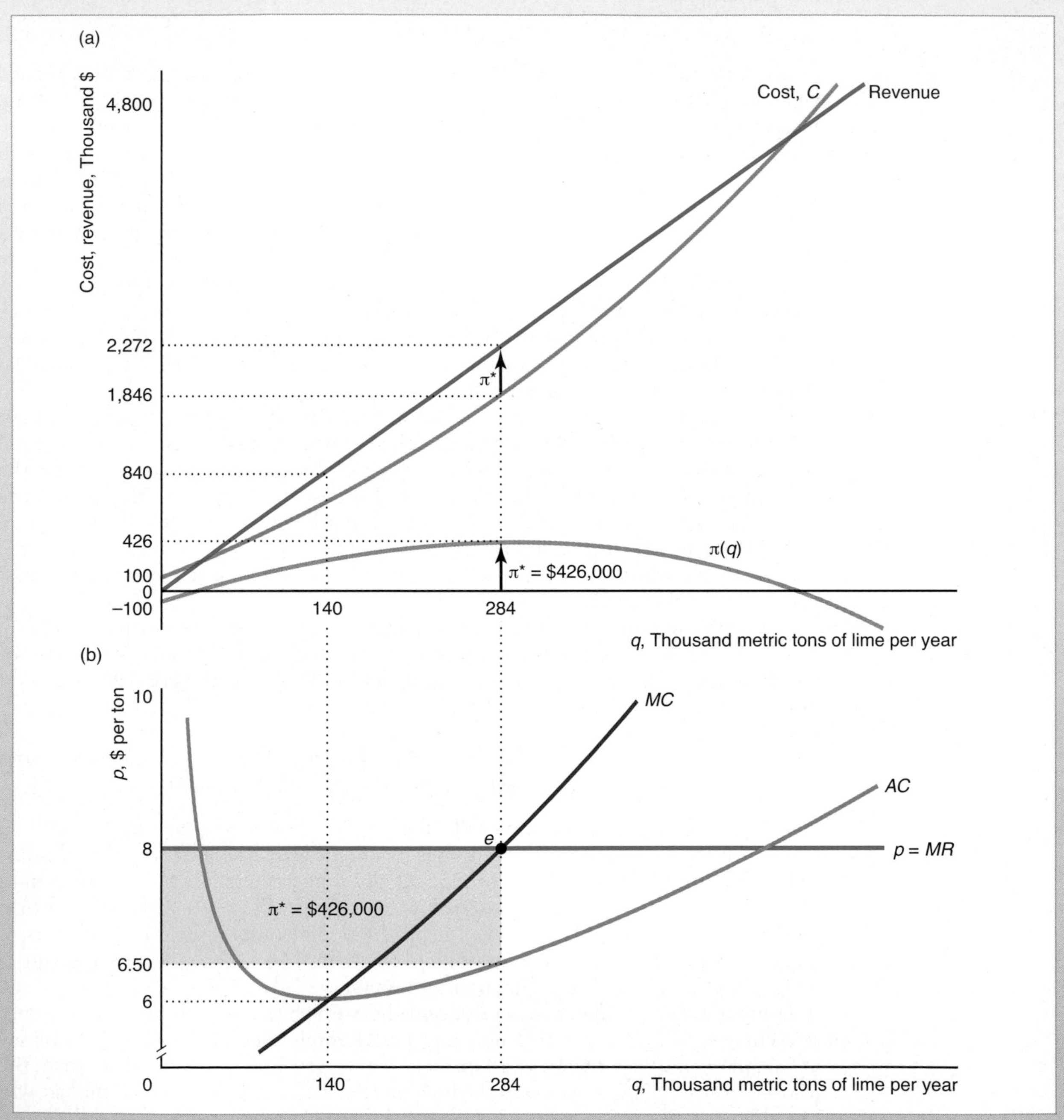

Solved Problem 8.1

If a specific tax of τ is collected from only one competitive firm, how should that firm change its output level to maximize its profit, and how does its maximum profit change?

Answer

1. *Show how the tax shifts the marginal cost and average cost curves.* The firm's before-tax marginal cost curve is MC^1 and its before-tax average cost curve is AC^1. Because the specific tax adds τ to the per-unit cost, it shifts the after-tax marginal cost curve up to $MC^2 = MC^1 + \tau$ and the after-tax average cost curve to $AC^2 = AC^1 + \tau$ (see Chapter 7).

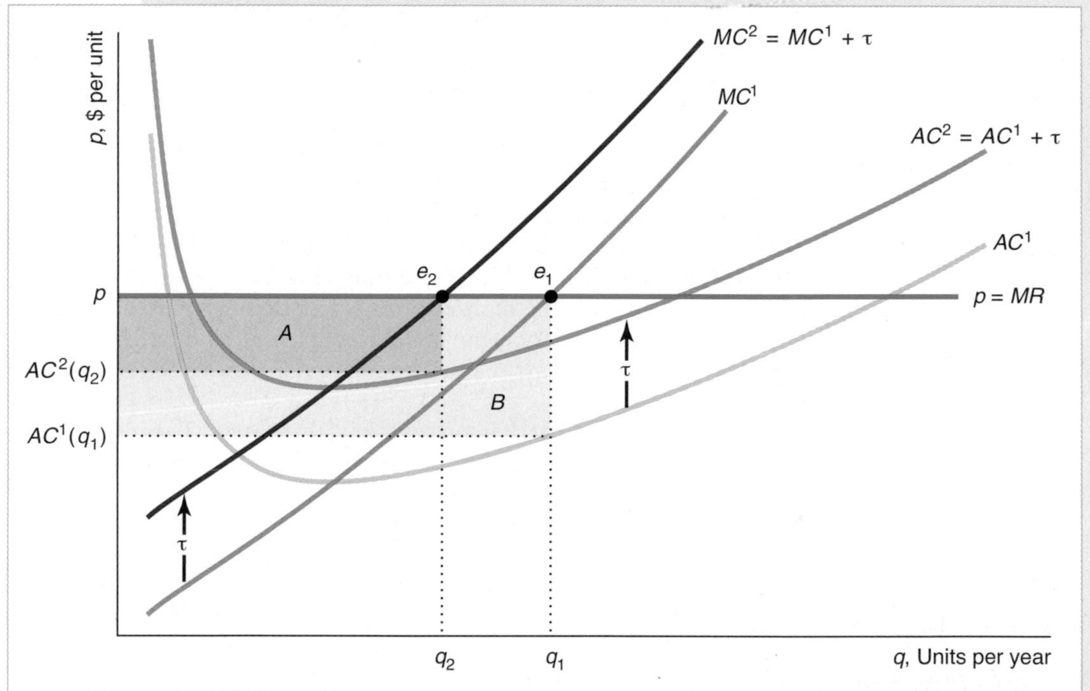

2. *Determine the before-tax and after-tax equilibria and the amount by which the firm adjusts its output.* Where the before-tax marginal cost curve, MC^1, hits the horizontal demand curve, p, at e_1, the profit-maximizing quantity is q_1. The after-tax marginal cost curve, MC^2, intersects the demand curve, p, at e_2 where the profit-maximizing quantity is q_2. Thus, in response to the tax, the firm produces $q_1 - q_2$ fewer units of output.

3. *Show how the profit changes after the tax.* Because the market price is constant but the firm's average cost curve shifts upward, the firm's profit at every output level falls. The firm sells fewer units (because of the increase in MC) and makes less profit per unit (because of the increase in AC). The after-tax profit is area $A = \pi_2 = [p - AC^2(q_2)]q_2$, and the before-tax profit is area $A + B = \pi_1 = [p - AC^1(q_1)]q_1$, so profit falls by area B due to the tax.

Short-Run Shutdown Decision. Does the competitive lime firm operate or shut down? At the market price of $8 in Figure 8.3, the lime firm is making an economic profit, so it chooses to operate.

If the market price falls below $6, which is the minimum of the average cost curve, the price does not cover average cost, so average profit is negative (using Equation 8.4), and the firm makes a loss. (A firm cannot "lose a little on every sale but make it up on volume.") The firm shuts down only if doing so reduces or eliminates its loss. This shutdown may be temporary. When the market price rises, the firm resumes producing.

The firm can gain by shutting down only if its revenue is less than its short-run variable cost:

$$pq < VC. \tag{8.5}$$

By dividing both sides of Equation 8.5 by output, we can write this condition as

$$p < AVC(q).$$

A competitive firm shuts down if the market price is less than the minimum of its short-run average variable cost curve.

We illustrate this rule in Figure 8.4 using the lime firm's cost curves. The minimum of the average variable cost, point a, is $5 at 50 units (one unit again being 1,000 metric tons). If the market price is less than $5 per ton, the firm shuts down. The firm stops hiring labor, buying materials, and paying for energy, thereby avoiding these variable costs. If the market price rises above $5, the firm starts operating again.

In this figure, the market price is $5.50 per ton. Because the minimum of the firm's average cost, $6 (point b), is more than $5.50, the firm loses money if it produces.

Figure 8.4 The Short-Run Shutdown Decision.

The competitive lime manufacturing plant operates if price is above the minimum of the average variable cost curve, point a, at $5. With a market price of $5.50, the firm produces 100 units because that price is above $AVC(100)$ = $5.14, so the firm more than covers its out-of-pocket, variable costs. At that price, the firm makes a loss of area A = $62,000 because the price is less than the average cost of $6.12. If it shuts down, its loss is its fixed cost, area $A + B$ = $98,000. Thus, the firm does not shut down.

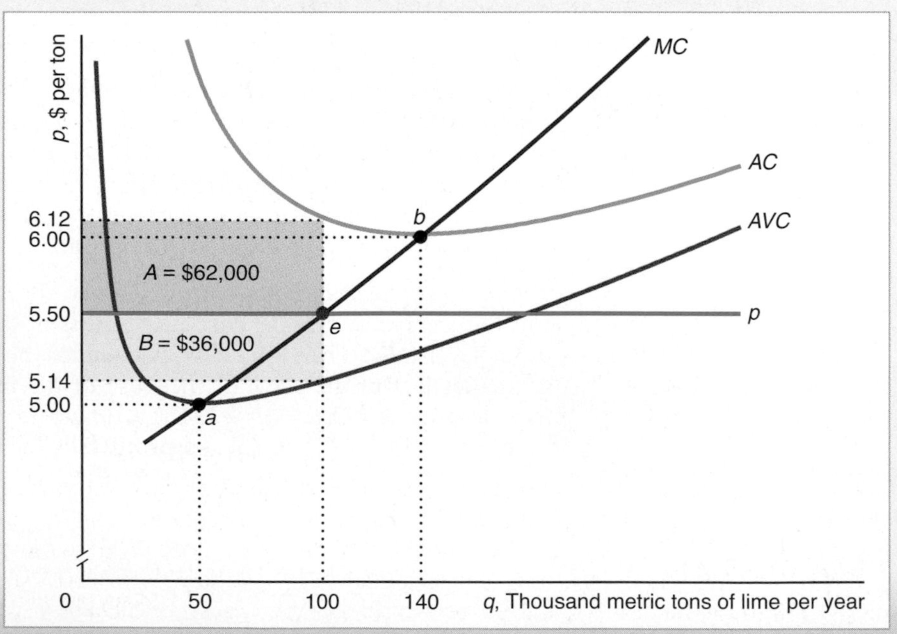

If the firm produces, it sells 100 units at *c*, where its marginal cost curve intersects its demand curve, which is horizontal at \$5.50. By operating, the firm loses area *A*, or \$62,000. The length of *A* is 100 units, and the height is the average loss per ton, or 62¢, which equals the price of \$5.50 minus the average cost at 100 units of \$6.12.

The firm is better off producing than shutting down. If the firm shuts down, it has no revenue or variable cost, so its loss is the fixed cost, \$98,000, which equals area $A + B$. The length of this box is 100 units, and its height is the lost average fixed cost of 98¢, which is the difference between the average variable cost and the average cost at 100 units.

The firm saves \$36,000 (area *B*) by producing rather than shutting down. This amount is the money left over from the revenue after paying for the variable cost, which helps cover part of the fixed cost. Thus, even if $p < AC$, so that the firm is making a loss, the firm continues to operate if $p > AVC$, so that it is more than covering its variable costs.

In summary, a competitive firm uses a two-step decision-making process to maximize its profit. First, the competitive firm determines the output that maximizes its profit or minimizes its loss when its marginal cost equals the market price (which is its marginal revenue): $MC = p$. Second, the firm chooses to produce that quantity unless it would lose more by operating than by shutting down. The firm shuts down only if the market price is less than the minimum of its average variable cost, $p < AVC$.

Solved Problem 8.2

A competitive firm's bookkeeper, upon reviewing the firm's books, finds that the firm spent twice as much on its plant, a fixed cost, as the firm's manager had previously thought. Should the manager change the output level because of this new information? How does this new information affect profit?

Answer

1. *Show that a change in fixed costs does not affect the firm's decisions.* How much the firm produces and whether it shuts down in the short run depend only on the firm's variable costs. (The firm picks its output level so that its marginal cost—which depends only on variable costs—equals the market price, and it shuts down only if market price is less than its minimum average variable cost.) Learning that the amount spent on the plant was greater than previously believed should not change the output level that the manager chooses.
2. *Show that the change in how the bookkeeper measures fixed costs does not affect economic profit.* The change in the bookkeeper's valuation of the historical amount spent on the plant may affect the firm's short-run business profit but does not affect the firm's true economic profit. The economic profit is based on opportunity costs—the amount for which the firm could rent the plant to someone else—and not on historical payments.

APPLICATION

Oil, Oil Sands, and Oil Shale Shutdowns

Oil production starts and stops as prices fluctuate. In 1998–1999, 74,000 of the 136,000 oil wells in the United States were temporarily shut down or permanently abandoned. At the time, Terry Smith, the general manager of Tidelands Oil Production Company, who had shut down 327 of his company's 834 wells, said that he would operate these wells again when price rose above \$10 a

barrel—his minimum average variable cost. Getting oil from oil wells is relatively easy. It is harder and more costly to obtain oil from other sources, so firms that use those alternative sources have higher shutdown points.

One such alternate source is in Canada. You probably know that Saudi Arabia has the most (259 billion barrels) "proven" crude oil reserves of any country in the world. But did you know that Canada has the second-largest known reserves, 180 billion barrels? Canada's reserves far exceed Iraq's third-place 113 billion (and the Arctic National Wildlife Refuge's estimated 10 billion). You rarely see discussions of Canada's vast oil reserves in newspapers because 97% of those reserves are oil sands, which cover an area the size of Florida.

Oil sands are a mixture of heavy petroleum (bitumen), water, and sandstone. Producing oil from oil sands is extremely expensive and polluting. To liberate four barrels of crude from the sands, a processor must burn the equivalent of a fifth barrel. With the technology available in 2006, two tons of sand yields a single barrel (42 gallons) of oil and produces more greenhouse gas emissions than do four cars operating for a day. Today's limited production draws from the one-fifth of the oil sands deposits that lie close enough to the surface to allow strip mining. Going after deeper deposits will be even more expensive.

The first large oil sands mining began in the 1960s, but as oil prices often were less than the $25-per-barrel average variable cost of recovering crude from the sand, production was frequently halted. In early 2008, a barrel of oil sells for more than $100 and technological improvements have lowered the average variable cost to $18 a barrel, so firms are producing oil from oil sands. Because they expect oil prices to remain high, virtually every large U.S. oil firm and one Chinese firm have Canadian oil sands projects, and their planned investments over the next decade exceed $25 billion.

Even these gigantic oil sands deposits may be exceeded by oil shale. According to some current estimates, oil shale deposits in Colorado and neighboring areas of Utah and Wyoming contain 800 billion recoverable barrels, the equivalent of 40 years of U.S. oil consumption. The United States has between 1 and 2 trillion recoverable barrels from oil shale, which is at least four times Saudi Arabia's proven reserves. A 2007 federal task force report concluded that the U.S. will be able to produce 3 million barrels of oil a day from oil shale and sands by 2035. Oil shale is much more difficult to extract and to transform into crude oil than are oil sands. Shell Oil now believes that it will be profitable to extract oil from shale at $30 a barrel. As soon as that occurs, if current oil prices stay as high as they currently are, oil shale production facilities will start operating, joining oil wells and oil sand producers.

See Questions 7–9.

Short-Run Firm Supply Curve

We just demonstrated how a competitive firm chooses its output for a given market price so as to maximize its profit. By repeating this analysis at different possible market prices, we learn how the amount the competitive firm supplies varies with the market price.

Tracing Out the Short-Run Supply Curve. As the market price increases from $p_1 = \$5$ to $p_2 = \$6$ to $p_3 = \$7$ to $p_4 = \$8$, the lime firm increases its output from 50 to 140 to 215 to 285 units per year in Figure 8.5. The equilibrium at each market price, e_1 through e_4, is determined by the intersection of the relevant demand curve—market price line—and the firm's marginal cost curve. That is, as the market price increases, the equilibria trace out the marginal cost curve.

If the price falls below the firm's minimum average variable cost at \$5, the firm shuts down. Thus, *the competitive firm's short-run supply curve is its marginal cost curve above its minimum average variable cost.*

The firm's short-run supply curve, *S*, is a thick line in the figure. At prices above \$5, the short-run supply curve is the same as the marginal cost curve. The supply is zero when price is less than the minimum of the *AVC* curve of \$5. (From now on, to keep the graph as simple as possible we will not show the supply curve at prices below minimum *AVC*.)

Factor Prices and the Short-Run Firm Supply Curve. An increase in factor prices causes the production costs of a firm to rise, shifting the firm's supply curve to the left. If all factor prices double, it costs the firm twice as much as before to produce a given level of output. If only one factor price rises, costs rise less than in proportion.

To illustrate the effect of an increase in a single factor price on supply, we examine a vegetable oil mill. This firm uses vegetable oil seed to produce canola and soybean oils, which customers use in commercial baking and soap making, as lubricants, and for other purposes. At the initial factor prices, a Canadian oil mill's average variable cost curve, AVC^1, reaches its minimum of \$7 at 100 units (where one unit is 100 metric tons) of vegetable oil, as in Figure 8.6 (based on the estimates

Figure 8.5 How the Profit-Maximizing Quantity Varies with Price.

As the market price increases, the lime manufacturing firm produces more output. The change in the price traces out the marginal cost curve of the firm.

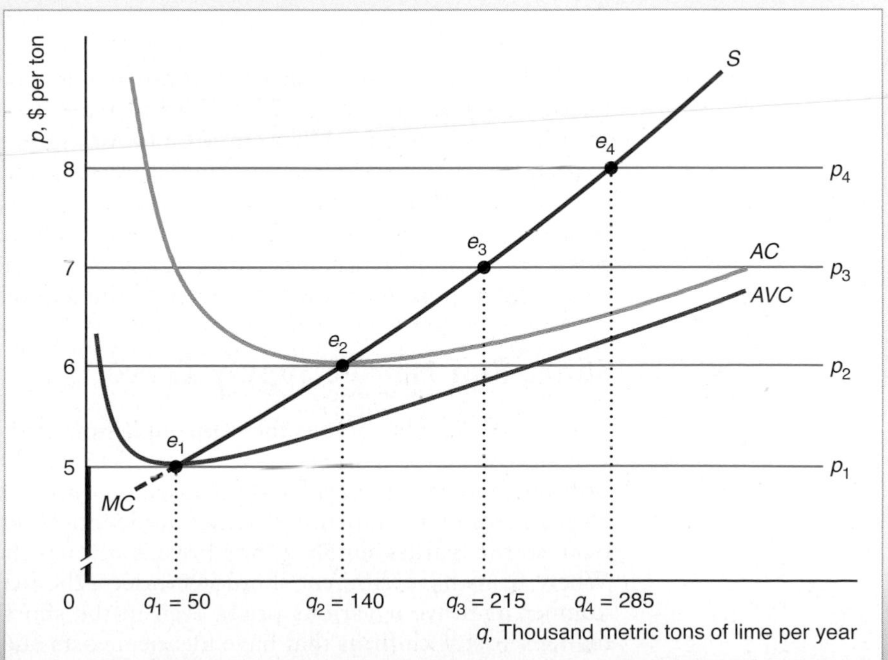

Figure 8.6 Effect of an Increase in the Cost of Materials on the Vegetable Oil Supply Curve.

Materials are 95% of variable costs, so when the price of materials rises by 25%, variable costs rise by 23.75% (95% of 25%). As a result, the supply curve of a vegetable oil mill shifts up from S^1 to S^2. If the market price is $12, the quantity supplied falls from 178 to 145 units.

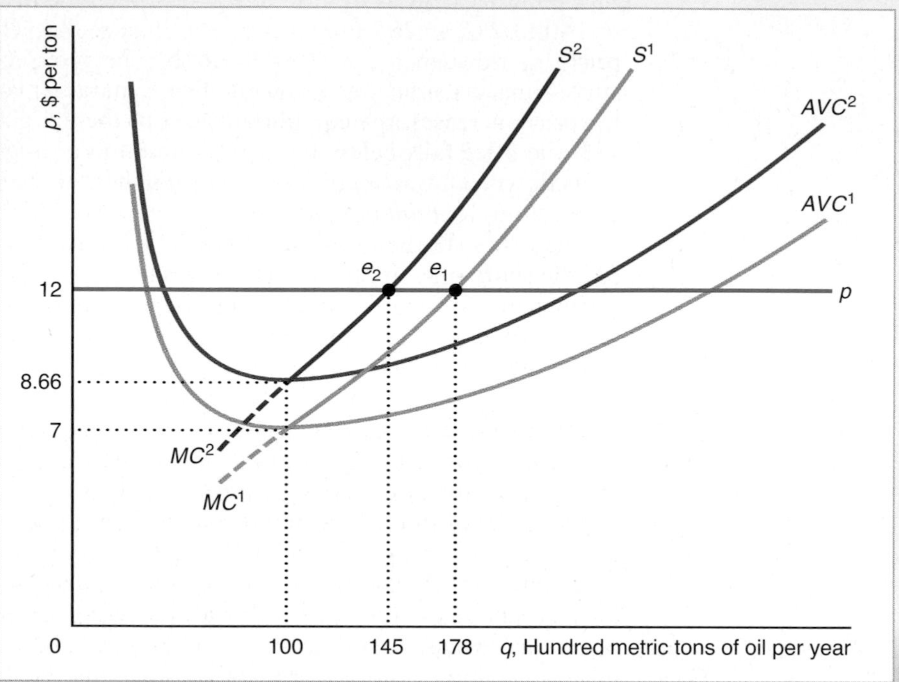

of the variable cost function for vegetable oil mills by Robidoux and Lester, 1988). As a result, the firm's initial short-run supply curve, S^1, is the initial marginal cost curve, MC^1, above $7.

If the wage, the price of energy, or the price of oil seeds increases, the cost of production rises for a vegetable oil mill. The vegetable oil mill cannot substitute between oil seeds and other factors of production. The cost of oil seeds is 95% of the variable cost. Thus, if the price of raw materials increases by 25%, variable cost rises by 95% × 25%, or 23.75%. This increase in the price of oil seeds causes the marginal cost curve to shift from MC^1 to MC^2 and the average variable cost curve to go from AVC^1 to AVC^2 in the figure. As a result, the firm's short-run supply curve shifts upward from S^1 to S^2. The price increase causes the shutdown price to rise from $7 per unit to $8.66. At a market price of $12 per unit, at the original factor prices, the firm produces 178 units. After the increase in the price of vegetable oil seeds, the firm produces only 145 units if the market price remains constant.

See Question 10.

Short-Run Market Supply Curve

The market supply curve is the horizontal sum of the supply curves of all the individual firms in the market (see Chapter 2). In the short run, the maximum number of firms in a market, n, is fixed because new firms need time to enter the market. If all the firms in a competitive market are identical, each firm's supply curve is identical, so the market supply at any price is n times the supply of an individual firm. Where firms have different shutdown prices, the market supply reflects a different number of firms at various prices even in the short run. We examine competitive markets first with firms that have identical costs and then with firms that have different costs.

Short-Run Market Supply with Identical Firms. To illustrate how to construct a short-run market supply curve, we suppose that the lime manufacturing market has $n = 5$ competitive firms with identical cost curves. Panel a of Figure 8.7 plots the short-run supply curve, S^1, of a typical firm—the *MC* curve above the minimum *AVC*—where the horizontal axis shows the firm's output, q, per year. Panel b illustrates the competitive market supply curve, the dark line S^5, where the horizontal axis is market output, Q, per year. The price axis is the same in the two panels.

If the market price is less than $5 per ton, no firm supplies any output, so the market supply is zero. At $5, each firm is willing to supply $q = 50$ units, as in panel a. Consequently, the market supply is $Q = 5q = 250$ units in panel b. At $6 per ton, each firm supplies 140 units, so the market supply is 700 ($= 5 \times 140$) units.

Suppose, however, that there were fewer than five firms in the short run. The light-color lines in panel b show the market supply curves for various other numbers of firms. The market supply curve is S^1 if there is one price-taking firm, S^2 with two firms, S^3 with three firms, and S^4 with four firms. The market supply curve flattens as the number of firms in the market increases because the market supply curve is the horizontal sum of more and more upward-sloping firm supply curves. As the number of firms grows very large, the market supply curve approaches a horizontal line at $5. Thus, *the more identical firms producing at a given price, the flatter (more elastic) the short-run market supply curve at that price.* As a result, the more firms in the market, the less the price has to increase for the short-run market supply to increase substantially. Consumers pay $6 per ton to obtain 700 units of lime if there are five firms but must pay $6.47 per ton to obtain that much with only four firms.

Short-Run Market Supply with Firms That Differ. If the firms in a competitive market have different minimum average variable costs, not all firms produce at every price, a situation that affects the shape of the short-run market supply curve. Suppose that the only two firms in the lime market are our typical lime firm with a

Figure 8.7 Short-Run Market Supply with Five Identical Lime Firms.

(a) The short-run supply curve, S^1, for a typical lime manufacturing firm is its *MC* above the minimum of its *AVC*. (b) The market supply curve, S^5, is the horizontal sum of the supply curves of each of the five identical firms. The curve S^4 shows what the market supply curve would be if there were only four firms in the market.

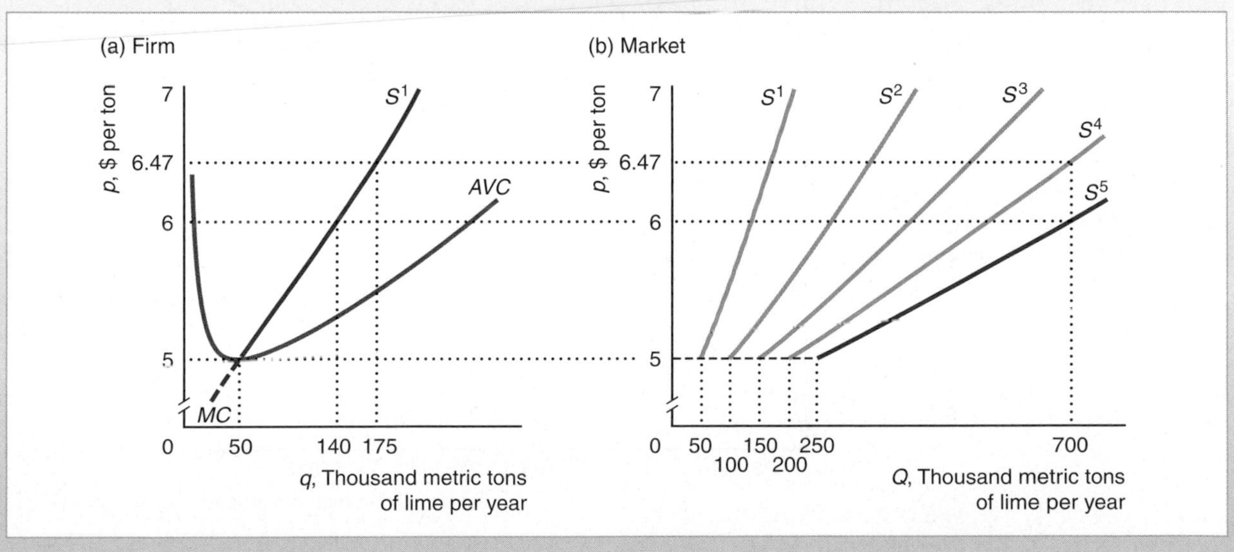

supply curve of S^1 and another firm with a higher marginal and minimum average cost with the supply curve of S^2 in Figure 8.8. The first firm produces at a market price of \$5 or above, whereas the second firm does not produce unless the price is \$6 or more. At \$5, the first firm produces 50 units, so the quantity on the market supply curve, *S*, is 50 units. Between \$5 and \$6, only the first firm produces, so the market supply, *S*, is the same as the first firm's supply, S^1. At and above \$6, both firms produce, so the market supply curve is the horizontal summation of their two individual supply curves. For example, at \$7, the first firm produces 215 units, and the second firm supplies 100 units, so the market supply is 315 units.

As with the identical firms, where both firms are producing, the market supply curve is flatter than that of either firm. Because the second firm does not produce at as low a price as the first firm, the short-run market supply curve has a steeper slope (less elastic supply) at relatively low prices than it would if the firms were identical.

Where firms differ, only the low-cost firm supplies goods at relatively low prices. As the price rises, the other, higher-cost firm starts supplying, creating a stairlike market supply curve. The more suppliers there are with differing costs, the more steps there are in the market supply curve. As price rises and more firms are supplying goods, the market supply curve flattens, so it takes a smaller increase in price to increase supply by a given amount. Stated the other way, the more firms differ in costs, the steeper the market supply curve at low prices. Differences in costs are one explanation for why some market supply curves are upward sloping.

Short-Run Competitive Equilibrium

By combining the short-run market supply curve and the market demand curve, we can determine the short-run competitive equilibrium. We first show how to deter-

Figure 8.8 Short-Run Market Supply with Two Different Lime Firms.

The supply curve S^1 is the same as for the typical lime firm in Figure 8.7. A second firm has a *MC* that lies to the left of the original firm's cost curve and a higher minimum of its *AVC*. Thus, its supply curve, S^2, lies above and to the left of the original firm's supply curve, S^1. The market supply curve, *S*, is the horizontal sum of the two supply curves. When prices are high enough for both firms to produce, \$6 and above, the market supply curve is flatter than the supply curve of either individual firm.

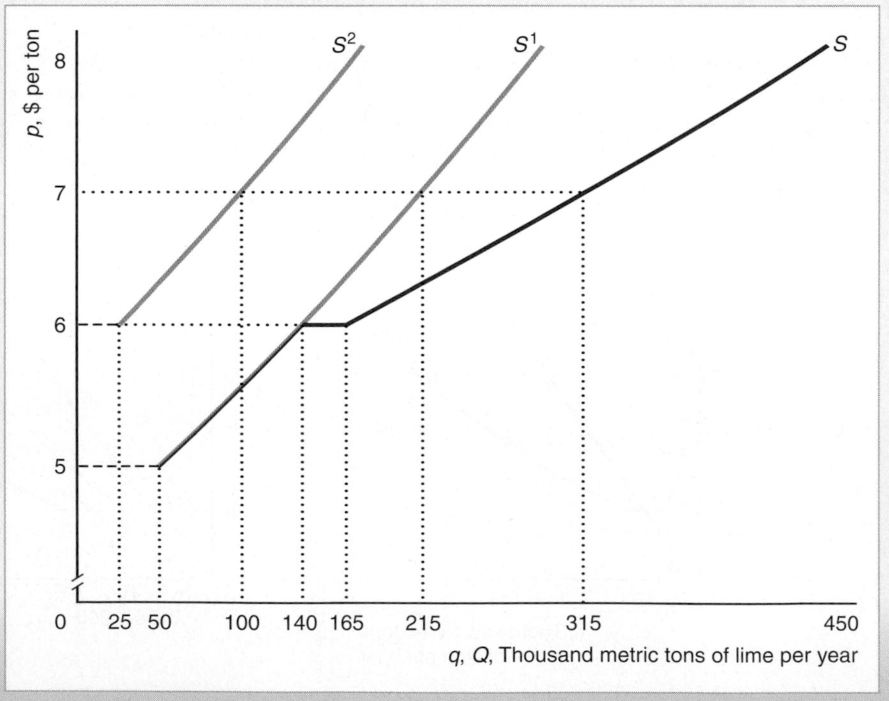

mine the equilibrium in the lime market, and we then examine how the equilibrium changes when firms are taxed.

Short-Run Equilibrium in the Lime Market. Suppose that there are five identical firms in the short-run equilibrium in the lime manufacturing industry. Panel a of Figure 8.9 shows the short-run cost curves and the supply curve, S^1, for a typical firm, and panel b shows the corresponding short-run competitive market supply curve, S.

In panel b, the initial demand curve D^1 intersects the market supply curve at E_1, the market equilibrium. The equilibrium quantity is $Q_1 = 1{,}075$ units of lime per year, and the equilibrium market price is \$7.

In panel a, each competitive firm faces a horizontal demand curve at the equilibrium price of \$7. Each price-taking firm chooses its output where its marginal cost curve intersects the horizontal demand curve at e_1. Because each firm is maximizing its profit at e_1, no firm wants to change its behavior, so e_1 is the firm's equilibrium. In panel a, each firm makes a short-run profit of area $A + B$ = \$172,000, which is the average profit per ton, $p - AC$ = \$7 – \$6.20 = 80¢, times the firm's output, q_1 = 215 units. The equilibrium market output, Q_1, is the number of firms, n, times the equilibrium output of each firm: $Q_1 = nq_1 = 5 \times 215$ units = 1,075 units (panel b).

Now suppose that the demand curve shifts to D^2. The new market equilibrium is E_2, where the price is only \$5. At that price, each firm produces q = 50 units, and market output is Q = 250 units. In panel a, each firm loses \$98,500, area $A + C$, because it makes an average per ton of $(p - AC)$ = (\$5 – \$6.97) = –\$1.97 and it sells q_2 = 50 units. However, such a firm does not shut down because price equals the firm's average variable cost, so the firm is covering its out-of-pocket expenses.

See Questions 11–18 and Problem 38.

Figure 8.9 Short-Run Competitive Equilibrium in the Lime Market.

(a) The short-run supply curve is the marginal cost above minimum average variable cost of \$5. At a price of \$5, each firm makes a short-run loss of $(p - AC)q$ = (\$5 – \$6.97) × 50,000 = –\$98,500, area $A + C$. At a price of \$7, the short-run profit of a typical lime firm is $(p - AC)q$ = (\$7 – \$6.20) × 215,000 = \$172,000, area $A + B$. (b) If there are five firms in the lime market in the short run, so the market supply is S, and the market demand curve is D^1, then the short-run equilibrium is E_1, the market price is \$7, and market output is Q_1 = 1,075 units. If the demand curve shifts to D^2, the market equilibrium is p = \$5 and Q_2 = 250 units.

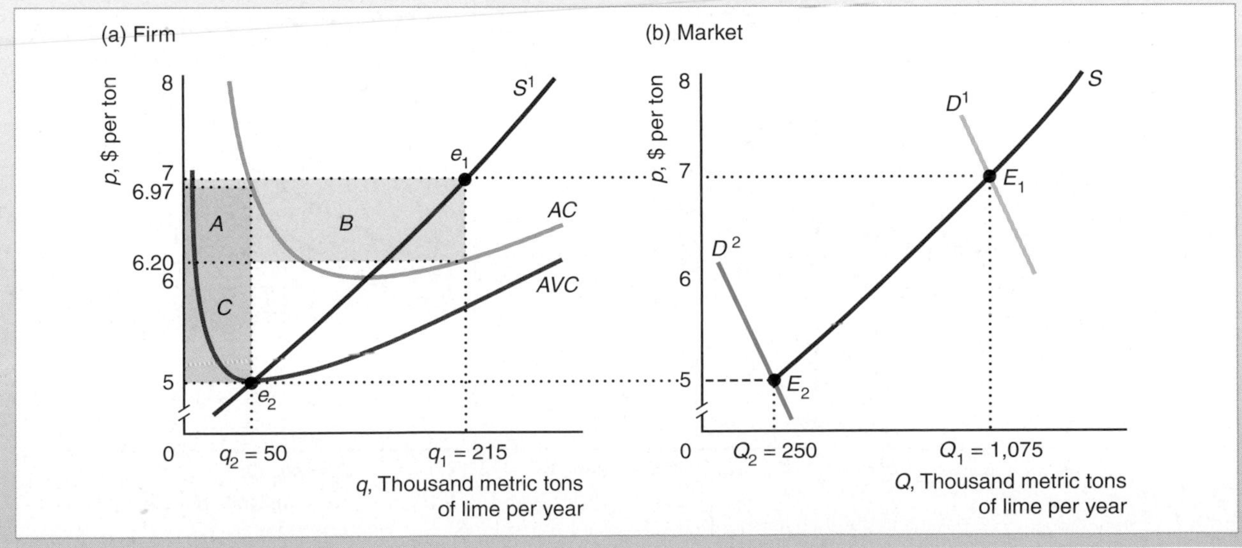

Solved Problem 8.3

What is the effect on the short-run equilibrium of a specific tax of τ per unit that is collected from all n firms in a market? What is the incidence of the tax?

Answer

1. *Show how the tax shifts a typical firm's marginal cost and average cost curves and hence its supply curve.* In Solved Problem 8.1, we showed that such a tax causes the marginal cost curve, the average cost curve, and (hence) the minimum average cost of the firm to shift up by τ, as illustrated in panel a of the figure. As a result, the short-run supply curve of the firm, labeled $S^1 + \tau$, shifts up by τ from the pretax supply curve, S^1.
2. *Show how the market supply curve shifts.* The market supply curve is the sum of all the individual firm supply curves, so it too shifts up by τ, from S to $S + \tau$ in panel b of the figure.
3. *Determine how the short-run market equilibrium changes.* The pretax, short-run market equilibrium is E_1, where the downward-sloping market demand curve D intersects S in panel b. In that equilibrium, price is p_1 and quantity is Q_1, which equals n (the number of firms) times the quantity q_1 that a typical firm produces at p_1. The after-tax, short-run market equilibrium, E_2, determined by the intersection of D and the after-tax supply curve, $S + \tau$, occurs at p_2 and Q_2. Because the after-tax price p_2 is above the after-tax minimum average variable cost, all the firms continue to produce, but they produce less than before: $q_2 < q_1$. Consequently the equilibrium quantity falls from $Q_1 = nq_1$ to $Q_2 = nq_2$.
4. *Discuss the incidence of the tax.* The equilibrium price increases, but by less than the full amount of the tax: $p_2 < p_1 + \tau$. The incidence of the tax is shared between consumers and producers because both the supply and the demand curves are sloped (Chapter 3).

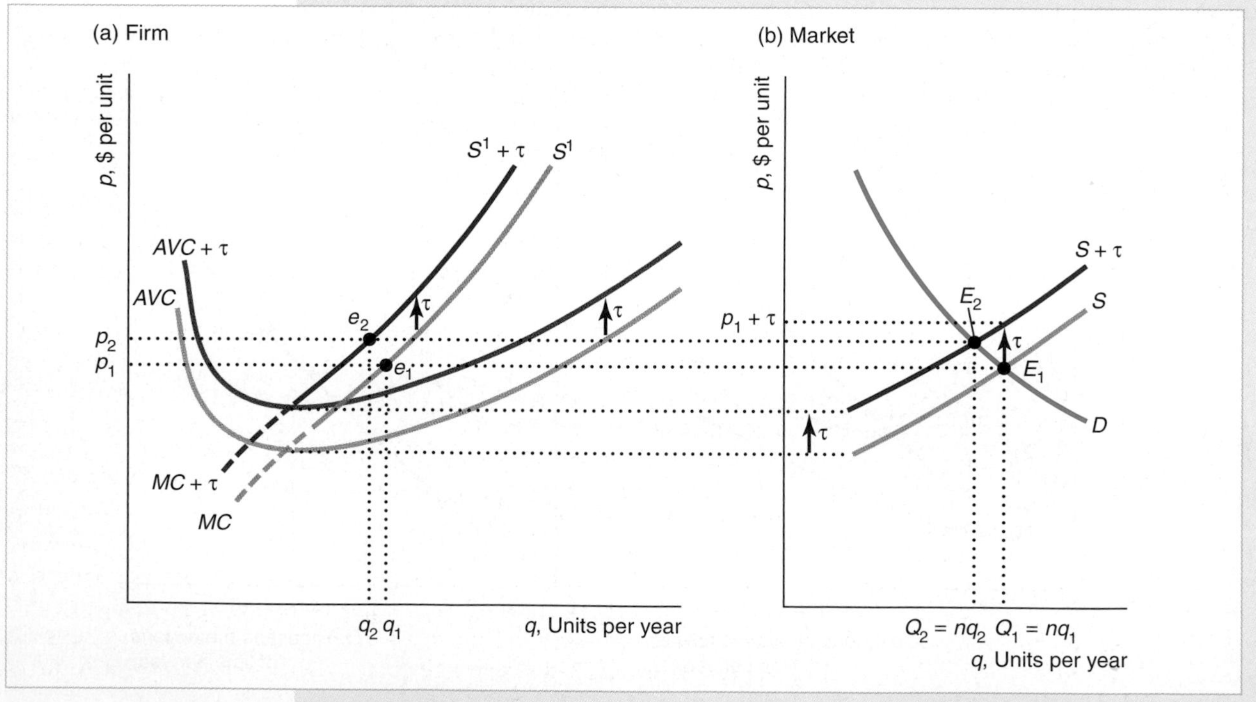

8.4 Competition in the Long Run

I think there is a world market for about five computers.
—Thomas J. Watson, IBM chairman, 1943

In the long run, competitive firms can vary inputs that were fixed in the short run, so the long-run firm and market supply curves differ from the short-run curves. After briefly looking at how a firm determines its long-run supply curve so as to maximize its profit, we examine the relationship between short-run and long-run market supply curves and competitive equilibria.

Long-Run Competitive Profit Maximization

The firm's two profit-maximizing decisions—how much to produce and whether to produce at all—are simpler in the long run than in the short run. In the long run, typically all costs are variable, so the firm does not have to consider whether fixed costs are sunk or avoidable.

Long-Run Output Decision. The firm chooses the quantity that maximizes its profit using the same rules as in the short run. The firm picks the quantity that maximizes long-run profit, the difference between revenue and long-run cost. Equivalently, it operates where long-run marginal profit is zero and where marginal revenue equals long-run marginal cost.

Long-Run Shutdown Decision. After determining the output level, q^*, that maximizes its profit or minimizes its loss, the firm decides whether to produce or shut down. The firm shuts down if its revenue is less than its avoidable or variable cost. In the long run, however, all costs are variable. As a result, in the long run, the firm shuts down if it would make an economic loss by operating.

Long-Run Firm Supply Curve

A firm's long-run supply curve is its long-run marginal cost curve above the minimum of its long-run average cost curve (because all costs are variable in the long run). The firm is free to choose its capital in the long run, so the firm's long-run supply curve may differ substantially from its short-run supply curve.

The firm chooses a plant size to maximize its long-run economic profit in light of its beliefs about the future. If its forecast is wrong, it may be stuck with a plant that is too small or too large for its level of production in the short run. The firm acts to correct this mistake in plant size in the long run.

The firm in Figure 8.10 has different short- and long-run cost curves. In the short run, the firm uses a plant that is smaller than the optimal long-run size if the price is \$35. (Having a short-run plant size that is too large is also possible.) The firm produces 50 units of output per year in the short run, where its short-run marginal cost, *SRMC*, equals the price, and makes a short-run profit equal to area *A*. The firm's short-run supply curve, S^{SR}, is its short-run marginal cost above the minimum, \$20, of its short-run average variable cost, *SRAVC*.

If the firm expects the price to remain at \$35, it builds a larger plant in the long run. Using the larger plant, the firm produces 110 units per year, where its long-run marginal cost, *LRMC*, equals the market price. It expects to make a long-run profit, area $A + B$, which is greater than its short-run profit by area *B* because it sells 60 more units and its equilibrium long-run average cost, $LRAC = \$25$, is lower than its short-run average cost in equilibrium, \$28.

Figure 8.10 The Short-Run and Long-Run Supply Curves.

See Question 19.

The firm's long-run supply curve, S^{LR}, is zero below its minimum average cost of \$24 and equals the long-run marginal cost, *LRMC*, at higher prices. The firm produces more in the long run than in the short run, 110 units instead of 50 units, and earns a higher profit, area $A + B$ instead of just area A.

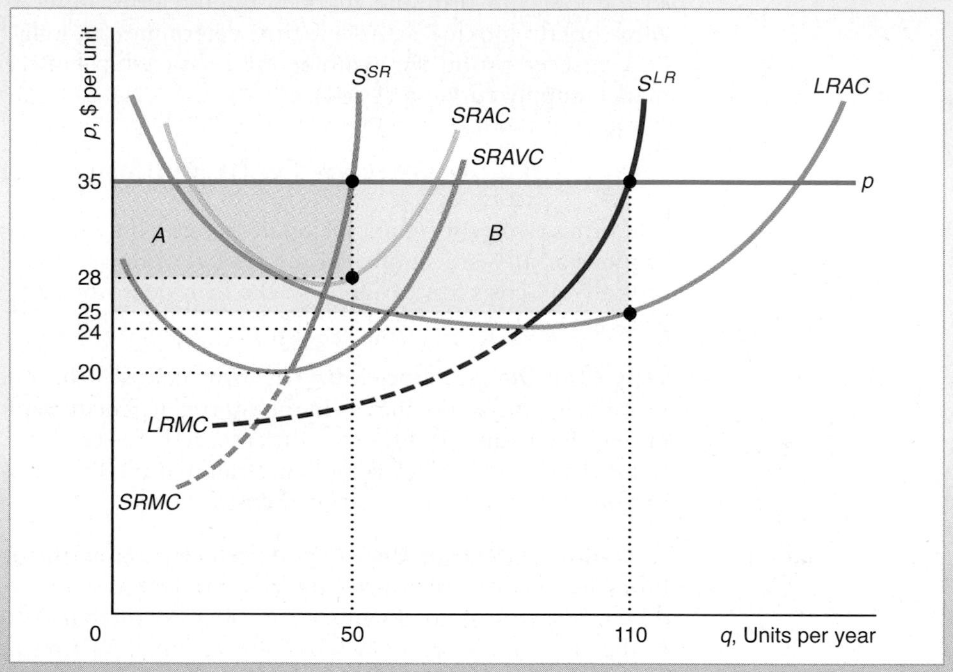

The firm does not operate at a loss in the long run when all inputs are variable. It shuts down if the market price falls below the firm's minimum long-run average cost of \$24. Thus, the competitive firm's long-run supply curve is its long-run marginal cost curve above \$24.

Long-Run Market Supply Curve

The competitive market supply curve is the horizontal sum of the supply curves of the individual firms in both the short run and the long run. Because the maximum number of firms in the market is fixed in the short run, we add the supply curves of a known number of firms to obtain the short-run market supply curve. The only way for the market to supply more output in the short run is for existing firms to produce more.

In the long run, firms can enter or leave the market. Thus, before we can add all the relevant firm supply curves to obtain the long-run market supply curve, we need to determine how many firms are in the market at each possible market price.

To construct the long-run market supply curve properly, we also have to determine how input prices vary with output. As the market expands or contracts substantially, changes in factor prices may shift firms' cost and supply curves. If so, we need to determine how such shifts in factor prices affect firm supply curves so that we can properly construct the market supply curve. The effect of changes in input prices is greater in the long run than in the short run because market output can change more dramatically in the long run.

We now look in detail at how entry and changing factor prices affect long-run market supply. We first derive the long-run market supply curve, assuming that the price of inputs remains constant as market output increases, so as to isolate the role of entry. We then examine how the market supply curve is affected if the price of inputs changes as market output rises.

Role of Entry and Exit. The number of firms in a market in the long run is determined by the *entry* and *exit* of firms. In the long run, each firm decides whether to enter or exit depending on whether it can make a long-run profit.

In many markets, firms face barriers to entry or must incur significant costs to enter. Many city governments limit the number of cab drivers, creating an insurmountable barrier that prevents additional firms from entering. To enter other markets, a new firm has to hire consultants to determine the profit opportunities, pay lawyers to write contracts, and incur other expenses. Typically, such costs of entry or exit are fixed costs.

Even if existing firms are making positive profits, no entry occurs in the short run if entering firms need time to find a location, build a new plant, and hire workers. In the long run, firms enter the market if they can make profits by so doing. The costs of entry are often lower, and hence the profits from entering are higher, if a firm takes its time to enter. As a result, firms may enter markets long after profit opportunities first appear.

In contrast, firms usually react faster to losses than to potential profits. We expect firms to shut down or exit the market quickly in the short run when price is below average variable cost.

In some markets, there are no barriers or fixed costs to entry, so firms can freely enter and exit. For example, many construction firms, which have no capital and provide only labor services, engage in *hit-and-run* entry and exit: They enter the market whenever they can make a profit and exit when they can't. These firms may enter and exit markets several times a year.

In such markets, a shift of the market demand curve to the right attracts firms to enter. For example, if there were no government regulations, the market for taxicabs would have free entry and exit. Car owners could enter or exit the market virtually instantaneously. If the demand curve for cab rides shifted to the right, the market price would rise, and existing cab drivers would make unusually high profits in the short run. Seeing these profits, other car owners would enter the market, causing the market supply curve to shift to the right and the market price to fall. Entry occurs until the last firm to enter—the *marginal firm*—makes zero long-run profit.

Similarly, if the demand curve shifts to the left so that the market price drops, firms suffer losses. Firms with minimum average costs above the new, lower market price exit the market. Firms continue to leave the market until the next firm considering leaving, the marginal firm, is again earning a zero long-run profit.

Thus, in a market with free entry and exit:

- A firm enters the market if it can make a long-run profit, $\pi > 0$.
- A firm exits the market to avoid a long-run loss, $\pi < 0$.

If firms in a market are making zero long-run profit, they are indifferent between staying in the market and exiting. We presume that if they are already in the market, they stay in the market when they are making zero long-run profit.

See Question 20.

Most transportation markets are thought to have free entry and exit unless governments regulate them. Relatively few airline, trucking, or shipping firms may serve a particular route, but they face extensive potential entry. Other firms can and will quickly enter and serve a route if a profit opportunity appears. Entrants shift their highly mobile equipment from less profitable routes to more profitable ones. See **www.myeconlab.com/perloff**, Chapter 8, "Threat of Entry in Shipping."

Evidence on Ease of Entry and Exit. Entry and exit are relatively difficult in many manufacturing, mining, and government-regulated industries, such as public utilities and insurance. Firms can enter and exit easily in many agriculture, construction, wholesale and retail trade, and service industries.

Table 8.1 lists the average annual entry rate (percentage of firms that enter per year relative to total firms) and exit rate for various U.S. industries. Rates range from a low of 4% for entry and 3% for exit in the highly regulated electricity, gas, and water public utility sector to a high of 12% for both entry and exit in the relatively competitive textile products, leather, and footwear industry. Industries with high entry rates tend to have high exit rates. That is, entry and exit barriers are likely to be related.

Table 8.1 Average Annual Entry and Exit Rates in Selected U.S. Industries, 1989–1996.

Industry	Entry Rate, %	Exit Rate, %
Total economy	10	8
Agriculture, hunting, forestry, and fishing	11	8
Construction	11	9
Services	10	8
Mining and quarrying	8	9
Total manufacturing	8	7
Textile products, leather, and footwear	12	12
Wood products	10	9
Paper products, printing, and publishing	8	8
Food products, beverages, and tobacco	8	7
Chemical, rubber, plastics, and fuel products	8	6
Electricity, gas, and water supply	4	3

Source: Calculations based on data from the OECD Firm-Level Data Project, **www.oecd.org**, as of 2005.

APPLICATION

Enter the Dragon: Masses Producing Art for the Masses

Chinese paintings are flooding the world's generic art market. These inexpensive renditions of puppies playing, flowers in a field, and classic Western artworks hang proudly in motels, restaurants, Florida condominiums, and dorm rooms. Many college students reason, "Why have a poster of van Gogh's *Sunflowers,* Hopper's *Nighthawks,* or the dreaded puppies on your dorm room wall when you can buy an oil-painted copy on eBay for only a few bucks more and have it shipped to you directly from China?" One young Chinese artist, Zhang Libing, 26, estimates that he has already painted up to 20,000 copies of van Gogh's works.

Internet sales and falling prices for communications and shipping have facilitated Chinese firms' entry into world markets. Chinese art factories not only pay low wages, but they are turning what has been an individual craft into a mass production industry, driving out of business independent artists who sold their works from Rome's Spanish Steps to Santa Monica's beach sidewalks and beyond.

The number of art graduates from Chinese universities zoomed 59% in 2004, to 20,031, and apprenticeship programs turn out many additional artists who are

willing to work for little pay. A typical artist earns less than $200 a month, plus modest room and board, or $360 a month without food and housing.

Chinese art factories exploit economies of scale and specialization, using a Henry Ford–like approach to production. The Internet allows them to sell assembly-line paintings all over the world. The Chaozhou Hongjia Arts and Crafts Company has two factories with a total of 10 designers who do original paintings, 250 painters, and more than 500 framers and assistant painters. In larger factories some artisans specialize in painting trees, skies, or flowers, with several working on a single painting.

U.S. and European firms like oilpaintings.com pay $25 to $30 for each Chinese painting, including the frames, and spend another $1 per painting in shipping charges. Bulk shipments of Chinese paintings to the United States nearly tripled from slightly over $10 million in 1996 to $30.5 million in 2004 (and 2005 sales were 50% above the corresponding period in 2004).

See Questions 21 and 22.

Long-Run Market Supply with Identical Firms and Free Entry. The *long-run market supply curve is flat* at the minimum long-run average cost *if firms can freely enter and exit* the market, an unlimited number of *firms have identical costs*, and *input prices are constant*. This result follows from our reasoning about the short-run supply curve, in which we showed that the market supply was flatter, the more firms there were in the market. With many firms in the market in the long run, the market supply curve is effectively flat. ("Many" is 10 firms in the vegetable oil market.)

The long-run supply curve of a typical vegetable oil mill, S^1 in panel a of Figure 8.11, is the long-run marginal cost curve above a minimum long-run average cost of $10. Because each firm shuts down if the market price is below $10, the long-run market supply curve is zero at a price below $10. If the price rises above $10, firms are making positive profits, so new firms enter, expanding market output until profits are driven to zero, where price is again $10. The long-run market supply curve in panel b is a horizontal line at the minimum long-run average cost of the typical firm, $10. At a price of $10, each firm produces $q = 150$ units (where one unit equals 100 metric tons). Thus, the total output produced by n firms in the market is $Q = nq = n \times 150$ units. Extra market output is obtained by new firms entering the market.

In summary, the long-run market supply curve is horizontal if the market has free entry and exit, an unlimited number of firms have identical costs, and input prices are constant. When these strong assumptions do not hold, the long-run market supply curve has a slope, as we now show.

Long-Run Market Supply When Entry Is Limited. If the number of firms in a market is limited in the long run, the market supply curve slopes upward. The number of firms is limited if the government restricts that number, if firms need a scarce resource, or if entry is costly. An example of a scarce resource is the limited number of lots on which a luxury beachfront hotel can be built in Miami. High entry costs restrict the number of firms in a market because firms enter only if the long-run economic profit is greater than the cost of entering.

Figure 8.11 Long-Run Firm and Market Supply with Identical Vegetable Oil Firms.

(a) The long-run supply curve of a typical vegetable oil mill, S^1, is the long-run marginal cost curve above the minimum average cost of $10. (b) The long-run market supply curve is horizontal at the minimum of the long-run minimum average cost of a typical firm. Each firm produces 150 units, so market output is 150n, where n is the number of firms.

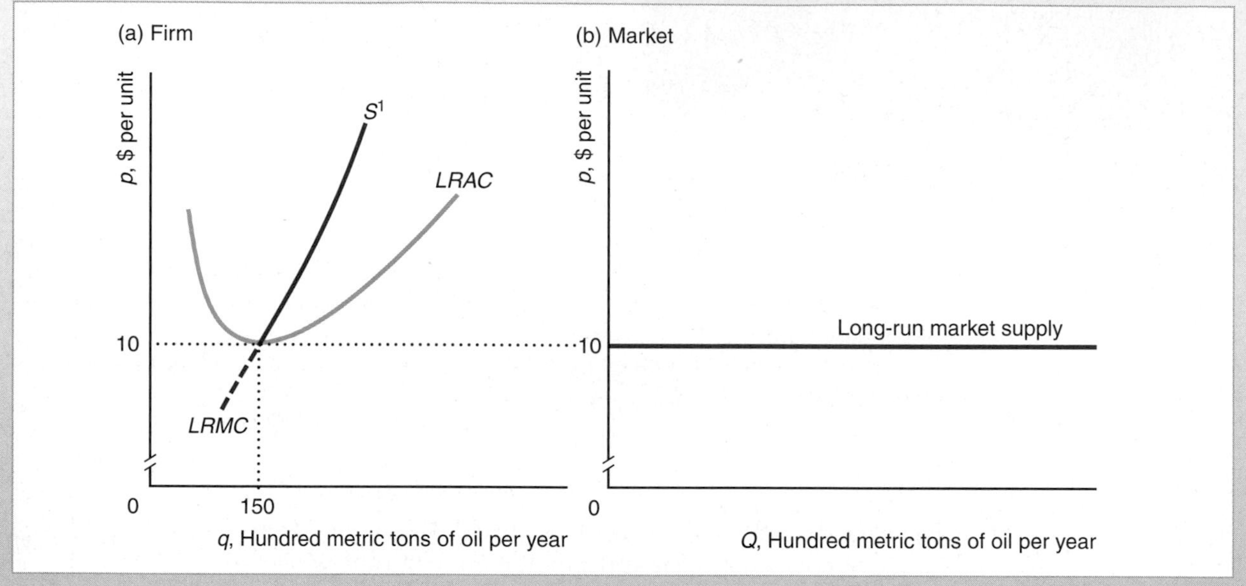

The only way to get more output if the number of firms is limited is for existing firms to produce more. Because individual firms' supply curves slope upward, the long-run market supply curve is also upward sloping. The reasoning is the same as in the short run, as panel b of Figure 8.7 illustrates, given that no more than five firms can enter. The market supply curve is the upward-sloping S^5 curve, which is the horizontal sum of the five firms' upward-sloping marginal cost curves above minimum average cost.

Long-Run Market Supply When Firms Differ. A second reason why some long-run market supply curves slope upward is that firms differ. Firms with relatively low minimum long-run average costs are willing to enter the market at lower prices than others, resulting in an upward-sloping long-run market supply curve.

The long-run supply curve is upward sloping because of differences in costs across firms *only* if the amount that lower-cost firms can produce is limited. If there were an unlimited number of the lowest-cost firms, we would never observe any higher-cost firms producing. Effectively, then, the only firms in the market would have the same low costs of production.

APPLICATION

Upward-Sloping Long-Run Supply Curve for Cotton

Many countries produce cotton. Production costs differ among countries because of differences in the quality of land, rainfall, costs of irrigation, costs of labor, and other factors.

The length of each steplike segment of the long-run supply curve of cotton in the graph is the quantity produced by the labeled country. The amount that the low-cost countries can produce must be limited, or we would not observe production by the higher-cost countries.

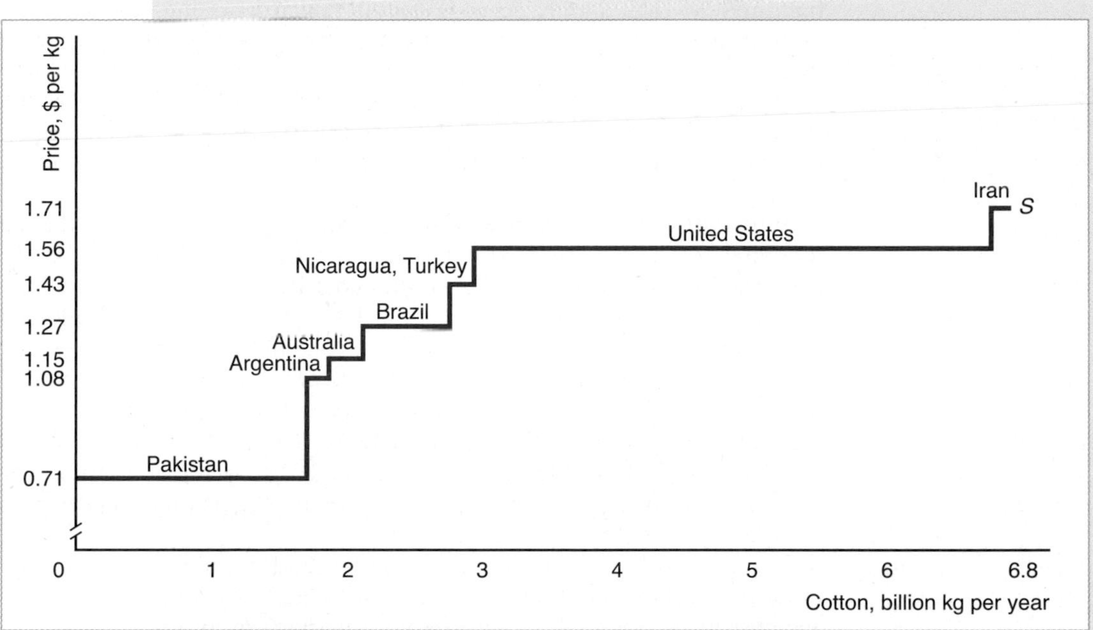

The height of each segment of the supply curve is the typical minimum average cost of production in that country. The average cost of production in Pakistan is less than half that in Iran. The supply curve has a steplike appearance because we are using an average of the estimate average cost in each country, which is a single number. If we knew the individual firms' supply curves in each of these countries, the market supply curve would have a smoother shape.

See Question 23.

As the market price rises, the number of countries producing rises. At market prices below \$1.08 per kilogram, only Pakistan produces. If the market price is below \$1.50, the United States and Iran do not produce. If the price increases to \$1.56, the United States supplies a large amount of cotton. In this range of the supply curve, supply is very elastic. For Iran to produce, the price has to rise to \$1.71. Price increases in that range result in only a relatively small increase in supply. Thus, the supply curve is relatively inelastic at prices above \$1.56.

Long-Run Market Supply When Input Prices Vary with Output. A third reason why market supply curves may slope is nonconstant input prices. In markets in which factor prices rise or fall when output increases, the long-run supply curve slopes even if firms have identical costs and can freely enter and exit.

If the market buys a relatively small share of the total amount of a factor of production that is sold, then, as market output expands, the price of the factor is unlikely to be affected. For example, dentists do not hire enough receptionists to affect the market wage for receptionists.

In contrast, if the market buys most of the total sales of a factor, the price of that input is more likely to vary with market output. As jet plane manufacturers expand and buy more jet engines, the price of these engines rises because the jet plane manufacturers are the sole purchaser of these engines.

To produce more goods, firms must use more inputs. If the prices of some or all inputs rise when more inputs are purchased, the cost of producing the final good also rises. We call a market in which input prices rise with output an *increasing-cost market*. Few steelworkers have no fear of heights and are willing to construct tall buildings, so their supply curve is steeply upward sloping. As more skyscrapers are built at one time, the demand for these workers shifts to the right, driving up their wage.

We assume that all firms in a market have the same cost curves and that input prices rise as market output expands. We use the cost curves of a representative firm in panel a of Figure 8.12 to derive the upward-sloping market supply curve in panel b.

When input prices are relatively low, each identical firm has the same long-run marginal cost curve, MC^1, and average cost curve, AC^1, in panel a. A typical firm produces at minimum average cost, e_1, and sells q_1 units of output. The market supply is Q_1 in panel b when the market price is p_1. The n_1 firms collectively sell $Q_1 = n_1 q_1$ units of output, which is point E_1 on the market supply curve in panel b.

If the market demand curve shifts outward, the market price rises to p_2, new firms enter, and market output rises to Q_2, causing input prices to rise. As a result, the marginal cost curve shifts from MC^1 to MC^2, and the average cost curve rises from AC^1 to AC^2. The typical firm produces at a higher minimum average cost, e_2. At this higher price, there are n_2 firms in the market, so market output is $Q_2 = n_2 q_2$ at point E_2 on the market supply curve.

Thus, in both an increasing-cost market and a constant-cost market—in which input prices remain constant as output increases—firms produce at minimum average cost in the long run. The difference is that the minimum average cost rises as market output increases in an increasing-cost market, whereas minimum average cost is constant in a constant-cost market. In conclusion, *the long-run supply curve is upward sloping in an increasing-cost market and flat in a constant-cost market.*

See Questions 24–27.

Figure 8.12 Long-Run Market Supply in an Increasing-Cost Market.

(a) At a relatively low market output, Q_1, the firm's long-run marginal and average cost curves are MC^1 and AC^1. At the higher market quantity Q_2, the cost curves shift upward to MC^2 and AC^2 because of the higher input prices. Given identical firms, each firm produces at minimum average cost, such as points e_1 and e_2. (b) Long-run market supply, S, is upward sloping.

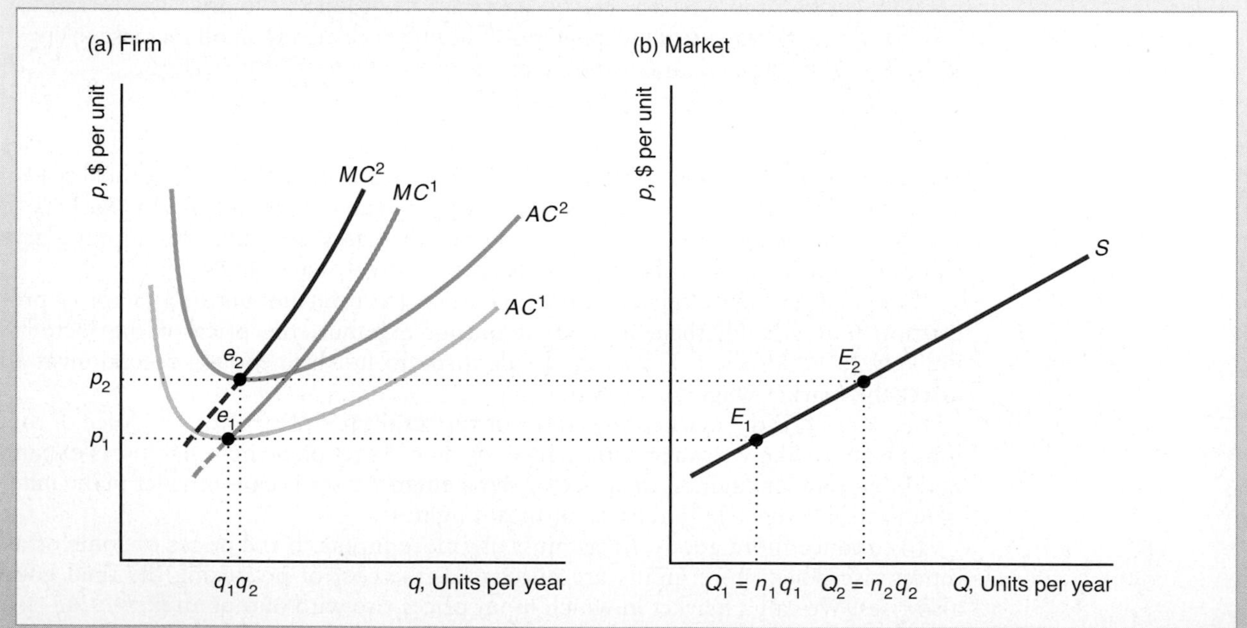

In decreasing-cost markets, as market output rises, at least some factor prices fall. As a result, *in a decreasing-cost market, the long-run market supply curve is downward sloping.*

Increasing returns to scale may cause factor prices to fall. For example, when the personal computer market was young, there was much less demand for CD or DVD drives than there is today. As a result, those drives were partially assembled by hand at relatively high cost. As demand for these drives increased, it became practical to automate more of the production process so that drives could be produced at lower per-unit cost. The decrease in the price of these drives lowers the cost of personal computers.

Figure 8.13 shows a decreasing-cost market. As the market output expands from Q_1 to Q_2 in panel b, the prices of inputs fall, so a typical firm's cost curves shift downward, and the minimum average cost falls from e_1 to e_2 in panel a. On the long-run market supply curve in panel b, point E_1, which corresponds to e_1, is above E_2, which corresponds to e_2. As a consequence, *a decreasing-cost market supply curve is downward sloping.*

To summarize, theory tells us that competitive long-run market supply curves may be flat, upward sloping, or downward sloping. If all firms are identical in a market in which firms can freely enter and input prices are constant, the long-run market supply curve is flat. If entry is limited, firms differ in costs, or input prices rise with output, the long-run supply curve is upward sloping. Finally, if input prices fall with market output, the long-run supply curve is downward sloping. (See **www.myeconlab.com/perloff**, Chapter 8, "Slope of Long-Run Market Supply Curves.")

Long-Run Market Supply Curve with Trade. Cotton, oil, and many other goods are traded on world markets. The world equilibrium price and quantity for a good

Figure 8.13 Long-Run Market Supply in a Decreasing-Cost Market.

(a) At a relatively low market output, Q_1, the firm's long-run marginal and average cost curves are MC^1 and AC^1. At the higher market quantity Q_2, the cost curves shift downward to MC^2 and AC^2 because of lower input prices. Given identical firms, each firm produces at minimum average cost, such as points e_1 and e_2. (b) Long-run market supply, S, is downward sloping.

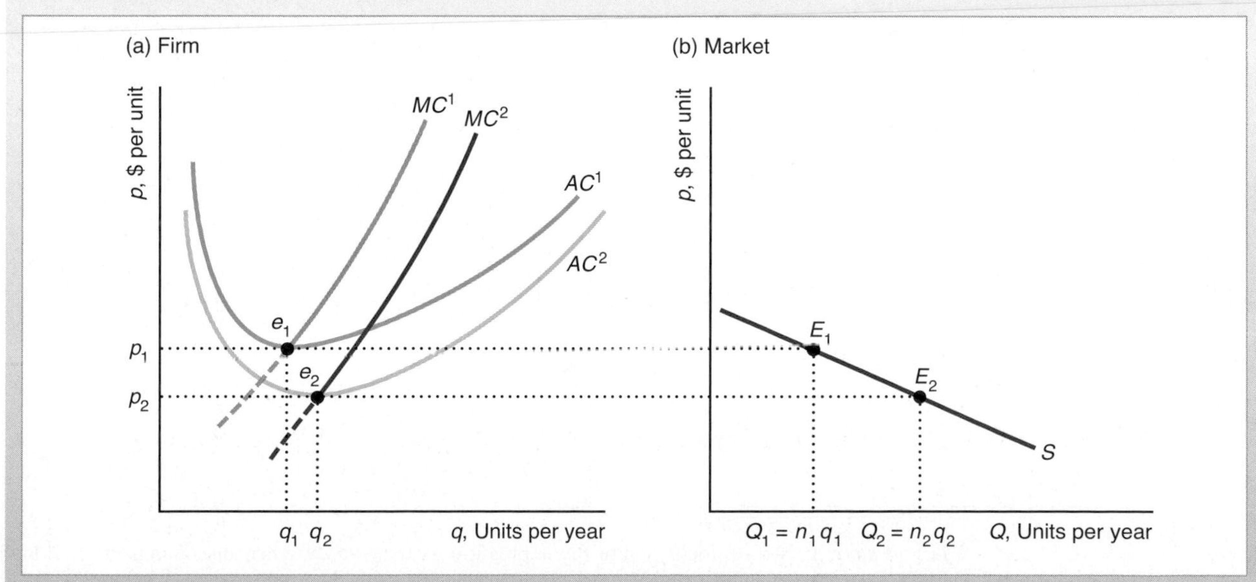

are determined by the intersection of the world supply curve—the horizontal sum of the supply curves of each producing country—and the world demand curve—the horizontal sum of the demand curves of each consuming country.

A country that imports a good has a supply curve that is the horizontal sum of its domestic industry's supply curve and the import supply curve. The domestic supply curve is the competitive long-run supply curve that we have just derived. However, we need to determine the import supply curve.

residual supply curve the quantity that the market supplies that is not consumed by other demanders at any given price

The country imports the world's residual supply, where the **residual supply curve** is the quantity that the market supplies that is not consumed by other demanders at any given price.[11] The country's import supply function is its residual supply function, $S^r(p)$, which is the quantity supplied to this country at price p. Because the country buys only that part of the world supply, $S(p)$, that is not consumed by any *other* demander elsewhere in the world, $D^o(p)$, its residual supply function is

$$S^r(p) = S(p) - D^o(p). \tag{8.6}$$

At prices so high that $D^o(p)$ is greater than $S(p)$, the residual supply, $S^r(p)$, is zero.

In Figure 8.14, we derive Japan's residual supply curve for cotton in panel a using the world supply curve, S, and the demand curve of the rest of the world, D^o, in panel b. The scales differ for the quantity axes in the two panels. At a price of \$850 per metric ton, the demand in other countries exhausts world supply (D^o intersects S at 32 million metric tons per year), so there is no residual supply for Japan. At a much higher price, \$935, Japan's excess supply, 4 million metric tons, is the difference between the world supply, 30 million tons, and the quantity demand elsewhere, 34 million tons. As the figure illustrates, the residual supply curve facing Japan is much closer to horizontal than is the world supply curve.

Figure 8.14 Excess or Residual Supply Curve.

Japan's excess supply curve, S^r, for cotton is the horizontal difference between the world's supply curve, S, and the demand curve of the other countries in the world, D^o.

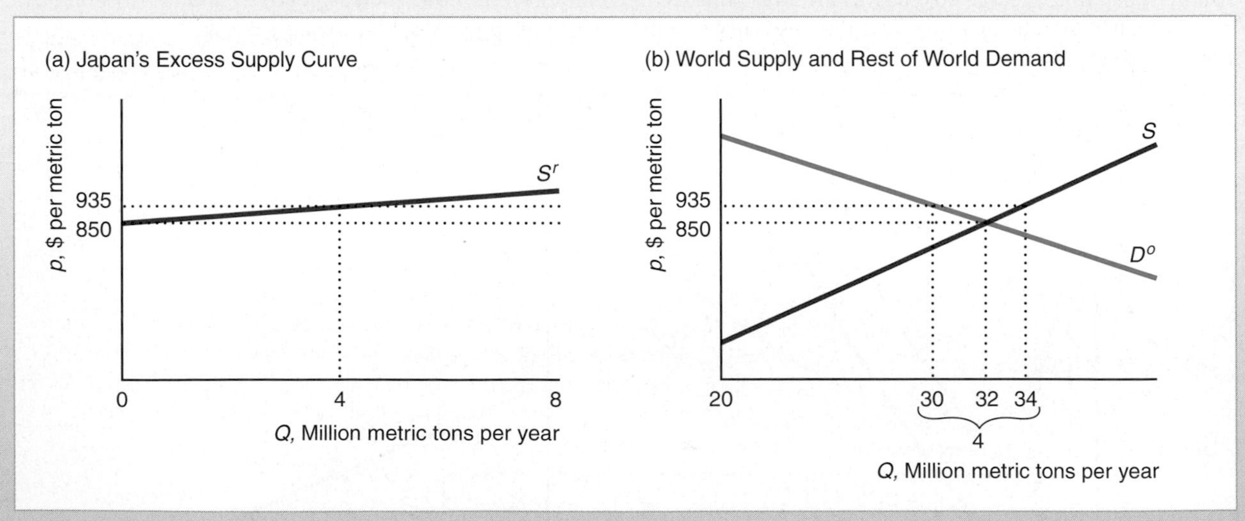

[11]*Jargon alert:* It is traditional to use the expression *excess supply* when discussing international trade and *residual supply* otherwise, though the terms are equivalent.

See Problem 39.

The elasticity of residual supply, η_r, facing a given country is (by a similar argument to that in Appendix 8A)

$$\eta_r = \frac{\eta}{\theta} - \frac{1-\theta}{\theta}\varepsilon_o, \tag{8.7}$$

where η is the market supply elasticity, ε_o is the demand elasticity of the other countries, and $\theta = Q_r/Q$ is the importing country's share of the world's output.

If a country imports a small fraction of the world's supply, we expect it to face a nearly perfectly elastic, horizontal residual supply curve. On the other hand, a relatively large consumer of the good might face an upward-sloping residual supply curve.

We can illustrate this difference for cotton, where $\eta = 0.5$ and $\varepsilon = -0.7$ (Green et al., 2005). The United States imports $\theta = 1\%$ of the world's cotton, so its residual supply elasticity is

$$\begin{aligned}\eta_r &= \frac{\eta}{0.001} - \frac{0.999}{0.001}\varepsilon_o \\ &= 1{,}000\eta - 999\varepsilon_o \\ &= (1{,}000 \times 0.5) - (999 \times [-0.7]) = 1{,}199.3,\end{aligned}$$

which is 2,398.6 times more elastic than the world's supply elasticity. Canada's import share is 10 times larger, $\theta = 1\%$, so its residual supply elasticity is "only" 119.3. Nonetheless, its residual supply curve is nearly horizontal: A 1% increase in its price would induce imports to more than double, rising by 119.3%. Even Japan's $\theta = 2.5\%$ leads to a relatively elastic $\eta_r = 46.4$. In contrast, China imports 18.5% of the world's cotton, so its residual supply elasticity is 5.8. Even though its residual supply elasticity is more than 11 times larger than the world's elasticity, it is still small enough that its excess supply curve is upward sloping.

Thus, if a country is "small"—imports a small share of the world's output—then it faces a horizontal import supply curve at the world equilibrium price. If its domestic supply curve is everywhere above the world price, then it only imports and faces a horizontal demand curve. If some portion of its upward-sloping domestic supply curve is below the world price, then its total supply curve is the upward-sloping domestic supply curve up to the world price, and then is horizontal at the world price (Chapter 9 shows such a supply curve for oil).

This analysis of trade applies to trade within a country too. The following application shows that it can be used to look at trade across geographic areas or jurisdictions such as states.

APPLICATION

Special Blends and Gasoline Supply Curves

You can't buy the gasoline sold in Milwaukee elsewhere in Wisconsin. Houston gas isn't the same as west Texas gas. California, Minnesota, and Nevada and most of America's biggest cities use one or more of 17 specialized blends, while the rest of the country uses regular gas. Because special blends usually are designed to cut air pollution, they are more likely to be used in areas with serious pollution problems.

The number of working U.S. refineries has dropped from 324 in 1981 to 145 in 2008. Many of these refiners produce regular gasoline, which is sold throughout most of the country. Wholesalers are willing to ship regular gas across state lines in response to slightly higher prices in neighboring states. If the price rises slightly in New Hampshire, firms will quickly send gasoline from Vermont or

Maine to New Hampshire. As a consequence, the residual supply curve for regular gasoline for a given state is close to horizontal.

In contrast, gasoline is usually not imported into jurisdictions that require special blends. Few refiners produce any given special blend. Only 13 of the 22 California refineries can produce California's special low-polluting blend of gasoline, California Reformulated Gasoline (CaRFG). Because refineries require expensive upgrades to produce a new kind of gas, they generally do not switch from producing one to another type of gas. Thus, if the price of gasoline starts rising in California, wholesalers in other states do not send gasoline to California, because they cannot legally sell regular gasoline in California and it would cost too much to start producing CaRFG.

As a result, the supply curve for California's special blend is eventually upward sloping. At relatively small quantities, refineries can produce more gasoline without incurring higher costs, so California's supply curve in this region is relatively flat. However, to produce much larger quantities of gasoline, refiners have to run their plants around the clock and convert a larger fraction of each gallon of oil into gasoline, incurring higher costs of production. Thus, they are willing to sell larger quantities in this range only at a higher price, so the supply curve slopes upward. When the refineries reach capacity, no matter how high the price gets, firms cannot produce more gasoline (at least until new refineries go online), so the supply curve becomes vertical. California normally operates in the steeply upward-sloping section of its supply curve. In 2003, the 14.8 billion gallons consumed nearly equaled refiners' 15-billion-gallon maximum capacity. Brown et al. (2008) finds that, on average, regulated areas' gasoline prices are 3¢ higher than in unregulated areas.

See Question 28 and Problem 40.

Solved Problem 8.4

In the short run, what happens to the competitive market price of gasoline if the demand curve in a state shifts to the right as more people move to the state or start driving gas-hogging SUVs? In your answer, distinguish between areas in which regular gasoline is sold and jurisdictions that require special blends.

Answer

1. *Show the effect of a shift of the demand curve in areas that use regular gasoline.* In an area that uses regular gasoline, the supply curve is horizontal, as panel a of the figure shows. Thus, as the demand curve shifts to the right from D^1 to D^2, the equilibrium shifts along the supply curve from e_1 to e_2 and the price remains at p_1.

2. *Show the effect of both a small and a large shift of the demand curve in a jurisdiction that uses a special blend.* The supply curve in panel b is drawn as described in the application. If the demand curve shifts slightly to the right from D^1 to D^2, the price remains unchanged at p_1 because the demand curve continues to intersect the supply curve in the flat region. However, if the demand curve shifts farther to the right to D^3, then the new intersection is in the upward-sloping section of the supply curve and the price increases to p_3. Consequently, unforeseen "jumps" in demand are more likely to cause a *price spike*—a large increase in price—in jurisdictions that use special blends.[12]

[12]The gasoline wholesale market may not be completely competitive, especially in areas where special blends are used. Moreover, gas can be stored. Hence, price differences across jurisdictions may be due to other factors as well (Borenstein et al., 2004).

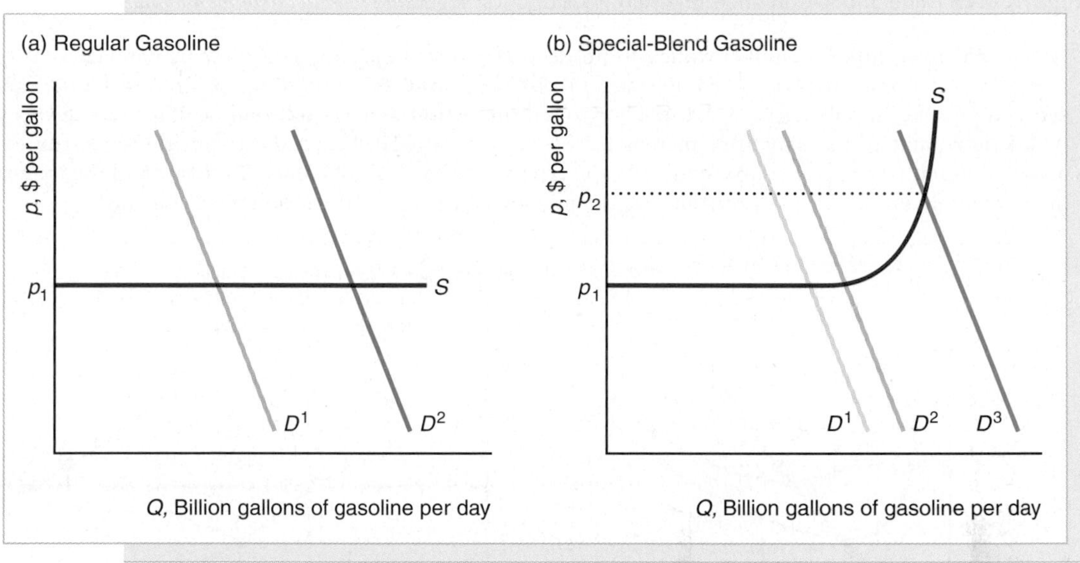

Long-Run Competitive Equilibrium

The intersection of the long-run market supply and demand curves determines the long-run competitive equilibrium. With identical firms, constant input prices, and free entry and exit, the long-run competitive market supply is horizontal at minimum long-run average cost, so the equilibrium price equals long-run average cost. A shift in the demand curve affects only the equilibrium quantity and not the equilibrium price, which remains constant at minimum long-run average cost.

The market supply curve is different in the short run than in the long run, so the long-run competitive equilibrium differs from the short-run equilibrium. The relationship between the short- and long-run equilibria depends on where the market demand curve crosses the short- and long-run market supply curves. Figure 8.15 illustrates this point using the short- and long-run supply curves for the vegetable oil mill market.

The short-run firm supply curve for a typical firm in panel a is the marginal cost above the minimum of the average variable cost, \$7. At a price of \$7, each firm produces 100 units, so the 20 firms in the market in the short run collectively supply 2,000 (= 20 × 100) units of oil in panel b. At higher prices, the short-run market supply curve slopes upward because it is the horizontal summation of the firm's upward-sloping marginal cost curves.

We assume that the firms use the same size plant in the short and long run so that the minimum average cost is \$10 in both the short and long run. Because all firms have the same costs and can enter freely, the long-run market supply curve is flat at the minimum average cost, \$10, in panel b. At prices between \$7 and \$10, firms supply goods at a loss in the short run but not in the long run.

If the market demand curve is D^1, the short-run market equilibrium, F_1, is below and to the right of the long-run market equilibrium, E_1. This relationship is reversed if the market demand curve is D^2.[13]

[13]Using data from Statistics Canada, I estimate that the elasticity of demand for vegetable oil is –0.8. Both D^1 and D^2 are constant –0.8 elasticity demand curves, but the demand at any price on D^2 is 2.4 times that on D^1.

Figure 8.15 The Short-Run and Long-Run Equilibria for Vegetable Oil.

(a) A typical vegetable oil mill is willing to produce 100 units of oil at a price of \$10, or 165 units at \$11. (b) The short-run market supply curve, S^{SR}, is the horizontal sum of 20 individual firms' short-run marginal cost curves above minimum average variable cost, \$7. The long-run market supply curve, S^{LR}, is horizontal at the minimum average cost, \$10. If the demand curve is D^1, in the short-run equilibrium, F_1, 20 firms sell 2,000 units of oil at \$7. In the long-run equilibrium, E_1, 10 firms sell 1,500 units at \$10. If demand is D^2, the short-run equilibrium is F_2 (\$11, 3,300 units, 20 firms) and the long-run equilibrium is E_2 (\$10, 3,600 units, 24 firms).

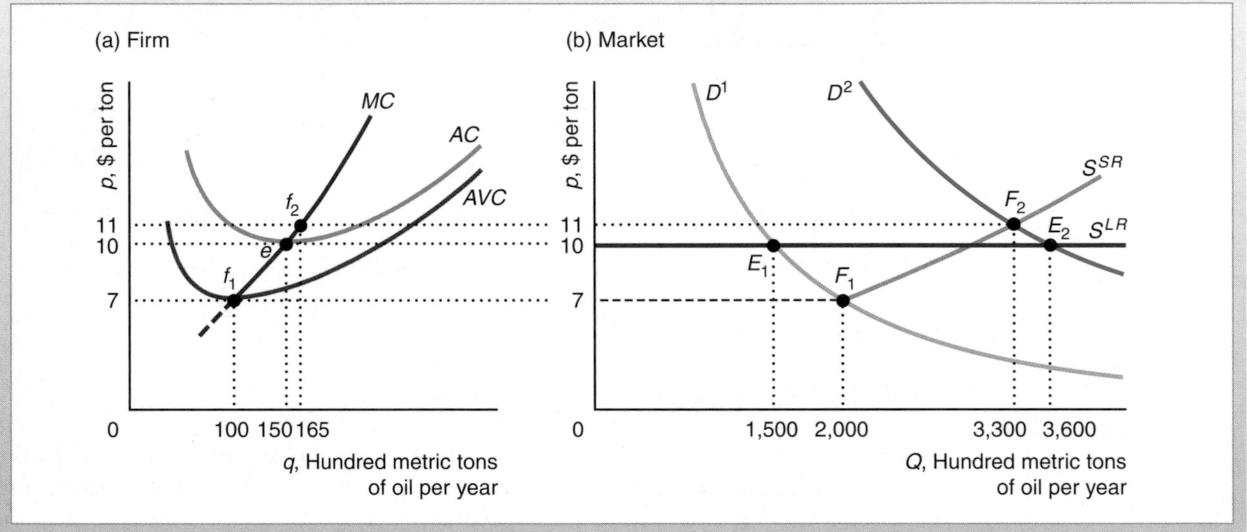

In the short run, if the demand is as low as D^1, the market price in the short-run equilibrium, F_1, is \$7. At that price, each of the 20 firms produces 100 units, at f_1 in panel a. The firms lose money because the price of \$7 is below average cost at 100 units. These losses drive some of the firms out of the market in the long run, so market output falls and the market price rises. In the long-run equilibrium, E_1, price is \$10, and each firm produces 150 units, e, and breaks even. As the market demands only 1,500 units, only 10 (= 1,500/150) firms produce, so half the firms that produced in the short run exit the market.[14] Thus, with the D^1 demand curve, price rises and output falls in the long run.

If demand expands to D^2, in the short run, each of the 20 firms expands its output to 165 units, f_2, and the price rises to \$11, where the firms make profits: The price of \$11 is above the average cost at 165 units. These profits attract entry in the long run, and the price falls. In the long-run equilibrium, each firm produces 150 units, e, and 3,600 units are sold by the market, E_2, by 24 (= 3,600/150) firms. Thus, with the D^2 demand curve, price falls and output rises in the long run.

See Question 29.

Because firms may enter and exit in the long run, taxes can have a counterintuitive effect on the competitive equilibrium. For example, as Solved Problem 8.5 shows, a lump-sum franchise tax causes the competitive equilibrium output of a firm to increase, although market output falls.

[14]How do we know which firms leave? If the firms are identical, the theory says nothing about which ones leave and which ones stay. The firms that leave make zero economic profit, and those that stay make zero economic profit, so firms are indifferent as to whether they stay or exit.

Solved Problem 8.5

If the government starts collecting a lump-sum franchise tax of $\mathcal{L}$ each year from each identical firm in a competitive market with free entry and exit, how do the long-run market and firm equilibria change?

Answer

1. *Show that the franchise tax causes the minimum long-run average cost to rise.* A typical firm's cost curves are shown in panel a and the market equilibrium in panel b. In panel a, a lump-sum, franchise tax shifts the typical firm's average cost curve upward from AC^1 to $AC^2 = AC^1 + \mathcal{L}/q$ but does not affect the marginal cost (see the answer to Solved Problem 7.1). As a result, the minimum average cost rises from e_1 to e_2.

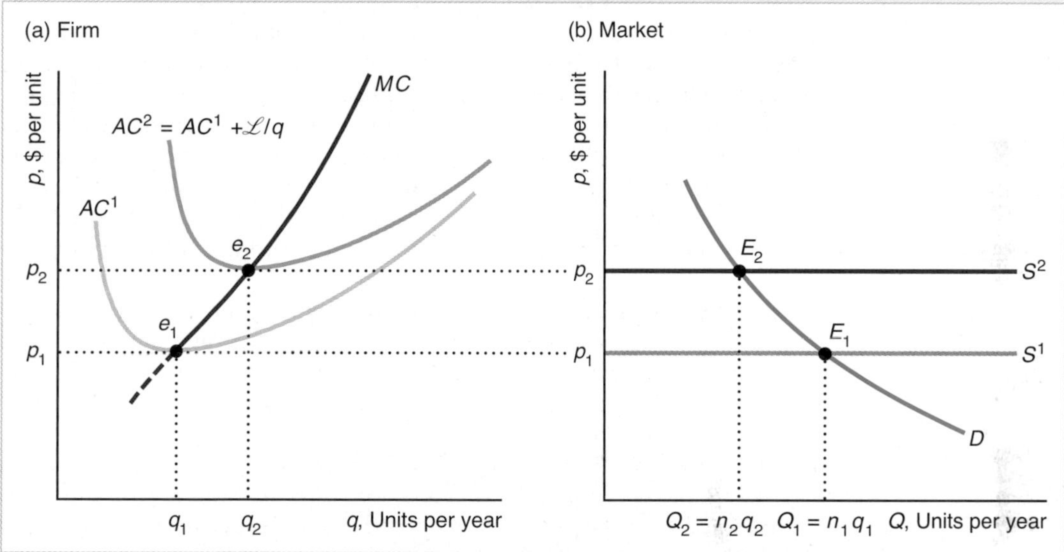

2. *Show that the shift in the minimum average cost causes the market supply curve to shift upward, equilibrium quantity to fall, and equilibrium price to rise.* The long-run market supply is horizontal at minimum average cost. Thus, the market supply curve shifts upward by the same amount as the minimum average cost increases in panel b. With a downward-sloping market demand curve, the new equilibrium, E_2, has a lower quantity, $Q_2 < Q_1$, and higher price, $p_2 > p_1$, than the original equilibrium, E_1.

3. *Show that the increase in the equilibrium price causes output of an individual firm to rise.* Because the market price rises, the quantity that a firm produces rises from q_1 to q_2. Therefore, if the firm remains in the market, it will produce more.

4. *Use the market quantity and individual firm quantity to determine how the number of firms changes.* At the initial equilibrium, the number of firms was $n_1 = Q_1/q_1$. The new equilibrium number of firms, $n_2 = Q_2/q_2$, must be smaller than n_1 because $Q_2 < Q_1$ and $q_2 > q_1$. Thus, there are fewer firms but each remaining firm produces more output at the new equilibrium.

See Questions 30 and 31.

8.5 Zero Profit for Competitive Firms in the Long Run

Competitive firms earn zero profit in the long run whether or not entry is completely free. As a consequence, competitive firms must maximize profit.

Zero Long-Run Profit with Free Entry

The long-run supply curve is horizontal if firms are free to enter the market, firms have identical cost, and input prices are constant. All firms in the market are operating at minimum long-run average cost. That is, they are indifferent between shutting down or not because they are earning zero profit.

One implication of the shutdown rule is that the firm is willing to operate in the long run even if it is making zero profit. This conclusion may seem strange unless you remember that we are talking about *economic profit*, which is revenue minus opportunity cost. Because opportunity cost includes the value of the next best investment, at a zero long-run economic profit, the firm is earning the normal business profit that the firm could earn by investing elsewhere in the economy.

For example, if a firm's owner had not built the plant the firm uses to produce, the owner could have spent that money on another business or put the money in a bank. The opportunity cost of the current plant, then, is the forgone profit from what the owner could have earned by investing the money elsewhere.

The five-year after-tax accounting return on capital across all firms was 10.5%, indicating that the typical firm earned a business profit of 10.5¢ for every dollar it invested in capital (*Forbes*). These firms were earning roughly zero economic profit but positive business profit.

Because business cost does not include all opportunity costs, business profit is larger than economic profit. Thus, *a profit-maximizing firm may stay in business if it earns zero long-run economic profit but shuts down if it earns zero long-run business profit.*

APPLICATION

Abortion Market

Abortion clinics operate in a nearly perfectly competitive market, close to their break-even point. Medoff (2007) estimates that the price elasticity of demand for abortions is −1.071 and the income elasticity is 1.24. However, in recent years the demand curve has shifted significantly to the left (as have the number of births). The number of abortions has fallen substantially over the last several decades. The abortion rate per 1,000 women of childbearing age dropped from 29 in 1981 to 21 in 2003.

This large shift in the number of abortions performed forced smaller clinics to shut down. However, the number of clinics performing 400 or more abortions a year—clinics responsible for more than 89% of all abortions—has remained steady at 690 since 1992.

Women in rural areas and in areas with fewer than 200,000 people who want abortions generally must travel to a major metropolitan area, where virtually all large clinics are located. These in-city abortion clinics fiercely compete with respect to price. Many doctors who perform abortions refuse to train others, so as to prevent them from entering the market.

As clinics fight for the diminishing business, they are forced to operate at the shutdown point and make zero economic profit. To stay in business, the clinics keep their variable costs as low as possible. A low-paid staff does everything but the actual surgery, from drawing blood to doing lab tests. Clinics have a doctor present only on days when they can schedule a steady stream of patients. Each first-trimester procedure takes only two to three minutes of the doctor's time.

See Problem 41.

The average price of an abortion has remained relatively constant over the last 25 years, in contrast to a fivefold increase in the price of other medical services. According to the Alan Guttmacher Institute in 2004, the average price (in 1997 dollars) was roughly \$372 from 1983 through 2001. That the price has remained relatively constant over time, despite major shifts in the demand curve and an 11% decline in abortion providers between 1996 and 2000, is consistent with a nearly horizontal supply curve for abortions.

Zero Long-Run Profit When Entry Is Limited

In some markets, firms cannot enter in response to long-run profit opportunities. One reason for the limited number of firms is that the supply of an input is limited. Only so much land is suitable for mining uranium, and only a few people have the superior skills needed to play professional basketball.

One might think that firms could make positive long-run economic profits in such markets; however, that's not true. The reason why firms earn zero economic profits is that firms bidding for the scarce input drive its price up until the firms' profits are zero.

Suppose that the number of acres suitable for growing tomatoes is limited. Figure 8.16 shows a typical farm's average cost curve if the rental cost of land is zero (the average cost curve includes only the farm's costs of labor, capital, materials, and energy—not land). At the market price p^*, the firm produces q^* bushels of tomatoes and makes a profit of π^*, the shaded rectangle in the figure.

Thus, if the owner of the land does not charge rent, the farmer makes a profit. Unfortunately for the farmer, the landowner rents the land for π^*, so the farmer

Figure 8.16 Rent.

If it did not have to pay rent for its land, a farm with high-quality land would earn a positive long-run profit of π^*. Due to competitive bidding for this land, however, the rent equals π^*, so the landlord reaps all the benefits of the superior land, and the farmer earns a zero long-run economic profit.

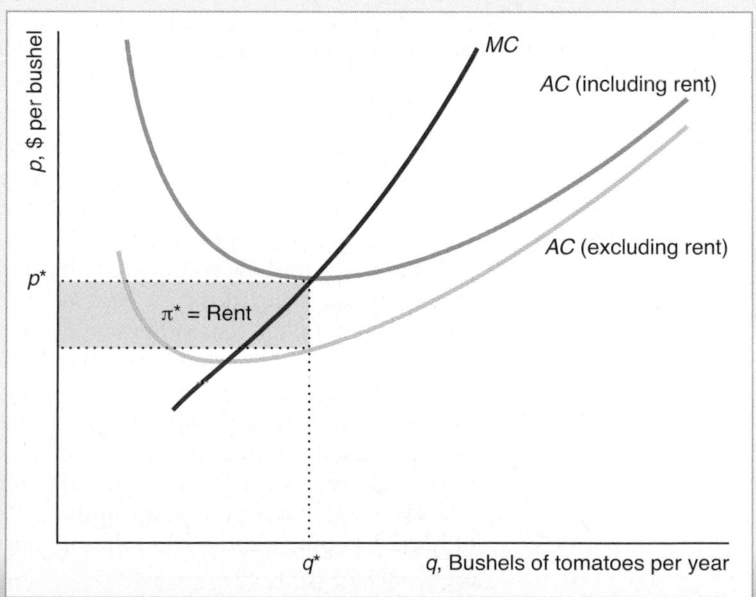

actually earns zero profit. Why does the landowner charge that much? The reason is that π^* is the opportunity cost of the land: The land is worth π^* to other potential farmers. These farmers will bid against each other to rent this land until the rent is driven up to π^*.

This rent is a fixed cost to the farmer because it doesn't vary with the amount of output. Thus, the rent affects the farm's average cost curve but not its marginal cost curve.

As a result, if the farm produces at all, it produces q^*, where its marginal cost equals the market price, no matter what rent is charged. The higher average cost curve in the figure includes a rent equal to π^*. The minimum point of this average cost curve is p^* at q^* bushels of tomatoes, so the farmer earns zero economic profit.

If a shift in the market demand curve causes the market price to fall, these farmers will make short-run losses. In the long run, the rental price of the land will fall enough that, once again, each firm earns zero economic profit.

Does it make a difference whether farmers own or rent the land? Not really. The opportunity cost to a farmer who owns superior land is the amount for which that land could be rented in a competitive land market. Thus, the economic profit of both owned and rented land is zero at the long-run equilibrium.

Good-quality land is not the only scarce resource. The price of any fixed factor will be bid up in the same way so that economic profit for the firm is zero in the long run.

Similarly, the government may require that a firm have a license to operate and then limits the number of licenses. The price of the license gets bid up by potential entrants, driving profit to zero. For example, the license fee is $326,000 a year for the hot dog stand on the north side of the steps of the Metropolitan Museum of Art in New York City.[15]

rent
a payment to the owner of an input beyond the minimum necessary for the factor to be supplied

A scarce input, such as a person with high ability or land, earns an extra opportunity value. This extra value is called a **rent**: a payment to the owner of an input beyond the minimum necessary for the factor to be supplied.

Bonnie manages a store for the salary of $30,000, which is what a typical manager is paid. Because she's a superior manager, however, the firm earns an economic profit of $50,000 a year. Other firms, seeing what a good job Bonnie is doing, offer her a higher salary. The bidding for her services drives her salary up to $80,000: her $30,000 base salary plus the $50,000 rent. After paying this rent to Bonnie, the store makes zero economic profit.

See Questions 32 and 33.

Similarly, people with unusual abilities can earn staggering rents. Though no law stops anyone from trying to become a professional entertainer, most of us do not have enough talent that others will pay to watch us perform. According to Forbes .com, Oprah Winfrey earned $260 million in 2007 (dwarfing the earnings of the second-highest celebrity earner, Tiger Woods at $100 million). To put these receipts in perspective, these amounts exceed many small nations' gross domestic product (value of total output): $15 (U.S. dollars) million, Tuvalu (11,636 people); $73 million, Kiribati (103,092 people); $109 million in Anguilla; $115 million, Marshall Islands (59,071 people); $125 million, Palau (20,303 people); $179 million, Tonga (112,422 people); and $183 million, Cook Islands (according to CIA.gov, 2008).

[15]In the hotdog stand photo, I'm the fellow in the blue shirt with the dopey expression.

In short, if some firms in a market make short-run economic profits due to a scarce input, the other firms in the market bid for that input. This bidding drives the price of the factor upward until all firms earn zero long-run profits. In such a market, the supply curve is flat because all firms have the same minimum long-run average cost.

The Need to Maximize Profit

The worst crime against working people is a company which fails to operate at a profit.

—Samuel Gompers, first president of the American Federation of Labor

In a competitive market with identical firms and free entry, if most firms are profit-maximizing, profits are driven to zero at the long-run equilibrium. Any firm that did not maximize profit—that is, any firm that set its output so that price did not equal its marginal cost or did not use the most cost-efficient methods of production—would lose money. Thus, *to survive in a competitive market, a firm must maximize its profit.*

SUMMARY

1. **Competition.** Competitive firms are price takers that cannot influence market price. Markets are likely to be competitive if all firms in the market sell identical products, firms can enter and exit the market freely, buyers and sellers know the prices charged by firms, and transaction costs are low. A competitive firm faces a horizontal demand curve at the market price.
2. **Profit Maximization.** Most firms maximize economic profit, which is revenue minus economic cost (explicit and implicit cost). Because business profit, which is revenue minus only explicit cost, does not include implicit cost, economic profit tends to be less than business profit. A firm earning zero economic profit is making as much as it could if its resources were devoted to their best alternative uses. To maximize profit, all firms (not just competitive firms) must make two decisions. First, the firm determines the quantity at which its profit is highest. Profit is maximized when marginal profit is zero or, equivalently, when marginal revenue equals marginal cost. Second, the firm decides whether to produce at all.
3. **Competition in the Short Run.** Because a competitive firm is a price taker, its marginal revenue equals the market price. As a result, a competitive firm maximizes its profit by setting its output so that its short-run marginal cost equals the market price. The firm shuts down if the market price is less than its minimum average variable cost. Thus, a profit-maximizing competitive firm's short-run supply curve is its marginal cost curve above its minimum average variable cost. The short-run market supply curve, which is the sum of the supply curves of the fixed number of firms producing in the short run, is flat at low output levels and upward sloping at larger levels. The short-run competitive equilibrium is determined by the intersection of the market demand curve and the short-run market supply curve. The effect of an increase in demand depends on whether demand intersects the market supply in the flat or upward-sloping section.
4. **Competition in the Long Run.** In the long run, a competitive firm sets its output where the market price equals its long-run marginal cost. It shuts down if the market price is less than the minimum of its average long-run cost because all costs are variable in the long run. Consequently, the competitive firm's supply curve is its long-run marginal cost above its minimum long-run average cost. The long-run supply curve of a firm may have a different slope than the short-run curve because it can vary its fixed factors in the long run. The long-run market supply curve is the horizontal sum of the supply curves of all the firms in the market. If all firms are identical, entry and exit are easy, and input prices are constant, the long-run market supply curve is flat at minimum average cost. If firms differ, entry is difficult or costly, or input prices vary with output, the long-run market supply curve has an upward slope. The long-run market supply curve slopes upward if input prices increase with output and slopes downward if input prices decrease with output. The long-run market equilibrium price and quantity are different from the short-run price and quantity.
5. **Zero Profit for Competitive Firms in the Long Run.** Although firms may make profits or losses in

the short run, they earn zero economic profit in the long run. If necessary, the prices of scarce inputs adjust to ensure that competitive firms make zero long-run profit. Because profit-maximizing firms just break even in the long run, firms that do not try to maximize profits will lose money. Competitive firms must maximize profit to survive.

QUESTIONS

■ = *exercise is available on MyEconLab;* * = *answer appears at the back of this book;* C = *use of calculus may be necessary;* W = *audio-slideshow answer by James Dearden is available in Textbook Resources on MyEconLab.*

1. A competitive firm faces a relatively horizontal residual demand curve. Do the following conditions make the demand curve flatter (and why)?
   a. Ease of entry
   b. A large number of firms in the market
   c. The market demand curve is relatively elastic at the equilibrium
   d. The supply curves of other firms are relatively elastic
2. Should a firm shut down (and why) if its revenue is $R = \$1{,}000$ per week,
   a. its variable cost is $VC = \$500$, and its sunk fixed cost is $F = \$600$?
   b. its variable cost is $VC = \$1{,}001$, and its sunk fixed cost $F = \$500$?
3. Should a firm shut down if its weekly revenue is \$1,000, its variable cost is \$500, and its fixed cost is \$800, of which \$600 is avoidable if it shuts down? Why?
4. ■ Should a competitive firm ever produce when it is losing money (making a negative economic profit)? Why or why not?
5. ■ In June 2005, Eastman Kodak announced that it no longer would produce black-and-white photographic paper—the type used to develop photographs by a traditional darkroom process. Kodak based its decision on the substitution of digital photography for traditional photography. In making its exit decision, does Kodak compare the price of its paper and average variable cost (at its optimal output)? Alternatively, does Kodak compare the price of its paper and average total cost (again at its optimal output)? W
6. ■ *Many marginal cost curves are U-shaped. As a result, it is possible that the *MC* curve hits the demand or price line at two output levels. Which is the profit-maximizing output? Why?
7. ■ According to the "Oil, Oil Sands, and Oil Shale Shutdowns" application, the minimum average variable cost of processing oil sands dropped from \$25 a barrel in the 1960s to \$18 today due to technological advances. In a figure, show how this change affects the supply curve of a typical competitive firm and the supply curve of all the firms producing oil from oil sands.
8. When natural gas prices rose in the first half of 2004, producers considered using natural gas fields that once had been passed over because of the high costs of extracting the gas (Russell Gold, "Natural Gas Is Likely to Stay Pricey," *Wall Street Journal,* June 14, 2004, A2).
   a. Show in a figure what this statement implies about the shape of the natural gas extraction cost function.
   b. Use the cost function you drew in part a to show how an increase in the market price of natural gas affects the amount of gas that a competitive firm extracts. Show the change in the firm's equilibrium profit. W
9. ■ *For Red Delicious apple farmers in Washington, 2001 was a terrible year (Linda Ashton, "Bumper Crop a Bummer for Struggling Apple Farmers," *San Francisco Chronicle,* January 9, 2001, C7). The average price for Red Delicious was \$10.61 per box, well below the shutdown level of \$13.23. Many farmers did not pick the apples off their trees. Other farmers bulldozed their trees, getting out of the Red Delicious business for good, taking 25,000 acres out of production. Why did some farms choose not to pick apples, and others to bulldoze their trees? (*Hint*: Consider the average variable cost and expectations about future prices.)
10. Mercedes-Benz of San Francisco advertises on the radio that it has been owned and operated by the same family in the same location for 46 years (as of 2008). It then makes two claims: first, that because it has owned this land for 46 years, it has lower overhead than other nearby auto dealers, and second, because of its lower overhead, it charges a lower price on its cars. Discuss the logic of these claims.

11. Carol Skonberg, a housewife and part-time piano teacher, thought she was filling a crying need with her wineglass jewelry ("Eve Tahmincioglu, "Even the Best Ideas Don't Sell Themselves," *New York Times,* October 9, 2003, C9). Her Wine Jewels are sterling silver charms of elephants, palm trees, and other subjects that hook on wineglass stems so that people don't lose their drinks at parties. In 2000, her first year, she signed up 90 stores in Texas to carry her charms. Then, almost overnight, orders disappeared as rival companies offered similar products—with names such as Wine Charms, Stemmies, and That Wine Is Mine—at lower prices. Ellen Petti started That Wine Is Mine in 1999. She set up a national network of sales representatives and got the product in national catalogs. Its sales surged from $250,000 the first year to $6 million in 2001, before falling to $4.5 million in 2002, when she sold the company. Tina Matte's firm started selling Stemmies in late 2000, making $90,000 in its first year, before sales fell to $75,000 the following year. Assume that this market is competitive and use side-by-side firm and market diagrams to show what happened to prices, quantities, number of firms, and profit as this market evolved over a couple of years. (*Hint*: Consider the possibility that firms' cost functions differ.)

12. Fierce storms in October 2004 caused TomatoFest Organic Heirlooms Farm to end its tomato harvest two weeks early. According to Gary Ibsen, a partner in this small business (Carlyn Said, "Tomatoes in Trouble," *San Francisco Chronicle,* October 29, 2004, C1, C2), TomatoFest lost about 20,000 pounds of tomatoes that would have sold for about $38,000; however, because he did not have to hire pickers and rent trucks during these two weeks, his net loss was about $20,000. In calculating the revenue loss, he used the post-storm price, which was double the pre-storm price. Assume that TomatoFest's experience was typical of that of many small tomato farms.

    a. Draw a diagram for a typical firm next to one for the market to show what happened as a result of the storm.

    b. Did TomatoFest suffer an economic loss? What extra information (if any) do you need to answer this question? How do you define "economic loss" in this situation?

13. The African country Lesotho gains most of its export earnings—90% in 2004—from its garment and textile factories. Your t-shirts from Wal-Mart and fleece sweats from J. C. Penney probably were made there. In 2005, the demand curve for Lesotho products shifted down precipitously due to increased Chinese supply with the end of textile quotas on China and the resulting increase in Chinese exports (see Chapter 2, Question 13) and the plunge of the U.S. dollar exchange rate against its currency. Lesotho's garment factories had to sell roughly $55 worth of clothing in the United States to cover a factory worker's monthly wage in 2002, but they had to sell an average of $109 to $115 in 2005. Consequently, in the first quarter of 2005, 6 of Lesotho's 50 clothes factories shut down, as the world price plummeted below their minimum average variable cost. These shutdowns eliminated 5,800 of the 50,000 garment jobs. Layoffs at other factories have eliminated another 6,000. Since 2002, Lesotho has lost an estimated 30,000 textile jobs.

    a. What is the shape of the demand curve facing Lesotho textile factories, and why? (*Hint*: They are price takers in the world market.)

    b. Use figures to show how the increase in Chinese exports affected the demand curve the Lesotho factories face.

    c. Discuss how the change in the exchange rate affected their demand curve, and explain why.

    d. Use figures to explain why the factories have temporarily or permanently shut down. How does a factory decide whether to shut down temporarily or permanently?

14. During the winter of 2004–2005, wholesale gasoline prices rose rapidly. Although retail gasoline prices increased, retailers' profit per gallon fell. The difference between price and average variable cost for self-serve regular gasoline averaged 7.7¢ a gallon in the first quarter of 2005 compared with 9.1¢ for all of 2004. In addition, many gasoline retailers exited the market. (Thaddeus Herrick, "Pumping Profits from Gas Sales Is Tough to Do," *Wall Street Journal,* May 25, 2005, B1).

    a. Show how an increase in wholesale gasoline prices affects the individual retailer's marginal cost and supply curves.

    b. Show how shifts in the individual retailer's supply curves affect the market supply curve.

    c. Show and explain why an $\$x$ per gallon increase in wholesale gasoline prices results in a retail market price increase that is less than $\$x$.

    d. Identify the effect of wholesale gasoline price increases on the profit margins of an individual gasoline retailer.

    e. Why has the increase in wholesale gasoline prices prompted many gasoline retailers to exit the market? W

15. Dairy farms can produce Grade A milk, which meets the highest sanitation standards designed for the fluid market, or Grade B milk, which meets lower sanitation standards designed for the cheese, butter, and nonfluid markets (Caputo and Paris, 2005). Substantial additional physical and human capital is necessary to produce Grade A rather than Grade B milk. From 1949 to 1999, the share of Grade A milk produced in the United States rose from 57% to 97%, as most dairy farms adopted the necessary technology. Use graphs to explain why Caputo and Paris conclude that "the rising relative price of Grade A milk gave dairy farmers the incentive to adopt the technology for Grade A milk production since such adoption resulted in higher future expected profits than did Grade B milk production." (*Note*: Federal and state governments limit entry into milk production.)

16. Americans used 33 million real Christmas trees and 40 million artificial trees in 1994. The number of tree producers fell by about a third over the previous 10 years, to about 2,000 in 1994, due to artificial tree sales. That year, trees sold for an average of \$26.50, about 50¢ more than the previous year. Retailers' average cost was \$20. In 1998, 33 million trees sold for an average of \$29.25. Use graphs to illustrate this information.

17. A few years ago, virtually every U.S. food company had seemed to "Atkinize," introducing low-carbohydrate foods by removing sugar and starch. In 1999, few food or beverage products were sold as "no-carb" or "low-carb." In 2003, some 500 products carried such labels, and by 2004, more than 3,000 products made such a claim (Melanie Warner, "Is the Low-Carb Boom Over?" *New York Times*, December 5, 2004, 3.1, 3.9). Low-carb product sales rose 6% in the 13 weeks ended September 24, 2004, compared to double-digit gains in the corresponding period in 2003 and triple-digit gains in the beginning of 2004. By 2005, low-carb products were disappearing rapidly. Assume that food firms can be properly viewed as being competitive. Use side-by-side firm and market diagrams to show why firms quickly entered and then quickly exited the low-carb market. Did the firms go wrong by introducing many low-carb products? (Answer in terms of fixed costs and expectations about demand.)

18. The Internet is affecting holiday shipping. In years past, the busiest shipping period was Thanksgiving week. Now as people have become comfortable with e-commerce, they put off purchases to the last minute and are more likely to have them shipped (rather than to purchase locally). In December 2004, FedEx handled a 40% increase in packages over the previous year (Pia Sakar, "Shippers Snowed Under," *San Francisco Chronicle*, December 21, 2004, D1, D8). FedEx, along with Amazon and other e-commerce firms, has to hire extra workers during this period, and many regular workers log substantial overtime hours (up to 60 a week).

    a. Are a firm's marginal and average costs likely to rise or fall with this extra business? (Discuss economies of scale and the slopes of marginal and average cost curves.)

    b. Use side-by-side firm-market diagrams to show the effects on the number of firms, equilibrium price and output, and profits of such a seasonal shift in demand for e-retailers in both the short run and the long run. Explain your reasoning.

19. Redraw Figure 8.10 showing a situation in which the short-run plant size is too large relative to the optimal long-run plant size.

*20. What is the effect on firm and market equilibrium of the U.S. law requiring a firm to give its workers six months' notice before it can shut down its plant?

21. Chinese art factories are flooding the world's generic art market (see the "Enter the Dragon" application). Using a step-like supply function (similar to the one in the "Upward-Sloping Long-Run Supply Curve for Cotton" application), show how the entry of the Chinese affects the world supply curve and how this change affects the equilibrium, including who produces art. Explain.

22. Cheap handheld video cameras revolutionized the hard-core pornography market. Previously, making movies required expensive equipment and some technical expertise. Now anyone with a thousand dollars and a moderately steady hand can buy and use a video camera to make a movie. Consequently, many new firms have entered the market, and the supply curve of porn movies has slithered substantially to the right. The number of video porn titles released annually in the United States grew from only 1,300 in 1988 to 2,200 in 1992, 3,200 in 1994, 10,300 in 1999, and 13,588 in 2005, or one new film produced every 38 minutes (**internet-filter-review.toptenreviews .com/internet-pornography-statistics.html**, March 2008). Use a side-by-side diagram to illustrate how this technological innovation affected the long-run supply curve and the equilibrium in this market.

23. The "Upward-Sloping Long-Run Supply Curve for Cotton" application shows a supply curve for cotton. Discuss the equilibrium if the world demand curve crosses this supply curve in either (a) a flat section labeled Brazil or (b) the following vertical section. What do farms in the United States do?

24. In 2007, the average price of renting a ship to carry raw materials from Brazil to China nearly tripled to $180,000 a day from $65,000 in the previous year (Robert Guy Matthews, "Ship Shortage Pushes Up Prices of Raw Materials," *Wall Street Journal*, October 22, 2007, A1).
    a. Use graphs to illustrate that this increase in the price of shipping is due to an increase in demand, particularly from the growing Chinese and Indian economies, and a fixed number of ships in the short run. In the long run, after an increase in the number of ships, shipping prices should drop.
    b. For some goods, ocean shipping can be more expensive than the cargo itself: Iron ore costs about $60 a ton, but it costs about $88 a ton to transport it from Brazil to Asia. Higher shipping rates are expected to increase commodity prices according to weight, with transportation fees making up a larger percentage of the cost of heavier products like iron ore and grain. The trend may force manufacturers to pay more for the basic ingredients they need to make their products. And those higher costs could be passed on to consumers, affecting the price of everything from automobiles and washing machines to bread. What effect will this increase in shipping costs have on marginal costs and supply curves for various types of finished products (e.g., those that use heavier inputs or inputs that come from distant lands)?
25. In late 2004 and early 2005, the price of raw coffee beans jumped as much as 50% from the previous year. In response, the price of roasted coffee rose about 14%. Why would firms increase the price less than in proportion to the rise in the cost of raw beans?
26. A San Francisco supervisor called for a tax on grocery store bags collected from the stores (Suzanne Herel, "Grocery Store Bag Fee Lacks Public Support; Supervisors Ponder Lower Charge, Other Ways to Reduce Use," *San Francisco Chronicle,* May 13, 2005, B1, B4). He said that he never intended that this surcharge be passed on to consumers. Does such a tax affect marginal cost? How much? How much of the tax is therefore likely to be passed on to consumers?
27. Navel oranges are grown in California and Arizona. If Arizona starts collecting a specific tax per orange from its firms, what happens to the long-run market supply curve? (*Hint*: You may assume that all firms initially have the same costs. Your answer may depend on whether unlimited entry occurs.)
28. To reduce pollution, the California Air Resources Board in 1996 required the reformulation of gasoline sold in California. In 1999, a series of disasters at California refineries substantially cut the supply of gasoline and contributed to large price increases. Environmentalists and California refiners (who had sunk large investments to produce the reformulated gasoline) opposed imports from other states, which would have kept prices down. To minimize fluctuations in prices in California, Severin Borenstein and Steven Stoft suggest setting a 15¢ surcharge on sellers of standard gasoline. In normal times, none of this gasoline would be sold, because it costs only 8¢ to 12¢ more to produce the California version. However, when disasters trigger a large shift in the supply curve of gasoline, firms could profitably import standard gasoline and keep the price in California from rising more than about 15¢ above prices in the rest of the United States. Use figures to evaluate Borenstein and Stoft's proposal.
29. The war in Iraq caused the Defense Department to greatly increase purchases from defense contractors, which include everything from ice cream vendors to armored vehicle manufacturers. Use side-by-side firm-market diagrams to show the effects (number of firms, price, output, profits) of such a shift in demand in one such industry in both the short run and the long run. Explain how your answer depends on whether the shift in demand is expected to be temporary or permanent.
30. In Solved Problem 8.5, would it make a difference to the analysis whether the franchise tax were collected annually or only once when the firm starts operation? How would each of these franchise taxes affect the firm's long-run supply curve? Explain your answer.
31. Answer Solved Problem 8.5 for the short run rather than for the long run. (*Hint*: The answer depends on where the demand curve intersects the original short-run supply curve.)
32. Is it true that the long-run supply curve for a good is horizontal only if the long-run supply curves of all factors are horizontal? Explain.
33. The reputations of some of the world's most prestigious museums have been damaged by accusations that they obtained antiquities that were looted or stolen in violation of international laws and treaties aimed at halting illicit trade in art and antiquities (Ron Stodghill, "Do You Know Where That Art Has Been?" *New York Times*, March 18, 2007). A new wariness among private and public collectors to buy works whose provenance has not been rigorously established jeopardizes the business of even the most established dealers. Conversely, this fear has increased the value of antiquities that have a solid ownership history. The Aboutaams brothers, who are

among the world's most powerful dealers of antiquities, back an international ban on trade in excavated antiquities. As Hicham Aboutaam said, "The more questionable works entering the antiquities market, the less their value and the larger the dark cloud that hangs over the field. That affects prices negatively. I think we could put an end to the new supply, and work comfortably with what we have."

a. What would be the effect of the ban on the current stock of antiquities for sale in the United States and Europe?

b. Would such a ban differentially affect established dealers and new dealers?

c. Why would established dealers back such a ban?

d. Discuss the implications of a ban using the concept of an economic rent.

34. Bribes paid by Swiss companies to foreign officials, which were tax deductible since 1946, are no longer deductible as of 1999. Use economic models from this chapter and Chapter 7 to show the likely effects of this ban on the bribing behavior of Swiss firms.

35. If we plot a firm's profit against the number of vacation days taken by its owner, Julia, we find that profit first rises with vacation days (a few days of vacation improve Julia's effectiveness as a manager the rest of the year) but eventually falls as she takes more vacation days. Use a diagram to determine if Julia takes the number of vacation days that maximizes profit given that she has usual-shaped indifference curves (see Chapters 4 and 5) between profit and vacation days. Explain.

PROBLEMS

36. If the cost function for John's shoe repair is $C(q) = 100 + 10q - q^2 + \frac{1}{3}q^3$, what is the firm's marginal cost function? What is its profit-maximizing condition? C

*37. If a competitive firm's cost function is $C(q) = a + bq + cq^2 + dq^3$, where a, b, c, and d are constants, what is the firm's marginal cost function? What is the firm's profit-maximizing condition? C

38. Each firm in a competitive market has a cost function of $C = 16 + q^2$. The market demand function is $Q = 24 - p$. Determine the long-run equilibrium price, quantity per firm, market quantity, and number of firms.

*39. Derive Equation 8.7. (*Hint*: Use a method similar to that used in Appendix 8A.)

*40. As of 2005, the federal specific tax on gasoline is 18.4¢ per gallon, and the average state specific tax is 20.2¢, ranging from 7.5¢ in Georgia to 25¢ in Connecticut (down from 38¢ in 1996). A statistical study (Chouinard and Perloff, 2004) finds that the incidence (Chapter 3) of the federal specific tax on consumers is substantially lower than that from state specific taxes. When the federal specific tax increases by 1¢, the retail price rises by about $\frac{1}{2}$¢ Retail consumers bear half the tax incidence. In contrast, when a state that uses regular gasoline increases its specific tax by 1¢, the incidence of the tax falls almost entirely on consumers: The retail price rises by nearly 1¢.

a. What are the incidences of the federal and state specific gasoline taxes on firms?

b. Explain why the incidence on consumers differs between a federal and a state specific gasoline tax assuming that the market is competitive. (*Hint*: Consider the residual supply curve facing a state compared to the supply curve facing the nation.)

c. Using the residual supply equation (Equation 8.6), estimate how much more elastic is the residual supply elasticity to one state than is the national supply elasticity. (For simplicity, assume that all 50 states are identical.)

*41. By how much would the market price of abortions and the number of abortions change if a lump-sum tax is assessed on abortion clinics that raises their minimum average cost by 10%? Use a figure to illustrate your answer. (*Hint*: See Solved Problem 8.3 and use the price elasticity and other information from the "Abortion Market" application.)

Applying the Competitive Model

9

No more good must be attempted than the public can bear.
—Thomas Jefferson

In 2007, the World Trade Organization (WTO), which referees global trade disputes, ruled in favor of Brazil and Canada against the United States. The WTO concluded that U.S. government subsidies to its farmers broke international trade laws, harming farmers elsewhere. This decision could result in billions of dollars in penalties against the United States.

How does such a trade war affect consumers and producers? In this chapter, we show how the competitive model can answer this type of question. One of the major strengths of the competitive market model is that it can predict how trade wars, changes in government policies, global warming, and major cost-saving discoveries affect consumers and producers.

This chapter introduces the measure that economists commonly use to determine whether consumers or firms gain or lose when the equilibrium of a competitive market changes. Using such a measure, we can predict whether a policy change benefits the winners more than it harms the losers. To decide whether to adopt a particular policy, policymakers can combine these predictions with their normative views (values), such as whether they are more interested in helping the group that gains or the group that loses.

To most people, the term *welfare* refers to the government's payments to poor people. No such meaning is implied when economists employ the term. Economists use *welfare* to refer to the well-being of various groups such as consumers and producers. They call an analysis of the impact of a change on various groups' well-being a study of *welfare economics*.

In this chapter, we examine six main topics

1. **Consumer Welfare.** How much consumers are helped or harmed by a change in the equilibrium price can be measured by using information from demand curves or utility functions.
2. **Producer Welfare.** How much producers gain or lose from a change in the equilibrium price can be measured by using information from the marginal cost curve or by measuring the change in profits.
3. **Competition Maximizes Welfare.** Competition maximizes a measure of social welfare based on consumer and producer welfare.
4. **Policies That Shift Supply Curves.** Government policies that limit the number of firms in competitive markets harm consumers and lower welfare.
5. **Policies That Create a Wedge Between Supply and Demand.** Government policies such as taxes, price ceilings, price floors, and tariffs that create a wedge between the

supply and demand curves reduce the equilibrium quantity, raise the equilibrium price to consumers, and lower welfare.

6. **Comparing Both Types of Policies: Imports.** Policies that limit supply (such as quotas or bans on imports) or create a wedge between supply and demand (such as *tariffs*, which are taxes on imports) have different welfare effects when both policies reduce imports by equal amounts.

9.1 Consumer Welfare

Economists and policymakers want to know how much consumers benefit from or are harmed by shocks that affect the equilibrium price and quantity. To what extent are consumers harmed if a local government imposes a sales tax to raise additional revenues? To answer such a question, we need some way to measure consumers' welfare. Economists use measures of welfare based on consumer theory (Chapters 4 and 5).

If we knew a consumer's utility function, we could directly answer the question of how an event affects a consumer's welfare. If the price of beef increases, the budget line facing someone who eats beef rotates inward, so the consumer is on a lower indifference curve at the new equilibrium. If we knew the levels of utility associated with the original indifference curve and the new one, we could measure the impact of the tax in terms of the change in the utility level.

This approach is not practical for a couple of reasons. First, we rarely, if ever, know individuals' utility functions. Second, even if we had utility measures for various consumers, we would have no obvious way to compare them. One person might say that he got 1,000 utils (units of utility) from the same bundle that another consumer says gives her 872 utils of pleasure. The first person is not necessarily happier—he may just be using a different scale.

As a result, *we measure consumer welfare in terms of dollars*. Instead of asking the rather silly question "How many utils would you lose if your daily commute increased by 15 minutes?" we could ask "How much would you pay to avoid having your daily commute grow a quarter of an hour longer?" or "How much would it cost you in forgone earnings if your daily commute were 15 minutes longer?" It is easier to compare dollars across people than utils.

We first present the most widely used method of measuring consumer welfare. Then we show how it can be used to measure the effect of a change in price on consumer welfare.

Measuring Consumer Welfare Using a Demand Curve

Consumer welfare from a good is the benefit a consumer gets from consuming that good minus what the consumer paid to buy the good. How much pleasure do you get from a good above and beyond its price? If you buy a good for exactly what it's worth to you, you are indifferent between making that transaction and not. Frequently, however, you buy things that are worth more to you than what they cost. Imagine that you've played tennis in the hot sun and are very thirsty. You can buy a soft drink from a vending machine for 75¢, but you'd be willing to pay much more because you are so thirsty. As a result, you're much better off making this purchase than not.

If we can measure how much more you'd be willing to pay than you did pay, we'd know how much you gained from this transaction. Luckily for us, the demand curve contains the information we need to make this measurement.

Marginal Willingness to Pay. To develop a welfare measure based on the demand curve, we need to know what information is contained in a demand curve. The demand curve reflects a consumer's *marginal willingness to pay*: the maximum amount a consumer will spend for an extra unit. The consumer's marginal willingness to pay is the *marginal value* the consumer places on the last unit of output.

David's demand curve for magazines per week, panel a of Figure 9.1, indicates his marginal willingness to buy various numbers of magazines. David places a marginal value of $5 on the first magazine. As a result, if the price of a magazine is

Figure 9.1 Consumer Surplus.

(a) David's demand curve for magazines has a steplike shape. When the price is $3, he buys three magazines, point *c*. David's marginal value for the first magazine is $5, areas $CS_1 + E_1$, and his expenditure is $3, area E_1, so his consumer surplus is $CS_1 = \$2$. His consumer surplus is $1 for the second magazine, area CS_2, and is $0 for the third (he is indifferent between buying and not buying it). Thus, his total consumer surplus is the shaded area $CS_1 + CS_2 + CS_3 = \$3$. (b) Steven's willingness to pay for trading cards is the height of his smooth demand curve. At price p_1, Steven's expenditure is $E\ (= p_1q_1)$, his consumer surplus is CS, and the total value he places on consuming q_1 trading cards per year is $CS + E$.

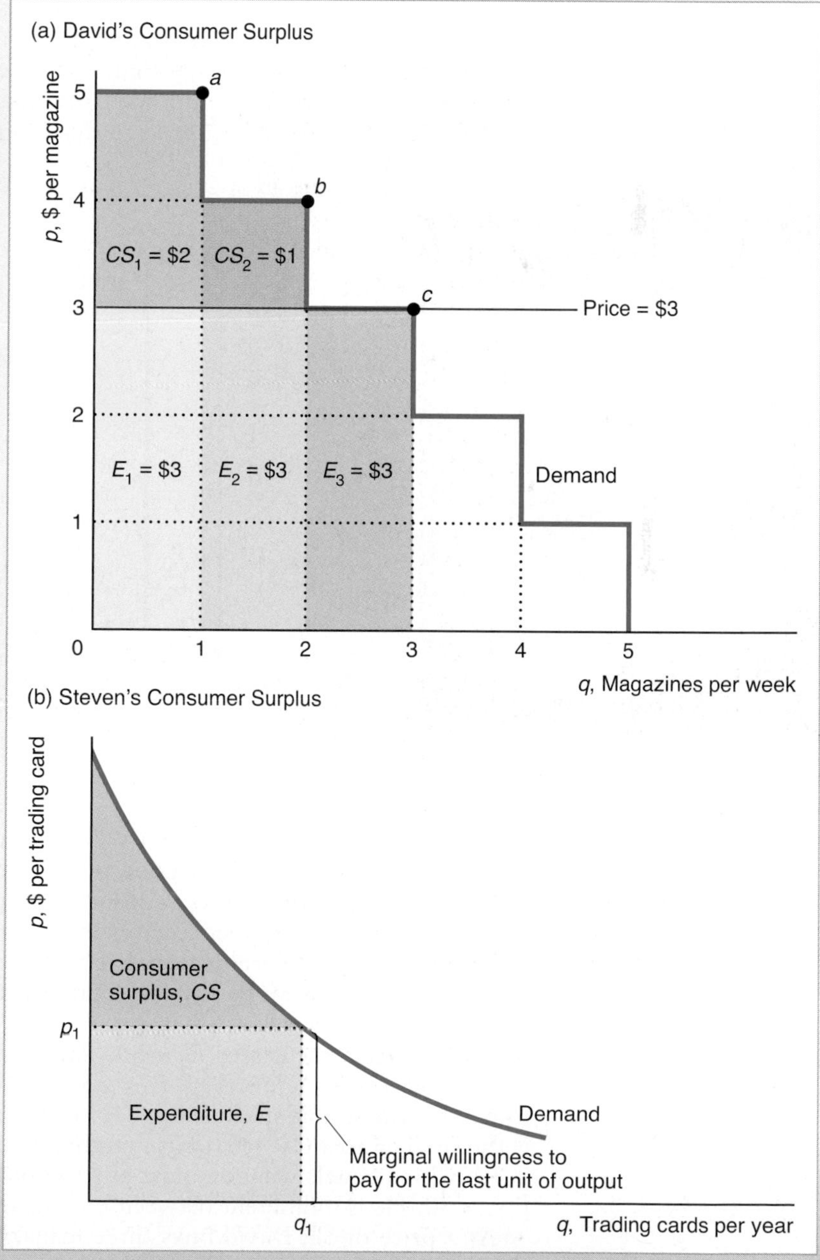

$5, David buys one magazine, point a on the demand curve. His marginal willingness to buy a second magazine is $4, so if the price falls to $4, he buys two magazines, b. His marginal willingness to buy three magazines is $3, so if the price of magazines is $3, he buys three magazines, c.

See Problems 32 and 33.

APPLICATION Willingness to Pay on eBay

People differ in their willingness to pay for a given item. We can determine individuals' willingness to pay for one Homer and Marge Simpson wedding cake topper on the basis of how much they bid in an eBay auction. As we show in Chapter 14, their best strategy was to bid their willingness to pay: the maximum value that they placed on the item. From what eBay reported, we know the maximum bid of each person except the winner: eBay uses a *second-price auction* where the winner pays the second-highest amount bid (plus a small increment—in the case of the cake topper, $1). In the figure, bids are arranged from highest to lowest. Because each bar on the graph indicates one cake topper, the figure shows how many units could have been sold to this group of bidders at various prices.

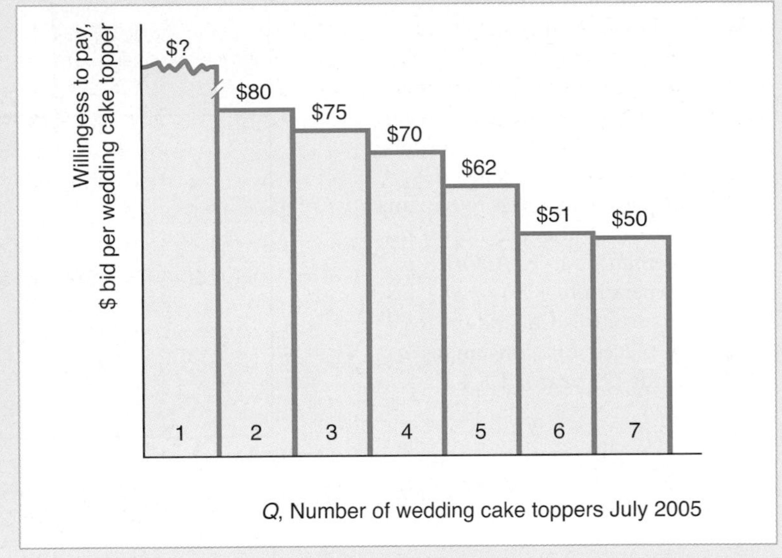

Consumer Surplus. The monetary difference between what a consumer is willing to pay for the quantity of the good purchased and what the good actually costs is called **consumer surplus** (*CS*). Consumer surplus is a dollar-value measure of the extra pleasure the consumer receives from the transaction beyond its price.

consumer surplus (*CS*) the monetary difference between what a consumer is willing to pay for the quantity of the good purchased and what the good actually costs

David's consumer surplus from each additional magazine is his marginal willingness to pay minus what he pays to obtain the magazine. His marginal willingness to pay for the first magazine, $5, is area $CS_1 + E_1$. If the price is $3, his expenditure to obtain the magazine is area $E_1 = \$3$. Thus, his consumer surplus on the first magazine is area $CS_1 = (CS_1 + E_1) - E_1 = \$5 - \$3 = \$2$. Because his marginal willingness to pay for the second magazine is $4, his consumer surplus for the second magazine is the smaller area $CS_2 = \$1$. His marginal willingness to pay for the third magazine is $3, which equals what he must pay to obtain it, so his consumer surplus is zero, $CS_3 = \$0$. He is indifferent between buying and not buying the third magazine.

At a price of $3, David buys three magazines. His total consumer surplus from the three magazines he buys is the sum of the consumer surplus he gets from each of these magazines: $CS_1 + CS_2 + CS_3 = \$2 + \$1 + \$0 = \$3$. This total consumer surplus of \$3 is the extra amount that David is willing to spend for the right to buy three magazines at \$3 each. Thus, *an individual's consumer surplus is the area under the demand curve and above the market price up to the quantity the consumer buys.*

David is unwilling to buy a fourth magazine unless the price drops to \$2 or less. If David's mother gives him a fourth magazine as a gift, the marginal value that David puts on that fourth magazine, \$2, is less than what it cost his mother, \$3.

We can determine consumer surplus for smooth demand curves in the same way as with David's unusual stairlike demand curve. Steven has a smooth demand curve for baseball trading cards, panel b of Figure 9.1. The height of this demand curve measures his willingness to pay for one more card. This willingness varies with the number of cards he buys in a year. The total value he places on obtaining q_1 cards per year is the area under the demand curve up to q_1, the areas CS and E. Area E is his actual expenditure on q_1 cards. Because the price is p_1, his expenditure is p_1q_1. Steven's consumer surplus from consuming q_1 trading cards is the value of consuming those cards, areas CS and E, minus his actual expenditures E to obtain them, or CS. Thus, his consumer surplus, CS, is the area under the demand curve and above the horizontal line at the price p_1 up to the quantity he buys, q_1.

Just as we measure the consumer surplus for an individual using that individual's demand curve, we measure the consumer surplus of all consumers in a market using the market demand curve. *Market consumer surplus is the area under the market demand curve above the market price up to the quantity consumers buy.*

To summarize, consumer surplus is a practical and convenient measure of consumer welfare. There are two advantages to using consumer surplus rather than utility to discuss the welfare of consumers. First, the dollar-denominated consumer surplus of several individuals can be easily compared or combined, whereas the utility of various individuals cannot be easily compared or combined. Second, it is relatively easy to measure consumer surplus, whereas it is difficult to get a meaningful measure of utility directly. To calculate consumer surplus, all we have to do is measure the area under a demand curve.

APPLICATION

Consumer Surplus from Television

Do you get consumer surplus from television? Fewer than one in four (23%) Americans say that they would be willing to "give up watching absolutely all types of television" for the rest of their lives in exchange for \$25,000. Almost half (46%) say that they'd refuse to give up TV for anything under \$1 million. One in four Americans wouldn't give it up for \$1 million. Indeed, one-quarter of those who earn under \$20,000 a year wouldn't give up TV for \$1 million—more than they will earn in 50 years.

Thus, if you ask how much consumer surplus people receive from television, you will get many implausibly high answers. For this reason, economists typically calculate consumer surplus by using estimated demand curves, which are based on actual observed behavior, or by conducting surveys that ask consumers to choose between relatively similar bundles of goods. A more focused survey of families in Great Britain and Northern Ireland in 2000 found that they were willing to pay £10.40 (\$20.80) per month to keep their current, limited television service (BBC1, BBC2, ITV, Channel 4, and Channel 5) and received £2 (\$4) per month of consumer surplus.

Today, many people pay a fee to receive television signals by cable, satellite, or broadband. However, some people still watch broadcast television. If such broadcasts were curtailed, Hazlett et al. (2007) estimate that consumer surplus would fall by \$77 billion.

See Question 1.

Effect of a Price Change on Consumer Surplus

If the supply curve shifts upward or a government imposes a new sales tax, the equilibrium price rises, reducing consumer surplus. We illustrate the effect of a price increase on market consumer surplus using estimated supply and demand curves for sweetheart and hybrid tea roses sold in the United States.[1] We then discuss which markets are likely to have the greatest loss of consumer surplus due to a price increase.

Consumer Surplus Loss from a Higher Price. Suppose that the introduction of a new tax causes the (wholesale) price of roses to rise from the original equilibrium price of 30¢ to 32¢ per rose stem, a shift along the demand curve in Figure 9.2. The consumer surplus is area $A + B + C = \$173.74$ million per year at a price of 30¢, and it is only area $A = \$149.64$ million at a price of 32¢.[2] Thus, the loss in consumer surplus from the increase in the price is $B + C = \$24.1$ million per year.

Figure 9.2 Fall in Consumer Surplus from Roses as Price Rises.

As the price of roses rises 2¢ per stem from 30¢ per stem, the quantity demanded decreases from 1.25 to 1.16 billion stems per year. The loss in consumer surplus from the higher price, areas *B* and *C*, is $24.1 million per year.

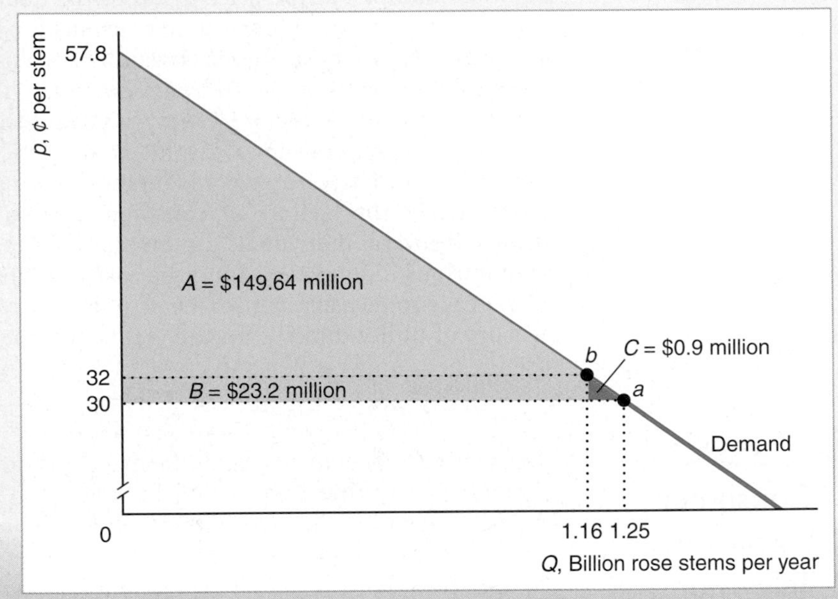

APPLICATION
Bruce Springsteen's Gift to His Fans

In 2002, the $75 that Bruce Springsteen and the E Street Band charged for their concerts that year was well below the market-clearing price. When the tickets went on sale at the Bradley Center in Milwaukee, 9,000 tickets sold in the first 10 minutes and virtually all were gone after 20 minutes.

---

[1] I estimated this model using data from the *Statistical Abstract of United States*, *Floriculture Crops*, *Floriculture and Environmental Horticulture Products*, and **usda.mannlib.cornell.edu/data-sets/crops/95917/sb917.txt.** The prices are in real 1991 dollars.

[2] The height of triangle *A* is 25.8¢ = 57.8¢ − 32¢ per stem and the base is 1.16 billion stems per year, so its area is $\frac{1}{2} \times \$0.258 \times 1.16$ billion = \$149.64 million per year. Rectangle *B* is $\$0.02 \times 1.16$ billion = \$23.2 million. Triangle *C* is $\frac{1}{2} \times \$0.02 \times 0.09$ billion = \$0.9 million.

Some tickets were available from scalpers, ticket brokers, and on the Internet at higher prices. One Web site offered tickets for the concert at the American Airlines Center in Dallas for $540 to $1,015. According to a survey, the average price of a resold ticket for the concert at the First Union Center in Philadelphia was $280. Mr. Springsteen said that he set the price relatively low to give value to his fans (in addition, he may have helped to promote his new album). Assuming that he could have sold all the tickets at $280, he gave almost $3 million of consumer surplus to his Philadelphia fans—double the ticket revenue for that concert.

See Question 2.

Markets in Which Consumer Surplus Losses Are Large. In general, as the price increases, consumer surplus falls more (1) the greater the initial revenues spent on the good and (2) the less elastic the demand curve (Appendix 9A). More is spent on a good when its demand curve is farther to the right so that areas like A, B, and C in Figure 9.2 are larger. The larger $B + C$ is, the greater is the drop in consumer surplus from a given percentage increase in price. Similarly, the less elastic a demand curve is (the closer it is to vertical), the less willing consumers are to give up the good, so consumers do not cut their consumption much as the price increases, with the result of greater consumer surplus losses.

Higher prices cause greater consumer surplus loss in some markets than in others. Consumers would benefit if policymakers, before imposing a tax, considered in which market the tax is likely to harm consumers the most.

We can use estimates of demand curves to predict for which good a price increase causes the greatest loss of consumer surplus. Table 9.1 shows the consumer surplus loss in billions of 2004 dollars from a 10% increase in the price of various goods. The table shows that the larger the loss in consumer surplus, the larger the initial revenue (price times quantity) that is spent on a good. A 10% increase in price causes a much greater loss of consumer surplus if it is imposed on medical services, $135 billion, than if it is imposed on alcohol and tobacco, $17 billion, because much more is spent on medical services.

At first glance, the relationship between elasticities of demand and the loss in consumer surplus in Table 9.1 looks backward: A given percent change in prices has a larger effect on consumer surplus for the relatively elastic demand curves. However, this relationship is coincidental: The large revenue goods happen to have

See Problem 34.

Table 9.1 Effect of a 10% Increase in Price on Consumer Surplus (Revenue and Consumer Surplus in Billions of 2007 Dollars).

	Revenue	Elasticity of Demand, ε	Change in Consumer Surplus, ΔCS
Medical	1,545	−0.604	−150
Housing	1,375	−0.633	−133
Food	670	−0.245	−67
Clothing	363	−0.405	−36
Transportation	335	−0.461	−32
Utilities	198	−0.448	−19
Alcohol and tobacco	195	−0.162	−19

Sources: Revenues are from National Income and Product Accounts (NIPA), **www.econstats.com**; elasticities are based on Blanciforti (1982). Appendix 9A shows how the change figures were calculated.

relatively elastic demand curves. The effect of a price change depends on both revenue and the demand elasticity. In this table, the relative size of the revenues is more important than the relative elasticities.

If we could hold revenue constant and vary the elasticity, we would find that consumer surplus loss from a price increase is larger as the demand curve becomes less elastic. If the demand curve for alcohol and tobacco were 10 times more elastic, −1.62, while the revenue stayed the same—the demand curve became flatter at the initial price and quantity—the consumer surplus loss would be nearly $1 million less.

Solved Problem 9.1

Suppose that two linear demand curves go through the initial equilibrium, e_1. One demand curve is less elastic than the other at e_1. For which demand curve will a price increase cause the larger consumer surplus loss?

Answer

1. *Draw the two demand curves, and indicate which one is less elastic at the initial equilibrium.* Two demand curves cross at e_1 in the diagram. The steeper demand curve is less elastic at e_1.[3]

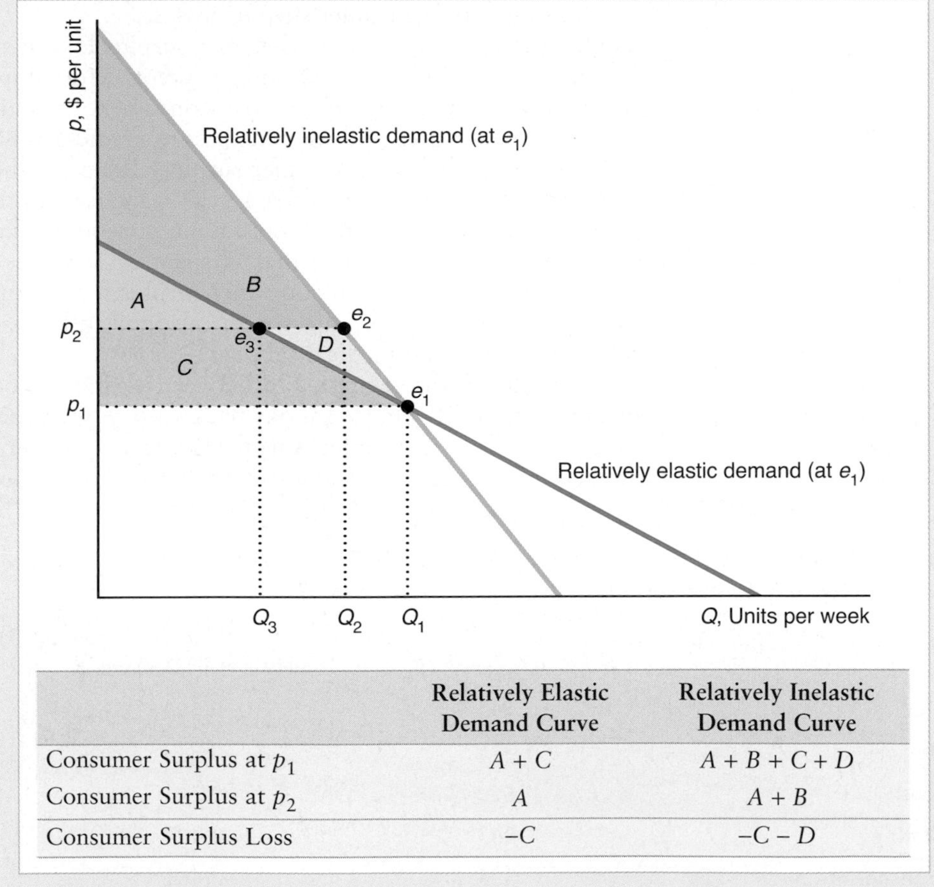

	Relatively Elastic Demand Curve	Relatively Inelastic Demand Curve
Consumer Surplus at p_1	$A + C$	$A + B + C + D$
Consumer Surplus at p_2	A	$A + B$
Consumer Surplus Loss	$-C$	$-C - D$

[3]As we discussed in Chapter 3, the price elasticity of demand, $\varepsilon = (\Delta Q/\Delta p)(p/Q)$, is 1 over the slope of the demand curve, $\Delta p/\Delta Q$, times the ratio of the price to the quantity. At the point of intersection where both demand curves have the same price, p_1, and quantity, Q_1, the steeper the demand curve, the lower the elasticity of demand.

See Question 3.

2. *Illustrate that a price increase causes a larger consumer surplus loss with the less elastic demand curve.* If the price rises from p_1 to p_2, the consumer surplus falls by only $-C$ with the relatively elastic demand curve and by $-C - D$ with the relatively inelastic demand curve.

9.2 Producer Welfare

producer surplus (*PS*) the difference between the amount for which a good sells and the minimum amount necessary for the seller to be willing to produce the good

A supplier's gain from participating in the market is measured by its **producer surplus** (*PS*), which is the difference between the amount for which a good sells and the minimum amount necessary for the seller to be willing to produce the good. The minimum amount a seller must receive to be willing to produce is the firm's avoidable production cost (the shutdown rule in Chapter 8).

Measuring Producer Surplus Using a Supply Curve

To determine a competitive firm's producer surplus, we use its supply curve: its marginal cost curve above its minimum average variable cost (Chapter 8). The firm's supply curve in panel a of Figure 9.3 looks like a staircase. The marginal cost of pro-

Figure 9.3 Producer Surplus.

(a) The firm's producer surplus, \$6, is the area below the market price, \$4, and above the marginal cost (supply curve) up to the quantity sold, 4. The area under the marginal cost curve up to the number of units actually produced is the variable cost of production. (b) The market producer surplus is the area above the supply curve and below the line at the market price, p^*, up to the quantity produced, Q^*. The area below the supply curve and to the left of the quantity produced by the market, Q^*, is the variable cost of producing that level of output.

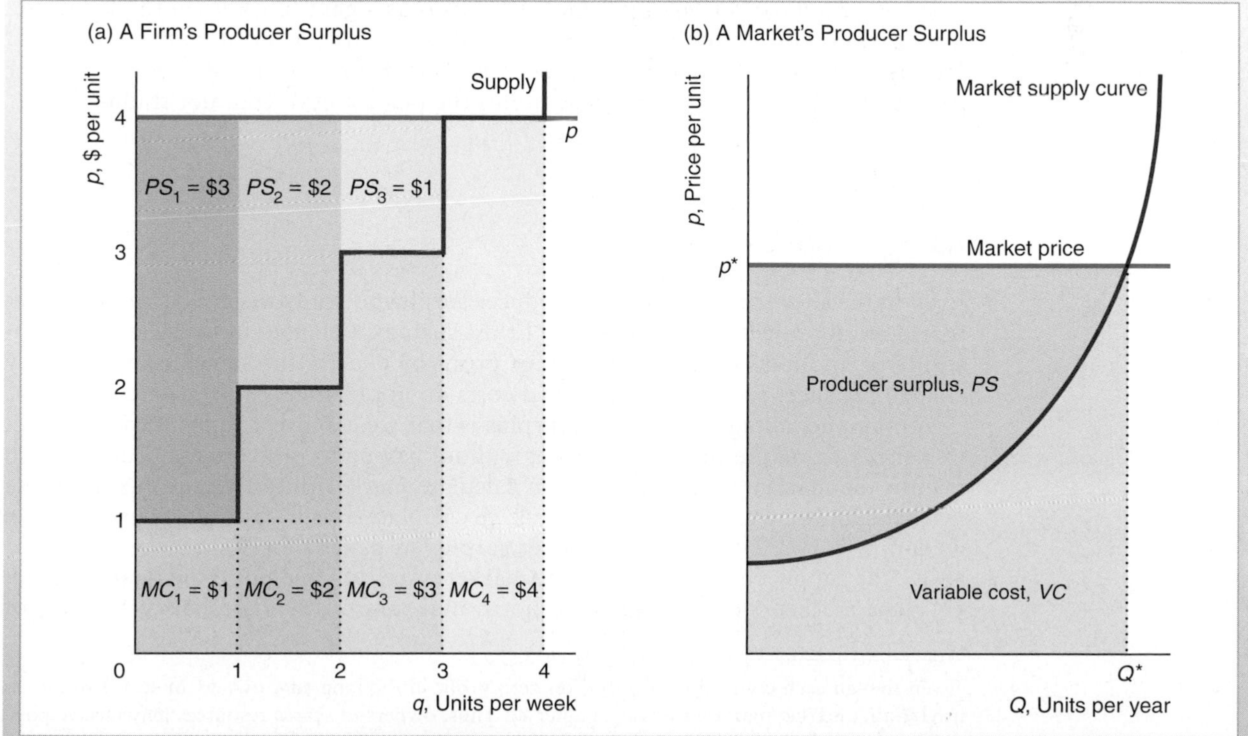

ducing the first unit is $MC_1 = \$1$, which is the area under the marginal cost curve between 0 and 1. The marginal cost of producing the second unit is $MC_2 = \$2$, and so on. The variable cost, VC, of producing four units is the sum of the marginal costs for the first four units:

$$VC = MC_1 + MC_2 + MC_3 + MC_4 = \$1 + \$2 + \$3 + \$4 = \$10.$$

If the market price, p, is \$4, the firm's revenue from the sale of the first unit exceeds its cost by $PS_1 = p - MC_1 = \$4 - \$1 = \$3$, which is its producer surplus on the first unit. The firm's producer surplus is \$2 on the second unit and \$1 on the third unit. On the fourth unit, the price equals marginal cost, so the firm just breaks even. As a result, the firm's total producer surplus, PS, from selling four units at \$4 each is the sum of its producer surplus on these four units:

$$PS = PS_1 + PS_2 + PS_3 + PS_4 = \$3 + \$2 + \$1 + \$0 = \$6.$$

See Problem 35.

Graphically, the total producer surplus is the area above the supply curve and below the market price up to the quantity actually produced. This same reasoning holds when the firm's supply curve is smooth.

The producer surplus is closely related to profit. Producer surplus is revenue, R, minus variable cost, VC:

$$PS = R - VC.$$

In panel a of Figure 9.3, revenue is $\$4 \times 4 = \$16$ and variable cost is \$10, so producer surplus is \$6.

Profit is revenue minus total cost, C, which equals variable cost plus fixed cost, F:

$$\pi = R - C = R - (VC + F).$$

Thus, the difference between producer surplus and profit is fixed cost, F. If the fixed cost is zero (as often occurs in the long run), producer surplus equals profit.[4]

See Question 4.

Another interpretation of producer surplus is as a gain to trade. In the short run, if the firm produces and sells its good—trades—it earns a profit of $R - VC - F$. If the firm shuts down—does not trade—it loses its fixed cost of $-F$. Thus, producer surplus equals the profit from trade minus the profit (loss) from not trading of

$$(R - VC - F) - (-F) = R - VC = PS.$$

Using Producer Surplus

Even in the short run, we can use producer surplus to study the effects of any shock that does not affect the fixed cost of firms, such as a change in the price of a substitute or an input. Such shocks change profit by exactly the same amount as they change producer surplus because fixed costs do not change.

A major advantage of producer surplus is that we can use it to measure the effect of a shock on *all* the firms in a market without having to measure the profit of each firm in the market separately. We can calculate market producer surplus using the market supply curve in the same way as we calculate a firm's producer surplus using its supply curve. The market producer surplus in panel b of Figure 9.3 is the area above the supply curve and below the market price, p^*, line up to the quantity sold, Q^*. The market supply curve is the horizontal sum of the marginal cost curves of

[4]Even though each competitive firm makes zero profit in the long run, owners of scarce resources used in that market may earn rents (Chapter 8). Thus, owners of scarce resources may receive positive producer surplus in the long run.

each of the firms (Chapter 8). As a result, the variable cost for all the firms in the market of producing Q is the area under the supply curve between 0 and the market output, Q.

Solved Problem 9.2

If the estimated supply curve for roses is linear, how much producer surplus is lost when the price of roses falls from 30¢ to 21¢ per stem (so that the quantity sold falls from 1.25 billion to 1.16 billion rose stems per year)?

Answer

1. *Draw the supply curve, and show the change in producer surplus caused by the price change.* The figure shows the estimated supply curve for roses. Point *a* indicates the quantity supplied at the original price, 30¢, and point *b* reflects the quantity supplied at the lower price, 21¢. The loss in producer surplus is the sum of rectangle *D* and triangle *E*.

2. *Calculate the lost producer surplus by adding the areas of rectangle D and triangle E.* The height of rectangle *D* is the difference between the original and the new price, 9¢, and its base is 1.16 billion stems per year, so the area of *D* (not all of which is shown in the figure because of the break in the quantity axis) is \$0.09 per stem × 1.16 billion stems per year = \$104.4 million per year. The height of triangle *E* is also 9¢, and its length is 0.9 billion stems per year, so its area is $\frac{1}{2}$ × \$0.09 per stem × 0.9 billion stems per year = \$4.05 million per year. Thus, the loss in producer surplus from the drop in price is \$108.45 million per year.

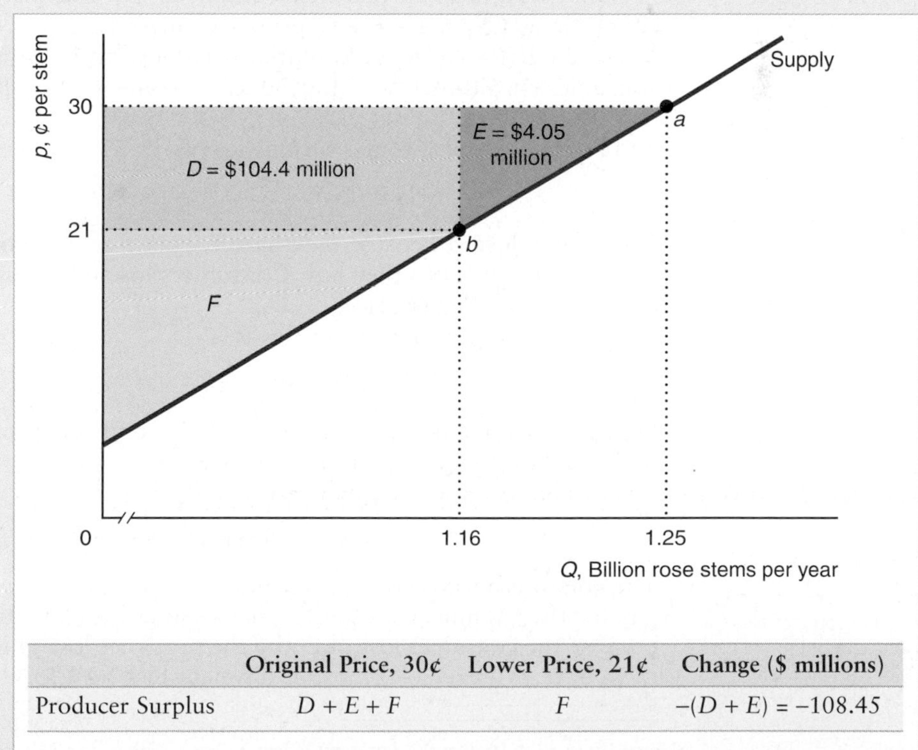

	Original Price, 30¢	Lower Price, 21¢	Change (\$ millions)
Producer Surplus	$D + E + F$	F	$-(D + E) = -108.45$

9.3 Competition Maximizes Welfare

How should we measure society's welfare? There are many reasonable answers to this question. One commonly used measure of the welfare of society, W, is the sum of consumer surplus plus producer surplus:

$$W = CS + PS.$$

This measure implicitly weights the well-being of consumers and producers equally. By using this measure, we are making a value judgment that the well-being of consumers and that of producers are equally important.

Not everyone agrees that society should try to maximize this measure of welfare. Groups of producers argue for legislation that helps them even if it hurts consumers by more than the producers gain—as though only producer surplus matters. Similarly, some consumer advocates argue that we should care only about consumers, so social welfare should include only consumer surplus.

We use the consumer surplus plus producer surplus measure of welfare in this chapter (and postpone a further discussion of other welfare concepts until the next chapter). One of the most striking results in economics is that competitive markets maximize this measure of welfare. If either less or more output than the competitive level is produced, welfare falls.

Why Producing Less than the Competitive Output Lowers Welfare

Producing less than the competitive output lowers welfare. At the competitive equilibrium in Figure 9.4, e_1, where output is Q_1 and price is p_1, consumer surplus equals areas $CS_1 = A + B + C$, producer surplus is $PS_1 = D + E$, and total welfare is $W_1 = A + B + C + D + E$. If output is reduced to Q_2 so that price rises to p_2 at e_2, consumer surplus is $CS_2 = A$, producer surplus is $PS_2 = B + D$, and welfare is $W_2 = A + B + D$.

The change in consumer surplus is

$$\Delta CS = CS_2 - CS_1 = A - (A + B + C) = -B - C.$$

Consumers lose B because they have to pay $p_2 - p_1$ more than at the competitive price for the Q_2 units they buy. Consumers lose C because they buy only Q_2 rather than Q_1 at the higher price.

The change in producer surplus is

$$\Delta PS = PS_2 - PS_1 = (B + D) - (D + E) = B - E.$$

Producers gain B because they now sell Q_2 units at p_2 rather than p_1. They lose E because they sell $Q_2 - Q_1$ fewer units.

deadweight loss (*DWL*) the net reduction in welfare from a loss of surplus by one group that is not offset by a gain to another group from an action that alters a market equilibrium

The change in welfare, $\Delta W = W_2 - W_1$, is[5]

$$\Delta W = \Delta CS + \Delta PS = (-B - C) + (B - E) = -C - E.$$

The area B is a transfer from consumers to producers—the extra amount consumers pay for the Q_2 units goes to the sellers—so it does not affect welfare. Welfare drops because the consumer loss of C and the producer loss of E benefit no one. This drop in welfare, $\Delta W = -C - E$, is a **deadweight loss** (DWL): the net reduction in welfare

[5]The change in welfare is $\Delta W = W_2 - W_1 = (CS_2 + PS_2) - (CS_1 + PS_1) = (CS_2 - CS_1) + (PS_2 - PS_1) = \Delta CS + \Delta PS$.

Figure 9.4 Why Reducing Output from the Competitive Level Lowers Welfare.

Reducing output from the competitive level, Q_1, to Q_2 causes price to increase from p_1 to p_2. Consumers suffer: Consumer surplus is now A, a fall of $\Delta CS = -B - C$. Producers may gain or lose: Producer surplus is now $B + D$, a change of $\Delta PS = B - E$. Overall, welfare falls by $\Delta W = -C - E$, which is a deadweight loss (DWL) to society.

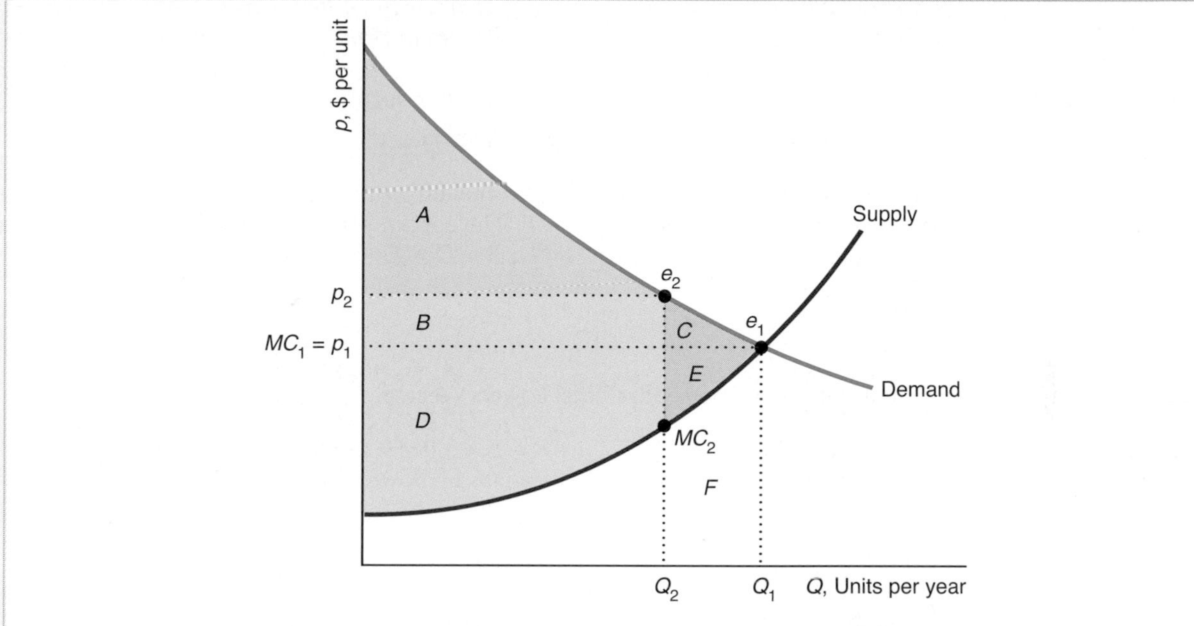

	Competitive Output, Q_1 (1)	Smaller Output, Q_2 (2)	Change (2) – (1)
Consumer Surplus, CS	$A + B + C$	A	$-B - C = \Delta CS$
Producer Surplus, PS	$D + E$	$B + D$	$B - E = \Delta PS$
Welfare, $W = CS + PS$	$A + B + C + D + E$	$A + B + D$	$-C - E = \Delta W = DWL$

from a loss of surplus by one group that is not offset by a gain to another group from an action that alters a market equilibrium.

The deadweight loss results because consumers value extra output by more than the marginal cost of producing it. At each output between Q_2 and Q_1, consumers' marginal willingness to pay for another unit—the height of the demand curve—is greater than the marginal cost of producing the next unit—the height of the supply curve. For example, at e_2, consumers value the next unit of output at p_2, which is much greater than the marginal cost, MC_2, of producing it. Increasing output from Q_2 to Q_1 raises firms' variable cost by area F, the area under the marginal cost (supply) curve between Q_2 and Q_1. Consumers value this extra output by the area under the demand curve between Q_2 and Q_1, area $C + E + F$. Thus, consumers value the extra output by $C + E$ more than it costs to produce it.

Society would be better off producing and consuming extra units of this good than spending this amount on other goods. In short, *the deadweight loss is the opportunity cost of giving up some of this good to buy more of another good.*

Why Producing More than the Competitive Output Lowers Welfare

Increasing output beyond the competitive level also decreases welfare because the cost of producing this extra output exceeds the value consumers place on it. Figure 9.5 shows the effect of increasing output from the competitive level Q_1 to Q_2 and letting the price fall to p_2, point e_2 on the demand curve, so consumers buy the extra output.

Because price falls from p_1 to p_2, consumer surplus rises by

$$\Delta CS = C + D + E,$$

which is the area between p_2 and p_1 to the left of the demand curve. At the original price, p_1, producer surplus was $C + F$. The cost of producing the larger output is the area under the supply curve up to Q_2, $B + D + E + G + H$. The firms sell this quan-

Figure 9.5 Why Increasing Output from the Competitive Level Lowers Welfare.

Increasing output from the competitive level, Q_1, to Q_2 lowers the price from p_1 to p_2. Consumer surplus rises by $C + D + E$, producer surplus falls by $B + C + D + E$, and welfare falls by B, which is a deadweight loss to society.

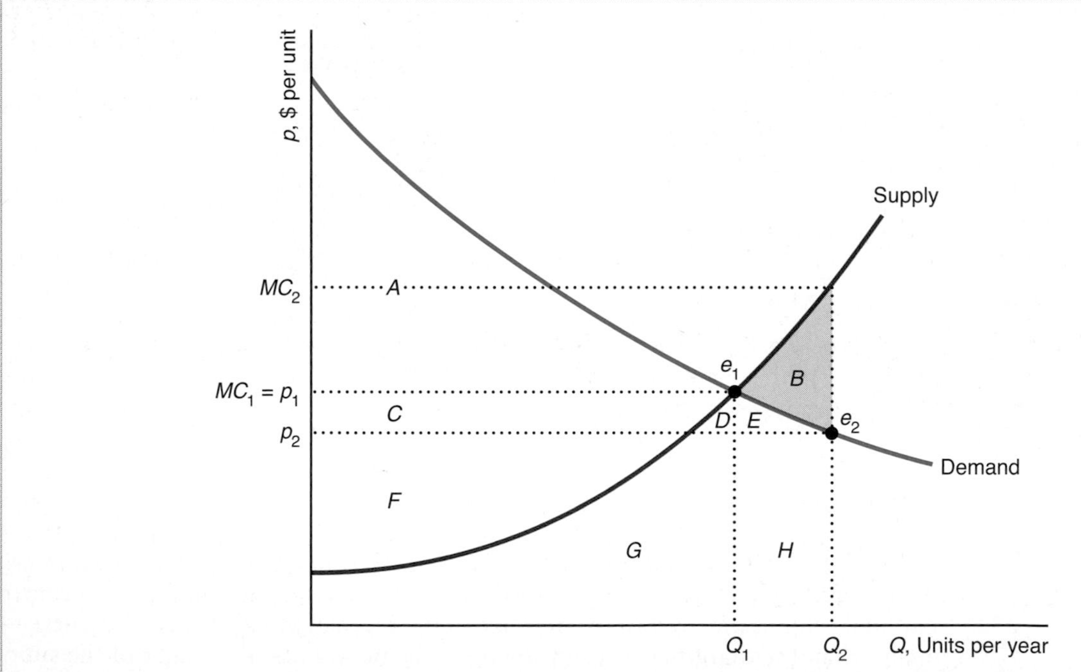

	Competitive Output, Q_1	Larger Output, Q_2	Change
Consumer Surplus, CS	A	$A + C + D + E$	$C + D + E = \Delta CS$
Producer Surplus, PS	$C + F$	$F - B - D - E$	$-B - C - D - E = \Delta PS$
Welfare, $W = CS + PS$	$A + C + F$	$A + C + F - B$	$-B = \Delta W = DWL$

tity for only p_2Q_2, area $F + G + H$. Thus, the new producer surplus is $F - B - D - E$. As a result, the increase in output causes producer surplus to fall by

$$\Delta PS = -B - C - D - E.$$

Because producers lose more than consumers gain, the deadweight loss is

$$\Delta W = \Delta CS + \Delta PS = (C + D + E) + (-B - C - D - E) = -B.$$

A net loss occurs because consumers value the $Q_2 - Q_1$ extra output by only $E + H$, which is less than the extra cost, $B + E + H$, of producing it. The new price, p_2, is less than the marginal cost, MC_2, of producing Q_2. Too much is being produced.

See *Question 5.*

The reason that competition maximizes welfare is that price equals marginal cost at the competitive equilibrium. At the competitive equilibrium, demand equals supply, which ensures that price equals marginal cost. When price equals marginal cost, consumers value the last unit of output by exactly the amount that it costs to produce it. If consumers value the last unit by more than the marginal cost of production, welfare rises if more is produced. Similarly, if consumers value the last unit by less than its marginal cost, welfare is higher at a lower level of production.

market failure
inefficient production or consumption, often because a price exceeds marginal cost

A **market failure** is inefficient production or consumption, often because a price exceeds marginal cost. In the next application, we show that the surplus for the recipient of a gift is often less than the giver's cost.

APPLICATION

Deadweight Loss of Christmas Presents

Just how much did you enjoy the expensive woolen socks with the dancing purple teddy bears that your Aunt Fern gave you last Christmas? Often the cost of a gift exceeds the value that the recipient places on it.

Only 10% to 15% of holiday gifts are money. A gift of cash typically gives at least as much pleasure to the recipient as a gift that costs the same but can't be exchanged for cash. (So what if giving cash is tacky?) Of course, it's possible that a gift can give more pleasure to the recipient than it costs the giver—but how often does that happen to you?

An "efficient" gift is one that the recipient values as much as the gift costs the giver. The difference between the price of the gift and its value to the recipient is a deadweight loss to society. Joel Waldfogel (1993) asked Yale undergraduates just how large this deadweight loss is. He estimated that the deadweight loss is between 10% and 33% of the value of gifts. Waldfogel (2005) finds that consumers value their own purchases at 10% to 18% more, per dollar spent, than items received as gifts. He found that gifts from friends and "significant others" are most efficient, while noncash gifts from members of the extended family are least efficient (one-third of the value is lost). Luckily, grandparents, aunts, and uncles are most likely to give cash.

Given holiday expenditures of about $40 billion per year in the United States, he concluded that a conservative estimate of the deadweight loss of Christmas, Hanukkah, and other holidays with gift-giving rituals is between a tenth and a third as large as estimates of the deadweight loss from inefficient income taxation.

People sometimes deal with a lame present by "regifting" it. Some families have been passing the same fruitcake among family members for decades. According to a survey just before Christmas in 2004, 33% of women and 19% of men admitted that they pass on an unwanted gift to someone else (and 28% of respondents said that they would not admit it if asked whether they had done so).

One compromise is to buy a gift card. More than half of all U.S. consumers said that they were going to buy gift cards in 2007. While recipients cannot buy as many goods as with cash, at least they have some choices, and a gift card is viewed as less crass than cash by many people. However, *Consumer Reports* found that 27% of recipients hadn't used them within a year. As of 2007, several Web sites such as **cardavenue.com** and **leveragecard.com** allow some cards to be exchanged for others. **Swapagift.com** will buy certain cards at 60% to 70% of the face value—which is the lost consumer surplus. Another option is branded gift cards with an American Express, Discover, MasterCard, or Visa brand logo that can be used anywhere. Then again, there's always eBay for unloading unusable gift cards and other unpopular gifts.

See Question 6.

The question remains why people don't give cash instead of presents. If the reason is that they get pleasure from picking the "perfect" gift, the deadweight loss that adjusts for the pleasure of the giver is lower than these calculations suggest. (Bah, humbug!)

9.4 Policies That Shift Supply Curves

I don't make jokes. I just watch the government and report the facts.
—Will Rogers

One of the main reasons that economists developed welfare tools was to predict the impact of government policies and other events that alter a competitive equilibrium, which we consider next. We focus on government policies rather than other shocks caused by random events or other members of society because we, as part of the electorate, can influence these decisions.

Virtually all government actions affect a competitive equilibrium in one of two ways. Some government policies, such as limits on the number of firms in a market, shift the supply or demand curve. Other government actions, such as sales taxes, create a wedge between price and marginal cost so that they are not equal, as they were in the original competitive equilibrium.

These government actions move us from an unconstrained competitive equilibrium to a new, constrained competitive equilibrium. Because welfare was maximized at the initial competitive equilibrium, the following examples of government-induced changes lower welfare. In later chapters, we examine markets in which welfare was not maximized initially, so government intervention may raise welfare.

Although government policies may cause either the supply curve or the demand curve to shift, we concentrate on policies that limit supply because they are frequently used and have clear-cut effects. The two most common types of government policies that shift the supply curve are limits on the number of firms in a market and quotas or other limits on the amount of output that firms may produce. We study restrictions on entry and exit of firms in this section and examine quotas later in the chapter.

Government policies that cause a decrease in supply at each possible price (shift the supply curve to the left) lead to fewer purchases by consumers at higher prices, an outcome that lowers consumer surplus and welfare. Welfare falls when governments restrict the consumption of competitive products that we all agree are *goods*, such as food and medical services. In contrast, if most of society wants to discourage the use of certain products, such as hallucinogenic drugs and poisons, policies that restrict consumption may increase some measures of society's welfare.

Governments, other organizations, and social pressures limit the number of firms in at least three ways. The number of firms is restricted explicitly in some markets, such as the one for taxi service. In other markets, some members of society are barred from owning firms or performing certain jobs or services. In yet other markets, the number of firms is controlled indirectly by raising the cost of entry.

Restricting the Number of Firms

A limit on the number of firms causes a shift of the supply curve to the left, which raises the equilibrium price and reduces the equilibrium quantity. Consumers are harmed: They don't buy as much as they would at lower prices. Firms that are in the market when the limits are first imposed benefit from higher profits.

To illustrate these results, we examine the regulation of taxicabs. Countries throughout the world regulate taxicabs. Many American cities limit the number of taxicabs. To operate a cab in these cities legally, you must possess a city-issued permit, which may be a piece of paper or a medallion.

Two explanations are given for such regulation. First, using permits to limit the number of cabs raises the earnings of permit owners—usually taxi fleet owners—who lobby city officials for such restrictions. Second, some city officials contend that limiting cabs allows for better regulation of cabbies' behavior and protection of consumers. (However, it would seem possible that cities could directly regulate behavior and not restrict the number of cabs.)

Whatever the justification for such regulation, the limit on the number of cabs raises the market prices. If the city doesn't limit entry, a virtually unlimited number of potential taxi drivers with identical costs can enter freely.

Panel a of Figure 9.6 shows a typical taxi owner's marginal cost curve, MC, and average cost curve, AC^1. The MC curve slopes upward because a typical cabbie's opportunity cost of working more hours increases as the cabbie works longer hours (drives more customers). An outward shift of the demand curve is met by new firms entering, so the long-run supply curve of taxi rides, S^1 in panel b, is horizontal at the minimum of AC^1 (Chapter 8). For the market demand curve in the figure, the equilibrium is E_1, where the equilibrium price, p_1, equals the minimum of AC^1 of a typical cab. The total number of rides is $Q_1 = n_1q_1$, where n_1 is the equilibrium number of cabs and q_1 is the number of rides per month provided by a typical cab.

Consumer surplus, $A + B + C$, is the area under the market demand curve above p_1 up to Q_1. There is no producer surplus because the supply curve is horizontal at the market price, which equals marginal and average cost. Thus, welfare is the same as consumer surplus.

Legislation limits the number of permits to operate cabs to $n_2 < n_1$. The market supply curve, S^2, is the horizontal sum of the marginal cost curves above minimum average cost of the n_2 firms in the market. For the market to produce more than n_2q_1 rides, the price must rise to induce the n_2 firms to supply more.

With the same demand curve as before, the equilibrium market price rises to p_2. At this higher price, each licensed cab firm produces more than before by operating longer hours, $q_2 > q_1$, but the total number of rides, $Q_2 = n_2q_2$, falls because there are fewer cabs, n_2. Consumer surplus is A, producer surplus is B, and welfare is $A + B$.

Thus, because of the higher fares (prices) under a permit system, consumer surplus falls by

$$\Delta CS = -B - C.$$

The producer surplus of the lucky permit owners rises by

$$\Delta PS = B.$$

Figure 9.6 Effect of a Restriction on the Number of Cabs.

A restriction on the number of cabs causes the supply curve to shift from S^1 to S^2 in the short run and the equilibrium to change from E_1 to E_2. The resulting lost surplus, C, is a deadweight loss to society. In the long run, the unusual profit, π, created by the restriction becomes a rent to the owner of the license. As the license owner increases the charge for using the license, the average cost curve rises to AC^2, so the cab driver earns a zero long-run profit. That is, the producer surplus goes to the permit holder, not to the cab driver.

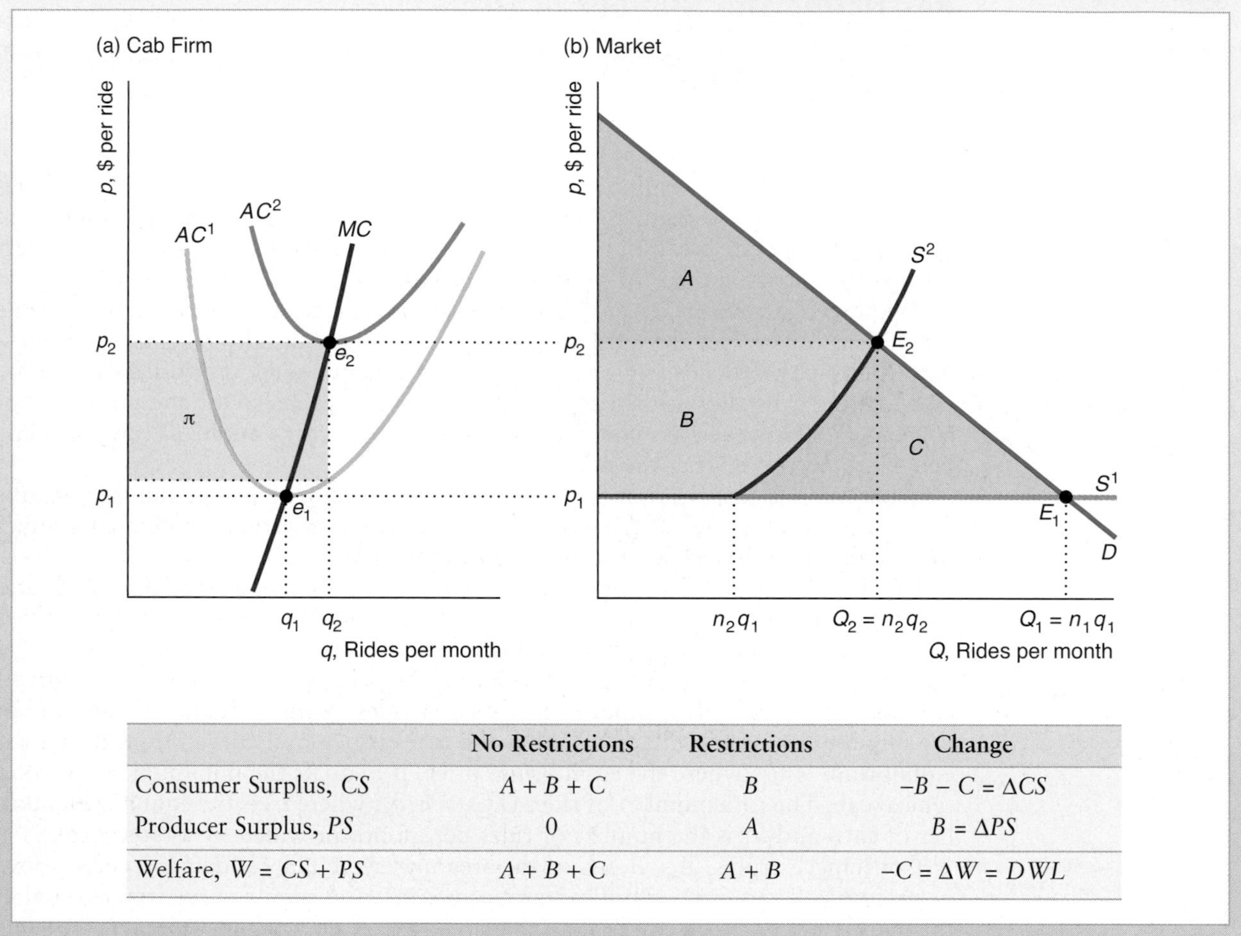

	No Restrictions	Restrictions	Change
Consumer Surplus, CS	$A + B + C$	B	$-B - C = \Delta CS$
Producer Surplus, PS	0	A	$B = \Delta PS$
Welfare, $W = CS + PS$	$A + B + C$	$A + B$	$-C = \Delta W = DWL$

As a result, total welfare falls:

$$\Delta W = \Delta CS + \Delta PS = (-B - C) + B = -C,$$

which is a deadweight loss.

By preventing other potential cab firms from entering the market, limiting cab permits creates economic profit, the area labeled π in panel a, for permit owners. In many cities, these permits can be sold or rented, so the owner of the scarce resource, the permit, can capture the unusual profit, or *rent* (Chapter 8). The rent for the permit or the implicit rent paid by the owner of a permit causes the cab driver's average cost to rise to AC^2. Because the rent allows the use of the cab for a certain period of time, it is a fixed cost that is unrelated to output. As a result, it does not affect the marginal cost.

Cab drivers earn zero economic profits because the market price, p_2, equals their average cost, the minimum of AC^2. The producer surplus, B, created by the limits on entry go to the original owners of the permits rather than to the current cab drivers. Thus, the permit owners are the *only* ones who benefit from the restrictions, and their gains are less than the losses to others. If the government collected the rents each year in the form of an annual license, then these rents could be distributed to all citizens instead of to just a few lucky permit owners.

See Questions 7 and 8.

In many cities, the rents and welfare effects that result from these laws are large. The size of the loss to consumers and the benefit to permit holders depend on how severely a city limits the number of cabs.

APPLICATION

Cab Fare

Too bad the only people who know how to run the country are busy driving cabs and cutting hair. —George Burns

Limiting the number of cabs has large effects in cities around the world. Some cities regulate the number of cabs much more strictly than others. Tokyo has five times as many cabs as New York City. San Francisco, which limits cabs, has only a tenth as many cabs as Washington, D.C., which has fewer people but does not restrict the number of cabs. The number of residents per cab is 757 in Detroit, 748 in San Francisco, 538 in Dallas, 533 in Baltimore, 350 in Boston, 301 in New Orleans, and 203 in Honolulu.

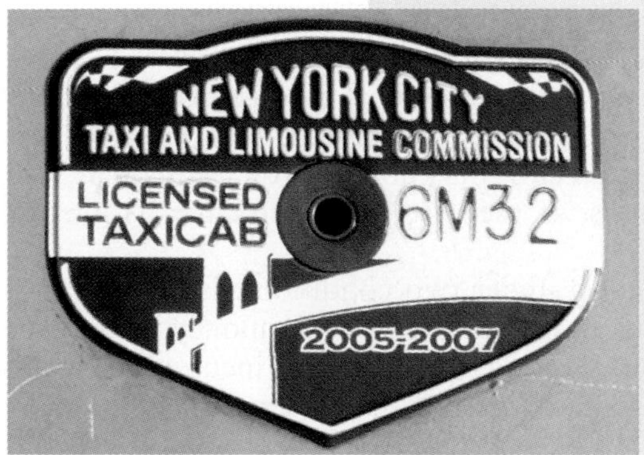

In San Francisco, permit holders lease their permits for up to \$3,500 a month to taxi companies, which own only about a quarter of all permits. Thus, each permit is worth up to \$42,000 a year. This rent is the extra producer surplus of the lucky permit holders that would be eliminated if anyone could supply taxi services.

In 1937, when New York City started regulating the number of cabs, all 11,787 cab owners could buy a permit, called a medallion, for \$10. Because New York City allows these medallions to be sold, medallion holders do not have to operate a cab to benefit from the restriction on the number of cabs. A holder can sell a medallion for an amount that captures the unusually high future profits from the limit on the number of cabs. Because the number of medallions has hardly increased, to 12,779 in 2006, this limit has become more binding over time, so the price of a medallion has soared. A license sold in a 2007 auction for \$384,990. The cumulative value of New York City licenses is \$4.9 billion—greater than the \$3.6 billion insured value of the World Trade Center.

Medallion systems in other cities have also generated large medallion values: for example, \$250,000 in Boston and \$135,000 in Chicago. Taxi licenses usually sell for £25,000 (\$50,000) in the United Kingdom and for more than \$100,000 in Rome as of 2005.

Cab drivers do not make unusual returns. New York City cab drivers who lease medallions earn as little as \$50 to \$115 a day. In Boston, cabbies average 72 hours a week driving someone else's taxi, to net maybe \$550.

A 1984 study for the U.S. Department of Transportation estimated consumers' annual extra cost from restrictions on the number of taxicabs throughout the United States at nearly \$1.9 billion (in 2005 dollars). The total lost consumer surplus is even greater because this amount does not include lost waiting time and other inconveniences associated with having fewer taxis. Movements toward liberalizing entry into taxi markets started in the United States in the 1980s and in Sweden, Ireland, the Netherlands, and the United Kingdom in the 1990s, but tight regulation remains common throughout the world.

See Question 9.

Raising Entry and Exit Costs

Instead of directly restricting the number of firms that may enter a market, governments and other organizations may raise the cost of entering, thereby indirectly restricting that number. Similarly, raising the cost of exiting a market discourages some firms from entering.

Entry Barriers. If its cost will be greater than that of firms already in the market, a potential firm might not enter a market even if existing firms are making a profit. Any cost that falls only on potential entrants and not on current firms discourages entry. A long-run **barrier to entry** is an explicit restriction or a cost that applies only to potential new firms—existing firms are not subject to the restriction or do not bear the cost.

barrier to entry
an explicit restriction or a cost that applies only to potential new firms—existing firms are not subject to the restriction or do not bear the cost

At the time they entered, incumbent firms had to pay many of the costs of entering a market that new entrants incur, such as the fixed costs of building plants, buying equipment, and advertising a new product. For example, the fixed cost to McDonald's and other fast-food chains of opening a new fast-food restaurant is about \$2 million. These fixed costs are *costs of entry* but are *not* barriers to entry because they apply equally to incumbents and entrants. Costs incurred by both incumbents and entrants do not discourage potential firms from entering a market if existing firms are making money. Potential entrants know that they will do as well as existing firms once they are in business, so they are willing to enter as long as profit opportunities exist.

Large sunk costs can be barriers to entry under two conditions. First, if capital markets do not work well, so new firms have difficulty raising money, new firms may be unable to enter profitable markets. Second, if a firm must incur a large *sunk* cost, which makes the loss if it exits great, the firm may be reluctant to enter a market in which it is uncertain of success.

See Question 10.

Exit Barriers. Some markets have barriers that make it difficult (though typically not impossible) for a firm to exit by going out of business. In the short run, exit barriers can keep the number of firms in a market relatively high. In the long run, exit barriers may limit the number of firms in a market.

Why do exit barriers limit the number of firms in a market? Suppose that you are considering starting a construction firm with no capital or other fixed factors. The firm's only input is labor. You know that there is relatively little demand for construction during business downturns and in the winter. To avoid paying workers when business is slack, you plan to shut down during those periods. If you can avoid losses by shutting down during those periods, you enter this market if your expected economic profits during good periods are zero or positive.

A law that requires that you give your workers six months' warning before laying them off prevents you from shutting down quickly. You know that you'll regularly suffer losses during business downturns because you'll have to pay your workers for up to six months during periods when you have nothing for them to do. Knowing that you'll incur these regular losses, you are less inclined to enter the market. Unless the economic profits during good periods are much higher than zero—high enough to offset your losses—you will not enter the market. See "Job Termination Laws" at **www.myeconlab.com/Perloff,** Chapter 9.

If exit barriers limit the number of firms, the same analysis that we used to examine entry barriers applies. Thus, exit barriers may raise prices, lower consumer surplus, and reduce welfare.

9.5 Policies That Create a Wedge Between Supply and Demand

The most common government policies that create a wedge between supply and demand curves are sales taxes (or subsidies) and price controls. Because these policies create a gap between marginal cost and price, either too little or too much is produced. For example, a tax causes price to exceed marginal cost—consumers value the good more than it costs to produce it—with the result that consumer surplus, producer surplus, and welfare fall.

Welfare Effects of a Sales Tax

A new sales tax causes the price consumers pay to rise (Chapter 3), resulting in a loss of consumer surplus, $\Delta CS < 0$, and a fall in the price firms receive, resulting in a drop in producer surplus, $\Delta PS < 0$. However, the new tax provides the government with new tax revenue, $\Delta T = T > 0$ (if tax revenue was zero before this new tax).

Assuming that the government does something useful with the tax revenue, we should include tax revenue in our definition of welfare:

$$W = CS + PS + T.$$

As a result, the change in welfare is

$$\Delta W = \Delta CS + \Delta PS + \Delta T.$$

Even when we include tax revenue in our welfare measure, a specific tax must lower welfare in a competitive market. We show the welfare loss from a specific tax of $\tau = 11¢$ per rose stem in Figure 9.7.

Without the tax, the intersection of the demand curve, D, and the supply curve, S, determines the competitive equilibrium, e_1, at a price of 30¢ per stem and a quantity of 1.25 billion rose stems per year. Consumer surplus is $A + B + C$, producer surplus is $D + E + F$, tax revenue is zero, and there is no deadweight loss.

The specific tax shifts the effective supply curve up by 11¢, creating an 11¢ wedge (Chapter 3) between the price consumers pay, 32¢, and the price producers receive, $32¢ - \tau = 21¢$. Equilibrium output falls from 1.25 to 1.16 billion stems per year.

The extra 2¢ per stem that buyers pay causes consumer surplus to fall by $B + C$ = \$24.1 million per year, as we showed earlier. Due to the 9¢ drop in the price firms receive, they lose producer surplus of $D + E$ = \$108.45 million per year (Solved Problem 9.2). The government gains tax revenue of τQ = 11¢ per stem × 1.16 billion stems per year = \$127.6 million per year, area $B + D$.

The combined loss of consumer surplus and producer surplus is only partially offset by the government's gain in tax revenue, so that welfare drops:

$$\Delta W = \Delta CS + \Delta PS + \Delta T = -\$24.1 - \$108.45 + \$127.6 = -\$4.95 \text{ million per year.}$$

Figure 9.7 Welfare Effects of a Specific Tax on Roses.

The $\tau = 11¢$ specific tax on roses creates an 11¢ per stem wedge between the price customers pay, 32¢, and the price producers receive, 21¢. Tax revenue is $T = \tau Q =$ \$127.6 million per year. The deadweight loss to society is $C + E =$ \$4.95 million per year.

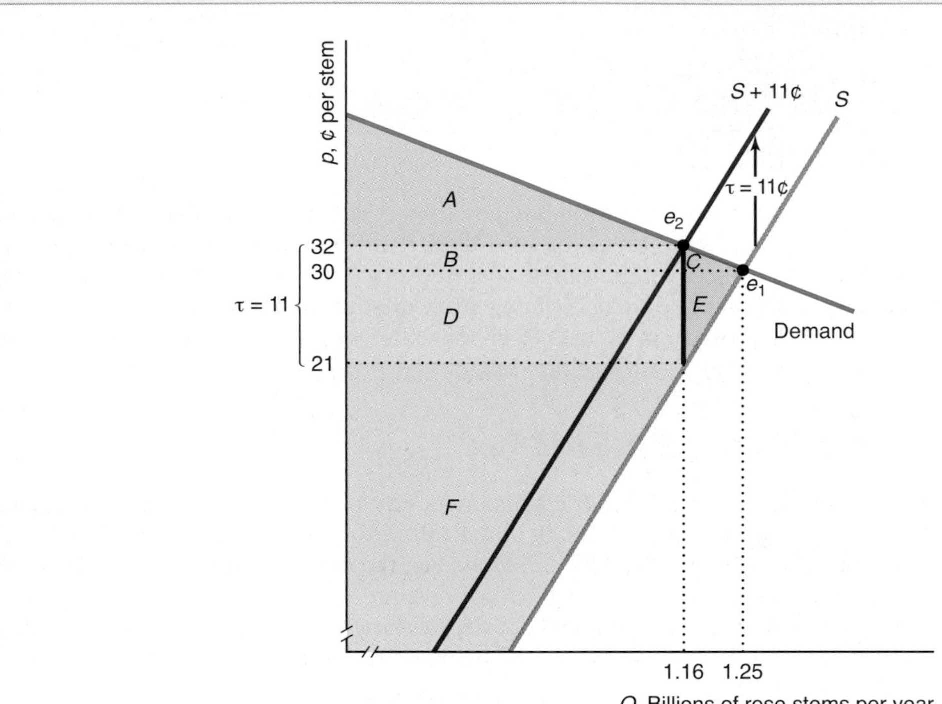

	No Tax	Specific Tax	Change (\$ millions)
Consumer Surplus, CS	$A + B + C$	A	$-B - C = -24.1 = \Delta CS$
Producer Surplus, PS	$D + E + F$	F	$-D - E = -108.45 = \Delta PS$
Tax Revenue, $T = \tau Q$	0	$B + D$	$B + D = 127.6 = \Delta T$
Welfare, $W = CS + PS + T$	$A + B + C + D + E + F$	$A + B + D + F$	$-C - E = -4.95 = DWL$

See Problems 36 and 37.

This deadweight loss is area $C + E$.

Why does society suffer a deadweight loss? The reason is that the tax lowers output from the competitive level where welfare is maximized. An equivalent explanation for this inefficiency or loss to society is that the tax puts a wedge between price and marginal cost. At the new equilibrium, buyers are willing to pay 32¢ for one more stem of roses, while the marginal cost to firms is only 21¢ (= the price minus τ). Shouldn't at least one more rose be produced if consumers are willing to pay nearly a third more than the cost of producing it? That's what our welfare study indicates.

See Questions 11–15.

APPLICATION

Deadweight Loss from Wireless Taxes

Federal, state, and local government taxes and fees on cell phone and other wireless services create deadweight loss by raising costs to consumers and reducing the quantity demanded. These fees vary substantially across jurisdictions. The median state tax is 10%, and the median combined state and federal tax is 14.5%, which corresponds to a yearly payment of about \$91. California and Florida have even higher state taxes of 21%, so their combined taxes are 25.5%, or \$185 per year (and New York is nearly as high). Overall, governments raise about \$4.8 billion in wireless taxes.

The marginal cost of supplying a minute of wireless service is constant at about 5¢. Thus, a tax inflicts consumer surplus loss but not producer surplus loss (see Solved Problem 3.2). Hausman (2000) estimates the deadweight loss (efficiency cost) to the economy from taxes to be about \$2.6 billion.[6] For every \$1 raised in tax revenue, the average efficiency cost is 53¢ and the loss in high-tax states is about 70¢. Moreover, for every additional tax dollar raised, the marginal efficiency cost is 72¢ for the typical state and about 93¢ for the high-tax states.

The wireless efficiency loss is large relative to that imposed by other taxes. For example, estimates of the marginal efficiency loss per dollar of income tax range from 26¢ to 41¢. One reason for the relatively large wireless efficiency losses is that the price elasticity of mobile telephones is about –0.7, which is more elastic than for other telecommunications services (see Solved Problem 9.1). In contrast, a tax on landlines creates almost no deadweight loss because the price elasticity for local landline phone service is virtually zero (–0.005).

See Question 16.

Solved Problem 9.3

Suppose that the government gives rose producers a specific subsidy of s = 11¢ per stem. What is the effect of the subsidy on the equilibrium prices and quantity, consumer surplus, producer surplus, government expenditures, welfare, and deadweight loss? (*Hint*: A subsidy is a negative tax, so we can use the same approach as with a tax.)

Answer

1. *Show how the subsidy shifts the supply curve and affects the equilibrium.* The specific subsidy shifts the supply curve, S in the figure, down by $s = 11$¢, to the curve labeled $S - 11$¢. Consequently, the equilibrium shifts from e_1 to e_2, so the quantity sold increases (from 1.25 to 1.34 billion rose stems per year), the price that consumers pay falls (from 30¢ to 28¢ per stem), and the amount that suppliers receive, including the subsidy, rises (from 30¢ to 39¢), so that the differential between what the consumer pays and the producer receives is 11¢.

2. *Show that consumers and producers benefit.* Consumers and producers of roses are delighted to be subsidized by other members of society. Because the price drops to customers, consumer surplus rises from $A + B$ to $A + B + D + E$. Because firms receive more per stem after the subsidy, producer surplus rises from $D + G$ to $B + C + D + G$ (the area under the price they receive and above the original supply curve).

[6]We can analyze the consumer surplus loss from taxes in both competitive and noncompetitive markets similarly. Hausman takes account of higher than competitive pretax prices in his analysis of the wireless market.

3. *Show how much government expenditures rise and determine the effect on welfare.* Because the government pays a subsidy of 11¢ per stem for each stem sold, the government's expenditures go from zero to the rectangle $B + C + D + E + F$. Thus, the new welfare is the sum of the new consumer surplus and producer surplus minus the government's expenses. As the table under the figure shows, welfare falls from $A + B + D + G$ to $A + B + D + G - F$. The deadweight loss, this drop in welfare, $\Delta W = -F$, results from producing too much: The marginal cost to producers of the last stem, 39¢, exceeds the marginal benefit to consumers, 28¢.

See Questions 17 and 18.

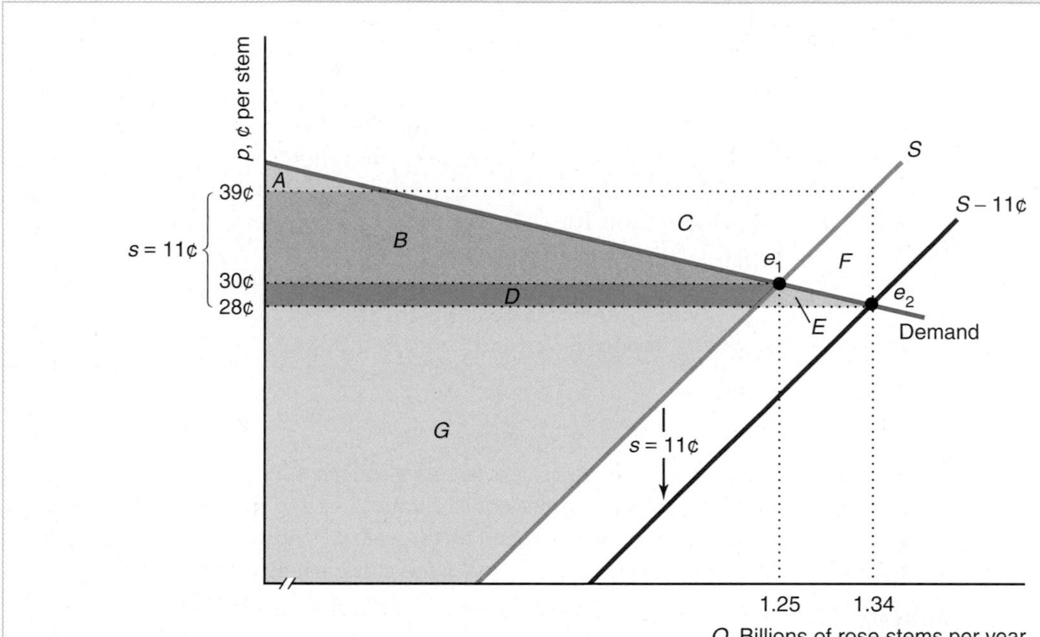

	No Subsidy	Subsidy	Change ($ millions)
Consumer Surplus, CS	$A + B$	$A + B + D + E$	$D + E = 116.55 = \Delta CS$
Producer Surplus, PS	$D + G$	$B + C + D + G$	$B + C = 25.9 = \Delta PS$
Government Expenses, X	0	$-B - C - D - E - F$	$-B - C - D - E - F = -147.4 = \Delta X$
Welfare, $W = CS + PS - X$	$A + B + D + G$	$A + B + D + G - F$	$-F = -4.95 = DWL$

Welfare Effects of a Price Floor

Amount the E.U. paid to businessmen in Serbia–Montenegro for sugar subsidies before realizing that there was no sugar industry there: $1.2 million.
—Harper's Index, 2004

In some markets, the government sets a *price floor*, or minimum price, which is the lowest price a consumer can pay legally for the good. For example, in most countries the government creates price floors under at least some agricultural prices to guarantee producers that they will receive at least a price of $\underline{p}$ for their good. If the market price is above $\underline{p}$, the support program is irrelevant. If the market price would be below $\underline{p}$, however, the government buys as much output as necessary to drive the price up to $\underline{p}$. Since 1929 (the start of the Great Depression), the U.S. government has used price floors or similar programs to keep prices of many agricultural products above the price that competition would determine in unregulated markets.

My favorite program is the wool and mohair subsidy. The U.S. government instituted wool price supports after the Korean War to ensure "strategic supplies" for uniforms. Congress later added mohair subsidies, though mohair has no military use. In some years, the mohair subsidy exceeded the amount consumers paid for mohair, and the subsidies on wool and mohair reached a fifth of a billion dollars over the first half-century of support. No doubt the Clinton-era end of these subsidies in 1995 endangered national security. Thanks to Senator Phil Gramm, a well-known fiscal conservative, and other patriots (primarily from Texas, where much mohair is produced), the subsidy was resurrected in 2000![7] Representative Lamar Smith took vehement exception to people who questioned the need to subsidize mohair: "Mohair is popular! I have a mohair sweater! It's my favorite one!" The 2008 budget calls for a \$10 million mohair subsidy.

We now show the effect of a price support using estimated supply and demand curves for the soybean market (Holt, 1992). The intersection of the market demand curve and the market supply curve in Figure 9.8 determines the competitive equilibrium, e, in the absence of a price support program, where the equilibrium price is $p_1 = \$4.59$ per bushel and the equilibrium quantity is $Q_1 = 2.1$ billion bushels per year.

With a price support on soybeans of $\underline{p} = \$5.00$ per bushel and the government's pledge to buy as much output as farmers want to sell, quantity sold is $Q_s = 2.2$ billion bushels.[8] At $\underline{p}$, consumers buy less output, $Q_d = 1.9$ billion bushels, than the Q_1 they would have bought at the market-determined price p_1. As a result, consumer surplus falls by $B + C = \$864$ million. The government buys $Q_g = Q_s - Q_d \approx 0.3$ billion bushels per year, which is the excess supply, at a cost of $T = \underline{p} \times Q_g = C + D + F + G = \$1.283$ billion.

The government cannot resell the output domestically because if it tried to do so, it would succeed only in driving down the price consumers pay. The government stores the output or sends it abroad.

Although farmers gain producer surplus of $B + C + D = \$921$ million, this program is an inefficient way to transfer money to them. Assuming that the government's purchases have no alternative use, the change in welfare is $\Delta W = \Delta CS + \Delta PS - T = -C - F - G = -\$1.226$ billion per year.[9] This deadweight loss reflects two distortions in this market:

- **Excess production.** More output is produced than is consumed, so Q_g is stored, destroyed, or shipped abroad.
- **Inefficiency in consumption.** At the quantity they actually buy, Q_d, consumers are willing to pay \$5 for the last bushel of soybeans, which is more than the marginal cost, $MC = \$3.60$, of producing that bushel.

See Questions 19 and 20 and Problem 38.

---

[7]As U.S. representative Lynn Martin said, "No matter what your religion, you should try to become a government program, for then you will have everlasting life."

[8]In 1985, the period Holt studied, the price support was \$5.02. The proposed 2008 farm bill sets the support at \$4.92.

[9]This measure of deadweight loss underestimates the true loss. The government also pays storage and administration costs. In 2005, the U.S. Department of Agriculture, which runs farm support programs, had 109,832 employees, or one worker for every eight farms that received assistance (although many of these employees have other job responsibilities).

Figure 9.8 Effect of Price Supports in Soybeans.

Without government price supports, the equilibrium is e, where p_1 = \$4.59 per bushel and Q_1 = 2.1 billion bushels of soybeans per year (based on estimates in Holt, 1992). With the price support at $\underline{p}$ = \$5.00 per bushel, output sold increases to Q_s and consumer purchases fall to Q_d, so the government must buy $Q_g = Q_s - Q_d$ at a cost of \$1.283 billion per year. The deadweight loss is $C + F + G$ = \$1.226 billion per year, not counting storage and administrative costs.

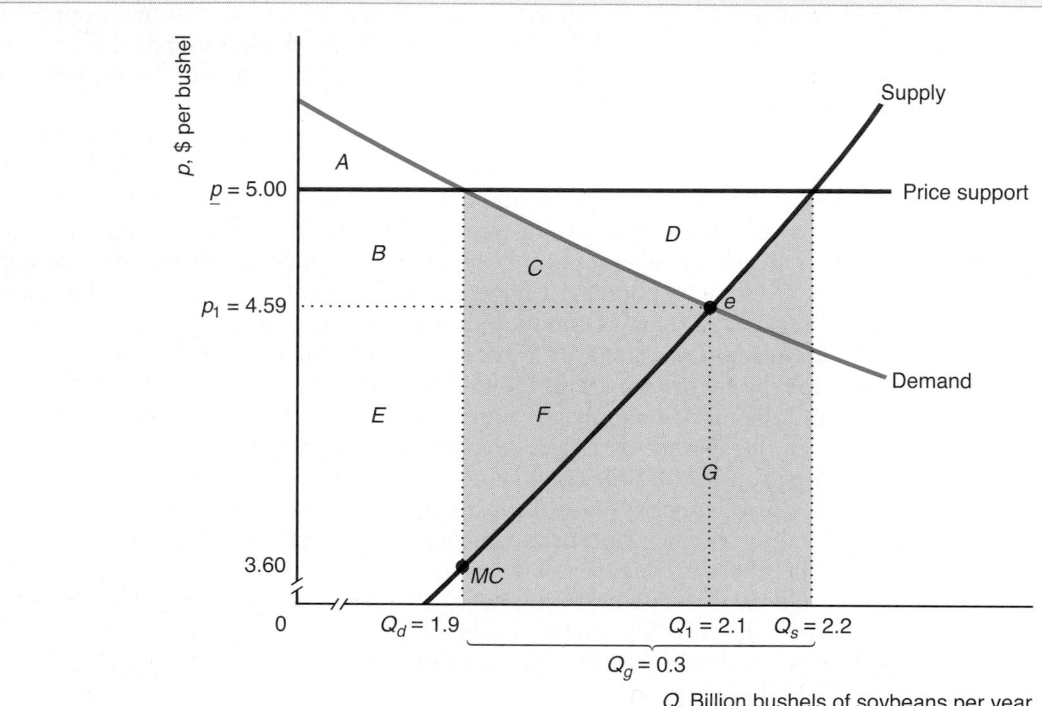

	No Price Support	Price Support	Change (\$ millions)
Consumer Surplus, CS	$A + B + C$	A	$-B - C = -864 = \Delta CS$
Producer Surplus, PS	$E + F$	$B + C + D + E + F$	$B + C + D = 921 = \Delta PS$
Government Expense, $-X$	0	$-C - D - F - G$	$-C - D - F - G = -1{,}283 = \Delta X$
Welfare, $W = CS + PS - X$	$A + B + C + E + F$	$A + B + E - G$	$-C - F - G = -1{,}226 = \Delta W = DWL$

Alternative Price Support. Because of price supports, the government was buying and storing large quantities of food, much of which was allowed to spoil. As a consequence, the government started limiting the amount farmers could produce. Because there is uncertainty about how much a farmer will produce, the government set quotas or limits on the amount of land farmers could use, so as to restrict their output. See **www.myeconlab.com/perloff**, Chapter 9, Solved Problem 2. Today, the government uses an alternative subsidy program. The government sets a support price, $\underline{p}$. Farmers decide how much to grow and sell all of their produce to consumers at the price, p, that clears the market. The government then gives the farmers a *deficiency* payment equal to the difference between the support and actual prices, $\underline{p} - p$ for every unit sold so that farmers receive the support price on their entire crop.

Solved Problem 9.4

What are the effects in the soybean market of a \$5-per-bushel price support using a deficiency payment on the equilibrium price and quantity, consumer surplus, producer surplus, and deadweight loss?

Answer

1. *Describe how the program affects the equilibrium price and quantity.* Without a price support, the equilibrium is e_1 in the figure, where the price is $p_1 = \$4.59$ and the quantity is 2.1 billion bushels per year. With a support price of \$5 per bushel, the new equilibrium is e_2. Farmers produce at the quantity where the price support line hits their supply curve at 2.2 billion bushels. The equilibrium price is the height of the demand curve at 2.2 billion bushels, or approximately \$4.39 per bushel. Thus, the equilibrium price falls and the quantity increases.

2. *Show the welfare effects.* Because the price consumers pay drops from p_1 to p_2, consumer surplus rises by area $D + E$. Producers now receive $\underline{p}$ instead of p_1, so their producer surplus rises by $B + C$. Government payments are the difference between the support price, $\underline{p}$ = \$5, and the price consumers pay,

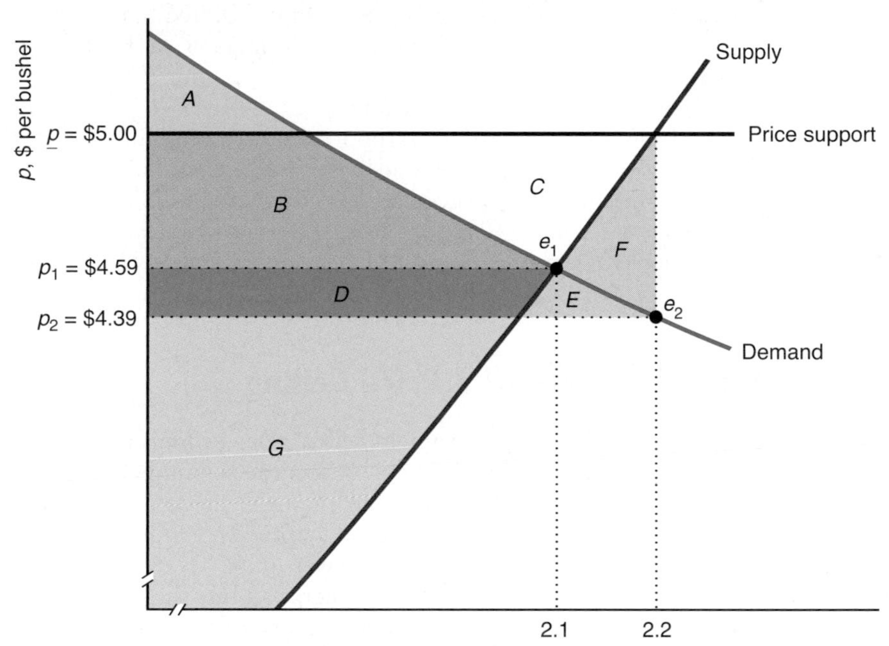

	No Price Support	Price Support	Change
Consumer Surplus, CS	$A + B$	$A + B + D + E$	$D + E = \Delta CS$
Producer Surplus, PS	$D + G$	$B + C + D + G$	$B + C = \Delta PS$
Government Expense, $-X$	0	$-B - C - D - E - F$	$-B - C - D - E - F = \Delta X$
Welfare, $W = CS + PS - X$	$A + B + D + G$	$A + B + D + G - F$	$-F = \Delta W = DWL$

$p_2 = \$4.39$, times the number of units sold, 2.2 billion bushels per year, or the rectangle $B + C + D + E + F$. Because government expenditures exceed the gains to consumers and producers, welfare falls by the deadweight loss triangle F.[10]

Who Benefits. Presumably, the purpose of these programs is to help poor farmers, not to hurt consumers and taxpayers. However, the lion's share of American farm subsidies goes to large agricultural corporations, not to poor farmers. Three-quarters of U.S. farms have sales of less than $50,000 per year, yet these farms received only 16% of the total direct government payments for agriculture in 2003. In contrast, farms with over half a million dollars in annual sales are only 3.5% of all farms, yet they received 29% of all direct government payments. Farms with over a quarter of a million dollars in sales (top 8% of all farms) received 50% of the payments.

APPLICATION

Farmer Subsidies

Virtually every country in the world showers its farmers with subsidies. For example, EU sugar producers receive three times the world price of sugar.

Government subsidies to farmers in 2006 equaled 1% of total farm sales in New Zealand, 6% in Australia, 11% in the United States, 17% in Mexico, 23% in Canada, 32% in the European Union, 53% in Japan, 63% in Korea and Switzerland, 65% in Norway, and 66% in Iceland. This share has fallen in most countries over the last two decades.

In 2006, total agricultural support was $49 billion in Japan, $97 billion in the United States, and $156 billion in the European Union. Nearly 1% of the U.S. gross domestic product goes to support agriculture. Each adult in the United States pays about $440 a year to support agriculture. Did you get full value for your money? (Cargill, Monsanto, and Archer Daniels Midland thank you.)

Welfare Effects of a Price Ceiling

In some markets, the government sets a *price ceiling*: the highest price that a firm can legally charge. If the government sets the ceiling below the precontrol competitive price, consumers demand more than the precontrol equilibrium quantity and firms supply less than that quantity (Chapter 2). Producer surplus must fall because firms receive a lower price and sell fewer units.

Because of the price ceiling, consumers can buy the good at a lower price but cannot buy as much of it as they'd like. Because less is sold than at the precontrol equilibrium, there is deadweight loss: Consumers value the good more than the marginal cost of producing extra units.

In the 1970s, the U.S. government used price controls to keep gasoline prices below the market price (Chapter 2). This policy led to long lines at gas stations and large deadweight losses. Frech and Lee (1987) estimate that the loss in consumer surplus in California in 2002 dollars was $2 billion during the December 1973 to March 1974 price controls and $1.3 billion during the May 1979 to July 1979 controls.

[10]Compared to the soybean price support program in Figure 9.8, the deficiency payment approach results in a smaller deadweight loss (less than a tenth of the original one) and lower government expenditures (though the expenditures need not be smaller in general).

Solved Problem 9.5

What is the effect on the equilibrium and welfare if the government sets a price ceiling, $\bar{p}$, below the unregulated competitive equilibrium price?

Answer

1. *Show the initial unregulated equilibrium.* The intersection of the demand curve and the supply curve determines the unregulated, competitive equilibrium e_1, where the equilibrium quantity is Q_1.

2. *Show how the equilibrium changes with the price ceiling.* Because the price ceiling, $\bar{p}$, is set below the equilibrium price of p_1, the ceiling binds. At this lower price, consumer demand increases to Q_d while the quantity firms are willing to supply falls to Q_s, so only $Q_s = Q_2$ units are sold at the new equilibrium, e_2. Thus, the price control causes the equilibrium quantity and price to fall, but consumers have excess demand of $Q_d - Q_s$.

3. *Describe the welfare effects.* Because consumers are able to buy Q_s units at a lower price than before the controls, they gain area *D*. Consumers lose consumer surplus of *C*, however, because they can purchase only Q_s instead of Q_1 units of output. Thus, consumers gain net consumer surplus of $D - C$. Because they sell fewer units at a lower price, firms lose producer surplus $-D - E$. Part of this loss, *D*, is transferred to consumers because of lower prices, but the rest, *E*, is a loss to society. The deadweight loss to society is at least $\Delta W = \Delta CS + \Delta PS = -C - E$.

See Question 21.

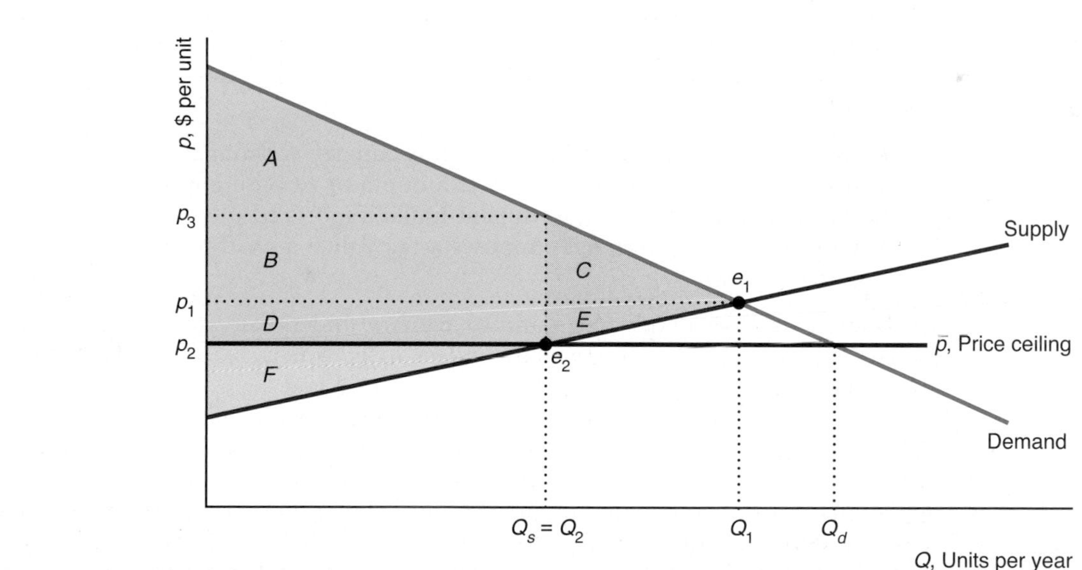

	No Ceiling	Price Ceiling	Change
Consumer Surplus, *CS*	$A + B + C$	$A + B + D$	$D - C = \Delta CS$
Producer Surplus, *PS*	$D + E + F$	F	$-D - E = \Delta PS$
Welfare, $W = CS + PS$	$A + B + C + D + E + F$	$A + B + D + F$	$-C - E = \Delta W = DWL$

Comment: This measure of the deadweight loss may *underestimate* the true loss. Because consumers want to buy more units than are sold, they may spend time searching for a store that has units for sale. This (unsuccessful) search activity is wasteful and hence a deadweight loss to society. (Such wasteful search does not occur if the good is efficiently but inequitably distributed to people of one race or one gender, people in the military, or attractive people, or if it is based on some other known discriminatory criterion.) Another possible inefficiency is that consumers who buy the good may value it less than those who are unable to find a unit to purchase. For example, someone might purchase the good who values it at p_2, while someone who values it at p_3 cannot find any to buy.

9.6 Comparing Both Types of Policies: Imports

Traditionally, most of Australia's imports come from overseas.
—Keppel Enderbery, former Australian cabinet minister

We've examined examples of government policies that shift supply or demand curves and policies that create a wedge between supply and demand. Governments use both types of policies to control international trade.

Allowing imports of foreign goods benefits the importing country. If a government reduces imports of a good, the domestic price rises; the profits of domestic firms that produce the good increase, but domestic consumers are hurt. Our analysis will show that the loss to consumers exceeds the gain to producers.

The government of the (potentially) importing country can use one of four import policies:

- **Allow free trade.** Any firm can sell in this country without restrictions.
- **Ban all imports.** The government sets a quota of zero on imports.
- **Set a positive quota.** The government limits imports to $\bar{Q}$.
- **Set a tariff.** The government imposes a tax called a **tariff** (or a *duty*) on only imported goods.

tariff (*duty*)
a tax on only imported goods

We compare welfare under free trade to welfare under bans and quotas, which change the supply curve, and to welfare under tariffs, which create a wedge between supply and demand.

To illustrate the differences in welfare under these various policies, we examine the U.S. market for crude oil.[11] We make two assumptions for the sake of simplicity. First, we assume that transportation costs are zero. Second, we assume that the supply curve of the potentially imported good is horizontal at the world price p^*. Given these two assumptions, the importing country, the United States, can buy as much of this good as it wants at p^* per unit: It is a price taker in the world market because its demand is too small to influence the world price.

[11]We assume that the market is competitive. Our figures are based on short-run, constant-elasticity supply and demand equations for crude oil in 1988 using the short-run supply and demand elasticities reported in Anderson and Metzger (1991).

Free Trade Versus a Ban on Imports

No nation was ever ruined by trade. —Benjamin Franklin

Preventing imports into the domestic market raises the price, as we illustrated in Chapter 2 for the Japan rice market. The estimated U.S. domestic supply curve, S^a, is upward sloping, and the foreign supply curve is horizontal at the world price of \$14.70 in 1988 in Figure 9.9. The total U.S. supply curve, S^1, is the horizontal sum of the domestic supply curve and the foreign supply curve. Thus, S^1 is the same as the upward-sloping domestic supply curve for prices below \$14.70 and is horizontal at \$14.70. Under free trade, the United States imports crude oil if its domestic price in the absence of imports would exceed the world price, \$14.70 per barrel.

The free-trade equilibrium, e_1, is determined by the intersection of S^1 and the demand curve, where the U.S. price equals the world price, \$14.70, and the quan-

Figure 9.9 Loss from Eliminating Free Trade.

Because the supply curve foreigners face is horizontal at the world price of \$14.70, the total U.S. supply curve of crude oil is S_1 when there is free trade. The free-trade equilibrium is e_1. With a ban on imports, the equilibrium e_2 occurs where the domestic supply curve, $S^a = S^2$, intersects D. The ban increases producer surplus by B = \$132.5 million per day and decreases consumer surplus by $B + C$ = \$163.7 million per day, so the deadweight loss is C = \$31.2 million per day or \$11.4 billion per year.

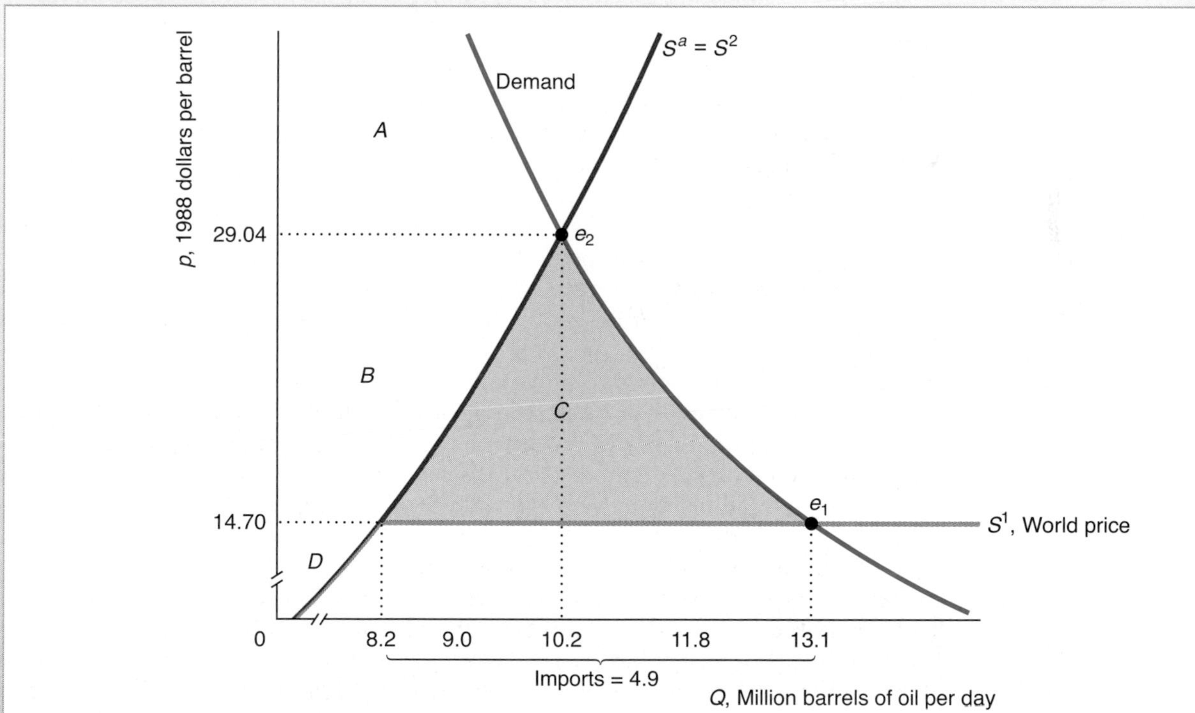

U.S.	Free Trade	U.S. Import Ban	Change (\$ millions)
Consumer Surplus, CS	$A + B + C$	A	$-B - C = -163.7 = \Delta CS$
Producer Surplus, PS	D	$B + D$	$B = 132.5 = \Delta PS$
Welfare, $W = CS + PS$	$A + B + C + D$	$A + B + D$	$-C = -31.2 = \Delta W = DWL$

tity is 13.1 million barrels per day. At the equilibrium price, domestic supply is 8.2, so imports are 4.9 (= 13.1 – 8.2). U.S. consumer surplus is $A + B + C$, U.S. producer surplus is D, and U.S. welfare is $A + B + C + D$. Throughout our discussion of trade, we ignore welfare effects in other countries.

If imports are banned, the total U.S. supply curve, S^2, is the American domestic supply curve, S^a. The equilibrium is at e_2, where S^2 intersects the demand curve. The new equilibrium price is $29.04, and the new equilibrium quantity, 10.2 million barrels per day, is produced domestically. Consumer surplus is A, producer surplus is $B + D$, and welfare is $A + B + D$.

The ban helps producers but harms consumers. Because of the higher price, domestic firms gain producer surplus of $\Delta PS = B =$ $132.5 million per day. The change in consumers' surplus is $\Delta CS = -B - C =$ –$163.7 million per day.

Does the ban help the United States? The change in total welfare, ΔW, is the difference between the gain to producers and the loss to consumers, $\Delta W = \Delta PS + \Delta CS$ = –$31.2 million per day or –$11.4 billion per year. This deadweight loss is 24% of the gain to producers. Consumers lose $1.24 for every $1 that producers gain from a ban.

See Questions 22–24.

Free Trade Versus a Tariff

TARIFF, n. A scale of taxes on imports, designed to protect the domestic producer against the greed of his customers. —Ambrose Bierce

There are two common types of tariffs: *specific tariffs*—τ dollars per unit—and *ad valorem tariffs*—α percent of the sales price. In recent years, tariffs have been applied throughout the world, most commonly to agricultural products.[12] American policymakers have frequently debated the optimal tariff on crude oil as a way to raise revenue or to reduce "dependence" on foreign oil.

You may be asking yourself, "Why should we study tariffs if we've already looked at taxes? Isn't a tariff just another tax?" Good point! Tariffs are just taxes. If the only goods sold were imported, the effect of a tariff in the importing country is the same as we showed for a sales tax. We study tariffs separately because a tariff is applied only to imported goods, so it affects domestic and foreign producers differently.

Because tariffs are applied to only imported goods, all else the same, they do not raise as much tax revenue or affect equilibrium quantities as much as taxes applied to all goods in a market. De Melo and Tarr (1992) find that almost five times more tax revenue would be generated by a 15% additional *ad valorem* tax on petroleum products ($34.6 billion) than by a 25% additional import tariff on oil and gas ($7.3 billion).

To illustrate the effect of a tariff, suppose that the government imposes a specific tariff of $\tau =$ $5 per barrel of crude oil. Given this tariff, firms will not import oil into the United States unless the U.S. price is at least $5 above the world price, $14.70. The tariff creates a wedge between the world price and the American price. This tariff causes the total supply curve to shift from S^1 to S^3 in Figure 9.10. Given that the

[12]After World War II, most trading nations signed the General Agreement on Tariffs and Trade (GATT), which limited their ability to subsidize exports or limit imports using quotas and tariffs. The rules prohibited most export subsidies and import quotas, except when imports threatened "market disruption" (the term that was, unfortunately, not defined). The GATT also required that any new tariff be offset by a reduction in other tariffs to compensate the exporting country. Modifications of the GATT and agreements negotiated by its successor, the World Trade Organization, have reduced or eliminated many tariffs.

Figure 9.10 Effect of a Tariff (or Quota).

A tariff of $\tau = \$5$ per barrel of oil imported or a quota of $\bar{Q} = 2.8$ drives the U.S. price of crude oil to \$19.70, which is \$5 more than the world price. Under the tariff, the equilibrium, e_3, is determined by the intersection of the S_3 total U.S. supply curve and the D demand curve. Under the quota, e_3 is determined by a quantity wedge of 2.8 million barrels per day between the quantity demanded, 9.0 million barrels per day, and the quantity supplied, 11.8 million barrels per day. Compared to free trade, producers gain B = \$42.8 million per day and consumers lose $B + C + D + E$ = \$61.9 million per day from the tariff or quota. The deadweight loss under the quota is $C + D + E$ = \$19.1 million per day. With a tariff, the government's tariff revenue increases by D = \$14 million a day, so the deadweight loss is only $C + E$ = \$5.1 million per day.

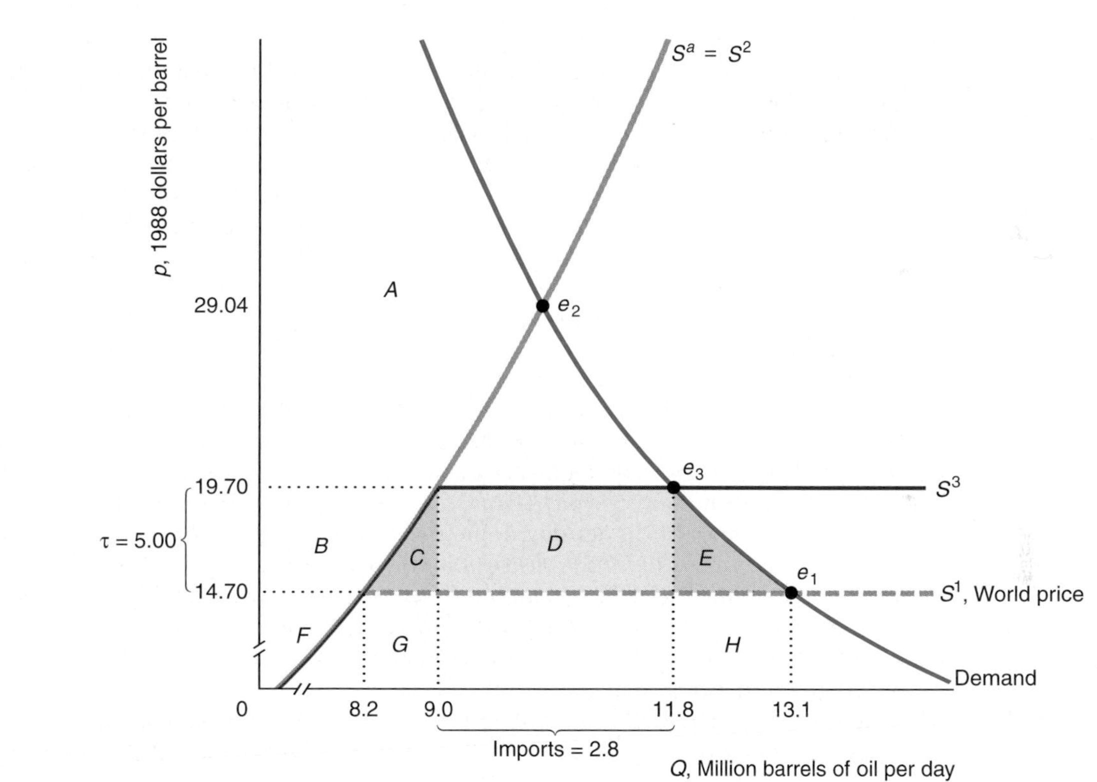

U.S.	Free Trade	U.S. Tariff or Quota	Change (\$ millions)
Consumer Surplus, CS	$A + B + C + D + E$	A	$-B - C - D - E = -61.9$
Producer Surplus, PS	F	$B + F$	$B = 42.8$
Tariff Revenues, T	0	D (tariff)	$D = 14.0$ (tariff)
		0 (quota)	0 (quota)
Welfare from a Tariff, $W = CS + PS + T$	$A + B + C + D + E + F$	$A + B + D + F$	$-C - E = -5.1 = DWL$
Welfare from a Quota, $W = CS + PS$	$A + B + C + D + E + F$	$A + B + F$	$-C - D - E = -19.1 = DWL$

world's excess supply curve to the United States is horizontal (see Chapter 8) at \$14.70, a tariff shifts this supply curve upward so that it is horizontal at \$19.70. As a result, the total U.S. supply curve with the tariff, S^3, equals the domestic supply curve for prices below \$19.70 and is horizontal at \$19.70.

The new equilibrium, e_3, occurs where S^3 intersects the demand curve. At this equilibrium, price is \$19.70 and quantity is 11.8 million barrels of oil per day. At this higher price, domestic firms supply 9.0 million barrels of oil per day, so imports are 2.8 million barrels of oil per day (= 11.8 – 9.0).

The tariff *protects* American producers from foreign competition. The larger the tariff, the less is imported, hence the higher the price that domestic firms can charge. (With a large enough tariff, nothing is imported, and the price rises to the no-trade level, \$29.04.) With a tariff of \$5, domestic firms' producer surplus increases by area B = \$42.8 million per day.

Because of the rise in the price from \$14.70 to \$19.70, consumer surplus falls by \$61.9 million per day. The government receives tariff revenues, T, equal to area D = \$14 million per day, which is τ = \$5 times the quantity imported, 2.8.

The deadweight loss is $C + E$ = \$5.1 million per day, or nearly \$1.9 billion per year.[13] This deadweight loss is almost 12% of the gain to producers. Consumers lose \$1.45 for each \$1 domestic producers gain. Because the tariff doesn't completely eliminate imports, the welfare loss is smaller than it is if all imports are banned.

See Question 25.

We can interpret the two components of this deadweight loss. First, C is the loss from producing 9.0 million barrels per day instead of 8.2 million barrels per day. Domestic firms produce this extra output because the tariff drove up the price from \$14.70 to \$19.70. The cost of producing this extra 0.8 million barrels of oil per day domestically is $C + G$, the area under the domestic supply curve, S^a, between 8.2 and 9.0. Had Americans bought this oil at the world price, the cost would have been only G = \$11.8 million per day. Thus, C is the extra cost from producing the extra 0.8 million barrels of oil per day domestically instead of importing it.

Second, E is a *consumption distortion loss* from American consumers' buying too little oil, 11.8 instead of 13.1 million barrels per day, because the price rose from \$14.70 to \$19.70 owing to the tariff. American consumers value this extra output as $E + H$, the area under their demand curve between 11.8 and 13.1, whereas the value in international markets is only H, the area below the line at \$14.70 between 11.8 and 13.1. Thus, E is the difference between the value at world prices and the value American consumers place on this extra 1.3 million barrels per day.

See Questions 26–30.

Free Trade Versus a Quota

The effect of a positive quota is similar to that of a tariff. If the government limits imports to $\bar{Q}$ = 2.8 million barrels per day, the quota is binding because 4.9 million barrels per day were imported under free trade. Given this binding quota, at the equilibrium price, the quantity demanded minus the quantity supplied by domestic producers equals 2.8 million barrels per day. In Figure 9.10, where the price is \$19.70, the gap between the quantity demanded, 11.8 million barrels per day, and the quantity supplied, 9.0 million barrels per day, is 2.8 million barrels per day. Thus, a quota on imports of 2.8 leads to the same equilibrium, e_3, as a tariff of \$5.

The gain to domestic producers, B, and the loss to consumers, $C + E$, are the same as those with a tariff. However, unlike with the tariff, with the quota the gov-

[13]If the foreign supply is horizontal, welfare in the importing country *must* fall. However, if the foreign supply is upward sloping, welfare in the importing country may rise.

ernment does not receive any revenue (unless the government sells import licenses). Area D may go to foreign exporters. As a result, the deadweight loss from the quota, \$19.1 million per day, or \$7.0 billion per year, is greater than under the tariff. This deadweight loss is nearly half (45%) of the gains to producers.

See Question 31.

Therefore, the importing country fares better using a tariff than setting a quota that reduces imports by the same amount. Consumers and domestic firms do as well under the two policies, but the government gains tariff revenues, D, only when the tariff is used.

Rent Seeking

Given that tariffs and quotas hurt the importing country, why do the Japanese, U.S., and other governments impose tariffs, quotas, or other trade barriers? The reason is that domestic producers stand to make large gains from such government actions; hence, it pays for them to organize and lobby the government to enact these trade policies. Although consumers as a whole suffer large losses, most individual consumers face a negligible loss. Moreover, consumers rarely organize to lobby the government about trade issues. Thus, in most countries, producers are often able to convince (cajole, influence, or bribe) legislators or government officials to aid them, even though consumers suffer more-than-offsetting losses.

If domestic producers can talk the government into a tariff, quota, or other policy that reduces imports, they gain extra producer surplus (rents), such as area B in Figures 9.9 and 9.10. Economists call efforts and expenditures to gain a rent or a profit from government actions **rent seeking**. If producers or other interest groups bribe legislators to influence policy, the bribe is a transfer of income and hence does not increase deadweight loss (except to the degree that a harmful policy is chosen). However, if this rent-seeking behavior—such as hiring lobbyists and engaging in advertising to influence legislators—uses up resources, the deadweight loss from tariffs and quotas understates the true loss to society. The domestic producers may spend up to the gain in producer surplus to influence the government.[14]

rent seeking
efforts and expenditures to gain a rent or a profit from government actions

Indeed, some economists argue that the government revenues from tariffs are completely offset by administrative costs and rent-seeking behavior. If so (and if the tariffs and quotas do not affect world prices), the loss to society from tariffs and quotas is all of the change in consumer surplus, such as areas $B + C$ in Figure 9.9 and areas $B + C + D + E$ in Figure 9.10.

Lopez and Pagoulatos (1994) estimate the deadweight loss and the additional losses due to rent-seeking activities in the United States in food and tobacco products. Table 9.2 summarizes their estimates for several industries. They estimate that the deadweight loss is \$13.8 billion, which is 2.6% of the domestic consumption of these products. The largest deadweight losses were in milk products and sugar manufacturing, which primarily use import quotas to raise domestic prices. The gain in producer surplus is \$49.9 billion, or 9.5% of domestic consumption. The government obtained \$2.0 billion in tariff revenues, or 0.4% of consumption. If all of producer surplus and government revenues were expended in rent-seeking behavior and other wasteful activities, the total loss is \$65.7 billion, or 12.5% of consumption, which is 4.75 times larger than the deadweight loss alone. In other words, the loss to society is somewhere between the deadweight loss of \$13.8 billion and \$65.7 billion.

[14]This argument is made in Tullock (1967) and Posner (1975). Fisher (1985) and Varian (1989) argue that the expenditure is typically less than the producer surplus.

Table 9.2 Welfare Cost of Trade Barriers (millions of 2007 dollars).

Industry	*DWL*	ΔPS	Government Revenues	ΔCS
Meat products	−33	2,777	80	−2,891
Dairy products[a]	−18,116	33,080	1,241	−48,514
Sugar confectionery[a]	−1,131	5,188	330	−6,646
Grain mill products	−12	1,350	12	−1,260
Fats and oils	−157	2,800	5	−2,964
Beverages	−11	1,295	173	−1,478
Tobacco	−242	4,521	112	−4,874
All food and tobacco	**−15,961**	**57,750**	**2,342**	**−76,050**

[a] Import quotas are the primary instrument of protection.

Notes: As estimated, $\Delta CS = DWL - \Delta PS$ − government revenue. Dollar amounts were adjusted using the Consumer Price Index.

Source: Lopez and Pagoulatos (1994).

SUMMARY

1. **Consumer Welfare.** The pleasure a consumer receives from a good in excess of its cost is called *consumer surplus*. Consumer surplus equals the area under the consumer's demand curve above the market price up to the quantity that the consumer buys. How much consumers are harmed by an increase in price is measured by the change in consumer surplus.

2. **Producer Welfare.** A firm's gain from trading is measured by its producer surplus. Producer surplus is the largest amount of money that could be taken from a firm's revenue and still leave the firm willing to produce. That is, the producer surplus is the amount the firm is paid minus its variable cost of production, which is profit in the long run. It is the area below the price and above the supply curve up to the quantity that the firm sells. The effect of a change in a price on a supplier is measured by the change in producer surplus.

3. **Competition Maximizes Welfare.** One standard measure of welfare is the sum of consumer surplus and producer surplus. The more price is above marginal cost, the lower this measure of welfare. In the competitive equilibrium, in which price equals marginal cost, welfare is maximized.

4. **Policies That Shift Supply Curves.** Governments frequently limit the number of firms in a market directly, by licensing them, or indirectly, by raising the costs of entry to new firms or raising the cost of exiting. A reduction in the number of firms in a competitive market raises price, hurts consumers, helps producing firms, and lowers the standard measure of welfare. This reduction in welfare is a deadweight loss: The gain to producers is less than the loss to consumers.

5. **Policies That Create a Wedge Between Supply and Demand.** Taxes, price ceilings, and price floors create a gap between the price consumers pay and the price firms receive. These policies force price above marginal cost, which raises the price to consumers and lowers the amount consumed. The wedge between price and marginal cost results in a deadweight loss: The loss of consumer surplus and producer surplus is not offset by increased taxes or by benefits to other groups.

6. **Comparing Both Types of Policies: Imports.** A government may use either a quantity restriction such as a quota, which shifts the supply curve, or a tariff, which creates a wedge, to reduce imports or achieve other goals. These policies may have different welfare implications. A tariff that reduces imports by the same amount as a quota has the same harms—a larger loss of consumer surplus than increased domestic producer surplus—but has a partially offsetting benefit—increased tariff revenues for the government. Rent-seeking activities are attempts by

firms or individuals to influence a government to adopt a policy that favors them. By using resources, rent seeking exacerbates the welfare loss beyond the deadweight loss caused by the policy itself. In a perfectly competitive market, government policies frequently lower welfare. As we show in later chapters, however, in markets that are not perfectly competitive, government policies may increase welfare.

QUESTIONS

■ = *exercise is available on MyEconLab;* * = *answer appears at the back of this book;* C = *use of calculus may be necessary;* W = *audio-slideshow answer by James Dearden is available in Textbook Resources on MyEconLab.*

1. In the "Consumer Surplus from Television" application, people are asked how much they would be willing to pay to watch television or how much they'd have to be paid never to watch again. Graph what is being measured. What alternative question could have been asked that would have provided more details on the value consumers place on watching an extra hour of television?
2. Use a graph to show what his fans received according to the "Bruce Springsteen's Gift to His Fans" application.
3. ■ The U.S. Department of Agriculture's (USDA's) minimum general recommendation is five servings of fruits and vegetables a day. Jetter et al. (2004) estimate that, if consumers followed that advice, the equilibrium price and quantity of most fruits and vegetables would increase substantially. For example, the price of salad would rise 7.2%, output would increase 3.5%, and growers' revenues would jump 7.3% (presumably, health benefits would occur too). Use a diagram to illustrate as many of these effects as possible and to show how consumer surplus and producer surplus change. Discuss how to calculate the consumer surplus (given that the USDA's recommendation shifts consumers' tastes or behavior).
4. For a firm, how does the concept of *producer surplus* differ from that of *profit*?
5. If society cared only about the well-being of consumers so that it wanted to maximize consumer surplus, would a competitive market achieve that goal given that the government cannot force or bribe firms to produce more than the competitive level of output? How would your answer change if society cared only about maximizing producer surplus?
6. Use an indifference curve diagram (gift goods on one axis and all other goods on the other) to illustrate that one is better off receiving cash than a gift. (*Hint*: See the discussion of gifts in this chapter and the discussion of food stamps in Chapter 4.) Relate your analysis to the "Deadweight Loss of Christmas Presents" application.
7. In 2002, Los Angeles imposed a ban on new billboards. Owners of existing billboards did not oppose the ban. Why? What are the implications of the ban for producer surplus, consumer surplus, and welfare? Who are the producers and consumers in your analysis? How else does the ban affect welfare in Los Angeles?
8. The park service wants to restrict the number of visitors to Yellowstone National Park to Q^*, which is fewer than the current volume. It considers two policies: (1) raising the price of admissions and (2) setting a quota. Compare the effects of these two policies on consumer surplus and welfare. Use a graph to show which policy is superior by your criterion.
9. There are many possible ways to limit the number of cabs in a city. The most common method is an explicit quota using a medallion that is kept forever and can be resold. One alternative is to charge a high license fee each year, which is equivalent to the city's issuing a medallion or license that lasts only a year. A third option is to charge a daily tax on taxicabs. Using figures, compare and contrast the equilibrium under each of these approaches. Discuss who wins and who loses from each plan, considering consumers, drivers, the city, and (if relevant) medallion owners.
10. Although 23 states barred the self-service sale of gasoline in 1968, most removed the bans by the mid-1970s. By 1992, self-service outlets sold nearly 80% of all U.S. gas, and only New Jersey and Oregon continued to ban self-service sales. Using predicted values for self-service sales for New Jersey and Oregon, Johnson and Romeo (2000) estimate that the ban in those two states raised the price by approximately 3¢ to 5¢ per gallon. Why did the ban affect the price? Illustrate using a figure and explain. Show the welfare effects in your figure. Use a table to show who gains or loses.
11. What is the welfare effect of an *ad valorem* sales tax, α, assessed on each competitive firm in a market?

12. How would the quantitative effect of a specific tax on welfare change as demand becomes more elastic? As it becomes less elastic? (*Hint*: See Solved Problem 9.1.)

13. Google, Yahoo, and other Internet search companies charge advertisers for each click on their ads (which sends the browser to the advertiser's Web site). Per-click advertising fees present an opportunity for "click fraud," an industry term describing someone (say, a rival firm or a hacker) clicking on a Web-search ad with ill intent. If the advertiser can demonstrate that a click was fraudulent, the search company does not bill for that click. A market for click-fraud detectives has developed to fight click fraud. The market demand for the detectives depends on the amount of fraud they can catch, which reduces the firm's advertising bill. Let p_C denote the per-click fee, n denote the number of clicks per month an advertiser generates, and X be the fraction of clicks that are fraudulent. Let Z represent the fraction of fraudulent clicks that a detective can prove are fraudulent.

    a. Show how much money the advertiser can save by hiring a click-fraud detective in terms of p_C, n, X, and Z. What is the advertiser's willingness to pay for the detective services?

    b. Suppose there are 500 advertisers with the following attributes: $p_C = \$5$, $n = 700$, $X = 0.2$, and $Z = 0.8$. There are 200 advertisers with the attributes $p_C = \$9$, $n = 600$, $X = 0.3$, and $Z = 0.8$. Finally, there are 300 advertisers with the attributes $p_C = \$12$, $n = 100$, $X = 0.1$, and $Z = 0.7$. Draw the inverse market demand curve for click-fraud detectives. (*Hint*: The demand curve is a "step" function (see Figure 9.1a).)

    c. Suppose the market supply curve for click-fraud detective services is perfectly price elastic with an intercept of \$500 on the price axis. What is the consumer surplus to the advertisers? W

*14. What is the long-run welfare effect of a profit tax (the government collects a specified percentage of a firm's profit) assessed on each competitive firm in a market?

*15. What is the welfare effect of a lump sum tax, $\$L$, assessed on each competitive firm in a market? (*Hint:* See Chapter 8.)

16. Using the information in the "Deadweight Loss from Wireless Taxes" application, draw graphs to illustrate why the tax on landlines creates almost no deadweight loss while the tax on cell phones creates more substantial deadweight loss.

17. Government policies affect who gets the scarce water in the western United States and how that water is used. In 2004, farmers in California's Central Valley paid as little as \$10 per acre-foot, while in urban San Jose, California, a water agency shelled out \$80 an acre-foot. Price differentials between agricultural and other uses can persist only if the groups cannot trade. Critics argue that eliminating the agricultural subsidy would encourage farmers to conserve water. The California Department of Water Resources estimates that doubling water prices would reduce agricultural water use by roughly 30% (Jim Carlton, "Is Water Too Cheap?" *Wall Street Journal,* March 17, 2004, B1). Further, farmers would use water more efficiently. (An alternative approach is to allow farmers to sell their cheap water in a competitive market—an approach some areas are using.)

    a. Based on the data in the description of this problem, what is the price elasticity of demand for water?

    b. What is the relationship between the price elasticity of demand for water and the effect of a price increase on water conservation? W

18. Ethanol, which is distilled from corn, is blended into gasoline, (allegedly) to burn cleaner and to increase the supply of fuel. Given that ethanol is a close substitute for gasoline, its price in a competitive market would be closely tied to the price of gasoline. However, ethanol usually costs more to make than gasoline, so its usage depends on federal incentives and clean-air legislation mandates for oil companies to use cleaner fuels.

    a. Suppose that without federal clean-air legislation mandates, ethanol and gasoline are perfect substitutes. Derive the wholesale-market demand function for ethanol. How does this market demand function depend on the price of gasoline?

    b. Suppose that federal clean-air legislation mandates that at least 5% of automobile fuel must contain ethanol. Derive the wholesale-market demand function for ethanol.

    c. Compare the wholesale-market demand functions of parts a and b.

    d. Suppose that for any refining plant output, q gallons per day, the marginal cost of ethanol refining, $MC_e(q)$, is greater than the marginal cost of gasoline refining, $MC_g(q)$. Compare the wholesale-market supply functions of ethanol and gasoline. Show that if the wholesale price of gasoline is sufficiently low, federal mandates are needed to ensure that ethanol is produced, but that if the price of gasoline is sufficiently high, federal mandates are not needed. W

19. The government wants to drive the price of soybeans above the equilibrium price, p_1, to p_2. It offers growers a payment of x to reduce their output from Q_1 (the equilibrium level) to Q_2, which is the quantity demanded by consumers at p_2. Show in a figure how large x must be for growers to reduce output to this level. What are the effects of this program on consumers, farmers, and total welfare? Compare this approach to (a) offering a price support of p_2, (b) offering a price support and a quota set at Q_1, and (c) offering a price support and a quota set at Q_2.

20. What are the welfare effects of a binding minimum wage? Use a graphical approach to show what happens if all workers are identical. Then verbally describe what is likely to happen to workers who differ by experience, education, age, gender, and race.

21. A mayor wants to help renters in her city. She considers two policies that will benefit renters equally. One policy is a *rent control*, which places a price ceiling, $\bar{p}$, on rents. The other is a government housing subsidy of s dollars per month that lowers the amount renters pay (to $\bar{p}$). Who benefits and who loses from these policies? Compare the two policies' effects on the quantity of housing consumed, consumer surplus, producer surplus, government expenditure, and deadweight loss. Does the comparison of deadweight loss depend on the elasticities of supply and demand? (*Hint*: Consider extreme cases.) If so, how?

22. Canada has 20% of the world's known freshwater resources, yet many Canadians believe that the country has little or none to spare. Over the years, U.S. and Canadian firms have struck deals to export bulk shipments of water to drought-afflicted U.S. cities and towns. Provincial leaders have blocked these deals in British Columbia and Ontario. Use graphs to show the likely outcome of such barriers to exports on the price and quantity of water used in Canada and in the United States if markets for water are competitive. Show the effects on consumer and producer surplus in both countries.

23. The U.S. Supreme Court ruled in May 2005 that people can buy wine directly from out-of-state vineyards. In the 5–4 decision, the Court held that state laws requiring people to buy directly from wine retailers located in the state violate the Constitution's commerce clause.

    a. Suppose the market for wine in New York is perfectly competitive both before and after the Supreme Court decision. Use the analysis in Section 9.6 to evaluate the effect of the Court's decision on the price of wine in New York.

    b. Evaluate the increase in New York consumer surplus.

    c. How does the increase in consumer surplus depend on the price elasticity of supply and demand? W

24. During the Napoleonic Wars, Britain blockaded North America, seizing U.S. vessels and cargo and impressing sailors. At President Thomas Jefferson's request, Congress imposed a nearly complete—perhaps 80%—embargo on international commerce from December 1807 to March 1809. Just before the embargo, exports were about 13% of GNP. Due to the embargo, U.S. consumers could not find good substitutes for manufactured goods from Europe, and producers could not sell farm produce and other goods for as much as in Europe. According to Irwin (2001), the welfare cost of the embargo was at least 8% of the U.S. gross national product (GNP) in 1807. Use graphs to show the effects of the embargo on a market for an exported good and one for an imported good. Show the change in equilibria and the welfare effects on consumers and firms.

25. Show that if the importing country faces an upward-sloping foreign supply curve (excess supply curve), a tariff may raise welfare in the importing country.

26. Given that the world supply curve is horizontal at the world price for a given good, can a subsidy on imports raise welfare in the importing country? Explain your answer.

27. The United States not only subsidizes producers of cotton (in several ways, including a water subsidy and a price support) but pays $1.7 billion to U.S. manufacturers to buy American cotton. It has paid $100 million each to Allenberg Cotton and Dunavant Enterprises and large amounts to more than 300 other firms (Elizabeth Becker, "U.S. Subsidizes Companies to Buy Subsidized Cotton," *New York Times*, November 4, 2003, C1, C2). Assume for simplicity that specific subsidies (dollars per unit) are used. Use a diagram to show how applying both subsidies changes the equilibrium from the no-subsidy case. Show who gains and who loses.

28. In 2004 the Bush administration ruled that China and Vietnam were dumping shrimp in the United States at below their costs, and proposed duties as high as 112%. Suppose that China and Vietnam were subsidizing their shrimp fishers. Show in a diagram who gains and who loses in the United States (compared to the equilibrium in which those nations do not subsidize their shrimp fishers). Now use your diagram to show how the large tariff would affect the

welfare of consumers and producers and government revenues.

29. After Mexico signed the North American Free Trade Agreement (NAFTA) with the United States in 1994, corn imports from the United States doubled within a year, and today U.S. imports are nearly one-third of the amount of corn consumed in Mexico. According to Oxfam (2003), the price of Mexican corn has fallen more than 70% since NAFTA took effect. Part of the reason for this flow south of our border is that the U.S. government subsidizes corn production to the tune of \$10 billion a year. According to Oxfam, the 2002 U.S. cost of production was \$3.08 per bushel, but the export price was \$2.69 per bushel, with the difference reflecting an export subsidy of 39¢ per bushel. The U.S. exported 5.3 metric tons. Use graphs to show the effect of such a subsidy on the welfare of various groups and on government expenditures in the United States and Mexico.

30. By 1996, the world price for raw sugar, 11.75¢ per pound, was about half the domestic price, 22.5¢ per pound, because of quotas and tariffs on sugar imports. As a consequence, American-made corn sweetener, which costs 12¢ a pound to make, can be profitably sold. Archer Daniels Midland made an estimated profit of \$290 million in 1994 from selling corn sweetener. The U.S. Commerce Department says that the quotas and price support reduce American welfare by about \$3 billion a year. If so, each dollar of Archer Daniels Midland's profit costs Americans about \$10. Model the effects of a quota on sugar in both the sugar and corn sweetener markets.

31. A government is considering a quota or a tariff, both of which will reduce imports by the same amount. Which does the government prefer, and why?

PROBLEMS

*32. If the inverse demand function for toasters is $p = 60 - Q$, what is the consumer surplus if price is 30?

33. If the inverse demand function for radios is $p = a - bQ$, what is the consumer surplus if price is $a/2$?

34. Use the numbers for the alcohol and tobacco category from Table 9.1 to draw a figure that illustrates the role that the revenue and the elasticity of demand play in determining the loss of consumer surplus due to an increase in price. Indicate how the various areas of your figure correspond to the equation derived in Appendix 9A.

35. If the supply function is $Q = Ap^{\eta}$, what is the producer surplus if price is p^*? C

36. If the inverse demand function for books is $p = 60 - Q$ and the supply function is $Q = p$, what is the initial equilibrium? What is the welfare effect of a specific tax of $\tau = \$2$?

37. Suppose that the demand curve for wheat is $Q = 100 - 10p$ and the supply curve is $Q = 10p$. The government imposes a specific tax of $\tau = 1$ per unit.
    a. How do the equilibrium price and quantity change?
    b. What effect does this tax have on consumer surplus, producer surplus, government revenue, welfare, and deadweight loss?

*38. Suppose that the demand curve for wheat is $Q = 100 - 10p$ and the supply curve is $Q = 10p$. The government imposes a price support at $\underline{p} = 6$ using a deficiency payment program.
    a. What are the quantity supplied, the price that clears the market, and the deficiency payment?
    b. What effect does this program have on consumer surplus, producer surplus, welfare, and deadweight loss?

39. Suppose that the demand curve for wheat is $Q = 100 - 10p$ and the supply curve is $Q = 10p$. The government imposes a price ceiling of $p = 3$.
    a. Describe how the equilibrium changes.
    b. What effect does this ceiling have on consumer surplus, producer surplus, and deadweight loss?

General Equilibrium and Economic Welfare

10

Capitalism is the astounding belief that the most wickedest of men will do the most wickedest of things for the greatest good of everyone.
—John Maynard Keynes

A change in government policies, a natural disaster, or other shocks often affect equilibrium price and quantity in more than one market. To determine the effects of such a change, we must examine the interrelationships among markets. In this chapter, we extend our analysis of equilibrium in a single market to equilibrium in all markets.

We then examine how a society decides whether a particular equilibrium (or change in equilibrium) in all markets is desirable. To do so, society must answer two questions: "Is the equilibrium efficient?" and "Is the equilibrium equitable?"

For the equilibrium to be efficient, both consumption and production must be efficient. Production is efficient only if it is impossible to produce more output at current cost given current knowledge (Chapter 7). Consumption is efficient only if goods cannot be reallocated across people so that at least someone is better off and no one is harmed. In this chapter, we show how to determine whether consumption is efficient.

Whether the equilibrium is efficient is a scientific question. It is possible that all members of society could agree on how to answer scientific questions concerning efficiency.

To answer the equity question, society must make a value judgment as to whether each member of society has his or her "fair" or "just" share of all the goods and services. A common view in individualistic cultures is that each person is the best—and possibly only legitimate—judge of his or her own welfare. Nonetheless, to make social choices about events that affect more than one person, we have to make interpersonal comparisons, through which we decide whether one person's gain is more or less important than another person's loss. For example, in Chapter 9 we argued that a price ceiling lowers a measure of total welfare given the value judgment that the well-being of consumers (consumer surplus) and the well-being of the owners of firms (producer surplus) should be weighted equally. People of goodwill—and others—may disagree greatly about equity issues.

As a first step in studying welfare issues, many economists use a narrow value criterion, called the *Pareto principle* (after an Italian economist, Vilfredo Pareto), to rank different allocations of goods and services for which no interpersonal comparisons need to be made. According to this principle, a change that makes one person better off without harming anyone else is desirable. An allocation is **Pareto efficient** if any possible reallocation would harm at least one person.

Pareto efficient
describing an allocation of goods or services such that any reallocation harms at least one person

Presumably, you agree that any government policy that makes all members of society better off is desirable. Do you also agree that a policy that makes some members better off without harming others is desirable? What about a policy that helps one group more than it hurts another group? What about a policy that hurts another group more than it helps your group? It is very unlikely that all members of society will agree on how to answer these questions—much less on the answers.

The efficiency and equity questions arise even in small societies, such as your family. Suppose that your family has gathered together in November and everyone wants pumpkin pie. How much pie you get will depend on the answer to efficiency and equity questions: "How can we make the pie as large as possible with available resources?" and "How should we divide the pie?" It is probably easier to get agreement about how to make the largest possible pie than about how to divide it equitably.

So far in this book (aside from Chapter 9's welfare analysis), we've used economic theory to answer the scientific efficiency question. We've concentrated on that question because the equity question requires a value judgment. (Strangely, most members of our society seem to believe that economists are no better at making value judgments than anyone else.) In this chapter, we examine various views on equity.

In this chapter, we examine five main topics

1. **General Equilibrium.** The welfare analysis in Chapter 9 (involving gains and losses in consumer and producer surplus) changes when a government policy change or other shock affects several markets at once.
2. **Trading Between Two People.** Where two people have goods but cannot produce more goods, both parties benefit from mutually agreed trades.
3. **Competitive Exchange.** The competitive equilibrium has two desirable properties: Any competitive equilibrium is Pareto efficient, and any Pareto-efficient allocation can be obtained by using competition, given an appropriate income distribution.
4. **Production and Trading.** The benefits from trade continue to hold when production is introduced.
5. **Efficiency and Equity.** Because there are many Pareto-efficient allocations, a society uses its views about equity to choose among them.

10.1 General Equilibrium

partial-equilibrium analysis
an examination of equilibrium and changes in equilibrium in one market in isolation

So far we have used a **partial-equilibrium analysis**: an examination of equilibrium and changes in equilibrium in one market in isolation. In a partial-equilibrium analysis in which we hold the prices and quantities of other goods fixed, we implicitly ignore the possibility that events in this market affect other markets' equilibrium prices and quantities.

When stated this baldly, partial-equilibrium analysis sounds foolish. It needn't be, however. Suppose that the government puts a specific tax on the price of hula hoops. If the tax is sizable, it will dramatically affect the sales of hula hoops. However, even a very large tax on hula hoops is unlikely to affect the markets for automobiles, doctor services, or orange juice. Indeed, it is unlikely to affect the demand for other toys greatly. Thus, a partial-equilibrium analysis of the effect of such a tax should serve us well. Studying all markets simultaneously to analyze this tax would be unnecessary at best and confusing at worst.

general-equilibrium analysis
the study of how equilibrium is determined in all markets simultaneously

Sometimes, however, we need to use a **general-equilibrium analysis:** the study of how equilibrium is determined in all markets simultaneously. For example, the discovery of a major oil deposit in a small country raises the income of its citizens, and the increased income affects all that country's markets. Economists sometimes model many markets in an economy and solve for the general equilibrium in all of them simultaneously, using computer models.

Frequently, economists look at equilibrium in several—but not all—markets simultaneously. We'd expect a tax on comic books to affect the price of comic books, which in turn affects the price of video games because video games are substitutes for comics. However, we would not expect that this tax on comics would have a measurable effect on the demand for washing machines. It's therefore reasonable to conduct a "general-equilibrium" analysis of the effects of a tax on comics by looking at just the markets for comics, video games, and a few other closely related markets such as those for movies and trading cards.

Markets are closely related if an increase in the price in one market causes the demand or supply curve in another market to shift measurably. Suppose that a tax on coffee causes the price of coffee to rise. The rise in the price of coffee causes the demand curve for tea to shift outward (more is demanded at any given price of tea) because tea and coffee are substitutes. The price increase in coffee also causes the demand curve for cream to shift inward because coffee and cream are complements.

Similarly, supply curves in different markets may be related. If a farmer produces both corn and soybeans, an increase in the price of corn will affect the relative amounts of both crops the farmer chooses to produce.

Markets may also be linked if the output of one market is an input in another market. A shock that raises the price of computer chips will also raise the price of computers.

Thus, an event in one market may have a *spillover effect* on other related markets for a number of reasons. Indeed, a single event may start a chain reaction of spillover effects that reverberates back and forth between markets.

Feedback Between Competitive Markets

To illustrate the feedback of spillover effects between markets, we examine the corn and soybean markets using supply and demand curves estimated by Holt (1992). Consumers and producers substitute between corn and soybeans, so the supply and demand curves in these two markets are related. The quantity of corn demanded and the quantity of soybeans demanded both depend on the price of corn, the price of soybeans, and other variables. Similarly, the quantities of corn and soybeans supplied depend on their relative prices.

Sequence of Events. We can demonstrate the effect of a shock in one market on both markets by tracing the sequence of events in the two markets. Whether these steps occur nearly instantaneously or take some time depends on how quickly consumers and producers react.

The initial supply and demand curves for corn, S_0^c and D_0^c, intersect at the initial equilibrium for corn, e_0^c, in panel a of Figure 10.1.[1] The price of corn is \$2.15 per bushel, and the quantity of corn is 8.44 billion bushels per year. The initial supply and demand curves for soybeans, S_0^s and D_0^s, intersect at e_0^s in panel b, where price is \$4.12

[1]Until recently, the corn and soybean markets were subject to price controls (Chapter 9). However, we use the estimated supply and demand curves to ask what would happen in these markets in the absence of price controls.

Figure 10.1 Relationship Between the Corn and Soybean Markets.

Supply and demand curves in the corn and soybean markets (as estimated by Holt, 1992) are related.

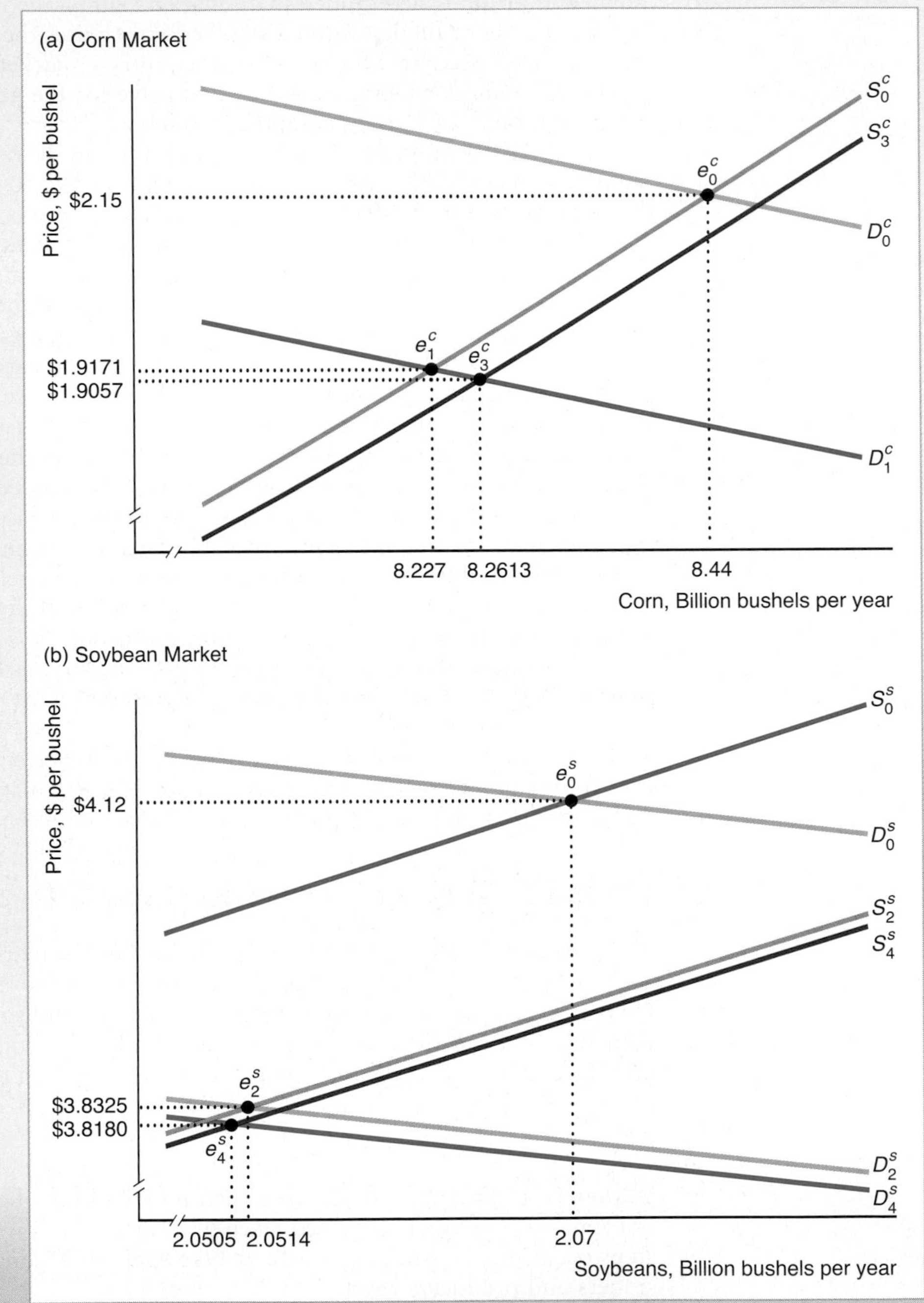

per bushel and quantity is 2.07 billion bushels per year. The first row of Table 10.1 shows the initial equilibrium prices and quantities in these two markets.

Now suppose that the foreign demand for American corn decreases, causing the export of corn to fall by 10% and the total American demand for corn to shift from D_0^c to D_1^c in panel a. The new equilibrium is at e_1^c, where D_1^c intersects S_0^c. The price

Table 10.1 Adjustment in the Corn and Soybean Markets.

	Corn		Soybeans	
Step	Price	Quantity	Price	Quantity
Initial (0)	2.15	8.44	4.12	2.07
1	1.9171	8.227		
2			3.8325	2.0514
3	1.9057	8.2613		
4			3.818	2.0505
5	1.90508	8.26308		
6			3.81728	2.05043
.	.	.	.	
.	.	.	.	.
.	.	.	.	.
Final	1.90505	8.26318	3.81724	2.05043

of corn falls by nearly 11% to \$1.9171 per bushel, and the quantity falls 2.5% to 8.227 billion bushels per year, as the Step 1 row of the table shows.

If we were conducting a partial-equilibrium analysis, we would stop here. In a general-equilibrium analysis, however, we next consider how this shock to the corn market affects the soybean market. Because this shock initially causes the price of corn to fall relative to the price of soybeans (which stays constant), consumers substitute toward corn and away from soybeans: The demand curve for soybeans shifts to the left from D_0^s to D_2^s in panel b.

In addition, because the price of corn falls relative to the price of soybeans, farmers produce more soybeans at any given price of soybeans: The supply curve for soybeans shifts outward to S_2^s. The new soybean demand curve, D_2^s, intersects the new soybean supply curve, S_2^s, at the new equilibrium e_2^s, where price is \$3.8325 per bushel, a fall of 7%, and quantity is 2.0514 billion bushels per year, a drop of less than 1% (Step 2 row).

As it turns out, this fall in the price of soybeans relative to the price of corn causes essentially no shift in the demand curve for corn (panel a shows no shift) but shifts the supply curve of corn, S_3^c, to the right. The new equilibrium is e_3^c, where S_3^c and D_1^c intersect. Price falls to \$1.9057 per bushel of corn and quantity to 8.2613 billion bushels per year (Step 3 row).

This new fall in the relative price of corn causes the soybean demand curve, D_4^s, to shift farther to the left and the supply curve, S_4^s, to shift farther to the right in panel b. At the new equilibrium at e_4^s, where D_4^s and S_4^s intersect, the price and quantity of soybeans fall slightly to \$3.818 per bushel and 2.0505 billion bushels per year, respectively (Step 4 row).

These reverberations between the markets continue, with additional smaller shifts of the supply and demand curves. Eventually, a final equilibrium is reached at which none of the supply and demand curves will shift further. The final equilibria in these two markets (last row of Table 10.1) are virtually the same as e_3^c in panel a and e_4^s in panel b.

See Question 1 and Problems 22 and 23.

Bias in a Partial-Equilibrium Analysis. Suppose that we were interested only in the effect of the shift in the foreign demand curve on the corn market. Could we rely on a partial-equilibrium analysis? According to the partial-equilibrium analysis, the price of corn falls 10.8% to $1.9171. In contrast, in the general-equilibrium analysis, the price falls 11.4% to $1.905, which is 1.2¢ less per bushel. Thus, the partial-equilibrium analysis underestimates the price effect by 0.6 percentage point. Similarly, the fall in quantity is 2.5% according to the partial-equilibrium analysis and only 2.1% according to the general-equilibrium analysis. In this market, then, the biases from using a partial-equilibrium analysis are small. For an example where the bias from using a partial-equilibrium analysis instead of a general-equilibrium analysis is large, see **www.myeconlab.com/perloff**, Chapter 10, "Sin Taxes."

Minimum Wages with Incomplete Coverage

We used a partial-equilibrium analysis in Chapter 2 to examine the effects of a minimum wage law that holds throughout the entire labor market. The minimum wage causes the quantity of labor demanded to be less than the quantity of labor supplied. Workers who lose their jobs cannot find work elsewhere, so they become unemployed.

The story changes substantially, however, if the minimum wage law covers workers in only some sectors of the economy, as we show using a general-equilibrium analysis. This analysis is relevant because the U.S. minimum wage law has not covered all workers historically.

When a minimum wage is applied to a covered sector of the economy, the increase in the wage causes the quantity of labor demanded in that sector to fall. Workers who are displaced from jobs in the covered sector move to the uncovered sector, driving down the wage in that sector. When the U.S. minimum wage law was first passed in 1938, some economists joked that its purpose was to maintain family farms. The law drove workers out of manufacturing and other covered industries into agriculture, which the law did not cover.

Figure 10.2 shows the effect of a minimum wage law when coverage is incomplete. The total demand curve, D in panel c, is the horizontal sum of the demand curve for labor services in the covered sector, D^c in panel a, and the demand curve in the uncovered sector, D^u in panel b. In the absence of a minimum wage law, the wage in both sectors is w_1, which is determined by the intersection of the total demand curve, D, and the total supply curve, S. At that wage, L_c^1 annual hours of work are hired in the covered sector, L_u^1 annual hours in the uncovered sector, and $L_1 = L_c^1 + L_u^1$ total annual hours of work.

If a minimum wage of $\underline{w}$ is set in only the covered sector, employment in that sector falls to L_c^2.To determine the wage and level of employment in the uncovered sector, we first need to determine how much labor service is available to that sector.

Anyone who can't find work in the covered sector goes to the uncovered sector. The supply curve of labor to the uncovered sector in panel b is a *residual supply curve*: the quantity the market supplies that is not met by demanders in other sectors at any given wage (see Chapter 8). With a binding minimum wage in the covered sector, the residual supply function in the uncovered sector is[2]

$$S^u(w) = S(w) - D^c(\underline{w}).$$

Thus, the residual supply to the uncovered sector, $S^u(w)$, is the total supply, $S(w)$, at any given wage w minus the amount of labor used in the covered sector, $L_c^2 = D^c(\underline{w})$.

[2]If there is no minimum wage, the residual supply curve for the uncovered sector is $S^u(w) = S(w) - D^c(w)$.

Figure 10.2 Minimum Wage with Incomplete Coverage.

In the absence of a minimum wage, the equilibrium wage is w_1. Applying a minimum wage, $\underline{w}$, to only one sector causes the quantity of labor services demanded in the covered sector to fall. The extra labor moves to the uncovered sector, driving the wage there down to w_2.

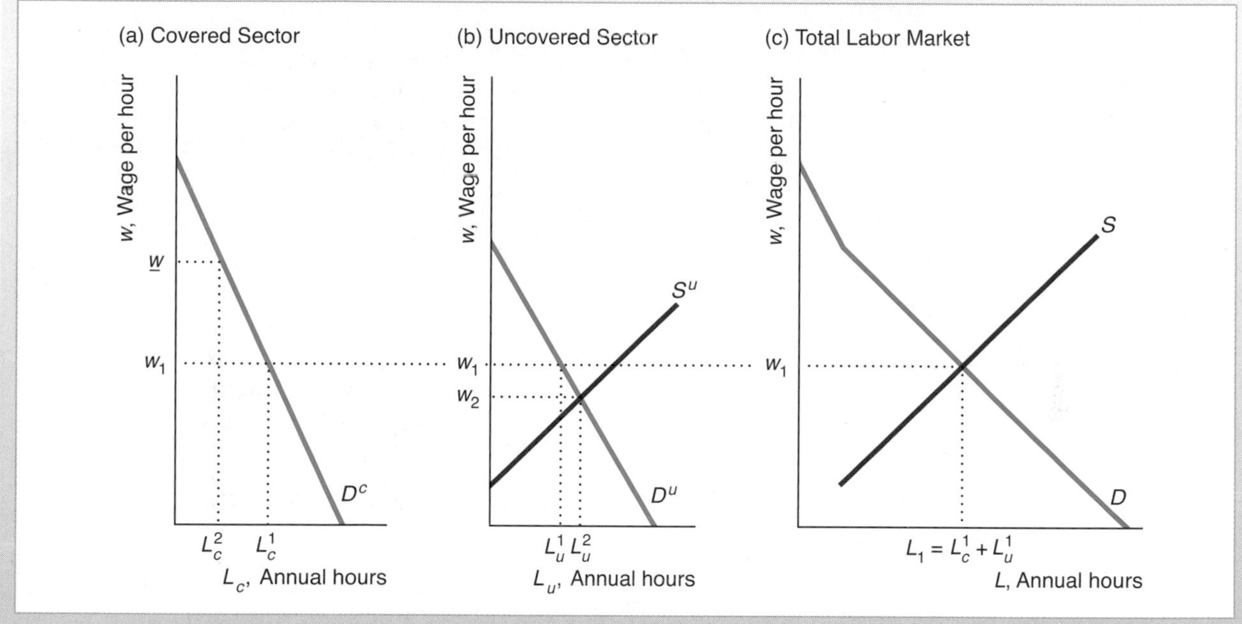

The intersection of D^u and S^u determines w_2, the new wage in the uncovered sector, and L_u^2 the new level of employment.[3] This general-equilibrium analysis shows that a minimum wage causes employment to drop in the covered sector, employment to rise (by a smaller amount) in the uncovered sector, and the wage in the uncovered sector to fall below the original competitive level. Thus, a minimum wage law with only partial coverage affects wage levels and employment levels in various sectors but need not create unemployment.

When the U.S. minimum wage was first passed in 1938, only 56% of workers were employed in covered firms (see **www.myeconlab.com/perloff**, Chapter 10, "U.S. Minimum Wage Laws and Teenagers"). Today, many state minimum wages provide incomplete coverage.

More than 100 U.S. cities and counties now have living-wage laws, a new type of minimum wage legislation where the minimum is high enough to allow a fully employed person to live above the poverty level in a given locale. Living-wage laws provide incomplete coverage, typically extending only to the employees of a government or to firms that contract with that government (see **www.myeconlab.com/perloff**, Chapter 10, "Living Wage Laws"). Chicago recently considered such a law for only employees of "big-box" stores such as Wal-Mart.

---

[3]This analysis is incomplete if the minimum wage causes the price of goods in the covered sector to rise relative to those in the uncovered sector, which in turn causes the demands for labor in those two sectors, D^c and D^u, to shift. Ignoring that possibility is reasonable if labor costs are a small fraction of total costs (hence the effect of the minimum wage is minimal on total costs) or if the demands for the final goods are relatively price insensitive.

Solved Problem 10.1

After the government starts taxing the cost of labor by τ per hour in a covered sector only, the wage that workers in both sectors receive is w, but the wage paid by firms in the covered sector is $w + \tau$. What effect does the subsidy have on the wages, total employment, and employment in the covered and uncovered sectors of the economy?

Answer

1. *Determine the original equilibrium.* In the diagram, the intersection of the total demand curve, D^1, and the total supply curve of labor, S, determines the original equilibrium, e_1, where the wage is w_1 and total employment is L_1. The total demand curve is the horizontal sum of the demand curves in the covered, D_1^c and uncovered, D^u, sectors.

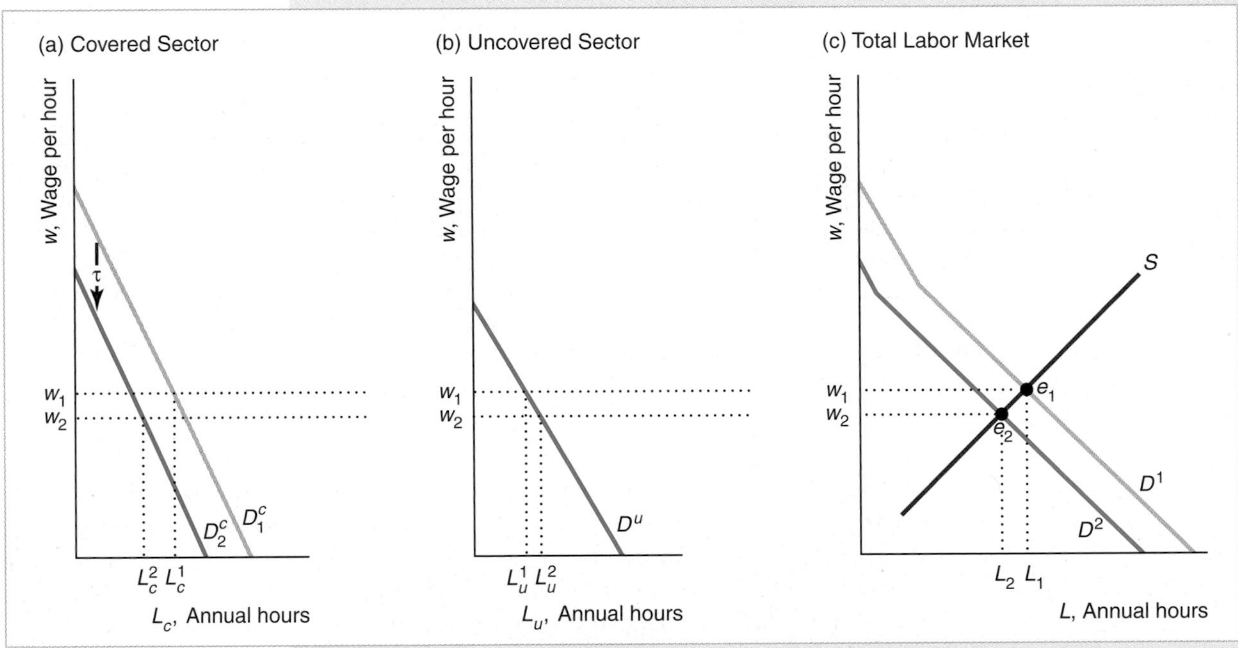

2. *Show the shift in the demand for labor in the covered sector and the resulting shift in the total demand curve.* The tax causes the demand curve for labor in the covered sector to shift downward from D_1^c to D_2^c. As a result, the total demand curve shifts inward to D^2.
3. *Determine the equilibrium wage using the total supply and demand curves, and then determine employment in the two sectors.* Workers shift between sectors until the new wage is equal in both sectors at w_2, which is determined by the intersection of the new total demand curve, D^2, and the total supply curve, S. Employment in the two sectors is L_2^c and L_2^u.
4. *Compare the equilibria.* The tax causes the wage, total employment, and employment in the covered sector to fall and employment in the uncovered sector to rise.

See Questions 2–8 and Problem 24.

APPLICATION

Urban Flight

Philadelphia and some other cities tax wages, while suburban areas do not (or set much lower rates). Philadelphia collects a wage tax from residents whether or not they work in the city and from nonresidents who work in the city. Unfortunately for Philadelphia, this approach drives people and jobs from the city to the suburbs. To offset such job losses, Philadelphia has engaged in a gradual wage tax reduction program. The wage tax on the city's workers declined from a high of 4.96% from 1983 to 1995 to 4.5635% in 2000, 4.4625% in 2003, 4.331% in 2005, and 4.26% in 2007.

The consulting firm Econsult (2003) conducted a study for Philadelphia and estimated that, if the city were to lower the wage tax by 0.4175 percentage points, 30,500 more people would work in the city. Local wage tax cuts are more effective than a national cut because employers generally cannot leave the country to avoid a tax, but they can move a few miles out of a city. As Crawford et al. (2004) noted, you can see how much more growth is taking place on the suburban side of City Line Avenue that runs along Philadelphia's border than on the city side.

See Questions 9 and 10.

10.2 Trading Between Two People

In Chapter 9, we learned that tariffs, quotas, and other restrictions on trade usually harm both importing and exporting nations. The reason is that both parties to a voluntary trade benefit from that trade or else they would not have traded. Using a general-equilibrium model, we will show that free trade is Pareto efficient: After all voluntary trades have occurred, we cannot reallocate goods so as to make one person better off without harming another person. We first demonstrate that trade between two people has this Pareto property. We then show that the same property holds when many people trade using a competitive market.

Endowments

Suppose that Jane and Denise live near each other in the wilds of Massachusetts. A snowstorm strikes, isolating them from the rest of the world. They must either trade with each other or consume only what they have at hand.

endowment
an initial allocation of goods

Collectively, they have 50 cords of firewood and 80 bars of candy and no way of producing more of either good. Jane's **endowment**—her initial allocation of goods—is 30 cords of firewood and 20 candy bars. Denise's endowment is 20 (= 50 − 30) cords of firewood and 60 (= 80 − 20) candy bars. So Jane has relatively more wood, and Denise has relatively more candy.

We show these endowments in Figure 10.3. Panels a and b are typical indifference curve diagrams (Chapters 4 and 5) in which we measure cords of firewood on the vertical axis and candy bars on the horizontal axis. Jane's endowment is e_j (30

Figure 10.3 Endowments in an Edgeworth Box.

(a) Jane's endowment is e_j; she has 20 candy bars and 30 cords of firewood. She is indifferent between that bundle and the others that lie on her indifference curve I_j^1. (b) Denise is indifferent between her endowment, e_d (60 candy bars and 20 cords of wood), and the other bundles on I_d^1. (c) Their endowments are at e in the Edgeworth box formed by combining panels a and b. Jane prefers bundles in A and B to e. Denise prefers bundles in B and C to e. Thus, both prefer any bundle in area B to e.

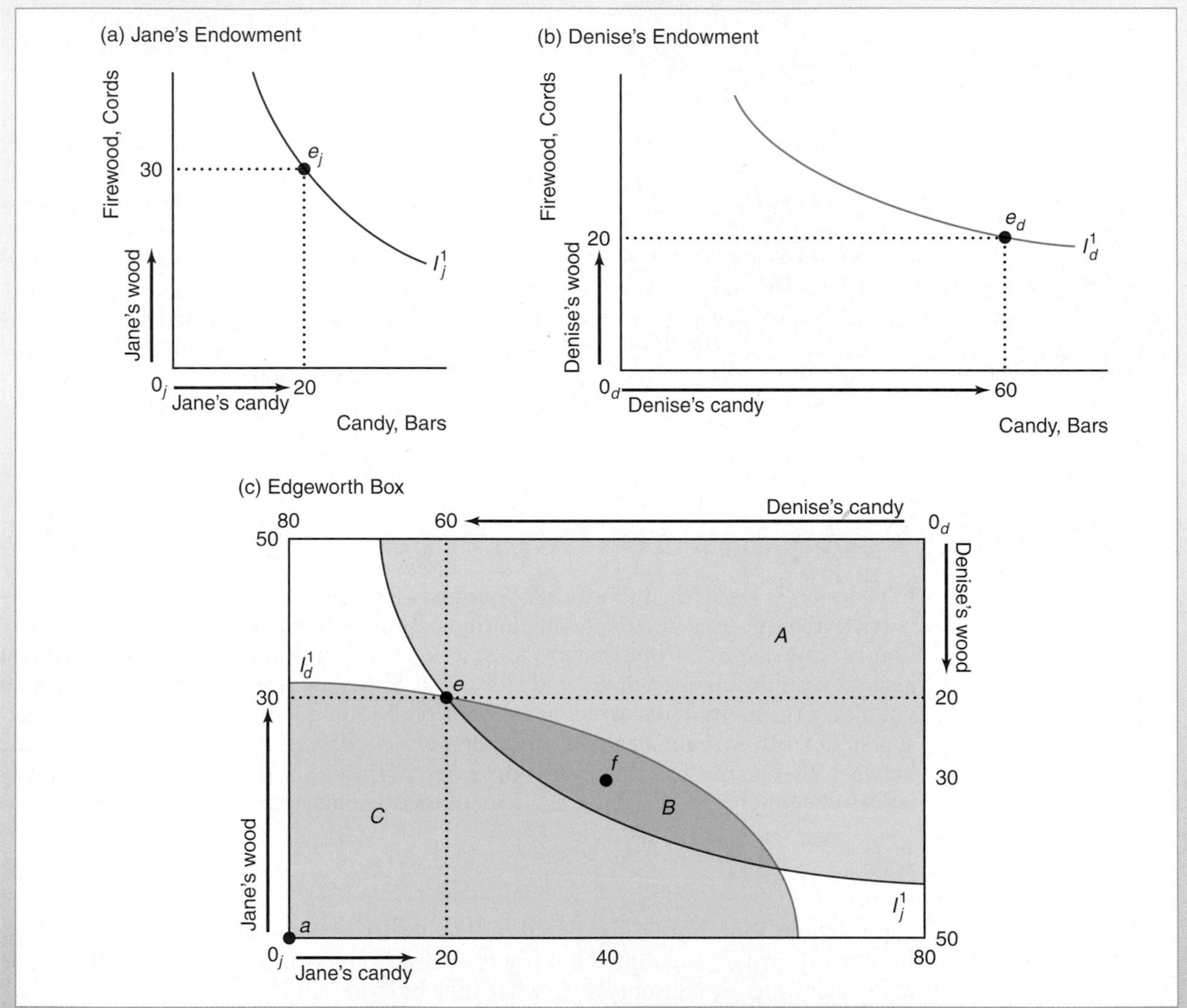

cords of firewood and 20 candy bars) in panel a, and Denise's endowment is e_d in panel b. Both panels show the indifference curve through the endowment.

If we take Denise's diagram, rotate it, and put it on Jane's diagram, we obtain the box in panel c. This type of figure, called an *Edgeworth box* (after an English economist, Francis Ysidro Edgeworth), illustrates trade between two people with fixed endowments of two goods. We use this Edgeworth box to illustrate a general-equilibrium model in which we examine simultaneous trade in firewood and in candy.

The height of the Edgeworth box represents 50 cords of firewood, and the length represents 80 candy bars, which are the combined endowments of Jane and Denise.

Bundle *e* shows both endowments. Measuring from Jane's origin, 0_j, at the lower left of the diagram, we see that Jane has 30 cords of firewood and 20 candy bars at endowment *e*. Similarly, measuring from Denise's origin, 0_d, at the upper-right corner, we see that Denise has 60 bars of candy and 20 cords of firewood at *e*.

Mutually Beneficial Trades

Should Jane and Denise trade? The answer depends on their tastes, which are summarized by thier indifference curves. We make four assumptions about their tastes and behavior:

- **Utility maximization.** Each person *maximizes* her *utility*.
- **Usual-shaped indifference curves.** Each person's indifference curves have the usual convex shape.
- **Nonsatiation.** Each person has strictly positive *marginal utility* for each good, so each person wants as much of the good as possible (neither person is ever satiated).
- **No interdependence.** Neither person's utility depends on the other's consumption (neither person gets pleasure or displeasure from the other's consumption), and neither person's consumption harms the other (one person's consumption of firewood does not cause smoke pollution that bothers the other person).

Figure 10.3 reflects these assumptions.

In panel a, Jane's indifference curve, I_j^1, through her endowment point, e_j, is convex to her origin, 0_j. Jane is indifferent between e_j and any other bundle on I_j^1. She prefers bundles that lie above I_j^1 to e_j and prefers e_j to points that lie below I_j^1. Panel c also shows her indifference curve, I_j^1. The bundles that Jane prefers to her endowment are in the shaded areas *A* and *B*, which lie above her indifference curve I_j^1.

Similarly, Denise's indifference curve, I_d^1, through her endowment is convex to her origin, 0_d, in the lower left of panel b. This indifference curve, I_d^1, is still convex to 0_d in panel c, but 0_d is in the upper right of the Edgeworth box. (It may help to turn this book around when viewing Denise's indifference curves in an Edgeworth box. Then again, possibly many points will be clearer if the book is held upside down.) The bundles Denise prefers to her endowment are in shaded areas *B* and *C*, which lie on the other side of her indifference curve I_d^1 from her origin 0_d (above I_d^1 if you turn the book upside down).

At endowment *e* in panel c, Jane and Denise can both benefit from a trade. Jane prefers bundles in *A* and *B* to *e*, and Denise prefers bundles in *B* and *C* to *e*, so *both* prefer bundles in area *B* to their endowment at *e*.

Suppose that they trade, reallocating goods from Bundle *e* to *f*. Jane gives up 10 cords of firewood for 20 more candy bars, and Denise gives up 20 candy bars for 10 more cords of wood. As Figure 10.4 illustrates, both gain from such a trade. Jane's indifference curve I_j^2 through allocation *f* lies above her indifference curve I_j^1 through allocation *e*, so she is better off at *f* than at *e*. Similarly, Denise's indifference curve I_d^2 through *f* lies above (if you hold the book upside down) her indifference curve I_d^1 through *e*, so she also benefits from the trade.

Now that they've traded to Bundle *f*, do Jane and Denise want to make further trades? To answer this question, we can repeat our analysis. Jane prefers all bundles above I_j^2, her indifference curve through *f*. Denise prefers all bundles above (when the book is held upside down) I_d^2 to *f*. However, there are no bundles that both prefer because I_j^2 and I_d^2 are tangent at *f*. Neither Jane nor Denise wants to trade from *f* to a bundle such as *e*, which is below both of their indifference curves. Jane would love to trade from *f* to *c*, which is on her higher indifference curve I_j^3, but such a

Figure 10.4 Contract Curve.

The contract curve contains all the Pareto-efficient allocations. Any bundle for which Jane's indifference curve is tangent to Denise's indifference curve lies on the contract curve, because no further trade is possible, so we can't reallocate goods to make one of them better off without harming the other. Starting at an endowment of *e*, Jane and Denise will trade to a bundle on the contract curve in area *B*: bundles between *b* and *c*. The table shows how they would trade to Bundle *f*.

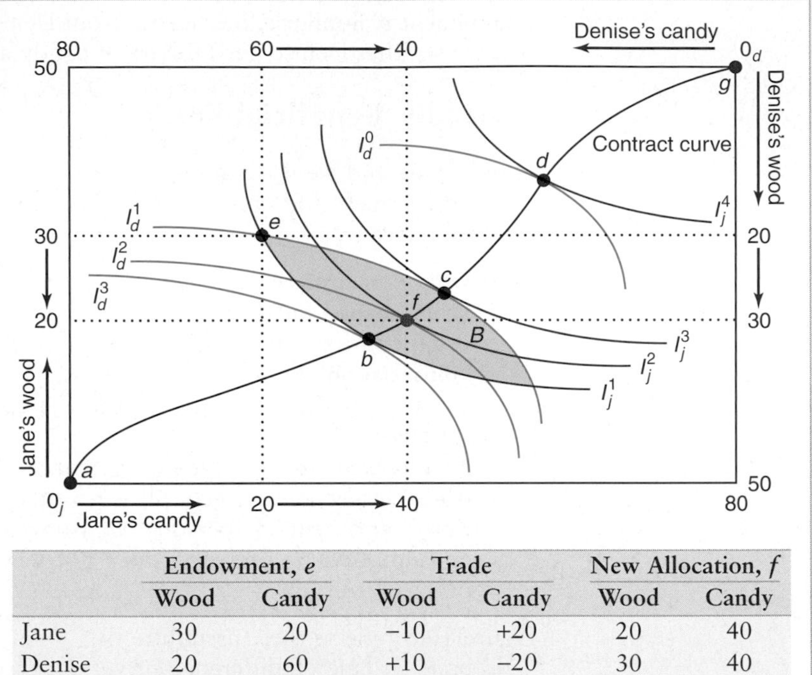

	Endowment, *e*		Trade		New Allocation, *f*	
	Wood	Candy	Wood	Candy	Wood	Candy
Jane	30	20	−10	+20	20	40
Denise	20	60	+10	−20	30	40

See Questions 11–13 and Problems 25 and 26.

trade would make Denise worse off because this bundle is on a lower indifference curve, I_d^1. Similarly, Denise prefers *b* to *f*, but Jane does not. Thus, *any* move from *f* harms at least one of them.

The reason no further trade is possible at a bundle like *f* is that Jane's marginal rate of substitution (the slope of her indifference curve), MRS_j, between wood and candy equals Denise's marginal rate of substitution, MRS_d. Jane's MRS_j is $-\frac{1}{2}$: She is willing to trade one cord of wood for two candy bars. Because Denise's indifference curve is tangent to Jane's, Denise's MRS_d must also be $-\frac{1}{2}$. When they both want to trade wood for candy at the same rate, they can't agree on further trades.

In contrast, at a bundle such as *e* where their indifference curves are not tangent, MRS_j does not equal MRS_d. Denise's MRS_d is $-\frac{1}{3}$, and Jane's MRS_j is −2. Denise is willing to give up one cord of wood for three more candy bars or to sacrifice three candy bars for one more cord of wood. If Denise offers Jane three candy bars for one cord of wood, Jane will accept because she is willing to give up one cord of wood for two candy bars. This example illustrates that trades are possible where indifference curves intersect because marginal rates of substitution are unequal.

To summarize, we can make four equivalent statements about allocation *f*:

1. The indifference curves of the two parties are tangent at *f*.
2. The parties' marginal rates of substitution are equal at *f*.
3. No further mutually beneficial trades are possible at *f*.
4. The allocation at *f* is Pareto efficient: One party cannot be made better off without harming the other.

contract curve the set of all Pareto-efficient bundles

Indifference curves are also tangent at Bundles *b*, *c*, and *d*, so these allocations, like *f*, are Pareto efficient. By connecting all such bundles, we draw the **contract curve**: the set of all Pareto-efficient bundles. The reason for this name is that only at these points are the parties unwilling to engage in further trades or contracts—these allocations are the final contracts. A move from any bundle on the contract curve must harm at least one person.

Solved Problem 10.2

Are allocations *a* and *g* in Figure 10.4 part of the contract curve?

Answer

By showing that no mutually beneficial trades are possible at those points, demonstrate that those bundles are Pareto efficient. The allocation at which Jane has everything, allocation *g*, is on the contract curve because no mutually beneficial trade is possible: Denise has no goods to trade with Jane. As a consequence, we cannot make Denise better off without taking goods from Jane. Similarly, when Denise has everything, *a*, we can make Jane better off only by taking wood or candy from Denise and giving it to Jane.

Bargaining Ability

For every allocation off the contract curve, there are allocations on the contract curve that benefit at least one person. If they start at endowment *e*, Jane and Denise should trade until they reach a point on the contract curve between Bundles *b* and *c* in Figure 10.4. All the allocations in area *B* are beneficial. However, if they trade to any allocation in *B* that is not on the contract curve, further beneficial trades are possible because their indifference curves intersect at that allocation.

Where will they end up on the contract curve between *b* and *c*? That depends on who is better at bargaining. Suppose that Jane is better at bargaining. Jane knows that the more she gets, the worse off Denise will be and that Denise will not agree to any trade that makes her worse off than she is at *e*. Thus, the best trade Jane can make is one that leaves Denise only as well off as at *e*, which are the bundles on I_d^1. If Jane could pick any point she wanted along I_d^1, she'd choose the bundle on her highest possible indifference curve, which is Bundle *c*, where I_j^3 is just tangent to I_d^1. After this trade, Denise is no better off than before, but Jane is much happier. By similar reasoning, if Denise is better at bargaining, the final allocation will be at *b*.

10.3 Competitive Exchange

Most trading throughout the world occurs without one-on-one bargaining between people. When you go to the store to buy a bottle of shampoo, you read its posted price and then decide whether to buy it or not. You've probably never tried to bargain with the store's clerk over the price of shampoo: You're a price taker in the shampoo market.

If we don't know much about how Jane and Denise bargain, all we can say is that they will trade to some allocation on the contract curve. If we know the exact trading process they use, however, we can apply that process to determine the final allocation. In particular, we can examine the competitive trading process to determine the competitive equilibrium in a pure exchange economy.

In Chapter 9, we used a partial-equilibrium approach to show that one measure of welfare, *W*, is maximized in a competitive market in which many voluntary trades occur. We now use a general-equilibrium model to show that a competitive market has two desirable properties:

- **The competitive equilibrium is efficient.** Competition results in a Pareto-efficient allocation—no one can be made better off without making someone worse off—in all markets.

- **Any efficient allocations can be achieved by competition.** All possible efficient allocations can be obtained by competitive exchange, given an appropriate initial allocation of goods.

Economists call these results the *First Theorem of Welfare Economics* and the *Second Theorem of Welfare Economics*, respectively. These results hold under fairly weak conditions.

Competitive Equilibrium

When two people trade, they are unlikely to view themselves as price takers. However, if there were a large number of people with tastes and endowments like Jane's and a large number of people with tastes and endowments like Denise's, each person would be a price taker in the two goods. We can use an Edgeworth box to examine how such price takers would trade.

Because they can trade only two goods, each person needs to consider only the relative price of the two goods when deciding whether to trade. If the price of a cord of wood, p_w, is \$2, and the price of a candy bar, p_c, is \$1, then a candy bar costs half as much as a cord of wood: $p_c/p_w = \frac{1}{2}$. An individual can sell one cord of wood and use that money to buy two candy bars.

At the initial allocation, *e*, Jane has goods worth \$80 = (\$2 per cord × 30 cords of firewood) + (\$1 per candy bar × 20 candy bars). At these prices, Jane could keep her endowment or trade to an allocation with 40 cords of firewood and no candy, 80 bars of candy and no firewood, or any combination in between as the price line (budget line) in panel a of Figure 10.5 shows. The price line is all the combinations of goods Jane could get by trading, given her endowment. The price line goes through point *e* and has a slope of $-p_c/p_w = -\frac{1}{2}$.

Given the price line, what bundle of goods will Jane choose? She wants to maximize her utility by picking the bundle where one of her indifference curves, I_j^2, is tangent to her budget or price line. Denise wants to maximize her utility by choosing a bundle in the same way.

In a competitive market, prices adjust until the quantity supplied equals the quantity demanded. An auctioneer could help determine the equilibrium. The auctioneer could call out relative prices and ask how much is demanded and how much is offered for sale at those prices. If demand does not equal supply, the auctioneer calls out another relative price. When demand equals supply, the transactions actually occur and the auction stops. At some ports, fishing boats sell their catch to fish wholesalers at a daily auction run in this manner.

Panel a shows that when candy costs half as much as wood, the quantity demanded of each good equals the quantity supplied. Jane (and every person like her) wants to sell 10 cords of firewood and use that money to buy 20 additional candy bars. Similarly, Denise (and everyone like her) wants to sell 20 candy bars and buy 10 cords of wood. Thus, the quantity of wood sold equals the quantity bought, and the quantity of candy demanded equals that supplied. We can see in the figure that the quantities demanded equal the quantities supplied because the optimal bundle for both types of consumers is the same, Bundle *f*.

At any other price ratio, the quantity demanded of each good would not equal the quantity supplied. For example, if the price of candy remained constant at $p_c =$ \$1 per bar but the price of wood fell to $p_w =$ \$1.33 per cord, the price line would be steeper, with a slope of $-p_c/p_w = -1/1.33 = -\frac{3}{4}$ in panel b. At these prices, Jane wants to trade to Bundle *j* and Denise wants to trade to Bundle *d*. Because Jane wants to buy 10 extra candy bars but Denise wants to sell 17 extra candy bars, the

Figure 10.5 Competitive Equilibrium.

The initial endowment is e. (a) If, along the price line facing Jane and Denise, p_w = \$2 and p_c = \$1, they trade to point f, where Jane's indifference curve, I_j^2 is tangent to the price line and to Denise's indifference curve, I_d^2. (b) No other price line results in an equilibrium. If p_w = \$1.33 and p_c = \$1, Denise wants to buy 12 (= 32 – 20) cords of firewood at these prices, but Jane wants to sell only 8 (= 30 – 22) cords. Similarly, Jane wants to buy 10 (= 30 – 20) candy bars, but Denise wants to sell 17 (= 60 – 43). Thus, these prices are not consistent with a competitive equilibrium.

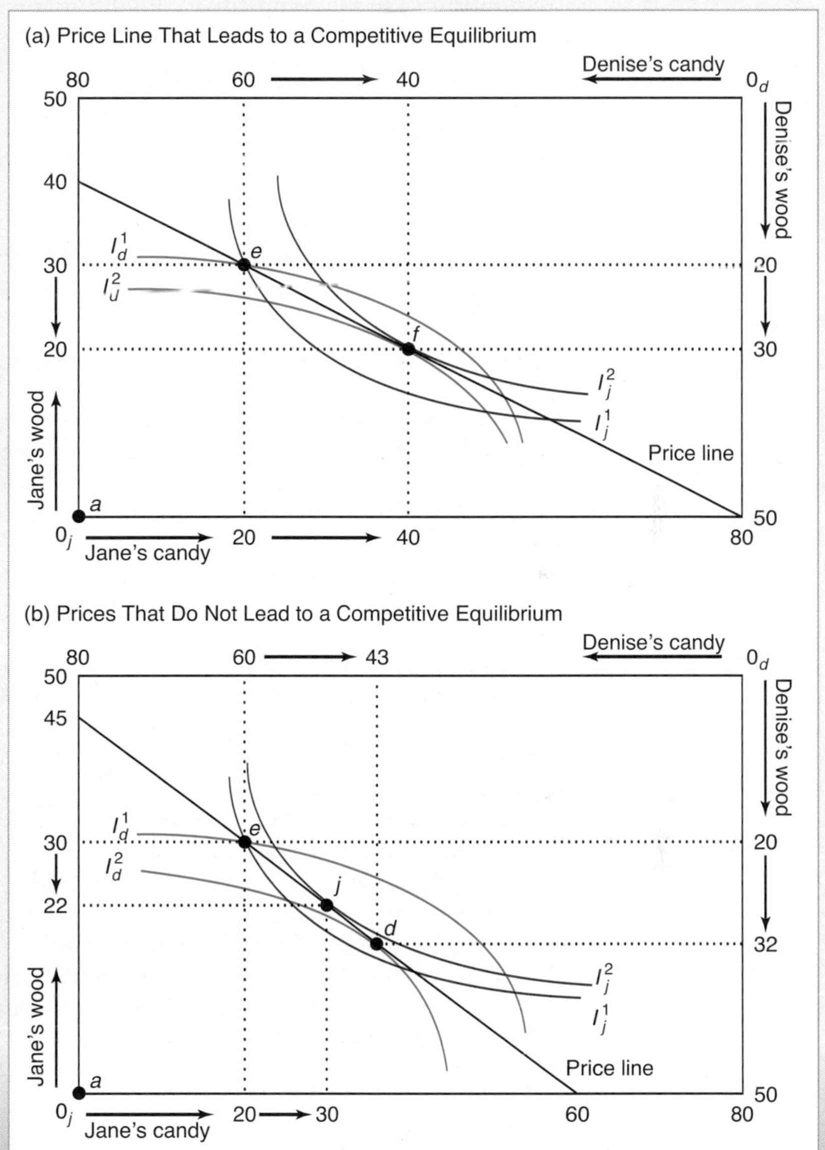

quantity supplied does not equal the quantity demanded, so this price ratio does not result in a competitive equilibrium when the endowment is e.

The Efficiency of Competition

In a competitive equilibrium, the indifference curves of both types of consumers are tangent at the same bundle on the price line. As a result, the slope (MRS) of each person's indifference curve equals the slope of the price line, so the slopes of the indifference curves are equal:

$$MRS_j = -\frac{p_c}{p_w} = MRS_d. \tag{10.1}$$

The marginal rates of substitution are equal across consumers in the competitive equilibrium, so the competitive equilibrium must lie on the contract curve. Thus, we have demonstrated the First Theorem of Welfare Economics:

Any competitive equilibrium is Pareto efficient.

The intuition for this result is that people (who face the same prices) make all the voluntary trades they want in a competitive market. Because no additional voluntary trades can occur, there is no way to make someone better off without making someone worse off in a competitive equilibrium. (If an involuntary trade occurs, at least one person is made worse off. A person who steals goods from another person—an involuntary exchange—gains at the expense of the victim.)

Obtaining Any Efficient Allocation Using Competition

Of the many possible Pareto-efficient allocations, the government may want to choose one. Can it achieve that allocation using the competitive market mechanism?

Our previous example illustrates that the competitive equilibrium depends on the endowment: the initial distribution of wealth. For example, if the initial endowment were *a* in panel a of Figure 10.5—where Denise has everything and Jane has nothing—the competitive equilibrium would be *a* because no trades would be possible.

Thus, for competition to lead to a particular allocation—say, *f*—the trading must start at an appropriate endowment. If the consumers' endowment is *f*, a Pareto-efficient point, their indifference curves are tangent at *f*, so no further trades occur. That is, *f* is a competitive equilibrium.

Many other endowments will also result in a competitive equilibrium at *f*. Panel a shows that the resulting competitive equilibrium is *f* if the endowment is *e*. In that figure, a price line goes through both *e* and *f*. If the endowment is any bundle along this price line—not just *e* or *f*—the competitive equilibrium is *f*, because only at *f* are the indifference curves tangent.

To summarize, any Pareto-efficient bundle x can be obtained as a competitive equilibrium if the initial endowment is x. That allocation can also be obtained as a competitive equilibrium if the endowment lies on a price line through x, where the slope of the price line equals the marginal rate of substitution of the indifference curves that are tangent at x. Thus, we've demonstrated the Second Theorem of Welfare Economics:

Any Pareto-efficient equilibrium can be obtained by competition, given an appropriate endowment.

The first welfare theorem tells us that society can achieve efficiency by allowing competition. The second welfare theorem adds that society can obtain the particular efficient allocation it prefers based on its value judgments about equity by appropriately redistributing endowments (income).

See Question 14.

10.4 Production and Trading

So far our discussion has been based on a pure exchange economy with no production. We now examine an economy in which a fixed amount of a single input can be used to produce two different goods.

Comparative Advantage

Jane and Denise can produce candy or chop firewood using their own labor. They differ, however, in how much of each good they produce from a day's work.

Production Possibility Frontier. Jane can produce either 3 candy bars or 6 cords of firewood in a day. By splitting her time between the two activities, she can produce various combinations of the two goods. If α is the fraction of a day she spends making candy and $1 - \alpha$ is the fraction cutting wood, she produces 3α candy bars and $6(1 - \alpha)$ cords of wood.

By varying α between 0 and 1, we trace out the line in panel a of Figure 10.6. This line is Jane's *production possibility frontier* (PPF^j; Chapter 7), which shows the maximum combinations of wood and candy that she can produce from a given amount of input. If Jane works all day using the best available technology (such as a sharp ax), she achieves *efficiency in production* and produces combinations of goods on PPF^j. If she sits around part of the day or does not use the best technology, she produces an inefficient combination of wood and candy inside PPF^j.

Marginal Rate of Transformation. The slope of the production possibility frontier is the *marginal rate of transformation* (MRT).[4] The marginal rate of transformation

Figure 10.6 Comparative Advantage and Production Possibility Frontiers.

(a) Jane's production possibility frontier, PPF^j, shows that in a day, she can produce 6 cords of firewood or 3 candy bars or any combination of the two. Her marginal rate of transformation (MRT) is –2. (b) Denise's production possibility frontier, PPF^d, has an MRT of $-\frac{1}{2}$. (c) Their joint production possibility frontier, PPF, has a kink at 6 cords of firewood (produced by Jane) and 6 candy bars (produced by Denise) and is concave to the origin.

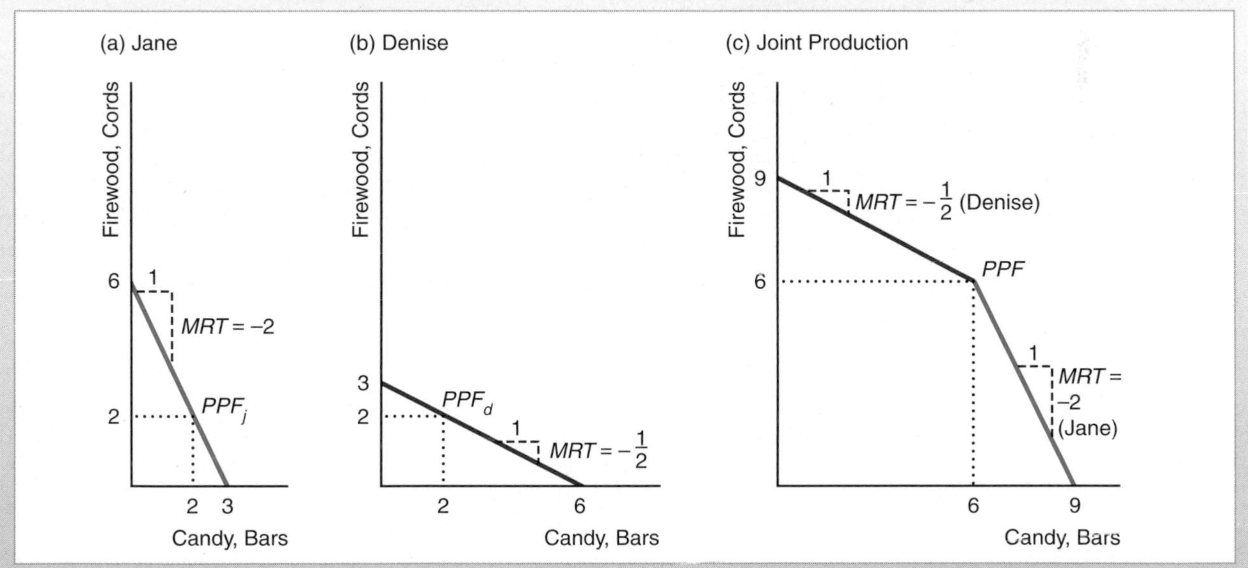

[4]In Chapter 4, we called the slope of a consumer's budget line the marginal rate of transformation. For a price-taking consumer who obtains goods by buying them, the budget line plays the same role as the production possibility frontier for someone who produces the two goods.

tells us how much more wood can be produced if the production of candy is reduced by one bar. Because Jane's PPF^j is a straight line with a slope of −2, her MRT is −2 at every allocation.

Denise can produce up to 3 cords of wood or 6 candy bars in a day. Panel b shows her production possibility function, PPF^d, with an $MRT = -\frac{1}{2}$. Thus, with a day's work, Denise can produce relatively more candy, and Jane can produce relatively more wood, as reflected by their differing marginal rates of transformation.

The marginal rate of transformation shows how much it costs to produce one good in terms of the forgone production of the other good. Someone with the ability to produce a good at a lower opportunity cost than someone else has a **comparative advantage** in producing that good. Denise has a comparative advantage in producing candy (she forgoes less in wood production to produce a given amount of candy), and Jane has a comparative advantage in producing wood.

comparative advantage
the ability to produce a good at a lower opportunity cost than someone else

By combining their outputs, they have the joint production possibility frontier PPF in panel c. If Denise and Jane spend all their time producing wood, Denise produces 3 cords and Jane produces 6 cords for a total of 9, which is where the joint PPF hits the wood axis. Similarly, if they both produce candy, they can jointly produce 9 bars. If Denise specializes in making candy and Jane specializes in cutting wood, they produce 6 candy bars and 6 cords of wood, a combination that appears at the kink in the PPF.

If they choose to produce a relatively large quantity of candy and a relatively small amount of wood, Denise produces only candy and Jane produces some candy and some wood. Jane chops the wood because that's her comparative advantage. The marginal rate of transformation in the lower portion of the PPF is Jane's, −2, because only she produces both candy and wood.

Similarly, if they produce little candy, Jane produces only wood and Denise produces some wood and some candy, so the marginal rate of transformation in the higher portion of the PPF is Denise's, $-\frac{1}{2}$. In short, the PPF has a kink at 6 cords of wood and 6 candy bars and is concave (bowed away from the origin).

See Questions 15–17.

Benefits of Trade. Because of the difference in their marginal rates of transformation, Jane and Denise can benefit from a trade. Suppose that Jane and Denise like to consume wood and candy in equal proportions. If they do not trade, each produces 2 candy bars and 2 cords of wood in a day. If they agree to trade, Denise, who excels at making candy, spends all day producing 6 candy bars. Similarly, Jane, who has a comparative advantage at chopping, produces 6 cords of wood. If they split this production equally, they can each have 3 cords of wood and 3 candy bars—50% more than if they don't trade.

They do better if they trade because each person uses her comparative advantage. Without trade, if Denise wants an extra cord of wood, she must give up two candy bars. Producing an extra cord of wood costs Jane only half a candy bar in forgone production. Denise is willing to trade up to two candy bars for a cord of wood, and Jane is willing to trade the wood as long as she gets at least half a candy bar. Thus, there is room for a mutually beneficial trade.

See Question 18 and Problem 27.

Solved Problem 10.3

How does the joint production possibility frontier in panel c of Figure 10.6 change if Jane and Denise can also trade with Harvey, who can produce 5 cords of wood, 5 candy bars, or any linear combination of wood and candy in a day?

Answer

1. *Describe each person's individual production possibility frontier.* Panels a and b of Figure 10.6 show the production possibility frontiers of Jane and Denise.

Harvey's production possibility frontier is a straight line that hits the firewood axis at 5 cords and the candy axis at 5 candy bars.

2. *Draw the joint PPF, by starting at the quantity on the horizontal axis that is produced if everyone specializes in candy and then connecting the individual production possibility frontiers in order of comparative advantage in chopping wood.* If all three produce candy, they make 14 candy bars (on the horizontal axis of the accompanying graph). Jane has a comparative advantage at chopping wood over Harvey and Denise, and Harvey has a comparative advantage over Denise. Thus, Jane's production possibility frontier is the first one (starting at the lower right), then comes Harvey's, and then Denise's. The resulting *PPF* is concave to the origin. (If we change the order of the individual frontiers, the resulting kinked line lies inside the *PPF*. Thus, the new line cannot be the joint production possibility frontier, which shows the maximum possible production from the available labor inputs.)

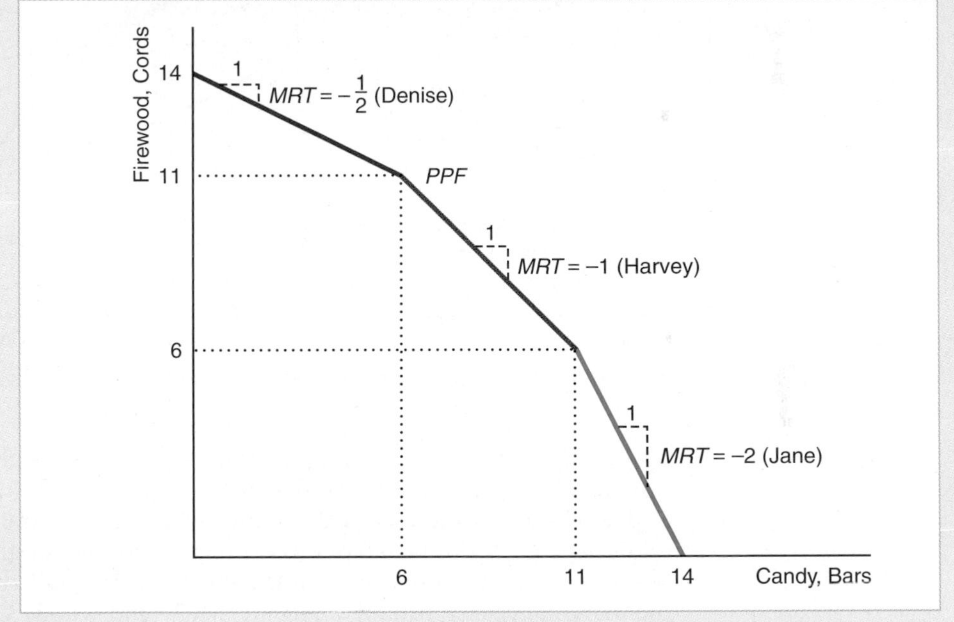

The Number of Producers. When there are only two ways of producing wood and candy—Denise's and Jane's methods with different marginal rates of transformation—the joint production possibility frontier has a single kink (panel c of Figure 10.6). If another method of production with a different marginal rate of transformation—Harvey's—is added, the joint production possibility frontier has two kinks (as in Solved Problem 10.3).

If many firms can produce candy and firewood with different marginal rates of transformation, the joint production possibility frontier has even more kinks. As the number of firms becomes very large, the *PPF* becomes a smooth curve that is concave to the origin, as in Figure 10.7.

Because the *PPF* is concave, the marginal rate of transformation decreases (in absolute value) as we move up the *PPF*. The *PPF* has a flatter slope at *a*, where the $MRT = -\frac{1}{2}$, than at *b*, where the $MRT = -1$. At *a*, giving up a candy bar leads to half a cord more wood production. In contrast, at *b*, where relatively more candy is

Figure 10.7 Optimal Product Mix.

The optimal product mix, *a*, could be determined by maximizing an individual's utility by picking the allocation for which an indifference curve is tangent to the production possibility frontier. It could also be determined by picking the allocation where the relative competitive price, p_c/p_f, equals the slope of the *PPF*.

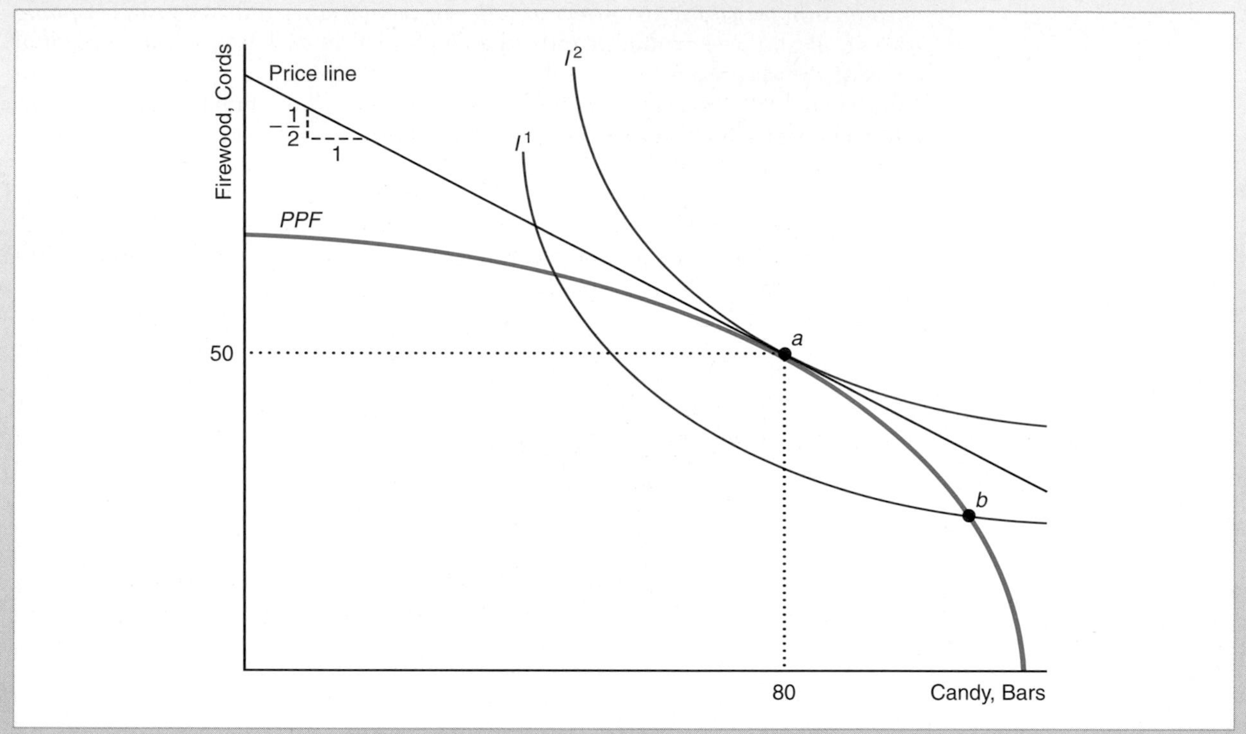

produced, giving up producing a candy bar frees enough resources that an additional cord of wood can be produced.

The marginal rate of transformation along this smooth *PPF* tells us about the marginal cost of producing one good relative to the marginal cost of producing the other good. The marginal rate of transformation equals the negative of the ratio of the marginal cost of producing candy, MC_c, and wood, MC_w:

$$MRT = -\frac{MC_c}{MC_w}. \tag{10.2}$$

Suppose that at point *a* in Figure 10.7, a firm's marginal cost of producing an extra candy bar is \$1 and its marginal cost of producing an additional cord of firewood is \$2. As a result, the firm can produce one extra candy bar or half a cord of wood at a cost of \$1. The marginal rate of transformation is the negative of the ratio of the marginal costs, $-(\$1/\$2) = -\frac{1}{2}$. To produce one more candy bar, the firm must give up producing half a cord of wood.

Efficient Product Mix

Which combination of products along the *PPF* does society choose? If a single person were to decide on the product mix, that person would pick the allocation of wood and candy along the *PPF* that maximized his or her utility. A person with the indifference curves in Figure 10.7 would pick Allocation *a*, which is the point where the *PPF* touches indifference curve I^2.

Because I^2 is tangent to the *PPF* at *a*, that person's marginal rate of substitution (the slope of indifference curve I^2) equals the marginal rate of transformation (the slope of the *PPF*). The marginal rate of substitution, *MRS*, tells us how much a consumer is willing to give up of one good to get another. The marginal rate of transformation, *MRT*, tells us how much of one good we need to give up to produce more of another good.

If the *MRS* doesn't equal the *MRT*, the consumer will be happier with a different product mix. At Allocation *b*, the indifference curve I^1 intersects the *PPF*, so the *MRS* does not equal the *MRT*. At *b*, the consumer is willing to give up one candy bar to get a third of a cord of wood ($MRT = -\frac{1}{3}$) but firms can produce one cord of wood for every candy bar not produced ($MRT = -1$). Thus, at *b*, too little wood is being produced. If the firms increase wood production, the *MRS* will fall and the *MRT* will rise until they are equal at *a*, where $MRS = MRT = -\frac{1}{2}$.

We can extend this reasoning to look at the product mix choice of all consumers simultaneously. Each consumer's marginal rate of substitution must equal the economy's marginal rate of transformation, $MRS = MRT$, if the economy is to produce the optimal mix of goods for each consumer. How can we ensure that this condition holds for all consumers? One way is to use the competitive market.

Competition

Each price-taking consumer picks a bundle of goods so that the consumer's marginal rate of substitution equals the slope of the consumer's price line (the negative of the relative prices):

$$MRS = -\frac{p_c}{p_w}. \tag{10.3}$$

Thus, if all consumers face the same relative prices, in the competitive equilibrium, all consumers will buy a bundle where their marginal rates of substitution are equal (Equation 10.1). Because all consumers have the same marginal rates of substitution, no further trades can occur. Thus, the competitive equilibrium achieves *consumption efficiency*: We can't redistribute goods among consumers to make one consumer better off without harming another one. That is, the competitive equilibrium lies on the contract curve.

If candy and wood are sold by competitive firms, each firm sells a quantity of a candy for which its price equals its marginal cost,

$$p_c = MC_c, \tag{10.4}$$

and a quantity of wood for which its price and marginal cost are equal,

$$p_w = MC_w. \tag{10.5}$$

Taking the ratio of Equations 10.4 and 10.5, we find that in competition, $p_c/p_w = MC_c/MC_w$. From Equation 10.2, we know that the marginal rate of transformation equals $-MC_c/MC_w$, so

$$MRT = -\frac{p_c}{p_w}. \tag{10.6}$$

We can illustrate why firms want to produce where Equation 10.6 holds. Suppose that a firm were producing at *b* in Figure 10.7, where its *MRT* is -1, and that

$p_c = \$1$ and $p_w = \$2$, so $-p_c/p_w = -\frac{1}{2}$. If the firm reduces its output by one candy bar, it loses \$1 in candy sales but makes \$2 more from selling the extra cord of wood, for a net gain of \$1. Thus, at b, where the $MRT < -p_c/p_w$, the firm should reduce its output of candy and increase its output of wood. In contrast, if the firm is producing at a, where the $MRT = -p_c/p_w = -\frac{1}{2}$, it has no incentive to change its behavior: The gain from producing a little more wood exactly offsets the loss from producing a little less candy.

Combining Equations 10.3 and 10.6, we find that in the competitive equilibrium, the *MRS* equals the relative prices, which equals the *MRT*:

$$MRS = -\frac{p_c}{p_w} = MRT.$$

Because competition ensures that the *MRS* equals the *MRT*, a competitive equilibrium achieves an *efficient product mix*: The rate at which firms can transform one good into another equals the rate at which consumers are willing to substitute between the goods, as reflected by their willingness to pay for the two goods.

By combining the production possibility frontier and an Edgeworth box, we can show the competitive equilibrium in both production and consumption. Suppose that firms produce 50 cords of firewood and 80 candy bars at a in Figure 10.8. The size of the Edgeworth box—the maximum amount of wood and candy available to consumers—is determined by point a on the *PPF*.

The prices consumers pay must equal the prices producers receive, so the price lines consumers and producers face must have the same slope of $-pc/pw$. In equilibrium, the price lines are tangent to each consumer's indifference curve at f and to the *PPF* at a.

Figure 10.8 Competitive Equilibrium.

At the competitive equilibrium, the relative prices firms and consumers face are the same (the price lines are parallel), so the $MRS = -p_c/p_w = MRT$.

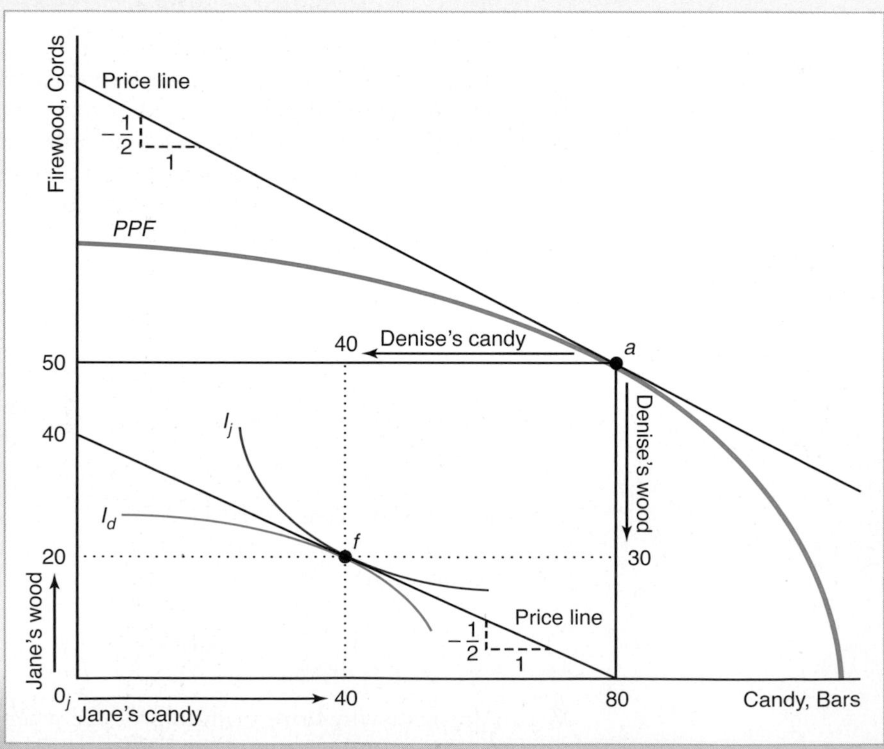

In this competitive equilibrium, supply equals demand in all markets. The consumers buy the mix of goods at *f*. Consumers like Jane, whose origin, 0_j, is at the lower left, consume 20 cords of firewood and 40 candy bars. Consumers like Denise, whose origin is *a* at the upper right of the Edgeworth box, consume 30 (= 50 − 20) cords of firewood and 40 (= 80 − 40) candy bars.

The two key results concerning competition still hold in an economy with production. First, a competitive equilibrium is Pareto efficient, achieving efficiency in consumption and in output mix.[5] Second, any particular Pareto-efficient allocation between consumers can be obtained through competition, given that the government chooses an appropriate endowment.

10.5 Efficiency and Equity

How well various members of society live depends on how society deals with efficiency (the size of the pie) and equity (how the pie is divided). The actual outcome depends on choices by individuals and on government actions.

Role of the Government

By altering the efficiency with which goods are produced and distributed and the endowment of resources, governments help determine how much is produced and how goods are allocated. By redistributing endowments or by refusing to do so, governments, at least implicitly, are making value judgments about which members of society should get relatively more of society's goodies.

Virtually every government program, tax, or action redistributes wealth. Proceeds from a British lottery, played mostly by lower-income people, support the "rich toffs" who attend the Royal Opera House at Covent Garden. Agricultural price support programs (Chapter 9) redistribute wealth to farmers from other taxpayers. Income taxes (Chapter 5) and food stamp programs (Chapter 4) redistribute income from the rich to the poor.

APPLICATION

Wealth Distribution in the United States

Since the United States was founded, changes in the economy have altered the share of the nation's wealth concentrated in the hands of the richest 1% of Americans (see the figure). An array of social changes—sometimes occurring during or after wars and often codified into new laws—have led to new equilibria and new distributions of wealth. For example, the emancipation of slaves in 1863 transferred vast wealth—the labor of the former slaves—from rich Southern landowners to the poor freed slaves. Anti-immigration laws have helped the domestic poor, because immigrant labor is typically a substitute for low-skilled domestic labor, and have hurt the middle and upper classes, because low-skilled immigrant labor is a complement to capital and high-skilled labor.

---

[5]Although we have not shown it here, competitive firms choose factor combinations so that their marginal rates of technical substitution between inputs equal the negative of the ratios of the relative factor prices (see Chapter 7). That is, competition also results in *efficiency in production*: We could not produce more of one good without producing less of another good.

Until the Great Depression, the share of wealth held by the richest 1% generally increased,[6] then declined through the mid-1970s, when the trend reversed dramatically. The share of income earned by the top 0.1% of the population doubled to 7.4% from 1980 to 2002. In 2004, the wealthiest 1% of the populace held 30% of total wealth, the next highest 9% had a third, and the remaining 90% owned 37%. As of 2004, 2.5 million Americans, or almost 1% of the population over the age of 15, had more than $1 million each in financial assets such as stocks, bonds, and bank accounts. An average chief executive officer (CEO) of a corporation received 821 times as much as a minimum wage earner in the firm (Mishel, 2006). Consequently, this CEO earns more before lunchtime on the first workday of the year than the minimum wage worker earns for the entire year.

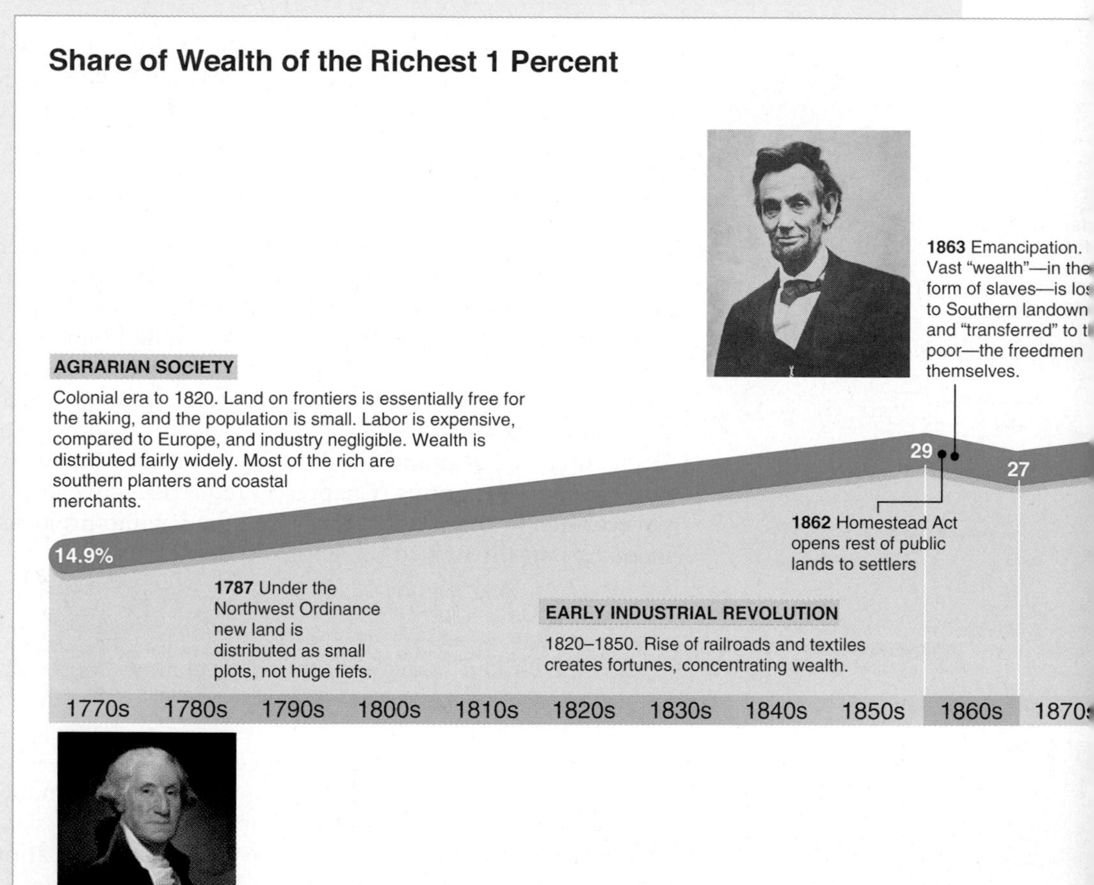

Share of Wealth of the Richest 1 Percent
AGRARIAN SOCIETY
Colonial era to 1820. Land on frontiers is essentially free for the taking, and the population is small. Labor is expensive, compared to Europe, and industry negligible. Wealth is distributed fairly widely. Most of the rich are southern planters and coastal merchants.
14.9%
1787 Under the Northwest Ordinance new land is distributed as small plots, not huge fiefs.
EARLY INDUSTRIAL REVOLUTION
1820–1850. Rise of railroads and textiles creates fortunes, concentrating wealth.
1862 Homestead Act opens rest of public lands to settlers
29
27
1770s
1780s
1790s
1800s
1810s
1820s
1830s
1840s
1850s
1860s

[6]According to *Forbes,* the wealth of Bill Gates, the wealthiest American, was $59 billion in 2007 (down from $85 billion in 1999). His wealth is 1/237th of the U.S. gross domestic product (down from 1/109th in 1999).

One reason for the increased concentration of wealth in recent decades was that the top income tax rate fell from 70% to less than 30% at the beginning of the Reagan administration, shifting more of the tax burden to the middle class. Since then, the top federal tax rate rose under the Clinton administration then fell under the Bush administration.

The federal government transfers 5% of total national household income from the rich to the poor: 2% using cash assistance such as general welfare programs and 3% using in-kind transfers such as food stamps and school lunch programs. Poor households receive 26% of their income from cash assistance and 18% from in-kind assistance.

The United States government gives only 0.1% of its gross national product to poor nations. In contrast, Britain gives 0.26% and the Netherlands 0.8%.

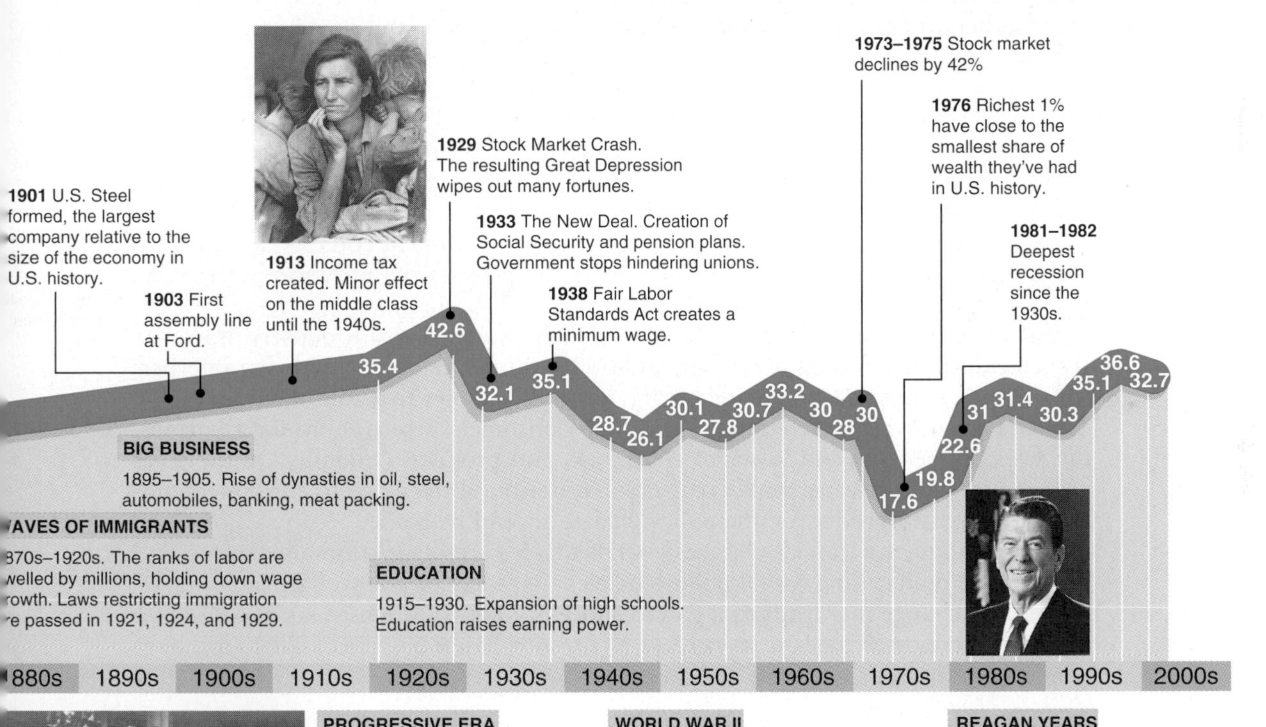

1901 U.S. Steel formed, the largest company relative to the size of the economy in U.S. history.
1903 First assembly line at Ford.
1913 Income tax created. Minor effect on the middle class until the 1940s.
1929 Stock Market Crash. The resulting Great Depression wipes out many fortunes.
1933 The New Deal. Creation of Social Security and pension plans. Government stops hindering unions.
1938 Fair Labor Standards Act creates a minimum wage.
1973–1975 Stock market declines by 42%
1976 Richest 1% have close to the smallest share of wealth they've had in U.S. history.
1981–1982 Deepest recession since the 1930s.
35.4
42.6
32.1
35.1
28.7
26.1
30.1
27.8
30.7
33.2
30
28
30
17.6
19.8
22.6
31
31.4
30.3
35.1
36.6
32.7
BIG BUSINESS
1895–1905. Rise of dynasties in oil, steel, automobiles, banking, meat packing.
AVES OF IMMIGRANTS
870s–1920s. The ranks of labor are welled by millions, holding down wage rowth. Laws restricting immigration e passed in 1921, 1924, and 1929.
EDUCATION
1915–1930. Expansion of high schools. Education raises earning power.
880s
1890s
1900s
1910s
1920s
1930s
1940s
1950s
1960s
1970s
1980s
1990s
2000s

PROGRESSIVE ERA

1900–1914. Inequality of wealth becomes a national political issue. Child labor laws, wage and hour laws, railroad rate controls created.

ROARING TWENTIES

1923–1929. Stock market boom expands richest people's fortunes.

WORLD WAR II

1941–1945. The draft dries up the labor supply, putting upward pressure on wages.

RAPID GROWTH

1950–1970. Helped by G.I. bill, many Americans get college educations, raising earning power. Strong unions and higher pay let the middle class buy homes and cars as never before, putting more wealth in their hands even as rising stock markets make the rich richer.

REAGAN YEARS

Top tax rate slashed from 70% to less than 30%, shifting tax burden to the middle class.

Efficiency

Many economists and political leaders make the value judgment that governments *should* use the Pareto principle and prefer allocations by which someone is made better off if no one else is harmed. That is, governments should allow voluntary trades, encourage competition, and otherwise try to prevent problems that reduce efficiency.

We can use the Pareto principle to rank allocations or government policies that alter allocations. The Pareto criterion ranks allocation x over allocation y if some people are better off at x and no one else is harmed. If that condition is met, we say that x is *Pareto superior* to y.

The Pareto principle cannot always be used to compare allocations. Because there are many possible Pareto-efficient allocations, however, a value judgment based on interpersonal comparisons must be made to choose between them. Issues of interpersonal comparisons often arise when we evaluate various government policies. If both allocation x and allocation y are Pareto efficient, we cannot use this criterion to rank them. For example, if Denise has all the goods in x and Jane has all of them in y, we cannot rank these allocations using the Pareto rule.

Suppose that when a country ends a ban on imports and allows free trade, domestic consumers benefit by many times more than domestic producers suffer. Nonetheless, this policy change does not meet the Pareto efficiency criterion that someone be made better off without anyone suffering. However, the government could adopt a more complex policy that meets the Pareto criterion. Because consumers benefit by more than producers suffer, the government could take enough of the gains from free trade from consumers to compensate the producers so that no one is harmed and some people benefit.

The government rarely uses policies by which winners subsidize losers, however. If such subsidization does not occur, additional value judgments involving interpersonal comparisons must be made before deciding whether to adopt the policy.

We've been using a welfare measure, W = consumer surplus + producer surplus, that weights benefits and losses to consumers and producers equally. On the basis of that particular interpersonal comparison criterion, if the gains to consumers outweigh the loss to producers, the policy change should be made.

Thus, calling for policy changes that lead to Pareto-superior allocations is a weaker rule than calling for all policy changes that increase the welfare measure W. Any policy change that leads to a Pareto-superior allocation must increase W; however, some policy changes that increase W are not Pareto superior: There are both winners and losers.

Equity

All animals are equal, but some animals are more equal than others.
—George Orwell

If we are unwilling to use the Pareto principle or if that criterion does not allow us to rank the relevant allocations, we must make additional value judgments to rank these allocations. A way to summarize these value judgments is to use a *social welfare function* that combines various consumers' utilities to provide a collective ranking of allocations. Loosely speaking, a social welfare function is a utility function for society.

We illustrate the use of a social welfare function using the pure exchange economy in which Jane and Denise trade wood and candy. There are many possible

Pareto-efficient allocations along the contract curve in Figure 10.4. Jane and Denise's utility levels vary along the contract curve. Figure 10.9 shows the *utility possibility frontier* (*UPF*): the set of utility levels corresponding to the Pareto-efficient allocations along the contract curve. Point *a* in panel a corresponds to the end of the contract curve at which Denise has all the goods, and *c* corresponds to the allocation at which Jane has all the goods.

The curves labeled W^1, W^2, and W^3 in panel a are *isowelfare curves* based on the social welfare function. These curves are similar to indifference curves for individuals. They summarize all the allocations with identical levels of welfare. Society maximizes its welfare at point *b*.

See Question 19.

Who decides on the welfare function? In most countries, government leaders make decisions about which allocations are most desirable. These officials may believe that transferring money from wealthy people to poor people raises welfare, or vice versa. When government officials choose a particular allocation, they are implicitly or explicitly judging which consumers are relatively deserving and hence should receive more goods than others.

Figure 10.9 Welfare Maximization.

Society maximizes welfare by choosing the allocation for which the highest possible isowelfare curve touches the utility possibility frontier, UPF. (a) The isowelfare curves have the shape of a typical indifference curve. (b) The isowelfare lines have a slope of −1, indicating that the utilities of both people are treated equally at the margin.

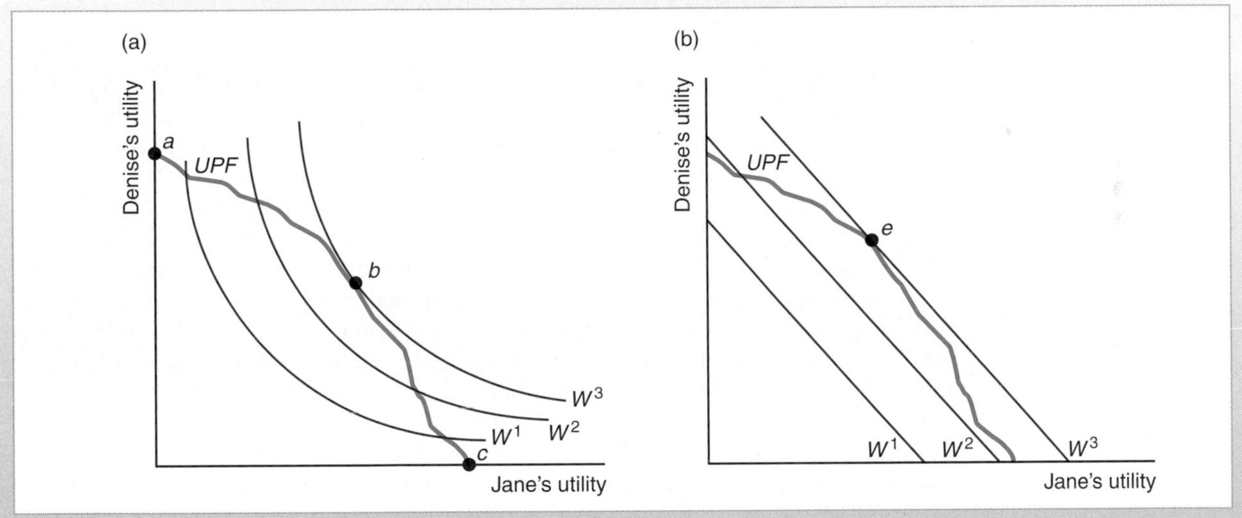

APPLICATION

An Unequal World

In most countries, the richest people control a very large share of the wealth, but the degree of inequality varies substantially across the world. If income were equally distributed, then the ratio of the share of income held by the "richest" 10% to that of the "poorest" 10% would equal 1. Instead, in 2007, the top 10% have 168 times the income of the bottom 10% in Bolivia, 16 times as much in the United States, but only 5 times as much in Japan.

	2007 Ratio of the Share of Income of the Richest 10% to the Poorest 10%
Bolivia	168
Namibia	129
Lesotho	105
Sierra Leone	87
Haiti	72
South Africa	65
Colombia	64
Mexico	25
China	22
United States	16
United Kingdom	14
Russian Federation	13
Australia	13
Canada	9
Germany	7
Pakistan	7
Sweden	6
Japan	5

Source: United Nations, *Human Development Reports*, **hdrstats.undp.org**, 2008.

Voting. In a democracy, important government policies that determine the allocation of goods are made by voting. Such democratic decision making is often difficult because people fundamentally disagree on how issues should be resolved and which groups of people should be favored.

In Chapter 4, we assumed that consumers could order all bundles of goods in terms of their preferences (completeness) and that their rank over goods was transitive.[7] Suppose now that consumers have preferences over allocations of goods across consumers. One possibility, as we assumed earlier, is that individuals care only about how many goods they receive—they don't care about how much others have. Another possibility is that because of envy, charity, pity, love, or other interpersonal feelings, individuals do care about how much everyone has.[8]

Let *a* be a particular allocation of goods that describes how much of each good an individual has. Each person can rank this allocation relative to Allocation *b*. For instance, individuals know whether they prefer an allocation by which everyone has equal amounts of all goods to another allocation by which people who work hard—or those of a particular skin color or religion—have relatively more goods than others.

Through voting, individuals express their rankings. One possible voting system requires that before the vote is taken, everyone agrees to be bound by the outcome in the sense that if a majority of people prefer Allocation *a* to Allocation *b*, then *a* is *socially preferred* to *b*.

[7]The transitivity (or *rationality*) assumption is that a consumer's preference over bundles is consistent in the sense that if the consumer weakly prefers Bundle *a* to Bundle *b* and weakly prefers Bundle *b* to Bundle *c*, the consumer weakly prefers Bundle *a* to Bundle *c*.

[8]To an economist, love is nothing more than interdependent utility functions. Thus, it's a mystery how each successive generation of economists is produced.

Using majority voting to determine which allocations are preferred by society sounds reasonable, doesn't it? Such a system might work well. For example, if all individuals have the same transitive preferences, the social ordering has the same transitive ranking as that of each individual.

Unfortunately, sometimes voting does not work well, and the resulting social ordering of allocations is not transitive. To illustrate this possibility, suppose that three people have the transitive preferences in Table 10.2. Individual 1 prefers Allocation *a* to Allocation *b* to Allocation *c*. The other two individuals have different preferred orderings. Two out of three of these individuals prefer *a* to *b*; two out of three prefer *b* to *c*; and two out of three prefer *c* to *a*. Thus, voting leads to nontransitive preferences, even though the preferences of each individual are transitive. As a result, there is no clearly defined socially preferred outcome. A majority of people prefers some other allocation to any particular allocation. Compared to Allocation *a*, a majority prefers *c*. Similarly, a majority prefers *b* over *c*, and a majority prefers *a* over *b*.

If people have this type of ranking of allocations, the chosen allocation will depend crucially on the order in which the vote is taken. Suppose that these three people first vote on whether they prefer *a* or *b* and then compare the winner to *c*. Because a majority prefers *a* to *b* in the first vote, they will compare *a* to *c* in the second vote, and *c* will be chosen. If instead they first compared *c* to *a* and the winner to *b*, then *b* will be chosen. Thus, the outcome depends on the political skill of various factions in determining the order of voting.

Similar problems arise with other types of voting schemes. Kenneth Arrow (1951), who received a Nobel Prize in Economics in part for his work on social decision making, proved a startling and depressing result about democratic voting. This result is often referred to as Arrow's Impossibility Theorem. Arrow suggested that a socially desirable decision making system, or social welfare function, should satisfy the following criteria:

- Social preferences should be complete (Chapter 4) and transitive, like individual preferences.
- If everyone prefers Allocation *a* to Allocation *b*, *a* should be socially preferred to *b*.
- Society's ranking of *a* and *b* should depend only on individuals' ordering of these two allocations, not on how they rank other alternatives.
- Dictatorship is not allowed; social preferences must not reflect the preferences of only a single individual.

Although each of these criteria seems reasonable—indeed, innocuous—Arrow proved that it is impossible to find a social decision-making rule that *always* satisfies all of these criteria. His result indicates that *democratic decision making* may fail—not that *democracy* must fail. After all, if everyone agrees on a ranking, these four criteria are satisfied.

If society is willing to give up one of these criteria, a democratic decision-making rule can guarantee that the other three criteria are met. For example, if we give up

Table 10.2 Preferences over Allocations of Three People.

	Individual 1	Individual 2	Individual 3
First choice	*a*	*b*	*c*
Second choice	*b*	*c*	*a*
Third choice	*c*	*a*	*b*

the third criterion, often referred to as the *independence of irrelevant alternatives*, certain complicated voting schemes in which individuals rank their preferences can meet the other criteria.

APPLICATION

How You Vote Matters

The 15 members of a city council must decide whether to build a new road (R), repair the high school (H), or install new street lights (L). Each councilor lists the options in order of preference. Six favor L to H to R; five prefer R to H to L; and four desire H over R over L.

One of the proponents of street lights suggests a plurality vote where everyone would cast a single vote for his or her favorite project. Plurality voting would result in six votes for L, five for R, and four for H, so that lights would win.

"Not so fast," responds a council member who favors roads. Given that H was the least favorite first choice, he suggests a run-off between L and R. Since the four members whose first choice was H prefer R to L, roads would win by nine votes to six.

A supporter of schools is horrified by these self-serving approaches to voting. She calls for pairwise comparisons. A majority of 10 would choose H over R, and nine would prefer H to L. Consequently, although the high school gets the least number of first-place votes, it has the broadest appeal in pairwise comparisons.

Finally, suppose the council uses a voting method developed by Jean-Charles de Borda in 1770 (to elect members to the Academy of Sciences in Paris), where, in an n-person race, a person's first choice gets n votes, the second choice gets $n - 1$, and so forth. (This method has been used in Australia and Slovenia.) Here H gets 34 votes, R receives 29, and L trails with 27, and so the high school project is backed. Thus, the outcome of an election or other vote may depend on the voting procedures used.

Social Welfare Functions. How would you rank various allocations if you were asked to vote? Philosophers, economists, newspaper columnists, politicians, radio talk show hosts, and other deep thinkers have suggested various rules that society might use to decide which allocations are better than others. Basically, all these systems answer the question of which individuals' preferences should be given more weight in society's decision making. Determining how much weight to give to the preferences of various members of society is usually the key step in determining a social welfare function.

Probably the simplest and most egalitarian rule is that every member of society is given exactly the same bundle of goods. If no further trading is allowed, this rule results in complete equality in the allocation of goods.

Jeremy Bentham (1748–1832) and his followers (including John Stuart Mill), the utilitarian philosophers, suggested that society should maximize the sum of the utilities of all members of society. Their social welfare function is the sum of the utilities of every member of society. The utilities of all people in society are given equal weight.[9] If U_i is the utility of Individual i and there are n people, the utilitarian welfare function is

$$W = U_1 + U_2 + \cdots + U_n.$$

[9]It is difficult to compare utilities across individuals because the scaling of utilities across individuals is arbitrary (Chapters 4 and 9). A rule that avoids this utility comparison is to maximize a welfare measure that equally weights consumer surplus and producer surplus, which are denominated in dollars.

This social welfare function may not lead to an egalitarian distribution of goods. Indeed, under this system, an allocation is judged superior, all else the same, if people who get the most pleasure from consuming certain goods are given more of those goods.

Panel b of Figure 10.9 shows some isowelfare lines corresponding to the utilitarian welfare function. These lines have a slope of –1 because the utilities of both parties are weighted equally. In the figure, welfare is maximized at *e*.

A generalization of the utilitarian approach assigns different weights to various individuals' utilities. If the weight assigned to Individual *i* is αi, this generalized utilitarian welfare function is

$$W = \alpha_1 U_1 + \alpha_2 U_2 + \cdots + \alpha_n U_n.$$

Society could give greater weight to adults, hardworking people, or those who meet other criteria. Under South Africa's former apartheid system, the utilities of people with white skin were given more weight than those of people with other skin colors.

John Rawls (1971), a philosopher at Harvard, believed that society should maximize the well-being of the worst-off member of society, who is the person with the lowest level of utility. In the social welfare function, all the weight should be placed on the utility of the person with the lowest utility level. The Rawlsian welfare function is

$$W = \min \{U_1, U_2, \cdots, U_n\}.$$

Rawls' rule leads to a relatively egalitarian distribution of goods.

One final rule, which is frequently espoused by various members of Congress and by wealthy landowners in less-developed countries, is to maintain the status quo. Exponents of this rule believe that the current allocation is the best possible allocation. They argue against any reallocation of resources from one individual to another. Under this rule, the final allocation is likely to be very unequal. Why else would the wealthy want it?

See Questions 20 and 21.

All of these rules or social welfare functions reflect value judgments in which interpersonal comparisons are made. Because each reflects value judgments, we cannot compare them on scientific grounds.

Efficiency Versus Equity

Given a particular social welfare function, *society might prefer an inefficient allocation to an efficient one*. We can show this result by comparing two allocations. In Allocation *a*, you have everything and everyone else has nothing. This allocation is Pareto efficient: We can't make others better off without harming you. In Allocation *b*, everyone has an equal amount of all goods. Allocation *b* is not Pareto efficient: I would be willing to trade all my zucchini for just about anything else. Despite Allocation *b*'s inefficiency, most people probably prefer *b* to *a*.

Although society might prefer an inefficient Allocation *b* to an efficient Allocation *a*, according to most social welfare functions, society would prefer some efficient allocation to *b*. Suppose that Allocation *c* is the competitive equilibrium that would be obtained if people were allowed to trade starting from Endowment *b*, in which everyone has an equal share of all goods. By the utilitarian social welfare functions, Allocation *b* might be socially preferred to Allocation *a*, but Allocation *c* is certainly socially preferred to *b*. After all, if everyone is as well off or better off in Allocation *c* than in *b*, *c* must be better than *b* regardless of weights on individuals' utilities. According to the egalitarian rule, however, *b* is preferred to *c* because only strict equality matters. Thus, by most of the well-known social welfare functions, but not all, *there is an efficient allocation that is socially preferred to an inefficient allocation.*

Competitive equilibrium may not be very equitable even though it is Pareto efficient. Consequently, societies that believe in equity may tax the rich to give to the poor. If the money taken from the rich is given directly to the poor, society moves from one Pareto-efficient allocation to another.

Sometimes, however, in an attempt to achieve greater equity, efficiency is reduced. For example, advocates for the poor argue that providing public housing to the destitute leads to an allocation that is superior to the original competitive equilibrium. This reallocation isn't efficient: The poor view themselves as better off receiving an amount of money equal to what the government spends on public housing. They could spend the money on the type of housing they like—rather than the type the government provides—or they could spend some of the money on food or other goods.[10]

Unfortunately, there is frequently a conflict between a society's goal of efficiency and the goal of achieving an equitable allocation. Even when the government redistributes money from one group to another, there are significant costs to this redistribution. If tax collectors and other government bureaucrats could be put to work producing rather than redistributing, total output would increase. Similarly, income taxes discourage people from working as hard as they otherwise would (Chapter 5). Nonetheless, probably few people believe that the status quo is optimal and that the government should engage in no redistribution at all (though some members of Congress seem to believe that we should redistribute from the poor to the rich).

SUMMARY

1. **General Equilibrium.** A shock to one market may have a spillover effect in another market. A general-equilibrium analysis takes account of the direct effects of a shock in a market and the spillover effects in other markets. In contrast, a partial-equilibrium analysis (such as we used in earlier chapters) looks only at one market and ignores the spillover effects in other markets. The partial-equilibrium and general-equilibrium effects can differ.
2. **Trading Between Two People.** If people make all the trades they want, the resulting equilibrium will be Pareto efficient: By moving from this equilibrium, we cannot make one person better off without harming another person. At a Pareto-efficient equilibrium, the marginal rates of substitution between people are equal because their indifference curves are tangent.
3. **Competitive Exchange.** Competition, in which all traders are price takers, leads to an allocation in which the ratio of relative prices equals the marginal rates of substitution of each person. Thus, *every competitive equilibrium is Pareto efficient.* Moreover, *any Pareto-efficient equilibrium can be obtained by competition, given an appropriate endowment.*
4. **Production and Trading.** When one person can produce more of one good and another person can produce more of another good using the same inputs, trading can result in greater combined production.
5. **Efficiency and Equity.** The Pareto efficiency criterion reflects a value judgment that a change from one allocation to another is desirable if it makes someone better off without harming anyone else. This criterion does not allow all allocations to be ranked, because some people may be better off with one allocation and others may be better off with another. Majority voting may not result in a consensus, transitive ordering of allocations either. Economists, philosophers, and others have proposed many criteria for ranking allocations, as summarized in welfare functions. Society may use such a welfare function to choose among Pareto-efficient (or other) allocations.

---

[10]Letting the poor decide how to spend their income is efficient by our definition, even if they spend it on "sin goods" such as cigarettes, liquor, or illicit drugs. A similar argument was made regarding food stamps in Chapter 4.

QUESTIONS

■ = *exercise is available on MyEconLab;* * = *answer appears at the back of this book;* C = *use of calculus may be necessary;* W = *audio-slideshow answer by James Dearden is available in Textbook Resources on MyEconLab.*

1. The market demand for medical checkups per day, Q_F, is $Q_F = 25(200 - p_F)$, where p_F represents the price of a checkup. The market demand for the number of dental checkups per day, Q_T, is $Q_T = 100(150 - p_T)/3$, where p_T represents the price of a dental checkup. The market supply of medical checkups is $Q_F = 50p_F - 10p_T$. The market supply of dentists is $Q_T = 50p_T - 10p_F$. The supplies are linked because people decide whether to be doctors and dentists on the basis of relative earnings.
   a. The quantity supplied of medical checkups depends on the price of dental checkups. What does the supply function property imply about the length of time medical doctors and dentists, as well as those considering entering each profession, have to respond to the price changes?
   b. What is the equilibrium number of medical and dental checkups? What are the equilibrium prices?
   c. Suppose that, instead of determining the price of medical checkups by a market process, large health insurance companies set their reimbursement rates, effectively determining the prices. A medical doctor receives $35 per checkup from the insurance company, and patients pay only $10. How many checkups do doctors offer? What are the equilibrium quantity and price of dental checkups?
   d. What is the effect on the equilibrium salaries of dentists of a shift from a competitive medical checkup market to a market in which insurance companies dictate medical doctor payments? W

*2. What is the effect of a subsidy of s per hour on labor in only one sector of the economy on the equilibrium wage, total employment, and employment in the covered and uncovered sectors?

3. Initially, all workers are paid a wage of w_1 per hour. The government taxes the cost of labor by t per hour only in the "covered" sector of the economy (if the wage received by workers in the covered sector is w_2 per hour, firms pay $w_2 + t$ per hour). Show how the wages in the covered and uncovered sectors are determined in the posttax equilibrium. Compared to the pretax equilibrium, what happens to total employment, L, employment in the covered sector, L_c, and employment in the uncovered sector, L_u?

4. Suppose that the government gives a fixed subsidy of T per firm in one sector of the economy to encourage firms to hire more workers. What is the effect on the equilibrium wage, total employment, and employment in the covered and uncovered sectors?

5. Competitive firms located in Africa sell their output only in Europe and the United States (which do not produce the good themselves). The industry's supply curve is upward sloping. Europe puts a tariff of t per unit on the good but the United States does not. What is the effect of the tariff on total quantity of the good sold, the quantity sold in Europe and in the United States, and equilibrium price(s)?

6. Peaches are sold in a competitive market. There are two types of demanders: consumers who eat fresh peaches and canners. If the government places a binding price ceiling on only peaches sold directly to consumers, what happens to prices and quantities sold for each use?

7. Initially, electricity is sold in New York at a competitive single price. Now suppose that New York restricts the quantity of electricity its citizens can buy. Show what happens to the price of electricity and the quantities sold in New York.

8. A competitive industry with an upward-sloping supply curve sells Q_h of its product in its home country and Q_f in a foreign country, so the total quantity it sells is $Q = Q_h + Q_f$. No one else produces this product. There is no cost of shipping. Determine the equilibrium price and quantity in each country. Now the foreign government imposes a binding quota, $\underline{Q}$ ($< Q_f$ at the original price). What happens to prices and quantities in both the home and the foreign markets?

9. Philadelphia collects an *ad valorem* tax of 4.26% on its residents' earnings (see the "Urban Flight" application), unlike the surrounding counties. Show the effect of this tax on the equilibrium wage, total employment, employment in Philadelphia, and employment in the surrounding areas.

10. A central city imposes a rent control law that places a binding ceiling on the rent that can be charged for an apartment. The suburbs of this city do not have a rent control law. What happens to the rental prices in the suburbs and to the equilibrium number of apartments in the total metropolitan area, in the city, and in the suburbs? (For simplicity, you may assume that people are indifferent as to whether they live in the city or the suburbs.)

11. Initially, Michael has 10 candy bars and 5 cookies, and Tony has 5 candy bars and 10 cookies. After trading, Michael has 12 candy bars and 3 cookies. In an Edgeworth box, label the initial Allocation A and the new Allocation B. Draw some indifference curves that are consistent with this trade being optimal for both Michael and Tony.

12. The two people in a pure exchange economy have identical utility functions. Will they ever want to trade?

13. Two people trade two goods that they cannot produce. Suppose that one consumer's indifference curves are bowed away from the origin—the usual type of curves—but the other's are concave to the origin. In an Edgeworth box, show that a point of tangency between the two consumers' indifference curves is not a Pareto-efficient bundle. (*Hint*: Identify another allocation that is Pareto superior.)

14. In an Edgeworth box, illustrate that a Pareto-efficient equilibrium, point a, can be obtained by competition, given an appropriate endowment. Do so by identifying an initial endowment point, b, located somewhere other than at point a, such that the competitive equilibrium (resulting from competitive exchange) is a. Explain.

*15. In panel c of Figure 10.6, the joint production possibility frontier is concave to the origin. When the two individual production possibility frontiers are combined, however, the resulting *PPF* could have been drawn so that it was convex to the origin. How do we know which of these two ways of drawing the *PPF* to use?

16. Suppose that Britain can produce 10 units of cloth or 5 units of food per day (or any linear combination) with available resources and Greece can produce 2 units of food per day or 1 unit of cloth (or any combination). Britain has an *absolute advantage* over Greece in producing both goods. Does it still make sense for these countries to trade?

*17. Pat and Chris can spend their nonleisure time working either in the marketplace or at home (preparing dinner, taking care of children, doing repairs). In the marketplace, Pat earns a higher wage, $w_p = \$20$, than Chris, $w_c = \$10$. Discuss how living together is likely to affect how much each of them works in the marketplace. In particular, discuss what effect the marriage has on their individual and combined budget constraint (Chapters 4 and 5) and their labor-leisure choice (Section 5.5, "Deriving Labor Supply Curves"). In your discussion, take into account the theory of comparative advantage.

18. If Jane and Denise have identical, linear production possibility frontiers, are there gains to trade? Why?

19. A society consists of two people with utilities U_1 and U_2, and the social welfare function is $W = \alpha_1 U_1 + \alpha_1 U_1$. Draw a utility possibilities frontier similar to the ones in Figure 10.9. When social welfare is maximized, show that as α_1/α_2 increases, Person 1 benefits and Person 2 is harmed. W

20. Give an example of a social welfare function that leads to the egalitarian allocation that everyone should be given exactly the same bundle of goods.

21. Suppose that society used the "opposite" of a Rawlsian welfare function: It tried to maximize the well-being of the best-off member of society. Write this welfare function. What allocation maximizes welfare in this society?

PROBLEMS

22. The demand functions for Q_1 and Q_2 are

$$Q_1 = 10 - 2p_1 + p_2,$$
$$Q_2 = 10 - 2p_2 + p_1,$$

and there are five units of each good. What is the general equilibrium?

23. The demands for two goods depend on the prices of Good 1 and Good 2, p_1 and p_2,

$$Q_1 = 15 - 3p_1 + p_2,$$
$$Q_2 = 6 - 2p_2 + p_1,$$

but each supply curve depends on only its own price:

$$Q_1 = 2 + p_1,$$
$$Q_2 = 1 + p_2.$$

Solve for the equilibrium: p_1, p_2, Q_1, and Q_2.

24. The demand curve in Sector 1 of the labor market is $L_1 = a - bw$. The demand curve in Sector 2 is $L_2 = c - dw$. The supply curve of labor for the entire market is $L = e + fw$. In equilibrium, $L_1 + L_2 = L$.

a. Solve for the equilibrium with no minimum wage.

b. Solve for the equilibrium at which the minimum wage is $\underline{w}$ in Sector 1 ("the covered sector") only.

c. Solve for the equilibrium at which the minimum wage $\underline{w}$ applies to the entire labor market.

*25. In a pure exchange economy with two goods, G and H, the two traders have Cobb-Douglas utility functions. Amos' utility is

$$U_a = (G_a)^{\alpha}(H_{\alpha})^{1-\alpha},$$

and Elise's is

$$U_e - (G_e)^{\beta}(H_e)^{1-\beta}.$$

What are their marginal rates of substitution? Between them, Amos and Elise own 100 units of G and 50 units of H. Thus, if Amos has G_a and H_a, Elise has $G_e = 100 - G_a$ and $H_e = 50 - H_a$. Solve for their contract curve.

26. Adrienne and Deepa consume pizza, Z, and cola, C. Adrienne's utility function is $U_A = Z_A C_A$, and Deepa's is

$$Z_D^{0.5} C_D^{0.5}.$$

Adrienne's marginal utility of pizza is

$$MU_A^Z = C_A.$$

Similarly,

$$MU_C^A = Z_A,$$

$$MU_Z^D = \tfrac{1}{2} Z_D^{-0.5} C_D^{0.5}$$

and

$$MU_C^D = \tfrac{1}{2} Z_D^{0.5} C_D^{-0.5}.$$

Their endowments are $Z_A = 10$, $C_A = 20$, $Z_D = 20$, $C_D = 10$.

a. What are the marginal rates of substitution for each person?

b. What is the formula for the contract curve? Draw an Edgeworth box and indicate the contract curve.

27. Mexico and the United States can both produce food and toys. Mexico has 100 workers and the United States has 300 workers. If they do not trade, the United States consumes 10 units of food and 10 toys; and Mexico consumes 5 units of food and 1 toy. The following table shows how many workers are necessary to produce each good:

	Mexico	United States
Workers per unit of food	10	10
Workers per toy	50	20

a. In the absence of trade, how many units of food and toys can the United States produce? How many can Mexico produce?

b. Which country has a comparative advantage in producing food? In producing toys?

c. Draw the production possibility for each country and show where the two produce without trade. Label the axes accurately.

d. Draw the production possibility frontier with trade.

e. Show that both countries can benefit from trade.

CROSS-CHAPTER ANALYSIS

Outsourcing and the World Trade Organization

One of the most hotly debated current issues concerns free trade and outsourcing. For years, protesters have made it very difficult for countries to hold meetings of the World Trade Organization (WTO). The WTO's objective is to promote free trade among its 151 member countries. World trade was $11.8 trillion in 2006. As part of this agreement, member countries are supposed to remove many domestic distortions, such as by eliminating subsidies to farmers and others. Protesters complain that the WTO contributes to world poverty and pollution, and they object to outsourcing jobs. (A firm *outsources* if it retains others to provide services that the firm would otherwise perform itself.)

Background

The U.S. Constitution guarantees free trade among the 50 U.S. states. However, free trade occurs between the United States and other countries only if the countries agree to it. International trade has become increasingly important for the U.S. economy. Today, trade is over a quarter of the U.S. gross domestic product, up from 10% in 1970—the largest such increase of any major developed country over this period.

The United States has signed free-trade agreements—which eliminate or reduce tariffs and quotas—and liberalized rules on foreign investment to increase trade. The North American Free Trade Agreement with Canada and Mexico has been in effect for over a decade. The United States also has pacts with Singapore, Israel, Jordan, and Chile. In 2004, it established agreements with Australia, Bahrain, and Morocco. In 2005, the United States signed the Central American Free Trade Agreement (with Nicaragua, El Salvador, Honduras, Costa Rica, and Guatemala). The United States signed an agreement with Peru in 2007.

Arguments for and Against. The basic result from economic theory is that in a perfectly competitive market, a country that engages in free trade gains enough to improve everyone's lot (see the discussion of trade in Chapter 9 and of comparative advantage in Chapter 10). Business and jobs lost in one sector are more than offset by gains in other sectors.

Nonetheless, the WTO has been attacked from both the left and the right. Many U.S. opponents criticize restrictions on the United States' ability to subsidize domestic groups. Some people complain because the WTO, a foreign body, is empowered to enforce global commerce rules with the imposition of economic sanctions on member countries, although a country can withdraw from the agreement.

WTO foes primarily raise three economic objections. They contend that (1) free trade harms some people, such as poor farmers in developing countries who suffer when world agricultural prices fall due to international trade; (2) the WTO weakens environmental, health, and other protections; and (3) WTO objectives lead to job loss.

As part of the WTO agreement, countries must not establish domestic policies that unreasonably block trade, including certain food safety laws and environmental policies. A country must show that a given food safety law really aims to protect public health rather than to serve as a backdoor method of excluding imports. A very large percentage of all food trade (by one estimate, 92% in 1986) was affected by such nontariff barriers before the formation of the WTO. For example, in 1997, a WTO panel declared that the European Union's public health ban on imports of beef produced with artificial growth hormones violated international trade rules. A 1997 article in *The Ecologist* claimed that 80% of U.S. environmental standards and legislation was threatened by the WTO. In 1996, in response to complaints by Venezuela and Brazil, the WTO ruled against one aspect of the U.S. Clean Air Act rules concerning mandatory gasoline cleanliness standards for conventional and reformulated gasoline.

Outsourcing. Many U.S. groups are incensed by the outsourcing of U.S. jobs, particularly workers in the service sector. By some reports, U.S. financial services firms saved $2 billion per year by outsourcing to India, giving this sector a strong incentive to outsource.

Harrison and McMillan (2006) report that multinational manufacturing firms shed more than 3 million U.S. jobs from 1977 to 1999. However, the amount of outsourcing of high-tech and other skilled jobs is still quite limited. U.S. jobs sent offshore over the past three years range from an estimated 250,000 to 500,000, a small fraction of the 140 million U.S. workers. In the first quarter of 2004, the U.S. Department of Labor reported that 4,633 U.S. workers were laid off because their jobs were sent overseas.

According to former WTO director Supachai Panitchpakdi, for every U.S. job threatened by imports, a growing number of high-paid, high-skill jobs are created by exports. Exports are responsible for 12 million U.S. jobs today, compared to only 7 million a decade ago. He also contends that many of those jobs are in aerospace, finance and information technology, and other sectors that pay 10% more than the average U.S. wage. These new jobs more than offset the jobs lost to international outsourcing. By one estimate (see Mankiw and Swagel, 2006), every dollar of outsourcing results in an increase of U.S. income of $1.12 to $1.14.

While the debate flames in the United States about jobs moving to India and other foreign countries, Europeans are protesting that high-paying R&D jobs are being outsourced to the United States from Europe. Indeed, *insourcing*, whereby foreign companies buy U.S. services, has grown substantially, and the United States had a $74 billion trade surplus in 2002. In 2001 foreign companies employed 6.4 million U.S. workers.

Compensating Losers. Regardless of their political views, most economists believe in free trade in principle. Due to comparative advantage (Chapter 10), trade leads to a more efficient market outcome (Chapters 9 and 10). So are people who attack free trade and outsourcing simply ignorant or venal? Not necessarily.

Once a nation starts trading, it reduces the production of some goods and services so that it can concentrate on those in which it has a comparative advantage (Chapter 10). As a consequence, some people gain and some people lose from free trade. Firms in noncompetitive sectors may lose sunk capital. Their workers may suffer from unemployment for a while. The gains in the other sectors are large enough to compensate the losers. However, if society fails to compensate them, they will be adamantly (and reasonably) opposed to free trade.

As economist Hal Varian (2004) and cartoonist Garry Trudeau (see the *Doonesbury* panels below) explain, we can see the gains from trade in services by imagining that workers can subcontract. Suppose that you are hired to perform a service, such as designing a Web page, for $20 an hour. Further, imagine that you can find a very competent, reliable worker in India or Russia who can do the job as well as you can for $5 an hour. You can subcontract with that other worker, pocket $15 an hour, and take on an additional job with your free time—or enjoy your extra leisure time. Clearly, you would favor this plan. However, if your firm fired you and outsourced your job to a foreign worker, you would be outraged over your loss. This example illustrates that the debate on outsourcing jobs concerns who reaps the benefits and who suffers the losses rather than whether or not there is a net gain to society. As with any desirable trade, the winners can compensate the losers so that everyone benefits.

Rather than giving up the benefits of free trade, both domestic proponents and opponents of free trade are now calling for more compensation for the losers. In 2008, the U.S. Trade Adjustment Assistance program provides $220 million to train workers who lost their jobs due to foreign competition for new jobs. However, the United States spends only 0.5% of its gross domestic product to assist displaced workers, compared to 0.9% in the United Kingdom, 3.1% in Germany, and 3.7% in Denmark (Farrell, 2006).

Market Imperfections and the Desirability of Free Trade. According to economic theory, everyone can gain from free trade if losers are compensated and if domestic markets are perfectly competitive—not distorted by taxes, tariffs, the absence of insurance markets, pollution, or other externalities (Chapter 18), or other market imperfections.

According to the Theory of the Second Best, if an economy has at least two market distortions, correcting one of them may either increase or decrease welfare. For example, if a country has two tariffs, eliminating only one may not increase welfare. In the following task, we illustrate this theory.

Task

A country that produces wheat is a price taker on the world wheat market: The world price is *pw*. Using an analysis similar to that in Section 9.6, show that the country's total welfare is greater if it permits rather than bans free trade. Now suppose that the home government subsidizes its agricultural sector with a payment of *s* per unit of output. What are the welfare effects of permitting trade?

Analysis

To analyze this question, we use the trade model from Chapter 9. Panel a of the figure shows the gain to trade in the usual case. The domestic supply curve, *S*, is upward sloping, but the home country can import as much as it wants at the world price, p_w. In the free trade equilibrium, e_1, the equilibrium quantity is Q_1 and the equilibrium price is the world price, p_w. With a ban on imports, the equilibrium is e_2, quantity falls to Q_2, and price rises to p_2. Consequently, the deadweight loss from the ban is area *D*. (See the discussion of Figure 9.10 for a more thorough analysis.)

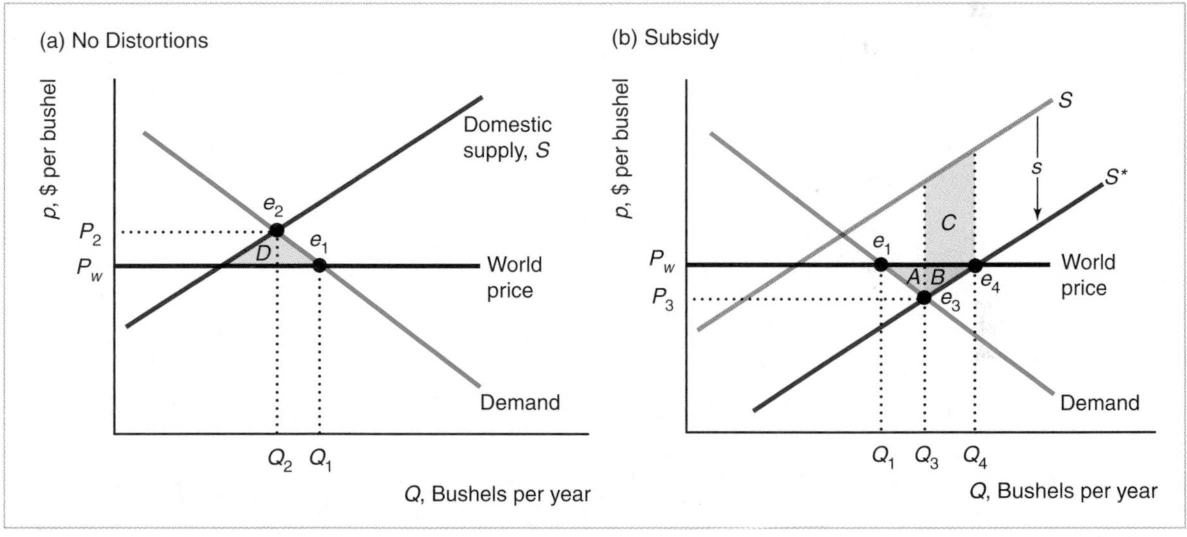

Now suppose that wheat is subsidized. The subsidy creates a distortion: excess production (Chapter 9). The per-unit subsidy *s* causes the supply curve to shift down from *S* to *S** in panel b. If there is a ban on trade, the equilibrium is at e_3, with a larger quantity, Q_3, than in the original free-trade equilibrium and a lower consumer price, p_3. Because the true marginal cost (the height of the *S* curve at Q_3) is above the consumer price, there is deadweight loss.

If free trade is permitted, the Theory of the Second Best tells us that welfare does not necessarily rise, because the country still has the subsidy distortion. The free-trade equilibrium is e_4. Firms sell all their quantity, Q_4, at the world price, with Q_1 going to domestic consumers and $Q_4 - Q_1$ to consumers elsewhere. The private gain to trade—ignoring the government's cost of providing the subsidy—is areas $A + B$ (see the discussion of Figure 9.10). However, the expansion of domestic output increases the government's cost of the subsidy by areas $B + C$ (the height of this area is the distance between the two supply curves, which is the subsidy, *s*, and the length is the extra output sold). Thus, if area *C* is greater than area *A*, there is a net welfare loss from permitting trade. As the diagram is drawn, C is greater than *A*, so allowing trade lowers welfare, given that the subsidy is provided.

Should the country prohibit free trade? No, the country should allow free trade and eliminate the subsidy in order to maximize welfare.

Questions

Answers are available at the back of the book.

1. If there are no distortions (the situation in panel a), how do we know that winners from trade can compensate losers and still have enough left over to benefit themselves?
2. Redraw panel b to show that it is possible for trade to increase welfare even with the subsidy.

Monopoly

Monopoly: one parrot.

A **monopoly** is the only supplier of a good for which there is no close substitute. Monopolies have been common since ancient times. In the fifth century B.C., the Greek philosopher Thales gained control of most of the olive presses during a year of exceptionally productive harvests. Similarly, the ancient Egyptian pharaohs controlled the sale of food. In England, until Parliament limited the practice in 1624, kings granted monopoly rights called royal charters or patents to court favorites. Today, virtually every country grants a *patent*—an exclusive right to sell that lasts for a limited period of time—to an inventor of a new product, process, substance, or design. Until 1999, the U.S. government gave one company the right to be the sole registrar of Internet domain names.

monopoly
the only supplier of a good for which there is no close substitute

A monopoly can *set* its price—it is not a price taker like a competitive firm. A monopoly's output is the market output, and the demand curve a monopoly faces is the market demand curve. Because the market demand curve is downward sloping, the monopoly (unlike a competitive firm) doesn't lose all its sales if it raises its price. As a consequence, the monopoly sets its price above marginal cost to maximize its profit. Consumers buy less at this high monopoly price than they would at the competitive price, which equals marginal cost.

In this chapter, we examine eight main topics

1. **Monopoly Profit Maximization.** Like all firms, a monopoly maximizes its profit by setting its price or output so that its marginal revenue equals its marginal cost.
2. **Effects of a Shift of the Demand Curve.** A shift of the demand curve may have a wider range of effects on a monopoly than on a competitive market.
3. **Market Power.** How much the monopoly's price is above its marginal cost depends on the shape of the demand curve it faces.
4. **Welfare Effects of Monopoly.** By setting its price above marginal cost, a monopoly creates a deadweight loss.
5. **Cost Advantages That Create Monopolies.** A firm can use a cost advantage over other firms (due, say, to control of a key input or economies of scale) to become a monopoly.
6. **Government Actions That Create Monopolies.** Governments create monopolies by establishing government monopoly firms, limiting entry of other firms to create a private monopoly, and issuing patents, which are temporary monopoly rights.
7. **Government Actions That Reduce Market Power.** The welfare loss of a monopoly can be reduced or eliminated if the government regulates the price the monopoly charges or allows other firms to enter the market.

8. **Network Externalities, Behavioral Economics, and Monopoly Decisions over Time.** If its current sales affect a monopoly's future demand curve, a monopoly that maximizes its long-run profit may choose not to maximize its short-run profit.

11.1 Monopoly Profit Maximization

All firms, including competitive firms and monopolies, maximize their profits by setting *marginal revenue equal to marginal cost* (Chapter 8). We already know how to derive the marginal cost curve of a monopoly from its cost curve (Chapter 7). We now derive the monopoly's marginal revenue curve and then use the marginal revenue and marginal cost curves to examine the monopoly's profit-maximizing behavior.

Marginal Revenue

A firm's marginal revenue curve depends on its demand curve. We will show that a monopoly's marginal revenue curve lies below its demand curve at any positive quantity because its demand curve is downward sloping.

Marginal Revenue and Price. A firm's demand curve shows the price, p, it receives for selling a given quantity, q. The price is the *average revenue* the firm receives, so a firm's revenue is $R = pq$.

A firm's *marginal revenue*, MR, is the change in its revenue from selling one more unit. A firm that earns ΔR more revenue when it sells Δq extra units of output has a marginal revenue (Chapter 8) of

$$MR = \Delta R/\Delta q.$$

If the firm sells exactly one more unit, $\Delta q = 1$, its marginal revenue is $MR = \Delta R$.

The marginal revenue of a monopoly differs from that of a competitive firm because the monopoly faces a downward-sloping demand curve unlike the competitive firm. The competitive firm in panel a of Figure 11.1 faces a horizontal demand curve at the market price, p_1. Because its demand curve is horizontal, the competitive firm can sell another unit of output without dropping its price. As a result, the marginal revenue it receives from selling the last unit of output is the market price.

Initially, the competitive firm sells q units of output at the market price of p_1, so its revenue, R_1, is area A, which is a rectangle that is $p_1 \times q$. If the firm sells one more unit, its revenue is $R_2 = A + B$, where area B is $p_1 \times 1 = p_1$. The competitive firm's marginal revenue equals the market price:

$$\Delta R = R_2 - R_1 = (A + B) - A = B = p_1.$$

A monopoly faces a downward-sloping market demand curve, as in panel b of Figure 11.1. (We've called the number of units of output a firm sells q and the output of all the firms in a market, or market output, Q. Because a monopoly is the only firm in the market, there is no distinction between q and Q, so we use Q to describe both the firm's and the market's output.) The monopoly, which is initially selling Q units at p_1, can sell one extra unit only if the price falls to p_2.

The monopoly's initial revenue, $p_1 \times Q$, is $R_1 = A + C$. When it sells the extra unit, its revenue, $p_2 \times (Q + 1)$, is $R_2 = A + B$. Thus, its marginal revenue is

$$\Delta R = R_2 - R_1 = (A + B) - (A + C) = B - C.$$

Figure 11.1 Average and Marginal Revenue.

The demand curve shows the average revenue or price per unit of output sold. (a) The competitive firm's marginal revenue, area B, equals the market price, p_1. (b) The monopoly's marginal revenue is less than the price p_2 by area C (the revenue lost due to a lower price on the Q units originally sold).

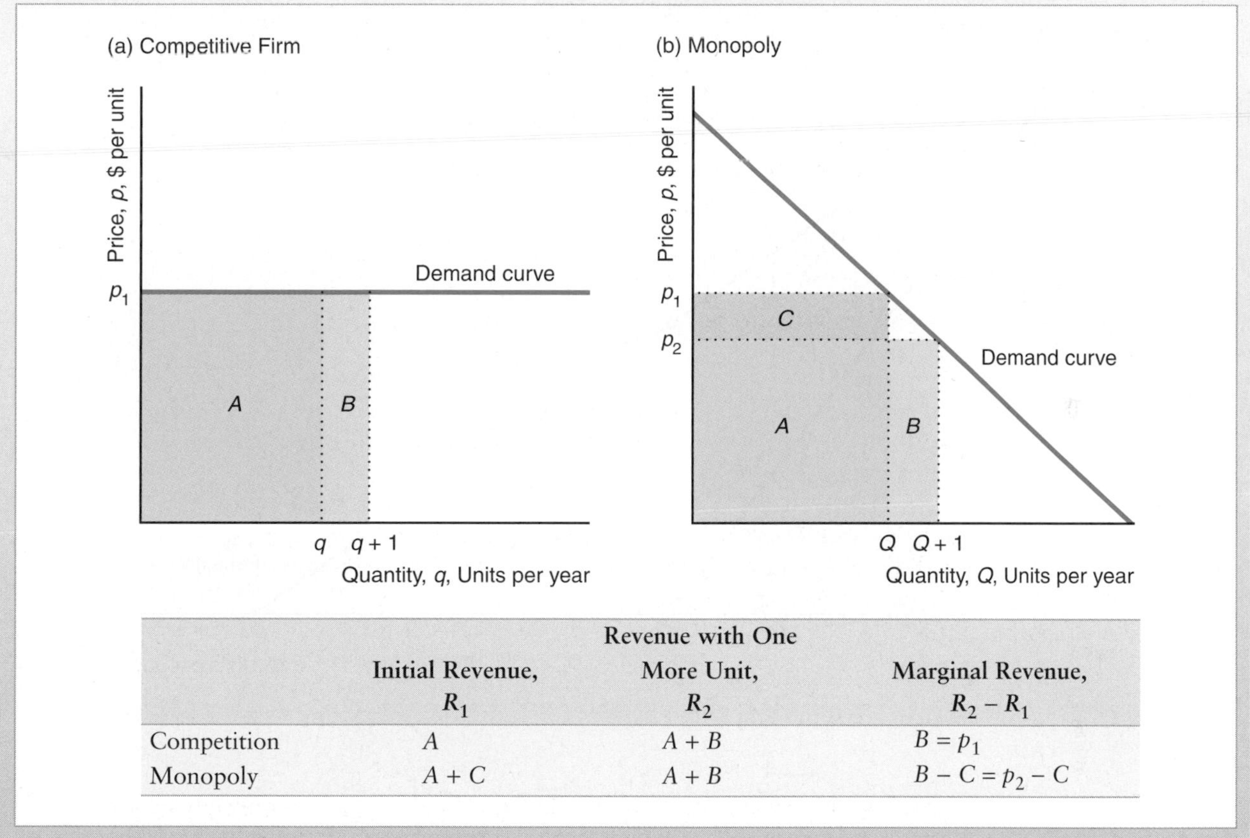

	Initial Revenue, R_1	Revenue with One More Unit, R_2	Marginal Revenue, $R_2 - R_1$
Competition	A	$A + B$	$B = p_1$
Monopoly	$A + C$	$A + B$	$B - C = p_2 - C$

The monopoly sells the extra unit of output at the new price, p_2, so its extra revenue is $B = p_2 \times 1 = p_2$. The monopoly loses the difference between the new price and the original price, $\Delta p = (p_2 - p_1)$, on the Q units it originally sold: $C = \Delta p \times Q$. Thus, the monopoly's marginal revenue, $B - C = p_2 - C$, is less than the price it charges by an amount equal to area C.

The competitive firm in panel a does not lose an area C from selling an extra unit because its demand curve is horizontal. It is the downward slope of the monopoly's demand curve that causes its marginal revenue to be less than its price.

Marginal Revenue Curve. Thus, *the monopoly's marginal revenue curve lies below the demand curve* at every positive quantity. In general, the relationship between the marginal revenue and demand curves depends on the shape of the demand curve.

For all *linear* demand curves, the relationship between the marginal revenue and demand curve is the same. The marginal revenue curve is a straight line that starts at the same point on the vertical (price) axis as the demand curve but has twice the slope of the demand curve, so the marginal revenue curve hits the horizontal (quantity) axis at half the quantity as the demand curve (see Appendix 11A). In Figure 11.2, the demand curve has a slope of -1 and hits the horizontal axis at 24 units, while the marginal revenue curve has a slope of -2 and hits the horizontal axis at 12 units.

Figure 11.2 Elasticity of Demand and Total, Average, and Marginal Revenue.

The demand curve (or average revenue curve), $p = 24 - Q$, lies above the marginal revenue curve, $MR = 24 - 2Q$. Where the marginal revenue equals zero, $Q = 12$, the elasticity of demand is $\varepsilon = -1$.

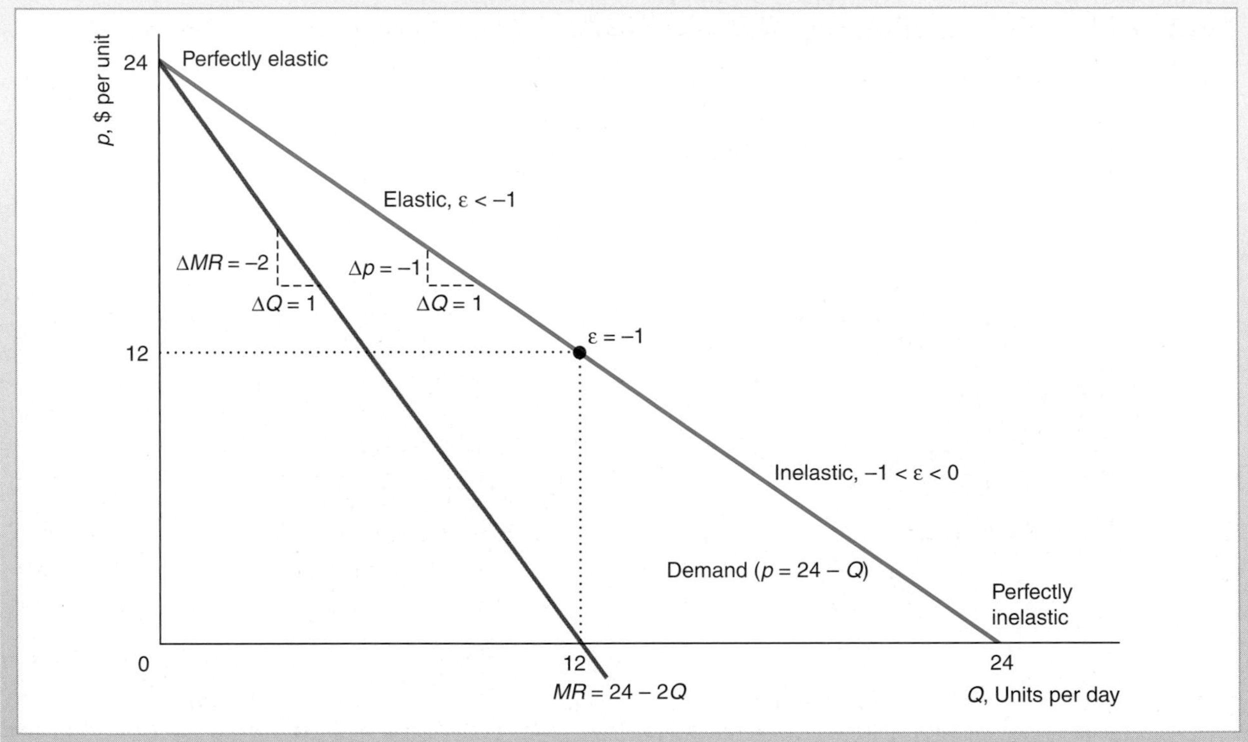

Deriving the Marginal Revenue Curve. To derive the monopoly's marginal revenue curve, we write an equation summarizing the relationship between price and marginal revenue that panel b of Figure 11.1 illustrates. (Because we want this equation to hold at all prices, we drop the subscripts from the prices.) For a monopoly to increase its output by ΔQ, the monopoly lowers its price per unit by $\Delta p/\Delta Q$, which is the slope of the demand curve. By lowering its price, the monopoly loses $(\Delta p/\Delta Q) \times Q$ on the units it originally sold at the higher price (area *C*), but it earns an additional *p* on the extra output it now sells (area *B*). Thus, the monopoly's marginal revenue is[1]

$$MR = p + \frac{\Delta p}{\Delta Q}Q. \tag{11.1}$$

Because the slope of the monopoly's demand curve, $\Delta p/\Delta Q$, is negative, the last term in Equation 11.1, $(\Delta p/\Delta Q)Q$, is negative. Equation 11.1 confirms that the price is greater than the marginal revenue, which equals *p* plus a negative term.

[1]Revenue is $R(Q) = p(Q)Q$, where $p(Q)$, the inverse demand function, shows how price changes as quantity increases along the demand curve. Differentiating, we find that the marginal revenue is

$$MR = dR(Q)/dQ = p(Q) + [dp(Q)/dQ]Q.$$

We now use Equation 11.1 to derive the marginal revenue curve when the monopoly faces the linear inverse demand function,

$$p = 24 - Q, \tag{11.2}$$

in Figure 11.2. Equation 11.2 shows that the price consumers are willing to pay falls \$1 if quantity increases by one unit. More generally, if quantity increases by ΔQ, price falls by $\Delta p = -\Delta Q$. Thus, the slope of the demand curve is $\Delta p/\Delta Q = -1$.

We obtain the marginal revenue function for this monopoly by substituting into Equation 11.1 the actual slope of the demand function, $\Delta p/\Delta Q = -1$, and replacing p with $24 - Q$ (using Equation 11.2):

$$MR = p + \frac{\Delta p}{\Delta Q}Q = (24 - Q) + (-1)Q = 24 - 2Q. \tag{11.3}$$

Figure 11.2 plots Equation 11.3. The slope of this marginal revenue curve is $\Delta MR/\Delta Q = -2$, so the marginal revenue curve is twice as steeply sloped as is the demand curve.

Marginal Revenue and Price Elasticity of Demand. The marginal revenue at any given quantity depends on the demand curve's height (the price) and shape. The shape of the demand curve at a particular quantity is described by the price elasticity of demand (Chapter 3), $\varepsilon = (\Delta Q/Q)/(\Delta p/p) < 0$, which tells us the percentage by which quantity demanded falls as the price increases by 1%.

At a given quantity, the marginal revenue equals the price times a term involving the elasticity of demand:[2]

$$MR = p\left(1 + \frac{1}{\varepsilon}\right). \tag{11.4}$$

According to Equation 11.4, marginal revenue is closer to price as demand becomes more elastic. Where the demand curve hits the price axis ($Q = 0$), the demand curve is perfectly elastic, so the marginal revenue equals price: $MR = p$.[3] Where the demand elasticity is unitary, $\varepsilon = -1$, marginal revenue is zero: $MR = p[1 + 1/(-1)] = 0$. Marginal revenue is negative where the demand curve is inelastic, $-1 < \varepsilon \le 0$.

With the demand function in Equation 11.2, $\Delta Q/\Delta p = -1$, so the elasticity of demand is $\varepsilon = (\Delta Q/\Delta p)(p/Q) = -p/Q$. Table 11.1 shows the relationship among quantity, price, marginal revenue, and elasticity of demand for this linear example. As Q approaches 24, ε approaches 0, and marginal revenue is negative. As Q approaches zero, the demand becomes increasingly elastic, and marginal revenue approaches the price.

Choosing Price or Quantity

Any firm maximizes its profit by operating where its marginal revenue equals its marginal cost. Unlike a competitive firm, a monopoly can adjust its price, so it has

---

[2]By multiplying the last term in Equation 11.1 by p/p (=1) and using algebra, we can rewrite the expression as

$$MR = p + p\frac{\Delta p}{\Delta Q}\frac{Q}{p} = p\left[1 + \frac{1}{(\Delta Q/\Delta p)(p/Q)}\right].$$

The last term in this expression is $1/\varepsilon$, because $\varepsilon = (\Delta Q/\Delta p)(p/Q)$.

[3]As ε approaches $-\infty$ (perfectly elastic demand), the $1/\varepsilon$ term approaches zero, so $MR = p(1 + 1/\varepsilon)$ approaches p.

Table 11.1 Quantity, Price, Marginal Revenue, and Elasticity for the Linear Inverse Demand Curve $p = 24 - Q$.

Quantity, Q	Price, p	Marginal Revenue, MR	Elasticity of Demand, $\varepsilon = -p/Q$	
0	24	24	$-\infty$	↑
1	23	22	−23	
2	22	20	−11	more elastic
3	21	18	−7	
4	20	16	−5	
5	19	14	−3.8	
6	18	12	−3	
7	17	10	−2.43	
8	16	8	−2	
9	15	6	−1.67	
10	14	4	−1.4	
11	13	2	−1.18	
12	**12**	0	**−1**	
13	11	−2	−0.85	
⋮	⋮	⋮	⋮	less elastic
23	1	−22	−0.043	
24	0	−24	0	↓

a choice of setting its price *or* its quantity to maximize its profit. (A competitive firm sets its quantity to maximize profit because it cannot affect market price.)

The monopoly is constrained by the market demand curve. Because the demand curve slopes downward, the monopoly faces a trade-off between a higher price and a lower quantity or a lower price and a higher quantity. The monopoly chooses the point on the demand curve that maximizes its profit. Unfortunately for the monopoly, it cannot set both its quantity and its price—thereby picking a point that is above the demand curve. If it could do so, the monopoly would choose an extremely high price and an extremely high output level and would become exceedingly wealthy.

If the monopoly sets its price, the demand curve determines how much output it sells. If the monopoly picks an output level, the demand curve determines the price. Because the monopoly wants to operate at the price and output at which its profit is maximized, it chooses the same profit-maximizing solution whether it sets the price or output. In the following, we assume that the monopoly sets quantity.

See Question 1.

Graphical Approach

All firms, including monopolies, use a two-step analysis to determine the output level that maximizes their profit (Chapter 8). First, the firm determines the output, Q^*, at which it makes the highest possible profit—the output at which its marginal revenue equals its marginal cost. Second, the firm decides whether to produce Q^* or shut down.

Profit-Maximizing Output. To illustrate how a monopoly chooses its output to maximize its profit, we continue to use the same linear demand and marginal revenue curves but add a linear marginal cost curve in panel a of Figure 11.3. Panel b shows the corresponding profit curve. The profit curve reaches its maximum at 6 units of output, where marginal profit—the slope of the profit curve—is zero. Because *marginal profit is marginal revenue minus marginal cost* (Chapter 8), marginal profit is zero where marginal revenue equals marginal cost. In panel a, marginal revenue equals marginal cost at 6 units. The price on the demand curve at

Figure 11.3 Maximizing Profit.

(a) At $Q = 6$, where marginal revenue, *MR*, equals marginal cost, *MC*, profit is maximized. The rectangle showing the maximum profit \$60 is average profit per unit, $p - AC = \$18 - \$8 = \$10$, times the number of units, 6. (b) Profit is maximized at a smaller quantity, $Q = 6$ (where marginal revenue equals marginal cost), than is revenue, $Q = 12$ (where marginal revenue is zero).

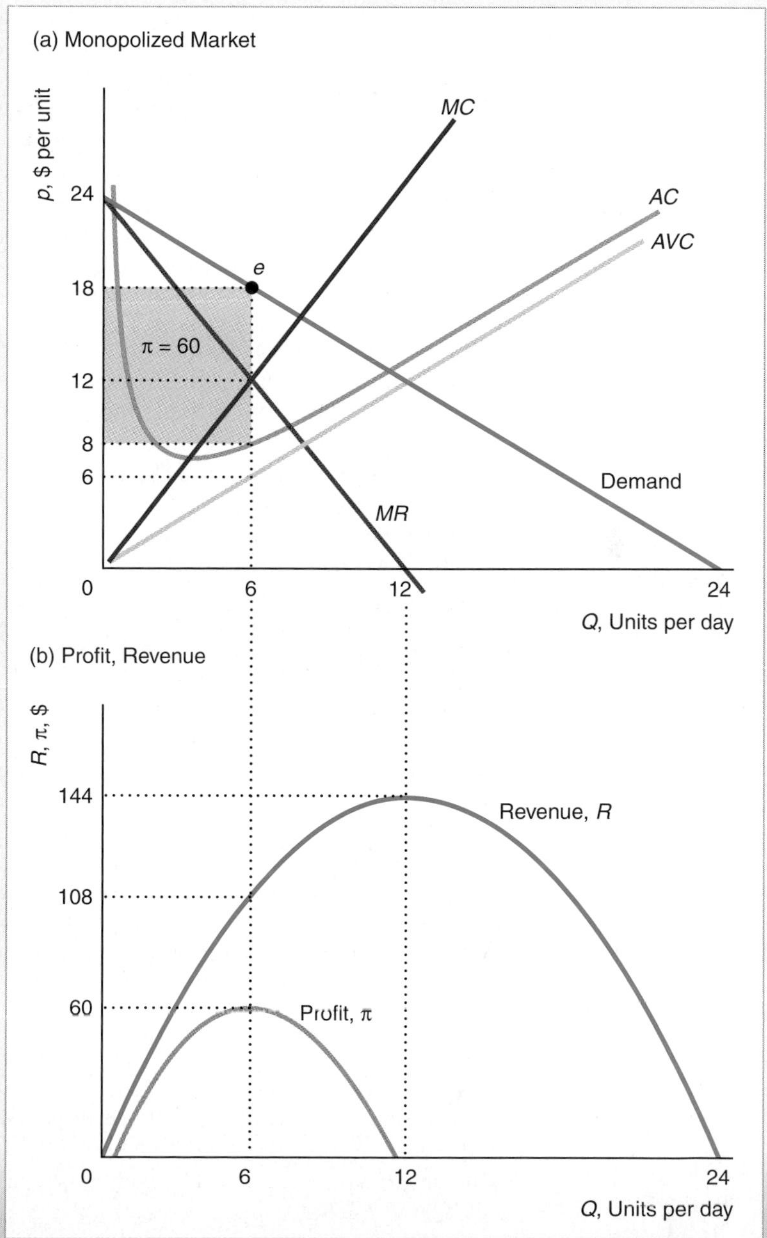

that quantity is \$18. Thus, the monopoly maximizes its profit at point e, where it sells 6 units per day for \$18 each.

Why does the monopoly maximize its profit by producing 6 units where its marginal revenue equals its marginal cost? At smaller quantities, the monopoly's marginal revenue is greater than its marginal cost, so its marginal profit is positive. By increasing its output, it raises its profit. Similarly, at quantities greater than 6 units, the monopoly's marginal cost is greater than its marginal revenue, so it can increase its profit by reducing its output.

The profit-maximizing quantity is smaller than the revenue-maximizing quantity. The revenue curve reaches its maximum at $Q = 12$, where the slope of the revenue curve, the marginal revenue, is zero (panel a). In contrast, the profit curve reaches its maximum at $Q = 6$, where marginal revenue equals marginal cost. Because marginal cost is positive, marginal revenue must be positive where profit is maximized. Because the marginal revenue curve has a negative slope, marginal revenue is positive at a smaller quantity than where it equals zero. Thus, the profit curve must reach a maximum at a smaller quantity, 6, than the revenue curve, 12.

As we already know, marginal revenue equals zero at the quantity where the demand curve has a unitary elasticity. Because a linear demand curve is more elastic at smaller quantities, *monopoly profit is maximized in the elastic portion of the demand curve.* (Here profit is maximized at $Q = 6$, where the elasticity of demand is -3.) Equivalently, *a monopoly never operates in the inelastic portion of its demand curve.*

Shutdown Decision. A monopoly shuts down to avoid making a loss in the long run if the monopoly-optimal price is below its average cost. In the short run, the monopoly shuts down if the monopoly-optimal price is less than its average variable cost. In our short-run example in Figure 11.3, the average variable cost, $AVC = \$6$, is less than the price, $p = \$18$, at the profit-maximizing output, $Q = 6$, so the firm chooses to produce.

See Questions 2–5.

Price is also above average cost at $Q = 6$, so the monopoly makes a positive profit.[4] At the profit-maximizing quantity of 6 units, the price is $p(6) = \$18$ and the average cost is $AC(6) = \$8$. As a result, the profit, $\pi = \$60$, is the shaded rectangle with a height equal to the average profit per unit, $p(6) - AC(6) = \$18 - \$8 = \$10$, and a width of 6 units.

Mathematical Approach

We can also solve for the profit-maximizing quantity mathematically. We already know the demand and marginal revenue functions for this monopoly. We need to determine its marginal cost curve. The monopoly's cost is a function of its output, $C(Q)$. In Figure 11.3, we assume the monopoly faces a short-run cost function of

$$C(Q) = Q^2 + 12, \tag{11.5}$$

where Q^2 is the monopoly's variable cost as a function of output and \$12 is its fixed cost (Chapter 7). Given this cost function, Equation 11.5, the monopoly's marginal cost function is[5]

$$MC = 2Q. \tag{11.6}$$

[4]Because profit is $\pi = p(Q)Q - C(Q)$, average profit is $\pi/Q = p(Q) - C(Q)/Q = p(Q) - AC$. Thus, average profit (and hence profit) is positive only if price is above average cost.

[5]By differentiating Equation 11.5 with respect to output, we find that the marginal cost is $MC = dC(Q)/dQ = 2Q$.

This marginal cost curve is a straight line through the origin with a slope of 2 in panel a. The average variable cost is $AVC = Q^2/Q = Q$, so it is a straight line through the origin with a slope of 1. The average cost is $AC = C/Q = (Q^2 + 12)/Q = Q + 12/Q$, which is U-shaped.

We determine the profit-maximizing output by equating the marginal revenue (Equation 11.3) and marginal cost (Equation 11.6) functions:

$$MR = 24 - 2Q = 2Q = MC.$$

Solving for Q, we find that $Q = 6$. Substituting $Q = 6$ into the inverse demand function (Equation 11.2), we find that the profit-maximizing price is

$$p = 24 - Q = 24 - 6 = \$18.$$

At that quantity, the average variable cost is $AVC = \$6$, which is less than the price, so the firm does not shut down. The average cost is $AC = \$(6 + 12/6) = \$8$, which is less than the price, so the firm makes a profit.

See Problems 25–28.

★ 11.2 Effects of a Shift of the Demand Curve

Shifts in the demand curve or marginal cost curve affect the monopoly optimum and can have a wider variety of effects in a monopolized market than in a competitive market. In a competitive market, the effect of a shift in demand on a competitive firm's output depends only on the shape of the marginal cost curve (Chapter 8). In contrast, the effect of a shift in demand on a monopoly's output depends on the shapes of both the marginal cost curve and the demand curve.

As we saw in Chapter 8, a competitive firm's marginal cost curve tells us everything we need to know about the amount that firm will supply at any given market price. The competitive firm's supply curve is its upward-sloping marginal cost curve (above its minimum average variable cost). A competitive firm's supply behavior does not depend on the shape of the market demand curve because it always faces a horizontal demand curve at the market price. Thus, if you know a competitive firm's marginal cost curve, you can predict how much that firm will produce at any given market price.

In contrast, a monopoly's output decision depends on the shapes of its marginal cost curve and its demand curve. Unlike a competitive firm, *a monopoly does not have a supply curve*. Knowing the monopoly's marginal cost curve is not enough for us to predict how much a monopoly will sell at any given price.

Figure 11.4 illustrates that the relationship between price and quantity is unique in a competitive market but not in a monopoly market. If the market is competitive, the initial equilibrium is e_1 in panel a, where the original demand curve D^1 intersects the supply curve, MC, which is the sum of the marginal cost curves of a large number of competitive firms. When the demand curve shifts to D^2, the new competitive equilibrium, e_2, has a higher price and quantity. A shift of the demand curve maps out competitive equilibria along the marginal cost curve, so for every equilibrium quantity, there is a single corresponding equilibrium price.

Now suppose there is a monopoly. As demand shifts from D^1 to D^2, the monopoly optimum shifts from E_1 to E_2 in panel b, so the price rises but the quantity stays constant, $Q_1 = Q_2$. Thus, *a given quantity can correspond to more than one monopoly-optimal price*. A shift in the demand curve may cause the monopoly-optimal price to stay constant and the quantity to change or both price and quantity to change.

See Question 6.

Figure 11.4 Effects of a Shift of the Demand Curve.

(a) A shift of the demand curve from D^1 to D^2 causes the competitive equilibrium to move from e_1 to e_2 along the supply curve (the horizontal sum of the marginal cost curves of all the competitive firms). Because the competitive equilibrium lies on the supply curve, each quantity corresponds to only one possible equilibrium price. (b) With a monopoly, this same shift of demand causes the monopoly optimum to change from E_1 to E_2. The monopoly quantity stays the same, but the monopoly price rises. Thus, a shift in demand does not map out a unique relationship between price and quantity in a monopolized market: The same quantity, $Q_1 = Q_2$, is associated with two different prices, p_1 and p_2.

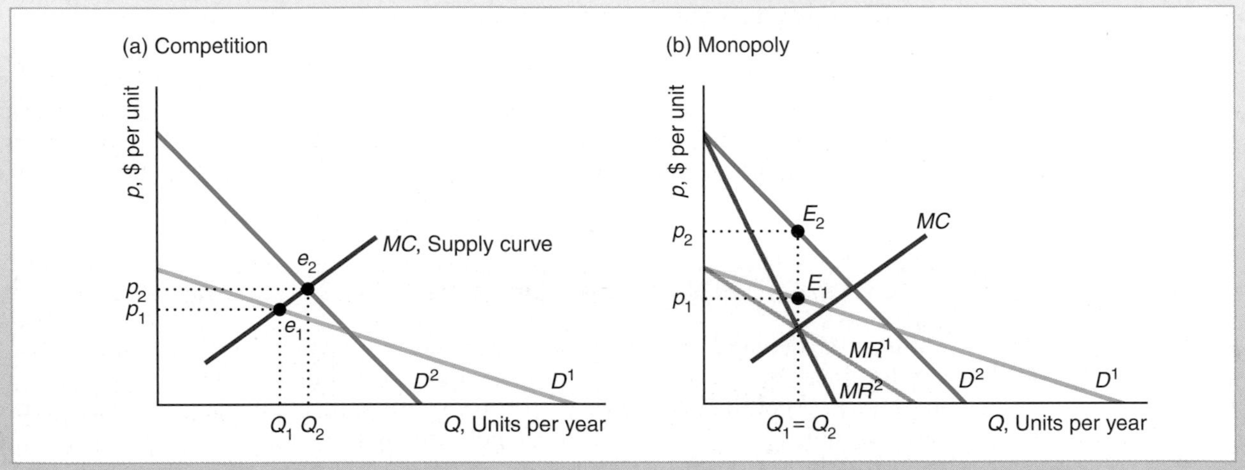

11.3 Market Power

market power
the ability of a firm to charge a price above marginal cost and earn a positive profit

A monopoly has **market power**: the ability of a firm to charge a price above marginal cost and earn a positive profit. We now examine the factors that determine how much above its marginal cost a monopoly sets its price.

Market Power and the Shape of the Demand Curve

The degree to which the monopoly raises its price above its marginal cost depends on the shape of the demand curve at the profit-maximizing quantity. If the monopoly faces a highly elastic—nearly flat—demand curve at the profit-maximizing quantity, it would lose substantial sales if it raised its price by even a small amount. Conversely, if the demand curve is not very elastic (relatively steep) at that quantity, the monopoly would lose fewer sales from raising its price by the same amount.

We can derive the relationship between market power and the elasticity of demand at the profit-maximizing quantity using the expression for marginal revenue in Equation 11.4 and the firm's profit-maximizing condition that marginal revenue equals marginal cost:

$$MR = p\left(1 + \frac{1}{\varepsilon}\right) = MC. \tag{11.7}$$

By rearranging terms, we can rewrite Equation 11.7 as

$$\frac{p}{MC} = \frac{1}{1 + (1/\varepsilon)}. \tag{11.8}$$

Equation 11.8 says that the ratio of the price to marginal cost depends *only* on the elasticity of demand at the profit-maximizing quantity.

In our linear demand example in panel a of Figure 11.3, the elasticity of demand is $\varepsilon = -3$ at the monopoly optimum where $Q = 6$. As a result, the ratio of price to marginal cost is $p/MC = 1/[1 + 1/(-3)] = 1.5$, or $p = 1.5MC$. The profit-maximizing price, \$18, in panel a is 1.5 times the marginal cost of \$12.

Table 11.2 illustrates how the ratio of price to marginal cost varies with the elasticity of demand. When the elasticity is -1.01, only slightly elastic, the monopoly's profit-maximizing price is 101 times larger than its marginal cost: $p/MC = 1/[1 + 1/(-1.01)] \approx 101$. As the elasticity of demand approaches negative infinity (becomes perfectly elastic), the ratio of price to marginal cost shrinks to $p/MC = 1$.[6]

This table illustrates that not all monopolies can set high prices. A monopoly that faces a horizontal, perfectly elastic demand curve sets its price equal to its marginal cost—just like a price-taking, competitive firm. If this monopoly were to raise its price, it would lose all its sales, so it maximizes its profit by setting its price equal to its marginal cost.

See Questions 7 and 8.

The more elastic the demand curve, the less a monopoly can raise its price without losing sales. All else the same, the more close substitutes for the monopoly's good there are, the more elastic the demand the monopoly faces. For example, Addison-Wesley has the monopoly right to produce and sell this textbook. Many other publishers, however, have the rights to produce and sell similar microeconomics textbooks (though you wouldn't like them as much). The demand Addison-Wesley faces is much more elastic than it would be if no substitutes were available. If you think this textbook is expensive, imagine the cost if no substitutes were published!

Table 11.2 Elasticity of Demand, Price, and Marginal Cost.

	Elasticity of Demand, ε	Price/Marginal Cost Ratio, $p/MC = 1/[1 + (1/\varepsilon)]$	Lerner Index, $(p - MC)/p = -1/\varepsilon$
↑ less elastic	-1.01	101	0.99
	-1.1	11	0.91
	-2	2	0.5
	-3	1.5	0.33
	-5	1.25	0.2
	-10	1.11	0.1
	-100	1.01	0.01
more elastic ↓	$-\infty$	1	0

APPLICATION

Cable Cars and Profit Maximization

Since San Francisco's cable car system started operating in 1873, it has been one of the city's main tourist attractions. In mid-2005, the cash-strapped Municipal Railway raised the one-way fare by two-thirds from \$3 to \$5. Not surprisingly, the number of riders dropped substantially, and many in the city called for a rate reduction.

[6]As the elasticity approaches negative infinity, $1/\varepsilon$ approaches zero, so $1/(1 + 1/\varepsilon)$ approaches $1/1 = 1$.

The rate increase prompted many locals to switch to buses or other forms of transportation, but most tourists have a relatively inelastic demand curve for cable car rides. Frank Bernstein of Arizona, who visited San Francisco with his wife, two children, and mother-in-law, said that there was no way they would visit San Francisco without riding a cable car: "That's what you do when you're here." But the round-trip \$50 cost for his family to ride a cable car from the Powell Street turnaround to Fisherman's Wharf and back "is a lot of money for our family. We'll do it once, but we won't do it again."

If the city ran the cable car system like a profit-maximizing monopoly, the decision to raise fares would be clear. The 67% rate hike resulted in a 23% increase in revenue to \$9,045,792 in the 2005–2006 fiscal year. Given that the revenue increased when the price rose, the city must have been operating in the inelastic portion of its demand curve ($\varepsilon > -1$), where $MR = p(1 + 1/\varepsilon) < 0$ prior to the fare increase. With fewer riders, costs stayed constant (they would have fallen if the city had decided to run fewer than its traditional 40 cars), so the city's profit increased given the increase in revenue. Presumably the profit-maximizing price is even higher in the elastic portion of the demand curve.

However, the city may not be interested in maximizing its profit on the cable cars. Mayor Gavin Newsom said that having fewer riders "was my biggest fear when we raised the fare. I think we're right at the cusp of losing visitors who come to San Francisco and want to enjoy a ride on a cable car." The mayor said that he believed keeping the price of a cable car ride relatively low helps attract tourists to the city, thereby benefiting many local businesses.[7] Newsom observed, "Cable cars are so fundamental to the lifeblood of the city, and they represent so much more than the revenue they bring in." The mayor decided to continue to run the cable cars at a price below the profit-maximizing level: The fare is still \$5 in 2008.

Lerner Index

Lerner Index
the ratio of the difference between price and marginal cost to the price: $(p - MC)/p$

Another way to show how the elasticity of demand affects a monopoly's price relative to its marginal cost is to look at the firm's **Lerner Index** (or *price markup*): the ratio of the difference between price and marginal cost to the price: $(p - MC)/p$. This measure is zero for a competitive firm because a competitive firm cannot raise its price above its marginal cost. The greater the difference between price and marginal cost, the larger the Lerner Index and the greater the monopoly's ability to set price above marginal cost.

If the firm is maximizing its profit, we can express the Lerner Index in terms of the elasticity of demand by rearranging Equation 11.8:

$$\frac{p - MC}{p} = -\frac{1}{\varepsilon}. \tag{11.9}$$

[7]That is, the mayor believes that cable cars provide a positive externality (see Chapter 18).

Because $MC \geq 0$ and $p \geq MC$, $0 \leq p - MC \leq p$, so the Lerner Index ranges from 0 to 1 for a profit-maximizing firm.[8] Equation 11.9 confirms that a competitive firm has a Lerner Index of zero because its demand curve is perfectly elastic.[9] As Table 11.2 illustrates, the Lerner Index for a monopoly increases as the demand becomes less elastic. If $\varepsilon = -5$, the monopoly's markup (Lerner Index) is $1/5 = 0.2$; if $\varepsilon = -2$, the markup is $1/2 = 0.5$; and if $\varepsilon = -1.01$, the markup is 0.99. Monopolies that face demand curves that are only slightly elastic set prices that are multiples of their marginal cost and have Lerner Indexes close to 1.

APPLICATION

Apple's iPod

Apple introduced its iPod on October 23, 2001. Although the iPod was not the first hard-drive music player, it was the most elegant one to date. Endowed with a tiny hard drive, it was about a quarter the size of its competitors, fit in one's pocket, and weighed only 6.5 ounces. Moreover, it was the only player to use a high-speed FireWire interface to transfer files. It held a thousand songs. Perhaps most importantly, iPod offered an intuitive interface and an attractive white case with unusual ear buds.

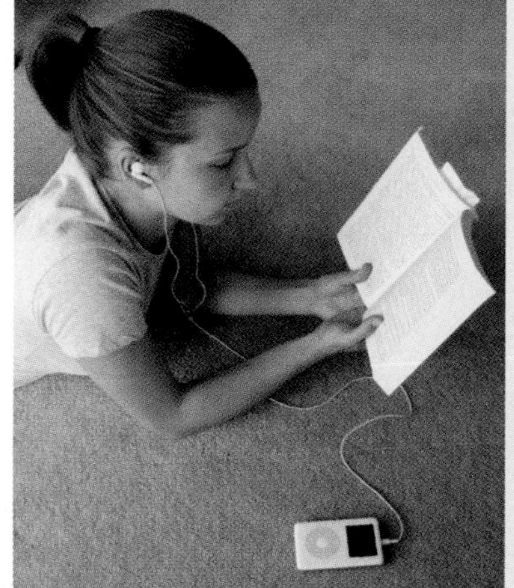

People loved the iPod. Even at its extremely high price of \$399, Apple had a virtual monopoly for several years. In 2004, the iPod had 95.6% of the hard-drive player market, and Apple believed that it still had more than 90% in 2005, though only 73% in 2007.

To keep ahead of potential competitors, Apple introduced subsequent generations of iPods in quick succession (though it sells its top-of-the-line model for \$399 or more). Its iTune proprietary media player software and its iTunes Music Store help Apple maintain its stranglehold on the market. At iTunes Music Store, users can easily download tracks for 99¢, burn them to a CD, play them using iTunes, or sync them with their MP3 player. However, iTunes supports copying music to the iPod and not from it, and songs purchased from the iTunes Music Store are copy protected with Apple's FairPlay digital rights management scheme, which prevents iTunes customers from using the purchased music on some portable digital music player other than the Apple iPod. Consequently, some current owners of iPods and iTunes are hesitant to switch to potential competitors because they will have to learn new software and may be unable to transfer some of their previously purchased songs to the new equipment.

See Problem 29.

Solved Problem 11.1

Apple's constant marginal cost of producing its top-of-the-line iPod is \$200, its fixed cost is \$736 million, and its inverse demand function is $p = 600 - 25Q$, where Q is units measured in millions.[10] What is Apple's average cost function? Assuming that Apple is maxi-

[8]For the Lerner Index to be above 1, ε would have to be a negative fraction, indicating that the demand curve was inelastic at the monopoly optimum. However, a profit-maximizing monopoly never operates in the inelastic portion of its demand curve.

[9]As the elasticity of demand approaches negative infinity, the Lerner Index, $-1/\varepsilon$, approaches zero.

[10]The marginal cost estimate comes from **www.eetimes.com/news/latest/showArticle.jhtml?articleID =18306938**. Though we assume that the marginal cost curve is constant, there is some evidence from Apple's other lines that it might be downward sloping. The quantity in 2004 is from In-Stat market research. We assumed that Apple's gross profit margin for 2004 held for the iPod line and used that to calculate the fixed cost. We derived the linear demand curve by assuming Apple maximizes profit and using the information on price, marginal cost, and quantity. Assuming that Apple maximizes its short-run profit may not be completely realistic, as we discuss in the last section of this chapter.

mizing short-run monopoly profit, what is its marginal revenue function? What are its profit-maximizing price and quantity, profit, and Lerner Index? What is the elasticity of demand at the profit-maximizing level? Show Apple's profit-maximizing solution in a figure.

Answer

1. *Derive the average cost function using the information about Apple's marginal and fixed costs.* Given that Apple's marginal cost is constant, its average variable cost equals its marginal cost, \$200. Its average fixed cost is its fixed cost divided by the quantity produced, $736/Q$. Thus, its average cost is $AC = 200 + 736/Q$.

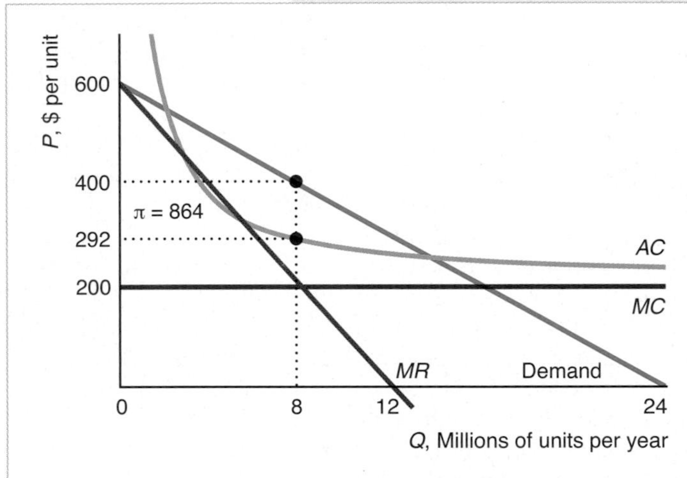

2. *Derive Apple's marginal revenue function using the information about its demand function.* Given that its demand function is linear, we know that its marginal revenue function is twice as steep as the demand function and has the same intercept on the price axis: $MR = 600 - 50Q$, as the figure shows.

3. *Derive Apple's profit-maximizing price and quantity by equating the marginal revenue and marginal cost functions and solving.* Apple maximizes its profit where

$$MR = 600 - 50Q = 200 = MC.$$

Solving this equation for the profit-maximizing output, we find that $Q = 8$ million units. By substituting this quantity into the inverse demand equation, we determine that the profit-maximizing price is $p = \$400$ per unit, as the figure shows.

4. *Calculate Apple's profit using the profit-maximizing price and quantity and the average cost.* The firm's profit is

$$\pi = (p - AC)Q = (400 - [200 + 736/8])8 = \$864 \text{ million.}$$

The figure shows that the profit is a rectangle with a height of $(p - AC)$ and a length of Q.

5. *Determine the Lerner Index using the formula.* Apple's Lerner Index is

$$(p - MC)/p = (400 - 200)/400 = \tfrac{1}{2}.$$

6. *Use Equation 11.9 to infer the elasticity.* According to that equation, a profit-maximizing monopoly operates where $(p - MC)p = -1/\varepsilon$. Substituting into this expression from the previous step, we learn that $\frac{1}{2} = -1/\varepsilon$, or $\varepsilon = -2$.

See Problems 30–35.

Sources of Market Power

When will a monopoly face a relatively elastic demand curve and hence have little market power? Ultimately, the elasticity of demand of the market demand curve depends on consumers' tastes and options. The more consumers want a good—the more willing they are to pay "virtually anything" for it—the less elastic is the demand curve.

All else the same, the demand curve a firm (not necessarily a monopoly) faces becomes more elastic as (1) *better substitutes* for the firm's product are introduced, (2) *more firms* enter the market selling the same product, or (3) firms that provide the same service *locate closer* to this firm. The demand curves for Xerox, the U.S. Postal Service, and McDonald's have become more elastic in recent decades for these three reasons.

When Xerox started selling its plain-paper copier, no other firm sold a close substitute. Other companies' machines produced copies on special slimy paper that yellowed quickly. As other firms developed plain-paper copiers, the demand curve that Xerox faced became more elastic.

The U.S. Postal Service (USPS) has a monopoly in first-class mail service. Today, phone calls, faxes, and e-mail are excellent substitutes for many types of first-class mail. The USPS had a monopoly in overnight delivery services until 1979. Now FedEx, United Parcel Service, and many other firms compete with the USPS in providing overnight deliveries. Because of this new competition, the USPS's share of business and personal correspondence fell from 77% in 1988 to 59% in 1996, and its overnight-mail market fell to 4%.[11] Thus, over time the demand curves the USPS faces for first-class mail and overnight service have shifted downward and become more elastic.

As you drive down a highway, you may notice that McDonald's restaurants are located miles apart. The purpose of this spacing is to reduce the likelihood that two McDonald's outlets will compete for the same customer. Although McDonald's can prevent its own restaurants from competing with each other, it cannot prevent Wendy's or Burger King from locating near its restaurants. As other fast-food restaurants open near a McDonald's, that restaurant faces a more elastic demand.

What happens as a profit-maximizing monopoly faces more elastic demand? It has to lower its price. See **www.myeconlab.com/perloff**, Chapter 11, "Airport Monopolies," for an illustration of how a monopoly adjusts its price as it changes its beliefs about the elasticity of demand it faces.

11.4 Welfare Effects of Monopoly

I think it's wrong that only one company makes the game Monopoly.
—Steven Wright

Welfare, W (here defined as the sum of consumer surplus, CS, and producer surplus, PS), is lower under monopoly than under competition. Chapter 9 showed that competition maximizes welfare because price equals marginal cost. By setting its price above its marginal cost, a monopoly causes consumers to buy less than the competitive level of the good, so a deadweight loss to society occurs.

Graphing the Welfare Loss

We illustrate this loss using our continuing example. If the monopoly were to act like a competitive market and operate where its inverse demand curve, Equation 11.2, intersects its marginal cost (supply) curve, Equation 11.6,

$$p = 24 - Q = 2Q = MC,$$

[11]Peter Passell, "Battered by Its Rivals," *New York Times*, May 15, 1997, C1. However, the USPS's share of air shipments rose to 38% by 2005 (**www.cygnusb2b.com**, January 13, 2007).

it would sell $Q_c = 8$ units of output at a price of \$16, as in Figure 11.5. At this competitive price, consumer surplus is area $A + B + C$ and producer surplus is $D + E$.

If the firm acts like a monopoly and operates where its marginal revenue equals its marginal cost, only 6 units are sold at the monopoly price of \$18, and consumer surplus is only A. Part of the lost consumer surplus, B, goes to the monopoly, but the rest, C, is lost.

By charging the monopoly price of \$18 instead of the competitive price of \$16, the monopoly receives \$2 more per unit and earns an extra profit of area B = \$12 on the $Q_m = 6$ units it sells. The monopoly loses area E, however, because it sells less than the competitive output. Consequently, the monopoly's producer surplus increases by $B - E$ over the competitive level. We know that its producer surplus increases, $B - E > 0$, because the monopoly had the option of producing at the competitive level and chose not to do so.

Figure 11.5 Deadweight Loss of Monopoly.

A competitive market would produce $Q_c = 8$ at p_c = \$16, where the demand curve intersects the marginal cost (supply) curve. A monopoly produces only $Q_m = 6$ at p_m = \$18, where the marginal revenue curve intersects the marginal cost curve. Under monopoly, consumer surplus is A, producer surplus is $B + D$, and the lost welfare or deadweight loss of monopoly is $-C - E$.

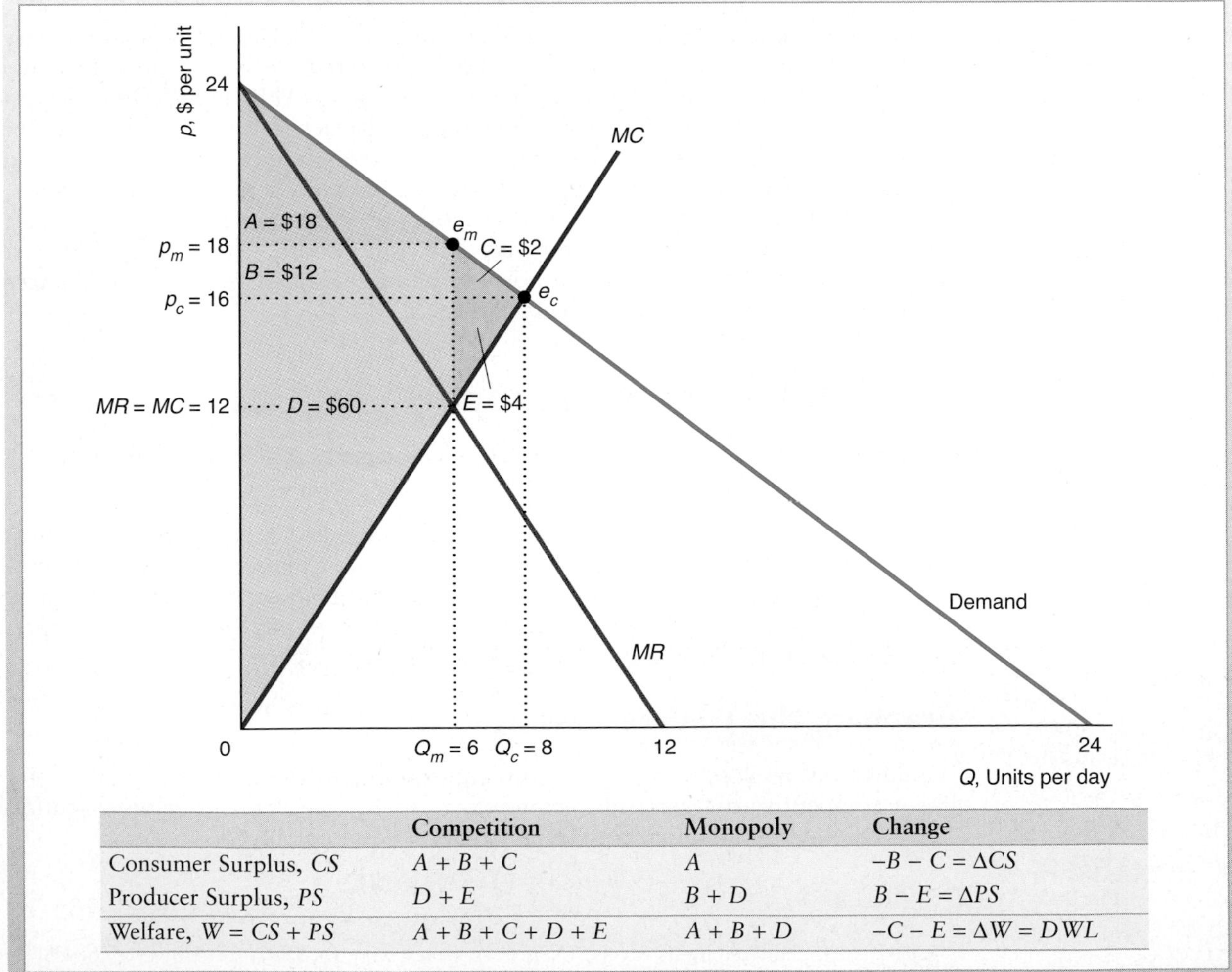

	Competition	Monopoly	Change
Consumer Surplus, CS	$A + B + C$	A	$-B - C = \Delta CS$
Producer Surplus, PS	$D + E$	$B + D$	$B - E = \Delta PS$
Welfare, $W = CS + PS$	$A + B + C + D + E$	$A + B + D$	$-C - E = \Delta W = DWL$

Monopoly welfare is lower than competitive welfare. The deadweight loss of monopoly is $-C - E$, which represents the consumer surplus and producer surplus lost because less than the competitive output is produced. As in the analysis of a tax in Chapter 9, the deadweight loss is due to the gap between price and marginal cost at the monopoly output. At $Q_m = 6$, the price, \$18, is above the marginal cost, \$12, so consumers are willing to pay more for the last unit of output than it costs to produce it. The calculated "Deadweight Loss of the U.S. Postal Service" is discussed in **www.myeconlab.com/perloff**, Chapter 11.

See Question 9.

Solved Problem 11.2

In the linear example in Figure 11.3, how does charging the monopoly a specific tax of τ = \$8 per unit affect the monopoly optimum and the welfare of consumers, the monopoly, and society (where society's welfare includes the tax revenue)? What is the incidence of the tax on consumers?

Answer

1. *Determine how imposing the tax affects the monopoly optimum.* In the accompanying graph, the intersection of the marginal revenue curve, *MR*, and

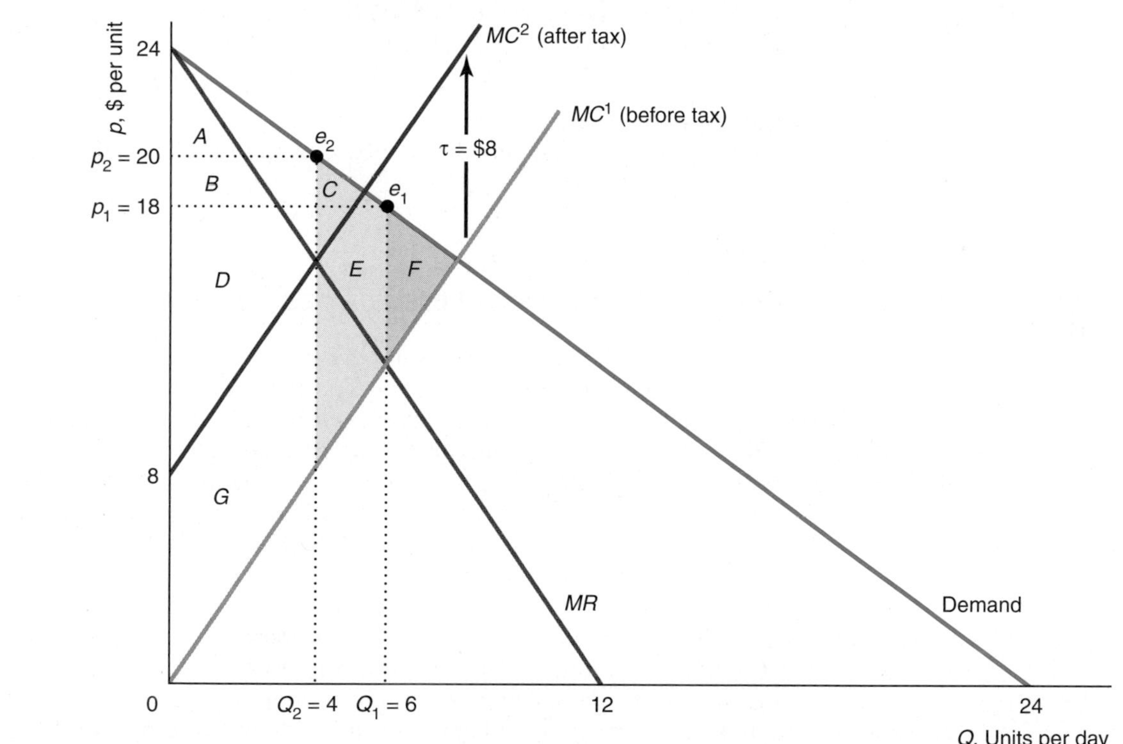

	Monopoly Before Tax	Monopoly After Tax	Change
Consumer Surplus, *CS*	$A + B + C$	A	$-B - C = \Delta CS$
Producer Surplus, *PS*	$D + E + G$	$B + D$	$B - E - G = \Delta PS$
Tax Revenues, $T = \tau Q$	0	G	$G = \Delta T$
Welfare, $W = CS + PS + T$	$A + B + C + D + E + G$	$A + B + D + G$	$-C - E = \Delta W$
Deadweight Loss, *DWL*	$-F$	$-C - E - F$	$-C - E = \Delta DWL$

the before-tax marginal cost curve, MC^1, determines the monopoly optimum quantity, $Q_1 = 6$. At the before-tax optimum, e_1, the price is $p_1 = \$18$. The specific tax causes the monopoly's before-tax marginal cost curve, $MC^1 = 2Q$, to shift upward by \$8 to $MC^2 = MC^1 + 8 = 2Q + 8$. After the tax is applied, the monopoly operates where $MR = 24 - 2Q = 2Q + 8 = MC^2$. In the after-tax monopoly optimum, e_2, the quantity is $Q_2 = 4$ and the price is $p_2 = \$20$. Thus, output falls by $\Delta Q = 2$ units and the price increases by $\Delta p = \$2$.

2. *Calculate the change in the various welfare measures.* The graph shows how the welfare measures change. Area G is the tax revenue collected by the government, $\tau Q = \$32$, because its height is the distance between the two marginal cost curves, $\tau = \$8$, and its width is the output the monopoly produces after the tax is imposed, $Q = 4$. The tax reduces consumer and producer surplus and increases the deadweight loss. We know that producer surplus falls because (a) the monopoly could have produced this reduced output level in the absence of the tax but did not because it was not the profit-maximizing output, so its before-tax profit falls, and (b) the monopoly must now pay taxes. The before-tax deadweight loss from monopoly is $-F$. The after-tax deadweight loss is $-C - E - F$, so the increase in deadweight loss due to the tax is $-C - E$. The table below the graph shows that consumer surplus changes by $-B - C$ and producer surplus by $B - E - G$.

3. *Calculate the incidence of the tax.* Because the tax goes from \$0 to \$8, the change in the tax is $\Delta\tau = \$8$. The incidence of the tax (Chapter 3) on consumers is $\Delta p/\Delta\tau = \$2/\$8 = \frac{1}{4}$. (The monopoly absorbs \$6 of the tax and passes on only \$2.)[12]

See Questions 10–12 and Problems 36–38.

★ Welfare Effects of *Ad Valorem* Versus Specific Taxes

Solved Problem 11.1 illustrates that a specific sales tax (the monopoly pays the government τ dollars per unit sold) provides tax revenue but reduces welfare below even the monopoly level. Governments use *ad valorem* taxes more often than specific taxes. Is there an advantage to using an *ad valorem* sales tax (the monopoly pays αp per unit of output, where α is a fraction and p is the price charged)? The answer is that a government raises more tax revenue with an *ad valorem* tax applied to a monopoly than with a specific tax when α and τ are set so that the after-tax output is the same with either tax, as we now show.[13]

In Figure 11.6, the before-tax market demand curve is D, and the corresponding marginal revenue is MR. The before-tax monopoly optimum is e_1. The MR curve intersects the MC curve at Q_1 units, which sell at a price of p_1.

If the government imposes a specific tax τ, the monopoly's after-tax demand curve is D^s, which is the market demand curve D shifted downward by τ dollars.[14] The corresponding marginal revenue curve, MR^s, intersects the marginal cost curve

[12]In contrast to a competitive market, when a monopoly is taxed, the incidence of the tax on consumers can exceed 100%, as Appendix 11B demonstrates.

[13]Chapter 3 shows that both taxes raise the same tax revenue in a competitive market. The taxes raise different amounts when applied to monopolies or other noncompetitive firms. See Delipalla and Keen (1992), Skeath and Trandel (1994), and Hamilton (1999).

[14]Instead, we could capture the effect of a specific tax by shifting the marginal cost curve upward by τ, as in our answer to Solved Problem 11.2.

Figure 11.6 *Ad Valorem* Versus Specific Tax.

A specific tax (τ) and an *ad valorem* tax (α) that reduce the monopoly output by the same amount (from Q_1 to Q_2) raise different amounts of tax revenues for the government. The tax revenue from the specific tax is area $A = \tau Q_2$. The tax revenue from the *ad valorem* tax is $A + B = \alpha p_2 Q_2$.

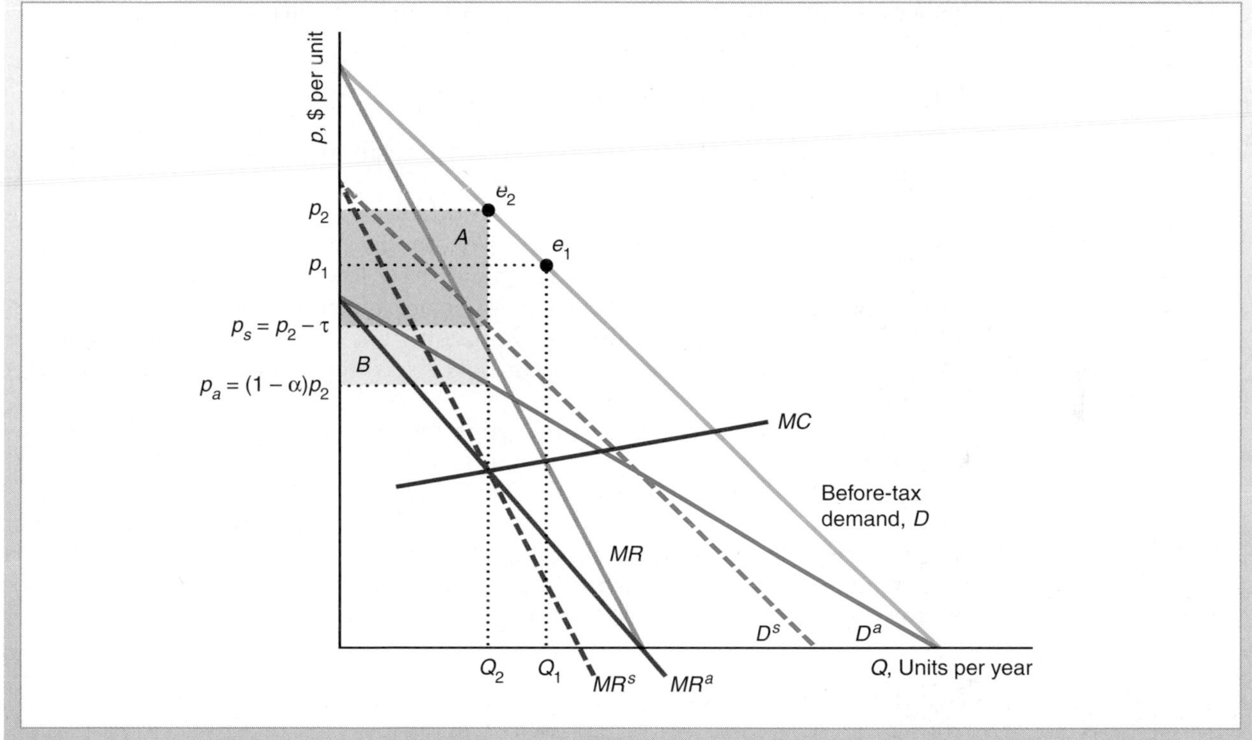

at Q_2. In this after-tax equilibrium, e_2, consumers pay p_2 and the monopoly receives $p_s = p_2 - \tau$ per unit. The government's revenue from the specific tax is area $A = \tau Q_2$.

If the government imposes an *ad valorem* tax α, the demand curve facing the monopoly is D^a. The gap between D^a and D, which is the tax per unit, αp, is greater at higher prices. By setting α appropriately, the corresponding marginal revenue curve, MR_a, intersects the marginal cost curve at Q_2, where consumers again pay p_2. Although the *ad valorem* tax reduces output by the same amount as the specific tax, the *ad valorem* tax raises more revenue, areas $A + B = \alpha p_2 Q_2$.

Both sales taxes harm consumers by the same amount because they raise the price consumers pay from p_1 to p_2 and reduce the quantity purchased from Q_1 to Q_2. The *ad valorem* tax transfers more revenue from the monopoly to the government, so the government prefers the *ad valorem* tax and the monopoly prefers the specific tax. (Equivalently, if the government set τ and α so that they raised the same amount of tax revenue, the *ad valorem* tax would reduce output and consumer surplus less than the specific tax.) Amazingly, it makes sense for government to employ an *ad valorem* tax, and most state and local governments use *ad valorem* taxes for most goods.[15]

[15]However, as Professor Stearns and his students at the University of Maryland inform me, the federal government uses many specific taxes (alcohol, tobacco products, gasoline and other fuels, international air travel, tires, vaccines, ship passengers, ozone-depleting chemicals) as well as *ad valorem* taxes (telephone service, transportation of property by air, sports fishing equipment, bow and arrow components, gas-guzzler autos, foreign insurance, and firearms).

11.5 Cost Advantages That Create Monopolies

Why are some markets monopolized? Two key reasons are that a firm has a cost advantage over other firms or that a government created the monopoly.[16] If a low-cost firm profitably sells at a price so low that other potential competitors with higher costs would make losses, no other firm enters the market.

Sources of Cost Advantages

A firm can have a cost advantage over potential rivals for a number of reasons. One reason is that the firm controls an *essential facility*: a scarce resource that a rival needs to use to survive. For example, a firm that owns the only quarry in a region is the only firm that can profitably sell gravel to local construction firms.

A second important reason why a firm may have lower costs is that the firm uses a superior technology or has a better way of organizing production. Henry Ford's methods of organizing production using assembly lines and standardization allowed him to produce cars at lower cost than rival firms until they copied his organizational techniques.

When a firm develops a better production method that provides an advantage—possibly enough of an advantage for the firm to be a monopoly—the firm must either keep the information secret or obtain a patent, which provides government protection from imitation. According to a survey of 650 research and development managers of U.S. firms (Levin, Klevorick, Nelson, and Winter, 1987), secrecy is more commonly used than patents to prevent duplication of new or improved processes by other firms but is less commonly used to protect new products.

Natural Monopoly

natural monopoly
situation in which one firm can produce the total output of the market at lower cost than several firms could

A market has a **natural monopoly** if one firm can produce the total output of the market at lower cost than several firms could. If the cost for any firm to produce q is $C(q)$, the condition for a natural monopoly is

$$C(Q) < C(q_1) + C(q_2) + \cdots + C(q_n), \qquad (11.10)$$

where $Q = q_1 + q_2 + \cdots + q_n$ is the sum of the output of any $n \geq 2$ firms. With a natural monopoly, it is more efficient to have only one firm produce than more firms.[17] Believing that they are natural monopolies, governments frequently grant

[16] In later chapters, we discuss three other means by which monopolies are created. One method is the merger of several firms into a single firm (Chapter 13). This method creates a monopoly if new firms fail to enter the market. A second method is for firms to coordinate their activities and set their prices as a monopoly would (Chapter 13). Firms that act collectively in this way are called a *cartel*. A third method is for a monopoly to use strategies that discourage other firms from entering the market (Chapter 14).

[17] A natural monopoly is the most efficient market structure only in the sense that the single firm produces at lowest cost. However, society's welfare may be greater with more than one firm in the industry producing at higher cost, because competition drives down the price from the monopoly level. A solution that allows society to maximize welfare is to have only one firm produce, but the government regulates that firm to charge a price equal to marginal cost (as we discuss later in this chapter).

monopoly rights to *public utilities* to provide essential goods or services such as water, gas, electric power, or mail delivery.

If a firm has economies of scale (Chapter 7) at all levels of output, its average cost curve falls as output increases for any observed level of output. If all potential firms have the same strictly declining average cost curve, this market has a natural monopoly, as we now illustrate.[18]

A company that supplies water to homes incurs a high fixed cost, F, to build a plant and connect houses to the plant. The firm's marginal cost, m, of supplying water is constant, so its marginal cost curve is horizontal and its average cost, $AC = m + F/Q$, declines as output rises. (An example is the iPod in Solved Problem 11.1.)

Figure 11.7 shows such marginal and average cost curves where m = \$10 and F = \$60. If the market output is 12 units per day, one firm produces that output at an average cost of \$15, or a total cost of \$180 (= \$15 × 12). If two firms each produce 6 units, the average cost is \$20 and the cost of producing the market output is \$240 (= \$20 × 12), which is greater than the cost with a single firm.

If the two firms divided total production in any other way, their cost of production would still exceed the cost of a single firm (as the following question asks you to prove). The reason is that the marginal cost per unit is the same no matter how many firms produce, but each additional firm adds a fixed cost, which raises the cost of producing a given quantity. If only one firm provides water, the cost of building a second plant and a second set of pipes is avoided.

Figure 11.7 Natural Monopoly.

This natural monopoly has a strictly declining average cost.

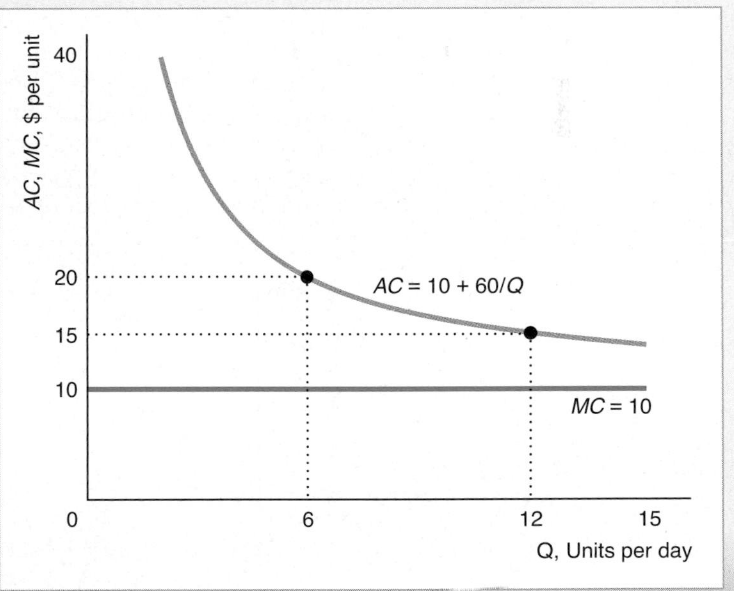

[18]A firm may be a natural monopoly even if its cost curve does not fall at all levels of output. If a U-shaped average cost curve reaches its minimum at 100 units of output, it may be less costly for only one firm to produce an output of 101 units even though average cost is rising at that output. Thus, a cost function with economies of scale everywhere is a sufficient but not a necessary condition for a natural monopoly.

Solved Problem 11.3

A firm that delivers Q units of water to households has a total cost of $C(Q) = mQ + F$. If any entrant would have the same cost, does this market have a natural monopoly?

Answer

Determine whether costs rise if two firms produce a given quantity. Let q_1 be the output of Firm 1 and q_2 be the output of Firm 2. The combined cost of these two firms producing $Q = q_1 + q_2$ is

$$C(q_1) + C(q_2) = (mq_1 + F) + (mq_2 + F) = m(q_1 + q_2) + 2F = mQ + 2F.$$

If a single firm produces Q, its cost is $C(Q) = mQ + F$. Thus, the cost of producing any given Q is greater with two firms than with one firm (the condition in Equation 11.10), so this market has a natural monopoly.

APPLICATION

Electric Power Utilities

According to the estimates of Christensen and Greene (1976), the average cost curve for U.S. electric-power-producing firms in 1970 was U-shaped, reaching its minimum at 33 billion kilowatt-hours (kWh) per year (see graph). Thus, whether an electric power utility was a natural monopoly depended on the demand it faced.

For example, if the demand curve for an electric utility was D on the graph, the quantity demanded was less than 33 billion kWh per year at any price, so the electric utility operated in the strictly declining section of its average cost curve and was a natural monopoly. In 1970, most electric companies were operating in regions of substantial economies of scale. Newport Electric produced only 0.5 billion kWh per year, and Iowa Southern Utilities produced 1.3 billion kWh per year.

A few of these firms operated in the upward-sloping section of the average cost curve and were not natural monopolies. The largest electric utility in 1970, Southern, produced 54 billion kWh per year. It was not a natural monopoly because two firms could produce that quantity at 3¢ less per thousand kWh than a single firm could. As the graph shows, two firms producing 33 billion kWh each have an average cost of \$4.79 per thousand kWh, while one firm producing 66 billion kWh has an average cost of \$4.85, or 6¢ more per thousand kWh.

See Questions 13–15.

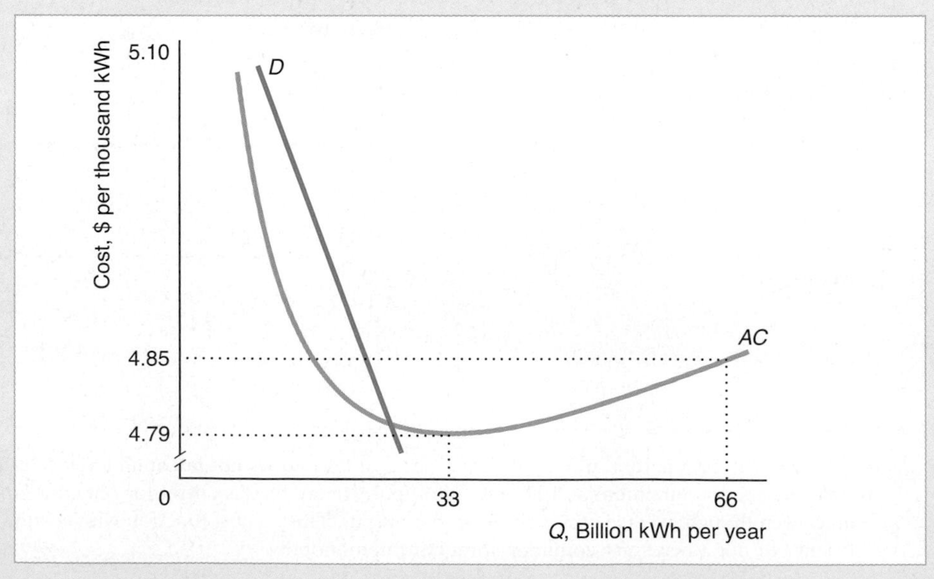

11.6 Government Actions That Create Monopolies

Governments create many monopolies. Sometimes governments own and manage monopolies. In the United States, as in most countries, the postal service is a government monopoly. Indeed, the U.S. Constitution explicitly grants the government the right to establish a postal service. Many local governments own and operate public utility monopolies that provide garbage collection, electricity, water, gas, phone services, and other utilities.

Frequently, however, governments create monopolies by preventing competing firms from entering a market. For example, when a government grants a patent, it limits entry and allows the patent-holding firm to earn a monopoly profit from an invention—a reward for developing the new product.

Barriers to Entry

By preventing other firms from entering a market, governments create monopolies. Typically, governments create monopolies in one of three ways: (1) by making it difficult for new firms to obtain a license to operate, (2) by granting a firm the rights to be a monopoly, or (3) by auctioning the rights to be a monopoly.

Frequently, firms need government licenses to operate. If governments make it difficult for new firms to obtain licenses, the first firm may maintain its monopoly. Until recently, many U.S. cities required that new hospitals or other inpatient facilities demonstrate the need for a new facility to obtain a certificate of need, which allowed them to enter the market.

Government grants of monopoly rights have been common for public utilities. Instead of running a public utility itself, a government gives a private company the monopoly rights to operate the utility. A government may capture some of the monopoly profits by charging a high rent to the monopoly. Alternatively, government officials may capture the rents for monopoly rights by means of bribes.

Governments around the world have privatized many state-owned monopolies in the past several decades. By selling its monopolies to private firms, a government can capture the value of future monopoly earnings today.[19] However, for political or other reasons, governments frequently sell at a lower price that does not capture all future profits. (See **www.myeconlab.com/perloff**, Chapter 11, "Iceland's Government Creates Genetic Monopoly.")

APPLICATION

Carlos Slim and the Mexican Monopolies

Starting in the late 1980s, Mexican President Carlos Salinas sold hundreds of state-owned companies intact, creating private monopolies. Today, Mexico has more monopolies than most countries, including beer brewing, television, cement, and phone services. As a consequence of monopolization, Mexicans shell out more money than consumers in wealthier nations for services such as electricity, phones, and bank fees.

As of 2007, the world's richest man is Carlos Slim. His fortune of $68 billion equals 6% of Mexico's gross national product. Over the last couple of years, Mr. Slim earned about $27 million a day, while a fifth of Mexicans made less than $2 a day.

Slim bought Mexico's telephone monopoly in a 1991 privatization. Slim's Teléfonos de México SA controls 92% of Mexico's fixed phone lines, and his América Móvil SA provides 73% of Mexico's cell phone service and operates in

---

[19]See **www.myeconlab.com/perloff**, Chapter 11, "Government Sales of Monopolies."

more than a dozen Latin American countries. He runs the firms efficiently and keeps phone rates much higher than in virtually any developed country in the world. As a consequence, in a country where the minimum wage is about 50¢ an hour, only half the homes have phones and only 4% have broadband Internet access.

He controls over 200 firms, including the Sanborns restaurant chain; an Internet provider; a brokerage house, part of his Grupo Financiero Inbursa group; a car insurance company; credit cards; and retail stores, among them Sears México and the Mixup record store chain. Slim also has shares in Televisa, the largest media company in the Spanish-speaking world, and one of his sons sits on Televisa's board.

Slim is not the only rich monopolist in Mexico; there are ten other billionaires who profited from the sales of monopolies in the 1980s. New President Felipe Calderón has promised to stop monopolistic practices. According to news reports, Mr. Calderón has tried to cut a backdoor deal with Mr. Slim, the nation's largest employer, to accept more competition. Good luck.

Patents

If a firm cannot prevent imitation by keeping its discovery secret, it may obtain government protection to prevent other firms from duplicating its discovery and entering the market. Virtually all countries provide such protection through a **patent:** an exclusive right granted to the inventor to sell a new and useful product, process, substance, or design for a fixed period of time. A patent grants an inventor the right to be the monopoly provider of the good for a number of years.

patent
an exclusive right granted to the inventor to sell a new and useful product, process, substance, or design for a fixed period of time

Patent Length. The length of a patent varies across countries. The U.S. Constitution explicitly gives the government the right to grant authors and inventors exclusive rights to their writings (copyrights) and to their discoveries (patents) for limited periods of time. Traditionally, U.S. patents lasted *17 years* from the date they were *granted*, but the United States agreed in 1995 to change its patent law as part of a GATT agreement. Now U.S. patents last for *20 years* after the date the inventor *files* for patent protection. The length of protection is likely to be shorter under the new rules, because it frequently takes more than three years after filing to obtain final approval of a patent.

Patents Stimulate Research. A firm with a patent monopoly sets a high price that results in deadweight loss. Why, then, do governments grant patent monopolies? The main reason is that inventive activity would fall if there were no patent monopolies or other incentives to inventors. The costs of developing a new drug or new computer chip are often hundreds of millions or even billions of dollars. If anyone could copy a new drug or chip and compete with the inventor, few individuals or firms would undertake costly research. Thus, the government is explicitly trading off the long-run benefits of additional inventions against the shorter-term harms of monopoly pricing during the period of patent protection.

APPLICATION

Botox Patent Monopoly

Ophthalmologist Dr. Alan Scott turned the deadly poison botulinum toxin into a miracle drug to treat two eye conditions: strabismus, which affects about 4% of children, and blepharospasm, an uncontrollable closure of the eyes. Blepharospasm left about 25,000 Americans functionally blind before Scott's discovery. His patented drug, Botox, is sold by Allergan, Inc.

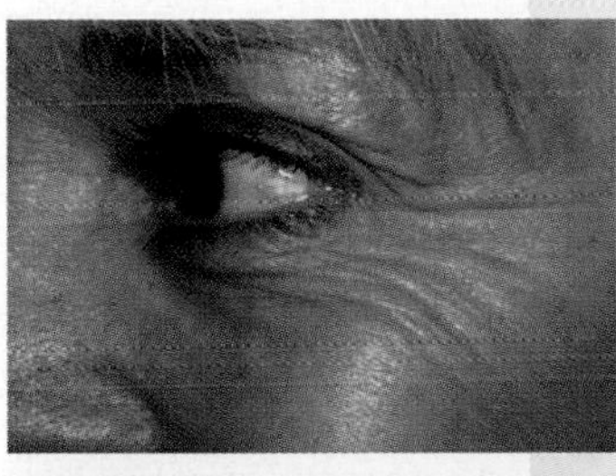

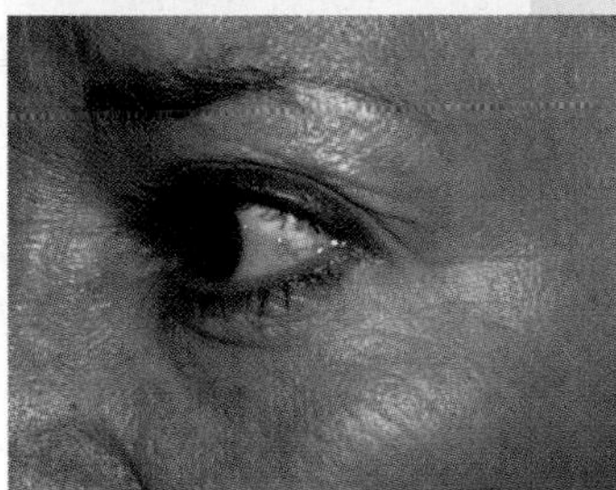

Dr. Scott has been amused to see several of the unintended beneficiaries of his research at the Academy Awards. Even before it was explicitly approved for cosmetic use, many doctors were injecting Botox into the facial muscles of actors, models, and others to smooth out their wrinkles. (The drug paralyzes the muscles, so those injected with it also lose the ability to frown—and, some would say, to act.) The treatment is only temporary, lasting up to 120 days, so repeated injections are necessary. Allergan had expected to sell $400 million worth of Botox in 2002. However, in April of that year, the Federal Food and Drug Administration approved the use of Botox for cosmetic purposes, a ruling that allows the company to advertise the drug widely.

Allergan had sales of $800 million in 2004 and $1.2 billion worth of Botox in 2007. Allergan has a near-monopoly in the treatment of wrinkles, although plastic surgery and collagen, Restylane, hyaluronic acids, and other filler injections provide limited competition. Between 2002 and 2004, the number of facelifts dropped 3% to about 114,000 according to the American Society of Plastic Surgeons, while the number of Botox injections skyrocketed 166% to nearly 3 million.

Dr. Scott says that he can produce a vial of Botox in his lab for about $25. Allergan then sells the potion to doctors for about $400. Assuming that the firm is setting its price to maximize its short-run profit, we can rearrange Equation 11.9 to determine the elasticity of demand for Botox:

$$\varepsilon = -\frac{p}{p - MC} = -\frac{400}{400 - 25} \approx -1.067.$$

Thus, the demand that Allergan faces is only slightly elastic: A 1% increase in price causes quantity to fall by only a little more than 1%.

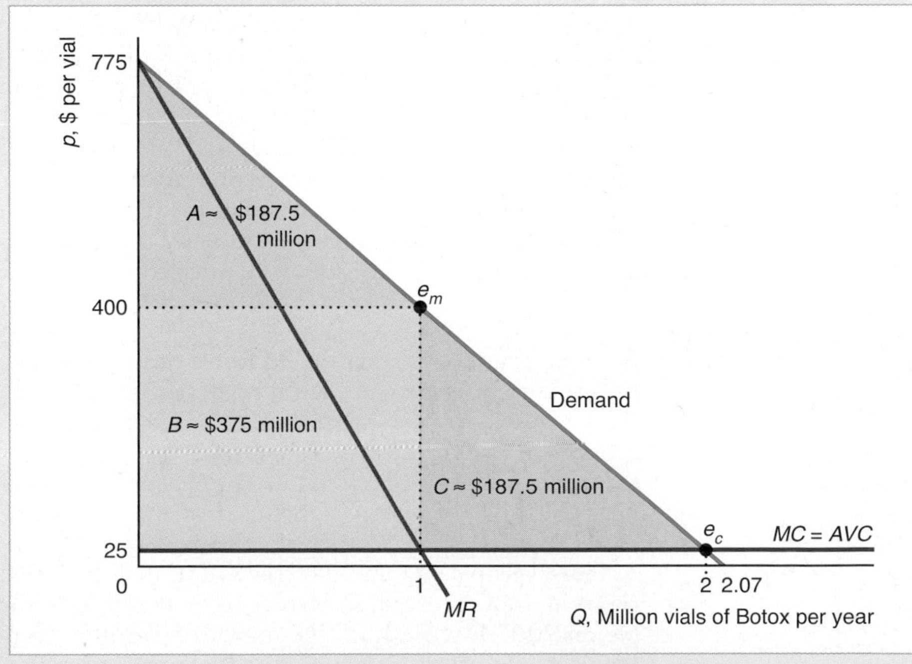

If we assume that the demand curve is linear and that the elasticity of demand is -1.067 at the 2002 monopoly optimum, e_m (one million vials sold at \$400 each, producing revenue of \$400 million), then Allergan's inverse demand function is

$$p = 775 - 375Q.$$

This demand curve (see graph) has a slope of -375 and hits the price axis at \$775 and the quantity axis at about 2.07 million vials per year. The corresponding marginal revenue curve,

$$MR = 775 - 750Q,$$

strikes the price axis at \$775 and has twice the slope, -750, as the demand curve.

The intersection of the marginal revenue and marginal cost curves,

$$MR = 775 - 750Q = 25 = MC,$$

determines the monopoly equilibrium at the profit-maximizing quantity of 1 million vials per year and a price of \$400 per vial.

Were the company to sell Botox at a price equal to its marginal cost of \$25 (as a competitive industry would), consumer surplus would equal areas $A + B + C =$ \$750 million per year. At the higher monopoly price of \$400, the consumer surplus is $A =$ \$187.5 million. Compared to the competitive solution, e_c, buyers lose consumer surplus of $B + C =$ \$562.5 million per year. Part of this loss, $B =$ \$375 million per year, is transferred from consumers to Allergan. The rest, $C =$ \$187.5 million per year, is the deadweight loss from monopoly pricing. Allergan's profit is its producer surplus, B, minus its fixed costs.

See Problems 39 and 40.

Alternatives to Patents. Instead of using patents to spur research, the government could give research grants or offer prizes. Rather than trying these alternative approaches, Congress has modified the patent system. In the 1960s and 1970s, the effective life of a patent on a drug shrank because of the additional time it took to get FDA approval to sell the drug. By 1978, the average drug had patent protection for fewer than ten years. The Drug Price Competition and Patent Term Restoration Act of 1984 restored up to three years of the part of the patent life that was lost while the firm demonstrated efficacy and safety to the FDA. As of 2007, a new drug averages 11.5 years of patent protection. At the same time, the act made it easier for generic products to enter at the end of the patent period. Thus, the law aimed both to encourage the development of new drugs by increasing the reward—the monopoly period—and to stimulate price competition at the end of the period.

APPLICATION

Property Rights and Piracy

A patent grants its owner the exclusive or monopoly right to sell a new and useful product, process, substance, or design for a fixed period. Similarly, a copyright gives its owner the exclusive production, publication, or sales rights to artistic, dramatic, literary, or musical works. The main purpose of providing these intellectual property rights is to encourage research and artistic creativity. Firms also have property rights to their brand names or symbol, called a trademark.

However, patents and copyrights are of little value to their owners if these rights are not enforced, so owners of these rights defend them fiercely. For example, in 2007 David Miller, the mayor of Toronto, wanted Canada's federal government to share some of the national sales tax—the general sales tax

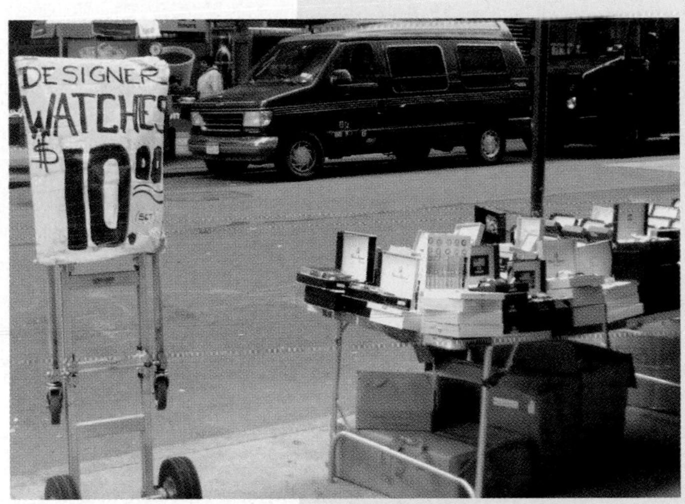

(GST)—with cities, so Toronto distributed posters, bumper stickers, and buttons with the slogan, "One Cent of the GST NOW" and a photo of a Canadian penny. All that happened was the Canadian mint sent the city a bill for $47,680 (Canadian) to compensate it for the use of its intellectual property: the photo of the penny.

Protecting intellectual property such as music and computer software from unauthorized copying has proved increasingly difficult over the past several years. Many users download music, movies, and books over the Internet without paying. Condemning these actions as piracy, music and software publishers have sued Napster and other firms that facilitate copying and have instituted copy protection schemes. These attempts to prevent copying have had limited success. In China, illegal copies of movies, music, and software openly sell for a fraction of the price—a fifth for many new DVDs—of the original price.

Owners of property rights turn to governments for help enforcing their rights. Colorful raids occur, but typically are of small scale and change little. For example, in 2007 federal customs agents raided 30 businesses and homes in 16 states looking for devices that allow pirated video games to play on Wiis, PlayStation 2s and Xboxes.

The Business Software Alliance's 2007 annual survey concluded that computer software piracy rates dropped in 63 countries but rose in 11 in 2006 compared to 2005. Moreover, in over half the countries, the piracy rate exceeds 62%. Armenia's rate is 95%. China's rate is 82%, but that reflects a 10 percentage point drop over the last three years. In the United States, 21% of software is pirated. The alliance concludes that 35% of software worldwide is illegal, costing firms $5 billion. By calculating the loss as the retail price times the number of illegal copies, however, they have an upward bias. Moreover, consumers who use pirated copies of a work may eventually decide to purchase legitimate copies of it or other related works. Thus, the effect of piracy on legitimate demand is an empirical question.

In the short run, artists and producers are harmed by piracy. If consumers benefit by being able to buy music or software for less or by stealing it, the overall short-run welfare effect of piracy is ambiguous. For example, in the extreme case where downloaders would not have bought the product, piracy raises welfare and harms no one.

Rob and Waldfogel (2004) surveyed college students at the University of Pennsylvania and elsewhere. They found that each album downloaded reduces purchases by at least 0.2% of an album. Students reported downloading almost as many albums as they purchased and admitted that if downloading had not been possible, they would have purchased 26% of the albums they downloaded. Among Penn undergrads, the researchers found that downloading reduced their personal expenditures on hit albums from $126 to $100 but raised their per capita consumer surplus by $70. Thus, for this group, the increase in consumer surplus more than offset the loss in revenues.

Regardless of the short-run welfare effects, the more serious harm occurs in the long run. Reduced copyright and patent protection lowers the drive to create or to innovate.

See Problem 41.

11.7 Government Actions That Reduce Market Power

Some governments act to reduce or eliminate monopolies' market power. Most Western countries have laws forbidding a firm from driving other firms out of the market so as to monopolize it. Many governments either regulate monopolies—especially those that the government has created—or destroy monopolies by breaking them up into smaller, independent firms or encouraging other firms to enter the market.

Regulating Monopolies

Governments limit monopolies' market power in a number of ways. Most utilities, for example, are subject to direct regulation. One method governments use to limit the harms of monopoly is to place a ceiling on the price that a monopoly charges.

Optimal Price Regulation. In some markets, the government can eliminate the deadweight loss of monopoly by requiring that a monopoly charge no more than the competitive price. We use our earlier linear example to illustrate this type of regulation in Figure 11.8.

If the government doesn't regulate the profit-maximizing monopoly, the monopoly optimum is e_m, at which 6 units are sold at the monopoly price of \$18. Suppose that the government sets a ceiling price of \$16, the price at which the marginal cost curve intersects the market demand curve. Because the monopoly cannot charge more than \$16 per unit, the monopoly's regulated demand curve is horizontal at \$16 (up to 8 units) and is the same as the market demand curve at lower prices. The marginal revenue, MR_r, corresponding to the regulated demand curve is horizontal where the regulated demand curve is horizontal (up to 8 units) and equals the marginal revenue curve, MR, corresponding to the market demand curve at larger quantities.

The regulated monopoly sets its output at 8 units, where MR_r equals its marginal cost, MC, and charges the maximum permitted price of \$16. The regulated firm still makes a profit, because its average cost is less than \$16 at 8 units. The optimally regulated monopoly optimum, e_o, is the same as the competitive equilibrium, where marginal cost (supply) equals the market demand curve.[20] Thus, setting a price ceiling where the MC curve and market demand curve intersect eliminates the deadweight loss of monopoly.

How do we know that this regulation is optimal? The answer is that this regulated outcome is the same as would occur if this market were competitive, where welfare is maximized (Chapter 9). As the table accompanying Figure 11.8 shows, the deadweight loss of monopoly, $C + E$, is eliminated by this optimal regulation.

Nonoptimal Price Regulation. Welfare is reduced if the government does not set the price optimally. Suppose that the government sets the regulated price below the optimal level, which is \$16 in our example. If it sets the price below the firm's minimum average cost, the firm shuts down. If that happens, the deadweight loss equals the sum of the consumer plus producer surplus under optimal regulation,

$$A + B + C + D + E.$$

[20]The monopoly produces at e_o only if the regulated price is greater than its average variable cost. Here the regulated price, \$16, exceeds the average variable cost at 8 units of \$8. Indeed, the firm makes a profit because the average cost at 8 units is \$9.50.

Figure 11.8 Optimal Price Regulation.

If the government sets a price ceiling at $16, where the monopoly's marginal cost curve hits the demand curve, the new demand curve the monopoly faces has a kink at 8 units, and the corresponding marginal revenue curve, MR_r, "jumps" at that quantity. The regulated monopoly sets its output where $MR_r = MC$, selling the same quantity, 8 units, at the same price, $16, as a competitive industry would. The regulation eliminates the monopoly deadweight loss, $C + E$. Consumer surplus, $A + B + C$, and producer surplus, $D + E$, are the same as under competition.

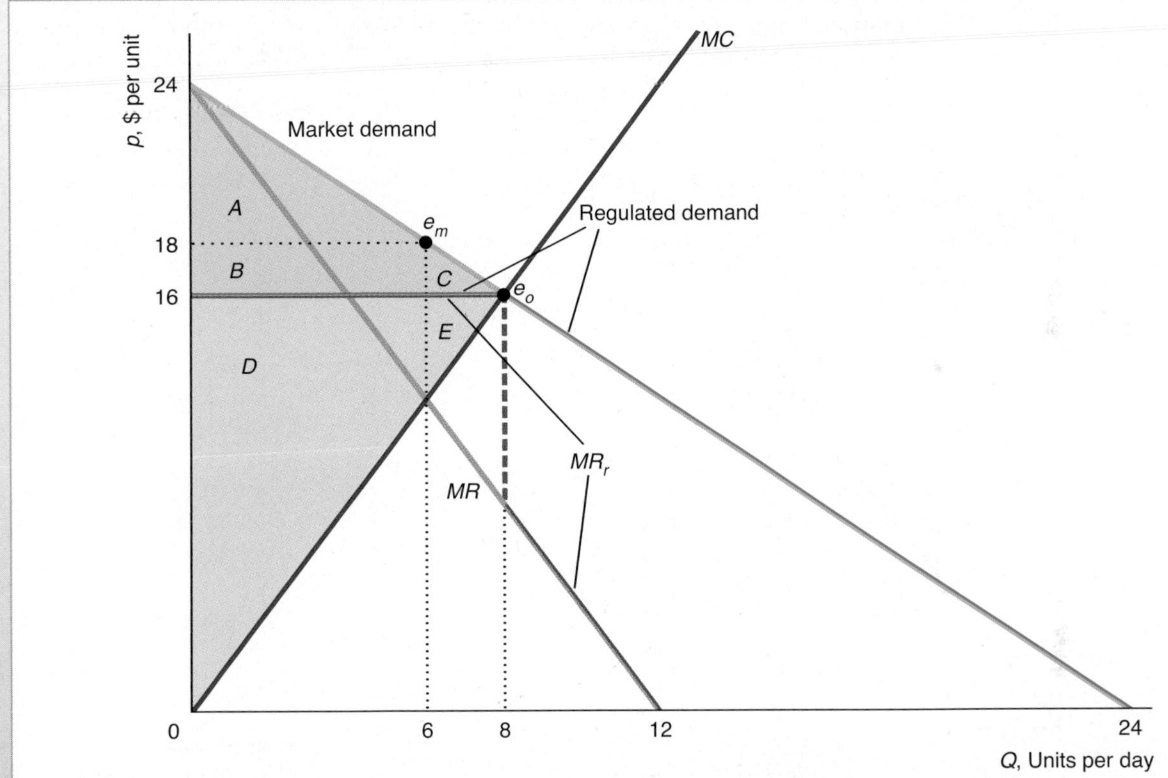

	Monopoly Without Regulation	Monopoly with Optimal Regulation	Change
Consumer Surplus, CS	A	$A + B + C$	$B + C = \Delta CS$
Producer Surplus, PS	$B + D$	$D + E$	$E - B = \Delta PS$
Welfare, $W = CS + PS$	$A + B + D$	$A + B + C + D + E$	$C + E = \Delta W$
Deadweight Loss, DWL	$-C - E$	0	$C + E = \Delta DWL$

If the government sets the price ceiling below the optimally regulated price but high enough that the firm does not shut down, consumers who are lucky enough to buy the good are better off because they can buy goods at a lower price than with optimal regulation. Some customers, however, are frustrated because the monopoly will not sell them the good, as we show next. There is a deadweight loss because less output is sold than with optimal regulation. (Question 16 at the end of the chapter asks you to determine the effects of a regulated price that is above the optimal level.)

Solved Problem 11.4

Suppose that the government sets a price, p_2, that is below the socially optimal level, p_1, but above the monopoly's minimum average cost. How do the price, the quantity sold, the quantity demanded, and welfare under this regulation compare to those under optimal regulation?

Answer

1. *Describe the optimally regulated outcome.* With optimal regulation, e_1, the price is set at p_1, where the market demand curve intersects the monopoly's marginal cost curve on the accompanying graph. The optimally regulated monopoly sells Q_1 units.

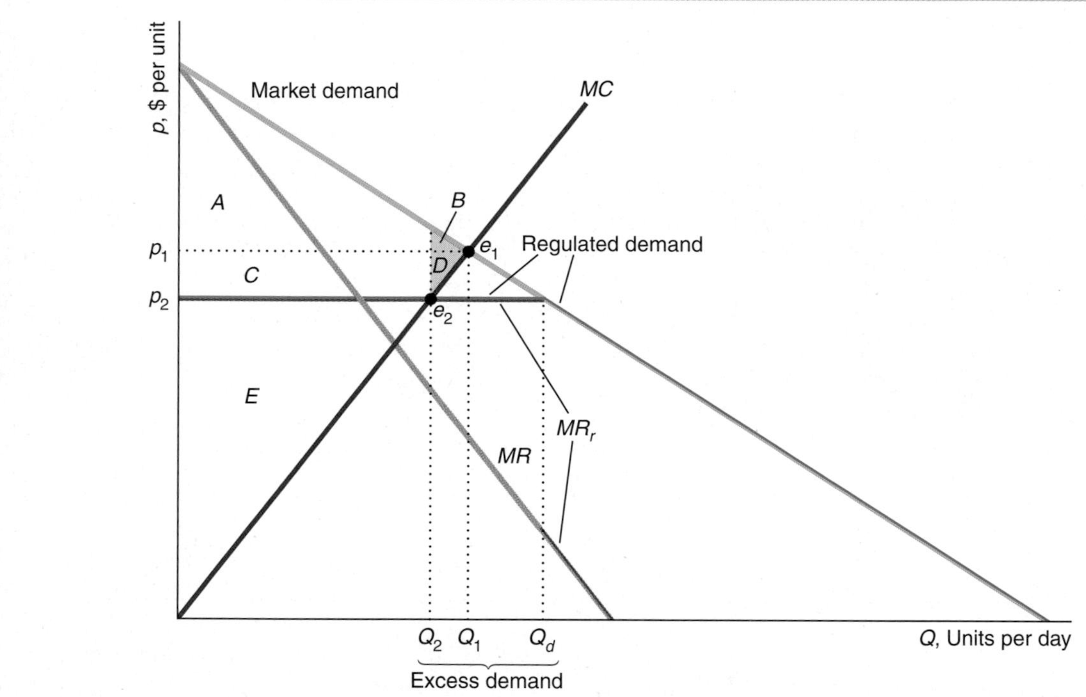

	Monopoly with Optimal Regulation	Monopoly with a Low Regulated Price	Change
Consumer Surplus, CS	$A + B$	$A + C$	$C - B = \Delta CS$
Producer Surplus, PS	$C + D + E$	E	$-C - D = \Delta PS$
Welfare, $W = CS + PS$	$A + B + C + D + E$	$A + C + E$	$-B - D = \Delta W = DWL$

2. *Describe the outcome when the government regulates the price at p_2.* Where the market demand is above p_2, the regulated demand curve for the monopoly is horizontal at p_2 (up to Q_d). The corresponding marginal revenue curve, MR_r, is kinked. It is horizontal where the regulated demand curve is horizontal. The MR_r equals the marginal revenue curve corresponding to the market demand curve, MR, where the regulated demand curve is downward sloping. The monopoly maximizes its profit by selling Q_2 units at p_2. The new regulated monopoly optimum is e_2, where MR_r intersects MC. The firm

does not shut down when regulated as long as its average variable cost at Q_2 is less than p_2.

3. *Compare the outcomes.* The quantity that the monopoly sells falls from Q_1 to Q_2 when the government lowers its price ceiling from p_1 to p_2. At that low price, consumers want to buy Q_d, so there is excess demand equal to $Q_d - Q_2$. Compared to optimal regulation, welfare is lower by at least $B + D$.

See Questions 16–20 and Problems 42 and 43.

Comment: The welfare loss is greater if unlucky consumers waste time trying to buy the good unsuccessfully or if goods are not allocated optimally among consumers. A consumer who values the good at only p_2 may be lucky enough to buy it, while a consumer who values the good at p_1 or more may not be able to obtain it.

Problems in Regulating. Governments face several problems in regulating monopolies. First, because they do not know the actual demand and marginal cost curves, governments may set the price at the wrong level. Second, many governments use regulations that are less efficient than price regulation. Third, regulated firms may bribe or otherwise influence government regulators to help the firms rather than society as a whole.

Because of limited information about the demand and marginal cost curves, governments may set a price ceiling above or below the competitive level. Moreover, a regulatory agency may have to set the price higher than is optimal because it cannot offer a subsidy.

If the regulatory agency were to set the price equal to a natural monopoly's marginal cost, the price would be below the firm's average cost. The monopoly would threaten to shut down unless the regulatory agency were to subsidize it or raise the price.

To illustrate this problem, we calculate how setting the price too low would affect a phone monopoly in Macon, Georgia (before deregulation in 1995 that allowed additional firms into the market).[21] In the absence of regulation and in light of the curves in Figure 11.9, this firm maximizes its profit by operating where its marginal cost equals its marginal revenue, e_1, where it provides 31,000 telephone lines at \$710 each annually. At that quantity, its average cost is \$248, so its profit is (\$710 – \$248)31,000 = \$14,322,000, area A.

Alternatively, the government may regulate the utility to behave like a price taker, e_3. The firm would lose money if it faced a price ceiling of \$160 annually, where the demand curve intersects the marginal cost curve at 63,000 lines. At that quantity, its average cost is \$204, so it loses (\$204 – \$160)63,000 = \$2,722,000, area B.

Typically, it is politically infeasible for a government regulatory agency to subsidize a firm. Instead, the agency might set the price at \$248, where the demand curve intersects the average cost curve and the monopoly breaks even. There is still a deadweight loss because that price is above marginal cost, but the deadweight loss is smaller than it would be if the monopoly were unregulated. The government may regulate the price so that the utility breaks even, e_2. If so, the government must subsidize the utility by area B = \$2,772,000 to keep it from shutting down.

---

[21]This example is based on Gasmi et al. (2002, Appendix A). We replaced their exponential demand curve with a linear demand curve, where both curves have a price elasticity of demand of –0.2 at point e_2.

Figure 11.9 Regulating a Telephone Utility.

If the phone utility is an unregulated, profit-maximizing monopoly, e_1, it provides 31,000 telephone lines at $710 each annually and makes a profit of $14,322,000, equal to area *A*. The government may regulate the price so that the utility breaks even, e_2. Alternatively, the government may regulate the utility to behave like a price taker, e_3. If so, the government must subsidize the utility by area B = $2,583,000 to keep it from shutting down.

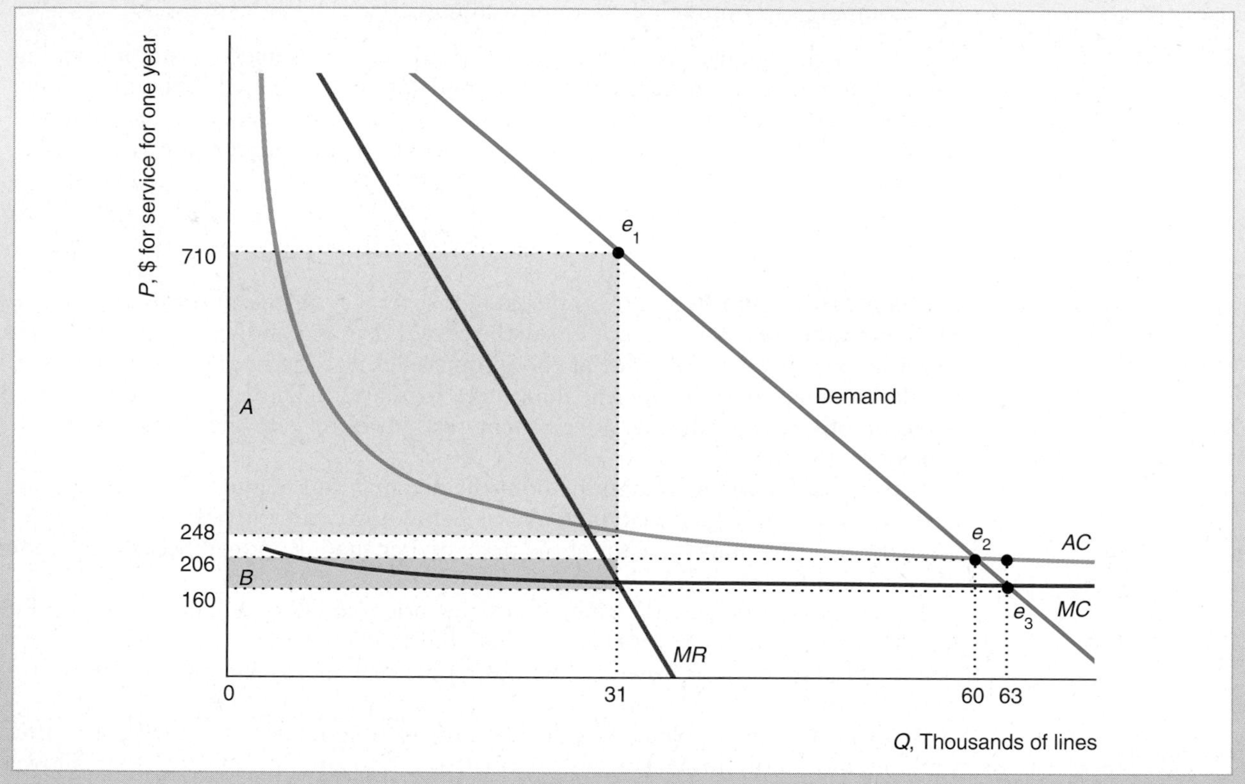

Unfortunately, regulation is often not effective when regulators are *captured*: influenced by the firms they regulate. Typically, this influence is more subtle than an outright bribe. Many American regulators have worked in the industry before they became regulators and hence are sympathetic to those firms. Many regulators hope to obtain good jobs in the industry eventually, so they don't want to offend potential employers. Other regulators, relying on industry experts for their information, may be misled or at least heavily influenced by the industry. For example, the California Public Utilities Commission urged telephone and cable companies to negotiate among themselves as to how they wanted to open local phone markets to competition by 1997. Arguing that these influences are inherent, some economists contend that price and other types of regulation are unlikely to result in efficiency.

Increasing Competition

Encouraging competition is an alternative to regulation as a means of reducing the harms of monopoly. When a government has created a monopoly by preventing entry, it can quickly reduce the monopoly's market power by allowing other firms to enter. As new firms enter the market, the former monopoly must lower its price to compete, so welfare rises. Many governments are actively encouraging entry into telephone, electricity, and other utility markets that were formerly monopolized.

Similarly, a government may end a ban on imports so that a domestic monopoly faces competition from foreign firms. If costs for the domestic firm are the same as costs for the foreign firms and there are many foreign firms, the former monopoly becomes just one of many competitive firms. As the market becomes competitive, consumers pay the competitive price, and the deadweight loss of monopoly is eliminated.

Governments around the world are increasing competition in formerly monopolized markets. For example, many U.S. and European governments are forcing former telephone and energy monopolies to compete. See **www.myeconlab.com/perloff**, Chapter 11, "Ending the Monopoly in Telephone Service."

Similarly, under pressure from the World Trade Organization, many countries are reducing or eliminating barriers that protected domestic monopolies. The entry of foreign competitive firms into a market can create a new, more competitive market structure. For example, see **www.myeconlab.com/perloff**, Chapter 11, "Dominant Firm and Competitive Fringe."

11.8 Network Externalities, Behavioral Economics, and Monopoly Decisions over Time

We have examined how a monopoly behaves in the current period, ignoring the future. For many markets, such an analysis is appropriate. However, in some markets, decisions today affect demand or cost in a future period. In such markets, the monopoly may maximize its long-run profit by making a decision today that does not maximize its short-run profit. For example, frequently a firm introduces a new product—such as a candy bar—by initially charging a low price or giving away free samples to generate word-of-mouth publicity or to let customers learn about its quality in hopes of getting their future business. We now consider an important reason why consumers' demand in the future may depend on a monopoly's actions in the present.

Network Externalities

network externality the situation where one person's demand for a good depends on the consumption of the good by others

The number of customers a firm has today may affect the demand curve it faces in the future. A good has a **network externality** if one person's demand depends on the consumption of a good by others.[22] If a good has a *positive* network externality, its value to a consumer grows as the number of units sold increases.

When a firm introduces a new good with a network externality, it faces a chicken-and-egg problem: It can't get Max to buy the good unless Sofia will buy it, but it can't get Sofia to buy it unless Max will. The firm wants its customers to coordinate or to make their purchase decisions simultaneously.

The telephone provides a classic example of a positive network externality. When the phone was introduced, potential adopters had no reason to get phone service

[22]In Chapter 18, we discuss the more general case of an *externality,* which occurs when a person's well-being or a firm's production capability is directly affected by the actions of other consumers or firms rather than indirectly through changes in prices. The following discussion on network externalities is based on Leibenstein (1950), Rohlfs (1974), Katz and Shapiro (1994), Economides (1996), Shapiro and Varian (1999), and Rohlfs (2001).

unless their family and friends did. Why buy a phone if there's no one to call? For Bell's phone network to succeed, it had to achieve a *critical mass* of users—enough adopters that others wanted to join. Had it failed to achieve this critical mass, demand would have withered and the network would have died. Similarly, the market for fax machines grew very slowly until a critical mass was achieved where many firms had them.

Direct Size Effect. Many industries exhibit positive network externalities where the customer gets a *direct* benefit from a larger network. The larger an ATM network such as the Plus network, the greater the odds that you will find an ATM machine when you want one, so the more likely it is that you will want to use that network. The more people who use a particular computer program, the more attractive it is to someone who wants to exchange files with other users.

Behavioral Economics. These examples of the direct effect of network externalities depend on the size of the network because customers want to interact with each other. However, sometimes consumers' behavior depends on beliefs or tastes that can be explained by psychological and sociological theories. These explanations are called *behavioral economics*.

One alternative explanation for a direct network externality effect is based on tastes. Harvey Leibenstein (1950) suggested that consumers sometimes want a good because "everyone else has it." A fad or other popularity-based explanation for a positive network externality is called a **bandwagon effect**: A person places greater value on a good as more and more other people possess it.[23] The success of the iPod today may be partially due to its early popularity. Ugg boots seem to be another example of a bandwagon effect.

bandwagon effect
the situation in which a person places greater value on a good as more and more other people possess it

The opposite, negative network externality is called a **snob effect**: A person places greater value on a good as fewer and fewer other people possess it. Some people prefer an original painting by an unknown artist to a lithograph by a star because no one else can possess that painting. (As Yogi Berra said, "Nobody goes there anymore; it's too crowded.")

snob effect
the situation in which a person places greater value on a good as fewer and fewer other people possess it

Indirect Effect. In some markets, positive network externalities are indirect and stem from complementary goods that are offered when a product has a critical mass of users. Why buy a computer if no software programs are available? The more extra devices and software that work with a particular computer, the more people want to buy that computer; however, these extra devices are available only if a critical mass of customers buys the computer. Similarly, the more people who drive diesel-powered cars, the more likely it is that gas stations will sell diesel fuel; and the more stations that sell the fuel, the more likely it is that someone will want to drive a diesel car. As a final example, once a critical mass of customers had broadband Internet service, more services provided downloadable music and movies and more high-definition Web pages become available; and once those killer apps appeared, more people signed up for broadband service.

Network Externalities as an Explanation for Monopolies

Because of the need for a critical mass of customers in a market with a positive network externality, we frequently see only one large firm surviving, as in the case of

[23]*Jargon alert*: Some economists use *bandwagon effect* to mean any positive network externality—not just those that are based on popularity.

eBay. Several online auctions started a few years ago, including eBay and Yahoo. However, all else being the same, sellers want to use the site that has the most potential buyers, and buyers want the largest choice of sellers. Thus, after eBay reached a critical mass, it grew rapidly, its rivals lost customers, and eventually eBay became a virtual monopoly.

Visa's ad campaign tells consumers that Visa cards are accepted "everywhere you want to be," including at stores that "don't take American Express." One could view its ad campaign as an attempt to convince consumers that its card has a critical mass and therefore everyone should switch to it.

But having achieved a monopoly, a firm does not necessarily keep it. History is filled with examples where one product knocks off another: "The king is dead; long live the king." Google replaced Yahoo as the predominant search engine. Explorer displaced Netscape as the big-dog browser (and Firefox lurks in the wings). Levi Strauss is no longer the fashion leader among the jeans set.

A Two-Period Monopoly Model

A monopoly may be able to solve the chicken-and-egg problem of getting a critical mass for its product by initially selling the product at a low introductory price. By doing so, the firm maximizes its long-run profit but not its short-run profit.

Suppose that a monopoly sells its good—say, root-beer-scented jeans—for only two periods (after that, the demand goes to zero as a new craze hits the market). If the monopoly sells less than a critical quantity of output, Q, in the first period, its second-period demand curve lies close to the price axis. However, if the good is a success in the first period—at least Q units are sold—the second-period demand curve shifts substantially to the right.

If the monopoly maximizes its short-run profit in the first period, it charges p^* and sells Q^* units, which is fewer than Q. To sell Q units, it would have to lower its first-period price to $\underline{p} < p^*$, which would reduce its first-period profit from π^* to $\underline{\pi}$.

In the second period, the monopoly maximizes its profit given its second-period demand curve. If the monopoly sold only Q^* units in the first period, it earns a relatively low second-period profit of π_l. However, if it sells Q units in the first period, it makes a relatively high second-period profit, π_h.

See Questions 21–23 and Problem 44.

Should the monopoly charge a low introductory price in the first period? Its objective is to maximize its long-run profit: the sum of its profit in the two periods.[24] If the firm has a critical mass in the second period, its extra profit is $\pi_h - \pi_l$. To obtain this critical mass by charging a low introductory price in the first period, it lowers its first period profit by $\pi^* - \underline{\pi}$. Thus, the firm chooses to charge a low introductory period in the first period if its first period loss is less than its extra profit in the second period. This policy must pay for some firms: A Google search found a third of a million cites to Web pages touting introductory prices.

[24]In Chapter 16, we discuss why firms place lower value on profit in the future than profit today, and how a firm can compare profit in the future to profit today. For now, we assume that the monopoly places equal value on profit in either period.

SUMMARY

1. **Monopoly Profit Maximization.** Like any firm, a monopoly—a single seller—maximizes its profit by setting its output so that its marginal revenue equals its marginal cost. The monopoly makes a positive profit if its average cost is less than the price at the profit-maximizing output.

2. **Effects of a Shift of the Demand Curve.** Because a monopoly does not have a supply curve, the effect of a shift in demand on a monopoly's output depends on the shapes of both its marginal cost curve and its demand curve. As a monopoly's demand curve shifts, price and output may change in the same direction or different directions.

3. **Market Power.** Market power is the ability of a firm to charge a price above marginal cost and earn a positive profit. The more elastic the demand the monopoly faces at the quantity at which it maximizes its profit, the closer its price to its marginal cost and the closer the Lerner Index or price markup, $(p - MC)/p$, to zero, the competitive level.

4. **Welfare Effects of Monopoly.** Because a monopoly's price is above its marginal cost, too little output is produced, and society suffers a deadweight loss. The monopoly makes higher profit than it would if it acted as a price taker. Consumers are worse off, buying less output at a higher price.

5. **Cost Advantages That Create Monopolies.** A firm may be a monopoly if it controls a key input, has superior knowledge about producing or distributing a good, or has substantial economies of scale. In markets with substantial economies of scale, the single seller is called a natural monopoly because total production costs would rise if more than one firm produced the good.

6. **Government Actions That Create Monopolies.** Governments may establish government-owned and -operated monopolies. They may also create private monopolies by establishing barriers to entry that prevent other firms from competing. Nations grant patents, which give inventors monopoly rights for a limited period of time.

7. **Government Actions That Reduce Market Power.** A government can eliminate the welfare harm of a monopoly by forcing the firm to set its price at the competitive level. If the government sets the price at a different level or otherwise regulates nonoptimally, welfare at the regulated monopoly optimum is lower than in the competitive equilibrium. A government can eliminate or reduce the harms of monopoly by allowing or facilitating entry.

8. **Network Externalities, Behavioral Economics, and Monopoly Decisions over Time.** If a good has a positive network externality so that its value to a consumer grows as the number of units sold increases, then current sales affect a monopoly's future demand curve. A monopoly may maximize its long-run profit—its profit over time—by setting a low introductory price in the first period that it sells the good and then later raising its price as its product's popularity ensures large future sales at a higher price. Consequently, the monopoly is not maximizing its short-run profit in the first period but is maximizing the sum of its profits over all periods.

QUESTIONS

■ = *exercise is available on MyEconLab;* * = *answer appears at the back of this book;* C = *use of calculus may be necessary;* W = *audio-slideshow answer by James Dearden is available in Textbook Resources on MyEconLab.*

1. Does it affect a monopoly's profit if it chooses price or quantity (assuming it chooses them optimally)? Why can't a monopoly choose both price and quantity?

2. When is a monopoly unlikely to be profitable in the long run? (*Hint*: Discuss the relationship between market demand and average cost.)

3. AT&T Inc., the biggest U.S. phone company and the one-time monopoly, is leaving the payphone business after 129 years because people are switching to wireless phones (Crayton Harrison, "AT&T to Disconnect Pay-Phone Business After 129 Years," Bloomberg.com, December 3, 2007). The number of wireless subscribers has quadrupled in the past decade: 80% of U.S. phone users now have mobile phones. Consequently, the number of payphones fell from 2.6 million at the peak in 1998 to 1 million in 2006. (But where will Clark Kent go to change into Superman now?) Use graphs to explain why a monopoly will exit a market as its demand curve shifts to the left.

4. Show why a monopoly may operate in the upward- or downward-sloping section of its long-run average cost curve but a competitive firm will operate only in the upward-sloping section.

5. Are major-league baseball clubs profit-maximizing monopolies? Some observers of this market have contended that baseball club owners want to maximize attendance or revenue. Alexander (2001) says that one test of whether a firm is a profit-maximizing monopoly is to check whether the firm is operating in the elastic portion of its demand curve (which he finds is true). Why is that a relevant test? What would the elasticity be if a baseball club were maximizing revenue?

6. Show that after a shift in the demand curve, a monopoly's price may remain constant but its output may rise.

7. When will a monopoly set its price equal to its marginal cost?

8. Draw an example of a monopoly with a linear demand curve and a constant marginal cost curve.

   a. Show the profit-maximizing price and output, p^* and Q^*, and identify the areas of consumer surplus, producer surplus, and deadweight loss. Also show the quantity, Q_c, that would be produced if the monopoly were to act like a price taker.

   b. Now suppose that the demand curve is a smooth concave-to-the-origin curve (whose ends hit the axes) that is tangent to the original demand curve at the point (Q^*, p^*). Explain why the monopoly equilibrium will be the same as with the linear demand curve. Show how much output the firm would produce if it acted like a price taker. Show how the welfare areas change.

   c. Repeat the exercises in part b if the demand curve is a smooth convex-to-the-origin curve (whose ends hit the axes) that is tangent to the original demand curve at the point (Q^*, p^*).

9. A monopoly has a constant marginal cost of production of $1 per unit and a fixed cost of $10. Draw the firm's *MC*, *AVC*, and *AC* curves. Add a downward-sloping demand curve, and show the profit-maximizing quantity and price. Indicate the profit as an area on your diagram. Show the deadweight loss.

10. What is the effect of a franchise (lump-sum) tax on a monopoly? (*Hint*: Consider the possibility that the firm may shut down.)

*11. Only Native American Indian tribes can run casinos in California. These casinos are spread around the state so that each is a monopoly in its local community. California governor Arnold Schwarzenegger negotiated with the state's tribes, getting them to agree to transfer a fraction of their profits to the state in exchange for concessions (Dan Morain and Evan Halper, "Casino Deals Said to Be Near," *Los Angeles Times*, June 16, 2004, 1). In 2004, he started with a proposal that the state get 25% of casino profits and then dropped the level to 15%. He announced a deal with two tribes at 10% in 2005. How does a profit tax affect a monopoly's output and price? How would a monopoly change its behavior if the profit tax were 10% rather than 25%? (*Hint*: You may assume that the profit tax refers to the tribe's economic profit.)

12. The heads of five major oil companies were forced to defend the industry's enormous post-Hurricane Katrina profits in a U.S. Senate hearing, in response to proposals for a windfall profit tax (which were not ultimately passed into law). Some ExxonMobil gas station operators complained that the company had raised the wholesale price of its gas by 24¢ a gallon within 24 hours of the hurricane and concluded that the increase was price gouging. Average oil industry profits were $24.3 billion from 2000–2004, but increased to $62.8 billion (at an annual rate) in the first quarter of 2005, immediately after the hurricane (Baker, 2005).

   a. What would be the short-run and long-run effects of a tax on economic profit?

   b. What would be the short-run and long-run effects of a tax on the windfall economic profit—the amount earned above the usual profit?

*13. Can a firm be a natural monopoly if it has a U-shaped average cost curve? Why or why not?

14. Can a firm operating in the upward sloping portion of its average cost curve be a natural monopoly? Explain.

15. Using the information in the "Electric Power Utilities" application, if a utility produced 34 billion kWh per year—which is on the upward-sloping section of the average cost curve—would it be a natural monopoly?

16. Describe the effects on output and welfare if the government regulates a monopoly so that it may not charge a price above $\bar{p}$ which lies between the unregulated monopoly price and the optimally regulated price (determined by the intersection of the firm's marginal cost and the market demand curve).

17. A monopoly drug company produces a lifesaving medicine at a constant cost of $10 per dose. The demand for this medicine is perfectly inelastic at prices less than or equal to the $100 (per day) income of the 100 patients who need to take this drug daily. At a higher price, nothing is bought. Show the equilibrium price and quantity and the consumer and producer surplus in a graph. Now the government imposes a price ceiling of $30. Show how the equilibrium, consumer surplus, and producer surplus

change. What is the deadweight loss, if any, from this price control?

18. The price of wholesale milk dropped by 30.3% in 1999 as the Pennsylvania Milk Marketing Board lowered the regulated price. The price to consumers fell by substantially less than 30.3% in Philadelphia. Why? (*Hint*: Show that a monopoly will not necessarily lower its price by the same percentage as its constant marginal cost drops.)

19. Bleyer Industries Inc., the only U.S. manufacturer of plastic Easter eggs, manufactures 250 million eggs each year. Over the past seven years, imports from China have cut into its business. In 2005, Bleyer filed for bankruptcy because the Chinese firms could produce the eggs at much lower costs ("U.S. Plastic Egg Industry a Shell of Its Former Self," *San Francisco Chronicle*, January 14, 2005). Use graphs to show how a competitive import industry could drive a monopoly out of business.

20. A country has a monopoly that is protected by a specific tariff, τ, on imported goods. (For example, Malaysia's monopoly auto manufacturer produces the Proton, which is protected from imports by tariffs.) The monopoly's profit-maximizing price is p^*. The world price of the good is p_w, which is less than p^*. Because the price of imported goods with the tariff is $p_w + \tau$, no foreign goods are imported. Under WTO pressure the government removes the tariff so that the supply of foreign goods to the country's consumers is horizontal at p_w. Show how much the former monopoly produces and what price it charges. Show who gains and who loses from removing the tariff. (*Hint*: Look at the effect of government price regulation on a monopoly's demand curve in Section 11.7.)

21. Hotels tend to charge a lot for phone calls from their rooms. Cell phones endangered this nice little "monopoly" business to the point that average telephone profit per available room at hotels in the United States fell from $637 in 2000 to $152 in 2003 (Christopher Elliott, "Mystery of the Cellphone That Doesn't Work at the Hotel," *New York Times*, September 7, 2004, C6). But now many travelers complain that their cell phones don't work in hotels. Though hotels deny that they are doing anything so nefarious as blocking signals, Netline Communications Technologies in Tel Aviv says that it has sold hundreds of cell phone jammers to hotels around the world. A Federal Communications Commission rule prohibits cell phone jammers, but it is unenforced. By one estimate, a device that could block all cell phone transmissions would cost $25,000 for a small hotel and $35,000 to $50,000 for a big chain hotel. Assume that the blocker lasts for one year. Under what conditions (in terms of profit per room, number of rooms, and so forth) would it pay for a hotel to install a jammer, assuming the law permits it? Explain your answer.

22. Once the copyright runs out on a book or music, it can legally be placed on the Internet for anyone to download. However, the U.S. Congress recently extended the copyright law to 95 years after the original publication. But in Australia and Europe, the copyright holds for only 50 years. Thus, an Australian Web site could post *Gone With the Wind*, a 1936 novel, or Elvis Presley's 1954 single "That's All Right," while a U.S. site could not. Obviously, this legal nicety won't stop American fans from downloading from Australian or European sites. Discuss how limiting the length of a copyright would affect the pricing used by the publisher of a novel.

23. A monopoly chocolate manufacturer faces two types of consumers. The larger group, the hoi polloi, loves desserts and has a relatively flat, linear demand curve for chocolate. The smaller group, the snobs, is interested in buying chocolate only if the hoi polloi do not buy it. Given that the hoi polloi do not buy the chocolate, the snobs have a relatively steep, linear demand curve. Show the monopoly's possible outcomes—high price, low quantity, low price, high quantity—and explain the condition under which the monopoly chooses to cater to the snobs rather than to the hoi polloi.

24. Suppose that many similar price-taking consumers (like Denise in Chapter 10) have a single good (candy bars). Jane has a monopoly in wood so she can set prices. Assume that no production is possible. Using an Edgeworth box, illustrate the monopoly optimum and show that it does not lie on the contract curve (isn't Pareto efficient).

PROBLEMS

25. The inverse demand curve a monopoly faces is

$$p = 100 - Q.$$

The firm's cost curve is $C(Q) = 10 + 5Q$ (so $MC = 5$). What is the profit-maximizing solution? How does your answer change if $C(Q) = 100 + 5Q$?

26. The inverse demand curve a monopoly faces is

$$p = 10Q^{-0.5}.$$

The firm's cost curve is $C(Q) = 5Q$. What is the profit-maximizing solution? C

27. A monopoly's production function is Cobb-Douglas: $p = L^{0.5}K^{0.5}$ where L is labor and K is capital. As a result, the marginal product functions are

$$MP_L = K^{0.5}/L^{0.5} \text{ and}$$
$$MP_K = \tfrac{1}{2}L^{0.5}/K^{0.5}.$$

The demand function is $p = 100 - Q$. The wage, w, is \$1 per hour, and the rental cost of capital, r, is \$4.

a. What is the equation of the (long-run) expansion path? Illustrate in a graph.

b. Derive the long-run total cost curve equation as a function of q.

c. What quantity maximizes this firm's profit?

d. Find the optimal input combination that produces the profit-maximizing quantity. Illustrate with a graph.

28. A monopoly manufactures its product in two factories with marginal cost functions $MC_1(Q_1)$ and $MC_2(Q_2)$, where Q_1 is the quantity produced in the first factory and Q_2 is the quantity manufactured in the second factory. The monopoly's total output is $Q = Q_1 + Q_2$. Use a graph (or math) to determine how much total output the monopoly produces and how much it produces at each factory. (*Hint*: Consider the cases where the factories have constant marginal costs—not necessarily equal—and where they have upward-sloping marginal cost curves.)

29. Suppose all iPod owners consider only two options for downloading music to their MP3 players: purchase songs from iTunes or copy songs from friends' CDs. With these two options, suppose the weekly inverse market demand for the Rolling Stones' song "Satisfaction" is $p = 1.98 - 0.00198Q$. The marginal cost to Apple Inc. of downloading a song is zero.

a. What is Apple's optimal price of "Satisfaction"? How many downloads of "Satisfaction" does Apple sell each week?

b. Now suppose that Apple sells a version of the iPod equipped with software in which songs played on the iPod must be downloaded from iTunes. For this iPod, the inverse market demand for "Satisfaction" is $p = 2.58 - 0.0129Q$. What is Apple's optimal price of downloads of "Satisfaction" for this new player? How many downloads of "Satisfaction" does Apple sell each week? W

30. In addition to the hard-drive-based iPod, Apple produces a flash-based audio player. Its 512MB iPod Shuffle (which does not have a hard drive) sold for \$99 in 2005. According to iSuppli, Apple's per-unit cost of manufacturing the Shuffle is \$45.37 (Brian Dipert, "Song Wars: Striking Back Against the iPod Empire," **www.reed-electronics.com**, June 9, 2005). What is Apple's price/marginal cost ratio? What is its Lerner Index? If we assume (possibly incorrectly) that Apple acts like a short-run profit-maximizing monopoly in pricing its iPod Shuffle, what elasticity of demand does Apple believe it faces?

*31. Humana hospitals in 1991 charged very high prices relative to their marginal costs. For example, Humana's Suburban Hospital in Louisville charged patients \$44.90 for a container of saline solution (salt water) that cost the hospital 81¢ (Douglas Frantz, "Congress Probes Hospital Costs—\$9 Tylenols, \$118 Heat Pads," *San Francisco Chronicle,* October 18, 1991, A2). Calculate the hospital's price/marginal cost ratio, its Lerner Index, and the demand elasticity, ε, that it faces for saline solution (assuming that it maximizes its profit).

32. According to the California Nurses Association, Tenet Healthcare hospitals mark up drugs substantially. At Tenet's Sierra Vista Regional Medical Center, drug prices are 1,840.80% of the hospital's costs (Chuck Squatriglia and Tyche Hendricks, "Tenet Hiked Drug Prices, Study Finds More Than Double U.S. Average," *San Francisco Chronicle,* November 24, 2002: A1, A10). Assuming Tenet is maximizing its profit, what is the elasticity of demand that Tenet believes it faces? What is its Lerner Index for drugs?

33. According to one estimate, the parts for a Segway Human Transporter—which has five gyroscopes, two tilt sensors, dual redundant motors, ten microprocessors, and can travel up to 12.5 mph—cost at least \$1,500 (Eric A. Taub, "Segway Transporter Slow to Catch On," *San Francisco Chronicle,* August 11, 2003, E4). Suppose that Segway's marginal cost is \$2,000. Given that the Segway's price is \$5,000, calculate the firm's price/marginal cost ratio, its Lerner Index, and the elasticity of demand it believes it faces (assuming that it is trying to maximize its short-run profit).

34. In 2005, Apple introduced the Mac mini G4, a miniature computer that weighs only 2.9 pounds but comes fully loaded with lots of memory and a large hard disk. According to one estimate, the cost of production was \$258 (Toni Duboise, "Low-cost Apple Mini Packs Punch, but BYO Peripherals," **www.eetimes.com**), while its suggested price was \$499. Although other firms produce computers, the Mac is viewed as a different product by aficionados. What is Apple's price/marginal cost ratio? What is its Lerner Index? If we assume that Apple is a profit-maximizing monopoly, what elasticity of demand does it believe it faces for this tiny computer?

35. The U.S. Postal Service (USPS) has a constitutionally guaranteed monopoly on first-class mail. In early 2008, it charges 41¢ for a stamp, which is probably not the profit-maximizing price, as the USPS goal, allegedly, is to break even rather than to turn a profit. Following the postal services in Australia, Britain, Canada, Switzerland, and Ireland, the USPS has allowed Stamps.com to sell a sheet of twenty 41¢ stamps with a photo of your dog, your mommy, or whatever image you want for \$18.99 in 2007 (that's 94.95¢ per stamp, or a 232% markup). Stamps.com keeps the extra beyond the 41¢ it pays the USPS. What is the firm's Lerner Index? If Stamps.com is a profit-maximizing monopoly, what elasticity of demand does it face for a customized stamp?

***36.** Show mathematically that a monopoly may raise the price to consumers by more than the specific tax imposed on it. (*Hint*: One approach is to consider a monopoly facing a constant-elasticity demand curve and a constant marginal cost, m.) C

37. If the inverse demand function facing a monopoly is $P(Q)$ and its cost function is $C(Q)$, show the effect of a specific tax, τ, on its profit-maximizing output. How does imposing τ affect its profit? C

38. In 1996, Florida voted on (and rejected) a 1¢-per-pound excise tax on refined cane sugar in the Florida Everglades Agricultural Area. Swinton and Thomas (2001) used linear supply and demand curves (based on elasticities estimated by Marks, 1993) to calculate the incidence from this tax given that the market is competitive. Their inverse demand curve was $p = 1.787 - 0.0004641Q$, and their inverse supply curve was $p = -0.4896 + 0.00020165Q$. Calculate the incidence of the tax that falls on consumers (Chapter 3) for a competitive market. If producers joined together to form a monopoly, and the supply curve is actually the monopoly's marginal cost curve, what is the incidence of the tax? (*Hint*: The incidence that falls on consumers is the difference between the equilibrium price with and without the tax divided by the tax. You should find that the incidence is 70% in a competitive market and 41% with a monopoly.)

39. In the Botox application, consumer surplus, triangle A, equals the deadweight loss, triangle C. Show that this equality is a result of the linear demand and constant marginal cost assumptions.

40. Based on the information in the "Botox Patent Monopoly" application, what would happen to the equilibrium price and quantity if the government had collected a specific tax of \$75 per vial of Botox? What welfare effects would such a tax have?

41. A monopoly sells music CDs. It has a constant marginal and average cost of 20. It faces two groups of potential customers: honest and dishonest people. The dishonest and the honest consumers' demand functions are the same: $p = 120 - Q$.

a. If it is not possible for the dishonest customers to steal the music, what are the monopoly's profit-maximizing price and quantity? What is its profit? What are the consumer surplus, producer surplus, and welfare?

b. Answer the same questions as in the previous part if the dishonest customers can pirate the music.

c. How do consumer surplus, producer surplus, and welfare change if piracy occurs?

42. Based on the information in the "Botox Patent Monopoly" application, what would happen to the equilibrium price and quantity if the government had set a price ceiling of \$200 per vial of Botox? What welfare effects would such a tax have?

43. The Commonwealth of Pennsylvania is the monopoly retailer of wine in the state. Suppose that Quaker Cabernet has no close substitutes and that the statewide inverse demand function for this wine is $p = 5 - 0.001Q$. The state purchases the wine on the wholesale market for \$2 per bottle, and the state-operated liquor stores incur no other expenses to sell this wine.

a. What are the state's profit-maximizing price and quantity?

b. Neighboring New Jersey permits private retailers to sell wine. They face the same statewide demand curve as in Pennsylvania. No interstate wine trade is permitted. Suppose the New Jersey market for Quaker Cabernet is perfectly competitive. What is the equilibrium price and quantity?

c. New Jersey taxes wine sales. While the retailers pay the taxes on wine sales, by raising prices they may pass on some or all of these taxes to consumers. Identify the specific tax (tax per bottle sold) for which New Jersey's equilibrium market price and quantity equal the Pennsylvania monopoly price and quantity. Given the quantity tax, show that New Jersey's tax revenue equals Pennsylvania's profit. W

***44.** A monopoly produces a good with a network externality at a constant marginal and average cost of 2. In the first period, its inverse demand curve is $p = 10 - Q$. In the second period, its demand is $p = 10 - Q$ unless it sells at least $Q = 8$ units in the first period. If it meets or exceeds this target, then the demand curve rotates out by α (it sells α times as many units for any given price), so that its inverse demand curve is $p = 10 - Q/\alpha$. The monopoly knows that it can sell no output after the second period. The monopoly's objective is to maximize the sum of its profits over the two periods. In the first period, should the monopoly set the output that maximizes its profit in that period? How does your answer depend on α? (*Hint*: See the discussion of the two-period monopoly model in Section 11.8 of this chapter.)

12 Pricing and Advertising

Everything is worth what its purchaser will pay for it.
—Publilius Syrus (1st century B.C.)

Why does Disneyland charge local residents $86 and out-of-towners $91 for a one-day pass? Why do the spiritualists and self-described mediums who live at the Wonewoc Spiritualist Camp give readings costing $40 for half an hour, but charge seniors only $35 on Wednesdays?[1] Why are airline fares less if you book in advance and stay over a Saturday night? Why are some goods, among them computers and software, sold bundled together at a single price? To answer these questions, we need to examine how monopolies set prices.

Monopolies (and other noncompetitive firms) can use information about individual consumers' demand curves to increase their profits. Instead of setting a single price, such firms use **nonuniform pricing**: charging consumers different prices for the same product or charging a single customer a price that depends on the number of units the customer buys. By replacing a single price with nonuniform pricing, the firm raises its profit.

nonuniform pricing
charging consumers different prices for the same product or charging a single customer a price that depends on the number of units the customer buys

Why can a monopoly earn a higher profit from using a nonuniform pricing scheme than from setting a single price? A monopoly that uses nonuniform prices can capture some or all of the consumer surplus and deadweight loss that results if the monopoly sets a single price. As we saw in Chapter 11, a monopoly that sets a high single price only sells to the customers who value the good the most, and those customers retain some consumer surplus. The monopoly loses sales to other customers who value the good less than the single price. These lost sales are a *deadweight loss*: the value of these potential sales in excess of the cost of producing the good. A monopoly that uses nonuniform pricing captures additional consumer surplus by raising the price to customers who value the good the most. By lowering its price to other customers, the monopoly makes additional sales, thereby changing what would otherwise be deadweight loss into profit.

We examine several types of nonuniform pricing including price discrimination, two-part tariffs, and tie-in sales. The most common form of nonuniform pricing is **price discrimination**, whereby a firm charges consumers different prices for the same good. Many magazines price discriminate by charging college students less for subscriptions than they charge older adults. If a magazine were to start setting a high price for everyone, many college student subscribers—who are sensitive to price increases (have relatively elastic demands)—would cancel their subscriptions. If the magazine were to let everyone buy at the college student price, it would gain few additional subscriptions because most potential older adult subscribers are relatively insensitive to the price, and it would earn less from those older adults who are willing to pay the higher price. Thus, the magazine makes more profit by price discriminating.

price discrimination
practice in which a firm charges consumers different prices for the same good

[1] **www.msnbc.msn.com/id/20377308/wid/11915829**, August 29, 2007.

Some noncompetitive firms that cannot practically price discriminate use other forms of nonuniform pricing to increase profits. One method is for a firm to charge a *two-part tariff*, whereby a customer pays one fee for the right to buy the good and another price for each unit purchased. Health club members pay an annual fee to join the club and then shell out an additional amount each time they use the facilities.

Another type of nonlinear pricing is a *tie-in sale*, whereby a customer may buy one good only if also agreeing to buy another good or service. Vacation package deals may include airfare and a hotel room for a single price. Some restaurants provide only full-course dinners: a single price buys an appetizer, a main dish, and a dessert. A firm may sell copiers under the condition that customers agree to buy all future copier service and supplies from it.

A monopoly may also increase its profit by advertising. A monopoly may advertise to shift its demand curve so as to raise its profit, taking into account the cost of advertising.

In this chapter, we examine seven main topics

1. **Why and How Firms Price Discriminate.** A firm can increase its profit by price discriminating if it has market power, can identify which customers are more price sensitive than others, and can prevent customers who pay low prices from reselling to those who pay high prices.
2. **Perfect Price Discrimination.** If a monopoly can charge the maximum each customer is willing to pay for each unit of output, the monopoly captures all potential consumer surplus, and the efficient (competitive) level of output is sold.
3. **Quantity Discrimination.** Some firms profit by charging different prices for large purchases than for small ones, which is a form of price discrimination.
4. **Multimarket Price Discrimination.** Firms that cannot perfectly price discriminate may charge a group of consumers with relatively elastic demands a lower price than other groups of consumers.
5. **Two-Part Tariffs.** By charging consumers a fee for the right to buy any number of units and a price per unit, firms earn higher profits than they do by charging a single price per unit.
6. **Tie-In Sales.** By requiring a customer to buy a second good or service along with the first, firms make higher profits than they do by selling the goods or services separately.
7. **Advertising.** A monopoly advertises to shift its demand curve and to increase its profit.

12.1 Why and How Firms Price Discriminate

The prince travels through the forest for many hours and comes upon an inn, where he is recognized immediately. He orders a light meal of fried eggs. When he finishes, the prince asks the innkeeper, "How much do I owe you for the eggs?" The innkeeper replies, "Twenty-five rubles." "Why such an exorbitant price?" asks the prince. "Is there a shortage of eggs in this area?" The innkeeper replies, "No, there is no shortage of eggs, but there is a shortage of princes."[2]

Until now, we've examined how a monopoly sets its price if it charges all its customers the same price. However, many noncompetitive firms increase their profits

[2]Thanks to Steve Salop.

by charging *nonuniform prices*, which vary across customers. We start by studying the most common form of nonuniform pricing: price discrimination.

Why Price Discrimination Pays

For almost any good or service, some consumers are willing to pay more than others. A firm that sets a single price faces a trade-off between charging consumers who really want the good as much as they are willing to pay and charging a low enough price that the firm doesn't lose sales to less enthusiastic customers. As a result, the firm usually sets an intermediate price. A price-discriminating firm that varies its prices across customers avoids this trade-off.

A firm earns a higher profit from price discrimination than from uniform pricing for two reasons. First, a price-discriminating firm charges a higher price to customers who are willing to pay more than the uniform price, capturing some or all of their consumer surplus—the difference between what a good is worth to a consumer and what the consumer paid—under uniform pricing. Second, a price-discriminating firm sells to some people who were not willing to pay as much as the uniform price.

We use a pair of extreme examples to illustrate the two benefits of price discrimination to firms—capturing more of the consumer surplus and selling to more customers. These examples are extreme in the sense that the firm sets a uniform price at the price the most enthusiastic consumers are willing to pay or at the price the least enthusiastic consumers are willing to pay, rather than at an intermediate level.

Suppose that the only movie theater in town has two types of patrons: college students and senior citizens. The college student will see the Saturday night movie if the price is \$10 or less, and the senior citizens will attend if the price is \$5 or less. For simplicity, we assume that there is no cost in showing the movie, so profit is the same as revenue. The theater is large enough to hold all potential customers, so the marginal cost of admitting one more customer is zero. Table 12.1 shows how pricing affects the theater's profit.

Table 12.1 A Theater's Profit Based on the Pricing Method Used.

(a) No Extra Customers from Price Discrimination

Pricing	Profit from 10 College Students	Profit from 20 Senior Citizens	Total Profit
Uniform, \$5	\$50	\$100	\$150
Uniform, \$10	\$100	\$0	\$100
Price discrimination*	\$100	\$100	\$200

(b) Extra Customers from Price Discrimination

Pricing	Profit from 10 College Students	Profit from 5 Senior Citizens	Total Profit
Uniform, \$5	\$50	\$25	\$75
Uniform, \$10	\$100	\$0	\$100
Price discrimination*	\$100	\$25	\$125

*The theater price discriminates by charging college students \$10 and senior citizens \$5.

Notes: College students go to the theater if they are charged no more than \$10. Senior citizens are willing to pay up to \$5. The theater's marginal cost for an extra customer is zero.

In panel a, there are 10 college students and 20 senior citizens. If the theater charges everyone $5, its profit is $150 = $5 × (10 college students + 20 senior citizens). If it charges $10, the senior citizens do not go to the movie, so the theater makes only $100. Thus, if the theater is going to charge everyone the same price, it maximizes its profit by setting the price at $5. Charging less than $5 makes no sense because the same number of people go to the movie as go when $5 is charged. Charging between $5 and $10 is less profitable than charging $10 because no extra seniors go and the college students are willing to pay $10. Charging more than $10 results in no customers.

At a price of $5, the seniors have no consumer surplus: They pay exactly what seeing the movie is worth to them. Seeing the movie is worth $10 to the college students, but they have to pay only $5, so each has a consumer surplus of $5, and their total consumer surplus is $50.

If the theater can price discriminate by charging senior citizens $5 and college students $10, its profit increases to $200. Its profit rises because the theater makes as much from the seniors as before but gets an extra $50 from the college students. By price discriminating, the theater sells the same number of seats but makes more money from the college students, capturing all the consumer surplus they had under uniform pricing. Neither group of customers has any consumer surplus if the theater price discriminates.

In panel b, there are 10 college students and 5 senior citizens. If the theater must charge a single price, it charges $10. Only college students see the movie, so the theater's profit is $100. (If it charges $5, both students and seniors go to the theater, but its profit is only $75.) If the theater can price discriminate and charge seniors $5 and college students $10, its profit increases to $125. Here the gain from price discrimination comes from selling extra tickets to seniors (not from making more money on the same number of tickets, as in panel a). The theater earns as much from the students as before and makes more from the seniors, and neither group enjoys consumer surplus. These examples illustrate that firms can make a higher profit by price discriminating, either by charging some existing customers more or by selling extra units. Leslie (1997) finds that Broadway theaters increase their profits 5% by price discriminating rather than using uniform prices.

See Questions 1–3.

Who Can Price Discriminate

Not all firms can price discriminate. For a firm to price discriminate successfully, three conditions must be met.

First, a firm must have *market power*; otherwise, it cannot charge any consumer more than the competitive price. A monopoly, an oligopoly firm, a monopolistically competitive firm, or a cartel may be able to price discriminate. A competitive firm cannot price discriminate.

Second, consumers must *differ* in their sensitivity to price (demand elasticities), and a firm must be able to *identify* how consumers differ in this sensitivity.[3] The movie theater knows that college students and senior citizens differ in their willingness to pay for a ticket, and Disneyland knows that tourists and natives differ in their willingness to pay for admission. In both cases, the firms can identify members of these two groups by using driver's licenses or other forms of identification.

[3]Even if consumers are identical, price discrimination is possible if each consumer has a downward-sloping demand curve for the monopoly's product. To price discriminate over the units purchased by a consumer, the monopoly has to know how the elasticity of demand varies with the number of units purchased.

Similarly, if a firm knows that each individual's demand curve slopes downward, it may charge each customer a higher price for the first unit of a good than for subsequent units.

Third, a firm must be able to *prevent or limit resales* to higher-price-paying customers by customers whom the firm charges relatively low prices. Price discrimination doesn't work if resales are easy because the firm would be able to make only low-price sales. A movie theater can charge different prices because senior citizens, who enter the theater as soon as they buy the ticket, do not have time to resell it.

Except for competitive firms, the first two conditions—market power and ability to identify groups with different price sensitivities—frequently hold. Usually, the biggest obstacle to price discrimination is a firm's inability to prevent resales. In some markets, however, resales are inherently difficult or impossible, so firms can take actions that prevent resales, or government actions or laws prevent resales.

See Questions 4–7.

APPLICATION

Disneyland Pricing

Disneyland, in southern California, is a well-run operation that rarely misses a trick when it comes to increasing profits. (Indeed, Disneyland mints money: When you enter the park, you can exchange U.S. currency for Disney dollars, which can be spent only in the park.)[4]

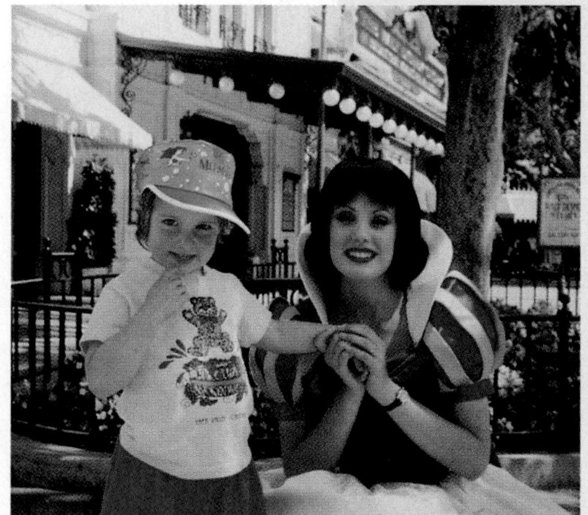

In 2008, Disneyland charged southern Californian adults \$86 for a park hopper ticket (good for both Disneyland and Disney's California Adventure park) but charged others \$91. This policy of giving locals discounts makes sense if visitors from afar are willing to pay more than locals. Imagine a Midwesterner who's never been to Disneyland before and wants to visit. Travel accounts for most of the cost of the trip, so an extra \$5 for entrance to Disneyland makes little percentage difference in the total cost of a visit and hence doesn't greatly affect that person's decision whether or not to go. In contrast, for a local who has gone to Disneyland many times and for whom the entrance price is a larger share of the cost of the visit, a slightly higher price might prevent a visit.

Charging both groups the same price is not in Disney's best interest. If Disney were to charge the higher price to everyone, many locals would stay away. If Disney were to use the lower price for everyone, it would be charging nonresidents much less than they are willing to pay. By setting different prices for the two groups, Disney increases its profit.

See Question 8.

Preventing Resales

Resales are difficult or impossible for most *services* and when *transaction costs are high*. If a plumber charges you less than your neighbor for clearing a pipe, you cannot make a deal with your neighbor to resell this service. The higher the transaction costs a consumer must incur to resell a good, the less likely that resales will occur. Suppose that you are able to buy a jar of pickles for \$1 less than the usual price. Could you practically find and sell this jar to someone else, or would the transaction costs be prohibitive? The more valuable a product or the more widely consumed it is, the more likely it is that transaction costs are low enough that resales occur.

[4]According to **www.babycenter.com**, it costs \$426,190 to raise a child from cradle through college. Parents can cut that total in half, however: They don't have to take their kids to Disneyland.

Some firms act to raise transaction costs or otherwise make resales difficult. If your college requires that someone with a student ticket must show a student identification card with a picture on it before being admitted to a sporting event, you'll find it difficult to resell your low-price tickets to nonstudents, who must pay higher prices. When students at some universities buy computers at lower-than-usual prices, they must sign a contract that forbids them to resell the computer. Disney prevents resales by locals who can buy a ticket at a lower price by checking a purchaser's driver's license and requiring that the ticket be used for same-day entrance.

Similarly, a firm can prevent resales by *vertically integrating*: participating in more than one successive stage of the production and distribution chain for a good or service. Alcoa, the former aluminum monopoly, wanted to sell aluminum ingots to producers of aluminum wire at a lower price than was set for producers of aluminum aircraft parts. If Alcoa did so, however, the wire producers could easily resell their ingots. By starting its own wire production firm, Alcoa prevented such resales and was able to charge high prices to firms that manufactured aircraft parts (Perry, 1980).

Governments frequently aid price discrimination by preventing resales. State and federal governments require that milk producers, under penalty of law, price discriminate by selling milk at a higher price for fresh use than for processing (cheese, ice cream) and forbid resales. Government *tariffs* (taxes on imports) limit resales by making it expensive to buy goods in a low-price country and resell them in a high-price country. In some cases, laws prevent such reselling explicitly. Under U.S. trade laws, certain brand-name perfumes may not be sold in the United States except by their manufacturers.

See *Question 9.*

APPLICATION

Preventing Resale of Designer Bags

It may not surprise you that during the holidays that stores limit how many of the hottest items—such as Wii game consoles in 2008—a customer can buy at one time. But it may surprise you that the Web sites of luxury retailers like Saks Fifth Avenue, Neiman Marcus, and Bergdorf Goodman limit how many designer handbags one can buy: "Due to popular demand, a customer may order no more than three units of these items every 30 days."

Why wouldn't they want to sell as many as they can? How many customers can even afford more than three of Prada's latest ruched nylon styles at $1,290, Bottega Veneta's signature woven leather hobos at $1,490, or the rectangular Yves Saint Laurent clutch that looks like a postcard addressed to the designer at $1,395?

The simple explanation is that the restriction has nothing to do with "popular demand"; it's designed to prevent resales that would enable manufacturers to price discriminate internationally. The manufacturers pressure the U.S. retailers to limit sales so as to prevent anyone from buying all the bags and reselling them in Europe or Asia where the same items in Prada and Gucci stores cost 20% to 40% more. For example, the Yves Saint Laurent Downtown bag that sells at Saks Fifth Avenue and Bergdorf Goodman in New York for $1,495, sells at Harvey Nichols in London for £910 ($1,777). The weakening U.S. dollar makes such international resales even more attractive.

Not All Price Differences Are Price Discrimination

Not every seller who charges consumers different prices is price discriminating. Hotels charge newlyweds more for bridal suites. Is that price discrimination? Some hotel managers say no. They contend that honeymooners, unlike other customers, always steal mementos, so the price differential reflects an actual cost differential.

The price for all issues of *TV Guide* magazine for a year is \$103.48 if you buy it at the newsstand, \$56.68 for a standard subscription, and \$39.52 for a college student subscription. The difference between the newsstand cost and the standard subscription cost reflects, at least in part, the higher cost of selling at a newsstand rather than mailing the magazine directly to customers, so this price difference does not reflect pure price discrimination (see the Cross-Chapter Analysis: Magazine Subscriptions, which follows this chapter). The price difference between the standard subscription rate and the college student rate reflects pure price discrimination because the two subscriptions are identical in every respect except price.

See Question 10.

Types of Price Discrimination

perfect price discrimination (*first-degree price discrimination*)
situation in which a firm sells each unit at the maximum amount any customer is willing to pay for it, so prices differ across customers and a given customer may pay more for some units than for others

quantity discrimination (*second-degree price discrimination*)
situation in which a firm charges a different price for large quantities than for small quantities but all customers who buy a given quantity pay the same price

There are three main types of price discrimination. With **perfect price discrimination**—also called *first-degree price discrimination*—the firm sells each unit at the maximum amount any customer is willing to pay for it, so prices differ across customers, and a given customer may pay more for some units than for others.

With **quantity discrimination** (*second-degree price discrimination*), the firm charges a different price for large quantities than for small quantities, but all customers who buy a given quantity pay the same price. With **multimarket price discrimination** (*third-degree price discrimination*), the firm charges different groups of customers different prices, but it charges a given customer the same price for every unit of output sold. Typically, not all customers pay different prices—the firm sets different prices only for a few groups of customers. Because this last type of discrimination is the most common, the phrase *price discrimination* is often used to mean *multimarket price discrimination*.

In addition to price discriminating, many firms use other, more complicated types of nonuniform pricing. Later in this chapter, we examine two other frequently used nonuniform pricing methods—two-part tariffs and tie-in sales—that are similar to quantity discrimination.

12.2 Perfect Price Discrimination

multimarket price discrimination (*third-degree price discrimination*)
a situation in which a firm charges different groups of customers different prices but charges a given customer the same price for every unit of output sold

reservation price
the maximum amount a person would be willing to pay for a unit of output

If a firm with market power knows exactly how much each customer is willing to pay for each unit of its good and it can prevent resales, the firm charges each person his or her **reservation price**: the maximum amount a person would be willing to pay for a unit of output. Such an all-knowing firm *perfectly price discriminates*. By selling each unit of its output to the customer who values it the most at the maximum price that person is willing to pay, the perfectly price-discriminating monopoly captures all possible consumer surplus. For example, the managers of the Suez Canal set tolls on an individual basis, taking into account many factors such as weather and each ship's alternative routes.

We first show how a firm uses its information about consumers to perfectly price discriminate. We then compare the perfectly price-discriminating monopoly to competition and single-price monopoly. By showing that the same quantity is produced as would be produced by a competitive market and that the last unit of output sells for the marginal cost, we demonstrate that perfect price discrimination is efficient. We then illustrate how the perfect price discrimination equilibrium differs from single-price monopoly by using the Botox application from Chapter 11. Finally, we discuss how firms obtain the information they need to perfectly price discriminate.

How a Firm Perfectly Price Discriminates

Suppose that a monopoly has market power, can prevent resales, and has enough information to perfectly price discriminate. The monopoly sells each unit at its reservation price, which is the height of the demand curve: the maximum price consumers will pay for a given amount of output.

Figure 12.1 illustrates how this perfectly price-discriminating firm maximizes its profit (see Appendix 12A for a mathematical treatment). The figure shows that the first customer is willing to pay \$6 for a unit, the next is willing to pay \$5, and so forth. This perfectly price-discriminating firm sells its first unit of output for \$6. Having sold the first unit, the firm can get at most \$5 for its second unit. The firm must drop its price by \$1 for each successive unit it sells.

A perfectly price-discriminating monopoly's marginal revenue is the same as its price. As the figure shows, the firm's marginal revenue is $MR_1 = \$6$ on the first unit, $MR_2 = \$5$ on the second unit, and $MR_3 = \$4$ on the third unit. As a result, *the firm's marginal revenue curve is its demand curve.*

This firm has a constant marginal cost of \$4 per unit. It pays for the firm to produce the first unit because the firm sells that unit for \$6, so its marginal revenue exceeds its marginal cost by \$2. Similarly, the firm certainly wants to sell the second

Figure 12.1 Perfect Price Discrimination.

The monopoly can charge \$6 for the first unit, \$5 for the second, and \$4 for the third, as the demand curve shows. Its marginal revenue is $MR_1 = \$6$ for the first unit, $MR_2 = \$5$ for the second unit, and $MR_3 = \$4$ for the third unit. Thus, the demand curve is also the marginal revenue curve. Because the firm's marginal and average cost is \$4 per unit, it is unwilling to sell at a price below \$4, so it sells 3 units, point *e*, and breaks even on the last unit.

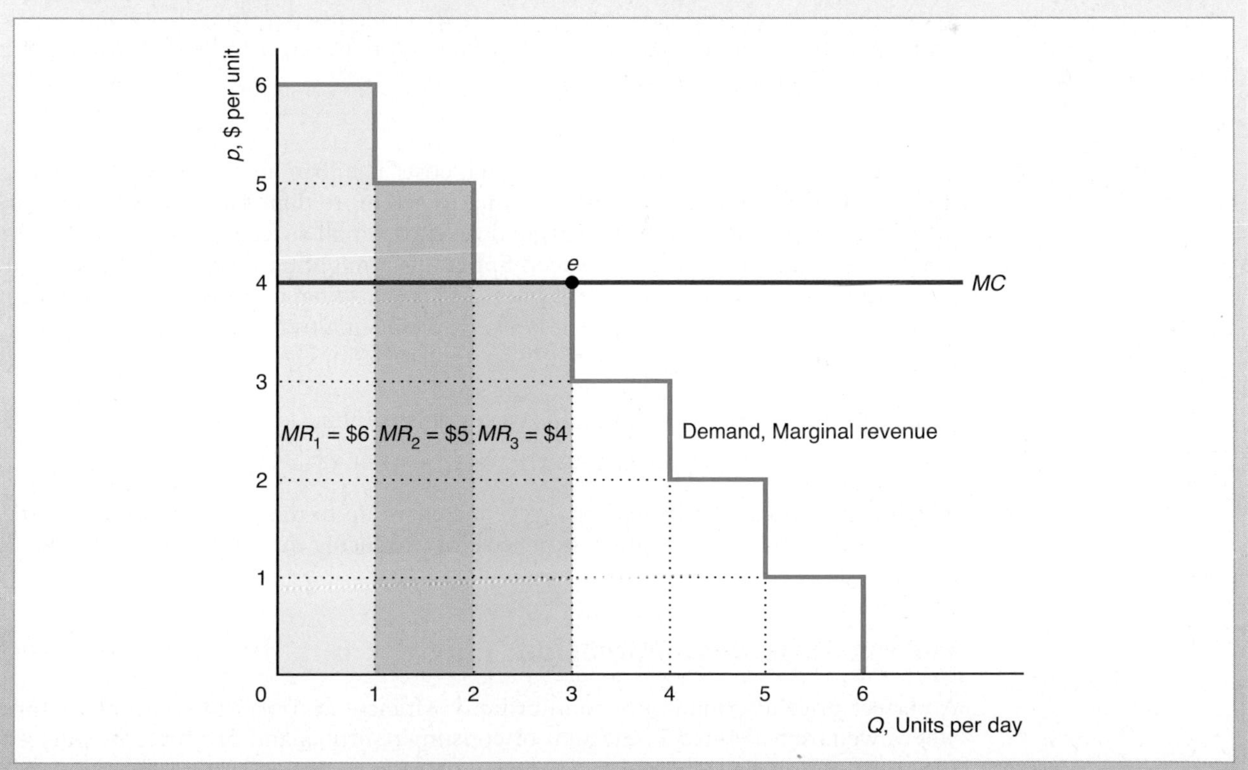

APPLICATION

Amazon Is Watching You

Amazon, a giant among e-commerce vendors, collects an enormous amount of information about its 23 million customers' tastes and willingness to buy. If you've shopped at Amazon, you've probably noticed that its Web site now greets you by name (thanks to a *cookie* it leaves on your computer, which provides information about you to Amazon's Web site).

In 2000, the firm decided to use this information to engage in *dynamic pricing*, where the price it charges its customers today depends on these customers' actions in the recent past—including what they bought, how much they paid, and whether they paid for high-speed shipping—and personal data such as where they live. Several Amazon customers discovered this practice. One man reported on the Web site DVDTalk.com that he had bought Julie Taylor's "Titus" for \$24.49. The next week, he returned to Amazon and saw that the price had jumped to \$26.24. As an experiment, he removed the cookie that identified him, and found that the price dropped to \$22.74.

Presumably, Amazon reasoned that a returning customer was less likely to compare prices across Web sites than was a new customer, and was pricing accordingly. Other DVDTalk.com visitors reported that regular Amazon customers were charged 3% to 5% more than new customers.

Amazon announced that its pricing variations stopped as soon as it started receiving complaints from DVDTalk members. It claimed that the variations were random and designed only to determine price elasticities. A spokesperson explained, "This was a pure and simple price test. This was not dynamic pricing. We don't do that and have no plans ever to do that." Right. An Amazon customer service representative called it dynamic pricing in an e-mail to a DVDTalk member, allowing that dynamic pricing was a common practice among firms. A 2003 experiment (see **www.managingchange.com/dynamic/survey/analysis.htm**) suggests that Amazon did not continue to use dynamic pricing. A 2007 examination found random fluctuations in price, but they did not appear to be tied to individuals' purchasing behavior.

See Question 11.

unit for \$5, which also exceeds its marginal cost. The firm breaks even when it sells the third unit for \$4. The firm is unwilling to sell more than three units because its marginal cost would exceed its marginal revenue on all successive units. Thus, like any profit-maximizing firm, a perfectly price-discriminating firm produces at point *e*, where its marginal revenue curve intersects its marginal cost curve. (If you find it upsetting that the firm is indifferent between producing two and three units, assume that the firm's marginal cost is \$3.99 so that it definitely wants to produce three units.)

This perfectly price-discriminating firm earns revenues of

$$MR_1 + MR_2 + MR_3 = \$6 + \$5 + \$4 = \$15,$$

which is the area under its marginal revenue curve up to the number of units, three, it sells. If the firm has no fixed cost, its cost of producing three units is $\$12 = \$4 \times 3$, so its profit is \$3.

Perfect Price Discrimination: Efficient But Hurts Consumers

A perfect price discrimination equilibrium is efficient and maximizes total welfare, where welfare is defined as the sum of consumer surplus and producer surplus. As such, this equilibrium has more in common with a competitive equilibrium than with a single-price-monopoly equilibrium.

If the market in Figure 12.2 is competitive, the intersection of the demand curve and the marginal cost curve, MC, determines the competitive equilibrium at e_c, where price is p_c and quantity is Q_c. Consumer surplus is $A + B + C$, producer surplus is $D + E$, and there is no deadweight loss. The market is efficient because the price, p_c, equals the marginal cost, MC_c.

With a single-price monopoly (which charges all its customers the same price because it cannot distinguish among them), the intersection of the MC curve and the single-price monopoly's marginal revenue curve, MC_s, determines the output, Q_s. The monopoly operates at e_s, where it charges p_s. The deadweight loss from monopoly is $C + E$. This efficiency loss is due to the monopoly's charging a price, p_s, that's above its marginal cost, MC_s, so less is sold than in a competitive market.

Figure 12.2 Competitive, Single-Price, and Perfect Discrimination Equilibria.

In the competitive market equilibrium, e_c, price is p_c, quantity is Q_c, consumer surplus is $A + B + C$, producer surplus is $D + E$, and there is no deadweight loss. In the single-price monopoly equilibrium, e_s, price is p_s, quantity is Q_s, consumer surplus falls to A, producer surplus is $B + D$, and deadweight loss is $C + E$. In the perfect discrimination equilibrium, the monopoly sells each unit at the customer's reservation price on the demand curve. It sells Q_d (= Q_c) units, where the last unit is sold at its marginal cost. Customers have no consumer surplus, but there is no deadweight loss.

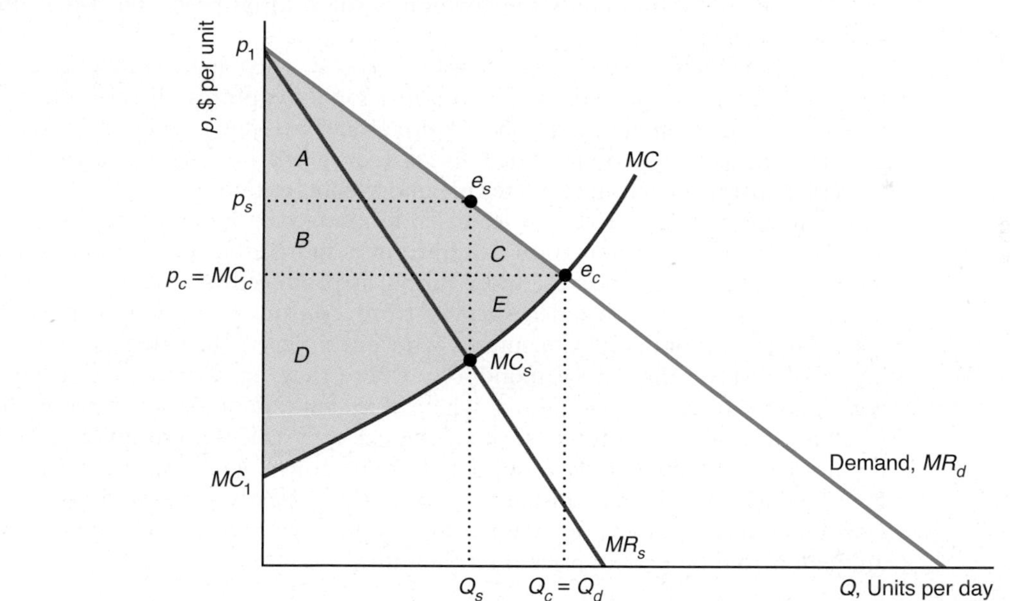

	Competition	Monopoly: Single Price	Monopoly: Perfect Price Discrimination
Consumer Surplus, CS	$A + B + C$	A	0
Producer Surplus, PS	$D + E$	$B + D$	$A + B + C + D + E$
Welfare, $W = CS + PS$	$A + B + C + D + E$	$A + B + D$	$A + B + C + D + E$
Deadweight Loss	0	$C + E$	0

A perfectly price-discriminating monopoly sells each unit at its reservation price, which is the height of the demand curve. As a result, the firm's marginal revenue curve, MR_d, is the same as its demand curve. The firm sells the first unit for p_1 to the consumer who will pay the most for the good. The firm's marginal cost for that unit is MC_1, so it makes $p_1 - MC_1$ on that unit. The firm receives a lower price and has a higher marginal cost for each successive unit. It sells the Q_d unit for p_c, where its marginal revenue curve, MR_d, intersects the marginal cost curve, MC, so it just covers its marginal cost on the last unit. The firm is unwilling to sell additional units because its marginal revenue would be less than the marginal cost of producing them.

The perfectly price-discriminating monopoly's total producer surplus on the Q_d units it sells is the area below its demand curve and above its marginal cost curve, $A + B + C + D + E$. Its profit is the producer surplus minus its fixed cost, if any. Consumers receive no consumer surplus because each consumer pays his or her reservation price. The perfectly price-discriminating monopoly's equilibrium has *no deadweight loss* because the last unit is sold at a price, p_c, that equals the marginal cost, MC_c, as in a competitive market. Thus, both a perfect price discrimination equilibrium and a competitive equilibrium are efficient.

The perfect price discrimination equilibrium differs from the competitive equilibrium in two ways. First, in the competitive equilibrium, everyone is charged a price equal to the equilibrium marginal cost, $p_c = MC_c$; however, in the perfect price discrimination equilibrium, only the last unit is sold at that price. The other units are sold at customers' reservation prices, which are greater than p_c. Second, consumers receive some welfare (consumer surplus, $A + B + C$) in a competitive market, whereas a perfectly price-discriminating monopoly captures all the welfare. Thus, perfect price discrimination doesn't reduce efficiency—the output and total welfare are the same as under competition—but it does redistribute income away from consumers: consumers are much better off under competition.

Is a single-price or perfectly price-discriminating monopoly better for consumers? The perfect price discrimination equilibrium is more efficient than the single-price monopoly equilibrium because more output is produced. A single-price monopoly, however, takes less consumer surplus from consumers than a perfectly price-discriminating monopoly. Consumers who put a very high value on the good are better off under single-price monopoly, where they have consumer surplus, than with perfect price discrimination, where they have none. Consumers with lower reservation prices who purchase from the perfectly price-discriminating monopoly but not from the single-price monopoly have no consumer surplus in either case. All the social gain from the extra output goes to the perfectly price-discriminating firm. Consumer surplus is greatest with competition, lower with single-price monopoly, and eliminated by perfect price discrimination.

APPLICATION

Botox Revisited

We illustrate how perfect price discrimination differs from competition and single-price monopoly using the application on Allergan's Botox from Chapter 11. The graph shows a linear demand curve for Botox and a constant marginal cost (and average variable cost) of \$25 per vial. If the market had been competitive (price equal to marginal cost at e_c), consumer surplus would have been triangle $A + B + C = \$750$ million per year, and there would have been no producer surplus or deadweight loss. In the single-price monopoly equilibrium, e_s, the Botox vials sell for \$400, and one million vials are sold. The corresponding consumer surplus is triangle $A = \$187.5$ million per year, producer surplus is rectangle $B = \$375$ million, and the deadweight loss is triangle $C = \$375$ million.

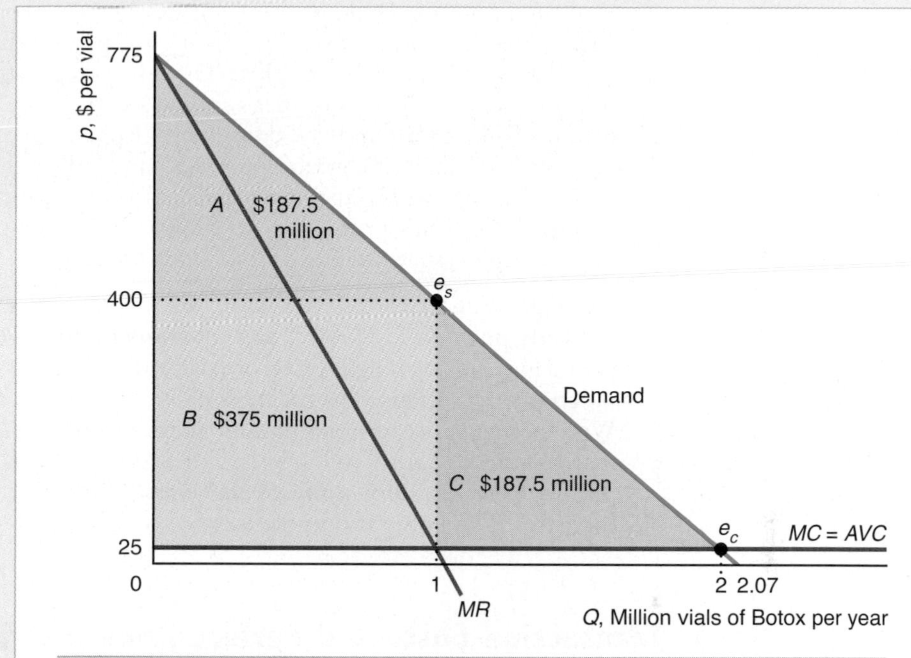

		Monopoly	
	Competition	Single Price	Perfect Price Discrimination
Consumer Surplus, *CS*	$A + B + C$	A	0
Producer Surplus, *PS*	0	B	$A + B + C$
Welfare, $W = CS + PS$	$A + B + C$	$A + B$	$A + B + C$
Deadweight Loss	0	C	0

If Allergan could perfectly price discriminate, its producer surplus would double to $A + B + C$ = $750 million per year, and consumers would obtain no consumer surplus. The marginal consumer would pay the marginal cost of $25, the same as in a competitive market.

Allergan's inability to perfectly price discriminate costs the company and society dearly. The profit of the single-price monopoly, B = $375 million per day, is lower than that of a perfectly price-discriminating monopoly by $A + C$ = $375 million per year. Similarly, society's welfare under single-price monopoly is lower than from perfect price discrimination by the deadweight loss, C, of $187.5 million per year.

See Questions 12 and 13.

Solved Problem 12.1

How does welfare change if the movie theater described in Table 12.1 goes from charging a single price to perfectly price discriminating?

Answer

1. *Calculate welfare for panel a (a) if the theater sets a single price and (b) if it perfectly price discriminates, and (c) compare them.* (a) If the theater sets the

profit-maximizing single price of \$5, it sells 30 tickets and makes a profit of \$150. The 20 senior citizen customers are paying their reservation price, so they have no consumer surplus. The 10 college students have reservation prices of \$10, so their consumer surplus is \$50. Thus, welfare is \$200: the sum of the profit, \$150, and the consumer surplus, \$50. (b) If the firm perfectly price discriminates, it charges seniors \$5 and college students \$10. Because the theater is charging all customers their reservation prices, there is no consumer surplus. The firm's profit rises to \$200. (c) Thus, *welfare is the same under both pricing systems where output stays the same.*

2. *Calculate welfare for panel b (a) if the theater sets a single price and (b) if it perfectly price discriminates, and (c) compare them.* (a) If the theater sets the profit-maximizing single price of \$10, only college students attend and have no consumer surplus. The theater's profit is \$100, so total welfare is \$100. (b) With perfect price discrimination, there is no consumer surplus, but profit increases to \$125, so welfare rises to \$125. (c) Thus, *welfare is greater with perfect price discrimination where output increases.* (The result that welfare increases if and only if output rises holds generally.)

Transaction Costs and Perfect Price Discrimination

Although some firms come close to perfect price discrimination, many more firms set a single price or use another nonlinear pricing method. Transaction costs are a major reason why these firms do not perfectly price discriminate: It is too difficult or costly to gather information about each customer's price sensitivity. Recent advances in computer technologies, however, have lowered these costs, causing hotels, car and truck rental companies, cruise lines, and airlines to price discriminate more often.

Private colleges request and receive financial information from students, which allows the schools to nearly perfectly price discriminate. The schools give partial scholarships as a means of reducing tuition to relatively poor students.

Many auto dealerships try to increase their profit by perfectly price discriminating, charging each customer the most that customer is willing to pay. These firms hire salespeople to ascertain potential customers' willingness to pay for a car and to bargain with them. Not all car companies believe that it pays to price discriminate in this way, however. As we saw in Chapter 1, Saturn charges all customers the same price, believing that the transaction costs (including wages of salespeople) of such information gathering and bargaining exceed the benefits to the firm of charging customers differential prices.

Many other firms believe that, taking the transaction costs into account, it pays to use quantity discrimination, multimarket price discrimination, or other nonlinear pricing methods rather than try to perfectly price discriminate. We now turn to these alternative approaches.

Solved Problem 12.2

Competitive firms are the customers of a union, which is the monopoly supplier of labor services. Show the union's "producer surplus" if it perfectly price discriminates. Then suppose that the union makes the firms a take-it-or-leave-it offer: They must guarantee to hire a minimum of H^* hours of work at a wage of w^*, or they can hire no one. Show that by setting w^* and H^* appropriately, the union can achieve the same outcome as if it could perfectly price discriminate.

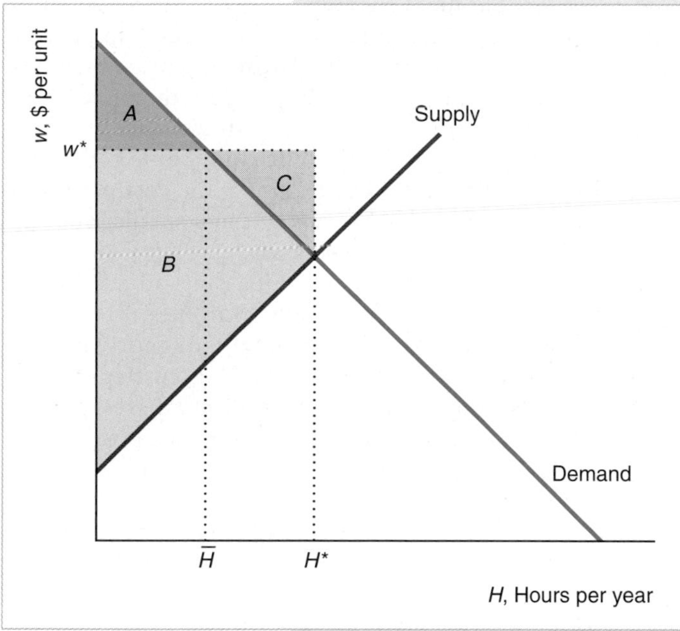

Answer

1. *Show the outcome and welfare areas if the union can perfectly price discriminate.* The figure shows the labor supply curve if the market were competitive. The union views this curve as its marginal cost curve. For each successive hour of labor service, the union sets the wage equal to the height of the demand curve and sells H^* total hours of labor services (see the discussion of Figure 12.2). Its producer surplus equals the total welfare: $A + B$.

2. *Show that the firms will agree to hire H^* at w^*, and the union will capture all the surplus.* If the union gives the firms a take-it-or-leave-it offer of hiring H^* hours at w^* or of hiring no one, the firms will accept the offer because area C is the same size as area A in the figure. At a wage of w^*, the firms have "consumer surplus" (the amount they are willing to pay above the wage for a given amount of labor services) of A for the first $\bar{H}$ hours of work, but they have negative consumer surplus of C for the remaining $H^* - \bar{H}$ hours of work. Thus, they have no consumer surplus overall, so they are indifferent between hiring the workers or not. The union's producer surplus is $B + C$, which equals its surplus if it perfectly price discriminated: $A + B$. Similarly, the number of hours of labor service provided, H^*, is the same under both pricing schemes.

See Questions 14 and 15.

APPLICATION

Unions That Have It All

Most unions act as a single-price monopoly of labor services. They set a wage and allow their customers to determine how many units of labor services to purchase. However, a few unions set both wages and a minimum number of work hours that employers must provide. Such contracts are common only in the transportation industry (excluding railroads and airplanes).

The International Longshore and Warehouse Union (ILWU) negotiates with the companies represented by the Pacific Maritime Association. The 10,500 union workers at West Coast ports handle $300 billion worth of goods per year. The registered union workers earn at least $80,000 (and some estimates set the figure at $100,000) per year with benefits and other perks worth about $42,000. The union contract in effect through 2008 guarantees a weekly income for each worker (it effectively sets the minimum number of hours). However, the number of dockworkers has shrunk over the years as firms have automated to become more efficient. Consequently, the union has insisted that the lost positions be replaced with new clerical positions.

12.3 Quantity Discrimination

Many firms are unable to determine which customers have the highest reservation prices. Such firms may know, however, that most customers are willing to pay more for the first unit than for successive units: The typical customer's demand curve is downward sloping. Such a firm can price discriminate by letting the price each customer pays vary with the number of units the customer buys. Here the price varies only with quantity: All customers pay the same price for a given quantity.

Not all quantity discounts are a form of price discrimination. Some reflect the reduction in a firm's cost with large-quantity sales. For example, the cost per ounce of selling a soft drink in a large cup is less than that of selling it in a smaller cup; the cost of cups varies little with size, and the cost of pouring and serving is the same. A restaurant offering quantity discounts on drinks may be passing on actual cost savings to larger purchasers rather than price discriminating. However, if the quantity discount is not due to cost differences, the firm is engaging in quantity discrimination. Moreover, a firm may quantity discriminate by charging customers who make large purchases more per unit than those who make small purchases.

Many utilities use *block-pricing* schedules, by which they charge one price for the first few units (a *block*) of usage and a different price for subsequent blocks. Both declining-block and increasing-block pricing are common.

The utility monopoly in Figure 12.3 faces a linear demand curve for each (identical) customer. The demand curve hits the vertical axis at \$90 and the horizontal axis at 90 units. The monopoly has a constant marginal and average cost of m = \$30. Panel a shows how this monopoly maximizes its profit if it can quantity discriminate by setting two prices. The firm uses declining-block prices to maximize its profit. The monopoly charges a price of \$70 on any quantity between 1 and 20—the first block—and \$50 on any units beyond the first 20—the second block. (The point that determines the first block, \$70 and 20 units, lies on the demand curve.) Given each consumer's demand curve, a consumer decides to buy 40 units and pays \$1,400 (= \$70 × 20) for the first block and \$1,000 (= \$50 × 20) for the second block. (See Appendix 12B for a mathematical analysis.)

If the monopoly can set only a single price (panel b), it produces where its marginal revenue equals its marginal cost, selling 30 units at \$60 per unit. Thus, by quantity discriminating instead of using a single price, the utility sells more units, 40 instead of 30, and makes a higher profit, B = \$1,200 instead of F = \$900. With quantity discounting, consumer surplus is lower, $A + C$ = \$400 instead of E = \$450; welfare (consumer surplus plus producer surplus) is higher, $A + B + C$ = \$1,600 instead of $E + F$ = \$1,350; and deadweight loss is lower, D = \$200 instead of G = \$450. Thus, in this example, the firm and society are better off with quantity discounting, but consumers as a group suffer.

See Question 16 and Problems 31–33.

The more block prices that the monopoly can set, the closer the monopoly can get to perfect price discrimination. The deadweight loss results from the monopoly setting a price above marginal cost so that too few units are sold. The more prices the monopoly sets, the lower the last price and hence the closer it is to marginal cost.

12.4 Multimarket Price Discrimination

Typically, a firm does not know the reservation price for each of its customers. But the firm may know which groups of customers are likely to have higher reservation prices than others. The most common method of multimarket price discrimination is to divide potential customers into two or more groups and set a different price for

Figure 12.3 Quantity Discrimination.

If this monopoly engages in quantity discounting, it makes a larger profit (producer surplus) than it does if it sets a single price, and welfare is greater. (a) With quantity discounting, profit is B = \$1,200 and welfare is $A + B + C$ = \$1,600. (b) If it sets a single price (so that its marginal revenue equals its marginal cost), the monopoly's profit is F = \$900, and welfare is $E + F$ = \$1,350.

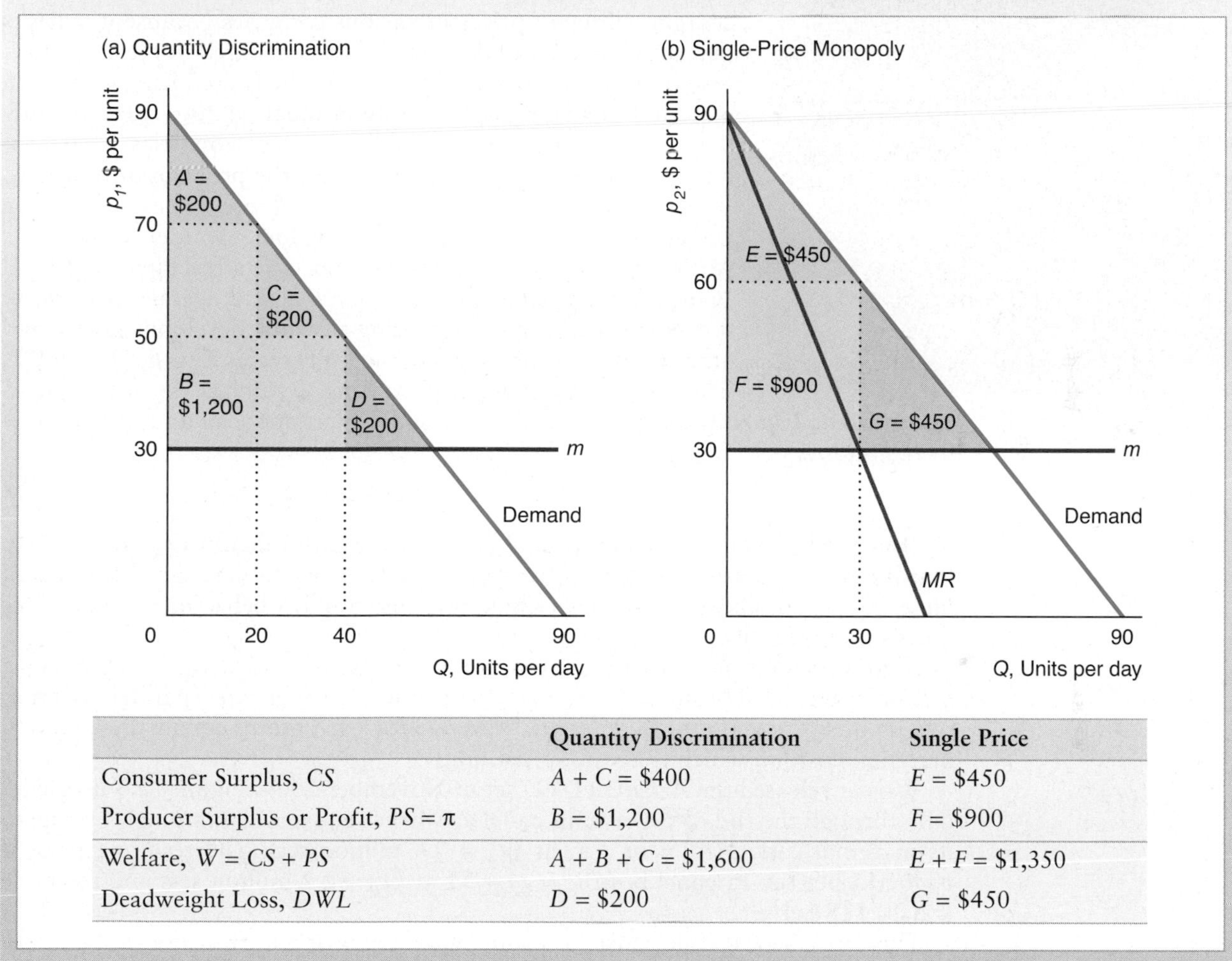

	Quantity Discrimination	Single Price
Consumer Surplus, CS	$A + C$ = \$400	E = \$450
Producer Surplus or Profit, $PS = \pi$	B = \$1,200	F = \$900
Welfare, $W = CS + PS$	$A + B + C$ = \$1,600	$E + F$ = \$1,350
Deadweight Loss, DWL	D = \$200	G = \$450

each group. All units of the good sold to customers within a group are sold at a single price. As with perfect price discrimination, to engage in multimarket price discrimination, a firm must have market power, be able to identify groups with different demands, and prevent resales.

For example, first-run movie theaters with market power charge senior citizens a lower price than they charge younger adults because senior citizens are not willing to pay as much as others to see a movie. By admitting people as soon as they demonstrate their age and buy tickets, the theater prevents resales.

Multimarket Price Discrimination with Two Groups

How does a monopoly set its prices if it sells to two (or more) groups of consumers with different demand curves and if resales between the two groups are impossible?

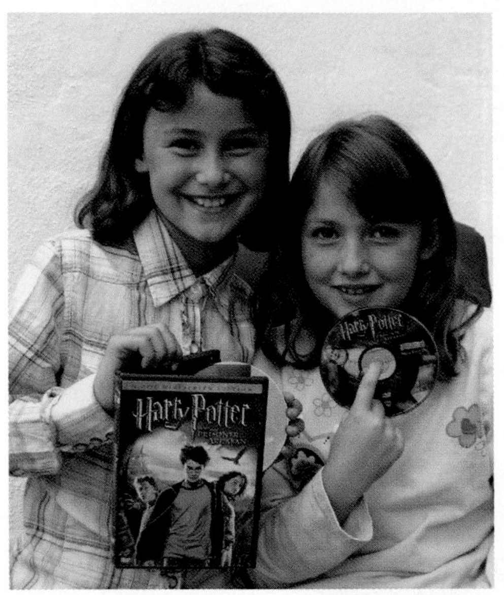

We examine this question for a firm that sells to groups of consumers in different countries.

A copyright gives Warner Home Entertainment the legal monopoly to produce and sell the *Harry Potter and the Prisoner of Azkaban* two-DVD movie set, which it released in November 2004. Warner engages in multimarket price discrimination by charging different prices in various countries because it believes that the elasticities of demand differ. Compared to the U.S. price, it sold this DVD set for 20% more in the United Kingdom, 33% more in Canada, and 66% more in Japan in 2005.[5] Presumably the cost to consumers of reselling across countries is so prohibitively high that Warner can ignore the problem of resales.[6]

For simplicity, we consider how Warner prices in just the United States and the United Kingdom. Warner charges its American consumers p_A for Q_A units, so its revenue is $p_A Q_A$. If Warner has the same constant marginal and average cost, m, in both countries, its profit (ignoring any sunk development cost and other fixed costs) from selling the DVD sets is $\pi_A = p_A Q_A - mQ_A$, where mQ_A is its cost of producing Q_A units. Warner wants to maximize its combined profit, π, which is the sum of its American and British profits, π_A and π_B:

$$\pi = \pi_A + \pi_B = [p_A Q_A - mQ_A] + [p_B Q_B - mQ_B].$$

How should Warner set its prices p_A and p_B—or equivalently Q_A and Q_B—so that it maximizes its combined profit? Appendix 12C gives a mathematical answer. Here we use our understanding of a single-price monopoly's behavior to answer this question graphically.

A multimarket-price-discriminating monopoly with a constant marginal cost maximizes its total profit by maximizing its profit to each group separately. Warner sets its quantities so that the marginal revenue for each group equals the common marginal cost, m, which is about $1 per unit.

Warner released the *Azkaban* DVD set in November 2004. Figure 12.4 uses sales data through the end of the year. In panel a, Warner equates its marginal revenue to its marginal cost, $MR^A = m = 1$, at $Q_A = 9.4$ million sets. The resulting price is $p_A = \$15$ per set. In panel b, $MR^B = m = \$1$ at $Q_B = 2.2$ million sets and the price is $p_B = \$18$ per set.

This price-setting rule must be profit maximizing if the firm doesn't want to change its price to either group. Would the monopoly want to lower its price and sell more output in the United States? If it did so, its marginal revenue would be below its marginal cost, so this change would reduce its profit. Similarly, if the monopoly sold less output in the United States, its marginal revenue would be above its marginal cost, which would reduce its profit. The same arguments can be made about its pricing in Britain. Thus, the price-discriminating monopoly maximizes its

[5]The sources for this section are **www.timewarner.com**, **Amazon.com** Web sites for each country, **www.ukfilmcouncil.org.uk**, **www.dvdexclusive.com**, and **www.leesmovieinfo.com**.

[6]Why don't customers in higher-price countries order the DVDs from a low-price country using Amazon.com or other Internet vendors? Explanations include consumers' lack of an Internet connection, their ignorance, higher shipping costs (though the price differentials slightly exceed this cost), language differences on the DVDs, desire for quick delivery, and legal restrictions.

Figure 12.4 Multimarket Pricing of Harry Potter DVD.

Warner Home Entertainment, the monopoly producer of the *Harry Potter and the Prisoner of Azkaban* DVD set, charges more in the United Kingdom, p_B = \$18, than in the United States, p_A = \$15, because the elasticity of demand is greater in the United States. Warner sets the quantity independently in each country where its relevant marginal revenue equals its common, constant marginal cost, m = \$1. As a result, it maximizes its profit by equating the two marginal revenues: $MR_A = 1 = MR_B$.

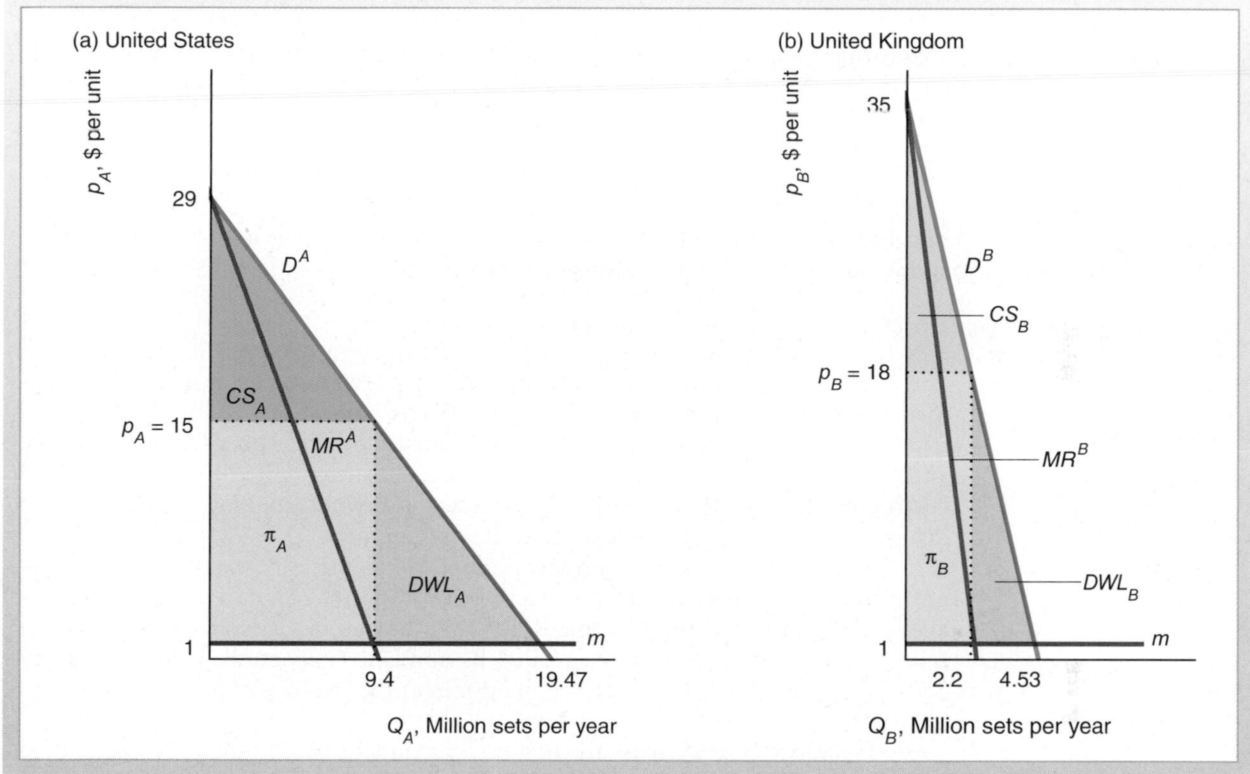

profit by operating where its marginal revenue for each country equals its common marginal cost.

Because the monopoly equates the marginal revenue for each group to its common marginal cost, $MC = m$, the marginal revenues for the two countries are equal:

$$MR^A = m = MR^B. \tag{12.1}$$

We can use Equation 12.1 to determine how the prices to the two groups vary with the price elasticities of demand at the profit-maximizing outputs. Each marginal revenue is a function of the corresponding price and the price elasticity of demand: $MR^A = p_A(1 + 1/\varepsilon_A)$, where ε_A is the price elasticity of demand for U.S. consumers, and $MR^B = p_B(1 + 1/\varepsilon_B)$, where ε_B is the price elasticity of demand for British consumers. Rewriting Equation 12.1 using these expressions for marginal revenue, we find that

$$MR^A = p_A\left(1+\frac{1}{\varepsilon_A}\right) = m = p_B\left(1+\frac{1}{\varepsilon_B}\right) = MR^B. \tag{12.2}$$

If m = \$1, p_A = \$15, and p_B = \$18 in Equation 12.2, Warner must believe that $\varepsilon_A = -15/14 \approx -1.07$ and $\varepsilon_B = -18/17 \approx -1.06$.[7]

By rearranging Equation 12.2, we learn that the ratio of prices in the two countries depends only on demand elasticities in those countries:

$$\frac{p_B}{p_A} = \frac{1 + 1/\varepsilon_A}{1 + 1/\varepsilon_B}. \tag{12.3}$$

Substituting the prices and the demand elasticities into Equation 12.3, we determine that

$$\frac{p_B}{p_A} = \frac{\$18}{\$15} = 1.2 = \frac{1 + 1/(-15/14)}{1 + 1/(-18/17)} = \frac{1 + 1/\varepsilon_A}{1 + 1/\varepsilon_B}.$$

See Questions 17–19 and 24–27 and Problems 34–39.

Thus, because Warner believes that the British demand curve is less elastic at its profit-maximizing prices, it charges British consumers 20% more than U.S. customers.

APPLICATION

Smuggling Prescription Drugs into the United States

A federal law forbids U.S. citizens from importing pharmaceuticals from Canada and other countries, but many U.S. citizens, city governments, and state governments openly flout this law. U.S. senior citizens have taken well-publicized bus trips across the Canadian and Mexican borders to buy their drugs at lower prices, and many Canadian, Mexican, and other Internet sites offer to ship drugs to U.S. customers. In a 2006 poll, 80% of Americans favored making importation of drugs easier. (European countries permit such imports.)

A U.S. citizen's incentive to import is great, as the prices of many popular drugs are substantially lower in virtually every other country. U.S. citizens paid an average of 81% more for brand-name drugs than buyers in Canada and six western European countries according to a 2004 Boston University study. U.S. citizens pay 75% more than Canada, which sets its prices at the median level of the countries it surveys.

So far, most U.S. citizens are not buying outside the country. According to Espicom, the U.S. expenditures on pharmaceuticals were \$270 billion in 2004, of which Canadian drug Internet imports were only \$1.2 billion. Thus, the ban appears to be relatively effective.

In contrast to many Democrats and some Republicans in Congress, President Bush opposes changing the importation law. The U.S. Food and Drug Administration (FDA) has raised the specter that imported brand-name drugs are not as safe as those purchased in the United States, although the FDA has not identified a single American injured by defective imported drugs.

Not surprisingly, U.S. pharmaceutical companies support the FDA's opposition to imports. They fear the possibility of resales, by which the drugs they sell at lower prices in other countries are then shipped to the United States. Such resales would drive down the drug firms' U.S. prices. The lower prices in other countries may reflect price discrimination by pharmaceutical firms, more competition due to differences in patent laws, price regulation by governments, or other causes.

Some drug companies, among them GlaxoSmithKline and Pfizer, are trying to reduce imports by cutting off Canadian pharmacies that ship south of the border.

---

[7]Rearranging the left side of Equation 12.2, we can obtain expressions of the form of Equation 11.9, which we can use to solve for the elasticity of demand. For example,

$$(p_A - m)/p_A = (15 - 1)/15 = -1/\varepsilon_A, \text{ so } \varepsilon_A = -15/14.$$

Wyeth and AstraZeneca report that they watch Canadian pharmacies and wholesale customers for spikes in sales volume that could indicate exports, and then restrict supplies to the Canadian pharmacies.

Many states and local governments provided Web site information about Canadian sources and planned to import the drugs. Starting in 2003, the FDA sent threatening letters to various state attorneys general warning that state agencies that imported Canadian prescription drugs were violating federal law. However, the agency has not sent a letter since 2006 (**www.fda.gov/importeddrugs** as of 2008).

The interesting question is not why many Democrats, Republicans, seniors, and most other U.S. citizens favor permitting such imports, but whether Canadians should oppose them. The following solved problem addresses these questions.

Solved Problem 12.3

A monopoly drug producer with a constant marginal cost of $m = 1$ sells in only two countries and faces a linear demand curve of $Q_1 = 12 - 2p_1$ in Country 1 and $Q_2 = 9 - p_2$ in Country 2. What price does the monopoly charge in each country, how much does it sell in each, and what profit does it earn in each with and without a ban against shipments between the countries?

Answer

If resales across borders are banned so that price discrimination is possible:

1. *Determine the profit-maximizing price that the monopoly sets in each country by setting the relevant marginal revenue equal to the marginal cost.* If the monopoly can price discriminate, it sets a monopoly price independently in each country (as Section 11.1 shows). By rearranging the demand function for Country 1, we find that the inverse demand function is $p_1 = 6 - \frac{1}{2}Q_1$ for quantities less than 6, and zero otherwise, as panel a shows. The marginal revenue curve is twice as steeply sloped as is the linear inverse demand curve (see Chapter 11): $MR_1 = 6 - Q_1$. The monopoly maximizes its profit where its marginal revenue equals its marginal cost,

$$MR_1 = 6 - Q_1 = 1 = m.$$

Solving, we find that its profit-maximizing output is $Q_1 = 5$. Substituting this expression back into the monopoly's inverse demand curve, we learn that its

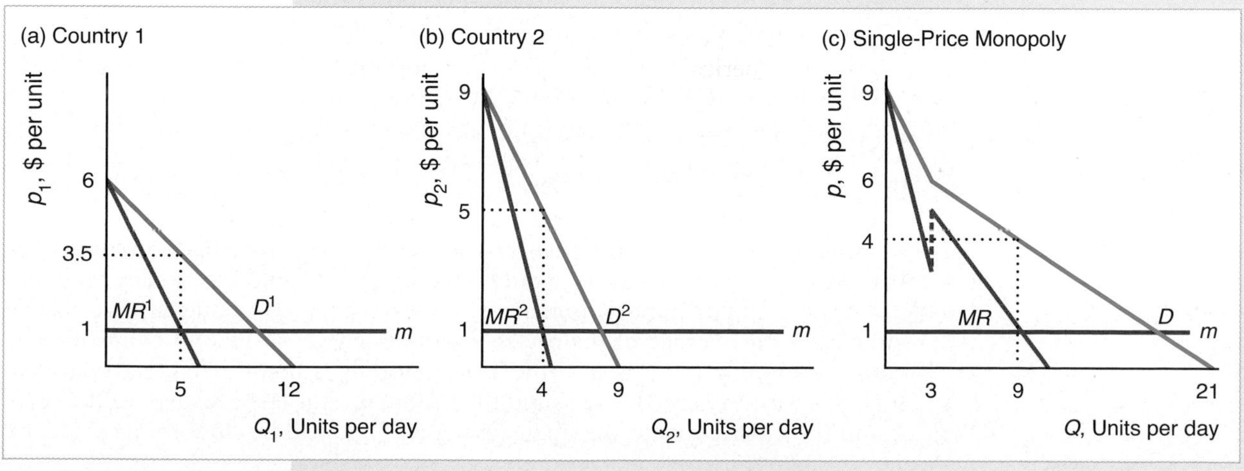

profit-maximizing price is $p_1 = 3.50$ (see panel a). In Country 2, the inverse demand curve is $p_2 = 9 - Q_2$, so the monopoly chooses Q_2 such that $MR_2 = 9 - 2Q_2 = 1 = m$. Thus, it maximizes its profit in Country 2 where $Q_2 = 4$ and $p_2 = 5$, as panel b shows.

2. *Calculate the profits.* The monopoly's profit in each country is the output times the difference between the price and its constant average cost, 1. The monopoly's profit in Country 1 is $\pi_1 = (3.50 - 1)5 = 12.50$. Its profit in Country 2 is $\pi_2 = (5 - 1)4 = 16$. Thus, its total profit is
$$\pi = \pi_1 + \pi_2 = 12.50 + 16 = 28.50.$$

If imports are permitted so that price discrimination is impossible:

3. *Derive the total demand curve.* If the monopoly cannot price discriminate, it charges the same price, p, in both countries. We can determine the aggregate demand curve it faces by horizontally summing the demand curves in each country at a given price (see Chapter 2). The total demand curve in panel c is the horizontal sum of the demand curves for each of the two countries in panels a and b. In the range of price where positive quantities are sold in each country ($p < 6$), the total demand function is
$$Q = (12 - 2p) + (9 - p) = 21 - 3p,$$
where $Q = q_1 + q_2$ is the total quantity that the monopoly sells.

4. *Determine the marginal revenue curve corresponding to the total demand curve.* Because no drugs are sold in Country 1 at prices above $p = 6$, the total demand curve (panel c) equals Country 2's demand curve (panel b) at prices above 6, and the total demand curve is the horizontal sum of the two countries' demand curves (panels a and b) at lower prices. Thus, the total demand curve has a kink at $p = 6$. Consequently, the corresponding marginal revenue curve has two sections. At prices above 6, the marginal revenue curve is that of Country 2. At prices below 6, where the total demand curve is the horizontal sum of the two countries' demand curves, the inverse demand curve is $p = 7 - (\frac{2}{3})Q$, so the marginal revenue curve is $MR = 7 - (\frac{1}{3})Q$. Panel c shows that the marginal revenue curve "jumps" (is discontinuous) at the point where we connect the two sections.

5. *Solve for the single-price monopoly solution.* The monopoly maximizes its profit where its marginal revenue equals its marginal cost. From inspecting panel c, we learn that the intersection occurs in the section where both countries are buying the good: $MR = 7 - (\frac{2}{3})Q = 1 = m$. Thus, the profit-maximizing output is $Q = 9$. Substituting that quantity into the inverse total demand function, we find that the monopoly charges $p = 4$.

6. *Calculate the profits.* The monopoly's profits are
See Question 20.
$$\pi_1 = (4 - 1)4 = 12,\ \pi_2 = (4 - 1)5 = 15, \text{ and } \pi = 12 + 15 = 27.$$

Comments: The monopoly's profit falls from 28.50 to 27 if it loses the ability to price discriminate. The price of the nondiscriminating monopoly, 4, lies between the two prices it would charge if it could price discriminate: $3.50 < 4 < 5$. The nondiscriminating monopoly charges a single price that is effectively the average of the prices it would charge in the two countries if it could discriminate. Consequently, if a monopoly wants to charge a relatively high price in the United States, and the U.S. market is large relative to the market in the other country, the single (average) price will be close to the price the monopoly would charge in the United States if it could price discriminate. U.S. consumers would benefit (slightly) and consumers in the other country would suffer. Hence, it is understandable why a low-price country might ban pharmaceutical exports, as Canadian officials announced in 2005 that they were considering. When the Canadian Government failed to act, the Canadian Pharmacist Association called for a ban in 2007.

Identifying Groups

Firms use two approaches to divide customers into groups. One method is to divide buyers into groups based on *observable characteristics* of consumers that the firm believes are associated with unusually high or low price elasticities. For example, movie theaters price discriminate using the age of customers. Similarly, some firms charge customers in one country higher prices than those in another country.[8] In 2008, Microsoft Office Home and Student Edition 2007 sells for $125 in the United States but sells for $130 in Britain, $169 in Canada, $231 in France, and $252 in Japan (based on Amazon.com sites in each country). A two-liter bottle of Coca-Cola costs 50% more in Britain than in other European Union nations. These differences are much greater than can be explained by shipping costs and reflect multimarket price discrimination.

Another approach is to identify and divide consumers on the basis of their *actions*: The firm allows consumers to self-select the group to which they belong. For example, customers may be identified by their willingness to spend time to buy a good at a lower price or to order goods and services in advance of delivery.

Firms use differences in the value customers place on their time to discriminate by using queues (making people wait in line) and other time-intensive methods of selling goods. Store managers who believe that high-wage people are unwilling to "waste their time shopping" may run sales by which consumers who visit the store and pick up the good themselves get a low price while consumers who order over the phone or by mail pay a higher price. This type of price discrimination increases profit if people who put a high value on their time also have less elastic demands for the good.

APPLICATION

Consumers Pay for Lower Prices

Firms draw on a variety of methods to induce consumers to indicate whether they have relatively high or low elasticities of demand. Each of these methods requires that to receive a discount, consumers incur some cost, such as their time. Otherwise, all consumers would get the discount. By spending extra time to obtain a discount, price-sensitive consumers are able to differentiate themselves from others.

Coupons. Many firms use discount coupons to multimarket price discriminate. By doing so, they divide customers into two groups, charging those who are willing to use coupons less than those who won't clip coupons. Providing coupons makes sense if people who don't use coupons are less price sensitive on

[8]A firm can charge a higher price for customers in one country than in another if the price differential is too small for many resales between the two countries to occur or if governments enforce import or export restrictions to prevent resales between countries. See **www.myeconlab.com/perloff**, Chapter 12, "Gray Markets."

average than those who clip.[9] People who are willing to spend their time clipping coupons buy cereals and other goods at lower prices than those who value their time more. Almost all (86%) of U.S. consumers use coupons (including 81% of those earning over $100,000 a year). They "saved" $2.6 billion on their purchases in 2006. However, manufacturers offered more than $330 billion in coupon savings that year.

Airline Tickets. By choosing between two different types of tickets, airline customers indicate whether they are likely to be business travelers or vacationers. Airlines give customers a choice between high-price tickets with no strings attached and low-price fares that must be purchased long in advance.

Airlines know that many business travelers have little advance warning before they book a flight and are usually unwilling to stay away over a Saturday night. These business travelers have relatively inelastic demand curves: They want to travel at a specific time even if the price is relatively high. In contrast, vacation travelers can usually plan in advance and stay over a Saturday night. Because vacation travelers can drive, take trains or buses, or postpone trips, they have relatively high elasticities of demand for air travel. The choice that airlines give customers ensures that vacationers with relatively elastic demands obtain cheap seats while most business travelers with relatively inelastic demands buy high-price tickets (often more than four times higher than the plan-ahead rate). The expected absolute difference in fares between two passengers on a route is 36% of the airline's average ticket price.

Reverse Auctions. Priceline.com and other online merchants use a name-your-own-price or reverse auction to identify price-sensitive customers. A customer enters a relatively low-price bid for a good or service, such as airline tickets. Then merchants decide whether to accept that bid or not. To keep their less price-sensitive customers from using those methods, airlines force successful Priceline bidders to be flexible: to fly at off hours, to make one or more connections, and to accept any type of aircraft. Similarly, when bidding on groceries, a customer must list "one or two brands you like." As Jay Walker, Priceline's founder explained, "The manufacturers would rather not give you a discount, of course, but if you prove that you're willing to switch brands, they're willing to pay to keep you."

Welfare Effects of Multimarket Price Discrimination

Multimarket price discrimination results in inefficient production and consumption. As a result, welfare under multimarket price discrimination is lower than that under competition or perfect price discrimination. Welfare may be lower or higher with multimarket price discrimination than with a single-price monopoly, however.

Multimarket Price Discrimination Versus Competition. Consumer surplus is greater and more output is produced with competition (or perfect price discrimination) than with multimarket price discrimination. In Figure 12.4, consumer surplus with multimarket price discrimination is CS_1 (for Group 1 in panel a) and CS_2 (for Group 2 in panel b). Under competition, consumer surplus is the area below the

[9]Firms post coupons on the Internet, and coupon clippers trade or sell their coupons to others using sites such as **www.coolsavings.com**.

demand curve and above the marginal cost curve: $CS_1 + \pi_1 + DWL_1$ in panel a and $CS_2 + \pi_2 + DWL_2$ in panel b.

Thus, multimarket price discrimination transfers some of the competitive consumer surplus, π_1 and π_2, to the monopoly as additional profit and causes the deadweight loss, DWL_1 and DWL_2, of some of the rest of the competitive consumer surplus. The deadweight loss is due to the multimarket-price-discriminating monopoly's charging prices above marginal cost, which results in reduced production from the optimal competitive level.

Multimarket Price Discrimination Versus Single-Price Monopoly. From theory alone, we can't tell whether welfare is higher if the monopoly uses multimarket price discrimination or if it sets a single price. Both types of monopolies set price above marginal cost, so too little is produced relative to competition. Output may rise as the firm starts discriminating if groups that did not buy when the firm charged a single price start buying. In the movie theater example in panel b of Table 12.1, welfare is higher with discrimination than with single-price monopoly because more tickets are sold when the monopoly discriminates (see Solved Problem 12.1).

The closer the multimarket-price-discriminating monopoly comes to perfectly price discriminating (say, by dividing its customers into many groups rather than just two), the more output it produces, so the less the production inefficiency there is. However, unless a multimarket-price-discriminating monopoly sells significantly more output than it would if it had to set a single price, welfare is likely to be lower with discrimination because of consumption inefficiency and time wasted shopping. These two inefficiencies don't occur with a monopoly that charges all consumers the same price. As a result, consumers place the same marginal value (the single sales price) on the good, so they have no incentive to trade with each other. Similarly, if everyone pays the same price, consumers have no incentive to search for low prices.

12.5 Two-Part Tariffs

We now turn to two other forms of second-degree price discrimination: *two-part tariffs* in this section and *tie-in sales* in the next one. Both are similar to the type of second-degree price discrimination we examined earlier because the average price per unit varies with the number of units consumers buy.

two-part tariff
a pricing system in which the firm charges a customer a lump-sum fee (the first tariff or price) for the right to buy as many units of the good as the consumer wants at a specified price (the second tariff)

With a **two-part tariff**, the firm charges a consumer a lump-sum fee (the first tariff) for the right to buy as many units of the good as the consumer wants at a specified price (the second tariff). Because of the lump-sum fee, consumers pay more per unit if they buy a small number of goods than if they buy a larger number.

To get telephone service, you may pay a monthly connection fee and a price per minute of use. Some car rental firms charge a per-day fee and a price per mile driven.

To buy season tickets to the Dallas Cowboys football games in the lower seating areas in 2009, a fan must pay a fee of between \$16,000 to \$150,000 for a *personal seat license* (PSL), which gives the fan the right to buy season tickets for the next 30 years at \$340 per game for 10 games, or \$3,400 per season. The Cowboys could make \$700 million just from the sale of PSLs if they can actually sell them at these prices. The Carolina Panthers introduced the PSL in 1993, and at least 13 NFL teams have used a PSL in 2008.

See Problem 40.

To profit from two-part tariffs, a firm must have market power, know how demand differs across customers or with the quantity that a single customer buys, and successfully prevent resales. We now examine two results. First, we consider how a firm uses a two-part tariff to extract consumer surplus (as in our previous price discrimination examples). Second, we see how, if the firm cannot vary its two-part tariff across its customers, its profit is greater the more similar the demand curves of its customers are.

We illustrate these two points for a monopoly that knows its customers' demand curves. We start by examining the monopoly's two-part tariff where all its customers have identical demand curves and then look at one where its customers' demand curves differ.

A Two-Part Tariff with Identical Consumers

If all the monopoly's customers are identical, a monopoly that knows its customers' demand curve can set a two-part tariff that has the same two properties as the perfect price discrimination equilibrium. First, the efficient quantity, Q_1, is sold because the price of the last unit equals marginal cost. Second, all consumer surplus is transferred from consumers to the firm.

Suppose that the monopoly has a constant marginal and average cost of $m = \$10$ (no fixed cost), and every consumer has the demand curve D^1 in panel a of Figure 12.5. To maximize its profit, the monopoly charges a price, p, equal to the constant marginal and average cost, $m = \$10$, and just breaks even on each unit sold. By setting price equal to marginal cost, it maximizes the *potential consumer surplus*: the consumer surplus if no lump-sum fee is charged. It charges the largest possible

Figure 12.5 Two-Part Tariff.

If all consumers have the demand curve in panel a, a monopoly can capture all the consumer surplus with a two-part tariff by which it charges a price, p, equal to the marginal cost, $m = \$10$, for each item and a lump-sum membership fee of $\mathcal{L} = A_1 + B_1 + C_1 = \$2{,}450$. Now suppose that the monopoly has two customers, Consumer 1 in panel a and Consumer 2 in panel b. If the monopoly can treat its customers differently, it maximizes its profit by setting $p = m = \$10$ and charging Consumer 1 a fee equal to its potential consumer surplus, $A_1 + B_1 + C_1 = \$2{,}450$, and Consumer 2 a fee of $A_2 + B_2 + C_2 = \$4{,}050$, for a total profit of \$6,500. If the monopoly must charge all customers the same price, it maximizes its profit at \$5,000 by setting $p = \$20$ and charging both customers a lump-sum fee equal to the potential consumer surplus of Consumer 1, $\mathcal{L} = A_1 = \$1{,}800$.

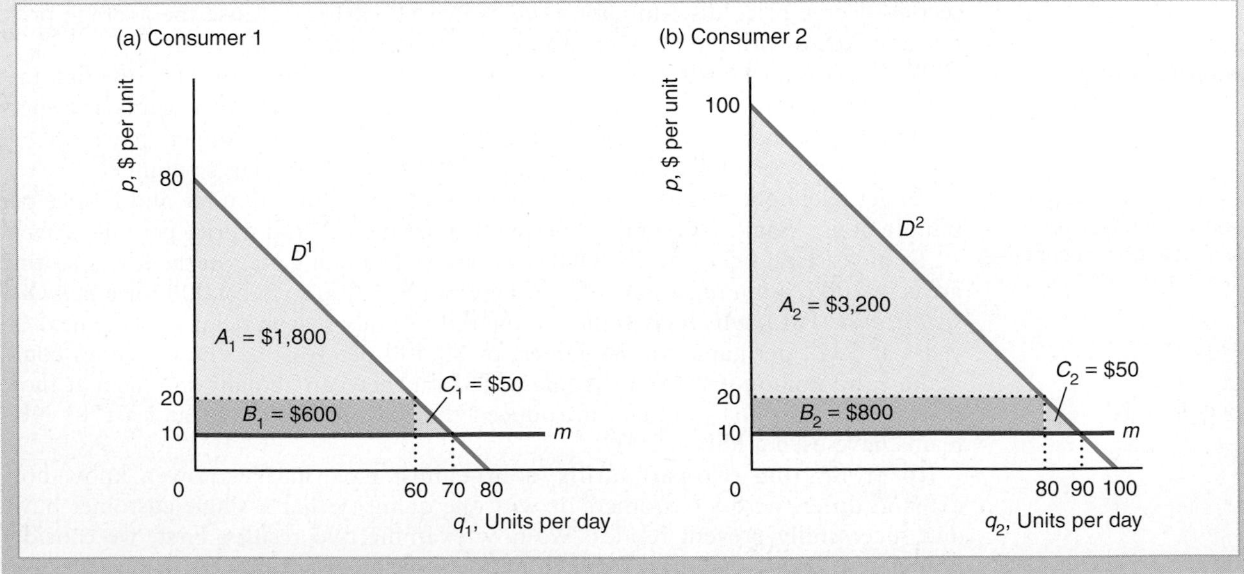

lump-sum fee, $\mathcal{L}$, which is the potential consumer surplus $A_1 + B_1 + C_1 = \$2,450$. Thus, its profit is \$2,450 times the number of customers.

Had the firm charged a higher per-unit price, it would sell fewer units and hence make a smaller profit. For example, if the monopoly charges $p = \$20$, it sells 60 units, making a profit from its unit sales of $B_1 = (\$20 - \$10)60 = \$600$. It must lower its fee to equal the new potential consumer surplus of $A_1 = \$1,800$, so its total profit per customer is only \$2,400. It loses area $C_1 = \$50$ by charging the higher price. Similarly, had the monopoly charged a lower per-unit price, its profit would be lower: It would sell too many units and make a loss on each unit because its price would be below its marginal cost.

Because the monopoly knows the demand curve, it could instead perfectly price discriminate by charging each customer a different price for each unit purchased: the price along the demand curve. Thus, this knowledgeable monopoly can capture all potential consumer surplus either by perfectly price discriminating or by setting its optimal two-part tariff.

If the monopoly does not know its customers' demand curve, it must guess how high a lump-sum fee to set. This fee will almost certainly be less than the potential consumer surplus. If the firm sets its fee above the potential consumer surplus, it loses all its customers.

A Two-Part Tariff with Nonidentical Consumers

Now suppose that there are two customers, Consumer 1 and Consumer 2, with demand curves D_1 and D_2 in panels a and b of Figure 12.5. If the monopoly knows each customer's demand curve and can prevent resales, it can capture all the consumer surplus by varying its two-part tariffs across customers. However, if the monopoly is unable to distinguish among the types of customers or cannot charge consumers different prices, efficiency and profitability fall.

Suppose that the monopoly knows its customers' demand curves. By charging each customer $p = m = \$10$ per unit, the monopoly makes no profit per unit but sells the number of units that maximizes the potential consumer surplus. The monopoly then captures all this potential consumer surplus by charging Consumer 1 a lump-sum fee of $\mathcal{L}_1 = A_1 + B_1 + C_1 = \$2,450$ and Consumer 2 a fee of $\mathcal{L}_2 = A_2 + B_2 + C_2 = \$4,050$. The monopoly's total profit is $\mathcal{L}_1 + \mathcal{L}_2 = \$6,500$. By doing so, the monopoly maximizes its total profit by capturing the maximum potential consumer surplus from both customers.

Now suppose that the monopoly has to charge each consumer the same lump-sum fee, $\mathcal{L}$, and the same per-unit price, p. For example, because of legal restrictions, a telephone company charges all residential customers the same monthly fee and the same fee per call, even though the company knows that consumers' demands vary. As with multimarket price discrimination, the monopoly does not capture all the consumer surplus.

The monopoly charges a lump-sum fee, $\mathcal{L}$, equal to either the potential consumer surplus of Consumer 1, CS_1, or of Consumer 2, CS_2. Because CS_2 is greater than CS_1, both customers buy if the monopoly charges $\mathcal{L} = CS_1$, whereas only Consumer 2 buys if the monopoly charges $\mathcal{L} = CS_2$. The monopoly sets either the low lump-sum fee or the higher one, depending on which produces the greater profit.

Any other lump-sum fee would lower its profit. The monopoly has no customers if it charges more than $\mathcal{L} = CS_2$. If it charges between CS_1 and CS_2, it loses money on Consumer 2 compared to what it could earn by charging CS_2, and it still does not sell to Consumer 1. By charging less than $\mathcal{L} = CS_1$, it earns less per customer and does not gain any additional customers.

In our example, the monopoly maximizes its profit by setting the lower lump-sum fee and charging a price p = \$20, which is above marginal cost (see Appendix 12D). Consumer 1 buys 60 units and Consumer 2 buys 80 units. The monopoly makes $(p - m)$ = (\$20 – \$10) = \$10 on each unit, so it earns $B_1 + B_2$ = \$600 + \$800 = \$1,400 from the units it sells. In addition, it gets a fee from both consumers equal to the consumer surplus of Consumer 1, A_1 = \$1,800. Thus, its total profit is 2 × \$1,800 + \$1,400 = \$5,000, which is \$1,500 less than if it could set different lump-sum fees for each customer. Consumer 1 has no consumer surplus, but Consumer 2 enjoys a consumer surplus of \$1,400 (= \$3,200 – \$1,800).

Why does the monopoly charge a price above marginal cost when using a two-part tariff? By raising its price, the monopoly earns more per unit from both types of customers but lowers its customers' potential consumer surplus. Thus, if the monopoly can capture each customer's potential surplus by charging different lump-sum fees, it sets its price equal to marginal cost. However, if the monopoly cannot capture all the potential consumer surplus because it must charge everyone the same lump-sum fee, the increase in profit from Customer 2 from the higher price more than offsets the reduction in the lump-sum fee (the potential consumer surplus of Customer 1).[10] (See **www.myeconlab.com/perloff**, Chapter 12, "Warehouse Stores.")

12.6 Tie-In Sales

tie-in sale
a type of nonlinear pricing in which customers can buy one product only if they agree to buy another product as well

requirement tie-in sale
a tie-in sale in which customers who buy one product from a firm are required to make all their purchases of another product from that firm

bundling (*package tie-in sale*)
a type of tie-in sale in which two goods are combined so that customers cannot buy either good separately

Another type of nonlinear pricing is a **tie-in sale**, in which customers can buy one product only if they agree to purchase another product as well. There are two forms of tie-in sales.

The first type is a **requirement tie-in sale**, in which customers who buy one product from a firm are required to make all their purchases of another product from that firm. Some firms sell durable machines such as copiers under the condition that customers buy copier services and supplies from them in the future. Because the amount of services and supplies each customer buys differs, the per-unit price of copiers varies across customers.

The second type of tie-in sale is **bundling** (or a *package tie-in sale*), in which two goods are combined so that customers cannot buy either good separately. For example, a Whirlpool refrigerator is sold with shelves, and a Hewlett-Packard ink-jet printer comes in a box that includes both black and color printer cartridges.

Most tie-in sales increase efficiency by lowering transaction costs. Indeed, tie-ins for efficiency purposes are so common that we hardly think about them. Presumably, no one would want to buy a shirt without buttons, so selling shirts with buttons attached lowers transaction costs. Because virtually everyone wants certain basic software, most companies sell computers with this software already installed. Firms also often use tie-in sales to increase profits, as we now illustrate.

Requirement Tie-In Sales

Frequently, a firm cannot tell which customers are going to use its product the most and hence are willing to pay the most for the good. These firms may be able to use a requirement tie-in sale to identify heavy users of the product and charge them more.

[10] If the monopoly lowers its price from \$20 to the marginal cost of \$10, it loses B_1 from Customer 1, but it can raise its lump-sum fee from A_1 to $A_1 + B_1 + C_1$, so its total profit from Customer 1 increases by C_1 = \$50. The lump-sum fee it collects from Customer 2 also rises by $B_1 + C_1$ = \$650, but its profit from unit sales falls by B_2 = \$800, so its total profit decreases by \$150. The loss from Customer 2, –\$150, more than offsets the gain from Customer 1, \$50. Thus, the monopoly makes \$100 more by charging a price of \$20 rather than \$10.

APPLICATION

IBM

In the 1930s, IBM increased its profit by using a requirement tie-in. IBM produced card punch machines, sorters, and tabulating machines (precursors of modern computers) that computed by using punched cards. Rather than selling its card punch machines, IBM leased them under the condition that the lease would terminate if any card not manufactured by IBM were used. (By leasing the equipment, IBM avoided resale problems and forced customers to buy cards from it.) IBM charged customers more per card than other firms would have charged. If we think of this extra payment per card as part of the cost of using the machine, this requirement tie-in resulted in heavy users' paying more for the machines than others did. This tie-in was profitable because heavy users were willing to pay more.[11]

Bundling

Firms that sell two or more goods may use bundling to raise profits. Bundling allows firms that can't directly price discriminate to charge customers different prices. Whether bundling is profitable depends on customers' tastes and the ability to prevent resales.

Imagine that you are in charge of selling season tickets for the local football team. Your stadium can hold all your potential customers, so the marginal cost of selling one more ticket is zero.

Should you bundle tickets for preseason (exhibition) and regular-season games, or should you sell books of tickets for the preseason and the regular season separately?[12] To answer this question, you have to determine how the fans differ in their desires to see preseason and regular-season games.

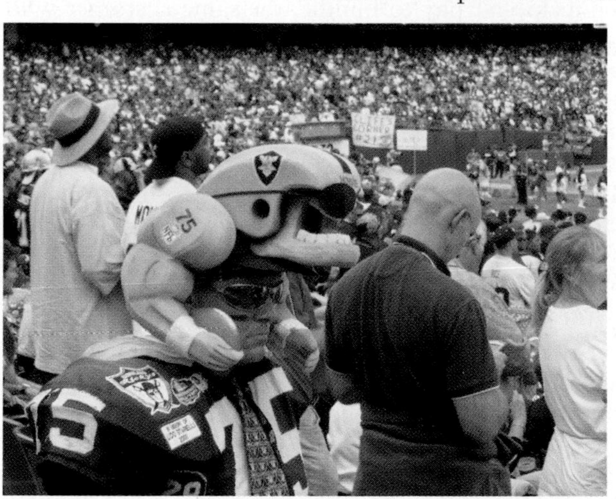

For simplicity, suppose that there are two customers (or types of customers). These football fans are so fanatical that they are willing to pay to see preseason exhibition games: There's no accounting for tastes!

Whether you should bundle depends on your customers' tastes. It does not pay to bundle in panel a of Table 12.2, in which Fan 1 is willing to pay more for both regular and preseason tickets than Fan 2. Bundling does pay in panel b, in which Fan 1 is willing to pay more for regular-season but less for exhibition tickets than Fan 2.

To determine whether it pays to bundle, we have to calculate the profit-maximizing unbundled and bundled prices. We start by calculating the profit-maximizing unbundled prices in panel a. If you charge

[11]The U.S. Supreme Court held that IBM's actions violated the antitrust laws because they lessened competition in the (potential) market for tabulating cards. IBM's defense was that its requirement was designed to protect its reputation. IBM claimed that badly made tabulating cards might cause its machines to malfunction and that consumers would falsely blame IBM's equipment. The Court did not accept IBM's argument. The Court apparently did not understand—or at least care about—the price discrimination aspect of IBM's actions.

[12]We assume that you don't want to sell tickets to each game separately. One reason for selling only season tickets is to reduce transaction costs. A second explanation is the same type of bundling argument that we discuss in this section.

Table 12.2 Bundling of Tickets to Football Games.

(a) Unprofitable Bundle			
	Regular Season	Preseason	Bundle
Fan 1	$2,000	$500	$2,500
Fan 2	$1,400	$100	$1,500
Profit-maximizing price	$1,400	$500	$1,500

(b) Profitable Bundle			
	Regular Season	Preseason	Bundle
Fan 1	$1,700	$300	$2,000
Fan 2	$1,500	$500	$2,000
Profit-maximizing price	$1,500	$300	$2,000

$2,000 for the regular-season tickets, you earn only $2,000 because Fan 2 won't buy tickets. It is more profitable to charge $1,400, sell tickets to both customers, and earn $2,800 for the regular season. By similar reasoning, the profit-maximizing price for the exhibition tickets is $500, at which you sell only to Fan 1 and earn $500. As a result, you earn $3,300 (= $2,800 + $500) if you do not bundle.

If you bundle and charge $2,500, you sell only to Fan 1. Your better option if you bundle is to set a bundle price of $1,500 and sell to both fans, earning $3,000. Nonetheless, you earn $300 more if you sell the tickets separately than if you bundle.

In this first example, in which it doesn't pay to bundle, the same customer who values the regular-season tickets the most also values the preseason tickets the most. In contrast, in panel b, the fan who values the regular-season tickets more values the exhibition season tickets less than the other fan does. Here your profit is higher if you bundle. If you sell the tickets separately, you charge $1,500 for regular-season tickets, earning $3,000 from the two customers, and $300 for preseason tickets, earning $600, for a total of $3,600. By selling a bundle of tickets for all games at $2,000 each, you'd earn $4,000. Thus, you earn $400 more by bundling than by selling the tickets separately.

By bundling, you can charge the fans different prices for the two components of the bundle. Fan 1 is paying $1,700 for regular-season tickets and $300 for exhibition tickets, while Fan 2 is paying $1,500 and $500, respectively.[13] If you could perfectly price discriminate, you'd charge each consumer his or her reservation price for the preseason and regular-season tickets and would make the same amount as you do by bundling.

See Questions 21–23.

These examples illustrate that bundling a pair of goods pays only if their demands are *negatively correlated*: Customers who are willing to pay relatively more for regular-season tickets are not willing to pay as much as others for preseason tickets, and vice versa. When a good or service is sold to different people, the price is determined by the purchaser with the *lowest* reservation price. If reservation prices differ substantially across consumers, a monopoly has to charge a relatively low price to make many sales. By bundling when demands are negatively correlated,

[13]As with price discrimination, you have to prevent resales for bundling to increase your profit. Someone could make a $198 profit by purchasing the bundle for $2,000, selling Fan 1 the regular-season tickets for $1,699, and selling Fan 2 the preseason tickets for $499. Each fan would prefer attending only one type of game at those prices to paying $2,000 for the bundle.

the monopoly reduces the dispersion in reservation prices, so it can charge more and still sell to a large number of customers.

12.7 Advertising

In addition to setting prices or quantities, choosing investments, and lobbying governments, firms engage in many other strategic actions to boost their profits. One of the most important is advertising.

Advertising is only one way to promote a product. Other promotional activities include providing free samples and using sales agents. Some promotional tactics are subtle. For example, grocery stores place sugary breakfast cereals on lower shelves so that they are at children's eye level. According to a survey of 27 supermarkets nationwide by the Center for Science in the Public Interest, the average position of ten child-appealing brands (44% sugar) was on the next-to-bottom shelf, while the average position of ten adult brands (10% sugar) was on the next-to-top shelf.

A monopoly advertises to raise its profit. A successful advertising campaign shifts the market demand curve by changing consumers' tastes or informing them about new products. The monopoly may be able to change the tastes of some consumers by telling them that a famous athlete or performer uses the product. Children and teenagers are frequently the targets of such advertising. (See **www.myeconlab.com/perloff**, Chapter 12, "Smoking-Gun Evidence?" for a discussion of cigarette advertising aimed at youths.) If the advertising convinces some consumers that they can't live without the product, the monopoly's demand curve may shift outward and become less elastic at the new equilibrium, at which the firm charges a higher price for its product (see Chapter 11). If the firm informs potential consumers about a new use for the product—for example, "Vaseline petroleum jelly protects lips from chapping"—demand at each price increases. (See **www.myeconlab.com/perloff**, Chapter 12, "Drug Commercials.")

The Decision Whether to Advertise

Even if advertising succeeds in shifting demand, it may not pay for the firm to advertise. If advertising shifts demand outward or makes it less elastic, the firm's *gross profit*, which ignores the cost of advertising, must rise. The firm undertakes this advertising campaign, however, only if it expects its *net profit* (gross profit minus the cost of advertising) to increase.

To illustrate a monopoly's decision making, in Figure 12.6, we use an estimate of Coca-Cola's market demand curve (Gasmi, Laffont, and Vuong, 1992). Suppose that Coke is a monopoly in the United States. If it does not advertise, it faces the demand curve D^1. If Coke advertises at its current level, its demand curve shifts from D^1 to D^2.

Coke's marginal cost, MC, is constant and equals its average cost, AC, at \$5 per unit (10 cases). Before advertising, Coke chooses its output, $Q_1 = 24$ million units, where its marginal cost equals its marginal revenue, MR^1, based on its demand curve, D^1. The profit-maximizing equilibrium is e_1, and the monopoly charges a price of $p_1 = \$11$. The monopoly's profit, π_1, is a box whose height is the difference between the price and the average cost, \$6 (= \$11 – \$5) per unit, and whose length is the quantity, 24 units (tens of millions of cases of twelve-ounce cans).

After its advertising campaign (involving dancing polar bears, talking lizards, or sincere celebrities) shifts its demand curve to D^2, Coke chooses a higher quantity, $Q_2 = 28$, where the MR^2 and MC curves intersect. In this new equilibrium, e_2, Coke

Figure 12.6 Advertising.

Suppose that Coke were a monopoly. If it does not advertise, its demand curve is D^1. At its actual level of advertising, its demand curve is D^2. Advertising increases Coke's gross profit (ignoring the cost of advertising) from π_1 to $\pi_2 = \pi_1 + B$. Thus, if the cost of advertising is less than the benefits from advertising, B, Coke's net profit (gross profit minus the cost of advertising) rises.

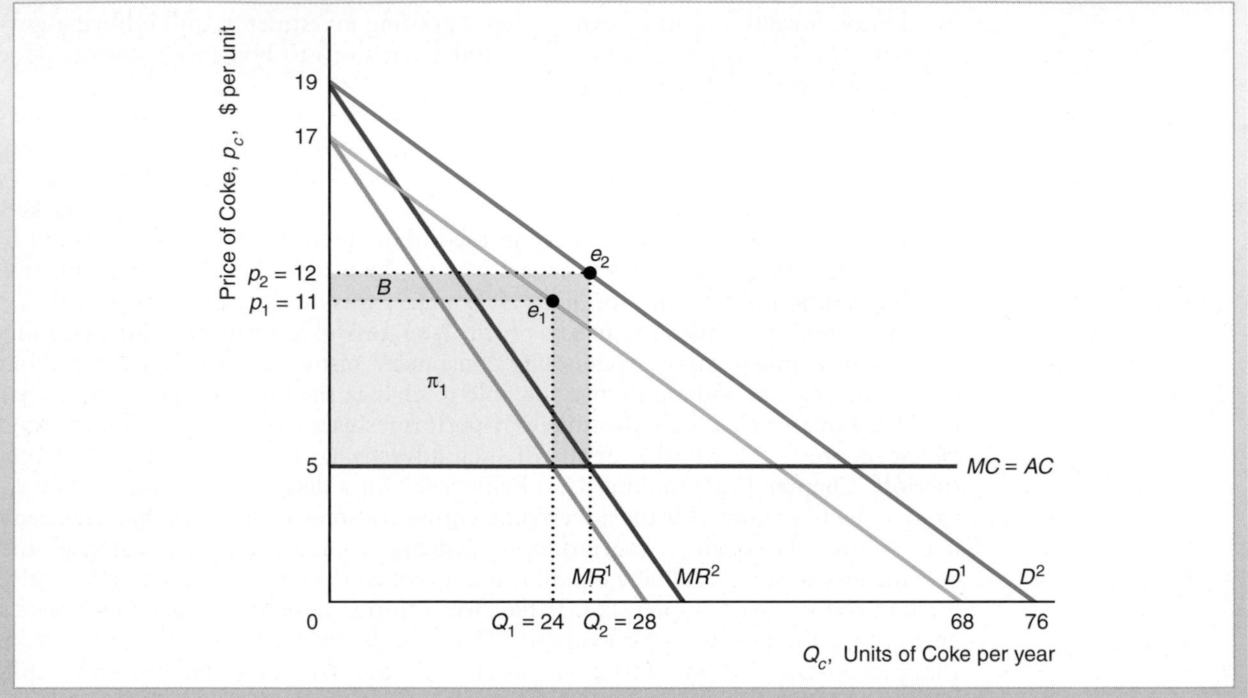

charges p_2 = \$12. Despite this higher price, Coke sells more cola after advertising because of the outward shift of its demand curve.

As a consequence, Coke's gross profit rises more than 36%. Coke's new gross profit is the rectangle $\pi_1 + B$, where the height of the rectangle is the new price minus the average cost, \$7, and the length is the quantity, 28. Thus, the benefit, B, to Coke from advertising at this level is the increase in its gross profit. If its cost of advertising is less than B, its net profit rises, and it pays for Coke to advertise at this level rather than not to advertise at all.

How Much to Advertise

How much should a monopoly advertise to maximize its net profit? To answer this question, we consider what happens if the monopoly raises or lowers its advertising expenditures by \$1, which is its marginal cost of an additional unit of advertising. If a monopoly spends one more dollar on advertising and its gross profit rises by more than \$1, its net profit rises, so the extra advertising pays. In contrast, the monopoly should reduce its advertising if the last dollar of advertising raises its gross profit by less than \$1, so its net profit falls. Thus, the monopoly's level of advertising maximizes its net profit if the last dollar of advertising increases its gross profit by \$1 (see Appendix 12E for an analysis using calculus). In short, the rule for setting the profit-maximizing amount of advertising is the same as that for setting the profit-maximizing amount of output: Set advertising or quantity where the marginal benefit (the extra gross profit from one more unit of advertising or the marginal revenue from one more unit of output) equals its marginal cost.

We can illustrate how firms use such marginal analysis to determine how much time to purchase from television stations for infomercials, those interminably long television advertisements sometimes featuring unique (and typically bizarre) plastic products: "Isn't that amazing?! It slices! It dices! ... But wait! That's not all!" As Figure 12.7 shows, the marginal cost per minute of broadcast time, MC, on small television stations is constant. The firm buys A_1 minutes of advertising time, where its marginal benefit, MB^1, equals its marginal cost.

See Questions 28–30 and Problems 41 and 42.

Figure 12.7 Shift in the Marginal Benefit of Advertising.

Before the Simpson trial, the marginal benefit of advertising is MB^1. The firm purchases A_1 minutes of advertising time, where MB^1 intersects the marginal cost per minute of broadcast time curve, MC. During the trial, the marginal benefit curve shifts to the left to MB^2. As a result, the firm reduces its purchase of advertising time to A_2.

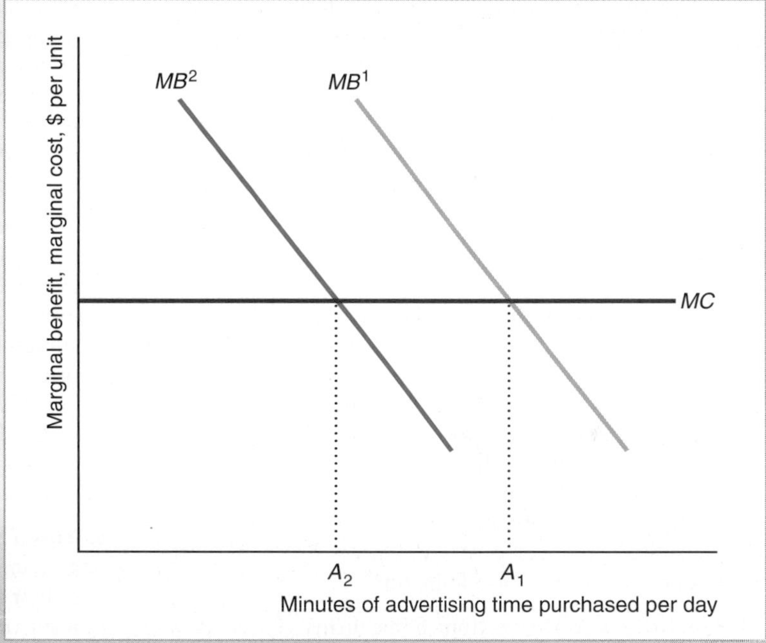

APPLICATION O. J. Trial Effect

Often a major event such as the Super Bowl affects TV watchers' viewing behavior and the benefits from advertising. A particularly dramatic event was O. J. Simpson's 1995 trial for murder, which many television and radio stations broadcast. The *O. J. Factor* cut the take from infomercials on other television stations. Sales sagged as viewers skipped program-length product pitches to watch trial coverage on weekday mornings.

The reason for the sales slump was that the marginal benefit curve for infomercials shifted. Where every \$1,000 spent on commercial time at 12:30 P.M. brought in an average of \$2,190 in sales in Charlotte, North Carolina, before the trial, it produced only \$1,790 (a drop of 18.3%) during the trial. The comparable figures for San Francisco at 9:30 A.M. were \$1,740 and \$790, a fall of 54.6%. Thus, for a given quantity (\$1,000 worth of advertising time), the marginal benefit for San Francisco shifted down by 54.6% from MB^1 to MB^2, as Figure 12.7 illustrates.

Because the marginal benefit curve shifted, a typical firm reduced the amount of advertising time it purchased from A_1 to A_2, where MB^2 intersects MC. Estimates of average infomercial sales declines due to the Simpson trial ranged from 10% to 60% across cities. It remains to be seen if Mr. Simpson's current legal proceedings will have as dramatic an effect on television advertising.

SUMMARY

1. **Why and How Firms Price Discriminate.** A firm can price discriminate if it has market power, knows which customers will pay more for each unit of output, and can prevent customers who pay low prices from reselling to those who pay high prices. A firm earns a higher profit from price discrimination than from uniform pricing because (a) the firm captures some or all of the consumer surplus of customers who are willing to pay more than the uniform price and (b) the firm sells to some people who would not buy at the uniform price.
2. **Perfect Price Discrimination.** To perfectly price discriminate, a firm must know the maximum amount each customer is willing to pay for each unit of output. If a firm charges customers the maximum each is willing to pay for each unit of output, the monopoly captures all potential consumer surplus and sells the efficient (competitive) level of output. Compared to competition, total welfare is the same, consumers are worse off, and firms are better off under perfect price discrimination.
3. **Quantity Discrimination.** Some firms charge customers different prices depending on how many units they purchase. If consumers who want more water have less elastic demands, a water utility can increase its profit by using declining-block pricing, in which the price for the first few gallons of water is higher than that for additional gallons.
4. **Multimarket Price Discrimination.** A firm that does not have enough information to perfectly price discriminate may know the relative elasticities of demand of groups of its customers. Such a profit-maximizing firm charges groups of consumers prices in proportion to their elasticities of demand, the group of consumers with the least elastic demand paying the highest price. Welfare is less under multimarket price discrimination than under competition or perfect price discrimination but may be greater or less than that under single-price monopoly.
5. **Two-Part Tariffs.** By charging consumers one fee for the right to buy and a separate price per unit, firms may earn higher profits than from charging only for each unit sold. If a firm knows its customers' demand curves, it can use two-part tariffs (instead of perfectly price discriminating) to capture all the consumer surplus. Even if the firm does not know each customer's demand curve or cannot vary the two-part tariffs across customers, it can use a two-part tariff to make a larger profit than it can get if it set a single price.
6. **Tie-In Sales.** A firm may increase its profit by using a tie-in sale that allows customers to buy one product only if they also purchase another one. In a requirement tie-in sale, customers who buy one good must make all of their purchases of another good or service from that firm. With bundling (a package tie-in sale), a firm sells only a bundle of two goods together. Prices differ across customers under both types of tie-in sales.
7. **Advertising.** A monopoly advertises or engages in other promotional activity to shift its demand curve to the right or make it less elastic so as to raise its profit net of its advertising expenses.

QUESTIONS

■ = *exercise is available on MyEconLab;* * = *answer appears at the back of this book;* C = *use of calculus may be necessary;* W = *audio-slideshow answer by James Dearden is available in Textbook Resources on MyEconLab.*

1. In the examples in Table 12.1, if the movie theater does not price discriminate, it charges either the highest price the college students are willing to pay or the one that the senior citizens are willing to pay. Why

doesn't it charge an intermediate price? (*Hint*: Discuss how the demand curves of these two groups are unusual.)

*2. Many colleges provide students from low-income families with scholarships, subsidized loans, and other programs so that they pay lower tuitions than students from high-income families. Explain why universities behave this way.

3. In 2002, seven pharmaceutical companies announced a plan to provide low-income elderly people with a card guaranteeing them discounts of 20% or more on dozens of prescription medicines. Why did the firms institute this program?

4. Alexx's monopoly currently sells its product at a single price. What conditions must be met so that he can profitably price discriminate?

*5. Spenser's Superior Stoves advertises a one-day sale on electric stoves. The ad specifies that no phone orders are accepted and that the purchaser must transport the stove. Why does the firm include these restrictions?

6. Each week, a department store places a different item of clothing on sale. Give an explanation based on price discrimination for why the store conducts such regular sales.

7. College students could once buy a computer at a substantial discount through a campus buying program. The discounts largely disappeared in the late 1990s, when PC companies dropped their prices. "The industry's margins just got too thin to allow for those [college discounts]," said the president of Educause, a group that promotes and surveys using technology on campus (David LaGesse, "A PC Choice: Dorm or Quad?" *U.S. News & World Report,* May 5, 2003, 64). Using the concepts and terminology discussed in this chapter, explain why shrinking profit margins are associated with the reduction or elimination of student discounts.

8. The 2002 production run of 25,000 new Thunderbirds included only 2,000 cars for Canada. Yet potential buyers besieged Ford dealers there. Many buyers hoped to make a quick profit by reselling the cars in the United States. Reselling was relatively easy, and shipping costs were comparatively low. When the Thunderbird with the optional hardtop first became available at the end of 2001, Canadians paid $56,550 Cdn. for the vehicle, while U.S. customers spent up to $73,000 Cdn. in the United States. Why? Why would a Canadian want to ship a T-Bird south? Why did Ford require that Canadian dealers sign an agreement with Ford that prohibited moving vehicles to the United States?

9. Disneyland price discriminates by charging lower entry fees for children than adults and for local residents than for other visitors. Why does it not have a resales problem?

10. On August 2, 2005, Hertz charged $141.06 a day to rent a Taurus in New York City but only $66.68 a day in Miami. Is this price discrimination? Why or why not?

11. As described in the "Amazon Is Watching You" application, some Amazon customers contended that Amazon used a dynamic pricing approach where the price offered depended on a customer's past purchases. What type of price discrimination is this?

12. Using the information in the "Botox Revisited" application, determine how much Allergan loses by being a single-price monopoly rather than a perfectly price-discriminating monopoly. Explain your answer.

13. A firm is a natural monopoly (Chapter 11). Its marginal cost curve is flat, and its average cost curve is downward sloping (because it has a fixed cost). The firm can perfectly price discriminate.

    a. In a graph, show how much the monopoly produces, Q^*. Will it produce to where price equals its marginal cost?

    b. Show graphically (and explain) what its profit is.

14. Consider a third pricing scheme that the union in Solved Problem 12.2 might use. It sets a wage, w^*, and lets the firms hire as many workers as they want (that is, the union does not set a minimum number of hours), but requires a lump-sum contribution to each worker's retirement fund. What is such a pricing scheme called? Can the union achieve the same outcome as it would if it perfectly price discriminated? (*Hint*: It could set the wage where the supply curve hits the demand curve.) Does your answer depend on whether the union workers are identical?

15. Ticketmaster Corp. used an Internet auction to sell tickets for a Sting concert (Leslie Walker, "Auctions Could Set Ticket Prices for Future Events," *San Francisco Chronicle,* October 13, 2003, E5).

    a. The floor seats were auctioned in a uniform price format where all winning bidders paid the same amount: the lowest bid ($90) at which all the seats were sold. Is this price discrimination? If so, what type?

    b. Suppose, instead, that each ticket was sold at the bid price to the highest bidder. Is this price discrimination? If so, what type?

16. Are all the customers of the quantity-discriminating monopoly in panel a of Figure 12.3 worse off than they would be if the firm set a single price (panel b)?

17. A firm charges different prices to two groups. Would the firm ever operate where it was suffering a loss from its sales to the low-price group? Explain.

18. A monopoly has a marginal cost of zero and faces two groups of consumers. At first, the monopoly could not prevent resales, so it maximized its profit by charging everyone the same price, $p = \$5$. No one from the first group chose to purchase. Now the monopoly can prevent resales, so it decides to price discriminate. Will total output expand? Why or why not? What happens to profit and consumer surplus?

19. Does a monopoly's ability to price discriminate between two groups of consumers depend on its marginal cost curve? Why or why not? [Consider two cases: (a) the marginal cost is so high that the monopoly is uninterested in selling to one group; (b) the marginal cost is low enough that the monopoly wants to sell to both groups.]

20. How would the analysis in Solved Problem 12.3 change if $m = 7$ or if $m = 4$? (*Hint*: Where $m = 4$, the marginal cost curve crosses the *MR* curve three times—if we include the vertical section. The single-price monopoly will choose one of these three points where its profit is maximized.)

21. A monopoly sells two products, of which consumers want only one. Assuming that it can prevent resales, can the monopoly increase its profit by bundling them, forcing consumers to buy both goods?

22. Abbott Laboratories, the patent holder of the anti-AIDS drug Norvir, raised the price from \$1.71 to \$8.57 a day in 2003 (Lauran Neergaard, "No Price Rollback on Costly AIDS Drug," *San Francisco Chronicle,* August 5, 2004, A4). The price was increased in the United States only when low doses of Norvir are used to boost the effects of other anti-HIV medicines—not in Abbott's own Kaletra, a medicine that includes Norvir. Why did Abbott raise one price but not others?

23. The publisher Reed Elsevier uses what economists call a mixed-bundling pricing strategy. The publisher sells a university access to a bundle of 930 of its journals for \$1.7 million for one year. It also offers the journals separately at individual prices. Because Elsevier offers the journals online (with password access), universities can track how often their students and faculty access journals and then cancel those journals that are seldom read. Suppose that a publisher offers a university only three journals—*A*, *B*, and *C*—at the unbundled, individual annual subscription prices of $p_A = \$1{,}600$, $p_B = \$800$, and $p_C = \$1{,}500$. Suppose a university's willingness to pay for each of the journals is $v_A = \$2{,}000$, $v_B = \$1{,}100$, and $v_C = \$1{,}400$.
    a. If the publisher offers the journals only at the individual subscription prices, to which journals does the university subscribe?
    b. Given these individual prices, what is the highest price that the university is willing to pay for the three journals bundled together?
    c. Now suppose that the publisher offers the same deal to a second university with willingness-to-pay $v_A = \$1{,}800$, $v_B = \$100$, and $v_C = \$2{,}100$. With the two universities, calculate the revenue-maximizing individual and bundle prices. W

24. In the spring of 2005, General Motors shifted its auto discounting policy to regionally targeted rebates in which the manufacturer offers varying discounts to different parts of the United States. Suppose that GM dealers offer all consumers in a given region the same posted price for a specific model (which is GM's pricing policy for its Saturn automobiles). Assume that it is unprofitable for a consumer to purchase an automobile in a low-price area and then to resell it in a high-price area.
    a. What form of price discrimination is GM's new policy?
    b. What is the relationship between a region's price and its price elasticity of demand?
    c. GM also eliminated a high-profile discount program "in an apparent effort to damp consumer expectation of big price cuts" (Lee Hawkins Jr., "GM Alters U.S. Discount Program with a Region-Specific Strategy," *Wall Street Journal,* March 7, 2005, A2). How do expected future prices of an automobile affect the current demand? Is a national discount program that is targeted to reduce slumping sales a form of price discrimination? Explain. W

25. In the 2003 Major League Baseball season, the New York Mets began charging fans up to twice as much to watch games involving the cross-town Yankees or other popular teams than less popular or less competitive teams. Other professional teams have adopted the same pricing strategy. While the Yankees increased the prices of popular games, they dropped the price of upper-deck seats for some weekday games against weak opponents.
    a. A Mets-Yankees game is more popular than a Mets-Marlins game. Is the Mets' policy of charging fans more to see the Yankees than the Marlins a form of price discrimination? If so, which type?
    b. What is the effect on the quantity of tickets demanded for the Yankees-Mets games if the Mets drop the price of the cheap seats for unpopular games? How do the Mets take this effect into account when setting ticket prices? In answering

the question, assume that the Mets choose two ticket prices—one for the Mets-Yankees game and the other for the Mets-Marlins game—to maximize the sum of revenues of the two games. W

26. Grocery stores often set consumer-specific prices by issuing frequent-buyer cards to willing customers and collecting information on their purchases. Grocery chains can use that data to offer customized discount coupons to individuals.
    a. Which type of price discrimination—first-degree, second-degree, or third-degree—are these personalized discounts?
    b. How should a grocery store use past-purchase data to set individualized prices to maximize its profit? (*Hint*: Refer to a customer's price elasticity of demand.) W

27. To promote her platinum-selling CD *Feels Like Home* in 2005, singer Norah Jones toured the country for live performances. However, she sold an average of only two-thirds of the tickets available for each show, T^* (Robert Levine, "The Trick of Making a Hot Ticket Pay," *New York Times*, June 6, 2005, C1, C4).
    a. Suppose that the local promoter is the monopoly provider of each concert. Each concert hall has a fixed number of seats. Assume that the promoter's cost is independent of the number of people who attend the concert (Ms. Jones received a guaranteed payment). Graph the promoter's marginal cost curve for the concert hall, where the number of tickets sold is on the horizontal axis (be sure to show T^*).
    b. If the monopoly can charge a single market price, does the concert's failure to sell out prove that the monopoly set too high a price? Explain.
    c. Would your answer in part b be the same if the monopoly can perfectly price discriminate? Use a graph to explain.

28. During the Superbowl, many firms present commercials with new slogans or themes. Those that are well-received according to polls are shown many times in later weeks, while others are rebroadcast infrequently. Use a marginal benefit-marginal cost diagram to explain why.

29. Cable operators and satellite providers whose set-top boxes give them direct access to viewers may soon subject customers to customized commercials, as the firms learn more about their viewing habits (Lorne Manly, "The Future of the 30-Second Spot," *New York Times*, March 27, 2005, 3.1, 3.4). How will this change affect the marginal benefit curve for an advertiser, and why?

30. Before the O. J. Simpson trial, if a firm spent \$1,000 on commercial television time at 12:30 P.M. in Charlotte, North Carolina, its sales rose by \$2,190. If the firm bought \$1,000 of advertising time during the trial, was it advertising optimally? If not, should it have increased or decreased the amount it spent on advertising?

PROBLEMS

31. In panel b of Figure 12.3, the single-price monopoly faces a demand curve of $p = 90 - Q$ and a constant marginal (and average) cost of m = \$30. Find the profit-maximizing quantity (or price) using math (Chapter 11). Determine the profit, consumer surplus, welfare, and deadweight loss.

32. The quantity-discriminating monopoly in panel a of Figure 12.3 can set three prices, depending on the quantity a consumer purchases. The firm's profit is

$$\pi = p_1Q_1 + p_2(Q_2 - Q_1) + p_3(Q_3 - Q_2) - mQ_3,$$

where p_1 is the high price charged on the first Q_1 units (first block), p_2 is a lower price charged on the next $Q_2 - Q_1$ units, p_3 is the lowest price charged on the $Q_3 - Q_2$ remaining units, Q_3 is the total number of units actually purchased, and m = \$30 is the firm's constant marginal and average cost. Use calculus to determine the profit-maximizing p_1, p_2, and p_3. C

33. In the quantity discrimination analysis in panel a of Figure 12.3, suppose that the monopoly can make consumers a take-it-or-leave-it offer (similar to the union in Solved Problem 12.2).
    a. Suppose the monopoly sets a price, p^*, and a minimum quantity, Q^*, that a consumer must pay to be able to purchase any units at all. What price and minimum quantity should it set to achieve the same outcome as it would if it perfectly price discriminated?
    b. Now suppose the monopolist charges a price of \$90 for the first 30 units and a price of \$30 for all subsequent units, but requires that a consumer must buy at least 30 units to be allowed to buy any. Compare this outcome to the one in part a and to the perfectly price discriminating outcome.

***34.** A patent gave Sony a legal monopoly to produce a robot dog called Aibo ("eye-BO"). The Chihuahuasize pooch robot can sit, beg, chase balls, dance, and play an electronic tune. When Sony started selling the toy in July 1999, it announced that it would sell 3,000 Aibo robots in Japan for about \$2,000 each and a limited litter of 2,000 in the United States for \$2,500 each. Suppose that Sony's marginal cost of producing Aibos is \$500. Its inverse demand curve is $p_j = 3{,}500 - \frac{1}{2}Q_j$ in Japan and $p_A = 4{,}500 - Q_A$ in the United States. Solve for the equilibrium prices and quantities (assuming that U.S. customers cannot buy robots from Japan). Show how the profit-maximizing price ratio depends on the elasticities of demand in the two countries. What are the deadweight losses in each country, and in which is the loss from monopoly pricing greater?

*35. A monopoly sells its good in the U.S. and Japanese markets. The American inverse demand function is $p_A = 100 - Q_A$, and the Japanese inverse demand function is $p_J = 80 - 2Q_J$, where both prices, p_A and p_J, are measured in dollars. The firm's marginal cost of production is $m = 20$ in both countries. If the firm can prevent resales, what price will it charge in both markets? (*Hint*: The monopoly determines its optimal (monopoly) price in each country separately because customers cannot resell the good.)

36. Warner Home Entertainment sells the *Harry Potter and the Prisoner of Azkaban* two-DVD movie set around the world. Warner charges 33% more in Canada and 66% more in Japan than in the United States. Using the information about Warner's marginal cost and U.S. sales in Section 12.4, determine what the elasticities of demand must be in Canada and in Japan if Warner is profit maximizing.

*37. Warner Home Entertainment sells the *Harry Potter and the Prisoner of Azkaban* two-DVD movie set in China for about \$3, which is only one-fifth the U.S. price, and has sold nearly 100,000 units. The price is extremely low in China because Chinese consumers are less wealthy than those in the other countries and because (lower-quality) pirated versions are available in China for 72¢–\$1.20, compared to the roughly \$3 required for the legal version (Jin Baicheng, "Powerful Ally Joins Government in War on Piracy," *China Daily*, March 11, 2005, 13). Assuming a marginal cost of \$1, what is the Chinese elasticity of demand? Derive the demand function for China and illustrate Warner's policy in China using a figure similar to panel a in Figure 12.4.

38. A monopoly sells its good in the United States, where the elasticity of demand is −2, and in Japan, where the elasticity of demand is −5. Its marginal cost is \$10. At what price does the monopoly sell its good in each country if resales are impossible?

39. A monopoly sells in two countries, and resales between the countries are impossible. The demand curves in the two countries are

$$p_1 = 100 - Q1,$$
$$p_2 = 120 - 2Q_2.$$

The monopoly's marginal cost is $m = 30$. Solve for the equilibrium price in each country.

40. Using math, show why a two-part tariff causes customers who purchase few units to pay more per unit than customers who buy more units. C

41. The demand a monopoly faces is

$$p = 100 - Q + A^{0.5},$$

where Q is its quantity, p is its price, and A is the level of advertising. Its marginal cost of production is 10, and its cost of a unit of advertising is 1. What is the firm's profit equation? Solve for the firm's profit-maximizing price, quantity, and level of advertising. (*Hint*: See Appendix 12E.)

42. What is the monopoly's profit-maximizing output, Q, and level of advertising, A, if it faces a demand curve of $p = a - bQ + cA^{\alpha}$, its constant marginal cost of producing output is m, and the cost of a unit of advertising is \$1? C

CROSS-CHAPTER ANALYSIS

Magazine Subscriptions

Special-interest publications should realize that if they are attracting enough advertising and readers to make a profit, the interest is not so special.

—Fran Lebowitz

You can get a subscription to *Esquire,* an award-winning magazine, for as little as \$7.97, or *Vanity Fair,* a fat folio of glamour, for \$11.95. A typical subscription costs \$1 per issue compared to \$2.95 or more at newsstands. Why are subscriptions relatively inexpensive? Are subscription prices likely to rise soon?

Background

Virtually all magazines—except *Consumer Reports*—carry ads. All else the same, the larger a magazine's circulation, the more the magazine charges advertisers per ad. Consequently, a magazine may drop its subscription price to boost its circulation, so as to increase its advertising revenue.

U.S. subscription sales rose 7.4% from 1996 to 2006 (*Magazine Handbook 2007/08*). In 2006, 87% of magazines were obtained by subscription rather than at a newsstand, compared to only 82% in 1996. Part of the reason for this shift toward subscriptions is that newsstand prices rose 46% from \$3.96 to \$4.46 from 1996 to 2006, while the average one-year subscription price fell 7% from \$29.44 to \$27.30.

Adjusting subscription prices is the key to increasing sales for most magazines. While subscription prices fell, advertising revenue rose, so the share of revenue from advertising increased. Magazine advertising revenues more than doubled from \$11 billion in 1996 to \$24 billion in 2006 (even as the share of magazine pages devoted to advertising dropped from 51% in 1996 to 47% in 2006). The percentage of advertising to overall consumer magazine revenue rose from 50% in 1996 to 71% in 2006.

New, highly specialized magazines target advertising to the optimal audience. In 2006, 324 new magazines launched, most aimed at fairly narrow consumer interests, including 53 on crafts, games, hobbies, or models. Perhaps because the advertising is better focused and less intrusive, consumers favor advertising in magazines than in other media. Sixty-one percent of magazine consumers had a very or somewhat positive attitude toward advertising, compared to 52% for television, 46% for radio, and 30% for the Internet.

Kaiser and Wright (2006) examined the market for magazine readership and advertising in Germany. Their findings support the view that readers are "subsidized" and that magazines make most of their money from advertisers. Moreover, they found that increased demand by magazine readers raises advertising rates, but that higher demand by advertisers decreases cover prices.

Task

Explain how advertising revenue affects the number of magazine subscriptions sold. Consider a magazine on costumes for dogs, *Canine Haute Couture*. Assume that this magazine acts like a monopoly (Chapter 11)—it has no close substitute (at least it shouldn't). The magazine's price for an ad is aQ, where a is the price per unit of circulation and Q is the number of subscriptions sold. Consequently, the more subscriptions sold, the more the magazine earns per ad.

Suppose that the n firms that produce costumes for dogs are each willing to place one ad per issue as long as the magazine charges no more than aQ. That is, a is determined by the advertising market.

The inverse demand curve for subscriptions is $p(Q)$, where p is the price of a subscription. The magazine's marginal cost per subscription is constant at m (primarily printing, paper, and mailing), and its fixed cost is F (office space, and payments to its editorial staff, authors, and photographers).

Analysis

The magazine's profit is

$$\pi = p(Q)Q + naQ - mQ - F,$$

where $p(Q)Q$ is the revenue the magazine receives from its subscribers, naQ is the advertising revenue, and mQ is its variable cost. We can think of the advertising revenue, naQ, as being much like a subsidy (negative tax), where na is the specific subsidy per subscription. Thus, the advertising revenue shifts up the demand curve (Chapter 14) as a subsidy would. (Because a specific tax has the opposite effect of a specific subsidy, Figure 3.6 shows that a specific tax shifts a demand curve downward.)

In the figure on the next page, the curves D^1 and MR^1 are the demand curve for magazines and the corresponding marginal revenue curve if no advertising were sold. The curves D^2 and MR^2 are the corresponding curves including advertising. Demand curve D^2 lies na units above D^1.

In the absence of advertising, the monopoly's optimum is determined by where its marginal revenue curve MR_1 (which corresponds to D^1) hits its marginal cost curve at m. It sells Q_1 subscriptions at a subscription price of p_1. With advertising, the monopoly operates where MR_2 (which corresponds to D^2) intersects its marginal cost curve. It provides Q_2 subscriptions at a price of p_2, which is the height of D^1 (the no-advertising demand curve) at that quantity. The firm receives $p^* = p^2 + na$ per subscription.

Questions

Answers appear at the back of the book.

1. Use calculus to show how a change in the advertising rate a affects the optimal number of subscriptions.

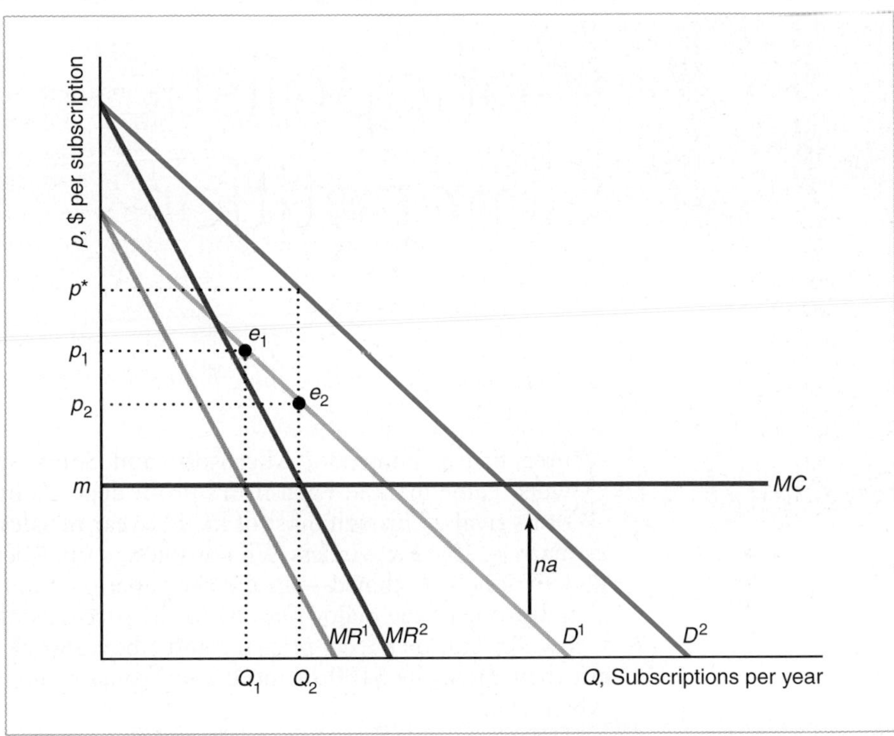

2. Why are newsstand prices higher than subscription prices for an issue?
3. Canada subsidizes Canadian magazines to offset the invasion of foreign (primarily U.S.) magazines, which take 90% of the country's sales. The Canada Magazine Fund provides a lump-sum subsidy to various magazines to "maintain a Canadian presence against the overwhelming presence of foreign magazines." Eligibility is based on high levels of investment in Canadian editorial content and reliance on advertising revenues. What effect will a lump-sum subsidy have on the number of subscriptions sold?

13 Oligopoly and Monopolistic Competition

Anyone can win unless there happens to be a second entry. —George Ade

Three firms—Nintendo, Microsoft, and Sony—dominate the $13 billion U.S. video game market. Each firm's profit depends on the actions it takes and those of its rivals. Through most of its first year of sales in 2007, Nintendo was selling as many of its new wireless Wii consoles as the Microsoft Xbox 360 and the Sony PlayStation 3 combined—despite the superior graphics of the other two consoles. Initially, one of the major reasons for its success was that Wii sold for $250, much below PlayStation's $599 price tag and Xbox 360's $399. To compete, both its rivals cut their prices by $100 or more and brought out popular new games such as the Xbox's Halo 3.[1]

oligopoly
a small group of firms in a market with substantial barriers to entry

The video game market is an **oligopoly**: a market with only a few firms and with substantial barriers to entry. Because relatively few firms compete in such a market, each can influence the price, and hence each affects rival firms. The need to consider the behavior of rival firms makes an oligopoly firm's profit-maximization decision more difficult than that of a monopoly or a competitive firm. A monopoly has no rivals, and a competitive firm ignores the behavior of individual rivals—it considers only the market price and its own costs in choosing its profit-maximizing output.

An oligopoly firm that ignores or inaccurately predicts its rivals' behavior is likely to suffer a loss of profit. For example, as its rivals produce more cars, the price Ford can get for its cars falls. If Ford underestimates how many cars its rivals will produce, Ford may produce too many automobiles and lose money.

cartel
a group of firms that explicitly agree to coordinate their activities

Oligopolistic firms may act independently or may coordinate their actions. A group of firms that explicitly agree (collude) to coordinate their activities is called a **cartel**. These firms may agree on how much each firm will sell or on a common price. By cooperating and behaving like a monopoly, the members of a cartel collectively earn the monopoly profit—the maximum possible profit. In most developed countries, cartels are generally illegal.

If oligopolistic firms do not collude, they earn lower profits. Yet because there are relatively few firms in the market, oligopolistic firms that act independently may earn positive economic profits in the long run, unlike competitive firms.

In an oligopolistic market, one or more barriers to entry keep the number of firms small. In a market with no barriers to entry, firms enter the market until profits are driven to zero. In perfectly competitive markets, enough entry occurs that firms face

[1]Elizabeth Millard, "Nintendo Wii Outsells Xbox 360 and PlayStation 3," *Sci-Tech Today*, March 16, 2007; Pia Sarkar, "Low Price, Unique Controller Make Nintendo Most Popular," *San Francisco Chronicle*, March 17, 2007; and Evelyn M. Rusli, "Nintendo's Wii Wonder," **Forbes.com**, December 14, 2007.

monopolistic competition
a market structure in which firms have market power but no additional firm can enter and earn positive profits

a horizontal demand curve and are price takers. However, in other markets, even after entry has driven profits to zero, each firm faces a downward-sloping demand curve. Because of this slope, the firm can charge a price above its marginal cost, creating a market failure: inefficient (too little) consumption (Chapter 9). **Monopolistic competition** is a market structure in which firms have market power (the ability to raise price profitably above marginal cost) but no additional firm can enter and earn positive profits.

In this chapter, we examine cartelized, oligopolistic, and monopolistically competitive markets in which firms set quantities or prices. As noted in Chapter 11, the monopoly equilibrium is the same whether a monopoly sets price or quantity. Similarly, if colluding oligopolies sell identical products, the cartel equilibrium is the same whether they set quantity or price. The oligopolistic and monopolistically competitive equilibria differ, however, if firms set prices instead of quantities.

In this chapter, we examine eight main topics

1. **Market Structures.** The number of firms, price, profits, and other properties of markets vary, depending on whether the market is monopolistic, oligopolistic, monopolistically competitive, or competitive.
2. **Cartels.** If firms successfully coordinate their actions, they can collectively behave like a monopoly.
3. **Noncooperative Oligopoly.** There are many different models of oligopoly in which firms act without colluding, and the equilibrium price and quantity range between competition at one extreme and monopoly at the other.
4. **Cournot Model.** In a Cournot model, in which firms choose their output levels without colluding, the market output and firms' profits lie between the competitive and monopoly levels.
5. **Stackelberg Model.** In a Stackelberg model, in which a *leader* firm chooses its output level before its identical-cost rivals, market output is greater than if all firms choose their output simultaneously, and the leader makes a higher profit than the other firms.
6. **Comparison of Collusive, Cournot, Stackelberg, and Competitive Equilibria.** Total market output declines from the competitive level to the Stackelberg level to the Cournot level and reaches a minimum with monopoly or collusion.
7. **Bertrand Model.** The oligopoly equilibrium in which firms set prices differs from the quantity-setting equilibrium and depends on the degree of product differentiation.
8. **Monopolistic Competition.** When firms can freely enter the market but, in equilibrium, face downward-sloping demand curves, firms charge prices above marginal cost but make no profit.

13.1 Market Structures

Markets differ according to the number of firms in the market, the ease with which firms may enter and leave the market, and the ability of firms in a market to differentiate their products from those of their rivals. Table 13.1 lists characteristics and properties of competition, monopoly, oligopoly, and monopolistic competition. For each of these market structures, we assume that the firms face many price-taking buyers.

Regardless of market structures, a firm maximizes its profit by setting quantity so that marginal revenue equals marginal cost (row 1 of Table 13.1). The four mar-

Table 13.1 Properties of Monopoly, Oligopoly, Monopolistic Competition, and Competition.

	Monopoly	Oligopoly	Monopolistic Competition	Competition
1. Profit-maximization condition	$MR = MC$	$MR = MC$	$MR = MC$	$p = MR = MC$
2. Ability to set price	Price setter	Price setter	Price setter	Price taker
3. Market power	$p > MC$	$p > MC$	$p > MC$	$p = MC$
4. Entry conditions	No entry	Limited entry	Free entry	Free entry
5. Number of firms	1	Few	Few or many	Many
6. Long-run profit	≥ 0	≥ 0	0	0
7. Strategy dependent on individual rival firms' behavior	No (has no rivals)	Yes	Yes	No (cares about market price only)
8. Products	Single product	May be differentiated	May be differentiated	Undifferentiated
9. Example	Local natural gas utility	Automobile manufacturers	Plumbers in a small town	Apple farmers

ket structures differ in terms of the market power of firms (ability to set price above marginal cost), ease of entry of new firms, and strategic behavior on the part of firms (taking account of rivals' actions). Monopolies, oligopolies, and monopolistically competitive firms are price setters rather than price takers (row 2) because they face downward-sloping demand curves. As a consequence, market failures occur in each of these market structures because price is above marginal revenue and hence above marginal cost (row 3). In contrast, a competitive firm faces a horizontal demand curve, so its price equals its marginal cost.

A monopoly or an oligopoly does not fear entry (row 4) because of insurmountable barriers to entry such as government licenses or patents. These barriers to entry restrict the number of firms so that there is only one firm (*mono-*) in a monopoly and, usually, a few (*oligo-*) in an oligopoly (row 5). The key difference between oligopolistic and monopolistically competitive markets is that firms are free to enter only in a monopolistically competitive market.

In both competitive and monopolistically competitive markets, entry occurs until no new firm can profitably enter (so the marginal firm earns zero profit, row 6). Monopolistically competitive markets have fewer firms than perfectly competitive markets do. Because they have relatively few rivals and hence are large relative to the market, each monopolistically competitive firm faces a downward-sloping demand curve.

Oligopolistic and monopolistically competitive firms pay attention to rival firms' behavior, in contrast to monopolistic or competitive firms (row 7). A monopoly has no rivals. A competitive firm ignores the behavior of individual rivals in choosing its output because the market price tells the firm everything it needs to know about its competitors.

Oligopolistic and monopolistically competitive firms may produce differentiated products (row 8). For example, Camry and Taurus automobiles differ in size, weight, and various other dimensions. In contrast, competitive apple farmers sell undifferentiated (homogeneous) products.

13.2 Cartels

People of the same trade seldom meet together, even for merriment and diversion, but the conversation ends in a conspiracy against the public, or some contrivance to raise prices. —Adam Smith, 1776

Firms have an incentive to form a cartel in which each firm reduces its output, which leads to higher prices and higher profits for individual firms and the firms collectively. Luckily for consumers' pocketbooks, cartels often fail because a government forbids them and because each firm in a cartel has an incentive to cheat on the cartel agreement by producing extra output. We now consider why cartels form, what laws prohibit cartels, why cartel members have an incentive to deviate from the cartel agreement, and what actions a cartel takes to maintain the cartel.

Why Cartels Form

A thing worth having is a thing worth cheating for. —W. C. Fields

A cartel forms if members of the cartel believe that they can raise their profits by coordinating their actions. Although cartels usually involve oligopolies, cartels may form in a market that would otherwise be competitive.

If a competitive firm is maximizing its profit, why should joining a cartel increase its profit? The answer involves a subtle argument. When a competitive firm chooses its profit-maximizing output level, it considers how varying its output affects its own profit only. The firm ignores the effect that changing its output level has on other firms' profits. A cartel, by contrast, takes into account how changes in any one firm's output affect the profits of all members of the cartel.

If a competitive firm lowers its output, it raises the market price very slightly—so slightly that the firm ignores the effect not only on other firms' profits but also on its own. If all the identical competitive firms in an industry lower their output by this same amount, however, the market price will change noticeably. Recognizing this effect of collective action, a cartel chooses to produce a smaller market output than is produced by a competitive market.

Figure 13.1 illustrates this difference between a competitive market and a cartel. There are n firms in this market, and no further entry is possible. Panel a shows the marginal and average cost curves of a typical firm. If all firms are price takers, the market supply curve, S, is the horizontal sum of the individual marginal cost curves above minimum average cost, as shown in panel b. At the competitive price, p_c, each price-taking firm produces q_c units of output (where MC intersects the line at p_c in panel a). The market output is $Q_c = nq_c$ (where S intersects the market demand curve in panel b).

Now suppose that the firms form a cartel. Should they reduce their output? At the competitive output, the cartel's marginal cost (which is the competitive industry supply curve, S in panel b) is greater than its marginal revenue, so the cartel's profit rises if it reduces output. The cartel's collective profit rises until output is reduced by enough that its marginal revenue equals its marginal cost at Q_m, the monopoly output. If the profit of the cartel increases, the profit of each of the n members of the cartel also increases. To achieve the cartel output level, each firm must reduce its output to $q_m = Q_m/n$, as panel a shows.

Why must the firms form a cartel to achieve these higher profits? A competitive firm produces q_c, where its marginal cost equals the market price. If only one firm reduces its output, it loses profit because it sells fewer units at essentially the same

Figure 13.1 Competition Versus Cartel.

(a) The marginal cost and average cost of one of the n firms in the market are shown. A competitive firm produces q_c units of output, whereas a cartel member produces $q_m < q_c$. At the cartel price, p_m, each cartel member has an incentive to increase its output from q_m to q^* (where the dotted line at p_m intersects the MC curve). (b) The competitive equilibrium, e_c, has more output and a lower price than the cartel equilibrium, e_m.

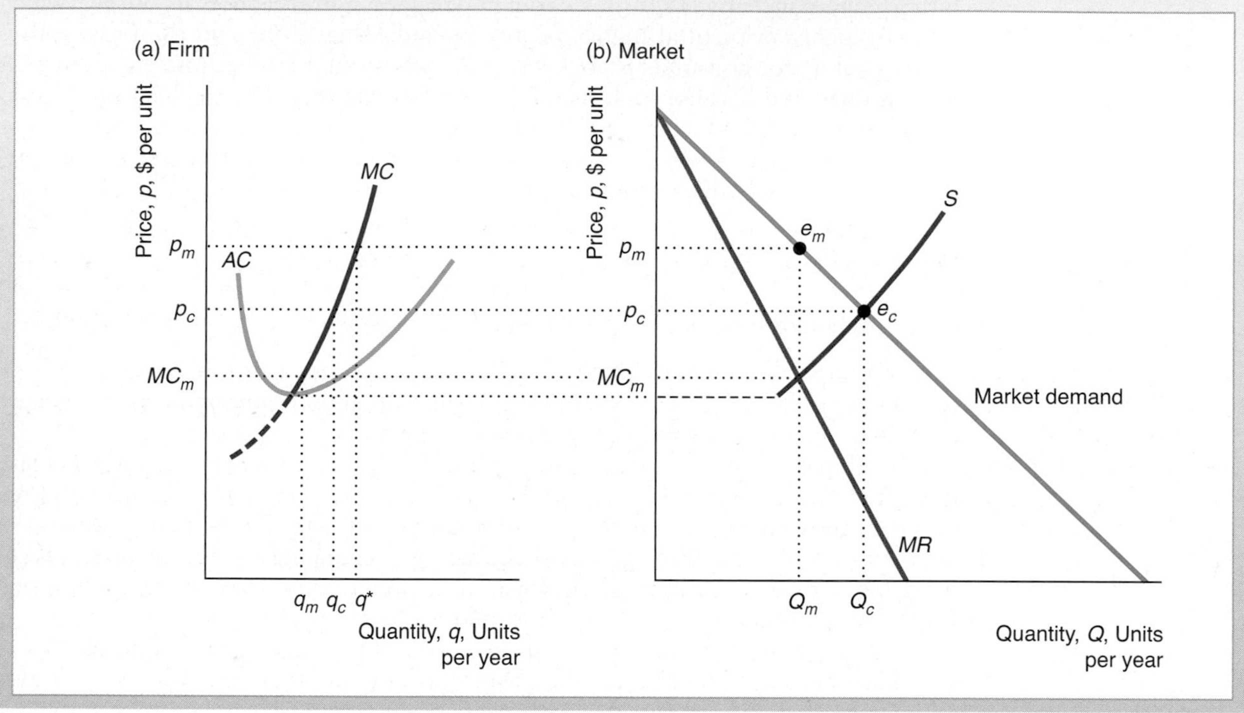

See Question 1.

price. By getting all the firms to lower their output together, the cartel raises the market price and hence individual firms' profits. The less elastic the market demand the potential cartel faces, all else the same, the higher the price the cartel sets (Chapter 11) and the greater the benefit from cartelizing. If the penalty for forming an illegal cartel is relatively low, some unscrupulous businesspeople may succumb to the lure of extra profits and join.

Laws Against Cartels

In the late nineteenth century, cartels (or, as they were called then, *trusts*) were legal and common in the United States. Oil, railroad, sugar, and tobacco trusts raised prices substantially above competitive levels.[2]

In response to the trusts' high prices, the U.S. Congress passed the Sherman Antitrust Act in 1890 and the Federal Trade Commission Act of 1914, which prohibit firms from *explicitly* agreeing to take actions that reduce competition. In particular, cartels that are formed for the purpose of jointly setting price are strictly

[2]Nineteenth century and early twentieth century robber barons who made fortunes due to these cartels include John Jacob Astor (real estate, fur), Andrew Carnegie (railroads, steel), Henry Clay Frick (steel), Jay Gould (finance, railroads), Mark Hopkins (railroads), J. P. Morgan (banking), John D. Rockefeller (oil), Leland Stanford (railroads), and Cornelius Vanderbilt (railroads, shipping).

prohibited. These laws reduce the probability that cartels form by imposing penalties on firms caught colluding. Virtually all industrialized nations have *antitrust laws*—or, as they are known in other countries, *competition policies*—that limit or forbid some or all cartels. In 2006, the U.S. Department of Justice, quoting the Supreme Court that collusion was the "supreme evil of antitrust," stated that prosecuting cartels was its "top enforcement priority."

However, cartels persist despite these laws for three reasons. First, international cartels and cartels within certain countries operate legally. Second, some illegal cartels operate believing that they can avoid detection or that the punishment will be insignificant. Third, some firms are able to coordinate their activity without explicitly colluding and thereby running afoul of competition laws.

Some international cartels organized by countries rather than firms are legal. The Organization of Petroleum Exporting Countries (OPEC) is an international cartel that was formed in 1960 by five major oil-exporting countries: Iran, Iraq, Kuwait, Saudi Arabia, and Venezuela. In 1971, OPEC members agreed to take an active role in setting oil prices.

Many illegal cartels flout the competition laws in major industrial countries. These firms apparently believe that they are unlikely to get caught or that the punishments they face are so negligible that it pays to collude anyway. At least until recently, they were correct. For example, in a cartel case involving the $9 billion American carpet industry, a firm with $150 million annual sales agreed with the U.S. Justice Department to plead guilty and pay a fine of $150,000. It is hard to imagine that a fine of one-tenth of 1% of annual sales significantly deters cartel behavior.

Even larger fines fail to discourage repeated collusion. In 1996, Archer Daniels Midland (ADM) paid to settle three civil price-fixing-related cases: $35 million in a case involving citric acid (used in many consumer products), $30 million to shareholders as compensation for lost stock value after the citric acid price-fixing scandal became public, and $25 million in a lysine (a feed additive) case. ADM paid a $100 million fine in a federal criminal case for fixing the price of lysine and citric acid in 1996, but only eight years later, ADM settled a fructose corn syrup price-fixing case for $400 million.

American antitrust laws use evidence of conspiracy (such as explicit agreements) rather than the economic effect of monopoly to determine guilt. Charging monopoly-level prices is not necessarily illegal—only the "bad behavior" of explicitly agreeing to raise prices is against the law. As a result, some groups of firms charge monopoly-level prices without violating the competition laws. These firms may *tacitly collude* without meeting by signaling to each other through their actions. Although the firms' actions may not be illegal, they behave much like cartels. For example, MacAvoy (1995) concluded that the major U.S. long-distance telephone companies tacitly colluded; as a result, each firm's Lerner Index (Chapter 11), $(p - MC)/p$, exceeded 60%, which is well above the competitive level, 0%. (See **www.myeconlab.com/perloff**, Chapter 13, "Tacit Collusion in Long-Distance Service.")

Over the past dozen years, the European Commission has been pursuing antitrust (competition) cases under laws that are similar to U.S. statutes. Recently the European Commission, the Department of Justice (DOJ), and the Federal Trade Commission (FTC) have become increasingly aggressive, prosecuting many more cases. Following the lead of the United States, which imposes both civil and criminal penalties, the British government introduced legislation in 2002 to criminalize certain cartel-related conduct. The European Union (EU) uses only civil penalties. However, EU and U.S. fines have increased dramatically in recent years.

In 1993, the DOJ introduced the Corporate Leniency Program, guaranteeing that whistle-blowing participants in cartels will receive immunity from federal prosecution. As a consequence, the DOJ has caught, prosecuted, and fined several gigantic cartels (see **www.myeconlab.com/perloff**, Chapter 13, "Vitamin Price Fixing"). In 2002, the European Commission adopted a similar policy. In 2004, Japan started more aggressively pursuing antitrust cases.

APPLICATION

Catwalk Cartel

Being thin, rich, and beautiful doesn't make you immune to exploitation. Some of the world's most successful models charged ten of New York's top modeling agencies—including Wilhelmina, Ford, Next, IMG, and Elite—with operating a sleazy cartel that cheated them out of millions of dollars in commissions.

Carolyn Fears—a 5′ 11″, redheaded former model who had earned up to $200,000 a year—initiated the suit when she learned that her agency not only charged her a 20% commission every time she was booked, but also extracted a 20% commission from her employers (mostly magazines). Her class-action lawsuit alleged that the agencies collectively fixed commissions for Claudia Schiffer, Heidi Klum, Gisele Bundchen, and thousands of other models over many years.

The agencies had formed an industry group, International Model Managers Association, Inc. (IMMA), which held repeated meetings. Monique Pillard, an executive at Elite Model Management, fired off a memo concerning one IMMA meeting, in which she "made a point . . . that we are all committing suicide, if we do not stick together. Pauline's agreed with me but as usual, Bill Weinberg [of Wilhelmina] cautioned me about price fixing. . . . Ha! Ha! Ha! . . . the usual (expletive)." As the trial judge, Harold Baer, Jr., observed, while "Wilhelmina objects to the outward discussion of price fixing, it is plausible from Pillard's reaction that Wilhelmina's objection was to the dissemination of information, not to the underlying price-fixing agreement."

The models argue that the association was little more than a front for helping agency heads keep track of each other's pricing policies. Documents show that shortly after association meetings, the agencies uniformly raised their commission rates from 10% to 15% and then to 20%. For example, at a meeting before the last increase, an Elite executive gave his competitors a heads up—but had not informed his clients—that Elite planned to raise its commissions to 20%. He said that at Elite, "we were also favorable to letting everyone know as much as possible about our pricing policies."

The trial started in 2004. Most of the parties settled in 2005. IMG alone paid the models $11 million.

Why Cartels Fail

Many cartels fail even without legal intervention. *Cartels fail if noncartel members can supply consumers with large quantities of goods.* For example, copper producers formed an international cartel that controlled only about a third of the noncommunist world's copper production and faced additional competition from firms that recycle copper from scrap materials. Because of this competition from noncartel members, the cartel was not successful in raising and keeping copper prices high.

In addition, *each member of a cartel has an incentive to cheat on the cartel agreement*. The owner of a firm may reason, "I joined the cartel to encourage others to reduce their output and increase profits for everyone. I can make more, however, if I cheat on the cartel agreement by producing extra output. I can get away with cheating if the other firms can't tell who's producing the extra output because I'm just one of many firms and because I'll hardly affect the market price." By this reasoning, it is in each firm's best interest for all *other* firms to honor the cartel agreement—thus driving up the market price—while it ignores the agreement and makes extra, profitable sales at the high price.

Figure 13.1 illustrates why firms want to cheat. At the cartel output, q_m in panel a, each cartel member's marginal cost is MC_m. The marginal revenue of a firm that violates the agreement is p_m because it is acting like a price taker with respect to the market price. Because the firm's marginal revenue (price) is above its marginal cost, the firm wants to increase its output. If the firm decides to violate the cartel agreement, it maximizes its profit by increasing its output to q^*, where its marginal cost equals p_m.

As more and more firms leave the cartel, the cartel price falls. The colluding firms act like a dominant firm facing a competitive fringe (Chapter 11). Eventually, if enough firms quit, the cartel collapses.

Maintaining Cartels

To keep firms from violating the cartel agreement, the cartel must be able to detect cheating and punish violators. Further, the members of the cartel must keep their illegal behavior hidden from customers and government agencies.

Detection. Cartels use many techniques to detect cheating. Some cartels, for example, give members the right to inspect each other's books. Similarly, governments often help cartels by reporting bids on government contracts, so that other firms learn if a cartel member bids below the agreed-on cartel price.

Cartels may divide the market by region or by customers, so that a firm that tries to steal another firm's customer is more likely to be detected. The two-country mercury cartel (1928–1972) allocated the Americas to Spain and Europe to Italy.

Other cartels use industry organizations to detect cheating. These organizations collect data on market share by firm and circulate their results. If a firm cheats on a cartel, its share would rise and other firms would know that it cheated.

You may have seen "low price" ads in which local retail stores guarantee to meet or beat the prices of any competitors. You may have thought that such a guarantee assured you of a low price. However, it may be a way for the firm to induce its customers to report cheating on a cartel agreement by other firms (Salop, 1986).

Enforcement. Many methods are used to enforce cartel agreements. For example, GE and Westinghouse, the two major sellers of large steam-turbine generators, included "most-favored-nation clauses" in their contracts. These contracts stated that the seller would not offer a lower price to any other current or future buyer without offering the same price decrease to that buyer. This type of rebate clause creates a penalty for cheating on the cartel: If either company cheats by cutting prices, it has to lower prices to all previous buyers as well. Another means of enforcing a cartel agreement is through threats of violence (see **www.myeconlab.com/perloff**, Chapter 13, "Bad Bakers").

Government Support. Sometimes governments help create and enforce cartels. For example, U.S., European, and other governments signed an agreement in

1944 to establish a cartel to fix prices for international airline flights and prevent competition.[3]

Professional baseball teams have been exempted from some U.S. antitrust laws since 1922. As a result, they can use the courts to help enforce certain aspects of their cartel agreement. Major league clubs are able to avoid competing for young athletes by means of a draft and contracts, limited geographic competition between teams, joint negotiations for television and other rights, and by acting collectively in many other ways.

Barriers to Entry. Barriers to entry that limit the number of firms help the cartel detect and punish cheating. The fewer the firms in a market, the more likely it is that other firms will know if a given firm cheats and the easier it is to impose costs on that firm. Cartels with a large number of firms are relatively rare, except those involving professional associations. Hay and Kelley (1974) examined Department of Justice price-fixing cases from 1963 to 1972 and found that only 6.5% involved 50 or more conspirators, the average number of firms was 7.25, and nearly half the cases (48%) involved 6 or fewer firms.

When new firms enter their market, cartels frequently fail. For example, when only Italy and Spain sold mercury, they were able to establish and maintain a stable cartel. When a larger group of countries joined them, their attempts to cartelize the world mercury market repeatedly failed (MacKie-Mason and Pindyck, 1986).

APPLICATION

Bail Bonds

The state of Connecticut sets a maximum fee that bail-bond businesses can charge for posting a given size bond (Ayres and Waldfogel, 1994). The bail-bond fee is set at virtually the maximum amount allowed by law in cities with only one active firm (Plainville, 99% of the maximum; Stamford, 99%; and Wallingford, 99%). The price is as high in cities with two firms (Ansonia, 99.6%; Meriden, 98%; and New London, 98%). In cities with three or more firms, however, the price falls well below the maximum permitted price, possibly because the difficulty of maintaining a cartel or tacit collusion rises with the number of firms. The fees are only 54% of the maximum in Norwalk with three firms, 64% in New Haven with eight firms, and 78% in Bridgeport with ten firms.

See Question 2.

Mergers

If antitrust or competition laws prevent firms from colluding, they may try to merge instead. Recognizing this potential problem, U.S. laws restrict the ability of firms to merge if the effect would be anticompetitive. Whether the Department of Justice or the Federal Trade Commission challenges a proposed merger turns on a large number of issues. Similarly, for the last 12 years, the European Commission has been active in reviewing and, when it felt it was necessary, blocking mergers. With only one exception (in 2002), none of the commission's decisions have been rejected by the courts. One reason why governments limit mergers is that all the firms in a market could combine and form a monopoly.

Then would it not be a good idea to ban all mergers? No, because some mergers result in more efficient production. Formerly separate firms may become more efficient because of greater scale, sharing trade secrets, or closing duplicative retail out-

[3]The European Court of Justice struck down the central provisions of aviation treaties among the United States and eight other countries in 2002. The European Commission plans to try to negotiate new treaties.

lets. For example, when Chase and Chemical banks merged, they closed or combined seven branches in Manhattan that were located within two blocks of other branches.

APPLICATION

Airline Mergers: Market Power Versus Flight Frequency

When duopoly airlines merge, the resulting monopoly may raise its price—due to its greater market power—and change its flight schedule. Consumers value both low prices and frequent, convenient flights. If the duopoly firms had similar departure times for their flights, the monopoly could schedule fewer but more convenient flights that would reduce costly travel delays for consumers.

Richard (2003) empirically examined United Airlines and American Airlines routes out of Chicago's O'Hare Airport. He concluded that airline mergers reduce passenger volume and cause consumer surplus to fall 20% on average, taking account of schedules. However, in one in nine markets, a gain from better schedules would increase consumer surplus by 19%.

13.3 Noncooperative Oligopoly

How do oligopolistic firms behave if they do not collude? Although there is only one model of competition and one model of monopoly, there are many models of noncooperative oligopolistic behavior with many possible equilibrium prices and quantities.

Which model is appropriate to use depends on the characteristics of a market, such as the type of *actions* firms take—such as setting quantity or price—and whether firms act simultaneously or sequentially. We examine the three best-known oligopoly models in turn. In the *Cournot model*, firms simultaneously choose quantities without colluding. In the *Stackelberg model*, a leader firm chooses its quantity and then the other, follower firms independently choose their quantities. In the *Bertrand model*, firms simultaneously and independently choose prices.

To illustrate these models as simply and clearly as possible, we start by making three restrictive assumptions, which we later relax. First, we initially assume that all firms are identical in the sense that they have the same cost functions and produce identical, *undifferentiated* products. We show how the market outcomes change if costs differ or if consumers believe that the products differ across firms.

duopoly
an oligopoly with two firms

Second, we initially illustrate each of these oligopoly models for a **duopoly**: an oligopoly with two (*duo-*) firms. Each of these models can be applied to markets with many firms. The Cournot and Stackelberg outcomes vary, whereas the Bertrand market outcome with undifferentiated goods does not vary, as the number of firms increases.

Third, we assume that the market lasts for only one period. Consequently, each firm chooses its quantity or price only once. In Chapter 14, we examine markets that last for more than one period.

To compare market outcomes under the various models, we need to be able to characterize the oligopoly equilibrium. In Chapter 2, we defined an *equilibrium* as a situation in which no one wants to change his or her behavior. For a competitive market to be in equilibrium, no firm wants to change its output level given what the other firms are producing. As oligopolistic firms may take many possible actions—such as setting price or quantity or choosing a level of advertising—the oligopoly equilibrium rule needs to refer to their behavior more generally than just setting output.

John Nash, a Nobel Prize-winning economist and mathematician, defined an equilibrium concept that has wide applicability including to oligopoly models (Nash

1951). We will give a general definition of a Nash equilibrium in Chapter 14. In this chapter we use a special case of that definition that is appropriate for the single-period oligopoly models where the only action that a firm can take is to set either its quantity or its price: A set of actions taken by the firms is a *Nash equilibrium* if, holding the actions of all other firms constant, no firm can obtain a higher profit by choosing a different action.

13.4 Cournot Model

The French economist and mathematician Antoine-Augustin Cournot introduced the first formal model of oligopoly in 1838. Cournot explained how oligopoly firms behave if they simultaneously choose how much they produce. The firms act independently and have imperfect information about their rivals. Each firm must choose its output level before knowing what the other firms will choose. The quantity one firm produces directly affects the profit of the other firms because the market price depends on total output. Thus, in choosing its strategy to maximize its profit, each firm takes into account its beliefs about the output its rivals will sell. Cournot introduced an equilibrium concept that is the same as the Nash definition where the action that firms take is to choose quantities.

We look at equilibrium in a market that lasts for only one period. Initially, we make four assumptions: (1) there are two firms and no other firms can enter the market, (2) the firms have identical costs, (3) they sell identical products, and (4) the firms set their quantities simultaneously. Later, we relax each of these assumptions in turn and examine how the equilibrium changes.

Cournot Model of an Airlines Market

To illustrate the basic idea of the Cournot model, we turn to an actual market where American Airlines and United Airlines compete for customers on flights between Chicago and Los Angeles.[4] The total number of passengers flown by these two firms, Q, is the sum of the number of passengers flown on American, q_A, and those flown on United, q_U. We assume that no other companies can enter, perhaps because they cannot obtain landing rights at both airports.[5]

How many passengers does each airline choose to carry? To answer this question, we determine the Nash equilibrium for this model. This Nash equilibrium, in which firms choose quantities, is also called a **Cournot equilibrium** or **Nash-Cournot equilibrium** (or *Nash-in-quantities equilibrium*): a set of quantities chosen by firms such that, holding the quantities of all other firms constant, no firm can obtain a higher profit by choosing a different quantity.

Cournot equilibrium (Nash-Cournot equilibrium)
a set of quantities sold by firms such that, holding the quantities of all other firms constant, no firm can obtain a higher profit by choosing a different quantity

To determine the Cournot equilibrium, we need to establish how each firm chooses its quantity. We start by using the total demand curve for the Chicago–Los Angeles route and a firm's belief about how much its rival will sell to determine its *residual demand curve*: the market demand that is not met by other sellers at any

---

[4]This example is based on Brander and Zhang (1990). They reported data for economy and discount passengers taking direct flights between the two cities in the third quarter of 1985. In calculating the profits, we assume that Brander and Zhang's estimate of the firms' constant marginal cost is the same as the firms' relevant long-run average cost.

[5]With the end of deregulation, existing firms were given the right to buy, sell, or rent landing slots. However, by controlling landing slots, existing firms can make entry difficult.

given price (Chapter 8). Next, we examine how a firm uses its residual demand curve to determine its best response: the output level that maximizes its profit, given its belief about how much its rival will produce. Finally, we use the information contained in the firms' best response functions to determine the Cournot equilibrium quantities.

Graphical Approach. The strategy that each firm uses depends on the demand curve it faces and its marginal cost. American Airline's profit-maximizing output depends on how many passengers it believes United will fly. Figure 13.2 illustrates two possibilities.

If American were a monopoly, it wouldn't have to worry about United's strategy. American's demand would be the market demand curve, D in panel a. To maximize its profit, American would set its output so that its marginal revenue curve, MR, intersected its marginal cost curve, MC, which is constant at $147 per passenger. Panel a shows that the monopoly output is 96 units (thousands of passengers) per quarter and the monopoly price is $243 per passenger (one way).

Because American competes with United, American must take account of United's behavior when choosing its profit-maximizing output. American's demand is not the entire market demand. Rather, American is concerned with its *residual demand curve*: the market demand that is not met by other sellers at any given price. (This concept is analogous to the *residual supply curve* discussed in Chapter 8.) In general, if the market demand function is $D(p)$, and the supply of other firms is $S^o(p)$, then the residual demand function, $D^r(p)$, is

$$D^r(p) = D(p) - S^o(p).$$

Figure 13.2 American Airlines' Profit-Maximizing Output.

(a) If American is a monopoly, it picks its profit-maximizing output, $q_A = 96$ units (thousand passengers) per quarter, so that its marginal revenue, MR, equals its marginal cost, MC. (b) If American believes that United will fly $q_U = 64$ units per quarter, its residual demand curve, D^r, is the market demand curve, D, minus q_U. American maximizes its profit at $q_A = 64$, where its marginal revenue, MR^r, equals MC.

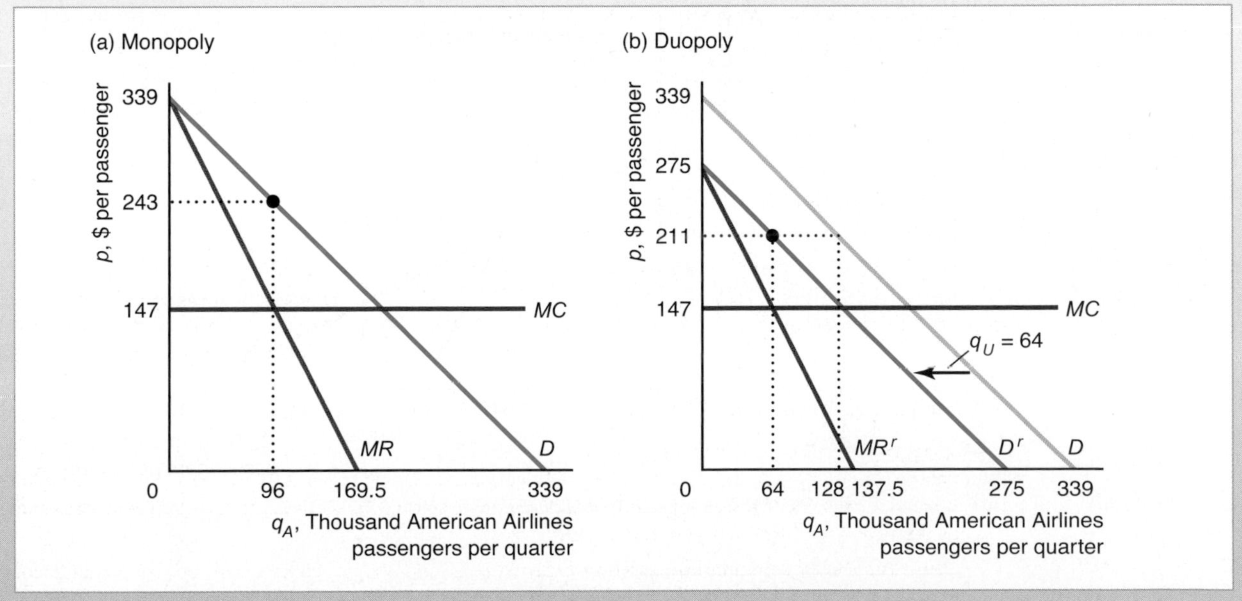

Thus, if United flies q_U passengers regardless of the price, American transports only the residual demand, $Q = D(p)$, minus the q_U passengers, so $q_A = Q - q_U$.

Suppose that American believes that United will fly $q_U = 64$. Panel b shows that American's residual demand curve, D^r, is the market demand curve, D, moved to the left by $q_U = 64$. For example, if the price is \$211, the total number of passengers who want to fly is $Q = 128$. If United transports $q_U = 64$, American flies $Q - q_U = 128 - 64 = 64 = q_A$.

What is American's best-response, profit-maximizing output if its managers believe that United will fly q_U passengers? American can think of itself as having a monopoly with respect to the people who don't fly on United, which its residual demand curve, D^r, shows. To maximize its profit, American sets its output so that its marginal revenue corresponding to this residual demand, MR^r, equals its marginal cost. Panel b shows that if $q_U = 64$, American's best response is $q_A = 64$.

By shifting its residual demand curve appropriately, American can calculate its best response to any given q_U using this type of analysis. Figure 13.3 plots American Airlines' best-response curve, which shows how many tickets American sells for each possible q_U.[6] As this curve shows, American will sell the monopoly number of tickets, 96, if American thinks United will fly no passengers, $q_U = 0$. The negative slope of the best-response curve shows that American sells fewer tickets, the more people American thinks that United will fly. American sells $q_A = 64$ if it thinks q_U will be 64. American shuts down, $q_A = 0$, if it thinks q_U will be 192 or more, because operating wouldn't be profitable.

Similarly, United's best-response curve shows how many tickets United sells if it thinks American will sell q_A. For example, United sells $q_U = 0$ if it thinks American will sell $q_A = 192$, $q_U = 48$ if $q_A = 96$, $q_U = 64$ if $q_A = 64$, and $q_U = 96$ if $q_A = 0$.

Figure 13.3 American and United's Best-Response Curves.

The best-response curves show the output each firm picks to maximize its profit, given its belief about its rival's output. The Cournot equilibrium occurs at the intersection of the best-response curves.

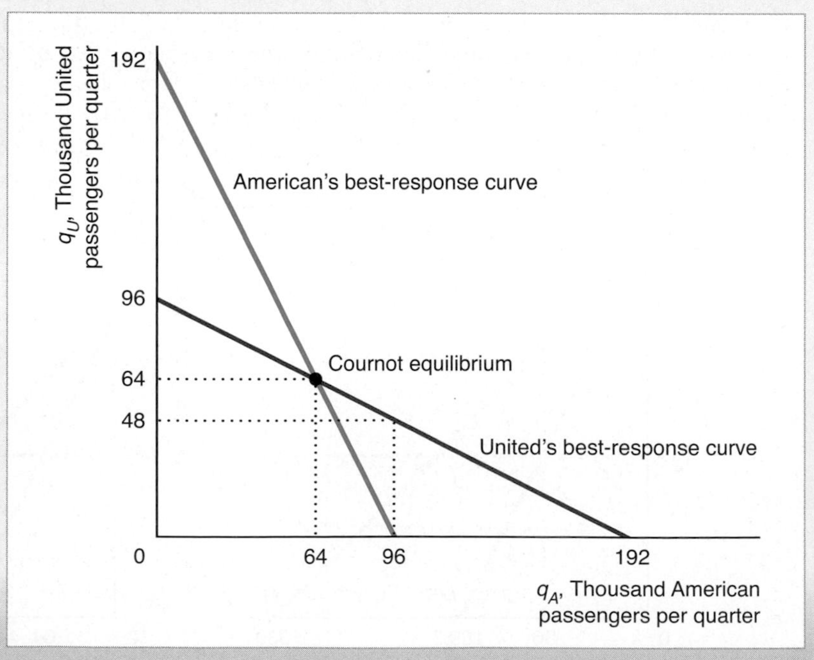

[6]*Jargon alert*: Some economists refer to the *best-response curve* as the *reaction curve*.

A firm wants to change its behavior if it is selling a quantity that is not on its best-response curve. In a Cournot equilibrium, neither firm wants to change its behavior. Thus, in a Cournot equilibrium, each firm is on its best-response curve: Each firm is maximizing its profit, given its correct belief about its rival's output.

These firms' best-response curves intersect at $q_A = q_U = 64$. If American expects United to sell $q_U = 64$, American wants to sell $q_A = 64$. Because this point is on its best-response curve, American doesn't want to change its output from 64. Similarly, if United expects American to sell $q_A = 64$, United doesn't want to change q_U from 64. Thus, this pair of outputs is a Cournot (Nash) equilibrium: Given its correct belief about its rival's output, each firm is maximizing its profit, and neither firm wants to change its output.

Any pair of outputs other than the pair at an intersection of the best-response functions is *not* a Cournot equilibrium. If either firm is not on its best-response curve, it changes its output to increase its profit. For example, the output pair $q_A = 96$ and $q_U = 0$ is not a Cournot equilibrium. American is perfectly happy producing the monopoly output if United doesn't operate at all: American is on its best-response curve. United, however, would not be happy with this outcome because it is not on United's best-response curve. As its best-response curve shows, if it knows that American will sell $q_A = 96$, United wants to sell $q_U = 48$. Only at $q_A = q_U = 64$ does neither firm want to change its behavior.

Algebraic Approach. We can also use algebra to solve for the Cournot equilibrium for these two airlines. (See Appendix 13A for the general case.) We use estimates of the market demand and firms' marginal costs to determine the equilibrium.

Our estimate of the market demand function is

$$Q = 339 - p, \tag{13.1}$$

where price, p, is the dollar cost of a one-way flight, and total quantity of the two airlines combined, Q, is measured in thousands of passengers flying one way per quarter. Panels a and b of Figure 13.2 show that this market demand curve, D, is a straight line that hits the price axis at \$339 and the quantity axis at 339 units (thousands of passengers) per quarter. Each airline has a constant marginal cost, MC, and average cost, AC, of \$147 per passenger per flight. Using only this information and our economic model, we can find the Cournot equilibrium for the two airlines.

If American believes that United will fly q_U passengers, American expects to fly only the total market demand minus q_U passengers. At a price of p, the total number of passengers, $Q(p)$, is given by the market demand function, Equation 13.1. Thus, the residual demand American faces is

$$q_A = Q(p) - q_U = (339 - p) - q_U.$$

Using algebra, we can rewrite this inverse residual demand function as

$$p = 339 - q_A - q_U. \tag{13.2}$$

In panel b, the linear residual demand, D^r, is parallel to the market demand, D, and lies to the left of D by $q_U = 64$.

If a demand curve is linear, the corresponding marginal revenue curve is twice as steep (Chapter 11). The slope of the residual demand curve, Equation 13.2, is $\Delta p/\Delta q_A = -1$, so the slope of the corresponding marginal revenue curve, MR^r in panel b in Figure 13.2, is –2. Therefore, the marginal revenue function is[7]

$$MR^r = 339 - 2q_A - q_U. \tag{13.3}$$

[7]American's revenue is $R = pq_A = (339 - q_A - q_U)q_A$. If American treats q_U as a constant and differentiates R with respect to its output, it finds that its marginal revenue is

$$MR = \partial R/\partial q_A = 339 - 2q_A - q_U.$$

American Airlines' best response—its profit-maximizing output, given q_U—is the output that equates its marginal revenue, Equation 13.3, and its marginal cost:

$$MR^r = 339 - 2q_A - q_U = 147 = MC. \tag{13.4}$$

By rearranging Equation 13.4, we can write American's best-response output, q_A, as a function of q_U:

$$q_A = 96 - \tfrac{1}{2}q_U. \tag{13.5}$$

Figure 13.3 shows American's best-response function, Equation 13.5. According to this best-response function, $q_A = 96$ if $q_U = 0$ and $q_A = 64$ if $q_U = 64$. By the same reasoning, United's best-response function is

$$q_U = 96 - \tfrac{1}{2}q_A. \tag{13.6}$$

A Cournot equilibrium is a pair of quantities, q_A and q_U, such that Equations 13.5 and 13.6 both hold: Each firm is on its best-response curve. This statement is equivalent to saying that the Cournot equilibrium is a point at which the best-response curves cross.

One way to determine the Cournot equilibrium is to substitute Equation 13.6 into Equation 13.5,

$$q_A = 96 - \tfrac{1}{2}\left(96 - \tfrac{1}{2}q_A\right),$$

and solve for q_A. Doing so, we find that $q_A = 64$ is the Cournot equilibrium quantity for American. Substituting $q_A = 64$ into Equation 13.6, we find that $q_U = 64$ is the Cournot equilibrium quantity for United. As a result, the total output in the Cournot equilibrium is $Q = q_A + q_U = 128$. Setting $Q = 128$ in the market demand Equation 13.1, we learn that the Cournot equilibrium price is \$211.

See Problem 21.

The Cournot Equilibrium and the Number of Firms

We've just seen that the price to consumers is lower if two firms set output independently than if they collude. The price to consumers is even lower if there are more than two firms acting independently in the market. We now show how the Cournot equilibrium varies with the number of firms.

Each Cournot firm maximizes its profit by operating where its marginal revenue equals its marginal cost. Chapter 11 shows that a firm's marginal revenue depends on the price and the elasticity of demand it faces where it maximizes its profit. The marginal revenue for a typical Cournot firm is $MR = p(1 + 1/\varepsilon_r)$, where ε_r is the elasticity of the residual demand curve the firm faces. Appendix 13A shows that $\varepsilon_r = n\varepsilon$, where ε is the market elasticity of demand and n is the number of firms with identical costs. Thus, we can write a typical Cournot firm's profit-maximizing condition as

$$MR = p\left(1 + \frac{1}{n\varepsilon}\right) = MC. \tag{13.7}$$

If $n = 1$, the Cournot firm is a monopoly, and Equation 13.7 is the same as the profit-maximizing monopoly condition, Equation 11.7. The more firms there are, the larger the residual demand elasticity, $n\varepsilon$, a single firm faces. As n grows very large, the residual demand elasticity approaches negative infinity ($-\infty$), and Equation 13.7 becomes $p = MC$, which is the profit-maximizing condition of a price-taking competitive firm.

The Lerner Index, $(p - MC)/p$, is a measure of market power: the firm's ability to raise price above marginal cost. By rearranging the terms in Equation 13.7, we find that a Cournot firm's Lerner Index depends on the elasticity the firm faces:

$$\frac{p - MC}{p} = -\frac{1}{n\varepsilon}. \tag{13.8}$$

Thus, a Cournot firm's Lerner Index equals the monopoly level, $-1/\varepsilon$, if there is only one firm: Setting $n = 1$ in Equation 13.8, we obtain the monopoly expression (Equation 11.9). Again, as the number of firms grows large, the residual demand elasticity a firm faces approaches $-\infty$, so the Lerner Index approaches zero, which is the same as with price-taking, competitive firms.

We can illustrate these results using our airlines example. Suppose that other airlines with identical marginal cost, $MC = \$147$, were to fly between Chicago and Los Angeles. Table 13.2 shows how the Cournot equilibrium price and the Lerner Index vary with the number of firms.[8]

As we already know, if there were only one "Cournot" firm, it would produce the monopoly quantity, 96, at the monopoly price, \$243. We also know that each duopoly firm's output is 64, so market output is 128 and price is \$211. The duopoly market elasticity is $\varepsilon = 1.65$, so the residual demand elasticity each duopolist faces is twice as large as the market elasticity, $2\varepsilon = -3.3$.

As the number of firms increases, each firm's output falls toward zero, but total output approaches 192, the quantity on the market demand curve where price equals marginal cost of \$147. Although the market elasticity of demand falls as the number of firms grows, the residual demand curve for each firm becomes increasingly horizontal (perfectly elastic). As a result, the price approaches the marginal cost, \$147. Similarly, as the number of firms increases, the Lerner Index approaches the price-taking level of zero.[9]

See Question 6 and Problems 22 and 23.

Table 13.2 Cournot Equilibrium Varies with the Number of Firms.

Number of Firms, n	Firm Output, q	Market Output, Q	Price, p, \$	Market Elasticity, ε	Residual Demand Elasticity, $n\varepsilon$	Lerner Index, $(p - m)/p = -1/(n\varepsilon)$
1	96	96	243	−2.53	−2.53	0.40
2	64	128	211	−1.65	−3.30	0.30
3	48	144	195	−1.35	−4.06	0.25
4	38.4	154	185.40	−1.21	−4.83	0.21
5	32	160	179	−1.12	−5.59	0.18
10	17.5	175	164.45	−0.94	−9.42	0.11
50	3.8	188	150.76	−0.80	−40.05	0.02
100	1.9	190	148.90	−0.78	−78.33	0.01
200	1.0	191	147.96	−0.77	−154.89	0.01

[8]In Appendix 13A, we derive the Cournot equilibrium quantity and price for a general linear demand. Given our particular demand curve, Equation 13.1, and marginal cost, \$147, each firm's Cournot equilibrium output is $q = (339 - 147)/(n + 1) = 192/(n + 1)$ and the Cournot market price is $p = (339 + 147n)/(n + 1)$.

[9]As the number of firms goes to infinity, the Cournot equilibrium goes to perfect competition only if average cost is nondecreasing (Ruffin, 1971).

The table shows that having extra firms in the market benefits consumers. When the number of firms rises from 1 to 4, the price falls by a quarter and the Lerner Index is cut nearly in half. At ten firms, the price is one-third less than the monopoly level, and the Lerner Index is a quarter of the monopoly level.

APPLICATION

Air Ticket Prices and Rivalry

The markup of price over marginal cost is much greater on routes in which one airline carries most of the passengers than on other routes. Unfortunately, a single firm is the only carrier or the dominant carrier on 58% of all U.S. domestic routes (Weiher et al., 2002).

The first column of the table identifies the market structure for U.S. air routes. The last column shows the share of routes. A single firm (monopoly) serves 18% of all routes. Duopolies control 19% of the routes, three-firm markets are 16%, four-firm markets are 13%, and five or more firms fly on 35% of the routes.

Although nearly two-thirds of all routes have three or more carriers, one or two firms dominate virtually all routes. We call a carrier a *dominant firm* if it has at least 60% of ticket sales by value but is not a monopoly. We call two carriers a *dominant pair* if they collectively have at least 60% of the market but neither firm is a dominant firm and three or more firms fly this route. All but 0.1% of routes have a monopoly (18%), a dominant firm (40%), or a dominant pair (42%).

The first row of the table shows that the price is slightly more than double (2.1 times) marginal cost on average across all U.S. routes and market structures. (This average price includes "free" frequent flier tickets and other below-cost tickets.) The price is 3.3 times marginal cost for monopolies and 3.1 times marginal cost for dominant firms. In contrast, over the sample period, the average price is only 1.2 times marginal cost for dominant pairs.

The markup of price over marginal cost depends much more on whether there is a dominant firm or dominant pair than on the total number of firms in the market. If there is a dominant pair, whether there are four or five firms, the price is between 1.3 times marginal cost for a four-firm route and 1.4 times marginal cost

Type of Market	p/MC	Share of All Routes (%)
All market types	2.1	100
Dominant firm	3.1	40
Dominant pair	1.2	42
One firm (monopoly)	3.3	18
Two firms (duopoly)	2.2	19
Dominant firm	2.3	14
No dominant firm	1.5	5
Three firms	1.8	16
Dominant firm	1.9	9
No dominant firm	1.3	7
Four firms	1.8	13
Dominant firm	2.2	6
Dominant pair	1.3	7
No dominant firm or pair	2.1	~0
Five or more firms	1.3	35
Dominant firm	3.5	11
Dominant pair	1.4	23
No dominant firm or pair	1.1	0.1

for a route with five or more firms. If there is a dominant firm, price is 2.3 times marginal cost on duopoly routes, 1.9 times on three-firm routes, 2.2 times on four-firm routes, and 3.5 times on routes with five or more firms.

Thus, preventing a single firm from dominating a route may substantially lower prices. Even if two firms dominate the market, the markup of price over marginal cost is substantially lower than if a single firm dominates.

★ The Cournot Model with Nonidentical Firms

We initially assumed that the firms were identical in the sense that they faced the same cost functions and produced identical products. However, costs often vary across firms, and firms often differentiate the products they produce from those of their rivals.

Unequal Costs. In the Cournot model, the firm sets its output so as to equate its marginal revenue to its marginal cost, which determines its best-response function. If the firms' marginal costs vary, then the firms' best-response functions will as well. In the resulting Cournot equilibrium, the relatively low-cost firm produces more. So long as the products are not differentiated, they both charge the same price.

We can illustrate the effect of unequal costs using our earlier duopoly airlines example. Suppose that American Airlines' marginal cost remains at \$147, but United's marginal cost drops to \$99. The firms continue to play Cournot, but the playing field is no longer level.[10] How does the Cournot equilibrium change? Your intuition probably tells you that United's output increases relative to that of American, as we now show.

Nothing changes for American, so its best-response function is unchanged. United's best response to any given American output is the output at which its marginal revenue corresponding to its residual demand, MR^r, equals its new, lower marginal cost. Because United's marginal cost curve fell, United wants to produce more than before for any given level of American's output.

Panel a of Figure 13.4 illustrates this reasoning. United's MR^r curve is unaffected, but its marginal cost curve shifts down from MC^1 to MC^2. Suppose we fix American's output at 64 units. Consequently, United's residual demand, D^r, lies 64 units to the left of the market demand, D. United's corresponding MR^r curve intersects its original marginal cost curve, $MC^1 = \$147$, at 64 and its new marginal cost, $MC^2 = \$99$, at 88. Thus, if we hold American's output constant at 64, United produces more as its marginal cost falls.

Because this reasoning applies for any level of output American picks, United's best-response function in panel b shifts outward as its marginal cost falls. United's best response to any given quantity that American sells is to sell more than at its previous, higher cost. As a result, the Cournot equilibrium shifts from the original e_1, at which both firms sold 64, to e_2, at which United sells 96 and American sells 48.

Using the market demand curve, Equation 13.1, we find that the market price falls from \$211 to \$195, benefiting consumers. United's profit increases from \$4.1 million to \$9.2 million, while American's profit falls to \$2.3 million.[11] Thus, United and consumers gain and American loses from the fall in United's marginal cost.

[10]Don't you think that anyone who uses the phrase "level playing field" should have to pay a fine?

[11]Each firm's profit per passenger is price minus average cost, $p - AC$, so the firm's profit is $\pi = (p - AC)q$, where q is the number of passengers the firm flies. The Cournot price is \$211 and the average cost is \$147, so the Cournot profit per firm is $\pi = (211 - 147) \times 64$ units per quarter = \$4.1 million per quarter.

Figure 13.4 Effect of a Drop in One Firm's Marginal Cost on a Duopoly Cournot Equilibrium.

(a) United's marginal cost falls from MC^1 = \$147 to MC^2 = \$99. If American produces $q_a = 64$, United's best response is to increase its output from $q_U = 64$ to 88 given its lower marginal cost. (b) If both airlines' marginal cost is \$147, the Cournot equilibrium is e_1. After United's marginal cost falls to \$99, its best-response function shifts outward. It now sells more tickets in response to any given American output than previously. At the new Cournot equilibrium, e_2, United sells $q_U = 96$, while American sells only $q_A = 48$.

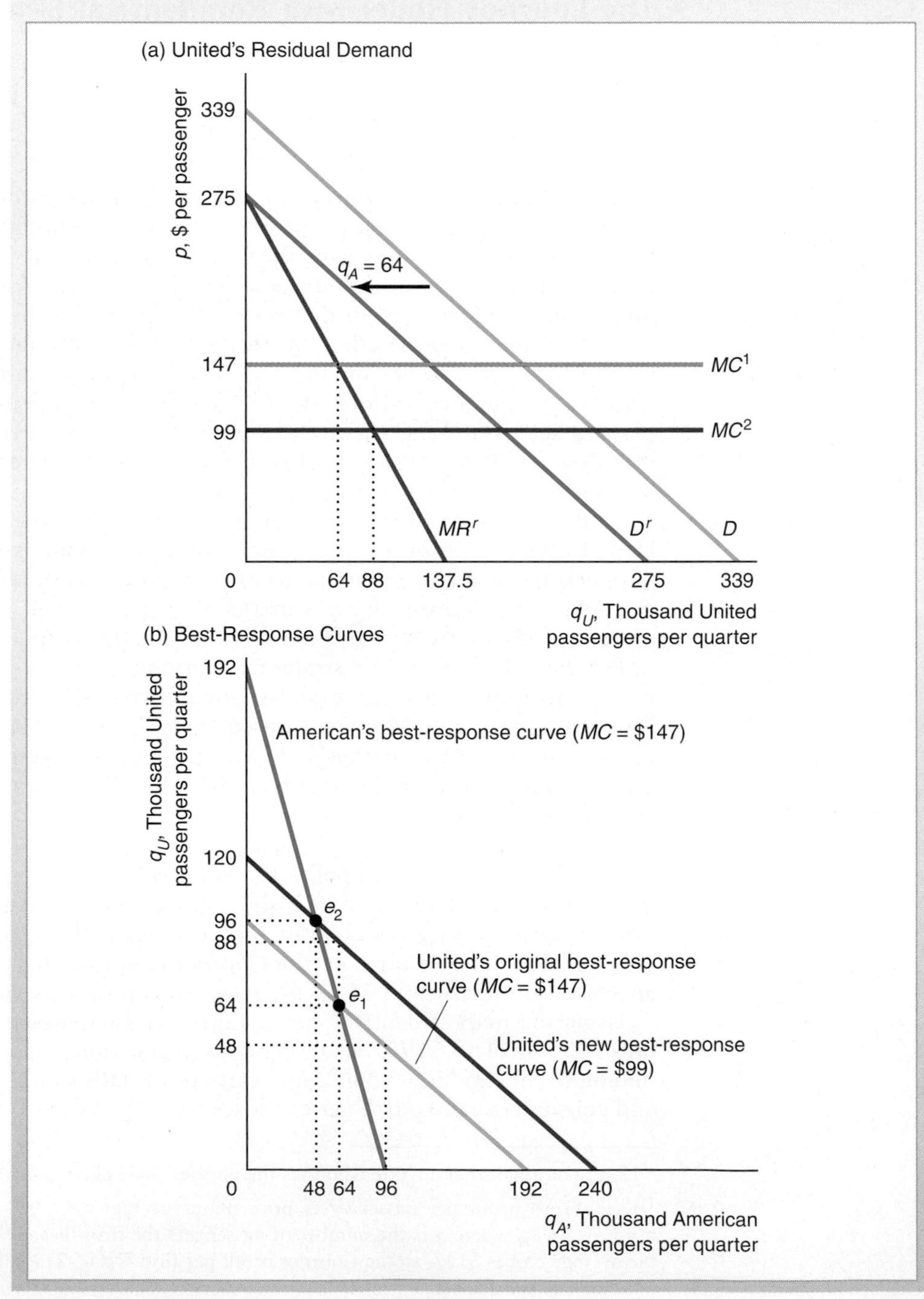

Solved Problem 13.1

Derive United Airlines' best-response function if its marginal cost falls to \$99 per unit.

Answer

1. *Determine United's marginal revenue function corresponding to its residual demand curve.* Luckily, we already know that. The shift in its marginal cost curve does not affect United's residual demand curve, hence its marginal revenue function is the same as before: $MR^r = 339 - 2q_U - q_A$. (The same expression as American's marginal revenue function in Equation 13.3, where the A and U subscripts are reversed.)

2. *Equate United's marginal revenue function and its marginal cost to determine its best-response function.* For a given level of American's output, q_A, United chooses its output, q_U, to equate its marginal revenue and its marginal cost, m:

$$MR^r = 339 - 2q_U - q_A = 99 = m.$$

We can use algebra to rearrange this expression for its best-response function to express q_U as a function of q_a:

$$q_U = 120 - \tfrac{1}{2}q_A.$$

This best-response function is the red line in panel b of Figure 13.4.

Comment: See Appendix 13A for a mathematical approach to a more general case.

See Questions 3 and 4 and Problems 24 and 25.

Differentiated Products. By differentiating its product from those of a rival, an oligopolistic firm can shift its demand curve to the right and make it less elastic. The less elastic the demand curve, the more that the firm can charge. Loosely speaking, consumers are willing to pay more for a product that they perceive as being superior.

One way to differentiate a product is to give it unique, "desirable" attributes, such as the Lexus car that parks itself. For example, after Heinz introduced funny-color ketchup—Blastin' Green, Funky Purple, and Stellar Blue—its share of all ketchup rose substantially, from 50% in 1999 to more than 60% by 2005. (Contrary to my wife's view, my purchases did not make a very major contribution to this increase.) However, its Kool Blue French fries were less successful.

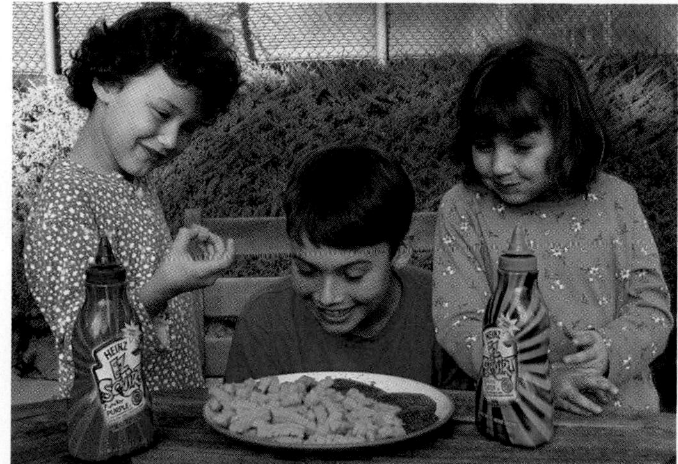

Alternatively, a firm can differentiate its product by advertising, using colorful labels, and engaging in other promotional activities to convince consumers that its product is superior in some (possibly unspecified) way even though it is virtually identical to its rivals physically or chemically. Economists call this practice *spurious differentiation*. Bayer charges more for its chemically identical aspirin than other brands because Bayer has convinced consumers that its product is safer or superior in some other way. Clorox's bottle may be superior, but the bleach inside is chemically identical to that from rival brands costing much less.

If consumers think products differ, the Cournot quantities and prices will differ across firms. Each firm faces a different inverse demand function and hence charges a different price. For example, suppose that Firm 1's inverse demand function is $p_1 = a - b_1q_1 - b_2q_2$, where $b_1 > b_2$ if consumers believe that Good 1 is different from Good 2 and $b_1 = b_2 = b$ if the goods are identical. Given that consumers view the products as differentiated and Firm 2 faces a similar inverse demand function, we replace the single market demand with these individual demand functions in the Cournot model. Solved Problem 13.2 shows how to solve for the Cournot equilibrium in an actual market with differentiated products.

See Question 5.

Solved Problem 13.2

Intel and Advanced Micro Devices (AMD) are the only two firms that produce central processing units (CPUs), which are the brains of personal computers. Both because the products differ physically and because Intel's advertising "Intel Inside" campaign has convinced some consumers' of its superiority, consumers view the CPUs as imperfect substitutes. Consequently, the two firms' inverse demand functions differ:

$$p_A = 197 - 15.1q_A - 0.3q_I, \tag{13.9}$$

$$p_I = 490 - 10q_I - 6q_A, \tag{13.10}$$

where price is dollars per CPU, quantity is in millions of CPUs, the subscript I indicates Intel, and the subscript A represents AMD.[12] Each firm faces a constant marginal cost of m = \$40 per unit. (For simplicity, we will assume there are no fixed costs.) Solve for the Cournot equilibrium quantities and prices.

Answer

1. *Using our rules for determining the marginal revenue for linear demand functions, calculate each firm's marginal revenue function.* For a linear demand curve, we know that the marginal revenue curve is twice as steeply slowed as is the demand curve. Thus, the marginal revenue functions that correspond to the inverse demand Equations 13.9 and 13.10 are[13]

$$MR^A = 197 - 30.2q_A - 0.3q_I, \tag{13.11}$$

$$MR^I = 450 - 20q_I - 6q_A. \tag{13.12}$$

2. *Equate the marginal revenue functions to the marginal cost to determine the best-response functions.* We determine AMD's best response function by equating MR^A from Equation 13.9 to its marginal cost of m = \$40,

$$MR^A = 197 - 30.2q_A - 0.3q_I = 40 = m,$$

and solving for q_A to obtain AMD's best-response function:

$$q_A = \frac{157 - 0.3\,q_I}{30.2}. \tag{13.13}$$

---

[12]I thank Hugo Salgado for estimating these inverse demand functions for me and for providing evidence that this market is well described by a Nash-Cournot equilibrium.

[13]We can use calculus to derive these marginal revenue functions. For example, by multiplying both sides of AMD's inverse demand function (13.9) by q_A, we learn that its revenue function is $R_A = p_Aq_A = 197q_A - 15.2(q_A)^2 - 0.3q_Iq_A$. Holding q_I constant and differentiating with respect to q_A, we obtain $MR^A = \mathrm{d}R_A/\mathrm{d}q_A = 197 - 30.2q_A - 0.3q_I$.

Similarly, Intel's best-response function is

$$q_I = \frac{450 - 6q_A}{20}. \quad (13.14)$$

3. *Use the best-response functions to solve for the Cournot equilibrium.* By simultaneously solving the system of best-response functions 13.13 and 13.14, we find that the Cournot equilibrium quantities are $q_A = 15{,}025/3{,}011 \approx 5$ million CPUs, and $q_I = 63{,}240/3{,}011 \approx 21$ million CPUs. Substituting these values into the inverse demand functions (13.9) and (13.10), we obtain the corresponding prices: $p_A = \$115.20$ and $p_I = \$250$ per CPU.

APPLICATION

Bottled Water

Perhaps the most dramatic recent example of spurious differentiation concerns the $11 billion U.S. bottled water industry. Pepsico's top-selling bottled water, Aquafina, has a colorful blue label and a logo showing the sun rising over the mountains. From that logo, consumers may guess that the water comes from some bubbling spring high in an unspoiled wilderness. If so, they're wrong. In 2007, Pepsi finally admitted that its best-selling bottled water comes from the same place as tap water: public-water sources. However, Pepsi insists that it filters the water using a state-of-the-art "HydRO-7 purification system," implying that such filtering (which removes natural minerals) is desirable. Coke has also admitted that its Dasani bottled water comes from public water sources.

13.5 Stackelberg Model

In the Cournot model, both firms make their output decisions at the same time. Suppose, however, that one of the firms, called the *leader*, can set its output before its rival, the *follower*, sets its output. This type of game, in which the players make decisions sequentially, arises naturally if one firm enters a market before another.

Would the firm that got to act first have an advantage? Heinrich von Stackelberg showed how to modify the Cournot model to answer this question.

How does the leader decide to set its output? The leader realizes that once it sets its output, the rival firm will use its Cournot best-response curve to pick a best-response output. Thus, the leader predicts what the follower will do before the follower acts. Using this knowledge, the leader manipulates the follower, thereby benefiting at the follower's expense.

We illustrate this model using our airlines market example (Appendix 13B analyzes the model mathematically). Although it is difficult to imagine that either American Airlines or United Airlines actually has an advantage that would allow it to act before its rival, we assume (arbitrarily) that American Airlines can act before United Airlines.

Stackelberg Graphical Model

Given that American Airlines chooses its output first, how does American decide on its optimal policy? American uses its residual demand curve to determine its profit-maximizing output. American knows that when it sets q_A, United will use its Cournot best-response function to pick its best-response q_U. Thus, American's residual demand curve, D^r (panel a of Figure 13.5), is the market demand curve, D (panel a) minus the output United will produce as summarized by United's best-response

Figure 13.5 Stackelberg Equilibrium.

(a) The residual demand the Stackelberg leader faces is the market demand minus the quantity produced by the follower, q_U, given the leader's quantity, q_A. The leader chooses $q_A = 96$ so that its marginal revenue, MR^r, equals its marginal cost. The total output, $Q = 144$, is the sum of the output of the two firms. (b) The quantity the follower produces is its best response to the leader's output, as given by its Cournot best-response curve.

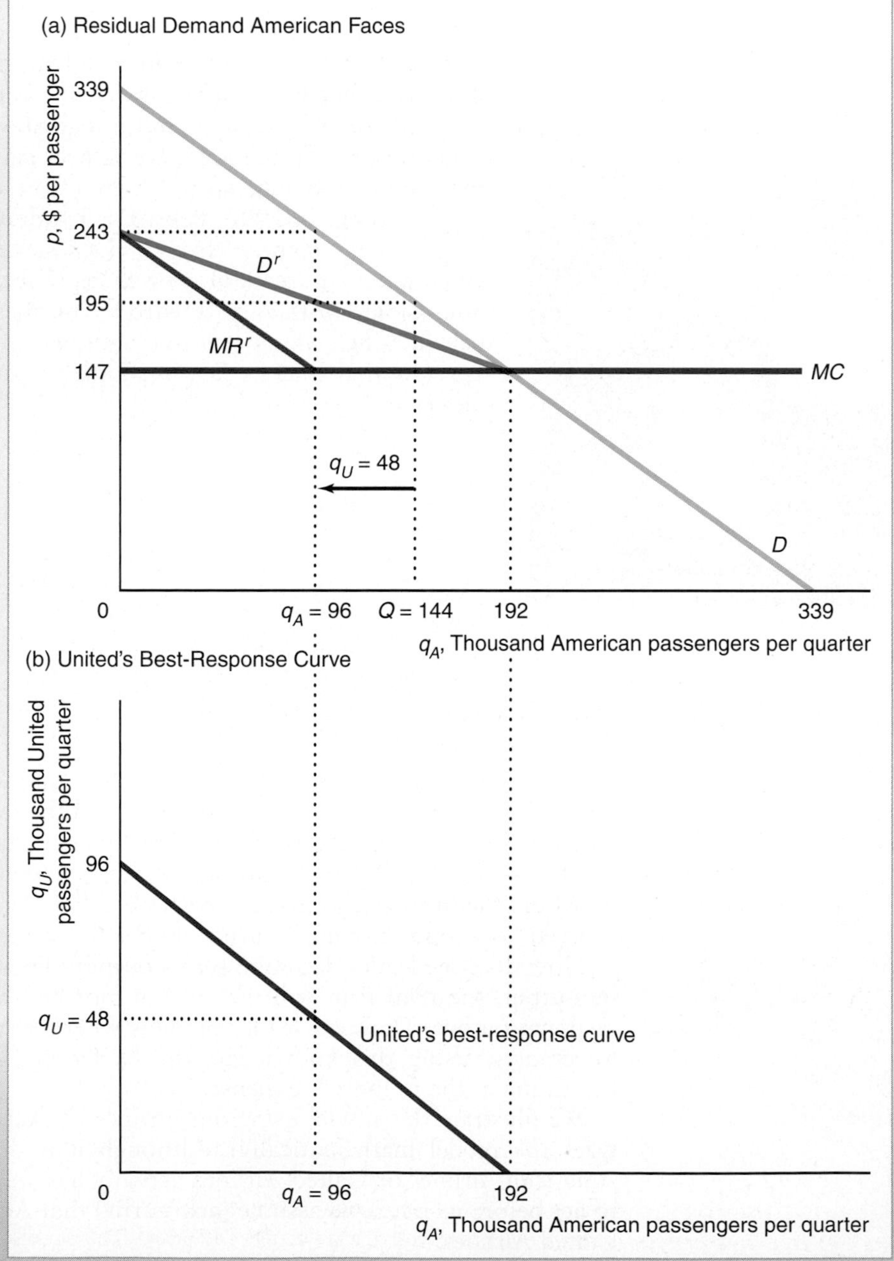

curve (panel b). For example, if American sets $q_A = 192$, United's best response is $q_U = 0$ (as shown by United's best-response curve in panel b). As a result, the residual demand curve and the market demand curve are identical at $q_A = 192$ (panel a).

Similarly, if American set $q_A = 0$, United would choose $q_U = 96$, so the residual demand at $q_A = 0$ is 96 less than demand. The residual demand curve hits the vertical axis, where $q_A = 0$, at $p = \$243$, which is 96 units to the left of demand at that price. When $q_A = 96$, $q_U = 48$, so the residual demand at $q_A = 96$ is 48 units to the left of the demand.

American chooses its profit-maximizing output, $q_A = 96$, where its marginal revenue curve that corresponds to the residual demand curve, MR^r, equals its marginal cost, \$147. At $q_A = 96$, the price, which is the height of the residual demand curve, is \$195. Total demand at \$195 is $Q = 144$. At that price, United produces $q_U = Q - q_A = 48$, its best response to American's output of $q_A = 96$.

Thus, in this Stackelberg equilibrium, the leader produces twice as much as the follower, as Figure 13.5 shows.[14] The total Stackelberg output, 144, is greater than the total Cournot, 128, output. As a result, the Stackelberg price, \$195, is less than the Cournot, \$211, price. Thus, consumers prefer the Stackelberg equilibrium to the Cournot equilibrium.

The Stackelberg leader earns \$4.6 million, which is more than it could earn in a Cournot game, \$4.1 million. Total Stackelberg profit is less than total Cournot profit because the Stackelberg follower, earning \$2.3 million, is much worse off than in the Cournot equilibrium.

Solved Problem 13.3

Use algebra to solve for the Stackelberg equilibrium quantities and market price if American Airlines were a Stackelberg leader and United Airlines were a follower. (*Hint*: As the graphical analysis shows, American Airlines, the Stackelberg leader, maximizes its profit as though it were a monopoly facing a residual demand function.)

Answer

1. *Determine the inverse residual demand function facing American Airlines.* The residual demand function facing American Airlines is the market demand function (Equation 13.1), $Q = 330 - p$, minus the best-response function of United Airlines (Equation 13.6), $q_U = 96 - \frac{1}{2}q_A$:

$$q_A(p) = Q(p) - q_U(q_A) = 339 - p - \left[96 - \tfrac{1}{2}q_A\right] = 243 - p - \tfrac{1}{2}q_A. \quad (13.15)$$

   Using algebra, we can rewrite Equation 13.10 as the inverse residual demand function (which is the D^r line in panel a of Figure 13.5):

$$p = 243 - \tfrac{1}{2}q_A. \quad (13.16)$$

2. *Solve for American Airlines' profit-maximizing output by equating its marginal revenue and marginal cost.* American Airlines, the Stackelberg leader, acts like a monopoly with respect to its residual demand. From Chapter 11, we know that its marginal revenue function is the same as its inverse residual demand function, Equation 13.16, except it has twice the slope: $MR_A = 243 - q_A$ (which is the MR^r line in panel a of Figure 13.5). To maximize its profit,

[14]Here the leader produces the same quantity as a monopoly would, and the follower produces the same quantity as it would in the cartel equilibrium. These relationships are due to the linear demand curve and the constant marginal cost—they do not hold more generally.

American Airlines picks its output so as to equate its marginal revenue to its marginal cost:

$$MR_A = 243 - q_A = 147 = MC. \qquad (13.17)$$

Solving Equation 13.17 for American Airlines' output, we find that $q_A = 96$.

3. *Use United Airlines' best-response function to solve for its quantity and the total output.* Substituting $q_A = 96$ into United Airlines' best-response function, Equation 13.6, we learn that United Airlines sells half as many seats as American Airlines: $q_U = 96 - \frac{1}{2}q_A = 48$. Thus, total output is

$$Q = q_A + q_U = 96 + 48 = 144.$$

4. *Use the market demand function to solve for the market price.* Substituting $Q = 144$, total output, into the market demand function, we determine that the market price is \$195.

See Problems 26 and 27.

Comment: See Appendix 13B for the solution to a more general case.

Why Moving Sequentially Is Essential

Why don't we get the Stackelberg equilibrium when both firms move simultaneously? Why doesn't one firm—say, American—announce that it will produce the Stackelberg leader output to induce United to produce the Stackelberg follower output level? The answer is that when the firms move simultaneously, United doesn't view American's warning that it will produce a large quantity as a *credible threat.*

If United believed that threat, it would indeed produce the Stackelberg follower output level. But United doesn't believe the threat because it is not in American's best interest to produce that large a quantity of output. If American were to produce the leader level of output and United produced the Cournot level, American's profit would be lower than if it too produced the Cournot level. Because American cannot be sure that United will believe its threat and reduce its output, American will actually produce the Cournot output level.

See Question 7.

Indeed, each firm may make the same threat and announce that it wants to be the leader. Because neither firm can be sure that the other will be intimidated and produce the smaller quantity, both produce the Cournot output level. In contrast, when one firm moves first, its threat to produce a large quantity is credible because it has already *committed* to producing the larger quantity, thereby carrying out its threat.

★ Strategic Trade Policy

Suppose that two identical firms in two different countries compete in a world market. Both firms act simultaneously, so neither firm can make itself the Stackelberg leader. A government may be tempted to intervene to make its firm a Stackelberg leader. The Japanese and French governments often help their domestic firms compete with international rivals; so do the U.S., British, Canadian, and many other governments. If only one government intervenes, it can make its domestic firm's threat to produce a large quantity of output credible, so foreign rivals will produce the Stackelberg follower level of output (Spencer and Brander, 1983).

Subsidizing an Airline. We'll modify our airline example to illustrate how one country's government can aid its firm. Suppose that United Airlines were based in one country and American Airlines in another. Initially, United and American are in a Cournot equilibrium. Each firm has a marginal cost of \$147 and flies 64 thousand passengers (64 units) per quarter at a price of \$211.

Now suppose that United's government gives United a \$48-per-passenger subsidy, but the other government doesn't help American. As a result, American's marginal cost remains at \$147, but United's marginal cost after the subsidy is only \$99.

Figure 13.4 illustrates how this subsidy changes the Cournot equilibrium. The subsidized firm, United, increases its output from 64 to 96, while American cuts its output from 64 to 48. As a result, total output rises from 128 to 144, causing the market price to fall from \$211 to \$195.

This example illustrates that a government subsidy to one firm *can* lead to the same outcome as in a Stackelberg equilibrium. Would a government *want* to give the subsidy that leads to the Stackelberg outcome?

The answer depends on the government's objective. Suppose that the government is interested in maximizing its domestic firm's profit net of (not including) the government's subsidy. The subsidy is a transfer from some citizens (taxpayers) to others (the owners of United). We assume that the government doesn't care about consumers—which is certainly true if they live in another country.

Table 13.3 shows the effects of various subsidies and a tax (a negative subsidy). If the subsidy is zero, we have the usual Cournot equilibrium. A \$48-per-passenger subsidy leads to the same outcome as in the Stackelberg equilibrium and maximizes the government's welfare measure. At a larger subsidy, such as \$60, United's profit rises, but by less than the cost of the subsidy to the government. Similarly, at smaller subsidies or taxes, welfare is also lower.

See Problem 28.

Problems with Intervention. Thus, in theory, a government may want to subsidize its domestic firm to make it produce the same output as it would if it were a Stackelberg leader. If such subsidies are to work as desired, however, five conditions must hold.

First, the government must be able to set its subsidy before the firms choose their output levels. The idea behind this intervention is that one firm cannot act before the other, but its government can act first.

Second, the other government must not retaliate. If both governments intervene, instead of having a game of strategies between firms, we have a game of strategies between governments, in which both countries may lose.

Table 13.3 Effects of a Subsidy Given to United Airlines.

Subsidy,	United			American	
s	q_U	π_U	Welfare, $\pi_U - sq_U$	q_A	π_A
60	104	\$10.8	\$4.58	44	\$1.9
48	**96**	**\$9.2**	**\$4.61**	**48**	**\$2.3**
30	84	\$7.1	\$4.50	54	\$2.9
0	64	\$4.1	\$4.10	64	\$4.1
–30	44	\$1.9	\$3.30	74	\$5.5

Notes:

The subsidy is in dollars per passenger (and is a tax if negative).

Output units are in thousands of passengers per quarter.

Profits and welfare (defined as United's profits minus the subsidy) are in millions of dollars per quarter.

Third, the government's actions must be credible. If the foreign firm's country doesn't believe that the government actually will subsidize its domestic firm, the foreign firm produces the Cournot level. Countries have difficulty in committing to long-term policies. For example, during the 1996 Republican presidential primaries, many candidates said that they would reverse President Clinton's trade policies if they were elected. Similarly, the 2004 and 2008 Democratic presidential candidates promised to change President Bush's trade policies.

Fourth, the government must know enough about how firms behave to intervene appropriately. If it doesn't know the demand function and the costs of all firms, the government may set its subsidy at the wrong level.

Fifth, the government must know which game the firms are playing. If they are not engaged in a Cournot game, the government would have to intervene in a different way.

Many economists who analyze strategic trade policies strongly oppose them because they are difficult to implement and mean-spirited, "beggar thy neighbor" policies. If only one government intervenes, another country's firm is harmed. If both governments intervene, both countries may suffer. For these reasons, the General Agreement on Tariffs and Trade and the World Trade Organization forbade the use of virtually all explicit export subsidies.

APPLICATION

Government Aircraft Subsidies

Governments consistently intervene in aircraft manufacturing markets. France, Germany, Spain, and the United Kingdom own and heavily subsidize Airbus, which competes in the widebody aircraft market with the U.S. firm Boeing. The U.S. government decries the European subsidies to Airbus, while directing lucrative military contracts to Boeing that the Europeans view as implicit subsidies. In 1992, the governments signed a U.S.–EU agreement on trade in civil aircraft that limits government subsidies (including a maximum direct subsidy limit of 33% of development costs and various limits on variable costs).

Irwin and Pavcnik (2004) found that aircraft prices increased by about 3.7% after the 1992 agreement. This price hike is consistent with a 5% increase in firms' marginal costs after the subsidy cuts.

In 2005 and 2007, Washington and the European Union traded countercomplaints to the World Trade Organization. Each again charged the other with illegally subsidizing its aircraft manufacturer. And the cycle of subsidies, charges, agreements, and new subsidies continues.

Solved Problem 13.4

If governments subsidize identical Cournot duopolies with a specific subsidy of s per unit of output, what is the qualitative effect (direction of change) on the equilibrium quantities and price? Assume that the before-subsidy best-response functions are linear.

Answer

1. *Show the initial, before-subsidy Cournot equilibrium.* We're told that the Cournot firms, labeled Firm *A* and Firm *B* on the graph, are identical. As a result, their best-response curves are mirror images of each other, and both firms produce the same quantity, q_1, at the Cournot equilibrium, e_1, where their best-response functions cross.

2. *Show how the best-response curves shift in response to the tax.* We've just seen that a subsidy lowers a firm's marginal cost, causing its best-response curve to shift away from the origin. Because both firms face the same specific subsidy,

marginal costs of both firms fall by the same amount. As a result, both after-subsidy best-response curves shift away from the origin by the same amount and remain mirror images of each other.

See Problem 29.

3. *Compare the two Cournot equilibria.* Each firm produces a larger quantity, q_2, at the new Cournot equilibrium, e_2, than in the original Cournot equilibrium. As a result, total equilibrium quantity rises and the equilibrium price falls.

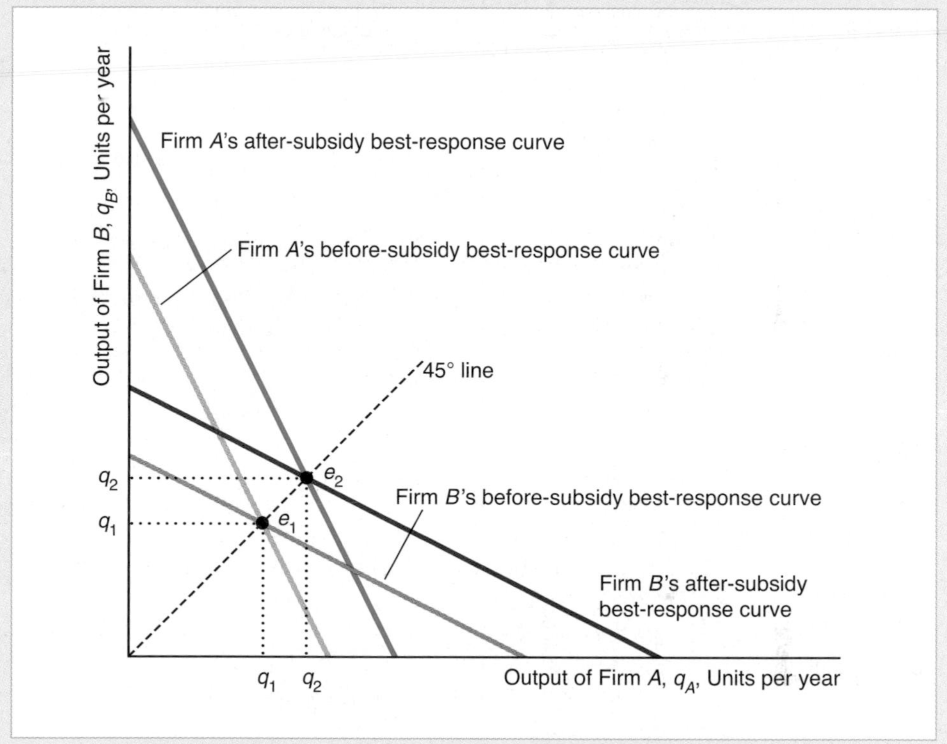

13.6 Comparison of Collusive, Cournot, Stackelberg, and Competitive Equilibria

The Cournot and Stackelberg equilibrium quantities, prices, and profits lie between those for the competitive (price taking) and collusive equilibria, as Figure 13.6 shows for our airline duopoly.

How would American and United behave if they colluded? They would maximize joint profits by producing the monopoly output, 96 units, at the monopoly price, \$243 per passenger (panel a of Figure 13.6). If the airlines collude, they could split the monopoly quantity in many ways. American could act as a monopoly and serve all the passengers, $q_A = 96$ and $q_U = 0$, and possibly give United some of the profits. Or they could reverse roles so that United served everyone: $q_A = 0$ and $q_U = 96$. Or the two airlines could share the passengers in any combination such that the sum of the airlines' passengers equals the monopoly quantity:

$$q_A + q_U = 96. \quad (13.18)$$

Figure 13.6 Duopoly Equilibria.

(a) The intersection of the best-response curves determines the Cournot equilibrium. The possible cartel equilibria lie on the contract curve. If the firms act as price takers, each firm produces where its residual demand equals its marginal cost. (b) The highest possible profit for the two firms combined is given by the profit possibility frontier. It reflects all the possible collusive equilibria, including the one indicated where the firms split the market equally. All equilibria except collusive ones lie within the profit possibility frontier.

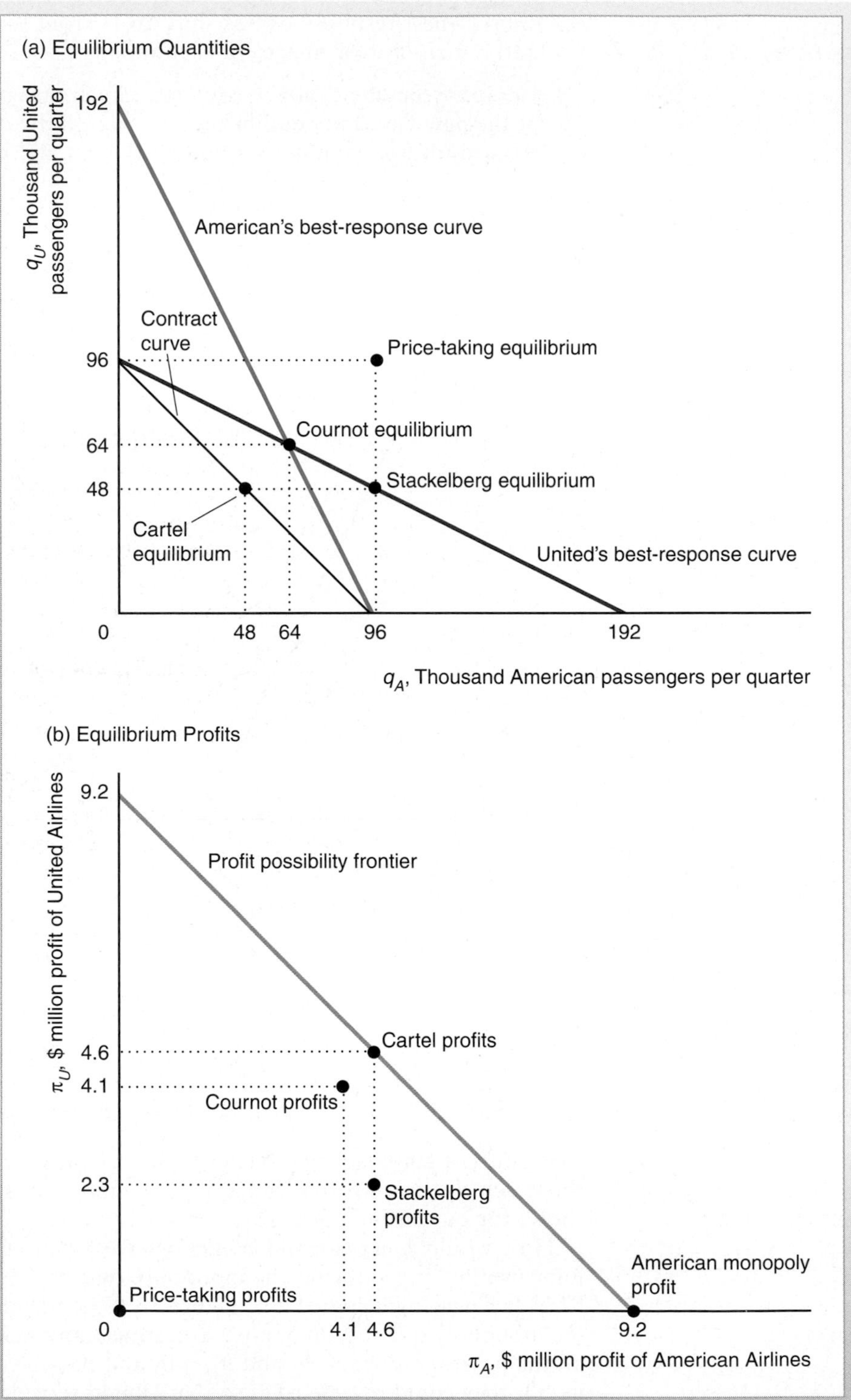

See Question 8 and Problems 30 and 31.

Panel a of Figure 13.6 shows the possible collusive output combinations in Equation (13.18) as a line labeled "Contract curve." Collusive firms could write a contract where they agree to produce at any of the points along this curve. In the figure, we assume that the collusive firms split the market equally so that $q_A = q_U = 48$.

If the firms were to act as price takers, they would each produce where their residual demand curve intersects their marginal cost curve, so price equals marginal cost of \$147. The price-taking equilibrium is $q_A = q_U = 96$.

The cartel profits are the highest-possible level of profits the firms can earn. The contract curve shows how the firms split the total monopoly-level profit. Panel b of Figure 13.6 shows the profit possibility frontier, which corresponds to the contract curve. At the upper left of the profit possibility frontier, United is a monopoly and earns the entire monopoly profit of approximately \$9.2 million per quarter. At the lower right, American earns the entire monopoly profit. At points in between, they split the profit. Where they split the profit equally, each earns approximately \$4.6 million.

In contrast, if the firms act independently, each earns the Cournot profit of \$4.1 million, as Table 13.4 shows. Because the Cournot price, \$211, is lower than the cartel price, \$243, consumers are better off if the firms act independently than if they collude. The Stackelberg leader earns \$4.6 million, which is more than it could earn in a Cournot outcome, \$4.1 million. Total Stackelberg profit, \$6.9 million, is less than total Cournot profit, \$8.2 million, because the Stackelberg follower, earning \$2.3 million, is much worse off than in the Cournot equilibrium.

Table 13.4 also shows how welfare measures vary with market structure. As we did in Chapter 9, we define welfare as consumer surplus plus producer surplus, which is the sum of the two firms' profits in our example.

At one extreme, if one firm has a monopoly or if the two firms form a cartel and split the market equally, total output is relatively low, price is high, consumer surplus

Table 13.4 Comparison of Airline Market Structures.

	Monopoly	Cartel	Cournot	Stackelberg	Price Taking
q_A	96	48	64	96	96
q_U	0	48	64	48	96
$Q = q_A + q_U$	96	96	128	144	192
p	\$243	\$243	\$211	\$195	\$147
π_A	\$9.2	\$4.6	\$4.1	\$4.6	\$0
π_U	\$0	\$4.6	\$4.1	\$2.3	\$0
Total profit $= \Pi = \pi_A + \pi_U$	\$9.2	\$9.2	\$8.2	\$6.9	\$0
Consumer surplus, CS	\$4.6	\$4.6	\$8.2	\$10.4	\$18.4
Welfare, $W = CS + \Pi$	\$13.8	\$13.8	\$16.4	\$17.3	\$18.4
Deadweight loss, DWL	\$4.6	\$4.6	\$2.0	\$1.2	\$0

Notes:

Passengers are in thousands per quarter.

Price is in dollars per passenger.

Profits, consumer surplus, welfare, and deadweight loss are in millions of dollars per quarter.

and welfare are low, and deadweight loss is high. At the other extreme, if American and United act as price takers, output is relatively high, price is low, consumer surplus and welfare are high, and society does not suffer a deadweight loss.

The duopoly Cournot and Stackelberg equilibria (in the table, American is the leader) lie between the extreme cases of monopoly or cartel and price taking. The Stackelberg equilibrium is closer to the price-taking equilibrium than the Cournot equilibrium in terms of total output, price, consumer surplus, welfare, and deadweight loss.

We showed that the Cournot equilibrium approaches the price-taking equilibrium as the number of firms grows. Similarly, we can show that the Stackelberg equilibrium approaches the price-taking equilibrium as the number of Stackelberg followers grows. As a result, the differences between the Cournot, Stackelberg, and price-taking market structures shrink as the number of firms grows.

APPLICATION

Deadweight Losses in the Food and Tobacco Industries

See Question 9.

Bhuyan and Lopez (1998) and Bhuyan (2000) estimated the deadweight loss for various U.S. food and tobacco manufacturing oligopolies and monopolistically competitive markets. Most of these industries have deadweight losses that are a relatively small percentage of sales (their prices and quantities are close to competitive levels). However, a few industries, such as cereal and flour and grain mills, have relatively large deadweight losses.

Industry	Loss, $ millions	Share of Sales, %
Cereal	2,192	33
Flour and grain mills	541	26
Poultry and eggs	1,183	8
Roasted coffee	440	7
Cigarettes	1,032	6
All food manufacturing	14,947	5

13.7 Bertrand Model

We have examined how oligopolistic set quantities to try to maximize their profits. However, many oligopolistic firms set prices instead of quantities and allow consumers to decide how much to buy. The market equilibrium is different if firms set prices rather than quantities.

In monopolistic and competitive markets, the issue of whether firms set quantities or prices does not arise. Competitive firms have no choice: They cannot affect price and hence can choose only quantity (Chapter 8). The monopoly equilibrium is the same whether the monopoly sets price or quantity (Chapter 11).

Bertrand equilibrium (Nash-Bertrand equilibrium)
a *Nash equilibrium* in prices; a set of prices such that no firm can obtain a higher profit by choosing a different price if the other firms continue to charge these prices

In 1883, Joseph Bertrand argued that oligopolies set prices and then consumers decide how many units to buy. The resulting Nash equilibrium is called a **Bertrand equilibrium or Nash-Bertrand equilibrium** (or Nash-in-prices equilibrium): a set of prices such that no firm can obtain a higher profit by choosing a different price if the other firms continue to charge these prices.

We will show that the price and quantity in a Bertrand equilibrium are different from those in a Cournot equilibrium. We will also show that a Bertrand equilibrium depends on whether firms are producing identical or differentiated products.

Bertrand Equilibrium with Identical Products

We start by examining a price-setting oligopoly in which firms have identical costs and produce identical goods. The resulting Bertrand equilibrium price equals the marginal cost, as in the price-taking equilibrium. To show this result, we use best-response curves to determine the Bertrand equilibrium, as we did in the Cournot model.

Best-Response Curves. Suppose that each of the two price-setting oligopoly firms in a market produces an identical product and faces a constant marginal and average cost of \$5 per unit. What is Firm 1's best response—what price should it set—if Firm 2 sets a price of $p_2 = \$10$? If Firm 1 charges more than \$10, it makes no sales because consumers will buy from Firm 2. Firm 1 makes a profit of \$5 on each unit it sells if it also charges \$10 per unit. If the market demand is 200 units and both firms charge the same price, we'd expect Firm 1 to make half the sales, so its profit is \$500.

Suppose, however, that Firm 1 slightly undercuts its rival's price by charging \$9.99. Because the products are identical, Firm 1 captures the entire market. Firm 1 makes a profit of \$4.99 per unit and a total profit of \$998. Thus, Firm 1's profit is higher if it slightly undercuts its rival's price. By similar reasoning, if Firm 2 charges \$8, Firm 1 also charges slightly less than Firm 2.

Now imagine that Firm 2 charges $p_2 = \$5$. If Firm 1 charges more than \$5, it makes no sales. The firms split the market and make zero profit if Firm 1 charges \$5. If Firm 1 undercuts its rival, it captures the entire market, but it makes a loss on each unit. Therefore, Firm 1 will undercut only if its rival's price is higher than Firm 1's marginal and average cost of \$5. By similar reasoning, if Firm 2 charges less than \$5, Firm 1 chooses not to produce.

Figure 13.7 shows that Firm 1's best response is to produce nothing if Firm 2 charges less than \$5. Firm 1's best response is \$5 if Firm 2 charges \$5. If Firm 2 charges prices above \$5, Firm 1's best response is to undercut Firm 2's price slightly. Above \$5, Firm 1's best-response curve is above the 45° line by the smallest amount possible. (The distance of the best-response curve from the 45° line is exaggerated in the figure for clarity.) By the same reasoning, Firm 2's best-response curve starts at \$5 and lies slightly below the 45° line.

See Question 10.

The two best-response functions intersect only at *e*, where each firm charges \$5. It does not pay for either firm to change its price as long as the other charges \$5, so *e* is a Nash or Bertrand equilibrium. In this equilibrium, each firm makes zero profit. Thus, *the Bertrand equilibrium when firms produce identical products is the same as the price-taking, competitive equilibrium.*

Bertrand Versus Cournot. The Bertrand equilibrium differs substantially from the Cournot equilibrium. We can calculate the Cournot equilibrium price for firms with constant marginal costs of \$5 per unit by rearranging Equation 13.8:

$$p = \frac{MC}{1 + 1/(n\varepsilon)} = \frac{\$5}{1 + 1/(n\varepsilon)}, \tag{13.19}$$

where n is the number of firms and ε is the market demand elasticity. If the market demand elasticity is $\varepsilon = -1$ and $n = 2$, the Cournot equilibrium price is $\$5/(1 - \frac{1}{2}) = \$10$ which is double the Bertrand equilibrium price.

When firms produce identical products and have a constant marginal cost, the Cournot model is more plausible than the Bertrand. The Bertrand model—unlike the Cournot model—appears inconsistent with real oligopoly markets in at least two ways.

Figure 13.7 Bertrand Equilibrium with Identical Products.

With identical products and constant marginal and average costs of \$5, Firm 1's best-response curve starts at \$5 and then lies slightly above the 45° line. That is, Firm 1 undercuts its rival's price as long as its price remains above \$5. The best-response curves intersect at *e*, the Bertrand or Nash equilibrium, where both firms charge \$5.

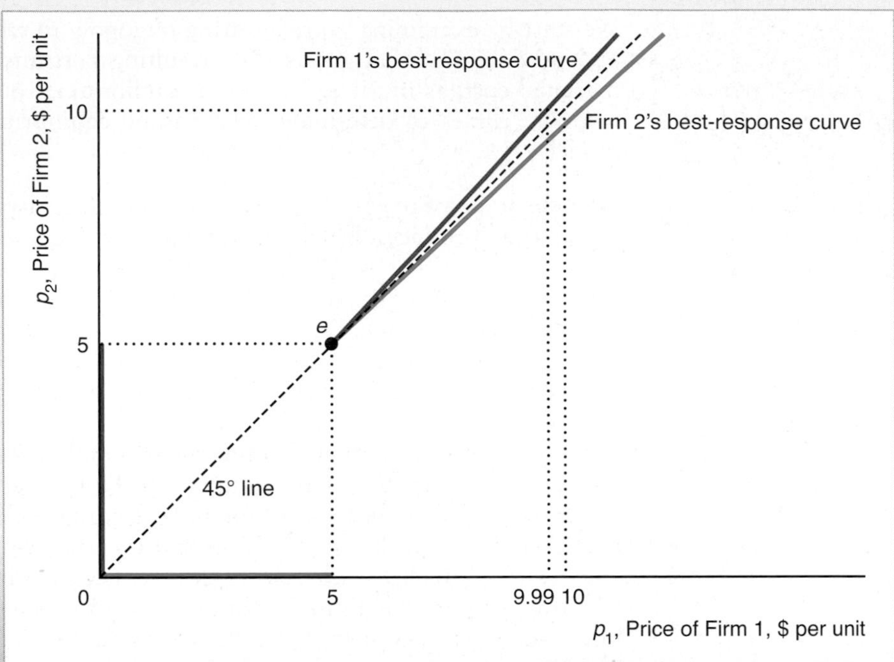

First, the Bertrand model's "competitive" equilibrium price is implausible. If there is only a small number of firms, why would they compete so vigorously that they would make no profit? In contrast, the Cournot equilibrium price with a small number of firms lies between the competitive price and the monopoly price. Because oligopolies typically charge a higher price than competitive firms, the Cournot equilibrium is more plausible.

Second, the Bertrand equilibrium price, which depends only on cost, is insensitive to demand conditions and the number of firms. In contrast, the Cournot equilibrium price, Equation 13.19, depends on the number of firms and demand and cost conditions. In our example, if the number of firms rises from two to three, the Cournot price falls from \$10 to $\$5/(1-\frac{1}{3}) = \$7.50$, but the Bertrand equilibrium price remains \$5. Again, the Cournot model is more plausible because we usually observe market price changing with the number of firms and demand conditions, not just with changes in costs.

See Question 11.

As a result, it seems more likely that when firms' products are identical, firms set quantities rather than prices. For these reasons, economists are much more likely to use the Cournot model than the Bertrand model to study markets in which firms produce identical goods.

Bertrand Equilibrium with Differentiated Products

Why don't they make mouse-flavored cat food? —Steven Wright

If most markets were characterized by firms producing homogeneous goods, the Bertrand model would probably have been forgotten. Markets with differentiated goods—automobiles, stereos, computers, toothpastes, and spaghetti sauces—however, are extremely common, as is price setting by firms. In such markets, the

Bertrand equilibrium is plausible, and the two "problems" of the homogeneous-goods model disappear: Firms set prices above marginal cost, and prices are sensitive to demand conditions.

Indeed, many economists believe that price-setting models are more plausible than quantity-setting models when goods are differentiated. If products are differentiated and firms set prices, then consumers determine quantities. In contrast, if firms set quantities, it is not clear how the prices of the differentiated goods are determined in the market.

Cola Market

We illustrate a Bertrand equilibrium with the differentiated products in the cola market. We use best-response curves in a figure to solve for the equilibrium.

Coke and Pepsi produce similar but not identical products; many consumers prefer one of these products to the other. If the price of Pepsi were to fall slightly relative to that of Coke, some consumers who prefer Coke to Pepsi would not switch. Thus, neither firm has to match exactly a price cut by its rival. As a result, neither firm's best-response curve in Figure 13.8 lies along a 45° line through the origin.[15]

Figure 13.8 Bertrand Equilibrium with Differentiated Products.

If both firms have a constant marginal cost of \$5, the best-response curves of Coke and Pepsi intersect at e_1, where each sets a price of \$13 per unit. If Coke's marginal cost rises to \$14.50, its best-response function shifts upward. In the new equilibrium, e_2, Coke charges a higher price, \$18, than Pepsi, \$14.

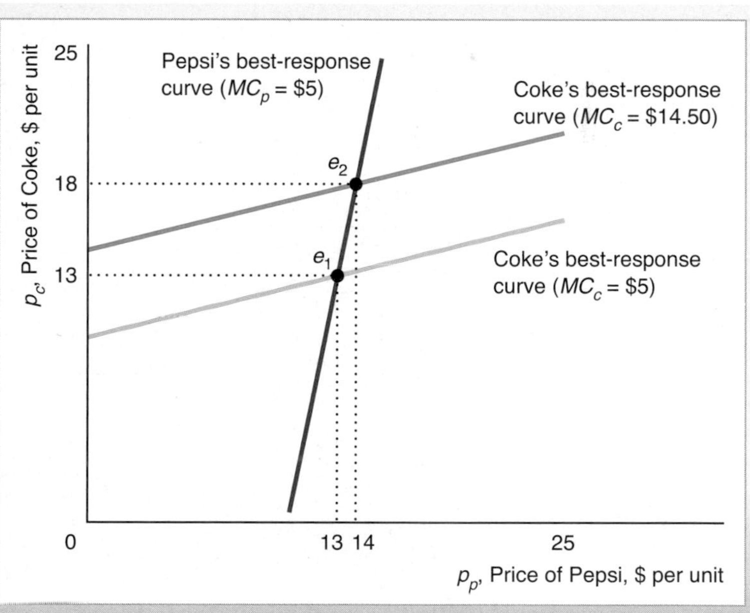

[15]The figure is based on Bertrand estimates from Gasmi, Laffont, and Vuong (1992). Their estimated model allows the firms to set both prices and advertising. We assume that the firms' advertising is held constant. The Coke equations are the authors' estimates (with slight rounding). The Pepsi equations are rescaled so that the equilibrium prices of Coke and Pepsi are equal. Quantities are in tens of millions of cases (a case consists of 24 twelve-ounce cans) per quarter, and prices (to retailers) and costs are in real 1982 dollars per 10 cases.

The Bertrand best-response curves have different slopes than the Cournot best-response curves in Figure 13.3. The Cournot curves—which plot relationships between quantities—slope downward, showing that a firm produces less the more its rival produces. In Figure 13.8, the Bertrand best-response curves—which plot relationships between prices—slope upward, indicating that a firm charges a higher price the higher the price its rival charges.

If both Pepsi and Coke have a constant marginal cost of $MC_p = MC_c = \$5$, the Bertrand equilibrium, e_1 in Figure 13.8, occurs where the price of each firm is \$13 per unit (10 cases). In this Nash equilibrium, each firm sets its best-response price *given the price the other firm is charging*. Neither firm wants to change its price because neither firm can increase its profit by so doing. (See Appendix 13C for a mathematical presentation.)

See Questions 12–14 and Problems 32–36.

Product Differentiation and Welfare. Because differentiation makes demand curves less elastic, prices are likely to be higher when products are differentiated than when they're identical. We also know that welfare falls as the gap between price and marginal cost rises. Does it follow that differentiating products lowers welfare? Not necessarily. Although differentiation leads to higher prices, which harm consumers, differentiation is desirable in its own right. Consumers value having a choice, and some may greatly prefer a new brand to existing ones.

One way to illustrate the importance of this second effect is to consider what the value is of introducing a new, differentiated product. This value reflects how much extra income consumers would require to be as well off without the good as with it.

APPLICATION

Welfare Gain from More Toilet Paper

An article in the *Economist* asked, "Why does it cost more to wipe your bottom in Britain than in any other country in the European Union?" The answer given was that British consumers are "extremely fussy" in demanding a soft, luxurious texture—in contrast to barbarians elsewhere. As a consequence, they pay twice as much for toilet paper as the Germans and French, and nearly 2.5 times as much as Americans.

Probably completely uninfluenced by this important cross-country research, Hausman and Leonard (2002) used U.S. data to measure the price effect and the extra consumer surplus from greater variety resulting from Kimberly-Clark's introduction of Kleenex Bath Tissue (KBT). Bath tissue products are divided into premium, economy, and private labels, with premium receiving more than 70% of revenue. Before KBT's entry, the major premium brands were Angel Soft, Charmin, Cottonelle, and Northern. ScotTissue was the leading economy brand.

Firms incur a sizeable fixed cost from capital investments. The marginal cost depends primarily on the price of wood pulp, which varies cyclically. Because KBT was rolled out in various cities at different times, Hausman and Leonard could compare the effects of entry at various times and control for variations in cost and other factors.

The prices of all rival brands fell after KBT entered; the price of the leading brand, Charmin, dropped by 3.5%, while Cottonelle's price plummeted 8.2%. In contrast, the price of ScotTissue, an economy brand, decreased by only 0.6%.

Hausman and Leonard calculated that the additional consumer surplus due to extra variety was \$33.4 million, or 3.5% of sales. When they included the gains due to lower prices, the total consumer surplus increase was \$69.2 million, or 7.3% of sales. Thus, the gains to consumers were roughly equally divided between the price effect and the benefit from extra variety.

13.8 Monopolistic Competition

We've assumed that the number of oligopoly firms is fixed because of barriers to entry. As a result, the oligopoly firms (such as the airlines) may earn economic profits. In contrast, monopolistically competitive markets do not have barriers to entry, so firms enter the market until no new firm can enter profitably.

If both competitive and monopolistically competitive firms make zero profits, what distinguishes these two market structures? In contrast to competitive firms (which face horizontal residual demand curves and charge prices equal to marginal cost), monopolistically competitive firms face downward-sloping residual demand curves, so they charge prices above marginal cost. Monopolistically competitive firms face downward-sloping residual demand because they have relatively few rivals or because they sell differentiated products.

The fewer monopolistically competitive firms, the less elastic the residual demand curve each firm faces. As we saw, the elasticity of demand for an individual Cournot firm is $n\varepsilon$, where n is the number of firms and ε is the market elasticity. Thus, the fewer the firms in a market, the less elastic the residual demand curve.

When monopolistically competitive firms benefit from economies of scale at high levels of output (the average cost curve is downward sloping), so that each firm is relatively large in comparison to market demand, there is room in the market for only a few firms. In the short run, if fixed costs are large and marginal costs are constant or diminishing, firms have economies of scale (Chapter 7) at all output levels, so there are relatively few firms in the market. In an extreme case with substantial enough economies of scale, the market may have room for only one firm: a natural monopoly (Chapter 11). The number of firms in equilibrium is smaller the greater the economies of scale and the farther to the left the market demand curve.

Monopolistically competitive firms also face downward-sloping residual demand curves if each firm sells a differentiated product. If some consumers believe that Tide laundry detergent is better than Cheer and other brands, Tide won't lose all its sales even if Tide has a slightly higher price than Cheer. Thus, Tide faces a downward-sloping demand curve—not a horizontal one.

Monopolistically Competitive Equilibrium

In a monopolistically competitive market, each firm tries to maximize its profit; however, each makes zero economic profit due to entry. Two conditions hold in a monopolistically competitive equilibrium: *Marginal revenue equals marginal cost* (because firms set output to maximize profit), and *price equals average cost* (because firms enter until no further profitable entry is possible).

Figure 13.9 shows a monopolistically competitive market equilibrium. A typical monopolistically competitive firm faces a residual demand curve D^r. To maximize its profit, the firm sets its output, q, where its marginal revenue curve corresponding to the residual demand curve intersects its marginal cost curve: $MR^r = MC$. At that quantity, the firm's average cost curve, AC, is tangent to its residual demand curve. Because the height of the residual demand curve is the price, at the point of tangency, price equals average cost, $p = AC$, and the firm makes zero profit.

If the average cost were less than price at that quantity, firms would make positive profits and entrants would be attracted. If average cost were above price, firms would lose money, so firms would exit until the marginal firm was breaking even.

minimum efficient scale *(full capacity)* the smallest quantity at which the average cost curve reaches its minimum

The smallest quantity at which the average cost curve reaches its minimum is referred to as *full capacity* or **minimum efficient scale**. The firm's full capacity or minimum efficient scale is the quantity at which the firm no longer benefits from

Figure 13.9 Monopolistically Competitive Equilibrium.

A monopolistically competitive firm, facing residual demand curve D^r, sets its output where its marginal revenue equals its marginal cost: $MR^r = MC$. Because firms can enter this market, the profit of the firm is driven to zero, so price equals the firm's average cost: $p = AC$.

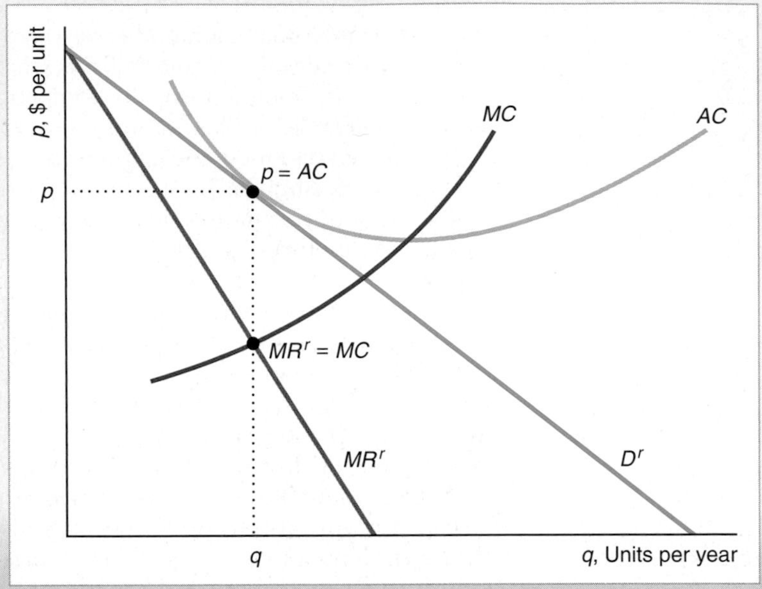

economies of scale. Because a monopolistically competitive equilibrium occurs in the downward-sloping section of the average cost curve (where the average cost curve is tangent to the downward-sloping demand curve), a monopolistically competitive firm operates at less than full capacity in the long run.

Fixed Costs and the Number of Firms

The number of firms in a monopolistically competitive equilibrium depends on firms' costs. The larger each firm's fixed cost, the smaller the number of monopolistically competitive firms in the market equilibrium.

Although entry is free, if the fixed costs are high, few firms may enter. In the automobile industry, just to develop a new fender costs \$8 to \$10 million.[16] Developing a new pharmaceutical drug may cost \$350 million or more.

We can illustrate this relationship using the airlines example, in which we modify our assumptions about entry and fixed costs. American and United are the only airlines providing service on the Chicago–Los Angeles route. Until now, we have assumed that a barrier to entry—such as an inability to obtain landing rights at both airports—prevented entry and that the firms had no fixed costs. If fixed cost is zero and marginal cost is constant at \$147 per passenger, average cost is also constant at \$147 per passenger. As we showed earlier, each firm in this oligopolistic market flies $q = 64$ per quarter at a price of $p = \$211$ and makes a profit of \$4.1 million per quarter.

[16] James B. Treece, "Sometimes, You Gotta Have Size," *Business Week*, Enterprise 1993, 200–201. Treece illustrates the role of fixed costs on entry in the following anecdote: "In 1946, steel magnate Henry J. Kaiser boasted to a Detroit dinner gathering that two recent stock offerings had raised a huge \$50 million to invest in his budding car company. Suddenly, a voice from the back of the room shot out: 'Give that man one white chip.'"

Now suppose that there are no barriers to entry, but each airline incurs a fixed cost, F, due to airport fees, capital expenditure, or other factors. Each firm's marginal cost remains \$147 per passenger, but its average cost,

$$AC = 147 + \frac{F}{q},$$

falls as the number of passengers rises, as panels a and b of Figure 13.10 illustrate for F = \$2.3 million.

If there are only two firms in a monopolistically competitive market, what must the fixed costs be so that the two firms earn zero profit? We know that these firms receive a profit of \$4.1 million per firm in the absence of fixed costs. As a result, the fixed cost must be \$4.1 million per firm for the firms to earn zero profit. With this fixed cost, the monopolistically competitive price and quantity are the same as in the oligopolistic equilibrium, $q = 64$ and p = \$211, and the number of firms is the same, but now each firm's profit is zero.

If the fixed cost is only \$2.3 million and there are only two firms in the market, each firm makes a profit, as panel a shows. Each duopoly firm faces a residual demand curve (labeled "D^r for 2 firms"), which is the market demand minus its rival's Cournot equilibrium quantity, $q = 64$. Given this residual demand, each firm produces $q = 64$, which equates its marginal revenue, MR^r, and its marginal cost, MC. At $q = 64$, the firm's average cost is AC = \$147 + (\$2.3 million)/(64 units) ≈ \$183, so each firm makes a profit of $\pi = (p - AC)q$ ≈ (\$211 – \$183) × 64 units per quarter ≈ \$1.8 million per quarter.

This substantial economic profit attracts an entrant. The entry of a third firm causes the residual demand for any one firm to shift to the left in panel b. In the new

Figure 13.10 Monopolistic Competition Among Airlines.

(a) If each identical airline has a fixed cost of \$2.3 million and there are two firms in the market, each firm flies q = 64 units (thousands of passengers) per quarter at a price of p = \$211 per passenger and makes a profit of \$1.8 million. This profit attracts entry. (b) After a third firm enters, the residual demand curve shifts, so each firm flies q = 48 units at p = \$195 and makes zero profit, which is the monopolistically competitive equilibrium.

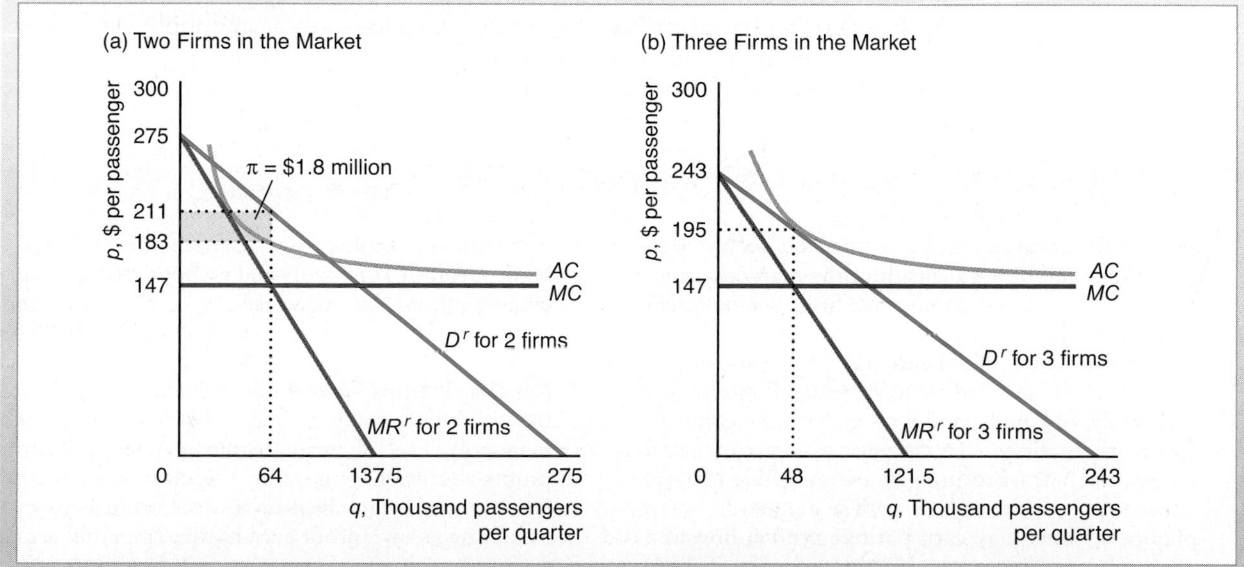

equilibrium, each firm sets $q = 48$ and charges $p = \$195$. At this quantity, each firm's average cost is \$195, so the firms break even. No other firms enter because if one did, the residual demand curve would shift even farther to the left and all the firms would lose money. Thus, if fixed cost is \$2.3 million, there are three firms in the monopolistically competitive equilibrium. This example illustrates a general result: *The lower the fixed costs, the more firms there are in the monopolistically competitive equilibrium.*

See Questions 15–18.

Solved Problem 13.5

What is the monopolistically competitive airline equilibrium if each firm has a fixed cost of \$3 million?

Answer

1. *Determine the number of firms.* We already know that the monopolistically competitive equilibrium has two firms if the fixed cost is \$4.1 million and three firms if the fixed cost is \$2.3 million. With a fixed cost of \$3 million, if there are only two firms in the market, each makes a profit of \$1.1 (= \$4.1 – 3) million. If another firm enters, though, each firm's loss equals –\$0.7 (= 2.3 – 3) million. Thus, the monopolistically competitive equilibrium has two firms, each of which earns a positive profit that is too small to attract another firm. This outcome is a monopolistically competitive equilibrium because no other firm wants to enter.

2. *Determine the equilibrium quantities and prices.* We already know that each duopoly firm produces $q = 64$, so $Q = 128$ and $p = \$211$.

APPLICATION

Virgin America's Fixed Costs

When Virgin America entered the airline business, it made a first quarter loss of \$35 million. The company was not surprised. As its spokesperson said, "You have incredibly high overhead costs when you start an airline." Virgin America's initial startup (fixed cost) expenditure was \$40 million. The airline secured \$177 million in funding to cover all its launch expenditures. Some of its fixed costs include \$100,000 to train each pilot, more than \$10,000 to train each flight attendant, capital for 43 planes, a headquarter building, landing rights at 8 airports, introductory advertising campaign, and large lawyer and lobbying fees to get regulatory approval.

SUMMARY

1. **Market Structures.** Prices, profits, and quantities in a market equilibrium depend on the market's structure. Because profit-maximizing firms set marginal revenue equal to marginal cost, price is above marginal revenue—and hence marginal cost—only if firms face downward-sloping demand curves. In monopoly, oligopoly, and monopolistically competitive markets, firms face downward-sloping demand curves, in contrast to firms in a competitive market. When entry is blocked, as with a monopoly or an oligopoly, firms may earn positive profits; however, when entry is free, as in competition or monopolistic competition, profits are driven toward zero. Noncooperative oligopoly and monopolistically competitive firms, in contrast to competitive and monopoly firms, must pay attention to their rivals.

2. **Cartels.** If firms successfully collude, they produce the monopoly output and collectively earn the monopoly level of profit. Although their collective profits rise if all firms collude, each individual firm has an incentive to cheat on a cartel arrangement so as to raise its own profit even higher. For cartel prices to remain high, cartel members must be able to detect

and prevent cheating, and noncartel firms must not be able to supply very much output. When antitrust laws or competition policies prevent firms from colluding, firms may try to merge if permitted by law.

3. **Noncooperative Oligopoly.** If oligopoly firms act independently, the equilibrium output, price, and total firm profits lie between those of competition and cartel (monopoly). The market outcome depends on the characteristics of the market, such as the number of firms, whether the firms produce differentiated products, and whether the firms act simultaneously or sequentially.

4. **Cournot Model.** If oligopoly firms act independently, the market output and firms' profits lie between the competitive and monopoly levels. In a Cournot model, each oligopoly firm sets its output at the same time. In the Cournot (Nash) equilibrium, each firm produces its best-response output—the output that maximizes its profit—given the output its rival produces. As the number of Cournot firms increases, the Cournot equilibrium price, quantity, and profits approach the price-taking levels.

5. **Stackelberg Model.** If one firm, the Stackelberg leader, chooses its output before its rivals, the Stackelberg followers, the leader produces more and earns a higher profit than each identical-cost follower firm. A government may subsidize a domestic oligopoly firm so that it produces the Stackelberg leader quantity, which it sells in an international market.

6. **Comparison of Collusive, Cournot, Stackelberg, and Competitive Equilibria.** Total market output is maximized and price is minimized under competition. For a given number of firms, the Stackelberg equilibrium output exceeds that of the Cournot equilibrium, which exceeds that of the collusive equilibrium (which is the same as a monopoly produces). Correspondingly, the Stackelberg price is less than the Cournot price, which is less than the collusive or monopoly price.

7. **Bertrand Model.** In many oligopolistic or monopolistically competitive markets, firms set prices instead of quantities. If the product is homogeneous and firms set prices, the Bertrand equilibrium price equals marginal cost (which is lower than the Cournot quantity-setting equilibrium price). If the products are differentiated, the Bertrand equilibrium price is above marginal cost. Typically, the markup of price over marginal cost is greater the more the goods are differentiated.

8. **Monopolistic Competition.** In monopolistically competitive markets, after all profitable entry occurs, there are few enough firms in the market that each firm faces a downward-sloping demand curve. Consequently, the firms charge prices above marginal cost. These markets are not perfectly competitive because there are relatively few firms—possibly because of high fixed costs or economies of scale that are large relative to market demand—or because the firms sell differentiated products.

QUESTIONS

■ = *exercise is available on MyEconLab;* * = *answer appears at the back of this book;* C = *use of calculus may be necessary;* W = *audio-slideshow answer by James Dearden is available in Textbook Resources on MyEconLab.*

1. At each Organization of Petroleum Exporting Countries (OPEC) meeting, Saudi Arabia, the largest oil producer, argues that the cartel should cut production. The Saudis complain that most OPEC countries, including Saudi Arabia (but not Indonesia or Venezuela), produce more oil than they are allotted under their cartel agreement (Simon Romero, "Saudis Push Plan for Cut in Production by OPEC," *New York Times,* March 31, 2004). Use a graph and words to explain why cartel members would produce more than the allotted amount given that they know that overproduction will drive down the price of their product.

2. In the "Bail Bonds" application, the price tends to fall as the number of firms rises above two, but prices are higher in New Haven (eight firms) and Bridgeport (ten firms) than in Norwalk (three firms). Give possible explanations for this pattern.

3. Southwest Airlines' cost to fly one seat one mile is 7.38¢ compared to 15.20¢ for USAir (*New York Times*, August 20, 2002, C4). Assuming that Southwest and USAir compete on a route, use a graph to show that their equilibrium quantities differ. (*Hint*: See Solved Problem 13.1.)

4. An audit by the U.S. Postal Service (USPS) determined that Netflix return envelopes jam automatic sorters, costing the agency $42 million in manual labor costs over the last two years. Consequently, the USPS may add a 17¢ surcharge per envelope. If Netflix incurs this surcharge and does not change its

behavior, its monthly operating income would fall by two-thirds from $1.05 per customer to 35¢, said Citibank analysts. These analysts observed that Netflix has more exposure to a USPS rate increase than does its main rival, Blockbuster, which does relatively more business in person than through the mail (Ned Randolph, "Netflix's Return Envelopes in a Jam," *Video Business*, December 5, 2007). Use a diagram to show how a USPS rate increase would affect the Cournot equilibrium, given that Netflix and Blockbuster engage in a Cournot game but have different marginal costs.

*5. Why does differentiating its product allow an oligopoly to charge a higher price?

6. In 2005, the prices for 36 prescription painkillers shot up as much as 15% after Merck yanked its once-popular arthritis drug Vioxx from the market due to fears that it caused heart problems ("Prices Climb as Much as 15% for Some Painkillers," *Los Angeles Times*, June 3, 2005, C3). Can this product's exit be the cause of the price increases if the prices reflect a Cournot equilibrium? Explain.

7. If two quantity-setting firms act simultaneously, is the Stackelberg outcome likely? Why or why not?

*8. Your college is considering renting space in the student union to one or two commercial textbook stores. The rent the college can charge per square foot of space depends on the profit (before rent) of the firms and hence on whether there is a monopoly or a duopoly. Which number of stores is better for the college in terms of rent? Which is better for students? Why?

9. The application "Deadweight Losses in the Food and Tobacco Industries" shows that the deadweight loss as a fraction of sales varies substantially across industries. One possible explanation is that the number of firms (degree of competition) varies across industries. Using the example in Table 13.3, show how the deadweight loss varies in this market as the number of firms increases from one to three.

10. What happens to the homogeneous-good Bertrand equilibrium price if the number of firms increases? Why?

*11. Will the price be lower if duopoly firms set price or if they set quantity? Under what conditions can you give a definitive answer to this question?

12. In the Coke and Pepsi example, what is the effect of a specific tax, τ, on the equilibrium prices? (*Hint*: What does the tax do to the firm's marginal cost? You do not have to use math to answer this problem.)

13. In 1998, California became the first state to adopt rules requiring many sport utility vehicles, pickups, and minivans to meet the same pollution standards as regular cars, effective in 2004. As the deadline drew near, a business group (which may have an incentive to exaggerate) estimated that using the new technology to reduce pollution would increase vehicle prices by as much as $7,000. A spokesperson for the California Air Resources Board, which imposed the mandate, said that the additional materials cost is only about $70 to $270 per vehicle. Suppose that the two major producers are Toyota and Ford, and these firms are price setters with differentiated products. Show the effect of the new regulation. Is it possible that the price for these vehicles would rise by substantially more than the marginal cost would? Explain your answer.

14. In the initial Bertrand equilibrium, two firms with differentiated products charge the same equilibrium prices. A consumer testing agency praises the product of one firm, causing its demand curve to shift to the right as new customers start buying the product. (The demand curve of the other product is not substantially affected.) Use a graph to illustrate how this new information affects the Bertrand equilibrium. What happens to the equilibrium prices of the two firms?

15. What is the effect of a government subsidy that reduces the fixed cost of each firm in an industry in a Cournot monopolistic competition equilibrium?

16. In the monopolistically competitive airlines model, what is the equilibrium if firms face no fixed costs?

17. In a monopolistically competitive market, the government applies a specific tax of $1 per unit of output. What happens to the profit of a typical firm in this market? Does the number of firms in the market change? Why?

18. Does an oligopoly or a monopolistically competitive firm have a supply curve? Why or why not? (*Hint*: See the discussion in Chapter 11 of whether a monopoly has a supply curve.)

19. According to a report from the Foundation for Taxpayer and Consumer Rights, U.S. drivers pay more for gasoline once taxes were taken out at the pump (Tom Doggett, "U.S, Drivers Subsidize European Pump Prices: Report," Reuters.com, August 31, 2006). Although gasoline costs more than $5 a gallon in Europe, most of that pump price reflects taxes. U.S. state and federal fuel taxes account for a much smaller share of the cost for gasoline. When taxes were removed, European drivers paid 24¢ a gallon less than their U.S. drivers. The report concludes that "U.S. motorists are essentially

subsidizing European drivers, who pay more for taxes but substantially less into oil company profits." Is this "subsidy" evidence of price discrimination by oligopolistic firms?

20. At the end of 2007, oil prices shot up to over $90 a barrel. American Airlines raised its round-trip fares by $20, while its rivals made similar adjustments (Melanie Trottman, "Higher Fuel Costs Emerge as a Test for AMR, Rivals In Now-Profitable Sector," *Wall Street Journal*, November 6, 2007, A2). The airlines have to consider how much of the oil increase to pass on to consumers in higher fares. Use theory to discuss the factors that determine the incidence of this price increase on consumers. (*Hint*: Refer to earlier discussions on the incidence of taxes in Chapters 3 and 11 and how the increase in one factor's price affects costs and supply in Chapter 8.)

PROBLEMS

*21. What is the duopoly Cournot equilibrium if the market demand function is

$$Q = 1{,}000 - 1{,}000p,$$

and each firm's marginal cost is $0.28 per unit?

*22. The viatical settlement industry enables terminally ill consumers, typically HIV patients, to borrow against equity in their existing life insurance contracts to finance their consumption and medical expenses. The introduction and dissemination of effective anti-HIV medication in 1996 reduced AIDS mortality, extending patients' lives and hence delaying when the viatical settlement industry would receive the insurance payments. However, viatical settlement payments (what patients can borrow) fell more than can be explained by greater life expectancy. The number of viatical settlement firms dropped from 44 in 1995 to 24 in 2001. Sood et al. (2005) found that an increase in market power of viatical settlement firms reduced the value of life insurance holdings of HIV-positive persons by about $1.0 billion. When marginal cost rises and the number of firms falls, what happens to Cournot equilibrium price? Use graphs or math to illustrate your answer. (*Hint*: If you use math, it may be helpful to assume that the market demand curve has a constant elasticity throughout.)

23. Show how the Cournot equilibrium for n firms given in Appendix 13A changes if each firm faces a fixed cost of F as well as a constant marginal cost per unit. (*Hint*: Very little, if any, formal math is needed, though it can be used.) C

24. How would the Cournot equilibrium change in the airline example if United's marginal cost was $100 and American's was $200?

*25. If the inverse market demand function facing a duopoly is $p = a - bQ$,what are the Nash-Cournot equilibrium quantities if the marginal cost of Firm 1 is m and that of Firm 2 is $m + x$, where $x > 0$? Which firm produces more and which has the higher profit?

*26. Duopoly quantity-setting firms face the market demand

$$p = 150 - q_1 - q_2.$$

Each firm has a marginal cost of $60 per unit.

a. What is the Cournot equilibrium?

b. What is the Stackelberg equilibrium when Firm 1 moves first?

27. Determine the Stackelberg equilibrium with one leader firm and two follower firms if the market demand curve is linear and each firm faces a constant marginal cost, m, and no fixed cost. (*Hint*: See Appendix 13B for the Stackelberg model with one follower.) C

28. Two firms, each in a different country, sell homogeneous output in a third country. Government 1 subsidizes its domestic firm by s per unit. The other government does not react. In the absence of government intervention the market has a Cournot equilibrium. Suppose demand is linear, $p = 1 - q_1 - q_2$, and each firm's marginal and average costs of production are constant at m. Government 1 maximizes net national income (it does not care about transfers between the government and the firm, so it maximizes the firm's profit net of the transfers). Show that Government 1's optimal s results in its firm producing the Stackelberg leader quantity and the other firm producing the Stackelberg follower quantity in equilibrium. C

29. Mathematically derive the equilibrium in the airline example in the chapter if both American and United receive a subsidy of $48 per passenger.

30. A duopoly faces a market demand of $p = 120 - Q$. Firm 1 has a constant marginal cost of $MC^1 = 20$. Firm 2's constant marginal cost is $MC^2 = 40$. Calculate the output of each firm, market output, and price if there is (a) a collusive equilibrium or (b) a Cournot equilibrium.

*31. To examine the trade-off between efficiency and market power from a merger, consider a market with two firms that sell identical products. Firm 1 has a constant marginal cost of 1, and Firm 2 has a constant marginal cost of 2. The market demand is $Q = 15 - p$.

a. Solve for the Cournot equilibrium price, quantities, profits, consumer surplus, and deadweight loss.

b. If the firms merge and produce at the lower marginal cost, how do the equilibrium values change?

c. Discuss the change in efficiency (average cost of producing the output) and welfare—consumer surplus, producer surplus (or profit), and deadweight loss.

*32. Suppose that identical duopoly firms have constant marginal costs of $10 per unit. Firm 1 faces a demand function of

$$q_1 = 100 - 2p_1 + p_2,$$

where q_1 is Firm 1's output, p_1 is Firm 1's price, and p_2 is Firm 2's price. Similarly, the demand Firm 2 faces is

$$q_2 = 100 - 2p_2 + p_1.$$

Solve for the Bertrand equilibrium. C

33. Solve for the Bertrand equilibrium for the firms described in Problem 32 if both firms have a marginal cost of $0 per unit.

34. Solve for the Bertrand equilibrium for the firms described in Problem 32 if Firm 1's marginal cost is $30 per unit and Firm 2's marginal cost is $10 per unit.

35. Firms in some industries with a small number of competitors earn normal economic profit. The *Wall Street Journal* (Lee Gomes, "Competition Lives On in Just One PC Sector," March 17, 2003, B1) reports that the computer graphics chips industry is one such market. Two chip manufacturers, NVIDIA and ATI, "both face the prospect of razor-thin profits, largely on account of the other's existence."

a. Consider the Bertrand model in which each firm has a positive fixed and sunk cost and a zero marginal cost. What are the Bertrand equilibrium prices? What are the Bertrand equilibrium profits?

b. Does this "razor-thin" profit result imply that the two manufacturers necessarily produce chips that are nearly perfect substitutes?

c. Assume that NVIDIA and ATI produce differentiated products and are Bertrand competitors. The demand for NVIDIA's chip is $q_V = \alpha - \beta p_V + \gamma p_A$; the demand for ATI's chip is $q_A = \alpha - \beta p_A + \gamma p_V$, where p_V is NVIDIA's price, p_A is ATI's price, and α, β, and γ are coefficients of the demand function. Suppose each manufacturer's marginal cost is a constant, m. What are values of α, β, and γ for which the equilibrium profit of each chip manufacturer is zero? In answering this question, show that despite differentiated products, duopolists may earn zero economic profit. W

36. In February 2005, the U.S. Federal Trade Commission (FTC) went to court to undo the January 2000 takeover of Highland Park Hospital by Evanston Northwestern Healthcare Corp. The FTC accused Evanston Northwestern of antitrust violations by using its post-merger market power in the Evanston hospital market to impose 40% to 60% price increases (Bernard Wysocki, Jr., "FTC Targets Hospital Merger in Antitrust Case," *Wall Street Journal,* January 17, 2005, A1). Hospitals, even within the same community, are geographically differentiated as well as possibly quality differentiated. The demand for an appendectomy at Highland Park Hospital is a function of the price of the procedure at Highland Park and Evanston Northwestern Hospital: $q_H = 50 - 0.01p_H + 0.005p_N$. The comparable demand function at Evanston Northwestern is $q_N = 500 - 0.01p_N + 0.005p_H$. At each hospital, the fixed cost of the procedure is $20,000 and the marginal cost is $2,000.

a. Use the product-differentiated Bertrand model to analyze the prices the hospitals set before the merger. Find the Bertrand equilibrium prices of the producers at the two hospitals.

b. After the merger, find the profit-maximizing monopoly prices of the procedure at each hospital. Include the effect of each hospital's price on the profit of the other hospital.

c. Does the merger result in increased prices?

*37. An incumbent firm, Firm 1, faces a potential entrant, Firm 2, with a lower marginal cost. The market demand curve is $p = 120 - q_1 - q_2$. Firm 1 has a constant marginal cost of $20, while Firm 2's is $10.

a. What are the Cournot equilibrium price, quantities, and profits if there is no government intervention?

b. To block entry, the incumbent appeals to the government to require that the entrant incur extra costs. What happens to the Cournot equilibrium if the legal requirement causes the marginal cost of the second firm to rise to that of the first firm, $20?

c. Now suppose that the barrier leaves the marginal cost alone but imposes a fixed cost. What is the minimal fixed cost that will prevent entry?

38. In the competition to attract athletes and produce champion teams, universities increased their spending on college athletics four times faster than overall university spending from 2001 through 2003. Schools have poured money into athletic programs even though studies show that this practice does not increase winning rates or alumni donations ("Review & Outlook," *Wall Street Journal,* May 27, 2005, W15). Nonetheless, suppose that money does matter in producing championships. University A spends m_A on its football team and University B spends m_B. The fraction of the time that University A wins is $w_A = m_A/(m_A + m_B)$, and the fraction that B wins is $w_B = 1 - w_A = m_B/(m_A + m_B)$. Suppose that each university wants to maximize its profit from having sports teams. The expected profit of University i, $i = A, B$, is $\pi_i = v_i m_i/(m_A + m_B)$, where v_i is the value to University i of winning a game.

a. Show that if $v_A = v_B$, in the Nash-Cournot equilibrium each school wins one-half of its games.

b. Show that if $v_A = v_B$ increases, each school spends more on its teams but continues to win one-half of its games.

c. Explain the result that schools are spending more on sports without affecting their win-loss ratios. W

CROSS-CHAPTER ANALYSIS

Frequent Flier Programs

Imagine that you are working for an airline company just before frequent flier programs take off, and the president of the firm asks you to analyze whether the firm should institute a frequent flier program (FFP). In particular, she asks you to predict how an FFP will affect the price your firm will charge and its profit. She understands that if only one airline adopts an FFP, it will gain many extra customers. However, she suspects that if all airlines introduce the program, none may gain a substantial number of extra customers and all will incur the extra costs of the program. Is she correct that airlines will necessarily lose money by using FFPs?

Background

In May 1981, American Airlines launched AAdvantage, the first frequent flier program. American Airlines' objective was to retain its best customers by rewarding their loyalty with free tickets and upgrades. American Airlines used its Sabre computer reservation system to compile a database of 150,000 of its top customers. The company searched Sabre bookings for recurring phone numbers, which were then connected to customers' names. These customers were the initial members of AAdvantage.

Had other airlines not responded, American Airlines would have attracted many of its rivals' best customers. Unfortunately for American Airlines, within days after it introduced AAdvantage, United Airlines announced its own FFP, Mileage Plus. Later in that same year, both Delta and TWA introduced FFPs.

Today, there are more than 150 frequent flier programs worldwide. A customer's main incentive to join an FFP is to get free tickets. Of critical importance to airlines is that 94% of business travelers belong to at least one FFP and 60% belong to three or more programs. Airlines adopted these programs because 80% of business travelers—those with the least elastic demands and who are charged the highest prices—report that FFPs influence their travel decisions.

According to Randy Petersen, editor of *Inside Flyer* magazine, FFPs had 430 million members worldwide in 2006. These members held more than 14.2 trillion frequent-flier miles (credits), or an average of 33,035 miles per member, which is enough for a free U.S. domestic round-trip ticket on some carriers. Since the programs began, an estimated 280 million free trips have been redeemed. The share of people flying free to paying customers on U.S. airlines' domestic flights was 7.7% for the six largest carriers in 2006. Globally, members flew about 25 million free trips in 2006, up from about 22 million in 2000.

According to United Airlines, about 14% to 17% of the accumulated miles go unclaimed, though that share rises to 70% for JetBlue, whose credits expire in a year. (In short, good luck using JetBlue miles!) In 2007, many airlines announced that accumulated credits would expire within a year if the member's account was inactive, so the share of unclaimed miles may rise.

Although some carriers, such as Southwest, were originally reluctant to adopt FFPs, all major carriers have these programs and none have reservations about frequent flier programs, as these programs are now worth enormous amounts of money. Airline rewards programs make money by selling miles to banks or hotels to give to customers. An independent frequent flier program sells points to carriers, banks, retailers, and other customers, and then buys airline seats and other rewards at a discount, pocketing the difference. Air Canada received $300 million for a 14.4% share of its Aeroplan frequent flier program in 2005, implying that this business was worth about $2 billion. In 2007, Aeroplan had a market value of $4.5 billion, substantially more than Air Canada's $2.8 billion value. Morgan Stanley estimates that American's AAdvantage program, with more than 57 million members, could sell for $5.7 billion, which is about American's market value.

Because the major airlines usually limit FFP award tickets to flights with unsold seats, a seat costs the airline only $10 to $20: the cost of a few additional gallons of jet fuel and an extra bag of peanuts. However, some smaller airlines join alliances with other airlines and must pay their partners if one of their customers uses an FFP reward ticket on another alliance airline.

Task

On your major route, you face only one competitor, American Airlines, which, before the introduction of the FFP, flies the same number of passengers as your airline and has the same costs.

Your firm conducts a marketing study and concludes that this market has a constant elasticity demand curve (Chapter 3) and that if both firms introduce FFP programs, the elasticity of demand would change from −2 to −1.75. Each firm's FFP would raise its marginal cost (extra meals, extra fuel) per passenger from $150 to $160 per trip.

For simplicity, we assume that both your airline and American Airlines set a single price for tickets—that is, they do not price discriminate (Chapter 12)—they engage in a Cournot, Nash-in-quantities game (Chapter 13), and each customer joins only one FFP. Before making your recommendation, you need to determine how equilibrium prices will change if both firms adopt the FFP.

Analysis

If only one of the airlines adopts an FFP, it gains many extra customers. However, if both airlines introduce the program, it's possible that none gains a substantial number of extra customers, yet both incur the extra costs of the program. Does it follow that airlines are likely to lose money by using FFPs? Not necessarily.

Introducing an FFP allows your firm to differentiate its service (see Chapter 13): All else the same, a customer who belongs only to your FFP will prefer to fly on your airline than on your rival's if both charge the same price for a ticket. The rise in variable cost and the product differentiation both lead to higher equilibrium prices.

In the absence of FFPs, Kathy, a typical customer, flies on whichever airline has the least expensive ticket. If both set the same fare, Kathy chooses randomly between them. If both airlines introduce an FFP and Kathy joins one of these programs, say American Airlines' AAdvantage program, Kathy now prefers buying a ticket from American Airlines even if she has to pay slightly more than she would have to pay for a ticket from its rival. Thus, due to this product differentiation, Kathy has a less elastic demand for American Airlines' services. All else being the same, American Airlines can charge a higher fare, the less elastic is its demand curve. Before, if American raised its price above its rival's even slightly, it would have lost Kathy's business. Consequently, if each airline has its own loyal customers who belong to its FFP, each airline can raise its price in equilibrium because each faces a less elastic demand curve.

We can use Equation 13.8 to determine the Cournot equilibrium price, p, that each airline initially sets:

$$p = \frac{MC}{1 + 1/(n\varepsilon)},$$

where $MC = \$150$ is its marginal cost, $n = 2$ is the number of identical firms, and the market elasticity of demand is $\varepsilon = -2$. Thus, each airline sets its price at

$$p = \frac{\$150}{1 + 1/(2 \times -2)} = \$200.$$

When the airlines introduce FFPs, the elasticity of demand facing each airline falls to $\varepsilon = -1.75$ and the marginal cost rises to \$160, so the equilibrium price rises to

$$p = \frac{\$160}{1 + 1/(2 \times -1.75)} = \$224.$$

Thus, the FFPs cause prices to rise both because each firm's demand has become less elastic and because its marginal cost has increased.

Have the airlines benefited? The answer depends on whether their total profits have increased. The airlines benefit from higher revenues because they now face less elastic demand curves. However, their costs (including possibly fixed costs) are also higher. Thus, it is possible, but not certain, that they are better off having frequent flier programs than not. Presumably, the larger airlines, whose costs have not risen substantially due to FFPs, have benefited. Some of the smaller airlines that must pay allies for FFP tickets, such as Alaska, may have suffered.

Questions

Answers appear at the back of the book.

1. How much would the equilibrium price have risen if only the elasticity of demand had changed and not the marginal cost? If only the marginal cost had changed?
2. How has the firm's profit changed? Suppose that the firm's weekly constant elasticity demand curve is $Q = 50{,}000{,}000p^{\varepsilon}$.

14 Game Theory

A camper awakens to the growl of a hungry bear and sees his friend putting on a pair of running shoes. "You can't outrun a bear," scoffs the camper. His friend coolly replies, "I don't have to. I only have to outrun you!"

In deciding how to price its video game controller, Nintendo takes into account the pricing of its rivals, Microsoft and Sony. When a small number of people or firms interact, they know that their actions significantly affect each other's welfare or profit, so they consider those actions carefully.

Firms compete on many fronts beyond setting quantity or price. To gain an edge over rivals, a firm makes many decisions, such as how much to advertise, whether to act to discourage a new firm from entering its market, how to differentiate its product, and whether to invest in new equipment.

Over the last half-dozen years, French tire maker Michelin SCA and its Japanese competitor, Bridgestone Corp., have competed for bragging rights that they produce the world's fastest Formula One racing tires. They pour huge amounts of money into racing—\$70 million a year for Michelin and \$100 million for Bridgestone—so that the winner can claim in their advertising that they produce the fastest tires.

Since 1999, when Westin Hotels and Resorts introduced the Heavenly Bed, the major hotel chains have been engaging in a "bed war." Marriott International, like virtually every rival chain, recently upgraded its bedding to feature 300-thread-count sheets, a feathered mattress topper, stylish pillow shams, a decorative bed scarf, and extra pillows. In 2006, Hilton Hotels announced a \$1 billion effort that included the addition of its branded Serenity Bed to many of its properties, with its signature mattress pads, down pillows, linens, decorative bed pillows, and bolsters.[1] A hotel that won't compete in the bed war will lose customers.

And it's not just firms that have to consider the actions of others. When deciding how and when to bid on eBay for that 1957 Mickey Mantle baseball card or those cow-shaped salt and pepper shakers, you have to think about how other bidders are likely to behave.

In this chapter, we use game theory (von Neumann and Morgenstern, 1944) to examine how a small number of firms or individuals interact. **Game theory** is a set of tools that economists, political scientists, military analysts, and others use to analyze players' strategic decision making. This chapter introduces the basic concepts of game theory.[2] *Games* are competitions between players, such as individuals or firms, in which each player is aware that the outcome depends on the actions of all players.

game theory
a set of tools that economists, political scientists, military analysts and others use to analyze decision making by players who use strategies

[1]Christopher Elliot, "Détente in the Hotel Bed Wars," *New York Times*, January 31, 2006.

[2]For more details, see, for example, Fudenberg and Tirole (1991) or Gibbons (1992). For an interesting, brief history, see **www.econ.canterbury.ac.nz/personal_pages/paul_walker/gt/hist.htm**.

line example, both Larry and Duncan confess even though they are better off if they both keep quiet.

Iterated Elimination of Strictly Dominated Strategies. In games where not all players have a dominant strategy, we cannot precisely identify the outcome of the game from what we know so far. Table 14.2 shows the normal-form representation of the game between United and American Airlines where they can each choose between three possible actions: fly 96, 64, or 48 thousand passengers per quarter between Chicago and Los Angeles.

Neither firm has a strictly dominant strategy in this game. As we showed before, if United chooses $q_U = 64$ or 48, American's profit is highest if it sets $q_A = 64$. However, if United selects $q_U = 96$, American's best action is to set $q_A = 48$.[3] Thus, none of American's possible strategies is a dominant strategy: a single strategy that always produces the highest profit regardless of United's actions. Rather, the strategy that maximizes American's payoff depends on United's action.

Nonetheless, we can determine the outcome of this game by generalizing our earlier logic. Because we know that a firm will not use a strategy that is strictly dominated by another strategy, we can eliminate any strictly dominated strategy. By eliminating such strategies repeatedly, we can predict a unique set of strategies.

In Table 14.2, American's strategy of $q_A = 96$ is strictly dominated by its alternative strategy of $q_A = 64$. Regardless of which strategy United uses, $q_A = 64$ produces a higher profit for American than does $q_A = 96$. Similarly, United's strategy of $q_U = 96$ is strictly dominated by its $q_U = 64$ strategy. Consequently, we draw a red line through the $q_A = 96$ column and through the $q_U = 96$ row to show that the firms will not use these strictly dominated strategies.

After we eliminate these strategies, the remaining payoff matrix is the same 2×2 matrix as in Table 14.1: The firms choose to fly either 64 or 48 thousand passengers per quarter. From our previous analysis, we know that choosing 48 is

Table 14.2 Profit Matrix for a Quantity-Setting Game: Iterated Dominance.

		American Airlines	
United Airlines	$q_A = 96$	$q_A = 64$	$q_A = 48$
$q_U = 96$	\$0 \$0	\$2.0 \$3.1	\$2.3 \$4.6
$q_U = 64$	\$3.1 \$2.0	\$4.1 \$4.1	\$3.8 \$5.1
$q_U = 48$	\$4.6 \$2.3	\$5.1 \$3.8	\$4.6 \$4.6

Note: Quantities are in thousands of passengers per quarter; (rounded) profits are in millions of dollars per quarter.

[3]Given that $q_U = 96$, American's profit is \$2.3 million if $q_A = 48$, \$2.0 million if $q_A = 64$, and \$0 if $q_A = 96$.

strictly dominated by the strategy of choosing 64, so we draw a green line through the dominated strategies within the 2 × 2 matrix. By this *iterated elimination of strictly dominated strategies*, we again predict that the firms will each choose to fly 64 thousand passengers per quarter.

The dominant strategy approach is a special case of the iterated elimination of strictly dominated strategies, because the dominant strategy was determined by eliminating all inferior strategies. The iterated approach is based on the belief that players will not choose strictly dominated strategies. However, to rely on this approach, we have to assume that the players possess common knowledge that they are payoff maximizing, that the players know that the other players are payoff maximizing, and that the players know that all the players know that the other players are payoff maximizing, and so forth.

Even given that we are willing to make these strong assumptions about common knowledge, iterative elimination of strictly dominated strategies does not always allow us to make precise predictions about the outcome of a game. In many games, we cannot eliminate all but one strategy for each player.

Best Response and Nash Equilibrium. When iterative elimination of strictly dominated strategies fails to predict a unique outcome, we can use a related concept. For any given set of strategies chosen by rivals, a player wants to use its **best response**—the strategy that maximizes a player's payoff given its beliefs about its rivals' strategies. A dominant strategy is one that is a best response to all possible strategies that a rival might use. However, a particular strategy might be a best response for some rival strategies but not for others. Given that firms always choose a best response, we can accurately forecast the outcome of many games that we cannot precisely predict using the iterated elimination of strictly dominated strategies.

best response
the strategy that maximizes a player's payoff given its beliefs about its rivals' strategies

Economists usually rely on a solution concept introduced by John Nash (1951) that is based on the belief that players use their best responses. Formally, a set of strategies is a **Nash equilibrium** if, when all other players use these strategies, no player can obtain a higher payoff by choosing a different strategy.[4] An appealing property of the Nash equilibrium is that it is self-enforcing. If each player uses a Nash equilibrium strategy, then no player wants to deviate by choosing another strategy.

Nash equilibrium
a set of strategies such that, when all other players use these strategies, no player can obtain a higher payoff by choosing a different strategy

The Nash equilibrium is a stronger solution conception than the iterated elimination of strictly dominated strategies. Not all Nash equilibria can be determined using the iterated elimination of strictly dominated strategies. However, if the iterated elimination of strictly dominated strategies produces a solution consisting of a single pair of strategies, then that combination of strategies is the unique Nash equilibrium in that game.

We can use the profit matrix in Table 14.1 to illustrate that the pair of strategies we chose using iterated elimination of strictly dominated strategies is a Nash equilibrium. By eliminating strictly dominated strategies, we concluded that both firms want to set output at 64. Would either firm want to deviate from that proposed outcome? If American knew that United would set $q_U = 64$, American would not switch to $q_A = 48$, because its profit would fall from \$4.1 million to \$3.8 million. By the same reasoning, United would not want change strategies either. That is, given that the other firm chooses 64, the strategy of 64 is a firm's best response. Because nei-

[4]In Chapter 13, we used a special case of this definition of a Nash equilibrium in which we referred to actions instead of strategies. An action and a strategy are the same if the players can move only once; however, later in this chapter, we will consider games that last for many periods and hence need a definition based on strategies.

ther firm wants to change its strategy given that the other firm is playing its Nash equilibrium strategy, the pair of strategies $q_A = q_U = 64$ is a Nash equilibrium.

Moreover, for any other combination of strategies, one or the other firm would want to change its behavior; hence, none of the other strategy pairs is a Nash equilibrium. At $q_A = q_U = 48$, either firm could raise its profit from $4.6 to $5.1 million by increasing its output to 64. At $q_A = 48$ and $q_U = 64$, American can raise its profit from $3.8 to $4.1 million by increasing its quantity to $q_A = 64$. Similarly, United would want to increase its output when $q_A = 64$ and $q_U = 48$.

See Questions 2–4 and Problem 23.

A similar analysis applies to the more general Cournot model (Chapter 13), where firms can pick any output they desire. That model can be presented as a normal-form game with n players (firms), a choice of strategies (any real-number, nonnegative quantity), and a payoff function that is common knowledge (that is, all firms know the profit function of each firm). We derived the Nash equilibrium to that game by finding those quantities that were best responses for all the firms. It is possible to obtain that Nash equilibrium in a linear, duopoly Cournot model by iterative elimination of strictly dominated strategies. With three or more firms, iterative elimination provides only the imprecise observation that each firm's quantity will not exceed the monopoly quantity (Gibbons, 1992). In Chapter 13, we showed that we could obtain the Nash equilibrium using best-response functions with three or more firms.

See Problems 24–26.

In games where iterated elimination of strictly dominated strategies does not determine a single pair of strategies, there may be a single Nash equilibrium (such as the Cournot model with three or more firms), multiple Nash equilibria, or no Nash equilibrium. We now turn to examples of the latter two possibilities.

Multiple Nash Equilibria, No Nash Equilibrium, and Mixed Strategies

In accordance with our principles of free enterprise and healthy competition, I'm going to ask you two to fight to the death for it. —Monty Python

pure strategy
each player chooses an action with certainty

mixed strategy
a firm (player) chooses among possible actions according to probabilities it assigns

In each of the games we have considered so far, there is only one Nash equilibrium, and the firms use a **pure strategy**: Each player chooses a single action. We now turn to an entry game that has more than one Nash equilibrium in pure strategies. Moreover, in addition to using a pure strategy, a firm in this entry game may employ a **mixed strategy** in which the player chooses among possible actions according to probabilities it assigns. A pure strategy assigns a probability of 1 to a single action, whereas a mixed strategy is a probability distribution over actions. That is, a pure strategy is a rule telling the player what action to take, whereas a mixed strategy is a rule telling the player which dice to throw, coin to flip, or other device to use to choose an action.

An entry game has both pure and mixed-strategy Nash equilibria. Suppose that two firms are considering opening gas stations at a highway rest stop that has no gas stations. There's enough physical space for at most two gas stations. The profit matrix in Table 14.3 shows that there is enough demand for only one station to operate profitably. If both firms enter, each loses $1 (hundred thousand). Neither firm has a dominant strategy. Each firm's best action depends on what the other firm does.

Pure Strategies. This game has two Nash equilibria in pure strategies: Firm 1 *enters* and Firm 2 *does not enter*, or Firm 2 *enters* and Firm 1 *does not enter*. The equilibrium in which only Firm 1 enters is Nash because neither firm wants to

Table 14.3 Simultaneous Entry Game.

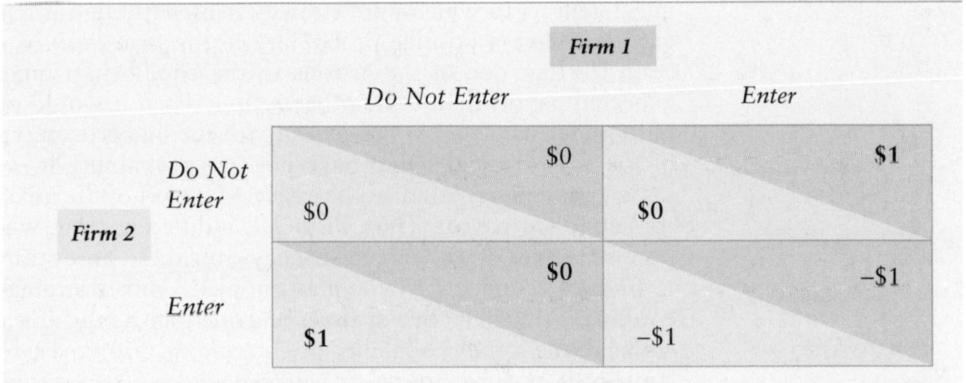

		Firm 1	
		Do Not Enter	*Enter*
Firm 2	*Do Not Enter*	$0 $0	$1 $0
	Enter	$0 $1	–$1 –$1

change its behavior. Given that Firm 2 does not enter, Firm 1 does not want to change its strategy from entering to staying out of the market. If it changed its behavior, it would go from earning $1 to earning nothing. Similarly, given that Firm 1 enters, Firm 2 does not want to switch its behavior and enter because it would lose $1 instead of making $0. Where only Firm 2 enters is also a Nash equilibrium by the same type of reasoning.

How do the players know which (if any) Nash equilibrium will result? They *don't* know. It is difficult to see how the firms choose strategies unless they collude and can enforce their agreement. For example, the firm that enters could pay the other firm to stay out of the market. Without an enforceable collusive agreement, even discussions between the firms before decisions are made are unlikely to help. These pure Nash equilibria are unappealing because they call for identical firms to use different strategies.

★ **Mixed Strategies.**[5] Both firms may use the same mixed strategy. When both firms enter with a probability of one-half—say, if a flipped coin comes up heads—there is a Nash equilibrium in mixed strategies because neither firm wants to change its strategy, given that the other firm uses its Nash equilibrium mixed strategy.

If both firms use this mixed strategy, each of the four outcomes in the payoff matrix in Table 14.3 is equally likely. Firm 1 has a one-fourth chance of earning $1 (upper-right cell), a one-fourth chance of losing $1 (lower-right cell), and a one-half chance of earning $0 (upper-left and lower-left cells).[6] Thus, Firm 1's expected profit—the firm's profit in each possible outcome times the probability of that outcome—is

$$(\$1 \times \tfrac{1}{4}) + (-\$1 \times \tfrac{1}{4}) + (\$0 \times \tfrac{1}{2}) = \$0.$$

Given that Firm 1 uses this mixed strategy, Firm 2 cannot achieve a higher expected profit by using a pure strategy. If Firm 2 uses the pure strategy of entering with probability 1, it earns $1 half the time and loses $1 the other half, so its expected profit is $0. If it stays out with certainty, Firm 2 earns $0 with certainty.

---

[5]This section requires an understanding of probabilities. It can be skipped without affecting one's understanding of other sections in this chapter.

[6]The probability that the outcome is a particular cell of the matrix is the product of the probability that each player chooses the relevant action. The probability that a player chooses a given action is $\frac{1}{2}$, so the probability that both players will choose the relevant actions is $\frac{1}{2} \times \frac{1}{2} = \frac{1}{4}$.

If Firm 2 believes that Firm 1 will use its equilibrium mixed strategy, Firm 2 is indifferent as to which pure strategy it uses (though it considers only those strategies that have a positive probability in the firm's mixed strategy). Suppose to the contrary that one of the actions in the equilibrium mixed strategy had a higher expected payoff than some other action. Then it would pay to increase the probability that Firm 2 takes the action with the higher expected payoff. However, if all of the pure strategies that have positive probability in a mixed strategy have the same expected payoff, then the expected payoff of the mixed strategy must also have that expected payoff. Thus, Firm 2 is indifferent as to whether it uses any of these pure strategies or any mixed strategy over these pure strategies.

In our example, why would a firm pick a mixed strategy where its probability of entering is one-half? In a symmetric game such as this one, we know that both players have the same probability of entering, θ. Moreover, for Firm 2 to use a mixed strategy, it must be indifferent between entering or not entering if Firm 1 enters with probability θ. Firm 2's payoff from entering is $[\theta \times (-1)] + [(1 - \theta) \times 1] = 1 - 2\theta$. Its payoff from not entering is $[\theta \times 0] + [(1 - \theta) \times 0] = 0$. Equating these two expected profits, $1 - 2\theta = 0$, and solving, we find that $\theta = \frac{1}{2}$. Thus, both firms using a mixed strategy where they enter with a probability of one-half is a Nash equilibrium.

Possible Equilibria. This game has two pure-strategy Nash equilibria—one firm employing the pure strategy of entering and the other firm pursuing the pure strategy of not entering—and a mixed-strategy Nash equilibrium. If Firm 1 decides to *enter* with a probability of one-half, Firm 2 is indifferent between choosing to enter with probability of 1 (the pure strategy of *enter*), 0 (the pure strategy of *do not enter*), or any fraction in between these extremes. However, for the firms' strategies to constitute a mixed-strategy Nash equilibrium, both firms must choose to enter with a probability of one-half.

See Question 6 and Problems 27–30.

One important reason for introducing the concept of a mixed strategy is that some games have no pure-strategy Nash equilibria (see Solved Problem 14.1). However, Nash (1950) proved that every static game with a finite number of players and a finite number of actions has at least one Nash equilibrium, which may involve mixed strategies.

Some game theorists argue that mixed strategies are implausible because firms do not flip coins to choose strategies. One response is that firms may only appear to be unpredictable. In this game with no dominant strategies, neither firm has a strong reason to believe that the other will choose a pure strategy. It may think about its rival's behavior as random. However, in actual games, a firm may use some information or reasoning that its rival does not observe in choosing a pure strategy. Another response is that a mixed strategy may be appealing in some games, such as the entry game or the similar game of chicken, where a random strategy and symmetry between players are plausible.

APPLICATION

Playing Chicken

Two cars simultaneously approach an intersection that has no stop signs or traffic lights. Which driver stops? Or do the cars collide?

This game is rarely played at U.S. intersections, where stop signs or traffic lights are common. Moreover, at U.S. intersections without traffic signs or signals, the traffic rule is that if two cars arrive simultaneously at the intersection, the car to the left yields to the car approaching from the first car's right. France also uses that rule, called *priorité de droite*.

In contrast, Belgium, which has few traffic signs or signals, does not currently use a yield-to-the-right rule. Even worse, a driver in Belgium who stops to look both ways at an intersection loses the legal right to proceed first. A driver who merely taps his brakes can find that his pause has sent a dangerous signal to other drivers: Any sign of hesitation often spurs other drivers to hit the gas in a race to get through the crossing first. The result is a game of chicken, where to slow down is to "show weakness," according to Belgian traffic court lawyer Virginie Delannoy.[7] Neither driver wants to lose the game, Delannoy says, adding: "And then, bam!" Formally, chicken is the same as the entry game: Disaster occurs if both players enter the intersection at the same time. Strangely, proposals to put signs at crossroads or to adopt the yield-to-the-right rule are very unpopular in Belgium.

The absence of signs and rules may explain the unusually high accident rate in Belgium. Failing to yield is the cause of more than two-thirds of the accidents at unmarked Belgian intersections that result in bodily injury. Last year, there were 11.2 deaths per 100,000 Belgians. In bordering countries with more stop signs and traffic lights and explicit rules about yielding the right of way, the accident death rate is much lower: only 4.6 per 100,000 in the Netherlands, 6.1 in Germany, and 8.7 in France.

See Problems 31 and 32.

Solved Problem 14.1

Mimi wants to support her son Jeff if he looks for work but not otherwise. Jeff wants to try to find a job only if Mimi will not support his life of indolence. Their payoff matrix is

		Jeff	
		Look for Work	*Loaf*
Mimi	*Support*	2 4	4 −1
	No Support	1 −1	0 0

If they choose actions simultaneously, what are the pure- or mixed-strategy equilibria?

Answer

1. *Check whether any of the four possible pairs of pure strategies is a Nash equilibrium.* The four possible pure-strategy equilibria are support/look, support/loaf, no support/look, and no support/loaf. None of these pairs of pure strategies is a Nash equilibrium because one or the other player would want

[7]Bertrand Russell observed that nuclear brinksmanship is essentially a game of chicken.

to change his or her strategy. The pair of strategies support/look is not a Nash equilibrium because, given that Mimi provides support, Jeff would have a higher payoff loafing, 4, than looking for work, 2. Support/loaf is not a Nash equilibrium because Mimi prefers not to support the bum, 0, to providing support, −1. We can reject no support/loaf because Jeff would prefer to search for work, 1, out of desperation rather than loaf, 0. Finally, no support/look is not a Nash equilibrium because Mimi would prefer to support her wonderful son, 4, rather than to feel guilty about not rewarding his search efforts, −1.

2. *By equating expected payoffs, determine the mixed-strategy equilibrium.* If Mimi provides support with probability θ_M, Jeff's expected payoff from looking for work is $2\theta_M + [1 \times (1 - \theta_M)] = 1 + \theta_M$, and his expected payoff from loafing is $4\theta_M + [0 \times (1 - \theta_M)] = 4\theta_M$. Thus, his expected payoffs are equal if $1 + \theta_M = 4\theta_M$, or $\theta_M = \frac{1}{3}$. Similarly, if Jeff looks for work with probability θ_J, then Mimi's expected payoff from supporting him is $4\theta_J + [(-1) \times (1 - \theta_J)] = 5\theta_J - 1$, and her expected payoff from not supporting him is $-\theta_J + [0 \times (1 - \theta_J)] = -\theta_J$. By equating her expected payoffs, $5\theta_J - 1 = -\theta_J$, we determine that his mixed-strategy probability is $\theta_J = \frac{1}{6}$.

Comment: Although this game has no pure-strategy Nash equilibria, it does have a mixed-strategy Nash equilibrium.

See Question 5.

Cooperation

Whether players cooperate in a static game depends on the payoff function. Table 14.4 shows an advertising game in which each firm can choose to advertise or not, with two possible payoff functions. The unique Nash equilibrium maximizes the collective payoff to the players in the second game, but the unique Nash equilibrium in the first game is not the cooperative outcome.

The game in panel a is a prisoners' dilemma game similar to the airline game in Table 14.4. Each firm has a dominant strategy: to advertise. In this Nash equilibrium, each firm earns \$1 million, which is less than the \$2 million it would make if neither firm advertised. Thus, *the sum of the firms' profits is not maximized in this simultaneous-choice one-period game.*

Many people are surprised the first time they hear this result. Why don't the firms cooperate and use the individually and jointly more profitable low-output strategies, by which each earns a profit of \$2 million instead of the \$1 million in the Nash equilibrium? The reason they don't cooperate is a lack of trust. Each firm uses the no-advertising strategy only if the firms have a binding (enforceable) agreement. The reason they do not trust each other is that each firm knows it is in the other firm's best interest to deviate from the actions that would maximize joint profits.

Suppose the two firms meet in advance and agree not to advertise. If the firms are going to engage in this game only once, each has an incentive to cheat on the agreement. If Firm 1 believes that Firm 2 will stick to the agreement and not advertise, Firm 1 can increase its profit from \$2 million to \$3 million by violating the agreement and advertising. Moreover, if Firm 1 thinks that Firm 2 will cheat on the agreement by advertising, Firm 1 wants to advertise (so that it will earn \$1 million rather than \$0). By this reasoning, each firm has a substantial profit incentive to cheat on the agreement. In this game, all else the same, if one firm advertises, its sales increase so that its profit rises, but its rival loses customers and hence the rival's profit falls.

In contrast, in panel b, when either firm advertises, the promotion attracts new customers to both firms. If neither firm advertises, both earn \$2 (million). If only

Table 14.4 Advertising Game.

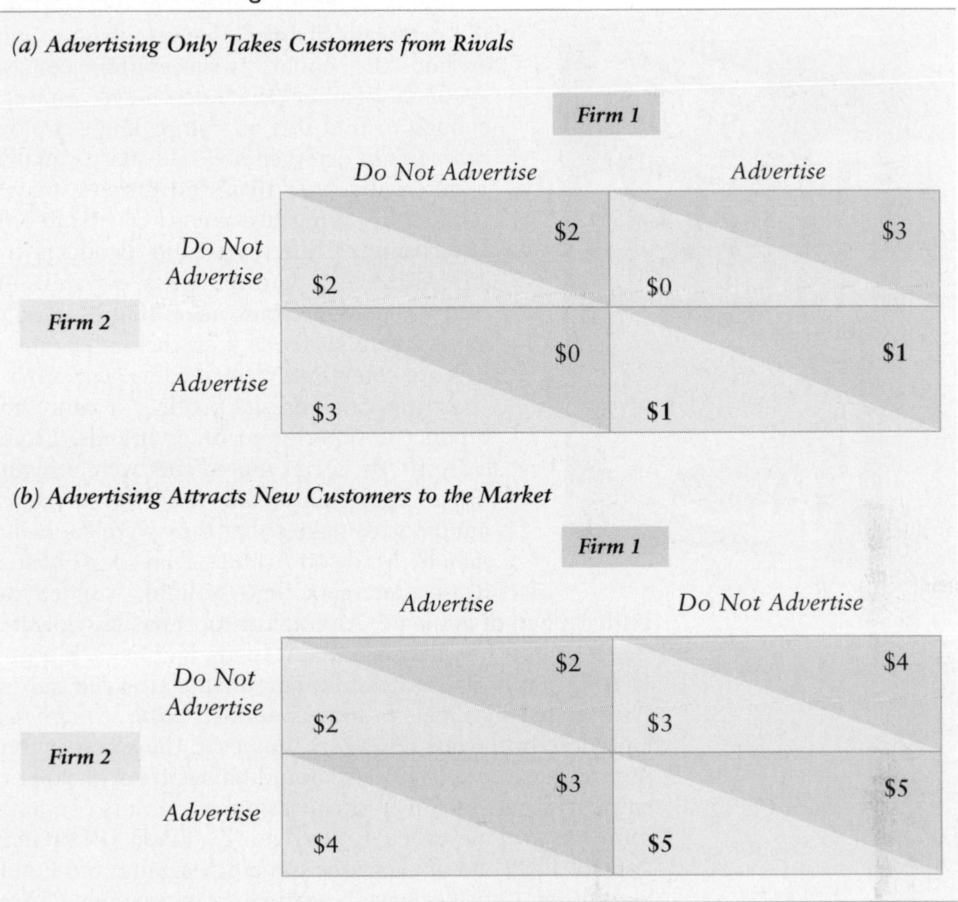

(a) Advertising Only Takes Customers from Rivals

Firm 2 \ Firm 1	*Do Not Advertise*	*Advertise*
Do Not Advertise	$2 / $2	$3 / $0
Advertise	$0 / $3	$1 / $1

(b) Advertising Attracts New Customers to the Market

Firm 2 \ Firm 1	*Advertise*	*Do Not Advertise*
Do Not Advertise	$2 / $2	$4 / $3
Advertise	$3 / $4	$5 / $5

See Question 7.

one firm advertises, its profit rises to $4, which is more than the $3 that the other firm makes. If both advertise, they are better off than if only one advertises or neither advertises. Again, advertising is a dominant strategy for both firms (as you are asked to prove in Question 7 at the end of the chapter). In the Nash equilibrium, both firms advertise.

Both firms advertise in the games in panel a and panel b. The distinction is that the Nash equilibrium in which both advertise is the same as the collusive equilibrium in panel b where advertising increases the market size, but it is not the collusive equilibrium in panel a. When advertising cannibalizes the sales of other firms in the market in panel a, the payoffs are lower in the equilibrium in which they advertise.

APPLICATION

Strategic Advertising

A firm may advertise to inform consumers about a new use for its product. Its advertising may cause the quantity demanded for its own *and* rival brands to rise.

Toothpaste ads provide an example. Before World War I, only 26% of Americans brushed their teeth. By 1926, in part because of ads like those in Ipana's "pink toothbrush" campaign, which detailed the perils of bleeding gums, the share of Americans who brushed rose to 40%. Ipana's advertising helped all manufacturers of toothbrushes and toothpaste.

Although it's difficult to believe, starting in the 1970s, Wisk liquid detergent claimed that it solved a major social problem: ring around the collar (**www.youtube.com/watch?v=H5ro68Xs4Lc**). Presumably, some consumers—even among those who were gullible enough to find this ad compelling—could generalize that applying other liquid detergents would work equally well.

Alternatively, a firm's advertising may increase demand for its product by taking customers away from other firms. A firm may use advertising to differentiate its products from those of rivals. The advertising may describe actual physical differences in the products or try to convince customers that essentially identical products differ. If a firm succeeds with this latter type of advertising, the products are sometimes described as *spuriously* differentiated.

A firm can raise its profit if it can convince consumers that its product is superior to other brands. From the 1930s through the early 1970s, *secret ingredients* were a mainstay of consumer advertising. These ingredients were given names combining letters and numbers to suggest that they were cooked up in laboratories rather than by Madison Avenue. Dial soap boasted that it contained AT-7. Rinso detergent had solium, Comet included Chlorinol, and Bufferin had di-alminate. Among the toothpastes, Colgate had Gardol, Gleem had GL-70, Crest had fluoristan, and Ipana had hexachlorophene and Durenamel.

About 30 years ago, secret ingredient claims fell out of favor, and manufacturers asserted that their brands contained *natural ingredients* such as baking soda and aloe. In the last few years, however, the secret ingredient approach has been reintroduced to differentiate brand names from cheaper competitors. Ads remind us that Clorets breath-freshening gum and mints contain Actizol. Cheer detergent touts an enzyme called Color Guard; Shade UVA Guard sunscreen lotion has Parasol 1789 and oxybenzone sun block agents; and Pond's Dramatic Results Skin Smoothing Capsules have Nutrium, "a miraculous oil-free complex."

Empirical evidence indicates that the impact of a firm's advertising on other firms varies across industries. At one extreme is cigarette advertising. Roberts and Samuelson (1988) found that cigarette advertising is cooperative in the sense that it increases the size of the market but does not change market shares substantially.[8] At the other extreme is cola advertising. Gasmi, Laffont, and Vuong (1992) reported that each firm's gain from advertising comes at the expense of its rivals; however, cola advertising has almost no effect on total market demand. Slade (1995) found results for saltine crackers that lie between these extremes.

If these empirical results are correct, cola firms would be delighted to have their advertising banned, but cigarette firms would oppose an advertising ban. In a more general model in which firms set the amount of advertising (rather than just decide whether to advertise or not), the amount of advertising depends critically on whether advertising increases the market size or only steals customers from rivals.

[8]However, the Centers for Disease Control and Prevention's evidence suggests that advertising may shift the brand loyalty of youths.

14.3 Dynamic Games

In static, normal-form games, players have imperfect information about how other players will act because everyone moves simultaneously and only once. In contrast, in *dynamic games* players move sequentially or move simultaneously repeatedly over time, so a player has perfect information about other players' previous moves. In this section, we show how to represent these static games diagrammatically and how to predict their outcomes.

extensive form
specifies the n players, the sequence in which they make their moves, the actions they can take at each move, the information that each player has about players' previous moves, and the payoff function over all the possible strategies

Rather than use the normal form, economists analyze dynamic games in their **extensive form**, which specifies the n players, the sequence in which they make their moves, the actions they can take at each move, the information that each player has about players' previous moves, and the payoff function over all possible strategies. In this section, we assume that players not only have complete information about the payoff function but also have perfect information about the play of the game to this point.

We consider two types of dynamic games. We start with a *two-stage game*, which is played once and hence can be said to occur in a "single period." In the first stage, Player 1 moves. In the second stage, Player 2 moves and the game ends with the players' receiving payoffs based on their actions. An example of such a game is the Stackelberg model.

We then examine a *repeated* or *multiperiod* game in which a single-period, simultaneous-move game, such as the airline prisoners' dilemma game, is repeated at least twice and possibly many times. Although the players move simultaneously in each period, they know about their rivals' moves in previous periods, so a rival's previous move may affect a player's current action. As a result, it is a dynamic game.

In games where players move sequentially, we have to clearly distinguish between an action and a strategy. An *action* is a move that a player makes at a specified point, such as how much output a firm produces this period. A *strategy* is a battle plan that specifies the action that a player will make conditional on the information available at each move. For example, American's strategy might state that it will fly 64 thousand passengers between Chicago and Los Angeles this quarter if United flew 64 thousand last quarter, but that it will fly only 48 thousand this quarter if United flew 48 thousand last quarter. This distinction between an action and a strategy is moot in a simultaneous-move, static game, where an action and a strategy are effectively the same.

Sequential Game

In solving a problem of this sort, the grand thing is to be able to reason backward. — Sherlock Holmes (Sir Arthur Conan Doyle)

We illustrate a sequential-move or two-stage game using the Stackelberg airline model (Chapter 13), where American chooses its output level before United does. For simplicity, we assume that American and United Airlines can choose only output levels of 96, 64, and 48 million passengers per quarter.

Game Tree. The normal-form representation of this game, Table 14.2, does not capture the sequential nature of the firms' moves. To demonstrate the role of sequential moves, we use an *extensive-form diagram* or *game tree*, Figure 14.1, which shows the order of the firms' moves, each firm's possible actions at the time of its move, and the resulting profits at the end of the game.

In the figure, each box is a point of decision by one of the firms, called a *decision node*. The name in the decision node box indicates that it is that player's turn to

Figure 14.1 Stackelberg Game Tree.

American, the leader firm, chooses its output level first. Given American's choice, United, the follower, picks an output level. The firms' profits that result from these decisions are shown on the right side of the figure. Two lines through an action line indicate that the firm rejects that action.

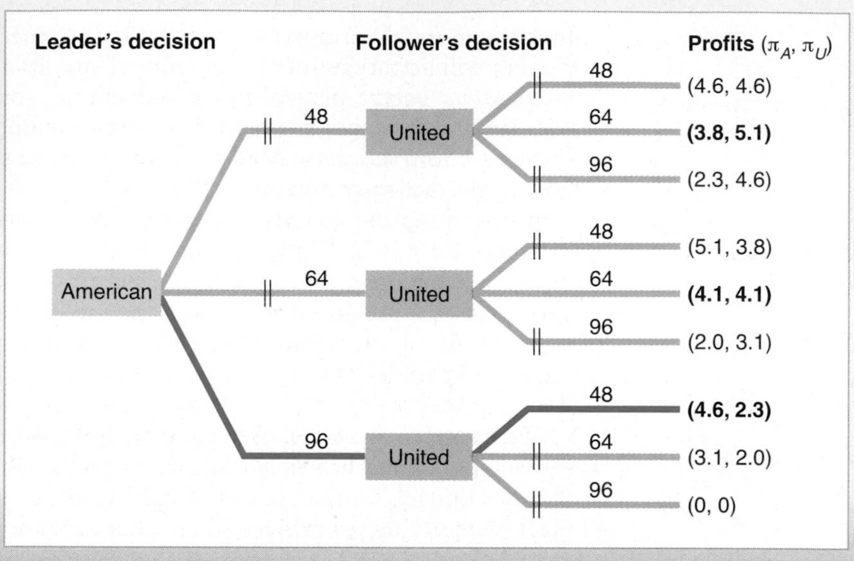

move. The lines or *branches* extending out of the box represent a complete list of the possible actions that the player can make at that point of the game. On the left side of the figure, American, the leader, starts by picking one of the three output levels. In the middle of the figure, United, the follower, chooses one of the three quantities after learning the output level American chose. The right side of the figure shows the profits that American and United earn, given that they sequentially took the actions to reach this final branch. For instance, if American selects 64 and then United chooses 96, American earns \$2.0 million profit per quarter and United earns \$3.1 million.

subgame
all the subsequent decisions that players may make given the actions already taken and corresponding payoffs

Within this game are *subgames*. At a given stage, a **subgame** consists of all the subsequent decisions that players may make given the actions already taken and corresponding payoffs. In the second stage where United makes a choice, there are three possible subgames. In Figure 14.1, if in the first stage American chooses q_A = 48, the relevant subgame is the top node in the second stage and its three branches. This game has four subgames. There are three subgames at the second stage where United makes a decision given each of American's three possible first-stage actions. There is an additional subgame at the time of the first-stage decision, which is the entire game.

subgame perfect Nash equilibrium
players' strategies are a Nash equilibrium in every subgame

Subgame Perfect Nash Equilibrium. To predict the outcome of this sequential game, we introduce a stronger version of the Nash equilibrium concept. A set of strategies forms a **subgame perfect Nash equilibrium** if the players' strategies are a Nash equilibrium in every subgame. As the entire dynamic game is a subgame, a subgame perfect Nash equilibrium is also a Nash equilibrium. In contrast, in a simultaneous-move game such as the static prisoners' dilemma, the only subgame is the game itself, so there is no important distinction between the Nash equilibrium and the subgame perfect Nash equilibrium.

Table 14.2 shows the normal-form representation of this game in which the Nash equilibrium to the simultaneous-move game is for each firm to choose 64. However, if the firms move sequentially, the subgame perfect Nash equilibrium results in a different outcome.

backward induction
first determine the best response by the last player to move, next determine the best response for the player who made the next-to-last move, then repeat the process back to the move at the beginning of the game

We can solve for the subgame perfect Nash equilibrium using **backward induction**, where we first determine the best response by the last player to move, next determine the best response for the player who made the next-to-last move, and then repeat the process until we reach the move at the beginning of the game. In our example, we work backward from the decision by the follower, United, to the decision by the leader, American, moving from the right to the left side of the game tree.

How should American, the leader, select its output in the first stage? For each possible quantity it can produce, American predicts what United will do and picks the output level that maximizes its own profit. Thus, to predict American's action in the first stage, American determines what United, the follower, will do in the second stage, given each possible output choice by American in the first stage. Using its conclusions about United's second-stage reaction, American makes its first-stage decision.

United, the follower, does not have a dominant strategy. The amount it chooses to produce depends on the quantity that American chose. If American chose 96, United's profit is $2.3 million if its output is 48, $2.0 million if it produces 64, and $0 if it picks a quantity of 96. Thus, if American chose 96, United's best response is 48. The double lines through the other two action lines show that United will not choose those actions.

Using the same reasoning, American determines how United will respond to each of American's possible actions, as the right side of the figure illustrates. American predicts that

- If American chooses 48, United will sell 64, so American's profit will be $3.8 million.
- If American chooses 64, United will sell 64, so American's profit will be $4.1 million.
- If American chooses 96, United will sell 48, so American's profit will be $4.6 million.

Thus, to maximize its profit, American chooses 96 in the first stage. United's strategy is to make its best response to American's first-stage action: United selects 64 if American chooses 48 or 64, and United picks 48 if American chooses 96. Thus, United responds in the second stage by selecting 48. In this subgame perfect Nash equilibrium, neither firm wants to change its strategy. Given that American Airlines sets its output at 96, United is using a strategy that maximizes its profit, $q_U = 48$, so it doesn't want to change. Similarly, given how United will respond to each possible American output level, American cannot make more profit than if it sells 96.

The subgame perfect Nash equilibrium requires players to believe that their opponents will act optimally—in their own best interests. No player has an incentive to deviate from the equilibrium strategies. The reason for adding the requirement of subgame perfection is that we want to explain what will happen if a player does not follow the equilibrium path. For example, if American does not choose its equilibrium output in the first stage, subgame perfection requires that United will still follow the strategy that maximizes its profit in the second stage conditional on American's actual output choice.

Not all Nash equilibria are subgame perfect Nash equilibria. For example, suppose that American's strategy is to pick 96 in the first stage, and United's strategy is to choose 96 if American selects 48 or 64, and 48 if American chooses 96. The outcome is the same as the subgame perfect Nash equilibrium we just derived because American selects 96, United chooses 48, and neither firm wants to deviate.[9] Thus,

[9]Given United's strategy, American does not have any incentive to deviate. If American chooses 48 it will get $2.3 million and if it chooses 64 it will get $2.0 million, both of which are less than the $4.6 million if it chooses 96. And given American's strategy, no change in United's strategy would raise its profit.

this set of strategies is a Nash equilibrium. However, this set of strategies is not a subgame perfect Nash equilibrium. Although this Nash equilibrium has the same equilibrium path as the subgame perfect Nash equilibrium, United's strategy differs out of the equilibrium path. If American had selected 48 (or 64), United's strategy would not result in a Nash equilibrium. United would receive a higher profit if it produced 64 rather than the 96 that this strategy requires. Therefore, this Nash equilibrium is not subgame perfect.

This subgame perfect Nash equilibrium, or Stackelberg equilibrium, differs from the simultaneous-move, Nash-Cournot equilibrium. American, the Stackelberg leader, sells 50% more than the Cournot quantity, 64, and earns $4.6 million, which is 15% more than the Cournot level of profit, $4.1 million. United, the Stackelberg follower, sells a quantity, 48, and earns a profit, $2.3 million, both of which are less than the Cournot levels. Thus, although United has more information in the Stackelberg equilibrium than it does in the Cournot model—it knows American's output level—it is worse off than if both firms chose their actions simultaneously.

Credibility. Why do the simultaneous-move and sequential-move games have different outcomes? Given the option to act first, American chooses a large output level to make it in United's best interest to pick a relatively small output level, 48. American benefits from moving first and choosing the Stackelberg leader quantity.

In the simultaneous-move game, why doesn't American announce that it will produce the Stackelberg leader's output to induce United to produce the Stackelberg follower's output level? The answer is that when the firms move simultaneously, United doesn't believe American's warning that it will produce a large quantity, because it is not in American's best interest to produce that large a quantity of output. For a firm's announced strategy to be a **credible threat**, rivals must believe that the firm's strategy is rational in the sense that it is in the firm's best interest to use it.[10] If American produced the leader's level of output and United produced the Cournot level, American's profit would be lower than if it too produced the Cournot level. Because American cannot be sure that United will believe its threat and reduce its output in the simultaneous-move game, American produces the Cournot output level. In contrast, in the sequential-move game, because American moves first, its commitment to produce a large quantity is credible.

credible threat
an announcement that a firm will use a strategy harmful to its rival and that the rival believes because the firm's strategy is rational in the sense that it is in the firm's best interest to use it

The intuition for why commitment makes a threat credible is that of "burning bridges." If the general burns the bridge behind the army so that the troops can only advance and not retreat, the army becomes a more fearsome foe—like a cornered animal. Similarly, by limiting its future options, a firm makes itself stronger.[11]

Not all firms can make credible threats, however, because not all firms can make commitments. Typically, for a threat to succeed, a firm must have an advantage that allows it to harm the other firm before that firm can retaliate. Identical firms that act simultaneously cannot credibly threaten each other. However, a firm may be able

---

[10]No doubt you've been in a restaurant and listened to an exasperated father trying to control his brat with such extreme threats as "If you don't behave, you'll have to sit in the car while we eat dinner" or "If you don't behave, you'll never see television again." The kid, of course, does not view such threats as credible and continues to terrorize the restaurant—proving that the kid is a better game theorist than the father.

[11]Some psychologists use the idea of commitment to treat behavioral problems. A psychologist may advise an author with writer's block to set up an irreversible procedure whereby if the author's book is not finished by a certain date, the author's check for $10,000 will be sent to the group the author hates most in the world—be it the Nazi Party, the Ku Klux Klan, or the National Save the Skeets Foundation. Such an irreversible commitment helps the author get the project done by raising the cost of failure. (We can imagine the author playing a game against the author's own better self.)

to make its threatened behavior believable if firms differ. An important difference is the ability of one firm to act before the other. For example, an incumbent firm could lobby for the passage of a law that forbids further entry.

Dynamic Entry Game. We can illustrate the use of laws as a form of commitment by using the entry game. One gas station, the incumbent, is already operating at a highway rest stop that has room for at most two gas stations. The incumbent decides whether to pay b dollars to the rest stop's landlord for the *exclusive right* to be the only gas station at the rest stop. If this amount is paid, the landlord will rent the remaining land only to a restaurant or some other business that does not sell gasoline. The incumbent's profit, π_i, is the monopoly profit, π_m, minus b. If the incumbent does not act to prevent entry, the potential entrant decides whether or not to enter. If entry does not occur, the incumbent's profit, π_i, equals the monopoly profit, π_m, and the other firm's profit, π_e, is zero. If entry occurs, both firms receive the duopoly profit, π_d, but the entrant's profit, π_e, is $\pi_d - F$ after paying the fixed cost, F, to build a station. Using a game tree, we can show that the subgame perfect Nash equilibrium depends on the values of the parameters π_m, π_d, b, and F.

To draw the extensive-form diagram, we need to determine which firm acts at each stage of the game, what options a firm has at each stage, and the payoffs contingent on the firm's actions, and use that information to draw the extensive-form game tree. In the first stage, the incumbent decides whether to incur b so as to prevent entry. In the second stage, the potential entrant decides whether to enter. Figure 14.2 shows the extensive-form game tree. If the incumbent incurs b, $\pi_i = \pi_m - b$ and $\pi_e = 0$. If the incumbent does not incur b but the second firm chooses not to enter, $\pi_i = \pi_m$ and $\pi_e = 0$. Finally, if the incumbent does not incur b and the second firm enters, $\pi_i = \pi_d$ and $\pi_e = \pi_d - F$.

To solve for the subgame perfect Nash equilibrium, we use backward induction. If the incumbent acts to prevent entry by paying b, the entrant has no possible action, so the payoffs are $\pi_i = \pi_m - b$ and $\pi_e = 0$. If the incumbent does not pay the landlord to prevent entry, in the resulting subgame the potential entrant either enters and earns $\pi_e = \pi_d - F$ or it does not enter and earns $\pi_e = 0$. The potential entrant decides to enter if $\pi_d - F \geq 0$ (assuming that it enters if it breaks even), and other-

Figure 14.2 Game Tree: Whether an Incumbent Pays to Prevent Entry.

If the potential entrant stays out of the market, it makes no profit, $\pi_e = 0$, and the incumbent firm makes the monopoly profit, $\pi_i = \pi_m$. If the potential entrant enters the market, the incumbent earns π_d and the entrant makes $\pi_d - F$. If the duopoly profit, π_d, is less than F, entry does not occur. Otherwise, entry occurs unless the incumbent acts to deter entry by paying for exclusive rights to be the only firm at the rest stop. The incumbent pays the landlord only if $\pi_m - b > \pi_d$.

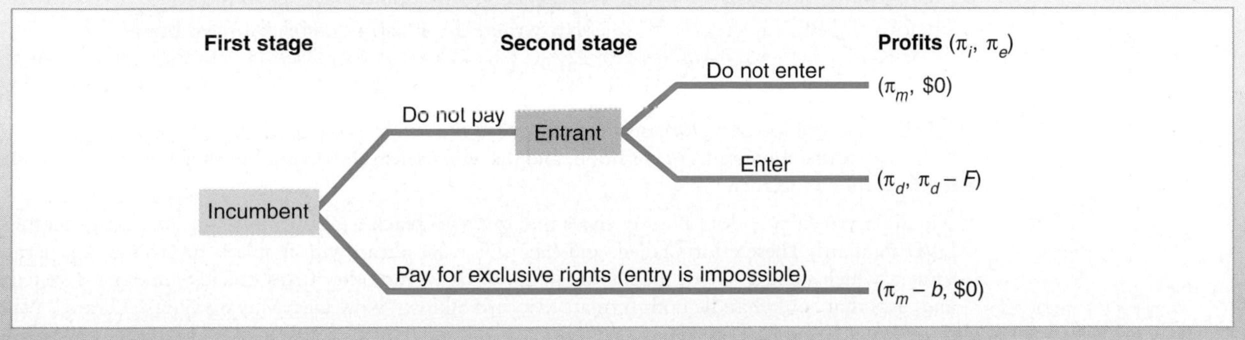

wise it stays out of the market. Thus, there are three possible subgame perfect Nash equilibria, depending on the parameters of the problem, π_m, π_d, b, and F:

- If $\pi_d - F < 0$, the potential entrant stays out of the market, the incumbent does not spend b, so $\pi_i = \pi_m$ and $\pi_e = 0$ (top line).
- If $\pi_d - F \geq 0$, then the potential entrant will enter unless the incumbent pays b. If $\pi_m - b < \pi_d$, the incumbent does not pay b, the other firm enters, and the payoffs are $\pi_i = \pi_d$ and $\pi_e = \pi_d - F$ (middle line).
- If $\pi_d - F \geq 0$ and $\pi_m - b \geq \pi_d$, the incumbent pays b so that the other firm stays out of the market, and the payoffs are $\pi_i = \pi_m - b$ and $\pi_e = 0$ (bottom line).

Solved Problem 14.2 makes use of all the methods that we've covered to this point. It first assumes that the players are engaged in a simultaneous-move game and solves for the pure and mixed strategies. It then assumes that they play a sequential-move game and solves for the subgame perfect Nash equilibrium.

See Questions 8–19 and Problem 33.

Solved Problem 14.2

See Question 34.

Recently, two groups of firms fought to determine the standard for the next generation of DVD players, which feature six-times-longer playing time and sharper images than previous models. A group led by Toshiba and NEC, with software from Microsoft, produced HD DVD discs. They were opposed by a group led by Sony that included Dell, Hewlett-Packard, Panasonic, Samsung, and Sharp, which championed Blu-ray technology. According to its proponents, the Microsoft-Toshiba approach was easier to use and cheaper and maintained continuity with the legacy standard, while Blu-ray technology stores more data and produces sharper images. Each group apparently believed that its product would be more successful if all DVD players could handle its format, but each group wanted to choose its own format. Suppose that the payoff matrix was[12]

		Blu-ray Group	
		HD DVD Standard	*Blu-ray Standard*
HD DVD Group	*HD DVD Standard*	HD DVD: 3; Blu-ray: 1	HD DVD: −1; Blu-ray: −1
	Blu-ray Standard	HD DVD: −1; Blu-ray: −1	HD DVD: 1; Blu-ray: 3

What are the pure- and mixed-strategy Nash equilibria if the firms had to set their standards simultaneously?[13] If the HD DVD group could have committed to a standard before the Blu-ray group chose, what would the Nash equilibrium have been?

[12]This game is of the same form as the game called *the battle of the sexes*. In that game, the husband likes to go to the mountains on vacation, and the wife prefers the ocean, but they both prefer to take their vacations together.

[13]In 2005, Toshiba and its Blu-ray rivals met to try to reach a compromise on the next-generation DVD standard. These efforts failed, and each side went ahead with its plans to produce a separate format, which started hitting the market in 2006. However, other firms quickly announced systems and discs that could handle both formats (Richard Siklos, "New Disc May Sway DVD Wars," *New York Times*, January 4, 2007).

Answer

1. *Determine the pure-strategy Nash equilibria if the firms decide simultaneously.* There are two Nash equilibria in which both groups choose the same standard. If both choose the HD DVD standard, neither group would change its strategy if it knew that the other was using the HD DVD standard. The HD DVD group's profit falls from 3 to −1 if it changes its strategy from the HD DVD to the Blu-ray standard, whereas the Blu-ray group's profit falls from 1 to −1 if it makes that change. Similarly, neither group would change its strategy from the Blu-ray standard if it believed that the other group would use the Blu-ray standard.

2. *Determine the mixed-strategy Nash equilibria if the firms decide simultaneously.* If the Blu-ray group chooses the HD DVD standard with a probability of θ_B, the HD DVD group's expected profit is $(3 \times \theta_B) + (-1 \times [1 - \theta_B]) = 4\theta_B - 1$ if it chooses the HD DVD standard and $(-1 \times \theta_B) + (1 \times [1 - \theta_B]) = 1 - 2\theta_B$ if it chooses the Blu-ray standard. For the HD DVD group to be indifferent between these two actions, its expected profits must be equal: $4\theta_B - 1 = 1 - 2\theta_B$. That is, if $\theta_B = \frac{1}{3}$, the HD DVD group is indifferent between choosing either standard. Similarly, if the HD DVD group selects the HD DVD standard with a probability of $\theta_H = \frac{2}{3}$, the Blu-ray group is indifferent between choosing either of the two standards.

3. *Determine the Nash equilibrium if the HD DVD group could commit to a strategy first.* The figure shows the extensive-form diagram given that the HD DVD group moves first. If it could commit first, the HD DVD group would choose the HD DVD standard. The HD DVD group knows that because the Blu-ray group realizes that the HD DVD group is using the HD DVD standard, the Blu-ray group will choose the HD DVD standard because it makes more (1) than if it chooses its own standard (−1). Thus, with a first-mover advantage, the HD DVD group would choose its own standard, which its rival accepts.

APPLICATION

Advantages and Disadvantages of Moving First

We've seen how a firm that enters the market first gains an advantage over potential rivals by moving first. The first-mover firm may prevent entry by building a reputation, committing to a large plant, raising costs to potential entrants, or getting an early start on learning by doing.

Toshiba, the main proponent of HD DVD, spent great sums of money to be the first to sell a next-generation DVD in 2006. It sold its initial HD DVD player for \$499 even though it apparently contained nearly \$700 worth of components, presumably to reinforce its first-to-market advantage by permeating the market with HD DVD units. In 2007, the backers of HD DVD reportedly paid Paramount and DreamWorks a combined \$150 million to adopt their format. However, when most content producers sided with Blu-ray, Toshiba stopped producing HD DVD in February 2008, conceding the market to Blu-ray.

The downsides of entering early are that the cost of entering quickly is higher, the odds of miscalculating demand are greater, and later entrants may build on the pioneer's research to produce a superior product. As the first of a new class of anti-ulcer drugs, Tagamet was extremely successful when it was introduced. However, the second entrant, Zantac, rapidly took the lion's share of the market. Zantac works similarly to Tagamet but has fewer side effects, could be taken less frequently when it was first introduced, and was promoted more effectively.

However, such examples of domination by second entrants are unusual. Urban, Carter, and Gaskin (1986) examined 129 successful consumer products and found that the second entrant gained, on average, only three-quarters of the market share of the pioneer and that later entrants captured even smaller shares.

Repeated Game

We now turn to static games that are repeated. In each period, there is a single stage: Both players move simultaneously. However, these are dynamic games because Player 1's move in period t precedes Player 2's move in period $t + 1$; hence, the earlier action may affect the later one. Such a repeated game is a *game of almost perfect information*: The players know all the moves from previous periods, but they do not know each other's moves within any one period because they all move simultaneously.

We showed that if American and United Airlines engage in a single-period prisoners' dilemma game, the two firms produce more than they would if they colluded. Yet cartels do form. What's wrong with this theory, which says that cartels won't occur? One explanation is that markets last for many periods, and collusion is more likely in a multiperiod game than in a single-period game.

In a single-period game, one firm cannot punish the other firm for cheating on a cartel agreement. But if the firms meet period after period, a wayward firm can be punished by the other.

Suppose now that the airlines' single-period prisoners' dilemma game is repeated quarter after quarter. If they play a single-period game, each firm takes its rival's strategy as a given and assumes that it cannot affect that strategy. When the same game is played repeatedly, the firms may devise strategies for this period that depend on rivals' actions in previous periods. For example, a firm may set a low output level this period only if its rival set a low output level in the previous period.

In a repeated game, a firm can influence its rival's behavior by *signaling* and *threatening to punish*. For example, one airline firm could use a low-quantity strategy for a couple of periods to signal to the other firm its desire that the two firms cooperate and produce that low quantity in the future. If the other firm does not respond by lowering its output in future periods, the first firm suffers lower profits for only a couple of periods. However, if the other firm responds to this signal and lowers its quantity, both firms can profitably produce at the low quantity thereafter.

In addition to or instead of signaling, a firm can threaten to punish a rival for not restricting output. The profit matrix in Table 14.1 illustrates how firms can punish rivals to ensure collusion. Suppose that American announces or somehow indicates to United that it will use the following two-part strategy:

- American will produce the smaller quantity each period as long as United does the same.
- If United produces the larger quantity in period t, American will produce the larger quantity in period $t + 1$ and all subsequent periods.

If United believes that American will follow this strategy, United knows that it will make \$4.6 million each period if it produces the lower quantity. Although United can make a higher profit, \$5.1 million, in period t by producing the larger quantity, by doing so it lowers its potential profit to \$4.1 million in each following period. Thus, United's best policy is to produce the lower quantity in each period unless it cares greatly about current profit and little about future profits. If United values future profits nearly as much as current ones, the one-period gain from deviating from the collusive output level will not compensate for the losses from reduced profits in future periods, which is the punishment American will impose. United may take this threat by American seriously because American's best response is to produce the larger quantity if it believes it can't trust United to produce the smaller quantity.[14] Thus, if firms play the same game *indefinitely*, they should find it easier to collude.

See Question 20.

Yet playing the same game many times does not necessarily help the firms cooperate. Suppose, for example, that the firms know that they are going to play the game for T periods. In the last period, they know that they're not going to play again, so they know they can cheat—produce a large quantity—without fear of punishment. As a result, the last period is like a single-period game, and both firms produce the large quantity. That makes the $T - 1$ period the last interesting period. By the same reasoning, the firms will cheat in $T - 1$ because they know that they will both cheat in the last period and hence no additional punishment can be imposed. Continuing this type of argument, we conclude that maintaining an agreement to produce the small quantity will be difficult if the game has a known stopping point. If the players know that the game will end but aren't sure when, cheating is less likely to occur. Cooperation is therefore more likely in a game that will continue forever or one that will end at an uncertain time.

See Question 21.

14.4 Auctions

To this point, we have examined games in which players have complete information about payoff functions. We now turn to an important game, the auction, in which players devise bidding strategies without knowing other players' payoff functions.

auction
a sale in which property or a service is sold to the highest bidder

An **auction** is a sale in which a good or service is sold to the highest bidder. A substantial amount of exchange takes place through auctions. Government contracts are typically awarded using procurement auctions. In recent years, governments have auctioned portions of the airwaves for radio stations, mobile phones, and wireless Internet access and have used auctions to set up electricity and transport markets. Other goods commonly sold at auction are natural resources such as timber, as well as houses, cars, agricultural produce, horses, antiques, and art. In this section, we first consider the various types of auctions and then investigate how the rules of the auction influence buyers' strategies.

Elements of Auctions

Before deciding what strategy to use when bidding in an auction, one needs to know the rules of the game. Auctions have three key components: the number of units being sold, the format of the bidding, and the value that potential bidders place on the good.

[14]American does not have to punish United forever to induce it to cooperate. All it has to do is punish it for enough periods that it does not pay for United to deviate from the low-quantity strategy in any period.

Number of Units. Auctions can be used to sell one or many units of a good. In 2004, Google auctioned its initial public offering of many identical shares of stock at one time. In many other auctions, a single good—such as an original painting—is sold. For simplicity in this discussion, we concentrate on auctions where a single, indivisible item is sold.

Format of Bidding. How auctions are conducted varies greatly. However, most approaches are variants of the *English auction*, the *Dutch auction*, or the *sealed-bid auction*.

- **English auction.** In the United States and Britain, almost everyone has seen an *English* or *ascending-bid auction*, at least in the movies. The auctioneer starts the bidding at the lowest price that is acceptable to the seller and then repeatedly encourages potential buyers to bid more than the previous highest bidder. The auction ends when no one is willing to bid more than the current highest bid: "Going, going, gone!" The good is sold to the last bidder for the highest bid. Sotheby's and Christie's use English auctions to sell art and antiques.
- **Dutch auction.** A *Dutch auction* or *descending-bid auction* ends dramatically with the first "bid." The seller starts by asking if anyone wants to buy at a relatively high price. The seller reduces the price by given increments until someone accepts the offered price and buys at that price. Variants of Dutch auctions are often used to sell multiple goods at once, such as in Google's initial public offering auction and the U.S. Treasury's sales of Treasury bills.
- **Sealed-bid auction.** In a *sealed-bid auction*, everyone submits a bid simultaneously without seeing anyone else's bid (for example, by submitting each bid in a sealed envelope), and the highest bidder wins. The price the winner pays depends on whether it is a first-price auction or a second-price auction. In a *first-price auction*, the winner pays its own, highest bid. Governments often use this type of auction. In a *second-price auction*, the winner pays the amount bid by the second-highest bidder. Many computer auction houses use a variant of the second-price auction.

For example, you bid on eBay by specifying the maximum amount you are willing to bid. If your maximum is greater than the maximum bid of other participants, eBay's computer places a bid on your behalf that is a small increment above the maximum bid of the second-highest bidder. This system differs from the traditional sealed-bid auction in that people can continue to bid until the official end-time of the auction, and potential bidders know the current bid price (but not the maximum that the highest bidder is willing to pay). Thus, eBay has some of the characteristics of an English auction.

Value. Auctioned goods are normally described as having a *private value* or a *common value*. Typically, this distinction turns on whether the good is unique.

- **Private value.** If each potential bidder places a different personal value on the good, we say that the good has a *private value*. Individual bidders know how much the good is worth to them but not how much other bidders value it. The archetypical example is an original work of art about which people differ greatly as to how much they value it.
- **Common value.** Many auctions involve a good that has the same fundamental value to everyone, but no buyer knows exactly what that *common value* is. For example, in a timber auction, firms bid on all the trees in a given area. All

firms know what the current price of lumber is; however, they do not know exactly how many board feet of lumber are contained in the trees.

In many actual auctions, goods have both private value and common value. For example, in the tree auction, bidding firms may differ not only in their estimates of the amount of lumber in the trees (common value), but also in their costs of harvesting (private value).

Bidding Strategies in Private-Value Auctions

A potential buyer's optimal strategy depends on the number of units, the format, and the type of values in an auction. For specificity, we examine auctions in which each bidder places a different private value on a single, indivisible good.

Second-Price Auction Strategies. According to eBay, if you choose to bid on an item in its second-price auction, you should "enter the maximum amount you are willing to spend" (**pages.ebay.com/education/gettingstarted/researching.html**). Is eBay's advice correct?

In a traditional sealed-bid, second-price auction, bidding your highest value *weakly dominates* all other bidding strategies: The strategy of bidding your maximum value leaves you *as well off* as, *or better off* than, bidding any other value. The amount that you bid affects whether you win, but it does not affect how much you pay if you win, which equals the second-highest bid.

Suppose that you value a folk art carving at $100. If the highest amount that any other participant is willing to bid is $85 and you place a bid greater than $85, you will buy the carving for $85 and receive $15 (= $100 – $85) of consumer surplus. Other bidders pay nothing and gain no consumer surplus.

Should you ever bid more than your value? Suppose that you bid $120. There are three possibilities. First, if the highest bid of your rivals is greater than $120, then you do not buy the good and receive no consumer surplus. This outcome is the same as what you would have received if you had bid $100, so bidding higher than $100 does not benefit you.

Second, if the highest alternative bid is less than $100, then you win and receive the same consumer surplus that you would have received had you bid $100. Again, bidding higher does not affect the outcome.

Third, if the highest bid by a rival were an amount between $100 and $120—say, $110—then bidding more than your maximum value causes you to win, but you purchase the good for more than you value it, so you receive negative consumer surplus: –$10 (= $100 – $110). In contrast, if you had bid your maximum value, you would not have won, and your consumer surplus would have been zero—which is better than losing $10. Thus, bidding more than your maximum value can never make you better off than bidding your maximum value, and you may suffer.

Should you ever bid less than your maximum value, say, $90? No, because you only lower the odds of winning without affecting the price that you pay if you do win. If the highest alternative bid is less than $90 or greater than your value, you receive the same consumer surplus by bidding $90 as you would by bidding $100. However, if the highest alternative bid lies between $90 and $100, you will lose the auction and give up positive consumer surplus by underbidding.

Thus, you do as well or better by bidding your value than by over- or underbidding. This argument does not turn on whether or not you know other bidders' valuation. If you know your own value but not other bidders' values, bidding your value is your best strategy. If everyone follows this strategy, the person who places the highest value on the good will win and will pay the second-highest value.

See Problem 35.

APPLICATION

Experienced Bidders

We've seen that bidding one's value is the dominant strategy in a sealed-bid, second-price auction. Economics professors conducting experimental sealed-bid, second-price auctions under "laboratory" settings using college students as subjects have been surprised to observe many overbids—bids that exceed the bidder's value—and few underbids. Garratt et al. (2007) provided an explanation. The students participating in these experiments had little prior experience bidding in auctions. Would experienced bidders use better strategies?

Garratt et al. repeated the experiment using people with extensive experience in eBay auctions. Auctions on eBay are second-price auctions that occur over time rather than sealed-bid auctions. The researchers found that even these experienced bidders did not always bid their values. However, unlike the inexperienced subjects, these bidders did not exhibit a systematic bias: They were just as likely to underbid as to overbid.

English Auction Strategy. Suppose instead that the seller uses an English auction to sell the carving to bidders with various private values. Your best strategy is to raise the current highest bid as long as your bid is less than the value you place on the good, \$100. If the current bid is \$85, you should increase your bid by the smallest permitted amount, say, \$86, which is less than your value. If no one raises the bid further, you win and receive a positive surplus of \$14. By the same reasoning, it always pays to increase your bid up to \$100, where you receive zero surplus if you win.

However, it never pays to bid more than \$100. The best outcome that you can hope for is to lose and receive zero surplus. Were you to win, you would have negative surplus.

See Question 22.

If all participants bid up to their value, the winner will pay slightly more than the value of the second-highest bidder. Thus, the outcome is essentially the same as in the sealed-bid, second-price auction.

Equivalence of Auction Outcomes. For Dutch or first-price sealed-bid auctions, one can show that participants will *shave* their bids to less than their value. The basic intuition is that you do not know the values of the other bidders. Reducing your bid reduces the probability that you win but increases your consumer surplus if you win. Your optimal bid, which balances these two effects, is lower than your actual value. Your bid depends on your beliefs about the strategies of your rivals. It can be shown that the best strategy is to bid an amount that is equal to or slightly greater than what you expect will be the second-highest bid, given that your value is the highest.

Thus, the expected outcome is the same under each format for private-value auctions: The winner is the person with the highest value, and the winner pays roughly the second-highest value. According to the Revenue Equivalence Theorem (Klemperer, 2004), under certain plausible conditions we would expect the same revenue from any auction in which the winner is the person who places the highest value on the good.

Winner's Curse

winner's curse
auction winner's bid exceeds the common-value item's value

A phenomenon occurs in common-value auctions that does not occur in private-value auctions. The **winner's curse** is that the auction winner's bid exceeds the common-value item's value. The overbidding occurs when there is uncertainty about the true value of the good.

When the government auctions off timber on a plot of land, potential bidders may differ in their estimates of how many board feet of lumber are available on that land. The higher one's estimate, the more likely that one will make the winning bid. If the average bid is accurate, then the high bid is probably excessive. Thus, the winner's curse is paying too much.

I can minimize the likelihood of falling prey to the winner's curse by *shading* my bid: reducing the bid below my estimate. I know that if I win, I am probably overestimating the value of the good. The amount by which I should shade my bid depends on the number of other bidders, because the more bidders, the more likely that the winning bid is an overestimate.

Because intelligent bidders shade their bids, sellers can do better with an English auction than with a sealed-bid auction. In an English auction, bidders revise their views about the object's value as they watch others bid.

SUMMARY

1. **An Overview of Game Theory.** The set of tools that economists use to analyze conflict and cooperation among players (such as firms) is called game theory. Each player adopts a strategy or battle plan to compete with other firms. Economists typically assume that players have *common knowledge* about the rules of the game, the payoff functions, and other players' knowledge about these issues. In many games, players have *complete information* about how payoffs depend on the strategies of all players. In some games, players have *perfect information* about players' previous moves.

2. **Static Games.** In a static game, such as in the Cournot model or the prisoners' dilemma game, players each make one move simultaneously. Economists use a normal-form representation or payoff matrix to analyze a static game. Typically, economists study static games in which players have complete information about the payoff function—the payoff to any player conditional on the actions all players take—but imperfect information about how their rivals behave because they act simultaneously. The set of players' strategies is a Nash equilibrium if, given that all other players use these strategies, no player can obtain a higher payoff by choosing a different strategy. Both pure-strategy and mixed-strategy Nash equilibria are possible in static games, and there may be multiple Nash equilibria for a given game. There is no guarantee that Nash equilibria in static games maximize the joint payoffs of all the players.

3. **Dynamic Games.** In dynamic games, a player takes the other players' previous moves into account when choosing a move. In sequential-move games, one player moves before the other player. Economists typically study sequential games of complete information about payoffs and perfect information about previous moves. The first mover may have an advantage over the second mover, such as in a Stackelberg game. An incumbent with first-mover advantage prevents entry by making a *credible threat*. For example, in a Stackelberg game, the leader *commits* to producing so much output that it is in the follower's best interest to produce a relatively small amount of output. In a repeated game, players replay a static game in which they move simultaneously within a period. The players have perfect information about other players' moves in previous periods but imperfect information within a period because the players move simultaneously. The best-known solution of a dynamic game is a subgame perfect Nash equilibrium, where the players' strategies are a Nash equilibrium in every subgame—the remaining game following a particular junction in the game. Players may use more complex strategies in dynamic games than in static games. Moreover, it is easier for players to maximize their joint payoff in a repeated game than in a single-period game.

4. **Auctions.** Auctions are games of incomplete information because bidders do not know the valuation others place on a good. Buyers' optimal strategies depend on the characteristics of an auction. Under fairly general conditions, if the auction rules result in a win by the person placing the highest value on a good that various bidders value differently, the expected price is the same in all auctions. For example, the expected price in various types of private-value auctions is the value of the good to the person who values it second-highest. In auctions where everyone values the good the same, though they may

differ in their estimates of that value, the successful bidder may suffer from the winner's curse—paying too much—unless bidders shade their bids to compensate for their overoptimistic estimation of the good's value.

QUESTIONS

■ = *exercise is available on MyEconLab;* * = *answer appears at the back of this book;* C = *use of calculus may be necessary;* W = *audio-slideshow answer by James Dearden is available in Textbook Resources on MyEconLab.*

*1. Show the payoff matrix and explain the reasoning in the prisoners' dilemma example where Larry and Duncan, possible criminals, will get one year in prison if neither talks; if one talks, one goes free and the other gets five years; and if both talk, both get two years. (*Note*: The payoffs are negative because they represent years in jail, which is a bad.)

■ 2. Two firms face the following payoff matrix:

Firm 2 \ Firm 1	Low Price	High Price
Low Price	$2, $0	$1, $2
High Price	$0, $7	$6, $6

Given these payoffs, Firm 2 wants to match Firm 1's price, but Firm 1 does not want to match Firm 2's price. What, if any, are the pure-strategy Nash equilibria of this game?

3. The *Wall Street Journal* (John Lippman, "The Producers: 'The Terminator' Is Back," March 8, 2002, A1) reported that Warner Bros. agreed to pay $50 million for its U.S. distribution rights, plus an additional $50 million in marketing costs, so that it could release *Terminator 3* (*T-3*) in the summer of 2003. It paid this large sum because it did not want anyone else to release *T-3* on the same weekend in 2003 that Warner Bros. released its movie *Matrix 2*. Suppose that Warner Bros. had not purchased the distribution rights to *T-3* and that the film's producer retained the rights. Warner Bros. decides whether to release *Matrix 2* on the July 4 weekend or on the July 18 weekend. Simultaneously, *T-3*'s producer decides which of those two weekends to release its film. The payoff matrix (in millions of dollars) of the simultaneous-moves game is:

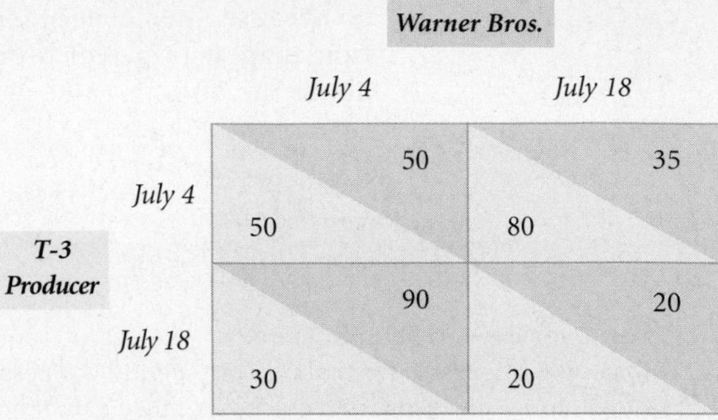

T-3 Producer \ Warner Bros.	July 4	July 18
July 4	50, 50	80, 35
July 18	30, 90	20, 20

a. What is the Nash equilibrium to this simultaneous-moves game?

b. Which release dates maximize the sum of the profits? Explain.

c. What is the greatest price Warner Bros. is willing to pay to purchase the distribution rights to *T-3*? What is the lowest price that *T-3*'s producer is willing to accept to sell the rights? Are there mutually beneficial prices at which the trade takes place?

d. If Warner Bros. purchases the distribution rights of *T-3*, when does it release the film and when does it release *Matrix 2*? Explain. W

*4. Suppose that Toyota and GM are considering entering a new market for electric automobiles and that their profits (in millions of dollars) from entering or staying out of the market are

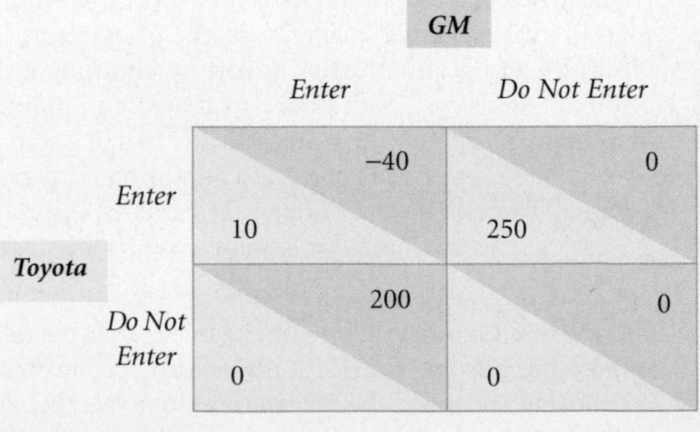

Toyota \ GM	Enter	Do Not Enter
Enter	10, −40	250, 0
Do Not Enter	0, 200	0, 0

If the firms make their decisions simultaneously, do either or both firms enter? How would your answer change if the U.S. government committed to paying GM a lump-sum subsidy of $50 million on the condition that it would produce this new type of car?

5. Lori employs Max. She wants him to work hard rather than to loaf. She considers offering him a bonus or not giving him one. All else the same, Max prefers to loaf.

		Max	
		Work	*Loaf*
Lori	*Bonus*	Lori: 1, Max: 2	Lori: −1, Max: 3
	No Bonus	Lori: 3, Max: −1	Lori: 0, Max: 0

If they choose actions simultaneously, what are their strategies?

6. Takashi Hashiyama, president of the Japanese electronics firm Maspro Denkoh Corporation, was torn between having Christie's or Sotheby's auction the company's $20 million art collection, which included a van Gogh, a Cézanne, and an early Picasso (Carol Vogel, "Rock, Paper, Payoff," *New York Times*, April 29, 2005, A1, A24). He resolved the issue by having the two auction houses' representatives compete in the playground game of rock-paper-scissors. A rock (fist) breaks scissors (two fingers sticking out), scissors cut paper (flat hand), and paper smothers rock. At stake were several million dollars in commissions. Christie's won: scissors beat paper.

   a. Show the profit or payoff matrix for this rock-paper-scissors game. (*Hint*: You may assume that the payoff is −1 if you lose, 0 if you tie, and 1 if you win.)

   b. Sotheby's expert in Impressionist and modern art said, "[T]his is a game of chance, so we didn't really give it much thought. We had no strategy in mind." In contrast, the president of Christie's in Japan researched the psychology of the game and consulted with the 11-year-old twin daughters of the director of the Impressionist and modern art department. One of these girls said, "Everybody knows you always start with scissors. Rock is way too obvious, and scissors beats paper." The other opined, "Since they were beginners, scissors was definitely the safest." Evaluate these comments on strategy. What strategy would you recommend if you knew that your rival was consulting with 11-year-old girls? In general, what pure or mixed strategy would you have recommended, and why?

7. Show that advertising is a dominant strategy for both firms in both panels of Table 14.4. Explain why that set of strategies is a Nash equilibrium.

8. In 2003, Microsoft spent $150 million on an advertising campaign to promote its then latest version of Microsoft Office (Nat Ives, "Advertising," *New York Times*, October 21, 2003, C6). That amount was five times as much as it spent promoting an upgrade in 2001. What are the possible explanations for its increase in expenditures? Does its action necessarily imply that Microsoft fears its competitors more than in previous years? Explain.

9. In Solved Problem 14.1, suppose that Mimi can move first. What are the equilibria, and why? Now repeat your analysis if Jeff can move first.

10. Suppose that Question 4 were modified so that GM has no subsidy but does have a head start over Toyota and can move first. What is the Nash equilibrium? Explain.

11. Two firms are planning to sell 10 or 20 units of their goods and face the following payoff matrix:

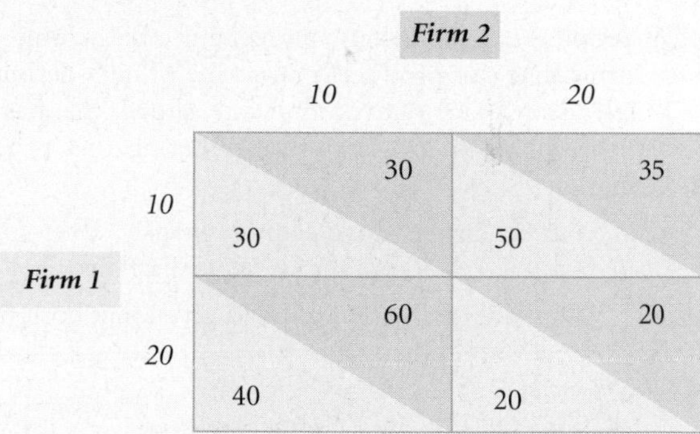

Firm 2
10
20
Firm 1
10
20
30
35
30
50
60
20
40
20

   a. What is the Nash equilibrium if both firms make their decisions simultaneously? Why? (What strategy does each firm use?)

   b. Suppose that Firm 1 can decide first. What is the outcome? Why?

   c. Suppose that Firm 2 can decide first. What is the outcome? Why?

12. How does your analysis in Question 11 change if the government imposes a lump-sum franchise tax of 40 on each firm (that is, the payoffs in the matrix are all reduced by 40). Now explain how your analysis

would change if the firms have an additional option of shutting down and avoiding the lump-sum tax rather than producing 10 or 20 units and paying the tax.

13. A thug wants the contents of a safe and is threatening the owner, the only person who knows the code, to open the safe. "I will kill you if you don't open the safe, and let you live if you do." Should the information holder believe the threat and open the safe? The table shows the value that each person places on the various possible outcomes.

	Thug	Safe's Owner
Open the safe, thug does not kill	4	3
Open the safe, thug kills	2	1
Do not open, thug kills	1	2
Do not open, thug does not kill	3	4

Such a game appears in many films, including *Die Hard*, *Crimson Tide*, and *The Maltese Falcon*.

a. Draw the game tree. Who moves first?

b. What is the equilibrium?

c. Does the safe's owner believe the thug's threat?

d. Does the safe's owner open the safe? W

14. Suppose that Panasonic and Zenith are the only two firms that can produce a new type of high-definition television. The matrix opposite shows the payoffs (in millions of dollars) from entering this product market.

a. If both firms move simultaneously, does either firm have a dominant strategy? Explain.

b. What are the Nash equilibria given that both firms move simultaneously?

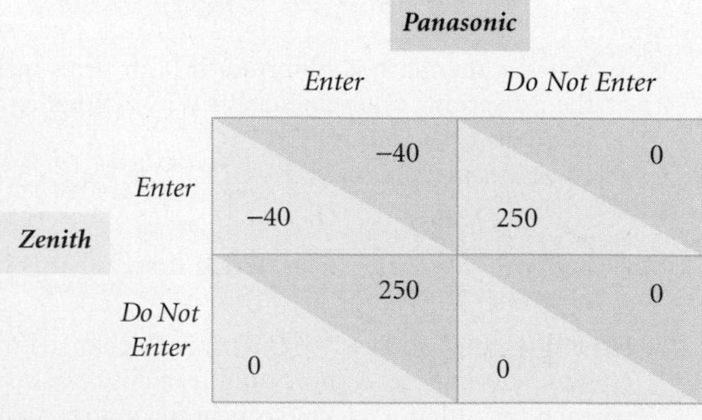

c. The U.S. government commits to paying Zenith a lump-sum subsidy of $50 million if it enters this market. What is the Nash equilibrium?

d. If Zenith does not receive a subsidy but has a head start over Panasonic, what is the Nash equilibrium?

15. The more an incumbent firm produces in the first period, the lower its marginal cost in the second period. If a potential entrant expects the incumbent to produce a large quantity in the second period, it does not enter. Draw a game tree to illustrate why an incumbent would produce more in the first period than the single-period profit-maximizing level. Now change the payoffs in the tree to show a situation in which the firm does not increase production in the first period.

16. From the ninth century B.C. until the proliferation of gunpowder in the fifteenth century A.D., the ultimate weapon of mass destruction was the catapult (John Noble Wilford, "How Catapults Married Science, Politics and War," *New York Times*, February 24, 2004, D3). Hero of Alexandria pointed out in the first century A.D. that it was not enough to have catapults. You needed your potential enemies to know that you had catapults so that they would not attack you in the first place. As early as the fourth century B.C., rulers set up what were essentially research and development laboratories to support military technology. However, unlike today, there was a conspicuous lack of secrecy. According to Alex Roland, a historian of technology at Duke University, "Rulers seemed to promote the technology for immediate payoff for themselves and had not yet worked through the notion that you ought to protect your investment with secrecy and restrictions. So engineers shopped their wares around, and information circulated freely among countries." Given this information, describe a ruler's optimal strategy with respect to catapult research, development, deployment, and public announcements. Should the strategy depend upon the country's wealth or size? What role does credibility of announcements play?

*17. A monopoly manufacturing plant currently uses many workers to pack its product into boxes. It can replace these workers with an expensive set of robotic arms. Although the robotic arms raise the monopoly's fixed cost substantially, they lower its marginal cost because it no longer has to hire as many workers. Buying the robotic arms raises its total cost: The monopoly can't sell enough boxes to make the machine pay for itself, given the market demand curve. Suppose the incumbent does not invest. If its rival does not enter, it earns $0 and the incumbent earns $900. If the rival enters, it earns $300 and the incumbent earns $400. Alternatively, the incumbent invests. If the rival does not enter, it earns $0 and the incumbent earns $500. If the rival enters, the rival loses $36 and the incumbent makes $132. Show the game tree. Should the monopoly buy the machine anyway?

*18. Suppose that an incumbent can commit to producing a large quantity of output before the potential entrant decides whether to enter. The incumbent chooses whether to commit to produce a small quantity, q_i, or a large quantity. The rival then decides whether to enter. If the incumbent commits to the small output level and if the rival does not enter, the rival makes $0 and the incumbent makes $900. If it does enter, the rival makes $125 and the incumbent earns $450. If the incumbent commits to producing the large quantity, and the potential entrant stays out of the market, the potential entrant makes $0 and the incumbent makes $800. If the rival enters, the best the entrant can make is $0, the same amount it would earn if it didn't enter, but the incumbent earns only $400. Show the game tree. What is the subgame perfect Nash equilibrium?

*19. Before entry, the incumbent earns a monopoly profit of π_m = $10 (million). If entry occurs, the incumbent and entrant each earn the duopoly profit, π_d = $3. Suppose that the incumbent can induce the government to require all firms to install pollution-control devices that cost each firm $4. Show the game tree. Should the incumbent urge the government to require pollution-control devices? Why or why not?

20. In the repeated-game airline example, what happens if the game is played forever but one or both firms care only about current profit?

21. In 2007, Italy announced that an Italian journalist, Daniel Mastrogiacomo, who had been held hostage for 15 days by the Taliban in Afghanistan, had been ransomed for 5 Taliban prisoners. Governments in many nations denounced the act as a bad idea because it rewarded terrorism and encouraged more abductions. Consequently, the Afghanistan government announced that it would no longer make such trades ("Afghanistan: Government Pledges End to Hostage Deals," Radio Free Europe, April 16, 2007). Use an extensive-form game tree to analyze the basic arguments. Can you draw any hard-and-fast conclusions about whether the Italians' actions were a good or bad idea? (*Hint*: Does your answer depend on the relative weight one puts on future costs and benefits relative to those today?)

22. At the end of performances of his Broadway play "Cyrano de Bergerac," Kevin Kline, who stars as Cyrano, the cavalier poet with a huge nose, auctions his prosthetic proboscis, which he and his co-star, Jennifer Garner, autograph (**www.nytimes.com/2007/12/09/business/09suits.html**) to benefit Broadway Cares in its fight against AIDS. An English auction is used. One night, a television producer grabbed the nose for $1,400, while the next night it fetched $1,600. On other nights it sold for $3,000 and $900. Why does the value fluctuate substantially from night to night? Which bidder's bid determines the sales price? How is the auction price affected by the audience's knowledge that the proceeds go to charity?

PROBLEMS

23. Two stars—the 100-meter gold medalist and the 200-meter gold medalist—from the last recent Olympic Games have agreed to a 150-meter duel. Before the race, each athlete decides whether to improve his performance by taking anabolic steroids. Each athlete's payoff is 20 from winning the race, 10 from tying, and 0 from losing. Furthermore, each athlete's utility of taking steroids is –6. Model this scenario as a game in which the players simultaneously decide whether to take steroids.

    a. What is the Nash equilibrium? Is the game a prisoners' dilemma? Explain.

    b. Suppose that one athlete's utility of taking steroids is –12, while the other's remains –6. What is the Nash equilibrium? Is the game a prisoners' dilemma? W

24. The town of Perkasie, Pennsylvania, has two diners: Emil's Diner and Bobby Ray's Diner. Both sell only chicken pies. Everyone who considers eating at the diners is aware that they sell the same chicken pies and knows the prices that they charge (p_E, p_{BR}). At precisely 5:00 P.M., each diner (simultaneously) sets its price of chicken pie for that evening. The market demand function for chicken pie is $Q = 120 - 20p$, where p is the lower of the two diners' prices. If there is a lower-priced diner, then people eat chicken pie at only that diner and the diner sells $120 - 20p$ chicken pies. If the two diners post the same price, then each sells to one-half of the market: $\frac{1}{2}(100 - 20p)$. Suppose that prices can be quoted in dollar units only (0, 1, 2, 3, 4, 5, or 6). Each diner's marginal cost is \$2 and the fixed cost is \$0.

a. Create a 7×7 payoff matrix and fill in the diners' profits.

b. Identify all Nash equilibria.

c. Suppose that Bobby Ray's Diner is out of business and that Emil's is a monopoly. Find Emil's profit-maximizing price.

d. Now return to the Emil's-versus-Bobby Ray's game. Pick one of the Nash equilibria that you identified in part b. Could the two diners collude—set prices different from the particular Nash equilibrium prices and increase both diners' profits? W

25. Acura and Volvo offer warranties on their automobiles, where w_A is the number of years of an Acura warranty and w_V is the number of years of a Volvo warranty. The revenue for Firm i, $i = A$ for Acura and V for Volvo, is $R_i = 27{,}000w_i/(w_A + w_V)$. Its cost of providing the warranty is $C_i = 2{,}000w_i$. Acura and Volvo participate in a warranty-setting game in which they simultaneously set warranties.

a. What is the profit function for each firm?

b. Suppose Acura and Volvo can set warranties in year lengths only, with a maximum of five years. Fill in a 5×5 payoff matrix with Acura's and Volvo's profits.

c. Determine the Nash equilibrium warranties.

d. Compare the Nash equilibrium warranties. If the two manufacturers offer the same warranty, explain why. If they offer different warranties, explain why.

e. Suppose Acura and Volvo collude in setting warranties. What warranties do they set?

f. Suppose Acura's cost of offering warranties decreases to $C_V = 1{,}000w_V$. What is the new Nash equilibrium? Explain the effect of the decrease in Volvo's cost function on the equilibrium warranties. W

26. In their study of cigarette advertising, Roberts and Samuelson (1988) found that the advertising of a particular brand affects overall market demand for cigarettes but does not affect the brand's share of market sales. Suppose the demand for brand i is $q_i = a + b(A_i + A_j)^{0.5}$, where A_i is brand i's advertising expenditure. The profit function of Brand i is $\pi_i = p_i(a + b(A_i + A_j)^{0.5}) - A_i$.

a. Does brand B's advertising expenditure affect A's market share, $q_A/(q_A + q_B)$?

b. In terms of a and b, what are the Nash equilibrium advertising expenditures? How does an increase in b affect the equilibrium expenditures? C, W

27. Suppose that you and a friend play a "matching pennies" game in which each of you uncovers a penny. If both pennies show heads or both show tails, you keep both. If one shows heads and the other shows tails, your friend keeps them. Show the payoff matrix. What, if any, is the pure-strategy Nash equilibrium to this game? Is there a mixed-strategy Nash equilibrium? If so, what is it?

***28.** What is the mixed-strategy Nash equilibrium for the game in Question 2.

29. In the AFC championship game between the Indianapolis Colts and the New England Patriots in 2007, the Colts had a fourth down and inches play. Rather than punt the ball and turn it over to their opponent, the Colts decided to go for a first down. Suppose the Colts have two play options: a fullback running up the middle or a screen pass to a wide receiver. The Patriots also have two play options: setting up to defend against the run or setting up to defend against the screen pass. The coaches of the two teams simultaneously choose their plays. If the Colts run the ball and the Patriots set up to defend against the run, then the Colts' payoff is –1 and the Patriots' payoff is 1. If the Colts pass and the Patriots set up to defend against the pass, then the Colts' payoff is –2 and the Patriots receive 2. If the Colts run and the Patriots set up to defend against the pass, the Colts' payoff is 6 and the Patriots' is –6. If the Colts pass and the Patriots set up to defend against the run, the Colts' payoff is 10 and the Patriots' is –10.

a. Show the payoff matrix for this simultaneous-moves game. What is the Nash equilibrium? Is it a pure-strategy or mixed-strategies Nash equilibrium?

b. Now suppose instead that if the Colts pass and the Patriots set up to defend again the pass, the Colts' payoff is 8 and the Patriots' is –8. Write the payoff matrix for this simultaneous-moves game. What is the Nash equilibrium? Does this Nash equilibrium involve pure or mixed strategies? W

30. In the novel and film *The Princess Bride*, the villain Vizzini kidnaps the princess. In an attempt to rescue her, the hero, Westley, challenges Vizzini to a battle of wits. Consider this variation on the actual plot. (I do not want to reveal the actual story.) In the battle, Westley puts two identical glasses of wine behind his back, out of Vizzini's view, and adds iocane powder to only one glass. (Iocane is "odorless, tasteless, dissolves instantly in liquid, and is among the more deadly poisons known to man.") Westley decides which glass to put on a table in front of Vizzini and which to put on the table in front of himself. Then, with Westley's back turned so that he cannot observe Vizzini's move, Vizzini decides whether to switch the two glasses. Assume the two simultaneously drink all the wine in their respective wine glasses. Assume also that each player's payoff from drinking the poisoned wine is −3 and the payoff from drinking the safe wine is +1. Write the payoff matrix for this simultaneous-moves game. Specify the possible Nash equilibria. Is there a pure-strategy Nash equilibrium? Is there a mixed-strategy Nash equilibrium? W

31. Two guys suffering from testosterone poisoning drive toward each other in the middle of a road. As they approach the impact point, each has the option of continuing to drive down the middle of the road or to swerve. Both believe that if only one driver swerves, that driver loses face (payoff = 0) and the other gains in self-esteem (payoff = 2). If neither swerves, they are maimed or killed (payoff = −10). If both swerve, no harm is done to either (payoff = 1). Show the payoff matrix for the two drivers engaged in this game of chicken. Determine the Nash equilibria for this game.

32. Modify the payoff matrix in the game of chicken in Problem 32 so that the payoff is −2 if neither driver swerves. How does the equilibrium change?

33. Xavier and Ying are partners in a course project. Xavier is the project leader and thus is the first to decide how many hours, h_X, to put into the project. After observing the amount of time that Xavier contributes, Ying decides how many hours, h_Y, to contribute. Xavier's utility function is

$$U_X = 18(h_X + h_Y)^{0.5} - h_X,$$

and Ying's utility function is

$$U_Y = 18(h_X + h_Y)^{0.5} - h_Y.$$

Ying threatens not to work on the project. For Ying's threat to be credible, what is the smallest number of hours that Xavier must contribute to the project? How much time does Xavier contribute? Does Ying work on the project? W

34. What are the Nash equilibria to the battle of the sexes game in footnote 12? Discuss whether this game and equilibrium concept make sense for analyzing a couple's decisions. How might you change the game's rules so that it makes more sense?

35. Suppose that Anna, Bill, and Cameron are the only three people interested in the paintings of the Bucks County artist Walter Emerson Baum. His painting *Sellers Mill* is being auctioned by a second-price sealed-bid auction. Suppose Anna's value of the painting is \$20,000, Bill's is \$18,500, and Cameron's is \$16,800. Each bidder's consumer surplus is $v_i - p$ if he or she wins the auction and 0 if he or she loses. The values are private. What is each bidder's optimal bid? Who wins the auction, and what price does he or she pay? W

15 Factor Markets and Vertical Integration

Work is of two kinds: first, altering the position of matter at or near the earth's surface relative to other matter; second, telling other people to do so.

—Bertrand Russell

To broadcast a television show, a local television station uses a variety of inputs. It builds or leases a studio, purchases or rents transmission equipment, hires labor, and buys or produces its own shows. The firm that owns the station may buy all these inputs from a market or produce some of them itself.

In the past few years, many media and communications companies have merged so that each could provide most of the services needed to bring entertainment into your home. Disney, Time Warner, and other major media firms are **vertically integrated**: They participate in more than one successive stage of the production or distribution of goods or services.

vertically integrated
describing a firm that participates in more than one successive stage of the production or distribution of goods or services

Disney is one of the most vertically integrated firms, with divisions that cover television production, film production, music, publishing, radio, broadcast TV, cable TV, the Internet, theme parks, and retail outlets. Rupert Murdoch's News Corporation's Fox Film Entertainment Group makes movies, TV shows, and animated features (including *The Simpsons*). The Fox network provides Fox-made shows to Fox-owned TV stations and affiliated stations in the United States and Australia. Fox delivers its shows directly via cable stations and satellite dishes around the world through companies that it partially or totally owns, such as fx, fxM, Fox Sports Net, Fox Sports International, ASkyB, and SkyMCI in the United States; BSkyB in the United Kingdom; Star TV, Zee TV, and JSkyB in Asia; Vox in Germany; Foxtel in Australia; and Sky Entertainment Latin American and Canal Fox in Latin America and the Caribbean. The parent company even owns *TV Guide*.

When does a firm buy factors from a market, and when does it produce those factors itself? The answer is that firms vertically integrate if the benefits outweigh the costs. Before we can examine the trade-off between these costs and benefits, we need to analyze how factor markets work.

We show that the factor market equilibrium price depends on the structure of factor markets and the output market. We first look at competitive factor and output markets. We then examine the effect of a monopoly in either or both markets.

We next consider markets in which there is a **monopsony**: the only buyer of a good in a market. A monopsony is the mirror image of a monopoly. Whereas a monopoly sells at a price higher than a competitive industry would charge, a monopsony buys at a lower price than a competitive industry would. Finally, we investigate when a firm vertically integrates to produce inputs itself and when it buys the inputs from a factor market.

monopsony
the only buyer of a good in a given market

In this chapter, we examine four main topics

1. **Competitive Factor Market.** The intersection of the factor supply curve and factor demand curve (which depends on firms' production functions and the market price for output) determines the equilibrium in a competitive factor market.
2. **Effect of Monopolies on Factor Markets.** If firms exercise market power in either factor or output markets, the quantities of inputs and outputs sold fall.
3. **Monopsony.** A monopsony maximizes its profit by paying a price below the competitive level, which creates a deadweight loss for society.
4. **Vertical Integration.** A firm may engage in many sequential stages of production itself, perform in only a few stages and rely on markets for others, or use contracts or other means to coordinate its activities with those of other firms, depending on which approach is the most profitable.

15.1 Competitive Factor Market

Virtually all firms rely on factor markets for at least some inputs. The firms that buy factors may be competitive price takers or noncompetitive price setters, such as a monopsony. Competitive, monopolistically competitive, oligopolistic, or monopolistic firms sell factors. Here we examine factor markets in which buying and selling firms are competitive price takers. In the next section, we consider noncompetitive factor markets.

Factor markets are competitive when there are many small buyers and sellers. The flower auction in Amsterdam that the Verenigde Bloemenveiling Aalsmeer cooperative holds daily (Chapter 8) typifies such a competitive market with many sellers and buyers. The sellers supply inputs (flowers in bulk) to buyers, who sell outputs (trimmed flowers in vases, wrapped bouquets) at retail to final customers.

Our earlier analysis of the competitive supply curve applies to factor markets. Chapter 5 derives the supply curve of labor by examining how individuals' choices between labor and leisure depend on tastes and the wage rate. Chapter 8 determines the competitive supply curves of firms in general, including those that produce factors for other firms. Given that we know the supply curve, all we need to do to analyze a competitive factor market is to determine the factor's demand curve.

Short-Run Factor Demand of a Firm

A profit-maximizing firm's demand for a factor of production is downward sloping: The higher the price of an input, the less the firm wants to buy. To understand what is behind a firm's factor demand, we examine a firm that uses capital and labor to produce output from factors. Using the theory of the firm (Chapters 6 and 7), we show how the amount of an input the firm demands depends on the prices of the factors and the price of the final output.

We start by considering the short-run factor demand for labor of a firm that can vary labor but not capital. Then we examine long-run factor demands when both inputs are variable.

In the short run, a firm has a fixed amount of capital, $\bar{K}$, and can vary the number of workers, L, it employs. Will the firm's profit rise if it hires one more worker? The answer depends on whether its revenue or labor costs rise more when output expands.

marginal revenue product of labor (MRP_L) the extra revenue from hiring one more worker

An extra worker per hour raises the firm's output per hour, q, by the marginal product of labor, $MP_L = \Delta q/\Delta L$ (Chapter 6). How much is that extra output worth to the firm? The extra revenue, R, from the last unit of output is the firm's marginal revenue, $MR = \Delta R/\Delta q$. As a result, the **marginal revenue product of labor (MRP_L)**, the extra revenue from hiring one more worker, is[1]

$$MRP_L = MR \times MP_L.$$

For a firm that is a competitive employer of labor, the marginal cost of hiring one more worker per hour is the wage, w. Hiring an extra worker raises the firm's profit if the marginal benefit—the marginal revenue product of labor—is greater than the marginal cost—the wage—from one more worker: $MRP_L > w$. If the marginal revenue product of labor is less than the wage, $MRP_L < w$, the firm can raise its profit by reducing the number of workers it employs. Thus, *the firm maximizes its profit by hiring workers until the marginal revenue product of the last worker exactly equals the marginal cost of employing that worker, which is the wage*:

$$MRP_L = w.$$

For now, we restrict our attention to competitive firms. A competitive firm faces an infinitely elastic demand for its output at the market price, p, so its marginal revenue is p (Chapter 8), and its marginal revenue product of labor is

$$MRP_L = p \times MP_L.$$

The marginal revenue product for a competitive firm is also called the *value of the marginal product* because it equals the market price times the marginal product of labor: the market value of the extra output. The competitive firm hires labor to the point at which its marginal revenue product of labor equals the wage:

$$MRP_L = p \times MP_L = w. \qquad (15.1)$$

Table 15.1 illustrates the relationship in Equation 15.1. If the firm hires $L = 3$ workers per hour, the marginal product from the third worker is 5 units of output per hour. Because the firm can sell the output at the market price $p = \$3$ per unit, the extra revenue from hiring the third worker is $MRP_L = p \times MP_L = \$3 \times 5 = \$15$.

Table 15.1 Marginal Product of Labor, Marginal Revenue Product of Labor, and Marginal Cost.

Labor, L	Marginal Product of Labor, MP_L	Marginal Revenue Product of Labor, $MRP_L = 3MP_L$	Output, q	Marginal Cost, $MC = 12/MP_L$
2	6	\$18	13	\$2
3	5	\$15	18	\$2.4
4	4	\$12	22	\$3
5	3	\$9	25	\$4
6	2	\$6	27	\$6

Notes: Wage, w, is \$12 per hour of work. Price, p, is \$3 per unit of output. Labor is variable, and capital is fixed.

---

[1]In the short run, output is a function of only labor, $q(L)$. The price the firm receives from selling q units of output is given by its demand function, $p(q)$. Thus, the revenue that the firm receives is $R(L) = p[q(L)]q(L)$. The extra revenue that the firm obtains from using an extra amount of labor services is derived using the chain rule of differentiation:

$$MRP_L \equiv \frac{dR}{dL} = \frac{dR}{dq} \times \frac{dq}{dL} \equiv MR \times MP_L.$$

By hiring this worker, the firm increases its profit because the wage of this worker is only w = \$12. If the firm hires a fourth worker, the marginal product of labor from this last worker falls to 4, and the marginal revenue product of labor falls to \$12. Thus, the extra revenue from the last worker exactly equals that worker's wage, so the firm's profit is unchanged. Were the firm to hire a fifth worker, the MRP_L = \$9 is less than the wage of \$12, so its profit would fall.

Panel a of Figure 15.1 shows the same relationship. The wage line, w = \$12, intersects the MRP_L curve at $L = 4$ workers per hour. *The wage line is the supply of labor the firm faces.* As a competitive buyer of labor services, the firm can hire as many workers as it wants at a constant wage of \$12. *The marginal revenue product of labor curve, MRP_L, is the firm's demand curve for labor* when other inputs are fixed. It shows the maximum wage a firm is willing to pay to hire a given number of workers. Thus, the intersection of the supply curve of labor facing the firm and the firm's demand curve for labor, Equation 15.1, determines the profit-maximizing number of workers.

A firm's labor demand curve is usually downward sloping because of the law of diminishing marginal returns (Chapter 6). The marginal product from extra workers, MP_L, of a firm with fixed capital eventually falls as the firm increases the amount of labor it uses. Table 15.1 illustrates that the marginal product of labor falls from 6 for the second worker to 2 for the sixth worker. Because the marginal product of labor declines as more workers are hired, the marginal revenue product of labor (which equals a constant price times the marginal product of labor) or demand curve must slope downward as well.

See Question 1.

Profit Maximization Using Labor or Output. Chapter 8 presents another profit-maximization condition: A competitive firm maximizes its profit by operating where the market price, p, equals the marginal cost of an extra unit of output, MC

Figure 15.1 The Relationship Between Labor Market and Output Market Equilibria.

(a) The firm's profit is maximized at $L = 4$ workers per hour where the wage line, w = \$12, crosses the marginal revenue product of labor, MRP_L, curve, which is also the demand curve for labor. (b) The firm's profit is maximized at 22 units of output (produced by 4 workers), for which its marginal cost, $MC = w/MP_L$, curve equals the market price, p = \$3.

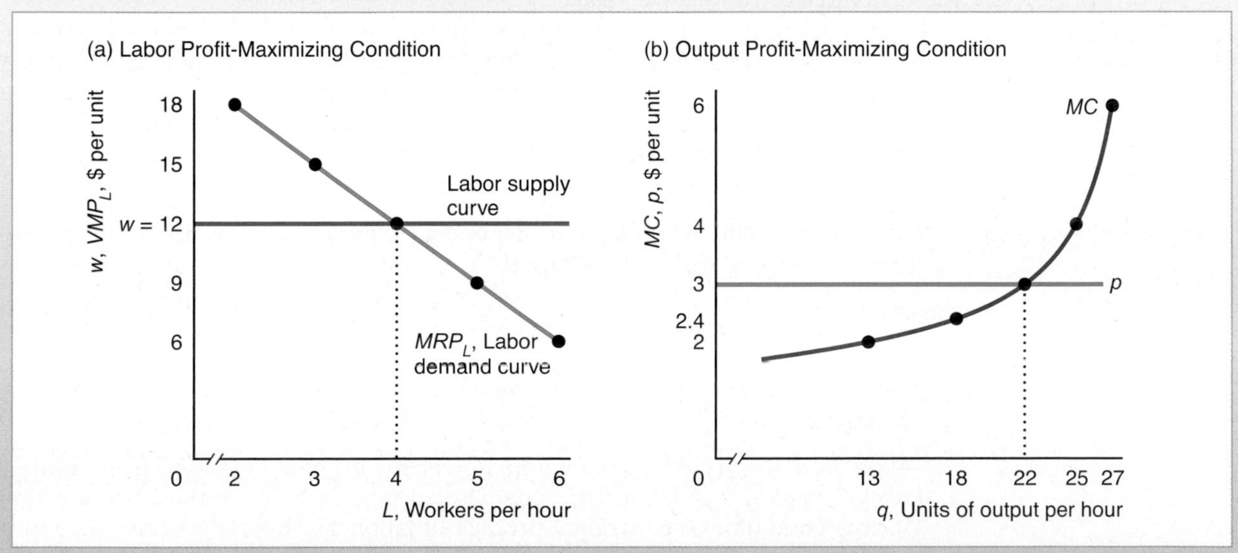

(Equation 8.3). This output profit-maximizing condition is equivalent to the labor profit-maximizing condition in Equation 15.1. Dividing Equation 15.1 by MP_L, we find that

$$p = \frac{w}{MP_L} = MC.$$

As Chapter 7 shows, the marginal cost equals the wage, w, times 1 over the marginal product of labor, which is the extra labor, $\Delta L/\Delta q$, necessary to produce one more unit of output. The marginal cost is the cost of the extra labor, $w\Delta L$, needed to produce the extra output, Δq.

Table 15.1 illustrates this relationship. The fourth column shows how the amount of output produced varies with the number of workers. Because 3 workers produce 18 units of output and 4 workers produce 22 units of output, the marginal product of the fourth worker is 4 units of output. With a wage of \$12, the marginal cost for the last unit of output is $MC = w/MP_L = \$12/4 = \$3$. The market price is also \$3, so the firm maximizes its profit by producing 22 units of output, as panel b of Figure 15.1 illustrates.

In summary, the two profit-maximizing equilibria in Figure 15.1 give the same answer: The firm maximizes its profit by hiring 4 workers to produce 22 units of output. Panel a shows that the firm maximizes its profit by hiring 4 workers, for which the marginal benefit or marginal revenue product from the last worker, MRP_L, equals the marginal cost of that worker, w. Panel b shows that the firm maximizes its profit by producing 22 units of output, for which the marginal benefit or marginal revenue from the last unit of output, $p = \$3$, equals the marginal cost of the last unit of output, MC.

How Changes in Wages and Prices Affect Factor Demand. The number of workers a firm hires depends on the wage and the price of the final good, as Equation 15.1 shows. Suppose that the supply of labor shifts so that the wage falls from $w_1 = \$12$ to $w_2 = \$6$ while the market price remains constant at \$3. The firm hires more workers because the cost of more labor falls while the incremental revenue from additional output is unchanged. Figure 15.2 shows that a fall in the wage due to a downward shift of the labor supply curve from S^1 to S^2 causes a shift along the labor demand curve D^1 from point a, where the firm hires 4 workers, to point b, where the firm hires 6 workers per hour.

If the market price falls from \$3 to \$2, the demand curve for labor shifts downward from D^1 to D^2. Demand D^2 is only $\frac{2}{3} = (2MP_L)/(3MP_L)$ as high as D^1 at any given quantity of labor. If the wage stays constant at $w_1 = \$12$, the firm reduces its demand for workers from 4, point a, to 2, point c. Thus, a shift in either the market wage or the market price affects the amount of labor that a firm employs.

Solved Problem 15.1

How does a competitive firm adjust its demand for labor when the government imposes a specific tax of τ on each unit of output?

Answer

1. *Give intuition.* The specific tax lowers the price per unit the firm receives, so we can apply the same type of analysis we just used for a fall in the market price.

2. *Show how the tax affects the marginal revenue product of labor.* The marginal revenue product of labor for a competitive firm is the price the firm receives for the good times the marginal product of labor. The tax reduces the price the

firm receives. The tax does not affect the relative prices of labor and capital, so it does not affect the marginal product of labor for a given amount of labor, $MP_L(L)$. For a given amount of labor, the marginal revenue product of labor falls from $p \times MP_L(L)$ to $(p - \tau) \times MP_L(L)$. The marginal revenue product of labor curve—the labor demand curve—shifts downward until it is only $(p - \tau)/p$ as high as the original labor demand curve at any quantity of labor.

See Question 2.

Figure 15.2 Shift of and Movement Along the Labor Demand Curve.

If the market price is \$3, the firm's labor demand curve is D^1. A fall in the wage causes a *shift of the supply curve* from S^1 to S^2 and a *movement along the demand curve for labor*. If the wage is $w_1 = \$12$, the firm hires 4 workers per hour, equilibrium point *a*. If the wage falls to $w_2 = \$6$, the firm hires 6 workers, point *b*. A fall in the market price to \$2 causes a *shift of the firm's demand curve for labor* from D^1 to D^2. If the market wage stays constant at $w_1 = \$12$, the fall in the market price causes a *movement along the supply curve* S^1: The number of workers the firm hires falls from 4, point *a* on D^1 and S^1, to 2, point *c* on D^2 and S^1.

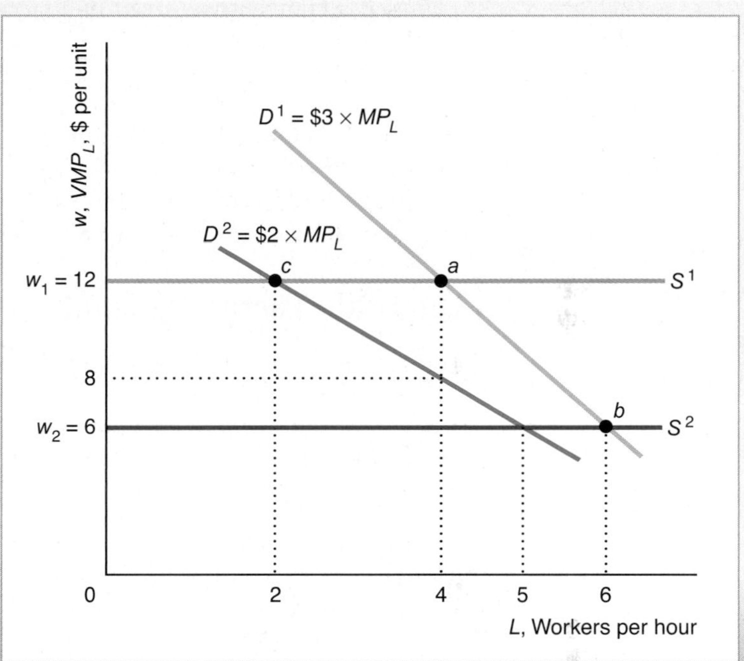

APPLICATION

Thread Mill

By calculating the marginal revenue product of labor, we can derive the labor demand curve for a Canadian thread mill. The firm has a Cobb-Douglas production function:[2]

$$q = L^{0.6}K^{0.2}. \tag{15.2}$$

Suppose that, in the short run, the mill's capital, K, is fixed at 32 units, so it can increase its output, q, only by increasing the amount of labor, L, it uses. To determine the firm's short-run production function, we set $K = 32$ in Equation 15.1:

$$q = L^{0.6}32^{0.2} = 2L^{0.6}.$$

The extra output or marginal product of labor from the last worker can be determined by using a calculator. We find that the extra output from the last worker when the firm goes from 31 to 32 workers is

$$\Delta q = (2 \times 32^{0.6}) - (2 \times 31^{0.6}) \approx 0.3.$$

[2]This production function is from the estimates of Baldwin and Gorecki (1986). The units of output are chosen appropriately so that the constant multiplier A in the general Cobb-Douglas, $q = AL^{\alpha}K^{\beta}$, equals 1.

The firm can sell its output at \$50 per unit. The firm's marginal revenue product of labor at $L = 32$ is

$$MRP_L = p \times MP_L = \$50 \times 0.3 = \$15.$$

Thus, when the price is \$50 and the wage is \$15, the firm hires 32 workers.

More generally, the marginal product of labor function, when we hold capital fixed at $K = 32$, is[3]

$$MP_L = 1.2L^{-0.4}.$$

Thus, if a competitive thread mill faces a market price of \$50, its labor demand curve is

$$MRP_L \equiv p \times MP_L = \$50 \times 1.2L^{-0.4} = \$60L^{-0.4}.$$

Figure 15.3 shows this MRP_L curve or short-run labor demand curve for the firm when capital is fixed at $K = 32$.

See Problems 28–30.

Long-Run Factor Demand

In the long run, the firm may vary all of its inputs. Now if the wage of labor rises, the firm adjusts both labor and capital. As a result, the short-run marginal revenue product of labor curve that holds capital fixed is not the firm's long-run labor demand curve. The long-run labor demand curve takes account of changes in the firm's use of capital as the wage rises.

In both the short run and the long run, the labor demand curve is the marginal revenue product curve of labor. In the short run, the firm cannot vary capital, so the short-run MP_L curve and hence the short-run MRP_L curve are relatively steep. In the long run, when the firm can vary all inputs, its long-run MP_L curve and MRP_L curves are flatter.

Figure 15.3 shows the relationship between the long-run and short-run labor demand curves for the thread mill.[4] In the short run, capital is fixed at $K = 32$, the wage is $w = \$15$, and the rental rate of capital is $r = \$5$. The firm hires 32 workers per hour, point *a* on its short-run labor demand curve, where $K = 32$. Using 32 workers and 32 units of capital is profit maximizing in the long run, so point *a* is also on the firm's long-run labor demand curve.

In the short run, if the wage fell to \$10, the firm could not increase its capital, so it would hire 88 workers, point *b* on the short-run labor demand curve, where

[3]We determine the marginal product of labor function holding capital fixed at $K = 32$ by differentiating the short-run production function, $q = 2L^{0.6}$, with respect to labor:

$$MP_L \equiv dq/dL = 0.6 \times 2 \times L^{0.6-1} = 1.2L^{-0.4}.$$

The calculator method, which compares a discrete change from 31 to 32 workers, gives approximately the correct MP_L. Using this exact formula, which is based on an infinitesimal change in labor, we find that the MP_L at $L = 32$ is exactly $0.3 = 1.2(32)^{-0.4}$.

[4]Appendix 15A formally shows that the long-run labor demand and capital demand functions for a Cobb-Douglas production function are functions of the market price, p; the wage rate, w; and the rental rate of capital, r. Substituting the parameters for the Canadian thread mill, $\alpha = 0.6$, $\beta = 0.2$, and $A = 1$, into Equation 15A.4, we find that the firm's long-run labor demand curve is $L = (0.6/w)^4(0.2/r)p^5$. Its long-run capital demand curve, Equation 15A.5, is $K = (0.6/w)^3(0.2/r)^2p^5$.

Figure 15.3 Labor Demand of a Thread Mill.

If the long-run market price is \$50 per unit, the rental rate of capital services is r = \$5, and the wage is w = \$15 per hour, a Canadian thread mill hires 32 workers (and uses 32 units of capital) at point a on its long-run labor demand curve. In the short run, if capital is fixed at K = 32, the firm still hires 32 workers per hour at point a on its short-run labor demand curve. If the wage drops to \$10 and capital remains fixed at K = 32, the firm would hire 88 workers, point b on the short-run labor demand curve. In the long run, however, it would increase its capital to K = 108 and hire 162 workers, point c on the long-run labor demand curve and on the short-run labor demand curve with K = 108.

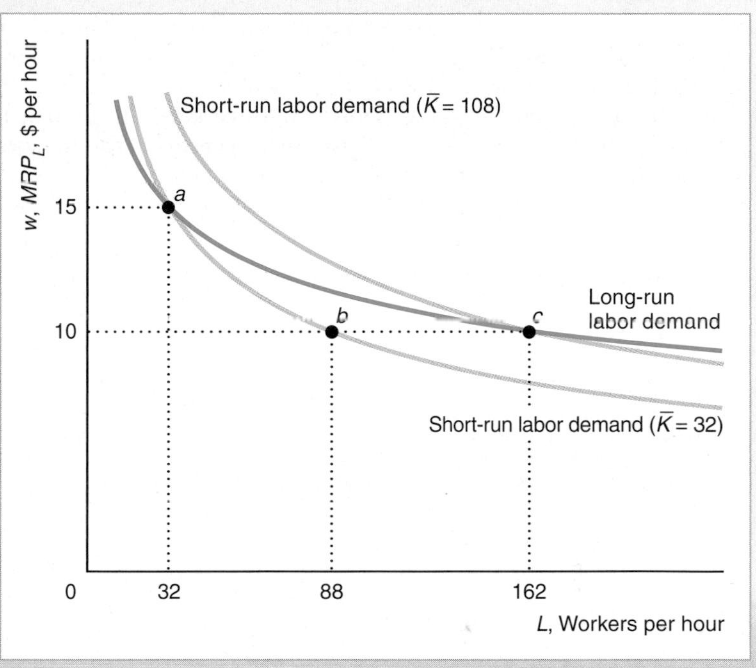

K = 32. In the long run, however, the firm would employ more capital and even more labor (because it can sell as much output as it wants at the market price). It would hire 162 workers and use 108 units of capital, which is point c on both the long-run labor demand curve and the short-run labor demand curve for K = 108.

Factor Market Demand

A factor market demand curve is the sum of the factor demand curves of the various firms that use the input. Determining a factor market demand curve is more difficult than deriving consumers' market demand for a final good. When horizontally summing the demand curves for individual consumers in Chapter 2, we were concerned with only a single market.

Inputs such as labor and capital are used in many output markets, however. Thus, to derive the labor market demand curve, we first determine the labor demand curve for each output market and then sum across output markets to obtain the factor market demand curve.

The Marginal Revenue Product Approach. Earlier we derived the factor demand of a competitive firm that took the output market price as given. The problem we face is that the output market price depends on the factor's price. As the factor's price falls, each firm, taking the original market price as given, uses more of the factor to produce more output. This extra production by all the firms in the market causes the market price to fall. As the market price falls, each firm reduces its output and hence its demand for the input. Thus, a fall in an input price causes less of an increase in factor demand than would occur if the market price remained constant, as Figure 15.4 illustrates.

Figure 15.4 Firm and Market Demand for Labor.

When the output price is $p = \$9$, the individual competitive firm's labor demand curve is $MRP_L(p = \$9)$. If $w = \$25$ per hour, the firm hires 50 workers, point *a* in panel a, and the 10 firms in the market demand 500 workers, point *A* on the labor demand curve $D(p = \$9)$ in panel b. If the wage falls to \$10, each firm would hire 90 workers, point *c*, if the market price stayed fixed at \$9. The extra output, however, drives the price down to \$7, so each firm hires 70 workers, point *b*. The market's demand for labor that takes price adjustments into account, *D*(price varies), goes through points *A* and *B*.

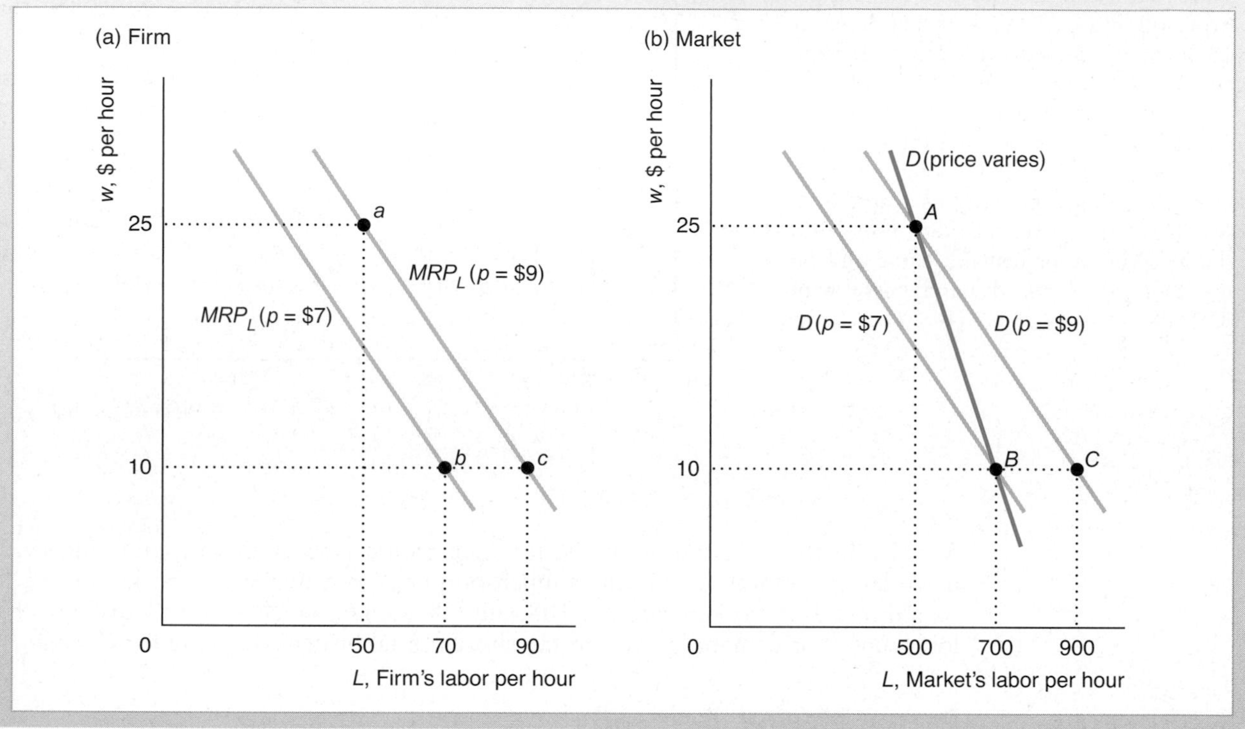

At the initial output market price of \$9 per unit, the competitive firm's labor demand curve (panel a) is $MRP_L(p = \$9) = \$9 \times MP_L$. When the wage is \$25 per hour, the firm hires 50 workers: point *a*. The 10 firms in the market (panel b) demand 500 hours of work: point *A* on the demand curve $D(p = \$9) = 100 \times \$9 \times MP_L$. If the wage falls to \$10 while the market price remains fixed at \$9, each firm hires 90 workers, point *c*, and all the firms in the market would hire 900 workers, point C. However, the extra output drives the price down to \$7, so each firm hires 70 workers, point *b*, and the firms collectively demand 700 workers, point *B*. The market labor demand curve for this output market that takes price adjustments into account, *D*(price varies), goes through points *A* and *B*. Thus, the market's demand for labor is steeper than it would be if output prices were fixed.

See Question 3.

An Alternative Approach. For certain types of production functions, it is easier to determine the market demand curve by using the output profit-maximizing equation rather than the marginal revenue product approach. Suppose that calculator manufacturers are competitive and use a fixed-proportions production function, producing each calculator using one microchip and one plastic case. Each plastic case costs p_p, and each microchip costs p_m. What is the calculator market's demand for microchips?

Figure 15.5 shows the demand both for calculators, Q, and microchips, M. Because the numbers of chips and calculators are equal, $Q = M$, the horizontal axes for chips and calculators are the same.

See Question 4.

Because each calculator requires one chip and one case, the marginal cost of producing a calculator is $MC = p_p + p_m$. Each competitive firm operates where the market price equals the marginal cost: $p = p_p + p_m = MC$. As a result, the most that any firm would pay for a silicon chip is $p_m = p - p_p$, the amount left over from selling a calculator after paying for the plastic case. Thus, the calculator market's demand curve for microchips lies p_p below the demand curve for calculators, as the figure shows.[5]

Competitive Factor Market Equilibrium

The intersection of the factor market demand curve and the factor market supply curve determines the competitive factor market equilibrium. We've just derived the factor market demand. There's nothing unusual about the factor supply curve. The long-run factor supply curve for each firm is its marginal cost curve above the minimum of its average cost curve, and the factor market supply curve is the horizontal sum of the firm supply curves (Chapter 8). As we've already analyzed competitive market equilibria for markets in general in Chapters 2, 3, 8, and 9, there's no point in repeating the analysis. (Been there. Done that.)

See Questions 5–7 and Problems 31 and 32.

Chapter 10 shows that factor prices are equalized across markets. For example, if wages were higher in one industry than in another, workers would shift from the low-wage industry to the high-wage industry until the wages were equalized. (See **www.myeconlab.com/perloff**, Chapter 15, "Why the Black Raises Wages.")

Figure 15.5 Demand for Microchips in Calculators.

It takes one microchip, which costs p_m, and one plastic case, which costs p_p, to produce a calculator, so the marginal cost of a calculator is $MC = p_m + p_p$. Competitive firms operate where the price of a calculator is $p = p_m + p_p$. Thus, the demand curve for a microchip lies p_p below that of a calculator.

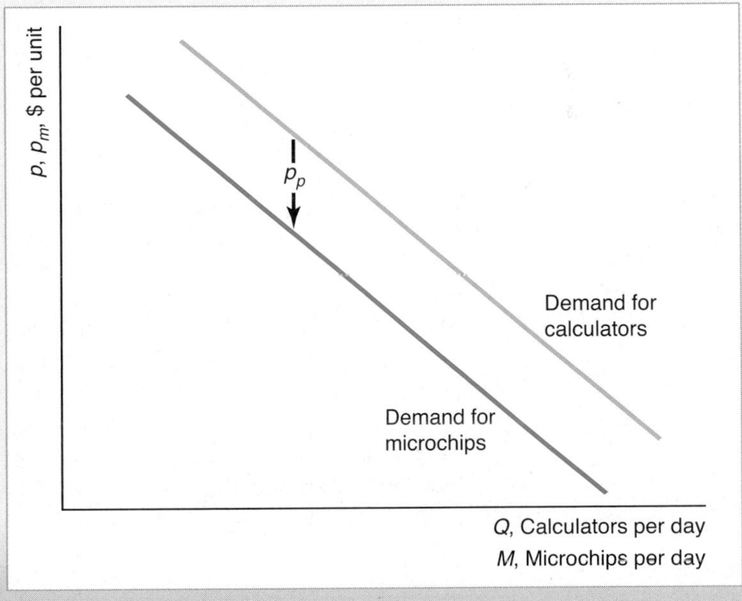

[5]The inverse demand function for calculators is a decreasing function of quantity, $p(Q)$. Similarly, the inverse demand function for microchips is $p_m(M)$. Because $Q = M$, we can write the profit-maximization condition as $p(Q) = p_m(M) + p_p$. Thus, the demand for chips lies p_p below the demand for calculators: $p_m(M) = p(Q) - p_p$.

15.2 Effect of Monopolies on Factor Markets

Having examined the factor market equilibrium where competitive firms sell a factor to a competitive output market, we now survey the effects of market power on factor market equilibrium. If firms in the output market *or* the factor market exercise market power by setting price above marginal cost, less of a factor is sold than would be sold if all firms were competitive.

Market Structure and Factor Demands

Factor demand curves vary with market power. As we saw in Chapters 11 and 12, the marginal revenue of a profit-maximizing firm, $MR = p(1 + 1/\varepsilon)$, is a function of the elasticity, ε, of its output demand curve and the market price, p. Thus, the firm's marginal revenue product of labor function is

$$MRP_L = p\left(1 + \frac{1}{\varepsilon}\right)MP_L.$$

The labor demand curve is $p \times MP_L$ for a competitive firm because it faces an infinitely elastic demand at the market price, so its marginal revenue equals the market price.

The marginal revenue product of labor or labor demand curve for a competitive market is above that of a monopoly or oligopoly firm. Figure 15.6 shows the short-run market factor demand for a thread mill if it is a competitive firm, one of two identical Cournot quantity-setting firms, or a monopoly.[6]

Figure 15.6 How Thread Mill Labor Demand Varies with Market Structure.

For all profit-maximizing firms, the labor demand curve is the marginal revenue product of labor: $MRP_L = MR \times MP_L$. Because marginal revenue differs with market structure, so does the MRP_L. At a given wage, a competitive thread firm demands more workers than a Cournot duopoly firm, which demands more workers than a monopoly.

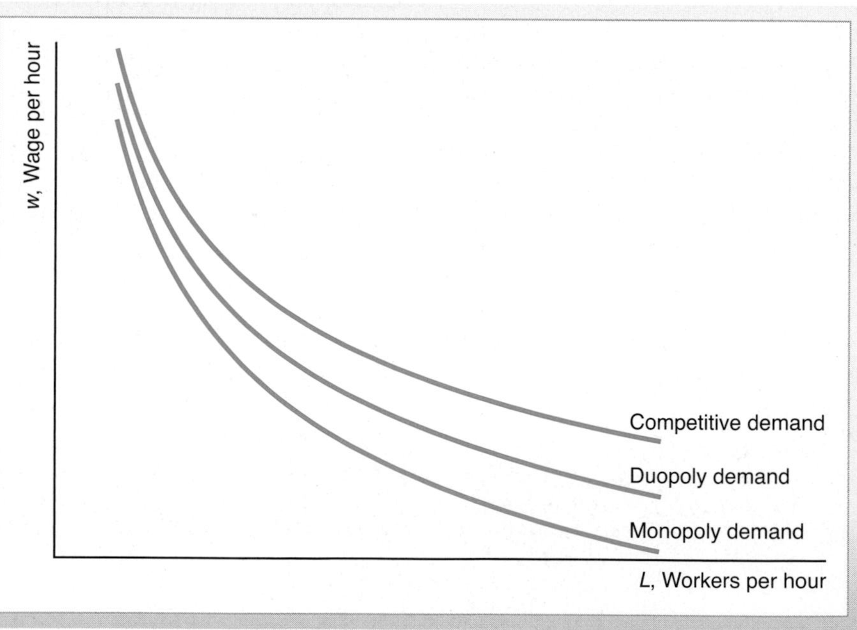

[6]In the short run, the thread mill's marginal product function is $MP_L = 1.2L^{-0.4}$. The labor demand is $p \times 1.2L^{-0.4}$ for a competitive firm, $p[1 + 1/(2\varepsilon)] \times 1.2L^{-0.4}$ for one of two identical Cournot duopoly firms, and $p(1 + 1/\varepsilon) \times 1.2L^{-0.4}$ for a monopoly.

A monopoly operates in the elastic section of its downward-sloping demand curve (Chapter 11), so its demand clasticity is less than −1 and finite: $-\infty < \varepsilon \leq -1$. As a result, at any given price, the monopoly's labor demand, $p(1 + 1/\varepsilon)MP_L$, lies below the labor demand curve, pMP_L, of a competitive firm with an identical marginal product of labor curve.

The elasticity of demand a Cournot firm faces is $n\varepsilon$, where n is the number of identical firms and ε is the market elasticity of demand (Chapter 13). Given that they have the same market demand curve, a duopoly Cournot firm faces twice as elastic a demand curve as a monopoly faces. Consequently, a Cournot duopoly firm's labor demand curve, $p[1 + 1/(2\varepsilon)]MP_L$, lies above that of a monopoly but below that of a competitive firm. From now on, we concentrate on the competitive and monopoly equilibria because the oligopoly and monopolistically competitive equilibria lie between these polar cases.

See Questions 8 and 9 and Problem 33.

A Model of Market Power in Input and Output Markets

When a firm with market power in either the factor or the output market raises its price, the price to final consumers rises. As a result, consumers buy fewer units, so fewer units of the input are demanded. We use a linear example to illustrate how monopolies affect factor market equilibrium. The inverse demand, $p(Q)$, for the final good is

$$p = 80 - Q. \tag{15.3}$$

Figure 15.7 plots this demand curve. An unlimited number of workers can be hired at \$20 an hour. Each unit of output, Q, requires one unit of labor, L, and no other factor, so the marginal product of labor is 1.

As a benchmark, we start our analysis with competitive factor and output markets. Then we ask how the factor market equilibrium changes if the output market is monopolized. Next, we examine a monopolized factor market and a competitive output market. Finally, we investigate the effect of market power in both markets.

Competitive Factor and Output Markets. The intersection of the relevant supply and demand curves determines the competitive equilibria in both input and output markets in Figure 15.7. Because $Q = L$, the figure measures both output and labor on the same horizontal axis.

The marginal product of labor is 1 because one extra worker produces one more unit of output. Thus, the competitive market's demand for labor, $MRP_L = p \times MP_L = p$, is identical to the output demand curve. The labor demand function is the same as the output demand function, where we replace p with w and Q with L:

$$w = 80 - L. \tag{15.4}$$

The competitive supply of labor is a horizontal line at \$20. Given a competitive output market, the intersection of this supply curve of labor and the competitive demand for labor (Equation 15.4) determines the labor market equilibrium, e_1, where $20 = 80 - L$. Thus, the competitive equilibrium amount of labor services is $L_1 = 60$, and the equilibrium wage is $w_1 = \$20$.

The cost of producing a unit of output equals the wage, so the supply curve of output is also horizontal at \$20. The intersection of this output supply curve and the output demand curve, Equation 15.3, occurs at $Q_1 = 60$ and $p_1 = \$20$. A competitive firm's average cost, w_1, exactly equals the price at which it sells its good, p_1, so the competitive firm breaks even.

Figure 15.7 Effect of Output Market Structure on Labor Market Equilibrium.

Because one unit of output is produced with one unit of labor, the marginal product of labor is 1, so the competitive labor demand curve is the same as the output demand curve. If both markets are competitive, the labor market equilibrium is e_1. A monopoly's labor demand curve is identical to its marginal revenue curve. An output monopoly charges final consumers a higher price, so it buys less labor. The new labor equilibrium is e_2. With a labor monopoly (union), the equilibrium is e_3.

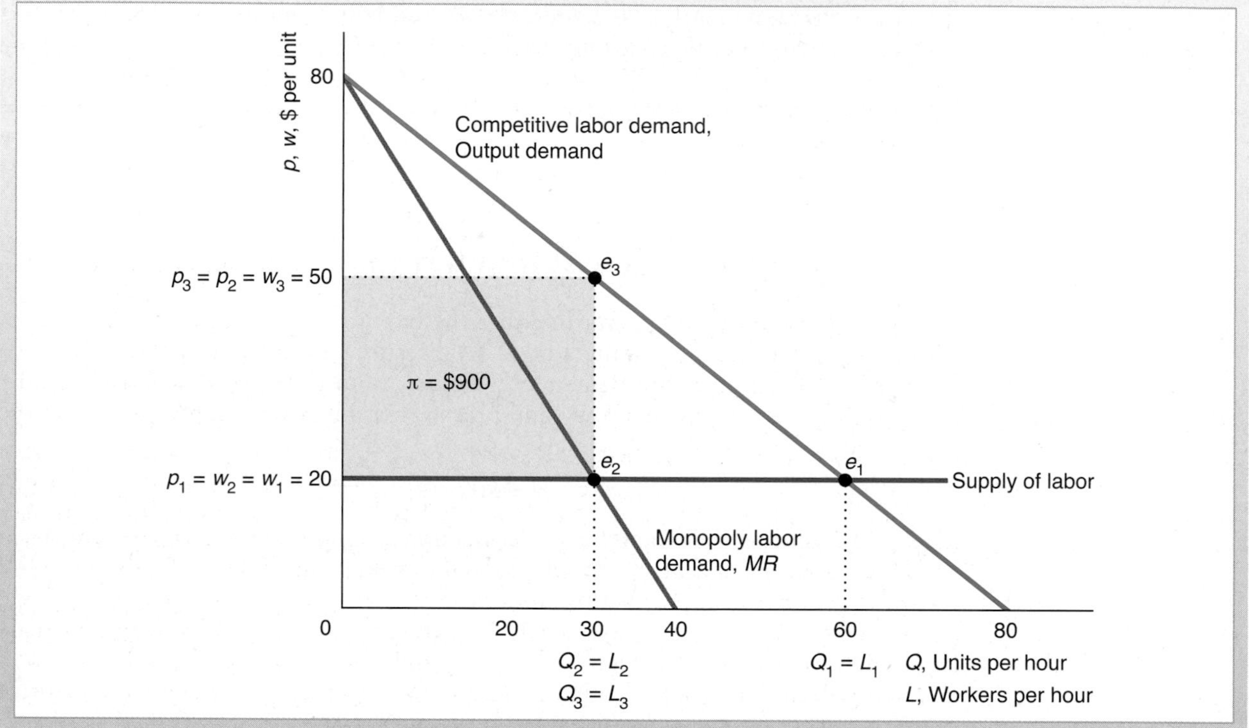

Competitive Factor Market and Monopolized Output Market. Because a monopoly in the output market charges a higher price than a competitive market would, it sells fewer units of output and hires fewer workers. The monopoly faces a competitive labor supply curve that is horizontal at the wage $w_2 = \$20$. Thus, the output monopoly's marginal cost is \$20 per unit.

The monopoly's marginal revenue curve is twice as steep as the linear output demand curve it faces (Chapter 11):

$$MR_Q = 80 - 2Q.$$

The monopoly maximizes its profit where its marginal revenue equals its marginal cost:

$$MR_Q = 80 - 2Q = 20 = MC.$$

Thus, the equilibrium quantity is $Q_2 = 30$. Substituting this quantity into the output demand, Equation 15.3, we find that the equilibrium price is \$50. The monopoly makes $p_2 - w_2 = \$50 - \$20 = \$30$ per unit. Its profit is $\pi = \$900$, as the shaded rectangle in Figure 15.7 shows.

Because the monopoly's marginal product of labor is 1, its demand curve for labor equals its marginal revenue curve:

$$MRP_L = MR_Q \times MP_L = MR_Q.$$

See Question 10.

We obtain its labor demand function by replacing Q with L and MR_Q with w in its marginal revenue function:

$$w = 80 - 2L.$$

The intersection of the competitive labor supply curve, w_2 = \$20, and the monopoly's demand for labor curve determines the labor market equilibrium, e_2, where $80 - 2L = 20$. Thus, the equilibrium amount of labor is $L_2 = 30$.

This example illustrates that a monopoly hurts final consumers and drives some sellers of the factor (workers) out of this market. Final consumers pay \$30 more per unit than they would pay if the market were competitive. Because of the higher price, consumers buy less output, $Q_2 = 30 < 60 = Q_1$. As a consequence, the monopoly demands less labor than a competitive market does: $L_2 = 30 < 60 = L_1$. If the supply curve of labor were upward sloping, this reduction in demand would also reduce workers' wages.

APPLICATION

Baseball Salaries and Ticket Prices

At a press conference in 1999, the Los Angeles Dodgers announced that they'd signed their star pitcher Kevin Brown to a new seven-year \$105 million contract, making Brown the first \$100 million player in baseball. (Under this contract, Brown, who was traded to the New York Yankees in 2003, was still the eleventh-highest-paid player in baseball at \$15.7 million in 2005—Barry Zito's 2007 seven-year contract for \$126 million is currently tops for a pitcher, while Alex Rodriguez has the largest contract for \$275 million.) When Mr. Brown was asked what effect his contract would have on ticket prices, he responded, "I have never believed that players' salaries are directly related to ticket prices." The reporters snickered.

Several of these newspaper pundits wrote that Mr. Brown's salary hike would drive up ticket prices to cover the expense. But their prediction doesn't make sense. If fans are willing to pay a higher price, it pays for the team to raise its price even if its players' salaries remain constant. The team sets its ticket price to maximize its profit given market demand and then negotiates with players to determine how they split the profit.

A baseball club's ticket price is determined by the intersection of its marginal revenue curve and its marginal cost curve. When a team raises a player's salary, it increases its fixed cost but not its marginal cost. The player's salary doesn't affect the cost of bringing one more fan to the stadium. Indeed, if there are unfilled seats in the stadium, the marginal cost of the last fan is essentially zero.

Ticket prices rise when a higher salary is paid only if the team hires a new star player, causing the demand curve to shift to the right. If the team has agreed to pay a higher salary to a current player, as in the Dodgers' case, the higher salary should have no effect on ticket prices.

But aren't player payrolls and ticket prices correlated? Sure, but higher ticket prices "cause" higher salaries rather than the other way around. Star players capture some of the rents. Indeed, the Dodgers raised their 1999 ticket prices before they signed Brown. Teams in cities where the demand is great tend to pay the highest salaries. The New York Yankees' cable television network had revenues of \$341 million in 2006, more than covering their payroll before a single fan enters Yankee Stadium. The five other highest payrolls are paid by teams with new, large stadiums that double as virtual cash registers and provide funds to hire players.

If salaries determined ticket prices, then we would expect changes in salaries to be correlated with changes in ticket prices. That doesn't happen. In 2002, of the 10 teams that reduced their payroll, 6 kept their ticket prices unchanged (as did 4 of the 20 teams that paid players more). Even though the Boston Red Sox cut their payroll and already sported the league's most expensive ticket, the team had the largest ticket price increase. Between 1990 and 2005, the average player salary increased 100% (to $2.5 million), while baseball ticket prices rose 120%.

See Question 11.

Monopolized Factor Market and Competitive Output Market. Now suppose that the output market is competitive and that there is a labor monopoly. One possibility is that the workers form a union that acts as a monopoly. Instead, for simplicity, we'll assume that the labor monopoly is the only firm that can supply the workers employed in the output market.[7]

The labor monopoly sets its marginal revenue equal to its marginal cost, which is $20. Because the competitive output market's labor demand curve is the same as the output demand curve, the marginal revenue curve this labor monopoly faces is the same as the marginal revenue curve of an output monopoly, where we replace Q with L:

$$MR_L = 80 - 2L.$$

The labor monopoly operates at e_3 in Figure 15.7, where its marginal revenue equals its marginal cost of $20:

$$80 - 2L = 20.$$

The labor monopoly sells $L_3 = 30$ hours of labor services. Substituting this quantity into the labor demand curve, Equation 15.4, we find that the monopoly wage is $w_3 = \$50$. Because the labor monopoly makes $w_3 - \$20 = \$30$ per hour of labor services and it sells 30 hours, its profit is $\pi = \$900$.

The competitive supply to the output market is horizontal at $w_3 = \$50$. The output equilibrium occurs where this supply curve hits the output demand curve, Equation 15.3: $50 = 80 - Q$. Thus, the equilibrium quantity is $Q_3 = 30$. The equilibrium price is the same as the wage, $p_3 = w_3 = \$50$. As a result, the output firms break even.

In our example, in which one unit of labor produces one unit of output, consumers fare the same whether the labor market or the output market is monopolized. Consumers pay $p_2 = p_3 = \$50$ and buy $Q_2 = Q_3 = 30$ units of output. The labor market equilibria are different: The wage is higher if the monopoly is in the labor market rather than the output market. The profit goes to the monopoly regardless of which market is monopolized.

APPLICATION

Union Monopoly Power

Workers acting collectively within a union can raise their wage much in the same manner as any other monopoly. A union's success in raising the wage depends on the elasticity of demand it faces, members' ability to act collectively, laws, and the share of the labor market that is unionized. Just as the entry of competitive firms reduces the power of a monopoly (Chapter 11), we expect that the markup of the union wage over the nonunion wage will be smaller, the smaller the fraction of the labor market controlled by unions.

---

[7]Many markets have firms that only supply labor to other firms. Manpower, Kelly Services, and Accountemps provide temporary office workers and other employees. Many construction firms supply only skilled craftspeople. Still other firms specialize in providing computer programmers.

The union markup in Britain has fallen over time. The table shows estimates of how much higher British union wages were than nonunion wages in various years for three labor-skill groups.

	1889–1890	1984	1990
Unskilled	25.2%	10.2%	7.2%
Semiskilled	17.4%	10.0%	6.3%
Skilled	19.3%	3.4%	1.5%

In the late nineteenth century, unions were thriving. Union membership more than doubled from 1888 to 1892, rising from 6.2% of the workforce to 13.0%. Most of the workers in the 1889–1890 survey reported in the table were employed in industries in which unions' share of the market was substantially higher (reaching up to 90% in some occupations and industries). Unions engaged in many strikes to demonstrate their market power aggressively.

In recent decades, the union wage markup has fallen. One estimate, by Blanchflower and Bryson (2004), of the overall U.K. markup in 2002 is 6.4%. (In comparison, they estimate the U.S. union wage markup at 16.5% in 2002.) Factors contributing to this decline include legislation that reduced the bargaining strength of trade unions, a drop in the share of union workers from 54% in 1980 to 38% in 1990 and 26% in 2006, and changes in the mix of occupations with strong union representation.

U.S. unions have exercised more union monopoly power than have their British counterparts. The average estimated U.S. markup was 14% based on many studies covering the 1967–1978 period (Lewis, 1986). The U.S. union markup was estimated to be 21.5% in 1993 (Eren, 2007) and 16.5% in 2002 (Blanchflower and Bryson, 2004).

Monopoly in Successive Markets. If the labor and output markets are both monopolized, consumers get hit with a double monopoly markup. The labor monopoly raises the wage, in turn raising the cost of producing the final output. The output monopoly then increases the final price even further.[8]

Figure 15.8 illustrates this double markup. The output monopoly's marginal revenue curve, $MR_Q = 80 - 2Q$, is the same as its labor demand curve, $w = 80 - 2L$. Because the labor demand curve is linear, the labor monopoly's marginal revenue curve is twice as steeply sloped:

$$MR_L = 80 - 4L.$$

The labor monopoly maximizes its profit by setting its marginal revenue equal to its marginal cost: $80 - 4L = 20$. Thus, at the labor market equilibrium, e_4, the labor monopoly provides $L_4 = 15$ workers. Substituting this quantity into the labor demand curve, $w = 80 - 2L$, we find that the labor monopoly's equilibrium wage is

[8]In our example, the labor monopoly has a constant marginal cost of $m = \$20$. It operates where its marginal cost equals its marginal revenue, $w(1 + 1/\varepsilon_L)$, where ε_L is the elasticity of labor demand. Thus, the wage is greater than marginal cost: $w = m\mu_L$, where $\mu_L = 1/(1 + 1/\varepsilon_L) > 1$ is the multiplicative labor monopoly markup. The wage is the output monopoly's marginal cost. The output monopoly further marks up the price: $p = w\mu_Q = m\mu_L\mu_Q$, where $\mu_Q = 1/(1 + 1/\varepsilon_Q) > 1$ is the multiplicative output monopoly markup and ε_Q is the output demand elasticity.

Figure 15.8 Double Monopoly Markup.

If there are two successive monopolies, consumers are hit with a double monopoly markup. The labor market equilibrium is e_4, where the wage, w_4, is \$30 above the labor market's marginal and average cost of \$20. The product market monopoly's price, p_4, is \$15 above its marginal cost, w_4. If the labor monopoly integrates vertically, consumers gain ($p_3 < p_4$), and total profit increases from $A + B$ to $B + C$.

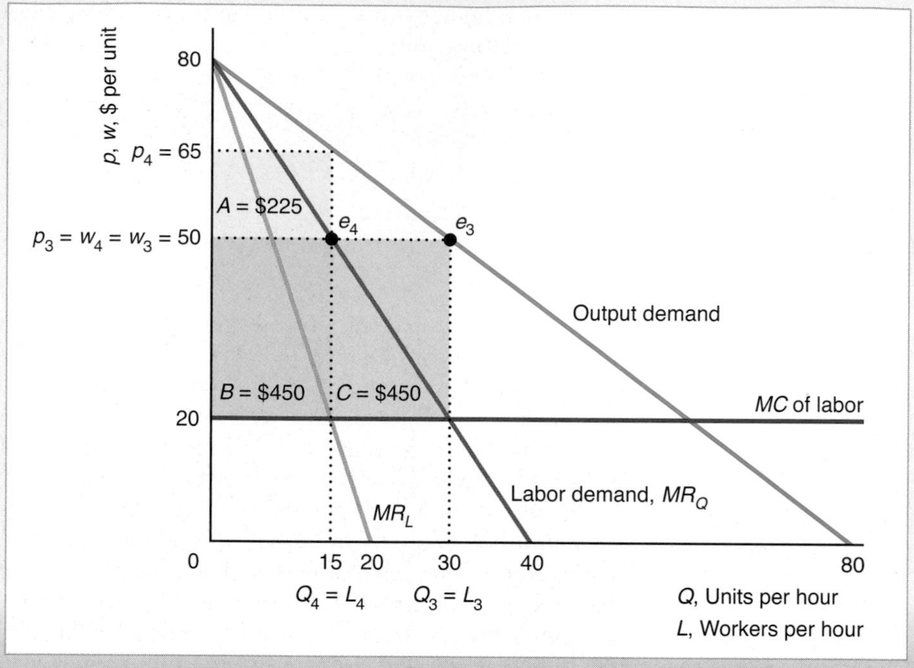

w_4 = \$50. Thus, the labor monopoly marks up its wage \$30 above its marginal cost. Its profit is area B = \$30 × 15 = \$450 in the figure.

To maximize its profit, the output monopoly sets its marginal revenue, $MR_Q = 80 - 2Q$, equal to its marginal cost, w_4 = \$50. It sells $Q_4 = 15$ units of output. Substituting this quantity into the output demand curve, we learn that the output monopoly's equilibrium price is p_4 = \$65. The output monopoly's markup is \$15 above its marginal cost. Its profit is area A = \$225.

See Question 12 and Problem 34.

This double markup harms consumers. They pay a higher price—\$65 rather than \$50—than they would pay if there were a monopoly in just one market or the other.

Solved Problem 15.2

How are consumers affected and how do profits change in the example if the labor monopoly buys the monopoly producer (integrates vertically)?

Answer

1. *Solve for the postmerger equilibrium.* The new merged monopoly's output demand is the market demand, and its marginal revenue from extra output is $MR_Q = 80 - 2Q$, as Figure 15.8 shows. Now that the firms are one, the former labor monopoly no longer marks up the labor to its production unit. Its marginal cost of an extra unit of output is \$20. The monopoly maximizes its profit by setting its marginal cost equal to MR_Q. The resulting output equilibrium is the same as it is when there was a single labor monopoly. Equilibrium output is $Q_3 = 30$ and p_3 = \$50. The integrated monopoly's profit is \$30 × 30 = \$900, area $B + C$.

2. *Compare the premerger and postmerger equilibria.* Consumers benefit from this merger. Because the price they pay falls from p_4 = \$65 to p_3 = \$50, they

buy 15 extra units of output. The firms also benefit. The combined profit with two monopolies is areas $A + B = \$675$, which is less than the profit of the integrated firm, areas $B + C = \$900$. The labor monopoly can offer the output monopoly more than it earns as a separate firm and still increase its own profit: The firms can split the extra \$225. Thus, everyone may gain from a vertical merger that eliminates one of the two monopoly markups.

APPLICATION

Is Limiting Entry into Casket Sales a Grave Restriction?

The average cost of U.S. funeral home services (not including payments at cemeteries or crematories) is \$6,500, according to the National Funeral Directors Association. The AARP reports that the final price for a burial can easily exceed \$10,000 once a burial plot, flowers, and other costs are included. Americans spend roughly as much at funeral homes as they do in the nation's movie theaters (and don't have nearly as much fun).

Entry into the funeral service business is regulated in all states, which may give funeral homes market power. Moreover, some states have laws that allow only licensed funeral service firms to sell funeral goods such as caskets, while other states allow competitive retailers to sell such goods.

Are consumers hurt by restrictions on entry into selling caskets? Chevalier and Scott Morton (2008) find that, the prices of funeral goods fall but the price of funeral services rise by nearly as much when courts have ended such sales restrictions.

Thus, they confirm what they call the "one monopoly rent" hypothesis: Because people buy one casket for each funeral, the total cost of the casket and the funeral service is the sum of the two individual fees. If the funeral home raises the price on caskets, it needs to lower the price on its services, or it will raise its total price so much that a consumer may go to another funeral home or choose a cheaper option, such as cremation.

15.3 Monopsony

In Chapter 11, we saw that a *monopoly*, a single *seller*, picks a point—a price and a quantity combination—on the market *demand curve* that maximizes its profit. A *monopsony*, a single *buyer* in a market, chooses a price-quantity combination from the industry *supply curve* that maximizes its profit. A monopsony is the mirror image of monopoly, and it exercises its market power by buying at a price *below* the price that competitive buyers would pay.

An American manufacturer of state-of-the-art weapon systems can legally sell only to the federal government. U.S. professional football teams, which act collectively, are the only U.S. firms that hire professional football players.[9] In many fisheries, there is only one buyer of fish (or at most a small number of buyers, an *oligopsony*).

Monopsony Profit Maximization

Suppose that a firm is the sole employer in town—a monopsony in the local labor market. The firm uses only one factor, labor (L), to produce a final good. The value

[9]Football players belong to a union that acts collectively, like a monopoly, in an attempt to offset the monopsony market power of the football teams.

the firm places on the last worker it hires is the marginal revenue product of that worker—the value of the extra output the worker produces—which is the height of the firm's labor demand curve for the number of workers the firm employs.

The firm has a downward-sloping demand curve in panel a of Figure 15.9. The firm faces an upward-sloping supply curve of labor: The higher its daily wage, w, the more people want to work for the firm. The firm's *marginal expenditure*—the additional cost of hiring one more worker—depends on the shape of the supply curve.

The supply curve shows the average expenditure, or wage, the monopsony pays to hire a certain number of workers. For example, the monopsony's average expenditure or wage is \$20 if it hires $L = 20$ workers per day. If the monopsony wants to obtain one more worker, it must raise its wage because the supply curve is upward sloping. Because it pays all workers the same wage, the monopsony must also pay more to each worker it was already employing. Thus, the monopsony's marginal expenditure on the last worker is greater than that worker's wage.[10] The marginal expenditure curve in the figure has twice as steep a slope as the linear supply curve.[11]

See Problem 35.

Figure 15.9 Monopsony.

(a) The marginal expenditure curve—the monopsony's marginal cost of buying one more unit—lies above the upward-sloping market supply curve. The monopsony equilibrium, e_m, occurs where the marginal expenditure curve intersects the monopsony's demand curve. The monopsony buys fewer units at a lower price, $w_m = \$20$, than a competitive market, $w_c = \$30$, would. (b) The supply curve is more elastic at the optimum than in (a), so the value that the monopsony places on the last unit (which equals the marginal expenditure of \$40) exceeds the price the monopsony pays, $w_m = \$30$, by less than in (a).

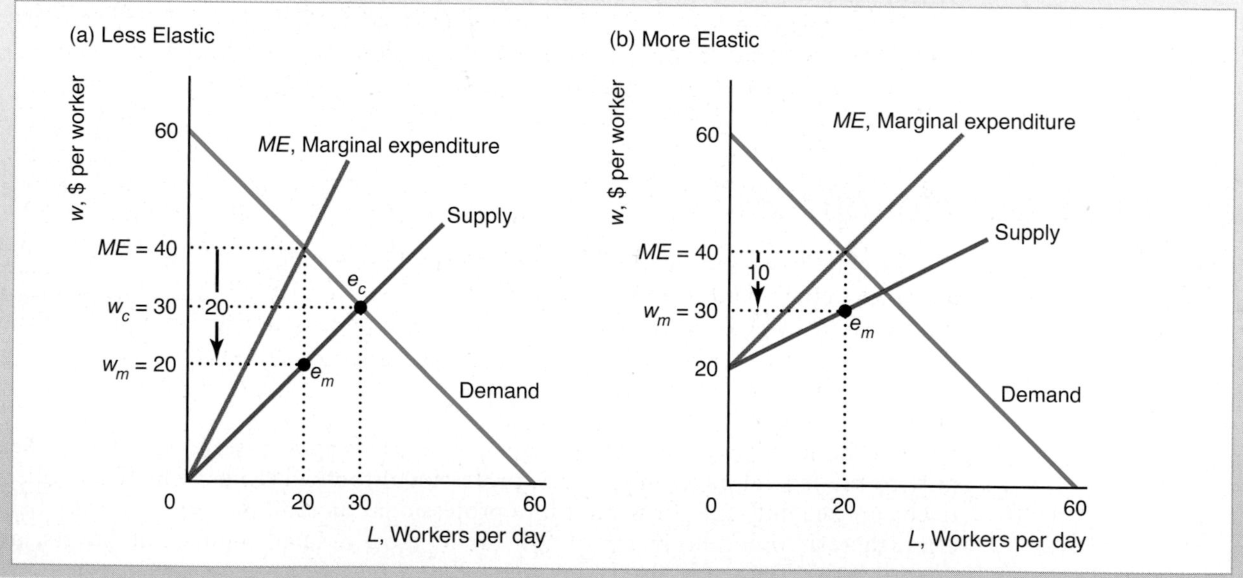

[10]The monopsony's total expenditure is $E = w(L)L$, where $w(L)$ is the wage given by the supply curve. Its marginal expenditure is $ME = dE/dL = w(L) + L[dw(L)/dL]$, where $w(L)$ is the wage paid the last worker and $L[dw(L)/dL]$ is the extra amount the monopsony pays the workers it was already employing. Because the supply curve is upward sloping, $dw(L)/dL > 0$, the marginal expenditure, ME, is greater than the average expenditure, $w(L)$.

[11]Appendix 15B shows that the ME curve is twice as steep as the labor supply curve for any linear labor supply curve.

See Question 13.

In contrast, if the firm were a competitive price taker in the labor market, it would face a supply curve that was horizontal at the market wage. Consequently, such a competitive firm's marginal expenditure to hire one more worker would be the market wage.

Any buyer—including a monopsony or a competitive firm—*buys labor services up to the point at which the marginal value of the last unit of a factor equals the firm's marginal expenditure* (Appendix 15B). If the last unit is worth more to the buyer than its marginal expenditure, the buyer purchases another unit. Similarly, if the last unit is less valuable than its marginal expenditure, the buyer purchases one less unit.

The monopsony buys 20 units of the factor. The intersection of its marginal expenditure curve and the demand curve determines the monopsony equilibrium, e_m. The monopsony values the labor services of the last worker at \$40 (height of its demand curve), and its marginal expenditure on that unit (height of its marginal expenditure curve) is \$40. It pays only \$20 (height of the supply curve). In other words, the monopsony values the last unit at \$20 more than it actually has to pay.

If the market in Figure 15.9 were competitive, the intersection of the market demand curve and the market supply curve would determine the competitive equilibrium at e_c, where buyers purchase 30 units at $p_c = \$30$ per unit. Thus, the monopsony hires fewer workers, 20 versus 30, than a competitive market would hire and pays a lower wage, \$20 versus \$30.

Monopsony power is the ability of a single buyer to pay less than the competitive price profitably. The size of the gap between the value the monopsony places on the last worker (the height of its demand curve) and the wage it pays (the height of the supply curve) depends on the elasticity of supply at the monopsony optimum. The markup of the marginal expenditure (which equals the value to the monopsony) over the wage is inversely proportional to the elasticity of supply at the optimum (Appendix 15B):

$$\frac{ME - w}{w} = \frac{1}{\eta}.$$

By comparing panels a and b in Figure 15.9, we see that the less elastic the supply curve is at the optimum, the greater the gap between marginal expenditure and the wage. At the monopsony optimum, the supply curve in panel b is more elastic than the supply curve in panel a.[12] The gap between marginal expenditure and wage is greater in panel a, $ME - w = \$20$, than in panel b, $ME - w = \$10$. Similarly, the markup in panel a, $(ME - w)/w = 20/20 = 1$, is much greater than that in panel b, $(ME - w)/w = 10/30 = \frac{1}{3}$. (See **www.myeconlab.com/perloff**, Chapter 15, "Monopsony Wage Setting.")

See Questions 14–19 and Problem 36.

APPLICATION
Company Towns

Most firms cannot act as a monopsony, paying low wages to their workers, because their employees could move to higher-paying firms. The only exception occurs when workers live in an isolated area with a single employer (or have jobs in an occupation with only one nearby employer).

Company towns—small communities where a single firm is the only major employer—were relatively common in the United States from the late 1800s

[12]The supply curve in panel a is $w = L$, while that in panel b is $w = 20 + \frac{1}{2}L$. The elasticity of supply, $\eta = (dL/dw)(w/L)$, at the optimum is $w/L = 20/20 = 1$ in panel a and $2w/L = 2 \times 30/20 = 3$ in panel b. Consequently, the supply curve at the optimum is three times as elastic in panel b as in panel a.

through the early 1900s. Typically, a company-town firm not only provided employment but also served as the purveyor of goods, the major landlord, the garbage collector, and the employer of police—the firm dispensed "justice."

Company towns were common in the coal mining industry in certain parts of the country. In the early 1920s, 65% to 80% of miners in southern Appalachia and in the Rocky Mountains lived in company towns, compared to 10% to 20% in most of the Midwest, 25% in Ohio, and 50% in Pennsylvania. Well-known examples are the Homestead Steel Mill in Homestead, Pennsylvania, and the Pullman Company that produced railroad cars in Pullman, Illinois.

The company town largely died out as automobiles and modern highways made workers more mobile. For example, in 2008, the bankrupt Pacific Lumber hopes to sell its company town, Scotia, California, which it has owned for 140 years. However, as the table shows, some company towns still exist. These modern-day firms can exercise monopsony power only if their workers cannot easily move to other employers.

Company	Town	Local Employees	Population	Percentage
Lands' End (catalog retailer)	Dodgeville, WI	4,354	4,220	103
Wal-Mart (retail stores)	Bentonville, AK	20,000	19,730	101
L. L. Bean (catalog retailer)	Freeport, ME	1,600	1,813	88
Smithfield Foods (pork)	Smithfield, VA	4,511	6,324	71
Adelphia Communications (cable TV)	Coudersport, PA	1,500	2,650	57
Hershey Foods (candy)	Hershey, PA	6,200	12,771	49
Corning (optical-fiber and cable)	Corning, NY	5,200	10,842	48
Pella (windows and doors)	Pella, Iowa	3,000	9,832	31
Maytag (appliances)	Newton, Iowa	4,000	15,579	26
Mohawk Industries (carpets)	Calhoun, GA	2,793	10,667	26
Whirlpool (appliances)	Benton Harbor, MI	2,700	11,182	24
Leggett & Platt (industrial materials)	Carthage, MO	2,169	12,668	17
Dow Chemical (chemicals)	Midland, MI	6,000	41,685	14
Timberland (boots and clothing)	Stratham, NH	730	5,810	13

Welfare Effects of Monopsony

By creating a wedge between the value to the monopsony and the value to the suppliers, the monopsony causes a welfare loss in comparison to a competitive market. In Figure 15.10, sellers lose producer surplus, $D + E$, because the monopsony price, p_m, for a good is below the competitive price, p_c. Area D is a transfer from the sellers to the monopsony and represents the savings of $p_c - p_m$ on the Q_m units the monopsony buys. The monopsony loses C because suppliers sell it less output, Q_m instead of Q_c, at the low price. Thus, the deadweight loss of monopsony is $C + E$. This loss is due to the wedge between the value the monopsony places on the Q_m

Figure 15.10 Welfare Effects of Monopsony.

By setting a price, p_m, below the competitive level, p_c, a monopsony causes too little to be sold by the supplying market, thereby reducing welfare.

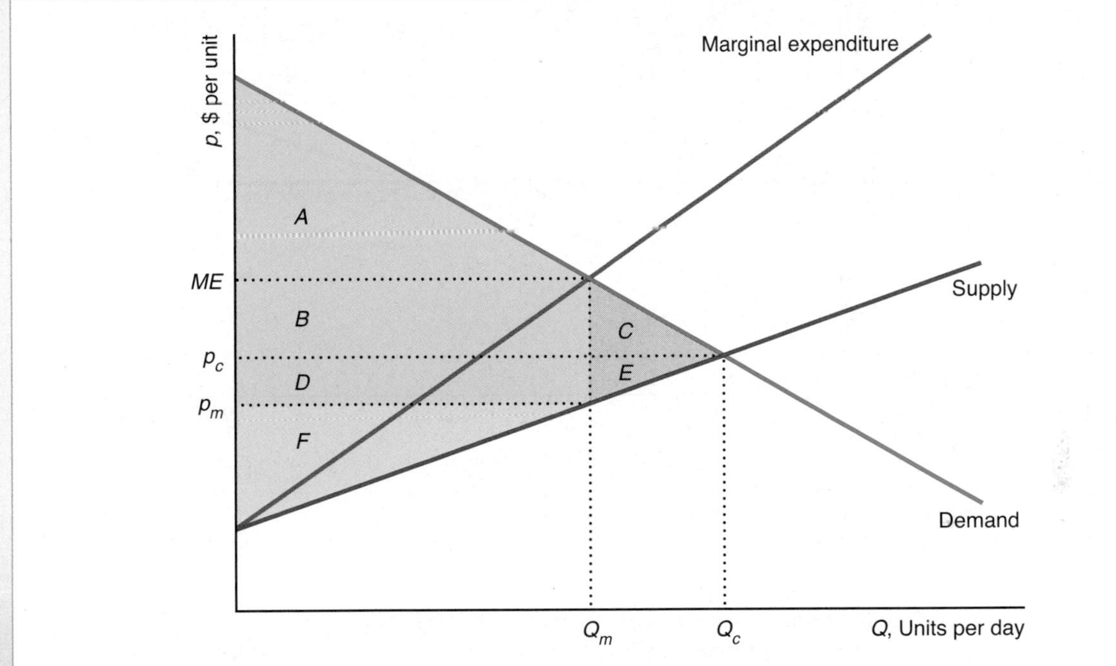

	Competition	Monopsony	Change
Consumer Surplus, *CS*	A + B + C	A + B + D	D − C = Δ*CS*
Producer Surplus, *PS*	D + E + F	F	−D − E = Δ*PS*
Welfare, *W* = *CS* + *PS*	A + B + C + D + E + F	A + B + D + F	−C − E = Δ*W* = *DWL*

See Question 20.

units, the monopoly expenditure *ME* in the figure, and the price it pays, p_m. The greater the difference between Q_c and Q_m and the larger the gap between *ME* and p_m, the greater the deadweight loss.

Solved Problem 15.3

How does the equilibrium in a labor market with a monopsony employer change if a minimum wage is set at the competitive level?

Answer

1. *Determine the original monopsony equilibrium.* Given the supply curve in the graph, the marginal expenditure curve is ME^1. The intersection of ME^1 and the demand curve determines the monopsony equilibrium, e_1. The monopsony hires L_1 workers at a wage of w_1.
2. *Determine the effect of the minimum wage on the marginal expenditure curve.* The minimum wage makes the supply curve, as viewed by the monopsony, flat in the range where the minimum wage is above the original supply curve (fewer than L_2 workers). The new marginal expenditure curve, ME^2, is flat

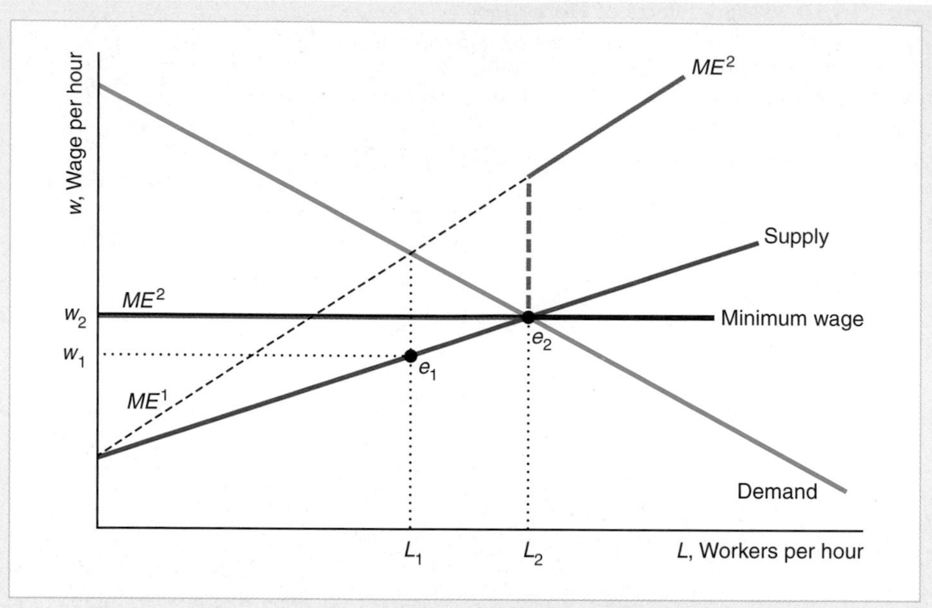

where the supply curve is flat. Where the supply curve is upward sloping, ME^2 is the same as ME^1.

3. *Determine the post-minimum-wage equilibrium.* The monopsony operates where its new marginal expenditure curve, ME^2, intersects the demand curve. With the minimum wage, the demand curve crosses the ME^2 curve at the end of the flat section. Thus, at the new equilibrium, e_2, the monopsony pays the minimum wage, w_2, and employs L_2 workers.

4. *Compare the equilibria.* The post-minimum-wage equilibrium is the same as the competitive equilibrium determined by the intersection of the supply and demand curves. Workers receive a higher wage, and more are employed than in the monopsony equilibrium. The minimum wage helps workers and hurts the monopsony.

See Questions 21 and 22.

Monopsony Price Discrimination

If some consumers have monopsony power while others do not, sellers offer those with monopsony power lower prices. The prices of organ transplants at the Cleveland Clinic, Duke University, and Johns Hopkins hospitals are 29% to 62% lower to health maintenance organizations (HMOs) than to fee-for-service patients. One explanation is that the HMOs threaten to take the business of their millions of members to other hospitals unless a hospital offers them a low, fixed-price contract. By getting bids from several hospitals, the HMOs convince each individual hospital that they have a higher elasticity of demand than other patients.

A monopsony may directly price discriminate in much the same way as a monopoly or an oligopoly. For example, suppose that a monopsony employer can hire either of two types of workers. One type is willing to move to any other firm that pays more. The second type is unwilling to move. The employer may pay those who are willing to move more than it pays other workers, all else the same (see **www.myeconlab.com/perloff**, Chapter 15, "Monopsony Price Discrimination.")

See Question 23.

15.4 Vertical Integration

To sell a good or service to consumers involves many sequential stages of production and sales activities. Profitability determines how many stages a firm performs itself.

Stages of Production

The turkey sandwiches you purchase at your local food stand are produced and delivered through the actions of many firms and individuals. Farmers grow wheat and raise turkeys using inputs they purchase from other firms; processors convert these raw inputs into bread and turkey slices; wholesalers transfer these products from the food processors to the food stand; and finally, employees at the food stand combine various foods to make a sandwich, wrap it, and sell it to you.

Figure 15.11 illustrates the sequential or *vertical* stages of production. First, firms use raw inputs (such as wheat) to produce semiprocessed materials (such as flour). Then the same or other firms use the semiprocessed materials and labor to produce the final good (such as bread). In the last stage, the final consumers buy the product.

In the nineteenth century, production often took place along a river. Early stages of production occurred upstream, and then the partially finished goods were shipped by barge downstream—going with the flow of the river—to other firms that finished the product. We still use anachronistic river terms to indicate the order of production: *Upstream* refers to factors of production, and *downstream* refers to final goods.

Figure 15.11 Vertical Organization.

Raw inputs produced upstream are combined using a production process, $Q = f(M, L)$, downstream to produce a final good, which is sold to consumers.

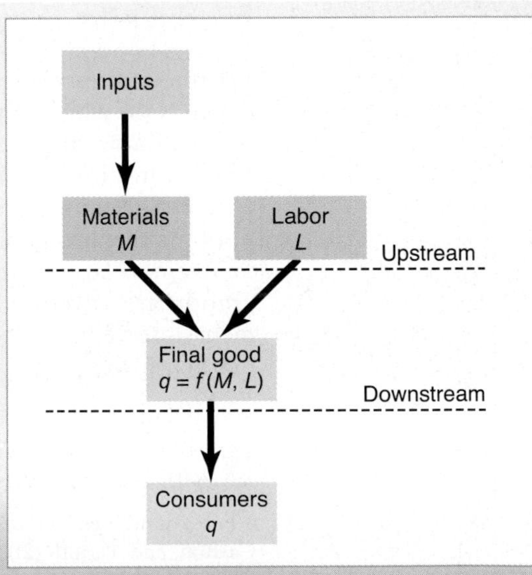

Degree of Vertical Integration

The number of separate firms involved in producing your turkey sandwich depends on how many steps of the process each handles. One possibility is that the food stand carries out many steps itself: making the sandwich, wrapping it, and selling it to you. Alternatively, one firm makes and wraps the sandwich and delivers it to another firm that sells it to you.

A firm that participates in more than one successive stage of the production or distribution of goods or services is *vertically integrated.* A firm may vertically integrate backward and produce its own inputs. For example, after years of buying its unique auto bodies from Fisher Body, General Motors purchased Fisher. Or a firm may vertically integrate forward and buy its former customer. In 1926, General Motors, a former supplier, purchased Hertz (the first car-rental company, founded in 1918). In 1954, Hertz went public. It was sold to a Ford Motor subsidiary in 1987 and became a fully owned Ford subsidiary in 1994.

All firms are vertically integrated to some degree, but they differ substantially as to how many successive stages of production they perform internally. Although you can't be a little bit dead, a firm *can* be partially vertically integrated. It may produce a good but rely on others to market it. Or it may produce some inputs itself and buy others from the market.

Some firms buy from a small number of suppliers or sell through a small number of distributors. These firms often control the actions of the firms with whom they deal by writing contracts that restrict the actions of those other firms. Such contractual *vertical restraints* approximate the outcome from vertically merging. Such tight relationships between firms are referred to as *quasi-vertical integration.*

For example, a franchisor and a franchisee have a close relationship that is governed by a contract. Some franchisors (such as McDonald's) sell a proven method of doing business to individual franchisees (owners of McDonald's outlets). A fast-food franchisor may dictate the types of raw products its franchisees buy, the franchisees' cooking methods, the restaurants' appearance, and the franchisees' advertising.

Produce or Buy

Whether a firm vertically integrates, quasi-vertically integrates, or relies on markets depends on which approach is the most profitable.[13] If a firm can perform most of the necessary stages of production at lower cost than it would incur buying from other firms, it vertically integrates.

When deciding whether to integrate vertically, the firm must take into account not only the direct costs of integrating, such as legal fees, but also the higher cost of managing a larger, more complex company. Five possible benefits from vertical integration are lowering transaction costs, ensuring a steady supply, avoiding government intervention, extending market power to another market, and eliminating market power.

---

[13]For a more detailed analysis of the pros and cons of vertical integration, see Perry (1989) and Carlton and Perloff (2005). The classic articles on vertical integration are Coase (1937) and Williamson (1975). See **www.myeconlab.com/perloff**, Chapter 15, "Vertical Integration of Auto Manufacturers," for a discussion of how Chrysler, Ford, and General Motors differ in the degree to which they are vertically integrated.

Lowering Transaction Costs. Probably the most important reason to integrate is to avoid *transaction costs*: the costs of trading with others besides the price, including the costs of writing and enforcing contracts. A firm that vertically integrates avoids many transaction costs, but its managerial costs rise as the firm becomes larger and more complex.

opportunistic behavior taking advantage of someone when circumstances permit

An important source of transaction costs is **opportunistic behavior:** taking advantage of someone when circumstances permit. When firms agree to a future transaction, each firm may try to interpret the terms of a contract to its advantage, especially when terms are vague or missing.

Opportunistic behavior is particularly likely when a firm deals with only one other firm. If an electronic game manufacturer can buy computer chips from only one firm, it is at the mercy of the chip supplier, a situation that could increase its price substantially just before the Christmas buying season.

Some firms vertically integrate to avoid the transaction costs imposed by opportunistic behavior. By manufacturing the chip itself, the electronic game company can avoid such opportunistic behavior.

Similarly, when one firm has more information than another—where there is *asymmetric information*—the knowledgeable firm may take advantage of the relatively ignorant firm. For example, a buyer may incur substantial transaction costs in monitoring the quality of the seller's product. If the buyer vertically integrates to ensure that critical components are built to a high standard, its quality-control problem changes from monitoring another firm to monitoring its own employees in ways that are not possible when firms are completely independent (see Chapters 19 and 20).

See Questions 24 and 25.

Ensuring a Steady Supply. Like the electronic game manufacturer, many firms are at the mercy of their suppliers. A supplier that delivers a crucial part late imposes substantial costs on these manufacturers. One possibility is for a manufacturer to replace unreliable suppliers in the long run.

Another possibility is quasi-vertical integration, in which the buyer signs a contract that rewards the supplier for prompt delivery and penalizes delays. Toyota and other Japanese manufacturers pioneered the *just-in-time* system of having suppliers deliver inputs at the time needed to process them, thus minimizing inventory costs and avoiding bottlenecks. If replacing unreliable suppliers or using quasi-vertical integration fails, a firm can ensure a steady supply and avoid costs from delays by vertically integrating.

APPLICATION

Aluminum

Opportunistic behavior and the need to ensure a steady supply explain why upstream vertical integration is common in the aluminum industry. Aluminum production has four main stages: mining, refining, smelting, and fabricating. After mining bauxite, a firm mixes it with caustic soda to refine it into alumina. Next, the firm uses electrolysis to produce primary aluminum metal from alumina. Finally, other firms fabricate the metal into foil, wire, cookware, airplane parts, and many other products.

The upstream activities of mining and refining bauxite are both oligopolistic. Bauxite mines and refineries require large capital investments, have large minimum efficient scales, and face substantial barriers to entry. There are only about 80 alumina refineries worldwide. Moreover, bauxite is expensive to ship, so the market for bauxite is regional. Thus, a mine or a refiner has few if any other firms with which it can deal.

To guarantee a steady supply, some refineries sign 20- to 25-year contracts with mines. Because these firms cannot foresee all possible contingencies during such

long periods, one trading party can inflict substantial costs on the other by refusing to deal with it (say, when prices are unusually high or low). These firms have no alternative uses for bauxite and the plants that mine and refine it.

To avoid the potential for such opportunistic behavior, many firms vertically integrate. Vertically integrated firms mine and refine most of the world's bauxite (91% in 1976) and alumina (75% in 2007).

Avoiding Government Intervention. Firms may also vertically integrate to avoid government price controls, taxes, and regulations. A vertically integrated firm avoids *price controls* by selling to itself. The federal government has set a maximum price that could be charged for steel products on several occasions since World War II. Under such price controls, steel producers did not want to sell as much steel as before the controls took effect. Consequently, they rationed steel, selling their longtime customers only a fraction of what they sold before the controls went into effect.

Because transactions within a company were unaffected by price controls, a buyer who really desired more steel could purchase a steel company and obtain all the steel it wanted (and at least one firm did so). Thus, purchasing a steel company allowed firms to avoid price controls. Were it not for the high transaction costs, firms could completely avoid price controls by vertically integrating.

Firms also integrate to lower their *taxes*. Tax rates vary by country, state, and type of product. A vertically integrated firm can shift profits from one of its operations to another simply by changing the *transfer price* at which it sells its internally produced materials from one division to another. By shifting profits from a high-tax jurisdiction to a low-tax jurisdiction, a firm can increase its after-tax profits. The Internal Revenue Service tries to restrict such behavior by requiring that firms use market prices for internal transfers where possible.

Government *regulations* create additional incentives for a firm to integrate vertically (or horizontally) when the profits of only one division of a firm are regulated. When the government restricts the profits that a local telephone company earns on local services but not its profits on other services, such as selling telephones in competition with other suppliers, the telephone company tries to shift profits from its regulated division to its unregulated division.

Extending Market Power. By vertically integrating, a firm may be able to increase its monopoly profits by price discriminating or by monopolizing. The Alcoa example in the "Preventing Resales" section of Chapter 12 shows how a monopoly supplier vertically integrates to prevent resales so that it can price discriminate.

An upstream monopoly supplier of a key input in a production process for a downstream competitive market may be able to boost its profit by vertically integrating forward to monopolize the production industry.[14] Similarly, a vertically integrated firm that supplies itself and others with inputs may be able to restrict essential inputs to potential competitors (see Chapter 14 and **www.myeconlab.com/perloff**, Chapter 15, "Vertical Integration and Essential Facilities: Barnes & Noble" and "Cutting Off Oxygen").

See Question 26.

Eliminating Market Power. A firm that faces a monopsony buyer or monopoly seller may try to eliminate that market power by vertically integrating. During the Great Depression, farms in a given area could sell their milk only to a single processor, who paid them a low monopsony price. Many farmers banded together to create cooperatives that processed their own milk. As we've seen, everyone may benefit from vertical integration if both buyer and seller have monopoly power.

See Question 27.

SUMMARY

1. **Competitive Factor Market.** Any firm maximizes its profit by choosing the quantity of a factor such that the marginal revenue product (MRP) of that factor—the marginal revenue times the marginal product of the factor—equals the factor price. The MRP is the firm's factor demand. A competitive firm's marginal revenue is the market price, so its MRP is the market price times the marginal product. The firm's long-run factor demand is usually flatter than its short-run demand because it can adjust more factors, thus giving it more flexibility. The market demand for a factor reflects how changes in factor prices affect output prices and hence output levels in product markets.
2. **Effect of Monopolies on Factor Markets.** If firms exercise market power to raise price above marginal cost in an output market or factor market, the quantity demanded by consumers falls. Because the quantity of output and the quantity of inputs are closely related, a reduction in the quantity of an input reduces output, and a reduction in output reduces the demand for inputs.
3. **Monopsony.** A profit-maximizing monopsony—a single buyer—sets its price so that the marginal value to the monopsony equals its marginal expenditure. Because the monopsony pays a price below the competitive level, fewer units are sold than in a competitive market, producers of factors are worse off, the monopsony earns higher profits than it would if it were a price taker, and society suffers a deadweight loss. A monopsony may also price discriminate.
4. **Vertical Integration.** A firm may vertically integrate (participate in more than one successive stage of the production or distribution of goods or services), quasi-vertically integrate (use contracts or other means to control firms with which it has vertical relations), or buy from a factor market. Depending on which is more profitable, a firm vertically integrates and produces an input itself or buys the input from others. Because vertical integration is costly, firms integrate only if there are significant benefits. Five possible benefits from vertically integrating are lowering transaction costs, ensuring a steady supply, avoiding government restrictions, extending market power to another market, and eliminating market power.

[14]If the downstream firms use a fixed-proportions production function (as in our earlier examples), a monopoly supplier does not gain additional market power by vertically integrating. See Carlton and Perloff (2005) for the relevant theory and a discussion of the empirical evidence.

QUESTIONS

■ = *exercise is available on MyEconLab;* * = *answer appears at the back of this book;* C = *use of calculus may be necessary;* W = *audio-slideshow answer by James Dearden is available in Textbook Resources on MyEconLab.*

1. What does a competitive firm's labor demand curve look like at quantities of labor such that the marginal product of labor is negative? Why?

*2. What effect does an *ad valorem* tax of α on the revenue of a competitive firm have on that firm's demand for labor?

3. How does a fall in the rental price of capital affect a firm's demand for labor in the long run?

4. If the firm uses a fixed-proportion production process where one unit of labor and one unit of capital produce one unit of output, what is the marginal revenue product of labor?

5. U.S. logging companies employ Canadian loggers to cut Maine trees. When the federal government restricted the number of temporary workers permitted in the United States, the logging companies had to use fewer Canadian loggers. Unable to find U.S. workers willing to cut trees, the logging companies had to lay off workers in complementary operations— truck drivers, for example. Suppose that a logging company needs exactly one truck driver for each six loggers it employs. Each truck driver and team of six loggers can cut and transport 80,000 tons of wood per day. What is the marginal revenue product function for truckers, and how does the function depend on the number of loggers employed? Show that with a decrease in the number of loggers, a logging company would hire fewer truckers. W

6. Suppose that a modern plague (AIDS, SARS, Ebola virus, avian flu) wipes out or incapacitates a major share of a small country's work force. If this country's labor market is competitive, what effect will this disaster have on wages in this country?

7. Oil companies, prompted by improvements in technology and increases in oil prices, are drilling in deeper and deeper water. Using a marginal revenue product and marginal cost diagram of drilling in deep water, show how improvements in drilling technology and increases in oil prices result in more deep-water drilling. W

8. How does a monopoly's demand for labor shift if a second firm enters its output market and the result is a Cournot duopoly equilibrium?

9. Does a shift in the supply curve of labor have a greater effect on wages if the output market is competitive or if it is monopolistic?

10. What is a monopoly's demand for labor if it uses a fixed-proportions production function in which each unit of output takes one unit of labor and one of capital?

11. The "Baseball Salaries and Ticket Prices" application points out that if a ball club raises a player's salary, it increases its fixed cost but not its variable cost. Use a formal model to show what effect such an increase has if (a) the firm is competitive or (b) the firm is a monopoly.

12. In 1998, four television networks (including ESPN) agreed to pay $17.6 billion for eight years of National Football League broadcast rights. In three of the deals, the price was more than double that of the previous contracts. What effect would you expect this deal to have on advertising rates and the number of commercials, and why?

13. Can a monopsony exercise monopsony power—profitably setting its price below the competitive level—if the supply curve it faces is horizontal?

14. Suppose that the original labor supply curve, S^1, for a monopsony shifts to the right to S^2 if the firm spends $1,000 in advertising. Under what condition should the monopsony engage in this advertising? (*Hint*: See the monopoly advertising analysis in Chapter 12.)

15. Some health reform proposals call for taxing firms to pay for workers' medical care. How is the incidence of a specific tax per worker shared between competitive firms and workers? How does your answer change if the firm is a monopsony?

16. Suppose that a modern plague (AIDS, SARS, Ebola virus, avian flu) wipes out or incapacitates a major share of a small country's work force. If this country's labor market is monopsonistic, what effect will this disaster have on wages in this country? Compare your answer to that in Question 6.

17. A firm is a monopoly in the output market and a monopsony in the input market. Its only input is the finished good, which it buys from a competitive market with an upward-sloping supply curve. The firm sells the same good to competitive buyers in the output market. Determine its profit-maximizing output. What price does it charge in the output market? What price does it pay to its suppliers?

18. Compare the equilibrium in a market in which a firm is both a monopoly and a monopsony (as in Question 17) to the competitive equilibrium.

19. Compare the equilibrium quantity and price in two markets: one in which a firm is both a monopsony and a monopoly (as in Question 17) and one in which the firm buys inputs competitively but has a monopoly in the output market.

20. Compare welfare in a market where a firm is both a monopsony and a monopoly to welfare in markets in which the firm has a monopsony in the input market but acts as a price taker in the output market.

21. What happens to the monopsony equilibrium if the minimum wage is set slightly above or below the competitive wage?

22. What effect does a price support have on a monopsony? In particular, describe the equilibrium if the price support is set at the price where the supply curve intersects the demand curve.

23. A health insurer monopsony may make physicians an "all-or-none" offer in which physicians must agree to see a certain minimum number of patients at a relatively low fee (Herndon, 2002). Show how, by so doing, the insurer can achieve the same outcome as it could if it could perfectly price discriminate. (*Hint*: Look at the "Unions That Have It All" application in Chapter 12.)

24. Is a firm more likely to be the victim of opportunistic behavior if it buys parts from (a) a single firm that it will not deal with again next year, (b) a single firm with which it has a long-term relationship, or (c) a market?

25. Auto insurers have vertically integrated into the auto-body and repair business. They claim they did so to reduce their costs of repairs, save customers' time and effort searching for reputable shops, and reduce customers' risk of shoddy repairs. Critics contend, however, that insurance companies do not act in the best interest of their customers when doing repairs; rather, they scrimp on quality to reduce their repair costs. Consider all of the costs of auto-body work and auto repair, including the costs of the repairs themselves, the opportunity cost of customer and insurance company appraiser time, and the cost of correcting shoddy work. Why is the cost of repairing an insured car less if the insurance company does the repairs than if the customer searches for and arranges with an independent shop to do the repairs? W

26. In 2007, Apple started selling the iPhone in the United States with the requirement that it be used only on the AT&T cell phone network. Indeed, Apple took a series of steps to prevent customers from "unlocking" the phone so that it could be used on other networks. The Orange network in France began selling the iPhone for €399 ($588) with a two-year subscription. Unlike in the United States, one can get an unlocked iPhone in France from the vendor. Orange will unlock an iPhone for an additional €100 ($144) if the customer will choose an iPhone service plan, €150 if the customer stays with the carrier and has a non-iPhone plan (which doesn't allow one to use the iPhone's special features), and €250 if the customer does not have a plan with Orange (Stan Beer, "Orange iPhone Unlock Starts Demise of Exclusive Carrier Model," *ITWire*, November 28, 2007). Give plausible explanations why Apple chooses to have an exclusive deal with AT&T, why AT&T wants Apple to enforce exclusivity, and why Orange is being more flexible. Is Apple or the phone service "extending monopoly power?"

27. Can a merger of an upstream and a downstream monopoly help consumers? Explain.

PROBLEMS

*28. A firm's production function is Cobb-Douglas: $Q = AL^{\alpha}K^{\beta}$. What is the firm's marginal revenue product of labor? (*Hint*: Use Appendix 6B.)

29. The Cobb-Douglas production function for a U.S. tobacco products firm is $q = L^{0.2}K^{0.3}$ ("Returns to Scale in U.S. Manufacturing" application, Chapter 6). Derive the marginal revenue product of labor for this firm.

*30. A competitive firm's production function is $q = L + 2LK + K$. What is its marginal revenue product of labor? (*Hint*: $MP_L = 1 + 2K$.)

31. Georges, the owner of Maison d'Ail, earned his coveted Michelin star by smothering his dishes in freshly minced garlic. Georges knows that he can save labor costs by using less garlic, albeit with a reduction in quality. If Georges puts g garlic cloves in a dish, the dish's quality, z, is $z = \frac{1}{2}g^{0.5}$. Georges always fills his restaurant to its capacity, 250 seats. He knows that he can raise the price of each dish by $0.40 for each unit increase in quality and continue to fill his restaurant. Jacqueline, who earns $10 per hour, minces Georges's garlic at a rate of 120 garlic cloves per hour.

a. What is Jacqueline's value of marginal revenue product?

b. How many hours per afternoon (while the kitchen prep work is being done) does Jacqueline work?

c. How many minced cloves of fresh garlic does Georges put in each dish? W

32. Suppose that a firm's production function is $q = L + K$. Can it be a competitive firm? Explain.

33. If a monopoly has a Cobb-Douglas production function, $Q = AL^{\alpha}K^{\beta}$, and faces a constant elasticity demand curve, what is its marginal revenue product of labor? C

34. Many grocery stores charge manufacturers a *slotting fee*: a one-time fee to place a given good on the shelf. Although stores sometimes claim that these fees are to cover their transaction costs of relabeling shelves and updating their computer files, the fees are too large—$50,000 or more—for that to be the only reason (Margaret Webb Pressler, "Grocery Stores Demanding Pay for Shelf Space," *San Francisco Chronicle,* January 20, 2004, B3). Suppose that both the manufacturer and the grocery stores were monopolies. What is the effect of a slotting fee on the manufacturer's wholesale price, the final price in the store, the number of units sold, and the two firms' profits?

35. A monopsony faces a supply curve: $p = 10 + Q$.

What is its marginal expenditure curve?

36. If the monopsony in Problem 35 has a demand curve of $p = 50 - Q$, what are the equilibrium quantity and price? How does this equilibrium differ from the competitive equilibrium?

Interest Rates, Investments, and Capital Markets

16

I'd gladly pay you Tuesday for a hamburger today. —Wimpy

This chapter examines *capital* and other *durable goods*: products that are usable for years. Firms use durable goods—such as manufacturing plants, machines, and trucks—to produce and distribute goods and services. Consumers spend one in every eight of their dollars on durable goods such as houses, cars, and refrigerators.

Until now, we have examined the choices between *nondurable* goods and services, which are consumed when they are purchased or soon thereafter. You eat an ice-cream cone or see a movie just after paying for it.

If a firm rents a durable good by the week, it faces a decision similar to buying a nondurable good or service. A firm demands workers' services (or other nondurable input) up to the point at which its *current* marginal cost (the wage) equals its *current* marginal benefit (the marginal revenue product of the workers' services). A firm that rents a durable good, such as a truck, by the month can use the same rule to decide how many trucks to employ per month. The firm rents trucks up to the point at which the *current* marginal rental cost equals its *current* marginal benefit—the marginal revenue product of the trucks.

If the capital good must be bought or built rather than rented, the firm cannot apply this rule on the basis of current costs and benefits alone. (There are many types of capital, such as factories or specialized pieces of equipment, that a firm *cannot* rent.) In deciding whether to build a long-lived factory, a firm must compare the *current* cost of the capital to the *future* higher profits it will make from using the plant.

Often such comparisons involve *stocks* and *flows*. A **stock** is a quantity or value that is measured independently of time. Because a durable good lasts for many periods, its stock is discussed without reference to its use within a particular time period. We say that a firm owns "an apartment building *this* year" (not "an apartment building *per* year"). If a firm buys the apartment house for $500,000, we say that it has a capital stock worth $500,000 today.

stock
a quantity or value that is measured independently of time

A **flow** is a quantity or value that is measured per unit of time. The consumption of nondurable goods, such as the number of ice-cream cones you eat per week, is a flow. Similarly, the stock of a durable good provides a flow of services. A firm's apartment house—its capital stock—provides a flow of housing services (apartments rented per month or year) to tenants. In exchange for these housing services, the firm receives a flow of rental payments from the tenants.

flow
a quantity or value that is measured per unit of time

Does it pay for the firm to buy the apartment house? To answer this question, we need to extend our analysis in two ways. First, we must develop a method of comparing a flow of dollars in the future to a dollar today, as we do in this chapter. Second, we need to consider the role of uncertainty about the future (can the firm rent all the apartments each month?), a subject that we discuss in Chapter 17.

In this chapter, we examine four main topics

1. **Comparing Money Today to Money in the Future.** Interest rates tell us how much more money is worth today than in the future.
2. **Choices over Time.** Investing money in a project pays if the return from that investment is greater than that on the best alternative when both returns are expressed on a comparable basis.
3. **Exhaustible Resources.** Scarcity, rising costs of extraction, and positive interest rates may cause the price of exhaustible resources like coal and gold to rise exponentially over time.
4. **Capital Markets, Interest Rates, and Investments.** Supply and demand in capital markets determine the market rate of interest, which affects how much people invest.

16.1 Comparing Money Today to Money in the Future

Even if there were no inflation—so a bundle of goods would sell for the same price today, next year, and 100 years from now—most people would still value receiving a dollar today more than a dollar to be received tomorrow. Wouldn't you rather eat a dollar's worth of chocolate today than wait ten years to eat that same amount of chocolate?

Interest Rates

Because virtually everyone values having a dollar today more than having a dollar in the future, getting someone to loan you a dollar today requires agreeing to pay back more than a dollar in the future. You may have borrowed money to pay for your college education in exchange for a credible promise to repay a greater amount after you graduate. How much more you must pay in the future is specified by an **interest rate**: the percentage more that must be repaid to borrow money for a fixed period of time.[1]

interest rate
the percentage more that must be repaid to borrow money for a fixed period of time

If you put money in a savings account, you are lending the bank your money, which it may in turn loan to someone who wants to buy a car or a house. For the use of your deposited funds for one year, the bank agrees to pay you an interest rate, i, of, say, 4%. That is, the bank promises to return to you \$1.04 (= $1 + i$) one year from now for every dollar you loan it. If you put \$100 in your savings account, you will have your \$100 plus interest of $\$100 \times 0.04 = \$4$ for a total of \$104 at the end of the year. (See **www.myeconlab.com/perloff**, Chapter 16, "Usury," for a discussion of ancient people's opposition to paying interest, and current restrictions on Islamic banks.)

See Questions 1 and 2.

Discount Rate. You may value future consumption more or less than other members of society. If you knew you had a fatal disease that would kill you within two years, you would place less value on payments three or more years in the future than most other people do. We call an individual's personal "interest" rate that person's **discount rate**: a rate reflecting the relative value an individual places on future consumption compared to current consumption.

discount rate
a rate reflecting the relative value an individual places on future consumption compared to current consumption

[1]For simplicity, we refer to *the* interest rate throughout this chapter, but in most economies there are many interest rates. For example, a bank charges a higher interest rate to loan you money than it pays you to borrow your money.

A person's willingness to borrow or lend depends on whether his or her discount rate is greater or less than the market interest rate. If your discount rate is nearly zero—you view current and future consumption as equally desirable—you would gladly loan money in exchange for a positive interest rate. Similarly, if your discount rate is high—current consumption is much more valuable to you than future consumption—you would be willing to borrow at a lower interest rate. In the following discussion, we assume for simplicity that an individual's discount rate is the same as the market interest rate unless we explicitly state otherwise.

Compounding. If you place \$100 in a bank account that pays 4%, at the end of a year, you can take out the interest payment of \$4 and leave your \$100 in the bank to earn more interest in the future. If you leave your \$100 in the bank indefinitely and the interest rate remains constant over time, you will receive a payment of \$4 each year. In this way, you can convert your \$100 stock into a flow of \$4-a-year payments forever.

In contrast, if you leave both your \$100 and your \$4 interest in the bank, the bank must pay you interest on \$104 at end of the second year. The bank owes you interest of \$4 on your original deposit of \$100 and interest of $\$4 \times 0.04 = \$0.16$ on your interest from the first year, for a total of \$4.16.

Thus, at the end of Year 1, your account contains

$$\$104.00 = \$100 \times 1.04 = \$100 \times 1.04^1.$$

By the end of Year 2, you have

$$\$108.16 = \$104 \times 1.04 = \$100 \times 1.04^2.$$

At the end of Year 3, your account has

$$\$112.49 \approx \$108.16 \times 1.04 = \$100 \times 1.04^3.$$

If we extend this reasoning, by the end of Year t, you have

$$\$100 \times 1.04^t.$$

In general, if you let your interest accumulate in your account, for every dollar you loan the bank, it owes you $1 + i$ dollars after one year, $(1 + i) \times (1 + i) = (1 + i)^2$ dollars after two years, $(1 + i) \times (1 + i) \times (1 + i) = (1 + i)^3$ after three years, and $(1 + i)^t$ dollars at the end of t years. This accumulation of interest on interest is called *compounding*.

Frequency of Compounding. To get the highest return on your savings account, you need to check both the interest rate and the frequency of compounding. We have assumed that interest is paid only at the end of the year. However, many banks pay interest more frequently than once a year. If you leave your interest in the bank for the entire year, you receive compounded interest—interest on the interest.

If a bank's annual interest rate is $i = 4\%$, but it pays interest two times a year, the bank pays you half a year's interest, $i/2 = 2\%$, after six months. For every dollar in your account, the bank pays you $(1 + i/2) = 1.02$ dollars after six months. If you leave the interest in the bank, at the end of the year, the bank must pay you interest on your original dollar and on the interest you received at the end of the first six months. At the end of the year, the bank owes you $(1 + i/2) \times (1 + i/2) = (1 + i/2)^2 = (1.02)^2 = \$1.0404$, which is your original \$1 plus 4.04¢ in interest.

If the bank were to compound your money more frequently, you would earn even more interest. Some banks offer continuous compounding, paying interest at every instant. Such compounding is only slightly better for you than daily compounding. Table 16.1 shows you that the amount you would earn after one year of investing

Table 16.1 Interest and the Frequency of Compounding.

	Interest Payments on a $10,000 Investment at the End of 1 Year, $	
Frequency of Compounding	4%	18%
Once a year	400.00	1,800.00
Twice a year	404.00	1,881.00
Four times a year	406.04	1,925.19
Daily	408.08	1,971.64
Continuous	408.11	1,972.17

$10,000 at a 4% or at an 18% annual rate of interest depends on the frequency of compounding.

Because most people cannot easily perform such calculations, the 1968 U.S. Truth-in-Lending Act requires lenders to tell borrowers the equivalent noncompounded annual percentage rate (APR) of interest. As the table shows, twice-a-year compounding at 4% has an APR of 4.04%. That is, over a year, an account with a noncompounded interest rate of 4.04% pays you the same interest as a 4% account that was compounded twice during the year.

Thus, when considering various loans or interest rates, you should compare the APRs; comparing rates that are compounded at different frequencies can be misleading. If you use credit cards to borrow money, it's particularly important that you compare APRs across accounts because credit card interest rates are usually high. If the interest rate on your card is 18%, a continuously compounded rate has an APR of over 19.7%. If you borrow $10,000 for a year, you'll owe $1,972.17 with continuous compounding, which is 9.6% more than the $1,800 you'd owe with annual compounding. From now on, we assume that compounding takes place annually.

See Problem 8.

Using Interest Rates to Connect the Present and Future

Interest rates connect the value of the money you put in the bank today, the *present value* (*PV*), and the *future value* (*FV*) that you are later repaid, which is the present value plus interest. Understanding this relationship allows us to evaluate the attractiveness of investments involving payments today for profits in the future and of purchases made today but paid for later. Knowing the interest rate and the present value allows us to calculate the future value. Similarly, we can determine the present value if we know the future value and the interest rate.

Future Value. If you deposit *PV* dollars in the bank today and allow the interest to compound for *t* years, how much money will you have at the end? The future value, *FV*, is the present value times a term that reflects the compounding of the interest payments:

$$FV = PV \times (1 + i)^t.$$

Table 16.2 shows how much $1 put in the bank today will be worth in the future at various annually compounded interest rates. For example, $1 left in the bank for 50 years will be worth only $1.64 at a 1% interest rate. However, that same investment is worth $7.11 at a 4% interest rate, $117.39 at a 10% rate, and $9,100.44 at a 20% rate.

See Problem 9.

Table 16.2 Future Value, *FV*, to Which $1 Grows by the End of Year *t* at Various Interest Rates, *i*, Compounded Annually, $.

t, Years	1%	4%	5%	10%	20%
1	1.01	1.04	1.05	1.10	1.20
5	1.05	1.22	1.28	1.61	2.49
10	1.10	1.48	1.63	2.59	6.19
25	1.28	2.67	3.39	10.83	95.40
50	1.64	7.11	11.47	117.39	9,100.44

Note: $FV = (1 + i)^t$, where *FV* is the future value of $1 invested for *t* years at an annual interest rate of *i*.

APPLICATION

Power of Compounding

One thousand dollars left to earn interest at 8% a year will grow to $43 quadrillion in 400 years, but the first 100 years are the hardest.

—Sidney Homer, Salomon Brothers analyst

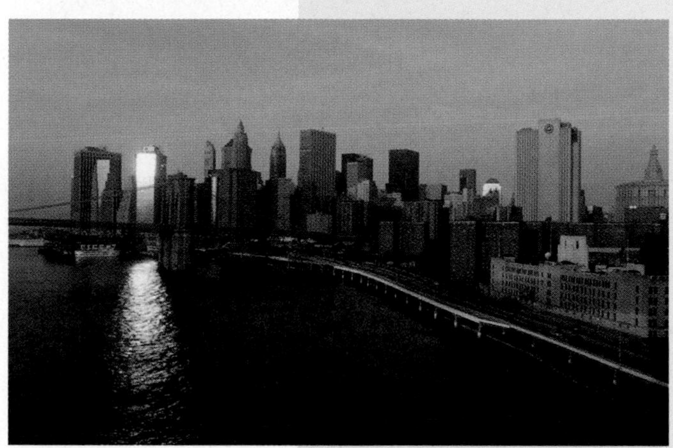

No doubt you've read that the Dutch got a good deal buying Manhattan from the original inhabitants in 1626 for about $24 worth of beads and trinkets. That conclusion may be wrong. If these native Americans had had the opportunity to sell the beads and invest in tax-free bonds with an APR of 7%, the bond would be worth $4 trillion in 2008, which is much more than the assessed value of Manhattan Island. On the other hand, if the United States had taken the $7.2 million it paid for the purchase of Alaska from Russia in 1867 and invested in the same type of bonds, that money would now be worth only $100 billion, which is much less than Alaska's current value.

Present Value. Instead of asking how much a dollar today is worth in the future, we can ask how much a dollar in the future is worth today, given the market interest rate. For example, we may want to know how much money, *PV*, we have to put in the bank today at an interest rate *i* to get a specific amount of money, *FV*, in the future. If we want to have $FV = \$100$ at the end of a year and the interest rate is $i = 4\%$, then from Equation 16.1 we know that $PV \times 1.04 = \$100$. Dividing both sides of this expression by 1.04, we learn that we need to put $PV = \$100/1.04 = \$96.15$ in the bank today to have $100 next year.

A more general formula relating money *t* periods in the future to money today is obtained by dividing both sides of Equation 16.1 by $(1 + i)^t$ to obtain

$$PV = \frac{FV}{(1 + i)^t}. \tag{16.2}$$

This equation tells us what *FV* dollars in year *t* are worth today at an interest *i* compounded annually. Table 16.3 and Figure 16.1 show what $1 in the future is worth

Table 16.3 Present Value, *PV*, of a Payment of $1 at the End of Year *t* at Various Interest Rates, *i*, Compounded Annually, $.

t, Years	1%	4%	5%	10%	20%
1	0.99	0.96	0.95	0.91	0.83
5	0.95	0.82	0.78	0.62	0.40
10	0.91	0.68	0.61	0.39	0.16
25	0.78	0.38	0.30	0.09	0.01
50	0.61	0.14	0.09	0.009	0.00011

Note: $PV = 1/(1 + i)^t$, where PV is the present value of $1 at the end of year t at an annual interest rate of i.

Figure 16.1 Present Value of a Dollar in the Future.

The present value of a dollar is lower the farther in the future it is paid. At a given time in the future, the present value is lower when the interest rate is higher.

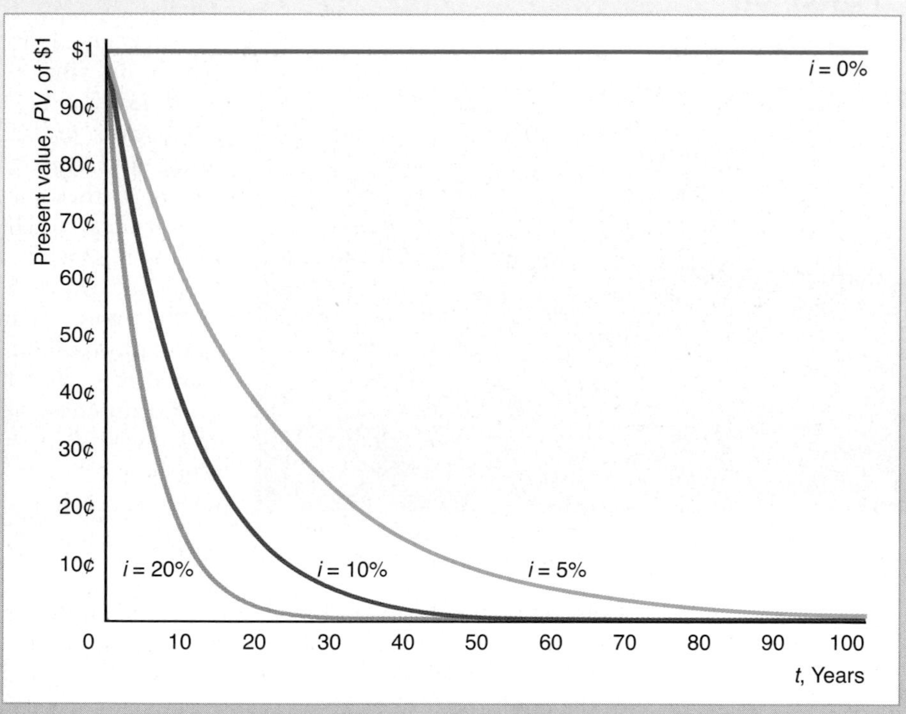

today at various interest rates. At high interest rates, money in the future is virtually worthless today: A dollar paid to you in 25 years is worth only 1¢ today at a 20% interest rate.

See Questions 3 and 4 and Problems 10–12.

Stream of Payments

Sometimes we need to deal with payments per period, which are flow measures, rather than a present value or future value, which are stock measures. Often a firm pays for a new factory or an individual pays for a house by making monthly mortgage payments. In deciding whether to purchase the factory or house, the decision maker compares the value of the stock (factory or home) to a flow of payments over time.

Present Value of Payments over Time. One way to make such an evaluation is to use our knowledge of the relationship between present and future value to determine the present value of the stream of payments. To do so, we calculate the present value of each future payment and sum them.

Payments for a Finite Number of Years. To motivate the general case, we start with a specific example. Suppose that you agree to pay \$10 at the end of each year for three years to repay a debt. If the interest rate is 10%, the present value of this series of payments is

$$PV = \frac{\$10}{1.1} + \frac{\$10}{1.1^2} + \frac{\$10}{1.1^3} \approx \$24.87.$$

More generally, if you make a *future payment* of f per year for t years at an interest rate of i, the present value (stock) of this flow of payments is

$$PV = f\left[\frac{1}{(1+i)^1} + \frac{1}{(1+i)^2} + \cdots + \frac{1}{(1+i)^t}\right]. \quad (16.3)$$

See Problem 13.

Table 16.4 shows that the present value of a payment of f = \$10 a year for five years is \$43 at 5%, \$38 at 10%, and \$30 at 20% annual interest.

Payments Forever. If these payments must be made at the end of each year forever, the present value formula is easier to calculate than Equation 16.3. If you put PV dollars into a bank account earning an interest rate of i, you can get an interest or future payment of $f = i \times PV$ at the end of the year. Dividing both sides of this expression by i, we find that to get a payment of f each year forever, you'd have to put

See Problem 14.

$$PV = \frac{f}{i} \quad (16.4)$$

in the bank. Thus, you'd have to deposit \$10/i in the bank to ensure a future payment of f = \$10 forever. (See Appendix 16A for a mathematical derivation.) Using

Table 16.4 Present Value, PV, of a Flow of \$10 a Year for t Years at Various Interest Rates, i, Compounded Annually, \$.

t, Years	5%	10%	20%
5	43	38	30
10	77	61	42
50	183	99	50*
100	198	100*	50*
∞	200	100	50

*The actual numbers are a fraction of a cent below the rounded numbers in the table. For example, the PV at 10% for 100 years is \$99.9927.

Note: The payments are made at the end of the year.

this formula, we determine that the present value of \$10 a year forever is \$200 at 5%, \$100 at 10%, and \$50 at 20%.[2]

Solved Problem 16.1

Melody Toyota advertises that it will sell you a Corolla for \$14,000 or lease it to you. To lease it, you must make a down payment of \$1,650 and agree to pay \$1,800 at the end of each of the next two years. After the last lease payment, you may buy the car for \$12,000. If you plan to keep the car until it falls apart (at least a decade) and the interest rate is 10%, which approach has a lower present value of costs?

Answer

1. *Calculate the present value of leasing.* The present value of leasing the car and then buying it is the sum of the down payment of \$1,650, the present value of paying $f = \$1,800$ at the end of each year for $t = 2$ years, and the present value of purchasing the car for $FV = \$12,000$ in $t = 2$ years. Using Equation 16.2, we find that the present value of buying the car at the end of the lease period is

$$PV = \frac{f}{i^2} = \frac{\$12,000}{1.1^2} \approx \$9,917.$$

Thus, the present value of leasing the car and then buying it is approximately

$$\$1,650 + \$3,124 + \$9,917 = \$14,691.$$

2. *Compare leasing to buying the car.* The present value of buying the car is \$14,000, which is \$691 less than the present value of leasing it.

Future Value of Payments over Time. We just calculated the present value of a stream of payments. This type of computation can help you decide whether to buy something today that you'll pay for over time. Sometimes, however, we want to know about the future value of a stream of payments.

For example, suppose that you want to know how much you'll have in your savings account, FV, at some future time if you save f each year. The first year, you place f dollars in your account. The second year, you add another f and you have the first year's payment plus its accumulated interest, $f(1 + i)^1$. Thus, at the end of the second year, your account has $f[1 + (1 + i)^1]$. In the third year, you have the third year's payment, f, plus the current value of the second year's payment, $f(1 + i)$, plus the current value of the first year's payment, $f(1 + i)^2$, for a total of $f[1 + (1 + i) + (1 + i)^2]$. Continuing in this way, we see that, at the end of t years, the account has[3]

$$FV = f[1 + (1 + i)^1 + (1 + i)^2 + \cdots + (1 + i)^{t-1}]. \tag{16.5}$$

[2]This payment-in-perpetuity formula, Equation 16.4, provides a good approximation of a payment for a large but finite number of years. As Table 16.4 shows, at a 5% interest rate, the present value of a payment of \$10 a year for 100 years, \$198, is close to the present value of a permanent stream of payments, \$200. At higher interest rates, this approximation is nearly perfect. At 10%, the present value of payments for 100 years is \$99.9927 compared to \$100 for perpetual payments. The reason this approximation works better at high rates is that a dollar paid more than 50 or 100 years from now is essentially worthless today, as Table 16.3 shows.

[3]This equation can be written as $FV = f[(1 + i)^0 + (1 + i)^1 + (1 + i)^2 + \dots + (1 + i)^{t-1}]$ because $(1 + i)^0 = 1$.

APPLICATION

Saving for Retirement

If all goes well, you'll live long enough to retire. Will you live like royalty off your savings, or will you depend on Social Security to provide enough income that you can avoid having to eat dog food to stay alive? (When I retire, I'm going to be a Velcro farmer.)

You almost certainly don't want to hear this, but it isn't too early to think about saving for retirement. Thanks to the power of compounding, if you start saving when you're young, you don't have to save as much per year as you would if you start saving when you're middle aged.

Suppose that you plan to work full time from age 22 until you retire at 70 and that you can earn 7% on your retirement savings account. Let's consider two approaches to savings:

- **Early bird.** You save $3,000 a year for the first 15 years of your working life and then let your savings accumulate interest until you retire.
- **Late bloomer.** After not saving for the first 15 years, you save $3,000 a year for the next 33 years until retirement.

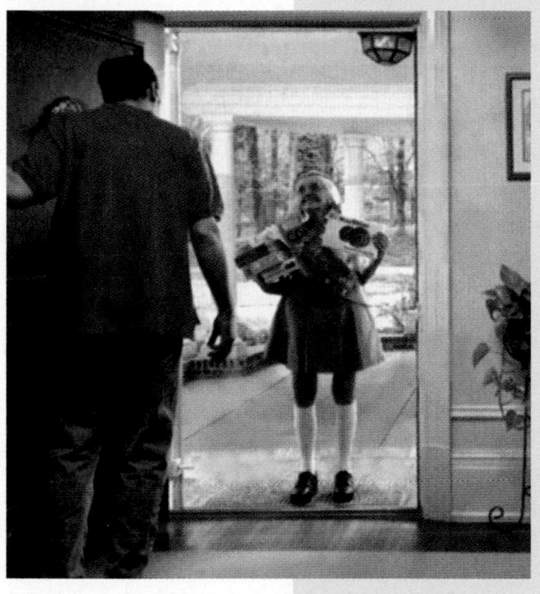

Which scenario leads to a bigger retirement nest egg? To answer this question, we calculate the future value at retirement of each of these streams of investments.

The early bird adds $3,000 each year for 15 years into a retirement account. Using Equation 16.5, we calculate that the account has

$$\$3{,}000(1 + 1.07^1 + 1.07^2 + \cdots + 1.07^{14}) = \$75{,}387$$

at the end of 15 years. This amount then grows as the interest compounds for the next 33 years. Using Equation 16.1, we determine that the fund grows about 9.3 times to

$$\$75{,}387.07 \times 1.07^{33} = \$703{,}010$$

by retirement.

The late bloomer makes no investments for 15 years and then invests $3,000 a year until retirement. Again using Equation 16.5, we calculate that the funds at retirement are

$$\$3{,}000(1 + 1.07 + 1.07^2 + \cdots + 1.07^{32}) = \$356{,}800.$$

Thus, even though the late bloomer contributes to the account for more than twice as long as the early bird, the late bloomer has saved only about half as much at retirement. Indeed, to have roughly the same amount at retirement as the early bird, the late bloomer would have to save nearly $6,000 a year for the 33 years. (By the way, someone who saved $3,000 each year for all 48 years would have $703,010 + $356,800 = $1,059,810 salted away by retirement.)

Inflation and Discounting

So far, we've ignored inflation (implicitly assumed an inflation rate of zero). Now we suppose that general inflation occurs so that *nominal prices*—actual prices that are not adjusted for inflation—rise at a constant rate over time. By adjusting for this rate of inflation (Chapter 5), we can convert nominal prices to *real prices*, which are constant prices that are independent of inflation. To calculate the real present value of future payments, we adjust for inflation and use interest rates to discount future real payments.

To illustrate this process, we calculate the real present value of a payment made next year. First, we adjust for inflation so as to convert next year's nominal payment to a real amount. Then we determine the real interest rate. Finally, we use the real interest rate to convert the real future payment to a real present value.

Adjusting for Inflation. Suppose that the rate of inflation is γ ("gamma") and the nominal amount you pay next year is $\tilde{f}$. This future debt in today's dollars—the real amount you owe—is $f = \tilde{f}/(1 + \gamma)$. If the rate of inflation is $\gamma = 10\%$, a nominal payment of $\tilde{f}$ next year is $\tilde{f}/1.1 \approx 0.909\tilde{f}$ in today's dollars.

Nominal and Real Rates of Interest. To calculate the present value of this future real payment, we discount using an interest rate. Just as we converted the future payments into real values by adjusting for inflation, we convert a nominal interest rate into a real interest rate by adjusting for inflation.

Without inflation, a dollar today is worth $1 + i$ next year, where i is the real interest rate. With an inflation rate of γ, a dollar today is worth $(1 + i)(1 + \gamma)$ nominal dollars tomorrow. If $i = 5\%$ and $\gamma = 10\%$, a dollar today is worth $1.05 \times 1.1 = 1.155$ nominal dollars next year.

Banks pay a nominal interest rate, $\tilde{i}$, rather than a real one. If they're going to get people whose real discount rate is i to save, banks' nominal interest rate must be such that a dollar pays $(1 + i)(1 + \gamma)$ dollars next year. Because $1 + \tilde{i} = (1 + i)(1 + \gamma) = 1 + i + i\gamma + \gamma$, the nominal rate is

$$\tilde{i} = i + i\gamma + \gamma.$$

By rearranging this equation, we see that the real rate of interest depends on the nominal rate of interest and the rate of inflation:

$$i = \frac{\tilde{i} - \gamma}{1 + \gamma}. \tag{16.6}$$

Equation 16.6 shows that the real rate of interest is less than the nominal rate in the presence of inflation.

If the inflation rate is small, the denominator of Equation 16.6, $1 + \gamma$, is close to 1. As a result, many people approximate the real rate of interest as the nominal rate of interest minus the rate of inflation:

$$\tilde{i} - \gamma.$$

If the nominal rate of interest is 15.5% and the rate of inflation is 10%, the real rate of interest is (15.5% − 10%)/1.1 = 5%. The approximation to the real rate, 15.5% − 10% = 5.5%, is above the true rate by half a percentage point. The lower the rate of inflation, the closer the approximation is to the real rate of interest. If the inflation rate falls to $\gamma = 2\%$ while the nominal rate remains 15.5%, the approximation to the real rate, 13.5%, is above the real rate, 13.24%, by only slightly more than a quarter of a percentage point.

Real Present Value. To obtain the real present value of a payment one year from now, we discount the future real payment of $f = \tilde{f}/(1 + \gamma)$ using the real interest rate:

$$PV = \frac{f}{1 + i} = \frac{\tilde{f}}{(1 + \gamma)(1 + i)}.$$

Thus, the real present value is obtained by adjusting for inflation and by discounting using the real interest rate.

Suppose that you sign a contract with a store to pay \$100 next year for a DVD player you get today. The rate of inflation is $\gamma = 10\%$, and the real rate of interest is

$i = 5\%$. We calculate the real present value by converting the future payment into real dollars and by using the real interest rate to discount. Next year's nominal payment of \$100 is only $\$100/1.1 \approx \$90.91$ in real dollars. Discounting by the real rate of interest, we find that the real present value of that payment is $\$90.91/1.05 \approx \$86.58$.

If everyone anticipates a particular inflation rate, γ, the nominal interest is roughly $i + \gamma$. Suppose, however, that the inflation rate turns out to be higher than the anticipated rate of γ. Such unanticipated inflation helps debtors because it lowers the real cost of future payments that are set in nominal rather than real terms.

Suppose that when you buy the DVD player, no one expects inflation ($\gamma = 0$), so both you and the store's owner believe that the present value of your future payment is $\$100/1.05 \approx \$95.24$. Immediately after you make the deal, the inflation rate suddenly increases to $\gamma = 10\%$, so the actual present value is only \$86.58. Thus, because of the unexpected inflation, the present value of what you owe is less than either you or the store owner initially expected.

See Problems 15 and 16.

APPLICATION

Winning the Lottery

Lottery: A tax on people who are bad at math.

Sheila Botelho won Rhode Island's November 28, 2007 Multi-State Powerball lottery jackpot. She was given the choice of a stream of annual payments over 30 years totaling \$151.9 million or a single, lump-sum payment of \$75.2 million. By extending these options, the lottery was implicitly acknowledging that money in the future is worth less than money today. Mrs. Botelho opted for the single, immediate payout. When asked why, Mrs. Botelho and her husband said that "At our age, we don't even buy green bananas."

Several states boast that their lottery pays a winner \$1 million. This claim is misleading (translation: They lie through their teeth). Typically, a lottery winner gets \$50,000 a year for 20 years, which means that the winner receives $20 \times \$50,000 = 1$ million nominal dollars over time. However, after adjustment for inflation and discounting, the real present value of these prize payments over time is much less than \$1 million.

What is a payment of \$50,000 for 20 years worth today? If the first payment is made today, its real present value is \$50,000, regardless of the inflation and interest rates. The later payments need to be adjusted for inflation and discounted to the present to be comparable to this year's payment.

If the rate of inflation is 5% and the real rate of interest is 4%, a \$50,000 payment next year is worth only $\$45,788 \approx \$50,000/(1.05 \times 1.04)$ this year. Generalizing, we determine that the real present value of a dollar t years from now is

$$\frac{1}{(1.05)^t(1.04)^t}.$$

The $(1.05)^t$ term in the denominator adjusts for inflation between now and the year t: It expresses the payment in the future in terms of today's dollars. The $(1.04)^t$ term in the denominator converts the payment in year t to a present value.

At these rates, the real present value of the 20 payments is less than half a million dollars: \$491,396. If there were no inflation ($\gamma = 0$), the real present value would be \$706,697. With 5% inflation and a real interest rate of 10%, the present value of the prize is only \$351,708.[4]

[4]This discussion of lottery prizes is not intended to encourage you to play the lottery. The important thing to remember about a lottery is that the probability of winning if you buy a ticket is almost exactly the same as the probability of winning if you don't buy a ticket: zero.

16.2 Choices over Time

Earlier chapters discuss how consumers and firms make choices that do not involve time. Often, however, such decisions involve comparisons over time. Individuals and firms must choose between two or more options—such as investments and contracts—that have different present and future values. A land speculator decides whether to sell a plot of land today for \$100,000 or next year for \$200,000. Margi decides among putting \$1,000 into a bank account, buying \$1,000 worth of stocks, paying \$1,000 for a course in computer programming, and consuming the \$1,000 now. MGM, a conglomerate, decides whether to produce a movie that stars a muscle-bound hero who solves the pollution problem by beating up an evil capitalist, to build a new hotel in Reno, to buy a television studio, or to put money in a long-term savings account.

One way to make a choice involving time is to *pick the option with the highest present value*. By borrowing or lending at the market interest rate, we can shift wealth from one period to another. Thus, if we choose the option that has the highest present value, we can shift our wealth between periods so that we have more money in every period than we'd have if we made a less attractive choice.

See Problems 17–25.

Investing

Investment decisions may be made by comparing present values. *A firm makes an investment if the expected return from the investment is greater than the opportunity cost* (Chapter 7). The opportunity cost is the best alternative use of its money, which is what it would earn in the next best use of the money.

Thus, to decide whether to make an investment, the firm needs to compare the potential outlay of money to the firm's best alternative. One possibility is that its best alternative is to put the money that it would otherwise spend on this investment in an interest-bearing bank account. We consider two methods for making this comparison: the *net present value* approach and the *internal rate of return* approach.

Net Present Value Approach. A firm has to decide whether to buy a truck for \$20,000. Because the opportunity cost is \$20,000, the firm should make the investment only if the present value of expected future returns from the truck is greater than \$20,000.

More generally, *a firm should make an investment only if the present value of the expected return exceeds the present value of the costs*. If R is the present value of the expected returns to an investment and C is the present value of the costs of the investment, the firm should make the investment if $R > C$.[5]

This rule is often restated in terms of the net present value, $NPV = R - C$, which is the difference between the present value of the returns, R, and the present value of the costs, C. *A firm should make an investment only if the net present value is positive*:

$$NPV = R - C > 0.$$

Assume that the initial year is $t = 0$, the firm's revenue in year t is R_t, and its cost in year t is C_t. If the last year in which either revenue or cost is nonzero is T, the net present value rule holds that the firm should invest if

[5]This rule holds when future costs and returns are known with certainty and investments can be reversed but cannot be delayed (Dixit and Pindyck, 1994).

$$NPV = R - C$$
$$= \left[R_0 + \frac{R_1}{(1+i)^1} + \frac{R_2}{(1+i)^2} + \cdots + \frac{R_T}{(1+i)^T}\right]$$
$$-\left[C_0 + \frac{C_1}{(1+i)^1} + \frac{C_2}{(1+i)^2} + \cdots + \frac{C_T}{(1+i)^T}\right] > 0.$$

Instead of comparing the present values of the returns and costs, we can examine whether the present value of the *cash flow* in each year (loosely, the annual *profit*), $\pi_t = R_t - C_t$, is positive. By rearranging the terms in the previous expression, we can rewrite the net present value rule as

$$NPV = \left(R_0 - C_0\right) + \frac{R_1 - C_1}{(1+i)^1} + \frac{R_2 - C_2}{(1+i)^2} + \cdots + \frac{R_T - C_T}{(1+i)^T}$$
$$= \pi_0 + \frac{\pi_1}{(1+i)^1} + \frac{\pi_2}{(1+i)^2} + \cdots + \frac{\pi_T}{(1+i)^T} > 0. \quad (16.7)$$

This rule does not restrict the firm to making investments only where its cash flow is positive each year. For example, a firm buys a piece of equipment for \$100 and spends the first year learning how to use it, so it makes no revenues from the machine and has a negative cash flow that year: $\pi_0 = -100$. The next year, its revenue is \$350 and the machine's maintenance cost is \$50, so its second year's cash flow is $\pi_1 = \$300$. At the end of that year, the machine wears out, so the annual cash flow from this investment is zero thereafter. Setting the interest rate at 5% in Equation 16.7, we learn that the firm's net present value is

$$NPV = -100 + 300/1.05 \approx \$185.71.$$

Because this net present value is positive, the firm makes the investment.

Solved Problem 16.2

Lewis Wolff and his investment group bought the Oakland A's baseball team for \$180 million in 2005. *Forbes* magazine estimates their net income for 2005 is \$5.9 million. If the new owners believed that they would continue to earn this annual profit (after adjusting for inflation), f = \$5.9 million, forever, was this investment more lucrative than putting the \$180 million in a savings account that pays a real interest rate of i = 3%?

Answer

Determine the net present value of the team. The net present value of buying the A's is positive if the present value of the expected returns, \$5.9 million/0.04 ≈ \$196.7 million, minus the present value of the cost, which is the purchase price of \$180 million, is positive:

$$NPV = \$196.7 \text{ million} - \$180 \text{ million} = \$16.7 \text{ million} > 0.$$

Thus, it paid for the investors to buy the A's if their best alternative investment paid 3%.

See Problem 26.

Internal Rate of Return Approach. Whether the net present value of an investment is positive depends on the interest rate. In Solved Problem 16.2, the investors buy the baseball team, given an interest rate of 3%. However, if the interest rate were 10%, the net present value would be \$5.9 million/0.1 – \$180 million = –\$121 million, and the investors would not buy the team.

internal rate of return (*irr*) the discount rate that results in a net present value of an investment of zero

At what discount rate (rate of return) is a firm indifferent between making an investment and not? The **internal rate of return** (*irr*) is the discount rate such that the net present value of an investment is zero. Replacing the interest rate, i, in Equation 16.7 with irr and setting the NPV equal to zero, we implicitly determine the internal rate of return by solving

$$NPV = \pi_0 + \frac{\pi_1}{1 + irr} + \frac{\pi_2}{(1 + irr)^2} + \cdots + \frac{\pi_T}{(1 + irr)^T} = 0$$

for irr.

It is easier to calculate irr when the investment pays a steady stream of profit, f, forever and the cost of the investment is PV. The investment's rate of return is found by rearranging Equation 16.4 and replacing i with irr:

$$irr = \frac{f}{PV}. \qquad (16.8)$$

Instead of using the net present value rule, we can decide whether to invest by comparing the internal rate of return to the interest rate. If the firm is borrowing money to make the investment, *it pays for the firm to borrow to make the investment if the internal rate of return on that investment exceeds that of the next best alternative* (which we assume is the interest rate):[6]

See Problems 27 and 28.

$$irr > i.$$

Solved Problem 16.3

A group of investors can buy the A's baseball team for PV = \$180 million. They expect an annual real flow of payments (profits) of f = \$5.9 million forever. If the interest rate is 3%, do they buy the team?

Answer

Determine the internal rate of return to this investment and compare it to the interest rate. Using Equation 16.8, we calculate that the internal rate of return from buying the A's is

$$irr = \frac{f}{PV} = \frac{\$5.9 \text{ million}}{\$180 \text{ million}} \approx 3.3\%.$$

See Problems 29 and 30.

Because this rate of return, 3.3%, is greater than the interest rate, 3%, the investors buy the team.

Rate of Return on Bonds

Instead of investing in capital or putting their money in a bank, firms or individuals may invest in a *bond*, a piece of paper issued by a government or a corporation that promises to repay the borrower with a payment stream. The amount borrowed is called the *face value* of the bond. Some bonds have a number of *coupons*. Each year, the holder of the bond clips one coupon, returns it to the issuer, and receives a payment of a fixed amount of money. At the *maturity date* shown on the bond—when no coupons remain—the borrower redeems the bond by returning the face value, the amount borrowed.

[6]The net present value approach always works. The internal rate of return method is inapplicable if irr is not unique. In Solved Problem 16.3, irr is unique, and using this approach gives the same answer as the net present value approach.

Some bonds, *perpetuities*, have no maturity date and the face value is never returned. Instead, the bondholder receives annual payments forever.

For example, last year Jerome paid PV = \$2,000 to buy a government-issued bond that guarantees the holder a payment of f = \$100 a year forever. According to Equation 16.8, the rate of return on Jerome's bond was 5% = \$100/\$2,000. At the time, banks were paying 5% on comparable accounts and were expected to do so in the future. As a result, Jerome was indifferent between buying a bond and keeping his money in a bank account.

This year, however, because of *unanticipated* inflation, the nominal interest rate that banks paid *unexpectedly* rose to 10%, and everyone expects this new interest rate to persist. If the bonds were to continue to sell for \$2,000, the rate of return would remain 5%, so everyone would prefer to keep their money in the bank. Thus, if Jerome wants to sell his bond, he must lower the price until the rate of return on the bond reaches 10%. As a result, the present value of Jerome's bond falls to \$1,000 = \$100/0.1 this year, according to Equation 16.4. In general, a bond's selling price falls from the face value of the bond if the nominal interest rate rises over time (and the price rises if the interest rate falls).

Similarly, the real return to a bond that pays a nominal rate of return varies with the inflation rate. During the high-inflation 1970s and early 1980s, holders of U.S. bonds lost much of their wealth for this reason. Following Canada, Britain, and other countries, the United States in 1997 started offering bonds that adjust for the inflation rate. These bonds are supposed to provide a constant, real rate of return.

Durability

Many firms must decide how durable to make the products they sell or those they produce for their own use. Should they make long-lasting products at a relatively high cost or less-durable goods at a lower cost?

Suppose that the company can vary the quality of a factor (a machine) that it uses in its own production process. If it needs exactly one machine, it must replace the machine when it wears out. Thus, *the firm should pick the durability level for the machine that minimizes the present discounted cost of having a machine forever.*

APPLICATION

Durability of Telephone Poles

Pacific Gas & Electric (PG&E), a western power utility, must decide how durable to make its 132 million wooden utility poles. The poles are a capital stock for PG&E, which uses them to provide a flow of services: supporting power and phone lines year after year. A wooden utility pole provides the same services each year for T years under normal use. After T years, the pole breaks and is replaced because it can't be repaired, but the flow of services must be maintained. Until recently, PG&E used poles with a life span of $T = 25$ years.

The constant marginal cost of manufacturing and installing the poles depends on how long they last, $m(T)$. For an additional cost, the firm can extend the life span of a pole by treating it with chemicals to prevent bug infestations and rot, reinforcing it with metal bands, varying its thickness, or using higher-quality materials. Because the marginal cost increases with the pole's expected life span, a pole that lasts 50 years costs more than one that lasts 25 years: $m(50) > m(25)$.

The replacement cost of a pole that lasts 25 years is $m(25)$ = \$1,500. Thus, replacing all of PG&E's poles today would come to \$198 billion—which is more than the cost of many of PG&E's giant power plants.

PG&E believes that it can save money by switching to a longer-lasting pole. The firm picks the duration, T, that minimizes its cost of maintaining its forest of poles. Because the utility keeps the same number of poles in place every year, after a pole wears out at T years, the firm incurs an expense of $m(T)$ to replace it. The present value of providing each pole is the cost of producing it today, $m(T)$, plus the discounted cost of producing another one in T years, $m(T)/(1 + i)^T$, plus the discounted cost of producing another one in $2T$ years, $m(T)/(1 + i)^{2T}$, and so on.

The table shows the present value of the cost of maintaining one pole for the next 100 years, given that the utility faces an interest rate of 5%. Because the cost of producing a pole that lasts for 25 years is $m(25) = \$1{,}500$, the present value of the cost of providing a pole for the next 100 years is \$2,112 (column 2). If the cost of a pole that lasts 50 years were $m(50) = \$1{,}943$ (column 4), the present value would be the same as that for the 25-year pole. If so, the utility would be indifferent between using poles that last 25 years and poles that last 50 years.

	25-Year Pole	50-Year Pole	
Marginal Cost, $m(T)$:	\$1,500	\$1,650	\$1,943
Year			
0	\$1,500	\$1,650	\$1,943
25	443	0	0
50	131	\$144	169
75	39	0	0
Present value of the cost of providing a pole for 100 years:	\$2,112	\$1,794	\$2,112

Note: Column 2 does not add to the present value due to rounding.

Thus, PG&E will not use 50-year poles if the extra cost is greater than \$443 = \$1,943 − \$1,500 but will use them if the difference in cost is less than that. The actual extra cost is less than \$150, so $m(50) = \$1{,}650$. Thus, the present value of the cost of a 50-year pole is only about \$1,794 (column 3 of the table). Because using the 50-year poles reduces the present value by \$318, or about 15% per pole, the utility wants to use the longer-lasting poles. By so doing, PG&E cuts the present value of the cost of maintaining all its poles for 100 years by about \$42 billion. Thus, the length of time one maintains a durable good depends on the alternatives and the rate of interest.

See Problem 25.

Human Capital

> *If a man is after money, he's money mad; if he keeps it, he's a capitalist; if he spends it, he's a playboy; if he doesn't get it, he's a ne'er-do-well; if he doesn't try to get it, he lacks ambition. If he gets it without working for it, he's a parasite; and if he accumulates it after a lifetime of hard work, people call him a fool who never got anything out of life.* —Vic Oliver

Just as a firm considers whether or not to invest in physical capital, individuals decide whether to invest in their own *human capital*. Where a firm chooses the durability of a piece of equipment, some people invest in lengthening their expected life spans by exercising or purchasing medical care. Where a firm buys machinery and other capital to produce more output and increase its future profits, individuals invest in education to raise their productivity and their future earnings.

One of the most important human capital decisions you've had to make is whether to attend college. If you opted to go to college solely for the purpose of increasing your lifetime earnings, have you made a good investment?[7]

Let's look back at your last year of high school. During that year, you have to decide whether to invest in a college education or go directly into the job market. If you venture straight into the job market, we assume that you work from age 18 until you retire at age 70.

If your motivation for attending college is to increase your lifetime earnings, you should start college upon finishing high school so that you can earn a higher salary for as long as possible. Let's assume that you graduate from college in four years, during which time you do not work and you spend $12,000 a year on tuition and other schooling expenses such as books and fees. When you graduate from college, you work from age 22 to 70. Thus, the opportunity cost of a college education includes the tuition payments plus the four years of forgone earnings for someone with a high school diploma. The expected benefit is the stream of higher earnings in the future.

See Question 5.

Figure 16.2 shows how much the typical person earns with a high school diploma and with a college degree at each age.[8] At age 22, a typical person earns $34,300

Figure 16.2 Annual Earnings of High School and College Graduates.

On the basis of a statistical analysis, the earnings of high school and college graduates vary by age. The cost of getting a college education is four years of forgone earnings (at the rate high school graduates earn) and tuition, which is assumed to be $12,000 a year. The benefit is that the college graduate earns more each year thereafter than a high school graduate.

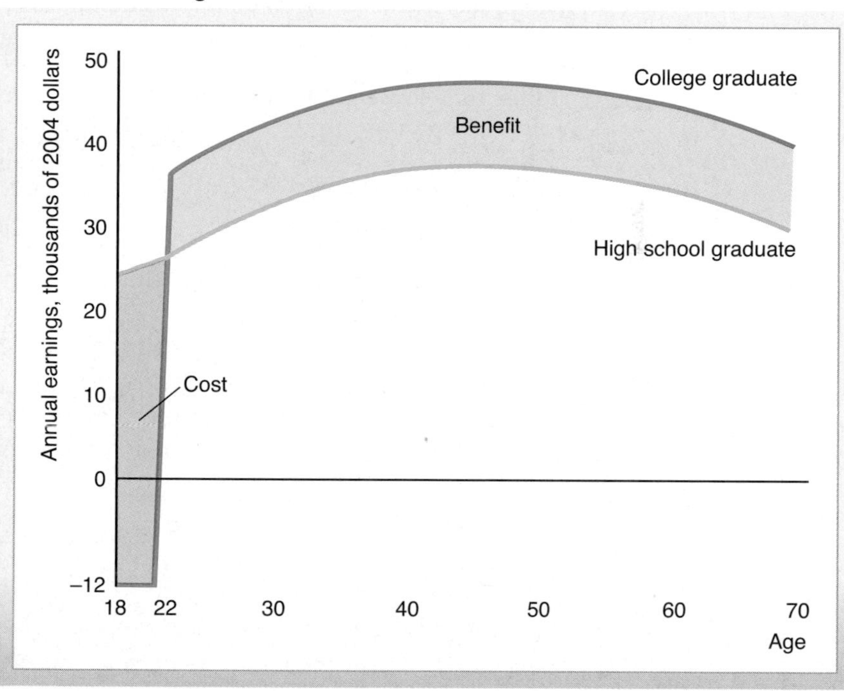

[7]"I have often thought that if there had been a good rap group around in those days, I would have chosen a career in music instead of politics." —Richard Nixon.

[8]Our figures are based on a statistical analysis of full-time weekly earnings from the March 2004 U.S. *Current Population Survey*, that controls for work experience, education, and demographic characteristics but not innate ability. We assume that people are paid for 52 weeks per year and that wages increase at the same rate as inflation, so real earnings are constant over time. No adjustment is made for the greater incidence of unemployment among high school graduates.

with a college degree but only $25,600 with a high school diploma. The college grad's earnings peak at 50 years of age, at $47,500. A high school grad's earnings reach a maximum at 50 years, at $35,400.

If one stream of earnings is higher than the other at every age, we would pick the higher stream. Because these streams of earnings cross at age 22, we cannot use that method. One way to decide whether investing in a college education pays is to compare the present values at age 18 of the two earnings streams. The present values depend on the interest rate used, as Table 16.5 shows.

If potential college students can borrow money at an interest rate of 0%, money in the future is worth as much as money today, so the present value equals the sum of earnings over time. According to the table, the sum of a college graduate's earnings (including the initial negative earnings) is $2.58 million, which is about 24% more than the earnings of a high school grad. Thus, it pays to go to college. The figure also illustrates that attending college pays at a 0% discount rate because the sum of the (negative) cost and (positive) benefit areas—the difference in earnings between going to college and going to work after high school—is positive.

See Problems 31 and 32.

Table 16.5 demonstrates that the present value of earnings for a college grad is greater than that of a high school grad for any interest rate below 5.1%. That is, the average internal rate of return to the college education is 5.1%. Thus, income-maximizing people with average characteristics go to college if the real interest rate at which they can borrow or invest is less than 5.1%.[9]

The decision whether to go to college is more complex for people for whom education has a consumption component. Somebody who loves school may go to col-

Table 16.5 Present Value of Earnings.

	Present Value, Thousands of 2004 Dollars	
Discount Rate, %	High School	College
0	2,088	2,583
1	1,506	1,807
2	1,126	1,302
3	871	965
4	694	733
5	568	569
5.1	560	560
6	475	450
7	406	362
8	352	295
9	310	243
10	276	202

[9]The nominal interest rate on federal Stafford loans, the most common type of educational loan, dropped to 4.06% in 2002, which was the lowest rate in its 37-year history. In 2008, the rate is 6.8% nominal. Real interest rates at which college students can loan money to a bank and the rates at which they can borrow using government loan programs are almost always lower than 5.1%. However, the commercial rates at which they can borrow money from banks may be higher than 5.1%. Some poor people who cannot borrow to pay for college at all—effectively, they face extremely high interest rates—do not go to college, unlike wealthier people with comparable abilities.

lege even if alternative investments pay more. Someone who hates going to school invests in a college education only if the financial rewards are much higher than those for alternative investments. If you do go to college, there is a higher payoff to majoring in economics than most other fields: see **www.myeconlab.com/Perloff**, Chapter 16, "Returns to Studying Economics."

★ Behavioral Economics: Time-Varying Discounting

Hard work pays off in the future. Laziness pays off now. —Steven Wright

People want immediate gratification.[10] We want rewards now and costs delayed until later: "Rain, rain, go away; Come again some other day; We want to go outside and play; Come again some other day."

Time Consistency. So far in this chapter, we have explained such impatience by assuming that people discount future costs or benefits by using *exponential discounting,* as in Equation 16.2: The present value is the future value divided by $(1 + i)^t$, where t is the exponent and the discount rate, i, is constant over time. If people use this approach, their preferences are *time consistent:* They will discount an event that occurs a decade from the time they're asked by the same amount today as they will one year from now.

However, many of us indulge in immediate gratification in a manner that is inconsistent with our long-term preferences: Our "long-run self" disapproves of the lack of discipline of our "short-run self." Even though we plan today not to overeat tomorrow, tomorrow we may overindulge. We have *present-biased preferences*: When considering the trade-off between two future moments, we put more weight on the earlier moment as it gets closer. For example, if you are offered \$100 in 10 years or \$200 in 10 years and a day, you will almost certainly choose the larger amount one day later. After all, what's the cost of waiting one extra day a decade from now? However, if you are offered \$100 today or \$200 tomorrow, you may choose the smaller amount today because an extra day is an appreciable delay when your planning horizon is short.

One explanation that behavioral economists (see Chapter 4) use for procrastination and other time-inconsistent behavior is that people's personal discount rates are smaller in the far future than in the near future. For example, suppose that you know that you can mow your lawn today in two hours, but if you wait until next week, it will take you two-and-a-quarter hours because the grass will be longer. Your displeasure (negative utility) from spending 2 hours mowing is –20 and from spending 2.25 hours mowing is –22.5. The present value of mowing next week is $-22.5/(1 + i)$, where i is your personal discount rate for a week. If today your discount rate is $i = 0.25$, then your present value of mowing in a week is $-22.5/1.25 = -18$, which is not as bad as –20, so you delay mowing. However, if you were asked six months in advance, your discount rate might be much smaller, say $i = 0.1$. At that interest rate, the present value is $-22.5/1.1 \approx -20.45$, which is worse than –20, so you would plan to mow on the first of the two dates. Thus, falling discount rates may explain this type of time-inconsistent behavior.

Falling Discount Rates and the Environment. A social discount rate that declines over time may be useful in planning for global warming or other future environmental disasters (Karp, 2005). Suppose that the harmful effects of greenhouse gases will not be felt for a century and that society used traditional, exponential dis-

[10]This section draws heavily on Rabin (1988), O'Donoghue and Rabin (1999), and Karp (2005).

counting. We would be willing to invest at most 37¢ today to avoid a dollar's worth of damages in a century if society's constant discount rate is 1%, and only 1.8¢ if the discount rate is 4%. Thus, even a modest discount rate makes us callous toward our distant descendants: We are unwilling to incur even moderate costs today to avoid large damages far in the future.

One alternative is for society to use a declining discount rate, although doing so will make our decisions time inconsistent. Parents today may care more about their existing children than their (not yet seen) grandchildren, and therefore may be willing to significantly discount the welfare of their grandchildren relative to that of their children. They probably have a smaller difference in their relative emotional attachment to the tenth future generation relative to the eleventh generation. If society agrees with such reasoning, our future social discount rate should be lower than our current rate. By reducing the discount rate over time, we are saying that the weights we place on the welfare of any two successive generations in the distant future are more similar than the weights on two successive generations in the near future.

APPLICATION

Falling Discount Rates and Self-Control

If people's discount rates fall over time, they have a *present bias* or a *self-control problem*, preferring immediate gratification to delayed gratification. Several recent studies argue that governments should help people with this bias by providing self-control policy.

Shapiro (2004) finds that food stamp recipients' caloric intake declines by 10% to 15% over the food stamp month, implying that they prefer immediate consumption. With a constant discount rate, they would be more likely to spread their consumption evenly over the month. Governments can help people with a present bias by delivering food stamps at two-week intervals instead of once a month, as several states do with welfare payments.

Kan (2007) examines inconsistent preferences with respect to cigarette smoking. Individuals with declining discount rates lack self-control and perpetually postpone quitting smoking. Consequently, a smoker who wants to quit may support the government's impositions of control devices. Based on a survey in Taiwan, Kan finds that a smoker who intends to quit is more likely to support a smoking ban and a cigarette tax increase.

★ 16.3 Exhaustible Resources

The meek shall inherit the earth, but not the mineral rights. —J. Paul Getty

exhaustible resources nonrenewable natural assets that cannot be increased, only depleted

Discounting plays an important role in decision making about how fast to consume oil, gold, copper, uranium, and other **exhaustible resources**: nonrenewable natural assets that cannot be increased, only depleted. An owner of an exhaustible resource decides when to extract and sell it so as to maximize the present value of the resource. Scarcity of the resource, mining costs, and market structure affect whether the price of such a resource rises or falls over time.

When to Sell an Exhaustible Resource

Suppose that you own a coal mine. In what year do you mine the coal, and in what year do you sell it to maximize the present value of your coal? To illustrate how to answer these questions, we assume that you can sell the coal only this year or next in a competitive market, that the interest rate is i, and that the cost of mining each pound of coal, m, stays constant over time.

Given the last two of these assumptions, the present value of mining a pound of coal is m if you mine this year and $m/(1 + i)$ if you mine next year. As a result, if you're going to sell the coal next year, you're better off mining it next year because you postpone incurring the cost of mining. You mine the coal this year only if you plan to sell it this year.

Now that you have a rule that tells you when to mine the coal—at the last possible moment—your remaining problem is when to sell it. That decision depends on how the price of a pound of coal changes from one year to the next. Suppose that you know that the price of coal will increase from p_1 this year to p_2 next year.

To decide in which year to sell, you compare the present value of selling today to that of selling next year. The present value of your profit per pound of coal is $p_1 - m$ if you sell your coal this year and $(p_2 - m)/(1 + i)$ if you sell it next year. Thus, to maximize the present value from selling your coal:

- *You sell all the coal this year* if the present value of selling this year is greater than the present value of selling next year: $p_1 - m > (p_2 - m)/(1 + i)$.
- *You sell all the coal next year* if $p_1 - m < (p_2 - m)/(1 + i)$.
- *You sell the coal in either year* if $p_1 - m = (p_2 - m)/(1 + i)$.

See Problem 33.

The intuition behind these rules is that storing coal in the ground is like keeping money in the bank. You can sell a pound of coal today, netting $p_1 - m$, invest the money in the bank, and have $(p_1 - m)(1 + i)$ next year. Alternatively, you can keep the coal in the ground for a year and then sell it. If the amount you'll get next year, $p_2 - m$, is less than what you can earn from selling now and keeping the money in a bank account, you sell the coal now. In contrast, if the price of coal is rising so rapidly that the coal will be worth more in the future than wealth left in a bank, you leave your wealth in the mine.

Price of a Scarce Exhaustible Resource

This two-period analysis generalizes to many time periods (Hotelling, 1931). We use a multiperiod analysis to show how the price of an exhaustible resource changes over time.

The resource is sold both this year, year t, and next year, $t + 1$, only if the present value of a pound sold now is the same as the present value of a pound sold next year: $p_t - m = (p_{t+1} - m)/(1 + i)$, where the price is p_t in year t and is p_{t+1} in the following year. Using algebra to rearrange this equation, we obtain an expression that tells us how price changes from one year to the next:

$$p_{t+1} = p_t + i(p_t - m). \quad (16.9)$$

If you're willing to sell the coal in both years, the price next year must exceed the price this year by $i(p_t - m)$, which is the interest payment you'd receive if you sold a pound of coal this year and put the profit in a bank that paid interest at rate i.

The gap between the price and the constant marginal cost of mining grows over time, as Figure 16.3 shows. To see why, we subtract p_t from both sides of Equation 16.9 to obtain an expression for the change in the price from one year to the next:

$$\Delta p \equiv p_{t+1} - p_t = i(p_t - m).$$

This equation shows that the gap between this year's price and next year's price widens as your cash flow this year, $p_t - m$, increases. Thus, the price rises over time, and the gap between the price line and the flat marginal cost of mining line grows, as the figure illustrates.

Figure 16.3 Price of an Exhaustible Resource.

The price of an exhaustible resource in year $t + 1$ is higher than the price in year t by the interest rate times the difference between the price in year t and the marginal cost of mining, $i(p_t - m)$. Thus, the gap between the price line and the marginal cost line, $p_t - m$, grows exponentially with the interest rate.

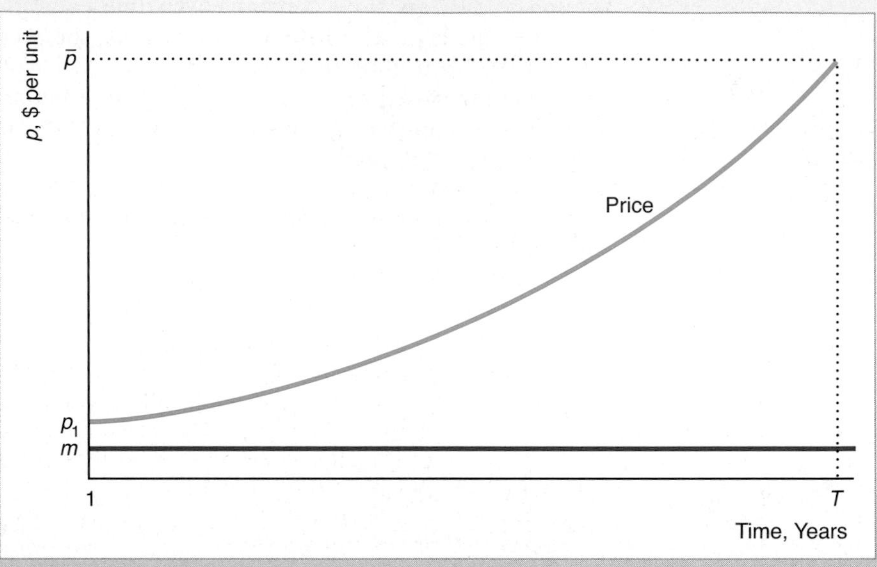

See Problem 34.

Although we now understand how price changes over time, we need more information to determine the price in the first year and hence in each subsequent year. Suppose that mine owners know that the government will ban the use of coal in year T (or that a superior substitute will become available that year). They want to price the coal so that all of it is sold by the year T, because any resource that is unsold by then is worthless. The restriction that all the coal is used up by T and Equation 16.9 determine the price in the first year and the increase in the price thereafter.

Price in a Two-Period Example. To illustrate how the price is determined in each year, we assume that there are many identical competitive mines, that no more coal will be sold after the second year because of a government ban, and that the marginal cost of mining is zero in each period. Setting $m = 0$ in Equation 16.9, we learn that the price in the second year equals the price in the first year plus the interest rate times the first-year price:

$$p_2 = p_1 + (i \times p_1) = p_1(1 + i). \tag{16.10}$$

Thus, the price increases with the interest rate from the first year to the second year.

The mine owners face a resource constraint: They can't sell more coal than they have in their mines. The coal they sell in the first year, Q_1, plus the coal they sell in the second year, Q_2, equals the total amount of coal in the mines, Q. The mine owners want to sell all their coal within these two years because any coal they don't sell does them no good.

Suppose that the demand curve for coal is $Q_t = 200 - p_t$ in each year t. If the amount of coal in the ground is less than would be demanded at a zero price, the sum of the amount demanded in both years equals the total amount of coal in the ground:

$$Q_1 + Q_2 = (200 - p_1) + (200 - p_2) = Q.$$

Substituting the expression for p_2 from Equation 16.10 into this resource constraint to obtain $(200 - p_1) + [200 - p_1(1 + i)] = Q$ and rearranging terms, we find that

$$p_1 = (400 - Q)/(2 + i). \tag{16.11}$$

Thus, the first-year price depends on the amount of coal in the ground and the interest rate.

If the mines initially contain $Q = 169$ pounds of coal, p_1 is \$110 at a 10% interest rate and only \$105 at a 20% interest rate, as Table 16.6 shows. At the lower interest rate, the difference between the first- and second-year price is smaller (\$11 versus \$21), so relatively more of the original stock of coal is sold in the second year (47% versus 44%).

See Problem 35.

Rents. If coal is a scarce good, its competitive price is above the marginal cost of mining the coal ($m = 0$ in our example). How can we reconcile this result with our earlier finding that price equals marginal cost in a competitive market? The answer is that when coal is scarce, it earns a *rent*: a payment to the owner of an input beyond the minimum necessary for the factor to be supplied (Chapter 8).

The owner of the coal need not be the same person who mines the coal. A miner could pay the owner for the right to take the coal out of the mine. After incurring the marginal cost of mining the coal, m, the miner earns $p_1 - m$. The owner of the mine, however, charges that amount in rent for the right to mine this scarce resource rather than giving any of this profit to the miner. Even if the owner of the coal and the miner are the same person, the amount beyond the marginal mining cost is a rent to scarcity.

If the coal were not scarce, no rent would be paid, and the price would equal the marginal cost of mining. Given the demand curve in the example, the most coal anyone would buy in a year is 200 pounds, which is the amount demanded at a price of zero. If there are 400 pounds of coal in the ground initially—enough to provide 200 pounds in each year—the coal is not scarce, so the price of coal in both years is zero (the marginal mining cost), as Table 16.6 shows.[11] As Figure 16.4 illustrates, the less coal there is in the ground initially, Q, the higher the initial price of coal.

Rising Prices. Thus, according to our theory, the price of an exhaustible resource rises if the resource (1) is scarce, (2) can be mined at a marginal cost that remains constant over time, and (3) is sold in a competitive market. The price of old-growth redwood trees rose as predicted by this theory.

Table 16.6 Price and Quantity of Coal Reflecting the Amount of Coal and the Interest Rate.

	$Q = 169$		$Q = 400$
	$i = 10\%$	$i = 20\%$	Any i
$p_1 = (400 - Q)/(2 + i)$	\$110	\$105	\$0
$p_2 = p_1(1 + i)$	\$121	\$126	\$0
$\Delta p \equiv p_2 - p_1 = i \times p_1$	11	21	0
$Q_1 = 200 - p_1$	90	95	200
$Q_2 = 200 - p_2$	79	74	200
Share sold in Year 2	47%	44%	50%

[11]Equation 16.11 holds only where coal is scarce: $Q \leq 400$. According to this equation, $p_1 = 0$ when $Q = 400$. If the quantity of coal in the ground is even greater, $Q > 400$, coal is not scarce—people don't want all the coal even if the price is zero—so the price in the first year equals the marginal mining cost of zero. That is, the price is not negative, as Equation 16.11 would imply if it held for quantities greater than 400.

Figure 16.4 First-Year Price in a Two-Period Model.

In a two-period model, the price of coal in the first year, p_1, falls as the amount of coal in the ground initially, Q, increases. This figure is based on an interest rate of 10%.

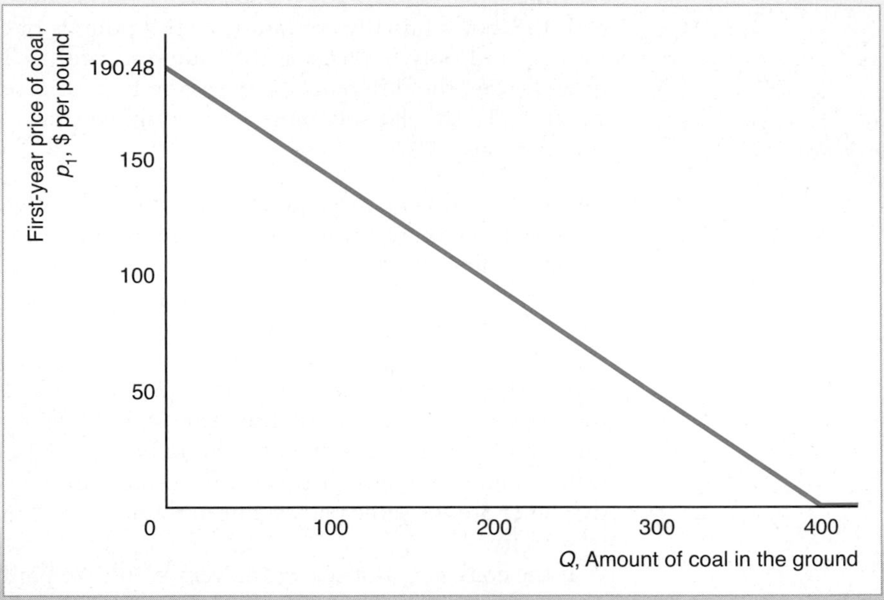

APPLICATION

Redwood Trees

Many of the majestic old-growth redwood trees in America's western forests are several hundred to several thousand years old. If a mature redwood is cut, young redwoods will not grow to a comparable size within our lifetime. Thus, an old-growth redwood forest, like fossil fuels, is effectively a nonrenewable resource, even though new redwoods are being created (very slowly). In contrast, many other types of trees, such as those grown as Christmas trees, are quickly replenished and therefore are renewable resources like fish.

The exponential trend line on the graph shows that the real price of redwoods rose from 1953 to 1983 at an average rate of 8% a year. By the end of this period, virtually no redwood trees were available for sale. The trees either had been harvested or were growing in protected forests. The last remaining privately owned stand was purchased by the U.S. government and the state of California from the Maxxam Corporation in 1996.

The unusually high prices observed in the late 1960s through the 1970s are in large part due to actions of the federal government, which used its power of eminent domain to buy a considerable fraction of all remaining old-growth redwoods for the Redwood National Park at the market price. The government bought 1.7 million million-board feet (MBF) in 1968 and 1.4 million MBF in 1978. The latter purchase represented about two and a quarter years of cutting at previous rates. These two government purchases combined equaled 43% of private holdings in 1978 of about 7.3 million MBF. Thus, the government purchases were so large that they moved up the time of exhaustion of privately held redwoods by several years, causing the price to jump to the level it would have reached several years later.

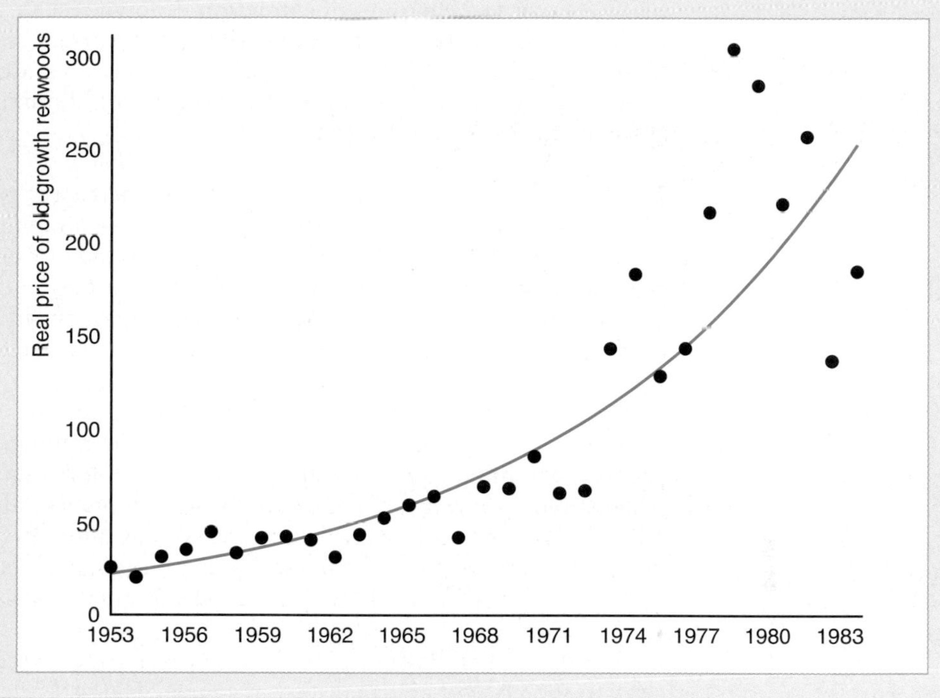

Why Price May Be Constant or Fall

If any one of the three conditions we've been assuming—*scarcity*, *constant marginal mining costs*, and *competition*—is not met, the price of an exhaustible resource may remain steady or fall.[12] Most exhaustible resources, such as aluminum, coal, lead, natural gas, silver, and zinc, have had decades-long periods of falling or constant real prices. Indeed, the real price of each major mineral, each metal, and oil was lower in 1998 than in 1980.

Abundance. As we've already seen, the initial price is set at essentially the marginal cost of mining if the exhaustible resource is not scarce. The gap between the price and the marginal cost grows with the interest rate. If the good is so abundant that the initial gap is zero, the gap does not grow and the price stays constant at the marginal cost. Further, if the gap is initially very small, it has to grow for a long time before the increase becomes noticeable.

Because of abundance, the real prices for many exhaustible resources have remained relatively constant for decades. Moreover, the price falls when the discovery of a large deposit of the resource is announced.

The amount of a resource that can be profitably recovered using current technology is called a *reserve*. Known reserves of some resources are enormous; others are more limited.[13] We have enough silicon (from sand) and magnesium to last vir-

[12]The following discussion of why prices of exhaustible resources may not rise and the accompanying examples are based on Berck and Roberts (1996) and additional data supplied by these authors. Their paper also shows that pollution and other environmental controls can keep resource prices from rising. Additional data are from Brown and Wolk (2000).

[13]Data are from **minerals.usgs.gov/minerals/pubs/mcs/2007/mcs2007.pdf.**

tually forever at 2006 rates of extraction. Known reserves of zinc will last 46 years; lead, 42 years; gold, 36 years; and silver, 29 years. Known reserves of aluminum (bauxite) will last 185 years, and additional reserves are constantly being discovered. Because of this abundance, the real price of aluminum has remained virtually constant for the past 50 years.

Technical Progress. Improved technology increased potential U.S. natural gas reserve estimates by 17% over the last 2 years—enough to last 82 years at current extraction rates.[14] Over long periods of time, steady technical progress has reduced the marginal cost of mining many natural resources and has thereby lowered the price of those exhaustible resources. A large enough drop in the marginal mining cost may more than offset the increase in the price due to the interest rate, so the price falls from one year to the next.[15]

The era spanning the end of the nineteenth century and the beginning of the twentieth century witnessed many advances in mining. As a result of technical progress in mining and discoveries of new supplies, the real prices of many exhaustible resources fell. For example, the real price of aluminum in 1945 was only 12% of the price 50 years earlier. Eventually, as mines play out, prospectors have to dig ever deeper to find resources, causing marginal costs to increase and prices to rise faster than they would with constant marginal costs.

Changing Market Power. Changes in market structure can result in either a rise or a fall in the price of an exhaustible resource. The real price of oil remained virtually constant from 1880 through 1972. But when the Organization of Petroleum Exporting Countries (OPEC) started to act as a cartel in 1973, the price of oil climbed rapidly. At its peak in 1981, the real price of oil was nearly five times higher than its nearly constant level during the period 1880–1972. When Iran and Iraq went to war in 1980, the OPEC cartel began to fall apart and the real price of oil sank to traditional levels, where it remained through the 1990s. Lately the price has increased substantially, presumably due to worldwide increases in demand.

16.4 Capital Markets, Interest Rates, and Investments

We've seen that an individual's decision about whether to make an investment depends on the market interest rate. As Figure 16.5 shows, the intersection of the supply and demand of loanable funds determines the equilibrium price or interest rate and the equilibrium quantity of funds in this capital market. In equilibrium, the amount borrowed (demanded) equals the amount loaned (supplied).

Funds are demanded by individuals buying homes or paying for a college education, governments borrowing money to build roads or wage wars, and firms investing in new plants or equipment. The demand curve, D, is downward sloping because more is borrowed as the interest rate falls.

---

[14]www.eenews.net/eenewspm/print/2007/09/13/1.

[15]When the marginal cost of mining is constant at m, Equation 16.9 shows that $p_{t+1} = p_t + i(p_t - m)$, so p_{t+1} must be above p_t. If we allow mining costs to vary from year to year, then

$$p_{t+1} = p_t + i(p_t - m_t) + (m_{t+1} - m_t).$$

Thus, if the drop in the mining costs, $m_{t+1} - m_t$, is greater than $i(p_t - m)$, the price in p_{t+1} *is less than* p_t.

Figure 16.5 Capital Market Equilibrium.

The initial equilibrium, e_1, is determined by the intersection of the demand curve for loans, D, and the initial supply curve, S^1. Changes in laws induce more people to save, shifting the supply curve to S^2. The interest rate, i_2, at the new equilibrium, e_2, is lower than the original interest rate, i_1. More funds are loaned than originally: $Q_2 > Q_1$.

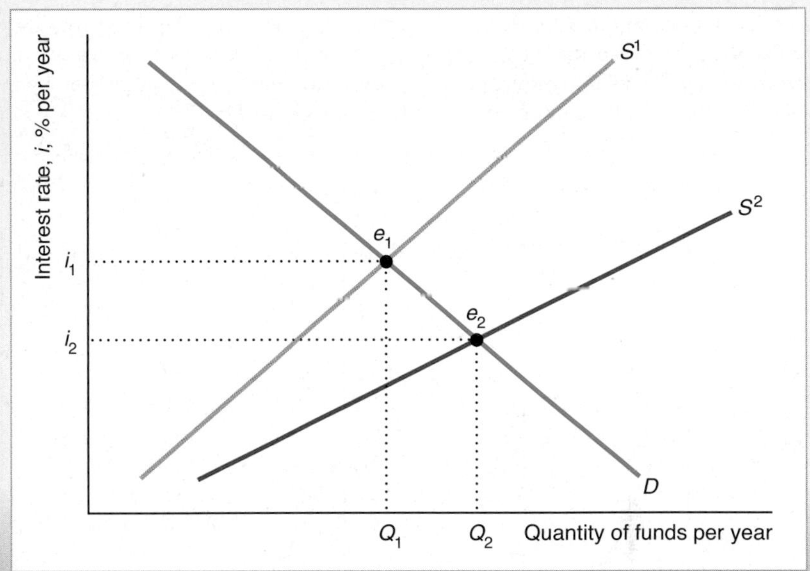

The supply curve reflects loans made by individuals and firms. Many people, when their earnings are relatively high, save money in bank accounts and buy bonds (which they convert back to money for consumption when they retire or during lean times). Firms that have no alternative investments with higher returns may also loan money to banks or others. Higher interest rates induce greater savings by both groups, so the initial supply curve, S^1, is upward sloping.

The initial equilibrium is e_1, with an equilibrium rate of interest of i_1 and an equilibrium quantity of funds loaned and borrowed of Q_1. As usual, this equilibrium changes if any of the variables—such as tastes and government regulations—that affect supply and demand shifts.

Increased Savings, More Investment

The supply curve of funds may shift to the right for many reasons. The government may remove a restriction on investment by foreigners. Or the government may make Individual Retirement Accounts (IRAs) tax exempt until retirement, a policy that induces additional savings at any given interest rate.

Such a change causes the supply curve to shift to the right to S_2 in Figure 16.5. The new equilibrium is e_2, with a lower interest rate, i_2. At the lower interest rate, firms and others undertake investment projects with lower rates of return than before the shift. They borrow more funds, so the new equilibrium is at $Q_2 > Q_1$.

See Question 6.

Increased Government Demand, Less Private Investment

Increased borrowing by the government raises the equilibrium interest rate, which discourages—*crowds out*—private investment. Figure 16.6 illustrates this effect. The total demand for funds, D^1 (panel c), is the horizontal sum of the demand from the private sector, D_p (panel a), and the initial demand from the public sector, D_g^1 (panel b). Given the market supply curve of funds S, the initial market equilibrium is e_1, with an equilibrium market interest rate of i_1 and quantity of Q_1.

Figure 16.6 How Government Borrowing Squeezes Out Private Investment.

(a) Private demand for funds for investment, D_p, remains constant. (b) Government demand for loans increases from D_g^1 to D_g^2 as the government borrows to finance a war. (c) As a result, total demand shifts from D^1 to D^2, and the equilibrium shifts from e_1 to e_2. At the new equilibrium, government borrowing increases, $Q_g^2 > Q_g^1$, while private borrowing falls, $Q_p^2 < Q_p^1$.

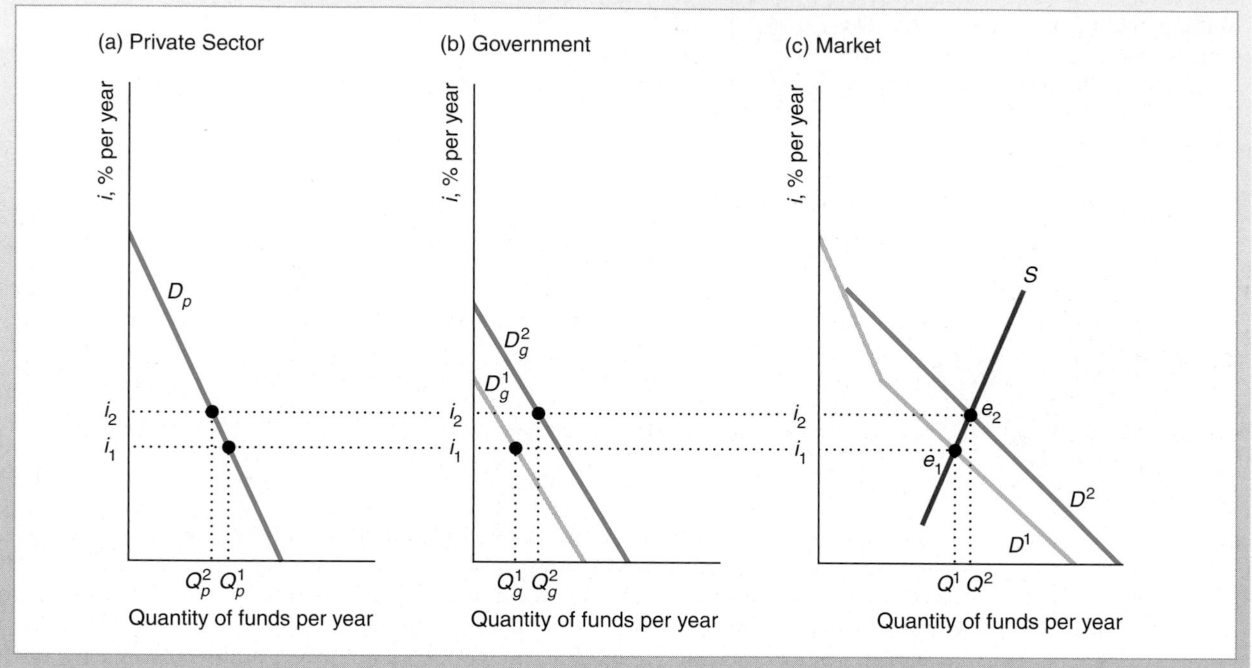

When the government borrows money to fight a war in a distant land, its demand for funds shifts outward to D_g^2. As a result, the market demand increases to D^2, which is the horizontal sum of D_p and D_g^2. At the new equilibrium, e_2, the market interest rate, i_2, is higher than the initial rate (panel c). The government borrows more than before in equilibrium: $D_g^2 > D_g^1$ (panel b). The higher market interest rate, however, causes private investment to fall from Q_p^1 to Q_p^2 (panel a).

See Question 7.

SUMMARY

1. **Comparing Money Today to Money in the Future.** Inflation aside, most people value money in the future less than money today. An interest rate reflects how much more people value a dollar today than a dollar in the future. To compare a payment made in the future to one made today, we can express the future payment in terms of current dollars by adjusting it using the interest rate. Similarly, a flow of payments over time is related to the present or future value of these payments by the interest rate.

2. **Choices over Time.** An individual or a firm may choose between two options with different cash flows over time by picking the one with the higher present value. Similarly, a firm invests in a project if its net present value is positive or its internal rate of return is greater than the interest rate. If people have a decreasing discount rate over time, they are not consistent in their behavior over time: They lack self-control and procrastinate.

3. **Exhaustible Resources.** Nonrenewable resources such as coal, gold, and oil are used up over time and cannot be replenished. If these resources are scarce, the marginal cost of mining them is constant or increasing, and the market structure remains

unchanged, their prices rise rapidly over time because of positive interest rates. However, if the resources are abundant, the marginal cost of mining falls over time, or the market becomes more competitive, nonrenewable resource prices may remain constant or fall over time.

4. **Capital Markets, Interest Rates, and Investments.** Supply and demand in capital markets determine the market rate of interest. A shock that shifts the supply curve to the left or the demand curve to the right raises the interest rate. As the interest rate increases, firms want to make fewer investments.

QUESTIONS

■ = *exercise is available on MyEconLab;* * = *answer appears at the back of this book;* C = *use of calculus may be necessary;* W = *audio-slideshow answer by James Dearden is available in Textbook Resources on MyEconLab.*

1. Some past and current civilizations, believing that interest should not be charged, passed usury laws forbidding it. What are the private and social benefits or costs of allowing interest to be charged?

2. What is the effect of a usury law on the market rate of interest if some potential lenders, hoping that the authorities do not catch them, are still willing to loan money?

*3. How does an individual with a zero discount rate weight current and future consumption? How does your answer change if the discount rate is infinite?

4. Discussing the $350 price of a ticket for one of her concerts, Barbra Streisand said, "If you amortize the money over 28 years, it's $12.50 a year. So is it worth $12.50 a year to see me sing? To hear me sing live?"[16] Under what condition is it useful for an individual to apply Ms. Streisand's rule to decide whether to go to the concert? What do we know about the discount rate of a person who made such a purchase?

5. If the interest rate is near zero, should an individual go to college, given the information in Figure 16.2? State a simple rule for determining whether this individual should go to college in terms of the areas labeled "Benefit" and "Cost" in the figure.

6. If the government bars foreign lenders from loaning money to its citizens, how does the capital market equilibrium change?

7. Suppose in Figure 16.6 that the government's demand curve remains constant at D_g^1 but the government starts to tax private earnings, collecting 1% of all interest earnings. How does the capital market equilibrium change? What is the effect on private borrowers?

PROBLEMS

8. The Web site **www.timetravelfund.com** discusses investing $1 at 5% interest, which it says will be worth $39,323,261,827.22 in 500 years. Is its calculation correct, and, if so, for what frequency of compounding? If you wish, you may also discuss how good an investment you think this site provides.

9. Many retirement funds charge an administrative fee equal to 0.25% on managed assets. Suppose that Alexx and Spenser each invest $5,000 in the same stock this year. Alexx invests directly and earns 5% a year. Spenser uses a retirement fund and earns 4.75%. After 30 years, how much more will Alexx have than Spenser?

10. If you buy a car for $100 down and $100 a year for two more years, what is the present value of these payments at a 5% rate of interest?

11. What is the present value of $100 paid a year from now and another $100 paid two years from now if the interest rate is *i*?

12. In 2002, Dell Computer made its suppliers wait 37 days on average to be paid for their goods; however, Dell was paid by its customers immediately. Thus, Dell earned interest on this *float*, the money that it was implicitly borrowing. If Dell can earn an APR of 4%, what is this float worth to Dell per dollar spent on inputs?

[16]"In Other Words . . ." *San Francisco Chronicle*, January 1, 1995, Sunday Section, p. 3. She divided the $350 ticket price by 28 years to get $12.50 as the payment per year.

13. What is the present value of a stream of payments of f per year for t years that starts T years from now if the interest rate is i?

14. How much money do you have to put into a bank account that pays 10% interest compounded annually to receive annual payments of $200 forever?

***15.** How much money do you have to put into a bank account that pays 10% interest compounded annually to receive perpetual annual payments of $200 in today's dollars if the rate of inflation is 5%?

***16.** You rent an apartment for two years. You owe a payment of $\tilde{f}$ today and another equal nominal payment next year. If the inflation rate is γ and the real interest rate is i, what is the present value of these rental payments?

***17.** Two different teams offer a professional basketball player contracts for playing this year. Both contracts are guaranteed, and payments will be made even if the athlete is injured and cannot play. Team A's contract would pay him $1 million today. Team B's contract would pay him $500,000 today and $2 million ten years from now. Assuming that there is no inflation, that our pro is concerned only about which contract has the highest present value, and that his personal discount rate (interest rate) is 5%, which contract does he accept? Does the answer change if the discount rate is 20%?

18. At a 10% interest rate, do you prefer to buy a phone for $100 or to rent the same phone for $10 a year? Does your answer depend on how long you think the phone will last?

19. Pacific Gas & Electric sent its customers a comparison showing that a person could save $80 per year in gas, water, and detergent expenses by replacing a traditional clothes washer with a new tumble-action washer. Suppose that the interest rate is 5%. You expect your current washer to die in five years. If the cost of a new tumble-action washer is $800, should you replace your washer now or in five years?

20. You plan to buy a used refrigerator this year for $200 and to sell it when you graduate in two years. Assuming that you can get $100 for the refrigerator at that time, there is no inflation, and the interest rate is 5%, what is the true cost (your current outlay minus the resale value in current terms) of the refrigerator to you?

21. You want to buy a room air conditioner. The price of one machine is $200. It costs $20 a year to operate. The price of the other air conditioner is $300, but it costs only $10 a year to operate. Assuming that both machines last 10 years, which is a better deal? (Do you need to do extensive calculations to answer this question?)

22. With the end of the Cold War, the U.S. government decided to "downsize" the military. Along with a pink slip, the government offered ex-military personnel their choice of $8,000 a year for 30 years or a lump sum payment of $50,000 immediately. The lump sum option was chosen by 92% of enlisted personnel and 51% of officers (Warner and Pleeter, 2001). What is the break-even personal discount rate at which someone would be indifferent between the two options? What can you conclude about the personal discount rates of the enlisted personnel and officers?

***23.** Your gas-guzzling car gets only ten miles to the gallon and has no resale value, but you are sure that it will last five years. You know that you can always buy a used car for $8,000 that gets 20 miles to the gallon. A gallon of gas costs $2.00 and you drive 6,000 miles a year. If the interest rate is 5% and you are interested only in saving money, should you buy a new car now rather than wait until your current car dies? Would you make the same decision if you faced a 10% interest rate?

24. You are buying a new $20,000 car and have the option to pay for the car with a 0% loan or to receive $500 cash back at the time of the purchase. With the loan, you pay $5,000 down when you purchase the car and then make three $5,000 payments, one at the end of each year of the loan. You currently have $50,000 in your savings account.

a. The rate of interest on your savings account is 4% and will remain so for the next three years. Which payment method should you choose?

b. What interest rate, i, makes you indifferent between the two payment methods? W

25. A resident of New York City, you are considering purchasing a new Toyota Prius. The Prius sells for $20,000. Your annual expense of owning and driving the car is $3,000 (most of which is the cost of parking the car in a Manhattan garage). If you do not purchase the car, you will spend $5,000 per year on public transportation and rental cars. The interest rate is 4%. What is the smallest number of years that you must own the car so that the discounted cost of owning the car is less than the discounted cost of the alternative? W

26. As discussed in Solved Problem 16.2, Lewis Wolff and his investment group bought the Oakland A's baseball team for $180 million in 2005. Reportedly Hall-of-Famer Reggie Jackson offered $25 million more but was rebuffed (*Forbes,* 2005). How would the calculations in Solved Problem 16.2 change if the sales price had been $205 million?

27. A firm's profit is π = revenue − labor costs − capital costs. Its capital cost can be stated as its rate of return on capital, *rr*, times the value of its capital, $p_K K$, where p_K is the price of a unit of capital and *K* is the number of units of capital. What is the firm's implicit rate of return on its capital? (*Hint*: Set profit equal to zero and solve the *irr*.)

***28.** A firm is considering an investment where its cash flow is $\pi_1 = \$1$ (million), $\pi_2 = -\$12$, $\pi_3 = \$20$, and $\pi_t = 0$ for all other *t*. The interest rate is 7%. Use the net present value rule to determine whether the firm should make the investment. Can the firm use the internal rate of return rule to make this decision?

29. To virtually everyone's surprise, the new Washington Nationals baseball team earned a pretax profit of $20 million in 2005, compared to a $10 million loss when the team was the Montreal Expos in 2004 (Thomas Heath, "Nationals' Expected '05 Profit Is $20 Million," *Washington Post*, June 21, 2005, A1). Major League Baseball, which bought the franchise for $120 million in 2002, sold the team for $450 million in 2006 (**washington.nationals.mlb.com**, 2008). If the Nationals are expected to earn $20 million each year in the future, what is the internal rate of return on a $400 million investment for this club?

30. A typical National Basketball Association (NBA) franchise would sell for $372 million—though the Knicks were worth $600 million in 2007 (**www.forbes.com/2007/12/06/business-basketball-nba-biz-07nba-cz_kb_mo_cs_1206nbaintro_print.html**). NBA teams posted average earnings (before interest, taxes, depreciation, and amortization) of $9.8 million. Assuming that the team can maintain this earnings flow indefinitely, does it pay for a profit-maximizing investor to buy such a franchise if the real interest rate is 3%? Answer using the methods in Solved Problems 16.2 and 16.3.

31. Which is worth more to you: (a) a $10,000 payment today or (b) a $1,000-per-year higher salary for as long as you work? At what interest rate would (a) be worth more to you than (b)? Does your answer depend on how many years you expect to work?

32. The Santa Cruz County fire department in California pays its employees with associate degrees $120 more a month than if they are high school graduates, $180 more for bachelor degrees, and $240 more for a master degrees (**santacruzsentinel.com**, December 3, 2006). Suppose you know that you want to work for this fire department and want to maximize how much you earn. Given that you want to be a firefighter, when you graduate from high school, should you go to college for four years at a cost of $12,000 per year or go directly into the fire department? In your calculations, assume that you'll work for 40 years and then retire and consider interest rates of 5% and 20%. Do you need to know how much a high school graduate earns to answer this question? (*Hint*: You can get a reasonable approximation to the answer by assuming that you work forever and use Equation 16.4 for part of your calculations.)

33. You have a barrel of oil that you can sell today for *p* dollars. Assuming no inflation and no storage cost, how high would the price have to be next year for you to sell the oil next year rather than now?

34. Trees, wine, and cattle become more valuable over time and then possibly decrease in value. Draw a figure with present value on the vertical axis and years (age) on the horizontal axis and show this relationship. Show in what year the owner should "harvest" such a good assuming that there is no cost to harvesting. [*Hint*: If the good's present value is P_0 and we take that money and invest it at interest rate *i* (a small number such as 2% or 4%), then its value in year *t* is $P_0(1 + i)^t$; or if we allow continuous compounding, $P_0 e^{it}$. Such a curve increases exponentially over time and looks like the curve labeled *Price* in Figure 16.3. Draw curves with different possible present values. Use those curves to choose the optimal harvest time.] How would your answer change if the interest rate were zero? Show in a figure.

35. If all the coal in the ground, *Q*, is to be consumed in two years and the demand for coal is $Q_t = A(p_t)^{-\varepsilon}$ in each year *t* where ε is a constant demand elasticity, what is the price of coal each year?

36. An economic consultant explaining the effect on labor demand of increasing health care costs, interviewed for the *Wall Street Journal*'s Capital column (David Wessel, "Health-Care Costs Blamed for Hiring Gap," March 11, 2004, A2), states, "Medical costs are rising more rapidly than anything else in the economy—more than prices, wages or profits. It isn't only current medical costs, but also the present value of the stream of endlessly high cost increases that retards hiring."

a. Why does the present value of the stream of health care costs, and not just the current health care costs, affect a firm's decision whether to create a new position?

b. Why should an employer discount the future health care costs in its decision whether to create a new position? W

17 Uncertainty

We must believe in luck. For how else can we explain the success of those we don't like?
—Jean Cocteau

Life's a series of gambles. Will you receive Social Security when you retire? Will you win the lottery tomorrow? Will your stock increase in value? Will you avoid disease, earthquakes, and fire? In this chapter, we extend the model of decision making by individuals and firms to include uncertainty. We look at how uncertainty affects consumption decisions (Chapters 4 and 5)—such as how much insurance to buy—as well as investment decisions (Chapter 16).

When making decisions about investments and other matters, you consider the possible *outcomes* under various circumstances, or *states of nature*. When deciding about whether to carry a new type of doll, a toy store owner considers how many dolls will be sold if the doll is popular and how many if it is unpopular—two possible outcomes—and how likely these two states of nature are.

risk
situation in which the likelihood of each possible outcome is known or can be estimated and no single possible outcome is certain to occur

Although we cannot know with certainty what the future outcome will be, we may know that some outcomes are more likely than others. When uncertainty can be quantified, it is sometimes called **risk**: The likelihood of each possible outcome is known or can be estimated, and no single possible outcome is certain to occur. All the examples in this chapter concern quantifiable or risky situations.[1]

Consumers and firms modify their decisions about consumption and investment as the degree of risk varies. Indeed, most people are willing to spend money to reduce risk by buying insurance or taking preventive measures. Moreover, most people will choose a riskier investment over a less risky one only if they expect a higher return from the riskier investment.

In this chapter, we examine five main topics

1. **Degree of Risk.** Probabilities are used to measure the degree of risk and the likely profit from a risky undertaking.
2. **Decision Making Under Uncertainty.** Whether people choose a risky option over a nonrisky one depends on their attitudes toward risk and on the expected payoffs of each option.
3. **Avoiding Risk.** People try to reduce their overall risk by not making risky choices, taking actions to lower the likelihood of a disaster, combining offsetting risks, insuring, and in other ways.

[1]*Jargon alert:* Many people do not distinguish between the terms *risk* and *uncertainty*. Henceforth, we use these terms interchangeably.

4. **Investing Under Uncertainty.** Whether people make an investment depends on the riskiness of the payoff, the expected return, attitudes toward risk, the interest rate, and whether it is profitable to alter the likelihood of a good outcome.
5. **Behavioral Economics of Risk.** Because some people do not choose among risky options the way that traditional economic theory predicts, some researchers have switched to new models that incorporate psychological factors.

17.1 Degree of Risk

In America, anyone can be president. That's one of the risks you take.
—Adlai Stevenson

You are thinking about buying lunch at a new restaurant. There are two possible outcomes: The lunch will or will not taste good to you. Knowing the likelihood of each of these outcomes would help you decide whether to try this new restaurant.

Before we can analyze decision making under uncertainty, we need a way to describe and quantify risk. A particular event—such as eating lunch at a new restaurant—has a number of possible outcomes: say, an enjoyable meal or an unenjoyable meal. Because you don't know whether you will enjoy the meal, eating at this new restaurant is risky. To describe how risky this activity is, we need to quantify the likelihood that each possible outcome occurs.

We can use our estimate of how risky each outcome is to estimate the most likely outcome. We then present measures of risk that reflect how much actual outcomes deviate from the most likely outcome.

Probability

A *probability* is a number between 0 and 1 that indicates the likelihood that a particular outcome will occur. You might, for example, have a 25% probability—a 1 in 4 chance—of enjoying the meal at the restaurant. How do we estimate a probability?

Frequency. If we have a history of the outcomes for an event, we can use the frequency with which a particular outcome occurred as our estimate of the probability. Let n be the number of times one particular outcome occurred during the N total number of times an event occurred. We set our estimate of the probability, θ (theta), equal to the frequency:

$$\theta = n/N.$$

See Problem 14.

A house either burns or does not burn. If $n = 13$ similar houses burned in your neighborhood of $N = 1{,}000$ homes last year, you might estimate the probability that your house will burn this year as $\theta = 13/1{,}000 = 1.3\%$.

Subjective Probability. Often we don't have a history that allows us to calculate the frequency. We use whatever information we have to form a *subjective probability*, which is our best estimate of the likelihood that an outcome will occur. We may use all available information—even information that is not based on a conscious, scientific estimation procedure.

How do you derive a subjective probability about the likelihood that you'll like the new restaurant? You might know that your friend liked the restaurant but your economics professor did not. If you're not sure whether either of these people likes the same food you do, you may estimate the probability that you'll like the restaurant at 50%. However, if you know that your friend usually likes the same type of food you do but you're less sure about whether your professor likes the same type of food, you might put more weight on your friend's report and estimate the probability that you'll like the restaurant as a number greater than half, perhaps 85%.[2]

Probability Distribution. A *probability distribution* relates the probability of occurrence to each possible outcome. Panel a of Figure 17.1 shows a probability distribution over five possible outcomes: zero to four days of rain per month in a relatively dry city. The probability that it rains no days during the month is 10%, as is the probability of exactly four days of rain. The chance of two rainy days is 40%, and the chance of one or three rainy days is 20% each. The probability that it rains five or more days a month is 0%.

These weather outcomes are *mutually exclusive*—only one of these outcomes can occur at a given time—and *exhaustive*—no other outcomes than those listed are

Figure 17.1 Probability Distribution.

The probability distribution shows the probability of occurrence for each of the mutually exclusive outcomes. Panel a shows five possible mutually exclusive outcomes. The probability that it rains exactly two days per month is 40%. The probability that it rains five or more days per month is 0%. The probability distributions in panels a and b have the same mean. The variance is smaller in panel b, where the probability distribution is more concentrated around the mean than the distribution in panel a.

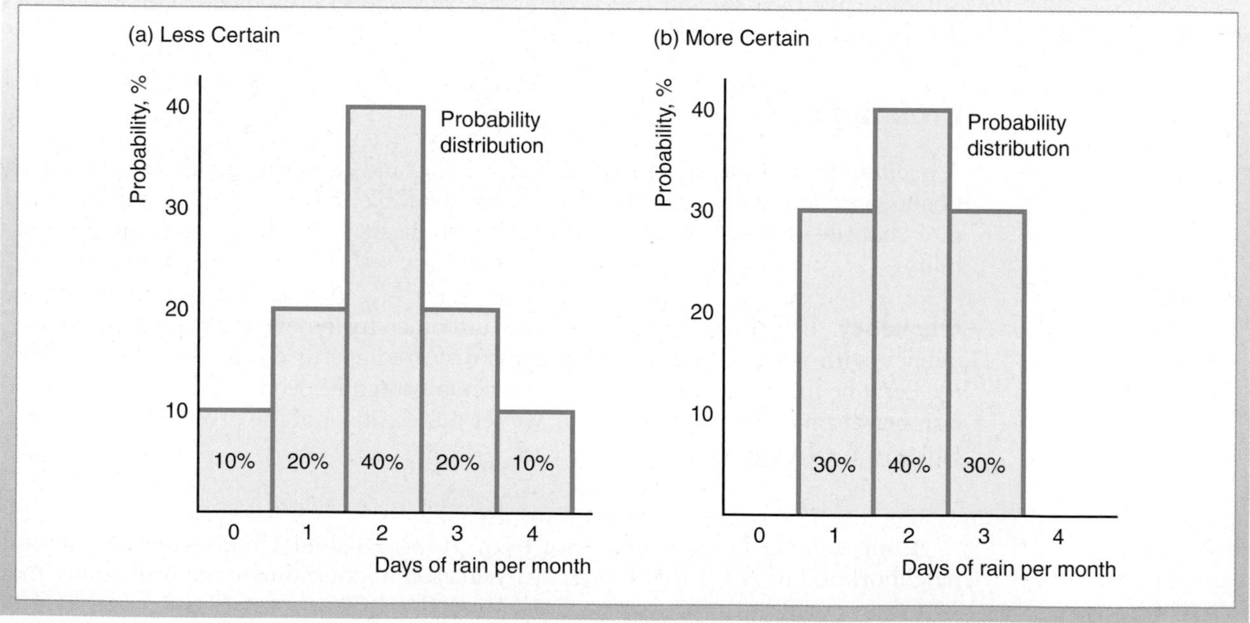

[2]When events are repeated, we can compare our subjective probabilities to observed frequencies. Your subjective probability (guess) that it rains 50% of the days in January can be compared to the frequency of rain in January during the recorded history for your city. If an event is not going to be repeated, however, it may not be possible to check whether your subjective probability is reasonable or accurate by comparing it to a frequency. You might believe that there's a 75% chance of dry weather tomorrow. If it does rain tomorrow, that doesn't mean you were wrong. Only if you believed that the probability of rain was 0% would observing rain tomorrow prove you wrong.

possible. Where outcomes are mutually exclusive and exhaustive, exactly one of these outcomes will occur with certainty, and the probabilities must add up to 100%. For simplicity, we concentrate on situations in which there are only two possible outcomes.

Expected Value

One of the common denominators I have found is that expectations rise above that which is expected. —George W. Bush

Gregg, a promoter, schedules an outdoor concert for tomorrow.[3] How much money he'll make depends on the weather. If it doesn't rain, his profit or value from the concert is $V = \$15$. (If it will make you happier—and it will certainly make Gregg happier—you can think of the profits in this example as \$15,000 instead of \$15.) If it rains, he'll have to cancel the concert and he'll lose $V = -\$5$, which he must pay the band. Although Gregg does not know what the weather will be with certainty, he knows that the weather department forecasts a 50% chance of rain.

The amount Gregg expects to earn is called his *expected value* (here, his *expected profit*). The expected value, EV, is the value of each possible outcome times the probability of that outcome:[4]

$$\begin{aligned} EV &= [Pr(\text{no rain}) \times \text{Value(no rain)}] + [Pr(\text{rain}) \times \text{Value(rain)}] \\ &= \left[\tfrac{1}{2} \times \$15\right] + \left[\tfrac{1}{2} \times (-\$5)\right] = \$5, \end{aligned}$$

where Pr is the probability of an outcome, so Pr(rain) is the "probability that rain occurs."

See Problem 15.

The expected value is the amount Gregg would earn on average if the event were repeated many times. If he puts on such concerts many times over the years and the weather follows historical patterns, he will earn \$15 at half of the concerts without rain, and he will get soaked for –\$5 at the other half of the concerts, at which it rains. Thus, he'll earn an average of \$5 per concert over a long period of time.

Solved Problem 17.1

How much more would Gregg expect to earn if he knew that he would obtain perfect information about the probability of rain far enough before the concert that he could book the band only if needed? How much does he gain from having this perfect information?

Answer

1. *Determine how much Gregg would earn if he had perfect information in each state of nature.* If Gregg knew with certainty that it would rain at the time of the concert, he would not book the band, so he would make no loss or profit. If Gregg knew that it would not rain, he would hold the concert and make \$15.

2. *Determine how much Gregg would expect to earn before he learns with certainty what the weather will be.* Gregg knows that he'll make \$15 with a 50%

---

[3]My brother Gregg, a successful concert promoter, wants me to inform you that the hero of the following story is some other Gregg who is a concert promoter.

[4]If there are n possible outcomes, the value of outcome i is V_i, and the probability of that outcome is Pr_i, then the expected value is $EV = Pr_1V_1 + Pr_2V_2 + \cdots + Pr_nV_n$.

probability and \$0 with a 50% probability, so his expected value, given that he'll receive perfect information in time to act on it, is

$$\left(\tfrac{1}{2} \times \$15\right) + \left(\tfrac{1}{2} \times \$0\right) = \$7.50.$$

3. *His gain from perfect information is the difference between his expected earnings with perfect information and with imperfect information.* Gregg expects to earn \$2.50 = \$7.50 – \$5 more with perfect information than with imperfect information. This answer can be reached more directly. Perfect weather information is valuable to him because he can avoid hiring the band unnecessarily when it rains. (Having information has no value if it doesn't alter behavior.) The *value of this information* is his expected savings from not hiring the band when it rains: $\tfrac{1}{2} \times \$5 = \$2.50$.

Variance and Standard Deviation

If Gregg would earn the same amount—the expected value—whether it rained or not, he would face no risk. We can measure the risk he faces in many different ways. One approach is to look at the degree by which actual outcomes vary from the expected value, EV.

The *difference* between his actual earnings and his expected earnings if it does not rain is \$10 = \$15 – \$5. The difference if it does rain is –\$10 = –\$5 – \$5. Because there are two differences—one difference for each state of nature—it is convenient to combine them in a single measure of risk.

One such measure of risk is the *variance*, which measures the spread of the probability distribution. For example, the variance in panel a of Figure 17.1, where the probability distribution ranges from zero to four days of rain per month, is greater than the variance in panel b, where the probability distribution ranges from one to three days of rain per month.

Formally, the variance is the probability-weighted average of the squares of the differences between the observed outcome and the expected value.[5] The variance of the value Gregg obtains from the outdoor concert is

$$\begin{aligned}\text{Variance} &= [Pr(\text{no rain}) \times (\text{Value(no rain)} - EV)^2] + [Pr(\text{rain}) \times (\text{Value(rain)} - EV)^2\\ &= \left[\tfrac{1}{2} \times (\$15 - \$5)^2\right] + \left[\tfrac{1}{2} \times (-\$5 - \$5)^2\right]\\ &= \left[\tfrac{1}{2} \times (\$10)^2\right] + \left[\tfrac{1}{2} \times (-\$10)^2\right] = \$100.\end{aligned}$$

Panel a of Table 17.1 shows how to calculate the variance of the profit from this concert step by step. The first column lists the two outcomes: rain and no rain. The next column gives the probability. The third column shows the value or profit of each outcome. The next column calculates the difference between the values in the third column and the expected value, $EV = \$5$. The following column squares these

[5]If there are n possible outcomes with an expected value of EV, the value of outcome i is V_i, and the probability of that outcome is Pr_i, then the variance is

$$Pr_1(V_1 - EV)^2 + Pr_2(V_2 - EV)^2 + \cdots + Pr_n(V_n - EV)^2.$$

The variance puts more weight on large deviations from the expected value than on smaller ones.

Table 17.1 Variance and Standard Deviation: Measures of Risk.

(a) Outdoor Concert					
Outcome	Probability	Value	Difference = Value – \$5	Difference^2	Difference^2 × Probability
No rain	$\frac{1}{2}$	\$15	\$10	\$100	\$50
Rain	$\frac{1}{2}$	–\$5	–\$10	\$100	\$50
				Variance	\$100
				Standard Deviation	\$10
(b) Indoor Concert					
Outcome	Probability	Value	Difference = Value – \$5	Difference^2	Difference^2 × Probability
No rain	$\frac{1}{2}$	\$10	\$5	\$25	\$12.50
Rain	$\frac{1}{2}$	\$0	–\$5	\$25	\$12.50
				Variance	\$25
				Standard Deviation	\$5

differences, and the last column multiplies these squared differences by the probabilities in the second column. The sum of these probability weighted differences, \$100, is the variance.

Instead of describing risk using the variance, economists and businesspeople often report the *standard deviation*, which is the square root of the variance. The usual symbol for the standard deviation is σ (sigma), so the symbol for variance is σ^2. For the outdoor concert, the variance is $\sigma^2 = \$100$ and the standard deviation is $\sigma = \$10$.

Holding the expected value constant, the smaller the standard deviation (or variance), the smaller the risk. Panel b of Table 17.1 illustrates that Gregg's expected value of profit is the same if he stages the concert indoors, but the standard deviation of his profit is less. The indoor theater does not hold as many people as the outdoor venue, so the most Gregg can earn if it does not rain is \$10. Rain discourages attendance even at the indoor theater, so he just breaks even, earning \$0. The expected value of the indoor concert,

$$EV = \left(\tfrac{1}{2} \times \$10\right) + \left(\tfrac{1}{2} \times \$0\right) = \$5,$$

See Problem 16.

is the same as that for the outdoor concert. Staging the concert indoors involves less risk, however. As panel b shows, the variance of the profit at the indoor concert is \$25, and the corresponding standard deviation is \$5.

17.2 Decision Making Under Uncertainty

There will be a rain dance Friday night, weather permitting.
—George Carlin

Will Gregg stage an indoor or outdoor concert? To answer such a question, we need to know his attitude toward bearing risk.

Although the indoor and outdoor concerts have the same expected value, the outdoor concert involves more risk. Gregg will earn more with good weather or lose more with bad weather by holding his concert outdoors instead of indoors. He'll book an outdoor concert only if he likes to gamble.

Even if he dislikes risk, Gregg may prefer a riskier option if it has a higher expected value. Suppose that he strikes a new agreement with the band by which he pays only if the weather is good and the concert is held. Gregg's expected value is \$7.50, the variance is \$56.25, and the standard deviation is \$7.50.[6] By holding the concert outdoors instead of inside, Gregg's expected value is higher (\$7.50 instead of \$5) and the standard deviation is higher (\$7.50 instead of \$5). He earns the same, \$0, from both types of concerts in bad weather. In good weather, he earns more from the outdoor concert. Because he always does as well with an outdoor concert as with an indoor show, Gregg clearly prefers the riskier outdoor concert with its higher expected value.

If he dislikes risk, Gregg won't necessarily stage the concert with the higher expected value. Suppose that his choice is between the indoor concert and an outdoor concert from which he earns \$100,015.50 if it doesn't rain and loses \$100,005 if it rains. His expected value is greater with the outside concert, \$5.25 instead of \$5, but he faces much more risk. The standard deviation of the outdoor concert is \$100,010.25 compared to \$5. Gregg might reasonably opt for the indoor concert with the lower expected value if he dislikes risk. After all, he may be loath to risk losing \$100,005 with a 50% probability.

Expected Utility

We can formalize this type of reasoning by extending our model of utility maximization (Chapter 4) to show how people's taste for risk affects their choice among options (investments, career choices, consumption bundles) that differ in both value and risk. If people made choices to maximize expected value, they would always choose the option with the highest expected value regardless of the risks involved. However, most people care about risk as well as expected value. Indeed, most people are *risk averse*—they dislike risk—and will choose a bundle with higher risk only if its expected value is substantially higher than that of a less-risky bundle.

In Chapter 4, we noted that we can describe an individual's preferences over various bundles of goods by using a utility function. John von Neumann and Oskar Morgenstern (1944) suggested an extension of this standard utility-maximizing model that includes risk.[7] In their reformulation, a rational person maximizes *expected utility*. Expected utility is the probability-weighted average of the utility

---

[6]The expected value is the same as in Solved Problem 17.1:

$$\left(\tfrac{1}{2}\times \$15\right)+\left(\tfrac{1}{2}\times \$0\right)=\$7.50.$$

The variance is

$$\tfrac{1}{2}(\$15-\$7.50)^2+\tfrac{1}{2}(\$0-\$7.50)^2=\$56.25,$$

so the standard deviation is \$7.50.

[7]This approach to handling choice under uncertainty is the most commonly used method. Schoemaker (1982) discusses the logic underlying this approach, the evidence for it, and several variants. Machina (1989) discusses a number of alternative methods. Here we treat utility as a cardinal measure rather than an ordinal measure as we did in Chapters 4 and 5.

from each possible outcome. For example, Gregg's expected utility, EU, from the outdoor concert is

$$EU = [Pr(\text{no rain}) \times U(\text{Value(no rain)})] + [Pr(\text{rain}) \times U(\text{Value(rain)})]$$
$$= \left[\tfrac{1}{2} \times U(\$15)\right] + \left[\tfrac{1}{2} \times U(-\$5)\right],$$

where his utility function, U, depends on his earnings. For example, $U(\$15)$ is the amount of utility Gregg gets from \$15. (People have preferences over the goods they consume. However, for simplicity, we'll say that a person receives utility from earnings or wealth, which can be spent on consumption goods.)

In short, the expected utility calculation is similar to the expected value calculation. Both are weighted averages in which the weights are the probability (Pr) that the state of nature will occur. The difference is that the expected value is the probability-weighted average of the monetary value, whereas the expected utility is the probability-weighted average of the utility from the monetary value.

If we know how an individual's utility increases with wealth, we can determine how that person reacts to risky propositions. We can classify people in terms of their willingness to make a **fair bet:** a wager with an expected value of zero. An example of a fair bet is one in which you pay a dollar if a flipped coin comes up heads and receive a dollar if it comes up tails. Because you expect to win half the time and lose half the time, the expected value of this bet is zero:

fair bet
a wager with an expected value of zero

$$\left[\tfrac{1}{2} \times (-\$1)\right] + \left[\tfrac{1}{2} \times \$1\right] = 0.$$

See Problem 17.

In contrast, a bet in which you pay \$1 if you lose the coin flip and receive \$2 if you win is an unfair bet that favors you, with an expected value of

$$\left[\tfrac{1}{2} \times (-\$1)\right] + \left[\tfrac{1}{2} \times \$2\right] = 50¢.$$

risk averse
unwilling to make a fair bet

risk neutral
indifferent about making a fair bet

risk preferring
willing to make a fair bet

Someone who is unwilling to make a fair bet is **risk averse**. A person who is indifferent about making a fair bet is **risk neutral**. A person who is **risk preferring** will make a fair bet.

Risk Aversion

We can use our expected utility model to examine how Irma, who is risk averse, makes a choice under uncertainty. Figure 17.2 shows Irma's utility function. The utility function is concave to the wealth axis, indicating that Irma's utility rises with wealth but at a diminishing rate.[8] She has *diminishing marginal utility of wealth*: The extra pleasure from each extra dollar of wealth is smaller than the pleasure from the previous dollar. An individual whose utility function is concave to the wealth axis is risk averse, as we now illustrate.

See Questions 1 and 2 and Problem 18.

A person whose utility function is concave picks the less risky choice if both choices have the same expected value. Suppose that Irma has an initial wealth of

[8]Irma's utility from W wealth is $U(W)$. She has positive marginal utility from extra wealth, $dU(W)/dW > 0$; however, her utility increases with wealth at a diminishing rate, $d^2U(W)/dW^2 < 0$.

Figure 17.2 Risk Aversion.

Initially, Irma's wealth is \$40, so her utility is $U(\$40) = 120$, point d. If she buys the vase and it's a Ming, she is at point c, where her utility is $U(\$70) = 140$. If the purchased vase is an imitation, she is at point a, where $U(\$10) = 70$. If her subjective probability that the vase is a Ming is 50%, her expected utility from buying the vase, point b, is $\frac{1}{2}U(\$10) + \frac{1}{2}U(\$70) = 105$, which is less than her utility with a certain wealth of \$40, $U(\$40) = 120$. Thus, she does not buy the vase. If Irma's subjective probability that the vase is a Ming is 90%, her expected utility from buying the vase is $0.1U(\$10) + 0.9U(\$70) = 133$, point f, which is more than her utility with a certain wealth of \$40, $U(\$40) = 120$, d, so she buys the vase.

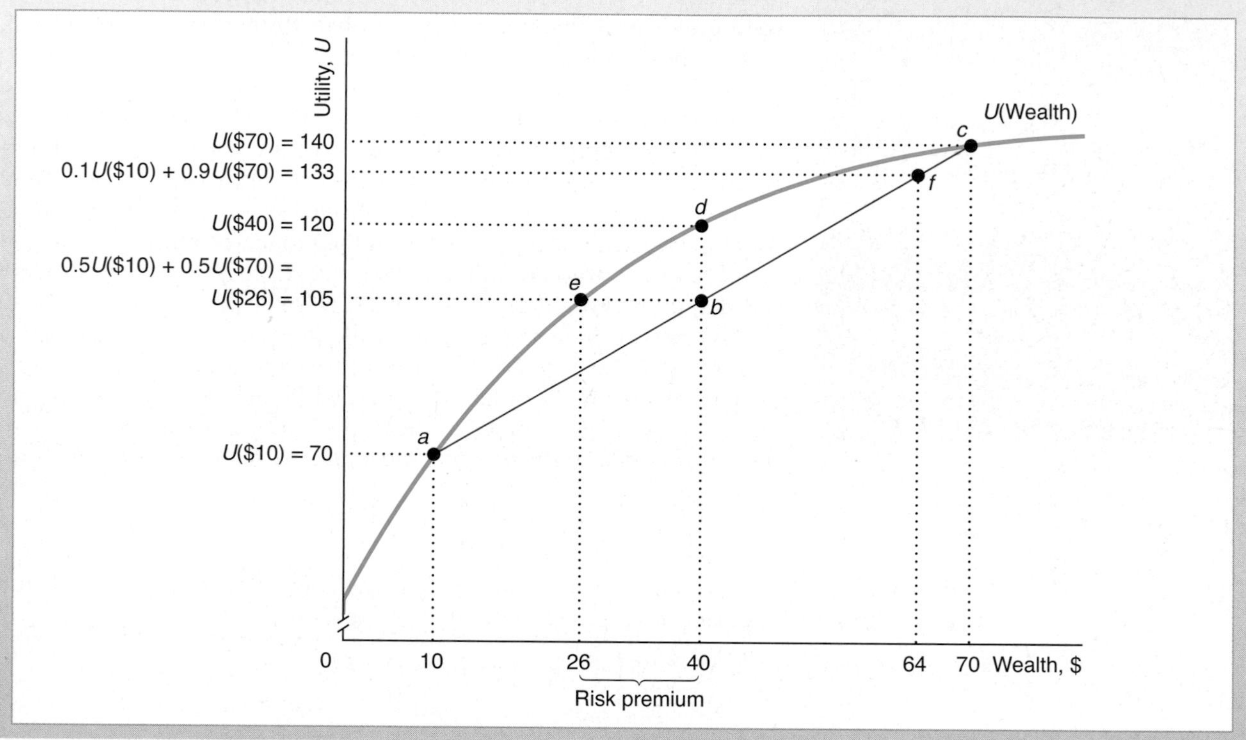

\$40 and has two options. One option is to do nothing and keep the \$40, so that her utility is $U(\$40) = 120$ (point d in Figure 17.2) with certainty.

Her other option is to buy a vase. Her wealth is \$70 if the vase is a Ming and \$10 if it is an imitation. Irma's subjective probability is 50% that it is a genuine Ming vase. Her expected value or wealth remains

$$\$40 = \left(\tfrac{1}{2} \times \$10\right) + \left(\tfrac{1}{2} \times \$70\right).$$

Thus, buying the vase is a fair bet because she has the same expected wealth whether she purchases the vase or not.

Irma prefers the certain wealth from not buying the vase because that option carries less risk. Her utility if the vase is a Ming is $U(\$70) = 140$, point c. If it's an imitation, her utility is $U(\$10) = 70$, point a. Thus, her expected utility is

$$\left[\tfrac{1}{2} \times U(\$10)\right] + \left[\tfrac{1}{2} \times U(\$70)\right] = \left[\tfrac{1}{2} \times 70\right] + \left[\tfrac{1}{2} \times 140\right] = 105.$$

The graph shows that her expected utility is point b, the midpoint of a line (called a *chord*) between a and c.[9]

Because Irma's utility function is concave, her utility from certain wealth, 120 at point d, is greater than her expected utility from the risky activity, 105 at point b. As a result, she does not buy the vase. Buying this vase, which is a fair bet, increases the risk she faces without changing her expected wealth.

risk premium
the amount that a risk-averse person would pay to avoid taking a risk

The **risk premium** is the amount that a risk-averse person would pay to avoid taking a risk. The figure shows how much Irma would be willing to pay to avoid this risk. Her certain utility from having a wealth of \$26, $U(\$26) = 105$, is the same as her expected utility if she buys the vase. Thus, Irma would be indifferent between buying the vase and having \$26 with certainty. Irma would be willing to pay a risk premium of $\$14 = \$40 - \$26$ to avoid bearing the risk from buying the vase.

A risk-averse person chooses a riskier option only if it has a sufficiently higher expected value. If Irma were much more confident that the vase were a Ming, her expected value would rise and she'd buy the vase, as Solved Problem 17.2 shows.[10]

Solved Problem 17.2

Suppose that Irma's subjective probability is 90% that the vase is a Ming. What is her expected wealth if she buys the vase? What is her expected utility? Does she buy the vase?

Answer

1. *Calculate Irma's expected wealth.* Her expected value or wealth is 10% times her wealth if the vase is not a Ming plus 90% times her wealth if the vase is a Ming:

$$(0.1 \times \$10) + (0.9 \times \$70) = \$64.$$

In Figure 17.2, \$64 is the distance along the wealth axis corresponding to point f.

2. *Calculate Irma's expected utility.* Her expected utility is the probability-weighted average of her utility under the two outcomes:

$$[0.1 \times U(\$10)] + [0.9 \times U(\$70)] = [0.1 \times 70] + [0.9 \times 140] = 133.$$

Her expected utility is the height on the utility axis of point f. Point f is nine-tenths of the distance along the line connecting point a to point c.

3. *Compare Irma's expected utility to her certain utility if she does not buy.* Irma's expected utility from buying the vase, 133 (point f), is greater than her certain utility, 120 (point d), if she does not. Thus, if Irma is this confident that the vase is a Ming, she buys it. Although the risk is greater from buying than from not buying, her expected wealth is enough higher (\$64 instead of \$40) that it's worth it to her to take the chance.

See Questions 3 and 4 and Problems 19–22.

[9]The chord represents all the possible weighted averages of the utility at point a and the utility at point c. When the probabilities of the two outcomes are equal, the expected value is the midpoint. If the probability that the vase is a Ming is greater than $\frac{1}{2}$, the expected value is closer to point c, as Solved Problem 17.2 illustrates.

[10]My colleague Irma Adelman visited an antique store and was offered a vase for \$10. In addition to being an outstanding economist, she's an art expert. At first glance, she thought that the vase was a Ming. Turning it over, she found marks on the bottom that convinced her that it was a Ming (I think it said "Made in China"). Because her subjective probability that the vase was a genuine Ming was very high, she bought it, even though she is risk averse. This lovely Ming vase graced her home until her !#@$! cat broke it.

Risk Neutrality

Someone who is risk neutral has a constant marginal utility of wealth: Each extra dollar of wealth raises utility by the same amount as the previous dollar. With constant marginal utility of wealth, the utility curve is a straight line in a utility and wealth graph.

Suppose that Irma is risk neutral and has the straight-line utility curve in panel a of Figure 17.3. She would be indifferent between buying the vase and not buying it if her subjective probability is 50% that it is a Ming. Her expected utility from buying the vase is the average of her utility at points a ($10) and c ($70):

$$\left[\tfrac{1}{2} \times U(\$10)\right] + \left[\tfrac{1}{2} \times U(\$70)\right] = \left[\tfrac{1}{2} \times 70\right] + \left[\tfrac{1}{2} \times 140\right] = 105.$$

Her expected utility exactly equals her utility with certain wealth of $40 (point b) because the line connecting points a and c lies on the utility function and point b is the midpoint of that line.

Here Irma is indifferent between buying and not buying the vase, a fair bet, because she doesn't care how much risk she faces. Because the expected wealth from both options is $40, she is indifferent between them.

In general, *a risk-neutral person chooses the option with the highest expected value, because maximizing expected value maximizes utility*. A risk-neutral person chooses the riskier option if it has even a slightly higher expected value than the less risky option. Equivalently, the risk premium for a risk-neutral person is zero.

Figure 17.3 Risk Neutrality and Risk Preference.

(a) If Irma's utility curve is a straight line, she is risk neutral and is indifferent as to whether or not to make a fair bet. Her expected utility from buying the vase, 105 at b, is the same as from a certain wealth of $40 at b. (b) If Irma's utility curve is convex to the horizontal axis, Irma has increasing marginal utility to wealth and is risk preferring. She buys the vase because her expected utility from buying the vase, 105 at b, is higher than her utility from a certain wealth of $40, 82 at d.

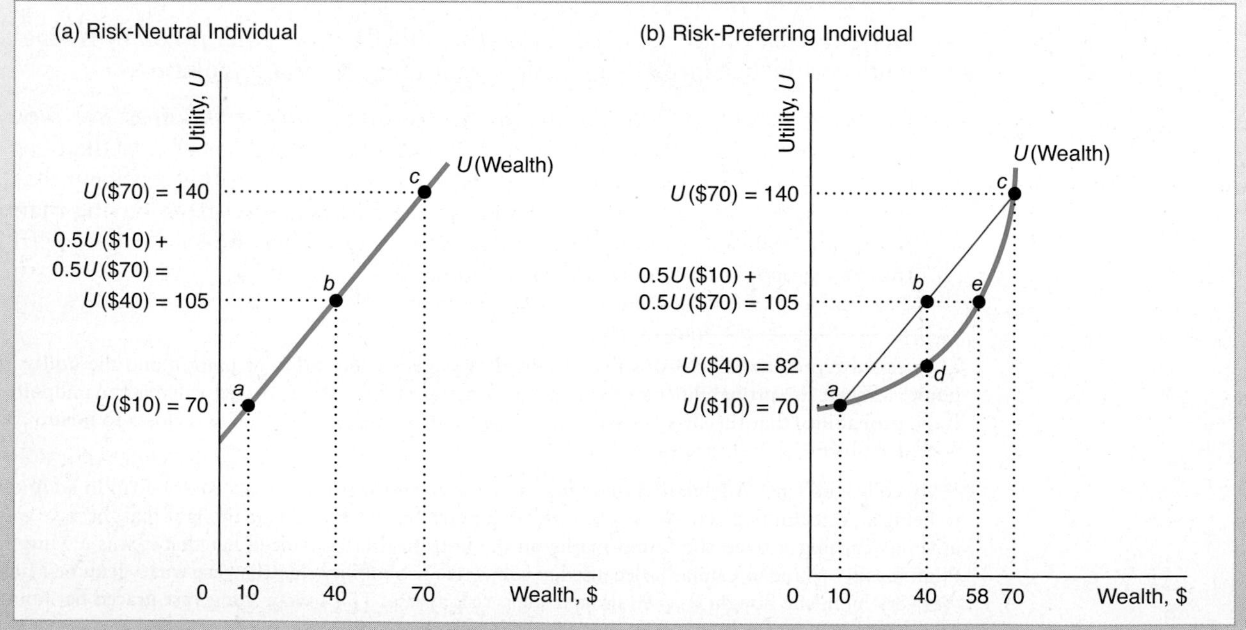

Risk Preference

An individual with an increasing marginal utility of wealth is risk preferring: willing to take a fair bet. If Irma has the utility curve in panel b of Figure 17.3, she is risk preferring. Her expected utility from buying the vase, 105 at *b*, is higher than her certain utility if she does not buy the vase, 82 at *d*. Therefore, she buys the vase.

A risk-preferring person is willing to pay for the right to make a fair bet (a negative risk premium). As the figure shows, Irma's expected utility from buying the vase is the same as the utility from a certain wealth of $58. Given her initial wealth of $40, if you offer her the opportunity to buy the vase or offer to give her $18, she is indifferent. With any payment smaller than $18, she prefers to buy the vase.

See Problem 23.

APPLICATION

Gambling

Horse sense is the thing a horse has which keeps it from betting on people.
—W. C. Fields

If you ask them, most people say that they don't like bearing risk. Consistent with such statements, they reduce the risk they face by buying insurance. Nonetheless, 80% of U.S. adults engage in games of chance at least once a year. Christiansen Capital Advisors estimate that U.S. gambling industry revenues were $91 billion in 2006 (roughly equal to IBM's revenues for that year).

Gambling on the Internet is growing rapidly in most of the world. U.S. Internet gambling was about $5.8 billion in 2006, though the United States banned Internet gambling starting in October 2006. Germany imposed a similar ban in 2008.

Over half of the countries in the world have lotteries with annual combined ticket sales well in excess of $205 billion, with Italy's Lottomatica taking in $13.3 billion in sales. The equity value of the 41 U.S. state lotteries would be $203 billion, if they could be sold.

Not only do many people gamble, but they make unfair bets, in which the expected value of the gamble is negative. That is, if they play the game repeatedly, they are likely to lose money in the long run.

For example, the British government keeps half of the total bet on its lottery. Americans lose at least $50 billion or 7% of the legal bets. A casino's *hold percentage*—the money the casino retains as a percentage of the amount of chips bought—for roulette wheels runs slightly over 20%; for the wheel of fortune about 45%; and for keno, nearly 30%.

See Problem 24.

Why do people take unfair bets? Some people gamble because they are risk preferring or because they have a compulsion to gamble. However, neither of these observations is likely to explain noncompulsive gambling by most people who exhibit risk-averse behavior in the other aspects of their lives (such as buying insurance). Risk-averse people may make unfair bets for three reasons: (1) They enjoy the game, (2) they have a utility curve with both risk-averse and risk-preferring regions, or (3) they falsely believe that the gamble favors them.

The first explanation is that gambling provides entertainment as well as risk. Risk-averse people insure their property, such as their house, because there's noth-

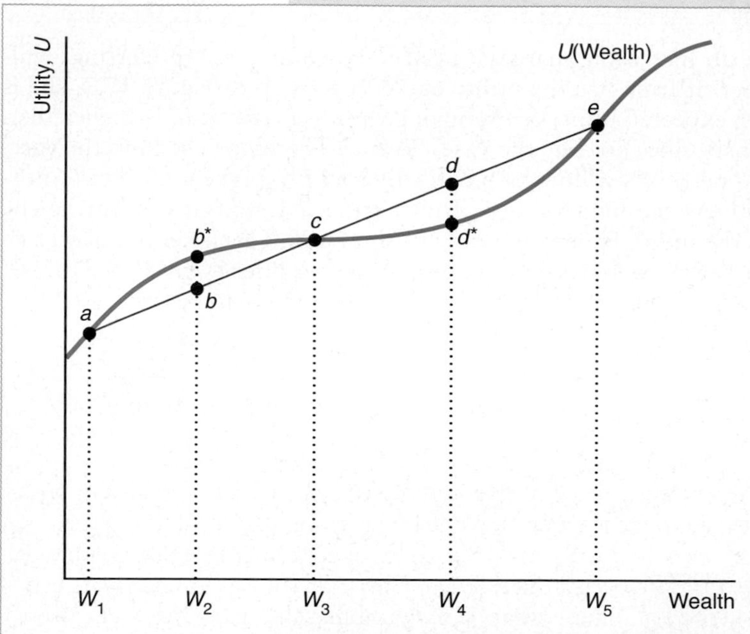

ing enjoyable about bearing the risk of theft, flooding, and fire. However, these same people may play poker or bet on horse races because they get enough pleasure from playing those games to put up with the financial risk and the expected loss.

People definitely like games of chance. One survey found that 65% of Americans say that they engage in games of chance, even when the games involve no money or only trivial sums (Brunk, 1981). That is, they play because they enjoy the games.[11]

The second explanation also involves tastes. Friedman and Savage (1948) suggested that gamblers place a high value on the chance to increase their wealth greatly. The graph shows Sylvia's utility curve, which has the shape that Friedman and Savage described. Sylvia is risk averse with respect to small gambles but risk preferring with respect to bets that allow for large potential winnings. Sylvia prefers receiving W_2 with certainty to engaging in a bet with an expected value of W_2, where she has an equal probability of receiving wealth W_1 or W_3. Sylvia chooses the certain wealth because her certain utility at b^* is above the expected utility at b. On the other hand, Sylvia prefers a bet with an equal chance of W_3 and W_5 to the certain wealth of W_4, which is the expected value of the bet, because the expected utility at d from the bet is greater than the certain utility at d^*.

The third explanation is that people make mistakes. Either people do not know the true probabilities or cannot properly calculate expected values, so they do not realize that they are participating in an unfair bet.

These three explanations are not mutually exclusive. A person could get entertainment value from gambling *and* have a Friedman-Savage utility *and* be unable to calculate odds correctly.[12]

[11]When I was an undergraduate at the University of Chicago, I lived in a dorm and saw overwhelming evidence that the "love of the game" is a powerful force. As the neighborhood provided few forms of entertainment, the dorm's denizens regularly watched the man from the vending company refill the candy machine with fresh candy. He took the old, stale, unpopular bars that remained in the machine and placed them in the "mystery candy" bin. Thanks to our careful study of stocking techniques, we all knew that buying the mystery candy was not a fair bet—who would want unpopular, stale candy bars at the same price as a fresh, popular bar? Nonetheless, one of the dorm dwellers always bought the mystery candy. When asked why, he responded, "I love the excitement of not knowing what'll come out." Life was very boring indeed on the South Side of Chicago.

[12]Economists, knowing how to calculate expected values and deriving most of their excitement from economic models, apparently are less likely to gamble than are real people. A number of years ago, a meeting of economists was held in Reno, Nevada. Reno hotels charge low room rates on the assumption that they'll make plenty from guests' gambling losses. However, the economists gambled so little that they were asked pointedly not to return.

17.3 Avoiding Risk

If 75% of all accidents happen within five miles of home, why not move ten miles away? —Steven Wright

Risk-averse people want to eliminate or reduce risk whether the bet is fair or biased against them. Risk-neutral people avoid unfair bets, and even risk-preferring people avoid very unfair bets.

Individuals can avoid optional risky activities, but often they can't escape risk altogether. Property owners, for instance, always face the possibility that their property will be damaged or stolen or will burn. They may be able to reduce the probability that bad states of nature occur, however.

Just Say No

The simplest way to avoid risk is to abstain from optional risky activities. No one forces you to bet on the lottery, go into a high-risk occupation, or buy stock in a start-up biotech firm. If one brand of a product you use comes with a warranty and an otherwise comparable brand does not, you lower your risk by buying the guaranteed product.

Even when you can't avoid risk altogether, you can take precautions to reduce the probability of bad states of nature or the magnitude of any loss that might occur. For example, you can maintain your car as the manufacturer recommends to reduce the probability that it will break down. By locking your apartment door, you lower the chance that your television will be stolen. Getting rid of your four-year-old collection of newspapers lessens the likelihood that your house will burn. Not only do these actions reduce your risk, but they also raise the expected value of your asset.

APPLICATION

Harry Potter's Magic

In addition to saving the world in books, Harry Potter protects his young fans from traumatic injuries on weekends. Stephen Gwilym of the John Radcliffe Hospital in Oxford and his colleagues found that only half as many 7- to 15-year-old children came to the emergency department on the weekends immediately after J. K. Rowling's books were released compared to other summer weekends. (Apparently your mom was trying to maim you when she said, "Stop reading and go outside and play on this lovely summer day!")

Obtain Information

Collecting accurate information before acting is one of the most important ways in which people can reduce risk and increase expected value and expected utility, as Solved Problem 17.1 illustrated. Armed with information, you may avoid a risky choice or you may be able to take actions that reduce the probability of a disaster or the size of the loss.

Before buying a car or refrigerator, many people read *Consumer Reports* to determine how frequently a particular brand is likely to need repairs. By collecting such information before buying, they can reduce the likelihood of making a costly mistake. See **www.myeconlab.com/perloff**, Chapter 17, "Bond Ratings," for a discussion of how the riskiness of bonds is expressed.

Diversify

Although it may sound paradoxical, individuals and firms often reduce their overall risk by making many risky investments instead of only one. This practice is called *risk pooling* or *diversifying*. Your grandparents may have put it this way: "Don't put all your eggs in one basket."

Correlation and Diversification. The extent to which diversification reduces risk depends on the degree to which various events are correlated over states of nature. The degree of correlation ranges from negatively correlated to uncorrelated to positively correlated.[13] If you know that the first event occurs, you know that the probability that the second event occurs is lower if the events are *negatively correlated* and higher if the events are *positively correlated*. The outcomes are *independent* or *uncorrelated* if knowing whether the first event occurs tells you nothing about the probability that the second event occurs.

Diversification can eliminate risk if two events are perfectly negatively correlated. Suppose that two firms are competing for a government contract and have an equal chance of winning. Because only one firm can win, the other must lose, so the two events are *perfectly negatively correlated*. You can buy a share of stock in either firm for \$20. The stock of the firm that wins the contract will be worth \$40, whereas the stock of the loser will be worth \$10. If you buy two shares of the same company, your shares are going to be worth either \$80 or \$20 after the contract is awarded. Thus, their expected value is

$$\$50 = \left(\tfrac{1}{2} \times \$80\right) + \left(\tfrac{1}{2} \times \$20\right)$$

with a variance of

$$\$900 = \left[\tfrac{1}{2} \times (\$80 - \$50)^2\right] + \left[\tfrac{1}{2} \times (\$20 - \$50)^2\right].$$

However, if you buy one share of each, your two shares will be worth \$50 no matter which firm wins, and the variance is zero.

Diversification reduces risk even if the two events are imperfectly negatively correlated, uncorrelated, or imperfectly positively correlated. *The more negatively correlated two events are, the more diversification reduces risk.*

Now suppose that the values of the two stocks are uncorrelated. Each of the two firms has a 50% chance of getting a government contract, and whether one firm gets a contract does *not* affect whether the other firm wins one. Because of this independence, the chance that each firm's share is worth \$40 is $\frac{1}{4}$, the chance that one is worth \$40 and the other is worth \$10 is $\frac{1}{2}$, and the chance that each is worth \$10 is $\frac{1}{4}$. If you buy one share of each firm, the expected value of these two shares is

$$\$50 = \left(\tfrac{1}{4} \times \$80\right) + \left(\tfrac{1}{2} \times \$50\right) + \left(\tfrac{1}{4} \times \$20\right),$$

---

[13]A measure of the *correlation* between two random variables x and y is

$$\rho = \mathrm{E}\left(\frac{x - \bar{x}}{\sigma_x}\,\frac{y - \bar{y}}{\sigma_y}\right),$$

where the $\mathrm{E}(\cdot)$ means "take the expectation" of the term in parentheses, $\bar{x}$ and $\bar{y}$ are the means, and σ_x and σ_y are the standard deviations of x and y. The two events are said to be uncorrelated if $\rho = 0$.

and the variance is

$$\$450 = \left[\tfrac{1}{4} \times (\$80 - \$50)^2\right] + \left[\tfrac{1}{2} \times (\$50 - \$50)^2\right] + \left[\tfrac{1}{4} \times (\$20 - \$50)^2\right].$$

The expected value is the same as buying two shares in one firm, but the variance is only half as large. Thus, diversification lowers risk when the values are uncorrelated.

In contrast, *diversification does not reduce risk if two events are perfectly positively correlated.* If the government will award contracts either to both firms or to neither firm, the risks are perfectly positively correlated. The expected value of the stocks and the variance are the same whether you buy two shares of one firm or one share of each firm.

Mutual Funds. Individual investors usually do not have the benefit of such detailed information about correlations. They know, however, that the value of the stock of most firms is not perfectly positively correlated with the value of other stocks, so buying stock in several companies tends to reduce risk. Many of these people effectively own shares in a number of companies at once by buying shares in a *mutual fund* of stocks. A mutual fund share is issued by a company that buys stocks in many other companies.

The *Standard & Poor's Composite Index of 500 Stocks* (S&P 500) is a value-weighted average of 500 large firms' stocks, most of them listed on the New York Stock Exchange (NYSE), though some are on the American Stock Exchange or are traded over the counter. The S&P 500 companies constitute only about 7% of all the publicly traded firms in the United States, but they represent approximately 80% of the total value of the U.S. stock market. The *New York Stock Exchange Composite Index* includes more than 1,500 common stocks traded on the NYSE. A number of "total market" funds have been introduced, such as the *Wilshire 5000 Index Portfolio*, which initially covered 5,000 stocks but now includes more than 7,200—virtually all of the U.S. stock market in terms of value. The retail assets in total market funds are relatively small: $11.1 billion versus $116.3 billion in S&P 500 index funds. Some other mutual funds are based on bonds or on a mixture of stocks, bonds, and other types of investments.[14]

Mutual funds allow you to reduce the risk associated with uncorrelated price movements across stocks. Suppose that two companies look very similar on the basis of everything you know about them. You have no reason to think that the stock in one firm will increase more in value or be riskier than the stock of the other firm. However, luck may cause one stock to do better than the other. You can reduce this type of random, unsystematic risk by diversifying and buying stock in both firms.

See Problem 25.

A stock mutual fund, however, has a systematic risk. The prices of all stocks tend to rise when the economy is expanding and to fall when the economy is contracting. By buying a diversified mutual stock fund, you are not able to avoid the systematic risks associated with shifts in the economy that affect all stocks at once.

---

[14]The Calvert, Domini Social Investments, Pax World Funds, and at least 200 other funds have portfolios consisting of only socially responsible firms (by their criteria). However, their investors must be willing to accept a lower return. Over the five years ending in February 2007, the total return of the Domini 400 index averaged 4.8% a year compared to the Standard & Poor's 500-stock index average of 6.81% (Alina Tugend, "Picking Stocks that Don't Sin," *New York Times*, March 17, 2007). If you want to invest in sin instead, go to **www.vicefund.com**.

Insure

I detest life-insurance agents; they always argue that I shall some day die, which is not so. —Stephen Leacock

As we've already seen, a risk-averse person is willing to pay money—a risk premium—to avoid risk. The demand for risk reduction is met by insurance companies, which bear the risk for anyone who buys an insurance policy. Many risk-averse individuals and firms buy insurance; global insurance premiums amounted to nearly $2.2 trillion in 1998.

How Much Insurance Individuals Want. The way insurance works is that a risk-averse person or firm gives money to the insurance company in the good state of nature, and the insurance company transfers money to the policyholder in the bad state of nature. This transaction allows the risk-averse person or firm to shift some or all of the risk to the insurance company.

Because Scott is risk averse, he wants to insure his house, which is worth $80 (thousand). There is a 25% probability that his house will burn next year. If a fire occurs, the house will be worth only $40.

With no insurance, the expected value of his house is

$$\left(\tfrac{1}{4}\times \$40\right)+\left(\tfrac{1}{4}\times \$80\right)=\$70.$$

Scott faces a good deal of risk. The variance of the value of his house is

$$\left[\tfrac{1}{4}\times(\$40-\$70)^2\right]+\left[\tfrac{3}{4}\times(\$80-\$70)^2\right]=\$300.$$

fair insurance
a bet between an insurer and a policyholder in which the value of the bet to the policyholder is zero

Now suppose that an insurance company offers a *fair bet*, or **fair insurance**: a bet between an insurer and a policyholder in which the value of the bet to the policyholder is zero. The insurance company offers to let Scott trade $1 in the good state of nature (no fire) for $3 in the bad state of nature (fire).[15] This insurance is fair because the expected value of this insurance to Scott is zero:

$$\left[\tfrac{1}{4}\times \$3\right]+\left[\tfrac{3}{4}\times(-\$1)\right]=\$0.$$

Because Scott is risk averse, he *fully insures* by buying enough insurance to eliminate his risk altogether. With this amount of insurance, he has the same amount of wealth in either state of nature.

Scott pays the insurance company $10 in the good state of nature and receives $30 in the bad state. In the good state, he has a house worth $80 less the $10 he pays the insurance company, for a net wealth of $70. If the fire occurs, he has a house worth $40 plus a payment from the insurance company of $30, for a net wealth, again, of $70.

Scott's expected value with fair insurance, $70, is the same as his expected value without insurance. The variance he faces drops from $300 without insurance to $0 with insurance. Scott is better off with insurance because he has the same expected value and faces no risk.

[15]As a practical matter, the insurance company collects money up front. If the fire doesn't occur, the company keeps the money. If the fire occurs, it gives back the amount paid originally plus additional funds. Scott's insurance company charges him $1 up front for every $4 it will pay him in the bad state. Thus, Scott effectively pays $1 in the good state of nature and receives a net payment of $3 in the bad state.

Solved Problem 17.3

The local government assesses a property tax of $4 (thousand) on Scott's house. If the tax is collected whether or not the house burns, how much fair insurance does Scott buy? If the tax is collected only if the house does not burn, how much fair insurance does Scott buy?

Answer

1. *Determine the after-tax expected value of the house without insurance.* The expected value of the house is

$$\$66 = \left(\tfrac{1}{4} \times \$36\right) + \left(\tfrac{3}{4} \times \$76\right)$$

if the tax is always collected and

$$\$67 = \left(\tfrac{1}{4} \times \$40\right) + \left(\tfrac{3}{4} \times \$76\right)$$

if the tax is collected only in the good state of nature.

2. *Calculate the amount of fair insurance Scott buys if the tax is always collected.* Because Scott is risk averse, he wants to be fully insured so that the after-tax value of his house is the same in both states of nature. If the tax is always collected, Scott pays the insurance company $10 in the good state of nature, so he has $76 – $10 = $66, and receives $30 in the bad state, so he has $36 + $30 = $66. That is, he buys the same amount of insurance as he would without any taxes. The tax has no effect on his insurance decision because he owes that amount regardless of the state of nature.

3. *Calculate the amount of fair insurance Scott buys if the tax is collected only if there is no fire.* If the tax is collected only in the good state of nature, Scott pays the insurance company $9 in the good state ($76 – $9 = $67) and receives $27 in the bad state ($40 + $27 = $67). Thus, he has the same after-tax income in both states of nature. Effectively, Scott is partially insured by the tax system, so he purchases less insurance than he otherwise would.

See Question 5 and Problem 26.

Fairness and Insurance. When fair insurance is offered, risk-averse people fully insure. If insurance companies charge more than the fair-insurance price, individuals buy less insurance.[16]

Because insurance companies do not offer fair insurance, most people do not fully insure. An insurance company could not stay in business if it offered fair insurance. With fair insurance, the insurance company's expected payments would equal the amount the insurance company collects. Because the insurance company has operating expenses—costs of maintaining offices, printing forms, hiring sales agents, and so forth—an insurance firm providing fair insurance would lose money. Insurance companies' rates must be high enough to cover their operating expenses, so the insurance is less than fair to policyholders.

How much can insurance companies charge for insurance? A monopoly insurance company could charge an amount up to the risk premium a person is willing to pay to avoid risk. For example, in Figure 17.2, Irma would be willing to pay up to $14 for an insurance policy that would compensate her if her vase were not a Ming. The more risk averse an individual is, the more a monopoly insurance company can

[16]As Solved Problem 17.3 shows, tax laws may act to offset this problem, so that some insurance may be fair or more than fair after tax.

charge. If there are many insurance companies competing for business, the price of an insurance policy is less than the maximum that risk-averse individuals are willing to pay—but still high enough that the firms cover their operating expenses.

APPLICATION

Air Insurance

If flying is so safe, why do they call the airport the terminal?

Insure America (IA) has brochures at many airports offering flight insurance. If I pay them $12 and die on a scheduled commercial flight, IA will pay my family $200,000. (IA also offers much larger amounts of insurance, but I figure there's no point in making myself worth more to my family dead than alive.)

If θ is my probability of dying on a flight, my family's expected value from this bet with IA is

$$[\theta \times \$200{,}000] + [(1 - \theta) \times (-12)].$$

For this insurance to be fair, this expected value must be zero, which is true if $\theta \approx 0.00006$, or one out of every 16,668 passengers dies. I'm not tempted by IA's offer because its insurance is not at all close to being fair. The chance that I'll die on a flight is much, much less than 0.00006.

How great *is* my danger of being in a fatal commercial airline crash? According to the National Transportation Safety Board, there were no fatalities on scheduled U.S. commercial airline flights in 1993, 1998, 2002, and 2007. In 2006, when 49 passengers died in 2 crashes, the probability that a passenger had a fatal accident was 0.00000018, or about one in 5.6 million. In 2001, the probability was much higher than average for the decade because of the deaths from the terrorist hijackings on September 11 and the subsequent sharp reduction in the number of flights. However, even in 2001, the probability was 0.00000086, or 1 in 1.1 million—still much lower than the probability that makes IA's insurance a fair bet.

Given the average rate for the last decade, 0.00000013, if I randomly choose a seat on a flight each day for 10 years, my probability of *not* being in a fatal accident is 99.95%. If I fly each day for 100 years, my probability of not being in a fatal accident is 99.5%. Indeed, I'd have to fly every day for about 15,000 years before my probability of being in a fatal crash would rise as high as 50%. (The greatest risk of an airplane trip for many people is the drive to and from the airport. Indeed, twice as many people are killed in vehicle-deer collisions as in plane crashes.)

Given that the chance of being in a fatal crash is 0.00000013, the fair rate to pay for $200,000 of flight insurance is about 2.6¢. IA is offering to charge me 462 times more than the fair rate for this insurance.

I'd have to be incredibly risk averse to be tempted by this offer. Indeed, I wouldn't buy this insurance even if I were that risk averse. Instead, I'd buy general life insurance, which is much less expensive than flight insurance and covers me for death from all types of accidents and diseases. (Remember: That airline that doesn't kill me makes me stronger.)

Insurance Only for Diversifiable Risks. Why is an insurance company willing to sell policies and take on risk? By pooling the risks of many people, the insurance company can lower its risk much below that of any individual. If the probability that one car is stolen is independent of whether other cars are stolen, the risk to an insurance company of insuring one person against theft is much greater than the average risk of insuring many people.

An insurance company sells policies only for risks that it can diversify. If the risks from disasters to its policyholders are highly positively correlated, an insurance company is not well diversified by holding many policies. A war affects all policyholders, so the outcomes that they face are perfectly correlated. Because wars are *nondiversifiable risks*, insurance companies do not offer policies insuring against wars.

APPLICATION

No Insurance for Natural Disasters

In recent years, many insurance companies have started viewing some major natural disasters as nondiversifiable risks because such catastrophic events cause many insured people to suffer losses at the same time. As more homes have been built in parts of the country where damage from storms or earthquakes is likely, the size of the potential losses to insurers from nondiversifiable risks has grown.

According to Pielke et al. (2008), the average annual hurricane damages from 1900 through 2005 was $10 billion, of which roughly half was covered by insurance. In one in four years, a hurricane caused at least $10 billion of damage. Damage of at least $50 billion occurred in only 5% of the years. During 2004 and 2005, the United States was struck by 7 of the 30 most damaging hurricanes since 1900. In 2005, Hurricane Katrina inflicted $81 billion in property losses; Hurricane Wilma, $21 billion; and Hurricane Rita, $10 billion.

Insurers paid out $12.5 billion in claims by residential homeowners after the 1994 Los Angeles earthquake. Farmers Insurance Group reported that it paid out three times as much for the Los Angeles earthquake as it collected in earthquake premiums over 30 years.

Insurance companies now refuse to offer hurricane or earthquake insurance in many parts of the country for these relatively nondiversifiable risks. From 2004 to 2007, more than three million homeowners received cancellation letters from their home-insurance companies, including about one million homeowners in the Mid-Atlantic and New England states. Allstate Corp., the nation's second-largest insurance carrier, ceased offering homeowners policies in Louisiana, Florida, and coastal parts of Texas and New York state, as well as earthquake coverage in California, Washington, Missouri, and Kansas. When Nationwide Insurance Company announced that it was sharply curtailing sales of new hurricane policies, a company official explained, "Prudence requires us to diligently manage our exposure to catastrophic losses."

See Questions 6 and 7.

In some of these areas, state-run pools—such as the Florida Joint Underwriting Association and the California Earthquake Authority—provide households with insurance. However, not only do these policies provide less protection, but their rates are often three times more than the previously available commercial rates, and they require large deductibles.

17.4 Investing Under Uncertainty

Don't invest money with any brokerage firm in which one of the partners is named Frenchy.
—Woody Allen

In Chapter 16, we ignored uncertainty when we analyzed how firms take account of discounting in making investment decisions. We now investigate how uncertainty affects the investment decision. In particular, we examine how attitudes toward risk affect individuals' willingness to invest, how people evaluate risky investments that last for many periods, and how investors pay to alter their probabilities of success.

In the following examples, the owner of a monopoly decides whether to open a new retail outlet. Because the firm is a monopoly, the owner's return from the investment does not depend on the actions of other firms. As a result, the owner faces no strategic considerations. The owner knows the cost of the investment but is unsure about how many people will patronize the new store; hence the profits are uncertain.

How Investing Depends on Attitudes Toward Risk

We start by considering a potential investment by the monopoly's owner that has an uncertain payoff this year. The owner must take risk into account but can ignore discounting. Whether the owner invests depends on how risk averse he or she is and on the risks involved.

See Question 8.

Risk-Neutral Investing. Chris, the owner of the monopoly, is risk neutral. She maximizes her expected utility by making the investment only if the expected value of the return from the investment is positive.

To determine whether to invest, Chris uses the *decision tree* in panel a of Figure 17.4. The rectangle, called a *decision node*, indicates that she must make a decision about whether to invest or not. The circle, a *chance node*, denotes that a random process determines the outcome (consistent with the given probabilities). If Chris does not open the new store, she makes \$0. If she does open the new store, she expects to make \$200 with 80% probability and to lose \$100 with 20% probability. The expected value from a new store (see the circle in panel a) is

$$EV = [0.8 \times \$200] + [0.2 \times (-\$100)] = \$140.$$

See Problems 27–29.

Because she is risk neutral, she prefers an expected value of \$140 to a certain one of \$0, so she invests. Thus, her expected value in the rectangle is \$140.

Risk-Averse Investing. Ken, who is risk averse, faces the same decision as Chris. Ken invests in the new store if his expected utility from investing is greater than his certain utility from not investing. Panel b of Figure 17.4 shows the decision tree for a particular risk-averse utility function. The circle shows that Ken's expected utility from the investment is

$$\begin{aligned} EU &= [0.2 \times U(-\$100)] + [0.8 \times U(\$200)] \\ &= (0.2 \times 0) + (0.8 \times 40) = 32. \end{aligned}$$

The certain utility from not investing is $U(\$0) = 35$. Thus, Ken does not invest. As a result, his expected utility (here, certain utility) in the rectangle is 35.

See Questions 9 and 10.

Figure 17.4 Investment Decision Tree with Risk Aversion.

The owner of a monopoly must decide whether to invest in a new store. (a) The expected value is $140, so it pays for a risk-neutral owner to invest. (b) The utility from not investing for this risk-averse owner is greater than the expected utility from investing, so the owner does not invest.

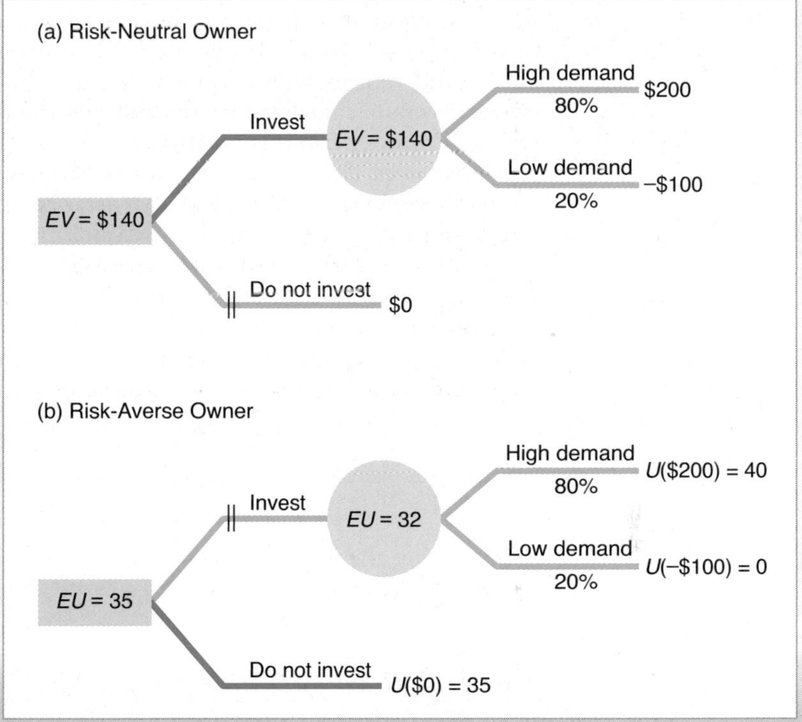

APPLICATION
Risk Premium

Risk-averse people will make risky investments only if these investments have an expected return that is sufficiently higher than that of a nonrisky investment, such as a U.S. government bond, as Figure 17.2 illustrates.[17] Because most people are risk averse, they will make risky investments only if *the expected rate of return on a risky investment exceeds the rate of return on a nonrisky investment by a risk premium.*

Most stock funds have more nondiversifiable risks—as reflected by a higher standard deviation in returns—than bond funds, even junk bond funds. The historical standard deviation varies substantially across a number of diversified stock and bond funds.

Because stocks are riskier than bonds, the rates of return on stocks exceed those on bonds over long periods of time. Of course, given the greater risk associated with equities, they may perform worse than bonds in any given period. For example, the S&P 500 had negative returns of –12% in 2001 and –22% in 2002, unlike bonds. Nonetheless, we expect equities to have a higher rate of return over a longer period. For the 20 years from March 1987 to March 2007, the average annual real rates of return (after adjusting for inflation, taxes, and expenses) were 9.9% on the S&P 500, 4.5% on U.S. Treasury bills, 4.1% on municipal bonds, and 1.2% on single-family homes.

---

[17]The Tappet brothers (the hosts of National Public Radio's *Car Talk*) offer a risk-free investment. Their Capital Depreciation Fund guarantees a 50% return. You send them $100 and they send you back $50.

Investing with Uncertainty and Discounting

Now suppose that the uncertain returns or costs from an investment are spread out over time. In Chapter 16, we derived an investment rule by which we know future costs and returns with certainty. We concluded that an investment pays if its *net present* value (calculated by discounting the difference between the return and cost in each future period) is positive.

How does this rule change if the returns are uncertain? A risk-neutral person chooses to invest if the *expected net present value* is positive. We calculate the expected net present value by discounting the difference between expected return and expected cost in each future period.

Sam is risk neutral. His decision tree, Figure 17.5, shows that his cost of investing is $C = \$25$ this year. Next year, he receives uncertain revenues from the investment of $125 with 80% probability or $50 with 20% probability. Thus, the expected value of the revenues next year is

$$EV = (0.8 \times \$125) + (0.2 \times \$50) = \$110.$$

With a real interest rate of 10%, the expected present value of the revenues is

$$EPV = \$110/1.1 = \$100.$$

Subtracting the $25 cost incurred this year, Sam determines that his expected net present value is $ENPV = \$75$. As a result, he invests.

Investing with Altered Probabilities

We have been assuming that nature dictates the probabilities of various states of nature. Sometimes, however, we can alter the probabilities, though usually at some expense.

Gautam, who is risk neutral, is considering whether to invest in a new store, as Figure 17.6 shows. After investing, he can increase the probability that demand will be high at the new store by advertising at a cost of $50.

If he makes the investment but does not advertise, he has a 40% probability of making $100 and a 60% probability of losing $100. His expected value without advertising is

$$[0.4 \times \$100] + [0.6 \times (-\$100)] = -\$20.$$

Thus, if he could not advertise, he would not make this investment.

Figure 17.5 Investment Decision Tree with Uncertainty and Discounting.

The risk-neutral owner invests if the expected net present value is positive. The expected value, *EV*, of the revenue from the investment next year is $110. With an interest rate of 10%, the expected present value, *EPV*, of the revenue is $100. The expected net present value, *ENPV*, is *EPV* = $100 minus the $25 cost of the investment this year, which is $75. The owner therefore invests.

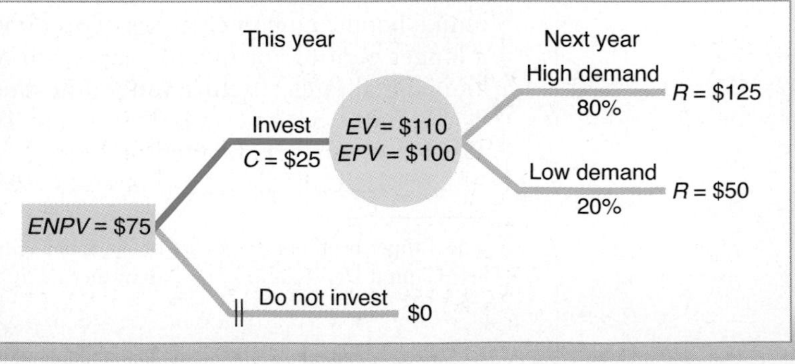

Figure 17.6 Investment Decision Tree with Advertising.

By advertising, the risk-neutral owner can alter the probability of high demand. The expected value of the investment is –$20 without advertising and $60 with advertising. Because the cost of advertising is $50, the expected value of investing and advertising is $10 (= $60 – $50). The owner therefore invests and advertises.

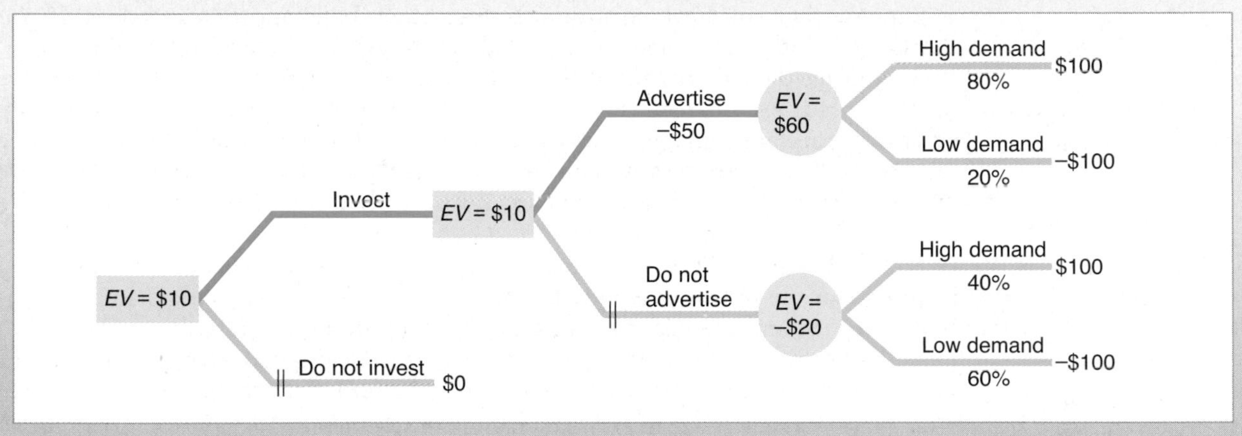

With advertising, the probability of his making $100 rises to 80%, so his expected value is

$$[0.8 \times \$100] + [0.2 \times (-\$100)] = \$60.$$

His expected value net of the cost of advertising is $10 (= $60 – $50). Thus, he is better off investing and advertising than not investing at all or investing without advertising.

See Questions 11 and 12.

17.5 Behavioral Economics of Risk

Many individuals make choices under uncertainty that are inconsistent with the predictions of expected utility theory. Researchers have established that some people have difficulty determining probabilities or making probability calculations. Through experiments, they've shown that many people behave differently under certain circumstances than others. New theories have been developed to explain behavior that is inconsistent with expected utility theory.

Difficulty Assessing Probabilities

People often have mistaken beliefs about the probability that an event will occur. These biases in estimating probabilities come from several sources, including false beliefs about causality and overconfidence.

Gambler's Fallacy. One common confusion, the *gambler's fallacy*, arises from the false belief that past events affect current, independent outcomes.[18] For example,

[18]The false belief that that one event affects another independent event is captured by the joke about a man who brings a bomb on board a plane whenever he flies because he believes that "The chance of having one bomb on a plane are very small, so the chance of having two bombs on a plane is near zero!"

suppose that you flip a fair coin and it comes up heads six times in a row. What are the odds that you'll get a tail on the next flip? Because past flips do not affect this one, the chance of a tail remains 50%, yet many people believe that a head is much more likely because they're on a "run." Others hold the opposite but equally false view that the chance of a tail is high because a tail is "due."

Suppose that you have an urn with three black balls and two red ones. If you draw a ball without looking, your probability of getting a black ball is 3/5 = 60%. If you replace the ball and draw again, the chance of a picking a black ball remains the same. However, if you draw a black ball and do not replace it, the probability of drawing a black ball again falls to 2/4 = 50%. Thus, the belief that a tail is due after several heads are tossed in a row is analogous to falsely believing that you are drawing without replacement when you are actually drawing with replacement.

Overconfidence. Another common explanation for why some people engage in gambles that the rest of us avoid like the plague is that these gamblers are overconfident. For example, Golec and Tamarkin (1995) found that football bettors tend to make low-probability bets because they greatly overestimated their probabilities of winning certain types of exotic football bets (an *exotic bet* depends on the outcome of more than one game). In a survey, gamblers estimated their chance of winning a particular bet at 45% when the objective probability was 20%.

APPLICATION

Biased Estimates?

Do newspaper stories, television, and movies encourage people to overestimate relatively rare events and underestimate relatively common ones? Newspapers are more likely to publish "man bites dog" stories—such as "Cobra Dies after Biting Priest of Snake Temple!" (*Express India,* July 11, 2005)—than the more common "dog bites man" events.

If you have seen the movie *Jaws*, you can't help but think about sharks before wading into the ocean. Newspapers around the world reported that an unfortunate 14-year-old girl was killed by a shark in waters off Florida in 2005 and that an Australian man survived an attack in 2007. Do you worry about shark attacks? You really shouldn't.

Only 55 people were killed by unprovoked shark attacks in U.S. waters from 1670 through 2006, an average of 0.16 per year. The rate is only slightly higher during the period 1990 through 2006 when 12 people died, an average of 0.7 a year. You're as likely to die from beanbag chair suffocation, more than twice as likely to die by being crushed by a soda machine toppling on you, and ten times more likely to meet your maker in a roller skating accident.

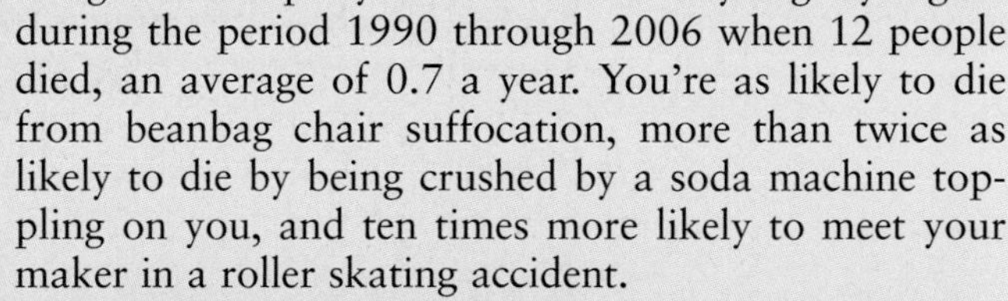

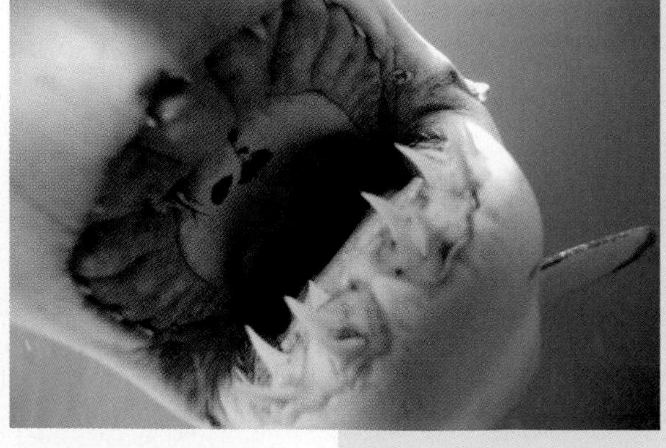

A typical American's chance of dying this year from a shark attack is 1 in 350 million; a terrorist attack, 1 in 9 million; a bee sting, 1 in 6 million; a commercial airline crash, 1 in 5.6 million; falling into a hole, 1 in 2.8 million; a handgun, 1 in 1.9 million; excessive cold, 1 in 643,000; lightning, 1 in 600,000; homicide, 1 in 15,000; flu, 1 in 3,025; cancer, 1 in 514; heart disease, 1 in 384; and any cause, 1 in 117.

Benjamin et al. (2001) reported that, when asked to estimate the frequency of deaths from various causes for the entire population, people overestimate the number of deaths from infrequent causes and underestimate those from more common causes such as cancer. In contrast, if they are asked to estimate the number of deaths among their own age group from a variety of causes, their estimates are almost completely unbiased. That is not to say that people know the true probabilities, but that their mistakes are not systematic. (However, you should know that, despite the widespread warnings issued every Christmas season, poinsettias are not poisonous.)

Behavior Varies with Circumstances

Over the years, economists and psychologists have shown that some people's choices vary with circumstances, which contradicts expected utility theory. Three of these strange results include responses to low-probability gambles, a bias toward relatively certain events, and sensitivity in making choices to how the choices are presented or *framed*.

Low-Probability Gambles. Earlier in this chapter, we noted that many otherwise risk-averse people—people who buy insurance—will accept an unfair gamble with low odds of winning a large amount, such as buying a lottery ticket. This result can be explained by expected utility theory only if people have a "funny" shaped utility function, where they are risk averse in some regions and risk preferring in others (see the application "Gambling").

Certainty Effect. Many people put excessive weight on outcomes that they consider to be certain relative to risky outcomes. This *certainty effect* (or *Allais effect*, after the French economist who first noticed it) can be illustrated using an example from Kahneman and Tversky (1979). First, a group of subjects were asked to choose between two options:

- *Option A.* You receive \$4,000 with probability 80% and \$0 with probability 20%.
- *Option B.* You receive \$3,000 with certainty.

The vast majority, 80%, chose the certain outcome, B.

Then, the subjects were given another set of options:

- *Option C.* You receive \$4,000 with probability 20% and \$0 with probability 80%.
- *Option D.* You receive \$3,000 with probability 25% and \$0 with probability 75%.

Now, 65% prefer C.

Kahneman and Tversky found that over half the respondents violated expected utility theory by choosing B in the first experiment and C in the second one. If $U(0) = 0$, then choosing B over A implies that the expected utility from B is greater than that of A, so that $U(3{,}000) > 0.8U(4{,}000)$, or $U(3{,}000)/U(4{,}000) > 0.8$. Choosing C over D implies that $0.2U(4{,}000) > 0.25U(3{,}000)$, or $U(3{,}000)/U(4{,}000) < 0.8$ $(= 0.2/0.25)$. Thus, these choices are inconsistent with each other, and hence inconsistent with expected utility theory.

See Problem 30.

Expected utility theory is based on gambles with known probabilities, whereas most real-world situations involve unknown or subjective probabilities. Ellsberg (1961) pointed out that expected utility theory cannot account for an ambiguous situation where many people are reluctant to put substantial decision weight on any outcome. He illustrated the problem in a "paradox." There are two urns, each with 100 red and black balls. In the first urn, you know that there are 50 red and 50 black balls. In the second urn, you do not know the ratio of red to black balls. Most of us would agree that the known probability of drawing a red from the first urn equals the subjective probability of drawing a red from the second urn. Yet, most people would prefer to bet that a red ball will be drawn from the first urn than from the second urn.

Framing. Many people reverse their preferences when a problem is presented or *framed* in different but equivalent ways. Tversky and Kahneman (1981) posed the problem that the United States expects an unusual disease (e.g., avian flu) to kill 600 people. The government is considering two alternative programs to combat the disease. The "exact scientific estimates" of the consequences of these programs are:

- If Program A is adopted, 200 people will be saved.
- If Program B is adopted, there is a $\frac{1}{3}$ probability that 600 people will be saved and a $\frac{2}{3}$ probability that no one will be saved.

When college students were asked to choose, 72% opted for the certain gains of Program A over the possibly larger but riskier gains of Program B.

A second group of students was asked to choose between an alternative pair of programs, and were told:

- If Program C is adopted, 400 people will die.
- If Program D is adopted, there is a $\frac{1}{3}$ probability that no one will die, and a $\frac{2}{3}$ probability that 600 people will die.

When faced with this choice, 78% chose the larger but uncertain losses of Program D over the certain losses of Program C. These results are surprising if people maximize their expected utility: Program A is identical to Program C and Program B is the same as Program D in the sense that these pairs have identical expected outcomes. Thus, expected utility theory predicts consistent choices for the two pairs of programs.

In many similar experiments, researchers have repeatedly observed this pattern, called the *reflection effect*: attitudes toward risk are reversed (reflected) for gains versus losses. People are often risk averse when making choices involving gains, but they are often risk preferring when making choices involving losses.

See Question 13.

Prospect Theory

Kahneman and Tversky's (1979) *prospect theory* is an alternative theory of decision-making under uncertainty that can explain some of the choices people make that are inconsistent with expected utility theory.

Comparing Expected Utility and Prospect Theories. We can illustrate the differences in the two theories by comparing how people would act under the two theories when facing the same situation. Both Muzhe and Rui have initial wealth W. They may choose a gamble where they get A dollars with probability θ or B dollars with probability $1 - \theta$. For example, A might be negative, reflecting a loss, and B might be a positive, indicating a gain.

Muzhe wants to maximize his expected utility. If he does not gamble, his utility is $U(W)$. To calculate his expected utility if he gambles, Muzhe uses the probabilities θ and $1 - \theta$ to weight the utilities from the two possible outcomes:

$$EU = \theta U(W + A) + (1 - \theta)U(W + B),$$

where $U(W + A)$ is the utility he gets from his after-gambling wealth if A occurs and $U(W + B)$ is the utility if he receives B. He chooses to gamble if his expected utility from gambling exceeds his certain utility from his initial wealth: $EU > U(W)$.

In contrast, Rui's decisions are consistent with prospect theory. According to *prospect theory*, people are concerned about gains and losses—the changes in wealth—rather than the level of wealth, as in expected utility theory. People start with a reference point and consider lower outcomes as losses and higher ones as gains, just as they use their initial endowment as a reference point in the behavioral economics section of Chapter 4.

Rui compares the gamble to her current reference point, which is her initial situation where she has W with certainty. The value she places on her reference point is $V(0)$, where 0 indicates that she has neither a gain nor a loss with this certain outcome. The (negative) value that she places on losing is $V(A)$, and the value from winning is $V(B)$.

To determine the value from taking the gamble, Rui does not calculate the expectation using the probabilities θ and $1 - \theta$, as she would with expected utility theory. Rather, she uses *decision weights* $w(\theta)$ and $w(1 - \theta)$, where the w function assigns different weights than the original probabilities. If people assign disproportionately high weights to rare events (see the application "Biased Estimates?"), the weight $w(\theta)$ exceeds θ for low values of θ and is less for high values of θ.

Rui gambles if the value from not gambling, $V(0)$, is less than her evaluation of the gamble, which is the weighted average of her values in the two cases:

$$V(0) < \left[w(\theta) \times V(A)\right] + \left[w(1-\theta) \times V(B)\right].$$

Thus, prospect theory differs from expected utility theory in both the valuation of outcomes and how they are weighted.

Properties of Prospect Theory. To resolve various choice mysteries, the prospect theory value function, V, has an S-shape, as in Figure 17.7. This curve has three properties. First, the curve passes through the reference point at the origin, because gains and losses are determined relative to the initial situation.

Second, both sections of the curve are concave to the horizontal, outcome axis. Because of this curvature, Rui is less sensitive to a given change in the outcome for large gains or losses than for small ones. For example, she cares more about whether she has a loss of \$1 rather than \$2 than she does about a loss of \$1,001 rather than \$1,002.

Third, the curve is asymmetric with respect to gains and losses. People treat gains and losses differently, in contrast to the predictions of expected utility theory. The S-curve in the figure shows a bigger impact to a loss than to a comparable size gain. That is, the value function reflects *loss aversion*: people hate making losses more than they like making gains.

Given the subjective weights, valuations based on gains and losses, and the shape of the value curve, prospect theory can resolve some of the behavioral mysteries.

Because prospect theory uses different weights than expected utility theory, prospect theory provides an alternative explanation to Friedman-Savage as to why some people engage in unfair lotteries: They put heavier weight on rare events than the true probability used in expected utility theory.

Similarly, we could use a weighting function to resolve the Ellsberg paradox. For example, with the urn containing an unknown ratio of black and red balls, an individual might put 40% on getting a black ball, 40% on getting a red ball, and leave

Figure 17.7 Prospect Theory Value Function.

The prospect theory value function has an S-shape. It passes through the reference point at the origin, because gains and losses are measured relative to the initial condition. Because both sections of the curve are concave to the outcome axis, decision makers are less sensitive to a given change in the outcome for large gains or losses than for small ones. Because the curve is asymmetric with respect to gains and losses, people treat gains and losses differently. This S-curve shows a bigger impact to a loss than to a comparable size gain, reflecting loss aversion.

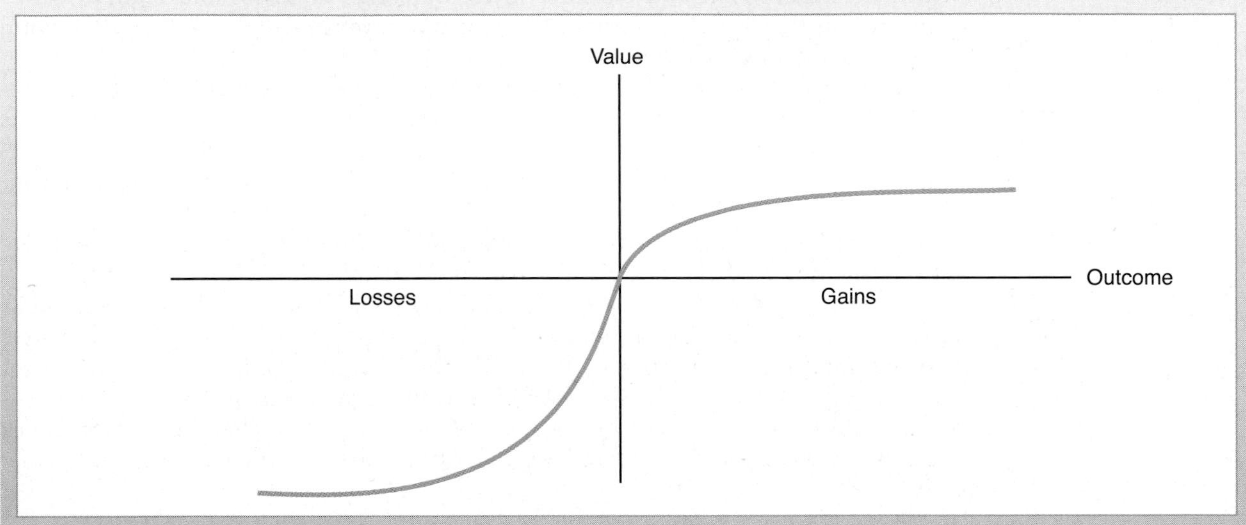

20% to capture an unwillingness to take a gamble when faced with substantial ambiguity. Doing so reduces the expected value of the gamble relative to that of the initial, certain situation where one does not gamble.

The S-shaped curve shows that people treat gains and losses differently. As such, it can explain the reflection effect in the disease experiment described earlier in this section.

SUMMARY

1. **Degree of Risk.** A probability measures the likelihood that a particular state of nature occurs. People may use historical frequencies, if available, to calculate a probability. Lacking detailed information, people form subjective estimates of the probability on the basis of available information. The expected value is the probability-weighted average of the values in each state of nature. One widely used measure of risk is the variance (or the standard deviation, which is the square root of the variance). The variance is the probability-weighted average of the squared difference of the value in each state of nature and the expected value.

2. **Decision Making Under Uncertainty.** Whether people choose a risky option over a nonrisky one depends on their attitudes toward risk and the expected payoffs of the various options. Most people are *risk averse* and will choose a riskier option only if its expected value is substantially higher than that of a less-risky option. *Risk-neutral* people choose whichever option has the higher rate of return because they do not care about risk. *Risk-preferring* people may choose the riskier option even if it has a lower rate of return. An individual's utility function reflects that person's attitude toward risk. People choose the option that provides the highest expected utility. Expected utility is the probability-weighted average of the utility from the outcomes in the various states of nature.

3. **Avoiding Risk.** People try in several ways to reduce the risk they face. They avoid some optional risks and take actions that lower the probabilities of bad events or reduce the harm from those events. By collecting information before acting, investors can make better choices. People can further reduce risk by pooling their risky investments, a strategy that is called

diversification. Unless returns are perfectly positively correlated, diversification reduces risk. Insurance companies offer policies for risks that they can diversify by pooling risks across many individuals. Risk-averse people fully insure if they are offered fair insurance, from which the expected return to the policyholder is zero. They may buy some insurance even if the insurance is not fair. When buying unfair insurance, they exchange the risk of a large loss for the certainty of a smaller loss.

4. **Investing Under Uncertainty.** Whether a person makes an investment depends on the uncertainty of the payoff, the expected return, the individual's attitudes toward risk, the interest rate, and the cost of altering the likelihood of a good outcome. For a risk-neutral person, an investment pays if the expected net present value is positive. A risk-averse person invests only if that person's expected utility is higher after investing. Thus, risk-averse people make risky investments if those investments pay higher rates of return than safer investments pay. If an investment takes place over time, a risk-neutral investor uses a real interest rate to discount expected future values and invests if the expected net present value is positive. People pay to alter the probabilities of various outcomes from an investment if doing so raises their expected utility.

5. **Behavioral Economics of Risk.** Economists and psychologists have identified behavior under uncertainty that is inconsistent with expected utility theory. These choices may be due to biased estimates of probabilities or different objectives than expected utility. For example, some people care more about losses than about gains. One alternative theory that is consistent with many of these puzzling choices is prospect theory, which allows people to treat gains and losses asymmetrically and to weight outcomes differently than with the probabilities used in expected utility theory.

QUESTIONS

■ = *exercise is available on MyEconLab;* * = *answer appears at the back of this book;* C = *use of calculus may be necessary;* W = *audio-slideshow answer by James Dearden is available in Textbook Resources on MyEconLab.*

1. Suppose that Maoyong's utility function with respect to wealth is $U(W) = \ln W$ (where "ln W" means the natural logarithm of W). Plot this utility function and illustrate in your figure why Maoyong is risk averse.

2. Jen's utility function is $U(W) = \sqrt{W}$ with respect to wealth. Plot this utility function and illustrate in your figure why Jen is risk averse.

*3. Given the information in Solved Problem 17.2, Irma prefers to buy the vase. Show graphically how high her certain income would have to be for her to choose not to buy the vase.

4. Suppose that an individual is risk averse and has to choose between $100 with certainty and a risky option with two equally likely outcomes: $\$100 - x$ and $\$100 + x$. Use a graph (or math) to show that this person's risk premium is smaller, the smaller x is (the less variable the gamble is).

5. Would risk-neutral people ever buy insurance that was not fair (that was biased against them)? Explain.

6. After Hurricane Katrina in 2005, the government offered subsidies to people whose houses were destroyed. How do these subsidies affect the probability that these people will buy insurance and the amount they buy? (*Hint*: Use a utility curve for a risk-averse person to illustrate your answer.)

7. Many people who live in areas where earthquakes and floods are common do not purchase insurance. One explanation is that they expect to receive aid from the government if a disaster occurs. Show how such aid affects a risk-averse individual's decision about whether to buy insurance.

8. What is the difference—if any—between an individual's gambling at a casino and buying a stock? What is the difference for society?

9. Use a decision tree to illustrate how a kidney patient would make a decision about whether to have a transplant operation. The patient currently uses a dialysis machine, which lowers her utility. If the operation is successful, her utility will return to its level before the onset of her kidney problems. However, there is a 5% probability that she will die if she has the operation. (If it will help, make up utility numbers to illustrate your answer.)

10. Robert Green repeatedly and painstakingly applied herbicides to kill weeds that would harm his beet crops in 2007. However, in 2008, he'll plant beets genetically engineered to withstand Monsanto's Roundup herbicide. Roundup will destroy the weeds but leave his crop unharmed, thereby saving him thousands of dollars in tractor fuel and labor (Andrew Pollack, "Round 2 for Biotech Beets," *New*

York Times, November 27, 2007). This policy is risky, however. In the past when beet breeders announced they were going to use Roundup-resistant seeds, sugar-using food companies like Hershey and Mars objected, fearing consumer resistance. Now, though, sensing that consumer concerns have subsided, many processors have cleared their growers to plant the Roundup-resistant beets. A Kellogg spokeswoman said her company was willing to use such beets, but Hershey and Mars declined to comment. Thus, a farmer like Mr. Green faces risks by switching to Roundup Ready beets. Use a decision tree to illustrate the analysis that a farmer in this situation needs to do.

*11. To discourage people from breaking the traffic laws, society can increase the probability that someone exceeding the speed limit will be caught and punished, or it can increase the size of the fine for speeding. Explain why either method can be used to discourage speeding. Which approach is a government likely to prefer, and why?

12. If criminals are rational, crime is deterred by large expected punishments, which are the product of the fine or the sentence if convicted and the probability of being caught and convicted. Thus, one can raise the expected value of the punishment by raising either the penalty or the odds of capture and conviction. Is the following argument logical?

"I propose executing one spammer per year. That way, even if we don't catch and convict many, the penalty will have substantial deterrent effect. Because the cost of executing them is much less than the cost of catching them, it is cost effective to increase the punishment rather than the odds of capture and conviction."

Explain your answer taking into account attitudes toward risk.

13. Draw a person's utility curve and illustrate that the person is risk averse with respect to a loss but risk preferring with respect to a gain.

PROBLEMS

14. In a neighborhood with 1,000 houses, 5 catch fire, 7 are damaged by high winds, and the rest are unharmed during a one-year period. What is the probability that a house is harmed by fire or high winds?

*15. Asa buys a painting. There is a 20% probability that the artist will become famous and the painting will be worth \$1,000. There is a 10% probability that the painting will be destroyed by fire or some other disaster. If the painting is not destroyed and the artist does not become famous, it will be worth \$500. What is the expected value of the painting?

*16. By next year, the stock you own has a 25% chance of being worth \$400 and a 75% probability of being worth \$200. What are the expected value and the variance?

17. Ryan offers to bet Kristin that if a six-sided die comes up with one or two dots showing, he will pay her \$3, but if it comes up with any other number of dots, she'll owe him \$2. Is that a fair bet for Kristin?

18. Suppose that Laura's utility function is $U(W) = W^{0.5}$, where W is wealth. Is she risk averse? Show mathematically.

19. Suppose that Laura has a utility function of $U(W) = W^{0.5}$ and an initial wealth of $W = \$100$. How much of a risk premium would she want to participate in a gamble that has a 50% probability of raising her wealth to \$120 and a 50% probability of lowering her wealth to \$80?

20. What is the risk premium if, in Problem 19, Laura's utility function were $\ln(W)$?

*21. Hugo has a concave utility function of $U(W) = W^{0.5}$. His only asset is shares in an Internet start-up company. Tomorrow he will learn the stock's value. He believes that it is worth \$144 with probability $\frac{2}{3}$ and \$225 with probability $\frac{1}{3}$. What is his expected utility? What risk premium would he pay to avoid bearing this risk?

22. After her final exam this semester, Sylvia must drive from her school in Philadelphia to her home in upstate New York and has two possible routes for her trip: through Pennsylvania (PA) or through New Jersey (NJ). Sylvia drives over the speed limit. In choosing her route, Sylvia's only concern is the probability that she will receive a speeding ticket and the amount of the fine on a given route. Prior to the trip, Sylvia's wealth is $Y = \$300$. Sylvia's utility of wealth function is $U(Y) = Y^{0.5}$. Sylvia has a probability of $\frac{1}{2}$ of receiving a \$200 speeding ticket on the PA route and a probability of $\frac{1}{4}$ of receiving a \$300 fine on the NJ route.

a. What are Sylvia's expected fine, expected wealth, and expected utility if she travels through NJ?

b. What are Sylvia's expected fine, expected wealth, and expected utility if she travels through PA?

c. Compare Sylvia's expected wealth and compare her expected utilities on the two routes. Comment on the comparison. W

23. Lisa just inherited a vineyard from a distant relative. In good years (when there is no rain or frost during harvest season), she earns \$100,000 from the sale of grapes from the vineyard. If the weather is poor, she loses \$20,000. Lisa's estimate of the probability of good weather is 60%.

a. Calculate the expected value and the variance of Lisa's income from the vineyard.

b. Lisa is risk averse. Ethan, a grape buyer, offers Lisa a guaranteed payment of \$70,000 each year in exchange for her entire harvest. Will Lisa accept this offer? Explain.

c. Why might Ethan make such an offer? Give three reasons, and explain each. One of these reasons should refer to his attitude toward risk. Illustrate this reason using a diagram that shows the general shape of Ethan's utility function over income.

24. Farrel et al. (2000) estimate that the elasticity of demand for lottery tickets is about −1. If the U.K. National Lottery is running its game to make money (it gets a percentage of the total revenues), is it running the lottery optimally? Explain your answer.

25. Lori, who is risk averse, has two pieces of jewelry, each worth \$1,000. She wants to send them to her sister in Thailand. She is concerned about the safety of shipping them. She believes that the probability that the jewelry won't arrive is θ. Is her expected utility higher if she sends the articles together or in two separate shipments?

26. An insurance agent (interviewed in Jonathan Clements, "Dare to Live Dangerously: Passing on Some Insurance Can Pay Off," *Wall Street Journal,* July 23, 2005, D1) states, "On paper, it never makes sense to have a policy with low deductibles or carry collision on an old car." But the agent notes that raising deductibles and dropping collision coverage can be a tough decision for people with a low income or little savings. Collision insurance is the coverage on a policyholder's own car for accidents where another driver is not at fault.

a. Suppose that the loss is \$4,000 if an old car is in an accident. During the six-month coverage period, the probability that the insured person is found at fault in an accident is $\frac{1}{36}$. Suppose that the price of the coverage is \$150. Should a wealthy person purchase the coverage? Should a poor person purchase the coverage? Do your answers depend on the policyholder's degree of risk aversion? Does the policyholder's degree of risk aversion depend on his or her wealth?

b. The agent advises wealthy people not to purchase insurance to protect against possible small losses. Why? W

*27. Andy and Kim live together. Andy may invest \$10,000 (possibly by taking on an extra job to earn the additional money) in Kim's education this year. This investment will raise Kim's future earnings by \$24,000 (in present value terms—see Chapter 16). If they stay together, they will share the benefit from the additional earnings. However, the probability is $\frac{1}{2}$ that they will split up in the future. If they were married (or in a civil union) and then split, Andy would get half of Kim's additional earnings. If they were living together without any legal ties and they split, then Andy would get nothing. Suppose that Andy is risk neutral. Will Andy invest in Kim's education? Does your answer depend on the couple's legal status?

28. Use a decision tree to illustrate how a risk-neutral plaintiff in a lawsuit decides whether to settle a claim or go to trial. The defendants offer \$50,000 to settle now. If the plaintiff does not settle, the plaintiff believes that the probability of winning at trial is 60%. If the plaintiff wins, the amount awarded is X. How large can X be before the plaintiff refuses to settle? How does the plaintiff's attitude toward risk affect this decision?

29. DVD retailers choose how many copies of a movie to purchase from a studio and to stock. The retailers have the right to return all unsold copies to the studio for a full refund, but the retailer pays the shipping costs for returned copies. A small mom-and-pop retailer will sell 1, 2, 3, or 4 copies with probabilities 0.2, 0.3, 0.3, and 0.2, respectively. Suppose that the retail market price of the DVD is \$15 and that the retailer must pay the studio \$8 for each copy. The studio's marginal cost is \$1. The retailer's marginal profit is \$7 for selling each copy, and the studio's marginal profit is \$7 for each nonreturned copy sold to the retailer. The cost of shipping each DVD back to the studio is \$2. The studio and retailer are risk neutral.

a. How many copies of the DVD will the retailer order from the studio? What is the studio's expected profit-maximizing number of copies for the retailer to order?

b. Alternatively, suppose that the studio pays the shipping costs to return unsold DVDs. How many copies would the retailer order?

c. Does the number of copies the retailer orders depend on which party pays the shipping costs? Why? W

30. First answer the following two questions about your preferences:

a. You are given \$5,000 and offered a choice between receiving an extra \$2,500 with certainty or flipping a coin and getting \$5,000 more if heads or \$0 if tails. Which option do you prefer?

b. You are given \$10,000 if you will make the following choice: return \$2,500 or flip a coin and return \$5,000 if heads and \$0 if tails. Which option do you prefer?

Most people choose the sure \$2,500 in the first case but flip the coin in the second. Explain why this behavior is not consistent. What do you conclude about how people make decisions concerning uncertain events?

31. Hal is considering applying to the Duke Law School. In light of Duke's reported information about acceptances and rejections based on GPAs (G) and LSAT scores (L), Hal estimates that his probability of being accepted, which is his utility, is a function:

$$U = \frac{1}{400} G^{0.36} L^{0.64}.$$

In this function, for example, a GPA of 4.00 is written as 400 and a GPA of 3.25 is written as 325. Hal calculates that for each one-point increase in his GPA (for example, from 350 to 351), he must study an additional eight minutes per week. So the opportunity cost or price (in minutes worked per week) of a unit increase in his GPA is $p_G = 8$. Similarly, the price of a unit increase in his LSAT score is $p_L = 32$. Hal has 8,650 minutes per week to study for either his classes or the LSATs.

a. Graph Hal's budget constraint.

b. Graph Hal's indifference curve for $U = 0.9$.

c. What is Hal's optimal ratio, G/L?

d. What is Hal's optimal choice, (G^*, L^*)?

e. What is Hal's equilibrium probability of being accepted by Duke?

f. If Hal has less than 8,650 minutes per week to study, will his probability of being accepted by Duke decrease?

Externalities, Open-Access, and Public Goods

18

There's so much pollution in the air now that if it weren't for our lungs there'd be no place to put it all.
—Robert Orben

In 2007, former U.S. Vice President Al Gore's documentary movie, *An Inconvenient Truth*, on the dangers of global warming from greenhouse gas emissions, won him an Academy Award and helped him to win the Nobel Peace Prize. A report at the United Nations-sponsored Intergovernmental Panel on Climate Change predicted catastrophic consequences—droughts, rising sea levels, heat waves, and disease—from pollution-created global warming. California's Republican governor Arnold Schwarzenegger backed legislation to combat global warming by regulating emissions into the atmosphere. One hundred physicians and public health scientists wrote a letter urging the U.S. Environmental Protection Agency (EPA) to set more restrictive standards for ground-level ozone, as the EPA's own formal science advisers recommended. All the major 2008 Democratic presidential candidates, the Republican presidential nominee John McCain, and most of the congressional Democrats called for much stiffer controls on pollution. Yet, President George W. Bush and many congressional Republicans argued that proposals such as these go too far and will impose excessive costs. At the 2007, 180-nation U.N. climate conference in Bali, President Bush directed American delegates to not endorse mandatory emissions controls. All the EU countries spent 2007 debating new plans to control greenhouse gas emissions from 2008–2012 and a possible EU-wide cap on emissions by 2013. Clearly pollution control will continue to be heatedly debated throughout the world for the foreseeable future.

This chapter examines why unregulated markets do not adequately control pollution and other externalities. An *externality* occurs if someone's consumption or production activities hurt or help others outside a market. For example, a manufacturing plant produces noxious fumes as a by-product of its production process. The emission of these fumes creates an externality that harms people in surrounding areas. If the government does not intervene, the firm is uninterested in the fumes—it does not sell the fumes, and it does not have to pay for the harm they cause. Because the firm has no financial incentive to reduce its level of pollution and it would be costly to do so, the firm pollutes excessively.

We start by examining externalities that arise as a by-product of production (such as water pollution from a factory) and consumption (such as air pollution from a car). We demonstrate that a competitive market produces more pollution than a market that is optimally regulated by the government and that a monopoly may not create as much of a pollution problem as a competitive market. Next we show that externalities are caused by a lack of clearly defined *property rights*, which allow owners to prevent others from using their resources.

We then turn to other issues arising from externalities. Externalities create problems for a *common property*, which is a resource available to anyone, such as a city park. Each person using the park causes an externality by crowding other people. Because no one has a property right to exclude others, such common property is overused.

When externalities benefit others, too little of the externality may be produced. A *public good*—a commodity or service whose consumption by one person does not preclude others from also consuming it—provides a positive externality if no one can be excluded from consuming it. National defense is an example of such a public good. Private firms cannot profitably charge people to provide national defense because people who did not pay would also benefit from it. Supplying anyone with a public good makes it available to others, so public goods provide a positive externality. Either markets for public goods do not exist or such markets undersupply the good.

When an externality problem arises, government intervention may be necessary. A government may directly regulate an externality such as pollution or may provide a public good. Alternatively, a government may indirectly control an externality through taxation or laws that make polluters liable for the damage they cause.

In this chapter, we examine six main topics

1. **Externalities.** By-products of consumption and production may benefit or harm other people.
2. **The Inefficiency of Competition with Externalities.** A competitive market produces too much of a harmful externality, but that overproduction can be prevented through taxation or regulation.
3. **Market Structure and Externalities.** With a harmful externality, a noncompetitive market equilibrium may be closer to the socially optimal level than a competitive equilibrium.
4. **Allocating Property Rights to Reduce Externalities.** Clearly assigning property rights allows exchanges that reduce or eliminate externality problems.
5. **Open-Access Common Property.** People overexploit resources when property rights are not clearly defined.
6. **Public Goods.** Private markets supply too few public goods, and governments have difficulty determining their optimal levels.

18.1 Externalities

Tragedy is when I cut my finger. Comedy is when you walk into an open sewer and die.
—Mel Brooks

externality
the direct effect of the actions of a person or firm on another person's well-being or a firm's production capability rather than an indirect effect through changes in prices

An **externality** occurs when a person's well-being or a firm's production capability is directly affected by the actions of other consumers or firms rather than indirectly through changes in prices. A firm whose production process lets off fumes that harm its neighbors is creating an externality for which there is no market. In contrast, the firm is not causing an externality when it harms a rival by selling extra output that lowers the market price.

Externalities may either help or harm others. An externality that harms someone is called a *negative externality*. You are harmed if your neighbors keep you awake by screaming at each other late at night. A chemical plant spoils a lake's beauty when it dumps its waste product into the water and in so doing also harms a firm that rents boats for use on that waterway. Government officials in Sydney, Australia, used loud Barry Manilow music to drive away late-night revelers from a suburban park—and in the process drove local residents out of their minds.[1]

A *positive externality* benefits others. By installing attractive shrubs and outdoor sculpture around its plant, a firm provides a positive externality to its neighbors.

A single action may confer positive externalities on some people and negative externalities on others. The smell of pipe smoke pleases some people and annoys others. Some people think that their wind chimes please their neighbors, whereas anyone with an ounce of sense would realize that those chimes make us want to strangle them! It was reported that efforts to clean up the air in Los Angeles, while helping people breathe more easily, caused radiation levels to increase far more rapidly than if the air had remained dirty.

See Questions 1–3.

APPLICATION

Negative Externality: SUVs Kill

U.S. drivers have set off an "arms race" by buying increasingly heavy vehicles such as sport utility vehicles (SUVs) and other light trucks. The replacement of cars with heavier vehicles has two offsetting effects. First, people feel better protected in larger, heavier vehicles—although Anderson (2008) finds that they are not safer. Second, a more massive vehicle may inflict greater harm—a negative externality—on the occupants of smaller vehicles, pedestrians, and bicyclists.

White (2004) concludes that light trucks and SUVs kill. For each 1 million light trucks that replace cars, between 34 and 93 additional car occupants, pedestrians, bicyclists, or motorcyclists are killed per year. That is, she finds that any safety gain to SUV and light truck owners comes at a very high cost: Each fatal crash that occupants of large vehicles avoid costs at least 4.3 additional fatal crashes involving others.

Similarly, Anderson (2008) calculates that the doubling of the share of light trucks from 1981 to 2004 caused annual traffic deaths to rise by 2,900. A one percentage point increase in light trucks' share raises annual traffic fatalities by 0.34%, or 143 deaths per year. Two-thirds to three-quarters of these deaths involve occupants of other vehicles and pedestrians. Friends don't let friends drive SUVs and light trucks.

APPLICATION

Positive Externality: Michael Jordan Effect

Basketball stars raise sales throughout the National Basketball Association (NBA), creating positive externalities. Controlling for team records, Hausman and Leonard (1997) showed that Michael Jordan's presence, when he played for the Chicago Bulls, increased ticket revenues at away games throughout the league by $2.5 million during the 1991–1992 regular season. (Jordan didn't affect gate receipts for playoff games because they would have sold out even without him.) Local television advertising revenues also rose by $2.4 million for these games. These increased ticket and local television advertising receipts reflected a positive externality because they went to the home team rather than to Jordan's employer, the Bulls.

Berri and Schmidt (2006) looked at the positive externality effects of 25 NBA stars during the 1996 season. They estimated that Jordan's presence was worth $931,000 in extra ticket sales alone for rival teams, compared to $723,000 for

[1]"Manilow Tunes Annoy Residents," **cnn.com**, July 17, 2006.

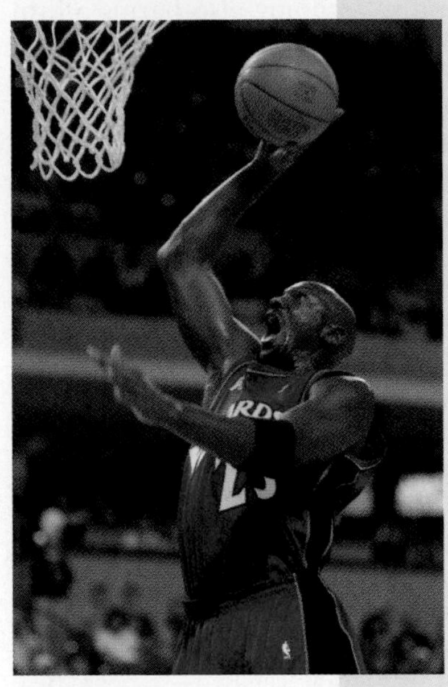

See Question 4.

Charles Barkley, $648,000 for Grant Hill, and $505,000 for Shaquille O'Neal.

Jordan's presence also increased national television advertising by $6.6 million during the regular season and by $13.9 million during the playoffs. From 1990 through 2001, NBA television ratings in the finals were 27% higher during the years in which he played than in his retirement years. Jordan also boosted the earnings of NBA Properties, which licenses NBA paraphernalia such as clothing and videos, by $15.1 million. National television revenues and NBA Properties' earnings are shared equally by all teams, so most of this increase was a positive externality for other teams.

Hausman and Leonard estimated the total value of Jordan's positive externalities at $40.3 million for the 1991–1992 season. When Michael Jordan returned from his second retirement to play for the lowly Washington Wizards in the 2001–2002 and 2002–2003 seasons, he again was the single biggest draw at away games. By various estimates, his return increased ticket sales by about 7% throughout the league, or about $8.2 million, and generated $20 million overall for the league.

18.2 The Inefficiency of Competition with Externalities

I shot an arrow in the air and it stuck.

Competitive firms and consumers do not have to pay for the harms of their negative externalities, so they create excessive amounts. Similarly, because producers are not compensated for the benefits of a positive externality, too little of such externalities is produced.

To illustrate why externalities lead to nonoptimal production, we examine a (hypothetical) competitive market in which firms produce paper and by-products of the production process—such as air and water pollution—that harm people who live near paper mills. We'll call the pollution *gunk*. Each ton of paper that is produced increases the amount of gunk by one unit, and the only way to decrease the volume of gunk is to reduce the amount of paper manufactured. No less-polluting technologies are available, and it is not possible to locate plants where the gunk bothers no one.

private cost
the cost of production only, not including *externalities*

social cost
the private cost plus the cost of the harms from *externalities*

Paper firms do not have to pay for the harm from the pollution they cause. As a result, each firm's **private cost**—the cost of production only, not including externalities—includes its direct costs of labor, energy, and wood pulp but not the indirect costs of the harm from gunk. The true **social cost** is the private cost plus the cost of the harms from externalities.

Supply-and-Demand Analysis

The paper industry is the major industrial source of water pollution. We use a supply-and-demand diagram for the paper market in Figure 18.1 to illustrate that *a competitive market produces excessive pollution because the firms' private cost is*

Figure 18.1 Welfare Effects of Pollution in a Competitive Market.

The competitive equilibrium, e_c, is determined by the intersection of the demand curve and the competitive supply or private marginal cost curve, MC^p, which ignores the cost of pollution. The social optimum, e_s, is at the intersection of the demand curve and the social marginal cost curve, $MC^s = MC^p + MC^g$, where MC^g is the marginal cost of the pollution (gunk). Private producer surplus is based on the MC^p curve, and social producer surplus is based on the MC^s curve.

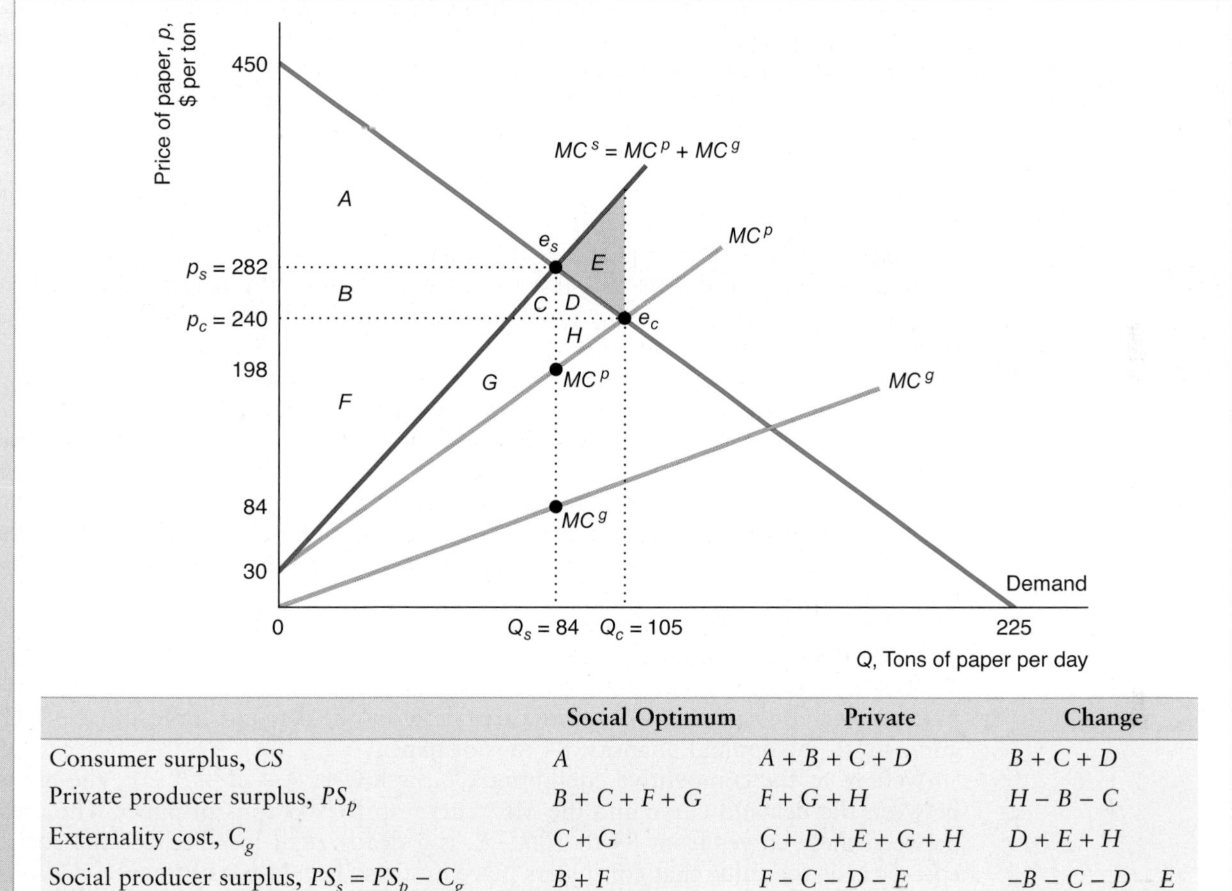

	Social Optimum	Private	Change
Consumer surplus, CS	A	$A + B + C + D$	$B + C + D$
Private producer surplus, PS_p	$B + C + F + G$	$F + G + H$	$H - B - C$
Externality cost, C_g	$C + G$	$C + D + E + G + H$	$D + E + H$
Social producer surplus, $PS_s = PS_p - C_g$	$B + F$	$F - C - D - E$	$-B - C - D - E$
Welfare, $W = CS + PS_s$	$A + B + F$	$A + B + F - E$	$-E = DWL$

less than their social cost.[2] In the competitive equilibrium, the firms consider only their private costs in making decisions and ignore the harms of the pollution externality they inflict on others. The market supply curve is the aggregate *private marginal cost* curve, MC^p, which is the horizontal sum of the private marginal cost curves of each of the paper manufacturing plants.

The competitive equilibrium, e_c, is determined by the intersection of the market supply curve and the market demand curve for paper. The competitive equilibrium quantity is $Q_c = 105$ tons per day, and the competitive equilibrium price is $p_c = \$240$ per ton.

[2]Appendix 18A uses algebra to analyze this model and derives the numbers in the figure. These numbers are not based on actual estimates.

The firms' *private producer surplus* is the producer surplus of the paper mills based on their *private marginal cost* curve: the area, $F + G + H$, below the market price and above MC^p up to the competitive equilibrium quantity, 105. The competitive equilibrium maximizes the sum of consumer surplus and private producer surplus (Chapter 9). If there were no externality, the sum of consumer surplus and private producer surplus would equal welfare, so competition would maximize welfare.

Because of the pollution, however, the competitive equilibrium does *not* maximize welfare. Competitive firms produce too much gunk because they do not have to pay for the harm from the gunk. This *market failure* (Chapter 9) results from competitive forces that equalize the price and *private marginal cost* rather than *social marginal cost*, which includes both the private costs of production and the externality damage.

For a given amount of paper production, the full cost of one more ton of paper to society, the *social marginal cost* (MC^s), is the cost of manufacturing one more ton of paper to the paper firms plus the additional externality damage to people in the community from producing this last ton of paper. Thus, the height of the social marginal cost curve, MC^s, at any given quantity equals the vertical sum of the height of the MC^p curve (the private marginal cost of producing another ton of paper) plus the height of the MC^g curve (the marginal externality damage) at that quantity.

The social marginal cost curve intersects the demand curve at the socially optimal quantity, $Q_s = 84$. At smaller quantities, the price—the value consumers place on the last unit of the good sold—is higher than the full social marginal cost. There the gain to consumers of paper exceeds the cost of producing an extra unit of output (and hence an extra unit of gunk). At larger quantities, the price is below the social marginal cost, so the gain to consumers is less than the cost of producing an extra unit.

Welfare is the sum of consumer surplus and *social producer surplus*, which is based on the *social marginal cost* curve rather than the *private marginal cost* curve. *Welfare is maximized where price equals social marginal cost.* At the social optimum, e_s, welfare equals $A + B + F$: the area between the demand curve and the MC^s curve up to the optimal quantity, 84 tons of paper.

Welfare at the competitive equilibrium, e_c, is lower: $A + B + F - E$, the areas between the demand curve and the MC^s curve up to 105 tons of paper. The area between these curves from 84 to 105, $-E$, is a deadweight loss because the social cost exceeds the value that consumers place on these last 21 tons of paper. *A deadweight loss results because the competitive market equates price with private marginal cost instead of with social marginal cost.*

Welfare is higher at the social optimum than at the competitive equilibrium because the gain from reducing pollution from the competitive to the socially optimal level more than offsets the loss to consumers and producers of the paper. The cost of the pollution to people who live near the factories is the area under the MC^g curve between zero and the quantity produced. By construction, this area is the same as the area between the MC^p and the MC^s curves. The total damage from the gunk is $-C - D - E - G - H$ at the competitive equilibrium and only $-C - G$ at the social optimum. Consequently, the extra pollution damage from producing the competitive output rather than the socially optimal quantity is $-D - E - H$.

The main beneficiaries from producing at the competitive output level rather than at the socially optimal level are the paper buyers, who pay \$240 rather than \$282 for a ton of paper. Their consumer surplus rises from A to $A + B + C + D$. The corresponding change in private producer surplus is $H - B - C$, which is negative in this figure.

The figure illustrates two main results with respect to negative externalities. First, *a competitive market produces excessive negative externalities*. Because the price of the pollution to the firms is zero, which is less than the marginal cost that the last unit of pollution imposes on society, an unregulated competitive market produces more pollution than is socially optimal.

Second, *the optimal amount of pollution is greater than zero*. Even though pollution is harmful and we'd like to have none of it, we cannot wipe it out without eliminating virtually all production and consumption. Making paper, dishwashers, and televisions creates air and water pollution. Fertilizers used in farming pollute the water supply. Delivery people pollute the air by driving to your home.

See Question 5.

Reducing Externalities. Because competitive markets produce too many negative externalities, government intervention may provide a social gain. Half a century ago in 1952, London suffered from a thick "peasouper" fog—pollution so dense that people had trouble finding their way home—that killed an estimated 4,000 to 12,000 people. Those dark days prompted the British government to pass its first Clean Air Act, in 1956. The United States passed a Clean Air Act in 1970.

Carbon dioxide (CO_2), which is primarily produced by burning fossil fuels, is a major contributor to global warming, damages marine life, and causes other harms. Rich countries tend to produce more CO_2 from energy consumption than do poorer countries, as Table 18.1 shows. The United States produces nearly a quarter of the world's CO_2. The United States has one of the world's highest rates of CO_2 per capita and a relatively high rate per thousand dollars of gross domestic product (GDP). The last column of the table shows that most countries have increased their production of CO_2 relative to GDP since 1990.

Developing countries spend little on controlling pollution, while many developing countries' public expenditures have fallen in recent years. In response, various protests have erupted, as in 2007 when hundreds of rioters in Chinese villages protested against pollution from nearby factories by destroying their machines.

Table 18.1 Industrial CO_2 Emissions, 2004.

	CO_2, Million Metric Tons	CO_2 Tons per Capita	CO_2 Tons per GDP	Percentage Change in CO_2 Tons per GDP Since 1990
United States	6,049	20.4	5.7	25
Canada	639	20.0	8.0	54
Australia	327	16.3	7.4	17
Russian Federation	1,525	10.5	46.4	NA
Japan	1,258	9.8	2.6	17
United Kingdom	587	9.8	3.7	1
Germany	809	9.8	4.2	–18
France	374	6.2	2.6	3
Mexico	438	4.2	7.1	6
China	5,010	3.8	29.2	109
World	27,246	4.2	NA	NA

Sources: CO_2 emissions in metric tons: **mdgs.un.org/unsd/mdg/Data.aspx** as of 2008; GDP, real (2000) hundred million U.S. dollars: **www.ers.usda.gov/Data/Macroeconomics**.

In 1992, representatives from more than 150 countries began negotiating an international emissions reduction policy. An agreement was reached in Kyoto, Japan, in 1997 that required most industrialized nations to reduce emissions by an average of 5.2% below 1990 levels by 2008–2012. To achieve this goal, the United States, Europe, and Japan need to curb their CO_2 emissions by 31%, 22%, and 35%, respectively, from the levels that would have been attained in the absence of a reduction policy. The Bush administration rejected this agreement.

If a government has sufficient knowledge about pollution damage, the demand curve, costs, and the production technology, it can force a competitive market to produce the social optimum. The government might control pollution directly by restricting the amount of pollution that firms may produce or by taxing them for pollution they create. A governmental limit on the amount of air or water pollution that may be released is called an *emissions standard*. A tax on air pollution is called an *emissions fee*, and a tax on discharges into the air or waterways is an *effluent charge*.

Frequently, however, a government controls pollution indirectly, through quantity restrictions or taxes on outputs or inputs. Whether the government restricts or taxes outputs or inputs may depend on the nature of the production process. It is generally better to regulate pollution directly rather than to regulate output. Direct regulation of pollution encourages firms to adopt efficient new technologies to control pollution (a possibility we ignore in our paper mill example).

Emissions Standard. We use the paper mill example in Figure 18.1 to illustrate how a government may use an *emissions standard* to reduce pollution. Here the government can achieve the social optimum by forcing the paper mills to produce no more than 84 units of paper per day. (Because output and pollution move together in this example, regulating either reduces pollution in the same way.)

Unfortunately, the government usually does not know enough to regulate optimally. For example, to set quantity restrictions on output optimally, the government must know how the marginal social cost curve, the demand for paper curve, and pollution vary with output. The ease with which the government can monitor output and pollution may determine whether it sets an output restriction or a pollution standard.

Even if the government knows enough to set the optimal regulation, it must enforce this regulation to achieve the social optimum. Though the U.S. Environmental Protection Agency (EPA) sets federal smog standards, it identified 474 counties in 31 states, home to 159 million people, as having excessive ozone (smog) in 2004. These counties have not met the new ozone standard of 0.085 parts per million, which replaced the older standard of 0.12 parts per million, set in 1979.[3]

See Question 6.

APPLICATION

Pulp and Paper Mill Pollution and Regulation

Pulp and paper mills are major sources of air and water pollution. Air pollution is generated primarily during the pulping process, in which the plant separates the wood fibers from the rest of the tree using various chemical and mechanical methods. Additional pollution occurs during the paper-making process if the paper is chemically treated to produce smoother surfaces.

[3]See **www.epa.gov/epahome/commsearch.htm** or **www.scorecard.org** for details on the environmental risks in your area.

For simplicity in our example, we assumed pollution is emitted in fixed ratio to output. H ever, in actuality, firms can choose less-pollut technologies, use additional pollution-controlli capital, and take other actions to lower the amou of pollution per unit of output.

Shadbegian and Gray (2003) found significantly lower air pollution emissions per unit of paper in plants using more capital designed to fight air pollution; specifically, a 10% increase in pollution-reducing capital reduces emissions by 6.9%. Each dollar spent on extra capital stock provides an annual return of about 75¢ in pollution reduction benefits.

Under the 1977 amendments to the 1970 Clean Air Act, U.S. counties are designated annually as in *attainment* (meeting ambient air quality standards) or *nonattainment* for each of several criteria pollutants. Because plants in nonattainment counties are substantially more stringently regulated than those in attainment counties, they have 43% lower emissions. The compliance rate of plants was 84% for air and 70% for water regulations.

Thus, politics and regulation matter. Gray and Shadbegian (2002) found that, all else the same, plants in areas where the perceived payoff to controlling pollution is greater produce less pollution. Plants near communities with more kids, more elderly people, and fewer poor people emit less pollution. Similarly, plants in areas with politically active, environmentally conscious populations emit less pollution.

Emissions Fee. The government may impose costs on polluters by taxing their output or the amount of pollution produced. (Similarly, a law could make a polluter liable for damages in a court.) In our paper mill example, taxing output works as well as taxing the pollution directly because the relationship between output and pollution is fixed. However, if firms can vary the output-pollution relationship by varying inputs or adding pollution-control devices, then the government should tax pollution.

In our paper mill example, if the government knows the marginal cost of the gunk, MC^g, it can set the output tax equal to this marginal cost curve: $t(Q) = MC^g$. (We write this tax as $t(Q)$ to show that it varies with output, Q.) Figure 18.2 illustrates the manufacturers' after-tax marginal cost, $MC^s = MC^p + t(Q)$.

internalize the externality
to bear the cost of the harm that one inflicts on others (or to capture the benefit that one provides to others)

The output tax causes a manufacturer to **internalize the externality**: to bear the cost of the harm that one inflicts on others (or to capture the benefit that one provides to others). The after-tax private marginal cost or supply curve is the same as the social marginal cost curve. As a result, the after-tax competitive equilibrium is the social optimum.

See Questions 7 and 8 and Problem 22.

Usually, the government sets a specific tax rather than a tax that varies with the amount of pollution, as MC^g does. As Solved Problem 18.1 shows, applying an appropriate specific tax results in the socially optimal level of production.

613

that ow- ing ng nt

...trol Pollution.

...rms equal to the harm from the ...auses them to internalize the exter- ...ate marginal cost is the same as the ...ost, MC^s. As a result, the competitive after-tax equilibrium is the same as the social optimum, e_s. Alternatively, applying a specific tax of $\tau = \$84$ per ton of paper, which is the marginal harm from the gunk at $Q_s = 84$, also results in the social optimum.

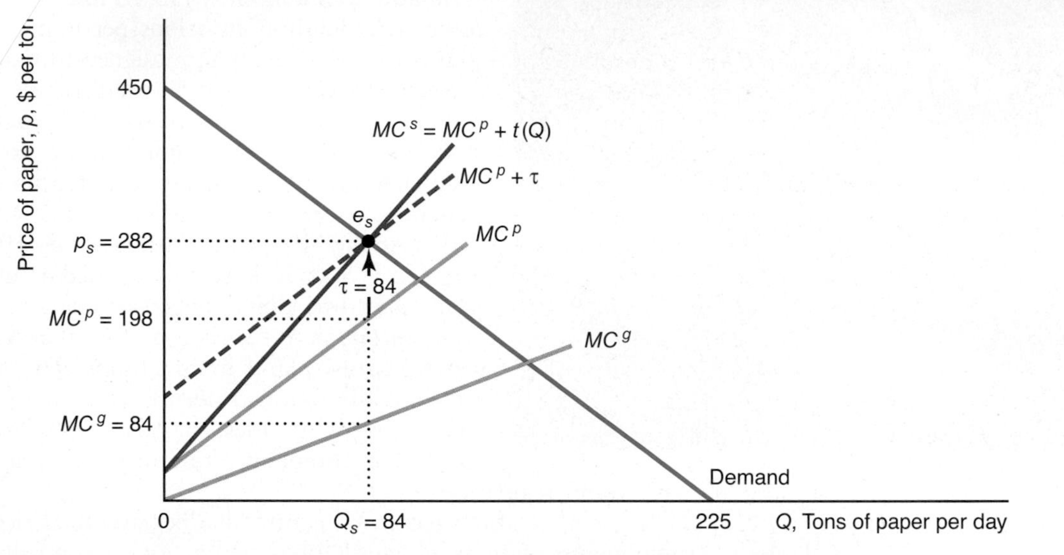

Solved Problem 18.1

For the market with pollution in Figure 18.1, what constant, specific tax, τ, on output could the government set to maximize welfare?

Answer

Set the specific tax equal to the marginal harm of pollution at the socially optimal quantity. At the socially optimal quantity, $Q_s = 84$, the marginal harm from the gunk is \$84, as Figure 18.2 shows. If the specific tax is $\tau = \$84$, the after-tax private marginal cost (after-tax competitive supply curve), $MC^p + \tau$, equals the social marginal cost at the socially optimal quantity. As a consequence, the after-tax competitive supply curve intersects the demand curve at the socially optimal quantity. By paying this specific tax, the firms internalize the cost of the externality at the social optimum. All that is required for optimal production is that the tax equals the marginal cost of pollution at the optimum quantity; it need not equal the marginal cost of pollution at other quantities.

See Questions 9 and 10 and Problems 23–25.

APPLICATION

Taxes to Reduce Auto Accidents

Extra drivers on the road, especially those who own SUVs or are drunk, cause auto accidents (as well as other negative externalities such as pollution and congestion). Governments can reduce auto accidents by imposing taxes or fees.

Edlin and Karaca-Mandic (2006) estimate auto accident externalities, which they measure as increases in the cost of insurance. These externalities are substantial in states with high traffic densities, though not in states with low densities. In California, a high-density state, an increase in traffic density from an additional driver increases total statewide insurance costs of other drivers by between $1,725 and $3,239 per year, and a 1% increase in driving raises insurer costs by between 3.3% and 5.4%. While the state could build more roads to lower density and hence accidents, a less expensive approach is to tax the externality. A tax equal to the marginal externality cost would raise $66 billion annually in California—more than the $57 billion raised by all existing state taxes—and over $220 billion nationally.

An alternative to a tax per driver is a tax per mile. For example, the government could raise the gas tax. Grabowski and Morrissey (2006) estimate that each 10% increase in the gasoline tax results in a 0.6% decrease in the traffic fatality rate.

Anderson (2008) finds that the probability of a serious accident from a single-vehicle frontal collision is 18% higher for light trucks than for cars. He calculates that the marginal externality cost of driving a light truck, such as an SUV, rather than a car is $3,850. Such a tax would raise $30 billion in tax revenue per year. A gas tax has a similar effect. The increase in real gasoline price by over a dollar in the last four years reduced the share of light trucks by about 10.3 percentage points, which explains part of the reason why high gasoline taxes reduce fatalities.

Similarly, Levitt and Porter (2001) estimate that to optimally mitigate the externality from drunk driving requires a tax of 30¢ per mile driven or $8,000 per drunk driving arrest. (See **www.myeconlab.com/perloff**, Chapter 18, "Sobering Drunk Drivers.")

Cost-Benefit Analysis

We've used a supply-and-demand analysis to show that *a competitive market produces too much pollution because the price of output equals the marginal private cost rather than the marginal social cost*. By using a cost-benefit analysis, we obtain another interpretation of the pollution problem in terms of the marginal cost and benefit of the pollution itself.

See Problem 26.

In the cost-benefit diagram, panel a of Figure 18.3 (which corresponds to Figure 18.1), the quantity on the horizontal axis starts at the competitive level, 105 tons, and *decreases to the right* (in contrast to the pattern in most of our graphs). Thus, a movement to the right indicates a reduction in paper and gunk, possibly due to a pollution abatement policy. Again, welfare peaks at the socially optimal quantity of output or gunk of 84 tons per day.

The benefit of reducing output is the reduced damage from gunk. The height of the benefit curve at a given quantity is the difference between the pollution harm at that quantity and the harm at the competitive quantity.

The cost of reducing output is that the consumer surplus and private producer surplus fall. The height of the cost curve at a given quantity is the sum of consumer surplus and private producer surplus at that quantity minus the corresponding value at the competitive quantity.

If society reduced output to 63 tons, the quantity at which the total benefit equals the total cost, society would be no better off than it is in the competitive equilibrium. To maximize welfare, we want to set output at 84 tons, the quantity for which the gap between the total benefit and total cost is greatest. At that quantity, the slope of the benefit curve, the marginal benefit, MB, equals the slope of the cost curve, the marginal cost, MC, as panel b of the figure shows.[4] Thus, *welfare is maximized by*

[4]This marginal cost curve, MC, reflects the social cost of removing the last unit of paper (gunk), whereas the social marginal cost curve, MC^s, in Figure 18.1 captures the extra cost to society from the last unit of paper (or gunk).

Figure 18.3 Cost-Benefit Analysis of Pollution.

(a) The benefit curve reflects the reduction in harm from pollution as the amount of gunk falls from the competitive level. The cost of reducing the amount of gunk is the fall in output, which reduces consumer surplus and private producer surplus. Welfare is maximized at 84 tons of paper and 84 units of gunk, the quantities at which the difference between the benefit and cost curves, the net benefit, is greatest. (b) The net benefit is maximized where the marginal benefit, *MB*, which is the slope of the benefit curve, equals the marginal cost, *MC*, the slope of the cost curve.

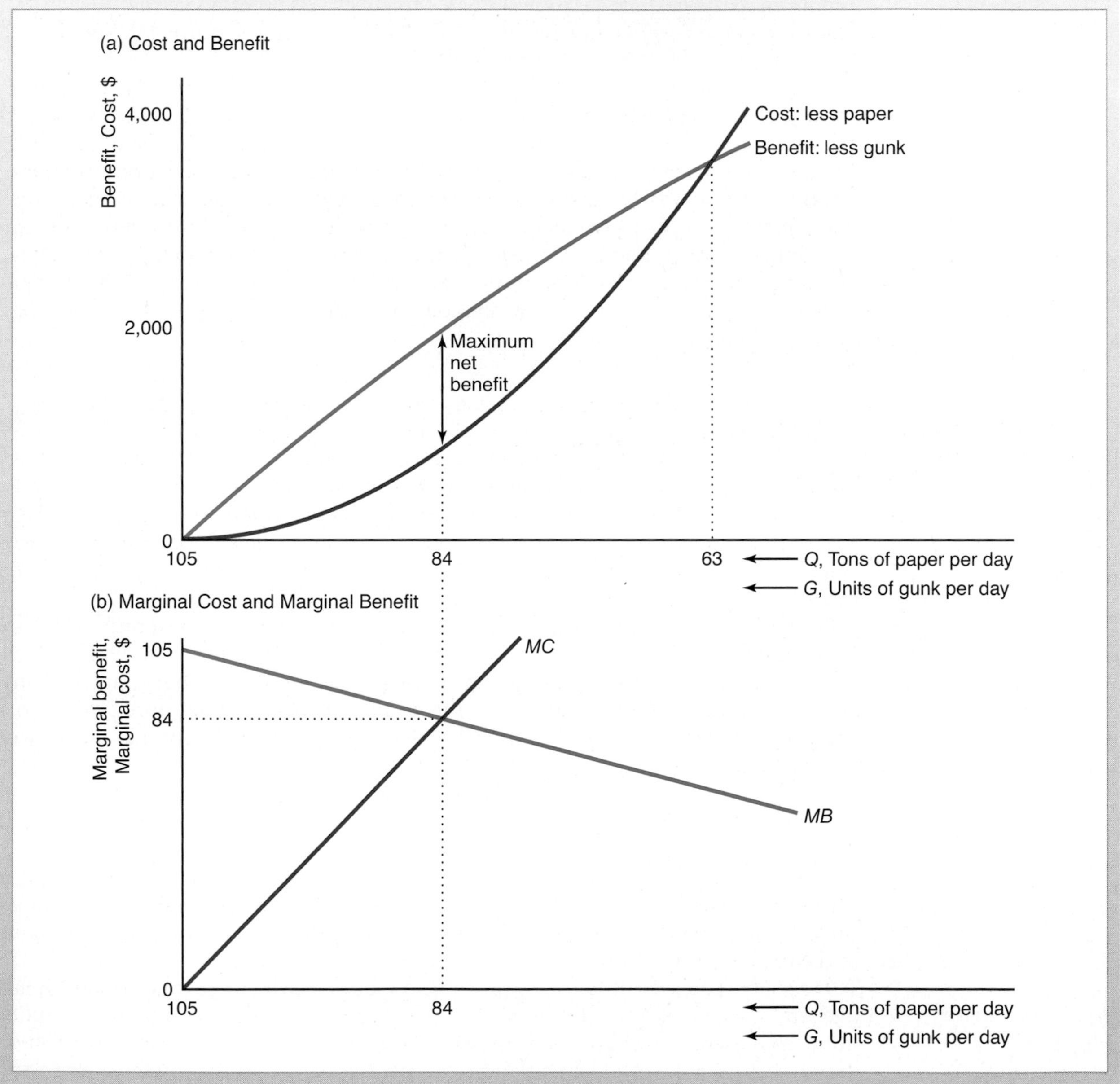

reducing output and pollution until the marginal benefit from less pollution equals the marginal cost of less output. See **www.myeconlab.com/perloff**, Chapter 18, "Emissions Standards for Ozone," and the Cross-Chapter Analysis that follows this chapter for examples of this type of analysis.

18.3 Market Structure and Externalities

Two of our main results concerning competitive markets and negative externalities—that too much pollution is produced and that a tax equal to the marginal social cost of the externality solves the problem—do not hold for other market structures. Although a competitive market always produces too many negative externalities, a noncompetitive market may produce more or less than the optimal level of output and pollution. If a tax is set so that firms internalize the externalities, a competitive market produces the social optimum, whereas a noncompetitive market does not.

Monopoly and Externalities

We use the paper-gunk example to illustrate these results. In Figure 18.4, the monopoly equilibrium, e_m, is determined by the intersection of the marginal revenue, *MR*, and private marginal cost, MC^p, curves. Like the competitive firms, the monopoly ignores the harm its pollution causes, so it considers just its direct, private costs in making decisions.

Figure 18.4 Monopoly, Competition, and Social Optimum with Pollution.

At the competitive equilibrium, e_c, more is produced than at the social optimum, e_s. As a result, the deadweight loss in the competitive market is *D*. The monopoly equilibrium, e_m, is determined by the intersection of the marginal revenue and the private marginal cost, MC^p, curves. The social welfare (based on the marginal social cost, MC^s, curve) under monopoly is $A + B$. Here the deadweight loss of monopoly, *C*, is less than the deadweight loss under competition, *D*.

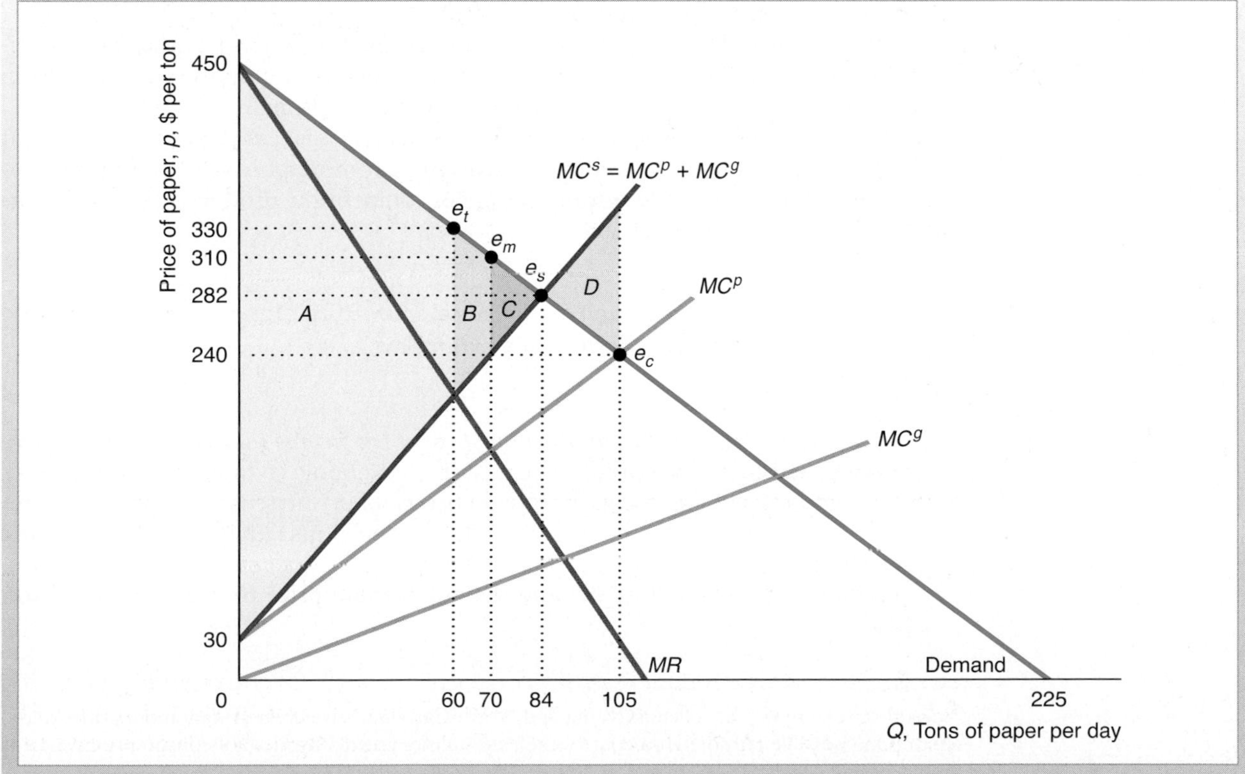

Output is only 70 tons in the monopoly equilibrium, e_m, which is less than the 84 tons at the social optimum, e_s. Thus, this figure illustrates that *the monopoly outcome may be less than the social optimum even with an externality.*

Although the competitive market with an externality always produces more output than the social optimum, a monopoly may produce more than, the same as, or less than the social optimum. The reason that a monopoly may produce too little or too much is that it faces two offsetting effects: The monopoly tends to produce too little output because it sets its price above its marginal cost, but the monopoly tends to produce too much output because its decisions depend on its private marginal cost instead of the social marginal cost.

Which effect dominates depends on the elasticity of demand for the output and on the extent of the marginal damage the pollution causes. If the demand curve is very elastic, the monopoly markup is small. As a result, the monopoly equilibrium is close to the competitive equilibrium, e_c, and greater than the social optimum, e_s. If extra pollution causes little additional harm—MC^g is close to zero at the equilibrium—the social marginal cost essentially equals the private marginal cost, and the monopoly produces less than the social optimum.

Monopoly Versus Competitive Welfare with Externalities

In the absence of externalities, welfare is greater under competition than under an unregulated monopoly (Chapter 11). However, with an externality, welfare may be greater with monopoly than with competition.[5]

If both monopoly and competitive outputs are greater than the social optimum, welfare must be greater under monopoly because the competitive output is larger than the monopoly output. If the monopoly produces less than the social optimum, we need to check which distortion is greater: the monopoly's producing too little or the competitive market's producing too much.

Welfare is lower at monopoly equilibrium, areas $A + B$, than at the social optimum, $A + B + C$, in Figure 18.4. The deadweight loss of monopoly, C, results from the monopoly's producing less output than is socially optimal.

In the figure, the deadweight loss from monopoly, C, is less than the deadweight loss from competition, D, so welfare is greater under monopoly. The monopoly produces only slightly too little output, whereas competition produces excessive output—and hence far too much gunk.

Solved Problem 18.2

In Figure 18.4, what is the effect on output, price, and welfare of taxing the monopoly an amount equal to the marginal harm of the externality?

Answer

1. *Show how the monopoly equilibrium shifts if the firm is taxed.* A tax equal to the marginal cost of the pollution causes the monopoly to internalize the externality and to view the social marginal cost as its private cost. The intersection of the marginal revenue, MR, curve and the social marginal cost, MC^s, curve determines the taxed-monopoly equilibrium, e_t. The tax causes the equilibrium quantity to fall from 70 to 60 and the equilibrium price to rise from \$310 to \$330.

[5]Several states, among them Pennsylvania and North Carolina, have created state monopolies to sell liquor. One possible purpose is to control the externalities created by alcohol consumption, such as drunk driving.

2. *Determine how this shift affects the deadweight loss of monopoly.* The sum of consumer and producer surplus is only A after the tax, compared to $A + B$ before the tax. Thus, welfare falls. The difference between A and welfare at the social optimum, $A + B + C$, is $-(B + C)$, which is the deadweight loss from the taxed monopoly. The tax exacerbates the monopoly's tendency to produce too little output. The deadweight loss increases from C to $B + C$. The monopoly produced too little before the tax; the taxed monopoly produces even less.

See Question 11 and Problem 27.

Taxing Externalities in Noncompetitive Markets

Many people recommend that the government tax firms an amount equal to the marginal harm of pollution on the grounds that such a tax achieves the social optimum in a competitive market. Solved Problem 18.2 shows that such a tax may lower welfare if applied to a monopoly. The tax definitely lowers welfare if the untaxed monopoly was producing less than the social optimum. If the untaxed monopoly was originally producing more than the social optimum, a tax may cause welfare to increase.

If the government has enough information to determine the social optimum, it can force either a monopolized or a competitive market to produce it. If the social optimum is greater than the unregulated monopoly output, however, the government has to subsidize (rather than tax) the monopoly to get it to produce as much output as is desired.

In short, trying to solve a negative externality problem is more complex in a noncompetitive market than in a competitive market. To achieve a social optimum in a competitive market, the government only has to reduce the externality, possibly by decreasing output. In a noncompetitive market, the government must eliminate problems arising from both externalities *and* the exercise of market power. Thus, the government needs more information to regulate a noncompetitive market optimally and may also require more tools, such as a subsidy. To the degree that the problems arising from market power and pollution are offsetting, however, the failure to regulate a noncompetitive market is less harmful than the failure to regulate a competitive market.

18.4 Allocating Property Rights to Reduce Externalities

property right
the exclusive privilege to use an asset

Instead of controlling externalities directly through emissions fees and emissions standards, the government may take an indirect approach by assigning a **property right**: an exclusive privilege to use an asset. By owning this textbook, you have a property right to read it and to stop others from reading or taking it.

If no one holds a property right for a good or a bad, the good or bad is unlikely to have a price. If you had a property right that assured you of the right to be free from noise pollution, you could get the courts to stop your neighbor from playing loud music. Or you could sell your right, permitting your neighbor to play the music. If you did not have this property right, no one would be willing to pay you a positive price for it.

In earlier chapters, we implicitly assumed that property rights were clearly defined and that no harmful by-products were created, so externalities did not arise. In those chapters, all goods had prices.

For many bads, such as pollution, and for some goods, property rights are not clearly defined. No one has exclusive property rights to the air we breathe. Because of this lack of a price, a polluter's private marginal cost of production is less than the full social marginal cost.

Coase Theorem

According to the *Coase Theorem* (Coase, 1960), the optimal levels of pollution and output can result from bargaining between polluters and their victims if property rights are clearly defined. Coase's contribution is not so much a practical solution to the pollution problem as a demonstration that a lack of clearly defined property rights is the root of the externality problem.

To illustrate the Coase Theorem, we consider two firms, a chemical plant and a boat rental company, that share a small lake. The chemical manufacturer dumps its waste by-products, which smell bad but are otherwise harmless, into the lake. The chemical company can reduce pollution only by restricting its output; it has no other outlet for this waste. The resulting pollution damages the boat rental firm's business. There are other lakes nearby where people can rent boats. Therefore, because they dislike the smell of the chemicals, people rent from this firm only if it charges a low enough price to compensate them fully for the smell.

No Property Rights. These two firms won't negotiate with each other unless property rights are clearly defined. After all, why would the manufacturer reduce its pollution if the boat rental firm has no legal right to clean water? Why would the boat rental firm pay the chemical company not to pollute if the courts may declare that the rental company has a right to be free from pollution?

If the firms do not negotiate, the chemical firm produces the output level that maximizes its profit, ignoring the effect on the boat rental firm. The profit matrix in panel a of Table 18.2 shows that the chemical firm makes \$0 if it produces nothing, \$10 if it produces 1 ton, and \$15 if it produces 2 tons regardless of what the boat rental firm does. Thus, the chemical company has a dominant strategy: It produces 2 tons. Knowing that the chemical company will produce 2 tons, the boat rental firm maximizes its profit with 1 boat.

Because nobody else is directly affected by this pollution, we call an outcome *efficient* if it maximizes the sum of the profits of the two firms.[6] The firms maximize their joint profits at \$20 when the chemical company produces 1 ton and the boat rental firm rents 1 boat. Thus, the no-property-rights equilibrium, with joint profits of \$17, is inefficient: Too much pollution is produced.

Property Right to Be Free of Pollution. If a court or the government grants the boat rental firm the property right to be free of pollution, the firm can prevent the chemical company from dumping at all. With no pollution, the boat company rents 2 boats and makes \$15. Rather than shut down, the chemical company offers to pay the boat company for the right to dump. The boat rental firm is willing to permit dumping only if it makes at least \$15, and it may hold out for more. The largest

[6]Because people who want to rent boats pay sufficiently less as compensation for putting up with the chemicals, they are not harmed by the pollution. Only the boat rental firm is harmed through lower prices.

Table 18.2 Property Rights and Bargaining.

(a) No Property Rights

		Boat Rental Firm: Boats Rented per Day		
		0	*1*	*2*
Chemical Firm: Tons per Day	*0*	$0, $0	$0, $14	$0, $15
	1	$10, $0	$10, $10	$10, $5
	2	$15, $0	$15, $2	$15, –$3

(b) Boat Rental Firm Has Property Right: Chemical company pays the boat rental firm $7 per ton for the right to dump

		Boat Rental Firm: Boats Rented per Day		
		0	*1*	*2*
Chemical Firm: Tons per Day	*0*	$0, $0	$0, $14	$0, $15
	1	$3, $7	$3, $17	$3, $12
	2	$1, $14	$1, $16	$1, $11

(c) Chemical Company Has Property Right: Boat rental firm pays the chemical company $6 for each ton by which it reduces its production below 2 tons

		Boat Rental Firm: Boats Rented per Day		
		0	*1*	*2*
Chemical Firm: Tons per Day	*0*	$12, –$12	$12, $2	$12, $3
	1	$16, –$6	$16, $4	$16, –$1
	2	$15, $0	$15, $2	$15, –$3

"bribe" the chemical company is willing to offer for the right to dump is one that leaves it with a positive profit. Panel b of Table 18.2 shows one possible compensation agreement: The chemical company offers the boat rental firm $7 per ton for the right to dump. If the firms agree to this deal, the chemical company's dominant strategy is to produce 1 ton, so the boat rental firm chooses to rent 1 boat. Both firms benefit. Indeed, in this equilibrium, their joint profits are maximized at $20.

In general, the chemical firm pays the boat rental firm between \$5 and \$10. The boat rental firm wants at least \$5 so that its profit when both produce one unit is at least \$15—the amount that it makes with no pollution. Any payment larger than \$10 would leave the chemical company with a negative profit, so that's the most it is willing to pay. The exact payment outcome depends on the firms' bargaining skills. Because both parties benefit from a deal, they should be able to reach an agreement if transaction costs are low enough that it pays to negotiate.

See Question 12.

Property Right to Pollute. Now suppose that the chemical company has the property right to dump in the lake (for example, by paying a pollution tax). Unless the boat rental company pays the chemical company not to pollute, the chemical company produces 2 tons, as in panel a of the table. The boat rental firm may bribe the chemical company to reduce its output so that both firms benefit. Again, the exact deal that is struck depends on their bargaining skills.

Panel c of Table 18.2 shows what happens if the boat rental firm pays the chemical company \$6 per ton for each ton less than 2 that it produces. The chemical company's dominant strategy is to produce 1 ton, and the boat rental firm rents 1 boat. The equilibrium is efficient as in the previous case. Now, however, the boat rental firm compensates the chemical company rather than the other way around.

To summarize the results from the Coase Theorem:

- If there are no impediments to bargaining, *assigning property rights results in the efficient outcome* at which joint profits are maximized.
- *Efficiency is achieved regardless of who receives the property rights.*
- Who gets the property rights affects the income distribution. *The property rights are valuable.* The party with the property rights may be compensated by the other party.

See Question 13.

Problems with the Coase Approach. To achieve the efficient outcome, the two sides must bargain successfully with each other. However, the parties may not be able to bargain successfully for at least three important reasons (Polinsky, 1979).

First, if transaction costs are very high, it might not pay for the two sides to meet. For example, if a manufacturing plant pollutes the air, thousands or even millions of people may be affected. The cost of getting them all together to bargain is prohibitive.

Second, if firms engage in strategic bargaining behavior, an agreement may not be reached. For instance, if one party says, "Give me everything I want" and will not budge, reaching an agreement may be impossible.

Third, if either side lacks information about the costs or benefits of reducing pollution, a nonefficient outcome may occur. It is difficult to know how much to offer the other party and to reach an agreement if you do not know how the polluting activity affects the other party.

For these reasons, Coasian bargaining is likely to occur in relatively few situations. Where bargaining cannot occur, the allocation of property rights affects the amount of pollution.

Markets for Pollution

If high transaction costs preclude bargaining, we may be able to overcome this problem by using a market that facilitates exchanges between individuals. Starting in the early 1980s, governments experimented with issuing permits to pollute that could be exchanged in a market, often by means of an auction. Today, many firms can buy the right to pollute—much as sinners bought indulgences in the Middle Ages.

Under this cap-and-trade system, the government gives firms permits, each of which confers the right to create a certain amount of pollution. Each firm may use its permits or sell them to other firms.

Firms whose products are worth a lot relative to the harm from pollution they create buy rights from firms that have less valuable products. Suppose that the cost in terms of forgone output from eliminating each ton of pollution is \$200 at one plant and \$300 at another. If the government tells both plants to reduce pollution by 1 ton, the total cost is \$500. With tradable permits, the first plant can reduce its pollution by 2 tons and sell its allowance to the second plant, so the total social cost is only \$400. The trading maximizes the value of the output for a given amount of pollution damage, thus increasing efficiency.

If the government knew enough, it could assign the optimal amount of pollution to each firm, and no trading would be necessary. By using a market, the government does not have to collect this type of detailed information to achieve efficiency. Its only decision concerns what total amount of pollution to allow.

APPLICATION

U.S. Cap-and-Trade Programs

The first large-scale U.S. cap-and-trade program was the Acid Rain Program in the 1990 Clean Air Act, which was designed to remove 10 million tons of sulfur dioxide (SO_2) and 2 million tons of nitrogen oxides, the primary components of acid rain. Under the law, the EPA issues SO_2 permits, each of which allows a firm to produce 1 ton of emissions of SO_2 annually, equal to the aggregate emissions cap. A firm that exceeds its pollution limit is fined \$2,000 per ton of emissions above its allowance. But at the end of a year, if a company's emissions are less than its allowance, it may sell the remaining allowance to another firm, thus providing the firm with an incentive to reduce emissions. The EPA holds an annual spot auction for permits that may be used in the current year and an advanced auction for permits effective in seven years. Anyone can purchase allowances. Some environmental groups, such as the Acid Rain Retirement Fund, have purchased permits and withheld them from firms to reduce pollution further. (You can see the outcome of the auctions at **www.epa.gov**.) According to some estimates, pollution reduction under this market program costs about a quarter to a third less than it would have cost if permits had not been tradable—a savings on the order of \$225 to \$375 million per year.

A 2006 EPA evaluation concluded that this program had reduced SO_2 emissions by more than 6.3 million tons from 1990 levels, or about 40% of total power sector emissions. Moreover, the EPA forecasted that the Acid Rain Program's annual benefits by 2010 will be approximately \$122 billion (in 2000 dollars), at an annual cost of about \$3 billion, or a 40-to-1 benefit-to-cost ratio.

In 2007, the U.S. Congress debated various measures to mitigate greenhouse gases and reduce the threat of global warming. Paltsev et al. (2007) analyzed a number of variants of the proposed cap-and-trade programs such as the Bingaman-Specter, McCain-Lieberman, Boxer-Sanders, and Kerry-Snowe bills, which were designed to reduce carbon dioxide emissions by as much as 50% to 80% below 1990 levels by 2050 so as to help prevent global warming. They concluded that these proposals would result in a price of between \$7 and \$53 per ton of carbon in 2015 and between \$39 to over \$210 by 2050. Their estimated welfare cost ranges from near zero in 2015 to 0.5% to 1.8% by 2050 (excluding one Bingaman-Specter variant). Auctioning pollution allowances in 2015 could raise between \$100 and \$400 billion annually. Those revenues would rise or fall over time depending on the speed with which the price increases relative to the decline in allowable emissions and permits.

18.5 Open-Access Common Property

open-access common property resources to which everyone has free access

So far we've examined externalities that arise as an undesired by-product of a production or consumption activity. Another important externality arises with **open-access common property**: resources to which everyone has free access and an equal right to exploit. Unlike private property, for which the owner can *exclude* others from using the property, open-access common property is not subject to such exclusion. For example, anyone can freely enter and enjoy urban parks such as Central Park in New York, Hyde Park in London, and the Boston Common.

Overuse of Open-Access Common Property

Because people do not have to pay to use open-access common property resources, they are overused. Parks with free entry often become crowded, an outcome that reduces everyone's enjoyment. Similarly, in less-developed economies, the sharing of public lands for hunting, grazing, or growing crops results in the overuse of common property. Other examples of common property problems are common pools, the Internet, roads, and fisheries.

Common Pools. Petroleum, water, and other fluids and gases are often extracted from a common pool. Owners of wells drawing from a common pool compete to remove the substance most rapidly, thereby gaining ownership of the good. This competition creates an externality by lowering fluid pressure, which makes further pumping more difficult. Iraq justified its invasion of Kuwait, which led to the Persian Gulf War in 1991, on the grounds that Kuwait was overexploiting common pools of oil underlying both countries.

The Internet. An important problem—one that may be inconveniencing you—is overcrowding on the Internet. If many people try to access a single Web site at one time, congestion may slow traffic to a crawl.

Roads. If you own a car, you have a property right to drive that car. But because you lack an exclusive property right to the highway on which you drive, you cannot exclude others from driving on the highway and must share it with them. Each driver, however, claims a temporary property right in a portion of the highway by occupying it (thereby preventing others from occupying the same space). Competition for space on the highway leads to congestion (a negative externality), which slows up every driver.

See Question 14 and Problem 28.

Fisheries. Many fisheries have common access such that anyone can fish and no one has a property right to a fish until it is caught. Each fisher wants to land a fish before others do to gain the property right to that fish. The lack of clearly defined property rights leads to overfishing. Fishers have an incentive to catch more fish than they would if the fishery were private property.

Suppose that each fisher owns a private lake. Because the property rights are clearly defined, there is no externality. Each owner is careful not to overfish in any one year so as to maintain the stock (or number) of fish in future years.[7]

---

[7]"There's a fine line between fishing and standing on the shore looking like an idiot." —Steven Wright

In contrast, most ocean fisheries are open-access common property. Like polluting manufacturers, ocean fishers look only at their private costs. In calculating these costs, fishers include the cost of boats, other equipment, a crew, and supplies. They do not include the cost that they impose on future generations by decreasing the stock of fish today, which reduces the number of fish in the sea next year. The fewer fish there are, the harder it is to catch any, so reducing the population today raises the cost of catching fish in the future. As a result, fishers do not forgo fishing now to leave fish for the future. The social cost is the private cost plus the externality cost from reduced future populations of fish. (See **www.myeconlab.com/perloff**, Chapter 18, "Emptying the Seas.")

See Question 15.

Solving the Commons Problem

There are two approaches to ameliorating the open-access commons problem. The first is direct government regulation through either taxation or restriction of access. The second is by clearly defining property rights.

Government Regulation of Commons. Overuse of a common resource occurs because individuals do not bear the full social cost. However, by applying a tax or fee equal to the externality harm that each individual imposes on others, a government forces each person to internalize the externality. For example, governments often charge an entrance fee to a park or a museum. However, if a government sets a fee that is less than the marginal externality harm, it reduces but does not eliminate the externality problem.

Alternatively, the government can restrict access to the commons. One typical approach is to grant access on a first-come, first-served basis. With quotas, people who arrive early gain access. In contrast, with taxes or fees, people who most heavily value the resource gain access. (See **www.myeconlab.com/perloff**, Chapter 18, "For Whom the Bridge Tolls.")

Assigning Property Rights. An alternative approach to resolving the commons problem is to assign private property rights. Converting common-access property to private property removes the incentive to overuse it. (See **www.myeconlab.com/perloff**, Chapter 18, "Claiming Lobster Fisheries," for an example.)

In developing countries over the past century, common agricultural land has been broken up into smaller private farms. Similarly, fish farming on private land is increasingly used as common-access fisheries are depleted.

18.6 Public Goods

We have seen that a competitive market produces too much output when a by-product creates a negative externality or when anyone can use a common property. That same competitive market may produce too little of a good in the presence of a positive externality. Positive externalities and too little production may occur when producers cannot restrict access to a **public good**: a commodity or service whose consumption by one person does not preclude others from also consuming it.

public good
a commodity or service whose consumption by one person does not preclude others from also consuming it

Types of Goods

Previous chapters discussed only *private goods*. *Private goods have the properties of rivalry and exclusion. Rivalry* means that only one person can consume the good:

The good is used up in consumption—it is *depletable*. If a second person is to consume a candy bar, the production of a second candy bar is required. *Exclusion* means that others can be prevented from consuming the good. Only the person who owns the candy bar may eat it.

Other types of goods lack rivalry or exclusion or both, as Table 18.3 shows. *Public goods lack rivalry*. Your consumption of a public good does not preclude others from also consuming it. There is no need to ration a public good—everyone can consume it. Indeed, excluding someone from consuming it harms that person without helping other consumers.

All public goods lack rivalry, but only some lack exclusion. Major problems occur when no one can be prevented from consuming a public good. National defense is an important example of a nonexclusive public good. The cost of protecting an extra person is literally zero when all people are protected (no rivalry), and no one in the country can be left unprotected (no exclusion). Clean air is also a public good without exclusion (and air pollution is a *public bad*). If the air is clean, we all benefit. If we clean up the air, we cannot prevent others who live nearby from benefiting from it. A *public good produces a positive externality*, and *excluding anyone from consuming a public good is inefficient*.

Other public goods are exclusive but lack rivalry in consumption. Security guards prevent people who don't have a ticket from entering a concert hall. Until the concert hall is filled, the cost of providing the concert to one extra person is zero. Thus, a concert in a hall that is not filled has elements of both a private good (exclusion) and a public good (no rivalry).

Such a concert is a special type of public good, called a *club good*. Although the marginal cost of providing the concert to one more person is zero as long as attendance is less than the seating capacity of the hall, adding another person creates congestion or other externalities that harm concertgoers once the concert hall is filled. Similarly, allowing more people to join a swim club doesn't inflict extra costs until members start getting in each other's way.

In addition to private goods, nonexclusive public goods, and club goods, there are resources with rivalry but without exclusion, such as an open-access common property resource. In an open-access fishery, anyone can fish (no exclusion), but once a fish is caught, no one else can catch it (rivalry).

Many goods differ in the degree to which they have rivalry and exclusion. Many goods are hybrids, with properties of both private and public goods. Telling your friend about something that you learned in a textbook provides a positive externality. A textbook is often viewed as a private good; however, the information in it is a public good. Because the cost of excluding people from a toll road is less than that of excluding people from an ocean fishery, a toll road may more closely resemble a private good than a fishery does.

See Questions 16 and 17.

Table 18.3 Rivalry and Exclusion.

	Exclusion	No Exclusion
Rivalry	*Private good*: candy bar, pencil, aluminum foil	*Open-access common property*: fishery, hunting, highway
No Rivalry	*Public good with exclusion*: cable television, *club good* (concert, tennis club)	*Public good without exclusion*: national defense, aerial spraying of pesticide, clean air

Markets for Public Goods

Markets for public goods exist only if nonpurchasers can be excluded from consuming them. Thus, markets do not exist for nonexclusive public goods. Usually, if the government does not provide a nonexclusive public good, no one provides it.

Because computer software use is nonrivalrous, computer software is virtually a public good. At almost no extra cost, a copy of the software program that you use can be supplied to another consumer. In countries where exclusion is impossible, computer software is pirated and widely shared, so it is not profitable to produce and sell software. In countries where intellectual property rights to software are protected by preventing piracy, a company such as Microsoft can sell software (very) profitably.

Microsoft makes a fortune by selling its software at a price that is well above its marginal cost, so too few units are sold. Markets tend to produce too little of an exclusive public good because of the lack of rivalry. In the absence of rivalry, the marginal cost of providing a public good to one extra person is (essentially) zero. Firms have no incentive to produce at a zero price. If firms set a price above zero, consumers buy too little of this public good.

Demand for Public Goods. The demand for a private good is different from that for a public good. The social marginal benefit of a private good is the same as the marginal benefit to the individual who consumes that good. The market demand or social marginal benefit curve for private goods is the *horizontal* sum of the demand curves of each individual (Chapter 2).

In contrast, the social marginal benefit of a public good is the sum of the marginal benefit to each person who consumes the good. Because a public good lacks rivalry, many people can get pleasure from the same unit of output. As a consequence, the *social demand curve* or *willingness-to-pay curve* for a public good is the *vertical* sum of the demand curves of each individual.

We illustrate this vertical summing by deriving the demand for guard services by stores in a mall that want to discourage theft. Guards patrolling the mall provide a service without rivalry: All the stores in the mall are simultaneously protected. Each store's demand for guards reflects its marginal benefit from a reduction in thefts due to the guards. The demand curve for the television store, which stands to lose a lot if thieves strike, is D^1 in Figure 18.5. The ice-cream parlor, which loses less from a theft, demands fewer guards at any given price, D^2.

Because a guard patrolling the mall protects both stores at once, the marginal benefit to society of an additional guard is the sum of the benefit to each store. The social marginal benefit of a fifth guard, \$10, is the sum of the marginal benefit to the television store, \$8 (the height of D^1 at five guards per hour), and the marginal benefit to the ice-cream store, \$2 (the height of D^2 at five guards per hour). Thus, the social demand is the vertical sum of the individual demand curves.

A competitive market supplies as many guards as the stores want at \$10 per hour per guard. At that price, the ice-cream store would not hire any guards on its own. The television store would hire four. If the stores act independently, four guards are hired at the private equilibrium, e_p. The sum of the marginal benefit to the two stores from four guards is \$13, which is greater than the \$10 marginal cost of an additional guard. If a fifth guard is hired, the social marginal benefit, \$10, equals the marginal cost of the last guard. Therefore, the social equilibrium, e_2, has five guards.

The ice-cream store can get guard services without paying because the guard service is a public good. Acting alone, the television store hires fewer guards than are socially optimal because it ignores the positive externality provided to the ice-cream

Figure 18.5 Inadequate Provision of a Public Good.

Security guards protect both tenants of the mall. If each guard costs \$10 per hour, the television store, with demand D^1, is willing to hire four guards per hour. The ice-cream parlor, with demand D^2, is not willing to hire any guards. Thus, if everyone acts independently, the equilibrium is e_p. The social demand for this public good is the vertical sum of the individual demand curves, D. Thus, the social optimum is e_s, at which five guards are hired.

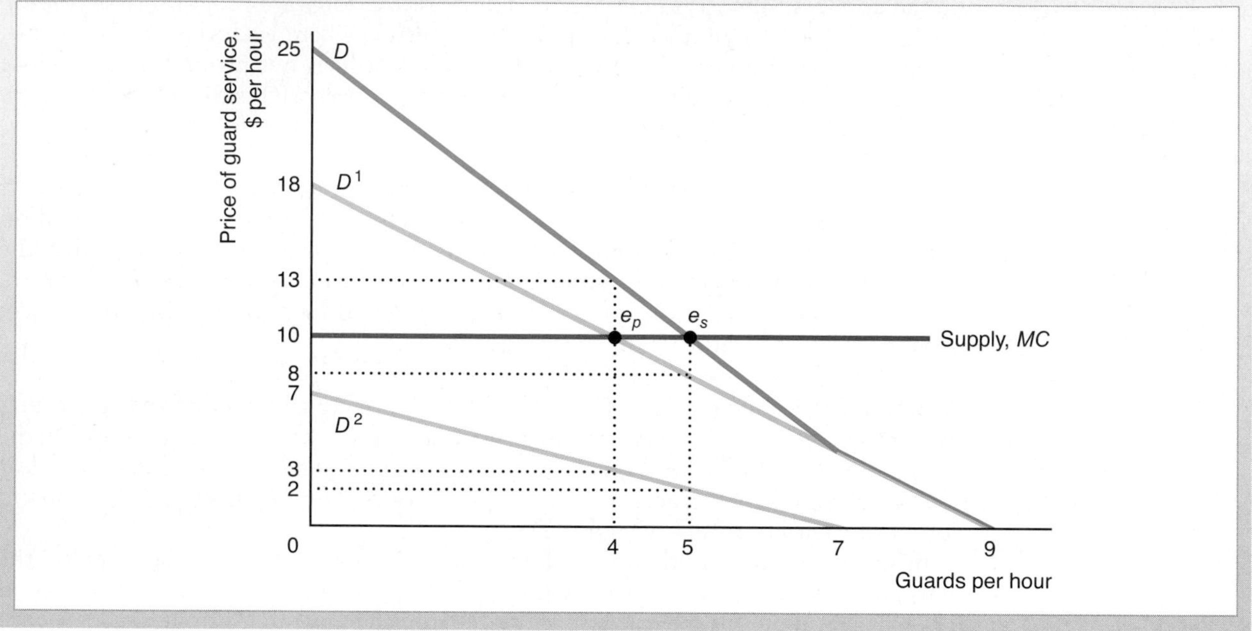

See Question 18 and Problem 29.

store, which the television store does not capture. Thus, the competitive market for guard services provides too little of this public good.

free ride
to benefit from the actions of others without paying

Free Riding. Many people are unwilling to pay for their share of a public good. They try to get others to pay for it, so they can get a **free ride**: benefit from the actions of others without paying. That is, they want to benefit from a positive externality.

To illustrate the problem of free riding, we examine a game between two stores in a mall that are deciding whether to hire one guard or none. (For now, we assume that hiring two guards does no more good than hiring one.) The cost of hiring a guard is \$10 per hour. The benefit to each store is \$8. Because the collective benefit, \$16, is greater than the cost of hiring a guard, the optimal solution is to hire the guard.

If the stores act independently, however, they do not achieve this optimal solution. Table 18.4 shows two games. In panel a, each store acts independently and pays \$10 to hire a guard on its own or does not hire a guard. If both decide to hire a guard, two guards are hired, but the benefit is still only \$8 per store.

In panel b, the stores split the cost of a guard if both firms agree to hire one. If only one firm wants to hire the guard, it must bear the full cost.

In each of these games, the Nash equilibrium is for neither store to hire a guard because of free riding. Each store has a dominant strategy. Regardless of what the other store does, each store is always as well off or better off not to hire a guard. The nonoptimal outcome occurs for the same reason as in other prisoners' dilemma games (Chapter 14): The stores don't do what is best for them collectively when they act independently.

See Questions 19–21 and Problem 30.

Table 18.4 Private Payments for a Public Good.

(a) ***Stores Decide Independently Whether to Hire a Guard***

		Television Store	
		Hire	*Do Not Hire*
Stereo Store	*Hire*	-$2 -$2	$8 -$2
	Do Not Hire	-$2 $8	$0 $0

(b) ***Stores Voting to Hire a Guard Split the Cost***

		Television Store	
		Hire	*Do Not Hire*
Stereo Store	*Hire*	$3 $3	$8 -$2
	Do Not Hire	-$2 $8	$0 $0

APPLICATION

Radiohead's "Public Good" Experiment

In 2007, the British rock band Radiohead sold its album *In Rainbows* by offering its fans a digital download without copy restriction software off the Internet at a price chosen by each fan for a three-month period. By so doing, the band faced a problem similar to that of society for a public good: Fans knew that the album could be theirs regardless of what they paid, so individuals were tempted to pay substantially less than their valuations of the album or the price of comparable albums.

The band did not release official figures about digital sales. According to comScore's estimates, 38% of fans paid an average of $6, while the rest paid nothing. Since approximately 1.2 million copies were downloaded, the band earned over $2.7 million.

After the initial three months, the band removed the digital version from the Internet and issued a traditional CD version with a list price of $13.98. In early 2008, despite all the downloads, *In Rainbows* topped the Billboard music chart of best sellers. Thus, the digital albums sold for much less than the CDs, but the early digital distribution did not kill all later CD sales. If at least those who paid something for the download would have paid full price for a CD, then the band lost millions. However, if the extra sales on the Internet were from people who would not have paid full price, the band came out ahead financially, and it received a great deal of free publicity from the news media.

Reducing Free Riding

Governmental or other collective actions can reduce free riding. Methods that may be used include social pressure, mergers, compulsion, and privatization.

Sometimes, especially when the group is small, *social pressure* eliminates free riding. Social pressure results in at least minimal provision of some public goods. Such pressure may cause most firms at a mall to contribute "voluntarily" to a fund to hire security guards.

A direct way to eliminate free riding by firms is for them to *merge* into a single firm and thereby internalize the positive externality. The sum of the benefit to the individual stores equals the benefit to the single firm, so an optimal decision is made to hire guards.

If the independent stores sign a contract that commits them to share the cost of the guards, they achieve the practical advantage from a merger. The question remains, however, as to why they would agree to sign the contract, given the prisoners' dilemma problem. One explanation is that firms are more likely to cooperate in a repeated prisoners' dilemma game (Chapter 14).

Another way to overcome free riding is through *compulsion*. Some outside entity such as the government may dictate a solution to a free-riding problem. For example, the management of a mall with many firms may require tenants to sign a rental contract committing them to pay "taxes" that are assessed through tenants' votes. If the majority votes to hire guards, all must share the cost. Although a firm might be unwilling to pay for the guard service if it has no guarantee that others will also pay, it may vote to assess everyone—including itself—to pay for the service.

With government enforcement—a form of compulsion—milk producers avoided free-rider problems by taxing themselves to produce the "Got Milk?" advertisements. In many cities, the restaurants and hotels tax themselves (or are taxed by the government) to advertise that their city is a place tourists should visit. Thus, actions by a group or government may overcome the free-rider problem so that a public service is provided.

Finally, privatization—exclusion—eliminates free riding. A good that would be a public good if anyone could use it becomes a private good if access to it is restricted. An example is water, the use of which is limited by individual meters.

APPLICATION

Free Riding on Water

Water is a private good for most households in Perth, Australia: They can consume it only if they pay the price for each unit. Others can be excluded from consuming the water because each household's consumption is individually metered. However, about 10% of the households share meters with one or more other households. Households in duplexes or apartments are likely to share meters. Perth's 20,545 flats have 1,800 meters between them, so on average, 11 households share each meter. Most group-metered households apportion the total bill equally among households.

How would you expect water consumption to vary between individually and collectively metered households? Because of free riding, you might expect households with individual meters to consume less water than households that draw from a common pool. Each member of the common pool has an incentive to free ride on the remaining members. As the household consumes a little more water, it receives all of the marginal benefits but only has to pay $1/n$ fraction of the marginal cost, where there are n households on a meter.

Moreover, you might expect that the incentive to free ride increases with the number of households sharing a meter. Not only is each household's share of the marginal cost smaller, but each household faces less effective social pressure to keep its free riding under control.

Grossman, Pirozzi, and Pope (1993) confirm these predictions. They find that collectively metered households consume 17% more water on average than households with private meters do.

The extra water consumption rises with the number of households sharing a meter. A household in a two-family duplex consumes only 0.05 kiloliter more per year than an individually metered household. Even a household in a block of ten housing units consumes only 1.3 kiloliters more. However, by the time the number in a housing block reaches 222 members (the largest in the sample), each household averages 640 extra kiloliters of water consumption.

Valuing Public Goods

To ensure that a nonexclusive public good is provided, a government usually produces it or compels others to do so. Issues that a government faces in providing such a public good include whether to provide it at all and, if so, how much to provide. To grapple with these questions, the government needs to know the cost—usually the easy part—and the value of the public good to many individuals—the hard part.

The government may try to determine the value that consumers place on the public good through surveys or voting results. One major problem with these methods is that most people do not know how much a public good is worth to them. How much would you pay to maintain the National Archives? How much does reducing air pollution improve your health? How much better do you sleep at night knowing that the army stands ready to protect you?

Even if people know how much they value a public good, they have an incentive to lie on a survey. Those who value the good greatly and want the government to provide it may exaggerate the value of the benefit. Similarly, people who place a low value on it may report too low a value—possibly even a negative one—to discourage government action.

Rather than rely on surveys, a government may have citizens vote directly on public goods. Suppose that a separate, majority-rule vote is held on whether to install a traffic signal—a public good—at each of several street corners. If a signal is installed, all voters are taxed equally to pay for it. An individual will vote to install a signal if the value of the signal to that voter is at least as much as the tax each must pay for the signal.

Whether the majority votes for the signal depends on the preferences of the *median voter*: the person with respect to whom half the populace values the project less and half values the project more. If the median voter wants to install a signal, then at least half the voters agree, so the vote carries. Similarly, if the median voter is against the project, at least half the voters are against it, so the vote fails.

It is *efficient* to install the signal if the value of the signal to society is at least as great as its cost. Does majority voting result in efficiency? The following examples illustrate that efficiency is not ensured.

Each signal costs $300 to install. There are three voters, so each individual votes for the signal only if that person thinks that the signal is worth at least $100, which is the tax each person pays if the signal is installed. Table 18.5 shows the value that each voter places on installing a signal at each of three intersections.

For each of the proposed signals, Hayley is the median voter, so her views signal the outcome. If Hayley, the median voter, likes the signal, then she and Asa, a majority, vote for it. Otherwise, Nancy and Hayley vote against it. The majority favors installing a signal at corners *A* and *C* and are against doing so at corner *B*. It would be efficient to install the signal at corner *A*, where the social value is $300, and at corner *B*, where the social value is $375, because each value equals or exceeds the cost of $300.

At corner *A*, the citizens vote for the signal, and that outcome is efficient. The other two votes lead to inefficient outcomes. No signal is installed at corner *B*,

Table 18.5 Voting on $300 Traffic Signals.

	Value to Each Voter, $				
Signal Location	Nancy	Hayley	Asa	Value to Society, $	Outcome of Vote*
Corner *A*	50	100	150	300	Yes
Corner *B*	50	75	250	375	No
Corner C	50	100	110	260	Yes

*An individual votes to install a signal at a particular corner if and only if that person thinks that the signal is worth at least $100, the tax that individual must pay if the signal is installed.

where society values the signal at more than $300, but a signal is installed at corner C, where voters value the signal at less than $300.

The problem with yes-no votes is that they ignore the intensity of preferences. A voter indicates only whether or not the project is worth more or less than a certain amount. Thus, such *majority voting fails to value the public good fully and hence does not guarantee that it is efficiently provided.*[8]

SUMMARY

1. **Externalities.** An externality occurs when a consumer's well-being or a firm's production capabilities are directly affected by the actions of other consumers or firms rather than indirectly affected through changes in prices. An externality that harms others is a negative externality, and one that helps others is a positive externality. Some externalities benefit one group while harming another.

2. **The Inefficiency of Competition with Externalities.** Because producers do not pay for a negative externality such as pollution, the private costs are less than the social costs. As a consequence, competitive markets produce more negative externalities than are optimal. If the only way to cut externalities is to decrease output, the optimal solution is to set output where the marginal benefit from reducing the externality equals the marginal cost to consumers and producers from less output. It is usually optimal to have some negative externalities, because eliminating all of them requires eliminating desirable outputs and consumption activities as well. If the government has sufficient information about demand, production cost, and the harm from the externality, it can use taxes or quotas to force the competitive market to produce the social optimum. It may tax or limit the negative externality, or it may tax or limit output.

3. **Market Structure and Externalities.** Although a competitive market produces excessive output and negative externalities, a noncompetitive market may produce more or less than the optimal level. With a negative externality, a noncompetitive equilibrium may be closer than a competitive equilibrium to the social optimum. A tax equal to the marginal social harm of a negative externality—which results in the social optimum when applied to a competitive market—may lower welfare when applied to a noncompetitive market.

4. **Allocating Property Rights to Reduce Externalities.** Externalities arise because property rights are not clearly defined. According to the Coase Theorem, allocating property rights to *either* of two parties results in an efficient outcome if the parties can bargain. The assignment of the property rights, however, affects income distribution, as the rights are valuable. Unfortunately, bargaining is usually not practical, especially when many people are involved. In such cases, markets for permits to produce externalities may overcome the externality problem.

[8]Although voting does not reveal how much a public good is worth, Tideman and Tullock (1976) and other economists have devised taxing methods that can sometimes induce people to reveal their true valuations. However, these methods are rarely used.

5. **Open-Access Common Property.** Externalities are a problem with open-access common property, which is a resource to which everyone has free access and an equal right to exploit. Such resources are overexploited. For example, if anyone can drive on a highway, too many people are likely to do so because they ignore the externality—delays due to congestion—that they impose on others. Taxes and quotas may reduce or eliminate overuse.

6. **Public Goods.** Public goods lack rivalry. Once a public good is provided to anyone, it can be provided to others at no additional cost. Excluding anyone from consuming a public good is inefficient. Markets provide too little of a nonexclusive public good. A government faces challenges in providing the optimal amount because it is difficult to determine how much people value the public good.

QUESTIONS

■ = *exercise is available on MyEconLab;* * = *answer appears at the back of this book;* C = *use of calculus may be necessary;* W = *audio-slideshow answer by James Dearden is available in Textbook Resources on MyEconLab.*

1. According to a study in the *New England Journal of Medicine*, your friendships or "social networks" are more likely than your genes to make you obese (Jennifer Levitz, "Can Your Friends Make You Fat?" *Wall Street Journal*, July 26, 2007, D1). If it is true that people who have overweight friends are more likely to be overweight all else the same, is that an example of a negative externality? Why? (*Hints*: Is this relationship a causal one, or do heavier people choose heavier friends? Also remember that people with thinner friends may be thinner.)

2. When *Star Wars Episode III: Revenge of the Sith* opened at 12:01 A.M., Thursday, May 19, 2005, the most fanatical *Star Wars* fans paid $50 million for tickets to stay up until 3:00 to 4:00 A.M. Businesses around the country, especially those tied to high-tech industries, suffered reduced productivity due to absent (suffering from Darth Vader flu) or groggy workers on Thursday and Friday. By one estimate, fan loyalty cost U.S. employers as much as $627 million (Josie Roberts, *Pittsburgh Tribune-Review,* May 19, 2005). On the other hand, this sum is chicken feed compared to the estimated $890 million loss during NCAA March Madness: 16 days of the virtually nonstop college basketball games (James Paton, "Hooky and Hoops—March Rituals," *Rocky Mountain News,* March 19, 2005, 3C). Are these examples of a negative externality? Explain.

3. Analyze the following statement. Is garbage a positive or negative externality? Why is a market solution practical here?

   Since the turn of the twentieth century, hog farmers in New Jersey fed Philadelphia garbage to their pigs. Philadelphia saved $3 million a year and reduced its garbage mound by allowing New Jersey farmers to pick up leftover food scraps for their porcine recyclers. The city paid $1.9 million to the New Jersey pig farmers for picking up the waste each year, which was about $79 a ton. Otherwise, the city would have had to pay $125 a ton for curbside recycling of the same food waste.

4. According to the "Positive Externality: Michael Jordan Effect" application, other teams benefited financially from having one team employ him. Do such positive externalities lower social welfare? If not, why not? If so, what could the teams do to solve that problem?

5. Why is zero pollution not the best solution for society? Can there be too little pollution? Why or why not?

6. Australia is requiring that incandescent light bulbs be phased out by 2010 in favor of the more fuel-efficient compact fluorescent bulbs. Ireland's ban starts in 2009, and the United States starts phasing out today's bulbs by 2012 (Brian M. Carney, "Bye Bye, Light Bulb," *Wall Street Journal*, January 2, 2008, A10). These restrictions are expected to reduce carbon and global warming. What alternative approaches could be used to achieve the same goals? What are the advantages and disadvantages of a ban relative to the alternatives?

7. In 2002, northern Victoria, Australia, imposed a vomit tax on pubs in the Greater Shepparton area that remain open between 3:00 A.M. and 6:00 A.M. The tax is to be used to pay for cleaning up the mess left by drunks who get sick in the street. Pub owners objected that politicians assume that hotel drinkers are responsible for the mess. Discuss the pros and cons of using such a tax to deal with this externality.

8. The state of Connecticut announced that commercial fleet operators would get a tax break if they converted vehicles from ozone-producing gasoline to what the state said were cleaner fuels such as natural gas and electricity. For every dollar spent on the conversion of their fleets or building alternative fueling stations, operators could deduct 50¢ from their corporate tax. Is this approach likely to be a cost-effective way to control pollution?

*9. In the paper market example in this chapter, what are the optimal emissions fee and the optimal tax on output (assuming that only one fee or tax is applied)?

10. In Figure 18.2, the government may optimally regulate the paper market using a tax on output. A technological change drives down the private marginal cost of production. Discuss the welfare implications if the output tax is unchanged.

11. Suppose that the only way to reduce pollution from paper production is to reduce output. The government imposes a tax equal to the marginal harm from the pollution on the monopoly producer. Show that the tax may raise welfare.

*12. Which allocation of property rights leads to the highest possible welfare level if firms cannot bargain with each other in Table 18.2?

13. To the dismay of business travelers, airlines now discretely cater to families with young children who fly in first class (Katherine Rosman, "Frequent Criers," *Wall Street Journal,* May 20, 2005, W1). Suppose the family's value is $4,500 from traveling in first class and $1,500 from traveling in coach. The total price of first-class tickets for the family is $4,000. Thus, the family's net value of traveling in first class is $500 = $4,500 – $4,000. Because the total price of coach tickets for the family is $1,200, the family's net value of traveling in coach is $300 = $1,500 – $1,200. A seasoned and weary business traveler who prefers to travel first class observes that the family is about to purchase first-class tickets. The business traveler quickly considers whether to offer to pay the family to fly in coach instead.

   a. Suppose that the business traveler knows the value that the family places on coach and first-class travel. What is the minimum price the traveler can offer the family not to travel in first class?

   b. Suppose the business traveler values peace and quiet at $600. Will the business traveler and family reach a mutually agreeable price for the family to move to coach?

   c. If instead the business traveler values peace and quiet at $200, can the business traveler and family reach a mutually agreeable price for the family to move to coach? W

14. Are heavily used bridges, such as the Brooklyn Bridge and the Golden Gate Bridge, commons? If so, what can be done to mitigate externality problems?

15. To prevent overfishing, could one set a tax on fish or on boats? Explain and illustrate with a graph.

16. Are broadcast television and cable television public goods? Is exclusion possible? If either is a public good, why is it privately provided?

17. Do publishers sell the optimal number of intermediate microeconomics textbooks? Discuss in terms of public goods, rivalry, and exclusion.

18. Guards patrolling a mall protect the mall's two stores. The television store's demand curve for guards is strictly greater at all prices than that of the ice-cream parlor. The marginal cost of a guard is $10 per hour. Use a diagram to show the equilibrium, and compare that to the socially optimal equilibrium. Now suppose that the mall's owner will provide a $$s$ per hour subsidy per guard. Show in your graph the optimal s that leads to the socially optimal outcome for the two stores.

19. Vaccinations help protect the unvaccinated from disease. Boulier et al. (2007) find that the marginal externality effect can be greater than one case of illness prevented among the unvaccinated. Is vaccination a public good? If so, what might the government do to protect society optimally?

20. You and your roommate have a stack of dirty dishes in the sink. Either of you would wash the dishes if the decision were up to you; however, neither will do it in the expectation (hope?) that the other will deal with the mess. Explain how this example illustrates the problem of public goods and free riding.

21. Under federal laws, firms in many agricultural industries can solve their public goods problems by forcing all industry members to contribute to collective activities if the majority agree. Under the Beef Promotion and Research Act, all beef producers must pay a $1-per-head fee on cattle sold in the United States. The $80 million thus raised finances research, education programs on mad cow disease, and collective advertising campaigns: "Beef: It's what's for dinner." Some farmers sued to end this program, arguing that they shouldn't have to pay for ads with which they disagree. In 2005, the U.S. Supreme Court rejected their argument, allowing cattlemen to continue this approach to solving their public goods challenge (Gina Holland, "Top Court Considers Challenge to Beef Ads," San Francisco Chronicle, December 9, 2004, C1, C4; **www.extension.iastate.edu/agdm/articles/mceowen/McEowJuly05.htm**). Supporters of collective advertising estimate that producers receive $5.67 in additional marginal revenue for every dollar they contribute. Is the industry advertising (see Chapter 12) optimally? Explain your answer. (*Hint*: Is there free riding?)

PROBLEMS

22. Universal Studios and Legoland California, among other theme parks, sell day passes that include line-cutting privileges for about twice the price of regular admission. Those who do not purchase the line-cutting privileges, however, are negatively affected by those who do. Perhaps your school can institute a similar policy. Suppose, for example, that Alan, Ben, and Clara are the only students who want to speak with Professor X during her office hours. All three show up at Professor X's door at the same time and must decide who goes first, second, and third. Alan's value of being first in line is $12, second is $5, and third is $0. Ben's values are $6, $3, and $0. Clara's values are $3, $2, and $0. Being clever, the three design a game to determine the order in which they speak with Professor X. The game has prices for the first two spaces in line: $6 for being first and $2 for being second. They decide to give the proceeds to Professor X. With these prices in place, each person announces, simultaneously with the others, a place in line. If only one person announces a given slot, that person receives the slot. If two or three announce the same slot, then these two or three are randomly assigned, with equal probability, to the desired slot and the unannounced slot(s), each paying the price of his or her randomly assigned slot.
   a. What is the Nash equilibrium of this game? Who purchases the right to be first?
   b. What is the marginal external cost of the purchase?
   c. Are the prices of the line-cutting privileges similar to a tax on the negative externality of line cutting? Explain.
   d. What is the sum of each person's value on his or her place in line in the Nash equilibrium? Is there any other line order with a greater sum of values? Explain. W

*23. Using the numerical example in Appendix 18A, determine the social optimum if the marginal harm of gunk is MC_g = $84 (instead of Equation 18A.3). Is there a shortcut that would allow you to solve this problem without algebra?

24. Let $H = \bar{G} - G$ be the amount that gunk, G, is reduced from the competitive level, $\bar{G}$. The benefit of reducing gunk is $B(H) = AH^{\alpha}$. The cost is $C(H) = H^{\beta}$. If the benefit is increasing but at a diminishing rate in H, and the cost is rising at an increasing rate, what are the possible ranges of values for A, α, and B?

25. In the model in Problem 24, use calculus to determine the optimal level of H. C

26. Using the numerical example of the model of the paper market in Appendix 18A, derive the equations for the benefit, cost, marginal benefit, and marginal cost curves in Figure 18.3.

27. Suppose that the inverse demand curve for paper is $p = 200 - Q$, the private marginal cost (unregulated competitive market supply) is $MC^p = 80 + Q$, and the marginal harm from gunk is $MC^g = Q$.
   a. What is the unregulated competitive equilibrium?
   b. What is the social optimum? What specific tax (per unit of output or gunk) results in the social optimum?
   c. What is the unregulated monopoly equilibrium?
   d. How would you optimally regulate the monopoly? What is the resulting equilibrium?

28. There are 240 automobile drivers per minute who are considering using the E-Z Pass lanes of the Interstate 78 bridge over the Delaware River that connects Easton, Pennsylvania and Phillipsburg, New Jersey. With that many autos, and a 5 mph speed restriction through the E-Z Pass sensors, there is congestion. We can divide the drivers of these cars into four groups: A, B, C, and D. Each group has 60 drivers. Each driver in Group i has the following value of crossing the bridge: v_i if 60 or fewer autos cross, $v_i - 1$ if between 61 and 120 autos cross, $v_i - 2$ if between 121 and 180 cross, and $v_i - 3$ if more than 180 cross. Suppose that $v_A = \$4$, $v_B = \$3$, $v_C = \$2$, and $v_D = \$1$. The marginal cost of crossing the bridge, not including the marginal cost of congestion, is zero.
   a. If the price of crossing equals a driver's marginal private cost—the price in a competitive market—how many cars per minute will cross? Which groups will cross?
   b. In the social optimum, which groups of drivers will cross? That is, which collection of groups crossing will maximize the sum of the drivers' utilities?

29. Two tenants of a mall are protected by the guard service, q. The number of guards per hour demanded by the television store is $q_1 = a_1 + b_1p$, where p is the price of one hour of guard services. The ice-cream store's demand is $q_2 = a_2 + b_2p$. What is the social demand for this service?

30. Anna and Bess are assigned to write a joint paper within a 24 hour period about the Pareto optimal provision of public goods. Let t_A denote the number of hours that Anna contributes to the project and t_B the number of hours that Bess contributes. The numeric grade that Anna and Bess earn is a function, 23 ln $(t_A + t_B)$, of the total number of hours that they contribute to the project. If Anna contributes t_A, then she has $(24 - t_A)$ hours in the day for leisure. Anna's utility function is $U_A = 23 \ln (t_A + t_B) + \ln (24 - t_A)$; and Bess's utility function is $U_B = 23 \ln (t_A + t_B) + \ln (24 - t_B)$. If they choose the hours to contribute simultaneously and independently, what is the Nash equilibrium number of hours that each will provide? What is the number of hours each should contribute to the project that maximizes the sum of their utilities?

CROSS-CHAPTER ANALYSIS

Emissions Fees Versus Standards Under Uncertainty

Frequently, European governments tax emissions or inputs, whereas the U.S. government sets emission standards (Chapter 18). Is it better to tax emissions or to set standards? In Chapter 18, we saw that the government can induce a firm to produce efficiently if it sets either a fee or a standard optimally. However, if the government is uncertain (Chapter 17) about the cost of pollution abatement, which approach produces more welfare depends on the shape of the marginal benefit and marginal cost curves for abating pollution.

Background

Cars that get more miles to the gallon tend to produce less pollution per mile driven. The U.S. government has mandated fuel-efficiency standard (Corporate Average Fuel Economy, CAFE) requiring that a manufacturer's cars must average 35 miles per gallon by 2020, up from 27.5 in 2008. Europe and Japan rarely set fuel-economy standards but impose gasoline taxes that are five to ten times as high as U.S. federal and state taxes combined (Chapter 3).

European countries impose environmental taxes to reduce carbon dioxide, sulfur dioxide, and other air pollutants, and some of these countries use taxes to control landfills. The taxes are returned to the economy by lowering personal income or social security taxes. Although the U.S. federal government occasionally takes an emission fee–like approach to control sulfur dioxide by using markets (Chapter 18), it generally sets standards on emissions and landfills.

Task

The following figure shows the government's knowledge about the shape and location of the marginal benefit, MB, curve of reducing gunk, a pollutant, and the marginal cost of abatement of gunk (Chapter 17). The government has no uncertainty about the MB curve. It believes that it is equally likely that the true marginal cost of abatement curve is MC^1 or MC^2.

First, suppose that the government uses its expected marginal cost of abatement curve, shown in the figure, to set an emission standard, s, on emissions (gunk) or an

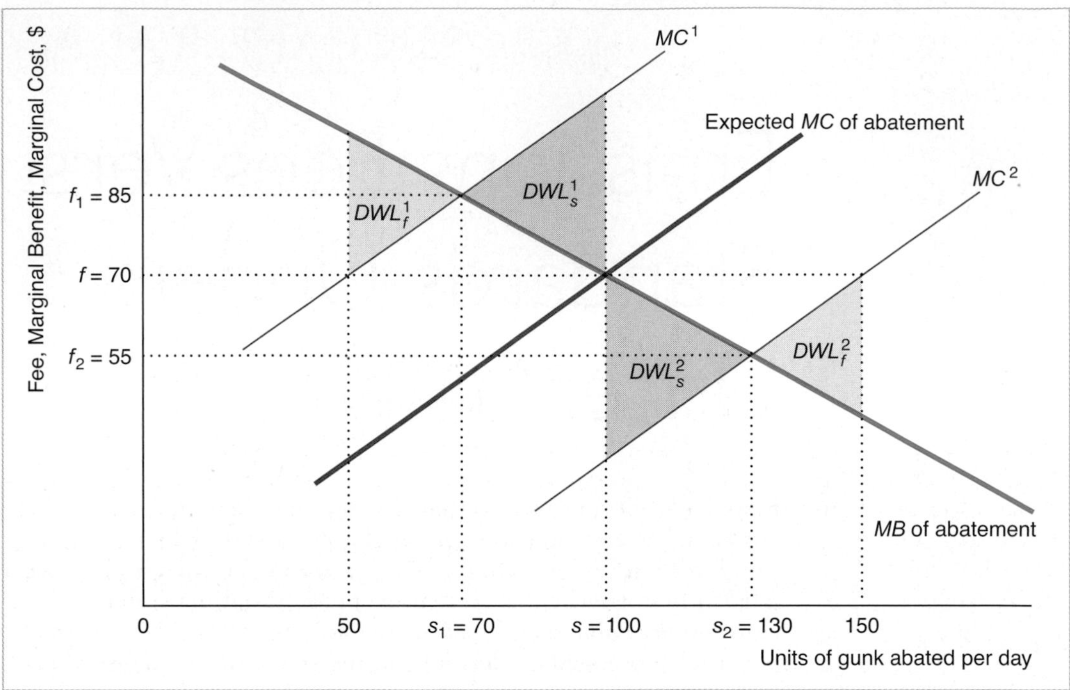

emissions fee, f per unit. What s and f will it choose? Second, should the government set a standard or a fee to maximize expected welfare, given the information in the figure?

Analysis

Using its expected marginal cost of abatement curve, the government sets an emission standard at $s = 100$ units or an emissions fee at $f = \$70$ per unit. If the true marginal cost of abatement is higher, MC^1, the optimal standard is $s_1 = 70$ and the optimal fee is $f_1 = \$85$. Thus, the government sets the emissions standard too high and the fee too low. The deadweight loss from too high an emissions standard, DWL_s^1 is greater than the deadweight loss from too low a fee, DWL_f^1.

If the true marginal cost is less than expected, MC^2, the government has set the standard too low and the fee too high. Again, the deadweight loss from the wrong standard, DWL_s^2, is greater than that from the wrong fee, DWL_f^2. Thus, given how this figure is drawn, the government should use the fee. (However, if we redraw the figure with a much steeper marginal benefit curve, the deadweight loss from the fee will be greater than that from the standard.)

Question

Answer appears at the back of the book.

1. Suppose that the government knows the marginal cost, MC, curve of reducing pollution (it is the same as the expected MC curve in the figure above) but is uncertain about the marginal benefit curve. With equal probability, it faces a relatively high or relatively low MB curve, so that its expected MB curve is the same as the one in the figure above. Should the government use an emissions fee or an emissions standard to maximize expected welfare? Explain.

Asymmetric Information

19

The buyer needs a hundred eyes, the seller not one. —George Herbert (1651)

So far we've examined models in which everyone is equally knowledgeable or equally ignorant. In the competitive model, everyone knows all relevant facts. In the uncertainty models in Chapter 17, the companies that sell insurance and the people who buy it are equally uncertain about future events. In contrast, in this chapter's models, people have **asymmetric information:** One party to a transaction knows a material fact that the other party does not. For example, the seller knows the quality of a product and the buyer does not.

asymmetric information
situation in which one party to a transaction knows a material fact that the other party does not

The more informed party may exploit the less-informed party. Such *opportunistic behavior* due to asymmetric information leads to market failures, destroying many desirable properties of competitive markets. In a competitive market in which everyone has full information, consumers can buy whatever quality good they want at its marginal cost. In contrast, when firms have information that consumers lack—when information is asymmetric—firms may sell only the lowest-quality good, the price may be above marginal cost, or other problems may occur.

If consumers do not know the quality of a good they are considering buying, some firms may try to sell them a dud at the price of a superior good. However, knowing that the chance of buying schlock is high, consumers may be unwilling to pay much for goods of unknown quality. As a result, firms that make high-quality products may not be able to sell them at prices anywhere near their cost of production. In other words, *bad products drive good ones out of the market*. The market failure is that the market for a good-quality product is reduced or eliminated, even though (knowledgeable) consumers value the high-quality product at more than the cost of producing it.

If consumers (unlike sellers) do not know how prices vary across firms, *firms may gain market power and set prices above marginal cost*. Suppose that you go to Store A to buy a television set. If you know that Store B is charging $299 for that set, you are willing to pay Store A at most $299 (or perhaps a little more to avoid having to go to Store B). *Knowledge is power*. However, if you don't know Store B's price for that set, Store A might sell you a television for much more than $299. *Ignorance costs*.

Market failures due to asymmetric information can be eliminated if consumers can inexpensively determine the quality of a product or learn the prices that various stores charge. In many markets, however, obtaining this information is prohibitively expensive.

In this chapter, we examine six main topics

1. **Problems Due to Asymmetric Information.** Informed people take advantage of uninformed people.
2. **Responses to Adverse Selection.** To reduce the harms from adverse selection—an informed person's benefiting from trading with an uninformed person who does not know about a characteristic of the informed person—government actions or contracts between involved parties may be used to prevent opportunistic behavior, or the information asymmetry may be reduced or eliminated.
3. **How Ignorance About Quality Drives Out High-Quality Goods.** If consumers cannot distinguish between good and bad products before purchase, it is possible that only bad products will be sold.
4. **Price Discrimination Due to False Beliefs About Quality.** If some consumers incorrectly think that quality varies across identical products, a firm may price discriminate.
5. **Market Power from Price Ignorance.** Consumers' ignorance about the price that each firm charges gives firms market power.
6. **Problems Arising from Ignorance When Hiring.** Attempts to eliminate information asymmetries in hiring may raise or lower social welfare.

19.1 Problems Due to Asymmetric Information

When both parties to a transaction have equally limited information, neither has an advantage over the other. If a roadside vendor sells a box of oranges to a passing motorist and neither person knows the quality of the oranges, neither has an advantage because both are operating with equal uncertainty.

In contrast, asymmetric information leads to problems of *opportunism*, whereby the informed person benefits at the expense of the person with less information. If only the vendor knows that the oranges are of low quality, the vendor may allege that the oranges are of high quality and charge a premium price for them.

adverse selection opportunism characterized by an informed person's benefiting from trading or otherwise contracting with a less-informed person who does not know about an unobserved characteristic of the informed person

The two major types of opportunistic behavior are *adverse selection* and *moral hazard*. **Adverse selection** is opportunism characterized by an informed person's benefiting from trading or otherwise contracting with a less-informed person who does not know about an *unobserved characteristic* of the informed person. For example, people who buy life insurance policies are better informed about their own health than insurance companies are. If an insurance company offers to insure people against death for ten years at a fixed rate, a disproportionately large share of unhealthy people will buy this policy. Because of this adverse selection, the insurance company will pay off on more policies than it would pay if healthy and unhealthy people bought the policy in proportion to their share in the population.

Similarly, if one firm starts offering an unusually generous maternity leave to mothers of newborn children, a disproportionate number of women planning to become mothers in the near future will apply for employment with that firm. The intention to have children is known to potential employees but not to the firm. As a result, the cost of this benefit is greater to the firm than its cost would be if the employees were a random sample of the entire population.

Adverse selection creates a market failure by reducing the size of a market or eliminating it, thereby preventing desirable transactions. Insurance companies have to charge higher rates for insurance due to adverse selection or choose not to offer insurance at all. Very few older people, regardless of their health, buy term life insurance because the rates are extremely high as a result of adverse selection. A parental leave benefit's higher cost due to adverse selection may discourage firms from offering the benefit, a decision that hurts both employees who are new parents (because they lose the benefit) and the firm (because it cannot use a benefit that would otherwise allow it to pay a lower wage).

moral hazard
opportunism characterized by an informed person's taking advantage of a less-informed person through an unobserved action

Moral hazard is opportunism characterized by an informed person's taking advantage of a less-informed person through an *unobserved action*. An employee may *shirk*—fail to fulfill job responsibilities—if not monitored by the employer. Similarly, insured people tend to take unobserved actions—engage in risky behaviors—that increase the probability of large claims against insurance companies, or they fail to take reasonable precautions that would reduce the likelihood of such claims. An insured homeowner may fail to remove fire hazards such as piles of old newspapers. Some insured motorists drive more recklessly than they would without insurance. Moral hazards such as shirking, failure to take care, and reckless behavior reduce output or increase accidents, which are market failures that harm society.

The distinction between adverse selection and moral hazard—between unobserved characteristics and unobserved actions—is not always simple. A life insurance company may face unusually high risks if it insures George and Marge, who, unknown to the company, skydive. George will skydive whether or not he has life insurance. Knowing the risks of skydiving, he's more likely to buy life insurance than other, similar people are. His unobserved characteristic—his love of plunging toward the earth at high speed—leads to adverse selection. Marge will skydive only if she has life insurance. Her unobserved action is a moral hazard for the insurance company.

See Questions 1 and 2 and Problem 17.

This chapter focuses on adverse selection and unobserved characteristics. We identify the problems that arise from adverse selection and discuss how they can sometimes be solved. Chapter 20 concentrates on moral hazard problems due to unobserved actions and on the use of contracts to deal with them.

19.2 Responses to Adverse Selection

The two main methods for solving adverse selection problems are to *restrict opportunistic behavior* and to *equalize information*. Responses to adverse selection problems increase welfare in some markets, but they may do more harm than good in others.

Controlling Opportunistic Behavior Through Universal Coverage

Adverse selection can be prevented if informed people have no choice. For example, a government can avoid adverse selection by providing insurance to everyone or by mandating that everyone buy insurance. Many states require that every driver carry auto insurance. They thereby reduce the adverse selection that would arise from having a disproportionate number of bad drivers buy insurance.

Similarly, firms often provide mandatory health insurance to all employees as a benefit, rather than paying a higher wage and letting employees decide whether to buy such insurance on their own. By doing so, firms reduce adverse selection problems for their insurance carriers: Both healthy and unhealthy people are covered. As a result, firms can buy medical insurance for their workers at a lower cost per person than workers could obtain on their own (because relatively more unhealthy individuals buy insurance).

Equalizing Information

screening
an action taken by an uninformed person to determine the information possessed by informed people

signaling
an action taken by an informed person to send information to an uninformed person

Either informed or uninformed parties can eliminate information asymmetries. **Screening** is an action taken by an uninformed person to determine the information possessed by informed people. A buyer may test-drive (screen) several used cars to determine which one starts and handles the best. **Signaling** is an action taken by an informed person to send information to a less-informed person. A firm may send a signal—such as widely distributing a favorable report on its product by an independent testing agency—to try to convince buyers that its product is of high quality. In some markets, government agencies or nonprofit organizations such as Consumers Union also provide consumers with information.

Screening. Uninformed people may try to eliminate their disadvantage by screening to gather information on the hidden characteristics of informed people. If the originally uninformed people obtain better information, they may refuse to sign a contract or insist on changes in contract clauses or in the price of a good.

"Good—very good! You qualify for our dental plan with no deductible whatsoever!"

Insurance companies try to reduce adverse selection problems by learning the health history of their potential customers—for example, by requiring medical exams. A life insurance company uses such information to better estimate the probability that it will have to pay off on a policy. The firm can then decide not to insure high-risk individuals or can charge high-risk people a higher premium as compensation for the extra risk.

It is costly to collect information on how healthy a person is and on whether that individual has dangerous habits (such as smoking and drinking). As a result, insurance companies collect information only up to the point at which the marginal benefit from extra information equals the marginal cost of obtaining it. Over time, insurance companies have increasingly concluded that it pays to collect information about whether individuals exercise, have a family history of dying young, or engage in potentially life-threatening activities. If individuals but not insurance companies know about these characteristics, individuals can better predict whether they'll die young, and adverse selection occurs.

APPLICATION
Risky Hobbies

To reduce the risk of adverse selection, life insurance companies no longer rely solely on information about age and general health in determining risk. They now also look into individuals' smoking and drinking habits and occupations and even their hobbies. Indeed, some hobbies or activities greatly affect the probability that an individual will die from an accident. Various sports add \$100 to \$2,500 in annual premiums for each \$100,000 of life insurance.

Steve Potter, a 40-year-old managing director at an executive recruiting firm, prepared to climb Mount Everest by buying a \$2 million life insurance policy. His firm took out an additional \$1 million on his life. Although Prudential Insurance Company of America would offer a typical healthy 40-year-old a \$1 million policy for \$1,000, the company wanted \$6,000 to cover the adventurous Mr. Potter.

Signaling. Signaling is used primarily by informed parties to try to eliminate adverse selection. If a buyer cannot tell a high-quality good or service from one of low quality, the buyer is unwilling to pay top dollar for the better good. Informed sellers of better goods and services may signal to potential buyers that their products are of high quality.

Likewise, potential employees use a variety of signals to convince firms of their abilities. For a job interview, serious candidates arrive on time, dress appropriately, don't chew gum, document their training and achievements, and show that they worked for long periods at other firms. Similarly, an applicant for life insurance could have a physical examination and then present an insurance company with a written statement from the doctor to signal good health.

Only people who believe that they can show that they are better than others want to send a signal. Moreover, signaling solves an information problem only if the signals are accurate. For example, if it is easy for people to find an unscrupulous doctor who will report falsely that they are in good health, insurance companies won't rely on such signals. Here screening may work better, and the insurance firms may require that potential customers go to a designated doctor for a checkup.

See Questions 3–5.

19.3 How Ignorance About Quality Drives Out High-Quality Goods

We now examine markets in which asymmetric information causes major problems due to adverse selection. In most of these situations, buyers know less than sellers.

Consumers often have trouble determining the quality of goods and services. Most people don't know how to judge the abilities of a professional such as a doctor, a lawyer, a plumber, an electrician, or an economist. Many of us have no reliable information about whether the processed foods we eat are safe. Is it safer to fly in a Boeing 747 than in a McDonnell Douglas DC-10?

Consumer ignorance about quality leads to a less-efficient use of resources than would occur if everyone had perfect information. Here we first show how limited consumer information leads to adverse selection. We demonstrate that adverse selection occurs whether or not a seller can alter the quality of the good. We then discuss how to ameliorate—though not necessarily eliminate—the adverse selection problem.

Lemons Market with Fixed Quality

Anagram for General Motors: or great lemons

When buyers cannot judge a product's quality before purchasing it, low-quality products—*lemons*—may drive high-quality products out of the market (Akerlof, 1970). This situation is common in used-car markets: Owners of lemons are more likely to sell their cars, leading to adverse selection.

Cars that appear to be identical on the outside often differ substantially in the number of repairs they will need. Some cars—*lemons*—are cursed. They have a variety of insidious problems that become apparent to the owner only after the car has been driven for a while. In contrast, the seller of a used car knows from experience whether the car is a lemon. We assume that the seller cannot alter the quality of the used car—at least not practically.

Suppose that there are many potential buyers for used cars. All are willing to pay $1,000 for a lemon and $2,000 for a good used car: The demand curve for lemons, D^L, is horizontal at $1,000 in panel a of Figure 19.1, and the demand curve for good cars, D^G, is horizontal at $2,000 in panel b.

Although the number of potential buyers is virtually unlimited, only 1,000 owners of lemons and 1,000 owners of good cars are willing to sell. The *reservation price* of owners of lemons—the lowest price at which they will sell their cars—is $750. Consequently, the supply curve for lemons, S^L in panel a, is horizontal at $750 up to 1,000 cars, where it becomes vertical (no more cars are for sale at any price). The reservation price of owners of high-quality used cars is v, which is less than $2,000. Panel b shows two possible values of v. If $v = \$1,250$, the supply curve for good cars, S^1, is horizontal at $1,250 up to 1,000 cars and then becomes vertical. If $v = \$1,750$, the supply curve is S^2.

Symmetric Information. If both sellers and buyers know the quality of all the used cars before any sales take place, all the cars are sold, and good cars sell for more than lemons. In panel a of Figure 19.1, the intersection of the lemons demand curve D^L and the lemons supply curve S^L determines the equilibrium at e in the lemons market, where 1,000 lemons sell for $1,000 each. Regardless of whether the supply curve for good cars is S^1 or S^2 in panel b, the equilibrium in the good-car market is E, where 1,000 good cars sell for $2,000 each.

This market is efficient because the goods go to the people who value them the most. All current owners, who value the cars less than the potential buyers, sell their cars.

Figure 19.1 Markets for Lemons and Good Cars.

If everyone has full information, the equilibrium in the lemons market is e (1,000 cars sold for $1,000 each), and the equilibrium in the good-car market is E (1,000 cars sold for $2,000 each). If buyers can't tell quality before buying but assume that equal numbers of the two types of cars are for sale, their demand in both markets is D^*, which is horizontal at $1,500. If the good car owners' reservation price is $1,250, the supply curve for good cars is S^1, and 1,000 good cars (point F) and 1,000 lemons (point f) sell for $1,500 each. If their reservation price is $1,750, the supply curve is S^2. No good cars are sold; 1,000 lemons sell for $1,000 each (point e).

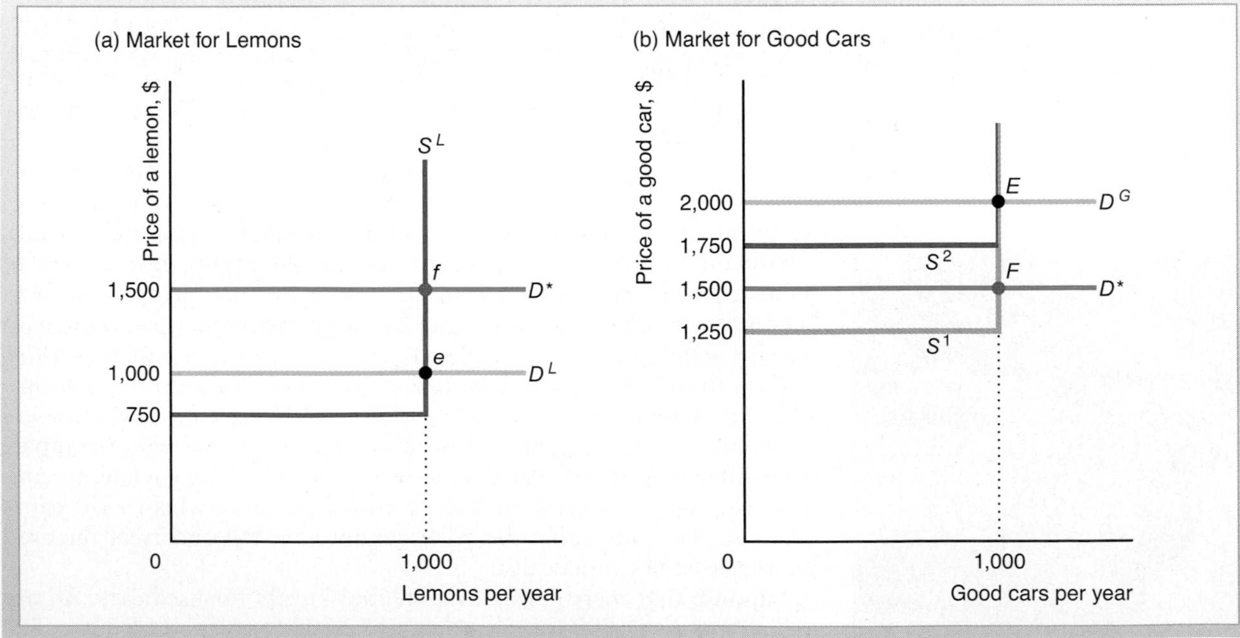

More generally, all buyers and sellers may have symmetric information by being equally informed or equally uninformed. *All the cars are sold if everyone has the same information.* It does not matter whether they all have full information or all lack information—it's the equality of information that matters. However, *the amount of information they have affects the price at which the cars sell.* With full information, good cars sell for \$2,000 and lemons for \$1,000.

If no one can tell a lemon from a good car at the time of purchase, both types of cars sell for the same price. Suppose that everyone is risk neutral (Chapter 17) and no one can identify the lemons: Buyers *and* sellers are equally ignorant. A buyer has an equal chance of buying a lemon or a good car. The expected value (Chapter 17) of a used car is

$$\$1,500 = \left(\tfrac{1}{2} \times \$1,000\right) + \left(\tfrac{1}{2} \times \$2,000\right).$$

A risk-neutral buyer would pay \$1,500 for a car of unknown quality. Because sellers cannot distinguish between the cars either, sellers accept this amount and sell all the cars.[1] Thus, this market is efficient because the cars go to people who value them more than their original owners.

Sellers of good-quality cars are implicitly subsidizing sellers of lemons. If only lemons were sold, they would sell for \$1,000. The presence of good-quality cars raises the price received by sellers of lemons. Similarly, if only good cars were sold, their owners would obtain \$2,000. The presence of lemons lowers the price that sellers of good cars receive.

Asymmetric Information. If sellers know the quality but buyers do not, this market may be inefficient: The better-quality cars may not be sold even though buyers value good cars more than sellers do. The equilibrium in this market depends on whether the value that the owners of good cars place on their cars, v, is greater or less than the expected value of buyers, \$1,500. *There are two possible equilibria: All cars sell at the average price, or only lemons sell for a price equal to the value that buyers place on lemons.*

Initially, we assume that the sellers of good cars value their cars at $v = \$1,250$, which is less than the buyers' expected value of the cars, so that transactions can occur. The equilibrium in the good-car market is determined by the intersection of S^1 and D^* at F, where 1,000 good cars sell at \$1,500. Similarly, owners of lemons, who value their cars at only \$750, are happy to sell them for \$1,500 each. The new equilibrium in the lemons market is f.

Thus, all cars sell at the same price. Consequently, *asymmetric information does not cause an efficiency problem, but it does have equity implications.* Sellers of lemons benefit and sellers of good cars suffer from consumers' inability to distinguish quality. Consumers who buy the good cars get a bargain, and buyers of lemons are left with a sour taste in their mouths.

Now suppose that the sellers of good cars place a value of $v = \$1,750$ on their cars and thus are unwilling to sell them for \$1,500. As a result, the *lemons drive good cars out of the market.* Buyers realize that, at any price less than \$1,750, they can buy only lemons. Consequently, in equilibrium, the 1,000 lemons sell for the expected (and actual) price of \$1,000, and no good cars change hands. This equilibrium is inefficient because high-quality cars remain in the hands of people who value them less than potential buyers do.

---

[1]Risk-neutral sellers place an expected value of $\left(\tfrac{1}{2} \times \$750\right) + \tfrac{1}{2}v = \$375 + \tfrac{1}{2}v < \$1,375$ (because $v < \$2,000$) on a car of unknown quality, so they are willing to sell their cars for \$1,500.

In summary, if buyers have less information about product quality than sellers do, the result might be a lemons problem in which high-quality cars do not sell even though potential buyers value the cars more than their current owners do. If so, the asymmetric information causes a competitive market to lose its desirable efficiency and welfare properties. The lemons problem does not occur if the information is symmetric. If buyers and sellers of used cars know the quality of the cars, each car sells for its true value in a perfectly competitive market. If, as with new cars, neither buyers nor sellers can identify lemons, both good cars and lemons sell at a price equal to the expected value rather than at their (unknown) true values.

See Questions 6–8 and Problems 18 and 19.

Solved Problem 19.1

Suppose that everyone in our used-car example is risk neutral, potential car buyers value lemons at $1,000 and good used cars at $2,000, the reservation price of lemon owners is $750, and the reservation price of owners of high-quality used cars is $1,750. The share of current owners who have lemons is θ [in our previous example, the share was $\theta = \frac{1}{2} = 1{,}000/(1{,}000 + 1{,}000)$]. For what values of θ do all the potential sellers sell their used cars? Describe the equilibrium.

Answer

1. *Determine how much buyers are willing to pay if all cars are sold.* Because buyers are risk neutral, if they believe that the probability of getting a lemon is θ, the most they are willing to pay for a car of unknown quality is

$$p = [\$2{,}000 \times (1 - \theta)] + (\$1{,}000 \times \theta) = \$2{,}000 - (\$1{,}000 \times \theta). \quad (19.1)$$

For example, $p = \$1{,}500$ if $\theta = \frac{1}{2}$ and $p = \$1{,}750$ if $\theta = \frac{1}{4}$.

2. *Solve for the values of* θ *such that all the cars are sold, and describe the equilibrium.* All owners will sell if the market price equals or exceeds their reservation price, $1,750. Using Equation 19.1, we know that the market (equilibrium) price is $1,750 or more if a quarter or fewer of the used cars are lemons, $\theta \le \frac{1}{4}$. Thus, for $\theta \le \frac{1}{4}$, all the cars are sold at the price given in Equation 19.1.

Lemons Market with Variable Quality

Many firms can vary the quality of their products. If consumers cannot identify high-quality goods before purchase, they pay the same for all goods regardless of quality. Because the price that firms receive for top-quality goods is the same as that for schlock, they do not produce top-quality goods. Such an outcome is inefficient if consumers are willing to pay sufficiently more for top-quality goods.

This unwillingness to produce high-quality products is due to an externality: *A firm does not completely capture the benefits from raising the quality of its product.* By selling a better product than what other firms offer, a seller raises the average quality in the market, so buyers are willing to pay more for all products. As a result, the high-quality seller shares the benefits from its high-quality product with sellers of low-quality products by raising the average price to all. *The social value of raising the quality*, as reflected by the increased revenues shared by all firms, *is greater than the private value*, which is only the higher revenue received by the firm with the good product.

To illustrate, suppose that it costs $10 to produce a low-quality book bag and $20 to produce a high-quality bag, consumers cannot distinguish between the products before purchase, there are no repeat purchases, and consumers value the bags at their cost of production. The five firms in the market produce 100 bags each. A firm produces only high-quality or only low-quality bags.

If all five firms make a low-quality bag, consumers pay \$10 per bag. If one firm makes a high-quality bag and all the others make low-quality bags, the expected value per bag to consumers is

$$\$12 = \left(\$10 \times \tfrac{4}{5}\right) + \left(\$20 \times \tfrac{1}{5}\right).$$

Thus, if one firm raises the quality of its product, all firms benefit because the bags sell for \$12 instead of \$10. The high-quality firm receives only a fraction of the total benefit from raising quality. It gets \$2 extra per high-quality bag sold, which is less than the extra \$10 it costs to make the better bag. The other \$8 is shared by the other firms. Because the high-quality firm incurs all the expenses of raising quality, \$10 extra per bag, and reaps only a fraction, \$2, of the benefits, it opts not to produce the high-quality bags. Therefore, *due to asymmetric information, the firms do not produce high-quality goods even though consumers are willing to pay for the extra quality.*

Limiting Lemons

In some markets, it is possible to avoid problems stemming from consumer ignorance. Laws might provide protection against being sold a lemon, consumers might screen by collecting the information themselves, the government or another third party might supply reliable information, or sellers might send credible signals.

Laws to Prevent Opportunism. Product liability laws protect consumers from being stuck with nonfunctional or dangerous products. Moreover, many state supreme courts have concluded that products are sold with an implicit understanding that they will safely perform their intended function. If they do not, consumers can sue the seller even in the absence of product liability laws. If consumers can rely on explicit or implicit product liability laws to force a manufacturer to make good on defective products, they need not worry about adverse selection.

An inherent problem with legal recourse, however, is that the transaction costs of going to court are very high. See **www.myeconlab.com/perloff**, Chapter 19, "Recycling Lemons," on laws in various countries to protect consumers with respect to cars that are lemons.

Consumer Screening. Consumers can avoid the lemons problem if they can obtain reliable information about quality (screen). When a consumer's cost of securing information is less than the private benefits, consumers obtain the information and markets function smoothly. However, if the cost exceeds the benefit, they do not gather the information and the market is inefficient. Consumers buy information from experts or infer product quality from sellers' reputations.

For many goods, consumers can buy reliable information from *objective experts*. For example, you can pay to have a mechanic appraise a used car. If the mechanic can reliably determine whether the car is a lemon, the information asymmetry is eliminated.

In some markets, consumers learn of a firm's *reputation* from other consumers or from observation. Consumers can avoid the adverse selection problem by buying only from firms that have reputations for providing high-quality goods. Consumers know that a used-car firm that expects repeat purchases has a strong incentive not to sell defective products.

Generally, in markets in which the same consumers and firms trade regularly, a reputation is easy to establish. In markets in which consumers buy a good only once, such as in tourist areas, firms cannot establish reputations as easily.

Third-Party Comparisons. Some nonprofit organizations, such as consumer groups, and for-profit firms publish expert comparisons of brands. To the degree that this information is credible, it may reduce adverse selection by enabling consumers to avoid buying low-quality goods.

If an outside organization is to provide believable information, it must convince consumers that it is trustworthy and is not deceiving them. Consumers Union, which publishes the product evaluation guide *Consumer Reports*, tries to establish its trustworthiness by refusing to accept advertising or other payments from firms.

Unfortunately, expert information is undersupplied because information is a *public good* (nonrivalrous and only sometimes exclusive—see Chapter 18). Consumers Union does not capture the full value of its information through sales of *Consumer Reports* because buyers lend their copies to friends, libraries stock the magazine, and newspapers report on its findings. As a result, Consumers Union conducts less research than is socially optimal.

See Question 9.

standard
a metric or scale for evaluating the quality of a particular product

certification
a report that a particular product meets or exceeds a given *standard* level

Standards and Certification. The government, consumer groups, industry groups, and others provide information based on a **standard**: a metric or scale for evaluating the quality of a particular product. For example, the R-value of insulation—a standard—tells how effectively insulation works. Consumers learn of a brand's quality through **certification**: a report that a particular product meets or exceeds a given standard level.

Many industry groups set their own standards and get an outside group or firm, such as Underwriters Laboratories (UL) or Factory Mutual Engineering Corporation (FMEC), to certify that their products meet specified standard levels. For example, by setting standards for the size of the thread on a screw, we ensure that screws work in products regardless of brand.

When standard and certification programs inexpensively and completely inform consumers about the relative quality of all goods in a market and do not restrict the goods available, the programs are socially desirable. Some of these programs have harmful effects, however.

Standard and certification programs that provide degraded information, for instance, may mislead consumers. Many standards use only a high- versus low-quality rating even though quality varies continuously. Such standards encourage the manufacture of products that have either the lowest possible quality (and cost of production) or the minimum quality level necessary to obtain the top rating.

If standard and certification programs restrict salable goods and services to those that are certified, such programs may also have anticompetitive effects. Many governments license only professionals and craftspeople who meet some minimum standards. People without a license are not allowed to practice their profession or craft. In most states, dozens, if not hundreds, of categories of professionals, craftspeople, and others are licensed, including public school teachers, electricians, plumbers, dentists, psychologists, contractors, and beauticians.

The restrictions raise the average quality in the industry by eliminating low-quality goods and services. They drive up prices to consumers for two reasons. First, the number of people providing services is reduced because the restrictions eliminate some potential suppliers. Second, consumers are unable to obtain lower-quality and less-expensive goods or services. As a result, welfare may go up or down, depending on whether the increased-quality effect or the higher-price effect dominates.

Whether such restrictions can be set properly and cost-effectively by government agencies is widely debated.

Moreover, licensing and mandatory standards and certification are often used for anticompetitive purposes such as erecting entry barriers to new firms and products. Doctors, lawyers, electricians, and other professionals establish their own licensing standards under government auspices. Frequently, these groups set standards that prevent entry of professionals from other states or those who have just finished their education so as to keep the wages of currently licensed professionals high. Such licensing is socially harmful because it excludes qualified professionals and raises consumers' costs. (Unfortunately, economists have not been clever enough to get their profession licensed so that they can act anticompetitively to limit supply and raise their earnings.)

APPLICATION

Finding a Good Surgeon

No one wants to be operated on by an incompetent surgeon. How can you ensure your own safety? Possibilities include consumer screening, third-party comparisons, and government certification.

Experience is a good signal of a surgeon's competence. When an experienced surgeon performs radical prostate surgery the prognosis is much better than with less-experienced surgeons. A 2007 study found that those patients with surgeons who had performed more than 250 prostate operations had a probability of recurrence within 5 years of 10%, compared to 17.9% for a surgeon who had operated only 10 times. Thus, a patient should screen potential surgeons by asking about their experience.

Many third-party Web sites rank physicians, such as **www.healthgrades.com**, **www.mdnationwide.org/surgeon_quality.htm**, **www.ratemds.com**. However, most of these appear to do little more than report unscientific surveys of patients.

More reliable government surgeon report cards may influence consumers directly or through the referring physician. New York, Pennsylvania, New Jersey, and other states issue report cards on coronary artery bypass graft surgeons. Their grading systems adjust for the difficulty of the cases facing a surgeon—hopefully not preventing surgeons from avoiding difficult cases. Although not all patients and referring cardiologists pay attention to these report cards, hospitals do. The grading apparently has contributed to reducing fatalities during operations. Improvement may stem from weeding out incompetent doctors and encouraging others to improve the quality of their care by emulating the techniques of more successful surgeons and hospitals. For example, more than 20% of the surgeons who scored in the bottom quarter of the New York state grades stopped practicing cardiac bypass surgery in the state within two years after the report was issued. Only 5% of surgeons who scored in the top quarter, and fewer than 7% of those with middling grades, dropped out.

Signaling by Firms. Producers of high-quality goods often try to signal to consumers that their products are of better quality than those of their rivals. If consumers believe their signals, these firms can charge higher prices for their goods. But if the signals are to be effective, they must be credible.

Firms use brand names as a signal of quality. For example, some farms brand their produce, while rivals sell their produce without labels. Shoppers may rely on this signal and choose only fruits and vegetables with brand labels. Presumably, a firm uses a brand name to enable buyers to identify its product only if the item's quality is better than that of a typical unbranded product.

Some firms provide guarantees or warranties as signals to convince consumers that their products are of high quality. Consumer durables such as cars and refrigerators commonly come with guarantees or warranties. Virtually all new cars have warranties. Moreover, one-third of used cars purchased from dealers include warranties (Genesove, 1993).

Signals solve the adverse selection problem only when consumers view them as credible (only high-quality firms find their use profitable). Smart consumers may place little confidence in unsubstantiated claims by firms. Would you believe that a used car runs well just because an ad tells you so? Legally enforceable guarantees and warranties are more credible than advertising alone.

Signaling will not solve an adverse selection problem if it is unprofitable for high-quality firms to signal or if both high- and low-quality firms send the same signal, so that the signal is worthless to consumers. For example, both low-quality and high-quality fruit and vegetable firms can use trademarks in tourist areas, where there are few repeat purchases. Similarly, all firms may provide guarantees for inexpensive goods, for which transaction costs are usually too high for consumers to use guarantees. (See **www.myeconlab.com/perloff**, Chapter 19, "Wholesale Market for Cherries," for an example of how firms use sorting of their products to signal quality.)

APPLICATION

Adverse Selection on eBay

When consumers buy over the Internet, they cannot directly observe quality, and shady sellers may misrepresent quality. In the worse-case lemons-market scenario, low-quality goods drive out high-quality ones. This adverse selection problem may be reduced or eliminated if warranties, brand names, and other means of establishing a reputation lower consumers' concerns about quality.

Philatelists can buy stamps at auctions on eBay or at a specialty stamps auction site, Michael Rogers, Inc. (MR). On eBay, a buyer has only the seller's description, possibly a photo, and the seller's eBay reputation, which is an index of the satisfaction of the previous trading partners. In contrast, MR takes possession of all stamps, inspects them, and provides standardized descriptions and photographic images. It also offers a 14-day refund guarantee on items if users were misled by inaccurate descriptions in their auction catalogs. Thus, bidders at MR should have very little uncertainty about quality.

Dewan and Hsu (2004) compared prices on particular stamps at the two sites. They concluded that adverse selection fears reduce eBay prices by 10% to 15% of the value of the goods relative to MR. Without eBay's reputation index, the adverse selection discount would be greater. On average, a 10% increase in seller rating is associated with a 0.44% increase in auction price.

19.4 Price Discrimination Due to False Beliefs About Quality

We've seen that bad products can drive out good products if consumers cannot distinguish lemons from good-quality products at the time of purchase. The market outcome also changes if consumers falsely believe that identical products differ in quality. Consumers pay more for a product that they believe is of higher quality.

If some consumers know that two products are identical while others believe that they differ in quality, a firm can profitably price discriminate. The firm takes advantage of the less-informed customers by charging them a high price for the allegedly superior product. The firm does not want to charge informed customers this same high price. Doing so would reduce profit because the resulting fall in sales would be greater than the gain from the higher price on sales that are made.

Asymmetric information on the part of some, but not all, consumers makes price discrimination possible. However, if all customers are informed or all are uninformed about the quality of different products, firms charge a single price.

By intentionally increasing consumer uncertainty, a firm may be better able to exploit ignorant consumers and earn a higher profit (Salop, 1977). One way in which firms confuse consumers is to create *noise* by selling virtually the same product under various brand names. Similarly, firms sometimes sell a product under their own brand name at a relatively high price and supply grocery or discount stores with a virtually identical product that is sold at a lower price under a *private-label* (house or store) brand. For example, the same processor produces Prego spaghetti sauce and similar house brands for various grocery stores.

See Question 10.

Brand proliferation pays if the cost of producing multiple brands is relatively low and the share of consumers who are willing to buy the higher-price product is relatively large. Otherwise, the firm makes a higher profit by selling a single product at a moderate price than by selling one brand at a low price and another at a high price.

Over time, as consumers have become familiar with private-label brands and recognized their quality, firms have reaped less advantage in maintaining multiple brands for many products. Indeed, private-label products are rapidly gaining market share. According to AC Nielsen, consumers across the 38 countries studied spent 17% of all grocery dollars on private-label packaged goods in 2005.

APPLICATION

Twin Brands

By selling the same product under more than one brand name, firms can charge ignorant consumers higher prices. For decades, outside firms have manufactured products that Sears, Roebuck & Company sells under its house brand names, Kenmore, Die-Hard, and Craftsman. Amana refrigerators are sold under their own brand name and under the Kenmore brand name. Similarly, Whirlpool sells its own washers and driers, but Sears also markets these products under the Kenmore name. Sears also places its label on Caloric, Frigidaire, GE, Gibson, Jenn-Air, and Toshiba products. (Want to know which firm made the product you bought at Sears? Go to **www.applianceaid.com/searscodes.html**.)

Frequently, the Kenmore product is identical to or even superior to the brand-name product and costs less. Knowledgeable consumers realizing that the two brands are identical except for the label, buy the Sears brand at the lower price. But customers who falsely believe that the name brand is better than the Kenmore product pay more for the name brand.

Similarly, auto manufacturers produce auto twins—or even as many as five related cars—using the same chassis and sharing most under-hood and interior components. These siblings have different styling features and are usually sold under different brand names. Manufacturers call this differentiation "badge engineering." The automaker creates a new model by putting a new set of badges or brand names and maybe a different grille on an existing model. In the past, the differentiated cars sold for similar prices and differed primarily in the packaging of standard features and options. The 2008 Pontiac Solstice and the Saturn SKY are nearly identical, but the SKY had a list price that was $3,060 more than the Solstice. One of the largest group of siblings consists of the Chevrolet TrailBlazer, GMC Envoy, Buick Rainier, Isuzu Ascender, and Saab 9-7X.

Recently, some twins have been substantially differentiated, with one selling as a luxury version of the other. The more luxurious Infiniti QX56 had a 2008 list price that was $16,750 more than the Nissan Armada, while the Cadillac XLR Roadster's list price was $26,075 more than the Chevrolet Corvette convertible.

See Question 11.

19.5 Market Power from Price Ignorance

We've just seen that consumer ignorance about quality can keep high-quality goods out of markets or lead to price discrimination. Consumer ignorance about how prices vary across firms has yet another effect: It gives firms market power. As a result, firms have an incentive to make it difficult for consumers to collect information about prices. For this reason, some stores won't quote prices over the phone.

We now examine why asymmetric information about prices leads to noncompetitive pricing in a market that would otherwise be competitive. Suppose that many stores in a town sell the same good. If consumers have *full information* about prices, all stores charge the full-information competitive price, p^*. If one store were to raise its price above p^*, the store would lose all its business. Each store faces a residual demand curve that is horizontal at the going market price and has no market power.

In contrast, if consumers have *limited information* about the price that firms charge for a product, one store can charge more than others and not lose all its customers. Customers who do not know that the product is available for less elsewhere keep buying from the high-price store.[2] Thus, each store faces a downward-sloping residual demand curve and has some market power.

Tourist-Trap Model

We now show that, if there is a single price in such a market, it is higher than p^*. You arrive in a small town near the site of the discovery of gold in California. Souvenir shops crowd the street. Wandering by one of these stores, you see that it sells the town's distinctive snowy: a plastic ball filled with water and imitation snow featuring a model of the Donner Party. You instantly decide that you must buy at least one of these tasteful mementos—perhaps more if the price is low enough. Your bus will leave very soon, so you can't check the price at each shop to find the lowest price. Moreover, determining which shop has the lowest price won't be useful to you in the future because you do not intend to return anytime soon.

Let's assume that you and other tourists have a guidebook that reports how many souvenir shops charge each possible price for the snowy, but the guidebook does not state the price at any particular shop.[3] There are many tourists in your position, each with an identical demand function.

It costs each tourist c in time and expenses to visit a shop to check the price or buy a snowy. Thus, if the price is p, the cost of buying a snowy at the first shop you visit is $p + c$. If you go to two souvenir shops before buying at the second shop, the cost of the snowy is $p + 2c$.

When Price Is Not Competitive. Will all souvenir shops charge the same price? If so, what price will they charge? We start by considering whether each shop charges the full-information, competitive price, p^*.

---

[2] A grave example concerns the ripping off of the dying and the survivors of the dead. A cremation arranged through a memorial society—which typically charges a nominal enrollment fee of \$10 to \$25—costs \$400 to \$600, compared with \$1,500 to \$2,000 for the same service when it is arranged through a mortuary. Consumers who know about memorial societies—which get competitive bids from mortuaries—can obtain a relatively low price. The less knowledgeable people who deal directly with mortuaries pay more. Mary Rowland, "Shedding Light on a Dark Subject," *New York Times*, July 24, 1994, 13.

[3] We make this assumption about the guidebook to keep the presentation as simple as possible. This assumption is not necessary to obtain the following result.

The full-information, competitive price is the equilibrium price only if no firm has an incentive to charge a different price. No firm would charge less than p^*, which equals marginal cost, because it would lose money on each sale.

However, a firm could gain by charging a higher price than p^*, so p^* is *not* an equilibrium price. If all other shops charge p^*, a firm can profitably charge $p_1 = p^* + \varepsilon$, where ε, a small positive number, is the shop's price markup. Suppose that you walk into this shop and learn that it sells the snowy for p_1. You know from your guidebook that all other souvenir shops charge only p^*. You say to yourself, "How unfortunate [or other words to that effect], I've wandered into the only expensive shop in town." Annoyed, you consider going elsewhere. Nonetheless, you do not go to another shop if this shop's markup, $\varepsilon = p_1 - p^*$, is less than c, the cost of going to another shop.

As a result, it pays for this shop to raise its price by an amount that is just slightly less than the cost of an additional search, thereby deviating from the proposed equilibrium where all other shops charge p^*. Thus, *if consumers have limited information about price, an equilibrium in which all firms charge the full-information, competitive price is impossible.*

Monopoly Price. We've seen that the market price cannot be lower than or equal to the full-information, competitive price. Can there be an equilibrium in which all stores charge the same price and that price is higher than the competitive price? In particular, can we have an equilibrium when all shops charge $p_1 = p^* + \varepsilon$? No, shops would deviate from this proposed equilibrium for the same reason that they deviated from charging the competitive price. A shop can profitably raise its price to $p_2 = p_1 + \varepsilon = p^* + 2\varepsilon$. Again, it does not pay for a tourist who is unlucky enough to enter that shop to go to another shop as long as $\varepsilon < c$. Thus, p_1 is not the equilibrium price. By repeating this reasoning, we can reject other possible equilibrium prices that are above p^* and less than the monopoly price, p_m.

However, the monopoly price may be an equilibrium price. No firm wants to raise its price above the monopoly level because its profit would fall due to reduced sales. When tourists learn the price at a particular souvenir shop, they decide how many snowies to buy. If the price is set too high, the shop's lost sales more than offset the higher price, so its profit falls. Thus, although the shop can charge a higher price without losing all its sales, it chooses not to do so.

The only remaining question is whether a shop would like to charge a lower price than p_m if all other shops charge that price. If not, p_m is an equilibrium price.

Should a shop reduce its price below p_m by less than c? If it does so, it does not pay for consumers to search for this low-price firm. The shop makes less on each sale, so its profits must fall. Thus, a shop should not deviate by charging a price that is only slightly less than p_m.

Does it pay for a shop to drop its price below p_m by more than c? If there are few shops, consumers may search for this low-price shop. Although the shop makes less per sale than the high-price shops, its profits may be higher because of greater sales volume. If there are many shops, however, consumers do not search for the low-price shop because their chances of finding it are low. As a result, when the presence of a large number of shops makes searching for a low-price shop impractical, no firm lowers its price, so p_m is the equilibrium price. Thus, *when consumers have asymmetric information and when search costs and the number of firms are large, the only possible single-price equilibrium is at the monopoly price.*

If the single-price equilibrium at p_m can be broken by a firm charging a low price, there is no single-price equilibrium. Either there is no equilibrium or there is an equilibrium in which prices vary across shops (see Stiglitz, 1979, or Carlton and Perloff, 2000). Multiple-price equilibria are common.

Solved Problem 19.2

Initially, there are many souvenir shops, each of which charges p_m (because consumers do not know the shops' prices), and buyers' search costs are c. If the government pays for half of consumers' search costs, can there be a single-price equilibrium at a price less than p_m?

Answer

Show that the argument we used to reject a single-price equilibrium at any price except the monopoly price did not depend on the size of the search cost. If all other stores charge any single price p, where $p^* \le p < p_m$, a firm profits from raising its price. As long as it raises its price by no more than $c/2$ (the new cost of search to a consumer), unlucky consumers who stop at this deviant store do not search further. This profitable deviation shows that the proposed single-price equilibrium is not an equilibrium. Again, the only possible single-price equilibrium is at p_m.[4]

Advertising and Prices

The U.S. Federal Trade Commission (FTC), a consumer protection agency, opposes groups that want to forbid price advertising; the FTC argues that advertising about price benefits consumers. If a firm informs consumers about its unusually low price, it may be able to gain enough extra customers to more than offset its loss from the lower price. If low-price stores advertise their prices and attract many customers, they can break the monopoly-price equilibrium that occurs when consumers must search store by store for low prices. The more successful the advertising, the larger these stores grow and the lower the average price in the market. If enough consumers become informed, all stores may charge the low price. Thus, without advertising, no store may find it profitable to charge low prices, but with advertising, all stores may charge low prices. See **www.myeconlab.com/perloff**, Chapter 19, "Advertising Lowers Prices."

See Question 12.

19.6 Problems Arising from Ignorance When Hiring

Asymmetric information is frequently a problem in labor markets. Prospective employees may have less information about working conditions than firms do. Firms may have less information about potential employees' abilities than the workers do.

Information asymmetries in labor markets lower welfare below the full-information level. Workers may signal and firms may screen to reduce the asymmetry in information about workers' abilities. Signaling and screening may raise or lower welfare, as we now consider.

Information About Employment Risks

Firms typically have more information than workers about job safety. This asymmetric information may lead to less than optimal levels of safety (Viscusi, 1979).

[4]If the search cost is low enough, however, the single-price equilibrium at p_m can be broken profitably by charging a low price so that only a multiple-price equilibrium is possible. If the search cost falls to zero, consumers have full information, so the only possible equilibrium is at the full-information, competitive price.

Prospective employees who do not know the injury rate at individual firms may know the average injury rates in an industry because these data are reported by the U.S. Bureau of Labor Statistics. People will work in a risky industry only if they are paid more than they would earn in less-risky industries.

Each firm must consider how safe to make its plant. Extra safety is costly. Safety investments—sprinkler systems, color-coded switches, fire extinguishers—by one firm provide an externality to other firms: That firm's lower incidence of accidents reduces the wage that all firms in the industry must pay. *Because each firm bears the full cost of its safety investments but derives only some of the benefits, the firms underinvest in safety.*

The prisoners' dilemma game in Table 19.1, which is played by the only two firms in an industry, illustrates this result. In the Nash equilibrium (upper left), neither firm invests and each earns $200.

An investment by only one firm raises safety levels at its plant. Workers in the industry do not know that safety has improved only at the plant of the investing firm. They realize only that it is safer to work in this industry, so both firms pay lower wages. The loss from the investment is greater than the wage savings, so the profit falls to $100 for the firm that invests. The wage savings causes its rival's profit to rise to $250.

If both firms invest (lower right), both earn $225, which is more than they would earn in the Nash equilibrium. However, investment by both firms is not an equilibrium, as each firm has an incentive to deviate.

This prisoners' dilemma would not occur if workers knew how safe each firm was. Only the firm that invested in safety would be able to pay a lower wage if workers knew the accident rate by firms. There would be no externality. Thus, a firm that can credibly convince workers that it is a relatively safe place to work can overcome this asymmetric information problem.[5]

In this example, the underinvestment problem could be avoided if the government provided the information, if the government set safety standards that would force both firms to invest, or if unions effectively lobbied both firms for higher levels of safety. For the government or unions to provide these useful functions practically, however, their cost of gathering the necessary information would have to be relatively low.

Table 19.1 Safety Investment Game.

		Firm 2	
		No Investment	*Investment*
Firm 1	*No Investment*	Firm 1: $200; Firm 2: $200	Firm 1: $250; Firm 2: $100
	Investment	Firm 1: $100; Firm 2: $250	Firm 1: $225; Firm 2: $225

[5]Because this information is a public good, others may obtain this information if the firm provides it to employees. The cost to the firm of having others, such as government regulators, obtain this information may exceed the lower-wage benefit from providing it to workers.

Cheap Talk

Honesty is the best policy—when there is money in it. —Mark Twain

We now consider situations in which workers have more information about their ability than firms do. We look first at inexpensive signals sent by workers, then at expensive signals sent by workers, and finally at screening by firms.

cheap talk
unsubstantiated claims or statements

When an informed person voluntarily provides information to an uninformed person, the informed person engages in **cheap talk**: unsubstantiated claims or statements (see Farrell and Rabin, 1996). People use cheap talk to distinguish themselves or their attributes at low cost. Even though informed people may lie when it suits them, it is often in their and everyone else's best interest for them to tell the truth. Nothing stops me from advertising that I have a chimpanzee for sale, but doing so serves no purpose if I actually want to sell my DVD player. One advantage of cheap talk, if it is effective, is that it is a less expensive method of signaling ability to a potential employer than paying to have that ability tested.

Suppose that a firm plans to hire Cyndi to do one of two jobs. The demanding job requires someone with high ability. The undemanding job can be done better by someone of low ability because the job bores more able people, who then perform poorly.

Cyndi knows whether her ability level is high or low, but the firm is unsure. It initially thinks that either level is equally likely. Panel a of Table 19.2 shows the payoffs to Cyndi and the firm under various possibilities.[6] If Cyndi has high ability, she

Table 19.2 Employee-Employer Payoffs.

(*a*) ***When Cheap Talk Works***

		Job That the Firm Gives to Cyndi			
		Demanding		*Undemanding*	
		Cyndi	Firm	Cyndi	Firm
Cyndi's Ability	*High*	3	2	1	1
	Low	1	1	2	4

(*b*) ***When Cheap Talk Fails***

		Job That the Firm Gives to Cyndi			
		Demanding		*Undemanding*	
		Cyndi	Firm	Cyndi	Firm
Cyndi's Ability	*High*	3	2	1	1
	Low	3	1	2	4

[6]Previously, we used a 2×2 matrix to show a simultaneous-move game (as in Table 19.1), in which both parties choose an action at the same time. Here only the firm can make a move. Cyndi does not take an action, because she cannot choose her ability level.

enjoys the demanding job: Her payoff is 3. If she has low ability, she finds the demanding job too stressful—her payoff is only 1—but she can handle the undemanding job. The payoff to the firm is greater if Cyndi is properly matched to the job: She is given the demanding job if she has high ability and the undemanding job if she has low ability.

We can view this example as a two-stage game. In the first stage, Cyndi tells the firm something. In the second stage, the firm decides which job she gets.

Cyndi could make many possible statements about her ability. For simplicity, though, we assume that she says either "My ability is high" or "My ability is low." This two-stage game has an equilibrium in which Cyndi tells the truth and the firm, believing her, assigns her to the appropriate job. If she claims to have high ability, the firm gives her the demanding job.

If the firm reacts to her cheap talk in this manner, Cyndi has no incentive to lie. If she did lie, the firm would make a mistake, and a mistake would be bad for both parties. Cyndi and the firm want the same outcomes, so cheap talk works.

In many other situations, however, cheap talk does not work. Given the payoffs in panel b, Cyndi and the firm do not want the same outcomes. The firm still wants Cyndi in the demanding job if she has high ability and in the undemanding job otherwise. But Cyndi wants the demanding job regardless of her ability. So she claims to have high ability regardless of the truth. Knowing her incentives, the firm views her statement as meaningless babbling—her statement does not change the firm's view that her ability is equally likely to be high or low.

Given that belief, the firm gives her the undemanding job, for which its expected payoff is higher. The firm's expected payoff is

$$\left(\tfrac{1}{2} \times 1\right) + \left(\tfrac{1}{2} \times 4\right) = 2.5$$

if it gives her the undemanding job and

$$\left(\tfrac{1}{2} \times 2\right) + \left(\tfrac{1}{2} \times 1\right) = 1.5$$

if it assigns her to the demanding job. Thus, given the firm's asymmetric information, the outcome is inefficient if Cyndi has high ability.

When the interests of the firm and the individual diverge, cheap talk does not provide a credible signal. Here an individual has to send a more expensive signal to be believed. We now examine such a signal.

Education as a Signal

No doubt you've been told that one good reason to go to college is to get a good job. Going to college may get you a better job because you obtain valuable training. Another possibility is that a college degree may land you a good job because it serves as a signal to employers about your ability. If high-ability people are more likely to go to college than low-ability people, schooling signals ability to employers (Spence, 1974).

To illustrate how such signaling works, we'll make the extreme assumptions that graduating from an appropriate school serves as the signal and that schooling provides no training that is useful to firms (Stiglitz, 1975). High-ability workers are θ share of the workforce, and low-ability workers are $1 - \theta$ share. The value of output that a high-ability worker produces for a firm is worth w_h, and that of a low-ability worker is w_l (over their careers). If competitive employers knew workers' ability levels, they would pay this value of the marginal product to each worker, so a high-ability worker receives w_h and a low-ability worker earns w_l.

We assume that employers cannot directly determine a worker's skill level. For example, when production is a group effort—such as in an assembly line—a firm cannot determine the productivity of a single employee.

pooling equilibrium
an equilibrium in which dissimilar people are treated (paid) alike or behave alike

Two types of equilibria are possible, depending on whether or not employers can distinguish high-ability workers from others. If employers have no way of telling workers apart, the outcome is a **pooling equilibrium**: Dissimilar people are treated (paid) alike or behave alike. Employers pay all workers the average wage:

$$\bar{w} = \theta w_h + (1 - \theta) w_l. \tag{19.2}$$

Risk-neutral, competitive firms expect to break even because they underpay high-ability people by enough to offset the losses from overpaying low-ability workers.

We assume that high-ability individuals can get a degree by spending c to attend a school and that low-ability people cannot graduate from the school (or that the cost of doing so is prohibitively high). If high-ability people graduate and low-ability people do not, a degree is a signal of ability to employers. Given such a clear signal, the outcome is a **separating equilibrium**: One type of people takes actions (such as sending a signal) that allow them to be differentiated from other types of people. Here a successful signal causes high-ability workers to receive w_h and the others to receive w_l, so wages vary with ability.

separating equilibrium
an equilibrium in which one type of people takes actions (such as sending a *signal*) that allows them to be differentiated from other types of people

We now examine whether a pooling or a separating equilibrium is possible. We consider whether anyone would want to change behavior in an equilibrium. If no one wants to change, the equilibrium is feasible.

Separating Equilibrium. In a separating equilibrium, high-ability people pay c to get a degree and are employed at a wage of w_h, while low-ability individuals do not get a degree and work for a wage of w_l. The low-ability people have no choice, as they can't get a degree. High-ability individuals have the option of not going to school. Without a degree, however, they are viewed as low ability once hired, and they receive w_l. If they go to school, their net earnings are $w_h - c$. Thus, it pays for a high-ability person to go to school if

$$w_h - c > w_l.$$

Rearranging terms in this expression, we find that a high-ability person chooses to get a degree if

$$w_h - w_l > c. \tag{19.3}$$

Equation 19.3 says that the benefit from graduating, the extra pay $w_h - w_l$, exceeds the cost of schooling, c. If Equation 19.3 holds, no worker wants to change behavior, so a separating equilibrium is feasible.

Suppose that $c = \$15,000$ and that high-ability workers are twice as productive as others: $w_h = \$40,000$ and $w_l = \$20,000$. Here the benefit to a high-ability worker from graduating, $w_h - w_l = \$20,000$, exceeds the cost by \$5,000. Thus, no one wants to change behavior in this separating equilibrium.

Pooling Equilibrium. In a pooling equilibrium, all workers are paid the average wage from Equation 19.2, $\bar{w}$. Again, because low-ability people cannot graduate, they have no choice. A high-ability person must choose whether or not to go to school. Without a degree, that individual is paid the average wage. With a degree, the worker is paid w_h. It does not pay for the high-ability person to graduate if the benefit from graduating, the extra pay $w_h - \bar{w}$, is less than the cost of schooling:

$$w_h - \bar{w} < c. \tag{19.4}$$

Thus, if Equation 19.4 holds, no worker wants to change behavior, so a pooling equilibrium persists.

For example, if $w_h = \$40,000$, $w_l = \$20,000$, and $\theta = \frac{1}{2}$, then

$$\bar{w} = \left(\tfrac{1}{2} \times \$40,000\right) + \left(\tfrac{1}{2} \times \$20,000\right) = \$30,000.$$

If the cost of going to school is $c = \$15,000$, the benefit to a high-ability person from graduating, $w_h - \bar{w} = \$10,000$ is less than the cost, so a high-ability individual does not want to go to school. As a result, there is a pooling equilibrium.

Solved Problem 19.3

For what values of θ is a pooling equilibrium possible in general? In particular, if $c = \$15,000$, $w_h = \$40,000$, and $w_l = \$20,000$, for what values of θ is a pooling equilibrium possible?

Answer

1. *Determine the values of θ for which it pays for a high-ability person to go to school.* From Equation 19.4, we know that a high-ability individual does not go to school if $w_h - \bar{w} < c$. Using Equation 19.2, we substitute for $\bar{w}$ in Equation 19.4 and rearrange terms to find that high-ability people do not go to school if

$$w_h - [\theta w_h + (1 - \theta) w_l] < c,$$

or

$$\theta > 1 - \frac{c}{w_h - w_l}. \tag{19.5}$$

If almost everyone has high ability, so θ is large, a high-ability person does not go to school. The intuition is that, as the share of high-ability workers, θ, gets large (close to 1), the average wage approaches w_h (Equation 19.2), so there is little benefit, $w_h - \bar{w}$, in going to school.

2. *Solve for the possible values of θ for the specific parameters.* If we substitute $c = \$15,000$, $w_h = \$40,000$, and $w_l = \$20,000$ into Equation 19.5, we find that high-ability people do not go to school—a pooling equilibrium is possible—if $\theta > \frac{1}{4}$.

Unique or Multiple Equilibria. Depending on differences in abilities, the cost of schooling, and the share of high-ability workers, only one type of equilibrium may be possible or both may be possible. In the following examples, using Figure 19.2, $w_h = \$40,000$ and $w_l = \$20,000$.

Only a pooling equilibrium is possible if schooling is very costly: $c > w_h - w_l = \$20,000$, so Equation 19.3 does not hold. A horizontal line in Figure 19.2 shows where $c = w_h - w_l = \$20,000$. Only a pooling equilibrium is feasible above that line, $c > \$20,000$, because it does not pay for high-ability workers to go to school.

Equation 19.5 shows that, if there are few high-ability people (relative to the cost and earnings differential), only a separating equilibrium is possible. The figure shows a sloped line where $\theta = 1 - c/(w_h - w_l)$. Below that line, $\theta < 1 - c/(w_h - w_l)$, relatively few people have high ability, so the average wage, $\bar{w}$, is low. A pooling equilibrium is not possible because high-ability workers would want to signal. Thus, below this line, only a separating equilibrium is possible. Above this line, Equation

19.5 holds, so a pooling equilibrium is possible. (The answer to Solved Problem 19.3 shows that no one wants to change behavior in a pooling equilibrium if $c = \$15{,}000$ and $\theta > \frac{1}{4}$, which are points to the right of x in the figure, such as y.)

Below the horizontal line where the cost of signaling is less than \$20,000 and above the sloped line where there are relatively many high-ability workers, either equilibrium may occur. For example, where $c = \$15{,}000$ and $\theta = \frac{1}{2}$, Equations 19.3 and 19.4 (or equivalently, Equation 19.5) hold, so both a separating equilibrium and a pooling equilibrium are possible. In the pooling equilibrium, no one wants to change behavior, so this equilibrium is possible. Similarly, no one wants to change behavior in a separating equilibrium.

See Problems 21–24.

A government could ensure that one or the other of these equilibria occurs. It achieves a pooling equilibrium by banning schooling (and other possible signals). Alternatively, the government creates a separating equilibrium by subsidizing schooling for some high-ability people. Once some individuals start to signal, so that firms pay either a low or high wage (not a pooling wage), it pays for other high-ability people to signal.

Efficiency. In our example of a separating equilibrium, high-ability people get an otherwise useless education solely to show that they differ from low-ability people. An education is privately useful to the high-ability workers if it serves as a signal that gets them higher net pay. In our extreme example, education is socially inefficient because it is costly and provides no useful training.

Signaling changes the distribution of wages: Instead of everyone getting the average wage, high-ability workers receive more pay than low-ability workers. Nonetheless, the total amount that firms pay is the same, so firms make zero expected profits in both equilibria.[7] Moreover, everyone is employed in both the pooling and the screening equilibrium, so total output is the same.

Nonetheless, everyone may be worse off in a separating equilibrium. At point y in Figure 19.2 ($w_h = \$40{,}000$, $w_l = \$20{,}000$, $c = \$15{,}000$, and $\theta = \frac{1}{2}$), either a pooling equilibrium or a separating equilibrium is possible. In the pooling equilibrium, each worker is paid $\bar{w} = \$30{,}000$ and there is no wasteful signaling. In the separating equilibrium, high-ability workers make $w_h - c = \$25{,}000$ and low-ability workers make $w_l = \$20{,}000$.

Here high-ability people earn less in the separating equilibrium, \$25,000, than they would in a pooling equilibrium, \$30,000. Nonetheless, if anyone signals, all high-ability workers will want to send a signal to prevent their wage from falling to that of a low-ability worker. The reason socially undesirable signaling happens is that the private return to signaling—high-ability workers net an extra \$5,000 [$= (w_h - c) - w_l = \$25{,}000 - \$20{,}000$]—exceeds the net social return to signaling. The gross social return to the signal is zero—the signal changes only the distribution of wages—and the net social return is negative because the signal is costly.

This inefficient expenditure on education is due to asymmetric information and the desire of high-ability workers to signal their ability. Here the government can increase total social wealth by banning wasteful signaling (eliminate schooling). Both low-ability and high-ability people benefit from such a ban.

In other cases, however, high-ability people do not want a ban. At point z (where $\theta = \frac{1}{2}$ and $c = \$5{,}000$), only a separating equilibrium is possible without government intervention. In this equilibrium, high-ability workers earn $w_h - c = \$35{,}000$ and low-ability workers make $w_l = \$20{,}000$. If the government bans signaling, both types of workers earn \$30,000 in the resulting pooling equilibrium, so high-ability

[7]Firms pay high-ability workers more than low-ability workers in a separating equilibrium, but the average amount they pay per worker is $\bar{w}$, the same as in a pooling equilibrium.

Figure 19.2 Pooling and Separating Equilibria.

If firms know workers' abilities, high-ability workers are paid w_h = \$40,000 and low-ability workers get w_l = \$20,000. The type of equilibrium depends on the cost of schooling, c, and the share of high-ability workers, θ. If c > \$20,000, only a pooling equilibrium, in which everyone gets the average wage, is possible. If there are relatively few high-ability people, $\theta < 1 - c/ \$20,000$, only a separating equilibrium is possible. Between the horizontal and sloped lines, either type of equilibrium may occur.

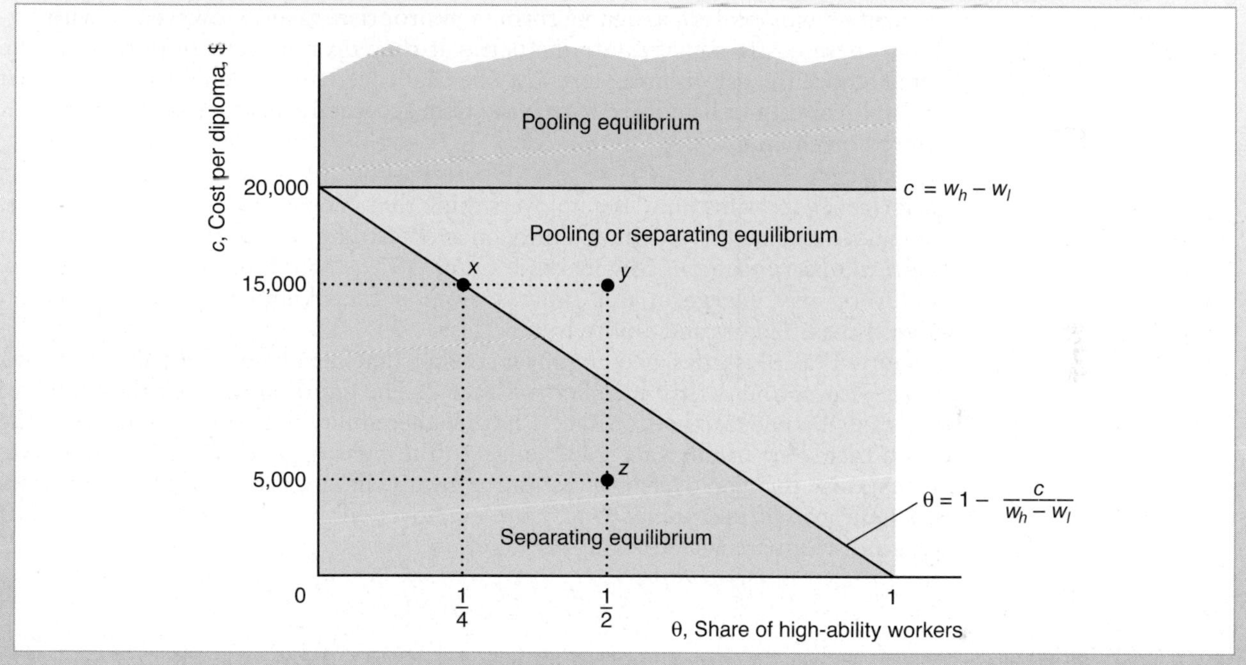

workers are harmed, losing \$5,000 each. So even though the ban raises efficiency (wasteful signaling is eliminated), high-ability workers oppose the ban.

In this example, efficiency can always be increased by banning signaling because signaling is unproductive. However, some signaling is socially efficient because it increases total output. Education may raise output because its signal results in a better matching of workers and jobs or because it provides useful training as well as serving as a signal. Education also may make people better citizens. In conclusion, *total social output falls with signaling if signaling is socially unproductive but may rise with signaling if signaling also raises productivity or serves some other desirable purpose.*

See Question 13.

Empirical evidence on the importance of signaling is mixed. Tyler, Murnane, and Willett (2000) find that, for the least skilled high school dropouts, passing the General Educational Development (GED) equivalency credential (the equivalent of a high school diploma) increases the white dropouts' earnings by 10% to 19% but has no statistically significant effect on minority dropouts. See **www.myeconlab.com/perloff**, Chapter 19, "Wages Rise with Education," for additional evidence that signaling raises wages.

Screening in Hiring

Firms screen prospective workers in many ways. An employer may base hiring on an individual's characteristic that the employer believes is correlated with ability, such as how a person dresses or speaks, or a firm may use a test. Further, some employers engage in *statistical discrimination*, believing that an individual's gender, race, religion, or ethnicity is a proxy for ability.

Interviews and Tests. Most societies accept the use of interviews and tests by potential employers. Firms commonly use interviews and tests as screening devices to assess abilities. If such screening devices are accurate, the firm benefits by selecting superior workers and assigning them to appropriate tasks. However, as with signaling, these costly activities are inefficient if they do not increase output. In the United States, the use of hiring tests may be challenged and rejected by the courts if the employer cannot demonstrate that the tests accurately measure skills or abilities required on the job.

See Question 14.

Statistical Discrimination. If employers think that people of a certain gender, race, religion, or ethnicity have higher ability on average than others, they may engage in *statistical discrimination* (Aigner and Cain, 1977) and hire only such people. Employers may engage in this practice even if they know that the correlation between these factors and ability is imperfect.

Figure 19.3 illustrates one employer's belief that members of Race 1 have, on average, lower ability than members of Race 2. The figure shows that the employer believes that some members of Race 1 have higher ability than some members of the second race: Part of the Race 1 curve lies to the right of part of the Race 2 curve. Still, because the employer believes that a group characteristic, race, is an (imperfect) indicator of individual ability, the employer hires only people of Race 2 if enough of them are available.

Figure 19.3 Statistical Discrimination.

This figure shows the beliefs of an employer who thinks that people of Race 1 have less ability on average than people of Race 2. This employer hires only people of Race 2, even though the employer believes that some members of Race 1 have greater ability than some members of Race 2. Because this employer never employs members of Race 1, the employer may never learn that workers of both races have equal ability.

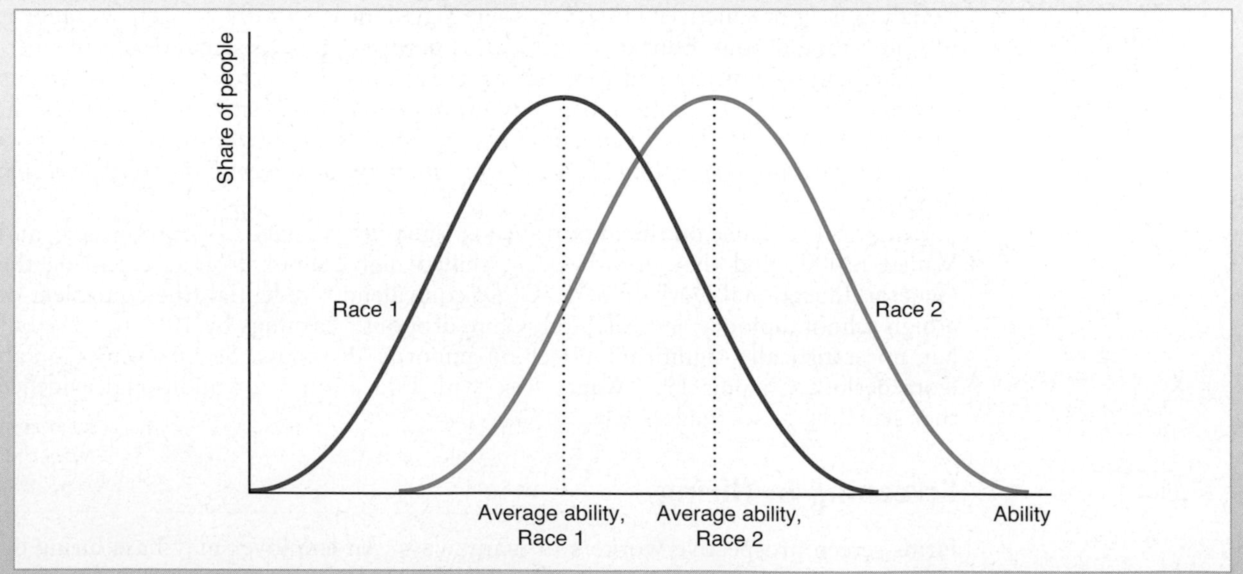

The employer may claim not to be prejudiced but to be concerned only with maximizing profit.[8] Nonetheless, this employer's actions harm members of Race 1 as much as they would if they were due to racial hatred.

It may be very difficult to eliminate statistical discrimination even though ability distributions are identical across races. If all employers share the belief that members of Race 1 have such low ability that it is not worth hiring them, people of that race are never hired, so employers never learn that their beliefs are incorrect. Thus, false beliefs can persist indefinitely. Such discrimination lowers social output if it keeps skilled members of Race 1 from performing certain jobs.

See Questions 15 and 16.

However, statistical discrimination may be based on true differences between groups. For example, insurance companies offer lower auto insurance rates to young women than to young men because young men are more likely, *on average*, to have an accident. The companies report that this practice lowers their costs of providing insurance by reducing moral hazard. Nonetheless, this practice penalizes young men who are unusually safe drivers and benefits young women who are unusually reckless drivers.

SUMMARY

1. **Problems Due to Asymmetric Information.** Asymmetric information causes market failures when informed parties engage in opportunistic behavior at the expense of uninformed parties. The resulting failures include the elimination of markets and pricing above marginal cost. Two types of problems arise from opportunism. Adverse selection is opportunism whereby only informed parties who have an unobserved characteristic that allows them to benefit from a deal agree to it, to the detriment of a less-informed party. Moral hazard is opportunism whereby an informed party takes advantage of a less-informed party through an unobserved action.
2. **Responses to Adverse Selection.** Avoiding adverse selection problems requires restricting the opportunistic behavior or eliminating the information asymmetry. To prevent the opportunism that occurs when information is asymmetric, governments may intervene in markets or the people involved may write contracts that restrict the behavior of informed people. To eliminate or reduce information asymmetries, uninformed people screen to determine the information of informed people, informed people send signals to uninformed people, or third parties such as the government provide information.
3. **How Ignorance About Quality Drives Out High-Quality Goods.** If consumers cannot distinguish between good and bad products before purchase, bad products may drive good ones out of the market. This lemons problem is due to adverse selection. Methods of dealing with the lemons problem include laws limiting opportunism, consumer screening (such as by using experts or relying on firms' reputations), the provision of information by third parties such as government agencies or consumer groups, and signaling by firms (including establishing brand names and providing guarantees or warranties).
4. **Price Discrimination Due to False Beliefs About Quality.** Firms may price discriminate if some consumers incorrectly think that quality varies across identical products. Because only some consumers collect information about quality, only those consumers know whether the quality differs between products in some markets. Firms can exploit ignorant consumers by creating noise: selling the same good under two different brand names at different prices.
5. **Market Power from Price Ignorance.** If consumers do not know how prices vary across firms, a firm can raise its price without losing all its customers. As a consequence, consumers' ignorance about price creates market power. In a market that would be competitive with full information, consumer ignorance about price may lead to a monopoly price or a distribution of prices.
6. **Problems Arising from Ignorance When Hiring.** Companies use signaling and screening to try to eliminate information asymmetries in hiring. Where prospective employees and firms share common interests—such as assigning the right worker to the right task—everyone benefits from eliminating

[8]Not all employment discrimination is due to statistical discrimination. Other common sources of discrimination are prejudice (Becker, 1971) and the exercise of monopsony power (Madden, 1973).

the information asymmetry by having informed job candidates honestly tell the firms—through *cheap talk*—about their abilities. When the two parties do not share common interests, cheap talk does not work. Potential employees may inform employers about their abilities by using expensive signals such as a college degree. If these signals are unproductive (as when education serves only as a signal and provides no training), they may be privately beneficial but socially harmful. If the signals are productive (as when education provides training or leads to greater output due to more fitting job assignments), they may be both privately and socially beneficial. Firms may also screen. Job interviews, objective tests, and other screening devices that lead to a better matching of workers and jobs may be socially beneficial. Screening by statistical discrimination, however, is harmful to discriminated-against groups. Employers who discriminate on the basis of a particular group characteristic may never learn that their discrimination is based on false beliefs because they never test these beliefs.

QUESTIONS

■ = *exercise is available on MyEconLab;* * = *answer appears at the back of this book;* C = *use of calculus may be necessary;* W = *audio-slideshow answer by James Dearden is available in Textbook Resources on MyEconLab.*

1. A grocery advertises a low price on its milk as a "loss leader" to induce customers to shop there. It finds that some people buy only milk there and do their other grocery shopping elsewhere. Is that an example of adverse selection or moral hazard?

2. According to a 2007 study by the Federal Trade Commission, 4.8 million U.S. consumers were victims of weight-loss fraud, ranging from a tea that promised to help you shed the pounds to fraudulent clinical trials and fat-dissolving injections. Do these frauds illustrate adverse selection or moral hazard?

3. Some states prohibit insurance companies from using car owners' home addresses to set auto insurance rates. Why do insurance companies use home addresses? What are the efficiency and equity implications of forbidding such practices?

*4. The state of California set up its own earthquake insurance program for homeowners in 1997. The rates vary by ZIP code, depending on the proximity of the nearest fault line. However, critics claim that the people who set the rates ignored soil type. Some houses rest on bedrock; others sit on unstable soil. What are the implications of such rate setting?

*5. A firm spends a great deal of money in advertising to inform consumers of the brand name of its mushrooms. Should consumers conclude that its mushrooms are likely to be of higher quality than unbranded mushrooms? Why or why not?

6. You want to determine whether there is a lemons problem in the market for single-engine airplanes. Can you use any of the following information to help answer this question? If so, how?
   a. Repair rates for original-owner planes versus planes that have been resold
   b. The fraction of planes resold in each year after purchase

7. If you buy a new car and try to sell it in the first year—indeed, in the first few days after you buy it—the price that you get is substantially less than the original price. Use Akerlof's lemons model to give one explanation for why.

8. Use Akerlof's lemons model to explain why restaurants that cater to tourists are likely to serve low-quality meals. Tourists will not return to this area, and they have no information about the relative quality of the food at various restaurants, but they can determine the relative price by looking at menus posted outside each restaurant.

9. In the world of French high cuisine, a three-star rating from the Michelin Red Guide is a widely accepted indicator of gastronomic excellence. French consumers consider Gault Milleau, another restaurant guide, not as authoritative as the Michelin guide because Gault Milleau, unlike Michelin, accepts advertising and its critics accept free meals (William Echikson, "Wish Upon a Star," *Wall Street Journal,* February 28, 2003, A8).
   a. Why are guides' ratings important to restaurant owners and chefs? Discuss the effect of a restaurant's rating on the demand for the restaurant.
   b. Why do advertising and free meals taint the credibility of Gault Milleau? Discuss the moral hazard problem of Gault Milleau's ratings.
   c. If advertising and free meals taint the credibility of Gault Milleau, why does the guide accept advertising and free meals?

10. Explain how a monopoly firm can price discriminate by advertising sales in newspapers or magazines that

only some of its customers see. Is it a noisy monopoly?

11. The "Twin Brands" application notes that an auto manufacturer may sell a luxury model for much more than another model that has the same internal components. Is the firm a noisy monopoly?

12. The Federal Trade Commission objected to the California Dental Association's prohibitions against its members engaging in advertising about prices, calling them restraints on trade. What effect should such restraints have on equilibrium prices?

13. Certain universities do not give letter grades. One rationale is that eliminating the letter-grade system reduces the pressure on students, thus enabling them to do better in school. Why might this policy help or hurt students?

14. In the ability signaling model, suppose that firms can pay c^* to have a worker's ability determined through a test. Does it pay for a firm to make this expenditure?

15. When is statistical discrimination privately inefficient? When is it socially inefficient? Does it always harm members of the discriminated-against group?

16. Some firms are willing to hire only high school graduates. On the basis of past experience or statistical evidence, these companies believe that high school graduates perform better than nongraduates, on average. How does this hiring behavior compare to statistical discrimination by employers on the basis of race or gender? Discuss the equity and efficiency implications of this practice.

PROBLEMS

17. While self-employed workers have the option to purchase private health insurance, many—especially younger—workers do not, due to adverse selection. Suppose that half the population is healthy and the other half is unhealthy. The cost of getting sick is \$1,000 for healthy people and \$10,000 for unhealthy people. In a given year, any one person (regardless of health) either becomes sick or does not. The probability that any one person gets sick is 0.4. Each person's utility of wealth function is $U(Y) = Y^{0.5}$, where Y is the person's wealth. Each worker's initial wealth is \$30,000. Although each person knows whether he or she is healthy, the insurance company does not know. The insurance company offers complete, actuarially fair insurance. Because the insurance company cannot distinguish whether a person is healthy, it must offer each person the same coverage at the same price. The only costs to the company are the medical expenses of the coverage. Under these conditions, the insurance company covers all medical expenses of its policyholders, and its expected profit is zero.
    a. If everyone purchases insurance, what is the price of the insurance?
    b. At the price you determined in part a, do healthy people purchase the optimal amount of insurance?
    c. If only unhealthy people purchase insurance, what is the price of the insurance?
    d. At the price you determined in part c, do unhealthy people optimally purchase insurance?
    e. Given that each person has the option to purchase insurance, which type actually purchases insurance? What is the price of the insurance? Discuss the adverse selection problem. W

*18. There are many buyers who value high-quality used cars at the full-information market price of p_1 and lemons at p_2. There are a limited number of potential sellers who value high-quality cars at $v_1 \le p_1$ and lemons at $v_2 \le p_2$. Everyone is risk neutral. The share of lemons among all the used cars that might potentially be sold is θ. Under what conditions are all cars sold? When are only lemons sold? Are there any conditions under which no cars are sold?

19. Suppose that the buyers in Problem 18 incur a transaction cost of \$200 to purchase a car. This transaction cost is the value of their time to find a car. What is the equilibrium? Is it possible that no cars are sold?

20. Many wineries of the Napa region of California have strong reputations for producing high-quality wines and want to protect those reputations. Fred T. Franzia, the owner of Bronco Wine Co., sells Napa-brand wines that do not contain Napa grapes (Julia Flynn, "In Napa Valley, Winemaker's Brands Divide an Industry," *Wall Street Journal*, February 22, 2005, A1). Other Napa wineries are involved in legal disputes with Mr. Franzia, contending that his wines, made from lower-quality grapes, are damaging the reputation of the Napa wines. Use the analysis in Section 19.3 to answer the following questions. The wine market in this problem has 2,000 wineries, in which each chooses to sell one bottle of wine. One thousand of the wineries have Napa grapes and can choose to turn the grapes into wine, and 1,000 wineries have Central Valley grapes and can turn those

grapes into wine. The marginal opportunity cost of selling a Napa wine is \$20 and the marginal opportunity cost of selling a Central Valley wine is \$5. A large number of risk-neutral consumers with identical tastes are willing to buy an unlimited number of bottles at their expected valuations. Each consumer values a wine made from Napa grapes at \$25 and values a wine made from Central Valley grapes at \$10. By looking at the bottles, the consumers cannot distinguish between the Napa and the Central Valley wines.

a. If all of the wineries choose to sell wine, what is a consumer's expected value of the wine? If only the wineries with Central Valley grapes choose to sell wine, what is a consumer's expected value of the wine?

b. What is the market equilibrium price? In the market equilibrium, which wineries choose to sell wine?

c. Suppose wine bottles clearly label where the grapes are grown. What are the equilibrium price and quantity of Napa wine? What are the equilibrium price and quantity of wine made from Central Valley grapes?

d. Does the market equilibrium exhibit a lemons problem? Include an analysis of whether clearly labeling the origin of the grapes solves the lemons problem. W

21. Suppose that you are given w_h, w_l, and θ in the signaling model in the chapter. For what value of c are both a pooling equilibrium and a separating equilibrium possible? For what value of c are both types of equilibria possible and do high-ability workers have higher net earnings in a separating equilibrium than in a pooling equilibrium?

22. Education is a continuous variable, where e_h is the years of schooling of a high-ability worker and e_l is the years of schooling of a lower-ability worker. The cost per period of education for these types of workers is c_h and c_l, respectively, where $c_l > c_h$. The wages they receive if employers can tell them apart are w_h and w_l. Under what conditions is a separating equilibrium possible? How much education will each type of worker get?

23. In Problem 22, under what conditions is a pooling equilibrium possible?

24. In Problems 22 and 23, describe the equilibrium if $c_l \leq c_h$.

20 Contracts and Moral Hazards

The contracts of at least 33 major league baseball players have incentive clauses providing a bonus if that player is named the Most Valuable Player in a Division Series. Unfortunately, no such award is given for a Division Series.[1]

An employee cruises the Internet for jokes instead of working when the boss is not watching. A driver of a rental car takes it off the highway and ruins the suspension. The dentist caps your tooth, not because you need it, but because he wants a new flat-screen TV.

Each of these examples illustrates an inefficient use of resources due to a *moral hazard*, whereby an informed person takes advantage of a less-informed person, often through an *unobserved action* (Chapter 19). In this chapter, we examine how to design contracts that *eliminate inefficiencies* due to moral hazard problems *without shifting risk to people who hate bearing it*—or contracts that at least reach a good compromise between these two goals.

For example, insurance companies face a trade-off between reducing moral hazards and increasing the risk of insurance buyers. Because an insurance company pools risks, it acts as though it is risk neutral (Chapter 17). The firm offers insurance contracts to risk-averse homeowners so that they can reduce their exposure to risk. If homeowners can buy full insurance so that they will suffer no loss if a fire occurs, some of them fail to take reasonable precautions. They store flammable liquids and old newspapers in their houses, increasing the chance of a catastrophic fire.

A contract that avoids this moral hazard problem specifies that the insurance company will not pay in the event of a fire if the company can show that the policyholders stored flammable materials in their home. If this approach is impractical, however, the insurance company might offer a contract that provides incomplete insurance, covering only a fraction of the damage from a fire. The less complete the coverage, the greater the incentive for policyholders to avoid dangerous activities but the greater the risk that the risk-averse homeowners must bear.

To illustrate methods of controlling moral hazards and the trade-off between moral hazards and risk, we focus in this chapter on contracts between a principal—such as an employer—and an agent—such as an employee. The *principal* contracts with the *agent* to take some *action* that benefits the principal. Until now, we have assumed that firms can produce efficiently. However, if a principal cannot practically monitor an agent all the time, the agent may steal, not work hard, or engage in other opportunistic behavior that lowers productivity.

Opportunistic behavior by an informed agent harms a less-informed principal. Sometimes the losses are so great that both parties would be better off if both had full information and opportunistic behavior were impossible.

[1]Tom FitzGerald, "Top of the Sixth," *San Francisco Chronicle*, January 31, 1997, C6.

In this chapter, we examine seven main topics

1. **Principal-Agent Problem.** How an uninformed principal contracts with an informed agent determines whether moral hazards occur and how risks are shared.
2. **Production Efficiency.** How much the agent produces depends on the type of contract used and the ability of the principal to monitor the agent's actions.
3. **Trade-Off Between Efficiency in Production and in Risk Bearing.** A principal and an agent may agree to a contract that does not eliminate moral hazards or optimally share risk but strikes a balance between these two objectives.
4. **Payments Linked to Production or Profit.** Employees work harder if they are rewarded for greater individual or group productivity.
5. **Monitoring.** Employees work harder if an employer monitors their behavior and makes it worthwhile for them to keep from being fired.
6. **Checks on Principals.** As a restraint against taking advantage of employees, an employer may agree to contractual commitments that make it in the employer's best interest to tell employees the truth.
7. **Contract Choice.** By observing which type of contract an agent picks when offered a choice, a principal may obtain enough information to reduce moral hazards.

20.1 Principal-Agent Problem

When you contract with people whose actions you cannot observe or evaluate, they may take advantage of you. If you pay someone by the hour to prepare your tax return, you do not know whether that person worked all the hours billed. If you retain a lawyer to represent you in a suit arising from an accident, you do not know whether the settlement the lawyer recommends is in your best interest or the lawyer's.

Of course, many people behave honorably even if they have opportunities to exploit others. Many people also honestly believe that they are putting in a full day's work even when they are not working as hard as they might. Aiko, who manages Pat's printing shop, is paid an hourly wage. She works every hour she is supposed to, even though Pat rarely checks on her. Nonetheless, Aiko may not be spending her time as effectively as possible. She politely (but impersonally) asks everyone who enters the shop, "May I help you?" If she were to receive the appropriate financial incentives—say, a share of the shop's profit—she would memorize the names of her customers, greet them enthusiastically by name when they enter the store, and check with nearby businesses to find out whether they would be interested in new services.

A Model

We can describe many principal-agent interactions using the following model. This model stresses that the output or profit from this relationship and the risk borne by the two parties depend on the actions of the agent and the state of nature.

In a typical principal-agent relationship, the principal, Paul, owns some property (such as a firm) or has a property right (such as the right to sue for damages from an injury). Paul hires or contracts with an agent, Amy, to take some action a that increases the value of his property or that produces profit, π, from using his property.

The principal and the agent need each other. If Paul hires Amy to run his ice-cream shop, Amy needs Paul's shop and Paul needs Amy's efforts to sell ice cream.

The profit from the ice cream sold, π, depends on the number of hours, a, that Amy works. The profit may also depend on the outcome of θ, which represents the *state of nature*:

$$\pi = \pi(a, \theta).$$

For example, profit may depend on whether the ice-cream machine breaks, $\theta = 1$, or does not break, $\theta = 0$. Or it may depend on whether it is a hot day, θ = the temperature.

In extreme cases, the profit function depends only on the agent's actions or only on the state of nature. At one extreme, profit depends only on the agent's action, $\pi = \pi(a)$, if there is only one state of nature: no uncertainty due to random events. In our example, the profit function has this form if demand does not vary with weather and if the ice-cream machine is reliable.

At the other extreme, profit depends only on the state of nature, $\pi = \pi(\theta)$, such as in an insurance market in which profit or value depends only on the state of nature and not on the actions of an agent. For instance, a couple buys insurance against rain on the day of their marriage. The value they place on their outdoor wedding ceremony is $\pi(\theta)$, which depends only on the weather, θ, because no actions are involved.

Types of Contracts

A verbal contract isn't worth the paper it's written on. —Samuel Goldwyn

Where a formal market exists, the principal may deal impersonally with an anonymous agent by buying a good or service of known quality at the market price. There is no opportunity for opportunism. In this chapter, we focus on situations for which either a formal market does not exist or a principal and an agent agree on a customized contract that is designed to reduce opportunism.

A contract between a principal and an agent determines how the outcome of their partnership (such as the profit or output) is split between them. Three common types of contracts are fixed-fee, hire, and contingent contracts.

In a *fixed-fee contract*, the payment to the agent, F, is independent of the agent's actions, a, the state of nature, θ, or the outcome, π. The principal keeps the *residual profit*, $\pi(a, \theta) - F$. Alternatively, the principal may get a fixed amount and the agent may receive the residual profit. For example, the agent may pay a fixed rent for the right to use the principal's property.[2]

In a *hire contract*, the payment to the agent depends on the agent's actions as they are observed by the principal. Two common types of hire contracts pay employees an *hourly rate*—a wage per hour—or a *piece rate*—a payment per unit of output produced. If w is the wage per hour (or the price per piece of output) and Amy works a hours (or produces a units of output), then Paul pays Amy wa and keeps the residual profit $\pi(a, \theta) - wa$.

In a *contingent contract*, the payoff to each person depends on the state of nature, which may not be known to the parties at the time they write the contract. For example, Penn agrees to pay Alexis a higher amount to fix his roof if it is raining than if it is not.

One type of contingent contract is a *splitting* or *sharing contract*, where the payoff to each person is a fraction of the total profit (which is observable). Alain sells

[2]Jefferson Hope says in the Sherlock Holmes mystery *A Study in Scarlet*, "I applied at a cab-owner's office, and soon got employment. I was to bring a certain sum a week to the owner, and whatever was over that I might keep for myself."

Pamela's house for her for $\pi(a, \theta)$ for a commission of 7% on the sales price. He receives $0.07\pi(a, \theta)$, and she keeps $0.93\pi(a, \theta)$.

Efficiency

The type of contract selected depends on what the parties can observe. A principal is more likely to use a hire contract if the principal can easily monitor the agent's actions. A contingent contract may be chosen, for example, if the state of nature can be observed after the work is completed. A fixed-fee contract does not depend on observing anything, so it can always be used.

efficient contract an agreement with provisions that ensures that no party can be made better off without harming the other party

efficiency in production situation in which the principal's and agent's combined value (profits, payoffs), π, is maximized

efficiency in risk bearing a situation in which risk sharing is optimal in that the person who least minds facing risk—the risk-neutral or less risk-averse person—bears more of the risk

Ideally, the principal and agent agree to an **efficient contract**: an agreement with provisions that ensure that no party can be made better off without harming the other party. Using an efficient contract results in *efficiency in production* and *efficiency in risk sharing*.

Efficiency in production requires that the principal's and agent's combined value (profits, payoffs), π, is maximized. We say that production is efficient if Amy manages Paul's firm so that the sum of their profits cannot be increased. In our examples, the moral hazard hurts the principal by more than it helps the agent, so total profit falls. Thus, achieving efficiency in production requires preventing the moral hazard.

Efficiency in risk bearing requires that risk sharing is optimal in that the person who least minds facing risk—the risk-neutral or less-risk-averse person—bears more of the risk. In Chapter 17, we saw that risk-averse people are willing to pay a risk premium to avoid risk, whereas risk-neutral people do not care if they face fair risk or not. Suppose that Arlene is risk averse and is willing to pay a risk premium of \$100 to avoid a particular risk. Peter is risk neutral and would bear the risk without a premium. Arlene and Peter can strike a deal whereby Peter agrees to bear *all* of Arlene's risk in exchange for a payment between \$0 and \$100. For simplicity, we concentrate on situations in which one party is risk averse and the other is risk neutral. (Generally, if both parties are risk averse, with one more risk averse than the other, both can be made better off if the less-risk-averse person bears more but not all of the risk.)

If everyone has full information—there is no uncertainty and no asymmetric information—efficiency can be achieved. The principal contracts with the agent to perform a task for some specified reward and observes whether or not the agent completes the task properly before paying, so no moral hazard problem arises.

Throughout the rest of this chapter, we examine what happens when the parties do not have full information. Production inefficiency is more likely when either the agent has more information than the principal or both parties are uncertain about the state of nature.

When the agent has more information than the principal and there is no risk because there is only one state of nature, contracts are used to achieve efficiency in production by conveying adequate information to the principal to eliminate moral hazard problems. Alternatively, incentives in the contract may discourage the informed person from engaging in opportunistic behavior. The contracts do not have to address efficiency in risk bearing because there is no risk.

Given that they face both asymmetric information and risk, the parties try to contract to achieve efficiency in production and efficiency in risk bearing. Often, however, both objectives cannot be achieved, so the parties must trade off between them.

See Questions 1–4.

20.2 Production Efficiency

The contract that an agent and principal use affects production efficiency. In the following example, production efficiency is achieved by maximizing *total* or *joint profit*: the sum of the principal's and the agent's individual profits. To isolate the production issues from risk bearing, we initially assume that there is only one state of nature, so the parties face no risk due to random events: Total profit, $\pi(a)$, is solely a function of the agent's action, a.

Efficient Contract

To be efficient and to maximize joint profit, the contract that a principal offers to an agent must have two properties. First, the contract must provide a large enough payoff that the agent is willing to *participate* in the contract. We know that the principal's payoff is adequate to ensure the principal's participation because the principal offers the contract.

incentive compatible referring to a contract's provision of inducements such that the agent wants to perform the assigned task rather than engage in opportunistic behavior

Second, the contract must be **incentive compatible** in that it provides inducements such that the agent wants to perform the assigned task rather than engage in opportunistic behavior. That is, it is in the agent's best interest to take an action that maximizes joint profit. If the contract is not incentive compatible—so the agent tries to maximize personal profit rather than joint profit—efficiency can be achieved only if the principal monitors the agent and forces the agent to act so as to maximize joint profit.

We use an example to illustrate why some types of contracts lead to efficiency and others do not. Paula, the principal, owns a store called Buy-A-Duck (located near a canal) that sells wood carvings of ducks. Arthur, the agent, manages the store. Paula and Arthur's joint profit is

$$\pi\,(a) = R(a) - 12a,$$

where $R(a)$ is the sales revenue from selling a carvings, and $12a$ is the cost of the carvings. It costs Arthur \$12 to obtain and sell each duck, including the amount he pays a local carver and the opportunity value (best alternative use) of his time.

Because Arthur bears the full marginal cost of selling one more carving, he wants to sell the joint-profit-maximizing output only if he also gets the full marginal benefit from selling one more duck. To determine the joint-profit-maximizing solution, we can ask what Arthur would do if he owned the shop and received all the profit so that he would have an incentive to maximize total profit.

How many ducks must Arthur sell to maximize the parties' joint profit? As panel a of Figure 20.1 shows, he would maximize profit by selling 12 carvings, for which his marginal revenue curve, MR, intersects his marginal cost curve, $MC = \$12$, at the equilibrium point e.[3] Panel b shows that total profit, π, reaches a maximum of \$72 at point E.

Which types of contracts lead to production efficiency? To answer this question, we first examine which contracts yield that outcome when both parties have full information and then consider which contracts bring the desired result when the

---

[3]The demand curve is $p = 24 - \frac{1}{2}a$, where p is the price and a is the number of carved ducks sold. Revenue is $R = 24a - \frac{1}{2}a^2$, and marginal revenue is $MR = 24 - a$. Profit is maximized where $MR = 24 - a = 12 = MC$ or $a = 12$.

Figure 20.1 Maximizing Joint Profit When the Agent Gets the Residual Profit.

(a) If the agent, Arthur, gets all the joint profit, π, he maximizes his profit by selling 12 carvings at e, where the marginal revenue curve intersects his marginal cost curve: $MR = MC = 12$. If he pays the principal, Paula, a fixed rent of \$48, he maximizes his profit by selling 12 carvings. (A fixed rent does not affect either his marginal revenue or his marginal cost.) (b) Joint profit at 12 carvings is \$72, point E. If Arthur pays a rent of \$48 to Paula, Arthur's profit is π – \$48. By selling 12 carvings and maximizing joint profit, Arthur also maximizes his profit.

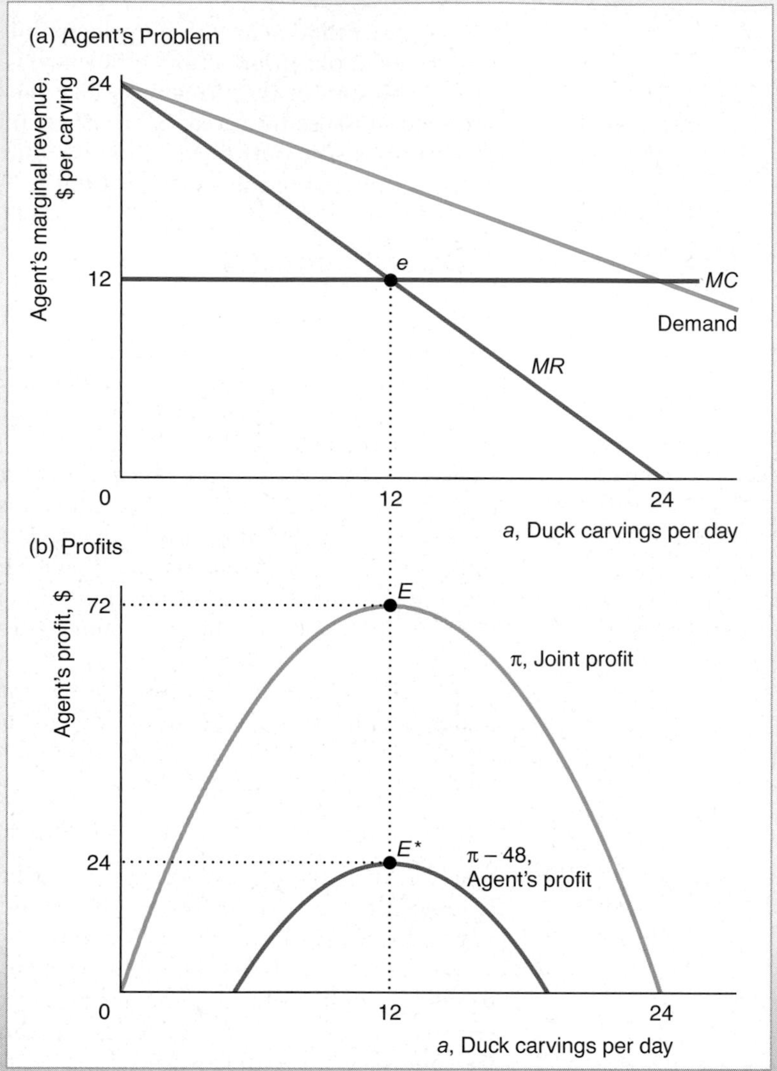

principal is relatively uninformed. It is important to remember that we are considering a special case: Contracts that work here may not work in some other settings, whereas contracts that do not work here may be effective elsewhere.

Full Information

Suppose that both Paula and Arthur have full information. Each knows the actions Arthur takes—the number of carvings sold—and the effect of those actions on profit. Because she has full information, Paula can dictate exactly what Arthur is to do. Are there incentive-compatible contracts that do not require such monitoring and supervision? To answer this question, we consider four kinds of contracts: a fixed-fee rental contract, a hire contract, and two types of contingent contracts.

Fixed-Fee Rental Contract. If Arthur contracts to rent the store from Paula for a fixed fee, F, joint profit is maximized. Arthur earns a residual profit equal to the joint profit minus the fixed rent he pays Paula, $\pi(a) - F$. Because the amount Paula makes is fixed, Arthur gets the entire marginal profit from selling one more duck. As a consequence, the amount, a, that maximizes Arthur's profit, $\pi(a) - F$, also maximizes joint profit, $\pi(a)$.

In Figure 20.1, Arthur pays Paula $F = \$48$ rent. This fixed payment does not affect his marginal cost. As a result, he maximizes his profit after paying the rent, $\pi - \$48$, by equating his marginal revenue to his marginal cost: $MR = MC = 12$ at point e in panel a.

Because Arthur pays the same fixed rent no matter how many units he sells, the agent's profit curve in panel b lies $48 below the joint-profit curve at every quantity. As a result, Arthur's net profit curve peaks (at point E^*) at the same quantity, 12, where the joint profit curve peaks (at E). Thus, the fixed-fee rental contract is incentive compatible. Arthur participates in this contract because he earns $24 after paying for the rent and the carvings (point E^*).

Hire Contract. Now suppose that Paula contracts to pay Arthur for each carving he sells. If she pays him $12 per carving, Arthur just breaks even on each sale. He is indifferent between participating and not. Even if he chooses to participate, he does not sell the joint-profit-maximizing number of carvings unless Paula supervises him. If she does supervise him, she instructs him to sell 12 carvings, and she gets all the joint profit of $72.

For Arthur to want to participate and to sell carvings without supervision, he must receive more than $12 per carving. If Paula pays Arthur $14 per carving, for example, he makes a profit of $2 per carving. He now has an incentive to sell as many carvings as he can, which does not maximize joint profit, so this contract is not incentive compatible.

Even if the contract calls for Arthur to get $14 per carving and for Paula to control how many carvings he sells, joint profit is not maximized. Paula keeps the revenue minus what she pays Arthur, $14 times the number of carvings,

$$R(a) - 14a.$$

Thus, her objective differs from the joint-profit-maximizing objective, $\pi = R(a) - 12a$. Joint profit is maximized when marginal revenue equals the marginal cost of $12. Because Paula's marginal cost, $14, is larger, she directs Arthur to sell fewer than the optimal number of carvings.[4]

Revenue-Sharing Contract. If Paula and Arthur use a *contingent contract* whereby they share the *revenue*, joint profit is not maximized. Suppose that Arthur receives three-quarters of the revenue, $\frac{3}{4}R$, and Paula gets the rest, $\frac{1}{4}R$. Panel a of Figure 20.2 shows the marginal revenue that Arthur obtains from selling an extra carving, $MR^* = \frac{3}{4}MR$. He maximizes his profit at $24 by selling 8 carvings, for which $MR^* = MC$ at e^*. Paula gets the remaining profit of $40, which is the difference between their total profit from selling 8 ducks per day, $\pi = \$64$, and Arthur's profit.

Thus, their joint profit in panel b at $a = 8$ is $64, which is $8 less than the maximum possible profit of $72 (point E). Arthur has an incentive to sell fewer than the

---

[4]Paula maximizes $R - 14a = \left(24a - \frac{1}{2}a^2\right) - 14a = 10a - \frac{1}{2}a^2$. Setting the derivative with respect to a equal to zero, $10 - a = 0$, we find that she maximizes her profit by selling 10 carvings. Joint profit is only $70 at 10 carvings, compared to $72 at the optimal 12 carvings.

Figure 20.2 Why Revenue Sharing Reduces Agent's Efforts.

(a) Joint profit is maximized at 12 carvings, where $MR = MC = 12$ at equilibrium point e. If Arthur gets three-quarters of the revenue and Paula gets the rest, Arthur maximizes his profit by selling 8 carvings, where his new marginal revenue curve $MR^* = \frac{3}{4}MR$ equals his marginal cost at point e^*. (b) Joint profit reaches a maximum of \$72 at E, where they sell 12 carvings per day. If they split the revenue, Arthur sells 8 ducks per day and gets \$24 at E^*, and Paula receives the residual, \$40 (= \$64 – \$24).

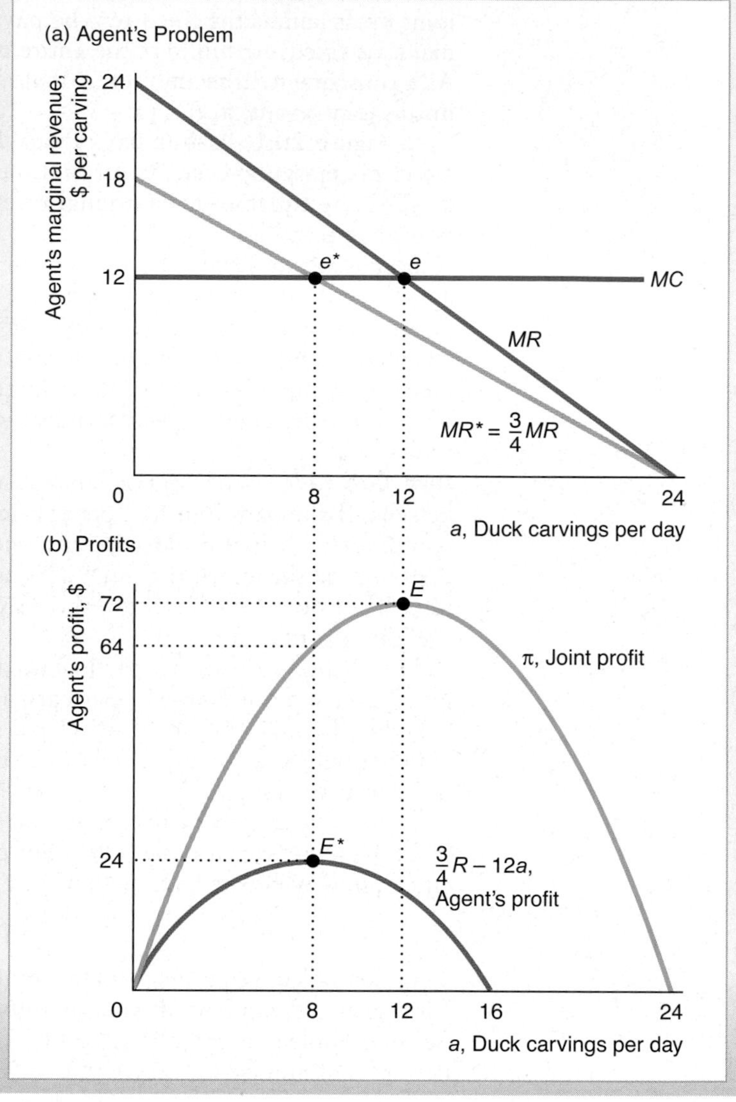

optimal number of ducks because he bears the full marginal cost of each carving he sells, \$12, but gets only three-quarters of the marginal revenue.[5]

Profit-Sharing Contract. Paula and Arthur may instead use a *contingent contract* by which they divide the *economic profit*, π. If they can agree that the true marginal and average cost is \$12 per carving (which includes Arthur's opportunity cost of time), the contract is incentive compatible because Arthur wants to sell the optimal

[5]Even if Paula controls how many carvings are sold, joint profit is not maximized. Because the amount she makes, $\frac{1}{4}R$, depends only on revenue and not on the cost of obtaining the carvings, she wants the revenue-maximizing quantity sold. Revenue is maximized where marginal revenue is zero at $a = 24$ (panel a). Arthur would not participate if the contract granted him only three-quarters of the revenue but required him to sell 24 carvings because he would lose money.

number of carvings. Only by maximizing total profit can he maximize his share of profit. As Figure 20.3 illustrates, Arthur receives one-third of the joint profit and chooses to produce the level of output, $a = 12$, that maximizes joint profit.[6] Arthur earns \$24, so he is willing to participate.

The second column of Table 20.1 summarizes our analysis. Whether efficiency in production is achieved depends on the type of contract the principal and the agent use. If the principal has full information (knows the agent's actions), the principal achieves production efficiency without having to supervise by using one of the incentive-compatible contracts: fixed-fee rental or profit-sharing.

See Questions 5 and 6 and Problem 18.

Asymmetric Information

Now suppose that the principal, Paula, has less information than the agent, Arthur. She cannot observe the number of carvings he sells or the revenue. Due to this asymmetric information, Arthur can steal from Paula without her detecting the theft.

As Table 20.1 shows, with asymmetric information, *the only contract that results in production efficiency and no moral hazard problem is the one whereby the principal gets a fixed rent.* All the other contracts result in inefficiency, and Arthur has an opportunity to take advantage of Paula.

Fixed-Fee Rental Contract. Arthur pays Paula the fixed rent that she is due because Paula would know if she were paid less. Arthur receives the residual profit, joint profit minus the fixed rent, so he wants to sell the joint-profit-maximizing number of carvings.

See Question 7.

Hire Contract. If Paula offers to pay Arthur the actual marginal cost of \$12 per carving and he is honest, he may refuse to participate in the contract because he

Figure 20.3 Why Profit Sharing Is Efficient.

If the agent, Arthur, gets a third of the joint profit, he maximizes his profit, $\frac{1}{3}\pi$, by maximizing joint profit, π.

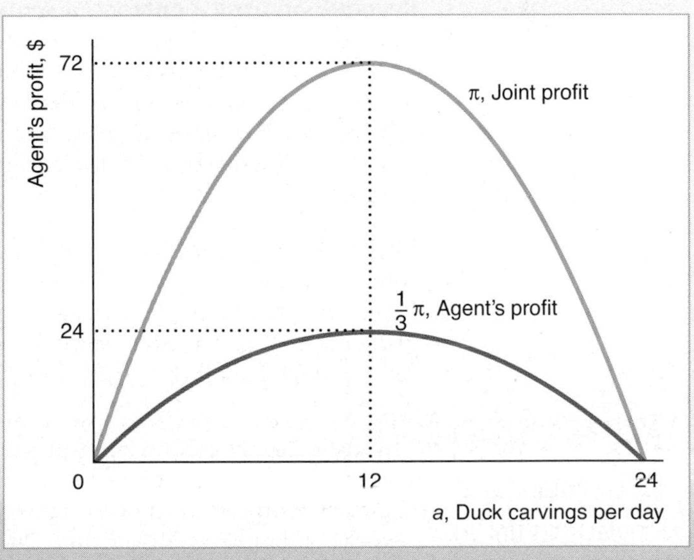

[6]Arthur gets one-third of profit, $\frac{1}{3}\pi = \frac{1}{3}(R - C) = \frac{1}{3}R - \frac{1}{3}C$, where R is revenue and C is cost. He maximizes his profit where $\frac{1}{3}MR = \frac{1}{3}MC$. Although he gets only one-third of the marginal revenue, $\frac{1}{3}MR$, he bears only one-third of the marginal cost. Dividing both sides of the equation by $\frac{1}{3}$, we find that this condition is the same as the one for maximizing total profit: $MR = MC$.

Table 20.1 Production Efficiency and Moral Hazard Problems for Buy-A-Duck.

	Full Information	Asymmetric Information	
Contract	Production Efficiency	Production Efficiency	Moral Hazard Problem
Fixed-fee rental contract			
Rent (to principal)	Yes	Yes	No
Hire contract, per unit pay			
Pay equals marginal cost	No[a]	No[b]	Yes
Pay is greater than marginal cost	No[c]	No	Yes
Contingent contract			
Share revenue	No	No[b]	Yes
Share profit	Yes	No[b]	Yes

[a]The agent may not participate and has no incentive to sell the optimal number of carvings. Efficiency can be achieved only if the principal supervises.

[b]Unless the agent steals all the revenue (or profit) from an extra sale, inefficiency results.

[c]The agent sells too many or the principal directs the agent to sell too few carvings.

makes no profit. Even if he participates, he has no incentive to sell the optimal number of carvings.

If he is dishonest, he may underreport sales and pocket some of the extra revenue. Unless he can steal all the extra revenue from an additional sale, he sells less than the joint-profit-maximizing quantity.

If Paula pays him more than the actual marginal cost per carving, he has an incentive to sell too many carvings, whether or not he steals. If he also steals, he has an even greater incentive to sell too many carvings.

Revenue-Sharing Contract. Even with full information, the revenue-sharing contract is inefficient. Asymmetric information adds a moral hazard problem: The agent may steal from the principal. If Arthur can steal a larger share of the revenues than the contract specifies, he has less of an incentive to underproduce than he does with full information. Indeed, if the agent can steal all the extra revenue from an additional sale, the agent acts efficiently to maximize joint profit, all of which the agent keeps.

Profit-Sharing Contract. If they use a contingent contract by which they agree to split the economic profit, Arthur has to report both the revenue and the cost to Paula so that they may calculate their shares. If he can overreport cost or underreport revenue, he has an incentive to produce a nonoptimal quantity. Only if Arthur can appropriate all the profit does he produce efficiently.

APPLICATION

Contracts and Productivity in Agriculture

In agriculture, landowners (principals) contract with farmers (agents) to work their land. Farmers may work on their own land (the principal and agent are the same person), work on land rented from a landowner (fixed-fee rental contract), work as employees for a time rate or a piece rate (hire contract), or sharecrop (contingent contract). A sharecropper splits the output (crop) with the landowner at the end of the growing season.[7]

[7]If a farmer is someone who is out standing in his field, a sharecropper is someone who is out standing in someone else's field.

Our analysis tells us that farmers' willingness to work hard depends on the type of contract that is used. Farmers who keep all the marginal profit from additional work—those who own the land or rent it for a fixed fee—work hard and maximize (joint) profit. Sharecroppers, who bear the full marginal cost of working an extra hour and get only a fraction of the extra revenue, put in too little effort. Hired farmworkers who are paid by the hour may not work hard unless they are very carefully supervised. That is, they may engage in **shirking**: a moral hazard in which agents do not provide all the services they are paid to provide.

shirking
a *moral hazard* in which agents do not provide all the services they are paid to provide

These predictions about contract type and agent effort were tested by using data on farmers in the Philippines. Foster and Rosenzweig (1994) could not directly monitor the work effort—any more than most landowners can. Rather, they ingeniously measured the effort indirectly. They contended that the harder people work, the more they eat and the more they use up body mass (defined as weight divided by height squared), holding calorie intake constant.

Foster and Rosenzweig estimated the effect of each compensation method on body mass and consumption (after adjusting for gender, age, type of activity, and other factors). They found that people who work for themselves or are paid by the piece use up 10% more body mass, holding calorie consumption constant, than time-rate workers and 13% more than sharecroppers. Foster and Rosenzweig also discovered that piece-rate workers consume 25% more calories per day and that people who work on their own farm consume 16% more than time-rate workers.

20.3 Trade-Off Between Efficiency in Production and in Risk Bearing

Writing an efficient contract is extremely difficult if the agent knows more than the principal, the principal never learns the truth, and both face risk. Usually, a contract does not achieve efficiency in production *and* in risk bearing. Contract clauses that increase efficiency in production may reduce efficiency in risk bearing, and vice versa. If these goals are incompatible, the parties may write imperfect contracts that reach a compromise between the two objectives. To illustrate the trade-offs involved, we consider a common situation in which it is difficult to achieve efficiency: contracting with an expert such as a lawyer.

We illustrate how contracts affect the outcome by using an example in which Pam, the principal, is injured in a traffic accident and is a plaintiff in a lawsuit, and Alfredo, the agent, is her lawyer. Pam faces uncertainty due to risk and to asymmetric information. The jury award at the conclusion of the trial, $\pi(a, \theta)$, depends on a, the number of hours Alfredo works before the trial, and θ, the state of nature due to the (unknown) attitudes of the jury. All else the same, the more time Alfredo spends working on the case, a, the larger the amount, π, that the jury is likely to award. Pam never learns the jury's attitudes, θ, so she cannot accurately judge Alfredo's efforts even after the trial. For example, if she loses the case, she doesn't know whether she lost because Alfredo didn't work hard (low a) or because the case was weak and the jury was prejudiced against her (bad θ).

Contracts and Efficiency

How hard Alfredo works depends on his attitudes toward risk and his knowledge of the payoff for his trial preparations. For any hour that he does not devote to Pam's case, Alfredo can work on other cases. The most lucrative of these forgone opportunities is his marginal cost of working on Pam's case.

The beneficiary of the extra payoff that results if Alfredo works harder depends on his contract with Pam. If Alfredo is risk neutral and gets the entire marginal benefit from any extra work, he puts in the optimal number of hours that maximizes their expected joint payoff. Alfredo collects the marginal benefit from the extra work and bears the marginal cost, so he sets his expected marginal benefit equal to his marginal cost, thus maximizing the expected joint payoff.

The choice of various possible contracts between Pam and Alfredo affects whether efficiency in production or in risk bearing is achieved. They choose among fixed-fee, hire (hourly wage), and contingent contracts. Table 20.2 summarizes the outcomes under each of these contracts.

Lawyer Gets a Fixed Fee. If Pam pays Alfredo a fixed fee, F, he gets paid the same no matter how much he works. Thus, he has little incentive to work hard on this case, and production is inefficient. His main incentive to work hard is to establish a reputation as a good lawyer so as to attract future clients. For simplicity, we will ignore this effect, as it applies for all types of contracts. Production efficiency could be achieved only if Pam could monitor Alfredo and force him to act optimally. Most individual plaintiffs, however, cannot monitor a lawyer and thus cannot determine whether the lawyer is behaving appropriately or not.

Whether the fixed-fee contract leads to efficiency in risk bearing depends on the attitudes toward risk on the part of the principal and the agent. Pam, the principal, bears all the risk. Alfredo's pay, F, is certain, while Pam's net payoff, $\pi(a, \theta) - F$, varies with the unknown state of nature, θ.

A lawyer who handles many similar cases may be less risk averse than an individual client whose financial future depends on a single case. If Alfredo has many cases like Pam's and if Pam's future rests on the outcome of this suit, their choice of this type of contract leads to inefficiency in both production and risk bearing. Not only is Alfredo not working hard enough, but Pam bears the risk even though she is more risk averse than Alfredo.

In contrast, suppose that Alfredo is a self-employed lawyer working on a major case for Pam, who runs a large insurance company with many similar cases. Alfredo is risk averse and Pam is risk neutral (because she is able to pool many similar cases). Here having the principal bear all the risk is efficient. If the insurance company can

Table 20.2 Efficiency of Client-Lawyer Contracts.

Type of Contract	Fixed Fee to Lawyer	Fixed Payment to Client	Lawyer Paid by the Hour	Contingent Contract
Lawyer's payoff	F	$\pi(a, \theta) - F$	wa	$\alpha\pi(a, \theta)$
Client's payoff	$\pi(a, \theta) - F$	F	$\pi(a, \theta) - wa$	$(1 - \alpha)\pi(a, \theta)$
Production efficiency	No*	Yes	No*	No*
Person bearing risk	Client	Lawyer	Client	Shared

*Production efficiency is possible if the client can monitor and enforce optimal effort by the lawyer.

monitor Alfredo's behavior, it is even possible to achieve production efficiency. Indeed, many insurance companies employ lawyers in this manner.

Plaintiff Gets a Fixed Payment. Instead, the two parties could agree to a contract by which Alfredo could pay Pam a fixed amount of money, F, for the right to try the case and collect the entire verdict less the payment to Pam, $\pi(a, \theta) - F$. With such a contract, Alfredo has an incentive to put in the optimal number of hours. He works until his marginal cost—the opportunity cost of his time—equals the marginal benefit—the extra amount he gets if he wins at trial. Because he has already paid Pam, all extra amounts earned at trial go to Alfredo.

Under this contract, Alfredo bears all the risk related to the outcome of the trial. No matter how risk averse Pam is, she may hesitate to agree to such a contract. Because she is not an expert on the law, she cannot easily predict the jury's likely verdict. Thus, she does not know how large a fixed fee she should insist on receiving. There is no practical way in which Alfredo's superior information about the likely outcome of the trial can be credibly revealed to her. She suspects that it is in his best interest to tell her that the likely payout is lower than he truly believes.[8]

Lawyer Is Hired by the Hour. In complicated cases, a lawyer's output is not easily measured, so it is not practical to pay the attorney by the piece. Pam could pay Alfredo a wage of w per hour for the a hours that he works. Doing so would create the potential for a serious moral hazard problem unless Pam could monitor Alfredo to determine how many hours he works. If she could not, Alfredo could bill her for more hours than he actually worked.[9] Even if Pam could observe how many hours he works, she would not know whether Alfredo worked effectively and whether the work was necessary. Thus, it would be difficult, if not impossible, for Pam to monitor Alfredo's work.

Here Pam bears all the risk. Alfredo's earnings, wa, are determined before the outcome is known. Pam's return, $\pi(a, \theta) - wa$, varies with the state of nature and is unknown before the verdict.

contingent fee
a payment to a lawyer that is a share of the award in a court case (usually after legal expenses are deducted) if the client wins and nothing if the client loses

Fee Is Contingent. Some lawyers offer plaintiffs a contract whereby the lawyer works for "free"—receiving no hourly payment—in exchange for splitting the compensation awarded in court or in a settlement before trial. The lawyer receives a **contingent fee**: a payment to a lawyer that is a share of the award in a court case (usually after legal expenses are deducted) if the client wins and nothing if the client loses. If the lawyer's share of the award is α and the jury awards $\pi(a, \theta)$, the lawyer receives $\alpha\pi(a, \theta)$ and the principal gets $(1 - \alpha)\pi(a, \theta)$. This approach is attractive to many plaintiffs because they cannot monitor how hard the lawyer works and are unable or unwilling to make payments before the trial is completed.

How they split the award affects the amount of risk each bears. If Alfredo gets one-quarter of the award, $\alpha = \frac{1}{4}$ and Pam gets three-quarters, Pam bears more risk

---

[8]Alfredo may be hesitant to offer Pam a fixed fee. How well they do in court depends on the merits of her case. At least initially, Alfredo does not know how good a case she has. Initially, she has an incentive to try to convince him that the case is very strong. Moreover, a lawyer may worry that if he pays the plaintiff a fixed fee, she will not fully cooperate in preparing the case (an issue that we've ignored in our example, in which only the actions of the lawyer matter).

[9]A lawyer dies in an accident and goes to heaven. A host of angels greet him with a banner that reads, "Welcome Oldest Man!" The lawyer is puzzled: "Why do you think I'm the oldest man who ever lived? I was only 47 when I died." One of the angels replied, "You can't fool us; you were at least 152 when you died. We saw how many hours you billed!"

than Alfredo does. Suppose that the award is either 0 or 40 with equal probability. Alfredo receives either 0 or 10, so his average award is 5. His variance (Chapter 17) is

$$\sigma_a^2 = \tfrac{1}{2}(0-5)^2 + \tfrac{1}{2}(10-5)^2 = 25.$$

Pam makes either 0 or 30, so her average award is 15 and her variance is

$$\sigma_p^2 = \tfrac{1}{2}(0-15)^2 + \tfrac{1}{2}(30-15)^2 = 225.$$

Thus, the variance in Pam's payoff is greater than Alfredo's.

Whether splitting the risk in this way is desirable turns on how risk averse each party is. If one is risk neutral and the other is risk averse, it is efficient for the risk-neutral person to bear all the risk. If they are equally risk averse, a splitting rule where $\alpha = \tfrac{1}{2}$, and they face equal risk may be optimal.[10]

A sharing contract encourages shirking: Alfredo is likely to put in too little effort. He bears the full cost of his labors—the forgone use of his time—but gets only α share of the returns from this effort. Thus, this contract results in production inefficiency and may or may not lead to inefficient risk bearing.

Choosing the Best Contract

Which contract is best depends on the parties' attitudes toward risk, the degree of risk, the difficulty in monitoring, and other factors. If Alfredo is risk neutral, they can achieve both efficiency goals if Alfredo gives Pam a fixed fee. He has the incentive to put in the optimal amount of work and does not mind bearing the risk.

However, if Alfredo is risk averse and Pam is risk neutral, they may not be able to achieve both objectives. Contracts by which Alfredo receives a fixed fee or a wage rate cause Pam to bear all the risk and lead to inefficiency in production because Alfredo has too little incentive to work hard.

Often when the parties find that they cannot achieve both objectives, they choose a contract that attains neither goal. For example, they may use a contingent contract that fails to achieve efficiency in production and may not achieve efficiency in risk bearing. The contingent contract strikes a compromise between the two goals. Alfredo has more of an incentive to work if he splits the payoff than he has if he receives a fixed fee. He is less likely to work excessive hours with the contingent fee than he would work if he were paid by the hour. Moreover, neither party has to bear all the risk—they share it under the contingent contract.

Lawyers usually work for a fixed fee only if the task or case is very simple, such as writing a will or handling an uncontested divorce. The client has some idea of whether the work is done satisfactorily, so monitoring is relatively easy and little risk is involved.

In riskier situations, the other types of contracts are more commonly used. When the lawyer is relatively risk averse or when the principal is very concerned that the lawyer works hard, an hourly wage may be used.

Contingent fee arrangements are particularly common for plaintiffs' lawyers who specialize in auto accidents, medical malpractice, product liability, and other *torts*: wrongful acts in which a person's body, property, or reputation is harmed and for which the injured party is entitled to compensation. Because these plaintiffs' lawyers

---

[10]If Pam and Alfredo split the award equally and each receives either 0 or 20 with equal probability, each has a variance of $\tfrac{1}{2}(0 - 10)^2 + \tfrac{1}{2}(20 - 10)^2 = 100$.

can typically pool risks across clients, they are less concerned than their clients about risk. As a consequence, these attorneys are willing to accept contingent fees (and might agree to pay a fixed fee to the plaintiff). Moreover, accident victims often lack the resources to pay for a lawyer's time before winning at trial, so they often prefer contingent contracts.

See Question 8 and Problem 19.

APPLICATION

Music Contracts: Changing Their Tunes

Ice Cube, Jackson Browne, the Eagles, Madonna, Pearl Jam, Prince, and Radiohead are no longer signing traditional contracts with major-label recording companies. In 2008, Robbie Williams and Coldplay were considering severing ties with EMI.

Traditional contracts obligate the artist to deliver a specific number of albums, the record company gives a cash advance and retains the lion's share (often 90%) of the revenue, and the artist receives a share (usually less than $2 a copy) only after the advance is paid back to the company. The record company owns the master recordings of the music, but pays to produce, promote, and distribute the recording.

Now, these stars are forgoing the upfront payments, bearing the recording and promotional costs, and retaining ownership of the recording, leaving only distribution to one of the major labels. The artist licenses the music to whichever major label offers the biggest share of sales. This rate is larger than in the past because the artist incurs more of the costs, as well as much more of the risk.

In 2006, Ice Cube chose to "bet on himself" and take the risk on his CD *Laugh Now, Cry Later*. EMI made and distributed the album, but Ice Cube paid for the recordings and, with his managers, oversaw most of the U.S. marketing. Pearl Jam sold its *Pearl Jam* album through a "partnership" agreement with Sony BMG's J Records, where the label received a percentage of sales for distribution and other services it provided. In 2007, the Eagles released their first album in nearly 30 years exclusively through Wal-Mart.

When Jackson Browne's contract with Warner Music Group Corporation's Elektra Records expired, he financed an album, *Solo Acoustic Vol. 1*, and licensed it to a Warner unit that distributes for independent record companies. It sold more copies than his last studio album for Elektra. Mr. Browne earned 7 to 10 times as much per copy sold under the new arrangement than under his previous contract.

Thus, these new contracts are changing production incentives and risk sharing. Because the artist bears more of the production and promotion costs and much more of the risk, only successful, wealthy artists are likely to use this new approach. However, as a consequence of this approach, some artists are releasing more albums, as their incentives to produce have increased. And some of these artists are earning substantial returns for bearing the extra costs and risks.

Solved Problem 20.1

Gary's demand for medical services (visits to his doctor) depends on his health. Half the time his health is good and his demand is D^1 on the graph. When his health is less good, his demand is D^2. Without medical insurance, he pays $50 a visit. Because Gary is risk averse, he wants to buy medical insurance. With full insurance, Gary pays a fixed fee at the beginning of the year, and the insurance company pays the full cost of any visit. Alternatively, with a contingent contract, Gary pays a smaller premium at the beginning of the year, and the insurance company covers only $20 per visit and Gary pays the remaining $30. How likely is a moral hazard problem to occur with each of these contracts? What is Gary's risk (variance of his medical costs) with each of the three types of insurance? Compare the contracts in terms of the trade-offs between risk and moral hazards.

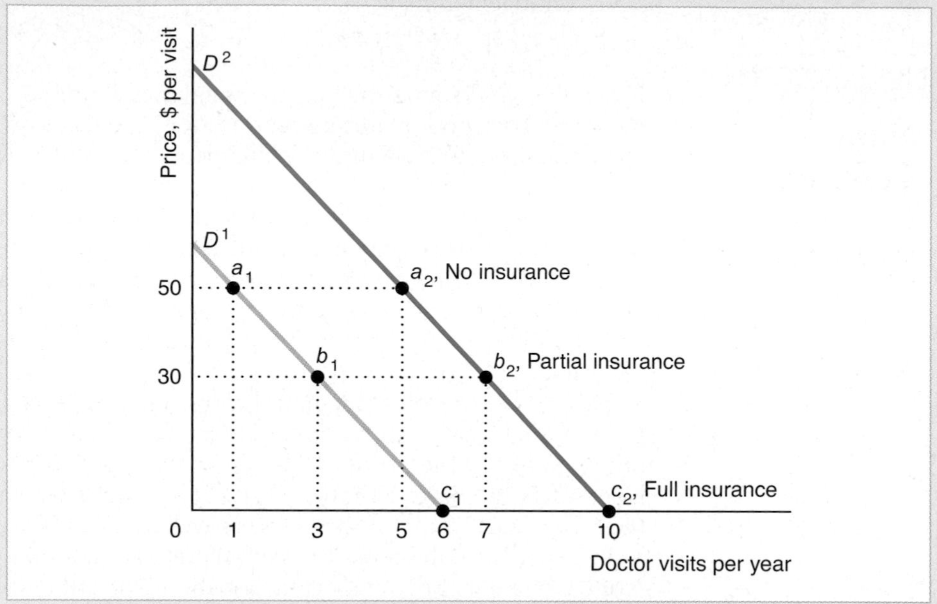

Answer

1. *Describe the moral hazard for each demand curve for each contract.* If Gary's health is good, he increases from one visit, a_1, with no insurance (where he pays \$50 a visit) to six visits, c_1, with full insurance (where he pays nothing per visit). Similarly, if his health is poor, he increases his visits from five, a_2, to ten, c_2. Thus, regardless of his health, he makes five extra visits a year with full insurance. These extra visits are the moral hazard. With a contingent contract whereby Gary pays \$30 a visit, the moral hazard is less because he makes only two extra visits instead of five (the difference between the number of visits at b_1 and a_1 and between b_2 and a_2).

2. *Calculate the variance of Gary's medical expenses with each level of insurance.* Without insurance, his average number of visits is

$$3\left[=\left(\tfrac{1}{2}\times 1\right)+\left(\tfrac{1}{2}\times 5\right)\right],$$

so his average annual medical cost is \$150. Thus, the variance of his medical expenses without insurance is

$$\begin{aligned}\sigma_n^2 &= \tfrac{1}{2}\left[(1\times \$50)-\$150\right]^2+\tfrac{1}{2}\left[(5\times 50)-\$150\right]^2\\ &= \tfrac{1}{2}(\$50-\$150)^2+\tfrac{1}{2}(\$250-\$150)^2\\ &= \$10{,}000.\end{aligned}$$

If he has full insurance, he makes a single fixed payment each year, so his payments do not vary with his health: His variance is $\sigma_f^2 = 0$. Finally, with partial insurance, he averages five visits with an average cost of \$150, and his variance is

$$\sigma_p^2 = \tfrac{1}{2}(\$90 - \$150)^2 + \tfrac{1}{2}(\$210 - \$150)^2 = \$3{,}600.$$

Thus, $\sigma_n^2 > \sigma_p^2 > \sigma_f^2$.

3. *Discuss the trade-offs.* Because Gary is risk averse, efficiency in risk bearing requires that the insurance company bear all the risk, as with full insurance. Full insurance, however, results in the largest moral hazard. Without insurance, there is no moral hazard but Gary bears all the risk. The contingent contract is a compromise whereby both the moral hazard and the degree of risk lie between the extremes.

See Questions 9 and 10.

20.4 Payments Linked to Production or Profit

We now examine how additional clauses are added to a contract to eliminate or reduce moral hazards. For simplicity, we ignore risk bearing. We focus on employer-employee contracts. Under most such contracts, employees are paid by the hour or given a fixed salary. The problem with such agreements is that the workers are not directly rewarded for productive, profit-enhancing actions, so they tend to shirk. Here rewarding agents for productive activities leads to greater efficiency.

There are two main ways to reward productive effort directly. One method is to link pay to a worker's individual output. Another is to link a worker's pay to the firm's output or profitability. However, employers who cannot monitor workers do not use incentive-compatible contracts.

Piece-Rate Hire Contracts

One direct approach to getting employees to work hard is to pay them by the *piece*—the output they produce—rather than by *time*—the number of hours they work. Piece rates are usually effective in increasing output, but they are not practical in all markets.

Greater Effort. Piece rates—by explicitly rewarding productivity—provide a greater incentive to employees to work hard than hourly wages do. For example, Billikopf (1995) found that employees who are paid by the piece prune a vineyard in only 19 hours of work per acre compared to 26 hours for employees paid by the hour. Shearer (2004) found that when tree planters were randomly assigned piece-rate pay or fixed hourly wages, they were 20% more productive when paid by the piece.

The increase in joint profit due to this greater productivity may be shared between the firm and the employees. Many workers, because they earn more with piece rates than they would earn with hourly pay, are pleased to be paid by the piece.

Problems with Piece Rates. Piece rates are not always practical. There are three chief difficulties with this system: measuring output, eliciting the desired behavior, and persuading workers to accept piece rates.

Paying piece rates is practical only if the employer can easily measure the output produced, such as the number of pieces of fruit picked or windshields installed. Employers do not use piece rates to compensate teachers, managers, and others whose output is difficult to measure. Thus, piece rates are more common for blue-collar jobs than for white-collar jobs. Roughly 15% of the labor force receives pay based on individual productivity, but most piecework is concentrated in a handful of low-paying industries such as agriculture (in which about a third of workers are paid by the piece) and apparel manufacturing or is confined to sales personnel, individual contractors, and other similar occupations.

Piece rates backfire if they encourage undesirable behavior. Sears, Roebuck & Company used to reward auto shop employees on the basis of the size of customers' repair bills. This system apparently led to overbilling of customers, which resulted in government actions and lawsuits.[11]

Some workers object to piece rates because they do not like to work hard or because they are concerned that firms will ratchet down workers' compensation after a while by lowering the pay per piece. In addition, piecework has a negative connotation in many people's minds because of its association with sweatshops, where workers toiled at repetitive tasks for 12 or more hours a day.

Contingent Contract Rewards Linked to a Firm's Success

> *I've always believed in writing without a collaborator, because where two people are writing the same book, each believes he gets all the worries and only half the royalties.*
> —Agatha Christie

Although companies can use piece rates with workers who produce easily measured output, they need alternative incentive schemes for managers, corporate directors, and others whose productivity is difficult to quantify, especially those who work as part of a team. Such workers may be rewarded if their team or the firm does well in general. Frequently, year-end bonuses are based on increases in the firm's profit or the value of its stock.

A common type of incentive is a lump-sum year-end bonus based on the firm's performance or that of a group of workers within the firm. Another incentive is a stock option, which gives managers (and increasingly other workers) the option of buying a certain number of shares of stock in the firm at a prespecified *exercise price*. If the stock's market price exceeds the exercise price during that period, an employee can exercise the option—buy the stock—and then sell it at the market price, in this way making an immediate profit. But if the stock's price stays below the exercise price, the option is worthless. Beyond motivating employees to work hard, these incentives also act as *golden handcuffs*: a deterrent to taking a job at a competing firm and forfeiting the stock option. See **www.myeconlab.com/perloff**, Chapter 20, "Increasing Use of Incentives."

See Questions 11 and 12 and Problems 20 and 21.

20.5 Monitoring

> *Washington, D.C.—According to a groundbreaking new study by the Department of Labor, working—the physical act of engaging in a productive job-related activity—may greatly increase the amount of work accom-*

[11]Barbara B. Buchholz, "The Bonus Isn't Reserved for Big Shots Anymore," *New York Times*, October 27, 1996.

plished during the workday, especially when compared with the more common practices of wasting time and not working.

—"Study Finds Working at Work Improves Productivity," *The Onion*, Issue 43–45, November 5, 2007.

On what was to be his last day on the job, Gus is caught asleep at the switch.

When using piece rates and rewarding workers for the success of the firm rather than individual output are not feasible, employers usually pay fixed-fee salaries or hourly wages. Employees who are paid a fixed salary have little incentive to work hard if the employer cannot observe shirking. If an employer pays employees by the hour but cannot observe how many hours they work, employees may inflate the number of hours they report working.

A firm can reduce such shirking by intensively supervising or monitoring its workers. Monitoring eliminates the asymmetric information problem: Both the employee and the employer know how hard the employee works. If the cost of monitoring workers is low enough, it pays to prevent shirking by carefully monitoring and firing employees who do not work hard.

Firms have experimented with various means of lowering the cost of monitoring. Requiring employees to punch a time clock and installing videocameras to record the work effort are examples of firms' attempts to use capital to monitor job performance. Similarly, by installing assembly lines that force employees to work at a pace dictated by the firm, employers can control employees' work rate.

According to a survey by the American Management Association, nearly two-thirds of employers record employees' voice mail, e-mail, or phone calls; review computer files; or videotape workers. A quarter of the firms that use surveillance don't tell their employees. The most common types of surveillance are tallying phone numbers called and recording the duration of the calls (37%), videotaping employees' work (16%), storing and reviewing e-mail (15%), storing and reviewing computer files (14%), and taping and reviewing phone conversations (10%). Monitoring and surveillance are most common in the financial sector, in which 81% of firms use these techniques. Rather than watching all employees all the time, companies usually monitor selected workers using spot checks.

For some jobs, however, monitoring is counterproductive or not cost effective. Monitoring may lower employees' morale, in turn reducing productivity. Several years ago, Northwest Airlines took the doors off bathroom stalls to prevent workers from slacking off there. When new management eliminated this policy (and made many other changes as well), productivity increased.

It is usually impractical for firms to monitor how hard salespeople work if they spend most of their time away from the main office. As telecommuting increases, monitoring workers may become increasingly difficult.

When direct monitoring is very costly, firms may use various financial incentives, which we consider in the next section, to reduce the amount of monitoring that is necessary. Each of these incentives—bonding, deferred payments, and efficiency (unusually high) wages—acts as a *hostage* for good behavior (Williamson, 1983). Workers who are caught shirking or engaging in other undesirable acts not only lose their jobs but give up the hostage too. The more valuable the hostage, the less monitoring the firm needs to use to deter bad behavior.

Bonding

A direct approach to ensuring good behavior by agents is to require that they deposit funds guaranteeing their good behavior, just as a landlord requires tenants to post security deposits to ensure that they will not damage an apartment. An employer may require an employee to provide a performance *bond*, an amount of money that will be given to the principal if the agent fails to complete certain duties or achieve certain goals. Typically, the agent *posts* (leaves) this bond with the principal or another party, such as an insurance company, before starting the job.

Many couriers who transport valuable shipments (such as jewels) or guards who watch over them have to post bonds against theft and other moral hazards. Similarly, bonds may be used to keep employees from quitting immediately after receiving costly training (Salop and Salop, 1976). Academics who take a sabbatical—a leave of absence that is supposed to be devoted to training or other activities that increase their future productivity—must typically sign an agreement to pay the college or university a certain sum if they quit within a year after returning from their sabbatical. Most of the other approaches we will examine as strategies for controlling shirking can be viewed as forms of bonding.

Bonding to Prevent Shirking. Some employers require a worker to post a bond that is forfeited if the employee is discovered shirking. For example, a professional athlete faces a specified fine (the equivalent of a bond) for skipping a meeting or game. The higher the bond, the less frequently the employer needs to monitor to prevent shirking.

Suppose that the value that a worker puts on the gain from taking it easy on the job is G dollars. If a worker's only potential punishment for shirking is dismissal if caught, some workers will shirk.

Suppose, however, that the worker must post a bond of B dollars that the worker forfeits if caught not working. Given the firm's level of monitoring, the probability that a worker is caught is θ. Thus, a worker who shirks expects to lose θB.[12] A risk-neutral worker chooses not to shirk if the certain gain from shirking, G, is less than or equal to the expected penalty, θB, from forfeiting the bond if caught: $G \leq \theta B$. Therefore, the minimum bond that discourages shirking is

$$B = \frac{G}{\theta}. \tag{20.1}$$

See Question 13.

Equation 20.1 shows that the bond must be larger for the higher the value that the employee places on shirking and the lower the probability that the worker is caught.

Trade-Off Between Bonds and Monitoring. Thus, the larger the bond, the less monitoring is necessary to prevent shirking. Suppose that a worker places a value of $G = \$1,000$ a year on shirking. A bond that is large enough to discourage shirking is \$1,000 if the probability of being caught is 100%, \$2,000 at 50%, \$5,000 at 20%, \$10,000 at 10%, and \$20,000 if the probability of being caught is only 5%.

[12]The expected penalty is $\theta B = (1 - \theta)0 = \theta B$, where the first term on the left side is the probability of being caught times the fine of B and the second term is the probability of not being caught and facing no fine.

Solved Problem 20.2

Workers post bonds of B that are forfeited if they are caught stealing (but no other punishment is imposed). Each extra unit of monitoring, M, raises the probability that a firm catches a worker who steals, θ, by 5%. A unit of M costs \$10. A worker can steal a piece of equipment and resell it for its full value of G dollars. What is the optimal M that the firm uses if it believes that workers are risk neutral? In particular, if B = \$5,000 and G = \$500, what is the optimal M?

Answer

1. *Determine how many units of monitoring are necessary to deter stealing.* The least amount of monitoring that deters stealing is the amount at which a worker's gain from stealing equals the worker's expected loss if caught. A worker is just deterred from stealing when the gain, G, equals the expected penalty, θB. Thus, the worker is deterred when the probability of being caught is $\theta = G/B$. The number of units of monitoring effort is $M = \theta/0.05$, because each extra unit of monitoring raises θ by 5%.
2. *Determine whether monitoring is cost effective.* It pays for the firm to pay for M units of monitoring only if the expected benefit to the firm is greater than the cost of monitoring, \$10 × M. The expected benefit if stealing is prevented is G, so monitoring pays if $G >$ \$10 × M, or $G/M >$ \$10.
3. *Solve for the optimal monitoring in the special case.* The optimal level of monitoring is

$$M = \frac{\theta}{0.05} = \frac{G/B}{0.05} = \frac{500/5{,}000}{0.05} = \frac{0.1}{0.05} = 2.$$

See Problems 22 and 23.

It pays to engage in this level of monitoring because G/M = \$500/2 = \$250 > \$10.

Problems with Bonding. Employers like the bond-posting solution because it reduces the amount of employee monitoring necessary to discourage moral hazards such as shirking and thievery. Nonetheless, firms use explicit bonding only occasionally to prevent stealing, and they rarely use it to prevent shirking.

Two major problems are inherent in posting bonds. First, to capture a bond, an unscrupulous employer might falsely accuse an employee of stealing. An employee who fears such employer opportunism might be unwilling to post a bond. One possible solution to this problem is for the firm to develop a reputation for not behaving in this manner. Another possible approach is for the firm to make the grounds for forfeiture of the bond objective and thus verifiable by others.

A second problem with bonds is that workers may not have enough wealth to post them. In our example, if the worker could steal \$10,000, and if the probability of being caught were only 5%, shirking would be deterred only if a risk-neutral worker were required to post a bond of at least \$200,000.

Principals and agents use bonds when these two problems are avoidable. Bonds are more common in contracts between firms than in those between an employer and employees. Moreover, firms have fewer problems than typical employees do in raising funds to post bonds.

Construction contractors sometimes post bonds to guarantee that they will satisfactorily finish their work by a given date. Both parties can verify whether the contract has been completed on time, so there is relatively little chance of opportunistic behavior by the principal.

Deferred Payments

Effectively, firms can post bonds for their employees through the use of deferred payments. For example, a firm pays new workers a low wage for some initial period of employment. Then, over time, workers who are caught shirking are fired, and those who remain get higher wages. In another form of deferred wages, the firm provides a pension that rewards only hard workers who stay with the firm until retirement. *Deferred payments serve the same function as bonds.* They raise the cost of being fired, so less monitoring is necessary to deter shirking.

Workers care about the present value (see Chapter 16) of their earnings stream over their lifetime. A firm may offer its workers one of two wage payment schemes. In the first, the firm pays w per year for each year that the worker is employed by the firm. In the second arrangement, the starting wage is less than w but rises over the years to a wage that exceeds w.

If employees can borrow against future earnings, those who work for one company for their entire career are indifferent between the two wage payment schemes if those plans have identical present values. The firm, however, prefers the second payment method because employees work harder to avoid being fired and losing the high future earnings.

Reduced shirking leads to greater output. If the employer and employee share the extra output in the form of higher profit and lifetime earnings, both the firm and workers prefer the deferred-payment scheme that lowers incentives to shirk.

A drawback of the deferred-payment approach is that, like bond posting, it can encourage employers to engage in opportunistic behavior. For example, an employer might fire nonshirking senior workers to avoid paying their higher wages and replace them with less expensive junior workers. However, if the firm can establish a reputation for not firing senior workers unjustifiably, the deferred-payment system can help prevent shirking.

Efficiency Wages

efficiency wage
an unusually high wage that a firm pays workers as an incentive to avoid shirking

As we've seen, the use of bonds and deferred payments discourages shirking by raising an employee's cost of losing a job. An alternative is for the firm to pay an **efficiency wage**: an unusually high wage that a firm pays workers as an incentive to avoid shirking.[13] If a worker who is fired for shirking can immediately go to another firm and earn the same wage, the worker risks nothing by shirking. However, a high wage payment raises the cost of getting fired, so it discourages shirking.[14]

How Efficiency Wages Act like Bonds. Suppose that a firm pays each worker an efficiency wage w, which is more than the *going wage* $\underline{w}$ that an employee would earn elsewhere after being fired for shirking. We now show that the less frequently the firm monitors workers, the greater the wage differential must be between w and $\underline{w}$ to prevent shirking.

---

[13]The discussion of efficiency wages is based on Yellen (1984), Stiglitz (1987), and especially Shapiro and Stiglitz (1984).

[14]There are other explanations for why efficiency wages lead to higher productivity. Some economists claim that in less-developed countries employers pay an efficiency wage—more than they need to hire workers—to ensure that workers can afford to eat well enough that they can work hard. Other economists (such as Akerlof, 1982) and management experts contend that the higher wage acts like a gift, making workers feel beholden or loyal to the firm, so that less (or no) monitoring is needed.

A worker decides whether to shirk by comparing the expected loss of earnings from getting fired to the value, G, that the worker places on shirking. A shirking worker expects to lose $\theta(w - \underline{w})$, where θ is the probability that a shirking worker is caught and fired and the term in parentheses is the lost earnings from being fired. A risk-neutral worker does not shirk if the expected loss from being fired is greater than or equal to the gain from shirking (see Appendix 20A):

$$\theta(w - \underline{w}) \geq G. \tag{20.2}$$

The smallest amount by which w can exceed $\underline{w}$ and prevent shirking is determined where this expression holds with equality, $\theta(w - \underline{w}) = G$, or

$$w - \underline{w} = \frac{G}{\theta}. \tag{20.3}$$

The extra earnings, $w - \underline{w}$, in Equation 20.3 serve the same function as the bond, B, in Equation 20.1 in discouraging bad behavior.

Suppose that the worker gets G = \$1,000 pleasure a year from not working hard and $\underline{w}$ is \$20,000 a year. If the probability that a shirking worker is caught is θ = 20%, then the efficiency wage w must be at least \$25,000 to prevent shirking. With greater monitoring, so that θ is 50%, the minimum w that prevents shirking is \$22,000. From the possible pairs of monitoring levels and efficiency wages that deter shirking, the firm picks the combination that minimizes its labor cost.

Efficiency Wages and Unemployment. We've argued that it is in a firm's best interest to pay more than the "going wage" to discourage shirking. The problem with this conclusion is that if it pays for one firm to raise its wage, it pays for all firms to do so. But if all firms raise their wages and pay the same amount, no one firm can discourage shirking by paying more than the others.

Nonetheless, the overall high wages do help prevent shirking. Because all firms are paying above the competitive wage, their labor demand falls, causing unemployment. Now if a worker is fired, the worker remains unemployed for a period of time while searching for a new job. Thus, the amount that the fired worker earns elsewhere, $\underline{w}$, is less than w because of this period of unemployment.[15] As a result, the (high) efficiency wages discourage shirking by creating unemployment.

One implication of this theory is that unemployment benefits provided by the government actually increase the unemployment rate. Such benefits raise $\underline{w}$, decrease the markup of w over $\underline{w}$, and thereby reduce the penalty of being fired. Thus, to discourage shirking, firms have to raise their efficiency wage even higher, and even more unemployment results. See **www.myeconlab.com/perloff**, Chapter 20, "Deferred Payments Versus Efficiency Wages in Fast-Food Restaurants."

See Question 14.

After-the-Fact Monitoring

So far we've concentrated on monitoring by employers looking for bad behavior as it occurs. If shirking or other bad behavior is detected after the fact, the offending employee is fired or otherwise disciplined. This punishment discourages shirking in the future.

Punishment. It is often very difficult to monitor bad behavior when it occurs but relatively easy to determine it after the fact. As long as a contract holds off payment

---

[15]If γ is the share of time that the fired worker remains unemployed, the worker's expected earnings are $\underline{w} = (1 - \gamma)w = \gamma 0 = (1 - \gamma)w$.

until after the principal checks for bad behavior, after-the-fact monitoring discourages bad behavior. For example, an employer can check the quality of an employee's work. If it is substandard, the employer can force the employee to make it right.

Insurance companies frequently use this approach in contracts with their customers. Insurance firms try to avoid extreme moral hazard problems by offering contracts that do not cover spectacularly reckless, stupid, or malicious behavior. If an insurance company determines after the fact that a claim is based on reckless behavior rather than chance, the firm refuses to pay.

For example, an insurance company will not pay damages for a traffic accident if the insured driver is shown to have been drunk at the time. A house insurance company disallows claims due to an explosion that is found to result from an illegal activity such as making methamphetamines. It will certainly disallow claims by arsonists who torch their own homes or businesses. Life insurance companies may refuse to pay benefits to the family of someone who commits suicide (as in the play *Death of a Salesman*).

See Question 15.

APPLICATION

Abusing Leased Cars

Because drivers of fleet automobiles such as rental cars do not own them, they do not bear all the cost from neglecting or abusing the vehicles, resulting in a moral hazard problem. These vehicles are driven harder and farther and depreciate faster than owner-operated vehicles. In 2007, about one-third of car shoppers leased their vehicles.

Using data from sales at used-car auctions, Dunham (1996), after controlling for mileage, found that fleet vehicles (not including taxis or police cars) depreciate 10% to 13% more rapidly than owner-driven vehicles.[16] The average auction price for a Pontiac 6000 was $5,200 for a fleet car and $6,500 for a nonfleet car. This $1,300 difference, which was one-fourth of the fleet car's price, reflects the increased depreciation of fleet cars.

To deal with this moral hazard, an automobile-leasing firm commonly writes contracts—open-ended leases—in which the driver's final payment for the vehicle depends on the selling price of the car. In this way, the contract makes the leasing driver responsible for at least some of the harm done to the car, to encourage the lessee to take greater care of the vehicle. Given the difference in auction prices, however, such leases apparently are not the full solution to this moral hazard.

No Punishment. Finding out about moral hazards after they occur is too late if wrongdoers cannot be punished at that time. Indeed, there's no point in monitoring after the fact if punishment is then impossible or impractical. Although it's upsetting to find that you've been victimized, there's nothing you can do beyond trying to prevent the situation from happening again.

APPLICATION

Subprime Borrowing

Although the average U.S. household has over $23,000 in nonmortgage debt, some households—particularly those with low incomes—have difficulty obtaining regular bank loans due to a lack of a credit history and collateral. These households participate in the subprime market, where they can get a loan only if they pay more than prime customers who are deemed creditworthy borrowers.

[16]According to National Public Radio's *Car Talk*—one of the world's most reliable sources of information—police cars have very few miles on them, but their engines are quickly shot because cops spend untold hours sitting in their cruisers in front of donut shops with the engine running and the air conditioner on high.

Cars. Adams et al. (2007) studied moral hazard and adverse selection using loan information from a large automobile sales company that specializes in the subprime market. Nearly a third of their loan applicants have neither a checking nor a savings account. The average person finances 90% of the price of the automobile, and the average loan is around $11,000.

Adams et al. presented two types of evidence that many of these households have trouble borrowing. First, they found that the availability of funds greatly affects demand for cars. For example, the quantity demanded is 50% higher during tax rebate season than at other times of the year.

Second, the demand for cars is highly sensitive to minimum down-payment requirements. An increase in the required down payment by $100 reduces the quantity demanded by 7%. This effect is large in the sense that car prices would have to rise nearly $1,000 to reduce the quantity demanded by that much.

This market has both moral hazard and adverse selection problems. The larger the loan, the more likely borrowers are to *default*—fail to repay the loan—because they do not bear the full cost of defaulting. Adams et al. find that a $1,000 increase in loan size increases the default rate by over 16%. Consequently, lenders want to cap the size of the loans to prevent overborrowing.

Adverse selection occurs because people who have a high risk of defaulting are more likely to apply for loans. The firm assigns buyers to a small number of credit categories based on their credit history and income. Adams et al. estimate that, all else the same, a buyer in the worst category wants to borrow $200 more than a buyer in the best category and is more than twice as likely to default for the same size loan. To avoid this problem, lenders use loan caps: The riskiest borrowers get smaller loans than others because they are required to make larger down payments. Within a given risk group, a buyer who pays an extra $1,000 down for unobservable reasons is 8% less likely to default than one who does not, given identical cars and loan liabilities.

Despite these actions by the firm, more than half of their customers default. Because of the high probability of default, the auto loan firm charges very high annual interest rates of 25% to 30%.

Homes. There are at least four important reasons (in addition to fraud) for the subprime mortgage market meltdown in 2007–2008. First, many mortgage-initiating firms failed to require down payments for subprime loans. In the California Bay Area, 69% of those families whose owner-occupied homes were in foreclosure had put down 0% at the time of purchase, and only 10% made the traditional 20% down payment in the first nine months of 2007.

Second, firms loaned to speculators who were more likely to walk away from a loan than would someone who lived in the mortgaged house. Speculators were a serious problem in Miami and Las Vegas. In Las Vegas during the first half of 2007, 74% of single-family homes in foreclosure were owned by absentee investors. The problem due to speculators was less severe nationwide, where nonowner-occupied homes accounted for 13% of prime defaults and 11% of subprime defaults.

Third, mortgages used adjustable rates that started very low and then rose rapidly. Because the implications of these escalator clauses were not made clear to borrowers, many poor people suddenly found themselves unable to make mortgage payments.

Fourth, many mortgage-originating firms failed to properly check borrowers' credit worthiness. Of the properties repossessed in the Bay Area, one in six was owned by people who had two or more foreclosures in their name, and some had five or more.

Thus, unlike the car loan firm, mortgage originators didn't take a number of obvious actions to mitigate adverse selection and moral problems. As a consequence, many borrowers defaulted on their loans.

Solved Problem 20.3

A savings & loan (S&L) association can make one of two types of loans. It can loan money on home mortgages, where it has a 75% probability of earning \$100 million and a 25% probability of earning \$80 million. Alternatively, it can loan money to oil speculators, where it has a 25% probability of earning \$400 million and a 75% probability of losing \$160 million (due to loan defaults by the speculators). The manager of the S&L, who will make the lending decision, receives 1% of the firm's earnings. He believes that if the S&L loses money, he can walk away from his job without repercussions, although without compensation. The manager and the shareholders of the company are risk neutral. What decision will the manager make if all he cares about is maximizing his personal expected earnings, and what decision would the stockholders prefer that he make?

Answer

1. *Determine the S&L's expected return on the two investments.* If the S&L makes home mortgage loans, its expected return is

$$(0.75 \times 100) + (0.25 \times 80) = 95$$

million dollars. Alternatively, if it loans to the oil speculator, its expected return is

$$(0.25 \times 400) = (0.75 \times [-160]) = -20$$

million dollars, an expected loss.

2. *Compare the S&L manager's expected profits on the two investments.* The manager expects to earn 1% of \$95 million, or \$950,000, from investing in mortgages. His take from investing in oil is 1% of \$400 million, or \$4 million, with a probability of 25% and no compensation with a probability of 75%. Thus, he expects to earn

$$(0.25 \times 4) = (0.75 \times 0) = 1$$

million dollars from investing in oil. As he is risk neutral and does not care a whit about anyone else, he invests in oil.

3. *Compare the shareholders' expected profits on the two investments.* The shareholders expect to receive 99% of the profit from the mortgages, or 0.99 × \$95 million = \$94.05 million. With the oil loans, they earn 99% of the \$400 million, \$396 million, if the investment is good, and bear the full loss in the case of defaults, \$160 million, so their expected profit (loss) is

$$(0.25 \times 396) = (0.75 \times [-160]) = -21$$

million dollars. Thus, the shareholders would prefer that the S&L invest in mortgages.

Comment: Given that the manager has the wrong incentives (and no integrity), he makes the investment that is not in the shareholders' interest. One possible solution to the problem of their diverging interests is to change the manager's compensation scheme.

20.6 Checks on Principals

To this point, we have concentrated on situations in which the agent knows more than the principal. Sometimes, however, the principal may have asymmetric information and engage in opportunistic behavior.

Because employers (principals) often pay employees (agents) after work is completed, employers have many opportunities to exploit workers. For example, a dishonest employer can underpay after falsely claiming that a worker took time off or that some of the worker's output was substandard. The employer can decrease piece rates over time, after employees are committed to this payment system. Employers who provide bonuses can underreport the firm's output or profit. An employer can dock earnings, claim that an employee bond was forfeited, or refuse to make deferred payments such as pensions after dishonestly claiming that a monitored worker engaged in bad behavior. Efficient contracts prevent or reduce such moral hazard problems created by employers as well as those caused by employees.

Requiring that a firm post a bond can be an effective method of deterring the firm's opportunistic behavior. For example, a firm may post bonds to ensure that it has the means of paying current wages and future pensions.

Another strategy for preventing a firm from acting opportunistically is to eliminate asymmetric information by requiring the employer to reveal relevant information to employees. For example, an employer can provide access to such information by allowing employee representatives to sit on the company board—from which vantage point they can monitor the firm's behavior. To induce workers to agree to profit sharing, a firm may provide workers with information about the company's profit by allowing them (or an independent auditor) to check its accounts. Alternatively, the firm may argue that its stock closely mirrors its profit and suggest that the known stock price be used for incentive payments.

As another means of conveying information to employees, firms may seek to establish a good reputation. For instance, a firm may publicize that it does not make a practice of firing senior employees to avoid paying pensions. The better the firm's reputation, the more likely workers are to accept a deferred payment scheme, which deters shirking.

See Question 16 and Problem 24.

When firms find these approaches infeasible, they may use inefficient contracts that might, for example, stipulate payments to employees on the basis of easily observed revenues rather than less reliable profit reports. The next application discusses a particularly damaging but common type of inefficient contract.

APPLICATION

Performance Termination Contracts

During economic downturns—recessions and depressions—demand for a firm's product falls. Many firms respond by laying off workers and reducing production rather than by lowering wages and keeping everyone employed. From January 1997 through November 2007, the average real wage steadily rose from \$16.59 (in 2007 dollars) to \$18.07 and rarely fluctuated more than a few cents from its trend from month to month. In contrast, the unemployment rate over this period dropped from 5.3% to 3.9%, rose back up to 6.3%, dropped to 4.4%, and rose to 5.0%.

If both sides agreed to it, a wage reduction policy would benefit firms and workers alike. Workers would earn more than they would if they were laid off. Because the firm's costs would fall, it could sell more during the downturn than it otherwise could, so its profits would be higher than they would be if there were layoffs. Firms that provide relatively low wages and then share profits with employees achieve this type of wage flexibility.

Why then are wage reductions less common than layoffs? One explanation involves asymmetric information: Workers, unlike the firm, don't know whether the firm is actually facing a downturn, so they don't agree to wage cuts. In short, they don't trust the firm to tell them the truth. They fear that the firm will falsely claim that economic conditions are bad to justify a wage cut. If the firm has to lay off workers—an action that hurts the firm as well as the workers—the firm is more likely to be telling the truth about economic conditions.

We illustrate this reasoning in the following matrix, which shows the payoffs if wages are reduced during downturns. The value of output produced by each worker is \$21 during good times and \$15 during bad times. The firm pays employees \$12 per hour if it reports that economic conditions are good and \$8 if it says that conditions are bad. If economic conditions are bad, the firm earns more by reporting these bad conditions, \$7, than it earns if it says that conditions are good, \$3. Similarly, if conditions are good, the firm earns more if it claims that conditions are bad, \$13, than if it says that they are good, \$9. Thus, regardless of the true state, the firm always claims that conditions are bad.

Wage Cut

		Firm's Claim About Conditions	
		Bad	*Good*
Actual Conditions	*Bad*	8, 7	12, 3
	Good	8, 13	12, 9

To shield themselves from such systematic lying, employees may insist that the firm lay off workers whenever it says that conditions are bad. This requirement provides the firm with an incentive to report the true conditions. In the next matrix, the firm must lay off workers for half of each period if it announces that times are bad, causing the value of output to fall by one-third. Because they now work only half the time, workers earn only half as much, \$6, as they earn during good times, \$12. If conditions are bad, the firm makes more by telling the truth, \$4, than by claiming that conditions are good, \$3. In good times, the firm makes

Worker Layoff (for half of any period the firm claims is bad)

		Firm's Claim About Conditions	
		Bad	*Good*
Actual Conditions	*Bad*	6, 4	12, 3
	Good	6, 8	12, 9

more by announcing that conditions are good, \$9, than by claiming that they are bad, \$8. Thus, the firm reports conditions truthfully.

With the wage-cut contract in which the firm always says that conditions are bad, workers earn \$8 regardless of actual conditions. If economic conditions are good half the time, the firm earns an average of $\$10 = (\frac{1}{2} \times \$7) + (\frac{1}{2} \times \$13)$. Under the contract that requires layoffs, the workers earn an average of $\$9 = (\frac{1}{2} \times \$6) + (\frac{1}{2} \times \$12)$ and the firm earns an average of $\$6.50 = (\frac{1}{2} \times \$4) + (\frac{1}{2} \times \$9)$.

Therefore, the firm prefers the wage-cut contract and the workers favor the layoff contract. However, if the workers could observe actual conditions, both parties would prefer the wage-cut contract. Workers would earn an average of $\$10 = (\frac{1}{2} \times \$8) + (\frac{1}{2} \times \$12)$, and the firm would earn $\$8 = (\frac{1}{2} \times \$7) + (\frac{1}{2} \times \$9)$. With the layoff contract, total payoffs are lower because of lost production. Thus, socially inefficient layoffs may be used because of the need to keep relatively well-informed firms honest.

20.7 Contract Choice

We have examined how to construct a single contract so as to prevent moral hazards. Often, however, a principal gives an agent a choice of contract. By observing the agent's choice, the principal obtains enough information to prevent agent opportunism.

Firms want to avoid hiring workers who will shirk. Employers know that not all workers shirk, even when given an opportunity to do so. So rather than focusing on stopping lazy workers from shirking, an employer may concentrate on hiring only industrious people. With this approach, the firm seeks to avoid *moral hazard* problems by preventing *adverse selection*, whereby lazy employees falsely assert that they are hardworking.

As discussed in Chapter 19, employees may *signal* to employers that they are productive. For example, if only nonshirking employees agree to work long hours, a commitment to work long hours serves as a reliable signal. In addition, employees can signal by developing a reputation as hard workers. To the degree that employers can rely on this reputation, sorting is achieved.

When workers cannot credibly signal, firms may try to *screen out* bad workers. One way in which firms can determine which prospective employees will work hard and which will shirk is to give them a choice of contracts. If job candidates who are hard workers select a contingent contract whereby their pay depends on how hard they work and if job applicants who are lazy workers choose a fixed-fee contract, the firm can tell the applicants apart by their choices.

Suppose that a firm wants to hire a salesperson who will run its Cleveland office and that the potential employees are risk neutral. A hardworking salesperson can sell \$100,000 worth of goods a year, but a lazy one can sell only \$60,000 worth (see Table 20.3). A hard worker can earn \$30,000 from other firms, so the firm considers using a contingent contract that pays a salesperson a 30% commission on sales.

If the firm succeeds in hiring a hard worker, the salesperson makes $\$30,000 = \$100,000 \times 0.30$. The firm's share of sales is \$70,000. The firm has no costs of production (for simplicity), but maintaining this branch office costs the firm \$50,000 a year. The firm's profit is therefore \$20,000. If the firm hires a lazy salesperson under the same contract, the salesperson makes \$18,000, the firm's share of sales is \$42,000, and the firm loses \$8,000 after paying for the office.

Table 20.3 Firm's Spreadsheet.

	Contingent Contract (30% of Sales), $	Fixed-Fee Contract ($25,000 Salary), $
Hard Worker		
Sales	100,000	100,000
– Salesperson's pay	–30,000	–25,000
= Firm's net revenue	70,000	75,000
– Office expenses	–50,000	–50,000
= Firm's profit	20,000	25,000
Lazy Worker		
Sales	60,000	60,000
– Salesperson's pay	–18,000	–25,000
= Firm's net revenue	42,000	35,000
– Office expenses	–50,000	–50,000
= Firm's profit	–8,000	–15,000

Thus, the firm wants to hire only a hard worker. Unfortunately, the firm does not know in advance whether a potential employee is a hard worker. To acquire this information, the firm offers a potential employee a choice of contracts:

- **Contingent contract.** No salary and 30% of sales
- **Fixed-fee contract.** Annual salary of $25,000, regardless of sales

A prospective employee who doesn't mind hard work would earn $5,000 more by choosing the contingent contract. In contrast, a lazy candidate would make $7,000 more from a salary than from commissions. If an applicant chooses the fixed-fee contract, the firm knows that the person does not intend to work hard and decides not to hire that person.

The firm learns what it needs to know by offering this contract choice as long as the lazy applicant does not pretend to be a hard worker by choosing the contingent contract. Under the contingent contract, the lazy person makes only $18,000, but that offer may dominate others available in the market. If this pair of contracts fails to sort workers, the firm may try different pairs. If all these choices fail to sort, the firm must use other means to prevent shirking.

See Question 17.

SUMMARY

1. **Principal-Agent Problem.** A principal contracts with an agent to perform some task. The size of their joint profit depends on any assets that the principal contributes, the actions of the agent, and the state of nature. If the principal cannot observe the agent's actions, the agent may engage in opportunistic behavior. This moral hazard reduces the joint profit. An efficient contract leads to efficiency in production (joint profit is maximized by eliminating moral hazards) and efficiency in risk bearing (the less-risk-averse party bears more of the risk). Three common types of contracts are *fixed-fee contracts*, whereby one party pays the other a fixed fee and the other keeps the rest of the profits; *hire contracts*, by which the principal pays the agent a wage or by the piece of output produced; and *contingent contracts*, wherein the payoffs vary with the amount of output produced or in some other way. Because a contract that reduces

the moral hazard may increase the risk for a relatively risk-averse person, a contract is chosen to achieve the best trade-off between the twin goals of efficiency in production and in risk bearing.

2. **Production Efficiency.** Whether efficiency in production is achieved depends on the contract that the principal and the agent use and the degree to which their information is asymmetric. For the agent to put forth the optimal level of effort in our example, the agent must get the full marginal profit from that effort or the principal must monitor the agent. When the parties have full information, an agent with a fixed-fee rental or profit-sharing contract gets the entire marginal profit and produces optimally without monitoring. If the principal cannot monitor the agent or does not observe profit and cost, only a fixed-fee rental contract prevents moral hazard problems and achieves production efficiency.

3. **Trade-Off Between Efficiency in Production and in Risk Bearing.** A principal and an agent may agree to a contract that strikes a balance between reducing moral hazards and allocating risk optimally. Contracts that eliminate moral hazards require the agent to bear the risk. If the agent is more risk averse than the principal, the parties may trade off a reduction in production efficiency to lower risk for the agent.

4. **Payments Linked to Production or Profit.** To reduce shirking, employers may reward employees for greater individual or group productivity. Piece rates, which reward faster individual work, are practical only when individual output can be easily measured and the quality of work is not critical. Bonuses and stock options that reward workers for increases in group effort provide less of an incentive than piece rates but still may reduce shirking.

5. **Monitoring.** Because of asymmetric information, an employer must normally monitor workers' efforts to prevent shirking. Less monitoring is necessary as the employee's interest in keeping the job increases. The employer may require the employee to post a large bond that is forfeited if the employee is caught shirking, stealing, or otherwise misbehaving. If an employee cannot afford to post a bond, the employer may use deferred payments or efficiency wages—unusually high wages—to make it worthwhile for the employee to keep the job. Employers may also be able to prevent shirking by engaging in after-the-fact monitoring. However, such monitoring works only if bad behavior can be punished after the fact.

6. **Checks on Principals.** Often both agents and principals can engage in opportunistic behavior. If a firm must reveal its actions to its employees, it is less likely to be able to take advantage of the employees. To convey information, an employer may let employees participate in decision-making meetings or audit the company's books. Alternatively, an employer may make commitments so that it is in the employer's best interest to tell employees the truth. These commitments, such as laying off workers rather than reducing wages during downturns, may reduce moral hazards but lead to nonoptimal production.

7. **Contract Choice.** A principal may be able to obtain valuable information from an agent by offering a choice of contracts. Employers avoid moral hazard problems by preventing adverse selection. For example, they may present potential employees with a choice of contracts, prompting hardworking job applicants to choose one contract and lazy candidates to choose another.

QUESTIONS

■ = *exercise is available on MyEconLab;* * = *answer appears at the back of this book;* C = *use of calculus may be necessary;* W = *audio-slideshow answer by James Dearden is available in Textbook Resources on MyEconLab.*

1. More than 3 million lead-tainted toys from China were recalled worldwide June through August of 2007. At the time, it was predicted that U.S. consumers would face price increases of up to 10% to pay for the industry's increased third-party testing by manufacturers and sellers (Anne D'Innocenzio, "Consumers Could Face Higher Toy Prices," *San Francisco Chronicle*, September 14, 2007). Suppose instead that toys could be reliably labeled "tested" or "untested," and untested toys sold at a discount. Would consumers buy cheaper, untested goods or would they fear a moral hazard problem? Discuss.

*2. A promoter arranges for many different restaurants to set up booths to sell Cajun-Creole food at a fair. Appropriate music and other entertainment are provided. Customers can buy food using only "Cajun Cash," which is scrip with the same denominations as actual cash sold by the promoter at the fair. Why aren't the food booths allowed to sell food directly for cash?

■ 3. The state of California set up its own earthquake insurance program. Because the state agency in charge has few staff members, it pays private insurance carriers to handle claims for earthquake damage. These insurance firms receive 9% of each approved claim. Is this compensation scheme likely to lead to opportunistic behavior by insurance companies? What would be a better way to handle the compensation?

***4.** Some sellers offer to buy back a good later at some prespecified price. Why would a firm make such a commitment?

***5.** When I was in graduate school, I shared an apartment with a fellow who was madly in love with a woman who lived in another city. They agreed to split the costs of their long-distance phone calls equally, regardless of who placed the call. What is the implication of this fee-sharing arrangement?

***6.** In the duck-carving example with full information (which the second column of Table 20.1 summarizes), is a contract efficient if it requires that Paula give Arthur a fixed-fee salary of $168 and leaves all decisions to Arthur? If so, why? If not, are there any additional steps that Paula can take to ensure that Arthur sells the optimal number of carvings?

7. In the duck-carving example with asymmetric information (summarized in the third and fourth columns of Table 20.1), is a fixed-fee contract efficient? If so, why? If not, are there any additional steps that Paula can take to ensure efficiency?

8. Fourteen states have laws that limit a franchisor's ability to terminate a franchise agreement. What effects would such laws have on production efficiency and risk bearing?

9. A health insurance company tries to prevent the moral hazard of "excessive" dentist visits by limiting the visits per person per year to a specific number. How does such a restriction affect moral hazard and risk bearing? Show these results in a graph.

10. Traditionally, doctors have been paid on a fee-for-service basis. Now doctors are increasingly paid on a capitated basis (they get paid for treating a patient for a year, regardless of how much treatment is required), though a patient may still have to pay a small fee each visit. In this arrangement, doctors form a group and sign a capitation contract whereby they take turns seeing a given patient. What are the implications of this change in compensation for moral hazards and for risk bearing?

11. According to a flyer from Schwab *Advisor-Source*, "Most personal investment managers base their fees on a percentage of assets managed. We believe this is in your best interest because your manager is paid for investment management, not solely on the basis of trading commissions charged to your account. You can be assured your manager's investment decisions are guided by one primary goal—increasing your assets." Is this policy in a customer's best interest? Why?

***12.** Zhihua and Pu are partners in a store in which they do all the work. They split the store's *business profit* equally (ignoring the opportunity cost of their own time in calculating this profit). Does their business profit-sharing contract give them an incentive to maximize their joint economic profit if neither can force the other to work? (*Hint*: Imagine Zhihua's thought process late one Saturday night when he is alone in the store, debating whether to keep the store open a little later or to go out on the town.)

13. Many law firms consist of partners who share profits. On being made a partner, a lawyer must post a bond, a large payment to the firm that will be forfeited on bad behavior. Why?

14. Explain why full employment may be inconsistent with no shirking.

15. Starting in 2008, Medicare won't cover the cost of a surgeon leaving an instrument in a patient, giving a patient transfusions of the wrong blood type, certain types of hospital-acquired infections, or other "preventable" mistakes (Liz Marlantes, "Medicare Won't Cover Hospital Mistakes: New Rules Aimed at Promoting Better Hospital Care and Safety," *ABC News*, August 19, 2007). Hospitals will have to cover these costs and cannot bill the patient. These changes are designed to provide hospitals with a stronger incentive to prevent those mistakes, particularly infections. The Centers for Disease Control and Prevention estimates that 2 million patients are annually infected in hospitals, costing society more than $27 billion. Nearly 100,000 of those infections are fatal. Many of these infections could be prevented if hospitals more rigorously follow basic infection control procedures, including having doctors and nurses wash their hands between every patient. Is Medicare's new policy designed to deal with adverse selection or moral hazard? Is it likely to help? Explain.

16. List as many ways as possible that a principal can reassure an agent that it will avoid opportunistic behavior.

17. In 2005, the co-founders of Google, Larry Page and Sergey Brin, asked that their annual pay be reduced to $1 (from $150,000 with bonuses of $206,556 in 2003, and $43,750 plus bonuses of $1,556 in 2004). Chief executive Eric Schmidt made the same request

(Verne Kopytoff, "Google's Execs Paid \$1 a Year," *San Francisco Chronicle*, April 9, 2005, C1, C2). Their compensation would be based on increases in the value of the vast amounts of Google stock each owned (as of March 28, 2005, Page had 36.5 million Google shares; Brin, 36.4 million; and Schmidt, 13.9 million). How would you feel about this offer if you were a shareholder? What are the implications for moral hazard, efficiency, and risk sharing? Can their decision be viewed as a form of signaling? If so, what are they signaling and to whom?

PROBLEMS

18. Warner Bros. Studios sells DVD copies of its films to Blockbuster, and the studio has revenue-sharing arrangements with the rental chain for VCR tapes of its films (Bruce Orwall, Martin Peers, and Ann Zimmerman, "DVD Gains on Tape, but Economics Have Hollywood in a Tizzy," *Wall Street Journal*, February 5, 2002, A1.) Suppose that Blockbuster is the only place where Perkasie, PA, residents can rent movies and that the Saturday night demand function to rent *L.A. Confidential* on either DVD or VHS is $p = 10 - Q/2$.

a. Suppose that the Perkasie Blockbuster purchased ten copies of *L.A. Confidential* under the studio sales arrangement. What is the Blockbuster outlet's optimal rental price?

b. Suppose that the Blockbuster outlet pays the studio \$2 per copy rented under the revenue-sharing arrangement, and the outlet has ten copies in stock. What is the Blockbuster outlet's optimal rental price?

c. Compare your answers to parts a and b. W

19. Book retailers can return unsold copies to publishers. Effectively, retailers pay for the books they order only after they sell the books. Dowell's Books believes it will sell, with $\frac{1}{2}$ probability each, either 0 or 1 copies of *The Fool's Handbook of Macroeconomics*. The bookstore also believes it will sell, with $\frac{1}{2}$ probability each, either 0 or 1 copies of the *Genius' Handbook of Microeconomics*. The retail price of each book is \$25. Suppose the marginal cost of manufacturing another copy of a book is \$6. The publisher's value of a returned copy is zero. The *Microeconomics* publisher charges a \$13 wholesale price and offers a full refund if an unsold book is returned. While the *Macroeconomics* publisher charges a low \$10.50 wholesale price, it pays a retailer only \$8 if it returns an unsold book. Dowell's places an order for one copy of each title. When the two books arrive, Dowell's has space to shelve only one. Which title does Dowell's return? Comment on how Dowell's decision about which title to return depends on the wholesales prices and its compensation from the publishers for returned unsold books. W

20. In the National Basketball Association (NBA), the owners share revenue but not their costs. Suppose that one team, the L. A. Clippers, sells only general-admission seats to a home game with the visiting Philadelphia 76ers (Sixers). The inverse demand for the Clippers-Sixers tickets is $p = 100 - 0.004Q$. The Clippers' cost function of selling Q tickets and running the franchise is $C(Q) = 10Q$.

a. Find the Clippers' profit-maximizing number of tickets sold and the price if the Clippers must give 50% of their revenue to the Sixers. At the maximum, what are the Clippers' profit and the Sixers' share of the revenues?

b. Instead, suppose that the Sixers set the Clippers' ticket price based on the same revenue-sharing rule. What price will the Sixers set, how many tickets are sold, and what revenue payment will the Sixers receive? Explain why your answers to parts a and b differ.

c. Now suppose that the Clippers must share their profit rather than their revenue. The Clippers keep 45% of their profit and share 55% with the Sixers. The Clippers set the price. Find the Clippers' profit-maximizing price and determine how many tickets the team sells and its share of the profit.

d. Compare your answers to parts a and c using marginal revenue and marginal cost in your explanation. W

21. Suppose that a textbook author is paid a royalty of α share of the revenue from sales where the revenue is $R = pq$, p is the competitive market price for textbooks, and q is the number of copies of this textbook (which is similar to others on the market) sold. The publisher's cost of printing and distributing the book is $C(q)$. Determine the equilibrium, and compare it to the outcome that maximizes the sum of the payment to the author plus the firm's profit. Answer using both math and a graph.

***22.** In Solved Problem 20.2, a firm calculated the optimal level of monitoring to prevent stealing. If $G = \$500$ and $\theta = 20\%$, what is the minimum bond that deters stealing?

23. In Problem 22, suppose that for each extra $1,000 of bonding that the firm requires a worker to post, the firm must pay that worker $10 more per period to get the worker to work for the firm. What is the minimum bond that deters stealing?

24. Suppose now that the textbook publisher in Problem 21 faces a downward-sloping demand curve. The revenue is $R(Q)$, and the publisher's cost of printing and distributing the book is $C(Q)$. Compare the equilibria for the following compensation methods in which the author receives the same total compensation from each method:

a. The author is paid a lump sum, $\mathcal{L}$.

b. The author is paid α share of the revenue.

c. The author receives a lump-sum payment and a share of the revenue.

Chapter Appendixes

Appendix 2A: Regressions

An economist's guess is as likely to be as good as anyone else's. —Will Rogers

Economists use a *regression* to estimate economic relationships such as demand curves and supply curves. A regression analysis allows us to answer three types of questions:

- How can we best fit an economic relationship to actual data?
- How confident are we in our results?
- How can we determine the effect of a change in one variable on another if many other variables are changing at the same time?

Estimating Economic Relations

We use a demand curve example to illustrate how regressions can answer these questions. The points in Figure 2A.1 show eight years of data on Nancy's annual purchases of candy bars, q, and the prices, p, she paid.[1] For example, in the year when candy bars cost 20¢, Nancy bought q_2 candy bars.

Because we assume that Nancy's tastes and income did not change during this period, we write her demand for candy bars as a function of the price of candy bars and unobservable random effects. We believe that her demand curve is linear and want to estimate the demand function:

$$q = a + bp + e,$$

where a and b are coefficients we want to determine and e is an error term. This *error term* captures random effects that are not otherwise reflected in our function. For instance, in one year, Nancy broke up with her longtime boyfriend and ate more candy bars than usual, resulting in a relatively large positive error term for that year.

The data points in the figure exhibit a generally downward-sloping relationship between quantity and price, but the points do not lie strictly on a line because of the error terms. There are many possible ways in which we could draw a line through these data points.

---

[1]We use a lowercase q for the quantity demanded for an individual instead of the uppercase Q that we use for a market. Notice that we violated the rule economists usually follow of putting quantity on the horizontal axis and price on the vertical axis. We are now looking at this relationship as statisticians who put the independent or explanatory variable, price, on the horizontal axis and the dependent variable, quantity, on the vertical axis.

Figure 2A.1 Regression.

The circles show data on how many candy bars Nancy bought in a year at several different prices. The regression line minimizes the sum of the squared residuals, e_1 through e_8.

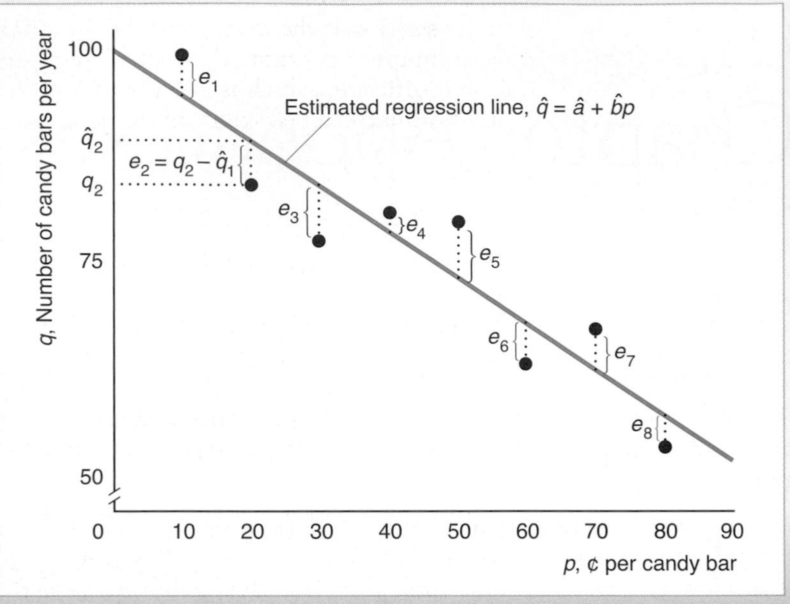

The way we fit the line in the figure is to use the standard criterion that our estimates *minimize the sum of squared residuals*, where a residual, $e = q - \hat{q}$, is the difference between an actual quantity, q, and the fitted or predicted quantity on the estimated line, $\hat{q}$. That is, we choose estimated coefficients $\hat{a}$ and $\hat{b}$ so that the estimated quantities from the regression line,

$$\hat{q} = \hat{a} + \hat{b}p,$$

make the sum of the squared residuals, $e_1^2 + e_2^2 + \cdots + e_8^2$, as small as possible. By summing the square of the residuals instead of the residuals themselves, we treat the effects of a positive or negative error symmetrically and give greater weight to large errors than to small ones.[2] In the figure, the regression line is

$$\hat{q} = 99.4 - 0.49p,$$

where $\hat{a} = 99.4$ is the intercept of the estimated line and $\hat{b} = -0.49$ is the slope of the line.

Confidence in Our Estimates

Because the data reflect random errors, so do the estimated coefficients. Our estimate of Nancy's demand curve depends on the *sample* of data we use. If we were to use data from a different set of years, our estimates, $\hat{a}$ and $\hat{b}$, of the true coefficients, a and b, would differ.

[2]Using calculus, we can derive the $\hat{a}$ and $\hat{b}$ that minimize the sum of squared residuals. The estimate of the slope coefficient is a weighted average of the observed quantities, $\hat{b} = \Sigma_i w_i q_i$, where $w_i = (p_i - \bar{p}) / \Sigma_i (p_i - \bar{p})^2$, $\bar{p}$ is the average of the observed prices, and Σ_i indicates the sum over each observation i. The estimate of the intercept, $\hat{a}$, is the average of the observed quantities.

If we had many estimates of the true parameter based on many samples, the estimates would be distributed around the true coefficient. These estimates are *unbiased* in the sense that the average of the estimates would equal the true coefficients.

Computer programs that calculate regression lines report a *standard error* for each coefficient, which is an estimate of the dispersion of the estimated coefficients around the true coefficient. In our example, a computer program reports

$$\begin{aligned}\hat{q} = \; & 99.4 \; - \; 0.49p, \\ & (3.99) \quad (0.08)\end{aligned}$$

where, below each estimated coefficient, its estimated standard error appears between parentheses.

The smaller the estimated standard error, the more precise the estimate, and the more likely it is to be close to the true value. As a rough rule of thumb, there is a 95% probability that the interval that is within two standard errors of the estimated coefficient contains the true coefficient.[3] Using this rule, the *confidence interval* for the slope coefficient, $\hat{b}$, ranges from $-0.49 - (2 \times 0.08) = -0.65$ to $-0.49 + (2 \times 0.08) = -0.33$.

If zero were to lie within the confidence interval for $\hat{b}$, we would conclude that we cannot reject the hypothesis that the price has no effect on the quantity demanded. In our case, however, the entire confidence interval contains negative values, so we are reasonably sure that the higher the price, the less Nancy demands.

Multiple Regression

We can also estimate relationships involving more than one explanatory variable using a *multiple regression*. For example, Moschini and Meilke (1992) estimate a pork demand function, Equation 2.2, in which the quantity demanded is a function of income, Y, and the prices of pork, p, beef, p_b, and chicken, p_c:

$$Q = 171 - 20p + 20p_b + 3p_c + 2Y.$$

The multiple regression is able to separate the effects of the various explanatory variables. The coefficient 20 on the p variable says that an increase in the price of pork by \$1 per kg lowers the quantity demanded by 20 million kg per year, holding the effects of the other prices and income constant.

Appendix 3A: Effects of a Specific Tax on Equilibrium

The government collects a specific or unit tax, τ, from sellers, so sellers receive $p - \tau$ when consumers pay p. We now determine the effect of the tax on the equilibrium.

In the new equilibrium, the price that consumers pay is determined by the intersection of supply and demand after taxes:

$$D(p) - S(p - \tau) = 0, \tag{3A.1}$$

[3]The confidence interval is the coefficient plus or minus 1.96 times its standard error for large samples (at least hundreds of observations) in which the coefficients are normally distributed. For smaller samples, the confidence interval tends to be larger.

where the supply equals demand equation is written in implicit function form (the right side of the equation is zero).

We determine the effect of a small tax on price by totally differentiating Equation 3A.1 with respect to p and τ:

$$\frac{dS}{dp}d\tau + \left(\frac{dD}{dp} - \frac{dS}{dp}\right)dp = 0.$$

Rearranging terms, it follows that the change in the price that consumers pay with respect to a change in the tax is

$$\frac{dp}{d\tau} = \frac{dS/dp}{dS/dp - dD/dp}. \tag{3A.2}$$

We know that $dD/dp < 0$ from the Law of Demand. If the supply curve slopes up, $dS/dp > 0$, then $dp/d\tau > 0$. The higher the tax, the greater the price consumers pay. If $dS/dp < 0$, the direction of change is ambiguous.

By multiplying both the numerator and denominator of the right side of Equation 3A.2 by p/Q, we can express this derivative in terms of elasticities:

$$\frac{dp}{d\tau} = \frac{(dS/dp)(p/Q)}{(dS/dp)(p/Q) - (dD/dP)(p/Q)} = \frac{\eta}{\eta - \varepsilon},$$

where the last equality follows because dS/dp and dD/dp are the changes in the quantities supplied and demanded as price changes and the consumer and producer prices are identical when $\tau = 0$. The change in price, Δp, equals $[\eta/(\eta - \varepsilon)]\Delta\tau$. This expression holds for any size change in $\Delta\tau$ if both the demand and supply curves are linear. The expression only holds for small changes $\Delta\tau$ for other curves.

To determine the effect on quantity, we can combine the price result from Equation 3A.2 with information from either the demand or supply curve. Differentiating the demand function with respect to τ, we know that

$$\frac{dQ}{d\tau} = \frac{dD}{dp}\frac{dp}{d\tau} = \frac{(dD/dP)(dS/dp)}{dS/dp - dD/dP},$$

which is negative if the supply curve is upward sloping.

Appendix 4A: Utility and Indifference Curves

We now use calculus to examine the relationship between utility and indifference curves and some properties of indifference curves. Suppose that Lisa's utility function is $U(B, Z)$, where B is the number of burritos and Z is the number of pizzas. Lisa's marginal utility for burritos, MU_B, is the amount of extra pleasure she would get from extra burritos, holding her consumption of pizza constant. Formally, her marginal utility for burritos, B, is the partial derivative of utility, $U(B, Z)$, with respect to B holding Z constant:

$$MU_B(B, Z) = \lim_{\Delta B \to 0} \frac{U(B + \Delta B, Z) - U(B, Z)}{\Delta B} = \frac{\partial U(B, Z)}{\partial B}.$$

By assumption, marginal utility is always nonnegative: A little more of a good makes you better off or at least doesn't harm you. The marginal utility depends on the current levels of B and Z.

Which combinations of B and Z leave Lisa with a given level of pleasure, say, $\overline{U}$? We can write those combinations as

$$\overline{U} = U(B, Z). \tag{4A.1}$$

Equation 4A.1 is the equation for an indifference curve with utility level $\bar{U}$.

We can express the slope of an indifference curve—the marginal rate of substitution, *MRS*—in terms of the marginal utilities. The slope of the indifference curve is found by determining the changes in *B* and *P* that leave utility unchanged. Totally differentiating Equation 4A.1, we find that

$$d\bar{U} = 0 = \frac{\partial U(B, Z)}{\partial B} dB + \frac{\partial U(B, Z)}{\partial Z} dZ \equiv MU_B\, dB + MU_Z\, dZ. \quad (4A.2)$$

This equation says that a little extra utility, MU_B, times the change in *B*, d*B*, plus the extra utility, MU_Z, times the change in *Z*, d*Z*, must add to zero. If we increase one of the goods, we must decrease the other to hold utility constant so that we stay on the same indifference curve. In Equation 4A.2, $d\bar{U} = 0$ because we are holding utility constant so that we stay on the same indifference curve. Rearranging the terms in Equation 4A.2, we find that

$$\frac{dB}{dZ} = -\frac{MU_Z}{MU_B}.$$

The slope of the indifference curve is the negative of the ratio of the marginal utilities.

Suppose that Lisa has the following utility function, known as a *Cobb-Douglas utility function*:

$$U(B,Z) = AB^{\alpha}Z^{\beta}. \quad (4A.3)$$

Her marginal utility of burritos is

$$MU_B(B, Z) = \alpha AB^{\alpha-1}Z^{\beta} = \alpha \frac{U(B, Z)}{B},$$

and her marginal utility of pizza is

$$MU_Z(B, Z) = \beta AB^{\alpha}Z^{\beta-1} = \beta \frac{U(B, Z)}{Z}.$$

Suppose that $\alpha = \beta = \frac{1}{2}$ and $A = 20$. If $B = Z = 4$, then $U(4, 4) = 80$ and $MU_B(4, 4) = MU_Z(4, 4) = 10$. If $B = 1$ and $Z = 4$, however, $U(1, 4) = 40$, $MU_B(1, 4) = 20$, and $MU_Z(1, 4) = 5$. The extra pleasure that Lisa gets from an extra burrito is greater, the fewer burritos she initially has, all else the same.

The slope of her indifference curve is

$$MRS = \frac{dB}{dZ} = -\frac{MU_Z}{MU_B} = -\frac{\beta AB^{\alpha}Z^{\beta-1}}{\alpha AB^{\alpha-1}Z^{\beta}} = -\frac{\beta B}{\alpha Z}.$$

The slope of the indifference curve differs with the levels of *B* and *Z*. If $\alpha = \beta = \frac{1}{2}$, $B = 4$, and $Z = 1$, $MRS(4, 1) = -(\frac{1}{2} \times 4)/(\frac{1}{2} \times 1) = -4$. At $B = Z = 4$, $MRS(4, 4) = -1$.

Appendix 4B: Maximizing Utility

Lisa's objective is to maximize her utility, *U*(*B*, *Z*), subject to (s.t.) a budget constraint:

$$\max_{B,Z} U(B, Z)$$
$$\text{s.t.} \quad Y = p_B B + p_Z Z, \quad (4B.1)$$

where *B* is the number of burritos she buys at price p_B, *Z* is the number of pizzas she buys at price p_Z, *Y* is her income, and $Y = p_B B + p_Z Z$ is her budget constraint (her spending on burritos and pizza can't exceed her income). The mathematical statement of her problem shows that her *control variables* (what she chooses) are B and Z, which appear under the "max" term in the equation. We assume that Lisa has no control over the prices she faces or her budget.

To solve this type of constrained maximization problem, we use the Lagrangian method:

$$\max_{B,Z,\lambda} \mathcal{L} = U(B, Z) - \lambda(p_B B + p_Z Z - Y), \tag{4B.2}$$

where λ is called the Lagrange multiplier. With normal-shaped utility functions, the values of B, Z, and λ determined by the first-order conditions of this Lagrangian problem are the same as the values that maximize the original constrained problem. The first-order conditions of Equation 4B.2 with respect to the three control variables, B, Z, and λ are:[4]

$$\frac{\partial \mathcal{L}}{\partial B} = MU_B(B, Z) - \lambda p_B = 0, \tag{4B.3}$$

$$\frac{\partial \mathcal{L}}{\partial Z} = MU_Z(B, Z) - \lambda p_Z = 0, \tag{4B.4}$$

$$\frac{\partial \mathcal{L}}{\partial \lambda} = Y - p_B B - p_Z Z = 0, \tag{4B.5}$$

where $MU_B(B, Z) \equiv \partial U(B, Z)/\partial B$ is the partial derivative of utility with respect to B (the marginal utility of B) and $MU_Z(B, Z)$ is the marginal utility of Z. Equation 4B.5 is the budget constraint. Equations 4B.3 and 4B.4 say that the marginal utility of each good equals its price times λ.

What is λ? If we equate Equations 4B.3 and 4B.4 and rearrange terms, we find that

$$\lambda = \frac{MU_B}{p_B} = \frac{MU_Z}{p_Z}. \tag{4B.6}$$

Because the Lagrangian multiplier, λ, equals the marginal utility of each good divided by its price, λ equals the extra pleasure one gets from one's last dollar of expenditures. Equivalently, λ is the value of loosening the budget constraint by one dollar.[5] Equation 4B.6 tells us that, to maximize her utility, Lisa should pick a B and

[4]To make our presentation as simple as possible, we assume that we have an interior solution, B and Z are infinitely divisible, and $U(B, Z)$ is continuously differentiable at least twice (so that the second-order condition is well defined). The first-order conditions give us the necessary conditions for an interior solution in which positive quantities of both goods are consumed. We assume that the second-order (sufficient) conditions hold, which is true if the utility function is quasiconcave or if the indifference curves are convex to the origin. That is, Lisa is maximizing rather than minimizing her utility when she chooses the levels of B and Z given by the first-order conditions.

[5]Differentiating utility with respect to Y, we find that

$$\frac{dU}{dY} = MU_B(B, Z)\frac{dB}{dY} + MU_Z(B, Z)\frac{dZ}{dY}.$$

Substituting from Equation 4B.6 into this expression, we obtain

$$\frac{dU}{dY} = \lambda p_B \frac{dB}{dY} + \lambda p_Z \frac{dZ}{dY} = \lambda \frac{p_B\, dB + p_Z\, dZ}{dY}.$$

Totally differentiating the budget constraint, we learn that

$$dY = p_B\, dB + p_Z\, dZ.$$

Substituting this expression into the previous expression gives us

$$\frac{dU}{dY} = \frac{\lambda p_B\, dB + \lambda p_Z\, dZ}{p_B\, dB + p_Z\, dZ} = \lambda.$$

Thus, λ equals the extra utility one gets from one more dollar of income.

Z so that, if she got one more dollar, spending that dollar on B or on Z would give her the same extra utility.

There is an alternative interpretation of this condition for maximizing utility. Taking the ratio of Equations 4B.3 and 4B.4 (or rearranging 4B.6), we find that

$$\frac{MU_Z}{MU_B} = \frac{p_Z}{p_B}. \tag{4B.7}$$

The left side of Equation 4B.7 is the absolute value of the marginal rate of substitution, $MRS = -MU_Z/MU_B$, and the right side is the absolute value of the marginal rate of transformation, $MRT = -p_Z/p_B$. Thus, the calculus approach gives us the same condition for an optimum that we derived using graphs. The indifference curve should be tangent to the budget constraint: The slope of the indifference curve, MRS, should equal the slope of the budget constraint, MRT.

For example, suppose that the utility is Cobb-Douglas, as in Equation 4A.3: $U = AB^{\alpha}Z^{\beta}$. The first-order condition, Equation 4B.5, the budget constraint, stays the same, and Equations 4B.3 and 4B.4 become

$$\frac{\partial \mathcal{L}}{\partial B} = \alpha \frac{U(B, Z)}{B} - \lambda p_B = 0, \tag{4B.8}$$

$$\frac{\partial \mathcal{L}}{\partial Z} = \beta \frac{U(B, Z)}{Z} - \lambda p_Z = 0. \tag{4B.9}$$

Using Equations 4B.8 and 4B.9, we can write Equation 4B.6 as

$$\lambda = \alpha \frac{U(B, Z)}{p_B B} = \beta \frac{U(B, Z)}{p_Z Z}.$$

Taking the ratio of Equations 4B.8 and 4B.9 and rearranging terms, we find that

$$\beta p_B B = \alpha p_Z Z. \tag{4B.10}$$

Substituting $Y - p_B B$ for $p_Z Z$, using Equation 4B.5, into Equation 4B.10 and rearranging terms, we get

$$B = \frac{\alpha}{\alpha + \beta} \frac{Y}{p_B}. \tag{4B.11}$$

Similarly, by substituting Equation 4B.11 into Equation 4B.10, we find that

$$Z = \frac{\beta}{\alpha + \beta} \frac{Y}{p_Z}. \tag{4B.12}$$

Thus, knowing the utility function, we can solve the expression for the B and Z that maximize utility in terms of income and prices.

Equations 4B.11 and 4B.12 are the consumer's demand curves for B and Z, respectively. (We derive demand curves using graphs in Chapter 5.)

If $\alpha = \beta = \frac{1}{2}$, $A = 20$, $Y = 80$, and $p_Z = p_B = 10$, then $B = Z = 4$ and the value of loosening the budget constraint is $\lambda = MU_B/p_B = MU_Z/p_Z = 10/10 = 1$. If p_B rises to 40, then $Z = 4$, $B = 1$, and $\lambda = 20/40 = 5/10 = \frac{1}{2}$.

Appendix 5A: The Slutsky Equation

The total effect on the quantity demanded when the price of a good rises equals the sum of the substitution and income effects. The Slutsky equation (named after its discoverer, the Russian economist Eugene Slutsky) explicitly shows the relationship among the price elasticity of demand, e, the pure substitution elasticity of demand, e*, and the income elasticity of demand, x:

Total effect	=	substitution effect	+	income effect
ε	=	ε^*	+	$(-\theta\xi)$

where θ is the budget share of this good: the amount spent on this good divided by the total budget.

We now sketch the derivation of the Slutsky equation (for a formal derivation, see a graduate microeconomics textbook such as Varian, 1992). The total effect, $\Delta q/\Delta p$, is the change in the quantity demanded, Δq, for a given change in the good's price, Δp. The substitution effect is the change in quantity demanded for a change in price, holding utility constant, which we label $(\Delta q/\Delta p)_{U\ constant}$.

A change in the price affects how much the consumer can buy and acts like a change in income. The income effect is the change in quantity as income changes times the change in income as price changes, $(\Delta q/\Delta Y)(\Delta Y/\Delta p)$, where ΔY is the change in income. The change in income from a change in price is $\Delta Y/\Delta p = -q$. For example, if price rises by \$1, income falls by the number of units purchased. From this last result, the income effect is $-q(\Delta q/\Delta Y)$.

Using these expressions, we write the identity that the total effect equals the substitution plus the income effect as

$$\Delta q/\Delta p = (\Delta q/\Delta p)_{U\ constant} - q(\Delta q/\Delta Y).$$

Multiplying this equation through by p/q, multiplying the last term by Y/Y, and rearranging terms, we obtain

$$\frac{\Delta q}{\Delta p}\frac{p}{q} = \left(\frac{\Delta q}{\Delta p}\right)_{U\ constant}\frac{p}{q} - \frac{\Delta q}{\Delta Y}\frac{Y}{q}\frac{pq}{Y}.$$

Substituting $\varepsilon = (\Delta q/\Delta p)(p/q)$, $\varepsilon^* = (\Delta q/\Delta p)_{U\ constant}(p/q)$, $\xi = (\Delta q/\Delta Y)(Y/q)$, and $\theta = pq/Y$ into this last expression, we have the Slutsky equation:

$$\varepsilon = \varepsilon^* - \theta\xi.$$

Appendix 5B: Labor-Leisure Model

Jackie's utility, U, is a function,

$$U = U(Y, N), \tag{5B.1}$$

of her leisure, N, and her income, Y, which she uses to buy all other goods and services. Jackie maximizes her utility, Equation 5B.1, subject to two constraints. The first, imposed by the clock, is that the number of hours she works, H, equals her total hours in a day minus her hours of leisure:

$$H = 24 - N. \tag{5B.2}$$

The second constraint is that her earned income (earnings), Y, equals her wage, w, times the hours she works:

$$Y = wH. \tag{5B.3}$$

For now, we assume that her unearned income is zero.

Although we can maximize Equation 5B.1 subject to Equations 5B.2 and 5B.3 using Lagrangian techniques, it is easier to do so by substitution. By substituting

Equations 5B.2 and 5B.3 into Equation 5B.1, we can convert this constrained problem into an unconstrained maximization problem:

$$\max_{H} U = U(wH, 24 - H). \tag{5B.4}$$

By using the chain rule of differentiation, we find that the first-order condition for an interior maximum to the problem in Equation 5B.4 is

$$\frac{dU}{dH} = MU_Y w - MU_N = 0,$$

where MU_Y, the marginal utility of goods or income, is the partial derivative of utility with respect to income, $\partial U/\partial Y$, and MU_N, the marginal utility of leisure, is the partial derivative with respect to leisure, $\partial U/\partial N$.[6] This expression can be rewritten as $w = MU_N/MU_Y$.

If we use the terminology from Chapter 4 to maximize her utility, Jackie must set her marginal rate of substitution of income for leisure, $MRS = -MU_N/MU_Y$, equal to her marginal rate of transformation of income for leisure, $MRT = -w$, in the market:

$$MRS = -\frac{MU_N}{MU_Y} = -w = MRT.$$

Suppose that Jackie's utility is

$$U = Y^{\alpha}N^{1-\alpha} = (wH)^{\alpha}(24 - H)^{1-\alpha},$$

which is a Cobb-Douglas utility function (Appendix 4A). Differentiating this utility function with respect to H, setting the derivative equal to zero, and rearranging terms, we find that $H = 24\alpha$. With this particular utility function, an individual's hours of leisure and work are fixed regardless of the wage. If $\alpha = \frac{1}{2}$, the individual works 12 hours a day (and has 12 hours of leisure) whether the wage is 50¢ an hour or \$500 an hour.

Appendix 6A: Properties of Marginal and Average Product Curves

We can use calculus to show that the MP_L curve crosses the AP_L curve at its peak. Because capital is fixed, we can write the production function solely in terms of labor: $q = f(L)$. In Figure 6.1, $df/dL > 0$ and $d^2f/dL^2 < 0$. Thus, $MP_L = dq/dL = df/dL > 0$ and $AP_L = q/L = f(L)/L > 0$. A necessary condition to identify the amount of labor where the AP_L curve reaches a maximum is that the derivative of AP_L with respect to L equals zero:

$$\frac{dAP_L}{dL} = \left(\frac{dq}{dL} - \frac{q}{L}\right)\frac{1}{L} = 0.$$

[6]The second-order condition for an interior maximum is

$$\frac{d^2U}{dH^2} = \frac{\partial^2 U}{\partial Y^2}w^2 - 2\frac{\partial^2 U}{\partial Y\,\partial N}w + \frac{\partial^2 U}{\partial N^2} < 0.$$

(At the L determined by this first-order condition, AP_L is maximized if the second-order condition is negative: $d^2AP_L/dL^2 = d^2f/dL^2 < 0$.) From the first-order condition, $MP_L = dq/dL = q/L = AP_L$ at the peak of the AP_L curve.

Appendix 6B: Cobb-Douglas Production Function

Economists frequently estimate production functions. The Cobb-Douglas production function (named after its inventors, Charles W. Cobb, a mathematician, and Paul H. Douglas, an economist and U.S. senator) is probably the most commonly estimated one. The Cobb-Douglas production function is

$$q = AL^{\alpha}K^{\beta}. \tag{6B.1}$$

Economists use statistical means to estimate A, α, and β, which determine the exact shape of the production function. The larger A is, the more output the firm gets from a given amount of labor and capital. A 1% increase in labor, holding capital constant, causes an α% increase in output. Similarly, a 1% increase in capital, holding labor constant, causes a β% increase in output.

For a tobacco firm, $\alpha = 0.18$ and $\beta = 0.33$ (Hsieh, 1995). Thus, a 1% increase in labor, holding capital fixed, causes output to increase by 0.18%.

The α term tells us the relationship between the average product of labor and the marginal product of labor. By differentiating the Cobb-Douglas production function with respect to L, holding K constant, we find that the marginal product of labor is

$$MP_L = \frac{\partial q}{\partial L} = \alpha AL^{\alpha-1}K^{\beta} = \alpha \frac{AL^{\alpha}K^{\beta}}{L} = \alpha \frac{q}{L}.$$

The marginal product of labor equals α times the average product of labor, $AP_L = q/L$. Thus, a tobacco firm's marginal product of labor is 0.18 times its average product of labor. Using similar reasoning, the marginal product of capital is $MP_K = \beta q/K$.

The marginal rate of technical substitution is $MRTS = -MP_L/MP_K = -(\alpha q/L)/(\beta q/K) = -(\alpha/\beta)K/L$. For a tobacco firm, $MRTS = -(0.18/0.33)K/L \approx -0.54K/L$.

Appendix 7A: Minimum of the Average Cost Curve

To determine the output level q where the average cost curve, $AC(q)$, reaches its minimum, we set the derivative of average cost with respect to q equal to zero:

$$\frac{dAC(q)}{dq} = \frac{d(C(q)/q)}{dq} = \left(\frac{dC(q)}{dq} - \frac{C(q)}{q}\right)\frac{1}{q} = 0.$$

This condition holds at the output q where $dC(q)/dq = C(q)/q$, or $MC = AC$. If the second-order condition holds at that q, the average cost curve reaches its minimum at that quantity. The second-order condition requires that the average cost curve be falling to the left of this q and rising to the right.

Appendix 7B: Furniture Manufacturer's Short-Run Cost Curves

We can use math to derive the various short-run cost curves for a typical furniture firm. Based on the estimates of Hsieh (1995), its production function is

$$q = 1.52L^{0.6}K^{0.4},$$

where labor, L, is measured in hours, K is the number of units of capital, and q is the amount of output. (*Note*: The coefficient 1.52 was chosen to produce round numbers.)

In the short run, the firm's capital is fixed at $\overline{K} = 100$. If the rental rate of a unit of capital is \$8, the fixed cost, F, is \$800. The figure in Chapter 7's application, "Short-Run Cost Curves for a Furniture Manufacturer," shows that the average fixed cost,

$$AFC = F/q = 800/q,$$

falls as output increases.

We can use the production function to derive the variable cost. First, we determine how output and labor are related. Setting capital, K, at 100 units in the production function, we find that the output produced in the short run is solely a function of labor:

$$q = 1.52L^{0.6}100^{0.4} \approx 9.59L^{0.6}.$$

Rearranging this expression, we can write the number of workers per year, L, needed to produce q units of output, as a function solely of output:

$$L(q) = \left(\frac{q}{1.52 \times 100^{0.4}}\right)^{\frac{1}{0.6}} \approx 0.023q^{1.67}. \tag{7B.1}$$

Now that we know how labor and output are related, we can calculate variable cost directly. The only variable input is labor, so if the wage is \$24, the firm's variable cost is

$$VC(q) = wL(q) = 24L(q).$$

Substituting for $L(q)$ using Equation 7B.1, we see how variable cost varies with output:

$$VC(q) = 24L(q) = 24\left(\frac{q}{1.52 \times 100^{0.4}}\right)^{\frac{1}{0.6}} \approx 0.55q^{1.67}. \tag{7B.2}$$

Using this expression for variable cost, we can construct the other cost measures.

We obtain the average variable cost as a function of output, $AVC(q)$, by dividing both sides of Equation 7B.2 by q:

$$AVC(q) = \frac{VC(q)}{q} = \frac{24L(q)}{q} \approx 24\left(\frac{0.023q^{1.67}}{q}\right) = 0.55q^{0.67}.$$

As the figure in the application shows, the average variable cost is strictly increasing.

To obtain the equation for marginal cost as a function of output, we differentiate the variable cost, $VC(q)$, with respect to output:

$$MC(q) = \frac{dVC(q)}{dq} \approx \frac{d(0.55q^{1.67})}{dq} = 1.67 \times 0.55q^{0.67} \approx 0.92q^{0.67}.$$

Thus, to construct all the cost measures of the printing firm, we need only the production function and the prices of the inputs.

Appendix 7C: Minimizing Cost

We can use calculus to derive the cost minimization conditions, Equations 7.6 and 7.7, discussed in the chapter. The problem the firm faces in the long run is to choose the level of labor, L, and capital, K, that will minimize the cost of producing a particular level of output, $\bar{q}$, given a wage of w and a rental rate of capital of r.

The relationship between inputs and output is summarized in the firm's production function: $q = f(L, K)$. The marginal product of labor, which is the extra output the firm produces from a little more labor, holding capital constant, is $MP_L(L, K) = \partial f(L, K)/\partial L$, which is positive. There are diminishing marginal returns to labor, however, so the marginal product of labor falls as labor increases: $\partial MP_L(L, K)/\partial L = \partial^2 f(L, K)/\partial L^2 < 0$. The marginal product of capital has the same properties: $\partial f(L, K)/\partial K > 0$ and $\partial MP_K(L, K)/\partial K < 0$.

The firm's problem is to minimize its cost, C, of production, through its choice of labor and capital,

$$\min_{L,K} C = wL + rK,$$

subject to the constraint that a given amount of output, $\bar{q}$, is to be produced:

$$f(L, K) = \bar{q}. \tag{7C.1}$$

Equation 7C.1 is the $\bar{q}$ isoquant.

We can change this constrained minimization problem into an unconstrained problem by using the Lagrangian technique. The firm's unconstrained problem is to minimize the Lagrangian, $\mathcal{L}$, through its choice of labor, capital, and the Lagrange multiplier, λ:

$$\min_{L,K,\lambda} \mathcal{L} = wL + rK - \lambda(f(L, K) - \bar{q}).$$

The necessary conditions for a minimum are obtained by differentiating $\mathcal{L}$ with respect to L, K, and λ and setting the derivatives equal to zero:

$$\partial\mathcal{L}/\partial L = w - \lambda MP_L(L, K) = 0, \tag{7C.2}$$

$$\partial\mathcal{L}/\partial K = r - \lambda MP_K(L, K) = 0, \tag{7C.3}$$

$$\partial\mathcal{L}/\partial\lambda = f(L, K) - \bar{q} = 0. \tag{7C.4}$$

We can rewrite Equations 7C.2 and 7C.3 as $w = \lambda MP_L(L, K)$ and $r = \lambda MP_K(L, K)$. Taking the ratio of these two expressions, we obtain

$$\frac{w}{r} = \frac{MP_L(L, K)}{MP_K(L, K)} = -MRTS, \tag{7C.5}$$

which is the same as Equation 7.6. This condition states that cost is minimized when the rate at which firms can exchange capital for labor in the market, w/r, is the same as the rate at which capital can be substituted for labor along an isoquant. That is, the isocost line is tangent to the isoquant.

We can rewrite Equation 7C.5 to obtain the expression

$$\frac{MP_L(L,K)}{w} = \frac{MP_K(L,K)}{r}.$$

This equation tells us that the last dollar spent on labor should produce as much extra output as the last dollar spent on capital; otherwise, the amount of factors used should be adjusted.

We can rearrange Equations 7C.2 and 7C.3 to obtain an expression for the Lagrangian multiplier:

$$\lambda = \frac{w}{MP_L(L,K)} = \frac{r}{MP_K(L,K)}. \tag{7C.6}$$

Equation 7C.6 says that the Lagrangian multiplier, λ, equals the ratio of the factor price to the marginal product for each factor. The marginal product for a factor is the extra amount of output one gets by increasing that factor slightly, so the reciprocal of the marginal product is the extra input it takes to produce an extra unit of output. By multiplying the reciprocal of the marginal product by the factor cost, we learn the extra cost of producing an extra unit of output by using more of this factor. Thus, the Lagrangian multiplier equals the marginal cost of production: It measures how much the cost increases if we produce one more unit of output.

If a firm has a Cobb-Douglas production function, $Q = AL^{\alpha}K^{\beta}$, the marginal product of capital is $MP_K = \beta q/K$ and the marginal product of labor is $MP_L = \alpha q/L$ (see Appendix 6B), so the *MRTS* is $\alpha K/(\beta L)$. Thus, the tangency condition, Equation 7C.5, requires that

$$\frac{w}{r} = \frac{\alpha K}{\beta L}. \tag{7C.7}$$

Using algebra, we can rewrite Equation 7C.7 as

$$K = \frac{\beta w}{\alpha r} L, \tag{7C.8}$$

which is the expansion path for a Cobb-Douglas production function and given w and r. According to Equation 7C.8, the expansion path of a firm with a Cobb-Douglas production function is an upward-sloping straight line through the origin with a slope of $\beta w/(\alpha r)$.

Appendix 8A: The Elasticity of the Residual Demand Curve

Here we derive the expression for the elasticity of the residual demand curve given in Equation 8.2. Differentiating the residual demand (Equation 8.1),

$$D^r(p) = D(p) - S^o(p),$$

with respect to p, we obtain

$$\frac{dD^r}{dp} = \frac{dD}{dp} = \frac{dS^o}{dp}.$$

Because the firms are identical, the quantity produced by each is $q = Q/n$, and the total quantity produced by all the other firms is $Q_o = (n - 1)q$. Multiplying both sides of the expression by p/q and multiplying and dividing the first term on the right side by Q/Q and the second term by Q_o/Q_o, this expression may be rewritten as

$$\frac{dD^r}{dp}\frac{p}{q} = \frac{dD}{dp}\frac{p}{Q}\frac{Q}{q} - \frac{dS^o}{dp}\frac{p}{Q_o}\frac{Q_o}{q},$$

where $q = D^r(p)$, $Q = D(p)$, and $Q_o = S^o(p)$. This expression can in turn be rewritten as Equation 8.2,

$$\varepsilon_i = n\varepsilon - (n - 1)\eta_o,$$

by noting that $Q/q = n$, $Q_o/q = (n - 1)$, $(dD^r/dp)(p/q) = \varepsilon_i$, $(dD/dp)(p/Q) = \varepsilon$, and $(dS^o/dp)(p/Q_o) = \eta_o$.

Appendix 8B: Profit Maximization

In general, a firm maximizes its profit, $\pi(q) = R(q) - C(q)$, by its choice of output q. A *necessary condition* for a maximum at a positive level of output is found by differentiating profit with respect to q and setting the derivative equal to zero:

$$\frac{d\pi}{dq} = \frac{dR(q^*)}{dq} - \frac{dC(q^*)}{dq} = 0. \tag{8B.1}$$

where q^* is the profit-maximizing output. Because $dR(q)/dq$ is the marginal revenue, $MR(q)$, and $dC(q)/dq$ is the marginal cost, $MC(q)$, Equation 8B.1 says that marginal revenue equals marginal cost at q^*:

$$MR(q^*) = MC(q^*). \tag{8B.2}$$

A *sufficient condition* for profit to be maximized at $q^* > 0$ is that the second-order condition holds:

$$\frac{d^2\pi}{dq^2} = \frac{d^2R(q^*)}{dq^2} - \frac{d^2C(q^*)}{dq^2} = \frac{dMR(q^*)}{dq} - \frac{dMC(q^*)}{dq} < 0. \tag{8B.3}$$

Equation 8B.3 can be rewritten as

$$\frac{dMR(q^*)}{dq} < \frac{dMC(q^*)}{dq}. \tag{8B.4}$$

Thus, a sufficient condition for a maximum is that the slope of the marginal revenue curve is less than that of the marginal cost curve and that the MC curve cuts the MR curve from below at q^*.

For a competitive firm, $\pi(q) = pq - C(q)$, so the necessary condition for profit to be maximized, Equation 8B.1 or 8B.2, can be written as

$$p = MC(q^*). \tag{8B.5}$$

Equation 8B.5 says that a profit-maximizing, competitive firm sets its output at q^* where its marginal cost equals its price.

Because a competitive firm's marginal revenue, p, is a constant, $\mathrm{d}MR/\mathrm{d}q = \mathrm{d}p/\mathrm{d}q = 0$. Thus, the sufficient condition for profit to be maximized, Equation 8B.4, can be rewritten as

$$0 < \frac{\mathrm{d}MC(q^*)}{\mathrm{d}q} \tag{8B.6}$$

for a competitive firm. Equation 8B.6 shows that a sufficient condition for a competitive firm to be maximizing its profit at q^* is that its marginal cost curve is upward sloping at the equilibrium quantity.

Appendix 9A: Demand Elasticities and Surplus

If the demand curve is linear, as in Figure 9.2, the lost consumer surplus, area $B + C$, equals the sum of the area of a rectangle, $Q\Delta p$, with length Q and height Δp, plus the area of a triangle, $\frac{1}{2}\Delta Q\Delta p$, of length ΔQ and height Δp. We can approximate any demand curve with a straight line, so that $\Delta CS = Q\Delta p + \frac{1}{2}\Delta Q\Delta p$ is a reasonable approximation to the true change in consumer surplus. We can rewrite this expression for ΔCS as

$$\begin{aligned}\Delta p\left(Q + \tfrac{1}{2}\Delta Q\right) &= Q\Delta p\left[1 + \tfrac{1}{2}\left(\frac{\Delta Q}{Q}\frac{p}{\Delta p}\right)\frac{\Delta p}{p}\right]\\ &= (pQ)\frac{\Delta p}{p}\left(1 + \tfrac{1}{2}\varepsilon\frac{\Delta p}{p}\right)\\ &= Rx\left(1 + \tfrac{1}{2}\varepsilon x\right),\end{aligned}$$

where $x = \Delta p/p$ is the percentage increase in the price, R $(= pQ)$ is the total revenue from the sale of good Q, and ε is the elasticity of demand. (This equation is used to calculate the last column in Table 9.1.)

Appendix 11A: Relationship Between a Linear Demand Curve and Its Marginal Revenue Curve

When the demand curve is linear, its marginal revenue curve is twice as steep and hits the horizontal axis at half the quantity of the demand curve. A linear demand curve can be written generally as

$$p = a - bQ.$$

The monopoly's revenues are quadratic, $R = pQ = aQ - bQ^2$. Differentiating revenue with respect to quantity, we find that the marginal revenue, $\mathrm{d}R(Q)/\mathrm{d}Q$, is linear,

$$MR = a - 2bQ.$$

The demand and MR curves hit the price axis at a. The slope of the demand curve, $\mathrm{d}p/\mathrm{d}Q = -b$, is half (in absolute value) the slope of the marginal revenue curve, $\mathrm{d}MR/\mathrm{d}Q = -2b$. The MR curve hits the quantity axis at half the distance, $a/(2b)$, of the demand curve, a/b.

Appendix 11B: Incidence of a Specific Tax on a Monopoly

In a monopolized market, the incidence of a specific tax falling on consumers can exceed 100%: The price may rise by an amount greater than the tax. To demonstrate this possibility, we examine a market where the demand curve has a constant elasticity of ε and the marginal cost is constant at $MC = m$.

Suppose that the inverse demand curve the monopoly faces is

$$p = Q^{1/\varepsilon}. \tag{11B.1}$$

The monopoly's revenue is $R = pQ = Q^{1+1/\varepsilon}$. By differentiating, we learn that the monopoly's marginal revenue is $MR = (1 + 1/\varepsilon)Q^{1/\varepsilon}$.

To maximize its profit, the monopoly operates where its marginal revenue equals its marginal cost:

$$MR = (1 + 1/\varepsilon)Q^{1/\varepsilon} = m = MC.$$

By solving this equation for the profit-maximizing output, we find that $Q = [m/(1 + 1/\varepsilon)]^{\varepsilon}$. Substituting that value of Q into Equation 11B.1, we find that

$$p = m/(1 + 1/\varepsilon)$$

A specific tax of τ per unit raises the marginal cost to $m + \tau$, so that the monopoly price increases to

$$p_t = (m + \tau)/(1 + 1/\varepsilon).$$

Consequently, the increase in price is $\tau/(1 + 1/\varepsilon)$. The incidence of the tax that falls on consumers is $\Delta p/\Delta\tau = [\tau/(1 + 1/\varepsilon)]/\tau = 1/(1 + 1/\varepsilon) > 1$, because $\varepsilon < -1$ (a monopoly never operates in the inelastic portion of its demand curve).

Appendix 12A: Perfect Price Discrimination

A perfectly price-discriminating monopoly charges each customer the reservation price $p = D(Q)$, where $D(Q)$ is the inverse demand function and Q is total output. The discriminating monopoly's revenue, R, is the area under the demand curve up to the quantity, Q, it sells:

$$R = \int_0^Q D(z)\,\mathrm{d}z,$$

where z is a placeholder for quantity. Its objective is to maximize its profit through its choice of Q:

$$\max_Q \pi = \int_0^Q D(z)\,\mathrm{d}z - C(Q). \tag{12A.1}$$

Its first-order condition for a maximum is found by differentiating Equation 12A.1 to obtain

$$\frac{\mathrm{d}\pi}{\mathrm{d}Q} = D(Q) - \frac{\mathrm{d}C(Q)}{\mathrm{d}Q} = 0. \tag{12A.2}$$

According to Equation 12A.2, the discriminating monopoly sells units up to the quantity, Q, where the reservation price for the last unit, $D(Q)$, equals its marginal cost, $\mathrm{d}C(Q)/\mathrm{d}Q$. (This quantity is $Q_c = Q_d$ in Figure 12.2.)

For this solution to maximize profits, the second-order condition must hold: $d^2\pi/dQ^2 = dD(Q)/dQ - d^2C(Q)/dQ^2 < 0$. Thus, the second-order condition holds if the marginal cost curve has a nonnegative slope (because the demand curve has a negative slope). More generally, the second-order condition holds if the demand curve has a greater (absolute) slope than the marginal cost curve.

The perfectly price-discriminating monopoly's profit is

$$\pi = \int_0^Q D(z)\,dz - C(Q).$$

For example, if $D(Q) = a - bQ$,

$$\pi = \int_0^Q (a - bz)\,dz - C(Q) = aQ - \frac{b}{2}Q^2 - C(Q). \tag{12A.3}$$

The monopoly finds the output that maximizes the profit by setting the derivative of the profit in Equation 12A.3 equal to zero:

$$a - bQ - \frac{dC(Q)}{dQ} = 0.$$

By rearranging terms, we find that $D(Q) = a - bQ = dC(Q)/dQ = MC$, as in Equation 12A.2. Thus, the monopoly produces the quantity at which the demand curve hits the marginal cost curve.

Appendix 12B: Quantity Discrimination

In the block-pricing example in the chapter, we assume that the utility monopoly faces an inverse demand curve $p = 90 - Q$ and that its marginal and average cost is $m = 30$. Consequently, the quantity-discounting utility's profit is

$$\begin{aligned}\pi &= p(Q_1)Q_1 + p(Q_2)(Q_2 - Q_1) - mQ_2\\ &= (90 - Q_1)Q_1 + (90 - Q_2)(Q_2 - Q_1) - 30Q_2,\end{aligned}$$

where Q_1 is the largest quantity for which the first-block rate, $p_1 = 90 - Q_1$, is charged and Q_2 is the total quantity a consumer purchases. The utility chooses Q_1 and Q_2 to maximize its profit. It sets the derivative of profit with respect to Q_1 equal to zero, $Q_2 - 2Q_1 = 0$, and the derivative of profit with respect to Q_2 equal to zero, $Q_1 - 2Q_2 + 60 = 0$. By solving these two equations, the utility determines its profit-maximizing quantities, $Q_1 = 20$ and $Q_2 = 40$. The corresponding block prices are $p_1 = 90 - 20 = 70$ and $p_2 = 50$.

Appendix 12C: Multimarket Price Discrimination

Suppose that a monopoly can divide its customers into two groups, as in Figure 12.4. It sells Q_1 to the first group and earns revenues of $R_1(Q_1)$, and it sells Q_2 units to the second group and earns $R_2(Q_2)$. Its cost of producing total output $Q = Q_1 + Q_2$ units is $C(Q)$. The monopoly can maximize its profit through its choice of prices or quantities to each group. We examine its problem when it chooses quantities:

$$\max_{Q_1, Q_2} \pi = R_1(Q_1) + R_2(Q_2) - C(Q_1 + Q_2). \tag{12C.1}$$

The first-order conditions corresponding to Equation 12C.1 are obtained by differentiating with respect to Q_1 and Q_2 and setting the partial derivative equal to zero:

$$\frac{\partial \pi}{\partial Q_1} = \frac{dR_1(Q_1)}{dQ_1} - \frac{dC(Q)}{dQ}\frac{\partial Q}{\partial Q_1} = 0, \tag{12C.2}$$

$$\frac{\partial \pi}{\partial Q_2} = \frac{dR_2(Q_2)}{dQ_2} - \frac{dC(Q)}{dQ}\frac{\partial Q}{\partial Q_2} = 0. \tag{12C.3}$$

Equation 12C.2 says that the marginal revenue from sales to the first group, $MR^1 = dR_1(Q_1)/dQ_1$, should equal the marginal cost of producing the last unit of total output, $MC = dC(Q)/dQ$, because $\partial Q/\partial Q_1 = 1$. Similarly, Equation 12C.3 says that the marginal revenue from the second group, MR^2, should also equal the marginal cost. By combining Equations 12C.2 and 12C.3, we find that the two marginal revenues are equal where the monopoly is profit maximizing:

$$MR^1 = MR^2 = MC.$$

Appendix 12D: Two-Part Tariffs

In the example of a two-part tariff with nonidentical consumers, the demand curves for Consumers 1 and 2 are $q_1 = 80 - p$ and $q_2 = 100 - p$. The consumer surplus for Consumer 1 is $CS_1 = \frac{1}{2}(80 - p)q_1 = \frac{1}{2}(80 - p)^2$. Similarly, $CS_2 = \frac{1}{2}(100 - p)^2$. If the monopoly charges the lower fee, $\mathcal{L} = CS_1$, it sells to both consumers and its profit is

$$\pi = 2\mathcal{L} + (p - m)(q_1 + q_2) = (80 - p)^2 + (p - 10)(180 - 2p).$$

Setting the derivative of π with respect to p equal to zero, we find that the profit-maximizing price is $p = 20$. The monopoly charges a fee of $\mathcal{L} = CS_1 = \$1{,}800$ and makes a profit of \$5,000. If the monopoly charges the higher fee, $\mathcal{L} = CS_2$, it sells only to Consumer 2, and its profit is

$$\pi = \mathcal{L} + (p - m)q_2 = \tfrac{1}{2}(100 - p)^2 + (p - 10)(100 - p).$$

The monopoly's profit-maximizing price is $p = 10$, and its profit is $\mathcal{L} = CS_2 = \$4{,}050$. Thus, the monopoly makes more by setting $\mathcal{L} = CS_1$ and selling to both customers.

Appendix 12E: Profit-Maximizing Advertising and Production

To maximize its profit, a monopoly must optimally set its advertising, A, and quantity, Q. Suppose that advertising affects only current sales, so the demand curve the monopoly faces is

$$p = p(Q, A).$$

As a result, the firm's revenue is

$$R = p(Q, A)Q = R(Q, A).$$

The firm's cost of production is the function $C(Q)$. Its cost of advertising is A, because each unit of advertising costs \$1 (we chose the units of measure appropriately). Thus, its total cost is $C(Q) + A$.

The monopoly maximizes its profit through its choice of quantity and advertising:

$$\max_{Q,A} \pi = R(Q, A) - C(Q) - A. \tag{12E.1}$$

Its necessary (first-order) conditions are found by differentiating the profit function in Equation 12E.1 with respect to Q and A in turn:

$$\frac{\partial \pi(Q, A)}{\partial Q} = \frac{\partial R(Q, A)}{\partial Q} - \frac{dC(Q)}{dQ} = 0, \tag{12E.2}$$

$$\frac{\partial \pi(Q, A)}{\partial A} = \frac{\partial R(Q, A)}{\partial A} - 1 = 0. \tag{12E.3}$$

The profit-maximizing output and advertising levels are the Q^* and A^* that simultaneously satisfy Equations 12E.2 and 12E.3. Equation 12E.2 shows that output should be chosen so that the marginal revenue, $\partial R(Q, A)/(\partial Q)$, equals the marginal cost, $dC(Q)/(dQ)$. According to Equation 12E.3, the monopoly advertises to the point where its marginal revenue from the last unit of advertising, $\partial R(Q, A)/(\partial A)$, equals the marginal cost of the last unit of advertising, $1.

Appendix 13A: Cournot Equilibrium

Here we use calculus to determine the Cournot equilibrium for n identical oligopolistic firms. We first solve for the equilibrium using general demand and cost functions, which are identical for all firms. Then we apply this general solution to a linear example. Finally, using the linear example, we determine the equilibrium when two firms have different marginal costs.

General Model

Suppose that the market demand function is $p(Q)$ and that each firm's cost function is the same $C(q_i)$. To analyze a Cournot market of identical firms, we first examine the behavior of a representative firm. Firm 1 tries to maximize its profits through its choice of q_1:

$$\max_{q_1} \pi_1(q_1, q_2, \ldots, q_n) = q_1 p(q_1 + q_2 + \cdots + q_n) - C(q_1), \tag{13A.1}$$

where $q_1 + q_2 + \cdots + q_n = Q$, the total market output. Firm 1 takes the outputs of the other firms as fixed. If Firm 1 changes its output by a small amount, the price changes by $(dp(Q)/dQ)(dQ/dq_1) = dp(Q)/dQ$. Its necessary condition to maximize profit (first-order condition) is found by differentiating profit in Equation 13A.1 and setting the result equal to zero. After we rearrange terms, this necessary condition is

$$MR = p(Q) + q_1 \frac{dp(Q)}{dQ} = \frac{dC(q_1)}{dq_1} = MC, \tag{13A.2}$$

or marginal revenue equals marginal cost. Equation 13A.2 specifies the firm's best-response function: the optimal q_1 for any given output of other firms.

The marginal revenue expression can be rewritten as $p[1 + (q_1/p)(dp/dQ)]$. Multiplying and dividing the last term by n, noting that $Q = nq_1$ (given that all firms are identical), and observing that ε, the market elasticity of demand, is $(dQ/dp)(p/Q)$, we can rewrite Equation 13A.2 as

$$p\left(1 + \frac{1}{n\varepsilon}\right) = \frac{dC(q_1)}{dq_1}. \tag{13A.3}$$

The left side of Equation 13A.3 expresses Firm 1's marginal revenue in terms of the elasticity of demand of its residual demand curve, $n\varepsilon$, which is the number of firms, n, times the market demand elasticity, ε. Holding ε constant, the more firms, the more elastic the residual demand curve, and hence the closer a firm's marginal revenue to the price.

We can rearrange Equation 13A.3 to obtain an expression for the Lerner Index, $(p - MC)/p$, in terms of the market demand elasticity and the number of firms:

$$\frac{p - MC}{p} = -\frac{1}{n\varepsilon}. \tag{13A.4}$$

The larger the Lerner Index, the greater the firm's market power. As Equation 13A.4 shows, if we hold the market elasticity constant and increase the number of firms, the Lerner Index falls. As n approaches ∞, the elasticity any one firm faces approaches $-\infty$, so the Lerner Index approaches 0 and the market is competitive.

Linear Example

Now suppose that the market demand is linear,

$$p = a - bQ,$$

and each firm's marginal cost is m, a constant, and it has no fixed cost. Firm 1, a typical firm, maximizes its profits through its choice of q_1:

$$\max_{q_1} \pi_1(q_1, q_2, \cdots, q_n) = q_1[a - b(q_1 + q_2 + \cdots + q_n)] - mq_1. \tag{13A.5}$$

Setting the derivative of profit with respect to q_1, holding the output levels of the other firms fixed, equal to zero, and rearranging terms, we find that the necessary condition for Firm 1 to maximize its profit is

$$MR = a - b(2q_1 + q_2 + \cdots + q_n) = m = MC. \tag{13A.6}$$

Because all firms have the same cost function, $q_2 = q_3 = \cdots = q_n \equiv q$ in equilibrium. Substituting this expression into Equation 13A.6, we find that the first firm's best-response function is

$$q_1 = R_1(q_2, \cdots, q_n) = \frac{a - m}{2b} - \frac{n - 1}{2}q. \tag{13A.7}$$

The other firms' best-response functions are derived similarly.

All these best-response functions must hold simultaneously. The intersection of the best-response functions determines the Cournot equilibrium. Setting $q_1 = q$ in Equation 13A.7 and solving for q, we find that the Cournot equilibrium output for each firm is

$$q = \frac{a - m}{(n + 1)b}. \tag{13A.8}$$

Total market output, $Q = nq$, equals $n(a - m)/[(n + 1)b]$. The corresponding price is obtained by substituting this expression for market output into the demand function:

$$p = \frac{a + nm}{n + 1}. \tag{13A.9}$$

Setting $n = 1$ in Equations 13A.8 and 13A.9 yields the monopoly quantity and price. As n becomes large, each firm's quantity approaches zero, total output approaches $(a - m)/b$, and price approaches m, which are the competitive levels. In Equation 13A.9, the Lerner Index is

$$\frac{p - MC}{p} = \frac{a - m}{a + nm}.$$

As n grows very large, the denominator goes to ∞, so the Lerner Index goes to 0, and there is no market power.

Different Costs

In the linear example with two firms, how does the equilibrium change if the firms have different marginal costs? The marginal cost of Firm 1 is m_1, and that of Firm 2 is m_2. Firm 1 chooses output to maximize its profit:

$$\max_{q_1} \pi_1(q_1, q_2) = q_1[a - b(q_1 + q_2)] - m_1 q_1. \tag{13A.10}$$

Setting the derivative of Firm 1's profit with respect to q_1, holding q_2 fixed, equal to zero, and rearranging terms, we find that the necessary condition for Firm 1 to maximize its profit is $MR_1 = a - b(2q_1 + q_2) = m_1 = MC$. Using algebra, we can rearrange this expression to obtain Firm 1's best-response function:

$$q_1 = \frac{a - m_1 - bq_2}{2b}. \tag{13A.11}$$

By similar reasoning, Firm 2's best-response function is

$$q_2 = \frac{a - m_2 - bq_1}{2b}. \tag{13A.12}$$

To determine the equilibrium, we solve Equations 13A.11 and 13A.12 simultaneously for q_1 and q_2:

$$q_1 = \frac{a - 2m_1 + m_2}{3b}, \tag{13A.13}$$

$$q_2 = \frac{a - 2m_2 + m_1}{3b}. \tag{13A.14}$$

By inspecting Equations 13A.13 and 13A.14, we find that the firm with the smaller marginal cost has the larger equilibrium output. Similarly, the low-cost firm has a higher profit. If m_1 is less than m_2, then

$$\pi_1 = \frac{(a + m_2 - 2m_1)^2}{9b} > \frac{(a + m_1 - 2m_2)^2}{9b} = \pi_2.$$

Appendix 13B: Stackelberg Equilibrium

We use calculus to derive the Stackelberg equilibrium for the linear example given in Appendix 13A with two firms that have the same marginal cost, m. Because Firm 1, the Stackelberg leader, chooses its output first, it knows that Firm 2, the follower, will choose its output using its best-response function, which is (see Equation 13A.7, where $n = 2$)

$$q_2 = R_2(q_1) = \frac{a - m}{2b} - \frac{1}{2}q_1. \tag{13B.1}$$

The Stackelberg leader's profit, $\pi_1(q_1 + q_2)$, can be written as $\pi_1(q_1 + R_2(q_1))$, where we've replaced the follower's output with its best-response function. The Stackelberg leader maximizes its profit by taking the best-response function as given:

$$\max_{q_1} \pi_1(q_1, R_2(q_1)) = q_1\left[a - b\left(q_1 + \frac{a - m}{2b} - \frac{1}{2}q_1\right)\right] - mq_1. \tag{13B.2}$$

Setting the derivative of Firm 1's profit (in Equation 13B.2) with respect to q_1 equal to zero and solving for q_1, we find that the profit-maximizing output of the leader is

$$q_1 = \frac{a - m}{2b}. \tag{13B.3}$$

Substituting the expression for q_1 in Equation 13B.3 into Equation 13B.1, we obtain the equilibrium output of the follower:

$$q_2 = \frac{a - m}{4b}. \tag{13B.4}$$

Appendix 13C: Bertrand Equilibrium

We can use math to determine the cola market Bertrand equilibrium discussed in the chapter. First, we determine the best-response functions each firm faces. Then we equate the best-response functions to determine the equilibrium prices for the two firms.

Coke's best-response function tells us the price Coke charges that maximizes its profit as a function of the price Pepsi charges. We use the demand curve for Coke to derive the best-response function.

The reason Coke's price depends on Pepsi's price is that the quantity of Coke demanded, q_c, depends on the price of Coke, p_c, and the price of Pepsi, p_p. Coke's demand curve is

$$q_c = 58 - 4p_c + 2p_p. \tag{13C.1}$$

Partially differentiating Equation 13C.1 with respect to p_c (that is, holding the price of Pepsi fixed), we find that the change in quantity for every dollar change in price is $\partial q_c/\partial p_c = -4$, so a \$1-per-unit increase in the price of Coke causes the quantity of Coke demanded to fall by 4 units. Similarly, the demand for Coke rises by 2 units if the price of Pepsi rises by \$1, while the price of Coke remains constant: $\partial q_c/\partial p_p = 2$.

If Coke faces a constant marginal and average cost of m per unit, its profit is

$$\pi_c = (p_c - m)q_c = (p_c - m)(58 - 4p_c + 2p_p), \tag{13C.2}$$

where $p_c - m$ is Coke's profit per unit. To determine Coke's profit-maximizing price (holding Pepsi's price fixed), we set the partial derivative of the profit function, Equation 13C.2, with respect to the price of Coke equal to zero,

$$\frac{\partial \pi_c}{\partial p_c} = q_c + (p_c - m)\frac{\partial q_c}{\partial p_c} = q_c - 4(p_c - m) = 0, \tag{13C.3}$$

and solve for p_c as a function of p_p and m to find Coke's best-response function:

$$p_c = 7.25 + 0.25p_p + 0.5m. \tag{13C.4}$$

Equation 13C.4 shows that Coke's best-response price is 25¢ higher for every extra dollar that Pepsi charges and 50¢ higher for every extra dollar of Coke's marginal cost.

If Coke's average and marginal cost of production is \$5 per unit, its best-response function is

$$p_c = 9.75 + 0.25p_p, \tag{13C.5}$$

as Figure 13.8 shows. If $p_p = \$13$, then Coke's best response is to set $p_c = \$13$.

Pepsi's demand curve is

$$q_p = 63.2 - 4p_p + 1.6p_c. \tag{13C.6}$$

Using the same approach, we find that Pepsi's best-response function (for $m = \$5$) is

$$p_p = 10.4 + 0.2p_c. \tag{13C.7}$$

The intersection of Coke's and Pepsi's best-response functions (Equations 13C.5 and 13C.7) determines the Nash equilibrium. By substituting Pepsi's best-response function, Equation 13C.7, for p_p in Coke's best-response function, Equation 13C.5, we find that

$$p_c = 9.75 + 0.25(10.4 + 0.2p_c).$$

Solving this equation for p_c, we determine that the equilibrium price of Coke is \$13. Substituting $p_c = \$13$ into Equation 13C.6, we discover that the equilibrium price of Pepsi is also \$13.

Appendix 15A: Factor Demands

If a competitive firm hires L units of labor at a wage rate of w and K units of capital at a rental rate of r, it can produce $q = f(L, K)$ units of output. The firm sells its output at the market price of p. The firm picks L and K to maximize its profit:

$$\max_{L,K} \pi = pq - (wL + rK) = pf(L, K) - (wL + rK). \tag{15A.1}$$

Thus, the firm's revenue, pq, and cost both depend on L and K, so its profit depends on L and K.

Profit is maximized by setting the partial derivatives of profit (in Equation 15A.1) with respect to L and K equal to zero:

$$\frac{\partial \pi}{\partial L} = pMP_L - w = 0, \tag{15A.2}$$

$$\frac{\partial \pi}{\partial L} = pMP_K - r = 0, \tag{15A.3}$$

where $MP_L = \partial f(L, K)/\partial L$, the marginal product of labor, is the partial derivative of the production function with respect to L, and $MP_K = \partial f(L, K)/\partial K$ is the marginal product of capital. Solving Equations 15A.2 and 15A.3 simultaneously produces the factor demand equations.

Rearranging Equations 15A.2 and 15A.3, we can write these factor demand equations as

$$MRP_L \equiv pMP_L = w,$$

$$MRP_K \equiv pMP_K = r.$$

Thus, the firm maximizes its profit when it picks its inputs such that the marginal revenue product of labor equals the wage and the marginal revenue product of capital equals the rental rate of capital. For these conditions to produce a maximum, the second-order conditions must also hold. These second-order conditions say that the MRP_L and MRP_K curves slope downward.

If the production function is Cobb-Douglas, $q = AL^{\alpha}K^{\beta}$, then Equations 15A.2 and 15A.3 are

$$\frac{\partial \pi}{\partial L} = p\alpha AL^{\alpha-1}K^{\beta} - w = 0,$$

$$\frac{\partial \pi}{\partial K} = p\beta AL^{\alpha}K^{\beta-1} - r = 0.$$

Solving these equations for L and K, we find that the factor demand functions are

$$L = \left(\frac{\alpha}{w}\right)^{(1-\beta)/\delta}\left(\frac{\beta}{r}\right)^{\beta/\delta}(Ap)^{1/\delta}, \tag{15A.4}$$

$$K = \left(\frac{\alpha}{w}\right)^{\alpha/\delta}\left(\frac{\beta}{r}\right)^{(1-\alpha)/\delta}(Ap)^{1/\delta}, \tag{15A.5}$$

where $\delta = 1 - \alpha - \beta$. By differentiating Equations 15A.4 and 15A.5, we can show that the demand for each factor decreases with w or r and increases with p.

If the Cobb-Douglas production function has constant returns to scale, $\delta = 0$, then Equations 15A.4 and 15A.5 are not helpful. The problem is that with constant returns to scale, a competitive firm with a Cobb-Douglas production function does not care how much it produces (and hence how many inputs it uses) as long as the market price and input prices are consistent with zero profit.

A competitive firm with a Cobb-Douglas production function pays labor the value of its marginal product, $w = p \times MP_L = p \times \alpha AL^{\alpha-1}K^{\beta} = \alpha pQ/L$. As a result, the share of the firm's revenues that is paid to labor is $\omega_L = wL/(pQ) = \alpha$. Similarly, $\omega_K = rK/(pQ) = \beta$. Thus, with a Cobb-Douglas production function, the shares of labor and of capital are fixed and independent of prices.

Appendix 15B: Monopsony

If only one firm can hire labor in a town, the firm is a monopsony. It chooses how much labor to hire to maximize its profit,

$$\pi = p(Q(L))Q(L) - w(L)L,$$

where $Q(L)$ is the production function, the amount of output produced using L hours of labor, and $w(L)$ is the labor supply curve, which shows how the wage varies with the amount of labor the firm hires. The firm maximizes its profit by setting the derivative of profit with respect to labor equal to zero (if the second-order condition holds):

$$\left(p + Q(L)\frac{dp}{dQ}\right)\frac{dQ}{dL} - w(L) - \frac{dw}{dL}L = 0. \tag{15B.1}$$

Rearranging terms in Equation 15B.1, we find that the maximization condition is that the marginal revenue product of labor,

$$MRP_L = p \times MPL = \left(p + Q(L)\frac{dp}{dQ}\right)\frac{dQ}{dL} = p\left(1 + \frac{1}{\varepsilon}\right)\frac{dQ}{dL},$$

equals the marginal expenditure,

$$ME = w(L) + \frac{dw}{dL}L = w(L)\left(1 + \frac{w}{L}\frac{dw}{dL}\right) = w(L)\left(1 + \frac{1}{\eta}\right), \tag{15B.2}$$

where η is the supply elasticity of labor.

If the supply curve is linear, $w(L) = g + hL$, the monopsony's expenditure is $E = w(L)L = gL + hL^2$, and the monopsony's marginal expenditure is $ME = dE/dL = g + 2hL$. Thus, the slope of the marginal expenditure curve, $2h$, is twice as great as that of the supply curve, h.

By rearranging the terms in Equation 15B.2, we find that

$$\frac{ME - w}{w} = \frac{1}{\eta}.$$

Thus, the markup of the marginal expenditure (and the value to the monopsony) to the wage, $(ME - w)/w$, is inversely proportional to the elasticity of supply. If the firm is a price taker, so η is infinite, the wage equals the marginal expenditure.

Appendix 16A: Perpetuity

We derive Equation 16.4, $PV = f/i$, which gives the present value, PV, of a stream of payments f that lasts forever if the interest rate is i. Using Equation 16.3, where the number of periods is infinite, we know that the present value is

$$PV = \frac{f}{1+i} + \frac{f}{(1+i)^2} + \frac{f}{(1+i)^3} + \cdots. \tag{16A.1}$$

Factoring Equation 16A.1, we can factor $1/(1 + i)$ out and rewrite the equation as

$$PV = \frac{1}{1+i}\left[f + \frac{f}{1+i} + \frac{f}{(1+i)^2} + \frac{f}{(1+i)^3} + \cdots\right]. \tag{16A.2}$$

The term in the brackets in Equation 16A.2 is $f + PV$ as given in Equation 16A.1. When we make this substitution, Equation 16A.2 becomes

$$PV = \frac{1}{1+i}(f + PV). \tag{16A.3}$$

Rearranging terms in Equation 16A.3, we obtain Equation 16A.4:

$$PV = \frac{f}{i}. \tag{16A.4}$$

Appendix 18A: Welfare Effects of Pollution in a Competitive Market

We now show the welfare effects of a negative externality in a competitive market where demand and marginal costs are linear, as in Figure 18.1. The inverse demand curve is

$$p = a - bQ, \tag{18A.1}$$

where p is the price of the output and Q is the quantity. The private marginal cost is the competitive supply curve if pollution is an externality:

$$MC^p = c + dQ. \tag{18A.2}$$

The marginal cost to people exposed to the pollution (gunk) is

$$MC^g = eQ. \tag{18A.3}$$

Equation 18A.3 shows that there is no pollution harm if output is zero and that the marginal harm increases linearly with output. The social marginal cost is the sum of the private marginal cost and the marginal cost of the externality:

$$MC^s = c + (d + e)Q. \tag{18A.4}$$

The intersection of the demand curve, Equation 18A.1, and the supply curve, Equation 18A.2, determines the competitive equilibrium where pollution is an externality:

$$p_c = a - bQ_c = c + dQ_c = MC^p. \tag{18A.5}$$

If we solve Equation 18A.5 for Q, the competitive equilibrium quantity is

$$Q_c = \frac{a - c}{b + d}.$$

Substituting this quantity into the demand curve, we find that the competitive price is $p_c = a - b(a - c)/(b + d)$.

If the externality is taxed at a rate equal to its marginal cost, so the externality is internalized, the market produces the social optimum. We find the social optimum by setting p in Equation 18A.1 equal to MC^s in Equation 18A.4 and solving for the resulting quantity:

$$Q_s = \frac{a - c}{b + d + e}.$$

The corresponding price is $p_s = a - b(a - c)/(b + d + e)$.

If output is sold only by a monopoly, the monopoly's revenue is found by multiplying both sides of Equation 18A.1 by quantity: $R = aQ - bQ^2$. Differentiating with respect to quantity, we find that the monopoly's marginal revenue is

$$MR = a - 2bQ. \tag{18A.6}$$

If the monopoly is unregulated, its equilibrium is found by setting MR, Equation 18A.6, equal to private marginal cost, Equation 18A.2, and solving for output:

$$Q_m = \frac{a - c}{2b + d}.$$

The corresponding price is $p_m = a - b(a - c)/(2b + d)$. If the monopoly internalizes the externality due to a tax equal to MC^g, the equilibrium quantity is

$$Q_m^* = \frac{a - c}{2b + d + e}.$$

The price is $p_m^* = a - b(a - c)/(2b + d + e)$.

In Figure 18.1, $a = 450$, $b = 2$, $c = 30$, $d = 2$, and $e = 1$. Substituting these values into the equations, we solve for the following equilibrium values:

	Quantity	Price
Competition	105	240
Social optimum (competition with a tax)	84	282
Monopoly	70	310
Monopoly with a tax	60	330

Appendix 20A: Nonshirking Condition

An efficiency wage acts like a bond to prevent shirking. An employee who never shirks is not fired and earns the efficiency wage, w. A fired worker goes elsewhere and earns the lower, going wage, $\underline{w}$. The expected value to a shirking employee is

$$\theta \underline{w} + (1 - \theta)w + G,$$

where the first term is the probability of being caught shirking, θ, times earnings elsewhere if caught and fired; the second term is the probability of not being caught times the efficiency wage; and the third term, G, is the value a worker derives from shirking. The worker chooses not to shirk if the certain high wage from not shirking exceeds the expected return from shirking:

$$w \geq (1 - \theta)w + \theta \underline{w} + G,$$

which simplifies to Equation 20.2, $\theta(w - \underline{w}) \geq G$. That is, a risk-neutral worker does not shirk if the expected loss from being fired is greater than or equal to the gain from shirking.

Answers to Selected Questions and Problems

I know the answer! The answer lies within the heart of all mankind! The answer is twelve? I think I'm in the wrong building. —Charles Schultz

Chapter 2

1. The statement "Talk is cheap because supply exceeds demand" makes sense if we interpret it to mean that the *quantity supplied* of talk exceeds the *quantity demanded* at a price of zero. Imagine a downward-sloping demand curve that hits the horizontal, quantity axis to the left of where the upward-sloping supply curve hits the axis. (The correct aphorism is "Talk is cheap until you hire a lawyer.")

15. A ban has no effect if foreigners supply nothing at the pre-ban, equilibrium price. Thus, if imports occur only at prices above those actually observed, a ban has no practical effect.

20. The law would create a price ceiling (at 110% of the pre-emergency price). Because the supply curve shifts substantially to the left during the emergency, the price control will create a shortage: A smaller quantity will be supplied at the ceiling price than will be demanded.

22. The demand curve for pork is $Q = 171 - 20p + 20p_b + 3p_c + 2Y$, where quantity is measured in millions of kg per year and income is measured in thousands of dollars per year. As a result, a ΔY change in income causes the quantity demanded to change by $\Delta Q = 2\Delta Y$. That is, a \$1,000 increase in income causes the quantity demanded to increase by 2 million kg per year, and a \$100 increase in income causes the quantity demanded to increase by a tenth as much, 0.2 million kg per year.

24. $Q - Q_1 + Q_2 = (120 - p) + (60 - \frac{1}{2}p) = 180 - 1.5p$.

27. In equilibrium, the quantity demanded, $Q = a - bp$, equals the quantity supplied, $Q = c + ep$, so

$$a - bp = c + ep.$$

By solving this equation for p, we find that the equilibrium price is $p = (a - c)/(b + e)$. By substituting this expression for p into either the demand curve or the supply curve, we find that the equilibrium quantity is $Q = (ae + bc)/(b + e)$.

33. Equating the right sides of the supply and demand functions and using algebra, we find $\ln(p) = 3.2 + 0.2\ln(p_t)$. We then set $p_t = 110$, solve for $\ln(p)$, and exponentiate $\ln(p)$ to obtain the equilibrium price: $p \approx \$61.62$/ton. Substituting p into the supply curve and exponentiating, we determine the equilibrium quantity: $Q \approx 11.78$ million short tons/year.

Chapter 3

5. According to Equation 3.1, the elasticity of demand is ε = (percentage change in quantity demanded) ÷ (percentage change in price) = −3.8% ÷ 10% = −0.38, which is inelastic.

23. The incidence of the tax on consumers is zero if the demand curve is perfectly elastic or the supply curve is perfectly inelastic (see Questions 19 and 20).

24. We showed that, in a competitive market, the effect of a specific tax is the same whether it is placed on suppliers or demanders. Thus, if the market for milk is competitive, consumers will pay the same price in equilibrium regardless of whether the government taxes consumers or stores.

28. Differentiating the demand function as $Q = Ap^{\varepsilon}$ with respect to p, we find that $dQ/dp = \varepsilon Ap^{\varepsilon - 1}$. To get the elasticity, we multiply dQ/dp by $p/Q = p/Ap^{\varepsilon} = 1/Ap^{\varepsilon - 1}$. That is, the elasticity is $\varepsilon Ap^{\varepsilon - 1} \times 1/Ap^{\varepsilon - 1} = \varepsilon$. Because this result holds for any p, the elasticity is the same, ε, at every point along the demand curve.

30. Because the linear supply function is $Q = g + hp$, a change in price of Δp causes a $\Delta Q = h\Delta p$ change in quantity. Thus, $\Delta Q/\Delta p = h$, and the elasticity of supply is $\eta = (\Delta Q/\Delta p)(p/Q) = hp/Q$. By substituting for Q using the supply function, we find that $\eta = hp/(g + hp)$. By using the supply function to substitute for p, we learn that $\eta = (Q - g)/Q$.

31. The elasticity of demand is (slope) × (p/Q) = $(\Delta Q/\Delta p)(p/Q)$ = (−9.5 thousand metric tons per year per cent) × (45¢/1,275 thousand metric tons per year) ≈ −0.34. That is, for every 1% fall in the price, a third of a percent more coconut oil is demanded. The cross-price elasticity of demand for coconut oil with respect to the price of palm oil is $(\Delta Q/\Delta p_p)(p_p/Q) = 16.2 \times (31/1{,}275) \approx 0.39$.

33. If the quantity changes by 10.4% and the price elasticity of demand is −1.6, then we would expect the price to

change by $-1.6 \times 10.4\% = -16.64\%$ (which is close to the 15% drop actually observed in the first month after the announcement).

34. Industry revenue is $R = p(Q)Q$, where $p(Q)$ is the inverse demand function (price as a function of quantity). Differentiating both sides of the revenue identity with respect to quantity, we find that $dR/dQ = p + (dp/dQ)Q$. The elasticity of revenue with respect to quantity is $(dR/dQ)(Q/R) = (dR/dQ)(Q/p) = 1 + (dp/dQ)(Q/p) = (1 + 1/\varepsilon)$. Thus, if demand is inelastic, $0 > \varepsilon > -1$, the elasticity of revenue with respect to quantity is negative.

41. By dividing both the numerator and the denominator of the right side of Equation 3.7 by η, we can rewrite that incidence equation as

$$\frac{\eta}{\eta - \varepsilon} = \frac{1}{1 - \varepsilon / \eta}.$$

As η goes to infinity, ε/η goes to zero, so the incidence approaches 1.

42. Differentiating quantity, $Q(p(\tau))$, with respect to the specific tax τ, we learn that the change in quantity as the tax changes is $dQ/d\tau = (dQ/dp)(dp/d\tau)$. Multiplying and dividing this expression by p/Q, we find that the change in quantity as the tax changes is $\varepsilon(Q/p)(dp/d\tau)$. Thus, the closer ε is to zero, the less the quantity falls, all else being the same. The tax causes revenue to change by

$$\frac{dR}{d\tau} = \left(Q + p\frac{dQ}{dp}\right)\frac{dp}{d\tau} = (1 + \varepsilon)Q\frac{dp}{d\tau}.$$

The closer ε is to zero, the larger the tax revenue effect.

Chapter 4

3. If the neutral product is on the vertical axis, the indifference curves are parallel vertical lines.

5. Sofia's indifference curves are right angles (as in panel b of Figure 4.4). Sophia's utility function is $U = \min(H, W)$, where *min* means the minimum of the two arguments, H is the number of units of hot dogs, and W is the number of units of whipped cream.

10. Suppose that Dale purchases two goods at prices p_1 and p_2. If her original income is Y, the intercept of the budget line on the Good 1 axis (where the consumer buys only Good 1) is Y/p_1. Similarly, the intercept is Y/p_2 on the Good 2 axis. A 50% income tax lowers income to half its original level, $Y/2$. As a result, the budget line shifts inward toward the origin. The intercepts on the Good 1 and Good 2 axes are $Y/(2p_1)$ and $Y/(2p_2)$, respectively. The opportunity set shrinks by the area between the original budget line and the new line.

12. See **www.myeconlab.com/perloff**, Chapter 4, Solved Problems.

23. If a wealthy person spends more on food than a poor person before the subsidy, then the wealthy person is more likely to be spending more than the value of the food stamps prior to receiving them and hence is less likely to have a tangency at a point like f in Figure 4.10.

36. Andy's marginal utility of apples divided by its price is $\frac{3}{2} = 1.5$. The marginal utility for kumquats is $\frac{5}{4} = 1.2$. That is, a dollar spent on apples gives him more extra utils than a dollar spent on kumquats. Thus, he maximizes his utility by spending all his money on apples and buying $40/2 = 20$ pounds of apples.

37. If we plot B on the vertical axis and Z on the horizontal axis, the slope of David's indifference curve is $-MU_Z/MU_B = -2$. The marginal utility from one extra unit of Z is twice that from one extra unit of B. Thus, if the price of Z is less than twice as much as that of B, David buys only Z (the optimal bundle is on the Z axis at Y/p_Z, where Y is his income and p_Z is the price of Z). If the price of Z is more than twice that of B, David buys only B. If the price of Z is exactly twice as much as that of B, he is indifferent between buying any bundle along his budget line.

40. Using Equations 4B.11 and 4B.12, we find that the necessary conditions for a utility maximum are $B = 100\alpha/[2(\alpha + \beta)]$ and $Z = 100\beta/(\alpha + \beta)$.

Chapter 5

2. An opera performance must be a normal good for Don because he views the only other good he buys as an inferior good. To show this result in a graph, draw a figure similar to Figure 5.3, but relabel the vertical "Housing" axis as "Opera performances." Don's equilibrium will be in the upper-left quadrant at a point like a in Figure 5.3.

6. The CPI accurately reflects the true cost of living because Alix does not substitute between the goods as the relative prices change.

8. On the following graph, L^f is the budget line at the factory store and L^o is the constraint at the outlet store. At the factory store, the consumer maximum occurs at e_f on indifference curve I^f. Suppose that we increase the income of a consumer who shops at the outlet store to

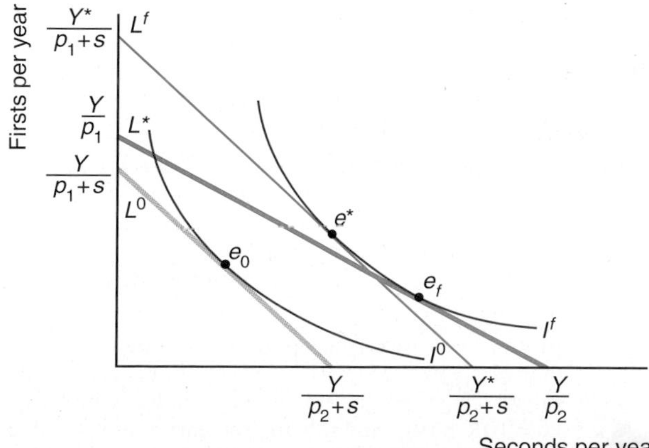

Y^*, so that the resulting budget line L^* is tangent to the indifference curve I^f. The consumer would buy Bundle e^*. That is, the pure substitution effect (the movement from e_f to e^*) causes the consumer to buy relatively more firsts. The total effect (the movement from e_f to e_o) reflects both the substitution effect (firsts are now relatively less expensive) and the income effect (the consumer is worse off after paying for shipping).

28. As the marginal tax rate on income increases, people substitute away from work due to the pure substitution effect. However, the income effect can be either positive or negative, so the net effect of a tax increase is ambiguous. Also, because wage rates differ across countries, the initial level of income differs, again adding to the theoretical ambiguity. If we know that people work less as the marginal tax rate increases, we can infer that the substitution effect and the income effect go in the same direction or the substitution effect is larger. However, Prescott's (2004) evidence alone about hours worked and marginal tax rates does not allow us to draw such an inference because U.S. and European workers may have different tastes and face different wages.

29. If the price of Coke, p_C, is greater than the price of Pepsi, p_P, Madeline buys only Pepsi. If the two prices are equal, $p_C = p_P = p$, she buys Y/p cans of either Coke or Pepsi. Finally, if $p_C < p_P$, she buys Y/p_C cans of Coke. Hence, as the price approaches zero, her Coke demand curve approaches the quantity axis asymptotically, as the figure below shows.

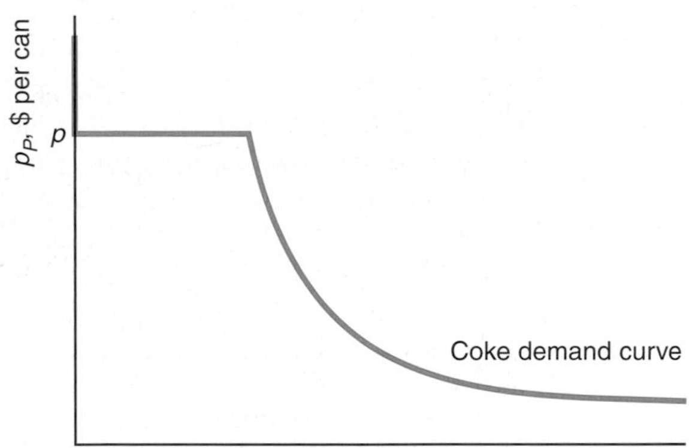

31. We can solve this problem by noting that Nadia determines her optimal bundle by equating the ratios of each good's marginal utility to its price.

    a. At the original prices, this condition is $MU_R/10 = 2RC = 2R^2 = MU_C/5$. Thus, by dividing both sides of the middle equality by $2R$, we know that her optimal bundle has the property that $R = C$. Her budget constraint is $90 = 10R + 5C$. Substituting C for R, we find that $15C = 90$, or $C = 6 = R$.

    b. At the new price, the optimum condition requires that $MU_R/10 = 2RC = R^2 = MU_C/10$, or $2C = R$. By substituting this condition into her budget constraint, $90 = 10R + 10C$, and solving, we learn that $C = 3$ and $R = 6$. Thus, as the price of chickens doubles, she cuts her consumption of chicken in half but does not change how many slabs of ribs she eats.

37. The consumer's budget constraint is

$$p_1q_1 + p_2q_2 + \cdots + p_nq_n = Y,$$

where Y is income and p_i is the price and q_i is the quantity of Good i. Differentiating with respect to Y, we find that

$$p_1\frac{dp_1}{dY} + p_2\frac{dq_2}{dY} + \cdots + p_n\frac{dq_n}{dY} = \frac{dY}{dY} = 1.$$

Multiplying and dividing each term by q_iY, we rewrite this last equation as

$$\frac{p_1q_1}{Y}\frac{dq_1}{dY}\frac{Y}{q_1} + \frac{p_2q_2}{Y}\frac{dq_2}{dY}\frac{Y}{q_2} + \cdots + \frac{p_nq_n}{Y}\frac{dq_n}{dY}\frac{Y}{q_n} = 1,$$

or

$$\omega_1\eta_1 + \omega_2\eta_2 + \cdots + \omega_n\eta_n = 1,$$

where η_i, the income elasticity for each Good i, equals $(dq_i/dY)(Y/q_i)$, and the budget share of Good i is $\omega_i = p_iq_i/Y$. That is, the weighted sum of the income elasticities equals 1. For this equation to hold, at least one of the goods must have a positive income elasticity; hence, not all the goods can be inferior.

Chapter 6

1. One worker produces one unit of output, two workers produce two units of output, and n workers produce n units of output. Thus, the total product of labor equals the number of workers: $q = L$. The total product of labor curve is a straight line with a slope of 1. Because we are told that each extra worker produces one more unit of output, we know that the marginal product of labor, $\Delta q/\Delta L$, is 1. By dividing both sides of the production function, $q = L$, by L, we find that the average product of labor, q/L, is 1.

6. The isoquant looks like the "right angle" ones in panel b of Figure 6.3 because the firm cannot substitute between disks and machines but must use them in equal proportions: one disk and one hour of machine services.

10. The isoquant for $q = 10$ is a straight line that hits the B axis at 10 and the G axis at 20. The marginal product of B is 1 everywhere along the isoquant. The marginal rate of technical substitution is 2 if B is on the horizontal axis.

19. Not enough information is given to answer this question. If we assume that Japanese and American firms have identical production functions and produce using the same ratio of factors during good times, Japanese firms will have a lower average product of labor during recessions because they are less likely to lay off workers. However, it is not clear how Japanese and American

firms expand output during good times (do they hire the same number of extra workers?). As a result, we cannot predict which country has the higher average product of labor.

22. The production function is $q = L^{0.75}K^{0.25}$.

a. As a result, the average product of labor, holding capital fixed at $\bar{K}$ is

$$AP_L = q/L = L^{-0.25}\bar{K}^{0.25} = (\bar{K}/L)^{0.25}.$$

b. The marginal product of labor is

$$MP_L = dq/dL = 0.75(\bar{K}/L)^{0.25}$$

c. If we double both inputs, output doubles to

$$(2L)^{0.75}(2K)^{0.25} = 2L^{0.75}K^{0.25} = 2q,$$

where q is the original output level. Thus, this production function has constant returns to scale.

25. Using Equation 6.3, we know that the marginal rate of technical substitution is $MRTS = MP_L / MP_K = \frac{2}{3}$.

26. This production function is a Cobb-Douglas. Even though it has three inputs instead of two, the same logic applies. Thus, we can calculate the returns to scale as the sum of the exponents:

$$\gamma = 0.27 + 0.16 + 0.61 = 1.04.$$

Thus, it has (nearly) constant returns to scale. The marginal product of material is

$$\partial q/\partial M = 0.61L^{0.27}K^{0.16}M^{-0.39} = 0.61q/M$$

(as Appendix 6B shows).

30. The marginal product of labor of Firm 1 is only 90% of the marginal product of labor of Firm 2 for a particular level of inputs. Using calculus, we find that the MP_L of Firm 1 is

$$\partial q_1/\partial L = 0.9\partial f(L, K)/\partial L = 0.9\partial q_2/\partial L.$$

Chapter 7

2. If the plane cannot be resold, its purchase price is a sunk cost, which is unaffected by the number of times the plane is flown. Consequently, the average cost per flight falls with the number of flights, but the total cost of owning and operating the plane rises because of extra consumption of gasoline and maintenance. Thus, the more frequently someone has reason to fly, the more likely that flying one's own plane costs less per flight than a ticket on a commercial airline. However, by making extra ("unnecessary") trips, Mr. Agassi raises his total cost of owning and operating the airplane.

6. The total cost of building a 1-cubic-foot crate is \$6. It costs four times as much to build an 8-cubic-foot crate, \$24. In general, as the height of a cube increases, the total cost of building it rises with the square of the height, but the volume increases with the cube of the height. Thus, the cost per unit of volume falls.

11. You produce your output, exam points, using as inputs the time spent on Question 1, t_1, and the time spent on Question 2, t_2. If you have diminishing marginal returns to extra time on each problem, your isoquants have the usual shapes: They curve away from the origin. You face a constraint that you may spend no more than 60 minutes on the two questions: $60 = t_1 + t_2$. The slope of the 60-minute isocost curve is −1: For every extra minute you spend on Question 1, you have one less minute to spend on Question 2. To maximize your test score, given that you can spend no more than 60 minutes on the exam, you want to pick the highest isoquant that is tangent to your 60-minute isocost curve. At the tangency, the slope of your isocost curve, −1, equals the slope of your isoquant, $-MP_1/MP_2$. That is, your score on the exam is maximized when $MP_1 = MP_2$, where the last minute spent on Question 1 would increase your score by as much as spending it on Question 2 would. Therefore, you've allocated your time on the exam wisely if you are indifferent as to which question to work on during the last minute of the exam.

12. From the information given and assuming that there are no economies of scale in shipping baseballs, it appears that balls are produced using a constant returns to scale, fixed-proportion production function. The corresponding cost function is $C(q) = [w + s + m]q$, where w is the wage for the time period it takes to stitch one ball, s is the cost of shipping one ball, and m is the price of all material to produce a ball. As the cost of all inputs other than labor and transportation are the same everywhere, the cost difference between Georgia and Costa Rica depends on $w + s$ in both locations. As firms choose to produce in Costa Rica, the extra shipping cost must be less than the labor savings in Costa Rica.

13. According to Equation 7.7, if the firm were minimizing its cost, the extra output it gets from the last dollar spent on labor, $MP_L/w = 50/200 = 0.25$, should equal the extra output it derives from the last dollar spent on capital, $MP_K/r = 200/1{,}000 = 0.20$. Thus, the firm is not minimizing its costs. It would do better if it used relatively less capital and more labor, from which it gets more extra output from the last dollar spent.

16. If $-w/r$ is the same as the slope of the line segment connecting the wafer-handling stepper and stepper technologies, then the isocost will lie on that line segment, and the firm will be indifferent between using either of the two technologies (or any combination of the two). In all the isocost lines in the figure, the cost of capital is the same, and the wage varies. The wage such that the firm is indifferent lies between the relatively high wage on the C^2 isocost line and the lower wage on the C^3 isocost line.

27. Let w be the cost of a unit of L and r be the cost of a unit of K. Because the two inputs are perfect substitutes in the production process, the firm uses only the less expensive of the two inputs. Therefore, the long-run cost function is $C(q) = wq$ if $w \le r$; otherwise, it is $C(q) = rq$.

33. The firm chooses its optimal labor/capital ratio using Equation 7.7: $MP_L/w = MP_K/r$. That is,

$$\tfrac{1}{2}q/(wL) = \tfrac{1}{2}q/(rK),$$

or $L/K = r/w$. Thus, in the United States where $w = r = 10$, the optimal $L/K = 1$, or $L = K$. Thus, the firm produces where $q = 100 = L^{0.5}K^{0.5} = K^{0.5}K^{0.5} = K$. Therefore, $K = 100 = L$. The cost is $C = wL + rK = 10 \times 100 + 10 \times 100 = 2{,}000$. At its Asian plant, the optimal input ratio is $L^*/K^* = 1.1r/(w/1.1) = 11/(10/1.1) = 1.21$. That is, $L^* = 1.21K^*$. Thus, $q = (1.21K^*)^{0.5}(K^*)^{0.5} = 1.1K^*$. Therefore, $K^* = 100/1.1$ and $L^* = 110$. The cost is $C^* = [(10/1.1) \times 110] + [11 \times (100/1.1)] = 2{,}000$. That is, the firm will use a different factor ratio in Asia, but the cost will be the same. If the firm could not substitute toward the less expensive input, its cost in Asia would be $C^{**} = [(10/1.1) \times 100] + [11 \times 100] = 2{,}009.09$.

35. The average cost of producing one unit is α (regardless of the value of β). If $\beta = 0$, the average cost does not change with volume. If learning by doing increases with volume, $\beta < 0$, so the average cost falls with volume. Here the average cost falls exponentially (a smooth curve that asymptotically approaches the quantity axis).

Chapter 8

6. Suppose that a U-shaped marginal cost curve cuts a competitive firm's demand curve (price line) from above at q_1 and from below at q_2. By increasing output to $q_2 + 1$, the firm earns extra profit because the last unit sells for price p, which is greater than the marginal cost of that last unit. Indeed, the price exceeds the marginal cost of all units between q_1 and q_2, so it is more profitable to produce q_2 than q_1. Thus, the firm should either produce q_2 or shut down (if it is making a loss at q_2). We can derive this result using calculus. The second-order condition, Equation 8B.3, for a competitive firm requires that marginal cost cut the demand line from below at q^*, the profit-maximizing quantity:

$$\mathrm{d}MC(q^*)/\mathrm{d}q > 0.$$

9. Some farms did not pick apples so as to avoid incurring the variable cost of harvesting apples. These farmers left open the question of whether they will harvest in the future if the price rises above the shutdown level. Other more pessimistic farmers did not expect price to rise anytime soon, so they bulldozed their trees, leaving the market for good. (Most planted alternative apples such as Granny Smith and Gala that are more popular with the public and sell at a price above the minimum average variable cost.)

20. The shutdown notice reduces the firm's flexibility, which matters in an uncertain market. If conditions suddenly change, the firm may have to operate at a loss for six months before it can shut down. This potential extra expense of shutting down may discourage some firms from entering the market initially.

37. The competitive firm's marginal cost function is found by differentiating its cost function with respect to quantity: $\mathrm{d}C(q)/\mathrm{d}q = b + 2cq + 3dq^2$. The firm's necessary profit-maximizing condition is $p = MC = b + 2cq + 3dq^2$. The firm solves this equation for q for a specific price to determine its profit-maximizing output.

39. To derive the expression for the elasticity of the residual or excess supply curve in Equation 8.7, we differentiate the residual supply curve (Equation 8.6), $S^r(p) = S(p) - D^o(p)$, with respect to p to obtain

$$\frac{\mathrm{d}S^r}{\mathrm{d}p} = \frac{\mathrm{d}S}{\mathrm{d}p} - \frac{\mathrm{d}D^o}{\mathrm{d}p}.$$

Let $Q_r = S^r(p)$, $Q = S(p)$, and $Q_o = D(p)$. We multiply both sides of the differentiated expression by p/Q_r, and for convenience, we also multiply the second term by $Q/Q = 1$ and the last term by $Q_o/Q_o = 1$:

$$\frac{\mathrm{d}S^r}{\mathrm{d}p}\frac{p}{Q_r} = \frac{\mathrm{d}S}{\mathrm{d}p}\frac{p}{Q_r}\frac{Q}{Q} - \frac{\mathrm{d}D^o}{\mathrm{d}p}\frac{p}{Q_r}\frac{Q_o}{Q_o}.$$

We can rewrite this expression as Equation 8.7,

$$\eta_r = \frac{\eta}{\theta} - \frac{1-\theta}{\theta}\varepsilon_o,$$

where $\eta_r = (\mathrm{d}S^t/\mathrm{d}p)(p/Q_r)$ is the residual supply elasticity, $\eta = (\mathrm{d}S/\mathrm{d}p)(p/Q)$ is the market supply elasticity, $\varepsilon_o = (\mathrm{d}D^o/\mathrm{d}p)(p/Q_o)$ is the demand elasticity of the other countries, and $\theta = Q_r/Q$ is the residual country's share of the world's output (hence $1 - \theta = Q_o/Q$ is the share of the rest of the world). *Note*: If there are n countries with equal outputs, then $1/\theta = n$, so this equation can be rewritten as $\eta_r = n\eta - (n-1)\varepsilon_o$.

40. See the answer to Problem 39 for details on the residual supply elasticity:

   a. The incidence of the federal specific tax is shared equally between consumers and firms, whereas the firms bear virtually none of the incidence of the state tax (they pass the tax on to consumers).

   b. From Chapter 3, we know that the incidence of a tax that falls on consumers in a competitive market is approximately $\eta/(\eta - \varepsilon)$. Although the national elasticity of supply may be a relatively small number, the residual supply elasticity facing a particular state is very large. Using the analysis about residual supply curves, we can infer that the supply curve to a particular state is likely to be nearly horizontal—nearly perfectly elastic. For example, if the price rises even slightly in Maine relative to Vermont, suppliers in Vermont will be willing to shift up to their entire supply to Maine. Thus, we expect the incidence on consumers to be nearly one from a state tax but less from a federal tax, consistent with the empirical evidence.

   c. If all 50 states were identical, we could write the residual elasticity of supply equation as

$$\eta_r = 50\eta - 49\varepsilon_o\,.$$

   Given this equation, the residual supply elasticity to one state is at least 50 times larger than the national elasticity of supply, $\eta_r \geq 50\eta$, because $\varepsilon_o < 0$, so the $-49\varepsilon_o$ term is positive and increases the residual supply elasticity.

41. Because the clinics are operating at minimum average cost, a lump-sum tax that caused the minimum average cost to rise by 10% would cause the market price of abortions to rise by 10%. Based on the estimated price elasticity of –1.07, the number of abortions would fall by nearly 11%.

Chapter 9

14. If the tax is based on *economic* profit, the tax has no long-run effect because the firms make zero economic profit. If the tax is based on *business* profit and business profit is greater than economic profit, the profit tax raises firms' after-tax costs and results in fewer firms in the market. The exact effect of the tax depends on why business profit is less than economic profit. For example, if the government ignores opportunity labor cost but includes all capital cost in computing profit, firms will substitute toward labor and away from capital.

15. Solved Problem 8.5 shows the long-run effect of a lump-sum tax in a competitive market. Consumer surplus falls by more than tax revenue increases, and producer surplus remains zero, so welfare falls.

32. The consumer surplus at a price of 30 is

$$450 = \tfrac{1}{2}(30 \times 30).$$

38. The answers are:

   a. The initial equilibrium is determined by equating the quantity demanded to the quantity supplied: $100 - 10p = 10p$. That is, the equilibrium is $p = 5$ and $Q = 50$. At the support price, the quantity supplied is $Q_s = 60$. The market-clearing price is $p = 4$. The deficiency payment was $D = (\underline{p} - p)Q_s = (6 - 4)60 = 120$.

   b. Consumer surplus rises from $CS_1 = \tfrac{1}{2}(10 - 5)50 = 125$ to $CS_2 = \tfrac{1}{2}(10 - 4)60 = 180$. Producer surplus rises from $PS_1 = \tfrac{1}{2}(5 - 0)50 = 125$ to $PS_2 = \tfrac{1}{2}(6 - 0)60 = 180$. Welfare falls from $CS_1 + PS_1 = 125 + 125 = 250$ to $CS_2 + PS_2 - D = 180 + 180 - 120 = 240$. Thus, the deadweight loss is 10.

Chapter 10

2. A subsidy is a negative tax. Thus, we can use the same analysis as in Solved Problem 10.1 to answer this question (reversing the signs of the effects).

15. If you draw the convex production possibility frontier on panel c of Figure 10.6, you will see that it lies strictly inside the concave production possibility frontier. Thus, more output can be obtained if Jane and Denise use the concave frontier. That is, each should specialize in producing the good for which she has a comparative advantage.

17. As Chapter 5 shows, the slope of the budget constraint facing an individual equals the negative of that person's wage. Panel a of the figure below illustrates that Pat's budget constraint is steeper than Chris' because Pat's wage is larger than Chris'. Panel b shows their combined budget constraint after they marry. Before they marry, each spends some time in the market earning money and other time at home cooking, cleaning, and consuming leisure. After they marry, one can specialize in earning money and the other at working at home. If they are both equally skilled at household work (or if Chris is better), then Pat has a comparative advantage (see Figure 10.6) in working in the market and Chris has a comparative advantage in working at home. Of course, if both enjoy consuming leisure, they may not fully specialize. As an example, suppose that before they lived together Chris and Pat each spent 10 hours a day in sleep and leisure activities, 5 hours working in the marketplace, and 9 hours working at home. Because Chris earns \$10 an hour and Pat earns \$20, they collectively earned \$150 a day and worked 18 hours a day at home. After they marry, they can benefit from specialization. If Chris works entirely at home and Pat works 10 hours in

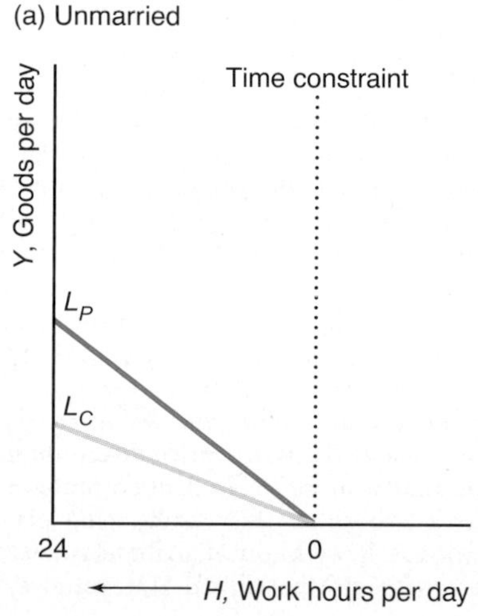

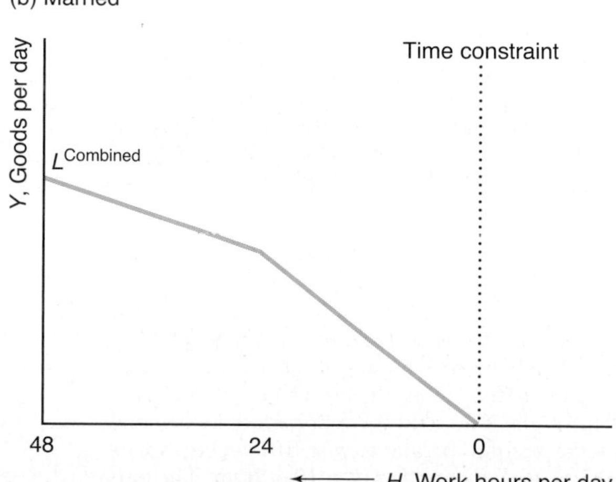

the market and the rest at home, they collectively earn \$200 a day (a one-third increase) and still have 18 hours of work at home. If they do not need to spend as much time working at home because of economies of scale, one or both could work more hours in the marketplace, and they will have even greater disposable income.

25. Amos' marginal rate of substitution is $MRS_a = [\alpha/(1-\alpha)]H_a/G_a$, and Elise's is $MRS_e = [\beta/(1-\beta)]\,H_e/G_e$. Along the contract curve, the two marginal rates of substitution are equal: $MRS_a = MRS_e$. Thus, to find the contract curve, we equate the right sides of the expressions for MRS_a and MRS_e. Using the information about the endowments and some algebra, we can write the (quadratic) formula for the contract curve as

$$(\beta - \alpha)G_aH_a + \beta(\alpha - 1)50G_a + \alpha(1 - \beta)100H_a = 0.$$

Chapter 11

11. A profit tax (of less than 100%) has no effect on a firm's profit-maximizing behavior. Suppose the government's share of the profit is γ. Then the firm wants to maximize its after-tax profit, which is $(1-\gamma)\pi$. However, whatever choice of Q (or p) maximizes π, will maximize $(1-\gamma)\pi$. Figure 20.3 gives a graphical example where $\gamma = \frac{1}{3}$. Consequently, the tribe's behavior is unaffected by a change in the share that the government receives. We can also answer this problem using calculus. The before-tax profit is $\pi_B = R(Q) - C(Q)$, and the after-tax profit is $\pi_A = (1-\gamma)[R(Q) - C(Q)]$. For both, the first-order condition is marginal revenue equals marginal cost: $R'(Q) = C'(Q)$.

13. Yes. As the electric power utility application illustrates, the demand curve could cut the average cost curve only in its downward-sloping section. Consequently, the average cost is strictly downward sloping in the relevant region.

31. See **www.myeconlab.com/perloff**, Chapter 11, "Humana Hospitals," for more examples. For saline solution, $p/MC \approx 55.4$ and the Lerner Index is $(p - MC)/p \approx 0.98$. From Equation 11.9, we know that $(p - MC)/p \approx 0.98 = -1/\varepsilon$, so $\varepsilon \approx 1.02$.

36. Suppose that the monopoly faces a constant-elasticity demand curve, with elasticity ε, and has a constant marginal cost, m, and that the government imposes a specific tax of τ. The monopoly sets its price such that $p = (m + \tau)/(1 + 1/\varepsilon)$. Thus, $dp/d\tau = 1/(1 + 1/\varepsilon) > 1$.

44. If the demand curve is $p = 10 - Q$, its marginal revenue curve is $MR = 10 - 2Q$. Thus, the output that maximizes the monopoly's profit is determined by $MR = 10 - 2Q = 2 = MC$, or $Q^* = 4$. At that output level, its price is $p^* = 6$ and its profit is $\pi^* = 16$. If the monopoly chooses to sell 8 units in the first period (it has no incentive to sell more), its price is 2 and it makes no profit. Given that the firm sells 8 units in the first period, its demand curve in the second period is $p = 10 - Q/\alpha$, so its marginal revenue function is $MR = 10 - 2Q/\alpha$. The output that leads to its maximum profit is determined by $MR = 10 - 2Q/\alpha = 2 = MC$, or its output is 4α. Thus, its price is 6 and its profit is 16α. It pays for the firm to set a low price in the first period if the lost profit, 16, is less than the extra profit in the second period, which is $16(\alpha - 1)$. Thus, it pays to set a low price in the first period if $16 < 16(\alpha - 1)$, or $2 < \alpha$.

Chapter 12

2. The colleges may be providing scholarships as a form of charity, or they may be price discriminating by lowering the final price to less wealthy families (with presumably higher elasticities of demand).

5. This policy allows the firm to maximize its profit by price discriminating if people who put a lower value on their time (are willing to drive to the store and move their purchases themselves) have a higher elasticity of demand than people who want to order over the phone and have the goods delivered.

34. See **www.myeconlab.com/perloff**, Chapter 12, Supplemental Material, "Aibo," for more details. The two marginal revenue curves are $MR_J = 3{,}500 - Q_J$ and $MR_A = 4{,}500 - 2Q_A$. Equating the marginal revenues with the marginal cost of \$500, we find that $Q_J = 3{,}000$ and $Q_A = 2{,}000$. Substituting these quantities into the inverse demand curves, we learn that $p_J = \$2{,}000$ and $p_A = \$2{,}500$. Rearranging Equation 11.9, we know that the elasticities of demand are $\varepsilon_J = p/(MC - p) = 2{,}000/(500 - 2{,}000) = -\frac{4}{3}$ and $\varepsilon_A = 2{,}500/(500 - 2{,}500) = -\frac{5}{4}$. Thus, using Equation 12.3, we find that

$$\frac{p_J}{p_A} = \frac{2{,}000}{2{,}500} = 0.8 = \frac{1 + 1/(-\frac{5}{4})}{1 + 1/(-\frac{4}{3})} = \frac{1 + 1/\varepsilon_A}{1 + 1/\varepsilon_J}.$$

The profit in Japan is $(p_J - m)Q_J = (\$2{,}000 - \$500) \times 3{,}000 = \$4.5$ million, and the U.S. profit is \$4 million. The deadweight loss is greater in Japan, \$2.25 million $(= \frac{1}{2} \times \$1{,}500 \times 3{,}000)$, than in the United States, \$2 million $(= \frac{1}{2} \times \$2{,}000 \times 2{,}000)$.

35. The marginal revenue function corresponding to a linear inverse demand function has the same intercept and twice as steep a slope (see Chapter 11). Thus, the American marginal revenue function is $MR_A = 100 - 2Q_A$, and the Japanese one is $MR_J = 80 - 4Q_J$. To determine how many units to sell in the United States, the monopoly sets its American marginal revenue equal to its marginal cost, $MR_A = 100 - 2Q_A = 20$, and solves for the optimal quantity, $Q_A = 40$ units. Similarly, because $MR_J = 80 - 4Q_J = 20$, the optimal quantity is $Q_J = 15$ units in Japan. Substituting $Q_A = 40$ into the American demand function, we find that $p_A = 100 - 40 = \$60$. Similarly, substituting $Q_J = 15$ units into the Japanese demand function, we learn that $p_J = 80 - (2 \times 15) = \$50$. Thus, the price-discriminating monopoly charges 20% more in the United States than in Japan. We can also show this result using elasticities. From Equation 3.3, we know that the elasticity of demand is $\varepsilon_A = -p_A/Q_A$ in the United States and $\varepsilon_J = -\frac{1}{2}p_J/Q_J$ in

Japan. In the equilibrium, $\varepsilon_A = -\frac{60}{40} = -\frac{3}{2}$ and $\varepsilon_J = 50/(2 \times 15) = -\frac{5}{3}$. As Equation 12.3 shows, the ratio of the prices depends on the relative elasticities of demand:

$$p_A/p_J = \tfrac{60}{50} = (1 + 1/\varepsilon_J)/(1 + 1/\varepsilon_A) = (1 - \tfrac{3}{5})/(1 - \tfrac{2}{3}) = \tfrac{6}{5}.$$

37. From the problem, we know that the profit-maximizing Chinese price is $p = 3$ and the quantity is $Q = 0.1$ (million). The marginal cost is $m = 1$. Using Equation 11.9, $(p_C - m)/p_C = (3 - 1)/3 = -1/\varepsilon_C$, so $\varepsilon_C = -3/2$. If the Chinese inverse demand curve is $p = a - bQ$, then the corresponding marginal revenue curve is $MR = a - 2bQ$. Warner maximizes its profit where $MR = a - 2bQ = m = 1$, so its optimal $Q = (a - 1)/(2b)$. Substituting this expression into the inverse demand curve, we find that its optimal $p = (a + 1)/2 = 3$, or $a = 5$. Substituting that result into the output equation, we have $Q = (5 - 1)/(2b) = 0.1$ (million). Thus, $b = 20$, the inverse demand function is $p = 5 - 20Q$, and the marginal revenue function is $MR = 5 - 40Q$. Using this information, you can draw a figure similar to Figure 12.4.

Chapter 13

5. By differentiating its product, a firm makes the residual demand curve it faces less elastic everywhere. For example, no consumer will buy from that firm if its rival charges less and the goods are homogeneous. In contrast, some consumers who prefer this firm's product to that of its rival will still buy from this firm even if its rival charges less. As the chapter shows, a firm sets a higher price, the lower the elasticity of demand at the equilibrium.

8. The monopoly will make more profit than the duopoly will, so the monopoly is willing to pay the college more rent. Although granting monopoly rights may be attractive to the college in terms of higher rent, students will suffer (lose consumer surplus) because of the higher prices.

11. Given that the duopolies produce identical goods, the equilibrium price is lower if the duopolies set price rather than quantity. If the goods are heterogeneous, we cannot answer this question definitively.

21. The inverse demand curve is $p = 1 - 0.001Q$. The first firm's profit is $\pi_1 = [1 - 0.001(q_1 + q_2)]q_1 - 0.28q_1$. Its first-order condition is

$$d\pi_1/dq_1 = 1 - 0.001(2q_1 + q_2) - 0.28 = 0.$$

If we rearrange the terms, the first firm's best-response function is $q_1 = 360 - \frac{1}{2}q_2$. Similarly, the second firm's best-response function is $q_2 = 360 - \frac{1}{2}q_1$. By substituting one of these best-response functions into the other, we learn that the Cournot-Nash equilibrium occurs at $q_1 = q_2 = 240$, so the equilibrium price is 52¢.

22. One approach is to show that the effect a rise in marginal cost or a fall in the number of firms tends to cause the price to rise. Solved Problem 13.4 shows the effect of a decrease in marginal cost (the opposite effect). The section titled "The Cournot Equilibrium and the Number of Firms" shows that as the number of firms falls, market power increases and the markup of price over marginal cost increases. The two effects reinforce each other. Suppose the market demand curve has a constant elasticity of ε. We can rewrite Equation 13.7 as $p = m/[1 + 1/(n\varepsilon)] = m\mu$, where $\mu = 1/[1 + 1/(n\varepsilon)]$ is the markup factor. Suppose that marginal cost increases to $(1 + \alpha)m$ and the drop in the number of firms causes the markup factor to rise to $(1 + \beta)\mu$; then the change in price is $[(1 + \alpha)m \times (1 + \beta)\mu] - m\mu = (\alpha + \beta + \alpha\beta)m\mu$. That is, price increases by the fractional increase in the marginal cost, α, plus the fractional increase in the markup factor, β, plus the interaction of the two, $\alpha\beta$.

25. Firm 1's profit is $\pi_1 = q_1[a - b(q_1 + q_2)] - mq_1$. Its best response function is $q_1 = (a - m - bq_2)/(2b)$, where we replace m_1 with m in Equation 13A.11. Firm 2's profit is $\pi_2 = q_2[a - b(q_1 + q_2)] - (m + x)q_2$. Simultaneously solving these best-response functions for q_1 and q_2, we get the equilibrium quantities in Equations 13A.13 and 13A.14, where we've substituted for the appropriate marginal costs:

$$q_1 = \frac{a - 2m + (m + x)}{3b} = \frac{a - m + x}{3b},$$

$$q_2 = \frac{a - 2(m + x) + m}{3b} = \frac{a - m - 2x}{3b}.$$

By inspection,

$$q_1 = [a - m + x]/[3b] > q_2 = [a - m - 2x]/[3b].$$

The low-cost firm, Firm 1, has the higher profit. The profits are $\pi_1 = (a + [m + x] - 2m)^2/[9b]$ and $\pi_2 = (a + m - 2[m + x])^2/[9b]$. Thus,

$$\pi_1 = \frac{(a - m + x)^2}{9b} > \frac{(a - m - 2x)^2}{9b} = \pi_2.$$

26. To answer these questions, we use Appendixes 13A (Cournot) and 13B (Stackelberg).

a. Using Equation 13A.8, the Cournot equilibrium quantity for each of the duopoly firms is $q = (a - m)/(3b) = (150 - 60)/3 = 30$. As a result, the Cournot price is $p = (a + 2m)/3 = (150 + 120)/3 = 90$ (using Equation 13A.9).

b. From Equation 13B.3, we know that the Stackelberg leader's quantity is $q_1 = (a - m)/(2b) = (150 - 60)/2 = 45$. The follower's quantity, from Equation 13B.4, is $q_2 = (a - m)/(4b) = (150 - 60)/4 = 22.5$. Thus, the Stackelberg equilibrium price is $p = 150 - 45 - 22.5 = 82.5$.

31. Appendix 13A shows the general formulas for the linear demand, constant marginal cost Cournot model.

a. For the duopoly, $q_1 = (15 - 2 + 2)/3 = 5$, $q_2 = (15 - 4 + 1)/3 = 4$, $p_d = 6$, $\pi_1 = (6 - 1)5 = 25$, $\pi_2 = (6 - 2)4 = 16$. Total output is $Q_d = 5 + 4 = 9$. Total profit is $\pi_d = 25 + 16 = 41$. Consumer surplus is

$$CS_d = \tfrac{1}{2}(15 - 6)9 = \tfrac{81}{2} = 40.5.$$

At the efficient price (equal to marginal cost of 1), the output is 14. The deadweight loss is

$$DWL_d = \tfrac{1}{2}(6 - 1)(14 - 9) = \tfrac{25}{2} = 12.5.$$

b. A monopoly equates its marginal revenue and marginal cost: $MR = 15 - 2Q_m = 1 = MC$. Thus,

$Q_m = 7$, $p_m = 8$, $\pi_m = (8 - 1)7 = 49$. Consumer surplus is $CS_m = \frac{1}{2}(15 - 8)7 = \frac{49}{2} = 24.5$. The deadweight loss is $DWL_m = \frac{1}{2}(8 - 1)(14 - 7) = \frac{49}{2} = 24.5$.

c. The average cost of production for the duopoly is $[(5 \times 1) + (4 \times 2)]/(5 + 4) = 1.44$, whereas the average cost of production for the monopoly is 1. The increase in market power effect swamps the efficiency gain so that consumer surplus falls while deadweight loss nearly doubles.

32. Firm 1 wants to maximize its profit:

$$\pi_1 = (p_1 - 10)q_1 = (p_1 - 10)(100 - 2p_1 + p_2).$$

Its first-order condition is

$$d\pi_1/dp_1 = 100 - 4p_1 + p_2 + 20 = 0,$$

so its best-response function is $p_1 = 30 + \frac{1}{4}p_2$. Similarly, Firm 2's best-response function is $p_2 = 30 + \frac{1}{4}p_1$. Solving, the Nash-Bertrand equilibrium prices are $p_1 = p_2 = 40$. Each firm produces 60 units.

37. The answers are:

a. The Cournot equilibrium in the absence of a government intervention is $q_1 = 30$, $q_2 = 40$, $p = 50$, $\pi_1 = 900$, and $\pi_2 = 1{,}600$.

b. The Cournot equilibrium is now $q_1 = 33.3$, $q_2 = 33.3$, $p = 53.3$, $\pi_1 = 1{,}108.9$, and $\pi_2 = 1{,}108.9$.

c. As Firm 2's profit was 1,600 in part a, a fixed cost slightly greater than 1,600 will prevent entry.

Chapter 14

1. The payoff matrix in this prisoners' dilemma game is

		Duncan: *Squeal*	Duncan: *Stay silent*
Larry	*Squeal*	Larry −2, Duncan −2	Larry 0, Duncan −5
	Stay silent	Larry −5, Duncan 0	Larry −1, Duncan −1

If Duncan stays silent, Larry gets 0 if he squeals and −1 (a year in jail) if he stays silent. If Duncan confesses, Larry gets −2 if he squeals and −5 if he does not. Thus, Larry is better off squealing in either case, so squealing is his dominant strategy. By the same reasoning, squealing is also Duncan's dominant strategy. As a result, the Nash equilibrium is for both to confess.

4. We start by checking for dominant strategies. Given the payoff matrix, Toyota always does at least as well by entering the market. If GM enters, Toyota earns 10 by entering and 0 by staying out of the market. If GM does not enter, Toyota earns 250 if it enters and 0 otherwise. Thus, entering is Toyota's dominant strategy. GM does not have a dominant strategy. It wants to enter if Toyota does not enter (earning 200 rather than 0), and it wants to stay out if Toyota enters (earning 0 rather than −40). Because GM knows that Toyota will enter (entering is Toyota's dominant strategy), GM stays out of the market. Toyota's entering and GM's not entering is a Nash equilibrium. Given the other firm's strategy, neither firm wants to change its strategy.

Next we examine how the subsidy affects the payoff matrix and dominant strategies. The subsidy does not affect Toyota's payoff, so Toyota still has a dominant strategy: It enters the market. With the subsidy, GM's payoffs if it enters increase by 50: GM earns 10 if both enter and 250 if it enters and Toyota does not. With the subsidy, entering is a dominant strategy for GM. Thus, both firms' entering is a Nash equilibrium.

17. The game tree below illustrates why the incumbent may install the robotic arms to discourage entry even though its total cost rises. If the incumbent fears that a rival is poised to enter, it invests to discourage entry. The incumbent can invest in equipment that lowers its marginal cost. With the lowered marginal cost, it is credible that the incumbent will produce larger quantities of output, which discourages entry. The incumbent's monopoly (no-entry) profit drops from \$900 to \$500 if it makes the investment because the investment raises its total cost. If the incumbent doesn't buy the robotic arms, the rival enters because it makes \$300 by entering and nothing if it stays out of the market. With entry, the incumbent's profit is \$400. With the investment, the rival loses \$36 if it enters, so it stays out of the market, losing nothing. Because of the investment, the incumbent earns \$500. Nonetheless, earning \$500 is better than earning only \$400, so the incumbent invests.

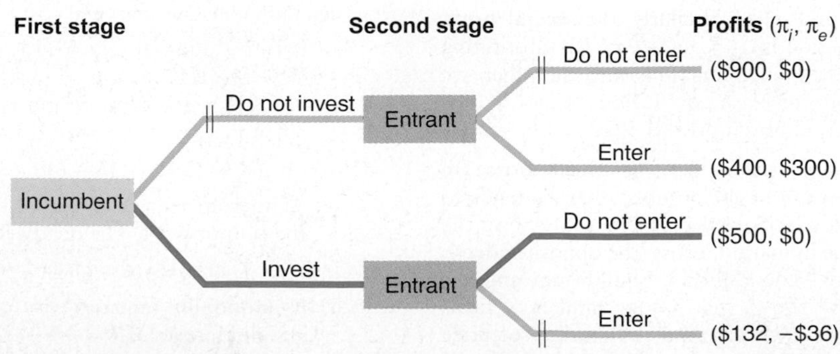

18. The incumbent firm has a *first-mover advantage*, as the game tree illustrates. Moving first allows the incumbent or leader firm to *commit* to producing a relatively large quantity. If the incumbent does not make a commitment before its rival enters, entry occurs and the incumbent earns a relatively low profit. By committing to produce such a large output level that the potential entrant decides not to enter because it cannot make a positive profit, the incumbent's commitment discourages entry. Moving backward in time (moving to the left in the diagram), we examine the incumbent's choice. If the incumbent commits to the small quantity, its rival enters and the incumbent earns \$450. If the incumbent commits to the larger quantity, its rival does not enter and the incumbent earns \$800. Clearly, the incumbent should commit to the larger quantity because it earns a larger profit and the potential entrant chooses to stay out of the market. Their chosen paths are identified by the darker blue in the figure below.

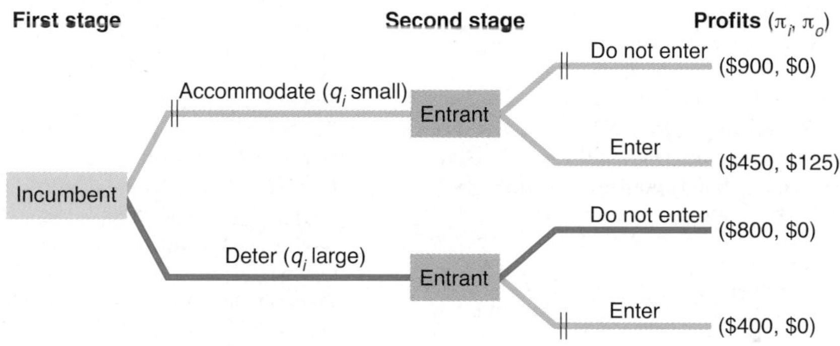

19. It is worth more to the monopoly to keep the potential entrant out than it is worth to the potential entrant to enter, as the figure shows. Before the pollution-control device requirement, the entrant would pay up to \$3 to enter, whereas the incumbent would pay up to $\pi_m - \pi_d =$ \$7 to exclude the potential entrant. The incumbent's profit is \$6 if entry does not occur, and it loses \$1 if entry occurs. Because the new firm would lose \$1 if it enters, it does not enter. Thus, the incumbent has an incentive to raise costs by \$4 to both firms. The incumbent's profit is \$6 if it raises costs rather than \$3 if it does not.

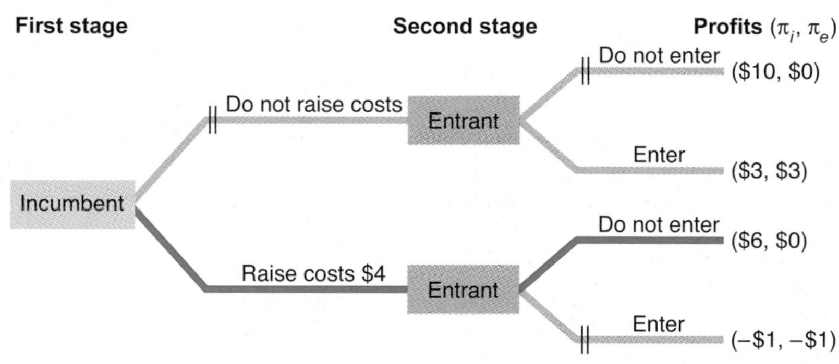

28. Let the probability that a firm sets a low price be θ_1 for Firm 1 and θ_2 for Firm 2. If the firms choose their prices independently, then $\theta_1\theta_2$ is the probability that both set a low price, $(1 - \theta_1)(1 - \theta_2)$ is the probability that both set a high price, $\theta_1(1 - \theta_2)$ is the probability that Firm 1 prices low and Firm 2 prices high, and $(1 - \theta_1)\theta_2$ is the probability that Firm 1 prices high and Firm 2 prices low. Firm 2's expected payoff is

$$E(\pi_2) = 2\theta_1\theta_2 + (0)\theta_1(1 - \theta_2) + (1 - \theta_1)\theta_2 + 6(1 - \theta_1)(1 - \theta_2)$$
$$= (6 - 6\,\theta_1) - (5 - 7\,\theta_1)\theta_2.$$

Similarly, Firm 1's expected payoff is

$$E(\pi_1) = (0)\theta_1\theta_2 + 7\,\theta_1(1 - \theta_2) + 2(1 - \theta_1)\theta_2 + 6(1 - \theta_1)(1 - \theta_2)$$
$$= (6 - 4\theta_2) - (1 - 3\,\theta_2)\theta_1.$$

Each firm forms a belief about its rival's behavior. For example, suppose that Firm 1 believes that Firm 2 will choose a low price with a probability $\hat{q}_2$. If $\hat{q}_2$ is less than $\frac{1}{3}$ (Firm 2 is relatively unlikely to choose a low price), it pays for Firm 1 to choose the low price because the second term in $E(\pi_i)$, $(1 - 3\hat{q}_2)q_1$, is positive, so that as θ_1 increases, $E(\pi_1)$ increases. Because the highest possible θ_1 is 1, Firm 1 chooses the low price with certainty. Similarly, if Firm 1 believes $\hat{q}_2$ is greater than $\frac{1}{3}$ it sets a high price with certainty ($\theta_1 = 0$).

If Firm 2 believes that Firm 1 thinks $\hat{q}_2$ is slightly below $\frac{1}{3}$, Firm 2 believes that Firm 1 will choose a low price with certainty, and hence Firm 2 will also choose a low price. That outcome, $\theta_2 = 1$, however, is not consistent with Firm 1's expectation that $\hat{q}_2$ is a fraction. Indeed, it is only rational for Firm 2 to believe that Firm 1 believes Firm 2 will use a mixed strategy if Firm 1's belief about Firm 2 makes Firm 1 unpredictable. That is, Firm 1 uses a mixed strategy only if it is *indifferent* between setting a high or a low price. It is only indifferent if it believes $\hat{q}_2$ is exactly $\frac{1}{3}$. By similar reasoning, Firm 2 will use a mixed strategy only if its belief is that Firm 1 chooses a low price with probability $\hat{q}_1 = \frac{5}{7}$. Thus, the only possible Nash equilibrium is $q_1 = \frac{5}{7}$ and $q_2 = \frac{1}{3}$.

Chapter 15

2. Before the tax, the competitive firm's labor demand was $p \times MP_L$. After the tax, the firm's effective price is $(1 - \alpha)p$, so its labor demand becomes $(1 - \alpha)p \times MP_L$.

28. The answer is given in Appendix 15A.

30. The competitive firm's marginal revenue of labor is $MRP_L = p(1 + 2K)$.

Chapter 16

3. An individual with a zero discount rate views current and future consumption as equally attractive. An individual with an infinite discount rate cares only about current consumption and puts no value on future consumption.

15. If the interest rate is set in real terms, putting $2,000 in the bank today results in an annual flow of $200 in real terms. If the interest rate is set in nominal terms, the real payment will shrink over time, so you cannot receive a real payment of $200 annually. (If the nominal rate were set at 15.5%, an initial $2,000 investment would ensure an annual flow of $200 in real terms.)

16. The real payment this year is the same as the nominal payment: $f = \tilde{f}$. The real payment next year is obtained by adjusting the nominal payment for inflation: $f = \tilde{f}/(1 + \tau) = \tilde{f}/1.1$. Thus, the real present value of the two payments is this year's real payment plus next year's real payment discounted by the real interest rate: $f + f/(1 + i) = \tilde{f} + \tilde{f}/[(1 + \gamma)(1 + i)]$, which is less than $2\tilde{f}$ because nominal future payments are worth less than current ones because of both inflation and discounting.

17. As the first contract is paid immediately, its present value equals the contract payment of $1 million. Our pro can use Equation 16.2 and a calculator to determine the present value of the second contract (or hire you to do the job for him). The present value of a $2 million payment 10 years from now is $\$2,000,000/(1.05)^{10} \approx \$1,227,827$ at 5% and $\$2,000,000/(1.2)^{10} \approx \$323,011$ at 20%. Consequently, the present values are:

	Present Value at 5%	Present Value Payment at 20%
$500,000 today	$50,000	$500,000
$2 million in 10 years	$1,227,827	$323,011
Total	$1,727,827	$823,011

Thus, at 5%, he should accept Contract B, with a present value of $1,727,827, which is much greater than the present value of Contract A, $1 million. At 20%, he should sign Contract A.

23. Currently, you are buying 600 gallons of gas at a cost of $1,200 per year. With a more gas-efficient car, you would spend only $600 per year, saving $600 per year in gas payments. If we assume that these payments are made at the end of each year, the present value of this savings for five years is $2,580 at a 5% annual interest rate and $2,280 at 10% (using Table 16.4). The present value of the amount you must spend to buy the car in five years is $6,240 at 5% and $4,960 at 10% (using Table 16.3). Thus, the present value of the additional cost of buying now rather than later is $1,760 (= $8,000 – $6,240) at 5% and $3,040 at 10%. The benefit from buying now is the present value of the reduced gas payments. The cost is the present value of the additional cost of buying the car sooner rather than later. At 5%, the benefit is $2,580 and the cost is $1,760, so you should buy now. However, at 10%, the benefit, $2,280, is less than the cost, $3,040, so you should buy later.

28. Solving for *irr*, we find that *irr* equals 1 or 9. This approach fails to give us a unique solution, so we should use the *NPV* approach instead.

Chapter 17

3. As the graph on the next page shows, Irma's expected utility of 133 at point f (where her expected wealth is $64) is the same as her utility from a certain wealth of Y.

11. The expected punishment for violating traffic laws is θV, where θ is the probability of being caught and fined and V is the fine. If people care only about the expected punishment (there's no additional psychological pain from the experience), increasing the expected punishment by increasing θ or V works equally well in discouraging bad behavior. The government prefers to increase the fine, V, which is costless, rather than to raise θ, which is costly due to the extra police, district attorneys, and courts required.

15. Assuming that the painting is not insured against fire, its expected value is

$$\$550 = (0.2 \times \$1{,}000) + (0.1 \times \$0) + (0.7 \times \$500).$$

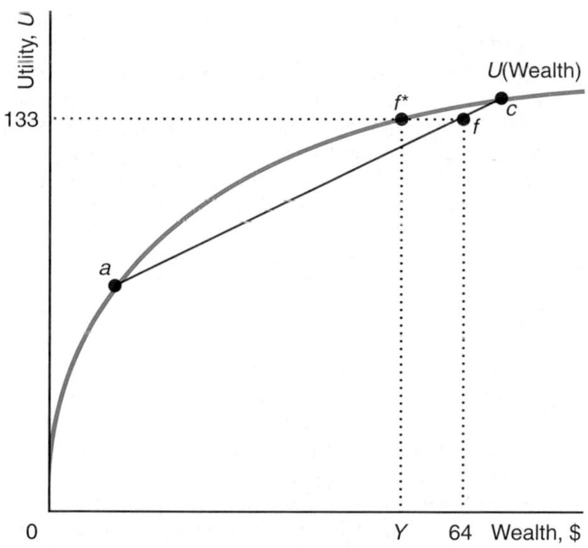

16. The expected value of the stock is

$$\left(\tfrac{1}{4}\times 400\right)+\left(\tfrac{3}{4}\times 200\right)=150.$$

The variance is

$$\tfrac{1}{4}(400-150)^2+\tfrac{3}{4}(200-150)^2=$$

$$\tfrac{1}{4}(150)^2+\tfrac{3}{4}(-50)^2=5{,}625+1{,}875=2{,}500.$$

21. Hugo's expected wealth is

$$\text{EW}=\left(\tfrac{2}{3}\times 144\right)+\left(\tfrac{1}{3}\times 225\right)=96+75=171.$$

His expected utility is

$$\begin{aligned}EU &= [\tfrac{2}{3}\times U(144)]+[\tfrac{1}{3}\times U(225)]\\ &= [\tfrac{2}{3}\times \sqrt{144}]+[\tfrac{1}{3}\times \sqrt{225}]\\ &= [\tfrac{2}{3}\times 12]+[\tfrac{1}{3}\times 15]=13.\end{aligned}$$

He would pay up to an amount P to avoid bearing the risk, where $U(\text{EW} - P)$ equals his expected utility from the risky stock, EU. That is,

$$U(\text{EW}-P)=U(171-P)=\sqrt{171-P}=13=\text{EU}.$$

Squaring both sides, we find that that $171 - P = 169$, or $P = 2$. That is, Hugo would accept an offer for his stock today of \$169 (or more), which reflects a risk premium of \$2.

27. If they were married, Andy would receive half the potential earnings whether they stayed married or not. As a result, Andy will receive \$12,000 in present-value terms from Kim's additional earnings. Because the returns to the investment exceed the cost, Andy will make this investment (unless a better investment is available). However, if they stay unmarried and split, Andy's expected return on the investment is the probability of staying together, $\frac{1}{2}$ times Kim's half of the returns if they stay together, \$12,000. Thus, Andy's expected return on the investment, \$6,000, is less than the cost of the education, so Andy is unwilling to make that investment (regardless of other investment opportunities).

Chapter 18

9. As Figure 18.2 shows, a specific tax of \$84 per ton of output or per unit of emissions (gunk) leads to the social optimum.

12. Granting the chemical company the right to dump 1 ton per day results in that firm dumping 1 ton and the boat company maintaining one boat, which maximizes joint profit at \$20.

23. Use the model in Appendix 18A to determine the equilibrium if the marginal harm of gunk is MC^g = \$84 (instead of Equation 18A.3). We care only about the marginal harm of gunk at the social optimum, which we know is MC^g = \$84 (because it is the same at every level of output). That is the same marginal cost as in the table at the end of Appendix 18A. Thus, the social optimum is the same as in that example (and no algebra is necessary). Using algebra, we set the demand curve equal to the new social marginal cost, $MC^2 = c + dQ + 84$, and we find that the socially optimal quantity is $Q_s = (a - c - 84)/(b + d) = (450 - 30 - 84)/(2 + 2) = 84$.

Chapter 19

4. Because insurance costs do not vary with soil type, buying insurance is unattractive for houses on good soil and relatively attractive for houses on bad soil. These incentives create a moral hazard problem: Relatively more homeowners with houses on poor soil buy insurance, so the state insurance agency will face disproportionately many bad outcomes in the next earthquake.

5. Brand names allow consumers to identify a particular company's product in the future. If a mushroom company expects to remain in business over time, it would be foolish to brand its product if its mushrooms are of inferior quality. (Just ask Babar's grandfather.) Thus, all else the same, we would expect branded mushrooms to be of higher quality than unbranded ones.

18. Because buyers are risk neutral, if they believe that the probability of getting a lemon is θ, the most they are willing to pay for a car of unknown quality is $p = p_1(1 - \theta) + p_2\theta$. If p is greater than both v_1 and v_2, all cars are sold. If $v_1 > p > v_2$, only lemons are sold. If p were less than both v_1 and v_2, no cars would be sold. However, we know that $v_2 < p_2$ and $p_2 < p$, so owners of lemons are certainly willing to sell them. (If sellers bear a transaction cost of c and $p < v_2 + c$, no cars are sold.)

Chapter 20

2. Presumably, the promoter collects a percentage of the revenue at each restaurant. If customers can pay cash, the restaurants may lie to the promoter as to the amount of food they sold. The scrip makes such opportunistic behavior difficult.

4. By making this commitment, the company may be trying to assure customers who cannot judge how quickly the product will deteriorate that the product is durable enough to maintain at least a certain value in the future. The firm is trying to eliminate asymmetric information to increase the demand for its product.

5. This agreement led to very long conversations. Whichever of them was enjoying the call more apparently figured that he or she would get the full marginal benefit of one more minute of talking while having to pay only half the marginal cost. What I learned from this experience was not to open our phone bill so as to avoid being shocked by its size.

6. If Paula pays Arthur a fixed-fee salary of \$168, Arthur has no incentive to buy any carvings for resale, as the \$12 per carving cost comes out of his pocket. Thus, Arthur sells no carvings if he receives a fixed salary and can sell as many or as few carvings as he wants. The contract is not incentive compatible. For Arthur to behave efficiently, this fixed-fee contract must be modified. For example, the contract could specify that Arthur gets a salary of \$168 and that he must obtain and sell 12 carvings. Paula must monitor his behavior. (Paula's residual profit is the joint profit minus \$168, so she gets the marginal profit from each additional sale and wants to sell the joint-profit-maximizing number of carvings.) Arthur makes \$24 = \$168 – \$144, so he is willing to participate. Joint profit is maximized at \$72, and Paula gets the maximum possible residual profit of \$48.

12. A partner who works an extra hour bears the full opportunity cost of this extra hour but gets only half the marginal benefit from the extra business profit. The opportunity cost of extra time spent at the store is the partner's best alternative use of time. A partner could earn money working for someone else or use the time to have fun. Because a partner bears the full marginal cost but gets only half the marginal benefit (the extra business profit) from an extra hour of work, each partner works only up to the point at which the marginal cost equals half the marginal benefit. Thus, each has an incentive to put in less effort than the level that maximizes their joint profit, where the marginal cost equals the marginal benefit.

22. The minimum bond that deters stealing is \$2,500 (= \$500/0.2).

Answers to Questions for Cross-Chapter Analyses

Child-Care Subsidies

1. Parents who do not receive subsidies prefer that poor parents receive lump-sum payments rather than a subsidized hourly rate for child care. If the supply curve for day care services is upward sloping, by shifting the demand curve farther to the right, the price subsidy raises the price of day care for these other parents.

2. The government could give a smaller lump-sum subsidy that shifts the L^{LS} curve down so that it is parallel to the original curve but tangent to indifference curve I^2. This tangency point is to the left of e_2, so the parents would consume fewer hours of child care than with the original lump-sum payment.

Outsourcing and the World Trade Organization

1. See Figure 9.10 (which corresponds to panel a). Going from no trade to free trade, consumers gain areas B and C, while domestic firms lose B. Thus, if consumers give firms an amount between B and $B + C$, both groups will be better off than with no trade.

2. There are several ways to demonstrate that welfare can go up despite the subsidy. For example, one could redraw panel b with flatter supply curves so that area C became smaller than A (area A remains unchanged). Similarly, if the subsidy is very small, then we are very close to the no-distortion case, so that welfare will increase.

Magazine Subscriptions

1. The magazine's profit is $\pi = R(Q) + naQ - mQ - F$, where $R(Q) = p(Q)Q$. Consequently, the magazine uses its first-order condition to determine the Q that maximizes its profit: $d\pi/dQ = R'(Q) + na - m = 0$. That is, its profit is maximized where its marginal revenue, $R'(Q) + na$, equals its marginal cost, m. To determine how a change in a affects its optimal number of subscriptions, we totally differentiate its first-order condition with respect to Q and a: $R''dQ + nda = 0$. Thus, the magazine's optimal number of subscriptions changes with a according to $dQ/da = -n/R''$. Because R'' is negative, $-n/R'' > 0$, so the magazine sells more subscriptions as the advertising rate increases.

2. People who buy a single copy often have a relatively less elastic demand than those who subscribe. If you are

about to board a plane and have nothing to read, you are willing to pay a relatively high price for your favorite magazine. As mentioned in Chapter 12, the magazine's cost of providing a newsstand copy and a subscription differ. The cost of providing newsstand copies is higher than the subscription cost if the magazine must accept returns of unsold copies. Thus, both the relatively less elastic demand and higher costs would cause the newsstand price to exceed the subscription price.

3. A fixed subsidy has no effect on the price or number of subscriptions sold. However, it might keep a magazine from shutting down (see Chapter 11).

Frequent Flier Programs

1. For the given values, the equilibrium price would be

$$p = \$150/[1 + 1/(2 \times -1.75)] = \$210$$

if only the elasticity had changed. If only the marginal cost changed, the equilibrium price would be

$$p = \$160/[1 + 1/(2 \times -2)] \approx \$213.3.$$

Thus, the change in both the marginal cost and the elasticity contributes to the increase in the equilibrium price.

2. In this example, profit increases substantially. Given that the marginal cost equals the average cost, the profit is $\pi = (p - MC)Q = (p - MC)50{,}000{,}000p^{\varepsilon}$. Prior to the FFP, the firm's profit is

$$(\$200 - \$150)1{,}250 = \$62{,}500.$$

After the FFP, the profit is approximately

$$(\$224 - \$160)3{,}855 = \$246{,}727.$$

Emissions Fees Versus Standards Under Certainty

1. In the following figure, the government uses its expected marginal benefit curve to set a standard at S or a fee at f. If the true marginal benefit curve is MB^1, the optimal standard is S_1 and the optimal fee is f_1. The deadweight loss from setting either the fee or the standard too high is the same, DWL_1. Similarly, if the true marginal benefit curve is MB^2, both the fee and the standard are set too low, but both have the same deadweight loss, DWL_2. Thus, the deadweight loss from a mistaken belief about the marginal benefit does not depend on whether the government uses a fee or a standard. When the government sets an emissions fee or standard, the amount of gunk actually produced depends only on the marginal cost of abatement and not on the marginal benefit. Because the standard and fee lead to the same level of abatement, at e, they cause the same deadweight loss.

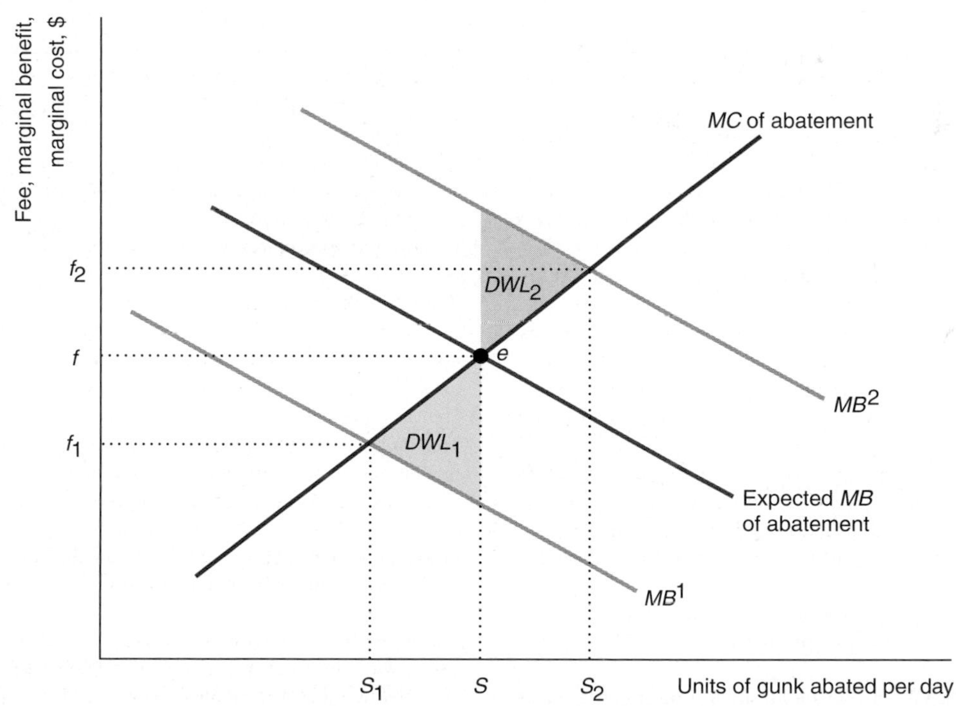

Definitions

I hate definitions. —Benjamin Disraeli

action: a move that a player makes at a specified stage of a game, such as how much output a firm produces in the current period. (14)*

adverse selection: opportunism characterized by an informed person's benefiting from trading or otherwise contracting with a less informed person who does not know about an unobserved characteristic of the informed person. (19)

asymmetric information: situation in which one party to a transaction knows a material fact that the other party does not. (19)

auction: a sale in which property or a service is sold to the highest bidder. (14)

average cost (*AC*): the total cost divided by the units of output produced: $AC = C/q$. (7)

average fixed cost (*AFC*): the fixed cost divided by the units of output produced: $AFC = F/q$. (7)

average product of labor (AP_L): the ratio of output, q, to the number of workers, L, used to produce that output: $AP_L = q/L$. (6)

average variable cost (*AVC*): the variable cost divided by the units of output produced: $AVC = VC/q$. (7)

backward induction: first determine the best response by the last player to move, next determine the best response for the player who made the next-to-last move, and then repeat the process back to the move at the beginning of the game. (14)

bad: something for which less is preferred to more, such as pollution. (4)

bandwagon effect: the situation in which a person places greater value on a good as more and more other people possess it. (11)

barrier to entry: an explicit restriction or a cost that applies only to potential new firms—existing firms are not subject to the restriction or do not bear the cost. (9)

behavioral economics: by adding insights from psychology and empirical research on human cognition and emotional biases to the rational economic model, economists try to better predict economic decision making. (4)

Bertrand equilibrium: a *Nash equilibrium* in prices; a set of prices such that no firm can obtain a higher profit by choosing a different price if the other firms continue to charge these prices. (13)

best response: the strategy that maximizes a player's payoff given its beliefs about its rivals' strategies. (14)

bounded rationality: people have a limited capacity to anticipate, solve complex problems, or enumerate all options. (4)

budget line (or *budget constraint*): the bundles of goods that can be bought if the entire budget is spent on those goods at given prices. (4)

bundling (*package tie-in sale*): a type of tie-in sale in which two goods are combined so that customers cannot buy either good separately. (12)

cartel: a group of firms that explicitly agree to coordinate their activities. (13)

certification: a report that a particular product meets or exceeds a given *standard* level. (19)

cheap talk: unsubstantiated claims or statements. (19)

common knowledge (in a game): what all players know about the rules of the game, that each player's payoff depends on actions taken by all players, and that all players want to maximize their payoffs; all players know that all players know the payoffs and that their opponents are payoff maximizing; and so on. (14)

common property: resources that everyone has an equal right to exploit. (18)

comparative advantage: the ability to produce a good at a lower opportunity cost than someone else. (10)

complete information (in a game): the situation where the payoff function is common knowledge among all players. (14)

constant returns to scale (*CRS*): property of a production function whereby when all inputs are increased by a certain percentage, output increases by that same percentage. (6)

consumer surplus (*CS*): the monetary difference between what a consumer is willing to pay for the quantity of the good purchased and what the good actually costs. (9)

contingent fee: a payment to a lawyer that is a share of the award in a court case (usually after legal expenses are deducted) if the client wins and nothing if the client loses. (20)

*Numbers refer to the chapter where the term is defined.

contract curve: the set of all Pareto-efficient bundles. (10)
cost (*total cost*, *C*): the sum of a firm's variable cost and fixed cost: $C = VC + F$. (7)
Cournot equilibrium (*Nash-Cournot equilibrium*): a set of quantities chosen by firms such that, holding the quantities of all other firms constant, no firm can obtain a higher profit by choosing a different quantity. (13)
credible threat: an announcement that a firm will use a strategy harmful to its rival and that the rival believes because the firm's strategy is rational in the sense that it is in the firm's best interest to use it. (14)
cross-price elasticity of demand: the percentage change in the *quantity demanded* in response to a given percentage change in the price of another good. (3)
deadweight loss (*DWL*): the net reduction in welfare from a loss of surplus by one group that is not offset by a gain to another group from an action that alters a market equilibrium. (9)
decreasing returns to scale (*DRS*): property of a production function whereby output increases less than in proportion to an equal percentage increase in all inputs. (6)
demand curve: the *quantity demanded* at each possible price, holding constant the other factors that influence purchases. (2)
discount rate: a rate reflecting the relative value an individual places on future consumption compared to current consumption. (16)
diseconomies of scale: property of a cost function whereby the average cost of production rises when output increases. (7)
dominant strategy: a strategy that strictly dominates (gives higher profits than) all other strategies, regardless of the actions chosen by rival firms. (14)
duopoly: an oligopoly with two firms. (13)
durable good: a product that is usable for years. (7)
dynamic game: game in which players move either sequentially or repeatedly. (14)
economic cost (*opportunity cost*): the value of the best alternative use of a resource. (7)
economic profit: revenue minus *economic cost*. (8)
economically efficient: minimizing the cost of producing a specified amount of output. (7)
economies of scale: property of a cost function whereby the average cost of production falls as output expands. (7)
economies of scope: situation in which it is less expensive to produce goods jointly than separately. (7)
efficiency in production: situation in which the principal's and agent's combined value (profits, payoffs), π, is maximized. (20)
efficiency in risk bearing: a situation in which risk sharing is optimal in that the person who least minds facing risk—the risk-neutral or less risk-averse person— bears more of the risk. (20)
efficiency wage: an unusually high wage that a firm pays workers as an incentive to avoid shirking. (20)
efficient contract: an agreement with provisions that ensures that no party can be made better off without harming the other party. (20)
efficient production (*technological efficiency*): situation in which the current level of output cannot be produced with fewer inputs, given existing knowledge about technology and the organization of production. (6)
elasticity: the percentage change in a variable in response to a given percentage change in another variable. (3)
endowment: an initial allocation of goods. (10)
endowment effect: people place a higher value on a good if they own it than they do if they are considering buying it. (4)
Engel curve: the relationship between the quantity demanded of a single good and income, holding prices constant. (5)
equilibrium: a situation in which no one wants to change his or her behavior. (2)
essential facility: a scarce resource that a rival must use to survive. (14)
excess demand: the amount by which the *quantity demanded* exceeds the *quantity supplied* at a specified price. (2)
excess supply: the amount by which the *quantity supplied* is greater than the *quantity demanded* at a specified price. (2)
exhaustible resources: nonrenewable natural assets that cannot be increased, only depleted. (16)
expansion path: the cost-minimizing combination of labor and capital for each output level. (7)
extensive form (of a game): specifies the *n* players, the sequence in which they make their moves, the actions they can take at each move, the information that each player has about players' previous moves, and the payoff function over all possible strategies. (14)
externality: the direct effect of the actions of a person or firm on another person's well-being or a firm's production capability rather than an indirect effect through changes in prices. (18)
fair bet: a wager with an expected value of zero. (17)
fair insurance: a bet between an insurer and a policyholder in which the value of the bet to the policyholder is zero. (17)
firm: an organization that converts inputs such as labor, materials, energy, and capital into outputs, the goods and services that it sells. (6)
fixed cost (*F*): a production expense that does not vary with output. (7)
fixed input: a factor of production that cannot be varied practically in the short run. (6)
flow: a quantity or value that is measured per unit of time. (16)
free ride: to benefit from the actions of others without paying. (18)
game: any competition between players (firms) in which strategic behavior plays a major role. (14)
game theory: a set of tools that economists, political scientists, military analysts, and others use to analyze decision making by players who use strategies. (14)
general-equilibrium analysis: the study of how equilibrium is determined in all markets simultaneously. (10)
Giffen good: a commodity for which a decrease in its price causes the quantity demanded to fall. (5)

good: a commodity for which more is preferred to less, at least at some levels of consumption. (4)

incentive compatible: referring to a contract's provision of inducements such that the agent wants to perform the assigned task rather than engage in opportunistic behavior. (20)

incidence of a tax on consumers: the share of the tax that falls on consumers. (3)

income effect: the change in the quantity of a good a consumer demands because of a change in income, holding prices constant. (5)

income elasticity of demand (or ***income elasticity***)**:** the percentage change in the *quantity demanded* in response to a given percentage change in income. (3)

increasing returns to scale (***IRS***)**:** property of a production function whereby output rises more than in proportion to an equal increase in all inputs. (6)

indifference curve: the set of all bundles of goods that a consumer views as being equally desirable. (4)

indifference map (or ***preference map***)**:** a complete set of indifference curves that summarize a consumer's tastes or preferences. (4)

inferior good: a commodity of which less is demanded as income rises. (5)

interest rate: the percentage more that must be repaid to borrow money for a fixed period of time. (16)

internal rate of return (***irr***)**:** the discount rate that results in a net present value of an investment of zero. (16)

internalize the externality: to bear the cost of the harm that one inflicts on others (or to capture the benefit that one provides to others). (18)

isocost line: all the combinations of inputs that require the same (*iso-*) total expenditure (*cost*). (7)

isoquant: a curve that shows the efficient combinations of labor and capital that can produce a single (*iso-*) level of output (*quant*ity). (6)

Law of Demand: consumers demand more of a good the lower its price, holding constant tastes, the prices of other goods, and other factors that influence consumption. (2)

learning by doing: the productive skills and knowledge that workers and managers gain from experience. (7)

Lerner Index: the ratio of the difference between price and marginal cost to the price: $(p - MC)/p$. (11)

limited liability: condition whereby the personal assets of the owners of the corporation cannot be taken to pay a corporation's debts if it goes into bankruptcy. (6)

long run: a lengthy enough period of time that all inputs can be varied. (6)

marginal cost (***MC***)**:** the amount by which a firm's cost changes if the firm produces one more unit of output. (7)

marginal product of labor (***MP_L***)**:** the change in total output, Δq, resulting from using an extra unit of labor, ΔL, holding other factors constant: $MP_L = \Delta q/\Delta L$. (6)

marginal profit: the change in profit a firm gets from selling one more unit of output. (8)

marginal rate of substitution (***MRS***)**:** the maximum amount of one good a consumer will sacrifice to obtain one more unit of another good. (4)

marginal rate of technical substitution: the number of extra units of one input needed to replace one unit of another input that enables a firm to keep the amount of output it produces constant. (6)

marginal rate of transformation (***MRT***)**:** the trade-off the market imposes on the consumer in terms of the amount of one good the consumer must give up to obtain more of the other good. (4)

marginal revenue (***MR***)**:** the change in revenue a firm gets from selling one more unit of output. (8)

marginal revenue product of labor (***MRP_L***)**:** the extra revenue from hiring one more worker. (15)

marginal utility: the extra utility that a consumer gets from consuming the last unit of a good. (4)

market: an exchange mechanism that allows buyers to trade with sellers. (1)

market failure: inefficient production or consumption, often because a price exceeds marginal cost. (9)

market power: the ability of a firm to charge a price above marginal cost and earn a positive profit. (11)

market structure: the number of firms in the market, the ease with which firms can enter and leave the market, and the ability of firms to differentiate their products from those of their rivals. (8)

microeconomics: the study of how individuals and firms make themselves as well off as possible in a world of scarcity and the consequences of those individual decisions for markets and the entire economy. (1)

minimum efficient scale (***full capacity***)**:** the smallest quantity at which the average cost curve reaches its minimum. (13)

mixed strategy: a firm (player) chooses among possible actions according to probabilities it assigns. (14)

model: a description of the relationship between two or more economic variables. (1)

monopolistic competition: a market structure in which firms have market power but no additional firm can enter and earn a positive profit. (13)

monopoly: the only supplier of a good for which there is no close substitute. (11)

monopsony: the only buyer of a good in a given market. (15)

moral hazard: opportunism characterized by an informed person's taking advantage of a less-informed person through an unobserved action. (19)

multimarket price discrimination (***third-degree price discrimination***)**:** a situation in which a firm charges different groups of customers different prices but charges a given customer the same price for every unit of output sold. (12)

Nash equilibrium: a set of strategies such that, holding the strategies of all other firms constant, no firm can obtain a higher profit by choosing a different strategy. (14)

Nash-Bertrand equilibrium (***Bertrand equilibrium*** **or** ***Nash-in-prices equilibrium***)**:** a set of prices such that no firm can obtain a higher profit by choosing a different price if the other firms continue to charge these prices. (13)

Nash-Cournot equilibrium (***Cournot equilibrium*** **or a** ***Nash-in-quantities equilibrium***)**:** a set of quantities sold by firms such that, holding the quantities of all other firms constant, no firm can obtain a higher profit by choosing a different quantity. (13)

natural monopoly: situation in which one firm can produce the total output of the market at lower cost than several firms could. (11)

network externality: the situation where one person's demand for a good depends on the consumption of the good by others. (11)

nonuniform pricing: charging consumers different prices for the same product or charging a customer a price that depends on the number of units the customer buys. (12)

normal form (of a game): representation of a static game of complete information, where the number of players is n, each player has a set of possible strategies, and the payoff function states the payoff for any combination of possible strategies among the players. (14)

normal good: a commodity of which as much or more is demanded as income rises. (5)

normative statement: a conclusion as to whether something is good or bad. (1)

oligopoly: a small group of firms in a market with substantial barriers to entry. (13)

open-access common property: resources to which everyone has free access and equal rights to exploit. (18)

opportunistic behavior: taking advantage of someone when circumstances permit. (15)

opportunity cost (*economic cost*): the value of the best alternative use of a resource. (7)

opportunity set: all the bundles a consumer can buy, including all the bundles inside the budget constraint and on the budget constraint. (4)

Pareto efficient: describing an allocation of goods or services such that any reallocation harms at least one person. (10)

partial-equilibrium analysis: an examination of equilibrium and changes in equilibrium in one market in isolation. (10)

patent: an exclusive right granted to the inventor to sell a new and useful product, process, substance, or design for a fixed period of time. (11)

payoffs (of a game): players' valuations of the outcome of the game, such as profits for firms or utilities for individuals. (14)

perfect complements: goods that a consumer is interested in consuming only in fixed proportions. (4)

perfect information: the situation where the player who is about to move knows the full history of the play of the game to this point, and that information is updated with each subsequent action. (14)

perfect price discrimination (*first-degree price discrimination*): situation in which a firm sells each unit at the maximum amount any customer is willing to pay for it, so prices differ across customers and a given customer may pay more for some units than for others. (12)

perfect substitutes: goods that a consumer is completely indifferent as to which to consume. (4)

pooling equilibrium: an equilibrium in which dissimilar people are treated (paid) alike or behave alike. (19)

positive statement: a testable hypothesis about cause and effect. (1)

price discrimination: practice in which a firm charges consumers different prices for the same good. (12)

price elasticity of demand (or *elasticity of demand*, ε): the percentage change in the *quantity demanded* in response to a given percentage change in the price. (3)

price elasticity of supply (or *elasticity of supply*, η): the percentage change in the *quantity supplied* in response to a given percentage change in the price. (3)

prisoners' dilemma: a game in which all players have dominant strategies that result in profits (or other payoffs) that are inferior to what they could achieve if they used cooperative strategies. (14)

private cost: the cost of production only, not including *externalities*. (18)

producer surplus (*PS*): the difference between the amount for which a good sells and the minimum amount necessary for the seller to be willing to produce the good. (9)

production function: the relationship between the quantities of inputs used and the maximum quantity of output that can be produced, given current knowledge about technology and organization. (6)

production possibility frontier: the maximum amount of outputs that can be produced from a fixed amount of input. (7)

profit (π): the difference between revenues, R, and costs, C: $\pi = R - C$. (6)

property right: the exclusive privilege to use an asset. (18)

public good: a commodity or service whose consumption by one person does not preclude others from also consuming it. (18)

pure strategy: players choose actions with certainty. (14)

quantity demanded: the amount of a good that consumers are willing to buy at a given price, holding constant the other factors that influence purchases. (2)

quantity discrimination (*second-degree price discrimination*): situation in which a firm charges a different price for large quantities than for small quantities but all customers who buy a given quantity pay the same price. (12)

quantity supplied: the amount of a good that firms *want* to sell at a given price, holding constant other factors that influence firms' supply decisions, such as costs and government actions. (2)

quota: the limit that a government sets on the quantity of a foreign-produced good that may be imported. (2)

rent: a payment to the owner of an input beyond the minimum necessary for the factor to be supplied. (8)

rent seeking: efforts and expenditures to gain a rent or a profit from government actions. (9)

requirement tie-in sale: a tie-in sale in which customers who buy one product from a firm are required to make all their purchases of another product from that firm. (12)

reservation price: the maximum amount a person would be willing to pay for a unit of output. (12)

residual demand curve: the market demand that is not met by other sellers at any given price. (8)

residual supply curve: The market supply that is not consumed by other demanders at any given price. (8)
risk: situation in which the likelihood of each possible outcome is known or can be estimated and no single possible outcome is certain to occur. (17)
risk averse: unwilling to make a fair bet. (17)
risk neutral: indifferent about making a fair bet. (17)
risk preferring: willing to make a fair bet. (17)
risk premium: the amount that a risk-averse person would pay to avoid taking a risk. (17)
rules of the game: regulations that determine the timing of players' moves and the actions that players can make at each move. (14)
screening: an action taken by an uninformed person to determine the information possessed by informed people. (19)
separating equilibrium: an equilibrium in which one type of people takes actions (such as sending a *signal*) that allows them to be differentiated from other types of people. (19)
shirking: a *moral hazard* in which agents do not provide all the services they are paid to provide. (20)
short run: a period of time so brief that at least one factor of production cannot be varied practically. (6)
shortage: a persistent excess demand. (2)
signaling: an action taken by an informed person to send information to an uninformed person. (19)
snob effect: the situation in which a person places greater value on a good as fewer and fewer other people possess it. (11)
social cost: the private cost plus the cost of the harms from *externalities*. (18)
standard: a metric or scale for evaluating the quality of a particular product. (19)
static game: game in which each player acts only once and the players act simultaneously (or, at least, each player acts without knowing rivals' actions). (14)
stock: a quantity or value that is measured independently of time. (16)
strategic behavior: a set of actions a firm takes to increase its profit, taking into account the possible actions of other firms. (14)
strategic interdependence: a player's optimal strategy depends on the actions of others. (14)
strategy: a battle plan that specifies the action that a player will make conditional on the information available at each move and for any possible contingency. (14)
subgame: all the subsequent decisions that players may make given the actions already taken and corresponding payoffs. (14)
subgame perfect Nash equilibrium: players' strategies are a Nash equilibrium in every subgame. (14)
substitution effect: the change in the quantity of a good that a consumer demands when the good's price changes, holding other prices and the consumer's *utility* constant. (5)
sunk cost: an expenditure that cannot be recovered. (7)
supergame: a game that is played repeatedly, allowing players to devise strategies for one period that depend on rivals' actions in previous periods. (13)
supply curve: the *quantity supplied* at each possible price, holding constant the other factors that influence firms' supply decisions. (2)
tariff (*duty*): a tax on only imported goods. (9)
technical progress: an advance in knowledge that allows more output to be produced with the same level of inputs. (6)
technological efficiency (*efficient production*): property of a production function such that the current level of output cannot be produced with fewer inputs, given existing knowledge about technology and the organization of production. (6)
tie-in sale: a type of nonlinear pricing in which customers can buy one product only if they agree to buy another product as well. (12)
total cost (C): the sum of a firm's variable cost and fixed cost: $C = VC + F$. (7)
total product of labor: the amount of output (or total product) that can be produced by a given amount of labor. (6)
transaction costs: the expenses of finding a trading partner and making a trade for a good or service beyond the price paid for that good or service. (2)
two-part tariff: a pricing system in which the firm charges a consumer a lump-sum fee (the first tariff or price) for the right to buy as many units of the good as the consumer wants at a specified price (the second tariff). (12)
utility: a set of numerical values that reflect the relative rankings of various bundles of goods. (4)
utility function: the relationship between *utility* values and every possible bundle of goods. (4)
variable cost (VC): a production expense that changes with the quantity of output produced. (7)
variable input: a factor of production whose quantity can be changed readily by the firm during the relevant time period. (6)
vertically integrated: describing a firm that participates in more than one successive stage of the production or distribution of goods or services. (15)
winner's curse: auction winner's bid exceeds the common-value item's value. (14)

Sources for Applications

Chapter 1

Flu Vaccine Shortage: "State Accuses Lauderdale Firm of Price Gouging for Flu Vaccine," sun-sentinel.com, October 13, 2004; Patrick O'Neill, "CDC Hopes to Inoculate against Recurrence of Flu-shot Shortage," *The Oregonian,* September 7, 2005; "Maine Health Officials Don't Foresee Flu Vaccine Shortage," **WMTW.com**, September 8, 2005; **www.cidrap.umn.edu/cidrap/content/influenza/general/news/mar0807asthma-jw.html**, 2007; **www.cdc.gov/flu/about/qa/0607season.htm**, January 2008, de Janvry et al. (2007).

Twinkie Tax: Jacobson and Brownell (2000); Bruce Bartlett, "The Big Food Tax," *National Review Online*, April 3, 2002; Pierre Lemieux, "It's the Fat Police," *National Post*, April 6, 2002; Helen Tobler, "Call for Tax War on Obesity," *Australian IT*, August 16, 2002; "Soda Pop to Be Banned in L.A. Schools," **CBSNEWS.com**, August 28, 2002; Chouniard et al. (2007).

Income Threshold Model and China: "Next in Line: Chinese Consumers," *Economist*, 326(7795), January 23, 1993:66–67; Jeff Pelline, "U.S. Businesses Pour into China," *San Francisco Chronicle*, May 17, 1994:B1–B2; *China Statistical Yearbook* (Beijing: China Statistical Publishing House, 2000); **www.uschina.org/info/forecast/2007/foreign-investment.html**; Jiang Wei, "FDI Doubles Despite Tax Concerns," *China Daily*, February 19, 2008.

Putting Saturn in Orbit: Martin Edwards, "We're Not Dealing: Fixed-Price Sales Find Fans," *Business Journal of North Carolina*, 7(33), November 30, 1992:20; Jeff Pelline, "No-Dicker Stickers for New Cars," *San Francisco Chronicle*, April 15, 1993:D1; Jeff Pelline, "GM Sold on New Pricing," *San Francisco Chronicle*, July 2, 1993:D1; "Automakers Urge Dealers to Quit Haggling," *Plain Dealer*, February 20, 1994:43K; Mark Glover, "There's No Haggling over GM Sales Jump," *Sacramento Bee*, February 4, 1994:D1; Tim Martin, "'No-Dicker' Sticker Has Mixed Success," *Nashville Tennessean*, April 12, 1994; Michael Levy, "Auto Sales Undergoing a Revolution: New Pricing, Mega-Dealerships Change Business," *Buffalo News*, April 24, 1994:Business, 15; Jim Kenzie, "Saturn Homecoming Celebrated First Decade," *Toronto Star*, August 14, 1999; Skip Kaltenheuser, "At Car Dealers, a No-Haggle Policy Sets Off a Battle," *New York Times*, August 29, 1999:4; Dana Flavelle, "Tiny, Tough Cynthia Trudell in Driver's Seat," *Toronto Star*, September 11, 1999; **www.ens-newswire.com/ens/jan2008/2008-01-16-03.asp**.

Chapter 2

Aggregating the Demand for Broadband Service: Duffy-Deno (2003).

Mad Cow: Shifting Supply and Demand Curves: Jason Henderson, "FAQs about Mad Cow Disease and Its Impacts," *The Main Street Economist,* December 2003; "Japan Deems Beef Standards Lax in Canada and U.S." *San Francisco Chronicle,* January 20, 2004:D3; George Raine, "Beef Sales Up Despite Mad Cow," *San Francisco Chronicle*, January 14, 2004:B1, B2; Jon Ortiz, "More Mad Cows Likely," *Sacramento Bee,* February 8, 2004; Peggy Hernandez, "Ban on U.S. Beef Leaves Japanese with a Craving," *Boston Globe,* February 20, 2004:A10; Carter and Huie (2004); Ouchi et al. (2004); George Raine, "Staging a Comeback," *San Francisco Chronicle,* January 1, 2005:D1, D4; Schlenker and Villas-Boas (2007); "Japan Halts Beef Imports From US Plant," *Houston Chronicle*, October 17, 2007.

American Steel Quotas: Robert W. Crandall, "The Effects of U.S. Trade Protection for Autos and Steel," *Brookings Papers on Economic Activity*, 1, 1987:271–288; James B. Burnham, *American Steel and International Trade: The Challenge of Globalization*, Center for the Study of American Business Contemporary Issues Series 95 (Center for the Study of American Business Contemporary Issues, September 1999); Alison Mitchell, "By a Wide Margin, the House Votes Steel Import Curb," *New York Times*, March 18, 1999:A1, C23; "EU Retaliates with Its Own Steel Tariffs," *San Francisco Chronicle*, March 26:2002: B3; Edmund L. Andrews, "Panel Rejects Effort to Add a Steel Tariff," *New York Times*, August 28, 2002:A1; David Hammer, "U.S. Regulators Revoke Steel Tariffs," *San Francisco Chronicle*, December 14, 2006; Christopher S. Rugaber, "Steel Makers Succeed in Keeping Tariffs," **biz.yahoo.com/ap/071010/steel_tariffs.html?.v=1**, October 10, 2007.

Price Controls Kill: "Mugabe's Election Victory May Be Short-Lived," *The Daily News*, March 15, 2002; "Smuggling Results in Sugar Shortages in Zimbabwe," *Harare*, April 21, 2002; "Construction Industry Faces Bleak Future," *Zimbabwe Standard*, May 5, 2002; "Zimbabwe Raises Cement Prices to Ease Shortage," *Harare*, May 7, 2002; "Makoni Admits Price Controls to Blame for Thriving Black Market," *The Daily News*, May 10, 2002; "Supermarkets Adjust Price of Chicken," *The Daily News*, May 17, 2002;

James, Stanley, "Bakeries Scale Down Operations," *The Independent*, September 6, 2002; "Zimbabwe Faces Food Shortages," **cnn.com**, May 24, 2005; "Zim Slaps Price Control on Food," News24, **finance24.com**, June 4, 2005; Fanuel Jongwe, "Watchdog Unlikely to Get Teeth into Zimbabwe Inflation," *Business Report*, November 13, 2006, **www.busrep.co.za/index.php?fArticleId=3534401**; Jan Raath, "Mugabe Cuts the Price of Basics as Bread Runs Out," *The Times*, July 3, 2007; Michael Wines, "Caps on Prices Only Deepen Zimbabweans' Misery," *New York Times*, August 2, 2007; "Zimbabwe Arrests Over Price Curbs," *Al Jazeera*, July 9, 2007, **english.aljazeera.net/NR/exeres/81D1350D-2D57-40C9-871F-EC95C875D5FC.htm**; **www.theaustralian.news.com.au/story/0,25197,23351335-2703,00.html** (March 11, 2008).

Chapter 3

Turning Off the Faucet: Nataraj (2007).

Substitution May Save Endangered Species: Von Hippel and von Hippel (2002, 2004), von Hippel et al. (2005).

The Big Freeze: Carman and Sexton (2007); **usda.mannlib.cornell.edu/usda/nass/AgriPric//2000s/2007/AgriPric-09-27-2007.txt.**

Oil Drilling in the Arctic National Wildlife Refuge: Dwight Lee, "To Drill or Not to Drill: Let the Environmentalists Decide," *The Independent Review,* Fall 2001, pp. 217–226; Energy Information Administration, "The Effects of Alaska Oil and Natural Gas Provisions of H.R. 4 and S. 1776 on U.S. Energy Markets," February 2002; United States Geological Survey, "Arctic National Wildlife Refuge, 1002 Area, Petroleum Assessment, 1998, Including Economic Analysis." **pubs.usgs.gov/fs/fs-0028-01/fs-0028-01.pdf**; "Oil Companies Could Benefit from Alaska Drilling," VNU Business Media, In., November 22, 2004; Severin Borenstein, "ANWR Oil and the Price of Gasoline," U.C. Energy Institute, *Energy Notes,* 3(2), June 2005, Kotchen and Burger (2007), **tonto.eia.doe.gov/dnav/pet/hist/wtotworldw.htm** (October 25, 2007).

Taxing to Stop Smoking and Raise Revenue: Keeler, Hu, Barnett, and Manning (1993); "A Tax We Can Live With," *University of California at Berkeley Wellness Letter*, 9(9), June 1993:7; "Tobacco: Armageddon and Appalachia," *Economist*, 32(7820), July 17, 1993:25; "In Canada, They're Cutting Sin Taxes," *Business Week*, February 21, 1994:44; Christopher Farrell, "This Sin Tax Is Win-Win," *Business Week*, April 11, 1994:31; Jonathan Marshall, "Life Is Very Good for Silicon Valley Residents," *San Francisco Chronicle*, January 13, 1997:B3; **www.ash.org**; Besley and Rosen (1998); "Government Announces Tobacco Tax Increases to Discourage Smoking," Canada NewsWire, June 17, 2002; Gruber, Sen, and Stabile (2002); Jha and Chaloupka (2000); Keeler et al. (2004); Levy and Meara (2005); U.S.D.A., "Tobacco Outlook—Summary," ERS-TBS-258, April 2005; **www.cdc.gov/mmwr/preview/mmwrhtml/mm5114a2.htm**; **www.cdc.gov/mmwr/preview/mmwrhtml/mm5425a1.htm** (2005); **www.who.int/tobacco/statistics/tobacco_atlas/en/** (2007); **tobaccofreekids.org/reports/prices/NationalTobaccoTaxMemo.pdf** (2007); **www.cdc.gov/tobacco/data_statistics/index.htm**; **www.taxfoundation.org/blog/topic/103.html** (2007).

Chapter 4

Indifference Curves Between Food and Clothing: Eastwood and Craven (1981).

Rationing: **www.washingtonpost.com/wp-dyn/content/article/2007/07/02/AR2007070201103.html** (2007); **www.walb.com/Global/story.asp?S=7273374&nav=5kZQ** (2007).

U.S. Versus EU SUVs: Stephen Power and Jo Wrighton, "In Europe, SUVs May Face Taxes Amid Drive to Penalize Emissions," *Wall Street Journal,* June 30, 2004; Gareth Harding, "Europe's SUV Backlash Begins," *Washington Times,* July 8, 2004; Rebecca Goldsmith, "In Europe, SUVs are Autos Non Grata," *San Francisco Chronicle,* September 28, 2004; Royal Ford, "Resurgent Sedan Muscling Past SUV," *Boston Globe,* September 29, 2004, 1; **www.selfemployedweb.com/suv-tax-deduction-changes.htm**; "SUV Tax Write-Offs Last Until End of Year," *Tulsa World,* December 15, 2004; "Tax-Law Change Real Cause of Drop in Sales of SUVs," *Palm Beach Post,* June 23, 2005, 21A; **masetto.sourceoecd.org/vl=2524937/cl=18/nw=1/rpsv/cgibin/fulltextew.pl?prpsv=/ij/oecdjournals/02562332/v2007n3/s1/p1l.idx**; Thomas Wagner, "London to Triple the Toll for Gas Guzzlers in Town," *San Francisco Chronicle*, February 13, 2008, A19.

Effects of Food Stamps: Whitmore (2002); "U.S. Converting Food Stamps into Debit-Card Benefits," *Chattanooga Times Free Press,* June 23, 2004; Kaushal (2007); Hoynes and Schanzenbach (2007); Kaushale (2007); **www.fns.usda.gov/oane/menu/Published/FSP/FILES/Participation/Trends1999-2005Sum.pdf** (2007).

Should Youths Be Allowed to Drink?: Carpenter and Dobkin (2007), **www.icap.org/PolicyIssues/YoungPeoplesDrinking/AgeLawsTable/tabid/219/Default.aspx** (2007), **www.ama-assn.org/ama/pub/category/13246.html** (2007), **www.grsproadsafety.org/themes/default/pdfs/Drinking%20Age%20Limits.pdf** (2007), **www.everything2.com/index.pl?node=legal%20drinking%20age** (2007).

How You Ask the Question Matters: Madrian and Shea (2001, 2002); Robert Powell, "Meet the Investments That Will Be Your Default 401(k) Choices," *MarketWatch*, October 31, 2007; Jesse J. Holland, "Pension Law Addresses Auto-Enrollment," Associated Press, October 22, 2007.

Chapter 5

Going Up in Smoke: Busch et al. (2004); **www.ers.usda.gov/briefing/tobacco/Data/table07.pdf** (2007).

Shipping the Good Stuff Away: Hummels and Skiba (2004).

Fixing the CPI Substitution Bias: Hausman (1997); "Who's Afraid of the Big Bad Deficit?" *Economist*, 336(7934), September 30, 1995:25–26; Louis Uchitelle, "Balancing Quantity, Quality and Inflation," *New York Times*, December 18, 1996: C1, C6; Jonathan Marshall, "Figuring

Inflation Is a Truly Tough Job," *San Francisco Chronicle*, December 9, 1996:C1, C2; Boskin et al. (1997); Alan G. White, "Measurement Biases in Consumer Price Indexes," *International Statistical Review*, 67(3), December 1999:301–325; Boskin and Jorgenson (1997); symposium in *Journal of Economic Perspectives*, Winter 1998; **www.bls.gov/cpi/home.htm** (2002); *Statistical Abstract of the United States* (Washington, D.C.: U.S. Bureau of the Census, 2007); **www.bls.gov/news.release/empsit.t14.htm** (2008).

Leisure-Income Choices of Textile Workers: Dunn (1977, 1978, 1979).

Winning the Good Life: Imbens, Rubin, and Sacerdote (2001).

Effect of a Tax Cut on Tax Revenue: Fullerton (1982); Stuart (1984); Goolsbee (2000); Fullerton and Gan (2004); Heijman and van Ophem (2005).

Chapter 6

Malthus and the Green Revolution: Luther Tweeten, *Farm Policy Analysis* (Boulder, CO: Westview Press, 1989); Donald N. Duvick, "Genetic Contributions to Advances in Yield of U.S. Maize," *Maydica*, 37(1), 1992:69–79; Crossette, "How to Fix a Crowded World: Add People," *New York Times*, November 2, 1997:sec.4: 1, 3; Brander and Taylor (1998); Michael M. Phillips, "Greenspan Credits New Technology for Helping Farmers Weather Crisis," *Wall Street Journal*, March 17, 1999; *Statistical Abstract of the United States* (Washington, D.C.: U.S. Bureau of the Census, 1999); *FAO Quarterly Bulletin of Statistics* (New York: United Nations, 1999); Alan Barkema, "Ag Biotech," *The Main Street Economist*, October 2000; Marc Levy, "Robots Do the Milking at Some U.S. Dairy Farms," *San Francisco Chronicle*, March 4, 2002:E3; **www.unep.org/aeo/251.htm; www.fao.org/NEWS/2000/000704-e.htm**; Norman Borlaug, "Nobel Lecture," December 11, 1970, **Nobelprize.org;** Gregg Easterbrook, "Forgotten Benefactor of Humanity," *Atlantic Monthly*, February 1997; "Biotechnology and the Green Revolution: Interview with Norman Borlaug," November 2002, **ActionBioscience.org; www.ers.usda.gov/Data/AgProductivity** (2007).

A Semiconductor Integrated Circuit Isoquant: Nile Hatch, personal communications; Roy Mallory, personal communications; "PC Processor War Rages On," Deutsche Presse-Agentur, September 1, 2002.

Returns to Scale in U.S. Manufacturing: Hsieh (1995).

Dell Computer's Organizational Innovations: Marc L. Songini, "Just-In-Time Manufacturing," *Computerworld*, November 20, 2000; Stacy Perman, "Automate or Die," *Business 2.0*, July 2001; Crayton Harrison, "Innovative Manufacturing Gives Dell an Advantage," *Dallas Morning News*, July 24, 2002; Larry Dignan, "Is Dell Hitting the Efficiency Wall?" *c/net* **News.Com**, July 29, 2002; John Pletz, "Dell Turns Productivity Gains into Market Share," *Austin American Statesman*, August 26, 2002: D1; Gary Rivlin, "Who's Afraid of China? How Dell Became the World's Most Efficient Computer Maker," *New York Times*, December 19, 2004:3:1 and 3:4; and "Five Top Tips," *The Manufacturer*, March 8, 2005; "Dell On Dell: 'Steady Progress,'" *Investor's Business Daily*, November 14, 2007.

Chapter 7

Opportunity Cost of Going to Church: Gruber and Hungerman (2006).

Swarthmore College's Cost of Capital: Peter Passell, "One Top College's Price Tag: Why So Low, and So High?" *New York Times*, July 27, 1994:A1; correspondence with Professor Mark Kuperberg; adjustments in costs to bring them to 2008 levels.

Short-Run Cost Curves for a Furniture Manufacturer: Hsieh (1995).

The Internet and Outsourcing: Matt Richetel, "Outsourced All the Way," *New York Times,* June 21, 2005.

Innovations and Economies of Scale: Stuart F. Brown, "Robotic Assembly Lines Help Drive Tire Innovation," *New York Times*, January 13, 2007.

Long-Run Cost Curves in Furniture Manufacturing and Oil Pipelines: Exxon (1975); Hsieh (1995).

Choosing an Ink-Jet or a Laser Printer: Various advertisements.

Learning by Doing in Computer Chips: Gruber (1992); Irwin and Klenow (1994); Chung (2001).

Scope: Friedlaender, Winston, and Wang (1983), Kim (1987) Ida and Kuwahara (2004), Asai (2006).

Chapter 8

Breaking Even on Christmas Trees: "How They Do It: Breaking Even in a Seasonal Business," *New York Times*, December 25, 1993:21.

Oil, Oil Sands, and Oil Shale Shutdowns: Agis Salpukas, "Low Prices Have Sapped Little Oil Producers," *New York Times,* April 3, 1999:B1, B4; Robert Collier, "Oil's Dirty Future," *San Francisco Chronicle,* May 22, 2005:A1, A14, A15; Robert Collier, "Coaxing Oil from Huge U.S. Shale Deposits," *San Francisco Chronicle*, September 4, 2006:A1; Jon Birger, "Oil Shale May Finally Have Its Moment," *Fortune*, November 1, 2007; Judith Kohler, "Energy Firms Cautious on Oil Shale," OCRegister, November 3, 2007; Neil Reynolds, *Globe and Mail*, November 21, 2007; Ben Geman, "Canada Warns U.S. Against Using Energy Law to Bar Fuel from Oil Sands," *Greenwire*, February 28, 2008.

Enter the Dragon: Masses Producing Art for the Masses: Keith Bradsher, "Own Original Chinese Copies of Real Western Art!" *New York Times,* July 15, 2005:A1, C4.

Upward-Sloping Long-Run Supply Curve for Cotton: International Cotton Advisory Committee, *Survey of the Cost of Production of Raw Cotton*, September 1992:5; *Cotton: World Statistics*, April 1993:4–5. The figure shows the supply of the major producing countries for which we have cost information. The only large producers for whom cost data are missing are India and China.

Special Blends and Gasoline Supply Curves: Borenstein, Bushnell, and Lewis (2004); David R. Baker, "Rules Fuel Patchwork Quilt of Gas Blends Nationwide," *San Francisco Chronicle,* June 19, 2005:B1, B3.

Abortion Market: Medoff (2007); **www.guttmacher.org** (2005); **www.cdc.gov** (2005); Erin McClam, "Abortions Less Common in U.S. but Rise among Low-Income Women," Associated Press, October 8, 2002.

Chapter 9

Willingness to Pay on eBay: Data from eBay.

Consumer Surplus from Television: Michel Delsol, "Would You Give Up TV for a Million Bucks?" *TV Guide*, October 10, 1992: 11; Aegis System Ltd., "Survey to Determine Consumers' Surplus Accruing TV Viewers and Radio Listeners," Prepared for the Radiocommunications Agency, October 2000; Hazlett et al. (2007).

Bruce Springsteen's Gift to His Fans: Kevin C. Johnson, "As Concert Tickets Rise Sharply, Attendance Falls Flat But Big-Name Acts May Yet Produce Record Profits for Industry," *St. Louis Post-Dispatch*, July 29, 2002:A1; Alan B. Krueger, "Economic Scene: Music Sales Slump, Concert Ticket Costs Jump and Rock Fans Pay the Price," *New York Times*, October 17, 2002:C2.

Deadweight Loss of Christmas Presents: Waldfogel (1993); "Help! What Do We Do With All This Stuff? 'Regift,' of Course," *New York Times,* December 26, 2004:3.2; **www.paymentsnews.com/2006/11/branded_gift_ca.html**, posted November 6, 2006; Sandra M. Jones, "Gift Card Fatigue?" *Chicago Tribune*, November 13, 2007; Andrea Chang, "Keeping Tabs on Gift Cards," *Los Angeles Times*, December 1, 2007; Marshall Loeb, "How to Offload Unwanted Gift Cards," South Florida Sun-Sentinel.com, December 2, 2007; Alan Krauss, "Gift Cards Go Philanthropic," *New York Times*, December 5, 2007:12.

Cab Fare: Ian Fisher, "A Bumpier Ride for New York Taxis," *New York Times*, October 6, 1991:7; Jonathan Marshall, "Cab Companies Hailed into Court," *San Francisco Chronicle*, July 1, 1993:A1, A11; Sheryl Fragin, "Taxi!" *Atlantic Monthly*, May 1994:30f; Emerald Yeh and Christine McMurry, "Are San Francisco Cabs a Bit Too Rare?" *San Francisco Chronicle*, September 15, 1996:4; Catherine Bowman, "Why San Francisco Taxis Are Catch as Catch Can," *San Francisco Chronicle*, September 16, 1995:A1, A11; Kathleen Harrington, "Bottom Line: 300 More Cabs Needed," *San Francisco Chronicle*, July 28, 1998:A19; Victoria Coliver, "Taxi Turmoil," *San Francisco Examiner*, June 13, 1999:B1, B7; Edward Epstein, "S.F. Tax Deal Rejected by Board of Supervisors," *San Francisco Chronicle*, April 13, 1999: A16; Broski and Mildner (1998); Pau Tharp, "He's Driven by Yellow Cabs," *New York Post*, June 30, 2002:31 Steven Oberbeck, "Medallion Financial Looks to Utah to Expand Taxi Licenses," *Salt Lake Tribune*, August 13, 2002:B5; Schaller (2004); Chris Berdik, "Fare Game," *Boston,* 42(9) September 2004:98–105; Hansu Kim, "Taxi Medallions—Why Given S.F. Assets Away?" *San Francisco Chronicle,* March 29, 2005:B7; Schaller Consulting (2006); **www.nyc.gov/html/tlc/downloads/pdf/press_release_11_01_07.pdf.**

Deadweight Loss from Wireless Taxes: "Hausman" (2000).

Farmer Subsidies: *Agricultural Policies, Markets and Trade: Monitoring and Outlook* (Geneva: Organization for Economic Cooperation and Development, 1994–1999); Edmund L. Andrews, "No Agreement on Reducing Europe Farm Subsidies," *New York Times*, February 27, 1999:B1, B2; **OECD.org** (2007).

Chapter 10

Urban Flight: Econsult (2003); Crawford et al. (2004); **www.bassman.com/01_06.html**, December 2007.

Wealth Distribution in the United States: Sylvia Nasar, "The Rich Get Richer, but Never the Same Way Twice," *New York Times*, August 16, 1992:3; Elise Golan and Mark Nord, "How Government Assistance Affects Income," *Food Review*, 21(1), January–April 1998:2–7; David Cay Johnston, "Gap Between Rich and Poor Bigger than Ever," *San Francisco Examiner*, September 5, 1999:B4; "*Forbes*' List of the Wealthy Finds Richest Even Richer," *San Francisco Chronicle*, September 24, 1999:A2; Kennickell (2001, 2003, 2006); David Cay Johnston, "Richest Are Leaving Even the Rich Far Behind," *New York Times,* June 5, 2005:A1, A17; Carolyn Said, "Number of Millionaires Rises in Bay Area, U.S. and World," *San Francisco Chronicle,* June 10, 2005:C1, C5; **www.epi.org/printer.cfm?id=2406&content_type=1&nice_name=webfeatures_snapshots_20060627**, 2007; **forbes.com**, 2007.

An Unequal World: United Nations, *Human Development Reports*, **hdrstats.undp.org**, 2008.

How You Vote Matters: "The Mathematics of Voting: Democratic Symmetry," *The Economist*, March 4, 2000:83; **www.sfelections.org/demo**, December 2007.

Chapter 11

Cable Cars and Profit Maximization: Rachel Gordon, "A Fare Too Steep?" *San Francisco Chronicle*, September 12, 2006:B-1; **www.sfmta.com/cms/mfares/fareinfo.htm#cable**, 2008.

Apple's iPod: "The History of Apple's iPod," **osviews.com/modules.php?op=modload&name=News&file=article&sid=4259**; Brad Gibson, "First on TMO," **www.macobserver.com**, November 3, 2004, and May 4, 2005; "A Brief History of the iPod," **www.uberreview.com/history.htm**, 2004–2005; **en.wikipedia.org/wiki/Ipod**, July 28, 2005; **en.wikipedia.org/wiki/Ipod**, July 28, 2005; **www.bloomberg.com/apps/news?pid=conewsstory&refer=conews&tkr=AAPL:US&sid=ap0bqJw2VpwI** , 2008.

Electric Power Utilities: Christensen and Greene (1976).

Carlos Slim and the Mexican Monopolies: "Mexico's Richest Man Casts Controversial Shadow," **www.cnn.com/2007/WORLD/americas/03/12/mexico.slim.ap/index.html**, March 13, 2007; **www.forbes.com/business/2007/04/11/billionaires -helu-telecom-biz-cz_hc_0411helu.html**; David

Luhnow, "The Secrets of the World's Richest Man," *Wall Street Journal*, August 4, 2007.

Botox Patent Monopoly: Mike Weiss, "For S.F. Doctor, Drug Botox Becomes a Real Eye-Opener," *San Francisco Chronicle*, April 14, 2002:A1, A19; Reed Abelson, "F.D.A. Approves Allergan Drug for Fighting Wrinkles," *New York Times*, April 16:2002; Harriet Tramer, "Docs Detecting How to Boost Botox Profitability," *Crain's Cleveland Business*, March 7, 2005:17; Natasha Singer, "Botox Plus: New Mixes for Plumping and Padding," *New York Times*, July 14, 2005; **www.forums.pharma-mkting.com/showthread.php?t=921**, 2007. The graph shows an inverse linear demand curve of the form $p = a - bQ$. Such a linear demand curve has an elasticity of $\varepsilon = -(1/b)(p/Q)$. Given that the elasticity of demand is $-400/375 = -(1/b)(400/1)$, where Q is measured in millions of vials, then $b = 375$. Solving $p = 400 = a - 375 \times 1$, we find that $a = 775$. The height of triangle $A + B + C$ is \$750 = \$775 − \$25, and its length is 2 million vials, so its area is \$750 million.

Property Rights and Piracy: Joseph Kahn, "The Pinch of Piracy Wakes China Up On Copyright Issue," *New York Times*, November 1, 2002:C1, C5; Benny Evangelista and Nick Wingfield, "Online Swapping of Music Declines in Wake of Suits," *Wall Street Journal*, January 5, 2004:B4; Connolly and Krueger (2005); Jane Wardell, "Software Piracy Rate Is Steady," *San Francisco Chronicle*, May 19, 2005; Carrie Kirby, "Survey Shows Little Progress in Effort to Halt Pirated Software," *San Francisco Chronicle*, May 19, 2005; Deborah Charles, "U.S. Court Rules against Grokster in File-Share Case," Reuters, June 27, 2005; Carolyn Said, "Pay to Play—Or Else," *San Francisco Chronicle*, June 28, 2005; "Raids in 16 States Seek to Thwart Video Game Piracy," *New York Times*, August 2, 2007; BSA, *Piracy Study*, 2007, **w3.bsa.org/globalstudy//upload/2007-Global-Piracy-Study-EN.pdf**; Ian Austen, "Tax Campaign by Toronto Brings a Bill from the Mint," *The New York Times*, October 15, 2007.

Chapter 12

Disneyland Pricing: **www.Disneyland.com**, 2008.

Preventing Resale of Designer Bags: Eric Wilson, "Retailers Limit Purchases of Designer Handbags," *New York Times*, January 10, 2008.

Amazon Is Watching You: David Streitfeld, "Amazon Pays a Price for Marketing Test," *Los Angeles Times*, October 2, 2000:C1; **www.managingchange.com/dynamic/survey/analysis.html**; David Streitfeld, "Amazon Mystery: Pricing of Books," *Los Angeles Times*, January 2, 2007.

Botox Revisited: See Chapter 11, "Botox Patent Monopoly."

Unions That Have It All: Peter Sleeth and Jim Lynch, "Lockout Disaster Averted," *Sunday Oregonian*, October 13, 2002:F1; George Raine, "Port Talks Turn Positive," *San Francisco Chronicle*, November 2, 2002:A1, A16; David Moberg, "What's Up on the Docks?" *These Times*, November 11, 2002:12; **www.ilwu.org**; Carl Biers and Marsha Niemeijer, "Members Angry Over Multi-Tier Wage and Benefit System," **www.labornotes.org**, June 2004; *Pacific Coast Longshore Contract Document*, July 1, 2002–July 1, 2008.

Smuggling Prescription Drugs into the United States: Tim Harper, "Canada's Drugs 'Dangerous,'" *Toronto Star*, August 28, 2003:A12; Christopher Rowland, "FDA Sting Targets Medicine Supplier Springfield," *Boston Globe*, August 28, 2003; Tony Pugh, "Canadian Online Pharmacies Struggle to Find Suppliers," *San Diego Union-Tribune*, September 7, 2003:A-3; Gardiner Harris, "U.S. Moves to Halt Import of Drugs from Canada," *New York Times*, September 10, 2003:C2; Ceci Connolly, "Hopefuls Back Drug Reimports," *Washington Post*, October 8, 2003:A6; Lolita C. Baldor, "FDA Questions Canada Drug Import Safety," Associated Press Online, December 23, 2003; "Survey: U.S. Families Struggle to Pay for Drugs," MSNBC News, February 23, 2004; Robert Pear, "U.S. to Study Importing Canada Drugs," *New York Times*, February 26, 2004:A16; Victoria Colliver, "U.S. Drug Prices 81% Higher than in 7 Western Nations," *San Francisco Chronicle*, October 29, 2004:C1, C6; Heather Timmons, "Court Refuses to Hear Case on European Drug Pricing," *New York Times*, June 1, 2005:C7; "Canada pharmacists seek ban on drug exports to U.S.," January 15, 2007, **www.reuters.com/articlePrint?articleId=USN1542065920070115**.

Consumers Pay for Lower Prices: Borenstein and Rose (1994); Hal Varian, "Priceline's Magic Show," *Industry Standard*, April 17, 2000; "PMA Coupon Council Celebrates September as National Coupon Month," *PR Newswire*, September 3, 2002; **www.couponmonth.com/pages/allabout.htm** (2007); **www.pmalink.org/press_releases/default.asp?p=pr_09062007** (2007).

IBM: *IBM* v. *United States*, 298 U.S. 131 (1936).

O. J. Trial Effect: Stuart Elliott, "Advertising: The 'O. J. Factor' Takes a Toll on Producers of Infomercials," *New York Times*, March 24, 1995:C4.

Chapter 13

Catwalk Cartel: William Sherman, "Catwalk Rocked by Legal Catfight," *Daily News*, March 14, 2004; Warren St. John, "Behind the Catwalk, Suspicion and Suits," *New York Times*, April 18, 2004:sec.9, 1, 12; Neil Chandler, "Models in GBP 28m Wage Battle," *Daily Star*, June 6, 2004:8; *Carolyn Fears et al.* v. *Wilhelmina Model Agency, Inc. et al.*, 02 Civ. 4911 (HB), United States District Court for the Southern District of New York, 2004 U.S. Dist. Lexis 4502; 2004–1 Trade Cas. (CCH) P74,351, March 23, 2004.

Bail Bonds: Ayres and Waldfogel (1994).

Air Ticket Prices and Rivalry: Weiher, Sickles, and Perloff (2002).

Bottled Water: David Lazarus, "How Water Bottlers Tap Into All Sorts of Sources," *San Francisco Chronicle*, January 19, 2007; Vinnee Tong, "What's in that Bottle?" **suntimes.com**, July 28, 2007; Kevin Cowherd, "Bottled-Water Labeling: A Source of Irritation,"**baltimoresun.com**, August 1, 2007; **www.myspringwater.com/SpringWaterInformation/LeadingWaterBrands.aspx?CMP=KNC-SRCH_MSW_WTR** (2007).

Government Aircraft Subsidies: Irwin and Pavcnik (2004); Constant Brand, "EU, Washington Resume Battle Over Boeing," *San Francisco Chronicle*, May 31, 2005.

Deadweight Losses in the Food and Tobacco Industries: Bhuyan and Lopez (1998).

Virgin America's Fixed Costs: George Raine, "Virgin America $35 Million in the Red in First Quarter of Operation," *San Francisco Chronicle*, December 18, 2007:D1; **www.emotrans.com/emo-usa/news/newsletter-0206.htm**, 2007.

Welfare Gain from More Toilet Paper: "Going Soft?" *The Economist*, March 4, 2000:59; Hausman and Leonard (2002).

Chapter 14

Playing Chicken: Mary Jacoby, "As Cars Collide, Belgian Motorists Refuse to Yield," *Wall Street Journal*, September 25, 2006:A1.

Strategic Advertising: "50 Years Ago …," *Consumer Reports*, January 1986; Roberts and Samuelson (1988); Gasmi, Laffont, and Vuong (1992); Elliott, Stuart, "Advertising," *New York Times*, April 28, 1994:C7; Slade (1995).

Advantages and Disadvantages of Moving First: The cost estimates are based on an iSuppli "teardown" analysis: Dylan McGrath, "'Teardown' Finds Toshiba Taking a Loss on HD DVD Player," *EE Times*, June 23, 2006, **www.eetimes.com/showArticle.jhtml?articleID=189600999**; Urban, Carter, and Gaskin (1986); Dylan McGrath, "Analyst Predicts Stalemate in Next-Gen DVD War," *EE Times*, June 23, 2006, **www.eetimes.com/showArticle.jhtml?articleID=189601178**; "Giants Shape Up in DVD Wars, November 24, 2007, **business.theage.com.au/giants-shape-up-in-dvd-wars/20071124-1cku.html#; money.cnn.com/news/newsfeeds/articles/newstex/IBD-0001-21882911.htm**, December 24, 2007; **www.nytimes.com/aponline/technology/AP-Dueling-DVD-Formats.html**, January 4, 2008.

Experienced Bidders: Garratt et al. (2005).

Chapter 15

Thread Mill: Baldwin and Gorecki (1986).

Baseball Salaries and Ticket Prices: Bill Shaikin, "Experts Say Demand, Not Higher Salaries, Drives Up Baseball Ticket Prices," *Los Angeles Times*, April 1, 1999; Chris Isidore, "Players' Pay Doesn't Hit Fans," *CNN/Money*, April 5, 2002; Bob Woodruff, "On the Sidelines Sticker Shock," *World News Tonight, ABC News Transcripts*, April 9, 2005; Chris Isidore, "Ticket Prices Going, Going…; Up," **CNNMoney.com**, April 4, 2005; **Forbes.com** (2005); **money.cnn.com/2007/08/01/news/companies/yes_sale.fortune/index.htm**.

Union Monopoly Power: Hatton, Boyer, and Bailey's (1994) estimates for 1889–1890 are based on data for individual workers, controlling statistically for age, skill level, industry, and other worker characteristics. Stewart's (1995) estimates for 1984 and 1990 reflect a comparison between union and nonunion firms that controls for firm attributes; Blanchflower and Bryson (2004), and DTI, *Employment Market Analysis and Research*, 2005.

Is Limiting Entry into Casket Sale a Grave Restriction?: Chevalier and Scott Morton (2008).

Company Towns: J. R. Romanko, "The Big Business of Small Towns," *New York Times*, September 22, 2002:sec.6, 20; Lawrence W. Boyd, "The Company Town," **www.eh.net**; Jesse McKinley, "Company Town, Losing a Landlord, Seeks a Mate," *New York Times*, July 6, 2006.

Aluminum: Hennart (1988), **www.globalalumina.com**, 2007.

Chapter 16

Power of Compounding: Helen Huntley, Kim Norris, and Robert Trigaux, "An Early Lesson in Investing for the Long Term," *St. Petersburg Times*, March 14, 1994:Business 3.

Saving for Retirement: Calculations by the author.

Winning the Lottery: "Baby Sitter from Chile Is Winner of Record $197 Million in Lottery," *San Francisco Chronicle*, April 16, 1999:A2; Holly Hunter, "Winning Lottery or a Pension: One Lump or Many?" *Portsmouth Herald*, August 22, 2004.

Durability of Telephone Poles: Marshall, Jonathan, "PG&E Cultivates Its Forest," *San Francisco Chronicle*, May 5, 1995:D1.

Falling Discount Rates and Self-Control: Shapiro (2004); Kan (2007).

Redwood Trees: Berck and Bentley (1997); Peter Berck, personal communications.

Chapter 17

Gambling: Friedman and Savage (1948); Brunk (1981); Golec and Tamarkin (1995); Meghan Cox Gurdon, "British Accuse Their Lottery of Robbing the Poor to Give to the Rich," *San Francisco Chronicle*, November 25, 1995:D1; Steve Coll, "Chances Are Brits Have Bet on It," *San Francisco Examiner*, July 10, 1994: 4; Andrew Pollack, "In the Gaming Industry, the House Can Have Bad Luck, Too," *New York Times*, July 25, 1999:Business, 4; Garrett and Sobel (1999); George Will, "Government's Hand in Surge of Gambling," *San Francisco Chronicle*, June 28, 1999:A21; Garrett (2001); Marsha Walton, "The Business of Gambling," **CNN.com**, July 6, 2005; **igwb.com/pdf/2006globallottery.pdf; igwb.com/pdf/2006grossgambling.pdf; igwb.com/enews-details.php?ida=3233&s=1**, December 4, 2007; **igwb.com/print.php?ida=774&cmag=IGWB**, 2008.

Harry Potter's Magic: Amanda Gardner, "Harry Potter Books Keep Kids Safe," **www.healthday.com**, December 22, 2005; "Harry Potter and the Injury-Free Children," *San Francisco Chronicle*, December 27, 2005, A2; Eric Nagourney, "Safety: with Harry Potter, Injuries Dip Like Magic," *New York Times*, January 3, 2006.

Air Insurance: Insure America brochure; National Transportation Safety Board; "U.S. Airlines Getting Safer, Statistics Show," *St. Petersburg Times Online*, January 4, 2005; **www.airlines.org**, 2008; **www.ntsb.gov/aviation/aviation.htm**, 2008.

No Insurance for Natural Disasters: Joseph B. Treaster, "Insurer Curbing Sales of Policies in Storm Areas," *New York Times*, October 10, 1996:A1, C4; Joseph B. Treaster, "Headed for Trouble," *New York Times*, September 18, 1998:B1, B14; "The New Protection Game," *Consumer Reports*, January 1999: 16–19; Joseph B. Treaster, "Why Insurers Shrink from Earthquake Risk," *New York Times*, November 21, 1999.sec.3: 1, 13; Tom Abate, "Storm May Be Costliest Ever in U.S.," *San Francisco Chronicle,* August 31, 2005:C1; James Sterngold, "Losses Could Total $100 Billion," *San Francisco Chronicle,* September 4, 2005:A7; **www.washingtonpost.com/wp-dyn/content/article/2006/04/29/AR2006042901364.html**; Paul Vitello, "Home Insurers Canceling in East," *New York Times*, October 16, 2007; Pielke et al. (2008).

Risk Premium: "The Cost of Looking," *Economist*, 328(7828), September 11, 1993:74; Leslie Eaton, "Assessing a Fund's Risk Is Part Math, Part Art," *New York Times*, April 2, 1995:sec.3: 9; Jagannathan, McGrattan, and Scherbina (2000); **www.standardandpoors.com; www.thornburginvestments.com/research/articles/real_real_0705.asp** (2005).

Biased Estimates?: Benjamin et al. (2001); Scott Wyman, "Fatal Shark Attack Highlights Need for Safety," Sun-Sentinel.com, June 27, 2005; International Shark Attack File, **www.arthurhu.com/index/health/death.htm#deathrank; www.findarticles.com/p/articles/mi_m0GER/is_2002_Fall/ai_93135768; www.nsc.org/lrs/statinfo/odds.htm**, 2008; **www.flmnh.ufl.edu/fish/sharks/statistics/GAttack/mapusa.htm**, 2008.

Chapter 18

Negative Externality: SUVs Kill: White (2004).

Positive Externality: Michael Jordan Effect: Hausman and Leonard (1997); *Harper's Index*, 1999; Mike Wise, "NBC Focuses on the Story Lines," *New York Times*, May 9, 1999; "Jordan Is No Slam Dunk," *CNNMoney*, September 28, 2001; "Old Man Wizard Keeps Rolling It In," *U.S. News & World Report*, October 8, 2001:10; Brad Weinstein, "No-Frills Free Agents Foiled by Impending Tax," *San Francisco Chronicle*, August 4, 2002:B3; Berri and Schmidt (2006).

Pulp and Paper Mill Pollution and Regulation: Gray and Shadbegian (2002); Shadbegian and Gray (2003).

Taxes to Reduce Auto Accidents: Grawboski and Morrisey (2006), Edlin and Karaca-Mandic (2006), Anderson (2007).

U.S. Cap-and-Trade Programs: Dallas Burtraw, "Trading Emissions to Clean the Air: Exchanges Few but Savings Many," *Resources*, 122, Winter 1996:3–6; Peter Passell, "For Utilities, New Clean-Air Plan," *New York Times*, November 18, 1994:C1, C6; Peter Passell, "Economic Scene," *New York Times*, January 4, 1996:C2; Boyce Rensberger, "Clean Air Sale," *Washington Post*, August 8, 1999:W7; Schmalensee et al. (1998); **www.epa.gov/region09/air/reclaim/index.html; www.epa.gov/airmarkt/progress/arpreport/acidrainprogress.pdf; www.emissionstrading.com; www.epa.com; www.epa.gov/airmarkt/progress/docs/2006-ARP-Report.pdf**; Paltsev et al. (2007).

Radiohead's "Public Good" Experiment: Jeff Leads, "Radiohead to Let Fans Decide What to Pay for Its New Album," *New York Times*, October 2, 2007; **blog.wired.com/music/2007/10/estimates-radio.html**, October 19, 2007; **www.daniweb.com/blogs/entry1785.html**, 2007; **djchall.com/2007/11/was_radioheads_name_your_own_p.html**, November 6, 2007; **www.eonline.com/news/article/index.jsp?uuid=a5676777-9992-4493-bc80-00a320f8a091&entry =index**, January 9, 2008.

Free Riding on Water: Grossman, Pirozzi, and Pope (1993).

Chapter 19

Risky Hobbies: Carol Marie Cropper, "Risk Takers Pay Dearly: It's the Danger of Living Fearlessly," *New York Times*, April 2, 1995:sec.3: 11.

Finding a Good Surgeon: David Wessel, "Grading Surgeons May Be Healthy Practice," *Wall Street Journal*, July 06, 2006; Epstein (2006); "Prostate patients fare better with experienced surgeons," *CBC News*, July 25, 2007.

Adverse Selection on eBay: Dewan and Hsu (2004).

Twin Brands: Marshall Schuon, "Twins, Triplets and Other Siblings," *New York Times*, November 7, 1993:sec.1:27; www.repairclinic.com; http://www.edmunds.com/advice/buying/articles/46969/article.html; www.answers.com/topic/toyota-camry.

Chapter 20

Contracts and Productivity in Agriculture: Foster and Rosenzweig (1994).

Music Contracts: Changing Their Tunes: Ethan Smith, "Bands on the Run," July 14, 2006, p. W8; **www.adweek.com/aw/magazine/article_display.jsp?vnu_content_id=1003686015**, December 24, 2007; **entertainment.howstuffworks.com/recording-contract.htm**, 2008.

Abusing Leased Cars: Dunham (1996); *Car Talk*, National Public Radio, May 1997; Peter Valdes-Dapena, "Car Leases are Back: Should You Bite?" *CNN/Money,* May 26, 2005; **finance.yahoo.com/print/expert/article/millionaire/43080**, August 27, 2007.

Subprime Borrowing: Adams et al. (2007); **riginatortimes.com/content/templates/default.aspx?a=2724&template=print-article.htm**, December 27, 2007; Erin McCormick and Carolyn Said, "Investors Own about One-Fifth of Bay Area Homes in Foreclosure," *San Francisco Chronicle*, December 16, 2007.

Performance Termination Contracts: Hall and Lilien (1979); **www.bls.gov**.

Cross-Chapter Analyses

Child Care Subsidies: Center for Law and Social Policy, **www.clasp.org/publications/ccdbgparticipation_2005.pdf; muse.jhu.edu/journals/future_of_children/v017/17.2greenberg.pdf; www.acf.dhhs.gov/programs/ccb/faq1/econom.htm; www.factsinaction.org/pageone/p1apr02.htm; www.now.org/nnt/03-98/legupdt.html;** Blau and Tekin (2001); Elena Cherney, "Giving Day-Care Cash to Stay-at-Home Parents Sounds Like Politics to Some Canadians," *Wall Street Journal*, July 3, 2006: A2; Terkin (2007); **clasp.org/WelfarePolicy/pdf/map100907us.pdf**(2007).

Outsourcing and the World Trade Organization: Edward Goldsmith, 1997, "Can the Environment Survive the Global Economy?" *The Ecologist,* 27(6); Larry Karp, 2003, "The Theory of the Second Best and the Principle of Targeting," **are.berkeley.edu/courses/EEP131/theoryofsecondbest.pdf;** "Bush Report: Sending Jobs Overseas Helps US," *Seattle Times* wire services, February 10, 2004, **seattletimes.nwsource.com/html/nationworld/2001854367_bushecon10.html;** Norman Ornstein, "In the Works: Trading Spaces at White House," *Houston Chronicle,* February 23, 2004; Paul Krugman, "Free Trade and Jobs," *New York Times,* February 28, 2004; David Armstrong, "It Takes a Global Village," *San Francisco Chronicle,* February 26, 2004:B1, B4; Hal R. Varian, "Economic Scene: With Free Trade, What Goes Abroad Usually Finds Its Way Back, To Everyone's Benefit," *New York Times,* March 11, 2004:C2; Paul Blustein, "Bush Team Relents on Aid for Outsource Workers," *San Francisco Chronicle,* March 14, 2004:A9; Saritha Rai, "An Outsourcing Giant Fights Back, *New York Times,* March 21, 2004: Money and Business, 1; Carolyn Lochhead, "Kerry Adviser Plays Down Impact of Offshoring Jobs; Ex-Clinton Aide Blames It for 'Small Fraction' of Job Losses," *San Francisco Chronicle,* March 30, 2004:A-9; Eduardo Porter, "Not Many Jobs Are Sent Abroad, U.S. Report Says," *New York Times,* June 11, 2004: C1, C6; Harrison and McMillan (2006); Mankiw and Swagel (2006); Farrell (2006); **wto.org**, 2008.

Magazine Subscriptions: "Magazine Fund Ensures Canadian Presence," *Montreal Gazette*, May 24, 2002:B2; David Carr, "Magazines: with Advertising in Deep Distress, Publishers Consider an End to the Era of Cheap Subscriptions," *New York Times*, October 28, 2002:C9; **http://www.pch.gc.ca/progs/ac-ca/progs/fcm-cmf/index_e.cfm;** "News Mags Drop in Circulation," NewsMax.com, August 16, 2005; Kaiser and Wright (2006); *The Magazine Handbook 2007/2008,* **www.magazines.org.**

Frequent Flier Programs: "Qatar Airways the Latest to Reward Frequent Fliers," Customer Loyalty Today, Vol 7, No. 7, July 2000, p. 5; Kyung M. Song, "Frequent-Flier Costs Clip Profit at Alaska Airlines Parent Firm," *Seattle Times*, July 15, 2000; Leah Beth Ward, "Airlines Compete for Business Travelers by Offering High-Tech Promotions," *The Dallas Morning News*, May 25, 2000; Scott Thurston, "Continental Airlines Tops among Frequent Fliers, Survey Shows," *Atlantic Journal and Constitution*, May 10, 2000; Sofia Reeves, "US Airways Cuts Fares, Increases Flier Miles in Wake of Averted Strike," *Pittsburgh Post-Gazette*, March 29, 2000; Bray, Roger, "Fast Lanes for Frequent Flyers," *Financial Times* (London), January 8, 2002:14; Joe Sharkey, "Reward Miles Are Piling Up; Fliers May Face Future Squeeze," *New York Times*, August 17, 2002:B1; Jane Engle, "As Airlines Change Rules, Passengers Hold the Bag," *Los Angeles Times*, September 15, 2002:L2; **http://frequentflier.com;** Philip Charlton, "Targeting—The Achilles' Heel of Frequent Flyer Programmes," **www.thewisemarketer.com/features/read.asp?id=42,** February 2004; "By the Numbers," July 26, 2005, **www.montrosetravel.com/print_version/75/FrequentFlyerPrograms-July26,2005.html; webflyer.com; www.usatoday.com/travel/flights/2007-01-29-air-miles-usat_x.htm; www.usatoday.com/travel/columnist/grossman/2006-05-01-grossman_x.htm; www.usatoday.com/travel/flights/2006-05-31-frequent-fliers_x.htm;** Susanna Ray and Hugo Miller, "American Airlines Investors Push for Sales of Frequent-Flier Plan," *Seattle Times*, November 23, 2007.

Emissions Fees Versus Standards Under Uncertainty: Weitzman (1974); Gary S. Becker, "A High Gas Tax, Not Fuel Efficiency Rules, Will Get Drivers to Conserve," *Wisconsin State Journal*, June 21, 2002:A12; "The Invisible Green Hand," *The Economist*, July 6, 2002; "Can the 'Environmental Tax Shift' Really Help?" *Green Living Magazine*, November 28, 2002:E3; **news.yahoo.com/;ylt=AhF8S9llDSWllDVfMrood_wGw_IE,** 2007. See Brozovic, Sunding, and Zilberman (2002) for an explanation of why real-world standards are more likely to dominate fees than this example suggests.

References

Adams, William, Liran Einav, and Jonathan Levin, "Liquidity Constraints and Imperfect Information in Subprime Lending," NBER Working Paper No. 13067, 2007.

Adelaja, Adesoji O., "Price Changes, Supply Elasticities, Industry Organization, and Dairy Output Distribution," *American Journal of Agricultural Economics*, 73(1), February 1991: 89–102.

Agcaoili-Sombilla, Mercedita C., *The World Rice Market: A Model of Imperfect Substitutes,* Ph.D. University of Minnesota, 1991.

Aigner, Dennis J., and Glen G. Cain, "Statistical Theories of Discrimination in Labor Markets," *Industrial and Labor Relations Review*, 30(2), January 1977:175–187.

Akerlof, George A., "The Market for 'Lemons': Quality Uncertainty and the Market Mechanism," *Quarterly Journal of Economics,* 84(3), August 1970:488–500.

Akerlof, George A., "Labor Contacts as Partial Gift Exchanges," *Quarterly Journal of Economics*, 97(4), November 1982:543–569.

Alexander, Donald L., "Major League Baseball," *Journal of Sports Economics,* 2(4), November 2001:341–355.

Allingham, M. G., "Progression and Leisure," *American Economic Review*, 62(3), June 1972:447–450.

Altonji, Joseph G., and Ernesto Villanueva, "The Marginal Propensity to Spend on Adult Children," *B.E. Journal of Economic Analysis & Policy*, Advances, 7(1), 2007, Article 14.

Anderson, Keith B., and Michael R. Metzger, *Petroleum Tariffs as a Source of Government Revenues*. Washington, D.C.: Bureau of Economics, Federal Trade Commission, 1991.

Anderson, Michael, "Safety for Whom? The Effects of Light Trucks on Traffic Fatalities," U.C. Berkeley Working Paper, December 2007.

Arrow, Kenneth, *Social Choice and Individual Values*. New York: Wiley, 1951.

Asai, Sumiko, "Scale Economies and Scope Economies in the Japanese Broadcasting Market," *Information Economics and Policy*, 18(3), April 2006:321–331.

Ayres, Ian, and Joel Waldfogel, "A Market Test for Race Discrimination in Bail Setting," *Stanford Law Review*, 46(5), May 1994:987–1047.

Baker, Dean, "Take Exxon's Windfall from Hurricane Katrina," CEPR Briefing Paper, September 2005.

Baldwin, John R., and Paul K. Gorecki, *The Role of Scale in Canada/U.S. Productivity Differences in the Manufacturing Sector, 1970–1979*. Toronto: University of Toronto Press, 1986.

Baldwin, Robert E., and Paul R. Krugman, "Industrial Policy and International Competition in Wide Bodied Jet Aircraft," in Robert E. Baldwin, ed., *Trade Policy Issues and Empirical Analysis*. Chicago: University of Chicago Press, 1988.

Bar-Ilan, Avner, and Bruce Sacerdote, "The Response to Fines and Probability of Detection in a Series of Experiments," NBER Working Paper 8638, December 2001.

Battalio, Raymond, John H. Kagel, and Carl Kogut, "Experimental Confirmation of the Existence of a Giffen Good," *American Economic Review*, 81(3), September 1991:961–970.

Becker, Gary S., *The Economics of Discrimination*, 2nd ed. Chicago: University of Chicago Press, 1971.

Benjamin, Daniel K., William R. Dougan, and David Buschena, *Journal of Risk and Uncertainty*, 22(1), January 2001:35–57.

Berck, Peter, and William R. Bentley, "Hotelling's Theory, Enhancement, and the Taking of the Redwood National Park," *American Journal of Agricultural Economics*, 79(2), May 1997:287–298.

Berck, Peter, and Michael Roberts, "Natural Resource Prices: Will They Ever Turn Up?" *Journal of Environmental Economics and Management*, 31(1), July 1996:65–78.

Berri, David J., and Martin B. Schmidt, "On the Road with the National Basketball Association's Superstar Externality," *Journal of Sports Economics*, 7(4), November 2006:347–358.

Besley, Timothy J., and Harvey S. Rosen, "Sales Taxes and Prices: An Empirical Analysis," *National Tax Journal*, 52(2), June 1999:157–178.

Besley, Timothy J., and Harvey S. Rosen, "Vertical Externalities in Tax Setting: Evidence from Gasoline and Cigarettes," *Journal of Public Economics*, 70(3), December 1998:383–398.

Bhuyan, Sanjib, and Rigoberto A. Lopez, "What Determines Welfare Losses from Oligopoly Power in the Food and Tobacco Industries?" *Agricultural and Resource Economics Review*, 27(2), October 1998:258–265.

Bhuyan, Sanjib, "Corporate Political Activities and Oligopoly Welfare Loss," *Review of Industrial Organization*, 17(4), December 2000:411–426.

Billikopf, Gregory Encina, "High Piece-Rate Wages Do Not Reduce Hours Worked," *California Agriculture*, 49(1), January–February 1995:17–18.

Bishai, David M., and Hui-Chu Lang, "The Willingness to Pay for Wait Reduction: The Disutility of Queues for Cataract Surgery in Canada, Denmark, and Spain," *Journal of Health Economics*, 19(2), March 2000:219–230.

Black, Dan A., Seth Sanders, and Lowell Taylor, "The Economic Rewards to Studying Economics," *Economic Inquiry,* 41(3), July 2003:365–377.

Blanchflower, David G., and Alex Bryson, "Union Relative Wage Effects in the United States and the United Kingdom," *Industrial Relations Research Association Proceedings*, 2004.

Blanciforti, Laura Ann, "The Almost Ideal Demand System Incorporating Habits: An Analysis of Expenditures on Food and Aggregate Commodity Groups." Doctoral thesis, University of California, Davis, 1982.

Blau, David, and Erdal Tekin, "The Determinants and Consequences of Child Care Subsidy Receipt by Low-Income Families," in Bruce Meyer and Greg Duncan, *The Incentives of Government Programs and the Well-Being of Families*, Joint Center for Poverty Research, 2001.

Bordley, Robert F., and James B. McDonald, "Estimating Aggregate Automotive Income Elasticities from the Population Income-Share Elasticity," *Journal of Business and Economic Statistics*, 11(2), April 1993:209–214.

Borenstein, Severin, James Bushnell, and Matthew Lewis, "Market Power in California's Gasoline Market," University of California Energy Institute, CSEM WP 132, May 2004, **www.ucei.berkeley.edu/PDF/csemwp132.pdf**.

Borenstein, Severin, and Nancy L. Rose, "Competition and Price Dispersion in the U.S. Airline Industry," *Journal of Political Economy*, 102(4), August 1994:653–683.

Borjas, George J., "The Labor Demand Curve Is Downward Sloping: Reexamining the Impact of Immigration on the Labor Market," *Quarterly Journal of Economics,* 118(4), November 2003:1335–1374.

Boroski, John W., and Gerard C. S. Mildner, "An Economic Analysis of Taxicab Regulation in Portland, Oregon," Cascade Policy Institute, **www.cascadepolicy.org**, 1998.

Boskin, Michael J., Ellen R. Dulberger, Robert J. Gordon, Zvi Griliches, and Dale W. Jorgenson, "The CPI Commission: Findings and Recommendations," *American Economic Review*, 87(2), May 1997:78–93.

Boskin, Michael J., and Dale W. Jorgenson, "Implications of Overstating Inflation for Indexing Government Programs and Understanding Economic Progress," *American Economic Review*, 87(2), May 1997:89–93.

Boulier, Bryan L., Tejwant S. Datta, and Robert S. Goldfarb, "Vaccination Externalities," *The B.E. Journal of Economic Analysis & Policy*, 7(1, Contributions), 2007:Article 23.

Bradbury, Hinton, and Karen Ross, "The Effects of Novelty and Choice Materials on the Intransitivity of Preferences of Children and Adults," *Annals of Operations Research*, 23(1–4), June 1990:141–159.

Brander, James A., and Anming Zhang, "Market Conduct in the Airline Industry: An Empirical Investigation," *Rand Journal of Economics*, 21(4), Winter 1990:567–583.

Brander, James A., and M. Scott Taylor, "The Simple Economics of Easter Island: A Ricardo-Malthus Model of Renewable Resource Use," *American Economic Review*, 88(1), March 1998:119–138.

Brown, Jennifer, Justine Hastings, Erin T. Mansur, and Sofia B. Villas-Boas, "Reformulating Competition: Gasoline Content Regulation and Wholesale Gasoline Prices," *Journal of Environmental Economics and Management*, 55(1), January 2008:1–19.

Brown, Robert W., "An Estimate of the Rent Generated by a Premium College Football Player," *Economic Inquiry*, 31(4), October 1993:671–684.

Brown, Stephen P. A., and Daniel Wolk, "Natural Resource Scarcity and Technological Change," *Economic and Financial Review* (Federal Reserve Bank of Dallas), First Quarter 2000:2–13.

Brownlee, Oswald, and George Perry, "The Effects of the 1965 Federal Excise Tax Reductions on Prices," *National Tax Journal*, 20(3), September 1967:235–249.

Brozovic, Nicholas, David L. Sunding, and David Zilberman, "Prices and Quantities Reconsidered," University of California, Berkeley, working paper, 2002.

Brunk, Gregory G., "A Test of the Friedman-Savage Gambling Model," *Quarterly Journal of Economics*, 96(2), May 1981:341–348.

Busch, Susan H., Mireia Jofre-Bonet, Tracy Falba, and Jody Sindelar, "Burning a Hole in the Budget: Tobacco Spending and its Crowd-out of Other Goods," *Applied Health Economics and Policy,* 3(4), 2004: 263–272.

Buschena, David E., and Jeffrey M. Perloff, "The Creation of Dominant Firm Market Power in the Coconut Oil Export Market," *American Journal of Agricultural Economics*, 73(4), November 1991:1000–1008.

Camerer, Colin F., George Lowenstein, and Matthew Rabin, eds., *Advances in Behavioral Economics*. New York: Russell Sage Foundation, 2004.

Caputo, Michael R., and Quirino Paris, "An Atemporal Microeconomic Theory and an Empirical Test of Price-Induced Technical Progress," *Journal of Productivity Analysis,* 1(3), November 2005:259–282.

Card, David, and Alan B. Krueger, *Myth and Measurement: The New Economics of the Minimum Wage*. Princeton, NJ: Princeton University Press, 1995.

Carlson, Steven, "An Overview of Food Stamp Cashout Research in the Food and Nutrition Service," in Nancy Fasciano, Darryl Hall, and Harold Beebout, eds., *New Directions in Food Stamp Policy Research*. Alexandria, VA: U.S. Department of Agriculture, Food and Nutrition Service, 1993.

Carlton, Dennis W., and Jeffrey M. Perloff, *Modern Industrial Organization*, 4th ed. Boston, MA: Addison-Wesley, 2005.

Carman, Hoy F., and Richard J. Sexton, "The 2007 Freeze: Tallying the Toll Two Months Later," *ARE Update*, Vol. 10, No. 4, March/April, 2007.

Carter, Colin A., and Jacqueline Huie, "Market Effects of Searching for Mad Cows," *ARE Update,* 8(1), September/October 2004:5–7.

Caves, Richard E., and David R. Barton, *Technical Efficiency in U.S. Manufacturing Industries*. Cambridge, MA: MIT Press, 1990.

Chetty, Raj, Adam Looney, and Kory Kroft, "Salience and Taxation: Theory and Evidence," NBER Working Paper No. 13330, 2007.

Chevalier, Judith, and Fiona Scott Morton, "State Casket Sales Restrictions: A Pointless Undertaking?" *Journal of Law and Economics*, August 2008.

Chouinard, Hayley, and Jeffrey M. Perloff, "Incidence of Federal and State Gasoline Taxes," *Economic Letters,* 83(1), April 2004:55–60.

Chouinard, Hayley H., David Davis, Jeffrey T. LaFrance, and Jeffrey M. Perloff, "Fat Taxes: Big Money for Small Change," *Forum for Health Economics & Policy,* 10(2, 2), 2007.

Christensen, Laurits R., and William H. Greene, "Economies of Scale in U.S. Electric Power Generation," *Journal of Political Economy*, 84(4, pt. 1), August 1976:655–676.

Chung, Sangho, "The Learning Curve and the Yield Factor: The Case of Korea's Semiconductor Industry," *Applied Economics*, 33(4), March 2001:472–483.

Coase, Ronald H., "The Nature of the Firm," *Economica*, 4(16), November 1937:386–405.

Coase, Ronald H., "The Problem of Social Cost," *Journal of Law and Economics*, 3, October 1960:1–44.

Connolly, Marie, and Alan B. Krueger, "Rockonomics: The Economics of Popular Music," NBER Working Paper 11282, **www.nber.org/papers/w11282**, 2005.

Crawford, David, John Del Roccili, and Richard Voith, "Comments on Proposed Tax Reforms," Econsult Corporation, June 9, 2004.

Deacon, Robert T., and Jon Sonstelie, "The Welfare Costs of Rationing by Waiting," *Economic Inquiry*, 27(2), April 1989:179–196.

Delipalla, Sophia, and Michael Keen, "The Comparison Between Ad Valorem and Specific Taxation Under Imperfect Competition," *Journal of Public Economics*, 49(3), December 1992:351–367.

de Janvry, Alain, Elisabeth Sadoulet, and Sofia B. Villas-Boas, "Short on Shots: Can Calls on Self-Restraint Be Effective in Managing the Scarcity of Flu Vaccines, and What Do They Reveal about Behavior," CUDARE working paper, July 16, 2007.

de Melo, Jaime, and David Tarr, *A General Equilibrium Analysis of U.S. Foreign Trade Policy*. Cambridge, MA: MIT Press, 1992.

de Melo, Jaime, and David Tarr, "VERs under Imperfect Competition and Foreign Direct Investment: A Case Study of the US–Japan Auto VER," *Japan and the World Economy,* 8(1), March 1996:11–33.

DellaVigna, Stefano, "Psychology and Economics: Evidence from the Field," NBER Working Paper No. 13420, 2007.

Dewan, Sanjeev, and Vernon Hsu, "Adverse Selection in Electronic Markets: Evidence from Online Stamp Auctions," *Journal of Industrial Economics,* LII(4), December 2004:497–516.

Diewert, W. Edwin, and Alice O. Nakamura, eds., *Essays in Index Number Theory*, Vol. 1. New York: North Holland, 1993.

Dixit, Avinash K., and Robert S. Pindyck, *Investment Under Uncertainty*. Princeton, NJ: Princeton University Press, 1994.

Duffy-Deno, Kevin T., "Business Demand for Broadband Access Capacity," *Journal of Regulatory Economics,* 24(3), 2003:359–372.

Dunham, Wayne R., *Moral Hazard and the Market for Used Automobiles*. Economic Analysis Group Discussion Paper 96–4. Washington, D.C.: U.S. Department of Justice, Antitrust Division, 1996.

Dunn, L. F., "Quantifying Nonpecuniary Returns," *Journal of Human Resources*, 2(3), Summer 1977:347–359.

Dunn, L. F., "An Empirical Indifference Function for Income and Leisure," *Review of Economics and Statistics*, 60(4), November 1978:533–540.

Dunn, L. F., "Measurement of Internal Income-Leisure Tradeoffs," *Quarterly Journal of Economics*, 93(3), August 1979:373–393.

Eastwood, David B., and John A. Craven, "Food Demand and Savings in a Complete, Extended, Linear Expenditure System," *American Journal of Agricultural Economics*, 63(3), August 1981:544–549.

Economides, Nicholas, "The Economics of Networks," *International Journal of Industrial Organization,* 14(6), October 1996:673–699.

Econsult Corporation, *Choosing the Best Mix of Taxes for Philadelphia: An Econometric Analysis of the Impacts of Tax Rates on Tax Bases, Tax Revenue, and the Private Economy,* Report to the Philadelphia Tax Reform Commission, 2003.

Edlin, Aaron S., and Pinar Karaca-Mandic, "The Accident Externality from Driving," *Journal of Political Economy*, 114(5), October 2006:931–955.

Ellsberg, Daniel, "Risk, Ambiguity, and the Savage Axioms," *Quarterly Journal of Economics*, 75(4), November 1961:643–669.

Epstein, Andrew J., "Do Cardiac Surgery Report Cards Reduce Mortality? Assessing the Evidence," *Medical Care Research Review*, 63(4), August 2006:403–426.

Exxon Company, U.S.A., *Competition in the Petroleum Industry*. Submission to the U.S. Senate Judiciary Subcommittee on Antitrust and Monopoly, January 21, 1975.

Farrell, Diana, "U.S. Offshoring: Small Steps to Make It Win-Win," *Economist Voice*, March 2006.

Farrell, Joseph, and Matthew Rabin, "Cheap Talk," *Journal of Economic Perspectives*, 10(3), Summer 1996:103–118.

Farrell, Lisa, Roger Hartley, Gauthier Lanot, and Ian Walker, "The Demand for Lotto," *Journal of Business & Economic Statistics,* 18(2), April 2000:228–241.

Fasciano, Nancy, Daryl Hall, and Harold Beebout, eds., *New Directions in Food Stamp Policy Research*. Alexandria, VA: U.S. Department of Agriculture, Food and Nutrition Service, 1993.

Federal Trade Commission, "Federal Trade Commission Advertising Cases Involving Weight Loss Products and Services," 1927, February 2003.

Fisher, Franklin M., "The Social Cost of Monopoly and Regulation: Posner Reconsidered," *Journal of Political Economy*, 93(2), April 1985:410–416.

Foster, Andrew D., and Mark R. Rosenzweig, "A Test for Moral Hazard in the Labor Market: Contractual Arrangements, Effort, and Health," *Review of Economics and Statistics*, 76(2), May 1994:213–227.

Fraker, Thomas M., "The Effects of Food Stamps on Food Consumption: A Review of the Literature," in Nancy Fasciano, Darryl Hall, and Harold Beebout, eds., *Current Perspectives on Food Stamp Program Participation*. Alexandria, VA: U.S. Department of Agriculture, Food and Nutrition Service, 1990.

Frech, H. E., III, and William C. Lee, "The Welfare Cost of Rationing-by-Queuing Across Markets: Theory and Estimates from the U.S. Gasoline Crisis," *Quarterly Journal of Economics*, 102(1), February 1987:97–108.

French, Ben C., and Gordon A. King, "Demand and Price-Markup Functions for Canned Cling Peaches and Fruit Cocktail," *Western Journal of Agricultural Economics*, 11(1), July 1986:8–18.

Friedlaender, Ann F., Clifford Winston, and Kung Wang, "Costs, Technology, and Productivity in the U.S. Automobile Industry," *Bell Journal of Economics and Management Science*, 14(1), Spring 1983:1–20.

Friedman, Milton, and Leonard J. Savage, "The Utility Analysis of Choices Involving Risk," *Journal of Political Economy*, 56(4), August 1948:279–304.

Fudenberg, Drew, and Jean Tirole, "A 'Signal-Jamming' Theory of Predation," *Rand Journal of Economics*, 17(3), Autumn 1986:366–376.

Fullerton, Don, "On the Possibility of an Inverse Relationship Between Tax Rates and Government Revenues," *Journal of Public Economy*, 19(1), October 1982:3–22.

Fullerton, Don, and Li Gan, "A Simulation-Based Welfare Loss Calculation for Labor Taxes with Piecewise-Linear Budgets," *Journal of Public Economics,* 88(11), September 2004:2339–2359.

Furnham, Adrian, "Understanding the Meaning of Tax: Young Peoples' Knowledge of the Principles of Taxation," *Journal of Socio-Economics*, 34(5), October 2005:703–713.

Gallini, Nancy T., "Demand for Gasoline in Canada," *Canadian Journal of Economics*, 16(2), May 1983:299–324.

Garratt, Rod, Mark Walker, and John Wooders, "Behavior in Second-Price Auctions by Highly Experienced eBay Buyers and Sellers," University of Arizona Economics Working Paper, 2007.

Gasmi, Farid, D., Mark Kennet, Jean-Jacques Laffont, and William W. Sharkey, *Cost Proxy Models and Telecommunications Policy,* Cambridge, MA: MIT Press, 2002.

Gasmi, Farid, Jean-Jacques Laffont, and Quang H. Vuong, "Econometric Analysis of Collusive Behavior in a Soft-Drink Market," *Journal of Economics and Management Strategy*, 1(2), Summer 1992, 277–311.

Genesove, David, "Adverse Selection in the Wholesale Used Car Market," *Journal of Political Economy*, 101(4), August 1993:644–665.

Gilbert, Richard J., "Patents, Sleeping Patents, and Entry Deterrence," in Steven C. Salop, ed., *Strategy, Predation, and Antitrust Analysis*. Washington, D.C.: Federal Trade Commission, 1979.

Golec, Joseph, and Maurry Tamarkin, "Do Bettors Prefer Long Shots Because They Are Risk Lovers, or Are They Just Overconfident?" *Journal of Risk and Uncertainty*, 11(1), July 1995:51–64.

Goolsbee, Austan, "What Happens When You Tax the Rich? Evidence from Executive Compensation," *Journal of Political Economy*, 108(2), April 2000:352–378.

Goolsbee, Austan, "In a World Without Borders: The Impact of Taxes on Internet Commerce," *Quarterly Journal of Economics*, 115(2), May 2000:561–576.

Goolsbee, Austan, "Competition in the Computer Industry: Online Versus Retail," *Journal of Industrial Economics*, XLIX(4), December 2001:487–499.

Grabowski, David C., and Michael A. Morrisey, "Do Higher Gasoline Taxes Save Lives?" *Economics Letters*, 90(1), January 2006:51–55.

Grabowski, Henry G., and John M. Vernon, "Brand Loyalty, Entry, and Price Competition in Pharmaceuticals After the 1984 Drug Act," *Journal of Law and Economics*, 35(2), October 1992:331–350.

Gray, Wayne B., and Ronald J. Shadbegian, "'Optimal' Pollution Abatement: Whose Benefits Matter, and How Much?," NBER Working Paper 9125, 2002, **www.nber.org/papers/w9125**.

Green, Richard, Richard Howitt, and Carlo Russo, "Estimation of Supply and Demand Elasticities of California Commodities," manuscript, May 2005.

Grossman, Michael, and Frank Chaloupka, "Demand for Cocaine by Young Adults: A Rational Addiction Approach," *Journal of Health Economics*, 17(4), August 1998:427–474.

Grossman, Philip J., Marco Pirozzi, and Jeff Pope, "An Empirical Test of Free-Rider Behaviour," *Australian Economic Papers*, 32(60), June 1993:152–160.

Gruber, Harald, "The Learning Curve in the Production of Semiconductor Memory Chips," *Applied Economics*, 24(8), August 1992:885–894.

Gruber, Jonathan, and Daniel M. Hungerman, "The Church vs. the Mall: What Happens When Religion Faces Increased Secular Competition?" NBER Working Paper No. 12410, July 2006.

Gruber, Jonathan, Anihdya Sen, and Mark Stabile, "Estimating Price Elasticities When There Is Smuggling: The Sensitivity of Smoking to Price in Canada," NBER Working Paper 8962, May 2002.

Guillickson, William, and Michael J. Harper, "Multifactor Productivity in U.S. Manufacturing, 1949–83," *Monthly Labor Review*, 110(10), October 1987:18–28.

Gundersen, Craig, and Victor Oliveira, "Food Stamp Program and Food Insufficiency," *American Journal of Agriculture Economics*, 83(4), November 2001:875–887.

Hahn, Robert W., Robert E. Litan, and Jesse Gurman, "Paying Less for Real Estate Brokerage: What Can Make It Happen?" AEI-Brookings Joint Center Working Paper 05-11, 2005.

Hall, Robert E., and David M. Lilien, "Efficient Wage Bargains Under Uncertain Supply and Demand," *American Economic Review*, 69(5), December 1979:868–879.

Hamilton, Stephen F., "The Comparative Efficiency of Ad Valorem and Specific Taxes Under Monopoly and Monopsony," *Economics Letters*, 63(2), May 1999:235–238.

Harkness, Joseph, and Sandra Newman, "The Interactive Effects of Housing Assistance and Food Stamps on Food Spending," *Journal of Housing Economics*, 12(3), September 2003:224–249.

Harrison, Ann E., and Margaret S. McMillan, "Outsourcing Jobs? Multinationals and U.S. Employment," NBER Working Papers: 12372, 2006.

Hatton, T. J., G. R. Boyer, and R. E. Bailey, "The Union Wage Effect in Late Nineteenth Century Britain," *Economica*, 61(244), November 1994:435–456.

Haughwout, Andrew F., Robert P. Inman, Steven Craig, and Thomas Luce, "Local Revenue Hills: Evidence from Four U.S. Cities," NBER Working Paper 9686, **www.nber.org/papers/w9686**, 2003.

Hausman, Jerry A., "Efficiency Effects on the U.S. Economy from Wireless Taxation," *National Tax Journal*, 52(3, part 2), September 2000:733–742.

Hausman, Jerry A., and Gregory K. Leonard, "The Competitive Effects of a New Product Introduction: A Case Study," *Journal of Industrial Economics*, 50(3), September 2002: 237–263.

Hausman, Jerry A., and Gregory K. Leonard, "Superstars in the NBA: Economic Value and Policy," *Journal of Labor Economics*, 14(4), October 1997:586–624.

Hay, George A., and Daniel Kelley, "An Empirical Survey of Price-Fixing Conspiracies," *Journal of Law and Economics*, 17(1), April 1974:13–38.

Hazlett, Thomas W., Jürgen Müller, and Roberto Muñoz, "The Social Value of TV Band Spectrum in European Countries," *Info*, 8(2), 2006:62–73.

Helland, Eric, and Alexander Tabarrok, "Contingency Fees, Settlement Delay, and Low-Quality Litigation: Empirical Evidence from Two Datasets," *Journal of Law, Economics, and Organization*, 19(2), Special Issue, October 2003:517–542.

Hennart, Jean-François, "Upstream Vertical Integration in the Aluminum and Tin Industries," *Journal of Economic Behavior and Organization*, 9(3), April 1988:281–299.

Herndon, Jill Boylston, "Health Insurer Monopsony Power: The All-or-None Model," *Journal of Health Economics*, 21(2), March 2002:197–206.

Holt, Matthew, "A Multimarket Bounded Price Variation Model Under Rational Expectations: Corn and Soybeans in the United States," *American Journal of Agricultural Economics*, 74(1), February 1992:10–20.

Hosoe, Nobuhiro, "Crop Failure, Price Regulation, and Emergency Imports of Japan's Rice Sector in 1993," *Applied Economics*, 36(10), June 2004:1051–1056.

Hotelling, Harold, "The Economics of Exhaustible Resources," *Journal of Political Economy*, 39(2), April 1931:137–175.

Houthakker, Hendrik S., "An International Comparison of Household Expenditures Patterns, Commemorating the Centenary of Engel's Law," *Econometrica*, 25(3), December 1957:532–551.

Hoynes, Hilary W., and Diane Schanzenbach, "Consumption Responses to In-Kind Transfers: Evidence from the Introduction of the Food Stamp Program," NBER Working Paper No. 13025, 2007.

Hsieh, Wen-Jen, "Test of Variable Output and Scale Elasticities for 20 U.S. Manufacturing Industries," *Applied Economics Letters*, 2(8), August 1995:284–287.

Hui, Kai-Lung, and Ivan P. L. Png, "Piracy and the Legitimate Demand for Recorded Music." *Contributions to Economic Analysis & Policy*, 2(1), 2003: article 11.

Hummels, David, and Alexandre Skiba, "Shipping the Good Apples Out? An Empirical Confirmation of the Alchian-Allen Conjecture," *Journal of Political Economy*, 112(6), December 2004:1384–1402.

Ida, Takanori, and Tetsuya Kuwahara, "Yardstick Cost Comparison and Economies of Scale and Scope in Japan's Electric Power Industry," *Asian Economic Journal*, 18(4), December 2004:423–438.

Imbens, Guido W., Donald B. Rubin, and Bruce I. Sacerdote, "Estimating the Effect of Unearned Income on Labor Earnings, Savings, and Consumption: Evidence from a Survey of Lottery Players," *American Economic Review*, 91(4), September 2001:778–794.

Irwin, Douglas A., and Peter J. Klenow, "Learning-by-Doing Spillovers in the Semiconductor Industry," *Journal of Political Economy*, 102(6), December 1994:1200–1227.

Irwin, Douglas A., and Nina Pavcnik, "Airbus versus Boeing Revisited: International Competition in the Aircraft Market," *Journal of International Economics*, 64(2), December 2004:223–245.

Ito, Harumi, and Darin Lee, "Assessing the Impact of the September 11 Terrorist Attacks on U.S. Airline Demand," *Journal of Economics and Business*, 57(1), January-February 2005:75–95.

Jacobson, Michael F., and Kelly D. Brownell, "Small Taxes on Soft Drinks and Snack Foods to Promote Health," *American Journal of Public Health*, 90(6), June 2000:854–857.

Jagannathan, Ravi, Ellen R. McGrattan, and Anna Scherbina, "The Declining U.S. Equity Premium," *Quarterly Review* (Federal Reserve Bank of Minneapolis), Fall 2000:3–19.

Jetter, Karen M., James A. Chalfant, and David A. Sumner, "Does 5-a-Day Pay?" *AIC Issues Brief*, No. 27, August 2004.

Jha, Prabhat, and Frank J. Chaloupka, "The Economics of Global Tobacco Control," BMJ, **bmj.com**, 321, August 2000:358–361.

Jha, Raghbendra, M. N. Murty, Satya Paul, and Balbir S. Sahni, "Cost Structure of the Indian Cement Industry," *Journal of Economics Studies*, 8(4), 1991:59–67.

Johnson, Ronald N., and Charles J. Romeo, "The Impact of Self-Service Bans in the Retail Gasoline Market," *Review of Economics and Statistics*, 82(4), November 2000:625–633.

Kahneman, Daniel, Jack L. Knetsch, and Richard H. Thaler, "Experimental Tests of the Endowment Effect and the Coase Theorem," *Journal of Political Economy*, 98(6), December 1990:1325–1348.

Kahneman, Daniel, and Amos Tversky, "Prospect Theory: An Analysis of Decision under Risk," *Econometrica*, 47(2), March, 1979:313–327.

Kaiser, Ulrich, and Julian Wright, "Price Structure in Two-Sided Markets: Evidence from the Magazine Industry," *International Journal of Industrial Organization*, 24(1), January 2006:1–28.

Kalirajan, K. P., and M. B. Obwona, "Frontier Production Function: The Stochastic Coefficient Approach," *Oxford Bulletin of Economics and Statistics*, 56(1), 1994:87–96.

Kan, Kamhon, "Cigarette Smoking and Self-Control, *Journal of Health Economics*, 26(1), January 2007:61–81.

Karp, Larry, "Global Warming and Hyperbolic Discounting," *Journal of Public Economics*, 89(2–3), February 2005: 261–282.

Karp, Larry S., and Jeffrey M. Perloff, "The Failure of Strategic Industrial Policies Due to the Manipulation by Firms," *International Review of Economics and Finance*, 4(1), 1995:1–16.

Katz, Michael L., and Carl Shapiro, "Systems Competition and Network Effects," *Journal of Economic Perspectives*, 8(2), 1994:93–115.

Kaushale, Neeraj, "Do Food Stamps Cause Obesity? Evidence from Immigrant Experience," NBER Working Paper No. 12849, 2007.

Keeler, Theodore E., Teh-Wei Hu, Paul G. Barnett, and Willard G. Manning, "Taxation, Regulation, and Addiction: A Demand Function for Cigarettes Based on Time-Series Evidence," *Journal of Health Economics*, 12(1), April 1993:1–18.

Keeler, Theodore E., Teh-Wei Hu, Michael Ong, and Hai-Yen Sung, "The U.S. National Tobacco Settlement: The Effects of Advertising and Price Changes on Cigarette Consumption," *Applied Economics*, 36(15), August 2004:1623–1629.

Kennickell, Arthur B., "An Examination of the Changes in the Distribution of Wealth from 1989 to 1998: Evidence from the Survey of Consumer Finances," Federal Reserve, 2001.

Kennickell, Arthur B., "A Rolling Tide: Changes in the Distribution of Wealth in the U.S., 1989–2001," Federal Reserve Board, 2003, **www.federalreserve.gov/pubs/oss/oss2/papers/asa2003.7.pdf.**

Kennickell, Arthur B., "Currents and Undercurrents: Changes in the Distribution of Wealth, 1989–2004," Federal Reserve Board, 2006.

Kennickell, Arthur B., and R. Louise Woodburn, "Consistent Weight Design for 1989, 1992, and 1995 SCPs, and the Distribution of Wealth," working paper, Board of Governors of the Federal Reserve System, August 1997.

Killingsworth, Mark R., *Labor Supply*, New York: Cambridge University Press, 1983.

Kim, E. Han, and Vijay Singal, "Mergers and Market Power: Evidence from the Airline Industry," *American Economic Review*, 83(3), June 1993:549–569.

Kim, H. Youn, "Economies of Scale and Scope in Multiproduct Firms: Evidence from U.S. Railroads," *Applied Economics*, 19(6), June 1987:733–741.

Kim, Hongjin, Gloria E. Helfand, and Richard E. Howitt, "An Economic Analysis of Ozone Control in California's San Joaquin Valley," *Journal of Agricultural and Resource Economics*, 23(1), July 1998:55–70.

Klein, Lawrence R., "The Use of the Input–Output Tables to Estimate the Productivity of IT," *Journal of Policy Modeling*, 25(5), July 2003:471–475.

Klemperer, Paul, *Auctions: Theory and Practice*, New Jersey: Princeton University Press, 2004.

Knetsch, Jack L., "Preferences and Nonreversibility of Indifference Curves," *Journal of Economic Behavior and Organization*, 1992, 17(1):131–139.

Kotchen, Matthew J., and Nicholas E. Burger, "Should We Drill in the Arctic National Wildlife Refuge? An Economic Perspective," NBER Working Paper No. 13211, July 2007.

Krattenmaker, Thomas G., and Steven C. Salop, "Anticompetitive Exclusion: Raising Rivals' Costs to Achieve Power over Price," *Yale Law Journal*, 96(2), December 1986:209–293.

Krupnick, A. J., and Paul R. Portney, "Controlling Urban Air Pollution: A Benefit-Cost Assessment," *Science*, 252, April 1991:522–528.

Lenard, Thomas M., "The Efficiency Costs of the Postal Monopoly: The Case of Third-Class Mail," *Journal of Regulatory Economics*, 6(4), December 1994:421–431.

Leslie, Phillip J., "A Structural Econometric Analysis of Price Discrimination in Broadway Theatre," working paper, Univ. of California, Los Angeles, November 15, 1997.

Levin, Richard C., Alvin K. Klevorick, Richard R. Nelson, and Sidney G. Winter, "Appropriating the Returns from Industrial Research and Development," *Brookings Papers on Economic Activity*, 3(Special Issue on Microeconomics), 1987:783–820.

Levitt, Steven D., and Jack Porter, "How Dangerous Are Drinking Drivers?" *Journal of Political Economy*, 109(6), December 2001:1198–1237.

Levy, Douglas E., and Ellen Meara, "The Effect of the 1998 Master Settlement Agreement on Prenatal Smoking," NBER Working Paper 11176, March 2005, **www.nber.org/papers/w11176.**

Liebenstein, Harvey, "Bandwagon, Snob, and Veblen Effects in the Theory of Consumers' Demand," *Quarterly Journal of Economics*, 64(2), May 1950:183–207.

List, John A., "Does Market Experience Eliminate Market Anomalies?" *Quarterly Journal of Economics*, 118(1), February 2003:41–71.

Lopez, Rigoberto A., and Emilio Pagoulatos, "Rent Seeking and the Welfare Cost of Trade Barriers," *Public Choice*, 79(1–2), April 1994:149–160.

MacAvoy, Paul W., "Tacit Collusion Under Regulation in the Pricing of Interstate Long-Distance Services," *Journal of Economics and Management Strategy*, 4(2), Summer 1995:147–185.

MacCrimmon, Kenneth R., and M. Toda, "The Experimental Determination of Indifference Curves," *Review of Economic Studies*, 56(3), July 1969:433–451.

Machina, Mark, "Dynamic Consistency and Non-Expected Utility Models of Choice Under Uncertainty," *Journal of Economic Literature*, 27(4), December 1989:1622–1668.

MacKie-Mason, Jeffrey K., and Robert S. Pindyck, "Cartel Theory and Cartel Experience in International Minerals Markets," in R. L. Gordon, H. D. Jacoby, and M. B. Zimmerman, eds., *Energy: Markets and Regulation: Essays in Honor of M. A. Adelman*. Cambridge, MA: MIT Press, 1986.

MaCurdy, Thomas, David Green, and Harry Paarsch, "Assessing Empirical Approaches for Analyzing Taxes and Labor Supply," *Journal of Human Resources*, 25(3), Summer 1990:415–490.

Madden, Janice F., *The Economics of Sex Discrimination*. Lexington, MA: Heath, 1973.

Maddock, Rodney, Elkin Castano, and Frank Vella, "Estimating Electricity Demand: The Cost of Linearizing the Budget Constraint," *Review of Economics and Statistics*, 74(2), May 1992:350–354.

Madrian, Brigitte C., and Dennis F. Shea, "The Power of Suggestion: Inertia in 401(k) Participation and Savings Behavior," *Quarterly Journal of Economics*, 116(4), November 2001: 1149–1187.

Madrian, Brigitte C., and Dennis F. Shea, "The Power of Suggestion: Inertia in 401(k) Participation and Savings Behavior: Erratum," *Quarterly Journal of Economics*, 117(1), February 2002: 377.

Mankiw, Gregory N., anad Phillip Swagel, "The Politics and Economics of Offshore Outsourcing," *Journal of Monetary Economics*, 53(5), July 2006: 1027–1056.

Marks, Steven V., "A Reassessment of Empirical Evidence on the U.S. Sugar Program," in S. V. Marks and K. Maskus, eds., *The Economics and Politics of World Sugar Policy*, Ann Arbor: University of Michigan Press, 1993.

McAfee, R. Preston, "The Real Lesson of Enron's Implosion: Market Makers Are in the Trust Business," 1(2), 2004: Article 4.

Medoff, Marshall H., "A Pooled Time-Series Analysis of Abortion Demand," *Population Research and Policy Review*, 16(6), December 1997:597–605.

Medoff, Marshall H., "Price, Restrictions and Abortion Demand," *Journal of Family and Economic Issues*, 28(4), December 2007:583–599.

Mishel, Lawrence, ed., *The State of Working America, 2006/2007*. New York: Cornell University Press, 2006.

Moffitt, Robert, "Estimating the Value of an In-Kind Transfer: The Case of Food Stamps," *Econometrica*, 57(2), March 1989:385–409.

Moschini, Giancarlo, and Karl D. Meilke, "Production Subsidy and Countervailing Duties in Vertically Related Markets: The Hog-Pork Case Between Canada and the United States," *American Journal of Agricultural Economics*, 74(4), November 1992:951–961.

Nash, John F., "Equilibrium Points in *n*-Person Games," *Proceedings of the National Academy of Sciences*, 36, 1950:48–49.

Nash, John F., "Non-Cooperative Games," *Annals of Mathematics*, 54(2), July 1951:286–295.

Nataraj, Shanthi, "Do Residential Water Consumers React to Price Increases? Evidence from a Natural Experiment in Santa Cruz," *Agricultural and Resource Economics Update*, 10(3), January/February 2007:9–11.

Nemoto, Jiro, Yasuo Nakanishi, and Seishi Madono, "Scale Economies and Over-Capitalization in Japanese Electric Utilities," *International Economic Review*, 34(2), May 1993:431–440.

Norman, G., "Economies of Scale in the Cement Industry," *Journal of Industrial Economics*, 27(4), June 1979: 317–337.

O'Donoghue, Ted, and Matthew Rabin, "Doing It Now or Later," *American Economic Review*, 89(1), March 1999:103–124.

Organization for Economic Cooperation and Development, *Agricultural Policies In OECD Countries: Monitoring and Evaluation 2007*, 2007.

Ouchi, Hiromi, Jill J. McCluskey, and Thomas I. Wahl, "Implications of the Consumer Response to Emerging Technologies and Diseases for International Trade: The Case of Japan," *Western Economics Forum*, 3(1), Spring 2004:11–16.

Oxfam, *Dumping Without Borders*, Oxfam Briefing Paper 50, 2003.

Paltsev, Sergey, John M. Reilly, Henry D. Jacoby, Angelo C. Gurgel, Gilbert E. Metcalf, Andrei P. Sokolov, and Jennifer F. Holak, "Assessment of U.S. Cap-and-Trade Proposals," NBER Working Paper, June 2007.

Panzar, John C., and Robert D. Willig, "Economies of Scale in Multi-Output Production," *Quarterly Journal of Economics*, 91(3), August 1977:481–493.

Panzar, John C., and Robert D. Willig, "Economies of Scope," *American Economic Review*, 71(2), May 1981:268–272.

Perry, Martin K., "Forward Integration by Alcoa: 1888–1930," *Journal of Industrial Economics*, 29(1), September 1980: 37–53.

Perry, Martin K., "Vertical Integration: Determinants and Effects," in Richard Schmalensee and Robert D. Willig, eds., *Handbook of Industrial Organization*. New York: North Holland, 1989.

Pielke, Roger A., Jr., Joel Gratz, Christopher W. Landsea, Douglas Collins, Mark A. Saunders, and Rade Musulin. "Normalized Hurricane Damages in the United States: 1900–2005." *Natural Hazards Review*, 9(1), February 2008:29–42.

Plott, Charles R., and Kathryn Zeiler, "The Willingness to Pay—Willingness to Accept Gap, the 'Endowment Effect,' Subject Misconceptions, and Experimental Procedures for Eliciting Values," *American Economic Review*, 95(3), June 2005:530–545.

Polinsky, A. Mitchell, "Controlling Externalities and Protecting Entitlements: Property Right, Liability Rule, and Tax-Subsidy Approaches," *Journal of Legal Studies*, 8(1), January 1979:1–48.

Pollak, Robert A., *The Theory of the Cost-of-Living Index*. New York: Oxford University Press, 1989.

Posner, Richard A., "The Social Cost of Monopoly and Regulation," *Journal of Political Economy*, 83(4), August 1975:807–827.

Prescott, Edward C., "Why Do Americans Work So Much More Than Europeans?" *Federal Reserve Bank of Minneapolis Quarterly Review,* 28(1), July 2004:2–13.

Rabin, Matthew, "Psychology and Economics," *Journal of Economic Literature,* 36(1), March 1998:11–46.

Ransom, Michael R., "Seniority and Monopsony in the Academic Labor Market," *American Economic Review*, 83(1), March 1993:221–233.

Rawls, John, *A Theory of Justice*. New York: Oxford University Press, 1971.

Reinstein, David A., and Christopher M. Snyder, "The Influence of Expert Reviews on Consumer Demand for Experience Goods: A Case Study of Movie Critics," *Journal of Industrial Economics,* 53(1), March 2005:27–51.

Richard, Oliver, "Flight Frequency and Mergers in Airline Markets," *International Journal of Industrial Organization,* 21(6), June 2003:907–922.

Rob, Rafael, and Joel Waldfogel, "Piracy on the High C's: Music Downloading, Sales Displacement, and Social Welfare in a Sample of College Students," NBER Working Paper 10874, 2004, **www.nber.org/papers/w10874**.

Roberts, Mark J., and Larry Samuelson, "An Empirical Analysis of Dynamic Nonprice Competition in an Oligopolistic Industry," *Rand Journal of Economics*, 19(2), Summer 1988:200–220.

Robidoux, Benoît, and John Lester, "Econometric Estimates of Scale Economies in Canadian Manufacturing," Working Paper No. 88-4, Canadian Dept. of Finance, 1988.

Robidoux, Benoît, and John Lester, "Econometric Estimates of Scale Economies in Canadian Manufacturing," *Applied Economics*, 24(1), January 1992:113–122.

Rohlfs, Jeffrey H., *Bandwagon Effects in High-Technology Industries,* Cambridge, MA: MIT Press, 2001.

Rohlfs, Jeffrey H., "A Theory of Interdependent Demand for a Communications Service," *Bell Journal of Economics and Management Science,* 5(1), Spring 1974:16–37.

Roth, Alvin E., and Axel Ockenfels, "Last-Minute Bidding and the Rules for Ending Second-Price Auctions: Evidence from eBay and Amazon Auctions on the Internet," *American Economic Review,* 92(4), September 2002:1093–1103.

Rosenberg, Howard R., "Many Fewer Steps for Pickers—A Leap for Harvestkind? Emerging Change in Strawberry Harvest Technology," *Choices,* 1st Quarter 2004:5–11.

Rousseas, S. W., and A. G. Hart, "Experimental Verification of a Composite Indifference Map," *Journal of Political Economy*, 59(4), August 1951:288–318.

Ruffin, R. J., "Cournot Oligopoly and Competitive Behavior," *Review of Economic Studies,* 38(116), October 1971: 493–502.

Salgado, Hugo, "A Dynamic Duopoly Model under Learning-by-Doing in the Computer CPU Industry," Working paper, 2007.

Salop, Joanne, and Steven C. Salop, "Self-Selection and Turnover in the Labor Market," *Quarterly Journal of Economics*, 90(4), November 1976:619–627.

Salop, Steven C., "The Noisy Monopolist: Imperfect Information, Price Dispersion, and Price Discrimination," *Review of Economic Studies*, 44(3), October 1977:393–406.

Salop, Steven C., "Strategic Entry Deterrence," *American Economic Review*, 69(2), May 1979:335–338.

Salop, Steven C., "Practices That (Credibly) Facilitate Oligopoly Coordination," in Joseph E. Stiglitz and G. Frank Mathewson, eds., *New Developments in the Analysis of Market Structure*. Cambridge, MA: MIT Press, 1986.

Salop, Steven C., and David T. Sheffman, "Cost-Raising Strategies," *Journal of Industrial Economics*, 36(1), September 1987:19–34.

Schaller Consulting, *The New York City Taxicab Fact Book,* 2004, **www.schallerconsult.com**.

Schaller Consulting, *New York City Taxicab Fact Book*, March 2006.

Scherer, F. M., "An Early Application of the Average Total Cost Concept," *Journal of Economic Literature,* 39(3), September 2001:897–901.

Schlenker, Wolfram, and Sofia B. Villas-Boas, "Consumer and Market Responses to Mad-Cow Disease," CUARE Working Paper 1023, 2007.

Schmalensee, Richard, Paul L. Joskow, A. Denny Ellerman, Juan Pablo Montero, and Elizabeth M. Bailey, "An Interim Evaluation of Sulfur Dioxide Emissions Trading," *Journal of Economic Perspectives*, 12(3) Summer 1998:53–68.

Schoemaker, Paul J. H., "The Expected Utility Model: Its Variants, Purposes, Evidence and Limitation," *Journal of Economic Literature*, 20(2), June 1982:529–563.

Shadbegian, Ronald J., and Wayne B. Gray, "What Determines Environmental Performance at Paper Mills? The Roles of Abatement Spending, Regulation and Efficiency," Center for Economic Studies working paper CES 03–10, 2003.

Shapiro, Carl, and Joseph E. Stiglitz, "Equilibrium Unemployment as a Worker Discipline Device," *American Economic Review*, 74(3), June 1984:434–444.

Shapiro, Carl, and Hal R. Varian, *Information Rules: A Strategic Guide to the Network Economy,* Boston: Harvard Business School Press, 1999.

Shapiro, Jesse M., "Is There a Daily Discount Rate? Evidence from the Food Stamp Nutrition Cycle," *Journal of Public Economics*, 89(2-3), February 2004:303–325.

Skeath, Susan E., and Gregory A. Trandel, "A Pareto Comparison of Ad Valorem and Unit Taxes in Noncompetitive Environments," *Journal of Public Economics*, 53(1), January 1994:53–71.

Slade, Margaret E., "Product Rivalry with Multiple Strategic Weapons: An Analysis of Price and Advertising Competition," *Journal of Economics and Management Strategy*," 4(3), Fall 1995:224–276.

Smiley, Robert, "Empirical Evidence on Strategic Entry Deterrence," *International Journal of Industrial Organization*, 6(2), June 1988:167–180.

Sood, Neeraj, Abby Alpert, and Jay Bhattacharya, "Technology, Monopoly, and the Decline of the Viatical Settlements Industry," NBER Working Paper 11164, March 2005, **www.nber.org/papers/w11164**.

Spence, A. Michael, *Market Signaling*. Cambridge, MA: Harvard University Press, 1974.

Spence, A. Michael, "The Learning Curve and Competition," *Bell Journal of Economics and Management Science*, 12(1), 1981:49–70.

Spencer, Barbara J., and James A. Brander, "International R&D Rivalry and Industrial Strategy," *Review of Economic Studies*, 50(4), October 1983:707–722.

Stewart, Mark B., "Union Wage Differentials in an Era of Declining Unionization," *Oxford Bulletin of Economics and Statistics*, 57(2), May 1995:143–166.

Stiglitz, Joseph E., "The Theory of 'Screening,' Education, and the Distribution of Income," *American Economic Review*, 65(3), June 1975:283–300.

Stiglitz, Joseph E., "Equilibrium in Product Markets with Imperfect Information," *American Economic Review*, 69(2), May 1979:339–345.

Stiglitz, Joseph E., "The Causes and Consequences of the Dependence of Quality on Price," *Journal of Economic Literature*, 25(1), March 1987:1–48.

Stuart, Charles, "Swedish Tax Rates, Labor Supply, and Tax Revenues," *Journal of Political Economy*, 89(5), October 1981:1020–1038.

Stuart, Charles, "Welfare Costs per Dollar of Additional Tax Revenue in the United States," *American Economic Review*, 74(3), June 1984:352–362.

Sullivan, Ashley F., and Eunyoung Choi, "Hunger and Food Insecurity in the Fifty States: 1998–2000," Center on Hunger and Poverty, Brandeis University, August 2002.

Sullivan, Daniel, "Monopsony Power in the Market for Nurses," *Journal of Law and Economics*, 32(2, pt. 2) October 1989:S135–S178.

Swinton, John R., and Christopher R. Thomas, "Using Empirical Point Elasticities to Teach Tax Incidence," *Journal of Economic Education*, 32(4), Fall 2001:356–368.

Tekin, Erdal, "Single Mothers Working at Night: Standard Work and Child Care Subsidies," *Economic Inquiry*, 45(2), April 2007:233–250.

Terrell, Katherine, "Technical Change and Factor Bias in Polish Industry (1962–1983)," *Review of Economics and Statistics*, 75(4), November 1993:741–747.

Tideman, T. Nicholaus, and Gordon Tullock, "A New and Superior Process for Making Social Choices," *Journal of Political Economy*, 84(6), December 1976:1145–1159.

Timmer, C. Peter, "Choice of Technique in Rice Milling on Java," in Carl K. Eicher and John M. Staatz, eds., *Agricultural Development in the Third World*. Baltimore: Johns Hopkins University Press, 1984.

Tullock, G., "The Welfare Cost of Tariffs, Monopolies, and Theft," *Western Economic Journal*, 5(3), June 1967:224–232.

Tversky, Amos, and Daniel Kahneman, "The Framing of Decisions and the Psychology of Choice," *Science*, 211(4481), January, 1981:453–458.

Tversky, Amos, and Daniel Kahneman, "Rational Choice and the Framing of Decisions," *Journal of Business*, 59(4, Part 2), October 1986: S251– S278.

Tyler, John H., Richard J. Murnane, and John B. Willett, "Estimating the Labor Market Signaling Value of the GED," *Quarterly Journal of Economics*, 115(2), May 2000:431–468.

Urban, Glen L., Theresa Carter, and Steven Gaskin, "Market Share Rewards to Pioneering Brands: An Empirical Analysis and Strategic Implications," *Management Science*, 32(6), June 1986:645–659.

Vandermeulen, Daniel C., "Upward Sloping Demand Curves Without the Giffen Paradox," *American Economic Review*, 62(3), June 1972:453–458.

Van Ravenstein, Ad, and Hans Vijlbrief, "Welfare Cost of Higher Tax Rates: An Empirical Laffer Curve for the Netherlands," *De Economist*, 136(2), 1988:205–219.

Varian, Hal R., "Measuring the Deadweight Cost of DUP and Rent-Seeking Activities," *Economics and Politics*, 1(1), Spring 1989:81–95.

Varian, Hal R., *Microeconomic Analysis*, 3rd ed. New York: Norton, 1992.

Varian, Hal R., "The Demand for Bandwidth," **www.sims.berkeley.edu/~hal/Papers/brookings.pdf**, February 2002.

Villegas, Daniel J., "The Impact of Usury Ceilings on Consumer Credit," *Southern Economic Journal*, 56(1), July 1989: 126–141.

Viscusi, W. Kip, *Employment Hazards*. Cambridge, MA: Harvard University Press, 1979.

Viscusi, W. Kip, *Pricing Environmental Risks*. Policy Study No. 112. St. Louis, Mo.: Center for the Study of American Business, Washington University, 1992.

Von Hippel, F. A., and W. F. Von Hipple, "Sex, Drugs and Animal Parts: Will Viagra Save Threatened Species?" *Environmental Conservation*, 29(3), 2002:277–281.

Von Hippel, F. A., and W. F. Von Hipple, "Is Viagra a Viable Conservation Tool? Response to Hoover, 2003," *Environmental Conservation*, 31(1), 2004:4–6.

von Hippel, William, Frank A. von Hippel, Norma Chan, and Clara Cheng, "Exploring the Use of Viagra in Place of Animal and Plant Potency Products in Traditional Chinese Medicine," *Environmental Conservation*, 32(3), September 2005:235–238.

von Neumann, John, and Oskar Morgenstern, *Theory of Games and Economic Behavior*. Princeton, NJ: Princeton University Press, 1944.

Waldfogel, Joel, "The Deadweight Loss of Christmas," *American Economic Review*, 83(5), December 1993:1328–1336.

Waldfogel, Joel, "Does Consumer Irrationality Trump Consumer Sovereignty?" working paper, 2004.

Walton, Clarence C., and Frederick W. Cleveland, *Corporations on Trial: The Electric Cases*. Belmont, CA: Wadsworth, 1964.

Warner, John T., and Saul Pleeter, "The Personal Discount Rate: Evidence from Military Downsizing Programs," *American Economic Review*, 91(1), March 2001:33–53.

Weiher, Jesse C., Robin C. Sickles, and Jeffrey M. Perloff, "Market Power in the U.S. Airline Industry," D. J. Slottje, ed., *Economic Issues in Measuring Market Power, Contributions to Economic Analysis*, Volume 255, Elsevier 2002 forthcoming.

Weinstein, Arnold A., "Transitivity of Preferences: A Comparison Among Age Groups," *Journal of Political Economy*, 76(2), March/April 1968:307–311.

Weitzman, Martin L., "Prices vs. Quantities," *Review of Economic Studies*, 41(4), October 1974:477–491.

Whinston, Michael D., and Scott C. Collins, "Entry and Competitive Structure in Deregulated Airline Markets: An Event Study Analysis of People Express," *Rand Journal of Economics*, 23(4), Winter 1992:445–462.

White, Michelle J., "The 'Arms Race' on American Roads," *Journal of Law and Economics,* 47(2), October 2004: 333–355.

Whitmore, Diane, "What Are Food Stamps Worth?" Princeton University Working Paper #468, July 2002, **www.irs.princeton.edu/pubs/pdfs/468.pdf**.

Williamson, Oliver E., *Markets and Hierarchies: Analysis and Antitrust Implications*. New York: Free Press, 1975.

Williamson, Oliver E., "Credible Commitments: Using Hostages to Support Exchange," *American Economic Review*, 73(4), September 1983:519–540.

Willis, Robert J., "A New Approach to the Economic Theory of Fertility Behavior," *Journal of Political Economy*, 81(2, pt. 2), March–April 1973:S14–S64.

Yellen, Janet L., "Efficiency Wage Models of Unemployment," *American Economic Review*, 74(2), May 1984:200–205.

Index

Credits

Chapter 1 p. 9: Jeffrey Perloff

Chapter 2 p. 29: Reuters/CORBIS
p. 33: Digital Vision
p. 34: U.S. Government Printing Office
p. 36: Getty Editorial

Chapter 3 p. 52, 57: CorbisRF

Chapter 4 p. 81: Universal Press Syndicate
p. 96: Jeffrey Perloff
p. 101: Courtesy USDA

Chapter 5 p. 127: PhotoDisc, Inc.
p. 138: Reprinted with permission of Malden Mills Industries, Inc., Lawrince, MA 01841.

Cross-Chapter Analysis
p. 148: Michael Newman/PhotoEdit

Chapter 6 p. 152: Reprinted with permission of Ghirardelli Chocolate Co.
p. 162: Library of Congress
p. 163: Norman Borlaug Institute for Plant Science Research.
p. 178: Courtesy of Dell inc.

Chapter 7 p. 185: Jeffrey Lott
p. 216: PhotoDisc, Inc.

Chapter 8 p. 238: Dan Lamont/Corbis
p. 262: Jeffrey Perloff

Chapter 9 p. 283, 287: Jeffrey Perloff

Chapter 10 p. 317: CorbisRF
p. 332, 333: Adapted from "The Rich Get Richer, but Never the Same Way Twice," *The New York Times*, August 16, 1992, Section 4, page E 3. Reprinted with permission. (Lincloln) Library of Congress; (woman with child) Libray of Congress; (Washington) National Portrait Gallery; (child workers) The National Archives; (Ronald Reagan) The Ronald Reagan Presidential Library

Cross-Chapter Analysis
p. 346: © 2004 Universal Press Syndicate

Chapter 11 p. 360, 362, 375: Jeffrey Perloff
p. 373: Courtesy of John W. Shore, M.D.

Chapter 12 p. 394, 406, 417: Jeffrey Perloff

Cross-Chapter Analysis
p. 428: AP Photo/Amy E. Conn

Chapter 13 p. 436: AP Wideworld
p. 449, 451: Jeffrey Perloff
p. 463: Lee Bennack

Cross-Chapter Analysis
p. 474: Jeffrey Perloff

Chapter 14 p. 487: Photographer's Choice/Getty Images
p. 490: Dorling Kindersley
p. 497: Jeffrey Perloff

Chapter 15 p. 530: John Springer Collection/Corbis
p. 536: Courtesy of Alcoa Inc.

Chapter 16 p. 545: PhotoDisc
p. 549: Shawn Michienzi/Ripsaw Photography
p. 564: Jeffrey Perloff

Chapter 17 p. 579, 583: Jeffrey Perloff
p. 580: William Cole and Mike Thaler, eds., The Classic cartoons, Cleveland, The World Publishing Co., © 1966 William Cole and Mike Thaler
p. 591: NOAA
p. 596: PhotoDisc Red

Chapter 18 p. 608: AP Wideworld Photos/Mary Ann Chastain
p. 613: Digital Vision

Cross-Chapter Analysis
p. 637: CorbisRF

Chapter 19 p. 642 (top): Tribune Media Services, Inc., All rights reserved. Reprinted with permission.
p. 642 (bottom): Mary Rich, art director; Cliff Leicht, writer; Craig Orsinni, photographer; Marc Ruggiero, Illustrator
p. 643: Beth Anderson

Chapter 20 p. 677: Carl and Ann Purcell/Corbis
p. 685: Garry Larson 8.15.90

Applications on the Perloff Web Site

www.myeconlab.com/perloff

Chapter 1
Tax on Fast-Food Containers

Chapter 2
Gas Lines
Minimum Wage Law in Puerto Rico
Sideways Wine

Chapter 3
Booze Sin Taxes
Condoms
Demanding Rail Safety
Gasoline Taxes as a Revenue Source
Incidence of Federal *Ad Valorem* Taxes
Incidence of Tax on Restaurant Meals
Specific Taxes
Why the Wealthy Buy More Houses
Willingness to Surf

Chapter 4
Substitution Effects in Canada
Taxes and Internet Shopping

Chapter 5
Christmas Price Index
Do Taxes Affect Click-versus-Brick Decisions?
Income Elasticities of Demand for Cars
International Comparison of Substitution and Income Effects
Quality Improvements, New Products, and the CPI
Wealth of Developing Countries
What to Do with Extra Income

Chapter 6
Does That Compute Down on the Farm?
German Versus British Productivity
More Productive Death
Nonneutral Technical Change in Pin Manufacturing
Rolls-Royce

Chapter 7
Average Cost of Cement Firms
Cost of Caring for Parents
Cost of Names
Depreciation
Lowering Transaction Costs for Used Goods at eBay and Abebooks
Quality and Factor Proportions
Rice Milling on Java
Tax Rules
Waiting for the Doctor

Chapter 8
Apple Crunch
Changes in Banking
Shutting Down Lesotho
Shutting Down Oil Wells
Slope of Long-Run Market Supply Curves
Threat of Entry in Shipping

Chapter 9
Barriers to Protect Our Way of Life
Discriminating Against Groups
Japanese Nontariff Barriers
Jefferson's Trade Embargo
Job Termination Laws
Occupational Licenses
Trucking
Unions and Guilds
Wal-Mart in Germany
Zoning

Chapter 10
Living-Wage Laws
Sin Taxes
U.S. Minimum Wage Laws and Teenagers

Chapter 11
A Drug Patent
Airport Monopolies
Banking Market Power
Competitive Versus Monopoly Sugar Tax Incidence
Creating and Destroying an Auto Monopoly
Deadweight Loss of the U.S. Postal Service
Ending the Monopoly in Telephone Service
Government Sales of Monopolies
Humana Hospitals
Iceland's Government Creates Genetic Monopoly
Near Monopolies

Chapter 12
A Hot Sale of Coke
Automatic Savings
Bundling Hardware with Software and Service
Flight of the Thunderbirds
Generics and Brand-Name Loyalty
Gray Markets
International Price Discrimination
Product Differentiation 1
Product Differentiation 2
Tagamet Revisited
Tailoring Credit Cards
Taking Women to the Cleaners
The Supreme Court's View on Tie-in Sales
Using Information to Perfectly Price Discriminate
Warehouse Stores

Chapter 13
A Government-Created Cartel
Airbus and Boeing
Bad Bakers
Blue Fries, Green Ketchup
Designer Glasses
Economists Prevent Collusion
European Cigarette Tax Incidence
Hospital Mergers
Insurance Price Wars
Oligopoly Competition Among Governments
Tacit Collusion in Long-Distance Service
The Art of Price Fixing
Toothbrushes
Vitamin Price Fixing

Chapter 14
Advertising Expenditures
Advertising Targets
Brand-Switching Advertising
Buttering Up Legislatures
Celebrities
Cleaning the Air
Drug Commercials
Evidence on Strategic Entry Deterrence
Exclusive Dealing
Generic Milk Promotions
Government Deterrence
Government's Helping Hand
Hitting Rivals Where It Hurts
Legislating Barriers to Entry
Nonprice Strategies
Phone Companies
Preventing Customers from Switching
Restroom Advertising
Smoking-Gun Evidence?
Splenda

Chapter 15
Black Death Raises Wages
Cutting Off Oxygen
Life Cycle of a Firm
Monopsony Price Discrimination
Monopsony Wage Setting
Outsourcing
Piggish Vertical Integration
Record Prices
Vertical Integration and Essential Facilities: Barnes & Noble
Vertical Integration of Auto Manufacturers

Chapter 16
Buying Versus Renting a Phone

Visit the Web site:
www.myeconlab.com/perloff